A Tutorial Guide to

AutoCAD® 2006

A Tutorial Guide to

AutoCAD® 2006

Shawna Lockhart
Montana State University

PEARSON
Prentice Hall

Upper Saddle River, New Jersey
Columbus, Ohio

Executive Editor: Debbie Yarnell
Managing Editor: Judith Casillo
Production Editor: Louise N. Sette
Production Supervision: Cindy Johnson
Design Coordinator: Diane Ernsberger
Cover Designer: Jim Hunter
Cover Art: Mark Gerisch — M&L Automotive
Production Manager: Deidra M. Schwartz
Marketing Manager: Jimmy Stephens

This book was set in Galliard by Publishing Services. It was printed and bound by Hamilton Printing Company. The cover was printed by Coral Graphic Services, Inc.

Pearson Education Ltd.
Pearson Education Singapore Pte. Ltd.
Pearson Education Canada, Ltd.
Pearson Education—Japan
Pearson Education Australia Pty. Limited
Pearson Education North Asia Ltd.
Pearson Educación de Mexico, S.A. de C.V.
Pearson Education Malaysia Pte. Ltd.

PEARSON
Prentice Hall

10 9 8 7 6 5 4 3
ISBN: 0-13-171383-3

For Rick, always

Contents in Brief

Chapter 1	**Preparing for the Tutorials 1**
Chapter 2	**AutoCAD Basics 13**
Tutorial 1	**Introduction to the AutoCAD Software 31**
Tutorial 2	**Basic Construction Techniques 79**
Tutorial 3	**Basic Editing and Plotting Techniques 111**
Tutorial 4	**Geometric Constructions 145**
Tutorial 5	**Template Drawings and More Plotting 185**
Tutorial 6	**2D Orthographic Drawings 229**
Tutorial 7	**Dimensioning 263**
Tutorial 8	**Advanced Dimensioning 303**
Tutorial 9	**Section and Auxiliary Views 323**
Tutorial 10	**Blocks, DesignCenter, and Tool Palettes 363**
Tutorial 11	**Introduction to Solid Modeling 393**
Tutorial 12	**Changing and Plotting Solid Models 443**
Tutorial 13	**Creating Assembly Drawings from Solid Models 465**
Tutorial 14	**Solid Modeling for Section and Auxiliary Views 501**
Tutorial 15	**Rendering 525**
	AutoCAD Command Summary 563
	Glossary 603
	Index 615
	Art Credits 643

Contents

PREFACE xxiii

CHAPTER 1
PREPARING FOR THE TUTORIALS 1
Introduction to the Tutorials 1
Basic Mouse Techniques 1
Recognizing Typographical Conventions 2
End-of-Tutorial Exercises 3
Configuring Windows for the Tutorials 3
Windows 2000/NT/XP 3
Screen Resolution 3
Backing Up AutoCAD Defaults 4
Customizable Support Files 5
Creating a Working Directory 6
Creating Multiple Shortcuts 6
Setting the Working Directory 7
Installing Data Files for the Tutorials 7
Configuring AutoCAD Software for the Tutorials 8
User Profiles 10
Changing the Configuration 11

CHAPTER 2
AUTOCAD BASICS 13
Introduction 13
Starting the AutoCAD 2006 Software 13
Microsoft Windows Conventions 13
Navigating in Windows 14
Basic Elements of the AutoCAD Graphics Window 14
Minimizing and Restoring an Application 14
Microsoft Windows Multitasking Options 15
AutoCAD Pointing Techniques 15
Picking Commands and Menu Options 15
Entering Points 15
Dragging 16

Object Selection 16
AutoCAD Commands and Menu Options 16
Typing Commands 17
Using the Toolbars 18
Dynamic Input 20
Backing Up and Backing Out of Commands 20
Repeating Commands 21
Using Pull-Down Menus 21
Working with Dialog Boxes 22
Accessing On-Line Help 25
Using a Scroll Bar 28
Working with Documents 28
Exiting an AutoCAD Session 29

TUTORIAL 1
INTRODUCTION TO THE AUTOCAD SOFTWARE 31
Introduction 31
Starting 31
The AutoCAD Screen 31
Canceling Commands 35
Picking Commands from the Menu Bar 35
Typing Commands 36
Command Aliasing 36
Using Dynamic Entry 36
Typing a Command Option Letter 38
Starting a New Drawing 38
Naming Drawing Files 39
Working with Multiple Drawings 40
Using Grid 42
Using Zoom 43
Using Zoom All 43
Using Snap 44
Grid and Snap Toggles 44
Drafting Settings 45
Using Line 45
Getting Help 46
Entering Coordinates 48
Using Absolute Coordinates 49
Drawing Using Grid and Snap 49
Using Last Point 50
Using Relative X- and Y-Coordinates 50
Using Polar Coordinates 51

Using Save 52
Using Erase 52
Erasing with Window or Crossing 53
Using Undo 56
Using Redo 57
Using Back 58
Setting the Units 58
Sizing Your Drawing 60
Using Limits 61
Using Rectangle 62
Saving Your Drawing 63
Drawing Circles 63
Adding Text 64
Using Special Text Characters 65
Copying Text 66
In Place Text Editing 67
Moving and Rotating Text 67
Setting the Text Style 67
Using Mtext 71
Spell Checking Your Drawing 72
Saving Your Drawing 73
Transferring Files 73
Key Terms & Commands 74
Exercises 75

TUTORIAL 2
BASIC CONSTRUCTION TECHNIQUES 79
Introduction 79
Starting 79
Opening an Existing Drawing 79
Saving as a New File 81
Using Layers 82
Current Layer 82
Controlling Layers 83
Controlling Colors 83
Layer Visibility 84
Freezing Layers 85
Locking Layers 85
Making Object's Layer Current 86
Using Layer 87
Color in Layers 88
Linetype in Layers 89
Using Object Snap 90

Using Arc 93
Arc 3 Points 93
Arc Start Center End 95
Arc Start End Angle 95
Arc Start Center Length 96
Arc Start End Radius 97
Continuing an Arc 97
Quick Selections for Arc 98
Using Zoom 98
Zooming Using Scale Factors 99
Zoom Window 99
Zoom Previous 101
Zoom Realtime 101
Zoom All 101
Using the Aerial Viewer 101
Using Pan Realtime 102
Using Circle Options 103
Circle 2 Point 103
Circle 3 Point 104
Circle Tangent Tangent Radius 105
Circle Tangent Tangent Tangent 105
Using Ellipse 105
Key Terms & Commands 107
Exercises 108

TUTORIAL 3
BASIC EDITING AND PLOTTING TECHNIQUES 111
Introduction 111
Starting 111
Starting from a Template Drawing 111
Using Trim 114
Using Offset 118
Trimming the Remaining Lines 119
Selecting All Edges to Use with Trim 119
Changing Object Properties 121
Using the Properties Palette 121
Using Fillet 123
Using Chamfer 124
Using Polyline 125
Edit Polyline 126
Using Spline 127
Getting Information about Your Drawing 128
Using List 129
Locating Points 130
Using Area 130

Using Multilines 131
Creating a Multiline Style 131
Drawing Multilines 132
The Plot Dialog Box 134
Plot Device 135
Key Terms & Commands 140
Exercises 140

TUTORIAL 4
GEOMETRIC CONSTRUCTIONS 145
Introduction 145
Starting 145
Setting the Units and Limits 145
Drawing the Wrench 146
Using Copy Object 146
Effective Use of Layers 147
Loading the Linetypes 148
Changing Properties 149
Setting the Global Linetype Scaling Factor 150
Changing an Object's Linetype Scale 151
Using Polygon 152
Drawing Hexagons 152
Using Polar Tracking 154
Using Object Snaps 156
Object Snap Overrides 157
Showing a Floating Toolbar 157
Snap to Endpoint 157
Snap to Quadrant 158
Snap to Center 158
Snap to Tangent 158
Snap to Intersection 159
Snap to Perpendicular 160
Snap to Parallel 160
Practicing with Running Mode Object Snaps 161
Using Break 162
Snap to Apparent Intersection 162
Snap to Nearest 162
Snap to Node 162
Snap to Insertion 163
Snap From 163
Snap to Extension 163
Object Tracking 163
Using Extend 163
Using Rotate 165

Using Move 166

Methods of Selecting Objects 166

Using Selection Filters 168

Using Quick Select 169

Closing the Coupler Drawing 169

Creating the Geneva Cam 169

Using Construction Line 171

Using Mirror 173

Using Array 174

Making Changes with Hot Grips 175

Activating an Object's Grips 176

Selecting the Base Grip 177

Using Stretch with Hot Grips 177

Using Move with Hot Grips 177

Using Move with the Copy Option 177

Using Rotate with Hot Grips 178

Using Scale with Hot Grips 179

Using Mirror with Hot Grips 179

Noun/Verb Selection 180

Key Terms & Commands 180

Exercises 181

TUTORIAL 5
TEMPLATE DRAWINGS AND MORE PLOTTING 185

Introduction 185

Starting 185

Using a Standard Template 186

Paper Space 187

Printer Area 188

Viewport 188

Switching to Model Space 188

Inserting an Existing Drawing 189

Properties of the Viewport 191

Setting the Viewport Zoom Scale 192

Using Pan Realtime 194

Creating a Second Floating Viewport 195

Making a Viewport Active 196

Making the Viewport Layer Non-Plotting 197

Adding Text and Notes to Paper Space 198

Using Irregularly Shaped Viewports 200

Plotting from Paper Space 201

Sheet Sets 202

Creating a Template Drawing 207

Creating Default Layers 208
Defining the Layers 209
Setting Up the Remaining Layers 210
Using the Drafting Settings Dialog Box 215
Selecting the Default Text Font 216
Setting the Viewres Default 217
Switching to a Paper Space Layout 217
Adding a Title Block and Text to Paper Space 219
Using Divide 221
Beginning a New Drawing from a Template Drawing 223
Changing the Title Block Text 224
Key Terms & Commands 225
Exercises 225

TUTORIAL 6
2D ORTHOGRAPHIC DRAWINGS 229
Introduction 229
The Front, Top, and Right-Side Orthographic Views 229
View Location 230
Starting 230
Switching to Model Space 231
Deciding the Model Space Limits 232
Viewing the Model Space Limits 232
Using Ortho 232
Drawing Construction Lines 233
Hidden Lines 236
Drawing Hidden Lines 237
Line Precedence 239
Slanted Surfaces 239
Top-View to Side-View Projection 241
Drawing the Miter Line 241
Using Object Tracking 241
Sizing and Positioning the Drawing 245
Locking the Viewport Scale 246
Drawing Holes 247
Drawing Centerlines and Centermarks 248
Breaking the Centerline 250
Setting the Global Linetype Scaling Factor 253
Projecting Slanted Surfaces on Cylinders 254
Key Terms & Commands 258
Exercises 258

TUTORIAL 7
DIMENSIONING 263

Introduction 263

Terminology and Conventions 263

Semiautomatic Dimensioning 264

Starting 265

Dimensioning a Shape 265

Using the DIM Layer 266

Dimension Standards 266

Drawing Scale and Dimensions 266

The Dimension Toolbar 267

Using Dimension Styles 267

Creating a Named Dimension Style 268

Setting the Line Features 269
Dimension Lines 269
Extension Lines 270
Symbols and Arrows 270
Centermark Size and Style 271
Text 271
Fit 273
The Dimension Scaling Factor 274
Primary Units 275
Measurement Scale 275
Zero Suppression for Linear Dimensions 275
Angular Dimensions 276
Zero Suppression for Angular Dimensions 276
Alternate Units 276
Tolerances 277
Setting the Current Style 278

Checking Your Dimension Settings 279

Associative Dimensioning 279
Adding Dimensions to the Layout or the Model 280

Adding Linear Dimensions 281

Creating a Diameter Dimension 281

Baseline Dimensioning 284

Using Xplode 285

Adding Text with Special Characters 286

Using Quick Dimension 287

Saving As a Template 288

Dimensioning the Adapter 288

Using Continue Dimension 290

Angular Dimensions 291

Setting a Child Style 291
Adding the Angular Dimension 291

Centering the Views 293
Adding the Tolerance Note 293
Updating Associative Dimensions 294
Using Stretch 294
Modifying Dimensions 296
Updating a Dimension Style 297
Key Terms & Commands 298
Exercises 298

TUTORIAL 8
ADVANCED DIMENSIONING 303
Tolerance 303
Tolerance Formats 303
Starting 304
Automatic Bilateral Tolerances 305
Setting the Tolerance Precision 307
Specifying Tolerance Values 307
Setting the Tolerance Text Height Scaling 307
Using Dimension Overrides 309
Using Limit Tolerances 311
Creating Feature Control Frames 313
Using Leader with Tolerances 316
Creating Datum Flags 318
Key Terms & Commands 320
Exercises 320

TUTORIAL 9
SECTION AND AUXILIARY VIEWS 323
Introduction 323
Section Views 323
Section View Conventions 323
Crosshatching 324
Starting 325
Creating 2D Section Views 325
Cutting Plane Lines 326
Creating Dashed Lines 326
Drawing the Leaders 326
Leader Command Options 327
Changing Hidden Lines to Visible 330
Using Hatch 331
Selecting the Hatch Pattern 332
Angling the Hatch Pattern 333

Scaling the Hatch Pattern 333
Options for Hatch Boundaries 333
Gradient Fills 334
Adding the Hatch Pattern 335
Creating the Side Section View 337
Changing the Viewport Scale 337
Reorienting and Hatching the View 337
Solid Fill 340
Using Draworder with Hatch 341
Changing Associative Hatches 341
Auxiliary Views 345
Drawing Auxiliary Views Using 2D 345
Aligning the UCS with the Angled Surface 347
Adding Visual Reference Lines 351
Linetype Conventions 351
Curved Surfaces 352
Rotating the Snap 353
Drawing the Ellipse 357
Key Terms & Commands 358
Exercises 359

TUTORIAL 10
BLOCKS, DESIGNCENTER, AND TOOL PALETTES 363
Introduction 363
Starting 364
Using the Block Command 364
Inserting a Block 367
Using Explode 368
Using Write Block 368
Using DesignCenter and Tool Palettes 370
Drawing the Half-Adder Circuit 374
Using Donut 374
Freezing the TEXT Layer 375
Creating Object Groups 376
Creating Custom Interfaces 377
Using Special Characters in Programmed Commands 380
Key Terms & Commands 387
Exercises 387

TUTORIAL 11
INTRODUCTION TO SOLID MODELING 393

Introduction 393
Starting 394
3D Coordinate Systems 394
Setting the Viewpoint 394
User Coordinate Systems 397
The UCS Icon 397
Showing the Solids Toolbar 398
Creating an Object 399
Creating Multiple Viewports 400
Selecting the Active Viewport 402
Changing the Viewpoint 404
Using the View Toolbar 404
Viewports Using Different UCSs 407
Setting Up the Right-Side View 408
Creating Cylinders 410
Setting Isolines 411
Building Complex Solid Models 412
Creating Wedges 413
Creating Cones 415
Creating User Coordinate Systems 416
Plotting Solid Models from Paper Space 418
Saving Your Multiview Setup as a Template 419
Creating Solid Models with Extrude and Revolve 420
Region Modeling 422
Extruding a Shape 423
Creating Solid Models by Revolution 424
Aligning the Views 425
Using the Boolean Operator Intersection 427
Creating Surface Models 432
Creating a Ruled Surface 434
Controlling Mesh Density 434
Creating an Edge Surface 436
Creating 3D Mesh 436
Key Terms & Commands 438
Exercises 438

TUTORIAL 12
CHANGING AND PLOTTING SOLID MODELS 443

Introduction 443
Starting 443
Using Fillet on Solids 444
Using Chamfer on Solids 444
Using Slice 445
Creating the Hole 451
Plotting with Hidden Lines 453
Controlling the Generated Layers 454
Setting the Linetypes and Colors for Generated Layers 455
Eliminating Unnecessary Hidden Lines 456
Adding the Centerlines 458
Using Freeze/Thaw in Current Viewport 459
Plotting 462
Key Terms & Commands 462
Exercises 463

TUTORIAL 13
CREATING ASSEMBLY DRAWINGS FROM SOLID MODELS 465

Introduction 465
Attaching Solid Models 465
Starting 466
Using External References 466
Layers and External References 468
Inserting the Solid Part Drawings 469
Checking for Interference 472
Determining Mass Properties 473
Creating an Exploded Isometric View 473
Creating a Dynamic Block for the Ball Tags 475
Dynamic Blocks 475
Defining Attributes 478
Attribute Modes 478
Attribute Tag 479
Attribute Prompt 479
Default Attribute Value 479
Attribute Text Options 479
Attribute Insertion Point 479
Defining the Parameters 481
Defining the Actions 482
Inserting the Ball Tags 483

Changing an Attribute Value 486
Changing an Externally Referenced Drawing 486
Creating the Parts List 488
Extracting Attribute Information 489
Key Terms & Commands 492
Exercises 493

TUTORIAL 14
SOLID MODELING FOR SECTION AND AUXILIARY VIEWS 501
Introduction 501
Creating Sections from a Solid Model 501
Using Solview and Soldraw 502
Setup Profile 504
Using Section and Slice 505
Using Section 507
Controlling Layer Visibility 509
Using Slice 510
Using Hide 511
Creating an Auxiliary View of a 3D Solid Model 511
Rotating the View 515
3 Point UCS 515
Using Plan 516
Using 3D Dynamic View 517
Using Solview 519
Key Terms & Commands 521
Exercises 521

TUTORIAL 15
RENDERING 525
Introduction 525
Starting 525
The Render Dialog Box 527
Rendering Algorithms 527
Scene to Render 528
Background 528
Fog/Depth Cue 528
Query for Selections 528
Crop Window 528
Destination 528
Rendering Options 529
Help 530

Adding Lights 531
Choosing Materials 535
Color/Pattern 539
Ambient 540
Reflection 540
Roughness 540
Transparency 540
Refraction 540
Bump Map 540
Adjusting Mapping 541
Rendering to a File 545
Using the Sun Angle Calculator 546
Adding Backgrounds 548
Using Landscape Objects 549
Exporting AutoCAD Files 550
Drawing Web Format 551
Plotting Shaded Views 551
Key Terms & Commands 554
Exercises 554

AUTOCAD COMMAND SUMMARY 563
GLOSSARY 603
INDEX 615
ART CREDITS 643

Preface

The AutoCAD® program is the most widely used design and drafting software in the world. The AutoCAD® 2006 release provides you with the capability to create complex and accurate drawings. Its position as the industry standard makes it an essential tool for anyone preparing for a career in engineering, design, or technology.

Because it is the industry standard, the AutoCAD program is the ideal cornerstone for your design and drafting skill set. With knowledge of the AutoCAD commands and capabilities, you will find it easy to add any number of a wide range of applications to create a complete design environment suited to your needs.

This tutorial-based guide will guide you step by step in using the AutoCAD 2006 software running under a Windows® 2000, Windows NT®, or Windows XP® operating system. You will learn to create 2D and 3D models and the engineering drawings that describe them. Written for the novice user, this guide uses a proven tutorial approach that steps you through the creation of actual drawings and models. AutoCAD information is presented in a need-to-know fashion that makes it easy to remember. Tips and shortcuts are included where appropriate to help you become an efficient and proficient AutoCAD user. A Command Summary and Glossary at the end of the book make it easy to review what you've learned and to use the manual as a reference.

This manual may be used in conjunction with a basic engineering graphics course, in introductory engineering, introductory architecture and/or design courses, in a short course, or independently for self-study. Completing this entire set of tutorials provides a solid foundation and enables you to apply AutoCAD techniques in a professional setting to create standard template files; use blocks, attributes, Xrefs, tool palettes, and the DesignCenter™; manage dimension styles; print and plot standard drawing views; use sheet sets; generate and render 3D solid models; create an AutoCAD parts list; customize your AutoCAD toolbars; use geometric dimensioning and tolerancing symbols, and even publish your drawings on the World Wide Web.

Key Features

To facilitate your AutoCAD 2006 studies, this tutorial guide includes:

- Step-by-step tutorials written for the novice user
- A complete chapter (Chapter 1) on configuring the AutoCAD software for performance and use with these tutorials
- Organization that parallels an introductory engineering graphics course

- Tips offering suggestions and warnings as you progress through the tutorials
- Exercises at the end of each tutorial providing challenges to a range of abilities in mechanical, electrical, and civil engineering, as well as architecture
- Key Terms and Key Commands listed to recap important topics and commands learned in each tutorial

Overview

The tutorials proceed in a logical fashion to guide you from drawing basic shapes to building three-dimensional models. Later tutorials introduce techniques for automatically generating 2D drawing views from your solid models and advanced dimensioning methods such as including geometric dimensioning and tolerancing symbols. The final tutorial shows you how to create photo-realistic renderings from 3D models.

Chapter 1 helps you configure the AutoCAD environment for the step-by-step instructions in this guide. Chapter 2 takes you on a guided tour of the AutoCAD 2006 screen display, help facility, and keyboard/mouse usage conventions.

The 15 tutorials introduce AutoCAD 2006 commands and capabilities in the context of technical drawing.

- Tutorials 1 and 2 introduce basic AutoCAD drawing commands and build proficiency with the menus, toolbars, and drawing aids.
- Tutorials 3 and 4 introduce editing commands and drawing construction and provide instruction on plotting a model space drawing.
- Tutorial 5 focuses on good drawing management with template drawings, layers, and plotting using layouts, including using the Sheet Set Manager.
- Tutorial 6 is devoted to the tools for projecting orthographic views.
- Tutorial 7 introduces dimensioning and the use of dimension styles.
- Tutorial 8 is devoted to advanced topics in dimensioning and tolerancing, such as geometric dimensioning and tolerancing (GD&T). It may be skipped and completed later, if desired.
- Tutorial 9 introduces how to create hatched sections and auxiliary views using 2D orthographic projection techniques.
- Tutorial 10 shows how to use blocks and how to create custom tool palettes and toolbars, as well as how to use the DesignCenter.
- Tutorials 11, 12, and 13 teach 3D solid modeling of a single part, editing parts, and adding parts to an assembly, respectively. You also learn to use the AutoCAD software to check for interference between parts.
- Tutorial 14 shows how to create section and auxiliary views using 3D techniques.
- Tutorial 15 shows how to render and shade 3D models. This tutorial may be completed any time after Tutorial 11 and then used to render models created in the other tutorials.

The Glossary defines key terms used in the tutorials.

The Command Summary lists the key commands used in the tutorials, defines them, and recaps their toolbar icon, menu location, and keyboard equivalent.

The Index identifies topics and helps you locate them throughout the manual.

Visit the text's Web page—*www.prenhall.com/lockhart*—to download drawings and other tools useful with this book.

Online Instructor's Manual

To access supplementary materials online, instructors need to request an instructor access code. Go to *www.prenhall.com*, click the **Instructor Resource Center** link, and then click **Register Today** for an instructor access code. Within 48 hours after registering you will receive a confirming e-mail including an instructor access code. Once you have received your code, go the site and log on for full instructions on downloading the materials you wish to use.

Autodesk Learning License

Through a recent agreement with the AutoCAD publisher, Autodesk®, Prentice Hall now offers the option of purchasing *A Tutorial Guide to AutoCAD 2006* with either a 180-day or a 1-year student software license agreement. This provides adequate time for a student to complete all the activities in this book. The software is functionally identical to the professional license, but is intended **for student or faculty personal use only**. It is not for professional use. For more information about this book and the Autodesk Learning License, contact your local Pearson Prentice Hall sales representative, or contact our National Marketing Manager, Jimmy Stephens at 1 (800) 228-7854 x3725 or at *Jimmy_Stephens@prenhall.com*. For the name and number of your sales rep, please contact Prentice Hall Faculty Services at 1 (800) 526-0485.

Other texts by Shawna Lockhart available from Prentice Hall:

Engineering Design Communication
—by Lockhart/Johnson

Modern Graphics Communication
—by Giesecke/Mitchell/Spencer/Hill/Dygdon/Novak/Lockhart

A Tutorial Guide to Mechanical Desktop®
—by Lockhart/Johnson

For examination copies, contact your local PH representative, or send an e-mail request to *EnGraphics@prenhall.com.*

Acknowledgments

I wish to thank the individuals who contributed to the conceptualization and implementation of these tutorials. Thanks to my many teaching colleagues who responded to inquiries and helped to shape the tutorials in this book. I cannot list all of the individuals who have made contributions of their encouragement, assistance, and ideas for this text, but I am grateful to the people listed below for their help in this and previous editions.

Special thanks go to Christopher R. Bowman, Marc Finseth, Amy E. Monte, *Michigan Technological State University*, Mary Tolle, *South Dakota State University*, Joseph A. Gosselin, *Central Connecticut State University*, S. Kant Vajpayee, *University of Southern Mississippi*, James G. Raschka, Reuben Aronovitz, John Matson,

Craig L. Miller, Michael H. Gregg, Steve Bachman, Tom Bryson, Karen Coen-Brown, Mary Ann Koen, D. Krall, Kim Manner, John Walker, Danny Hubbard, Edward C. Livingston; Denis Cadu and the many fine people at Autodesk; to Shannon Kyles and James Bethune, authors of previous editions of tutorial guides from which some material was adapted for this manual; and to James Earle, for permission to reprint several exercises from his text.

Editing, testing, and producing step-by-step tutorials requires expert publishing assistance and I would be remiss if I did not thank those who worked to make this book complete, technically accurate, and pleasing to look at, especially Cindy Johnson, Vickie Piercey, Kim Weaver, Katie Habib, Debbie Yarnell, Judith Casillo, Louise Sette, and Deidra Schwartz, for their enthusiasm, efficiency, and professionalism throughout this project.

Finally, I would like to once again thank all of the great students I have had the pleasure to teach at Montana State University and from whom I am still learning.

SHAWNA LOCKHART

Chapter

1 Preparing for the Tutorials

Objectives

This chapter describes how to prepare your computer system and the AutoCAD 2006 software for use with the tutorials in this manual. As you read this chapter, you will

1. Understand how to use a mouse during the completion of these tutorials.
2. Recognize the typographical conventions used in this book.
3. Create a separate shortcut for use with these tutorials.
4. Create and prepare data file and working directories.
5. Configure your copy of the AutoCAD software for use with these tutorials.

Introduction to the Tutorials

The tutorials in this guide will teach you to use the AutoCAD® 2006 software through a series of step-by-step exercises. You will learn its fundamental operating procedures and how to use drawing tools. As you progress through the tutorials, you will employ some more advanced features of the software to create, dimension, shade, and print drawings.

The tutorials in this guide are based on the assumption that you are using the software's default settings. If your system has been customized for other uses, some of the settings may not match those used in the step-by-step instruction in the tutorials. Please check your system against the configuration in this chapter so that you can work through the tutorials as instructed.

If you are using the AutoCAD software on a network at your school, ask your professor or system administrator about how the software is configured. You should not try to reconfigure the software unless instructed to do so by network personnel. Read about mouse techniques, typographical conventions, and end-of-tutorial exercises in this chapter, and then go on to Chapter 2, AutoCAD Basics.

To complete these tutorials, your system must be running Microsoft Windows 2000, NT 4.0, or Windows XP.

Basic Mouse Techniques

Tip

Your mouse may have more than one button. To click (or pick) in Windows and in the AutoCAD software, use the left mouse button. This button is also referred to as the pick button. To enter or return, click the right mouse button, also referred to as the return button. The middle or scroll button on your mouse is typically set to pan or zoom.

Tip

You can use the Mouse Properties selection in the Windows control panel to switch your mouse to a left-handed configuration. This will switch your pick button to the right button on the mouse. The left mouse button will then act as the enter or return button.

The tutorials in this guide are based on the assumption that you will be using a mouse or pointing device. The following terms will be used to streamline the instructions for use of the mouse.

Term	Meaning
Pick or Click	To press quickly and then release the left mouse button
Right-click	To quickly press and release the right mouse button
Double-click	To click the left mouse button twice in rapid succession
Drag	To press and hold down the left mouse button while you move the mouse
Point	To move the mouse until the mouse pointer on the screen is positioned over the item you want

Recognizing Typographical Conventions

When you work with the AutoCAD software, you'll use your keyboard and your pointing device to input information. As you read this book, you'll encounter special type styles that will help you determine the commands required and the information you must input.

Tip

The right button on your mouse and the spacebar often perform the same function as the ↵ key. Pressing the right mouse button can also pop up a context menu from which you can pick Enter.

Special symbols illustrate certain computer keys. For example, the Enter or Return key is represented by the symbol ↵.

The guide also employs special typefaces when it presents instructions for performing computer operations. Instructions are set off from the main text to indicate a series of actions or the AutoCAD command prompts. Boldface type (often in all capital letters) is used for the letters and numbers to be input by you. Bold italic type indicates actions you are to take. For example,

Command: **LINE**

instructs you to type "Line" to invoke the Line command.

From point: **pick point A**

instructs you to select point A on your screen by picking it with the mouse. The words "Command" and "From point" represent the AutoCAD command prompts that you would see on your screen. The command prompt line is always in regular type followed by a colon (:).

Instruction words, such as "pick," "type," "select," and "press," also appear as prompts. For example, "type" instructs you to strike or press several keys in sequence. For the following instruction,

Type: **4,4**

you would type 4,4 in that order on your keyboard. Remember to type exactly what you see, including spaces, if any.

"Pick" tells you to pick an object or an icon or to choose commands from the menu. For example,

Pick: **Line icon**

instructs you to use your pointing device to select the Line icon from the toolbar on your screen. To select an icon, move the pointer until the cursor is over the icon and press the pick button.

"Press" means to strike a key once. For example,

Press: ↵

means strike the Enter or Return key once. Sometimes "press" is followed by two keys, such as

Press: Ctrl-F1

In this case, press and hold down the first key, press the second key once and release it, and then release the first key.

Default values that are displayed as part of a command or prompt are represented in angle brackets: < >. For example,

Specify inside diameter of donut <0.5000>:

is the command prompt when the Donut command has a default value of 0.5 for the inside diameter.

New terms are in italics in the text when they are introduced and are defined in the Glossary at the end of the book.

End-of-Tutorial Exercises

Exercises at the end of the tutorials provide practice for you to apply what you have learned during the tutorial. To become proficient at using the AutoCAD software, it is important to gain independent practice creating drawings such as those in the exercises.

Configuring Windows for the Tutorials

The AutoCAD 2006 software takes advantage of common Windows file operations and allows you to run the AutoCAD software while running other applications.

Windows 2000/NT/XP

The AutoCAD 2006 software is designed to take full advantage of today's computers. It can be installed with Windows 2000, NT 4.0, or XP. The figures in this guide were captured in Windows XP using the XP theme. The screens in Windows NT 4.0 or Windows 2000 are similar to the screens that you will see in this guide. The steps are described in sufficient detail that you should be able to follow them on your own regardless of your operating system.

Screen Resolution

You can change your screen resolution from the Windows Control Panel. You can skip this step if you have already set up your system and do not need to make any changes.

Pick: **Start, Settings, Control Panel**
Double-click: **Display** (from the Control Panel)
Pick: **Settings** (in the dialog box that appears)

The Display Properties dialog box appears on your screen, as shown in Figure C1.1. You can change the color quality using the pull-down list of options.

Tip

Using a resolution higher than 1024 × 768 can allow more toolbars and drawing area to fit on your screen. You may want to use a higher resolution; if so, your AutoCAD screen will not match the book exactly.

Set your display to 256 Color palette (or higher).

You will very likely be able to select a higher color depth such as 16-bit or 32-bit color. You can change the screen resolution using the slider bar.

Select a resolution of 1024 × 768 pixels.

If your monitor is not capable of this resolution, use the closest resolution available to you. Be sure to test the setting to make sure it works. Not all monitors and video cards are capable of every resolution setting displayed in the Settings tab of the Display Properties dialog box. (Refer to your system documentation if you have trouble with your screen resolution settings.) If you have a monitor capable of higher resolution and want to use a higher setting, your screens will look slightly different from the ones captured for this book, but it should not affect the overall operation of the commands as described in the tutorials.

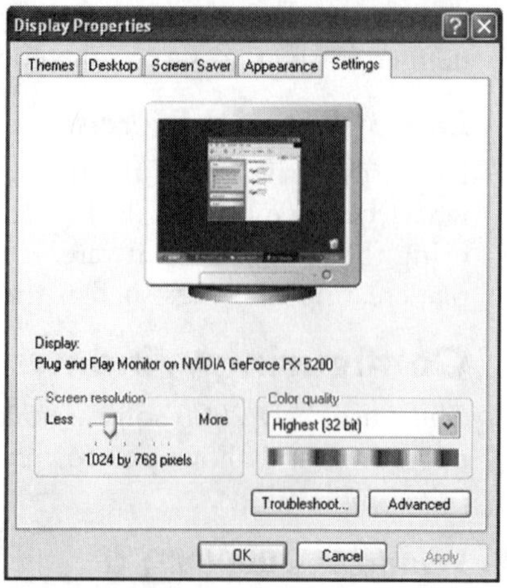

Figure C1.1

Pick: **OK** (to exit the Display Properties dialog box)

You may be prompted to restart Windows so that the change takes effect. If so, restart Windows now.

Backing Up AutoCAD Defaults

Before you begin to configure and customize the AutoCAD software for the purposes of these tutorials, you will want to back up your configuration and menu files to save the previous configuration. You can do this by copying the customizable files listed below to a floppy disk or to a safe location on your hard disk or a remote network drive where they will not be overwritten.

To locate these files, you must determine where they are stored on your computer. To do so,

Start the AutoCAD software.

Pick: **Tools, Options**

Pick: **the Files tab**

Expand the list by picking on the plus signs to see paths, settings, and file locations.

After you have located the files, return to Windows to copy them as you would any file.

If you want to restore the AutoCAD software defaults, you can copy them back to the directories where you found them or your working directory and overwrite the files there. If you are on a networked system, contact your network administrator about backing up these files.

Customizable Support Files

File	Description
**.chm*	AutoCAD Help files.
**.cif*	An *.xml* file that defines most user interface elements. The file *acad.cui* is automatically loaded when you start the AutoCAD program. This file type replaces the *.mnu*, *.mns*, and *.mnc* menu file types used in previous versions.
acad2006.cfg	AutoCAD device configuration file.
**.cus*	Custom dictionary files.
**.dcl*	AutoCAD Dialog Control Language (DCL) descriptions of dialog boxes.
acad.dcl	Describes the AutoCAD software standard dialog boxes.
**.lin*	AutoCAD linetype definition files.
acad.lin	The standard AutoCAD linetype library file.
**.lsp*	AutoLISP® program files.
acad.lsp	A user-defined AutoLISP routine that loads each time you start a drawing.
**.mln*	A multiline library file.
**.mnl*	AutoLISP routines used by AutoCAD menus. A *.mnl* file must have the same filename as the *.mnu* file it supports.
acad.mnl	AutoLISP routines used by the standard AutoCAD menu.
**.mnr*	AutoCAD menu resource files. Contain the bit maps used by AutoCAD menus.
**.pat*	AutoCAD hatch pattern definition files.
acad.pat	The standard AutoCAD hatch pattern library file.
**.pc3*	AutoCAD plot configuration parameters files. Each *.pc3* file stores configuration information for a specific plotter.
acad.pgp	The AutoCAD program parameters file. Contains definitions for external commands and command aliases.
acad.fmp	The AutoCAD Font Map file.
acad.psf	AutoCAD PostScript Support file; the master support file for the PSOUT and PSFILL commands.
acad.rx	Lists ARX applications that load when you start the AutoCAD software.
**.scr*	AutoCAD script files. A script file contains a set of AutoCAD commands processed as a batch.
**.shp*	AutoCAD shape/font definition files. Compiled shape/font files have the extension *.shx*.
acad.unt	AutoCAD unit definition file. Contains data that lets you convert from one set of units to another.

Creating a Working Directory

To make saving and opening files easier as you complete the tutorials, you will create and specify a new working directory for the AutoCAD software. The working directory is the default directory used to open and save files. By setting a working directory, you will not have to search through the computer's directories every time you are asked to save a file.

This is a good practice in general for organizing your files. You should not save your drawing files and other work files in the same directory as the AutoCAD software because doing so makes it likely that they will be overwritten or lost when you install software upgrades. It is also easier to organize and back up your project files and drawings if they are in a separate directory. Making subdirectories within this directory for different projects will organize your drawings even further.

You will create a new shortcut for launching the AutoCAD 2006 software that will use *c:\work* as the starting directory.

Before continuing, use your Windows Explorer to create a new directory, *c:\work.*

When you are finished, return to the Windows desktop.

Creating Multiple Shortcuts

In Windows, you will start the AutoCAD software from an icon on your desktop. Items on the desktop are shortcuts to the executable file in the AutoCAD software directory. You can create several shortcuts to the same file, each with different properties. If your network administrator has already set up the software, you may be able to skip these steps.

Tip

You can add a new shortcut to your Start menu by using the Settings option on the Start menu and choosing Taskbar & Start Menu.

Right-click on a blank area on your Windows desktop.
Pick: **New, Shortcut**

The Create Shortcut wizard appears on your screen similar to Figure C1.2.

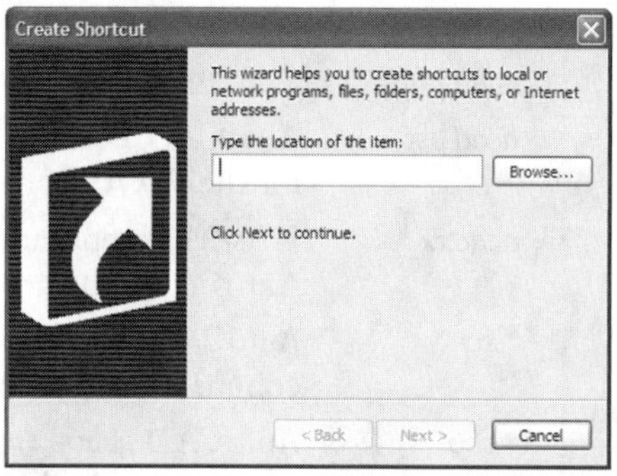

Figure C1.2

Pick: **Browse**

Locate the AutoCAD software directory in the list of directories in the dialog box that appears similar to Figure C1.3. The AutoCAD 2006 directory is probably inside the Program Files directory on your system, as this is the default installation.

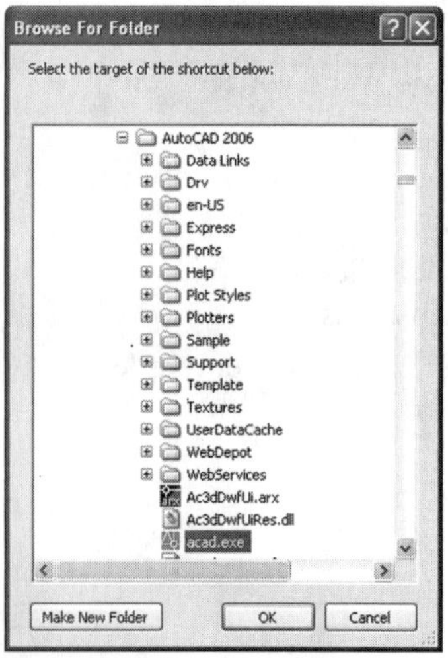

Figure C1.3

Pick: **to highlight *acad.exe***
Pick: **OK**
Pick: **Next**
Name the shortcut "**AutoCAD 2006 Tutorial**" on your own.

Tip

Depending on your operating system you may see a shortcut named "Copy of Shortcut to acad.exe."

Windows allows you to rename a file by picking on its name with the right mouse button and selecting Rename from the list in the resulting pop-up menu. (You can also rename the file by picking it twice, but NOT double-clicking. Pick on the shortcut once and then after a few seconds pick on it again; a cursor will start blinking to the right of the name allowing you to change it.)

You will now set *c:\work* as your working directory.

Setting the Working Directory

The AutoCAD session you start with this shortcut will save your drawings to *c:\work* by default if you set it as your working directory.

To set *c:\work* as your working directory, you will modify the settings stored with the new AutoCAD 2006 Tutorial shortcut.

Right-click: **the new AutoCAD 2006 Tutorial shortcut**
Pick: **Properties** (from the pull-down menu)
Pick: **the Shortcut tab at the top of the Properties dialog box**
Pick: **the text box labeled Start in and highlight the existing text**
Type: ***C:\WORK***

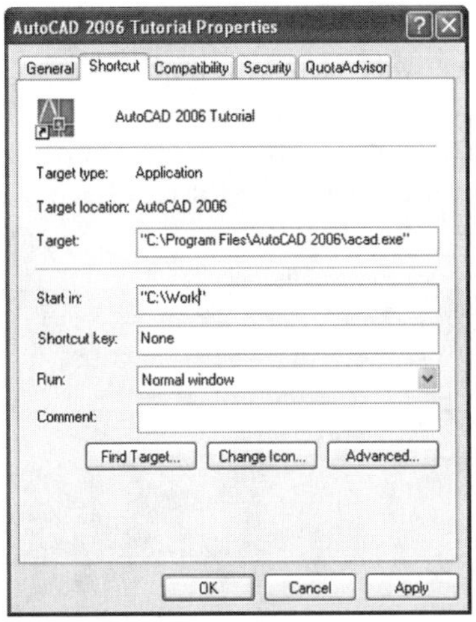

Figure C1.4

Your dialog box should look like Figure C1.4. If you have created your work directory on another drive, substitute the correct drive letter.

Pick: **OK** (to exit the Properties dialog box)

When you start the AutoCAD software from this shortcut, the drawings you save will be saved to *c:\work*. The settings necessary for running the AutoCAD software will not be affected by the change in the working directory. Those drive paths are laid out within the AutoCAD software's Preferences.

Installing Data Files for the Tutorials

The next step is to create a directory for the data files used in the tutorials and install them. Throughout the tutorials, you will be instructed to work with files already prepared for you. You will not be able to complete the tutorials without these files. You can download these files with a Web browser such as Netscape Navigator or Internet Explorer. Simply go to *http://www.prenhall.com/lockhart*, choose the section of the site dedicated to this book, and then follow instructions to download the files.

After you have retrieved the files, use Windows to create a new directory, *c:\datafile2006*. Copy *datafile2006.zip* into the directory and use a utility such as WinZip to decompress it. When the file is decompressed, you will see an assortment of files in the directory, most of which have the *.dwg* extension.

Now you are ready to customize your AutoCAD menus.

Warning

If you are working on a networked system or on a workstation in a classroom or lab, your system has already been configured for you. Please skip to Chapter 2, AutoCAD Basics.

Configuring AutoCAD Software for the Tutorials

The tutorials in this guide are based on the assumption that you are using the AutoCAD software's default settings. If your system has been customized for other uses, some of the settings may not match those in the step-by-step instructions in the tutorials. You will now set up your system so that you can work through the tutorials as instructed.

To start the AutoCAD software,

Pick: **AutoCAD 2006 Tutorial** shortcut from the Windows desktop

Tip

If you have configured your copy of the AutoCAD 2006 software to use settings other than the defaults, you may see a start up dialog box. If so, close the start up window using the Windows close button that looks like an X in the upper right corner.

The AutoCAD graphics window appears, as shown in Figure C1.5, with the following menus: File, Edit, View, Insert, Format, Tools, Draw, Dimension, Modify, Express (optional, see Tip), Window, and Help. The following toolbars are also showing: Draw and Modify (docked on the left and right side of the screen, respectively) and Layers, Properties, Standard, and Styles (docked on the upper part of the screen). The Sheet Set Manager and Tool Palettes are also shown by default when the AutoCAD software is first installed. Do not be concerned if you have them turned off; you will not use them for now.

Tip

When you install the AutoCAD software, you have the option to install the Express tools. These are unsupported productivity tools that you may find useful. They are not discussed in this guide.

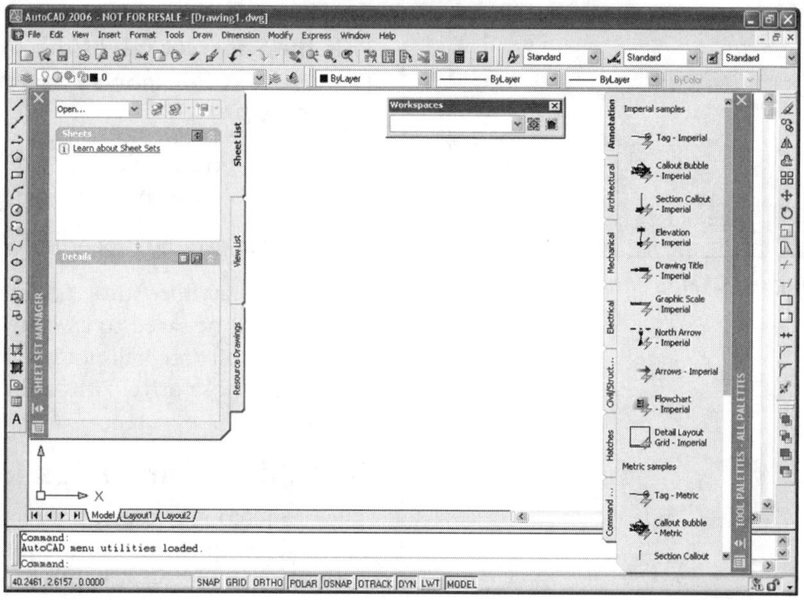

Figure C1.5

You will use the Tools menu to open the Options dialog box.

Pick: **Tools, Options**

The Options dialog box appears on your screen, as shown in Figure C1.6.

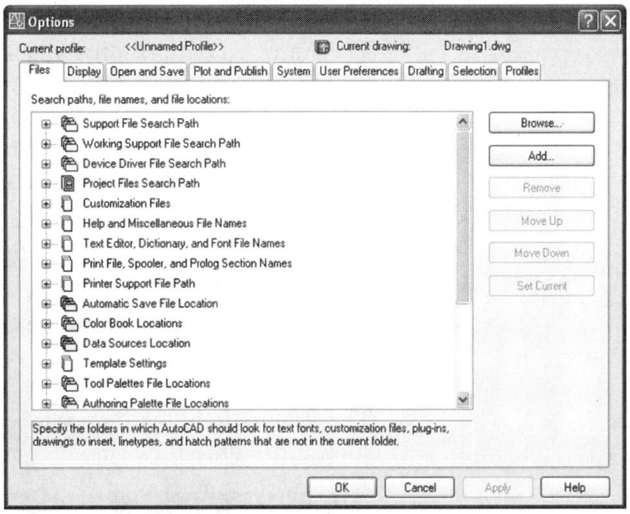

Figure C1.6

The tabs across the top represent "index cards" titled Files, Display, Open and Save, Plot and Publish, System, User Preferences, Drafting, Selection, and Profiles. The Options dialog box uses the Windows interface to set up the AutoCAD software's search paths, performance, display, pointer, and printer configurations, and various general items. When you make changes to the Options dialog box and pick Apply, the AutoCAD software will update the system registry.

To change from one card to the next, you will pick on the name on the tab. The card that you select will then appear on top of the stack.

The Files card shows the search paths that the AutoCAD software follows during particular operations. They are what the software uses to find the configuration, menu, and toolbar files. The Display card allows for changes to the display, including fonts and colors. You can use the Crosshair size slider to adjust the size of the cursor relative to the screen. The card labeled Open and Save allows you to change the default type of file created when you save, to set an automatic save time, and to control how externally referenced files are handled. The Plot and Publish card allows you to change the current printer and modify its settings. The System card allows you to select which video display driver is used and to select the pointing device, as well as other settings. The User Preferences tab lets you customize how objects are sorted and how selections are prioritized by the software, as well as how undefined units are handled. The Drafting tab lets you set snap and tracking features, and size the apertures and markers for these. You can use the Selection tab to control how objects are selected to be acted on by software commands.

Warning

Changes to the AutoCAD software's configuration can affect its performance greatly. If you are working on a networked system, you must check with the network administrator before creating your own profile. Whatever changes you make must be made only to your user Profile setting.

Do not change any of the settings in these cards at this time.

The Profiles card changes the AutoCAD environment to user-specified customizations. You will use this card to create your own Profile with the configuration settings used in this guide.

User Profiles

The AutoCAD 2006 software allows you to save multiple configuration profiles, making it possible to configure the software for different uses and peripherals. If you are working on a shared machine, you can create a special profile to use for these tutorials so that another user doesn't change your settings and defaults between sessions.

If you're working on a networked computer, your professor or system administrator has probably configured the system already. Ask which profile you should use.

To create a user-defined profile or configuration, first

Pick: **Profiles tab**

The Profiles index card appears on top of the other index cards, as shown in Figure C1.7.

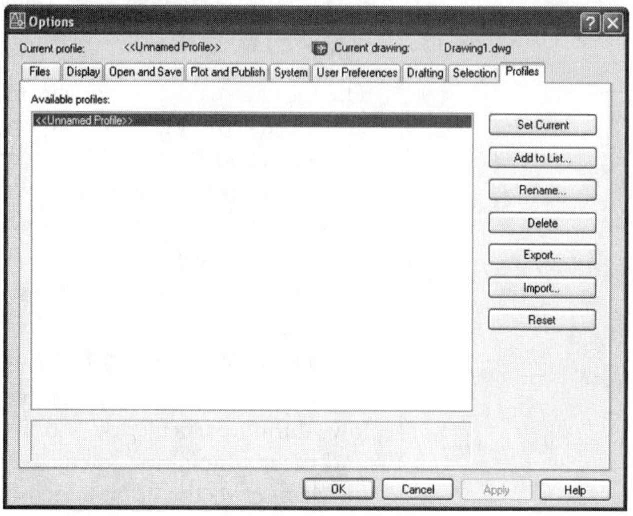

Figure C1.7

As you can see, the current profile is <Unnamed Profile>. Any changes made to the other cards will be stored in this Profile because it is selected as current. You will make a new profile for the tutorials, set it as current, and then make changes to the other cards.

Pick: **Add to List**

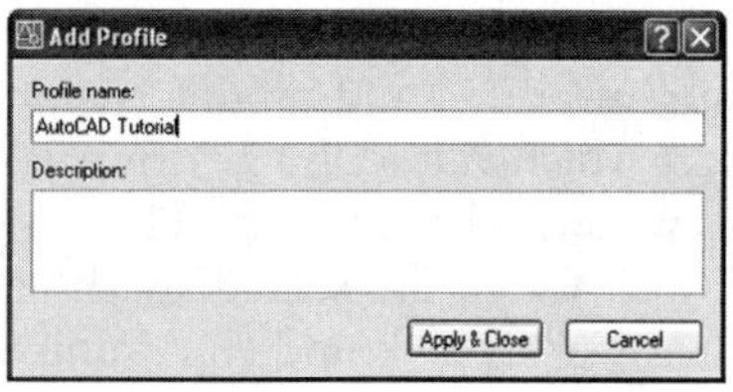

Figure C1.8

The Add Profile dialog box appears where you will type the name of your new Profile. A description is optional, but not necessary.

Type: **AUTOCAD TUTORIALS** (similar to Figure C1.8)

Pick: **Apply & Close**

You will see "AutoCAD Tutorials" appear in the list of profiles.

Pick: **to highlight the new profile named AutoCAD Tutorials**

Pick: **Set Current**

The software in the background should not change because the configuration settings for this Profile are the same as for the Unnamed Profile.

Changing the Configuration

Now you will make changes to the other cards, as necessary, to follow the tutorials in this guide.

Pick: **Display**

The Display card should appear. On your own, be sure that the settings are the same as those shown in Figure C1.9.

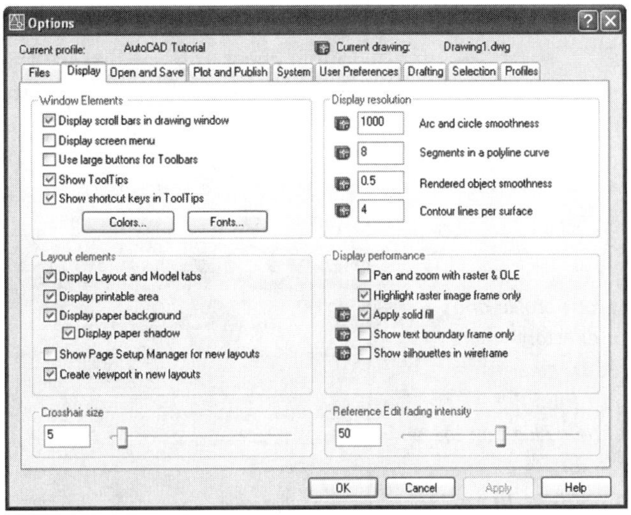

Figure C1.9

The background screen color for the tutorials is set to white. However, you do not have to change your background color to white. To see the available options, you can choose the Colors button.

When you have finished, choose the Plot and Publish tab.

Pick: **Plot and Publish**

The Plot and Publish card should appear, as shown in Figure C1.10.

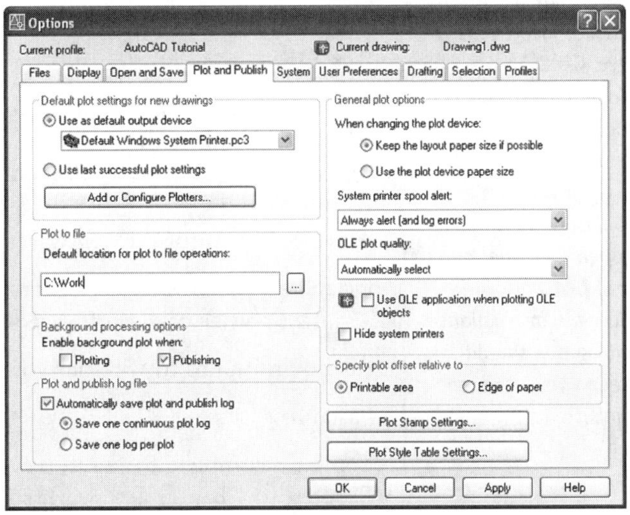

Figure C1.10

If you did not select a printer when you installed the AutoCAD software, the simplest way to print your drawings is to pick Add or Configure Plotters and then use the Add a Plotter Wizard to select the System Printer. Doing so allows you to use any printer that you have already set up to work with Windows. If you want to choose one of the other plotter options, refer to your documentation.

When you have finished, choose the System card.

Pick: **System**

Double check this card to see that you are using an appropriate pointing device. The default digitizer is the Current System Pointing Device (your mouse). The AutoCAD software can also support a tablet. To configure for a tablet, refer to your tablet documentation. On your own, be sure that the settings on your computer are similar to those shown in Figure C1.11.

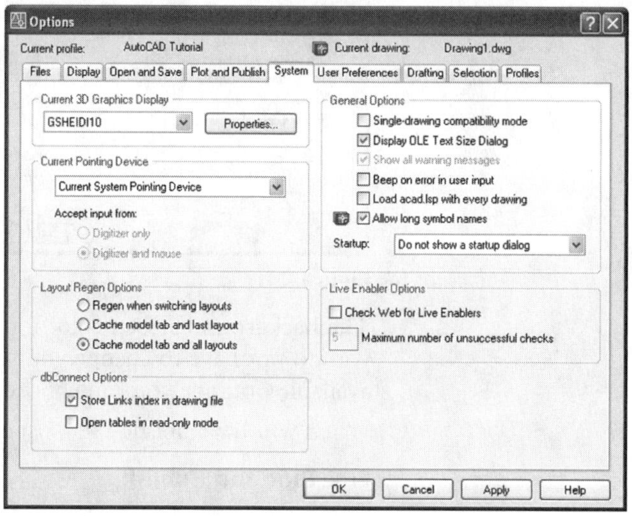

Figure C1.11

Tip

You can also export your profile and save it in a separate directory where it will not be changed by other users. To do this, pick Export from the Profiles tab and use the dialog box to save the file ending in .arg to a secure folder. When you need to restore it, pick Import from the Profiles tab and select your file ending in .arg to import.

Tip

The AutoCAD system variables control whether dialog boxes appear when certain commands are issued. FILEDIA controls the display of dialog boxes for file operations, such as New, Open, and Save. CMDDIA controls whether dialog boxes are displayed for some commands. Occasionally these variables can become set incorrectly. If you don't see dialog boxes appearing when you use commands or open files, check to see that FILEDIA and CMDDIA are set to 1. As you follow the instructions in the tutorials, a dialog box should appear on your screen every time one is used in the tutorials.

To accept the changes that you have just made (if any),

Pick: **OK**

The software screen appears again, with no significant changes. Now whenever you launch the AutoCAD software, you can go to the Options dialog box and select the AutoCAD Tutorials Profile to use with this guide.

To close the AutoCAD software,

Pick: **the Windows close button** (which appears like an X in the upper right corner of the software screen)

At the prompt as to whether you wish to save the drawing file.

Pick: **No**

You have completed the setup necessary to do the tutorials in this guide. Proceed to Chapter 2 to learn some basic operations.

Chapter

2 AutoCAD® Basics

Objectives

When you have completed this chapter, you will be able to

1. Minimize your drawing session and switch between other Windows applications.
2. Start a new drawing.
3. Recognize icons, menus, and commands.
4. Use the mouse to pick commands, menu options, and objects.
5. Work with a dialog box.
6. Access on-line help.
7. Save a drawing file.
8. Exit from the graphics window and return to the Windows operating system.

Tip

The Sheet Set Manager, Workspaces toolbar, and Tool Palettes may have already been turned off on your system. If this is the case, leave them off as you will not need them for this tutorial.

Warning

If you are working on a network, ask your technical support person about the software configuration. Changes from the standard configuration might have been made; for example, the program might be under a different directory name or require a special command or password to launch.

Introduction

In this chapter, you will learn the basics of the AutoCAD software's screen display, menus, and on-line help. The chapter also describes the type of instructions you'll encounter in the tutorials.

The tutorials in this manual are based on the assumption that you are using the standard configuration with the menus described in Chapter 1, Preparing for the Tutorials.

Starting the AutoCAD 2006 Software

Load the AutoCAD 2006 software as you did in Chapter 1.

The graphics window is displayed on your screen, as shown in Figure C2.1.

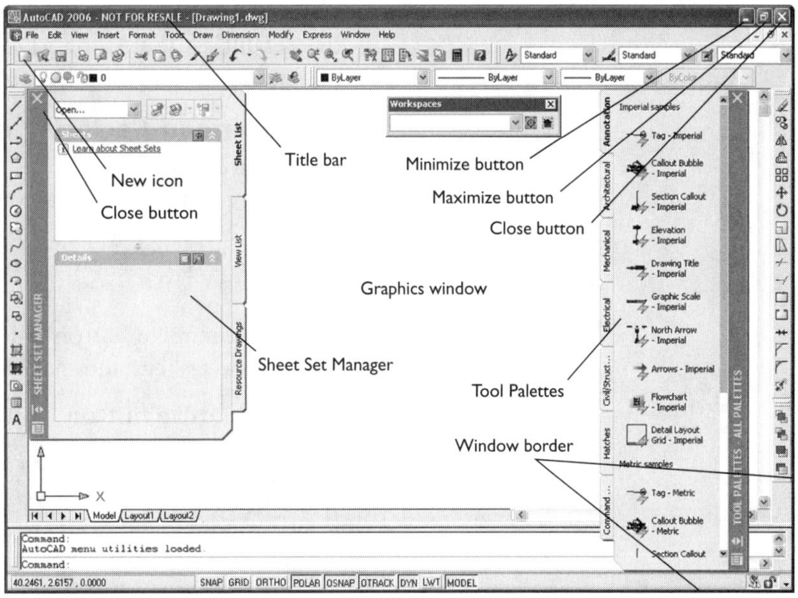

Figure C2.1

Microsoft Windows Conventions

The AutoCAD 2006 software uses many of the same conventions as other applications that run in Windows. This section will identify some of the techniques that you will be using to complete the tutorials in this manual.

The tutorials are based on the assumption that you will be using a mouse or pointing device to work with the AutoCAD 2006 software. If you are unfamiliar with mouse operations, refer to Chapter 1 or your on-line Microsoft Windows tutorial for basic mouse techniques.

Navigating in Windows

Using a mouse is usually easier than using the keyboard, although a combination of using the mouse and keyboard shortcuts is the most efficient way to navigate. For information on keyboard shortcuts in Windows, see your on-line Microsoft Windows tutorial.

Basic Elements of the AutoCAD Graphics Window

The AutoCAD graphics window is the main workspace. It has elements that are common to all applications written for the Windows environment. These elements are labeled in Figure C2.1 and described as follows.

- The close button is in the upper right corner of each window. Picking this button closes the window.
- The title bar shows the name of the application (in this case, AutoCAD 2006) followed by the document name (in this case, Drawing1).
- The window border is the outside edge of a window. You can change the window size by moving the cursor over the border until it becomes a double-ended arrow. Holding the mouse button down while you move the mouse (dragging) resizes the window.
- The maximize and minimize buttons are in the upper right corner of the window. Clicking the maximize button with the mouse enlarges the active window so that it fills the entire screen; this condition is the default for the AutoCAD software. You will learn to use the minimize button in the next section.

Minimizing and Restoring an Application

At times you may want to leave the AutoCAD software temporarily while you are in the middle of a work session, perhaps to access another application. Minimizing allows you to leave and return to the program more quickly than you could if you had to exit and start it all over again.

Picking the minimize button reduces the AutoCAD window to a title button on the taskbar and makes the Windows desktop accessible.

Pick: **the minimize button**

The AutoCAD software is reduced to a button at the bottom of your screen. (In a working AutoCAD session, you should always save your work before minimizing the program.)

The AutoCAD software is still running in the background, but other applications are accessible to you. When you are ready to return, pick the minimized AutoCAD 2006 button.

Pick: **the minimized AutoCAD 2006 button**

The AutoCAD graphics window returns to your screen.

Pick: **the Tool Palettes, Workspaces toolbar, and Sheet Set Manager's close buttons**

The Tool Palettes, Workspaces toolbar, and Sheet Set Manager windows are removed from your screen.

Microsoft Windows Multitasking Options

Microsoft Windows allows you to have several applications running and to switch between them. This feature is called multitasking. You will use multitasking in some of the tutorials in this manual to access your spreadsheet or word-processing application while you are still running the AutoCAD program. To switch between active applications, you press [Alt]-[Tab]. You will minimize the AutoCAD window and open another application to see how this works.

Pick: **the minimize button**

Pick: **to launch a different application from the Windows Start menu**

Press: [Alt]-[Tab] twice

A small window appears on your screen with the name of an application in it each time you press [Alt]-[Tab]. (Your AutoCAD drawing session should be on your screen. If it is not, continue pressing [Alt]-[Tab] until it appears.)

Press: [Alt]-[Tab]

You should have returned to your other application. (If not, continue pressing [Alt]-[Tab] until you do.)

Quit the other application now.

You will return to your AutoCAD drawing session automatically if it was the last application you were in. (If you do not see it on your screen, press [Alt]-[Tab] until you return to your AutoCAD session.)

AutoCAD Pointing Techniques

A drawing is made up of separate elements, called objects, that consist of lines, arcs, circles, text, and other elements that you access and draw by using AutoCAD commands and menu options.

The pointing device (usually a mouse) is the most common means of picking commands and menu options, selecting objects, or locating points in the AutoCAD software.

Picking Commands and Menu Options

The tutorials in this manual assume that you will be using a mouse or pointing device. The left mouse button is referred to as the pick button. The AutoCAD menus let you enter a command simply by pointing to the command and pressing the pick button to choose it. In this way you are instructed to "pick" specific commands. Recall that the right mouse button is referred to as the return button; it duplicates the action of the [↵] key when you are selecting objects or repeating commands.

Entering Points

You can specify points in a drawing either by typing in the coordinates from the keyboard or by using your mouse to locate the desired points in the graphics window.

When you move the mouse around on the mouse pad or table surface, "crosshairs" (the small intersecting vertical and horizontal lines on the screen) follow the motion of the mouse. These crosshairs form the

AutoCAD cursor in the graphics window. When you are selecting points during the execution of some commands, the location of the intersection of the crosshairs will be the selected point when you press the pick button. This is how you pick a point. In some AutoCAD modes the crosshairs change to arrows or boxes with target areas during the execution of certain commands. You will learn about these modes in the tuto-rials. The cursor on the screen always echoes the motion of the mouse.

Dragging

Many AutoCAD commands permit dynamic specification, or dragging, of an image of the object on the screen. You can use your mouse to move an object, rotate it, or scale it graphically. You will learn about drag mode in Tutorials 1 and 2. After you have selected an object in drag mode, the AutoCAD software draws tentative images as you move your pointing device. When you are satisfied with the appearance of the object, press the pick button to confirm it.

Object Selection

Many editing commands ask you to select one or more objects for processing. This collection of objects is called the *selection set*. You can use your mouse to add objects to the selection set or remove objects from it. You often use the cursor to point to objects in response to specific prompts. The objects highlight as you select them. You will learn about the various ways to select objects in the tutorials.

AutoCAD Commands and Menu Options

The AutoCAD software allows you several options for entering commands. You can select them from the toolbars, pick them from the pull-down menus, or type them at the command prompt. These elements are labeled in Figure C2.2. You can also use dynamic and pointer input, which you will learn about in Tutorial 1.

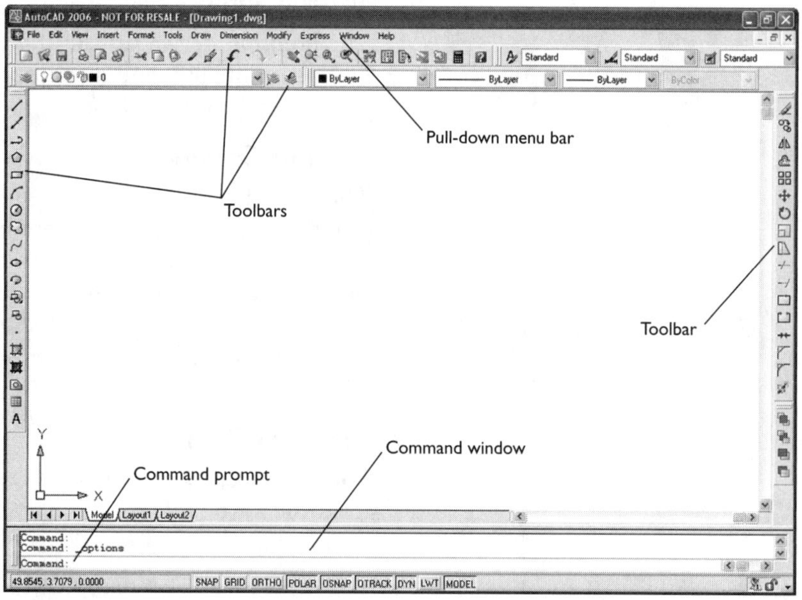

Figure C2.2

How you start a command may affect the order and wording of the prompts displayed on the screen. These differences offer you options for more efficient use of the software. Most AutoCAD commands can be typed at the command prompt, but picking them from a toolbar or a menu may be easier for you at first. For the purposes of the tutorials in this manual, you should pick or type commands exactly as instructed. The command selection location you should use will be indicated after the command. When you are supposed to type a command it will appear in all capital letters and bold (e.g., **NEW**). You must hit the ↵ key to activate the command. When you are supposed to invoke a command by picking its icon, the complete icon name, including the word icon, will appear in the instruction line (e.g., **New icon**). When you are supposed to invoke a command by selecting it from the pull-down menu, you will see the list of menu names at the instruction line (e.g., **File, New**).

As you progress through the tutorials, you will learn about the benefits of choosing commands in different ways in different situations. Remember, for the purposes of the tutorials in this manual, you should pick or type commands exactly as instructed.

Typing Commands

The command window at the bottom of your screen is very important for interacting with the AutoCAD software. All commands that you select by any means are echoed there, and additional prompts inform you what to do next. The prompt "Command:" in this window is a signal that the program is ready for a command. For commands with text output, you might need a larger command window display area. You can use the scroll arrows at the right of the command window to review the lines that may have been passed. You can also enlarge the window by positioning the cursor at the border of the window and dragging to enlarge the window so that it shows more lines.

Position the cursor at the top border of the command window.

Your cursor will change to a double-headed arrow.

Hold down the cursor and drag the mouse up to enlarge the command window to show more lines.

Your screen should look like Figure C2.3.

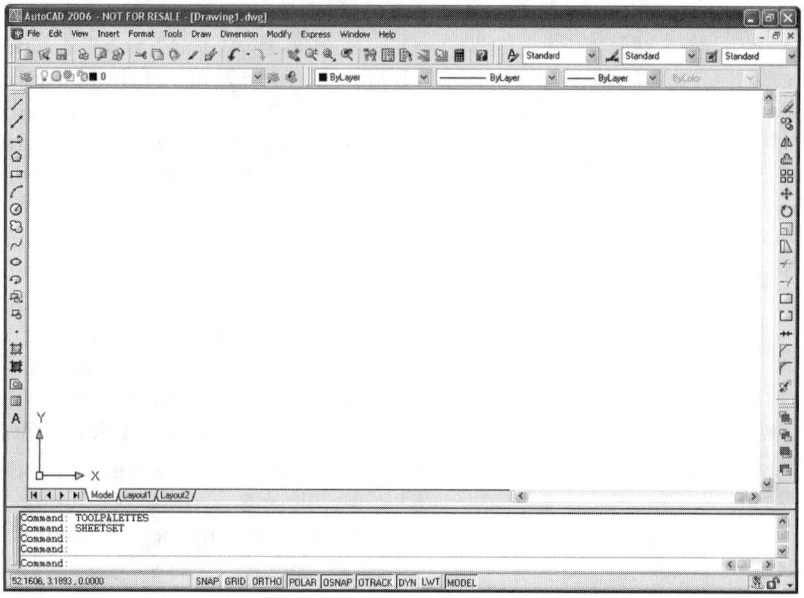

Figure C2.3

Return your command window to its original three-line display on your own, so that it will match the figures in the tutorials.

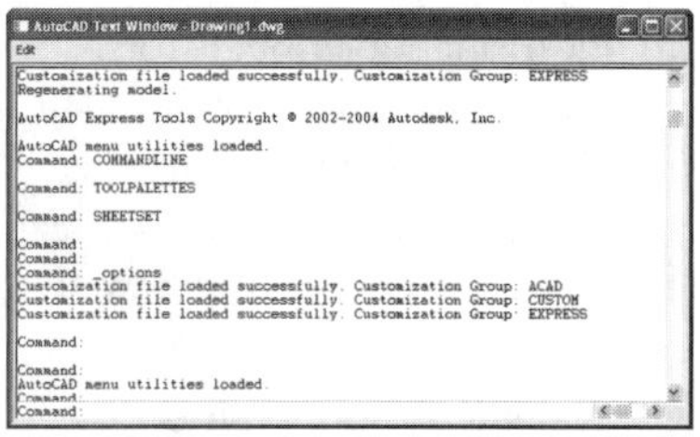

Figure C2.4

You can also review more lines of the command prompt by viewing an AutoCAD text window, as shown in Figure C2.4. You can use the [F2] key to toggle to a text window. Doing so will enlarge the command window and move it in front of your AutoCAD graphics window. To return to your graphics window, use the [F2] key again or close the text window with the Windows close button.

When you are supposed to type a command, it will appear in all capital letters (e.g., **LINE**). Watch the command line in the window as you type.

Command: **LINE** [Enter]

The Line command is activated when you press [Enter], and the Line command prompt "Specify first point:" is in the command window. This prompt tells you to enter the first point from which a line will be drawn. You will learn about the Line command in Tutorial 1. For now,

Press: [Esc] to cancel the command and return to the command prompt

Tip

You can also drag the command window to the top of the drawing area. This may make it easier for you to notice the command prompt.

Using the Toolbars

Toolbars contain icons that represent commands. The Standard, Layer, Properties, Styles, Draw, and Modify toolbars are visible by default, as shown in Figure C2.5. The Standard toolbar contains frequently used commands, such as New, Undo, and Zoom. The advantage of using icons to begin commands is that they are "heads-up"; that is, you do not need to look down at a digitizer to enter the command.

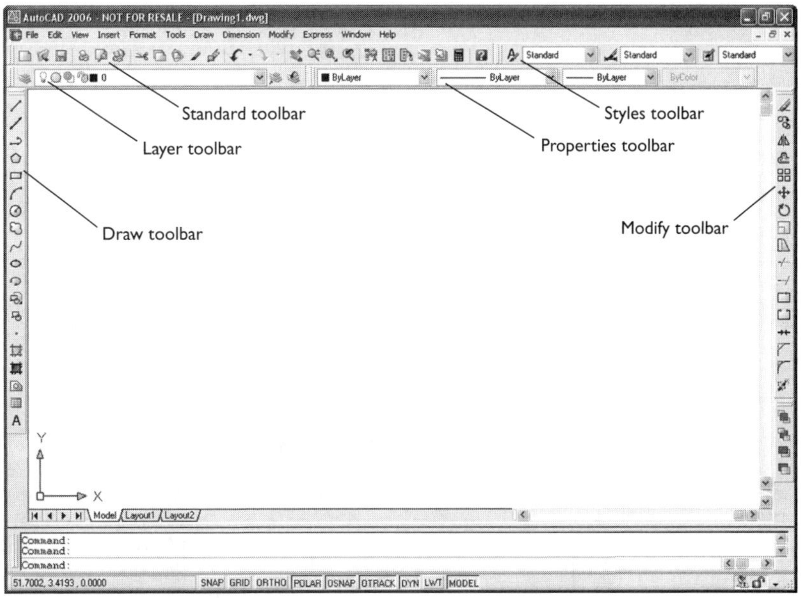

Figure C2.5

You can change the contents of toolbars, resize them, and dock or float them. A docked toolbar, such as the toolbars shown in Figure C2.5, attaches to any edge of the graphics window. A floating toolbar can lie anywhere on the application screen and can be resized. A docked toolbar cannot be resized and doesn't overlap the graphics window. You will learn to click and drag toolbars to reposition them in Tutorial 1.

When pointing to an icon, the cursor changes to an arrow that points up and to the left. You use this arrow to select command icons. When you move the pointing device over an icon, the name of the icon appears below the cursor, as shown in Figure C2.6. This feature is called a *tool tip* and is an easy way to identify icons.

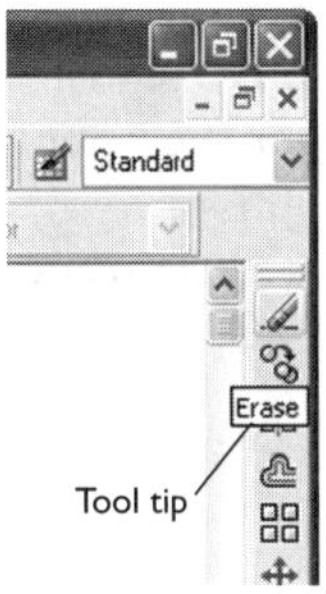

Figure C2.6

Icons with a small black triangle have *flyouts* that contain associated commands or subcommands. Hold the pick button down with the cursor over the Zoom Window icon on the Standard toolbar until the flyout appears, as shown in Figure C2.7.

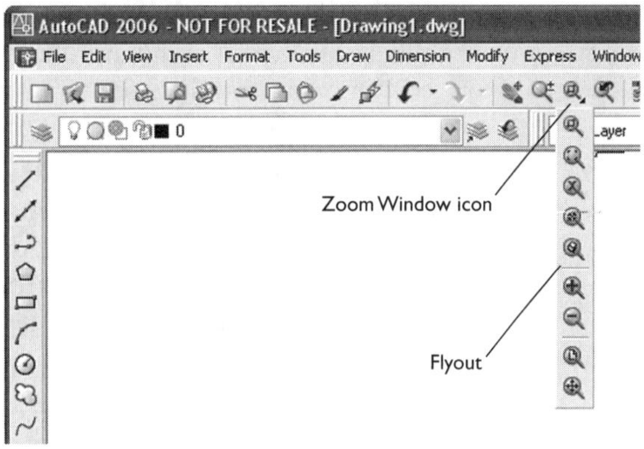

Figure C2.7

As new commands are introduced in the tutorials in this manual, their toolbar icons will appear at the beginning of the paragraph, as the Circle icon does here. Next you will pick the Circle icon from the Draw toolbar to see the options that appear. The icon looks like a circle with a radius drawn in it. As you move your mouse over the icons (you may need to pause), the command names are confirmed by the tool tips that appear below your cursor, and the icon's function appears in the status bar at the bottom of the graphics window; in this case, "Creates a circle using a specified radius: CIRCLE." (Sometimes the tool tip command name is slightly different from the name echoed at the command prompt or the command that you would type at the command prompt. If you are confused about a specific command name, check the AutoCAD Command Summary at the end of the manual.)

Pick: **Circle icon**

The following options appear at the command line.

Specify center point for circle or [3P/2P/Ttr (tan tan radius)]:

The letters that appear at the command prompt, 3P/2P/Ttr, are command options for the Circle command. Subcommands and command options work properly only when entered in response to the appropriate prompts on the command line. When a subcommand or option includes one or more uppercase letters in its name, it is a signal that you can type those letters at the prompt as a shortcut for the option name; for example, X for eXit. If a number appears in the option name—for example, 2P for Circle 2 Points—which creates a circle using two endpoints of the diameter—you need to type both the number and the capital letter(s).

Dynamic Input

Notice the dynamic input boxes appearing near the crosshairs, as shown in Figure C2.8. You can enter values by typing them into these boxes. Use the Tab key to change which input box is selected.

Figure C2.8

You can also use the dynamic input feature to select command options by pressing ↓.

Backing Up and Backing Out of Commands

When you type a command name or any data in response to a prompt on the command line, the typed characters "wait" until you press the spacebar or ↵ to act on the entered data.

If you have not already pressed ↵ or the spacebar, you can use the backspace key (generally located above and to the right of the ↵ key on standard IBM PC keyboards and represented by a long back arrow) to delete one character at a time from the command line. Pressing Ctrl-H has the same effect as pressing backspace.

Pressing Esc terminates the currently active command (if any) and reissues the Command: prompt. You can cancel a command at any time: while typing the command name, during command execution, or during any time-consuming process. A short delay may occur before the cancellation takes effect and the prompt *Cancel* confirms the cancellation.

Pressing [Esc] is also useful if you want to cancel a selection process. If you are in the middle of selecting an object, press [Esc] to cancel the selection process and discard the selection set. Any item that was highlighted because you selected it will return to normal.

If you complete a command and the result is not what you had expected or wanted, use the Undo command or type U to reverse the effect. You will learn more about Undo in Tutorial 1.

You will press [Esc] to cancel the Circle command.

Specify center point for circle or [3P/2P/Ttr (tan tan radius)]: [Esc]

Repeating Commands

You can press the spacebar or [↵] at the command prompt to repeat the previous command, regardless of the method you used to enter that command. You can also press the return button on your pointing device to repeat the command. You will try this now by starting a command and then pressing [Esc] to cancel it. Then you will repeat the command.

Type: **LINE** [↵]
Specify first point: [Esc]
Press: return mouse button (usually the right button)

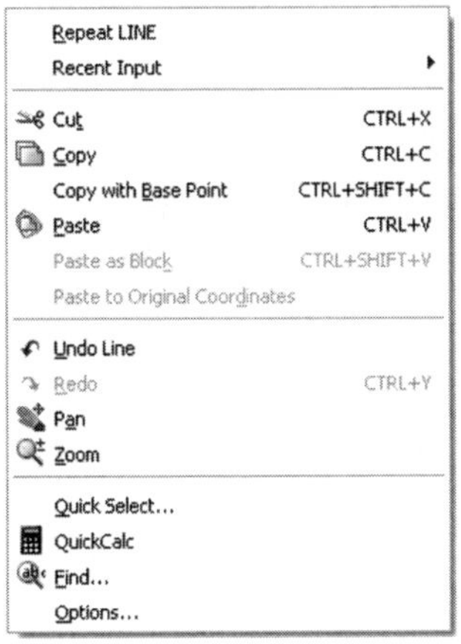

Figure C2.9

A menu will appear as shown in Figure C2.9. It can be used to repeat the command.

To remove the menu from your screen,

Press: [Esc]

Some commands, especially those that prompt you for settings when first invoked, assume default settings when repeated in this manner. You will try this now, and you will use the [Esc] key to cancel the command again.

Press: [↵]

The Line command is invoked again, and the prompt appears in the command window. You will cancel it with the [Esc] key.

Specify first point: [Esc]

Using Pull-Down Menus

The menu bar and its associated pull-down menus provide another way to select commands. The menu bar operates the same as in other Windows software. When in the menu area, the cursor changes to a selection arrow. To practice,

Pick: **Tools** (from the menu bar)

Picking a menu item executes the commands associated with it, opens a submenu of options, or opens a dialog box of options to be used to control the command. A triangle to the right of a menu item indicates that a submenu is associated with it. You will pick Inquiry to see its submenu.

Pick: **Inquiry** (from the Tools menu)

The Inquiry submenu shown in Figure C2.10 appears next to the Tools menu.

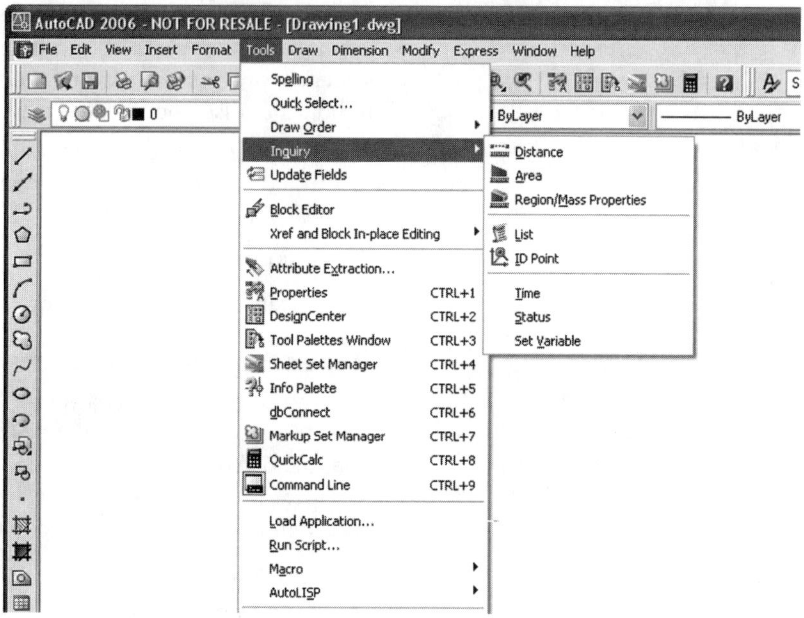

Figure C2.10

A pulled-down menu remains displayed until you

- pick an item from it,
- pick on the menu name again,
- pull down another menu by picking it from the menu bar,
- remove the menu by picking an unused area of the menu bar,
- pick a point in the graphics window,
- type a character on the keyboard, or
- pick an item from a tablet or button menu.

To remove the Tools and Inquiry menus from the screen,

Pick: **a point in the graphics window**

Working with Dialog Boxes

An ellipsis (...) after a pull-down menu item indicates that it will open a dialog box. Several commands let you set AutoCAD modes or perform operations by checking boxes or filling in fields in a dialog box.

When a dialog box is displayed, the cursor changes to an arrow. You use this arrow to select items from the dialog box.

You will open the Dimension Style Manager dialog box by picking Dimension Style from the Format menu.

Pick: **Format, Dimension Style**

The dialog box shown in Figure C2.11 appears on your screen.

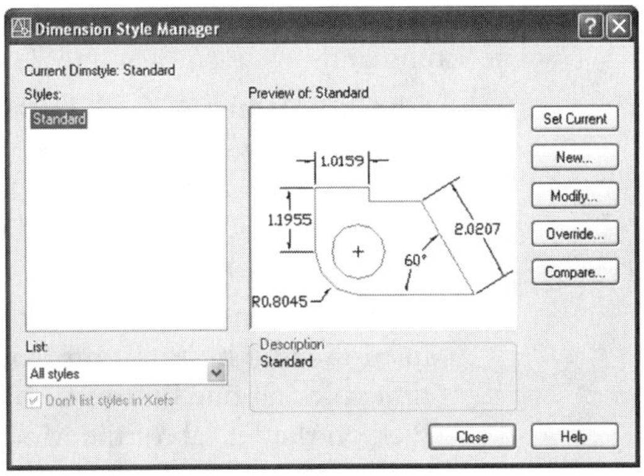

Figure C2.11

Warning

The term "button" used in conjunction with a dialog box refers to these selection options and should not be confused with the buttons on your mouse or digitizer.

Some dialog boxes have subboxes that pop up in front of them. When this occurs, you must respond to the "top" dialog box and close it before the underlying one can continue. The New, Modify, Override, and Compare buttons at the right of the dialog box bring up such subboxes.

Pick: **Modify**

The Modify Dimension Style dialog box shown in Figure C2.12 appears on your screen.

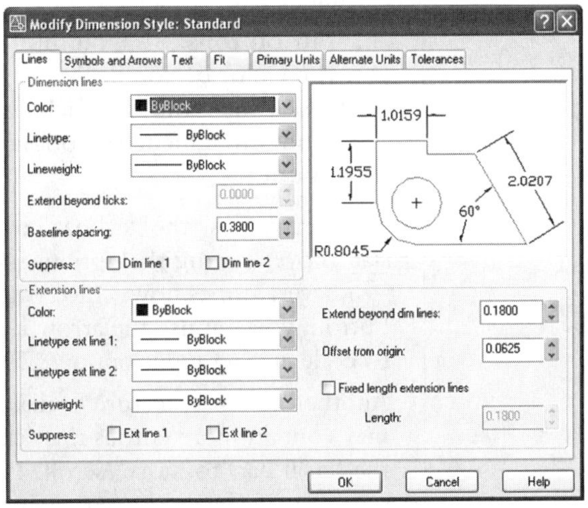

Figure C2.12

The modify Dimension Style Manager is a typical dialog box. Most dialog boxes have an OK (or Close) button that confirms the settings or options that you have selected in the dialog box. Picking it is analogous to pressing ↵ to send a command to the AutoCAD software. Picking the Cancel button disregards all changes made in the dialog box and closes the dialog box; it has the same effect as pressing Esc. You can use the Help button to get more information about a particular command.

Any item in a dialog box that is "grayed" cannot be picked, such as the Extend beyond ticks option in the Dimension Lines section.

Most dialog boxes have several types of buttons that control values or commands.

Check buttons: A check button is a small rectangle that is either blank or shows a check mark. Check buttons control an on/off switch—for example, turning Suppress Dim Line 1 on or off—or control a choice from a set of alternatives—for example, determining which modes are on. A blank check button is off.

Radio buttons: A radio button also turns an option on or off. A filled-in radio button is on. You can select only one radio button at a time; picking one button automatically turns any other button off. Pick on the Fit tab of the Modify Dimension Style dialog box to see radio buttons.

Action buttons: An action button doesn't control a value but causes an action. The OK action button causes the dialog box to close and all the selected options to go into effect. When an action button is highlighted (outlined with a heavy rule), you can press ↵ to activate it.

Text boxes: A text box allows you to specify a value, such as Baseline Spacing in Figure C2.12. Picking a text box puts the cursor in it and lets you type values in it or alter values already there. If you enter an invalid value, the OK button has no effect; you must highlight the value, correct it, and select OK again.

Input buttons: An input button chooses among preset options, such as the Color button in Figure C2.12. Input buttons have a small arrow at the right end. Picking the arrow causes the value area to expand into a menu of options that you can use to select the value for the button.

You can also use the keyboard to move around in dialog boxes. Pressing [Tab] moves among the options in the dialog box. Try this by pressing [Tab] several times now. Once you have highlighted a text box or input button, you can use the arrow keys to move the cursor in text boxes or to cycle among input options. The [spacebar] toggles options on and off.

Another common feature of dialog boxes is the scroll bar. A dialog box may contain more entries than can be displayed at one time. You use the scroll bars to move (scroll) the items up or down. You will use a scroll bar in the section Accessing On-Line Help.

Most dialog boxes save changes to the current drawing only. Two exceptions to this rule are the Options dialog box and the Plot dialog box; these dialog boxes change the way AutoCAD operates, not the appearance of the current drawing itself.

The Cancel button ignores all the selections that you made while this dialog box was open and returns you to the most recent settings. To return to the graphics window without making any changes,

Pick: **Cancel**
Pick: **Close**

You return to the graphics window.

Tip

A feature of many Windows dialog boxes allows you to double-click on the desired selection to select it and exit the dialog box in one action.

Accessing On-Line Help

The AutoCAD software has a context-sensitive on-line help facility. The tutorials in this manual explain the most efficient ways in which you can access a command. The Command Summary at the end of this manual also lists the various locations for a command, as well as the command names and aliases that you can enter at the command prompt. In addition, you can choose on-line help to find other ways of selecting a command.

You can get help in a number of ways. You can pick the Help icon, type HELP or ? at the command prompt, or press F1 to bring up the Help window.

You will use the Help icon, which looks like a question mark, from the Standard toolbar to open AutoCAD on-line help.

Pick: **Help icon**

The AutoCAD 2006 Help window is shown in Figure C2.13.

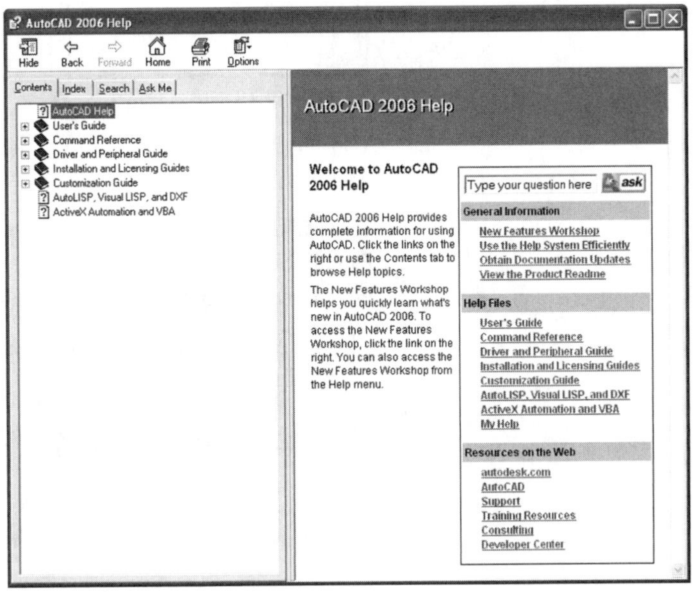

Figure C2.13

The window has four main tabs: Contents, Index, Search, and Ask Me. You may look under Contents for a list of general topics set up for you, search through an Index of topics, or use Search to locate help by referencing a single word. For now you will pick the Index tab.

Pick: **Index**

The Index portion of the dialog box appears on your screen, as shown in Figure C2.14. An alphabetical list of help topics appears in the Help window.

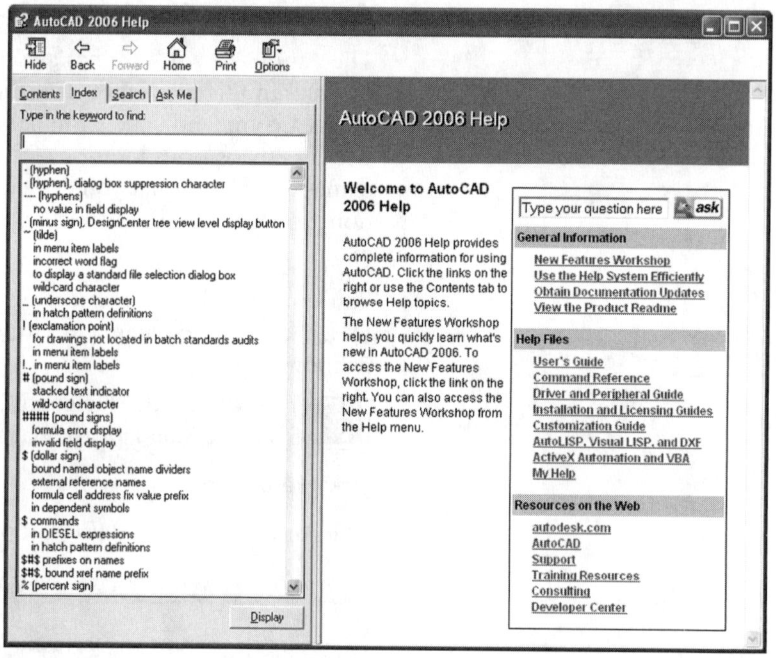

Figure C2.14

You will now type in an AutoCAD command instructing it to locate a particular topic in the Index.

Type: **ERASE ↵ (in the text box at the top left)**
Pick: **ERASE command from the list to highlight it**
Pick: **Display** (at the bottom of the dialog box)

The help screen for the Erase command appears on your screen, as shown in Figure C2.15.

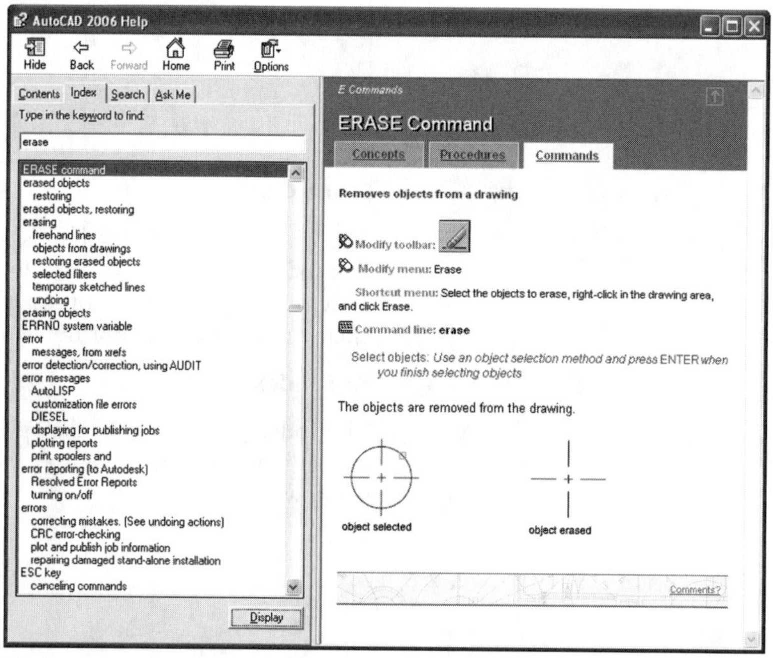

Figure C2.15

To return to the previous screen (if there was a previous screen), you can select Back from the menu bar.

Next, you will select the Search tab.

Pick: **Search tab**

You can type in a word that Help will try to find by accessing all the help functions available. This method is helpful when you do not know the exact function or topic to search for.

To get information about the Circle command, you will type the command in the box above the list of topics.

Type: **CIRCLE** (in the section titled "Type in the word(s) to search for")
Pick: **List Topics**
Double-click: **CIRCLE Command** (from the Select Topic list)

Help displays a text screen of information about the Circle command, as shown in Figure C2.16. If there is additional information that will not fit on the screen, you can use the scroll bar to move through it.

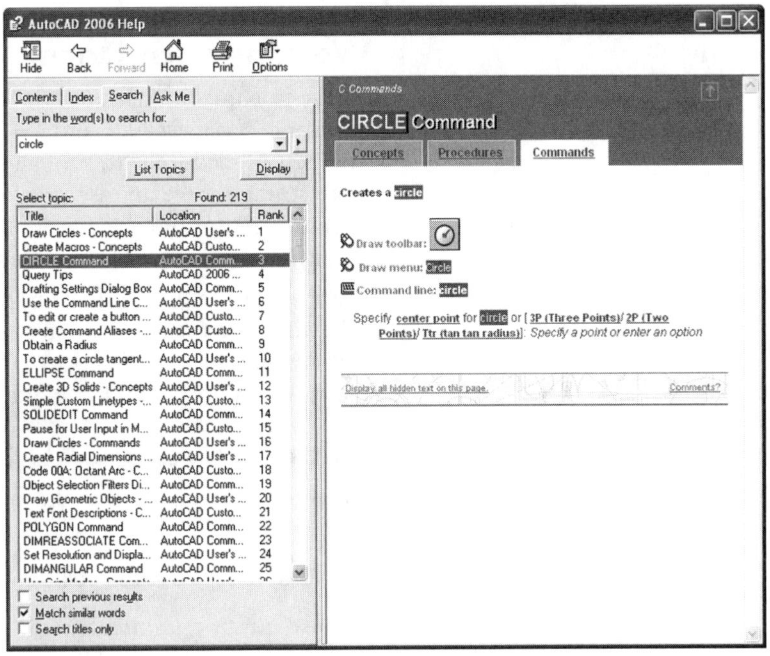

Figure C2.16

Using a Scroll Bar

A scroll bar allows you to access all items on a list that are too long to be fully displayed in the box. The up or down triangles are used to scroll in the desired direction. A slider box is located between the up and down triangles on the scroll bar. You can pick the slider box and drag it to move the entries up and down; with long lists this action is often faster than using the arrows.

Use the up and down triangles now to move through the topic list. Then place the cursor on the slider box and click and drag it up and down to move quickly through the list.

You will use the Windows close button to close the Help window and return to the AutoCAD graphics window.

Tip

For information on what's new in the AutoCAD 2006 software, you can select New Features Workshop from the Help menu.

Pick: **the Windows close button** in the top right of the Help window

On-line help is a great resource for learning how to use the powerful AutoCAD software. You should use help whenever you want more information about commands and options as you work through the tutorials.

Working with Documents

All the documents that you will be instructed to use are held in the directories *c:\datafile2006* and *c:\work*, which you created in Chapter 1. The best procedure is to save all files on your hard drive because it has more storage space and is faster than accessing a floppy disk drive. Saving directly from the AutoCAD program to your floppy disk can result in unrecoverable, corrupted drawing files.

You may have multiple drawing files open at the same time. If you have a drawing open when you select the Open or New commands, the current drawing file remains open until it is closed. You will learn more about working with multiple drawings in Tutorial 1.

Exiting an AutoCAD Session

When you have finished an AutoCAD session, you will exit the program by choosing File, Exit.

Pick: **File, Exit** (from the pull-down menu)

Because quitting unintentionally could cause the loss of a lengthy editing session, the AutoCAD software prompts you to save the changes if you want to. An AutoCAD dialog box appears that contains the message, Save Changes to *DRAWING1.dwg*? It gives you three options: Yes, No, and Cancel.

Pick: **Yes**

The Save Drawing As dialog box appears, as shown in Figure C2.17. (Your dialog box will not list any files because you have not saved anything to your work directory yet.)

Tip

If c:\work doesn't appear as your default directory, check to see that you have set the working directory as directed in Chapter 1. You can also set the project path by choosing ***Tools, Options*** *and using the Files tab to specify it as the project search path.*

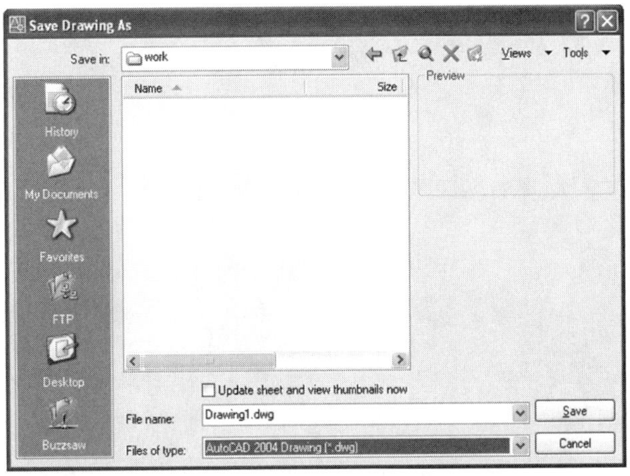

Figure C2.17

This dialog box is similar to other Windows dialog boxes for managing files. The Save in: box contains the directories available on the drives attached to your system; pressing the down arrow will display a list of these drives and directories. By double-clicking on a directory, you can open and select it as the place to store your file.

In Chapter 1, you created a working directory called *c:\work* in which to save your files. This directory should be open now. If it is not, refer to Setting the Working Directory in Chapter 1 to make *c:\work* your working directory. This change will eliminate the need to select the correct directory every time you create, open, or save a drawing file.

If you want to save your file to a disk, use the list that appears when you press the down arrow next to Save in: to select the floppy disk drive to be used for your drawing. Saving directly to your floppy disk isn't a good idea. However, if you have named your drawing so that it is on a floppy drive, such as drive *a:*, be sure to exit the AutoCAD program before you remove your disk from the drive. Always leave the same disk in the drive the entire time that you are in AutoCAD session. Otherwise, you can end up with part of your drawing not saved, which will result in an unrecoverable, corrupted drawing file. The best procedure is to create files and save them on your hard drive.

Now you need to give your file a name. The AutoCAD 2006 program supports long file names. (It will automatically add the drawing file suffix *.dwg* to your file name, so you need not type it. All file names in this manual will contain the appropriate suffix for clarity.) To continue practicing AutoCAD basics, name your file *basics.dwg*. The file name *Drawing1.dwg* should be highlighted in the File Name text box. (If it is not, click in the File Name text box and drag to highlight all the text.)

Tip

If you did not want to save your drawing, you would have picked No. If you have made some irreversible error and want to discard all changes made in an AutoCAD session, you can choose Exit from the File menu (or type QUIT at the command prompt) and select No so that the changes are not saved to your file.

Type: **BASICS**
Pick: **Save**

Your file is saved, and you are returned to Windows.

You are now ready to complete the tutorials in this manual.

Tutorial

1

Introduction to the AutoCAD® Software

Objectives

When you have completed this tutorial, you will be able to

1. Select commands from the AutoCAD menus.
2. Use AutoCAD toolbars.
3. Create an AutoCAD drawing file.
4. Work with multiple drawings.
5. Use the AutoCAD Help command.
6. Enter coordinates.
7. Draw lines, circles, and rectangles.
8. Erase drawing objects.
9. Select drawing objects, using implied Window and Crossing.
10. Add text to a drawing and edit it.
11. Save a drawing and transfer it from one drive to another.

Warning

If your screen does not look generally like Figure 1.1, be sure that you have configured the AutoCAD software properly for your computer system. Refer to Chapters 1 and 2 of this manual. You may not see the Sheet Set Manager, Workspace toolbar, and Tool Palettes as explained in Chapter 2, AutoCAD Basics.

Introduction

This tutorial introduces the fundamental operating procedures and drawing tools of the AutoCAD 2006 software. It explains how to create a new drawing; draw lines, circles, and rectangles; and save a drawing to a new name. You will learn how to erase items and select groups of objects. This tutorial also explains how to add text to a drawing.

Starting

Launch the AutoCAD 2006 software from your Windows Desktop.

If you need assistance with this, refer to Chapters 1 and 2.

A blank drawing area appears on your screen. By default, it is named *Drawing1.dwg*, as shown in its title bar.

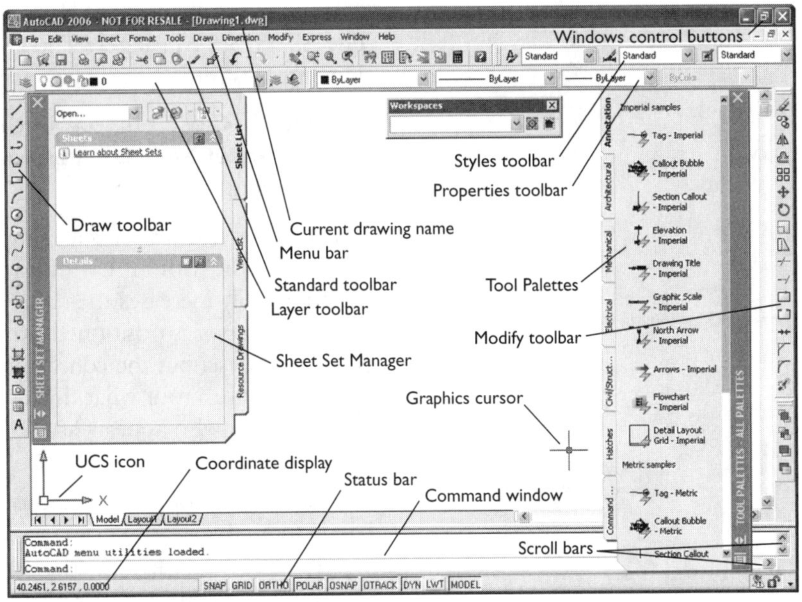

Figure 1.1

The AutoCAD Screen

Your computer display screen should look like Figure 1.1, which shows the AutoCAD drawing editor. When you first start, be sure to familiarize yourself with the main screen areas.

The Graphics Window: The *graphics window* is the central part of the screen, which you use to create and display drawings. The drawing's title bar appears above the blank area of the screen listing the drawing's name. *Windows control buttons* are located at the right of the title bar allowing you to minimize, maximize/tile, or close the drawing window.

The Graphics Cursor, or Crosshairs: The *graphics cursor*, or *crosshairs*, shows the location of your pointing device in the graphics window. You use the graphics cursor to draw, select, or pick menu items. The cursor's appearance depends on the command or option you select.

The Command Window: The *command window* is located at the bottom of the screen. It is called a *floating window* because you can move it anywhere on the screen. You can also resize it to show more or fewer command lines. Note that the command window also has *scroll bars* so that you can scroll to see commands that are not visible in the active area. Pay close attention to the command window because that's where you are prompted to enter information or make selections.

The User Coordinate System (UCS) Icon: The *UCS icon* helps you keep track of the current X-, Y-, Z-coordinate system that you are using and the direction from which the coordinates are being viewed in 3D drawings.

The Tool Palettes: *Tool palettes* can be used to organize hatches (shading patterns) and blocks (grouped symbols) for quick access. You will learn more about these in later tutorials.

The Sheet Set Manager: The *Sheet Set Manager* helps organize multiple drawing files into a single project sheet set.

Pick: **the X (Close button) in the upper right of the Tool Palettes and Sheet Set Manager windows to remove them from your screen at this time**

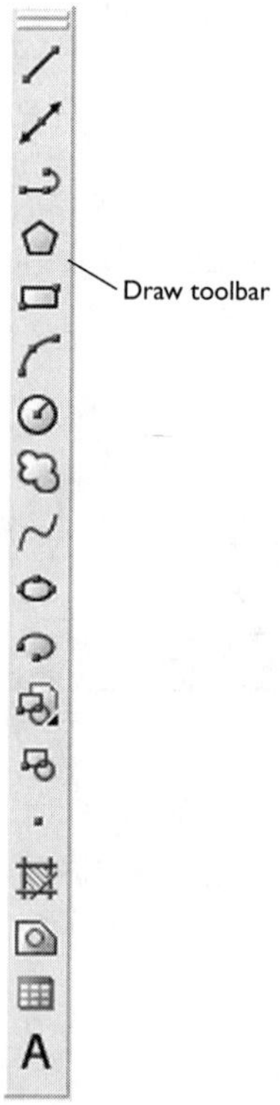

Figure 1.2

The Toolbars: A *toolbar* is a group of buttons that allow you to pick commands quickly, without having to search through a menu structure. This feature usually increases the speed with which you can select commands. When the cursor is positioned over a button, its tool tip appears. A *tool tip* is text that describes the command invoked by the button. It is useful if you are unsure about what the icon on the button represents. A help line for the button also appears at the bottom of the command window.

Toolbars can be *floating* or *docked* to the edge of the graphics window. You can float a toolbar around on your screen by picking on the gray bands that appear at its top (or side) when it is docked, and holding the pick button down as you *drag* the toolbar to its new location. Figure 1.2 shows the docked Draw toolbar. Notice the gray bands at one end.

Pick: **on the gray bands near the top of the Draw toolbar and hold the mouse's pick button down while you drag the toolbar near the center of the graphics area**

The *title bar* at the top of a floating toolbar helps to identify it. You can pick on a toolbar's title bar to drag it around on your screen. If you drag a toolbar near the edge of the window, the toolbar docks to the edge of the graphics window. When a toolbar is docked, its title bar does not appear. You can also change the shape of a toolbar. To do so, position the arrow cursor near the edge of the toolbar until the cursor changes to a double-headed arrow. While the cursor has this appearance,

Pick: **on the edge of the toolbar and, keeping the pick button depressed, drag the edge of the toolbar to reshape it**

Pick: **on the title bar of the Draw toolbar and hold the pick button down while you drag the toolbar to the left edge of the screen until it is docked**

You can customize the toolbars to show the commands you use most frequently and create new toolbars of your own. You will learn to do so in Tutorial 10.

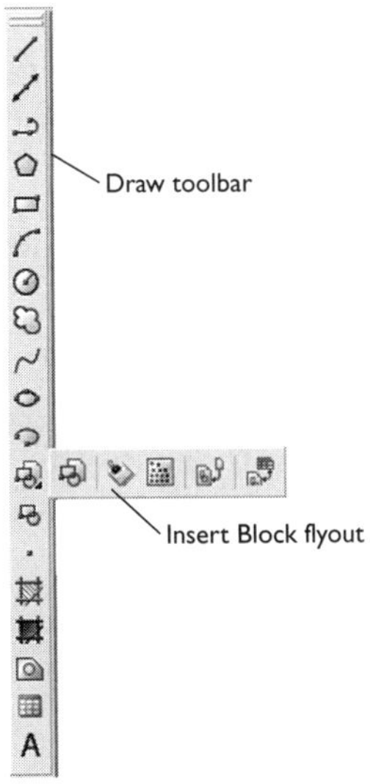

Figure 1.3

Flyouts: Items on the toolbar can also be ***flyouts***, where additional buttons are located and displayed when the icon is selected. Figure 1.3 shows the docked Draw toolbar and the Insert Block flyout. A flyout is identified by a small triangle in the button's lower right corner. To see the buttons that are located on a flyout, position the arrow cursor over the button that shows the flyout triangle and hold the pick button down. After you have held it down for a moment, you will see the additional buttons fly out. When you select a command from a flyout, that selection becomes the visible icon in the toolbar for the flyout. At first you may find this method confusing. However, once you become familiar with the flyouts, you'll find that it is a helpful feature because the most recently used command appears as the top button on the flyout, making it easy to select again.

Pick: **on the Insert Block flyout from the Draw toolbar, keeping the mouse button depressed until you see the additional buttons fly out**

Tip

Once you release the mouse button, the flyout should disappear from your screen. If you have selected a command by accident, press the Esc *key on your keyboard to cancel the command.*

The Standard Toolbar: The top of the screen displays the *Standard toolbar*, shown in Figure 1.4, which includes buttons for frequently used commands.

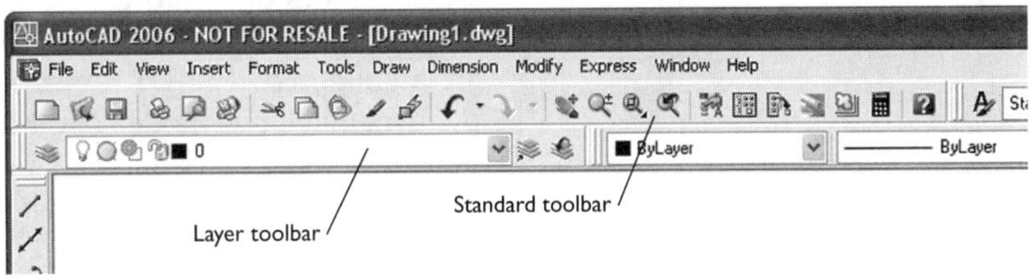

Figure 1.4

Move the graphics cursor up into the Standard toolbar area.

Note that the cursor changes from the crosshairs to an arrow when it moves out of the graphics window.

Position the arrow cursor over an item on the Standard toolbar, but do not press the pick button.

After the arrow cursor remains over a button for a few seconds, the button's tool tip appears below it.

Move the arrow cursor over each button in turn to familiarize yourself with the buttons on the Standard toolbar.

If you are unsure about which command an icon represents, use the help line at the bottom of the command window to help identify it. The Standard toolbar can float anywhere on the screen. Its default location is docked near the top of the screen.

The Layer Toolbar: The Layer toolbar controls the layers in your document. Its icons, from left to right, are: Layer Properties Manager, Layer Control, Make Object's Layer Current, and Layer Previous. The layer name 0 is shown in the Layer Control display, indicating that it is the current layer.

The Properties Toolbar: The Properties toolbar shown in Figure 1.5 contains tools to help you manipulate the properties, such as color, linetype, lineweight, and plot style of the graphical objects you create.

Tip

Generally you should leave the settings on the Properties toolbar set to Bylayer. You will learn how to use layers to control the color, linetype, and lineweight properties.

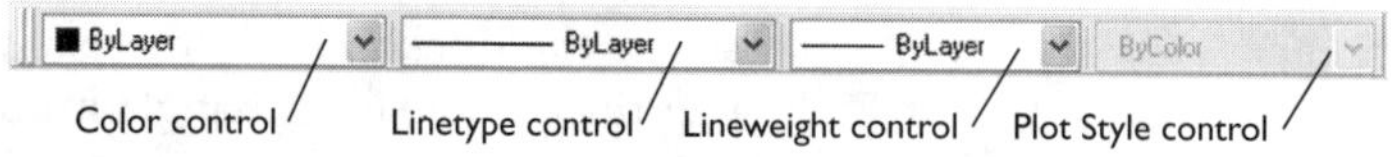

Figure 1.5

The word ByLayer is shown in the Color Control, Linetype Control, and Lineweight Control display. The Plot Style control is grayed out indicating that it cannot be selected at this time because no plot styles have been set. At this point, the properties of newly created drawing objects will be determined by the current layer 0. These tools will be covered more thoroughly in Tutorial 2.

The Status Bar: The *status bar* (Figure 1.6) at the bottom of the screen shows important settings and modes that may be in effect. The coordinate reference of the crosshairs' location appears in a box at the left of the status bar as three numbers with the general form X.XXXX, Y.YYYY, and Z.ZZZZ. The specific numbers displayed on your screen tell you the location of your crosshairs. The words SNAP, GRID, ORTHO, POLAR, OSNAP, OTRACK, DYN, LWT, and MODEL, appearing to the right of the coordinates, are buttons that you can pick to turn these special modes on and off. When the SNAP, GRID, ORTHO, POLAR, OSNAP, OTRACK, DYN and LWT modes are in effect, their buttons are highlighted. The DYN button allows you to quickly turn on and off the dynamic input mode. The MODEL button lets you quickly switch between model space and paper space, which you will learn to use in Tutorial 5. When you select paper space, the word PAPER replaces the word MODEL on the button. For now, leave the button set to MODEL.

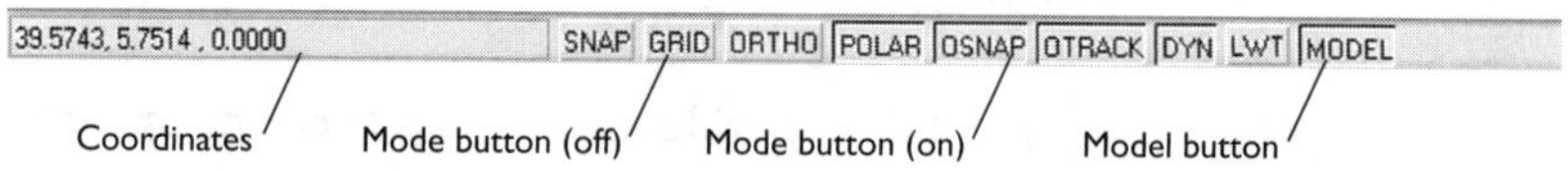

Figure 1.6

The Menu Bar: The row of words at the top of the screen is called the *menu bar*. The menu bar allows you to select commands by moving the cursor to the desired menu heading and pressing the pick button on your pointing device to pop down the available choices. To choose an item from the options that appear, position the cursor over the item and press the pick button. The menu bar shows the following headings.

File	Used to create new files, open and close existing files, save, export, print, recover, send drawings as email, and perform other file operations.

Edit	Contains editing commands for cutting and pasting operations similar to other Windows applications.
View	Lets you select commands that manipulate the view of your drawing on the screen, as well as turn on and off and customize the toolbars.
Insert	Used to insert blocks, 3D Studio® files, ACIS solids, Xrefs, and other object formats.
Format	Allows you to set color, linetype, text style, unit type, and other properties for new objects you create.
Tools	Contains the spell checker, display order, inquiry tools, user coordinate system tools, drafting settings, menu customization, and user options, among other tools.
Draw	Allows you to draw lines and circles and other drawing geometry, insert hatch patterns, input text, and create surfaces and solids.
Dimension	Allows you to dimension distances, lengths, and diameters and use many other dimensioning tools.
Modify	Contains commands allowing you to erase, copy, rotate, change properties such as layer or linetype, and make other object modifications.
Express	Optional tools that provide extra unsupported features. You may or may not have chosen to install these.
Window	Allows you to switch between and control the appearance of drawings that are open inside your AutoCAD session.
Help	Lets you find help for commands, toolbars, variables, plotting, and other information.

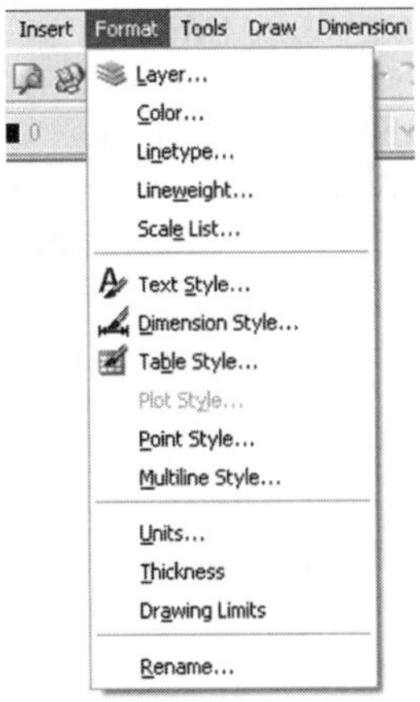

Figure 1.7

Tip

If you are unsure about which menu bar selection contains the command you want to use, move the cursor to the menu bar area and press the pick button. Move from selection to selection as you look for the command.

Canceling Commands

You can easily cancel commands by pressing Esc. If you make a selection by mistake, press Esc to cancel it. Sometimes you may have to press Esc twice to cancel a command, depending on where you are in the command sequence.

Picking Commands from the Menu Bar

Use your mouse to move the cursor to the menu bar.

Pick: **Format**

Figure 1.7 shows the Format menu pulled down from the menu bar. Items on the menu with three dots after them cause a dialog box to appear on the screen when picked. (Menu items with a triangle after the name activate another menu when picked.) Note that, as you move the cursor along the selections of the menu, the status bar at the bottom of your screen shows a help line describing the menu selection that is currently highlighted.

Move your mouse down the Format menu to see the help lines.

To remove the menu from the screen,

Pick: **in the graphics window**

Tip

Whenever you see the ↵ key in an instruction line in this manual you must press ↵, sometimes labeled Enter or Return on your keyboard, to enter the command or response. You can achieve the same result quickly by pressing the space bar on your keyboard or by pressing the return button on your pointing device (the right button on a two-button mouse) and then selecting Enter from the menu that pops up. When you are entering text during a text command you must press the actual ↵ key.

Alias	Command
A	Arc
C	Circle
D	Dimstyle
DI	Distance
E	Erase
F	Fillet
I	Insert
L	Line
LA	Layer
LS	List
LT	Linetype
M	Move
MS	Mspace
O	Offset
OS	Osnap
P	Pan
PE	Pedit
PS	Pspace
PL	Pline
R	Redraw
RE	Regen
RO	Rotate
T	Mtext
X	Explode
Z	Zoom

Typing Commands

You can type commands directly at the *command prompt* in the command window. To do so, you must type the exact command name or alias. Remember that many of the words on the menu bar are menu names, not commands. Only the actual command name, not menu names, when typed, activate a command. You will type the command, Line, in the command prompt area. You may type all capitals, capitals and lowercase, or all lowercase letters; AutoCAD commands are not *case-sensitive*.

Command: **LINE** ↵
Specify first point: [Esc]

Pressing [Esc] cancels the command. You will learn more about the Line command later in this tutorial.

Command Aliasing

You can type commands quickly through *command aliasing*. Many AutoCAD users feel that this is the fastest method of selecting commands. You can give any command a shorter name, called an *alias*. Many commands already have aliases assigned to them to help you get started. They are stored in the file *acad.pgp*, which is part of the AutoCAD software and is found in the directory that you have set in your support files search path. You can check this by picking Tools, Options and then the Files tab.

You can pick Tools, Customize, Edit Program Parameters (*acad.pgp*) to edit the file *acad.pgp* with a text editor and add lines with your own command aliases. (These lines take the form ALIAS, *COMMAND in the *acad.pgp* file.) After doing so, you can use the shortened name at the AutoCAD command prompt. The commands in the left margin are some for which aliases have already been created. When you need one of these commands, you can type its alias at the command prompt instead of the entire command name.

Remember these are only a few of the aliases available. For a more complete list, please reference the Command Summary at the end of this book. The Command Summary indicates where to find a command, its icon, the actual command name (which you can type to start the command) and its alias, if there is one. Try typing the alias for the Line command.

Command: **L** ↵
Specify first point: [Esc]

There are many different ways to select any command. After you have worked through the tutorials in this book, decide which methods work best for you. While you are working through the tutorials, however, be sure to select the commands from the locations specified. The subsequent command prompts and options may differ, depending on how you selected the command.

Using Dynamic Entry

Another way to give input and select command options is to enter values and options using the dynamic input boxes that appear near the cursor location. Dynamic input allows you to type input at your pointer location, specify dimensions during many draw commands and to select from command option prompts. Right-click the DYN button and pick Settings to control what is displayed by each component when Dynamic Input is on.

Right-click: **DYN button on the status bar**
Pick: **Settings**

The Drafting Settings dialog box appears on your screen with the Dynamic Input tab upppermost as shown in Figure 1.8. You can use this dialog box to customize which dynamic input options are shown at the cursor location. Do not change any settings now. To close the dialog box,

Pick: **Cancel**
Check to see that the DYN button on your status bar is on.
Command: **C** ↵

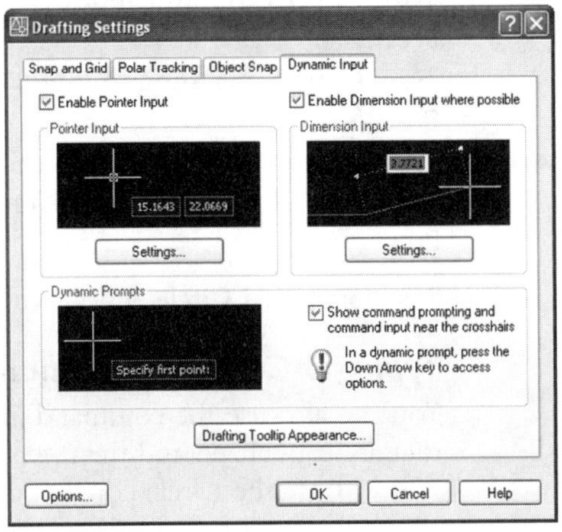

Figure 1.8

You should see the Circle command prompts appear on your screen along with the dynamic input boxes at the cursor location as shown in Figure 1.9.

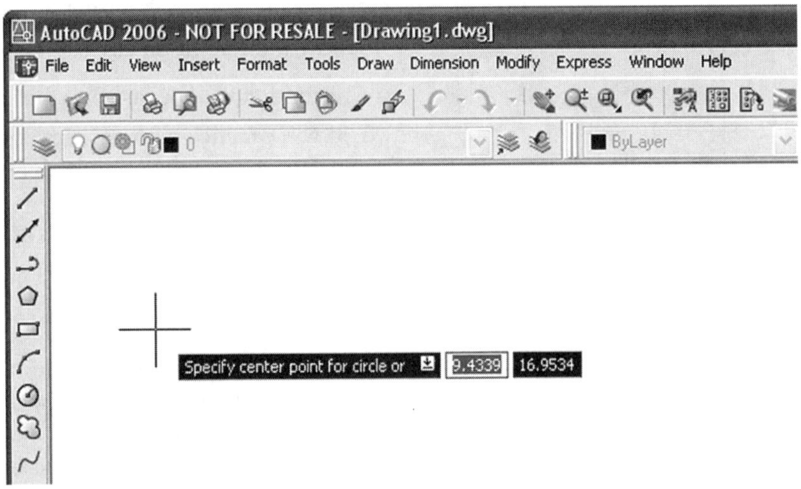

Figure 1.9

Once you have selected a command, a number of options may appear at the command prompt. To see them in the dynamic input menu,

Press: ↓ (the down arrow on your keyboard)

The options for the circle command appears near the cursor location as shown in Figure 1.10.

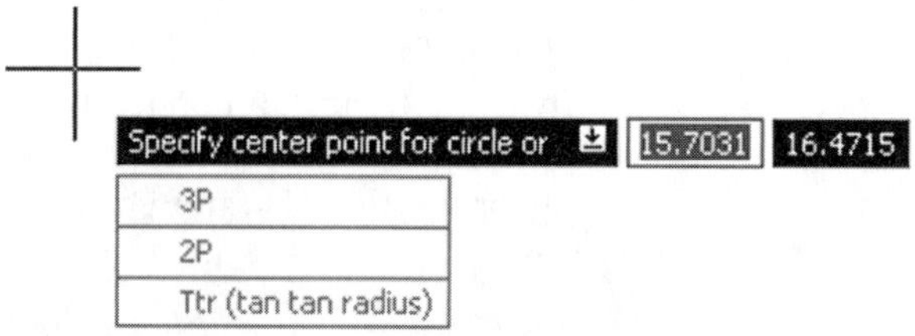

Figure 1.10

Pick: **2P from the options that appear dynamically**
Type: **10 into the first input box to specify the *x*-coordinate**
Press: Tab
Type: **10 into the second input box to specify the *y*-coordinate**
Press: ↵
Type: **8 into the input box that appears to specify the second endpoint of the circle's diameter**
Press: ↵

The completed Circle appears on your screen.

Typing a Command Option Letter

You can also use the command line to type the option letter or letters that are capitalized and then press ↵ to select the option you want. You will use the Circle command again and specify three points on the circumference of the circle to define it.

Pick to turn off the DYN button on your status bar.
Command: **C** ↵
Specify center point for circle or [3P/2P/Ttr (tan tan radius)]: **3P** ↵
Specify first point on circle: **pick a point from the screen**
Specify second point on circle: **pick a second point from the screen**
Specify third point on circle: **pick a third point from the screen**

A second circle appears on your screen.

You will practice with multiple drawings next by creating a second drawing. Do not close this circle drawing.

Starting a New Drawing

To start a new drawing,

Pick: **File, New**

The AutoCAD Select template dialog box (shown in Figure 1.11) allows you to select a pre-existing template file as a starting point for the new drawing. A *template* can contain useful settings, borders, and other items that then become a part of the new drawing. A number of standard templates are available and you can create your own from any AutoCAD drawing. You will learn more about creating and using templates in

Tutorial 5. The default option, *acad.dwt,* is a template with minimal settings for starting an essentially blank drawing.

Pick: ***acad.dwt*** (if it is not already highlighted), then **pick Open**

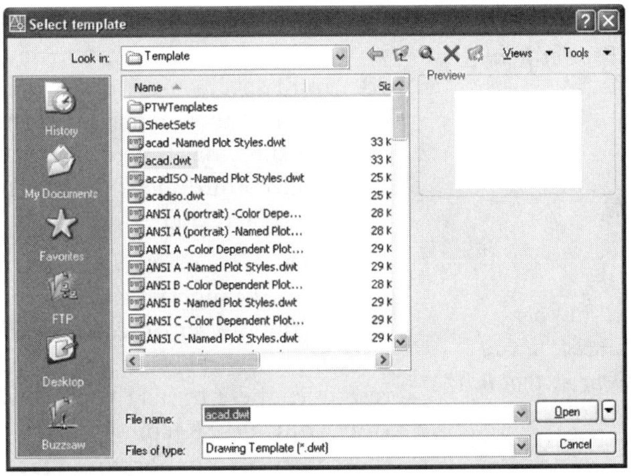

Figure 1.11

Naming Drawing Files

After the Select template dialog box disappears, you should see the new drawing named *Drawing2.dwg* on your screen. You will save the drawing under a new name. The drawing name *shapes.dwg* will serve as a good name for this sample drawing.

Pick: **File, Save**

The Save Drawing As dialog box shown in Figure 1.12 appears, which you can use to name your file and select the drive and directory.

Type: **SHAPES**

The AutoCAD software follows the Windows rules for naming a file. Names may include as many characters and/or numbers as you choose, along with other characters: underscores (_), dashes (-), commas (,), and periods (.). However, forward slashes (/) and backward slashes (\) aren't allowed in the drawing name.

Tip

It is not generally good practice to include periods (.) or spaces in your AutoCAD drawing names. Periods are generally used to divide the file name from the file extension (for example, shapes.dwg). Using a period within the name of the file may cause confusion with the extension and can make it difficult to use the file with other operating system versions, or inside other AutoCAD drawings.

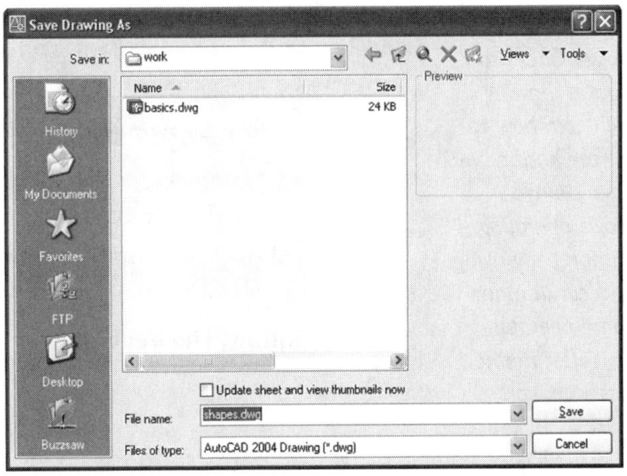

Figure 1.12

Tip

If you cannot open your drawing for use with the AutoCAD program because it is corrupted, you may be able to recover it with the selection File, Drawing Utilities, Recover from the menu bar.

Warning

Saving a drawing directly to your floppy disk is a poor practice. If you have named your drawing so that it is stored on a removable disk, such as a CD or floppy drive, be sure to exit the AutoCAD program before you remove your disk from the drive. Always leave the same disk in the drive for the entire AutoCAD session. Otherwise, you can end up with part of your drawing not saved, which will result in an unrecoverable, corrupted drawing file. Similar problems can occur when using removable zip disks and USB drives. As you create a drawing, more and more data are being stored in the drawing file. If the file size exceeds the remaining capacity of a disk, a FATAL ERROR may occur, resulting in the loss of the entire drawing file. To prevent problems with files that may become too large for a floppy, create all drawings on the hard drive or a network drive and then use your operating system to transfer them to another disk for storage after you exit the AutoCAD program. After completing the drawing for this tutorial, you will learn how to transfer drawings from the hard drive to a floppy disk or other storage media using the Windows operating system. File loss from improperly using removable media can occur in many programs and even some operating system operations. The safest method for preventing data loss is to work from your local hard disk.

All AutoCAD drawing files are automatically assigned the *file extension .dwg*, so typing the extension is unnecessary. The tutorials in this book use drawing names that are descriptive of the drawing being created. For example, the drawing that you will create for this first tutorial consists of basic shapes. Descriptive names make recognizing completed drawings easier. Drawing names can include a drive and directory specification. If you don't specify a drive, the drawing is saved in the *default directory*. In Chapter 1 of this manual, you should have already created a default working directory, called *c:\work*, where you will save your drawing files. If you have not done so, you may want to review Chapter 1.

On the the left side of the dialog box are icons for History, My Documents, Favorites, FTP, Desktop, and Buzzsaw that allow you to maneuver through your files and connect to Web resources. If you cannot see the full set of icons, use the scroll bars or enlarge the Save Drawing As window. If necessary, pick the Desktop icon and use the resources there to help you browse to the directory where you want to store your files. Keeping your files organized so that you can retrieve them later is an important aspect of using CAD.

Pick: **Save**

This action returns you to the drawing editor, where you can begin work on your drawing, called *shapes.dwg*. Unless you are using a different drive or working directory on your system, the entire default name of your drawing is *c:\work\shapes.dwg*. Note that the name *shapes.dwg* now appears in the title bar as the current file name. Depending on your system, the *.dwg* extension may not show up in the title bar; however, the AutoCAD software recognizes it as such.

Working with Multiple Drawings

You may have more than one drawing open in your AutoCAD 2006 session simultaneously. You should now have two open drawings: Shapes, the drawing you just created, and Drawing1, the previous drawing, where you experimented with picking from the AutoCAD menus and drew circles using the 2P and 3P options of the Circle command. You can use the Window selection from the menu bar to tile the drawings *horizontally* or *vertically*, cascade the drawings so that they appear in a neat stack, or switch between drawings that are currently open. The open drawings are listed at the bottom of the Window menu as you see in Figure 1.13. You can pick on a drawing name to make it the active drawing.

Pick: **Window, *Drawing1.dwg***

Drawing1 becomes the active drawing window. Notice its name is now in the AutoCAD title bar.

You can show both your new drawing, Shapes, and Drawing1 at the same time. To do this,

Pick: **Window, Tile Vertically**

Figure 1.13

Both drawings should now appear on your screen arranged side by side vertically as shown in Figure 1.14.

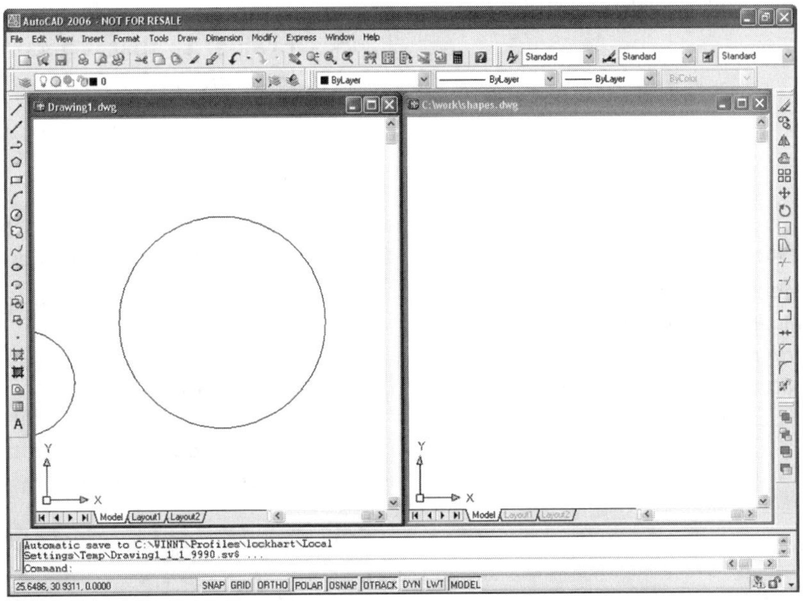

Figure 1.14

Pick: **Window, Cascade**

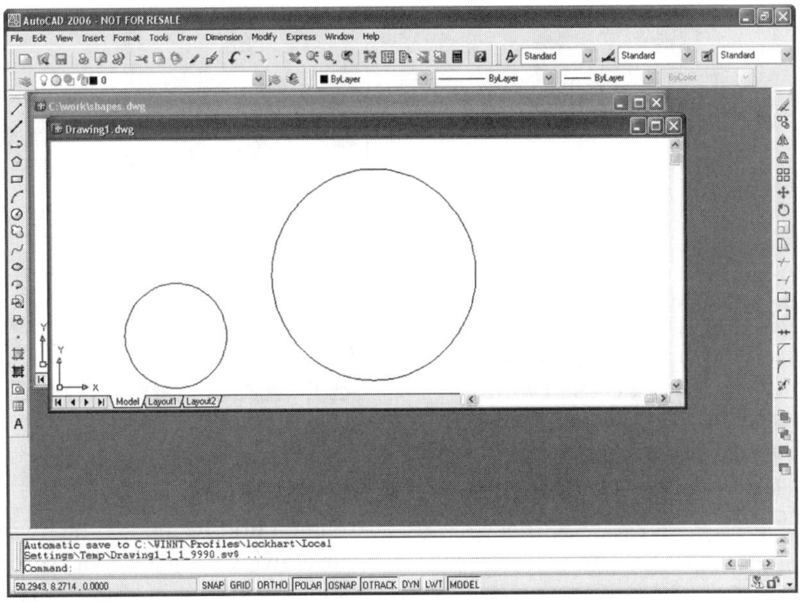

Figure 1.15

The drawings now appear as shown in Figure 1.15, arranged so that they appear stacked and so you can see the window controls for each drawing. Next you will pick on the title bar for *shapes.dwg* so that it becomes the active drawing.

Pick: **on the title bar for *shapes.dwg***

It will appear at the top of the cascaded stack of drawings. Next you will close Drawing1 by picking its Windows Close button (the × in the title bar).

Tip

You can cut and paste objects from one drawing window to another.

Pick: **Drawing1 so that it becomes active**
Pick: **Close button for *Drawing1.dwg***

A dialog box will appear prompting "Save changes to *Drawing1.dwg*?"

Pick: **No**

Drawing1.dwg should disappear from your screen leaving only *shapes.dwg*. Next you will maximize this drawing so that it fills the graphics area.

Warning

Make sure to close only the drawing window and not the AutoCAD program window. The uppermost Close button above the AutoCAD menu bar closes the entire program.

Pick: **the Maximize button in the title bar of *shapes.dwg***

Drawing Shapes should fill the graphics area as shown in Figure 1.16. Typically, you will work with the drawing maximized as you see now. Notice that the drawing no longer has a separate title bar and its window controls are below the controls to close, minimize, and maximize the AutoCAD program window.

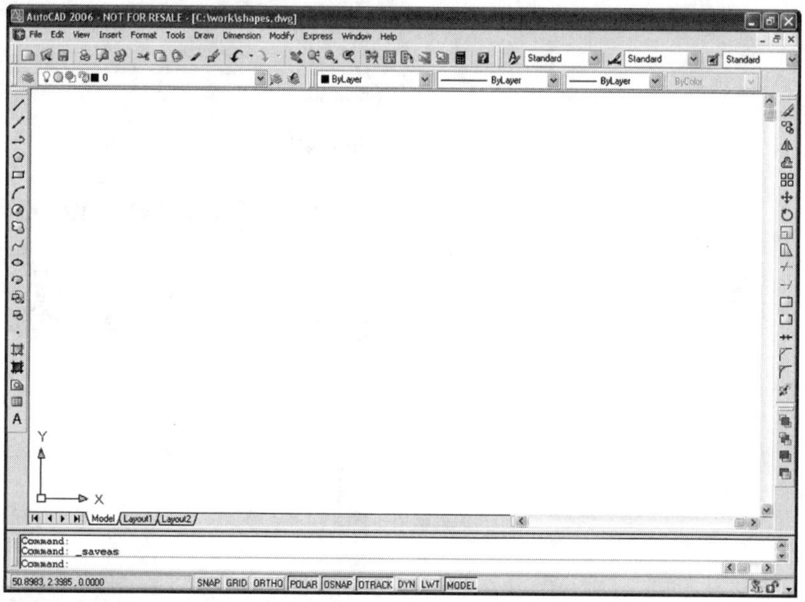

Figure 1.16

Using Grid

Adding a grid to the graphics window gives you a helpful reference for your drawing. A *grid* is a background of regularly spaced dots. The grid does not show up in your drawing when you print. You will turn on the background grid in the graphics window by picking it from the status bar.

Tip

You can turn off Multiple Document mode by selecting Tools, Options, the System tab, and then, under the General Options area, checking the Single Drawing Compatibility mode. Pick OK to exit the dialog box.

Pick: **Grid button** (from the status bar)

The grid appears on your screen. You can also type the Grid command which turns it on and shows you options for setting the grid spacing.

Command: **GRID** ↵

The grid spacing prompt displays the options available for the command. The default option, in this case <0.5000>, appears within *angle brackets*. Pressing ↵ on your pointing device accepts the default. To set the size of a grid, you type in the numerical value of the spacing and press ↵. You will change the grid spacing to 1 unit.

Specify grid spacing(X) or [ON/OFF/Snap/Aspect] <0.5000>:**1** ↵

> **Tip**
>
> *If you choose a grid size that is too small—so that it would effectively fill your graphics window with a solid pattern of grid dots—the error message "Grid too dense to display" appears. If that happens, restart the Grid command and change to a larger value. (You can simply press ↵ immediately after ending a command to restart it.) If the grid values are too large, nothing appears on the screen because the grid is beyond the visual limits of the screen.*

Using Zoom

The Zoom command enlarges or reduces areas of the drawing on your screen. It is different from the Scale command, which actually makes the selected items larger or smaller in your drawing database. You can use the Zoom command when you want to enlarge something on the screen so that you can more easily see details. You can also zoom out so objects appear smaller on your display. The Zoom command options are located on the Standard toolbar and on the View menu.

Using Zoom All

The *Zoom All* option displays the drawing limits (the area where the grid is displayed) or shows all the drawing objects on the screen, whichever is larger. Zoom All is located on the Zoom flyout on the Standard toolbar, which is described in greater detail in Tutorial 2. You will select View, Zoom All from the menu bar so that the grid area is larger on your display.

Pick: **View, Zoom, All**

Your screen should look like Figure 1.17, which shows a background grid drawn with 1-unit spacing. Note that GRID is now highlighted (with a dark shadow around the button) on the status bar to let you know that the grid is turned on.

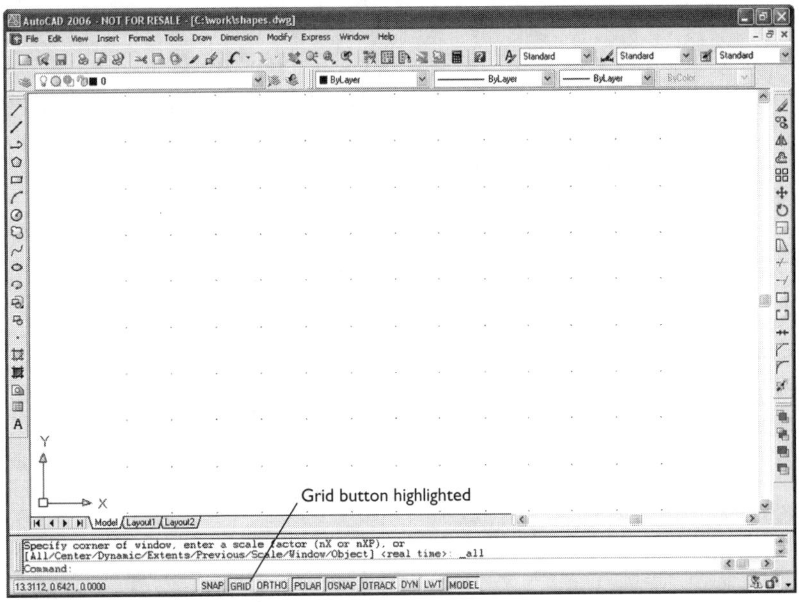

Figure 1.17

Using Snap

The *Snap* command restricts the movement of the cursor to make selecting locations with a specified spacing easier. When Snap is on, your cursor jumps to the specified intervals. Snap is a very helpful feature when you are locating objects or distances in a drawing. If each jump on the snap interval is exactly 0.5 unit (horizontally or vertically only, not diagonally), you could draw a line 2.00 units long by moving the cursor four snap intervals. You will activate Snap by typing the command.

Command: **SNAP** ↵

You should align the snap function with the grid size so that the snap spacing is the same as the grid spacing, at half the grid spacing, or some other even fraction of the grid spacing. The grid spacing is 1; you will accept the snap default value of <0.5000>, so the snap increment will be one-half of the grid spacing.

Snap spacing or [ON/OFF/Aspect/Rotate/Style/Type] <0.5000> : ↵

Tip

If you set the GRID spacing to 0.0000, and then set the SNAP, the grid spacing will automatically follow the same spacing as SNAP.

Note that SNAP is highlighted on the status bar to let you know that the Snap mode is in effect.

Move the crosshairs around on the screen.

Note that, instead of the smooth movement that you saw previously, the crosshairs jump or "snap" from point to point on the snap spacing.

Grid and Snap Toggles

You can quickly turn Grid and Snap on and off by clicking their respective buttons on the status bar. If their buttons on the status bar appear *highlighted* (with a darkened outline around the button), they are on; buttons that are solid gray are off. Each button on the status bar acts as a *toggle*: that is, clicking it once turns the function on; clicking it a second time turns the function off. You can toggle Grid and Snap on and off during the execution of other commands.

Pick: **SNAP button**

Move the crosshairs around on the screen. Note that they have been released from the snap constraint. To turn Snap on again,

Pick: **SNAP button**

The crosshairs jump from snap location to snap location again.

Pick: **GRID button**

Tip

Pressing [Ctrl]-G or [F7] also toggles the grid on and off; [Ctrl]-B or [F9] toggles the snap function.

The grid disappears from your screen, but the snap constraint remains. To show the grid again,

Pick: **GRID button**

Note how the command window keeps a visual record of all the commands.

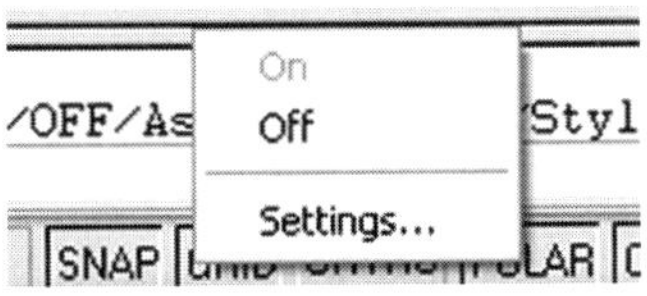

Figure 1.18

Drafting Settings

You can also adjust Snap and Grid by using the Drafting Settings dialog box. This dialog box appears when you right-click on the Snap or Grid button on the status bar and then pick Settings as shown in Figure 1.18.

Right-click: **Snap button**
Pick: **Settings**

The Drafting Settings dialog box appears on your screen as shown in Figure 1.19. The Snap and Grid tab should appear on top. You will learn about Polar Tracking and Object Snap in later tutorials.

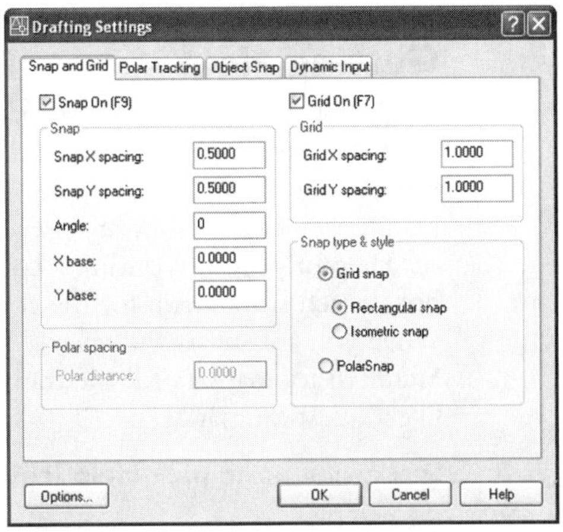

Figure 1.19

You will set the X spacing for the snap to 0.25. Use the input boxes on the left side of the dialog box.

Pick: **to highlight the text in the input box next to Snap X Spacing by dragging with your mouse button depressed**
Type: **.25**

Tip

Pressing ↵ automatically closes the Drafting Settings dialog box.
To quickly set a new snap or grid increment, type the value in the appropriate input box and then press ↵ to close the dialog box.

The Y Spacing box automatically changes to match the X Spacing box when you click in the Snap Y Spacing input box. If you want unequal spacing for X and Y, you can change the Y spacing separately.

Pick: **OK** (to exit from the dialog box)

As you move your mouse around on the screen, you should now notice the cursor jumping at an increment of one-fourth of the grid spacing.

Using Line

The *Line* command draws straight lines between endpoints that you specify. The Line command is located on the Draw toolbar, docked on the left-hand side of the screen. (AutoCAD toolbars and menus are organized according to spoken English syntax. This arrangement is helpful when you are trying to remember where commands are located. For example, you might say, "I want to draw a line.")

For the next sequence of commands, you will use the Draw toolbar to pick the Line command. When selecting the Line command, be sure to pick the icon that shows dots at both endpoints. This icon indicates that the command draws a line between the two points selected. You can

Tip

Using the toolbars and typing command aliases at the prompt are two of the fastest ways to select commands. You can also select the Line command by picking Draw, Line from the menu bar.

continue drawing lines from point to point until you press ↵ to end the command.

Leave the DYN button turned off for now.

Pick: **Line icon**

You are prompted for the starting point of the line. You can answer prompts requesting the input of a point in two different ways:

- By moving the cursor into the graphics window and choosing a screen location by pressing the pick button (Grid and Snap help to locate specifically defined points)
- By entering X-, Y-, and Z-coordinate values for the point

Tip

If you make an error when using any of the menu commands, press Esc to return to the command prompt.

Getting Help

You can get help during any command by using the AutoCAD transparent *Help* command. A ***transparent command*** is one that you can use during execution of another command. When transparent commands are entered, they are preceded by an apostrophe ('). If you type '? or 'Help or press F1 during a command, you will see the Help dialog box, which shows help for the command that you are currently using. While you are still at the Specify first point: prompt, you will use the Standard toolbar to pick the transparent Help command. Its icon looks like a question mark (?).

Specify first point: **pick Help icon**

The AutoCAD Help window with help for the Line command is shown in Figure 1.20. AutoCAD's Help feature is *context-sensitive*; it recognizes that you were using the Line command and therefore displays help for that command.

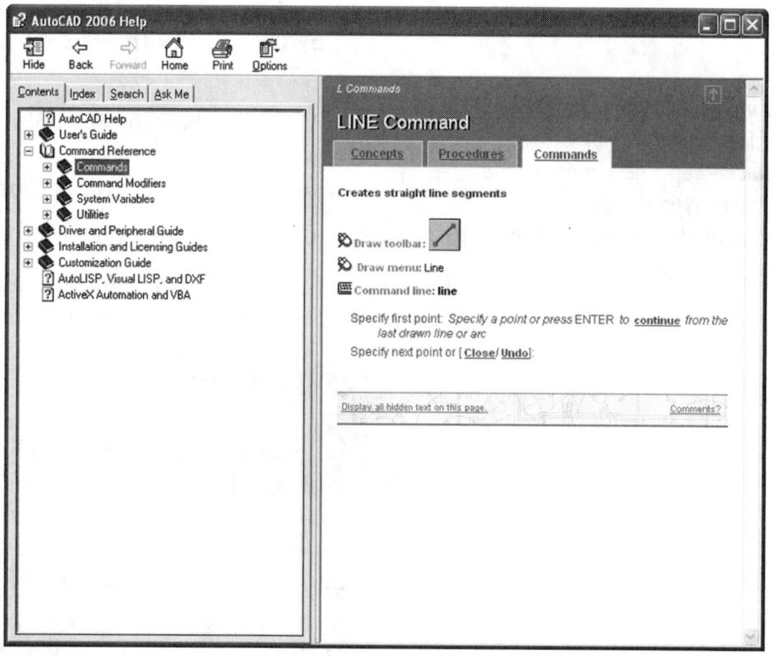

Tip

If the Help Window does not appear on your screen, check to see if it appears minimized on your Windows taskbar. If so, click on it to resume the Help window.

Figure 1.20

When you move the cursor over items displayed in a contrasting color on the right side of the window, the cursor changes to a hand. You can then select these items, changing to the related help window.

The left side of the Help window contains four different tabs: Contents, Index, Search, and Ask Me.

Select each tab to familiarize yourself with the options available and then pick the Index tab.

You have the option of typing the help topic you want or scrolling through all the help topics available.

Type: **GRID** ↵

Help either matches exactly what is typed or locates the closest option on the list. A list of topics related to grid appears in the window. The right side of the dialog box displays help for adjusting the grid and snap. If you pick the display button or double-click on a list item, new information about that option appears in the window at the right.

The help is divided into three categories: Concepts, Procedures, and Commands. These are represented by tabs across the top right.

Pick: **the Commands tab**

The commands and system variables that relate to the Grid command display in the Help Dialog box.

Pick: **Procedures tab**

The help dialog box changes as shown in Figure 1.21 to display procedures that you might find useful when using the grid.

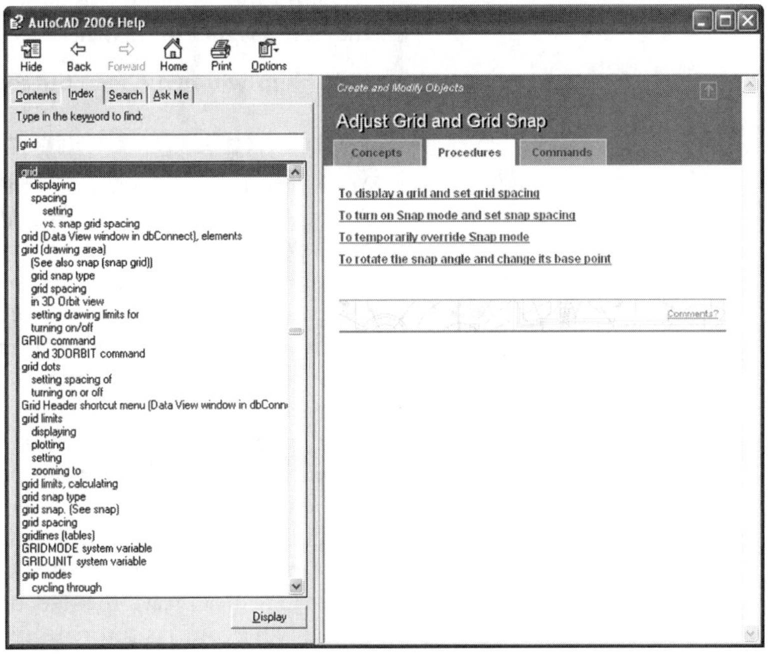

Figure 1.21

Pick: **To display a grid and set grid spacing**

Step-by-step information on how to set the grid spacing appears as in Figure 1.22. A lot of up-to-date information is available through using help. This is the first place you should turn to when you have questions about how to use your software.

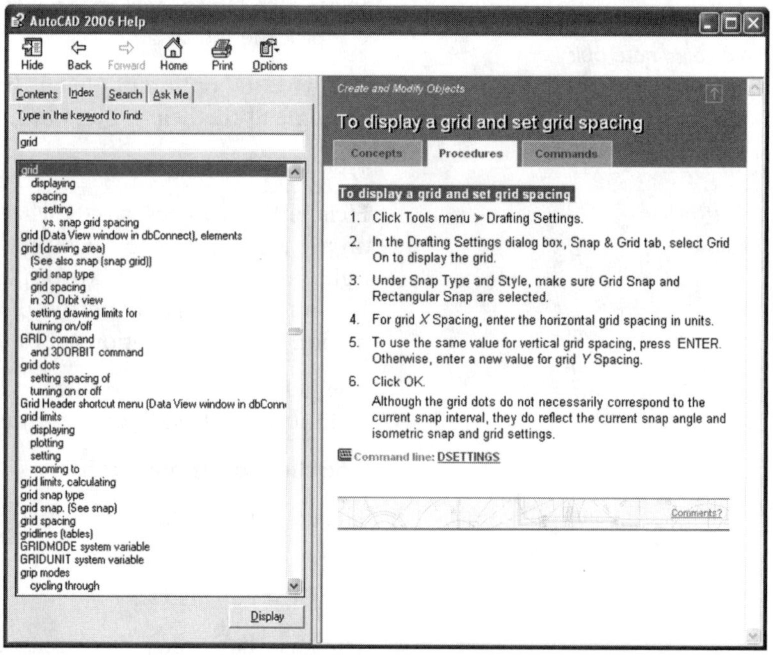

Figure 1.22

As with other Windows applications, you may use the Close button in the upper right-hand corner to close the Help window.

Pick: **Help window Close button**

Entering Coordinates

Your drawing geometry is stored using *World Coordinates*, which is the AutoCAD default *Cartesian coordinate system*, where X-, Y-, and Z-*coordinate values* specify locations in your drawing. The UCS icon near the bottom left corner of your screen shows the positive X- and positive Y-directions on the screen. You can think of the default orientation of the Z-axis as the location in front of the monitor for positive values and inside the monitor for negative values. The AutoCAD software uses the right-hand rule for coordinate systems. If you orient your right hand palm up and point your thumb in the positive X-direction and index finger in the positive Y-direction, the direction your other fingers curl will be the positive Z-direction. Use the right-hand rule and the UCS icon to figure out the directions of the coordinate system. You can specify a point explicitly by entering the X-, Y-, and Z-coordinates, separated by a comma. You can leave the Z-coordinate off when you are drawing in 2D, as you will be in this tutorial. If you do not specify the Z-coordinate, it is assumed to be the current elevation in the drawing, for which the default value is 0. For now, type only the X- and Y-values, and the default value of 0 for Z will be used.

Tip

Remember that the spacebar acts the same way as the ↵ key, to end a command. When typing in coordinates, enter only commas between them. Do not enter a space between the comma and the following coordinate of a coordinate pair because a space has the same effect as ↵. Recall that you can press the spacebar to enter commands quickly.

Tip

If you enter a wrong point while still in the Line command, you can back up one endpoint at a time with the Undo option by typing the letter U and pressing ↵.

Warning

Undo functions differently if you pick it as a command. If you select Undo at the command prompt, you may undo entire command sequences. If necessary, you can use Redo to return something that has been undone.

Tip

Be sure that Snap is highlighted on the status bar. If it is not, pick SNAP on the status bar or press F8 to turn it on.

Tip

Because Line was the last command used, you could restart the command by pressing the ↵ key, the spacebar, or the return button on your pointing device and then selecting Repeat Line from the pop-up menu. Using these shortcuts will help you produce drawings in less time. Keep in mind, however, that some commands selected from the toolbar do not always function the same when restarted at the command prompt. Restarting a command has the same effect as typing the command name at the prompt. Some toolbar and menu selections contain special programming to select certain options for you automatically.

Using Absolute Coordinates

You often need to type the exact location of specific points to represent the geometry of the object you are creating. To do so, type the X-, Y-, and Z-coordinates to locate the point on the current coordinate system. Called *absolute coordinates*, they specify a distance along the X-, Y-, Z-axes from the *origin* (or point (0, 0, 0) of the coordinate system).

Resume use of the Line command and use absolute coordinates to specify endpoints for the line you will draw. (Restart the Line command by picking the Line icon from the Draw toolbar if you do not see the Specify first point: prompt.)

Specify first point: **5.26,5.37** ↵

As you move your cursor, you will see a line rubberbanding from the point you typed to the current location of your cursor. The next prompt asks for the endpoint of the line.

Specify next point or [Undo]: **8.94,5.37** ↵

After you have entered the second point of a line, the line appears on the screen. The rubberband line continues to stretch from the last endpoint you selected to the current location of the cursor, and you are prompted for another point. This feature allows lines to be drawn end to end. Continue as follows:

Specify next point or [Undo]: **8.94,8.62** ↵
Specify next point or [Close/Undo]: **5.26,8.62** ↵

The Close option of the Line command joins the last point drawn to the first point drawn, thereby closing the lines and forming an area. To close the figure, you will type c in response to the prompt.

Specify next point or [Close/Undo]: **C** ↵

Drawing Using Grid and Snap

Use the grid and snap settings to draw another rectangle to the right of the one you just drew, as shown in Figure 1.23.

Pick: **Line icon**

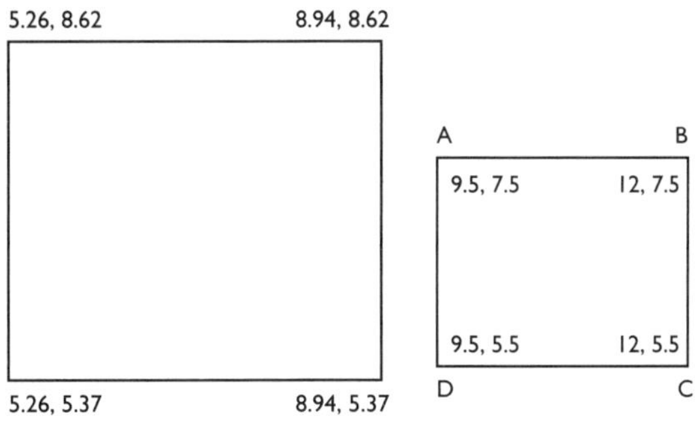

Figure 1.23

On your own, choose the starting point on the grid by moving the cursor to point A, as shown in Figure 1.23 and pressing the pick button. Remember to use the coordinate display on the status bar to help you select the points.

Create the 2.5-unit long horizontal line by moving the cursor 10 snap increments to the right and pressing the pick button to select point B.

Complete the rectangle by drawing a vertical line 8 snap increments (2.00 units) long to point C and another horizontal line 10 snap increments (2.5 units) long to point D.

Use the Close command option to complete the rectangle and end the Line command on your own.

Using Last Point

Tip

Once in the Line command, you can also press the spacebar or ↵ at the Specify first point: prompt to start your new line from the last point. You can also press the right mouse button.

The AutoCAD program always remembers the last point that you specified. Often you will need to specify a point that is exactly the same as the preceding point. The @ symbol on your keyboard is the AutoCAD name for the last point entered. You will use last point entry with the Line command. This time you will restart the Line command by pressing ↵ at the blank command prompt to restart the previous command.

Command: ↵
Specify first point: **2,5** ↵
Specify next point or [Undo]: **4,5** ↵
Specify next point or [Undo]: ↵
Press: ↵ (or the return button on your mouse and pick Repeat Line)
Specify first point: **@** ↵

Tip

When drawing, moving the cursor away from the point you have selected can help you see the effect of the selection. You will not notice rubberband lines if you leave the cursor over the previously selected point.

Your starting point is now the last point you entered in the previous step (4,5). Note the line rubberbanding from that point to the cursor.

Using Relative X- and Y-Coordinates

Relative coordinates allow you to select a point at a known distance from the last point specified. To do so, you must insert the @ symbol before your X- and Y-coordinate values. Now, continue the Line command.

Specify next point or [Undo]: **@0,3** ↵

Note that your line is drawn 0 units in the X-direction and 3 units (12 spaces on the grid) in the positive Y-direction from the last point specified (4,5). Complete the shape.

Specify next point or [Undo]: **@–2,0** ↵
Specify next point or [Close/Undo]: **@0,–3** ↵
Specify next point or [Close/Undo]: ↵

Your drawing should look like Figure 1.24. You may need to scroll your screen to see all three rectangles.

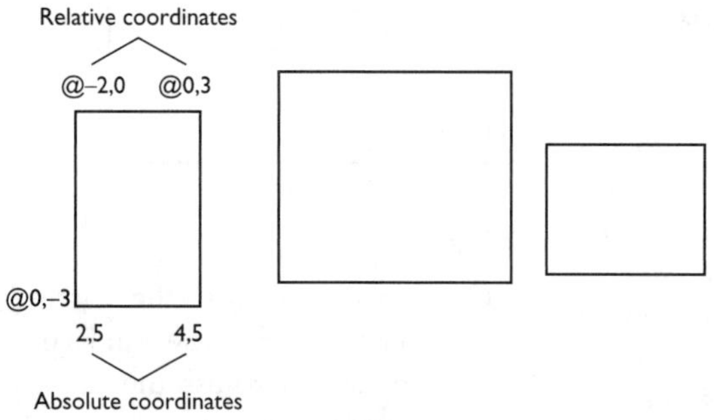

Figure 1.24

Using Polar Coordinates

When prompted to enter a point, you can specify the point by using *polar coordinates*. Polar coordinate values use the input format @DISTANCE<ANGLE. When using the default decimal units, you don't need to specify any units when typing the angle and length. Later in this tutorial, you will learn how to select different units of measure for lengths and angles. When you are using polar coordinates, each new input is calculated relative to the last point entered. The default AutoCAD system for measuring angles defines a horizontal line to the right of the current point as 0°. As shown in Figure 1.25, angular values are positive counterclockwise. Both distance and angle values may be negative.

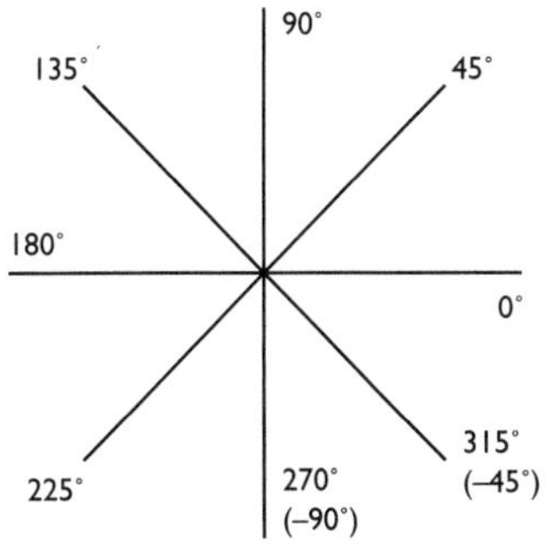

Figure 1.25

Figure 1.26 shows an example of lines drawn using relative coordinate entry. A line was drawn from the starting point to the distance and at the angle specified. In the figure, the line labeled 1 extends 3 units from the starting point at an angle of 30°. Remember that the default measures the angle from a horizontal line to the right of the starting point. Line 2 was begun at the last point of line 1 and extended 2 units at an angle of 135°, again measured from a horizontal line to the right of that line's starting point. Polar coordinates are very important for creating drawing geometry.

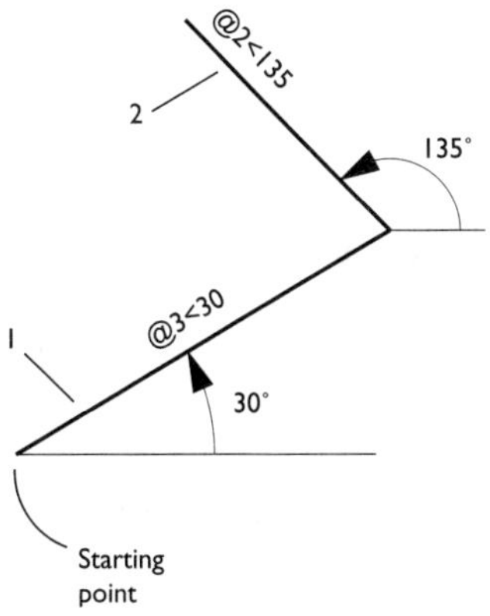

Figure 1.26

You will now draw a rectangle using polar coordinate values. The starting point for this rectangle is specified as point A in Figure 1.27. Use the toolbar to select the Line command. You will draw a horizontal line 3.5 units to the right of the starting point by responding to the prompts.

Pick: **Line icon**

Specify first point: **pick point A, coordinates 1.0,4.0**

Specify next point or [Undo]: **@3.5<0** ↵

You will draw the next segment using dynamic input.

Pick: **DYN button on the Status bar to toggle it on**

The dynamic entry inputs appear near the cursor location as shown in Figure 1.27.

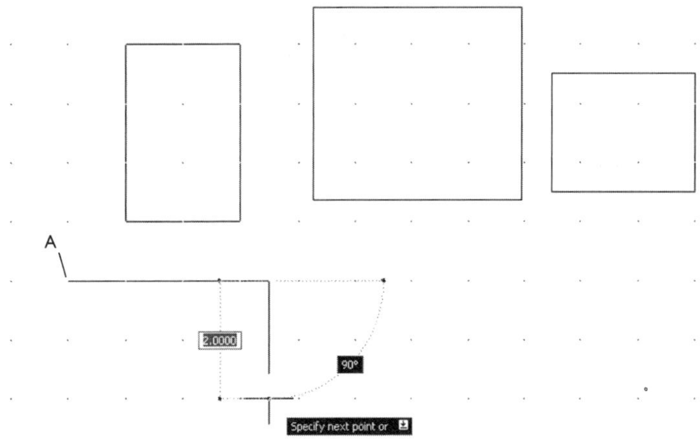

Figure 1.27

Tip

Clicking on the coordinates displayed on the status bar toggles their display; that is, you can toggle the coordinate display off and on. When you toggle the coordinate display off, the coordinates do not change when you move the crosshairs and they appear grayed out on the status bar. When you toggle the coordinates back on, they once again display the X-, Y-, and Z-location of the crosshairs. During execution of the commands a third toggle is available for the coordinate display: In a command such as Line, you can click the coordinate display to display the length and angle from the last point picked. This display can be very useful in helping you determine approximate distances and angles for polar coordinate entry. You can also toggle the coordinates by pressing [F6] *or* [Ctrl]*-D.*

In the highlighted input box, **type a distance of 2.00** and press [Tab]
Type: **90** (for the angle) ↵
Pick: **DYN button to toggle it off**

Complete the rectangle, using polar coordinate values.

Specify next point or [Close/Undo]: **@3.5<180** ↵
Specify next point or [Close/Undo]: **C** ↵

Your drawing should look like that in Figure 1.28.

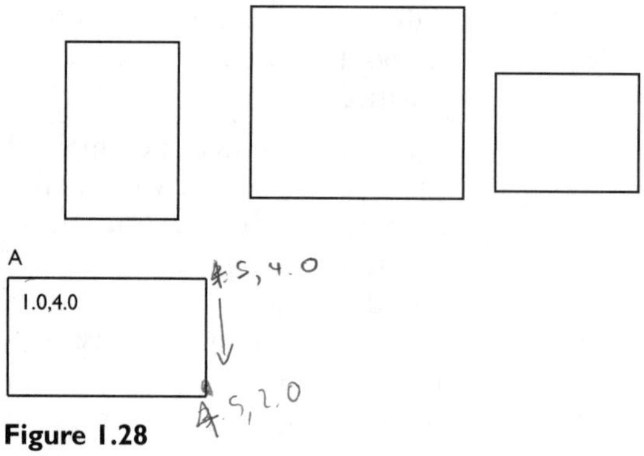

Figure 1.28

Using Save

The *Save* command lets you save your work to the file name you have previously specified, in this case *shapes.dwg*. You should save your work frequently. If the power went off or your computer crashed, you would lose all the work that you had not previously saved. If you save every ten minutes or so, you will never lose more than that amount of work. Save your work at this time by using the Standard toolbar to pick the Save icon, which looks like a floppy disk.

Pick: **Save icon**

Your work will be saved to *shapes.dwg*. If you had not previously named your drawing, the Save Drawing As dialog box would appear, allowing you to specify a name for the drawing. Save your work periodically as you work through these tutorials.

Using Erase

Tip

Typing E ↵ (the command alias) will also start the Erase command.

The *Erase* command removes objects from a drawing. The Erase command is located on the Modify toolbar.

Pick: **Erase icon**

Tip

If Snap is turned on, turning it off makes object selection easier.

A small square replaces the crosshairs, prompting you to select objects. To identify an object to be erased, place the cursor over the object and press the pick button. Each line that you have drawn is a separate drawing object, so now erase the objects A and B in Figure 1.29.

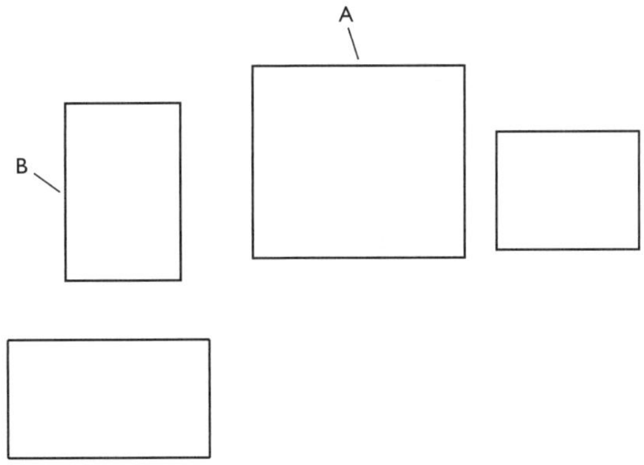

Figure 1.29

Select objects: **pick on line A**
Select objects: **pick on line B**

The lines you have selected are highlighted but are not erased. You can select more than one item to create a *selection set*. You will learn more ways to do so later in this tutorial. When you have finished selecting, you will press the return button on your pointing device or ↵ to indicate that you are done selecting. Pressing ↵ or the return button completes the selection set and erases the selected objects.

Press: ↵ (or the return button)

The selected lines are erased from the screen.

If you erase an object by mistake, you may activate the OOPS command at the command prompt.

Type: **OOPS** ↵

The lines last erased are restored on your screen. OOPS restores only the most recently erased objects. It won't restore objects beyond the last Erase command. However, it will work to restore erased objects even if other commands have been used in the meantime.

Tip

Don't position the selection cursor at a point where two objects cross because you cannot be certain which will be selected. The entire object is selected when you point to any part of it, so select the object at a point that is not ambiguous.

Tip

Redraw All works in all viewports to remove the blip marks *added to the drawing screen when you are drawing objects and to restore objects partially erased while you are editing other objects. Redraw All is located on the View menu. Redraw All has no prompts; it is simply activated when you pick it.*

You can also just type R ↵ at the command prompt; R is the command alias for Redraw.

Erasing with Window or Crossing

Next you will clear your graphics window to make room for new shapes by erasing all the rectangles on your screen. You can pick multiple objects by using the Window and Crossing selection modes.

To use implied Windowing mode, pick a point on the screen that is not on an object and move your pointing device from left to right. A window-type box will start to rubberband from the point you picked. In the *implied Windowing mode* (a box drawn from left to right), the window formed selects everything that is entirely enclosed in it. However, drawing the box from right to left causes the *implied Crossing mode* to be used. Everything that either crosses the box or is enclosed in the box is selected. You can use implied Windowing and implied Crossing to select objects during any command in which you are prompted to select objects.

You can turn implied Windowing on and off. Before using it, you will check to see that implied Windowing is turned on.

Tip

A helpful visual cue when you are drawing a crossing box (right to left) is that the box is drawn with a dashed line. When drawing a window box (left to right) the box is drawn with a solid line.

Pick: **Tools, Options**

The Options dialog box appears on your screen showing a number of tabs that can be used to control the way AutoCAD functions.

Pick: **the Selection tab**

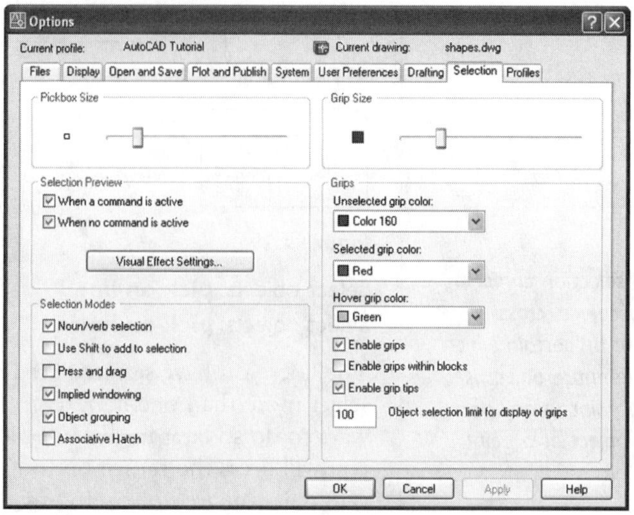

Figure 1.30

The Selection tab pops to the top of the stack as shown in Figure 1.30. For implied Windowing to work, it must be selected (a check must appear in the box to the left of Implied windowing).

On your own, select the Implied Windowing mode if it is not currently selected.

Pick: **Visual Effect Settings**

The Visual Effect Settings dialog box allows you to set the highlighting, window, and crossing box appearances. The default is that a window which selects only objects fully enclosed in the drawn box is colored blue, and a crossing selection box which selects any object the box crosses is shown with green. Leave the settings at the default colors for now as shown in Figure 1.31.

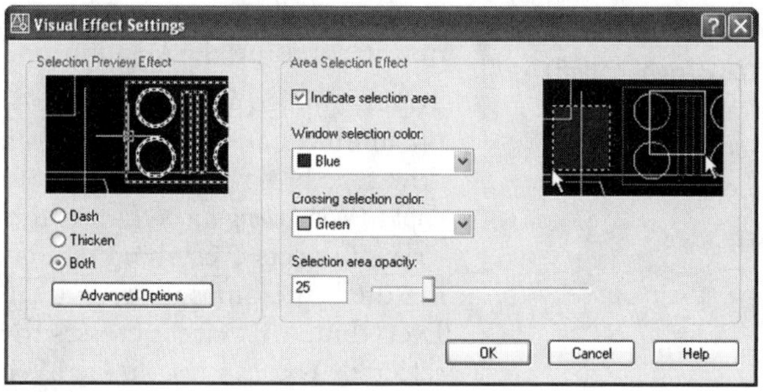

Figure 1.31

Pick: Cancel to exit each dialog box without making any changes if the settings were correct. If not correct them on your own.

Pick: **Erase icon**

Select objects: **pick a point above and to the left of your upper three rectangles,** identified as A in Figure 1.32

Other corner: **pick a point below and to the right of your upper three rectangles,** identified as B

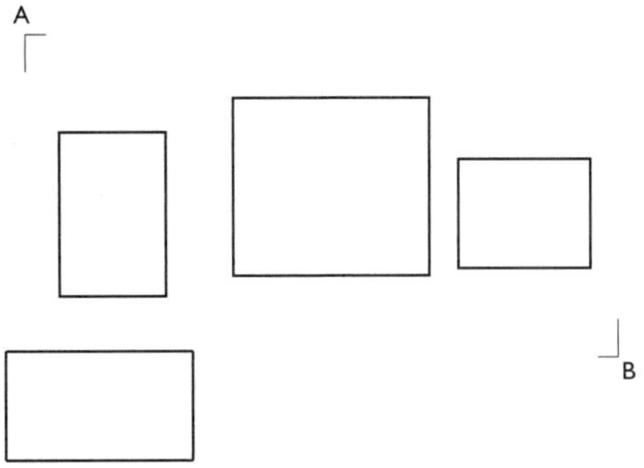

Figure 1.32

Note that a "window" box formed around the area specified by the upper left and lower right corners. Your screen should look like that in Figure 1.33.

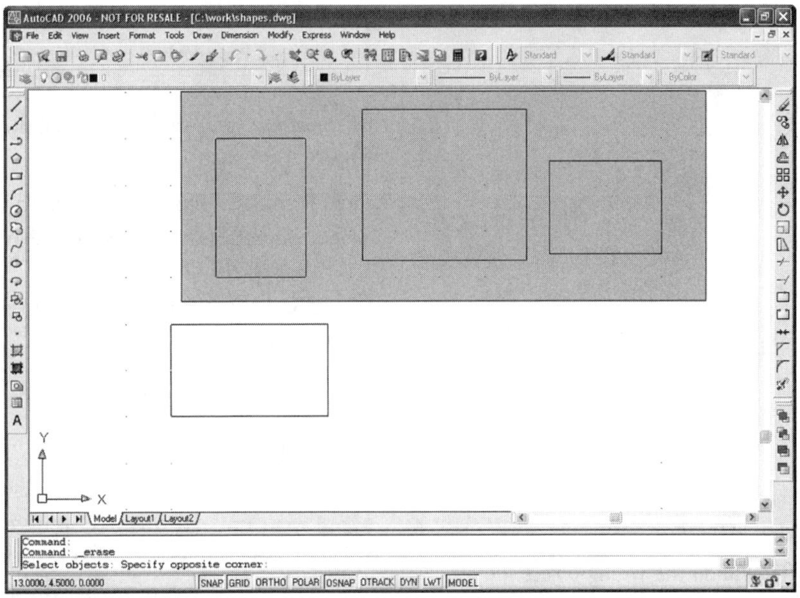

Figure 1.33

When you picked the second corner of the window (point B), the objects that were entirely enclosed in the window became highlighted. You will end the object selection by pressing ↵ and erasing the selected objects.

Select objects: ↵

Only objects that were entirely within the window were erased. The fourth rectangle (represented by four separate lines) was not completely enclosed and therefore was not erased.

Next, you will restart the Erase command and then use implied Crossing to erase the fourth rectangle. One way to restart a command is to use the right mouse button and pick anywhere in the blank area of the screen. This will pop up a *context-sensitive menu*.

Right-click: **anywhere in the blank area of the screen**

The context sensitive menu shown in Figure 1.34 pops up on the screen.

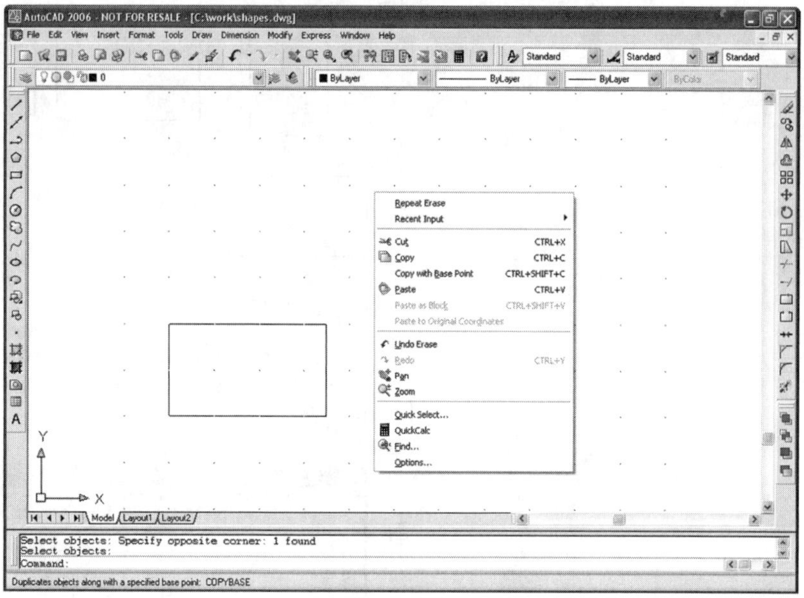

Figure 1.34

Pick: **Repeat Erase** (from the context menu)

Select objects: **pick a point below and to the right of the remaining rectangle**

Other corner: **pick a point above and to the left of the rectangle**

Select objects: ↵

The remaining rectangle is erased from the drawing.

Using Undo

The *Undo* command removes the effect of previous commands. If you make a mistake, pick the Undo command from the Standard toolbar, and the effect of the previous command will disappear.

You will try this now to see the last rectangle you erased reappear.

Pick: **Undo icon**

Line and other commands also include Undo as a command option that allows you to undo the last action within the command.

Pick: **Line icon**

Specify first point: **pick any point**

Specify next point or [Undo]: **pick any point**

Tip

If you undo the wrong object, the Redo command lets you restore the items you have undone. It is the icon to the right of Undo on the Standard toolbar.

Specify next point or [Undo]: **pick any point**
Specify next point or [Close/Undo]: **pick any point**
Specify next point or [Close/Undo]: **U** ↵
Specify next point or [Close/Undo]: ↵

One line segment disappeared while you remained within the Line command. Now, you will undo the entire Line command with the Undo command. You will pick Undo from the Standard toolbar.

Pick: **Undo icon**

All the line segments drawn with the last instance of the command disappear.

Typing Undo at the command prompt offers more options for undoing your work. You will draw some lines to have some objects to undo.

On your own, use Erase from the toolbar and erase all remaining objects in your graphics window. Use Line on your own to draw six parallel lines anywhere on your drawing screen. Use Snap and Grid as needed.

In the next step, you will type the Undo command to remove the last three lines that you drew.

Tip

Backing up one step at a time by using Undo from the Standard toolbar (the U command) often is the easiest way to undo previous steps. Some commands do several steps in one sequence, so you may not be sure of the exact number you want to back up.

Type: **UNDO** ↵
Enter the number of operations to undo or
[Auto/Control/BEgin/End/Mark/Back] <1>: **3** ↵

The last three lines drawn should disappear, corresponding to the last three instances of the Line command. You could have selected any number, depending on the number of command steps you wanted to undo.

The flyout symbol next to the Undo command lets you view the command history of selections you have made. You can undo them one by one using this option.

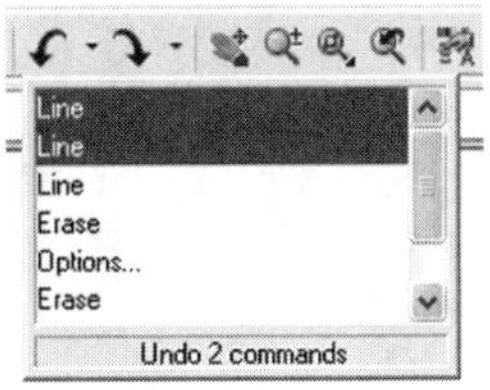

Figure 1.35

Pick: **on the flyout triangle next to the Undo icon**

The command history flies out as shown in Figure 1.35.

Pick: **on the Line command in the Undo flyout**

The line is undone from your screen.

Pick: **on the flyout triangle next to the Undo icon** to show the command history
Pick: **on the second Erase command listed in the history**

The Erase command is undone and the boxes that you erased earlier return to the screen.

Using Redo

If the last command undid something you really did not want to undo, you can use the *Redo* command to reverse the effects. The Redo icon appears on the Standard toolbar to the right of Undo.

Pick: **Redo icon**

The erased boxes reappear again as the Erase command is Redone.

Pick: the flyout triangle next to **Redo**

You should see a command history of the items that you have Undone. You can pick from the list to redo them.

Using Back

The Back option of the Undo command takes the drawing back to a mark that you set with the Mark option or to the beginning of the *drawing session* if you haven't set any marks. Be careful when selecting these options or you may undo too much.

Type: **UNDO** ↵

Enter the number of operations to undo or
[Auto/Control/BEgin/End/Mark/Back] <1>: **B** ↵

This will undo everything. OK? <Y>: ↵

All operations back to the beginning of the drawing session (or mark, if you had previously set one with the Mark option of the Undo command) will be undone. (You can use Help to find out what the remaining options, Auto, Control, Begin, and End, are used for.)

Pick: to flyout the command history next to **Redo**

The list of commands that you have selected in the drawing should appear in the command window.

On your own, select some of the commands from the list to Redo.

Next, close drawing Shapes.

Pick: **File, Close**

You will be prompted "Save changes to *c:\work\shapes.dwg?*"

Pick: **No**

The drawing will close, and the graphics area will appear gray to indicate that there is no drawing open. Notice that now there are only the New, Open, Sheet Set Manager and Help icons available on the standard toolbar.

Next, you will create a new drawing showing a plot plan. A plot plan is a plan view of a lot boundary and the location of utilities. You will set the units for this drawing, instead of using the defaults.

To start a new file, you will pick the *New* command from the Standard toolbar. It is the leftmost icon.

Pick: **New icon**

The Select template dialog box appears on your screen. The default template *acad.dwt* should be highlighted.

Pick: ***acad.dwt*** (if it is not already highlighted)

Pick: **Open**

Use File, Save As to save this drawing to a new name: ***plotplan.dwg.***

Be sure to create the new drawing in the ***c:\work*** directory.

Pick: **Save** (to exit the dialog box)

Setting the Units

The AutoCAD software allows you to work in the type of units that are appropriate for your drawing. The *default units* are decimal. You can

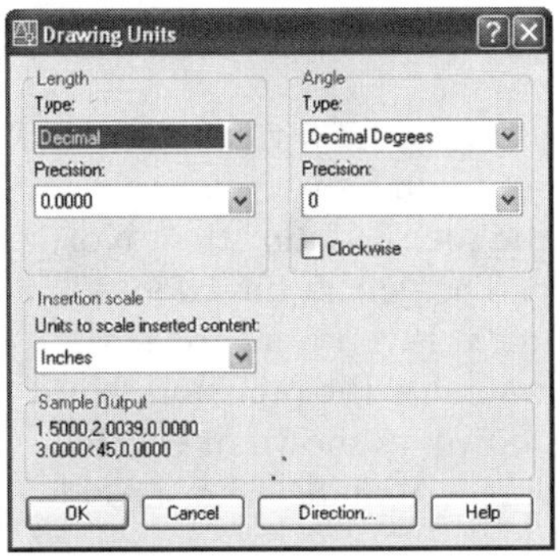

Figure 1.36

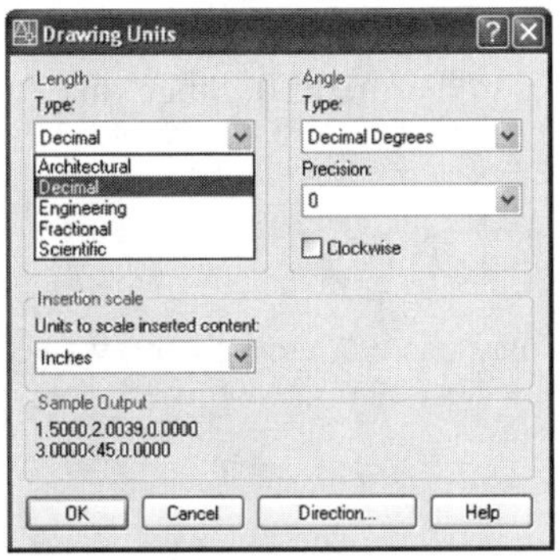

Figure 1.37

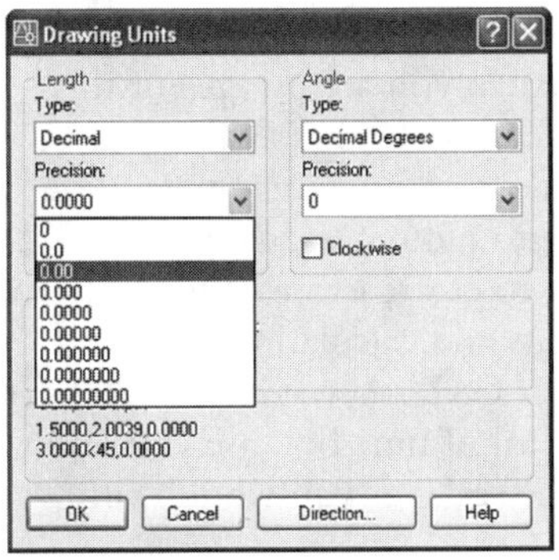

Figure 1.38

change the type of units for lengths to *architectural units* that appear in feet and fractional inches, *engineering units* that appear in feet and decimal inches, *scientific units* that appear in exponential format, or *fractional units* that are whole numbers and fractions. When you use architectural or engineering units, one drawing unit is equal to one inch; to specify feet you must type the feet mark after the numerical value (e.g., 50.5' or 20'2" or 35'-4"). You can think of the other types of units as representing any type of real-world measurement you want: decimal miles, furlongs, inches, millimeters, microns, or anything else. When the time comes to plot the drawing, you determine the final relationship between your drawing database, in which you create the object the actual size it is in the real world, and the paper plot.

Angular measurements can be given in decimal degrees; degrees, minutes, and seconds; gradians; radians; or *surveyor units*, such as the bearing N45°0'00"E.

You will use the Format selection from the menu bar to access the Units Control dialog box.

Pick: **Format, Units**

The Drawing Units dialog box appears on your screen, as shown in Figure 1.36.

In the Length area, the choices below Type pull down to allow you to select from the available length units for the drawing. Figure 1.37 shows the types of length units expanded.

Pick: **on the downward arrow near the word Decimal or in the box containing the word Decimal**

The length choices expand out below the current selection.

Pick: **Architectural** (from the available list)

Architectural appears as the type of units. You can select only one type at a time. Note that the units displayed under the heading Precision change to architectural units. Again use the Length Type area to:

Pick: **Decimal**

Note that the units in the Precision area change back to decimal units. The dimensions for the plot plan that you will create will be in decimal feet, so you will leave the units set to Decimal.

Pick: **on the number 0.0000** displayed in the box below Precision

The choices for unit precision pull down below the box, as shown in Figure 1.38.

Pick: **0.00**

Now the display precision is set to two decimal places. When specifying coordinates and lengths, you can still type a value from the keyboard with more precision and the AutoCAD drawing database will keep track of your drawing with this accuracy. However, because you have selected this precision, only two decimal places will be displayed. Units precision determines the *display* of the units on your screen and in the prompts, not the accuracy internal to the drawing. The AutoCAD software keeps track internally to at least fourteen decimal places, but only eight decimal places of accuracy will ever appear on the screen. You can change the type of unit and precision at any point during the drawing process.

The right side of the dialog box controls the type and precision of angular measurements. Remember that the default measurement of angles is counterclockwise, starting from a horizontal line to the right as 0°. You can change the default setting by picking on the Direction button and making a new selection. Leave the direction set at the default of 0 degrees toward East. Use the Type setting in the Angle area to:

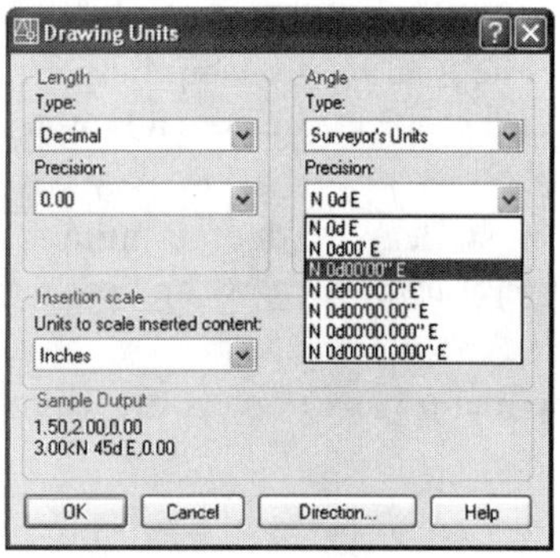

Figure 1.39

Pick: **Surveyor's Units**

Note that the display in this Precision area changes to list the angle as a bearing. When this mode is active, you can type in a surveyor angle and the program will measure the angle from the specified direction, North or South, toward East or West, as specified. The default direction, North, is straight toward the top of the screen. If you want to view greater angle precision, pick on the box containing the precision, N 0d E. The list of the available precisions pops down, as shown in Figure 1.39, allowing you to choose to display degrees, minutes, and seconds. To display degrees, minutes, and seconds:

Pick: **N0d00'00"E**

The Insertion scale area of the dialog box controls the scaling factor for blocks that are dragged into the current drawing from the Tool palettes. You will learn more about the Tool palettes in Tutorial 10. Since this drawing will be created in decimal feet,

Pick: **Feet**

Pick: **OK** (to exit the dialog box)

Look at the status bar: The coordinate display has changed to show two instead of four places after the decimal.

Sizing Your Drawing

You always create your AutoCAD drawing geometry in *real-world units*. In other words, if the object is 10" long, you make it exactly 10" long in the drawing database. If it is a few millimeters long, you create the drawing to those lengths. You can think of the decimal units as representing whatever decimal measurement system you are using. For this drawing, the units will represent decimal feet, so 10 units will equal 10 feet in the drawing. After you have created the drawing geometry, you can decide on the scale at which you want to plot your final printed drawing on the sheet of paper. The ability to create exact drawings from which you can make accurate measurements and calculations on the computer is one of the powerful features of CAD. Also, you can plot the final drawing to any scale, saving a great deal of time because you don't have to remake drawings just to change the scale, as you would with paper drawings.

For your plot plan drawing, you need to create a larger drawing area to accommodate the site plan shown in Figure 1.40.

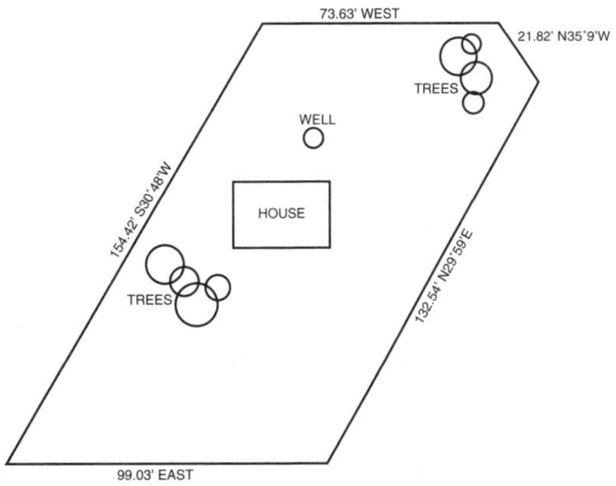

Figure 1.40

Using Limits

The *Limits* command sets the size of your drawing area. You can also turn off Limits if you do not want to preset the size of the drawing. Use the Drawing Limits selection from the Format menu to change the overall size of the drawing to reflect metric drawing units.

Pick: **Format, Drawing Limits**

Reset model space limits:

Specify lower left corner or [ON/OFF] <0.00,0.00>: ↵ (to accept default of 0,0)

Specify upper right corner <12.00,9.00>: **300,225** ↵

The default space in which you create your drawing geometry or model is called model space. It is where you accurately create real-world-size models. In Tutorial 5, you will learn to use paper space, where you lay out views, as you do on a sheet of paper. You can set different sizes for model space and paper space with the Limits command.

You will select View, Zoom All from the menu bar to show this larger area on your display.

Tip

If the coordinate display does not show a larger size, check to see that you set the limits correctly and that you picked Zoom All. Be sure that the coordinates are turned on by clicking on the coordinates located on the status bar until you see them change as you move the mouse.

Pick: **View, Zoom, All**

Move the crosshairs to the upper right-hand corner of the screen. You will see that the status bar displaying the coordinate location of the crosshairs indicates that the size of the graphics window has changed to reflect the limits of the drawing.

Now, you will set the grid spacing to a larger value so that you can see the grid on your screen.

Command: **GRID** ↵

Specify grid spacing(x) or [ON/OFF/Snap/Aspect] <0.50>: **10** ↵

To draw the site boundary, you will use absolute and polar coordinates as appropriate. You will be using surveyor angles to specify the directions for the lines. The AutoCAD surveyor angle selections, which you selected when setting the type of units, are given in bearings. *Bearings* give the angle to turn from the first direction stated toward the second direction stated. For example, a bearing of N29'59"E means to start at the direction North and turn an angle of 29'59" toward the East.

Now you are ready to start drawing the lines of the site boundary. Use the Draw toolbar.

Pick: **Line icon**

Specify first point: **50,30** ↵

Specify next point or [Undo]: **@99.03<E** ↵

Specify next point or [Close/Undo]: **@132.54<N29d59'E** ↵

Specify next point or [Close/Undo]: **@21.82<N35d9'W** ↵

Specify next point or [Close/Undo]: **@73.63<W** ↵

Specify next point or [Close/Undo]: **C** ↵

Your screen should look like Figure 1.41.

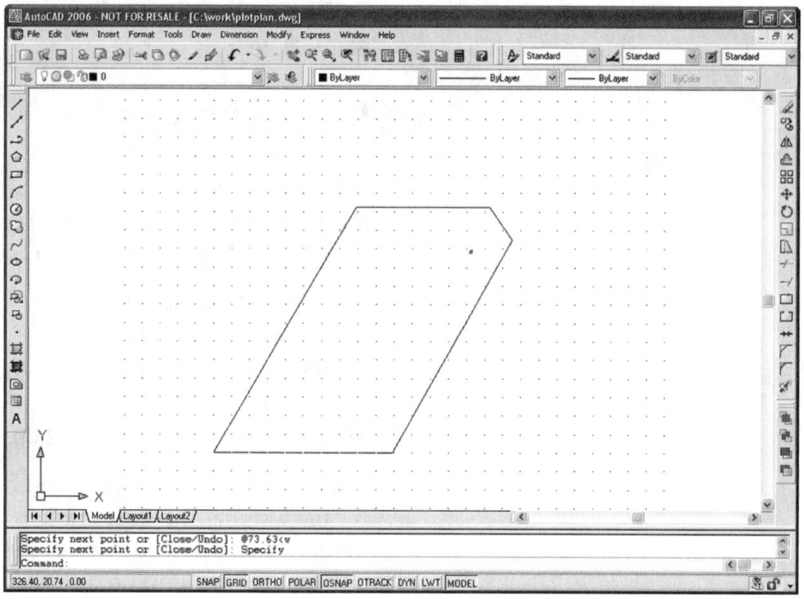

Figure 1.41

Using Rectangle

You are going to draw a rectangle to represent a house on the plot plan. Using coordinate values, you will place the rectangle roughly in the center of your plot plan.

The *Rectangle* command has several options: Chamfer, Elevation, Fillet, Thickness, and Width as well as a prompt for the corners of the rectangle. These options allow you to manipulate the appearance and placement of the rectangle before it is drawn. Chamfer and Fillet are options that change the corners of the rectangle (covered in Tutorial 3). Elevation and Thickness are options best used in 3D modeling. The Width option allows you to specify a width for the lines making up the rectangle.

You will pick Rectangle from the Draw toolbar and then type the command option letter W to change Width.

Pick: **Rectangle icon**

Specify first corner point or [Chamfer/Elevation/Fillet/Thickness/Width]: **W** ↵

Specify line width for rectangles <0.00>: **.5** ↵

Tip

You can also draw a rectangle by picking the corners directly from the screen using your mouse.

Specify first corner point or [Chamfer/Elevation/Fillet/Thickness/
Width]: **120,95** ↵
Specify other corner point or [Area/Dimensions/Rotation]: **150,115** ↵

Your drawing should be similar to the one in Figure 1.42.

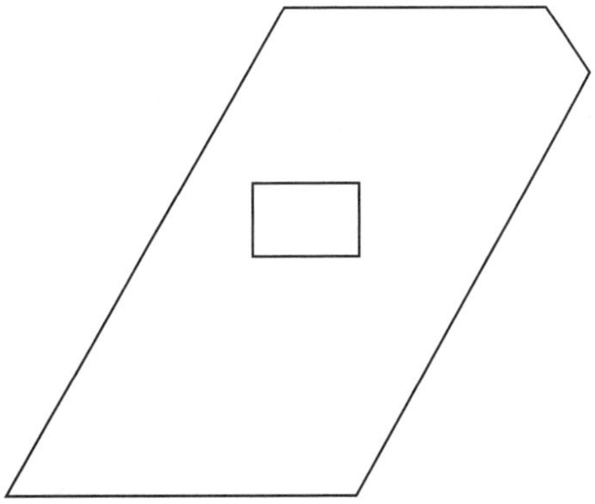

Figure 1.42

Saving Your Drawing

Having completed the site boundary, you should now save the drawing on your disk. You should save whenever you have completed a major step or every 10 to 15 minutes. This way, if your computer crashes, you will not have lost more than a few minutes worth of work. Also, if you make a mistake that you don't know how to correct, you can pick File, Close, discard your drawing changes, and open the saved version.

Pick: **Save icon**

Your file is saved to the name you assigned when you first saved the drawing.

Drawing Circles

You will draw a circle to represent the location of the well on the plot plan. You draw circles using the *Circle* command located on the Draw toolbar.

Pick: **Circle icon**
Command: Specify center point for circle or [3P/2P/
Ttr (tan tan radius)]: **145,128** ↵

As you move the cursor away from the center point, a circle continually re-forms, using the distance from the center to the cursor location as the radius value. You will type the value to specify the exact size for the circle's radius.

Specify radius of circle or [Diameter]: **3** ↵

Before continuing to draw more circles, you will turn off the Osnap, Polar, and Otrack buttons on the Status bar (if they are on). These buttons help you create objects that are aligned with other objects in your drawing. This can make it difficult to draw shapes freehand. You will turn them off now and learn more about them in Tutorial 4.

Pick: **to turn off Osnap, Otrack, Polar, and Ortho** (if necessary)

Now the only buttons that should appear highlighted are Grid and Model, as shown in Figure 1.43.

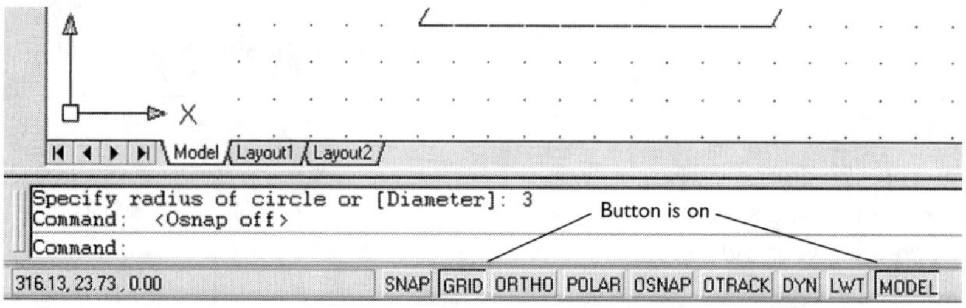

Figure 1.43

Now, draw some circles to represent trees or shrubs in the plot plan. You will specify the locations for the trees by picking them from the screen.

Pick: **Circle icon**

Specify center point for circle or [3P/2P/Ttr (tan tan radius)]: **pick a point for the center of circle 1** (as shown in Figure 1.44) ↵

Specify radius of circle or [Diameter]: **move the crosshairs away until the circle appears similar to that shown in Figure 1.44, then press the pick button** ↵

On your own, draw the remaining circles representing trees using this method, so that you are pleased with their appearance.

Your drawing should look like that in Figure 1.44.

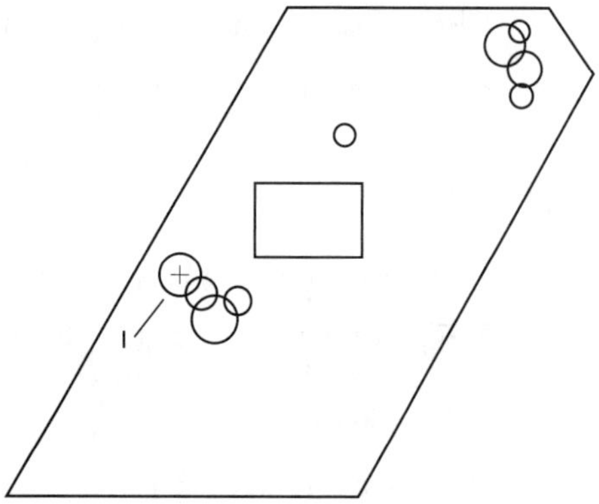

Figure 1.44

Adding Text

Use the Text (*formerly Dtext*) command to add single lines of text, words, or numbers to a drawing. Text, or Single Line Text, is located on the Draw menu, under Text. Unless you specify otherwise, text is added to the right of a designated starting point. You can also center text about a point or add it to the left of a point if you use the Justify option. To specify the starting point for the text, you will pick a point on the screen. (You can also type the coordinates of the location for the starting point.) You will label the lengths and bearings of the lot lines shown in the plot plan, starting with the bottom lot line. You will set the height for the text to 3 units because the default value of 0.20 is too small to be legible in model space on this drawing. The rotation prompt allows you to select a rotation angle for the text so that it appears angled

Tip

To determine the actual text height necessary, you must know the size of paper and scale you will use to plot the final drawing. In Tutorial 5 you will learn to use paper space to set up scaling and text for plotting. If you are unsure about what text height to use, move the crosshairs on the screen and read the coordinate display on the toolbar. Use the lengths shown to get an appropriate size for your text. You can also use the rubberband line that appears during the text height portion of the Text command to set the height visually.

on your screen. Typically, the best way to do this is by picking on the text using the rubberband line during the rotate portion of the prompt. Text on technical drawings is usually drawn horizontally and is called *uni-directional text*. Accept the default rotation angle of East to draw the text horizontally for the bottom lot line.

Pick: **Draw, Text, Single Line Text**

Specify start point of text or [Justify/Style]: **select a point at about coordinates 90,25**

Specify height <0.20>: **3** ↵

Specify rotation angle of text <E>: ↵

The AutoCAD software is now ready to accept typed-in text.

Type: **99.03' EAST** ↵ ↵

You can type the text just as you would with a word processing program. Text will not wrap text, so you must designate the end of each line by pressing ↵. If you make a mistake before exiting the Text command, backspace to erase the text. (After exiting the Text command, you can use Edit Text to make corrections to lines of text.) Press ↵ without entering any text (a null reply to the prompt) to end the Text command. (You must use the keyboard, not the return button on your pointing device.) When you exit Text, the text becomes a permanent object. Your drawing should look like that in Figure 1.45.

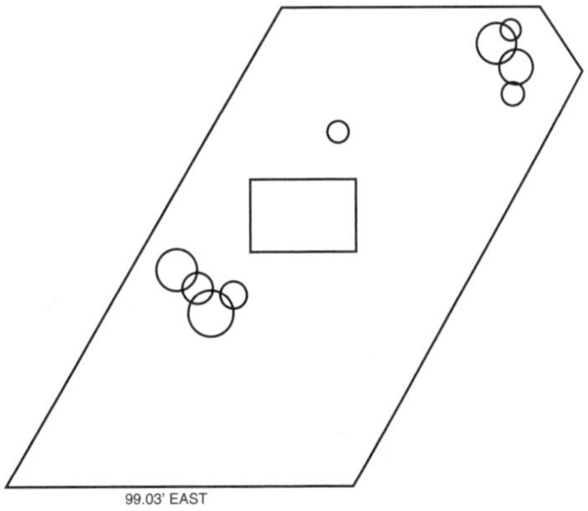

Figure 1.45

Using Special Text Characters

You will add the text labeling the length and angle for the right-hand lot line. When you are using the standard AutoCAD fonts, the special text item %%d creates the degree symbol. Type the line of text with %%d in place of the degree symbol. When you have finished typing in the text and press ↵, %%d will be replaced with a degree symbol. (You will use more special text characters in Tutorial 7.) You will also specify a rotation angle for the text so that it is aligned with the lot line. You will type Text to activate the command.

Type: **TEXT**

Specify start point of text or [Justify/Style]: **pick a point slightly to the right of the right-hand lot line**

Specify height <3.00>: ↵

Tip

You can also specify the rotation by picking when the line that rubber-bands from the point you picked for the text location is oriented at the rotation angle you desire. To easily add the rest of the text along the lot lines use this rubberband mode and drag a line parallel to the lot line at the Rotation angle prompt. If you do not want to type in bearings for the text angle, you can change the units at any time to return to degrees.

Specify rotation angle of text <E>: **N29d59'E** ↵
Type: **132.54' N29%%d59'E** ↵ ↵

The text should align with the lot line in your drawing.

Copying Text

Next you will learn how to copy a text object and edit it to quickly create labels for other items in your drawings. This is generally faster than placing text items one by one.

Pick: **Copy icon** (from the Modify toolbar)
Select objects: **pick the bottom text object 99.03' EAST** ↵
Specify base point or [Displacement] <Displacement>: **pick the middle of that text object**
Specify second point or <use first point as displacement>: **pick above the upper line** as shown in Figure 1.46

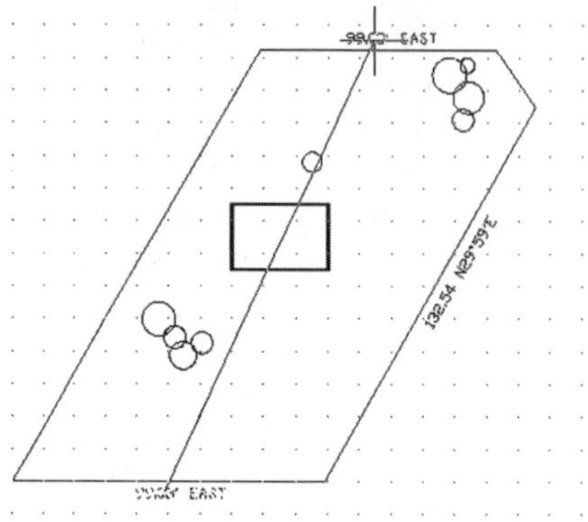

Figure 1.46

Specify second point or [Exit/Undo] <Exit>: **continue on your own to place the copied text items in the drawing** as shown in Figure 1.47
Press: ↵ when you are done

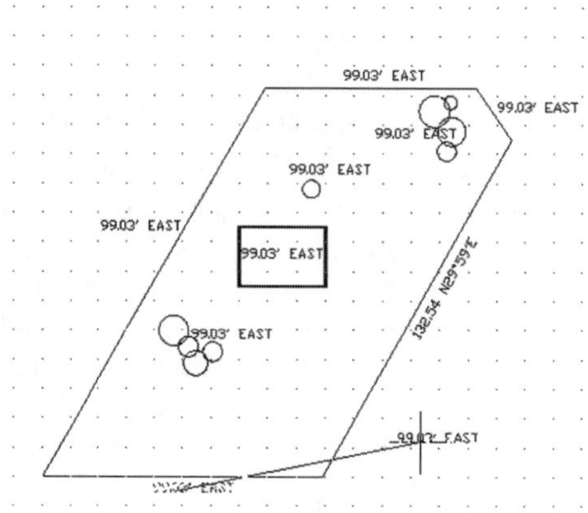

Figure 1.47

Tip

Most items in your drawing can be edited by double-clicking on them. Different editing commands launch depending on the type of entity you double-click.

Tip

You can also select Modify, Object, Text, Edit to use in place editing.

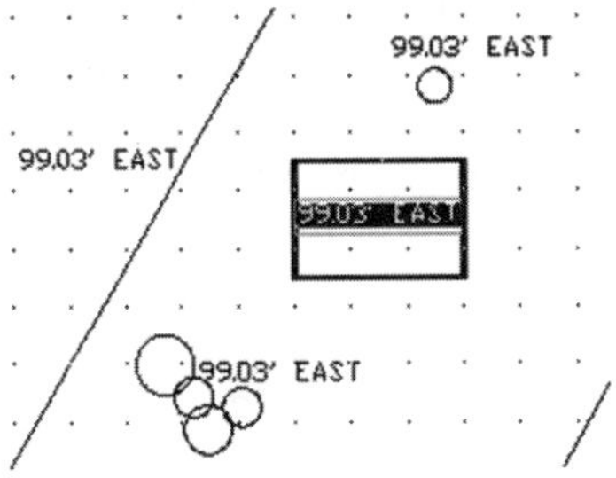

Figure 1.48

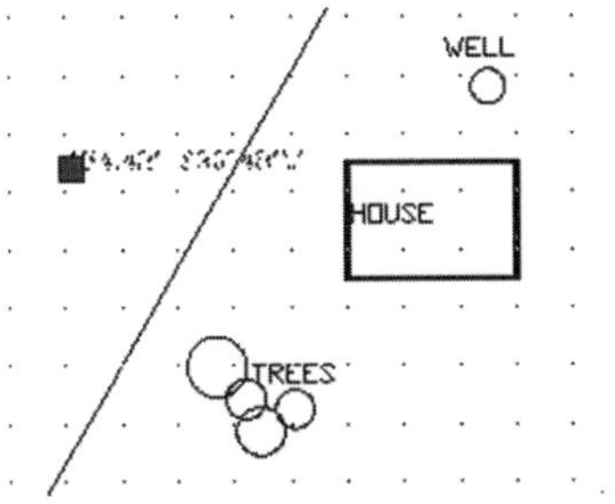

Figure 1.49

In Place Text Editing

Next you will change the text so that the drawing displays the correct information.

Double-click: **on the text in the rectangle** so that it appears in the text editor as shown in Figure 1.48

Type: **HOUSE** ⏎

On your own, change the text identifying the trees, well locations, and remaining bearings and distances. Press ⏎ to exit the command when done.

Moving and Rotating Text

Rotating and moving text is easy with the text object's grips.

Pick: **on the text along the left lot line** so that its grip appears as shown in Figure 1.49

Pick: **in the small grip box at the left of the text** so that it appears "hot" or active. Its color should change

Right-click: **with your mouse still over the grip** so that the grip editing menu appears as shown in Figure 1.50

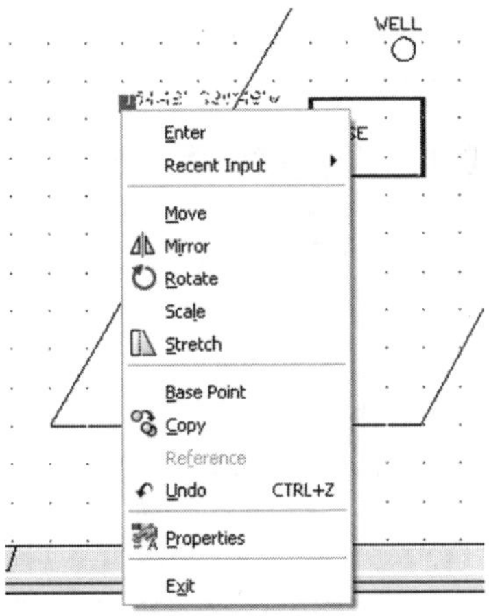

Figure 1.50

Pick: **Rotate**

On your own, use the mouse to rotate the text into alignment with the left lot line and pick to select the desired angle.

Press: Esc **to unselect the grips**

You can move items directly using the grips without selecting from the menu. To do this,

Pick: **the grip to make it active and then move it to a new location using your mouse.**

On your own, practice positioning the remaining text items for the plot plan.

Setting the Text Style

The *Style* command allows you to create a style specifying the font and other characteristics for the shapes of the text in your drawing. A *font* is a set of letters, numbers, punctuation marks, and symbols of a distinctive style and design. The AutoCAD software supplies several *shape-compiled fonts* that you can use to create text styles. In addition to these shape-compiled fonts, you can also use your own True Type, Type 1 Postscript, or Unicode fonts. Some sample True Type fonts are provided with the AutoCAD software.

Tip

If a drawing is opened on a system that does not have the same fonts used in the drawing, you may be asked to substitute a different font. This can wreak havoc with the way text is aligned. Unless your drawing requires special fonts, it is a good idea to use the .shx fonts provided with the AutoCAD software. These should be available on most systems. You can also load other fonts, but they can be expensive to purchase.

The Style command allows you to control the appearance of a font so that it is slanted (oblique), backwards, vertical, or upside-down. You can also control the height and proportional width of the letters.

If you don't use the default style, you must create the style you want to use before you add text to your drawing (or later change the properties of the text to that style).

To create a style, you will select Format, Text Style from the menu bar. After you have created (or selected) a style, that style will remain current for all text until you set a new style as the current one. An AutoCAD shape-compiled font that works well for engineering drawings is the Roman Simplex font.

Pick: **Format, Text Style**

The dialog box shown in Figure 1.51 appears on your screen. It is divided into four different sections: Style Name, Font, Effects, and Preview. You can set a new style in the Style Name section, and it will become the default style for any subsequently written text.

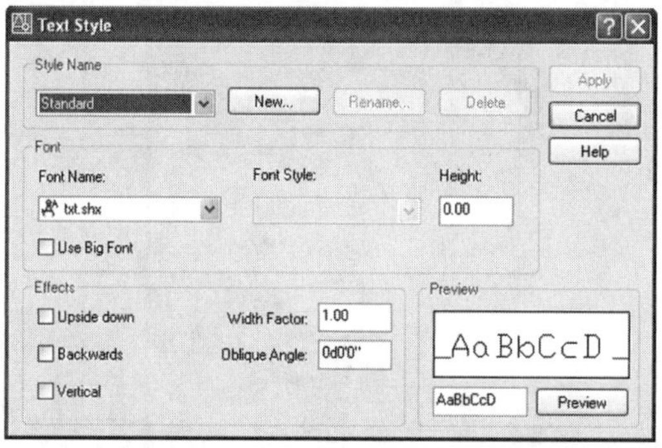

Figure 1.51

You will pick the New button, make a new style named MyStyle, and then give it the shape Romans.

Pick: **New**
Type: **MyStyle** (in the New Text Style dialog box)
Pick: **OK**

Next you will set the font for the new style, *Romans.shx*. Your system may have many fonts available in addition to the shape-compiled fonts.

Pick: **to expand the box below Font Name**
Pick: **on one of the fonts listed and note the changes in the Preview section of the dialog box**

The text in the Preview box will be underlined in red if it is a True Type font, as in Figure 1.52.

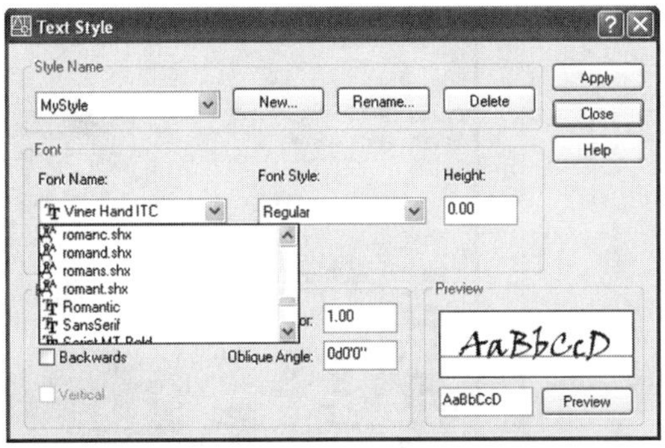

Figure 1.52

Scroll through the list until you see the ***romans.shx*** font, preceded by the calipers symbol, and select it.

Warning

Setting the text height in the Text Style dialog box causes you not to be prompted for the height of the text when you use the Text command.

The Font Style option only allows changes to True Type fonts, not to shape-compiled fonts (**.shx*) so it appears grayed out. Accept the default text height of 0.00.

At this point, you will make no changes to the Effects portion of the dialog box. To make the new text style current,

Pick: **Apply button**
Pick: **Close** (to exit the dialog box)

Any new text added to your drawing will apply the current text style until you set a different style as current. You will now add a title to the bottom of the drawing.

Command: **TEXT** ↵
Specify start point of text or [Justify/Style]: **J** ↵
Enter an option [Align/Fit/Center/Middle/Right/TL/TC/TR/ML/MC/MR/BL/BC/BR]: **C** ↵
Specify center point of text: **select a point near the middle bottom of the drawing**
Specify height <3.00>: ↵
Specify rotation angle of text<E>: **E** ↵ (be sure that your rotation angle is set to E)
Type: **PLOT PLAN** ↵ ↵

You can use the Help command to discover how the Justify options of the Text command work.

Pick: **Help icon**

The Help dialog box appears on your screen.

On your own, use the Search tab and type Text in the input box. Select to display the AutoCAD Command reference item for the TEXT command
Pick: **Concepts tab** (as in Figure 1.53)

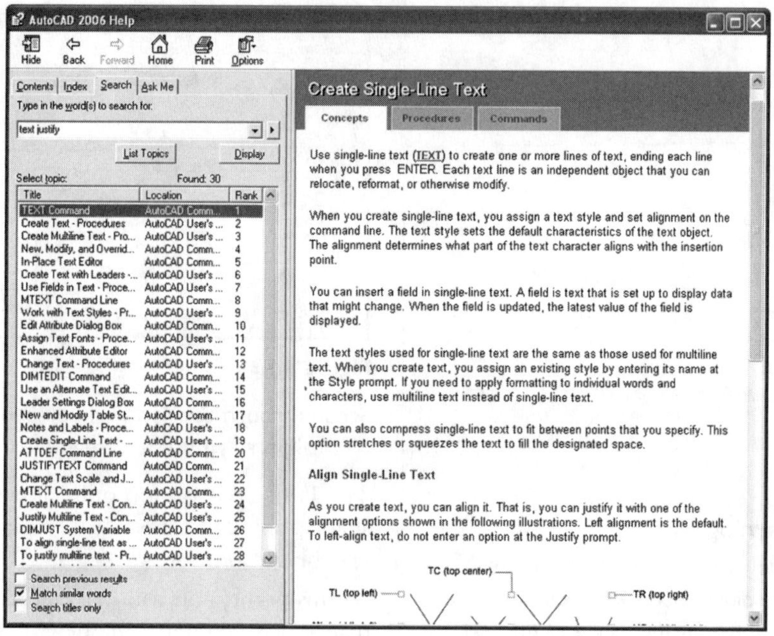

Figure 1.53

Scroll down to see the help for aligning text.

You should see additional help as shown in Figure 1.54 depicting the justification options. Take a minute to familiarize yourself with them. You can return to this help screen whenever you want more information about how a specific command works.

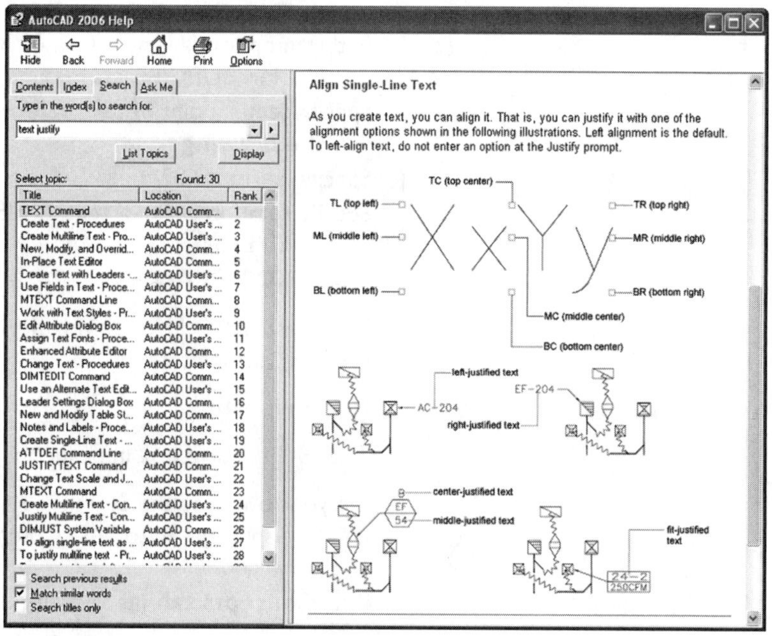

Figure 1.54

Pick: **to close the Help screen**

Using Mtext

Next you will use the *Multiline Text* (MText) feature to add a block of notes to your drawing. Unlike Text, the Mtext command automatically adjusts text within the width you specify. You can create text with your own text editor and then import it with the Mtext command, or you can create text with the Mtext command. As with Text, you can easily edit Mtext by using the DDEdit command after you have already placed the text in the drawing. You can select Mtext by picking the Text button from the Draw toolbar or choose Draw, Text, Multiline Text from the menu.

Pick: **Text icon**

Current text style: "MyStyle" Text height: **3.00**

Specify first corner: **pick a point to the right of the plot plan drawing where you want to locate the corner of the notes; a window will form**

Specify opposite corner or [Height/Justify/Line spacing/Rotation/Style/Width]: **pick the second corner of the window** to size the area for the notes

If you want to enter only the width of the text you will type in, type W at the preceding prompt instead of specifying the corners of the box, and then type the width you want to specify.

The Text Formatting dialog box appears on your screen, as shown in Figure 1.55. The ruler along the top of the blank area for text entry allows you to size the area where the text will appear in your drawing. The pointers on the left side of the ruler control the indent and margin. Holding down your mouse button and dragging the right end of the ruler controls the width of the box (corresponding to the width of the text area). The large blank area of the dialog box is where you will type in the notes for the plot plan.

Tip

Right-clicking in the blank text area of the Text formatting box pops-up a menu allowing you to Find and Replace, Select All, Change Case, Insert Symbols, Import Text, and other options.

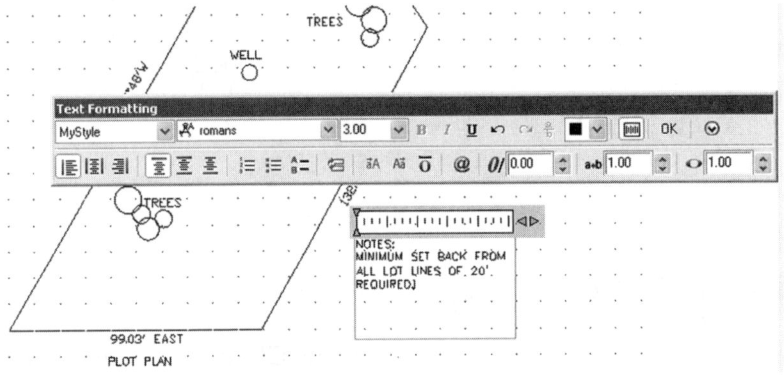

Figure 1.55

Type: **NOTES:** ⏎ **MINIMUM SET BACK FROM ALL LOT LINES OF 20' REQUIRED.**

You can use the standard Windows Control key combinations to edit text in the Text Formatting dialog box.

Ctrl-C	Copy selection to the Clipboard
Ctrl-V	Paste Clipboard contents over selection
Ctrl-X	Cut selection to the Clipboard
Ctrl-Z	Undo and Redo
Ctrl-Shift-Spacebar	Insert a nonbreaking space
↵	End the current paragraph and start a new line

You can create stacked fractions or stacked text with the Mtext command. To do so, separate the text to be stacked with either a forward slash (/), number sign (#), or the caret (^). Using / draws a line between the numerator and denominator of fractions. Separating numbers with /, #, or ^ and pressing ↵ pops up the Autostack Properties dialog box. This dialog box allows you to make stacked fractions using various options.

To change the current font, style of text (bold or italic), or color of text, use the text formatting menu bar options. These appear similar to that of your word processor.

You can also cut and paste text between the Text Formatting dialog box and your word processor.

Pick: **OK** (to exit the Text Formatting box)

The notes are placed in your drawing, which should now be similar to that in Figure 1.56.

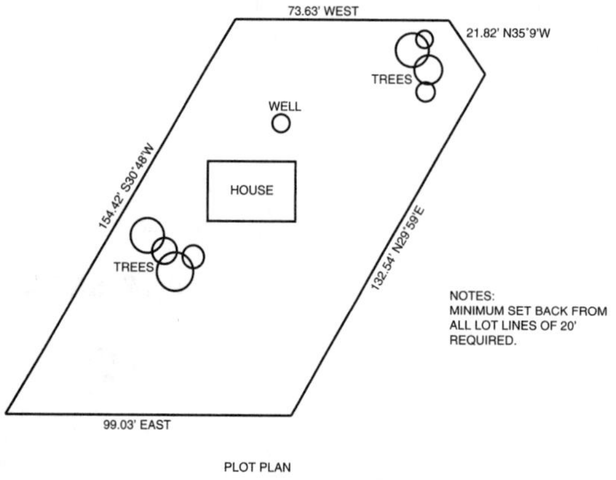

Figure 1.56

Spell Checking Your Drawing

You can use AutoCAD's spell checker to detect spelling errors in your drawing.

Pick: **Tools, Spelling**

Select objects: **pick on the notes you added ↵**

If the text contains spelling errors, the Check Spelling dialog box will appear, as shown in Figure 1.57. If your drawing does not contain any misspellings, the message "Spelling check complete" will appear.

Pick: **OK**

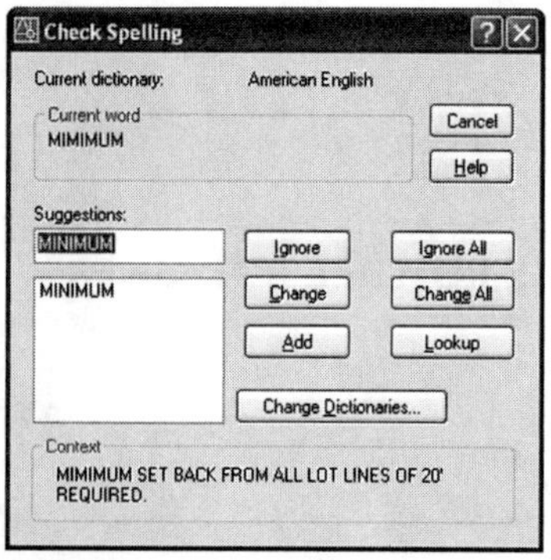

Figure 1.57

Saving Your Drawing

Now, save your drawing.

Pick: **Save icon**

The default file name is always the current drawing name. When you started the new drawing, you named it *plotplan.dwg*. The drawing is saved on the default drive because you did not specify a drive letter.

Transferring Files

Warning

To complete this section you will need a blank formatted floppy disk.

Warning

The appearance of Windows Explorer may depend on your operating system version and your individual settings.

You can transfer files from one drive to another. To transfer a file, place a blank formatted disk in drive *a*: (or substitute the appropriate drive letter for your system). To transfer the file named *plotplan.dwg* from the hard drive to a floppy disk in the drive selected, use Windows Explorer.

Pick: **to close the AutoCAD program**

If you have already saved your drawing, the close box causes an immediate exit. If you have not saved your changes and want to, pick on Save Changes in the dialog box. This will save your drawing to the file name *plotplan.dwg* that you selected when you began the new drawing.

You should now see the Windows desktop.

Double-click: **My Computer icon** on your Windows desktop

My Computer opens which you can use to copy your saved AutoCAD files from the hard drive to a specified drive.

The various directories and drives on your computer are located on the right side of the dialog box. The contents of a selected directory appear on the right side of the dialog box. To change the directory, position the arrow cursor over the name of the directory you want to select (in the list on the left) and double-click the pick button. If you need to step back out of a subdirectory to a directory one level closer to the root, or main, directory, click on the Back button. If you need to select a different drive, click on its name (*a*:, *b*:, *c*:, etc.) in the Other Places area. Select your hard drive and the Work directory where your files are stored.

Pick once to select and then right-click on the *plotplan.dwg* file.

Figure 1.58 shows the pop-up menu that you can use to copy your file.

On your own use this menu to copy the file to the drive where you want to save the file.

Tip

Use My Computer to check that your file has copied to the destination correctly.

You should see a box showing the file being copied.

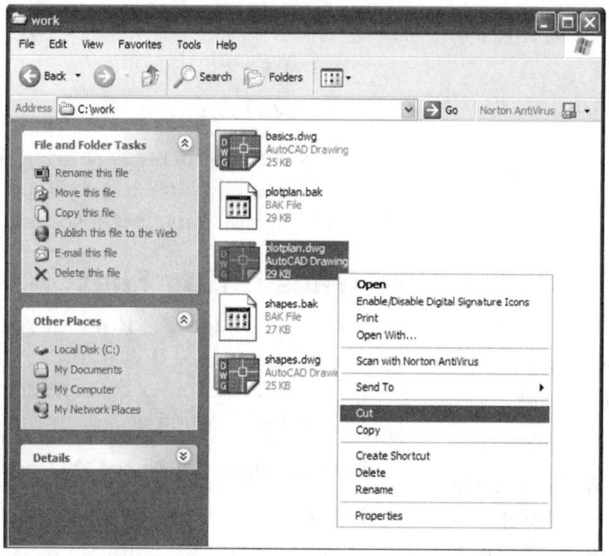

Figure 1.58

You have completed Tutorial 1.

Key Terms

absolute coordinates
alias
angle brackets
architectural units
bearing
Cartesian coordinate system
case-sensitive
command aliasing
command prompt
command window
context-sensitive
context-sensitive menu
coordinate values
default directory
default units
docked
drag
drawing session
engineering units
file extension
floating
floating window
flyout
font
fractional units
graphics cursor (crosshairs)
graphics window
grid
highlight
implied Crossing mode
implied Windowing mode
menu bar
origin
polar coordinates
real-world units
relative coordinates
scientific units
scroll bars
selection set
shape-compiled font
Sheet Set Manager
Standard toolbar
status bar
surveyor units
template
title bar
toggle
tool tip
tool palette
toolbar
transparent command
UCS icon
unidirectional text
Windows control buttons
World Coordinates

Key Commands

Circle 3 Points
Circle Center Radius
Copy
Dynamic Text
Erase
Grid
Help
Limits
Line
Multiline Text
New Drawing
OOPS
Rectangle
Redo
Redraw All
Save
Single Line Text
Snap
Style
Undo
Units
Window Cascade
Window Tile Horizontally
Window Tile Vertically
Zoom All

Exercises

Redraw the following shapes. If dimensions are provided, use them to create your drawing, showing the exact geometry of the part. The letter M after an exercise number means that the dimensions are in millimeters (metric units). If no letter follows the exercise number, the dimensions are in inches. The ∅ symbol indicates that the following dimension is a diameter. Do not include dimensions on the drawings.

1.1 Baseplate

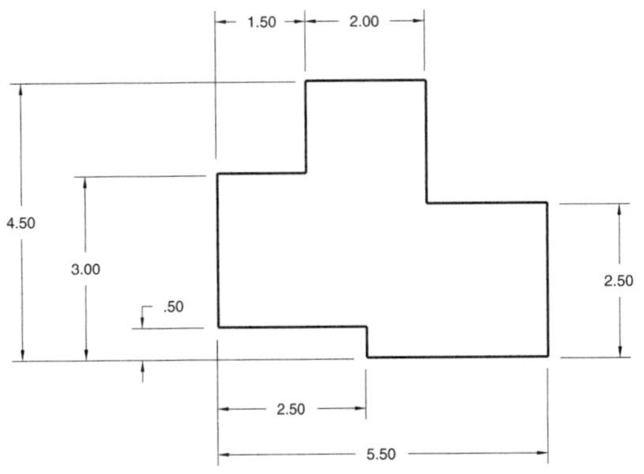

1.2 Bracket

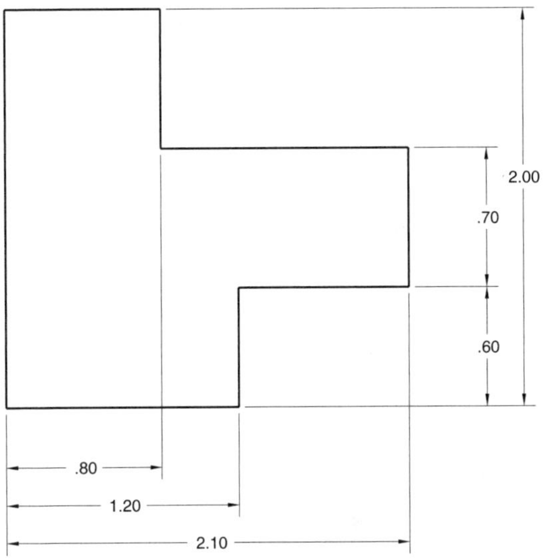

1.3 Site Boundary

Tip: *Solve angle relative to 0° toward East or use Help to set Polar into relative mode.*

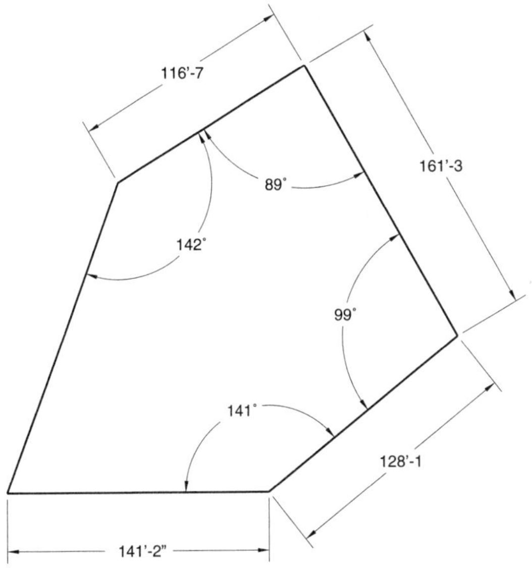

1.4 Filter Plate

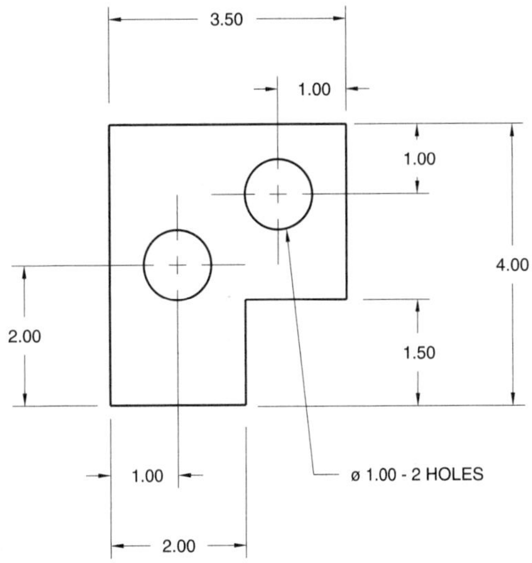

1.5M Gasket

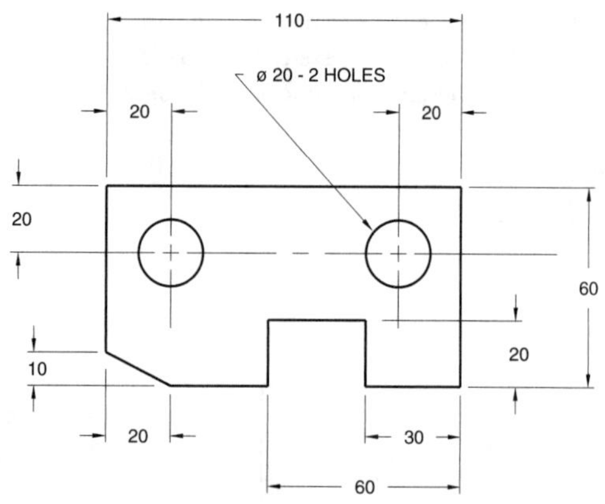

1.6 Spacer

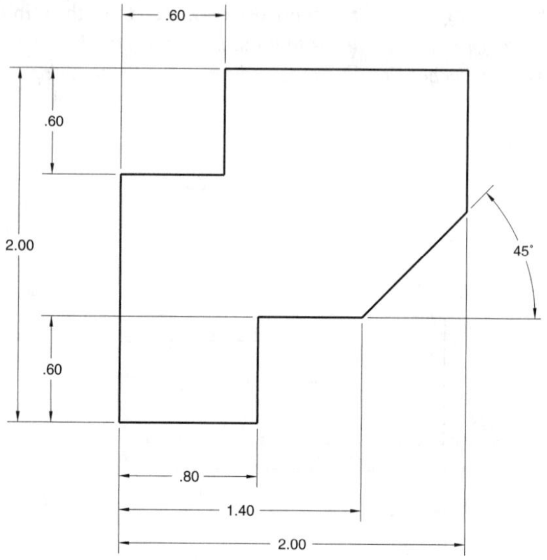

1.7M Guide Plate

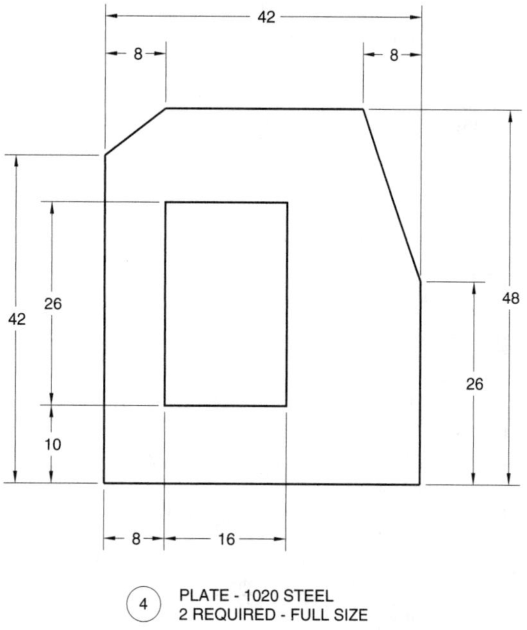

1.8 Amplifier

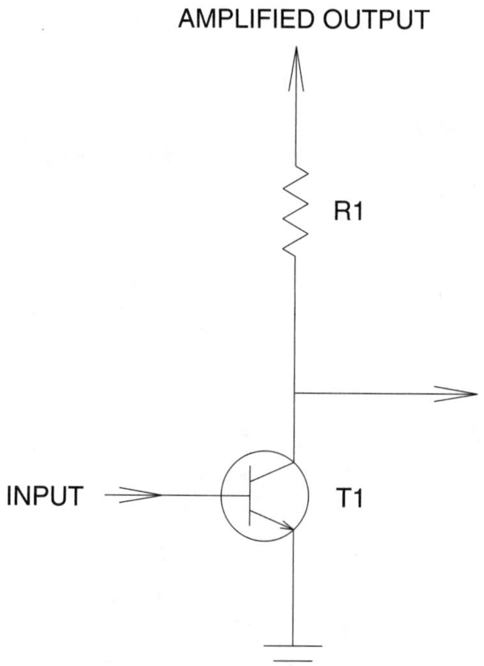

1.9 Dorm Room

Reproduce this drawing using Snap and Grid set to 0.25. The numerical values are for reference only. Use Text to label the items.

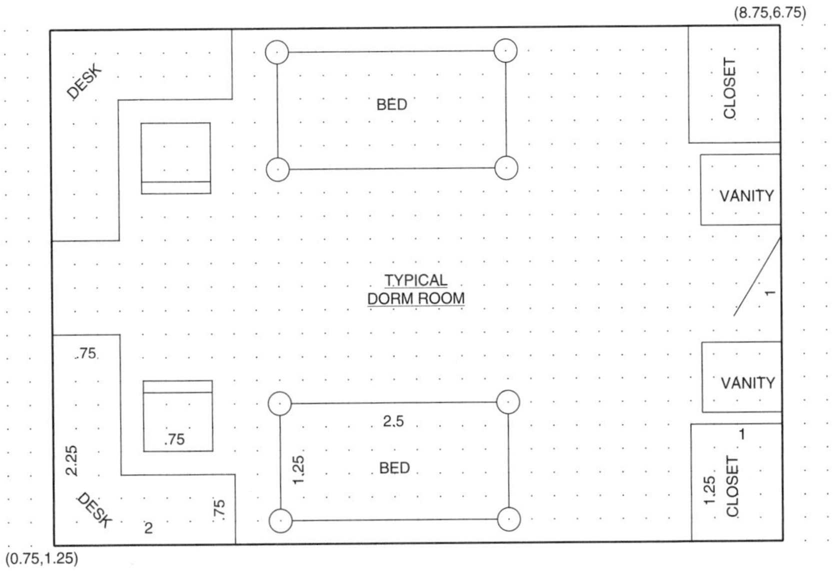

1.10 Template

Draw the shape using one grid square equal to 1/4" or 10 mm.

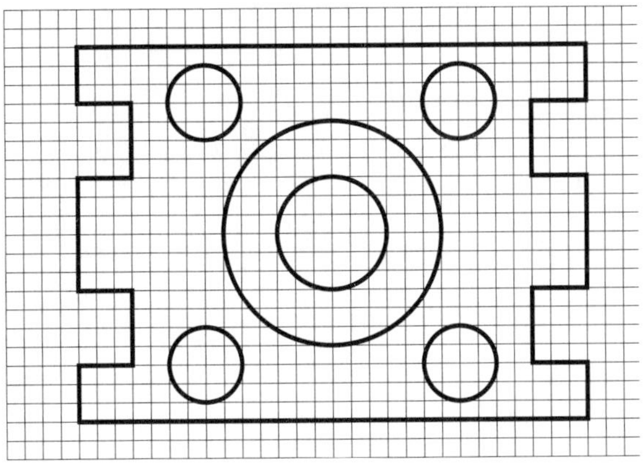

1.11 Bracket

Redraw the following shape. Use the dimensions to create your drawing showing the exact geometry of the part.

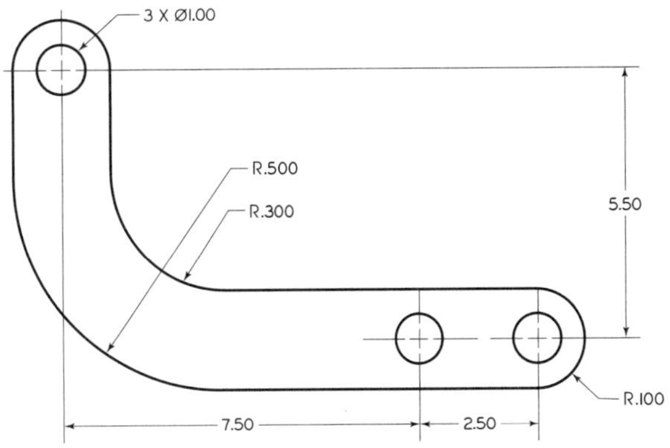

Tutorial

2 Basic Construction Techniques

Objectives

When you have completed this tutorial, you will be able to

1. Open existing drawings.
2. Work with new and existing layers.
3. Draw, using the Arc and Circle commands.
4. Set and use running Object snaps.
5. Change the display, using Zoom and Pan.
6. Use the Aerial Viewer.
7. Draw ellipses.

Warning

If the main AutoCAD screen, including the graphics window, Standard toolbar, Layer toolbar, Properties toolbar, status bar, command window, and menu bar, is not on your display screen, check to be sure that you have configured the AutoCAD software properly for your computer system. If you are still having difficulty, ask your technical support person for help.

Introduction

You usually create drawings by combining and modifying several different basic shapes called *primitives*, such as lines, circles, and arcs, to create more complex shapes. This tutorial will help you learn how to use the AutoCAD® software to draw some of the most common basic shapes. As you work through the tutorial, keep in mind that one of the advantages of using CAD over drawing on paper is that you are creating an accurate model of the drawing geometry. In Tutorial 3, you will learn to list information from the drawing database. Information extracted from the drawing is accurate only if you created the drawing accurately in the first place.

Starting

Before you begin, **launch the AutoCAD 2006 program.**

If you need assistance, refer to Chapters 1 and 2 of this guide.

Opening an Existing Drawing

This tutorial shows you how to add arcs and circles to the subdivision drawing provided with the datafiles that came with this guide. In Tutorial 3 you will finish the subdivision drawing so that the final drawing will look like Figure 2.1.

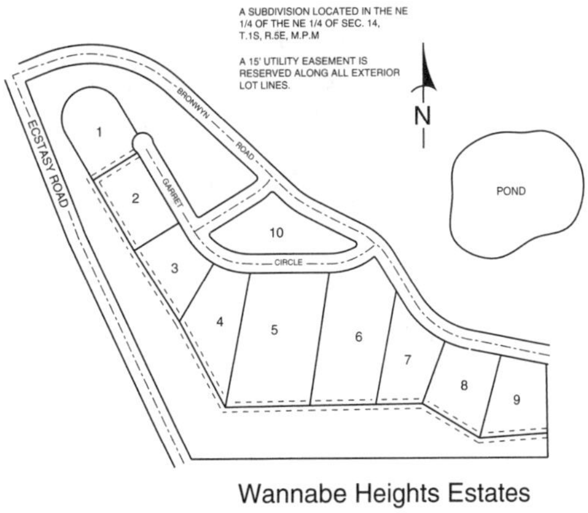

Figure 2.1

To open an existing drawing, you use the File, Open selection on the menu bar or pick the icon that looks like an open folder from the Standard toolbar.

Pick: **Open icon**

Tip

If you do not see a preview, pick Views from the dialog box's menu bar and make sure that Preview is checked.

The Select File dialog box appears on your screen. Use the center portion, which shows the default directory and drive, to select the location where your datafiles have been stored. In Chapters 1 and 2, you should have already created a directory called *c:\datafile2006*, and copied all the datafiles for this book into it. If you have not done so, you may want to review those chapters. If the correct directory is not showing in the Look In box, use the Up One Level icon or expand the choices by picking on the downward arrow for the Look In box. Use the scroll bars if necessary to scroll down the list of directories and open the appropriate one so the files appear in the dialog box as in Figure 2.2. Scroll down the list of files until you see the file named *subdivis.dwg*. When you select a file, a preview of the file appears in the box to the right. (Older files may not show a preview.)

Tip

Use the buttons at the left of the dialog box to show the History (recently used files), My Documents folder contents, or Favorites you have added. To add a favorite, find the folder and then right-click the Favorites button. Pick Add Current Folder from the pop-up menu that appears. To add a folder as a button, pick Tools, Add Current Folder to Places.

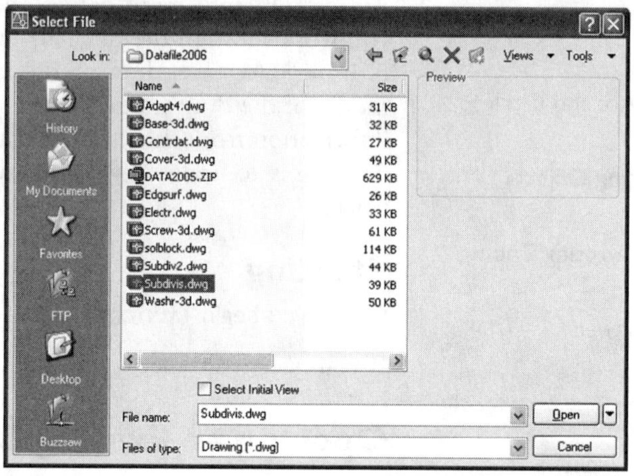

Figure 2.2

Menu choices at the top right of the Select File dialog box let you select different views to be displayed in the file list and other useful tools, such as a Find selection to search for files.

Pick: **Tools, Find**
Type: **subdivis** (in the Named area)
Pick: **Find Now button** (from upper right of dialog box)

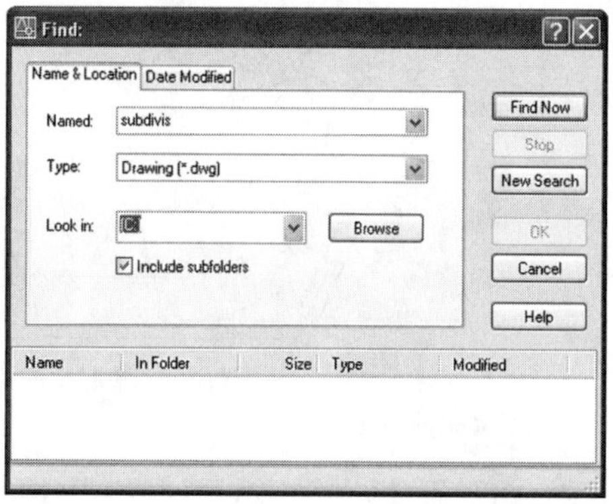

Figure 2.3

The Find dialog box displays the location for the file named Subdivis, as shown in Figure 2.3. You can type in a portion of the name to match if you cannot remember the entire name or pick the Date Modified tab if you want to search by date and time the file was created.

Double-click: ***Subdivis.dwg*** (from the list at the bottom)

You return to the Select File dialog box.

Pick: **Open**

When you have opened the file, it appears on your screen, as shown in Figure 2.4. Note that it opens with its own defaults for Grid, Snap, and other features. These settings are saved in the drawing file. When you open a drawing, its own settings are used.

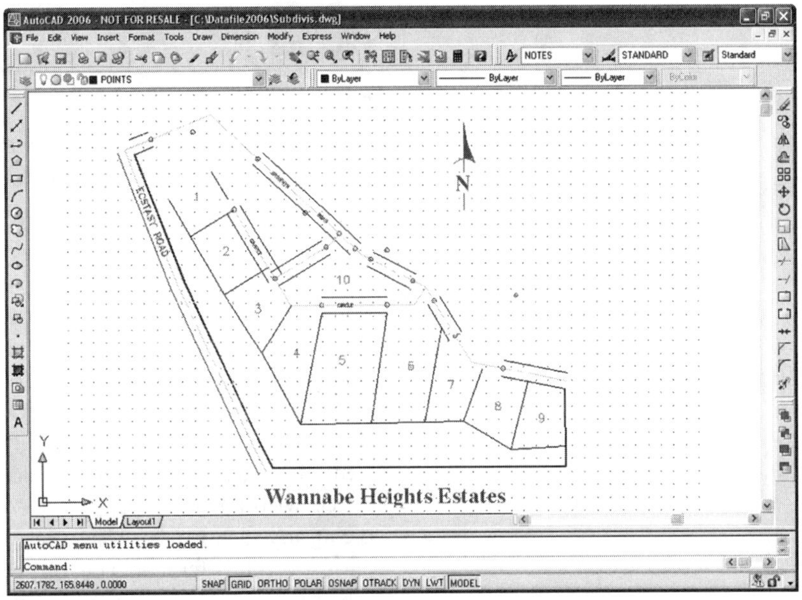

Figure 2.4

Saving as a New File

The Save As command allows you to save your drawing to a new file name and/or different drive or directory. You can select this command from the File selection on the menu bar. Don't use the Save command, because that will save your changes into the original datafile.

Pick: **File, Save As**

The Save Drawing As dialog box appears on your screen, similar to Figure 2.5.

On your own, use it to select the drive and directory *c:\work* as shown in Figure 2.5 and specify the name for your drawing, *subdivis.dwg*.

The new file name is the same as the previous file name, but the directory is different. Thus a new copy of drawing *subdivis.dwg* is saved in the directory *c:\work*.

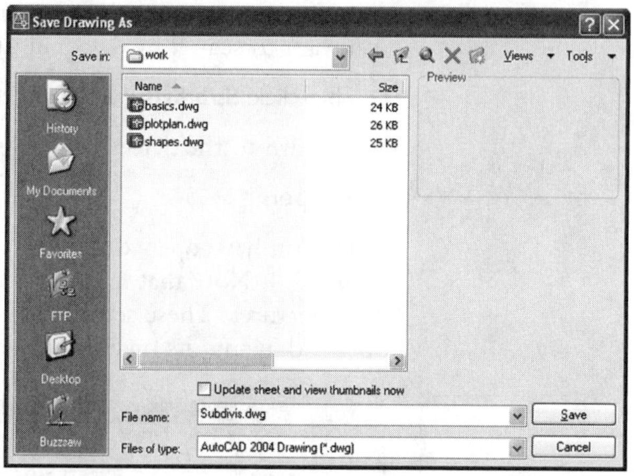

Figure 2.5

The original file *c:\datafile2006\subdivis.dwg* will remain unchanged on your drive. When you use the Save As command and specify a new file name, the AutoCAD software sets the newly saved file as current.

Using Layers

You can organize drawing information on different layers. Think of a *layer* as a transparent drawing sheet that you place over the drawing and that you can remove at will. The coordinate system remains the same from one layer to another, so graphical objects on separate layers remain aligned. You can create a virtually unlimited number of layers within the same drawing. The Layer command controls the color and linetype associated with a given layer and allows you to control which layers are visible at any given time. Using layers allows you to overlay a base drawing with several different levels of detail (such as wiring or plumbing schematics over the base plan for a building).

By using layers, you can also control which portions of a drawing are plotted, or remove dimensions or text from a drawing to make it easier to add or change objects. You can also lock layers, making them inaccessible but still visible on the screen. You can't change anything on a locked layer until you unlock it.

Current Layer

The *current layer* is the layer you are working on. Any new objects you draw are added to the current layer. The default current layer is Layer 0. If you do not create and use other layers, your drawing will be created on Layer 0. You used this layer when drawing the plot plan in Tutorial 1. Layer 0 is a special layer provided in the AutoCAD program. You cannot rename it or delete it from the list of layers. Layer 0 has special properties when used with the Block and Insert commands, which are covered in Tutorial 10.

Layer POINTS is the current layer in *subdivis.dwg*. There can be only one current layer at a time. The name of the current layer appears on the Layer toolbar.

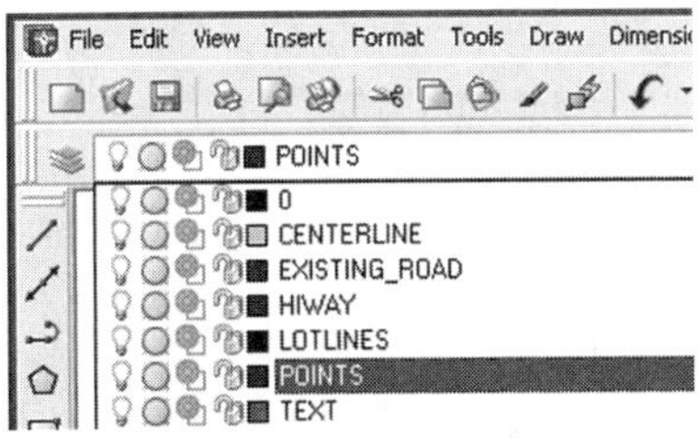

Figure 2.6

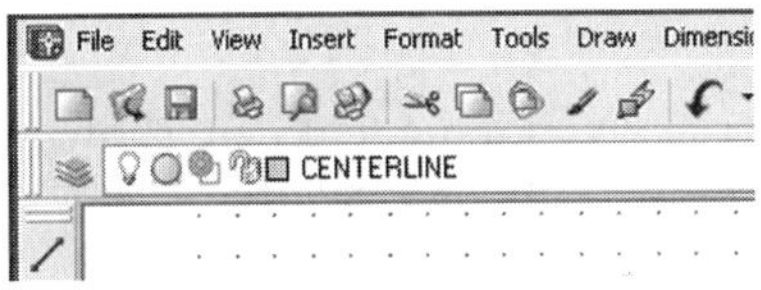

Figure 2.7

Controlling Layers

The Layer Control feature on the Layer toolbar is an easy way to control the visibility of existing layers in your drawing. You will learn more about creating and using layers in this tutorial. For now, you will use layers that have already been created for you.

To select the Layer Control pull-down feature,

Pick: **on the layer name POINTS, which appears on the Layer toolbar near the top of the screen**

The list of available layers pulls down, as shown in Figure 2.6. Notice the special layer 0 displayed near the top of the Layer Control list.

Pick: **on the layer name CENTERLINE from the Layer Control list**

It becomes the current layer shown on the toolbar. Any new objects will be created on this layer until you select a different current layer. The Layer Control now should look like Figure 2.7, showing the layer name CENTERLINE.

Use the Line command you learned in Tutorial 1 to draw a line off to the side of the subdivision drawing.

Note that it is green and has a centerline linetype (long dash, short dash, long dash). The line you drew is on Layer CENTERLINE.

Erase or Undo the line on your own.

Controlling Colors

Each layer can have a color associated with it. Using different colors for different layers helps you visually distinguish different types of lines in the drawing. An object's color also can control which pens are used during plotting. You can use layers of different colors to make setting pen colors and widths easy during plotting.

The AutoCAD program provides two different ways of selecting the color for objects on your screen. The best way is to set the layer color and draw the objects on the appropriate layer. This method keeps your drawing organized. The other method is to use the Color Control feature on the Properties toolbar. To select the Color Control pull-down feature,

Pick: **to pull down the Color Control by picking on the word ByLayer, to the right of the Layer toolbar**

The list of available colors pulls down, as shown in Figure 2.8.

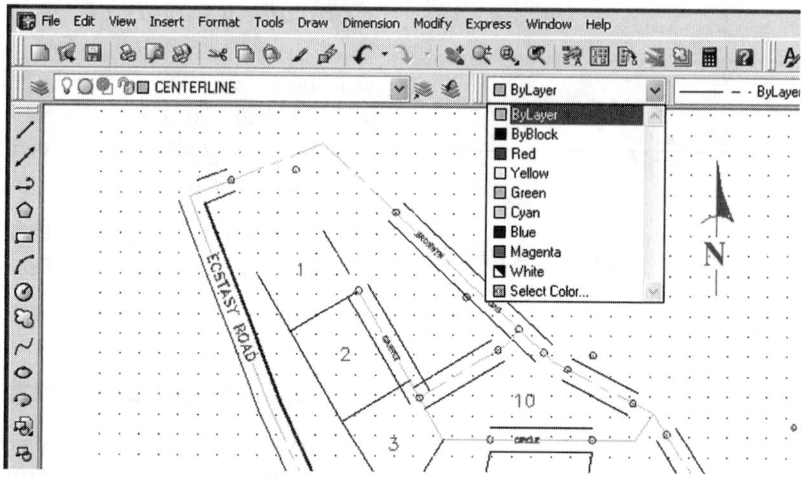

Figure 2.8

Note that the standard colors (yellow, red, green, blue, etc.) are shown. You can also choose Select Color to view the full color palette.

Pick: **Select Color**

The Select Color dialog box shown in Figure 2.9 appears on your screen, giving you a full range of colors from which to choose.

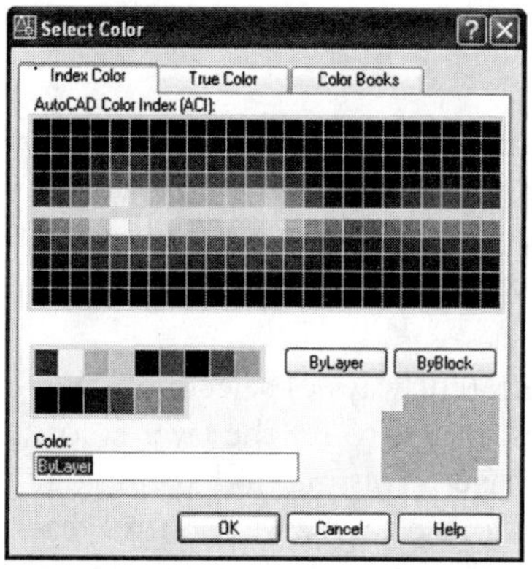

Figure 2.9

The three tabs of the Select Color dialog box allow you to choose among different methods to determine the color for your drawing entities.The True Color tab allows you to set color to either RGB, which stands for Red, Green, Blue, the primary colors of light, or HSL, which stands for the Hue, Saturation, and Luminance of the color. The Color Books tab lets you select from among different standard ink manufacturer's predefined colors so that you can match print colors very closely to the colors you choose on your screen. In this text you will use Index Color (AutoCAD Color Index) as the method for selecting color.

Make sure the **Index Color** tab is selected.

The default option for the Color (and also for the Linetype) command is BYLAYER. It's the best selection because, when you draw a line, the color and linetype will be those of the current layer. Otherwise, the color in your drawing can become very confusing. You will pick Cancel to exit the Select Color dialog box without making any changes. The colors for your new objects will continue to be determined by the layer on which they are created. Layers can have associated linetypes, as well as colors, as Layer CENTERLINE does.

Pick: **Cancel**

Layer Visibility

One of the advantages of using layers in the drawing is that you can choose not to display selected layers. That way, if you want to create projection lines or even notes about the drawing, you can draw them on a layer that you will later turn off, so that it isn't displayed or plotted. Or you may want to create a complex drawing with many layers, such as a building plan that contains the electrical plan on one layer and the mechanical plan on another, along with separate layers for the walls,

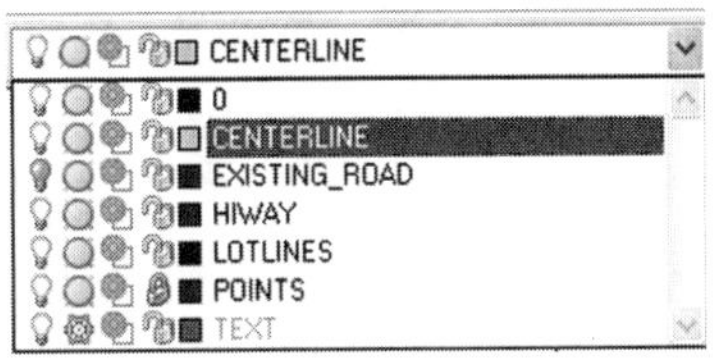

Figure 2.10

windows, and so on. You can store all the information in a single drawing, and then plot different combinations of layers to create the electrical layout, first-floor plan, and any other combination you want. Next, use the Layer Control to lock Layer POINTS, freeze Layer TEXT, and turn off Layer EXISTING_ROAD.

Pick: **on Layer CENTERLINE in the Layer Control**

The list of layers pulls down. Refer to Figure 2.10 as you make the following selections.

Pick: **the On/Off icon, which looks like a lightbulb, to the left of Layer EXISTING_ROAD**

Pick: **any blank area of the screen away from the Layer list**

Note that the blue roadway lines have been turned off so that they no longer appear. Invisible (off) layers are not printed or plotted, but objects on these layers are still part of the drawing. Next, you will freeze Layer TEXT.

Freezing Layers

Freezing a layer is similar to turning it off. You use the *freeze* option not only to make the layer disappear from the display, but also to cause it to be skipped when the drawing is regenerated. This feature can noticeably improve the speed with which the AutoCAD software regenerates a large drawing. You can never freeze the current layer because that would create a situation where you would be drawing objects that you couldn't see on the screen and that would not be generated for the drawing. The icon for freezing and thawing layers looks like a snowflake when frozen and a shining sun when thawed.

Tip

Make sure to use Freeze/Thaw and not Freeze/Thaw for the Current Viewport. The Freeze/Thaw icon is the one to the left that looks like a sun/snowflake. It does not have the box next to it.

Pick: **the Freeze/Thaw icon to the left of Layer TEXT**

Pick: **any blank area in the graphics window for the selection to take effect**

Layer TEXT is still on, but it is frozen and therefore invisible. A layer can both be turned off and frozen, but the effect is the same as freezing the layer. You should either freeze a layer or turn it off, but there is no point in doing both.

Locking Layers

You can see a *locked layer* on the screen, and you can add new objects to it. However, you can't make changes to the new or old objects on that layer. This constraint is useful when you need the layer for reference but do not want to change it. For example, you might want to move several items so that they line up with an object on the locked layer but prevent anything on the locked layer from moving. You will lock layer POINTS so that you cannot accidentally change the points already on the layer.

Pick: **the Lock/Unlock icon to the left of Layer POINTS**

Your screen should now be similar to Figure 2.11. Layer CENTERLINE is the current layer. (If for some reason it is not the current layer, set it current at this time.) Layer TEXT is frozen and does not appear. Layer EXISTING_ROAD is turned off and does not appear. Layer POINTS is locked so that you can see and add to it, but not change it.

On your own, try erasing one of the points. A message will appear, saying that the object is on a locked layer. The object won't be erased.

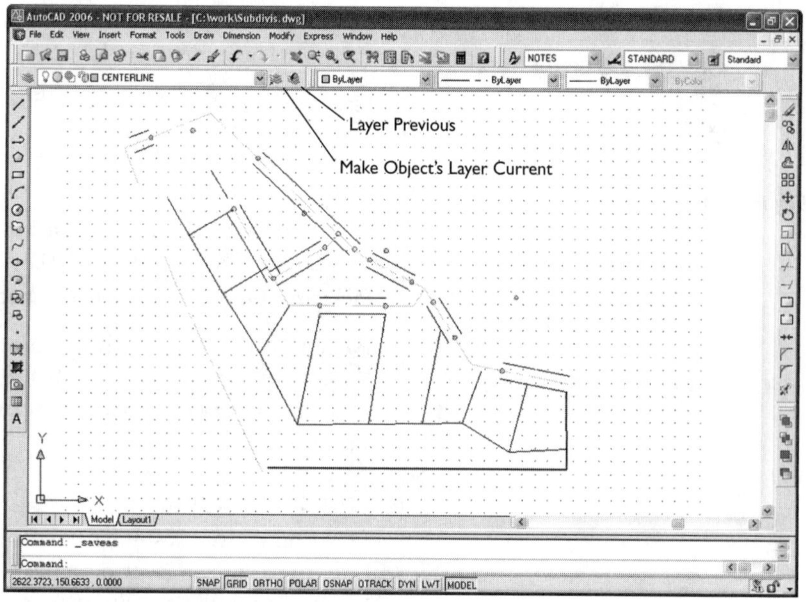

Figure 2.11

Making Object's Layer Current

The Make Object's Layer Current button located to the right of the Layer Control pull-down menu is labeled in Figure 2.11. This command lets you select an object and then pick on the icon to make that object's layer current. You will select a black lot line in your Subdivision drawing.

Pick: **a black lot line (white if your background color is black), representing a lot boundary**

Note that the Layer Control now shows LOTLINES, the layer of the line you selected. This name is only temporary, for if you draw a new line, the layer name changes back to the current layer (CENTERLINE). This is a useful feature when you are unsure which layer a particular object is on.

Next you will use the Make Object's Layer Current button to set LOTLINES as the current layer.

Pick: **the black lot line previously picked if it is not still highlighted**
Pick: **Make Object's Layer Current icon**

The current layer is changed to LOTLINES, and any new objects will be added to this layer. In the command prompt is the message: LOTLINES is now the current layer.

Now you will change the current layer back to CENTERLINE by using the Layer Previous icon on the Layer toolbar. It is identified in Figure 2.11.

Pick: **Layer Previous icon**

Layer CENTERLINE returns as the current layer.

Using Layer

The Layer command lets you create new layers and control the color and linetype associated with a layer. You can also use Layer to control which layers are visible or plotted at any one time and to set the current layer. Remember, only one layer at a time can be current. New objects are created on the current layer. Use the Layer Properties Manager icon on the Layer toolbar to create new layers and set their properties. (Its command alias is LA.)

Pick: **Layer Properties Manager icon**

The Layer Properties Manager appears on the screen, as shown in Figure 2.12.

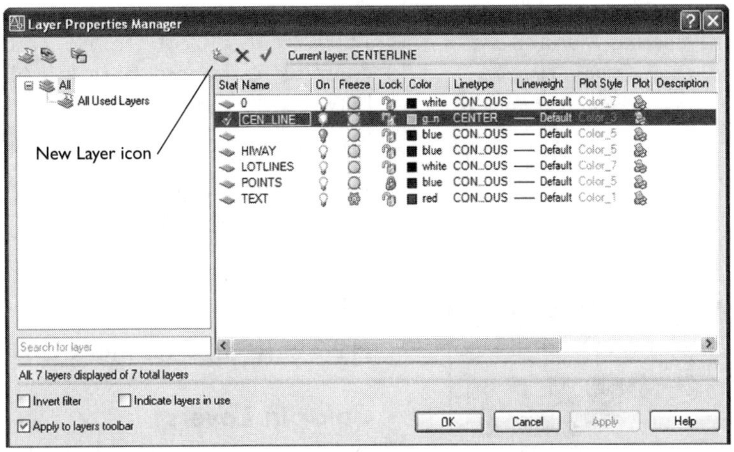

Figure 2.12

Figure 2.12 shows the list of the existing layers in the Layer Properties Manager. Notice that the layers you earlier turned off, locked, or froze are identified with those icons.

Next you will create a layer named EASEMENTS which you will use later in Tutorial 3. It will have a hidden linetype and the color cyan (a light blue shade)

Pick: **New Layer icon** (located at the top middle of the dialog box)

A new layer appears with the default name Layer1, which should be highlighted as shown in Figure 2.13.

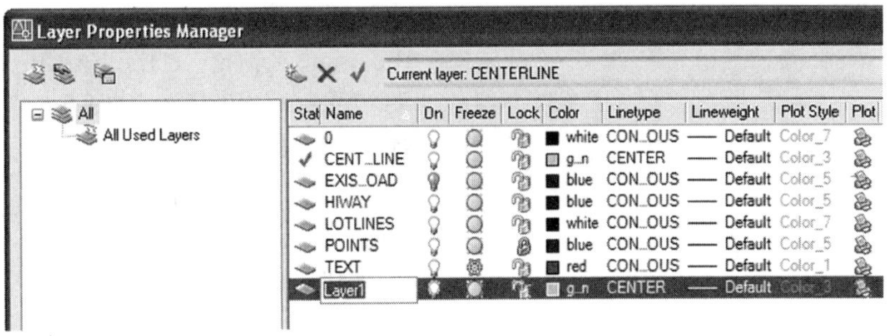

Figure 2.13

By default it has the same properties as the currently selected layer (CENTERLINE). You will change the layer name, color and linetype for the new layer next. Layer names can be as long as 255 characters. Layer names can contain almost any characters, except for restricted operating system characters like comma (,) and others like <>/”?:*|’=. Letters, numbers, spaces, and the characters dollar sign ($), period (.), number sign (#), underscore (_), and hyphen (-) are valid. While Layer1 is still highlighted,

Type: **EASEMENTS** ↵

Next, set the color for layer EASEMENTS. To the right of the layer names are the various layer controls mentioned previously. Each column title is labeled with the name of the function: On (light bulb), Freeze (sun), Lock/Unlock (lock), Color (small color box), Linetype, Lineweight, Plot Style, Plot, and Description. You can resize these columns to show more or less of the names by dragging the line between the name headings.

Tip

You can right-click on a heading in the Layer Properties Manager, and select Maximize Column Headings from the pop-up menu that appears.

To change the color for layer EASEMENTS,

Pick: **on the Color column box corresponding to layer EASEMENTS**

A dialog box containing color choices pops up on the screen. Figure 2.14 shows the Select Color dialog box.

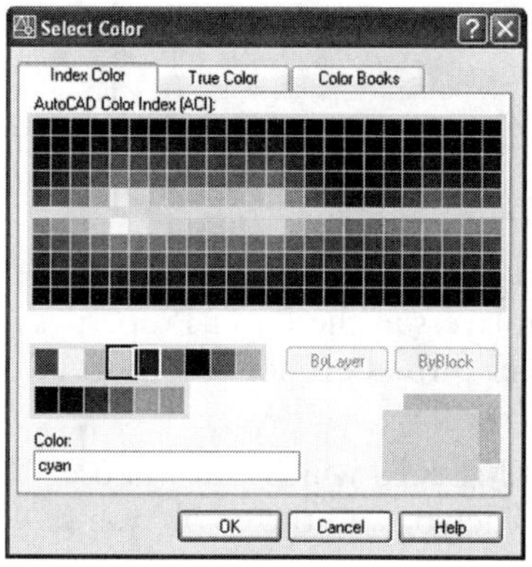

Figure 2.14

Make sure that the Index Color tab is uppermost.

Color in Layers

The Select Color dialog box allows you to specify the color for objects drawn on a layer. You will select the color cyan for the easement layer that you are creating. The color helps you visually distinguish linetypes and layers in drawings. You also use color to select the pen and pen width for your printer or plotter.

The Select Color dialog box has the choices BYLAYER and BYBLOCK on the right side. As you are specifying the color for layer EASEMENTS only, you can't select these choices, so they are shown grayed. Move the arrow cursor over the Standard Colors boxes, where cyan is the fourth color from the left.

Pick: **cyan** from the Standard Colors boxes left of the ByLayer button

The name of the color that you have selected appears in the Color: box at the bottom of the screen. (If you select one of the standard colors, the name appears in the box; if you select one of the other 255 colors from the palette, the color number appears.)

Pick: **OK**

Now the color for layer EASEMENTS is set to cyan. Check the listing of layer names and colors to verify that cyan has replaced green in the Color column to the right of the layer name EASEMENTS.

Linetype in Layers

The linetype column allows you to set the linetype drawn for the layer. You will select the linetype HIDDEN for your layer named EASEMENTS.

Pick: **on Center in the Linetype column across from layer EASEMENTS**

The Select Linetype dialog box shown in Figure 2.15 appears on your screen.

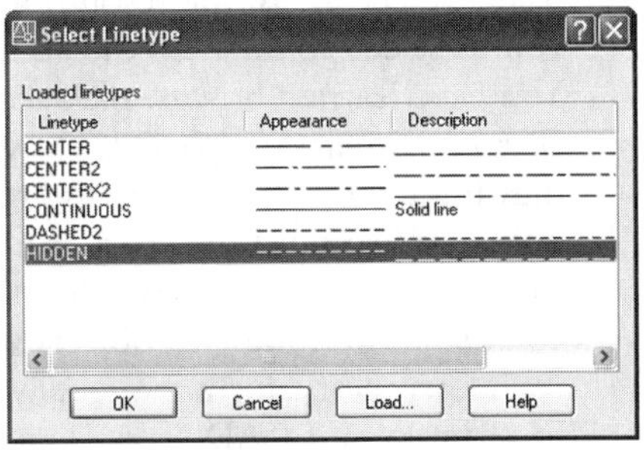

Figure 2.15

Pick: **HIDDEN** (so that the name becomes highlighted as you see in Figure 2.15)

Pick: **OK**

You return to the Layer Properties Manager. Layer EASEMENTS should have the properties set as shown in Figure 2.16.

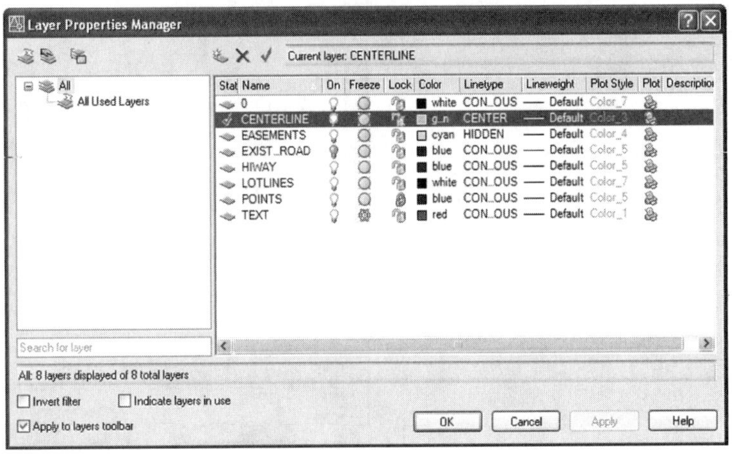

Figure 2.16

Pick: **OK** (to exit the dialog box)

CENTERLINE should still be the current layer on the Layer toolbar, showing a green square to the left of the layer name. You will use the EASEMENTS layer you created later in this tutorial.

Using layers to control the color and linetype of new objects that you create will work only if BYLAYER is active as the method for establishing object color, object linetype, and lineweight. To check,

Examine the Color Control, Linetype Control, and the Lineweight Control on the Properties Toolbar. All three should be set to BYLAYER.

Now that you know the basics of using and creating layers, you will begin creating the curved sections of the road centerline for the subdivision. The straight-line sections that the curves are tangent to have been drawn to get you started. First you will turn on the object snap for Node.

Using Object Snap

The object snap feature accurately selects locations based on existing objects in your drawing. When you pick points from the screen without using object snaps, the resolution of your screen makes it impossible for you to select points with the accuracy stored in the drawing database. You have learned how to pick accurately by snapping to a grid point. *Object snap* makes it possible for you to pick points accurately on your drawing geometry by snapping to an object's center, endpoint, midpoint, and so on. Whenever prompted to select a point or location, you can use an object snap to help make an accurate selection. Without this command, locating two objects with respect to each other in correct and useful geometric form is virtually impossible. Object snap is one of the most important CAD tools. The many specialized object snaps are listed on the Object Snap toolbar. You will use a right-click shortcut to turn on the toolbar.

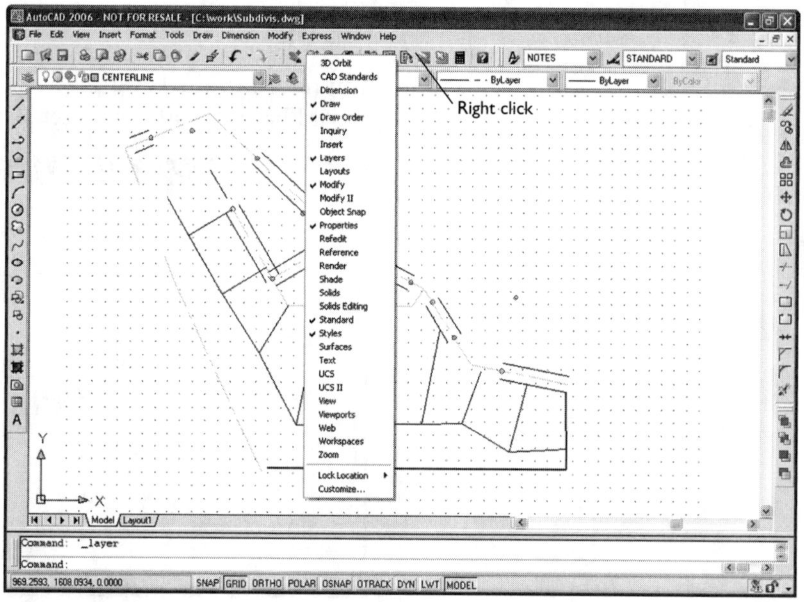

Figure 2.17

Right-click: (on the Properties toolbar or any other open toolbar)

A list of the available toolbars will expand from the location you picked as shown in Figure 2.17. The items shown with a check mark are the toolbars that are already open on your screen. To turn on the Object Snap toolbar,

Pick: **Object Snap** (from the popped up list)

The Object Snap toolbar should appear on your screen as shown in Figure 2.18.

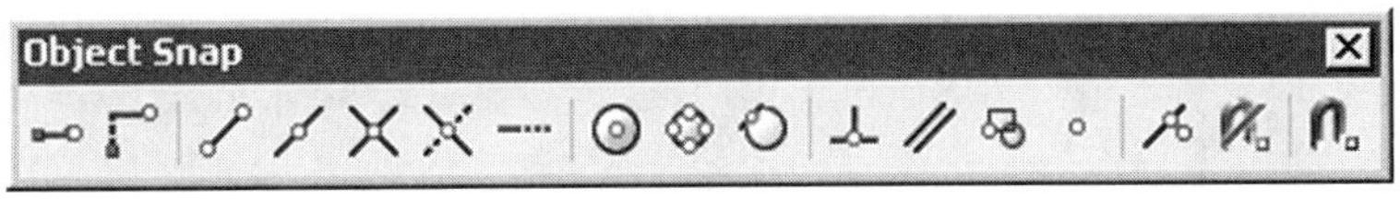

Figure 2.18

Object Snap can operate in two different ways. The first is called *override mode*. With this method, you select the object snap during a command. The object snap acts as a modifier within the command string to *target* the next point you select. You activate object snaps from within other commands by picking the appropriate icon from the Object Snap toolbar. The object locations they select are indicated by small circles on the icons. When you activate an object snap in this manner, it is active for one pick only. Remember, you can use this method only during a command that is prompting you to select points or objects.

Tip

You can also activate an object snap by typing the three-letter name any time you are prompted to enter points or select objects. Refer to the Command Summary for the three-letter codes.

A special AutoCAD feature called AutoSnap™ is active when Object Snap is in use. It displays a marker and description (SnapTip) when the cursor is placed near or on a snap point. This feature helps you to determine what location on the object will be selected.

The second method for using Object Snap is called *running mode*. With this method, you turn on the object snap and leave it on before you invoke any commands. When a running mode object snap is on, the marker box and SnapTip will appear during any future command when you are prompted for a point location, object selection, or other pick. The SnapTip will tell you which object snap location is being targeted.

Next you will turn on the running mode object snap by right-clicking on the OSNAP button on the status bar as shown in Figure 2.19.

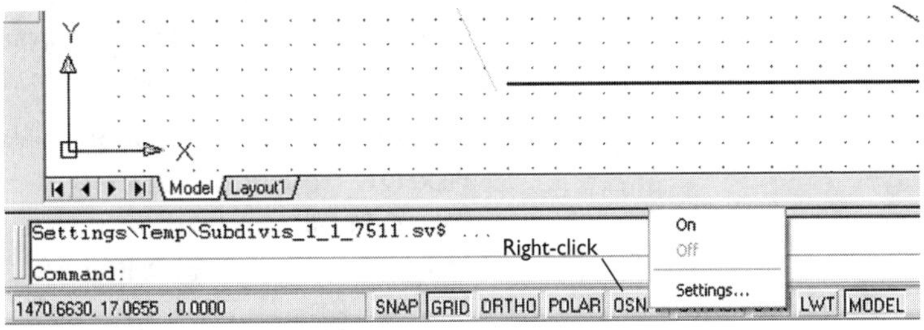

Figure 2.19

Right-click: **OSNAP button**
Pick: **Settings**

The Drafting Settings dialog box you used to set the snap and grid appears on your screen. Notice it has three tabs: Snap and Grid, Polar Tracking, and Object Snap. Object Snap should be on top.

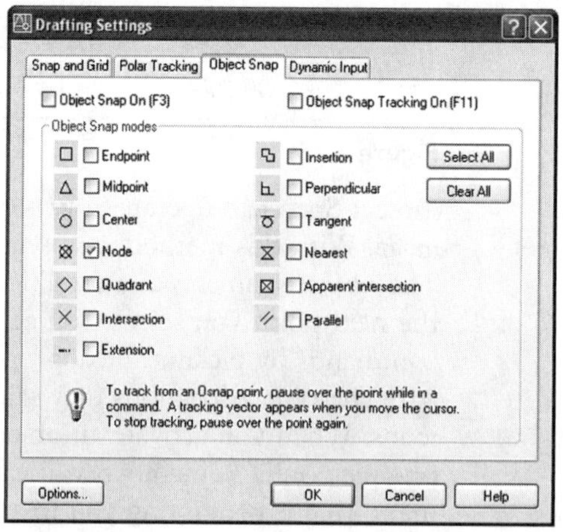

Figure 2.20

Pick: **Clear All** (to unselect the modes that are currently selected)
Pick: **Node**

A check appears in the box when it is selected, as shown in Figure 2.20. Node snaps to objects drawn with the AutoCAD Point command. The symbol next to the Node setting represents the AutoSnap marker shape that will appear in the drawing.

Pick: **Options** (from the lower left of the dialog box)

The Options dialog box appears on your screen as shown in Figure 2.21. You can use it to change Marker size, color, and settings. You may want to make the Marker box smaller or larger, depending on your drawing's complexity and size. On your own, try using the slider to make the box smaller and then larger. Next, you may want to change the Marker color to a more noticeable color, such as red. When you have finished,

Pick: **OK** (to exit the Options dialog box)
Pick: **OK** (to exit the Drafting Settings dialog box)
Pick: **OSNAP button** (to turn it on)
Make sure that ORTHO, POLAR, OTRACK and DYN are turned off.

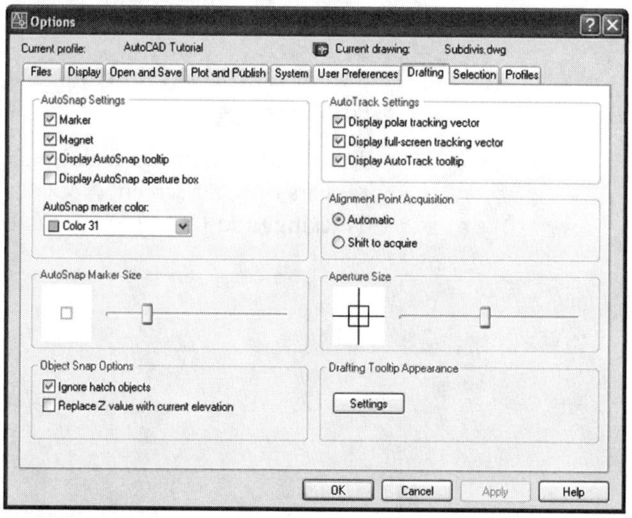

Figure 2.21

AutoSnap is a very useful tool and you will use it frequently throughout the rest of this guide. It can be very important to turn it on and off as needed. Notice that the OSNAP button on the Status bar is highlighted, meaning it is active. You may pick the OSNAP button to toggle the use of object snap on or off, similar to the SNAP and GRID buttons. Check your status bar to make sure that the OSNAP button is turned on. (It appears pressed in.)

Now you are ready to start creating arcs at accurate locations in the drawing. When you are prompted to select, look for the marker box on the crosshairs. When it's there, you know that Snap to Node is being used to select the points that were set previously in the drawing.

Using Arc

The Arc command is on the Draw toolbar, on the Draw menu, or you can type ARC at the command prompt. There are eleven different ways to create arcs; however, only one icon is on the Draw toolbar: the 3 Point Arc. To see the other options, choose Draw, Arc from the menu.

Each Arc command option requires that you input point locations. You can define those point locations by manually typing in the coordinate values or locating the points with the cursor and pressing the pick button on your pointing device. For the exercises presented in this tutorial, follow the directions carefully so that your drawing will turn out correctly. Keep in mind that if you were designing the subdivision, you might not use all the command options demonstrated in this tutorial. When you are using the AutoCAD program later for design, select the command options that are appropriate for the geometry in your drawing.

Arc 3 Points

The 3 Points option of the Arc command draws an arc through three points that you specify. The red dots located on the icon represent the three points of definition. This means that three point locations will be necessary for drawing that arc. Remember, to specify locations you can pick them or type in absolute, relative, or polar coordinates. You will draw an arc using the 3 Points option; refer to the points defined on Figure 2.22 as you select. The Snap to Node running object snap and AutoSnap feature will help you pick the points drawn in the datafile.

Pick: **Arc icon**

Specify start point of arc or [Center]: **select point 1, using the AutoSnap marker as shown in Figure 2.22**

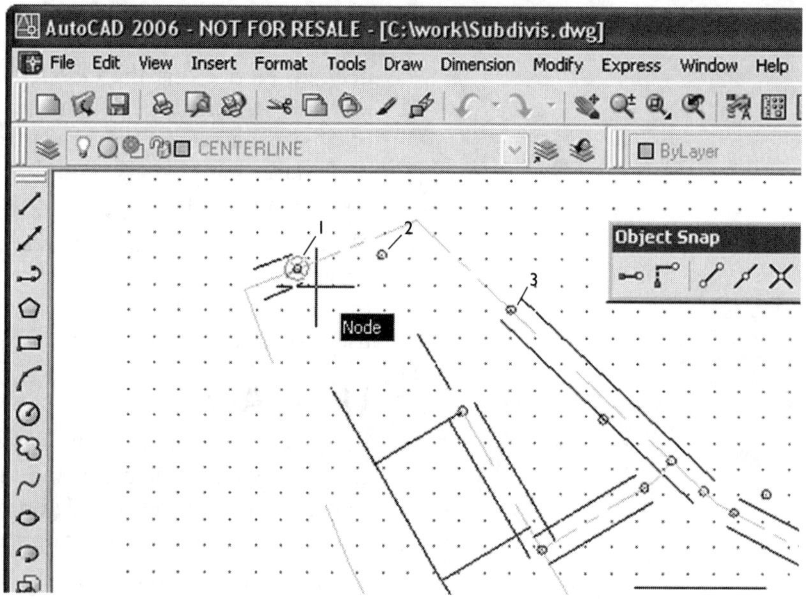

Figure 2.22

As can be seen in Figure 2.22, the AutoSnap marker for Node appears when the cursor is near a node point.

Now you will continue with selecting the points.

Specify second point of arc or [Center/End]: **select point 2**

The cursor enters drag mode, whereby you can see the arc move on the screen as you move the cursor. Many AutoCAD commands permit dynamic specification, or dragging, of the image on the screen.

Move the cursor around the screen to see how it affects the way the arc would be drawn. Recall your use of this feature to draw circles in Tutorial 1.

Specify end point of arc: **select point 3**

The third point defines the endpoint of the arc. The radius of the arc is calculated from the locations of the three points. Your drawing should now show the completed arc, as shown in the upper part of Figure 2.23.

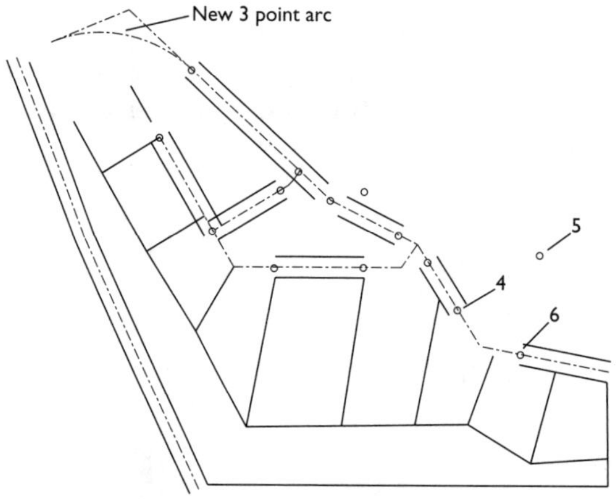

Figure 2.23

Arc Start Center End

Next, you will draw an arc by specifying the start, center, and endpoints. Figure 2.23 shows the points used to create this arc.

Pick: **Draw, Arc, Start Center End**

Specify start point of arc or [Center]: **select point 4 as the start point**

Specify center point of arc: **select point 5 to act as the arc's center**

Specify end point of arc or [Angle/chord Length]: **select point 6 to end the arc**

An arc is always drawn counterclockwise from the start point. Thus you need to define correctly the start point and the center point. Figure 2.23 shows the point locations needed to draw a *concave arc*. If the start point were located where the endpoint is, a *convex arc* outside the centerlines would have been drawn. When you have added the arc correctly, your arc should look like that in the lower part of Figure 2.24.

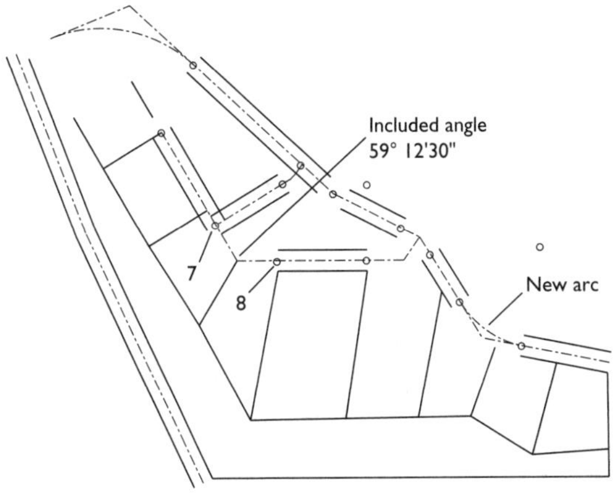

Figure 2.24

Tip

You can type the option letters at the command prompt to select an arc creation method. Pressing the spacebar, the right mouse button, or ⏎ to repeat the previous command will invoke the Arc command. Pressing the right mouse button pops up a menu that allows you to pick the same options for the Arc command that you selected previously (in this case Start Center End). Pressing the space bar or ⏎ key restarts the arc command in a more general way, where you must select the command options by typing in the option letter(s).

On your own, try drawing another arc with the Arc Start Center End option, this time picking point 6 first, then the center, and then point 4. Note that this arc is drawn counterclockwise, resulting in a convex arc. Undo this backward arc by typing U ⏎ at the command prompt.

Arc Start End Angle

Arc Start End Angle draws an arc through the selected start and endpoints by using the included angle you specify. Next, draw an arc with the Start End Angle option, referring to Figure 2.24. This time you will use dynamic entry.

Pick: **to turn on the DYN button on the Status Bar**

Pick: **Draw, Arc, Start End Angle**

Specify start point of arc or [Center]: **select point 7**

Specify end point of arc: **select point 8**

Specify included angle: **59d12'30"** ⏎

The arc is defined by the *included angular value* (often called the *delta angle* in survey drawings) from the start point to the endpoint. Positive angular values are measured counterclockwise. Negative angular values are measured clockwise. (Type d for the degree symbol when typing in surveyor angles. Use the single quote and double quote for minutes and seconds.)

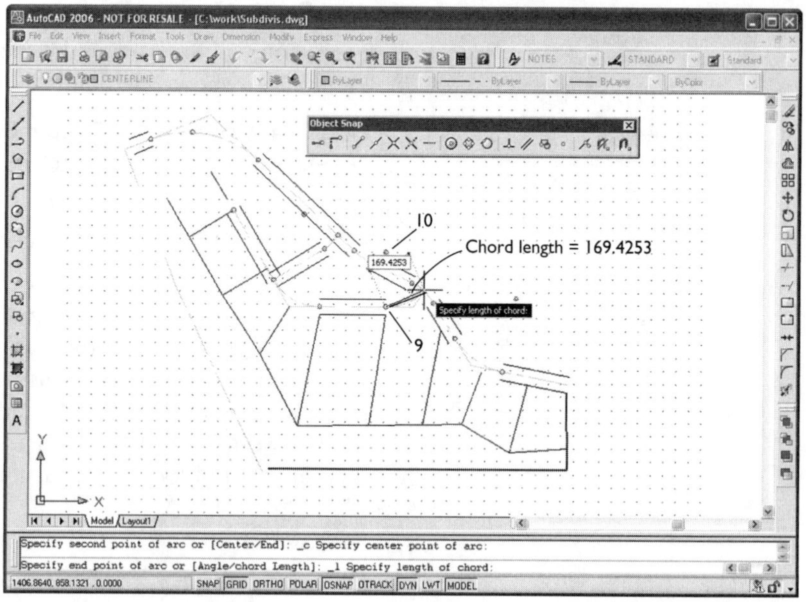

Figure 2.25

Arc Start Center Length

Arc Start Center Length draws an arc specified by the start and center points of the arc and the chord length. The *chord length* is the straight-line distance from the start point of the arc to the endpoint of the arc. You can enter negative values for the chord length to draw an arc in the opposite direction. Figure 2.26 shows a diagram describing the geometry of this type of arc.

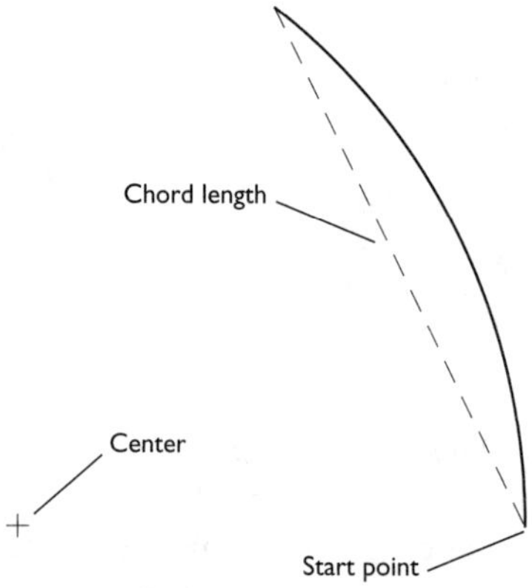

Figure 2.26

You will draw the next arc by using Arc Start Center Length. Figure 2.25 shows the dynamic entry to use for the chord length.

Pick: **Draw, Arc, Start Center Length**
Specify start point of arc or [Center]: **select point 9**
Specify center point of arc: **select point 10**
Specify length of chord: **169.4253** ↵

Your new arc should look like the one shown in Figure 2.27.

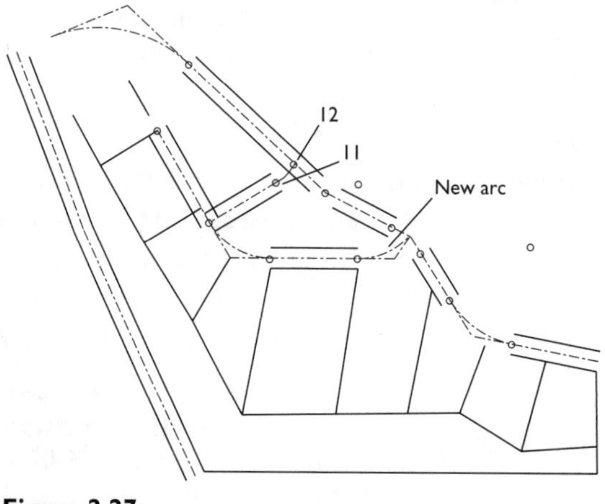

Figure 2.27

Arc Start End Radius

Draw the next arc by using Arc Start End Radius. The locations of the start and end points, 11 and 12, are shown in Figure 2.27.

Pick: **Draw, Arc, Start End Radius**
Specify start point of arc or [Center]: **select point 11**
Specify end point of arc: **select point 12**
Specify radius of arc: **154.87** ↵

Your drawing should be similar to that in Figure 2.28.

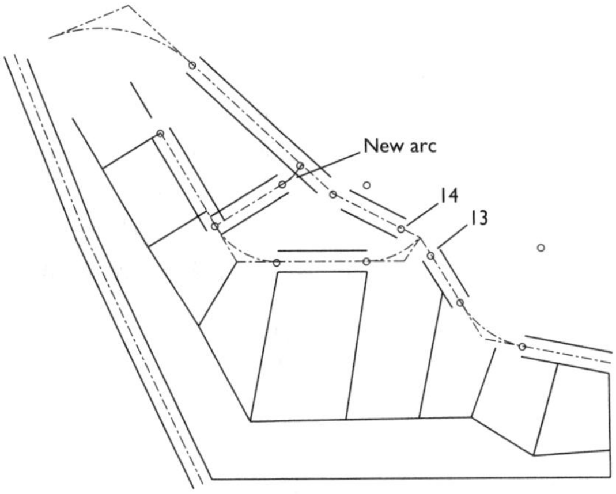

Figure 2.28

Continuing an Arc

Arc Continue allows you to join an arc to a previously drawn arc or line. You will give it a try off to the side of the subdivision drawing and then erase or undo it, as it is not a part of the drawing. To draw an arc that is the continuation of an existing line,

Pick: **Line icon**
Draw a line anywhere on your screen.
Pick: **Draw, Arc, Continue**

The last point of the line becomes the first point for the arc. The cursor is in drag mode, and an arc appears from the end of the line. You are prompted for an endpoint.

Specify end point of arc: **select an endpoint**

Next you will use Arc Start Center End to draw another arc. Then you will continue an arc from the endpoint of that arc.

Pick: **Draw, Arc, Start Center End**
Specify start point of arc or [Center]: **select a start point**
Specify center point of arc: **select a center point**
Specify end point of arc or [Angle/chord Length]: **select an endpoint**
Pick: **Draw, Arc, Continue**
Specify end point of arc: **select an endpoint**

Your drawings should look similar to those in Figure 2.29.

On your own, erase or undo the extra arcs and lines that you created.

Tip

After you draw an arc, restarting the command and then pressing the space bar or ↵ also engages the Continue option. You can use this method to continue a line from the previously drawn arc or line.

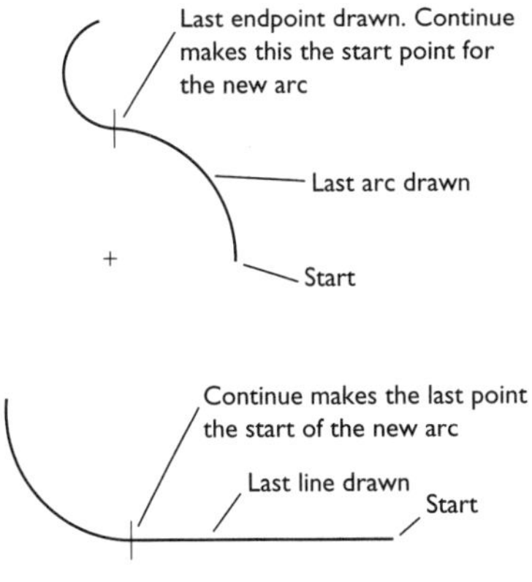

Figure 2.29

Tip

Recall that AutoCAD keyboard entry is not case-sensitive. You can type uppercase, lowercase, or mixed-case letters. In this book your keyboard entry is shown uppercase to help you identify easily what you are supposed to type, but the program does not require uppercase letters.

Quick Selections for Arc

To select the Arc command, you can also type the command alias, A, at the command prompt. When you start the Arc command this way, the default is the 3 Points option you used earlier. If you want to use another option, you can type the command option letter at the prompt. You will start the Arc command by typing its alias. You will then specify the start, end, and angle of the arc by typing the command option at the prompt. Refer to Figure 2.28 for the points, 13 and 14, to select.

Command: **A** ↵

The command Arc is echoed at the command prompt, followed by

Specify start point of arc or [Center]: **pick point 13**
Specify second point of arc or [Center/End]: **E** ↵
Specify end point of arc: **pick point 14**
Specify center point of arc or [Angle/Direction/Radius]: **A** ↵
Specify included angle: **30d54'04"** ↵
Pick: **to turn DYN button off**

The arc is added to your drawing. However, it may be hard to see because of the small size of the arc relative to the size of the screen and drawing. The AutoCAD Zoom commands change the size of the image on your display.

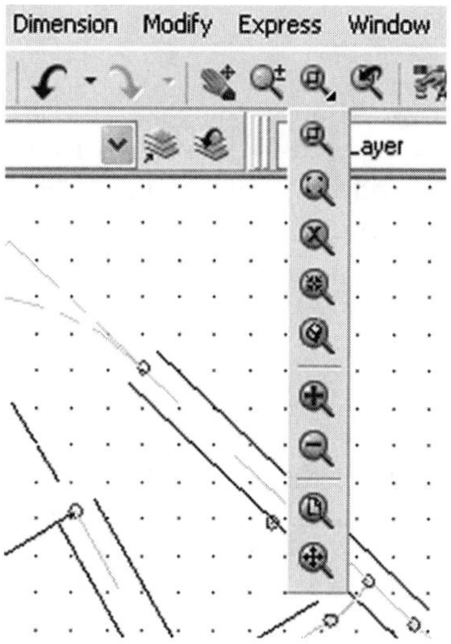

Figure 2.30

Using Zoom

The Zoom flyout is on the Standard toolbar, as shown in Figure 2.30.

To zoom in on an area of the drawing, you can select the Zoom In icon from the Zoom flyout.

Pick: **Zoom In icon**

Your drawing is enlarged to twice its previous size on the screen so that you can see more detail. Your screen should be similar to Figure 2.31.

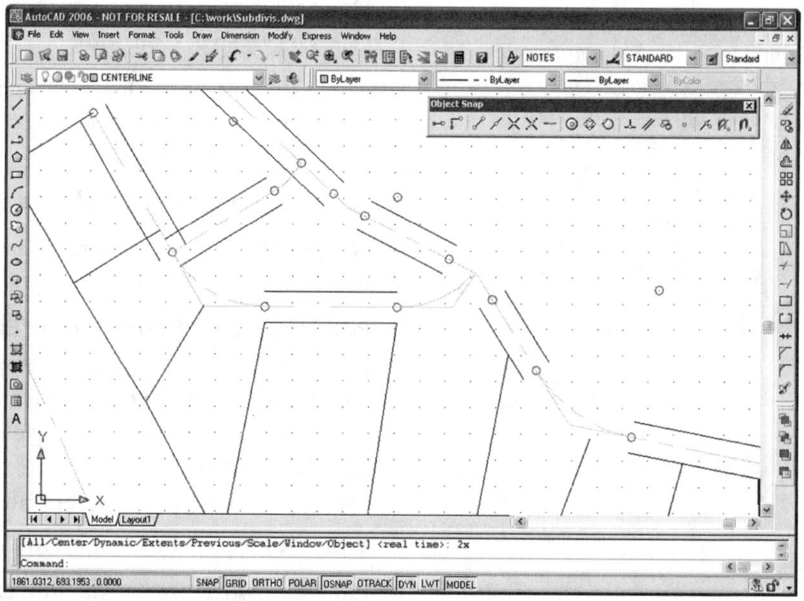

Figure 2.31

Next you will zoom back out, using the Zoom Out selection from the Zoom flyout.

Pick: **Zoom Out icon**

Your drawing should return to its original size on the screen. The Zoom In and Zoom Out options use the Scale feature of the Zoom command to zoom to a scale of 2X (twice the previous size) and 0.5X (half the previous size).

Zooming Using Scale Factors

You can also use *scale factors* to zoom when you pick the Scale option of the Zoom command. Scale factor 1.00 shows the drawing limits (where the grid is shown). Scale factor 0.5 shows the drawing limits half-size on the screen. Typing X after the scale factor makes the zoom scale relative to the previous view. For example, entering 2X causes the new view to be shown twice as big as the view established previously, as you saw when using Zoom In. A scale factor of 0.5X reduces the view to half the previous size, as you saw when using Zoom Out. Zoom Scale uses the current left corner or (0,0) coordinates as the base location for the zoom. Typing XP after the scale factor makes the new zoom scale relative to paper space. A scale factor of 0.5XP means that the object will be shown half-size when you are laying out your sheet of paper. You will learn more about paper space in Tutorial 5.

You will select the Zoom command by typing its alias at the command prompt.

Type: **Z** ↵
Specify corner of window, enter a scale factor (nX or nXP), or [All/Center/
Dynamic/Extents/Previous/Scale/Window/Object] <real time>: **2X** ↵

The objects are enlarged on the screen to twice the size of the previous view. Repeat the Zoom command.

Command: ↵
Specify corner of window, enter a scale factor (nX or nXP), or [All/Center/
Dynamic/Extents/Previous/Scale/Window/Object] <real time>: **.5** ↵

The drawing limits appear on the screen at half their original size. The area shown on the screen is twice as big as the drawing limits. Now, restore the original view.

Command: ↵
Specify corner of window, enter a scale factor (nX or nXP), or [All/Center/
Dynamic/Extents/Previous/Scale/Window/Object] <real time>: **1** ↵

Zoom Window

You can use Zoom Window to create a window around the area that you want to enlarge to fill the screen. This method lets you quickly enlarge the exact portion of the drawing that you are interested in seeing in detail. You will select this command by using the icon on the Zoom flyout. You will note that the Zoom command has an apostrophe in front of it in the command prompt area. Its presence means that the command is transparent and that you can select it during execution of another command. You will zoom in on the area shown in

Figure 2.32. To create the window, you will first select a point at the top left corner of the area to be zoomed and then select a point on the diagonal in the lower right corner.

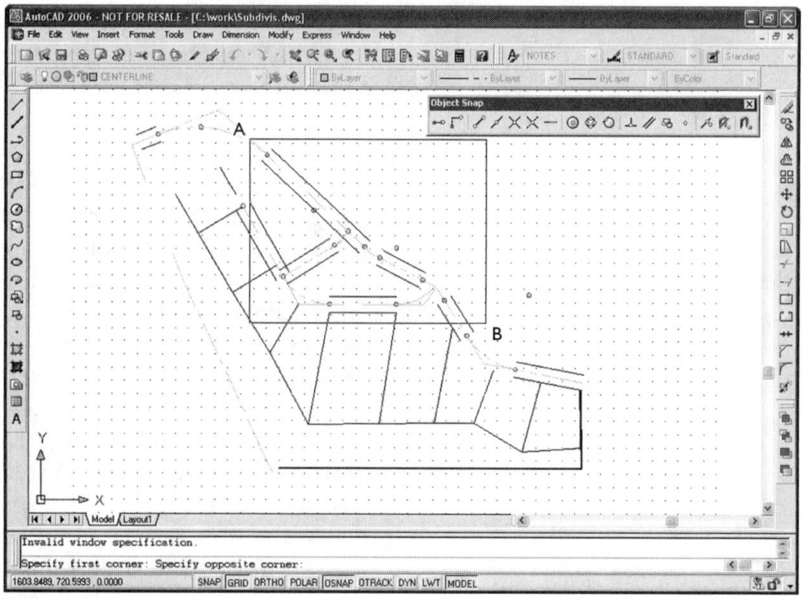

Figure 2.32

Pick: **Zoom Window icon**

Specify first corner: **select point A**

Specify opposite corner: **select point B**

The defined area is enlarged to the full screen size, as shown in Figure 2.33.

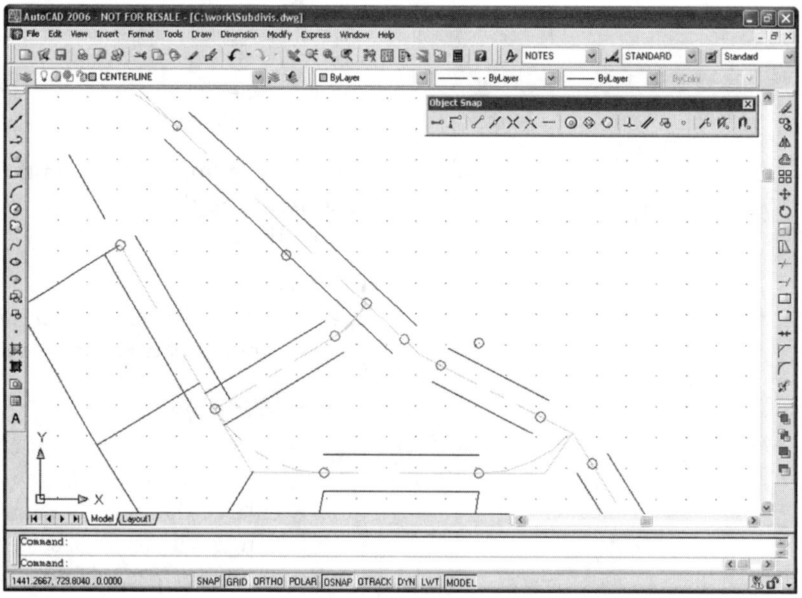

Figure 2.33

Zoom Previous

To return an area to its previous size, you will pick Zoom Previous from the Standard toolbar.

Pick: **Zoom Previous icon**

Your drawing is returned to its original size. Areas can be repeatedly zoomed, that is, you can zoom in on a zoomed area; in fact, you can continue to zoom until the portion shown on the display is ten trillion times the size of the original.

Tip

You can use your middle mouse scroll button for Zoom and Pan Realtime.

Zoom Realtime

An easy way to zoom your drawing to the desired size is to use the Zoom Realtime feature on the Standard toolbar.

Pick: **Zoom Realtime icon**

Select an arbitrary point in the middle of your drawing and hold down the pick button of your pointing device while dragging the cursor up and down. When you move the cursor upward, you zoom in closer to the drawing; when you move the cursor downward, you zoom out farther from the drawing.

Zoom All

Zoom All returns the drawing to its original size by displaying the drawing limits, or displaying the drawing extents (all of the drawing objects), whichever is larger. Select the Zoom All icon from the Zoom flyout.

Pick: **Zoom All icon**

Tip

If you open a drawing that you've saved with the view zoomed in, you can use Zoom All to return to the original drawing limits.

The drawing should return to its original size, that is, as it was before you began the Zoom command. Experiment on your own with the other options of the Zoom command and read about them in the Help window. The Vmax option lets you zoom out as far as possible without causing the drawing to ***regenerate***. The AutoCAD software uses the ***virtual screen***, a file from which the screen display is created. If you try to zoom out to areas that are not calculated in the current virtual screen file, the drawing is regenerated to calculate the display for the new area. Regenerating can take quite a while on a complex drawing, so being able to zoom out without causing a regeneration is useful.

Using the Aerial Viewer

To zoom in and move around in a large drawing quickly, use the AutoCAD Aerial Viewer. To select the Aerial Viewer, you will pick the command from the View menu.

Pick: **View, Aerial View**

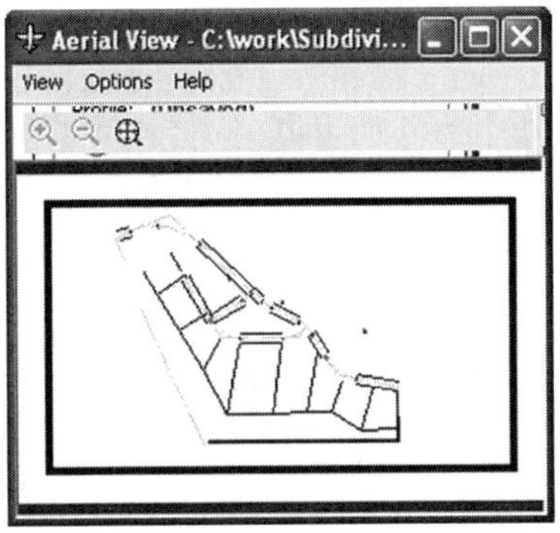

Figure 2.34

The Aerial Viewer appears on your screen, as shown in Figure 2.34. If the Aerial Viewer window is not as large as you would like, you can pick on its corners and drag to increase its size. You can move it around on your screen by picking on its title bar and moving it to a new location while holding down the pick button.

On your own, pick to position the locating box in the Aerial Viewer around the area you wish to select on your screen.

When the box contains an X in the center, it is in position mode. Move it to the location you desire and press the mouse pick button. Now an arrow will appear at the right edge of the box. Use this to enlarge the box as desired, and then press the pick button. You return to the position mode, so that you can move the box around again. When you are satisfied with the location of the box, press the return button on the mouse. The area enclosed in the box in the Aerial Viewer is enlarged to fill the graphics window, as shown in Figure 2.35. The thick border in the Aerial Viewer indicates the current view of which a portion is enlarged. The Aerial Viewer remains on your screen, available for continued use.

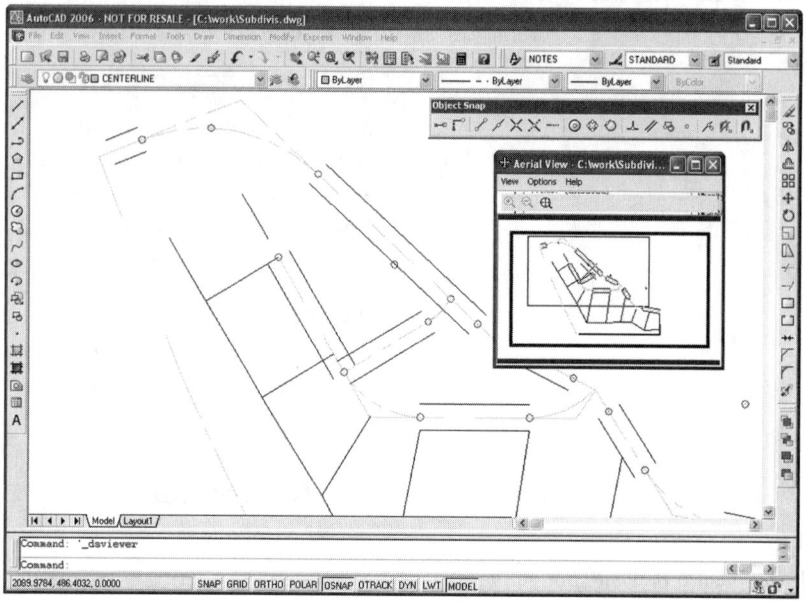

Figure 2.35

Zoom Dynamic works much the same way as the Aerial Viewer. Using Zoom Dynamic, you position and size a window on the area of the drawing you want to zoom. When you have the window positioned and sized the way you want it, press the return button or ↵ to select that area to zoom in on.

Using Pan Realtime

The Pan command lets you position the drawing view on the screen without changing the zoom factor. Unlike the Move command, which moves the objects in your drawing to different locations on the coordinate system, the Pan command does not change the location of the objects on the coordinate system. Rather, your view of the coordinate system and the objects changes to a different location on the screen.

Pick: **Pan Realtime icon**

You can now choose a location central to your drawing by holding down the pick button and dragging the drawing around the screen. The drawing should move freely about the drawing area until you let go of the pick button, at which point it will remain stationary.

Press: Esc or ↵ (to exit the command)

Using Circle Options

In Tutorial 1 you learned how to use the Circle command by specifying a center point and a radius value. You can also use the Circle command to draw circles by specifying any two points (Circle 2 Point), any three points (Circle 3 Point), or two tangent references and a radius (Circle Tan Tan Radius).

Before adding the next two circles, you will turn on the Endpoint running mode object snap so that the circles you create will line up exactly with the ends of the existing lot lines.

Right-click: **OSNAP button** (from status bar)
Pick: **Settings** (from context menu)
Pick: **to turn on Endpoint**
Pick: **OK**

The Endpoint and Node running mode object snaps are turned on. When you see the AutoSnap marker appear on the endpoint of a line, the crosshairs will snap to the marker point. If you see the Node marker, move the crosshairs until the endpoint you want is highlighted.

Pick: **LOTLINES** from the Layer Control to make it current

Circle 2 Point

You will draw a circle using Circle 2 Point. Select two points (1 and 2) to be the endpoints of the circle's diameter, as shown in Figure 2.36.

Pick: **Draw, Circle, 2 Points**
Specify first end point of circle's diameter: **select point 1**

Because you are in drag mode, you can see the circle being created on your screen as you move the cursor.

Specify second endpoint of circle's diameter: **select point 2**

The circle has been defined by the endpoints you selected for the diameter of the circle, which are also the endpoints of lot lines. Your screen should look like Figure 2.36.

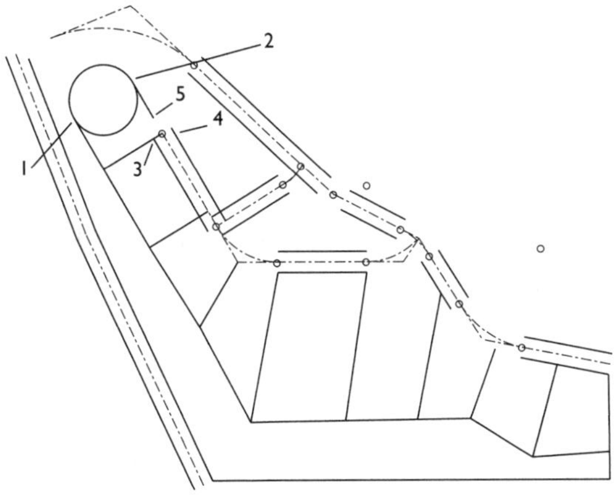

Figure 2.36

Circle 3 Point

To draw a circle using Circle 3 Point, specify any three points on the circle's circumference. Refer to Figure 2.36 for the points (3, 4, and 5) to select.

Pick: **Draw, Circle, 3 Points**
Specify first point on circle: **select point 3**
Specify second point on circle: **select point 4**

Because you are in drag mode again, you can see the circle being created on your screen as you move the cursor.

Specify third point on circle: **select point 5**

The three points on its circumference have defined the circle. Your screen should look like Figure 2.37.

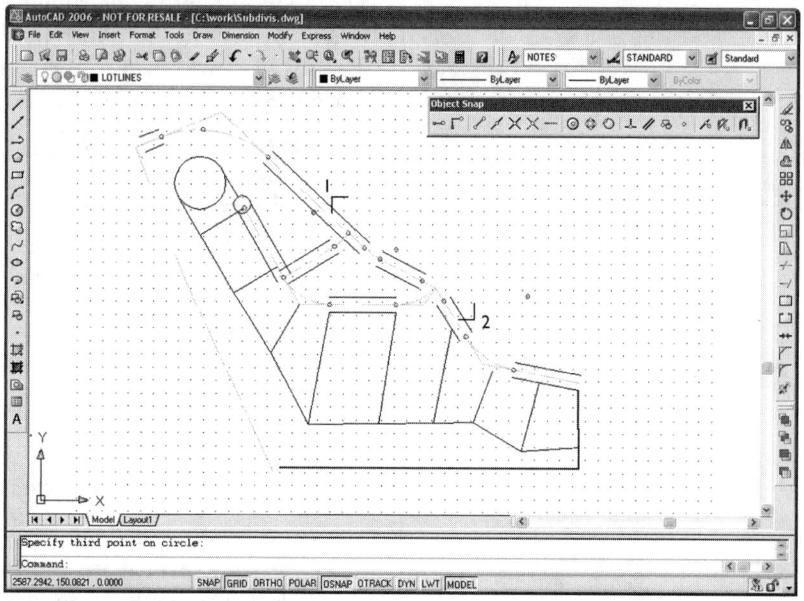

Figure 2.37

Next you will draw a circle tangent to two angled centerlines. First, you will set the current layer to CENTERLINE and then zoom up the area between points 1 and 2, shown in Figure 2.37.

Pick: **CENTERLINE** from the Layer Control list to make it current
Pick: **Zoom Window icon**
Specify first corner: **pick point 1**
Specify opposite corner: **pick point 2**

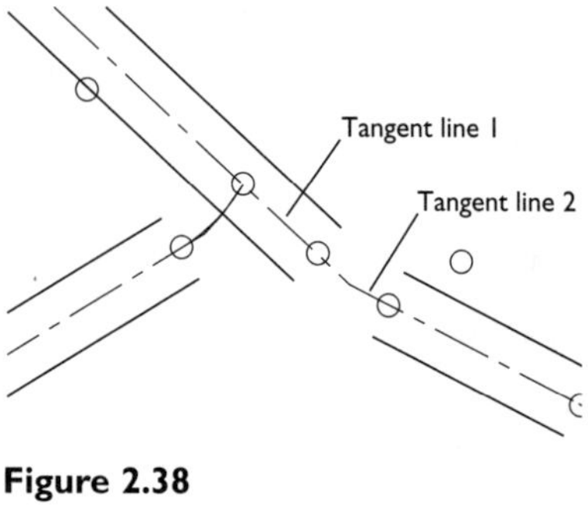

Figure 2.38

The area should be enlarged on your screen, as shown in Figure 2.38.

Next turn off the running object snaps by picking the OSNAP button on the Status bar.

Pick: **OSNAP button** (to turn it off)

The button should now appear unselected, meaning that all running mode object snaps are temporarily turned off. You should do so because sometimes object snaps can interfere with the selection of points and the operation of certain commands. You will use the Circle Tangent Tangent Radius option, which uses the Tangent object snap. This will not work well unless other object snaps are turned off.

Circle Tangent Tangent Radius

Circle Tangent Tangent Radius requires that you specify two objects to which the resulting circle will be *tangent* and the radius of the resulting circle. This method is frequently used in laying out road centerlines. It involves selecting the two straight sections of the road centerline to which the curve is tangent and then specifying the radius.

Pick: **Draw, Circle, Tan Tan Radius**

Note that the AutoSnap marker appears any time the cursor is near a line. Refer to Figure 2.38 for the lines to select. You can select either line first.

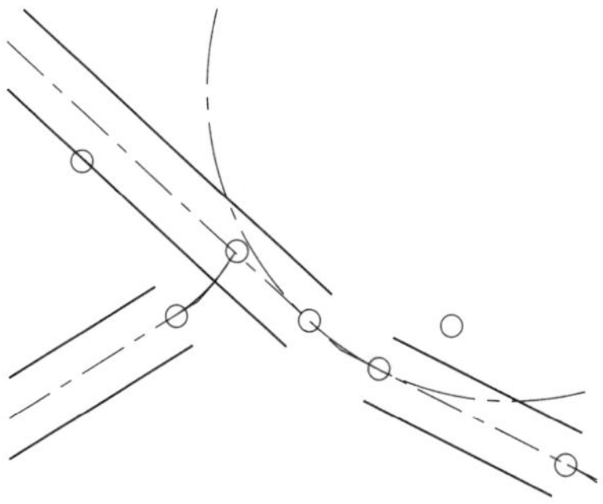

Figure 2.39

Specify point on object for first tangent of circle: **pick tangent line 1**
Specify point on object for second tangent of circle: **pick tangent line 2**
Specify radius of circle <34.0000>: **267.3098** ↵

A circle with a radius of 267.3098 is drawn tangent to both original lines, as shown in Figure 2.39.

You can also use Circle Tangent Tangent Radius to draw a circle tangent to two circles. You will try this by drawing two circles off to the side of the drawing and then adding a circle that is tangent to both of them.

On your own, draw two circles off to the side of your subdivision drawing.
Pick: **Draw, Circle, Tan Tan Radius**
Specify point on object for first tangent of circle: **select one of the circles you just drew**
Specify point on object for second tangent of circle: **select the other circle**
Specify radius of circle <267.3098>: **150** ↵

A circle with a radius of 150 is drawn tangent to both circles.

Tip

If you get the message, Circle does not exist, the radius you specified may be too small or too large to be tangent to both lines.

Tip

The value shown as the default radius for the circle depends on the size of the last circle you drew.

Circle Tangent Tangent Tangent

The Circle Tangent Tangent Tangent command lets you quickly define a circle that is tangent to three entities in the drawing.

Try it on your own by selecting Draw, Circle, Tan Tan Tan and then selecting three lot lines to draw a circle tangent to.
Now erase the extra circles on your own.

Using Ellipse

AutoCAD provides three different ways to specify an ellipse. The various methods can be found under Ellipse on the Draw menu. The Ellipse icon is on the Draw toolbar.

Next, you will practice using the Ellipse command by drawing some ellipses off to the side of the drawing. You will erase them when you are through. To draw an ellipse by specifying three points,

Pick: **Ellipse icon**
Specify axis endpoint of ellipse or [Arc/Center]: **select a point**

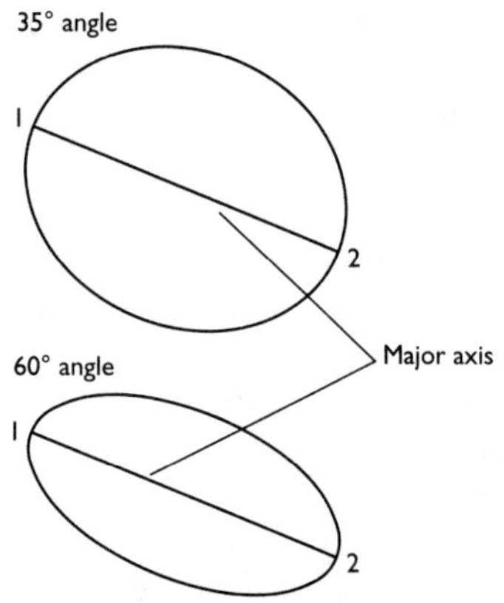

Figure 2.40

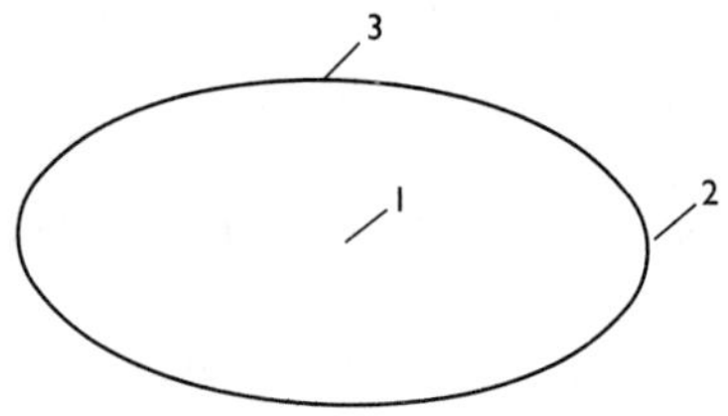

Figure 2.41

Specify other endpoint of axis: **select a point**
Specify distance to other axis or [Rotation]: **select a point**

An ellipse is created on your screen, using the three points that you selected. The ellipse has a *major axis* (the longest distance between two points on the ellipse) and a *minor axis* (the shorter distance across the ellipse). The AutoCAD program determines which axis is major and which is minor by examining the distance between the first pair of endpoints and comparing it to the distance specified by the third point.

One way to describe an ellipse is to create a circle and then tip the circle away from your viewing direction by a rotation angle. This method requires you to specify the angle of rotation instead of the endpoint of the second axis.

You will draw an ellipse using two endpoints and an angle of rotation. See Figure 2.40 to determine the location of the points.

Pick: **Ellipse icon**
Specify axis endpoint of ellipse or [Arc/Center]: **select point 1**
Specify other endpoint of axis: **select point 2**

This construction method defines the distance between points 1 and 2 as the major axis (diameter) of the ellipse. This circle will be rotated into the third dimension by the specified rotation angle.

Specify distance to other axis or [Rotation]: **R** ↵
Specify rotation around major axis: **35** ↵
On your own, **erase** from your screen the ellipses that you created.

The other two construction methods for ellipses are analogous to the two methods already described, but they use radius values rather than diameter values. That is, the center point of the ellipse is known and is used as a starting point instead of an endpoint. Next, you will draw an ellipse by specifying a center point and two axis points; refer to Figure 2.41 for the locations of the points.

Command: ↵ (to restart the command)
Specify axis endpoint of ellipse or [Arc/Center]: **C** ↵

The center of the ellipse is the intersection of the major and minor axes. You can enter a coordinate or use the cursor to select a point on the screen.

Specify center of ellipse: **select point 1**

Next, you provide the endpoint of the first axis. The angle of the ellipse is determined by the angle from the center point to this endpoint.

Specify endpoint of axis: **select point 2**

Now specify the distance measured from the center of the ellipse to the endpoint of the second axis (measured perpendicular to the first axis) or a rotation angle.

Specify distance to other axis or [Rotation]: **select point 3**

The point that you selected determined whether the first axis is a major or minor axis. The ellipse is drawn on your screen.

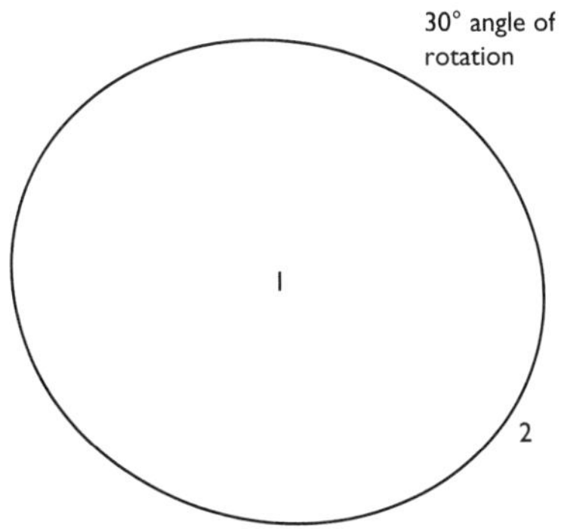

Figure 2.42

Tip

If you have older AutoCAD versions you can use the Save As command to save your drawing to the R12 or 2000 formats. In the Save Drawing As dialog box, scroll through the Save Drawing Type list for the various options.

Next, draw an ellipse by specifying a center point, one axis point, and an angle of rotation. Refer to Figure 2.42.

Pick: **Ellipse icon**
Specify axis endpoint of ellipse or [Arc/Center]: **C** ↵
Specify center of ellipse: **pick point 1 in Figure 2.42**
Specify endpoint of axis: **pick point 2**
Specify distance to other axis or [Rotation]: **R** ↵
Specify rotation around major axis: **30** ↵
Before you go on, **erase** the ellipses you drew when practicing.

Now that you have practiced with the Ellipse command,

Use Zoom All to return to the original view.
Save your drawing at this time.
Pick: to close the Object Snap toolbar by picking its Close button (X)

When you have successfully saved your drawing,

Pick: **File, Exit**

You are now back at the Windows desktop.
You will finish the subdivision drawing in Tutorial 3.

Key Terms

chord length	freeze	minor axis	running mode
concave arc	included angular value	object snap	scale factor
convex arc	layer	override mode	tangent
current layer	locked layer	primitives	target
delta angle	major axis	regenerate	virtual screen

Key Commands

Aerial Viewer	Circle 2 Point	Layer Control	Snap to Node
Arc 3 Points	Circle 3 Point	Object Snap	Zoom In
Arc Continue	Circle Tan Tan Radius	Open Drawing	Zoom Out
Arc Start Center End	Circle Tan Tan Tan	Pan Realtime	Zoom Previous
Arc Start Center Length	Color Control	Running Object Snap	Zoom Realtime
Arc Start End Angle	Ellipse	Save As	Zoom Scale
Arc Start End Radius	Layer	Snap to Endpoint	Zoom Window

Exercises

Redraw the following shapes. If dimensions are given, create your drawing geometry exactly to the specified dimensions. The letter M after an exercise number means that the dimensions are in millimeters (metric units). If no letter follows the exercise number, the dimensions are in inches. Do not include dimensions on the drawings. The ∅ symbol means diameter; R indicates a radius.

2.1M Bracket

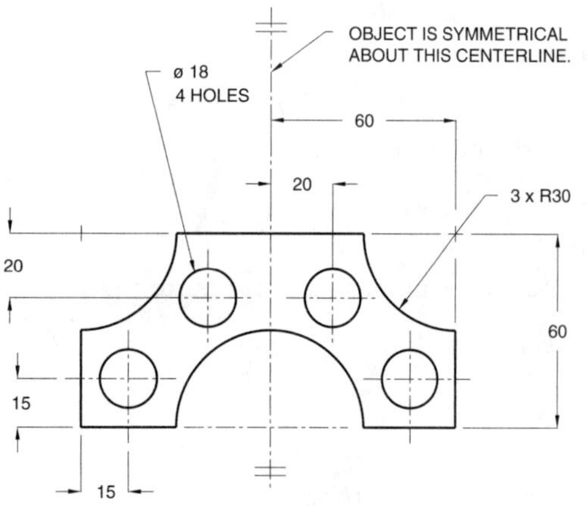

2.2 Gasket

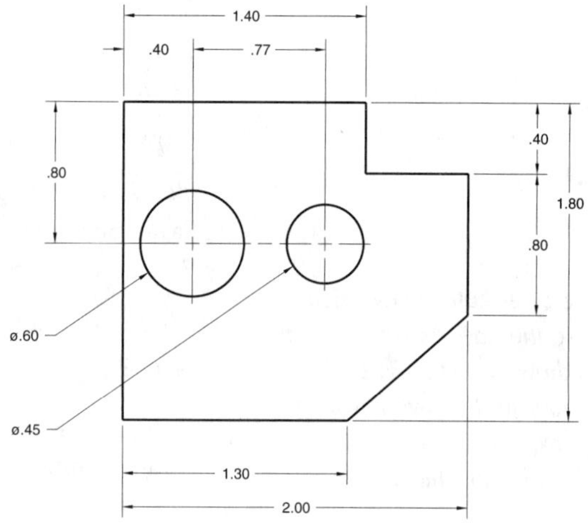

2.3M Flange

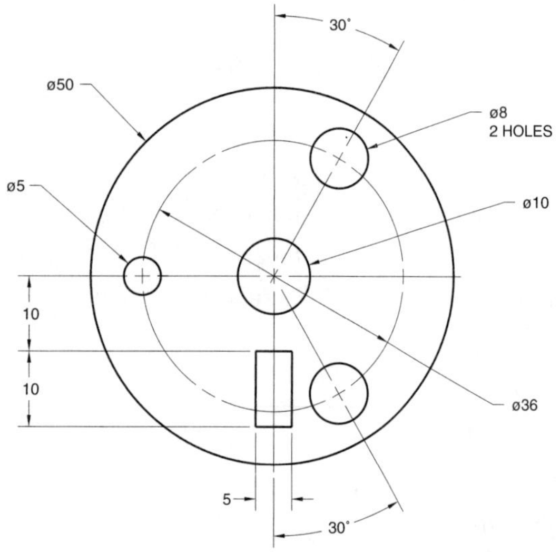

2.4M Puzzle

Draw the figure shown according to the dimensions provided. From your drawing determine what the missing distances must be (Hint: use DIST).

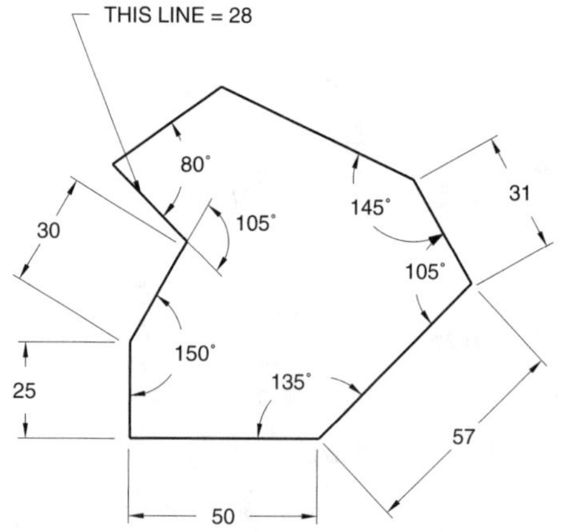

2.5 Plot Plan

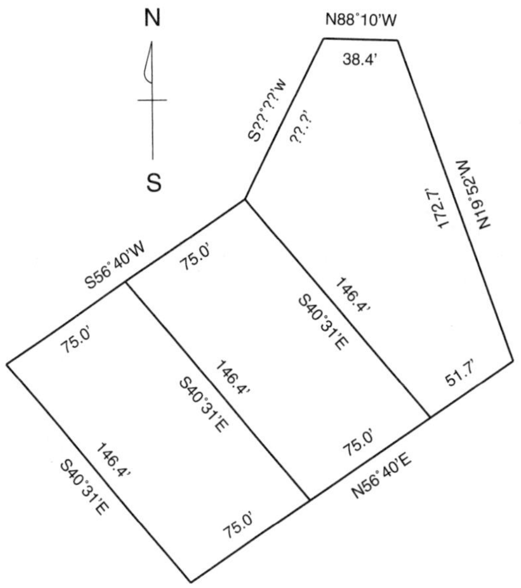

2.6 Link

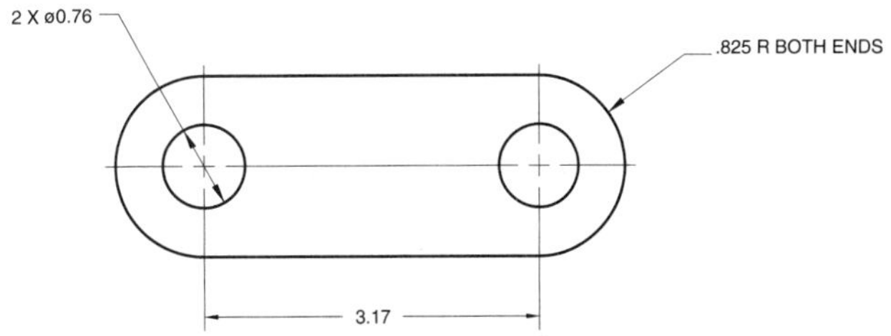

2.7 Power Supply

Draw this circuit, using the techniques you have learned.

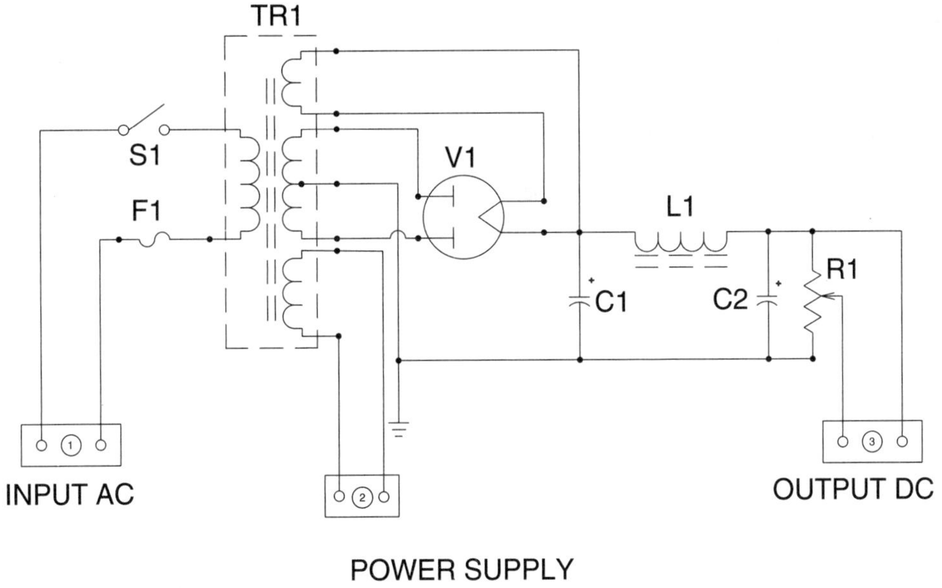

2.8 Gasket

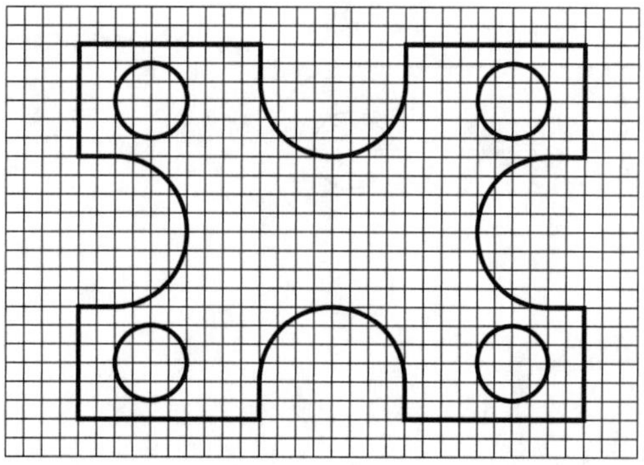

2.9 Shape

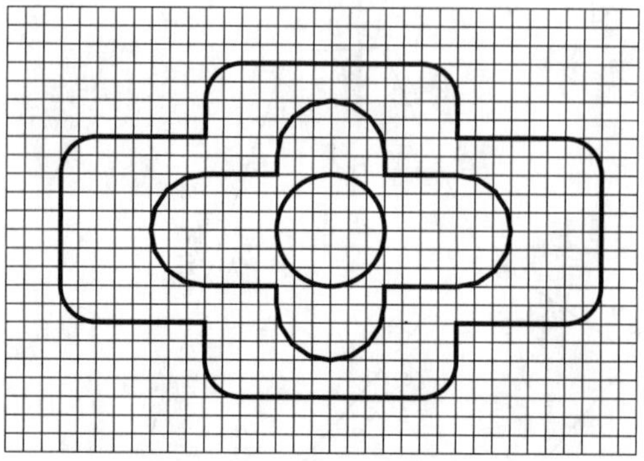

2.10M Lever Crank

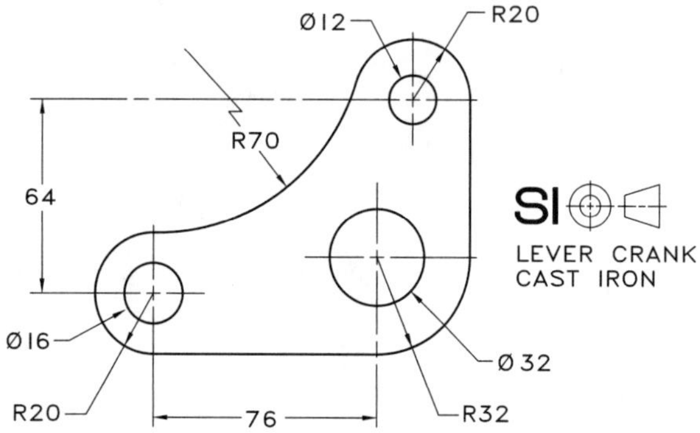

Tutorial

3 Basic Editing and Plotting Techniques

Objectives

When you have completed this tutorial, you will be able to

1. Modify your drawing, using the Fillet, Chamfer, Offset, and Trim commands.
2. Create and edit polylines and splines.
3. List graphical objects, locate points, and find areas from your drawing database.
4. Change properties of drawing objects.
5. Create multilines and multiline styles.
6. Print or plot your drawing.

Introduction

In this tutorial you will learn how to modify some of the basic shapes that you've drawn to create a wider variety of shapes required for technical drawings. As you work through the tutorial, keep in mind that one of the advantages of using CAD over drawing on paper is that you are creating an accurate model of the drawing geometry. You will see how to use this accurate drawing database to find areas, lengths, and other information. In later tutorials, you will also learn to use basic two-dimensional (2D) shapes as a basis for three-dimensional (3D) solid models.

In this tutorial you will finish drawing the subdivision that you started in Tutorial 2. A drawing has been provided with the datafiles that accompany this guide. You will start from it, in case the drawing that you created in Tutorial 2 has some settings that are different from the datafile. You will trim lines and arcs, and add fillets, multilines, and text to finish the subdivision drawing. When you've finished the drawing, you will plot your final result.

Starting

Launch the AutoCAD® 2006 software.

Starting from a Template Drawing

A template drawing is one designed to be used as the basis for new drawings. Any AutoCAD settings, preferences, and drawn objects in the template become part of the new drawing, while the original template remains unchanged. Files that can be used as templates have the extension *.dwt*. There is really no difference between them and drawings except for the file extension. Any drawing can be saved as a template file using Save As and then changing the file type to Drawing Template File (*.dwt*).

In order to continue with the subdivision drawing, you will start a new file, using the drawing file *subdiv2.dwt* as a template.

Pick: **File, New**

The Select Template dialog box should be showing, similar to that in Figure 3.1. You should see a list of premade templates to choose from; these are stored in the *Template* folder that was created when the software was installed.

Tip

You can pick Tools, Options and use the File tab of the Options dialog box to set a different default directory location for the template files.

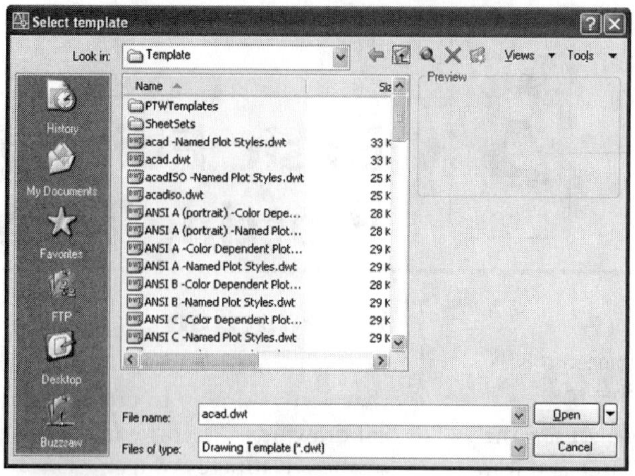

Figure 3.1

Pick: **to pull down the selections in the Look in box**

The storage devices connected to your computer appear similar to Figure 3.2.

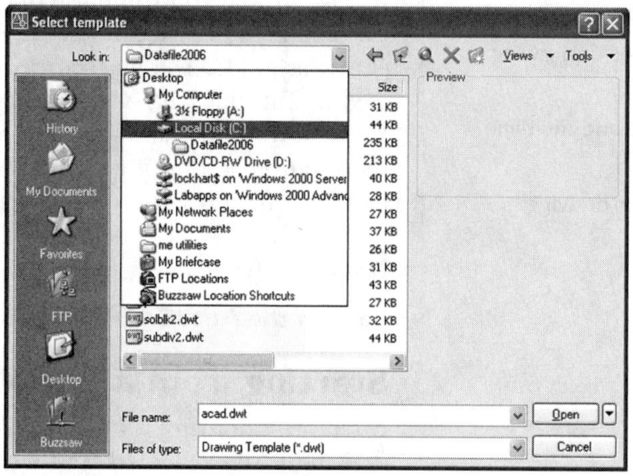

Figure 3.2

Choose the location of the *c:\datafile2006* folder so you can see the templates in it as shown in Figure 3.3.

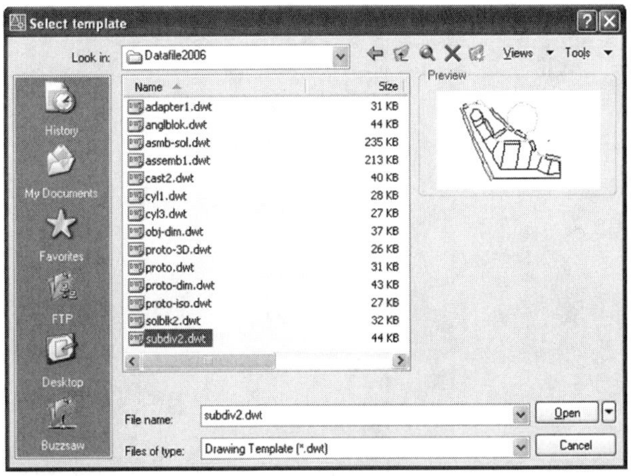

Figure 3.3

Select: **subdiv2.dwt**
Pick: **Open**

Tip

You may see Drawing followed by a different number depending on how many new drawings you have started in this AutoCAD session.

You should see the drawing on your screen with the AutoCAD default name "Drawing1", meaning that the actual *subdiv2.dwt* datafile will not be changed. Next you will save the drawing under the new name MYSUBDIV in your *c:\work* directory.

Pick: **File, Save As**
Change to the ***c:\work*** directory. For the file name,
Type: **MYSUBDIV**

The drawing on your screen should be similar to Figure 3.4.

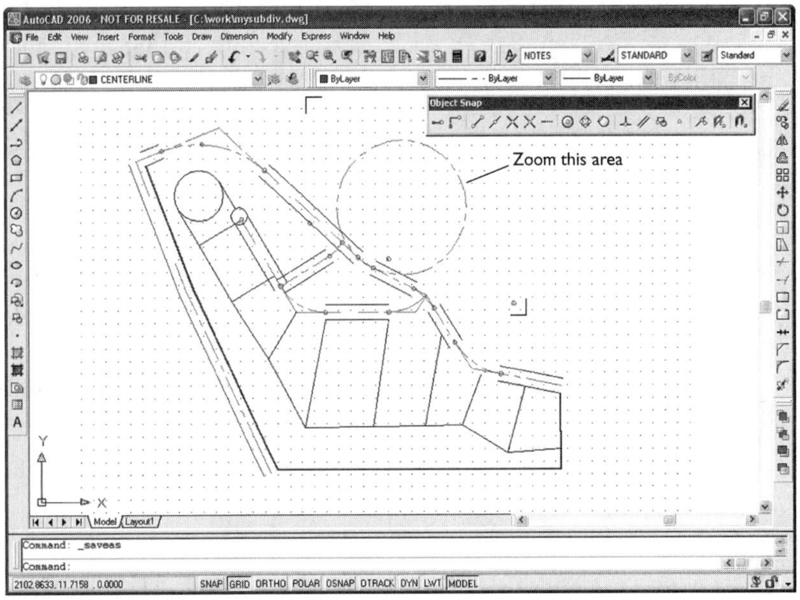

Figure 3.4

Use Zoom Window to enlarge the view of the area with the large circle indicated in Figure 3.4.

When you have finished zooming, your screen will look like Figure 3.5.

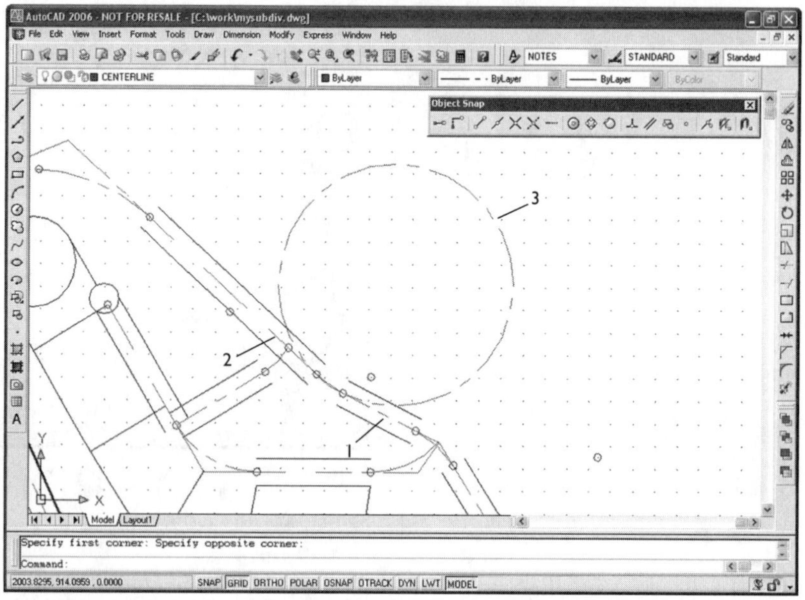

Figure 3.5

Using Trim

The Trim icon is located on the Modify toolbar, which is usually docked at the right side of the screen. Trim removes part of an object in two steps. First, you are prompted to select the objects that you will use as cutting edges. The ***cutting edges*** are drawing objects that you will use to cut off the portions that you want to trim. The cutting edge objects selected must cross the objects that you want to trim at the point at which you want to trim. Press ↵ to indicate that you have finished selecting cutting edges and want to begin the second step. After you press ↵, you are prompted to select the portions of the objects that you want to trim. Pick on the portions you want to remove. You can also hold down the shift key while selecting an object to extend that object to the cutting edge that you have selected.

The Trim command has several options. The Fence option lets you select items to trim by drawing a "fence" (an open ended series of line segments) across them.

The Crossing option lets you select the items to trim with a crossing box.

The Project option gives you three choices for the projection method used by the command.

View Trims objects where they intersect, as viewed from the current viewing direction.

None Trims objects only where they intersect in 3D space.

UCS Trims objects where they intersect in the current User Coordinate System.

The Edge option lets you decide whether to trim objects only where they intersect in 3D space or where they would intersect if the edge were extended. The Project and Edge options are very useful when you are working with 3D models as you will be in Tutorial 11.

The Erase option lets you erase unwanted items without leaving the Trim command.

The Undo option lets you undo the last trim without exiting the command; it's similar to the Undo option you used with the Line command.

You will pick the Trim command from the Modify toolbar and use it to remove the excess portion of the circle. Refer to Figure 3.5.

Pick: **Trim icon**
Current settings: Projection=UCS, Edge=None
Select cutting edges ...
Select objects or <select all>: **select lines 1 and 2**

The cutting edges selected will be highlighted. Note that the command line reported the projection mode set to UCS and the edge mode set to no extension.

Select objects: ↵

You have finished selecting the cutting edges. Next, select the portion of the circle to be removed.

Select object to trim or shift-select to extend or
[Fence/Crossing/Project/Edge/eRase/Undo]: **pick on the circle near point 3**

You will press ↵ to end the command,

Select object to trim or [Fence/Crossing/Project/Edge/eRase/Undo]: ↵

When you are done, your figure should be similar to Figure 3.6.

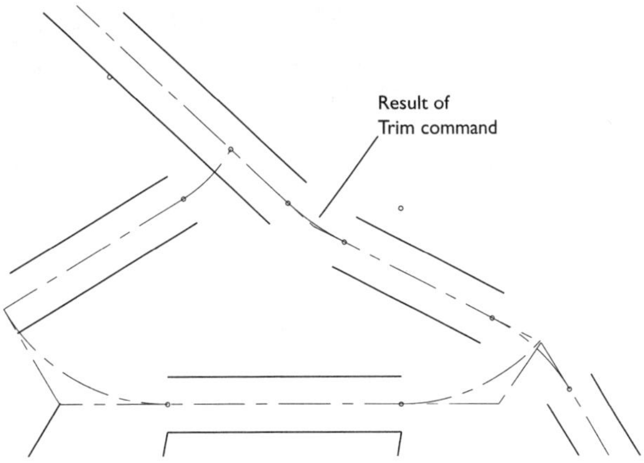

Figure 3.6

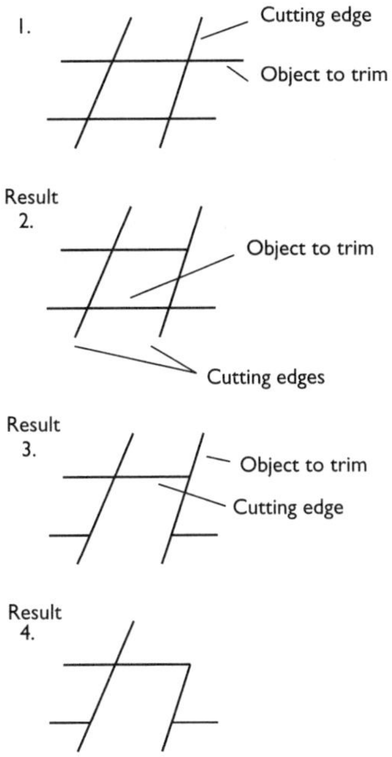

Figure 3.7

Refer to Figure 3.7 to understand how the cutting edge works in relation to the object to be trimmed.

When lines come together, as at a corner, you can select one or both of the lines as cutting lines, as shown in Figure 3.7, parts 1 and 3. Again, the cursor location determines which portion of the line is removed.

Next restore the previous zoom factor,

Pick: **View, Zoom Previous**

When you have finished these steps, your screen should look like Figure 3.8.

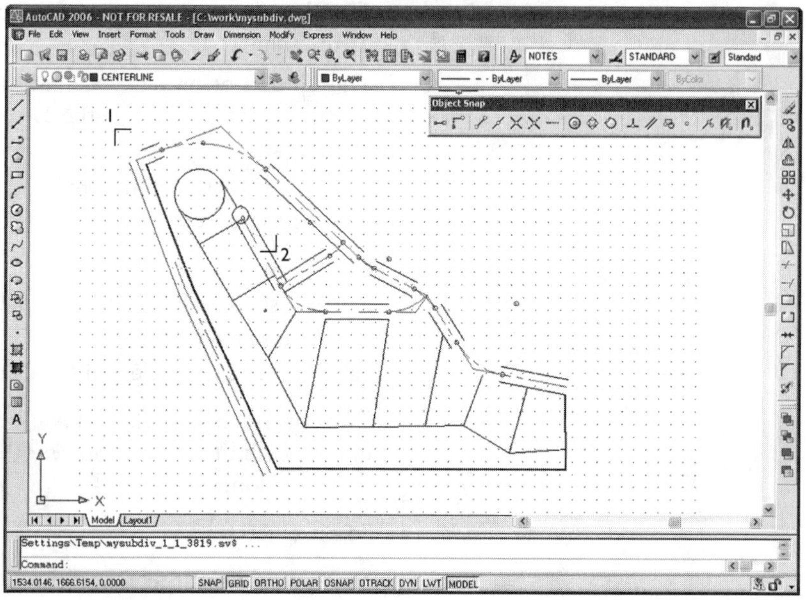

Figure 3.8

Next, enlarge the area shown in Figure 3.8 by picking near point 1 for the first corner of the window and near point 2 for the other corner.

Pick: **Zoom Window icon**
Specify first corner: **pick near 1**
Specify opposite corner: **pick near 2**

When you have finished, your screen should look like Figure 3.9.

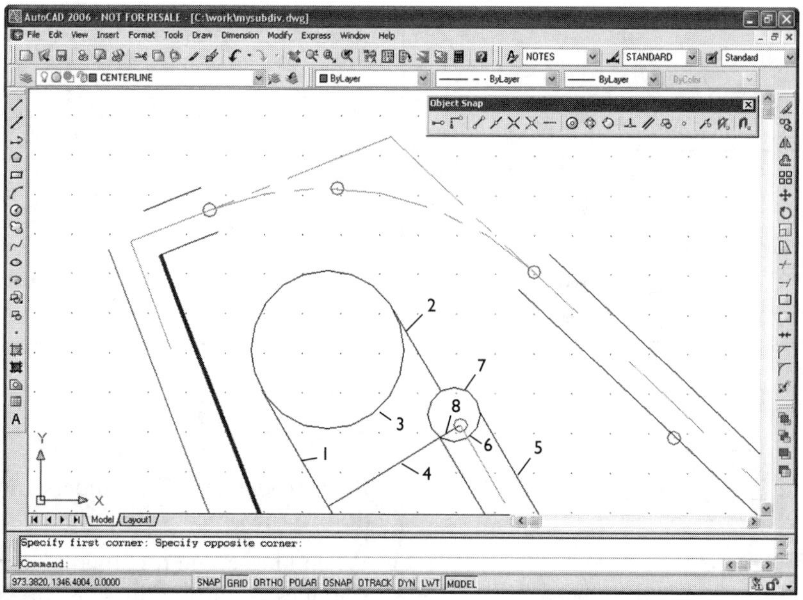

Figure 3.9

Next, you will trim the excess portions of the circles that you created with the 2 Point and 3 Point options. The arcs that remain when you have finished trimming will form the lot line and the cul-de-sac for the road.

Tip

When you zoom in on an area, circles may not be shown correctly. On the screen, circles are approximated with a number of straight-line segments. The number of segments used may look fine when the circle first appears on the screen, but when you zoom in on it, it may appear jagged. To eliminate this poor appearance, you can type REGEN at the command prompt, pick View, Regen, or type the command alias RE to cause the display to be recalculated from the drawing database and redisplayed on the screen correctly.

Pick: **Trim icon**

Current setting: Projection=UCS Edge=None

Select cutting edges ...

Select objects or <select all>: **select lines 1 and 2** identified in Figure 3.9

Select objects: ↵

Select object to trim or shift-select to extend or [Fence/Crossing/Project/Edge/eRase/Undo]: **pick the circle near point 3**

Select object to trim or shift-select to extend or [Fence/Crossing/Project/Edge/eRase/Undo]: ↵

Command: ↵ (to restart the Trim command)

Select objects or <select all>: **select lines 4 and 5**

Select objects: ↵

Select object to trim or shift-select to extend or [Fence/Crossing/Project/Edge/eRase/Undo]: **pick the circle near point 6**

Select object to trim or shift-select to extend or [Fence/Crossing/Project/Edge/eRase/Undo]: **Hold down the shift key and pick near point 8** to extend the line across the circle so that you can see how the extend feature works

Select object to trim or shift-select to extend or [Fence/Crossing/Project/Edge/eRase/Undo]: ↵

Command: ↵ (to restart the Trim command)

Select objects or <select all>: **select the circle near point 7**

Select objects: ↵

Select object to trim or shift-select to extend or [Fence/Crossing/Project/Edge/eRase/Undo]: **pick on the line near point 8**

Select object to trim or shift-select to extend or [Fence/Crossing/Project/Edge/eRase/Undo]: ↵

Tip

Lines that do not cross the cutting edge cannot be trimmed. Use the Erase option of the trim command to erase objects that no longer cross the cutting edge.

When you have finished trimming the circles, your screen should look like Figure 3.10. If it doesn't, change the drawing on your own so that it looks like the picture.

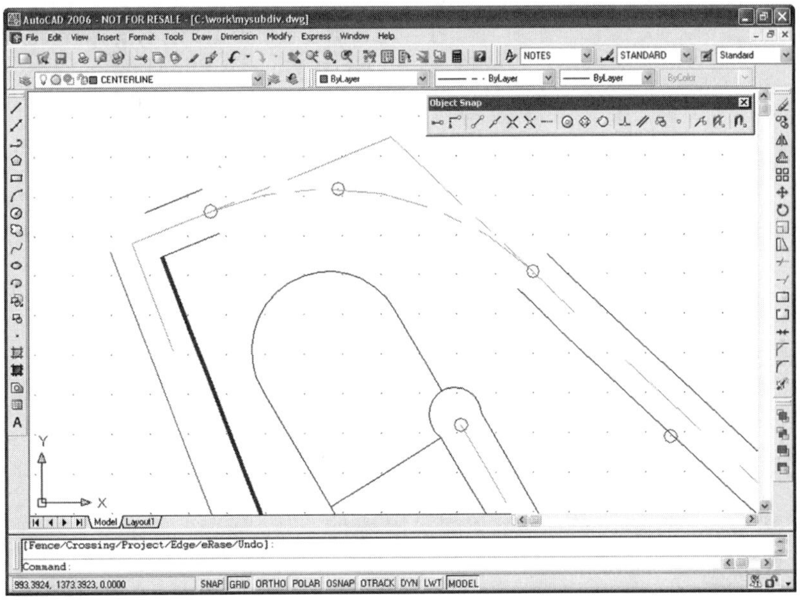

Figure 3.10

Pick: **Zoom Previous icon** to restore the previous zoom factor.

Using Offset

The Offset command creates a new object parallel to a given object. The Offset command is on the Modify toolbar and Modify menu. You will use Offset to create parallel curves 30 units from either side of the curved centerlines that you drew in Tutorial 2.

Pick: **Offset icon**

To offset an object, you need to determine the *offset distance* (the distance away from the original object) or the *through point* (the point through which the offset object is to be drawn). To specify the offset distance indicated in Figure 3.11,

Specify offset distance or [Through/Erase/Layer] <Through>: **30** ↵

Select object to offset or [Exit/Undo] <Exit>: **select curve 1**

Specify point on side to offset [Exit/Multiple/Undo]: **pick a point below the curve, like point A**

Select object to offset or [Exit/Undo] <Exit>: **select curve 1**

Specify point on side to offset [Exit/Multiple/Undo]: **pick a point above the curve, like point B**

Once you have defined the offset distance, the prompt *Select object to offset:* is repeated, allowing you to create additional parallel lines that have the same spacing.

On your own, repeat the steps just described to create lines offset 30 units from either side of the remaining curved centerlines so that your drawing looks like that shown in Figure 3.11. If necessary, use the Zoom commands to enlarge the smaller curves so that you can see them better on your screen when making selections. Use Zoom Previous to return to the previous view. Remember that the Zoom commands (with the exception of Zoom All) can be transparent so that you can select them during another command without canceling that command.

If you select the wrong item to offset, either erase the incorrect lines when you have finished or press Esc to cancel the command and then start again. When you have finished using the Offset command, press ↵ to end the command. Note that the new objects created by the Offset command are on the same layer as the object that you selected to offset. Which layer is current doesn't matter; the newly offset object will always be on the same layer as the original object that you selected.

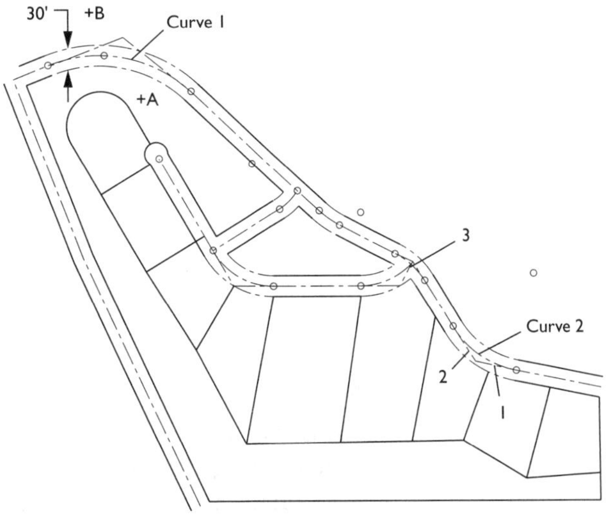

Figure 3.11

Trimming the Remaining Lines

On your own, refer to Figure 3.11 and select curve 2 as the cutting edge.

Be sure to press ↵ or the return button when you have finished selecting cutting edges.

Trim off the portions of the centerline that extend past the cutting edge by picking the points labeled 1 and 2.

Repeat this process and trim all remaining centerlines where they extend beyond the centerline arcs.

Note that line 3 doesn't extend past any cutting edges, so it cannot be trimmed. Use the Erase command to remove it.

Now zoom in on the center area of the drawing so that you can trim the excess lines where the roadways join.

The center portion of the drawing will be enlarged on your screen.

Selecting All Edges to Use with Trim

This time, instead of selecting one cutting edge at a time, you will press ↵ to select all the lines in that area as cutting edges. Refer to Figure 3.12 to make your selections.

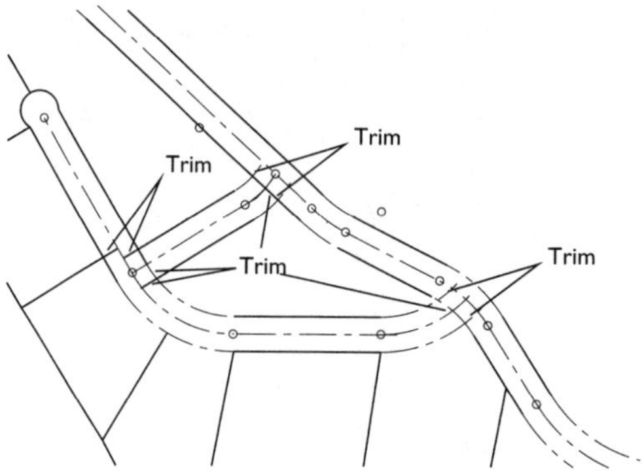

Figure 3.12

Pick: **Trim icon**
Current settings: Projection=UCS Edge=None
Select cutting edges ...
Select objects or <select all>: ↵

All objects become selected as cutting edges.

Select object to trim or shift-select to extend or
[Fence/Crossing/Project/Edge/eRase/Undo]: **select the extreme ends of the lines you want to remove and continue doing so until all the excess lines are trimmed**
Select object to trim or shift-select to extend or
[Fence/Crossing/Project/Edge/eRase/Undo]: ↵
Experiment with the Fence and Crossing options on your own.

Tip

If you pick something to trim by mistake, you can type the option letter U (for Undo) and press ↵ at the prompt. This restores the last object trimmed.

When you have finished trimming, use Zoom All on your own to show the entire drawing on the screen. If you have some short line segments left that no longer cross the cutting edges, use Erase to remove them on your own. Your drawing should now look like that shown in Figure 3.13.

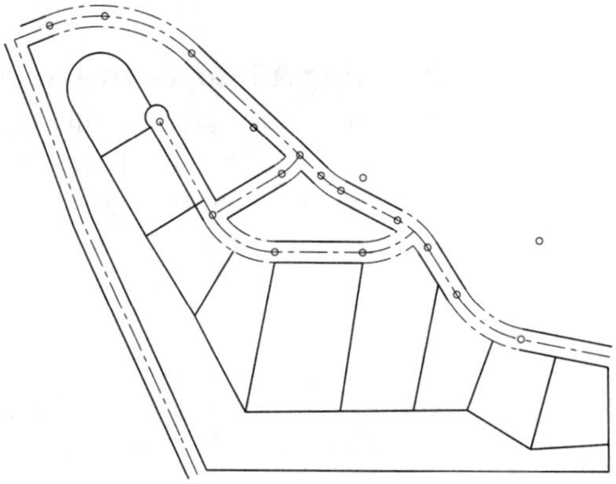

Figure 3.13

Changing Object Properties

Once you've drawn an object, changing the properties of the object or a group of objects may be useful. You will change the properties of the centerlines that you offset so that they are on the layer LOTLINES. The new offset lines are the edges of the road and should be on the same layer as the other lot lines.

A quick way to change objects to another layer is to use the Layer Control pull-down list. When you have objects selected and then pick a layer from the Layer Control list, the selected objects will be changed to the picked layer.

Tip

You can double-click on an object to quickly bring up its properties.

Pick: **some, but not all, of the roadway edges that appear as center-lines so that they become highlighted with small grip boxes**

Pick: **on the layer CENTERLINE** (in the Layer Control) to pull down available layers

Pick: **LOTLINES** (from the list of layers shown)

You will see the lines you selected change to the color and linetype for layer LOTLINES. Next you will press the escape key to unselect the lines.

Press: Esc

Notice that CENTERLINE once again shows as the current layer name in the Layer Control.

This same function applies to changing the color and linetype of an object, without having to change its layer. You would perform the same steps, only choose a different color or linetype from the Color Control or Linetype Control pull-down menus.

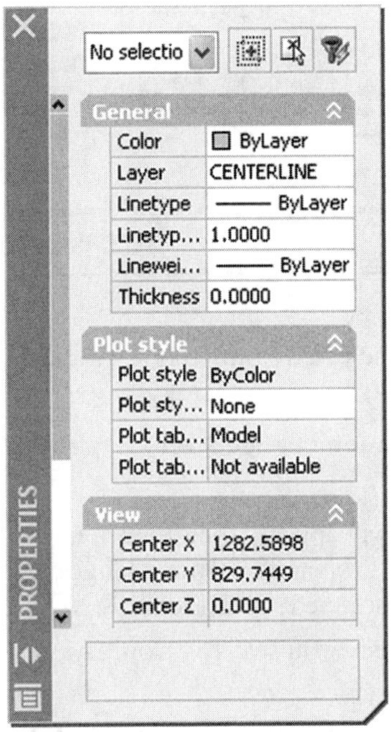

Figure 3.14

Using the Properties Palette

You can also use the Properties palette to view and change an object's properties. The Properties icon is on the Standard toolbar near the top of the screen. It is identified in Figure 3.15. The Properties palette lets you change the linetype, layer, lineweight, color, and geometric properties of the objects you select, as well as their linetype scale (which you will learn more about in Tutorial 4) and their thickness.

Pick: **Properties icon**

The Properties palette appears on your screen as shown in Figure 3.14.

It can dock to the edge of the screen like a toolbar and remain open for continued use. To anchor it on the edge of the screen,

Tip

You can right-click the title bar on the Properties palette and select Auto-hide. This will cause the Properties palette to only show the narrow toolbar title unless you hover your mouse over it, which causes it to expand. This only works when the palette is not docked.

Pick: **on the title bar, hold down the pick button and drag the Properties palette to the right edge of the screen so that it appears docked as shown in Figure 3.15**

Tip

You can resize the width of the Properties palette by moving your cursor over its vertical edges and then clicking and dragging when you see the cursor change to a double headed arrow symbol.

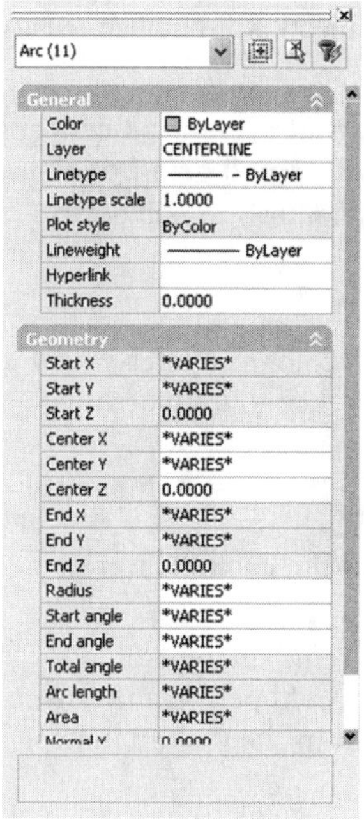

Figure 3.16

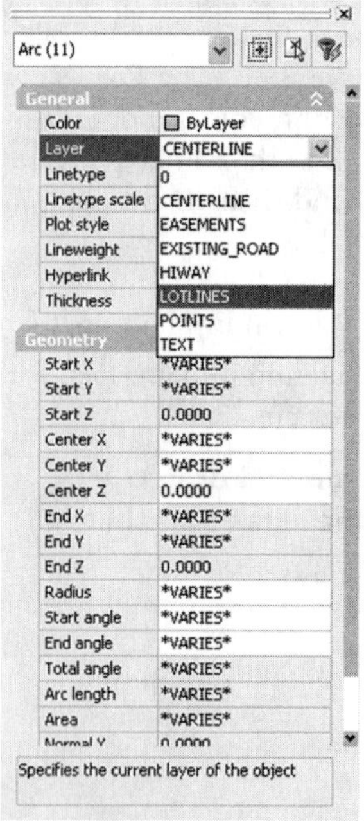

Figure 3.17

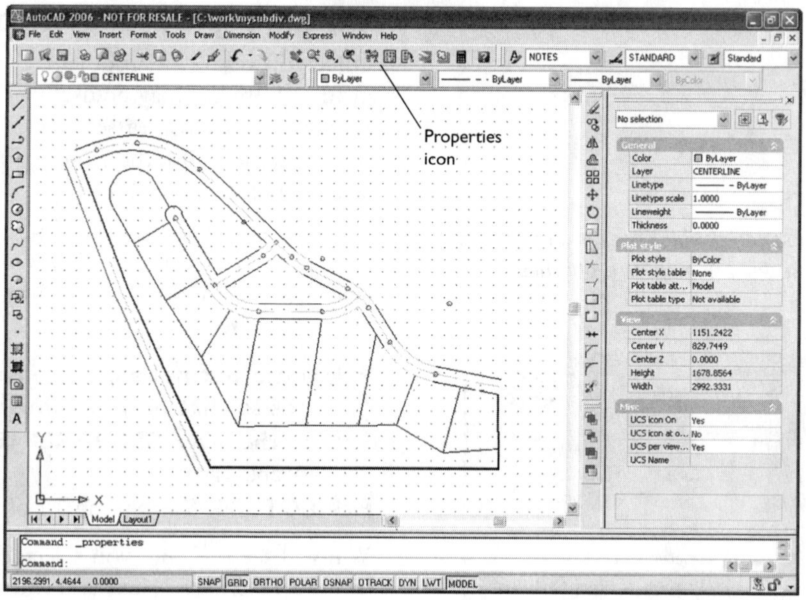

Figure 3.15

Currently there is no object selected, so the palette only reports general properties of the drawing.

Pick: **the roadway edges that have not been changed yet** (they appear green and with a centerline pattern)

The grip boxes for the objects you select will appear when they are selected. The information reported in the Properties palette changes to show the information for the objects you selected, as in Figure 3.16.

You will use the palette to change the objects you selected from layer CENTERLINE to layer LOTLINES.

Pick: **the box with the layer name CENTERLINE to the right of the word Layer**

The list of layers appears, as in Figure 3.17. From the list,

Pick: **LOTLINES**

Press: [Esc] [Esc] to unselect the arcs

Pick: **the Close button (X) in the upper right corner to close the Properties palette**

In your drawing, you will see the lines you selected change to black (or white, depending on your configuration) and linetype CONTINUOUS, as set by layer LOTLINES's properties.

Next, you will use the Fillet command to add *fillets*, or small rounded corners, to some of the lots. Before doing so, change your current layer to LOTLINES.

Pick: **one of the drawing lines on layer LOTLINES** (so that it becomes highlighted with grip boxes)

Pick: **Make Object's Layer Current icon**

The layer name LOTLINES should now appear on the toolbar as the current layer without any objects selected.

Tip

Be sure to save your drawing whenever you have finished a major step and you are satisfied with it. Take a minute to use the Save icon from the Standard toolbar and save your drawing on your own.

On your own, use Zoom Window to enlarge the center area of the drawing, as shown in Figure 3.18.

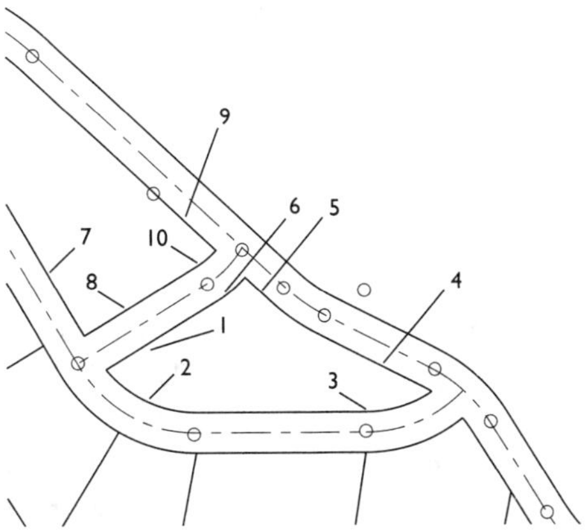

Figure 3.18

Using Fillet

The Fillet command connects lines, arcs, or circles with a smoothly fitted arc, or *fillet*. The Fillet command is on the Modify toolbar.

Pick: **Fillet icon**
Current settings: Mode = TRIM, Radius =0.0000
Select first object or [Undo/Polyline/Radius/Trim/Multiple]: **R** ↵

Typing R indicates that you want to enter a radius. You will enter a radius value of 10.

Specify fillet radius <0.0000>: **10** ↵

You are prompted to select the two objects. Refer to Figure 3.18 to select the lines.

Select first object or [Undo/Polyline/Radius/Trim/Multiple]: **select line 1**
Select second object: **select line 2**

A fillet should appear between the two lines, as shown in Figure 3.19.

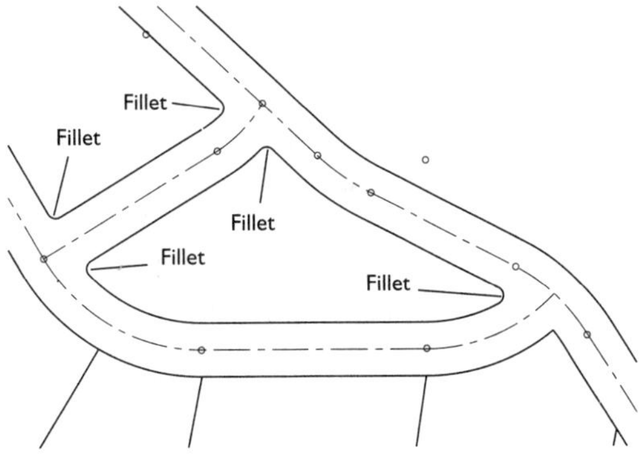

Figure 3.19

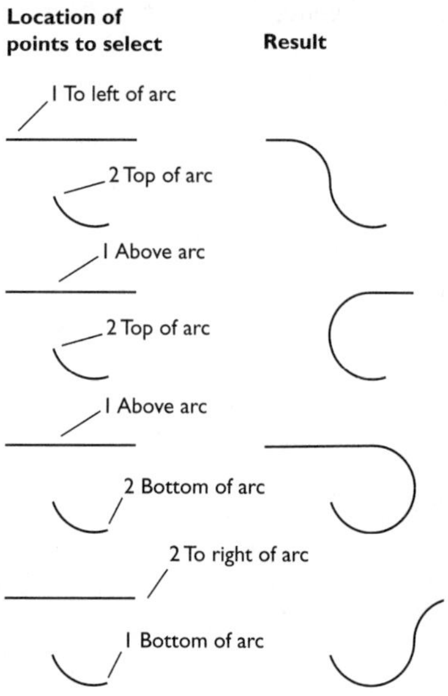

Figure 3.20

Tip

If you use a radius value of 0 with the Fillet command, you can use the command to make lines intersect that do not meet neatly at a corner. This method also works to make a neat intersection from lines that extend past a corner. You can also do so with the Chamfer command (which you will learn next) by setting both chamfer distances to 0.

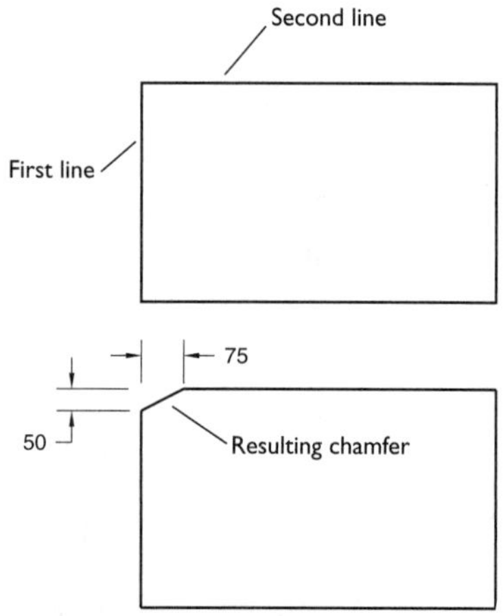

Figure 3.21

Command: ↵

The previous command restarts when you press ↵ or the spacebar at the blank command prompt. In this case, it returns to the original Fillet prompt, which allows you to repeat the selection process, drawing additional fillets of the same radius, or to type a command letter to select other fillet options. You will use the Multiple option to create multiple fillets of the same radius without having to restart the command. Create fillets between the lines shown in Figure 3.18.

Current settings: Mode = TRIM, Radius = 10.0000
Select first object or [Undo/Polyline/Radius/Trim/Multiple]: **M** ↵
Select first object or [Undo/Polyline/Radius/Trim/Multiple]: **select line 3**
Select second object: **select line 4**
Select first object or [Undo/Polyline/Radius/Trim/Multiple]: **continue to fillet lines 5 through 10 on your own**

You can use the Fillet command to fit a smooth arc between any combination of lines, arcs, or circles. Once you have defined the radius value, the direction of the fillet is determined by the cursor location used to identify the two objects.

Figure 3.20 shows some examples of how you can create fillets of different shapes by choosing different point locations. Each example starts with a line located directly above an arc, as shown in the column on the left. Picking the objects where indicated yields the results shown in the column on the right.

You can also set the Fillet command so that it does not automatically trim the lines to join neatly with the fillet, which is the default. You do so by selecting the command option Trim (typing the letter T at the command prompt) and then typing N to choose the option No trim. Experiment with this method on your own.

Using Chamfer

The Chamfer command draws a straight-line segment (called a chamfer) between two given lines. *Chamfer* is the name for the machining process of flattening a sharp corner of an object. Use the AutoCAD Help window to read about the options for the Chamfer command on your own. The Chamfer command is on the Modify toolbar and the Modify menu.

Use the Line command to draw a rectangle, off to the side of the subdivision drawing, as shown in Figure 3.21.
Pick: **Chamfer icon**
(TRIM mode) Current chamfer Dist1 = 0.0000, Dist2 = 0.0000
Select first line or [Undo/Polyline/Distance/Angle/Trim/mEthod/Multiple]: **D** ↵

Typing D indicates that you want to enter distance values.

Specify first chamfer distance <0.0000>: **50** ↵
Specify second chamfer distance <50.0000>: **75** ↵

The Chamfer command prompts you for selection of the first and second lines between which the chamfer is to be added. Refer to the upper part of Figure 3.21 to select the lines.

Select first line or [Undo/Polyline/Distance/Angle/Trim/mEthod/Multiple]: **select the first line**

Select second line or shift-select to apply corner: **select the second line**

A chamfer should appear on your screen that looks like the one shown in the lower part of Figure 3.21. The distance that each end of the chamfer is from the corner defines the size of the chamfer. As with the Fillet command, once you have entered these distances, you can draw additional chamfers of the same size by typing the M option for Multiple and pressing ↵ to enter the option. The command will then repeat until you press ↵ to end the command.

On your own, use the commands that you have learned to erase the chamfered rectangle from your drawing. Use Zoom All to restore the original appearance and then save the drawing.

In Tutorial 1 you learned how to draw a rectangle with the Rectangle icon, which had the options Fillet and Chamfer. The same Fillet and Chamfer principles that you just learned apply to using the Rectangle icon. At this point you may find it useful to practice with the Rectangle icon and changing the Chamfer and Fillet dimensions offered in the command prompt. When you have finished practicing drawing rectangles, erase them before moving on to the next section.

Using Polyline

The Polyline command draws a series of connected lines or arcs that AutoCAD treats as a single graphic object called a ***polyline***. The Polyline command is used on technical drawings to draw irregular curves and lines that have a width. An irregular curve is any curve that does not have a constant radius. (A circle and an arc have a constant radius.) The Polyline command is on the Draw toolbar and looks like an arc and line connected.

You will use the Polyline command to create the shape for a pond to add to the subdivision drawing. Before continuing, check to see that LOTLINES is the current layer.

Pick: **Polyline icon**

Specify start point: **select any point to the right of the subdivision where you want to locate the pond**

Current line-width is 0.0000

Specify next point or [Arc/Halfwidth/Length/Undo/Width]: **select 9 more points**

You will use the Close option as you did in Tutorial 1 when drawing closed figures with the Line command.

Specify next point or [Arc/Close/Halfwidth/Length/Undo/Width]: **C** ↵

Your screen should show a line made of multiple segments, similar to the one in Figure 3.22.

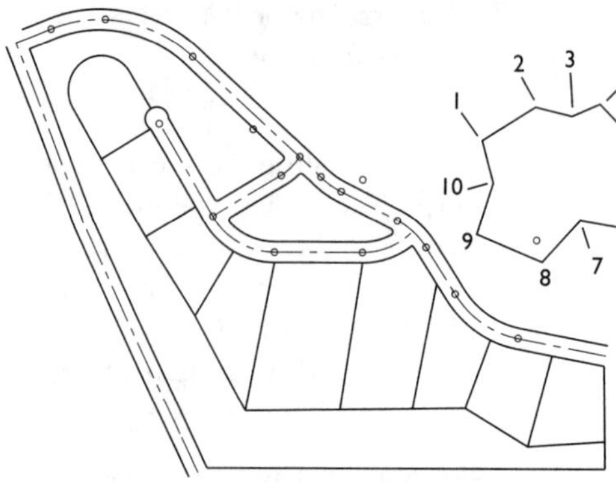

Figure 3.22

A shape drawn by using Polyline is different from a shape created by using the Line command, because the polyline is treated as one object. You cannot erase one of the polyline segments. If you try, the entire polyline is erased. Other Polyline options allow you to draw an arc as a polyline segment (Arc), specify the starting and ending width (or half-width) of a given segment (Width, Half-width), specify the length of a segment (Length), and remove segments already drawn (Undo).

Tip

You can use Edit Polyline to convert objects into polylines. At the Select polyline: prompt, pick the line or arc that you want to convert to a polyline. You will see the message ***Object selected is not a polyline. Do you want to turn it into one? <Y>:****. Press ↵ to accept the yes response to convert the selected object into a polyline and continue with the prompts for the Edit Polyline command.*

Edit Polyline

Once you have created a polyline, you can change it and its individual segments with Edit Polyline. The Edit Polyline (Pedit) command is on the Modify menu. You will use Modify, Object, Polyline to change the segmented line you just created to a smooth curve.

The Edit Polyline command provides two different methods of fitting curves. The Fit option joins every point you select on the polyline with an arc. The Spline option produces a smoother curve by using either a cubic or a quadratic B-spline approximation (depending on how the system variable Splinetype is set). You can think of the spline operation as working like a string stretched between the first and last points of your polyline. The vertices on your polyline act to pull the string in their direction, but the resulting spline does not necessarily reach those points.

Pick: **Modify, Object, Polyline**
Select polyline or [Multiple]: **select any part of the polyline**
Enter an option [Open/Join/Width/Edit vertex/Fit/Spline/Decurve/
Ltype gen/Undo]: **F** ↵

The straight-line segments change to a continuous curved line, as shown in Figure 3.23.

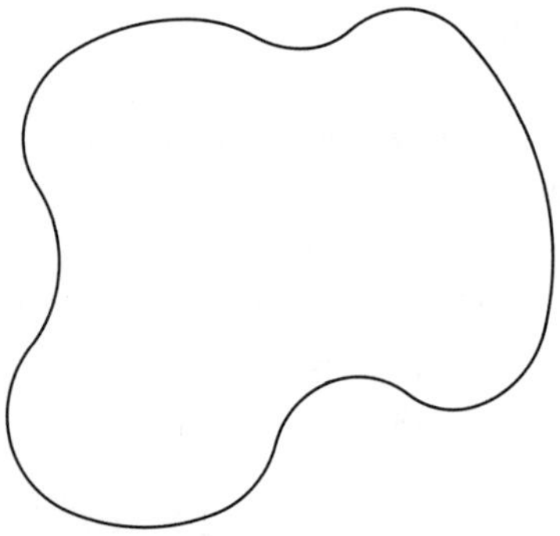

Figure 3.23

Fit curve connects all the vertices of a 2D polyline by joining each pair of vertices with an arc. You will use the Undo option of the command to return the polyline to its original shape.

Enter an option [Close/Join/Width/Edit vertex/Fit/Spline/Decurve/
Ltype gen/Undo]: **U** ↵

Tip

If you have a polyline that has already been curved with Fit or Spline, Decurve returns the original polyline.

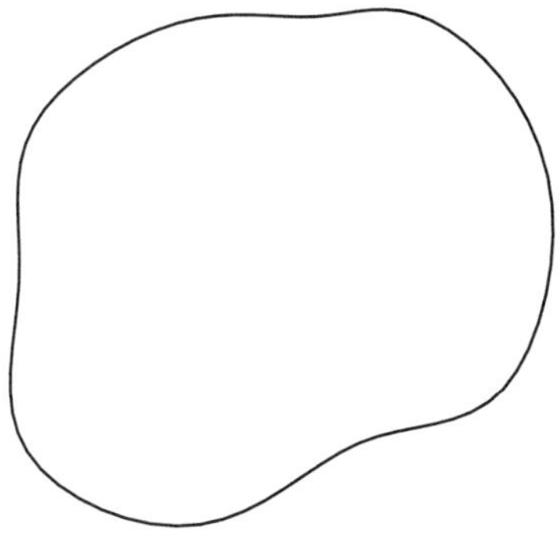

Figure 3.24

Tip

You can pick on the polyline and use it grips to stretch it to a different shape. To do this, pick the polyline and then pick again on one of the grips that appears. While the grip is highlighted move your mouse to drag the grip to a new location and then pick to place it there.

The original polyline returns on your screen. Now try the Spline option.

Enter an option [Close/Join/Width/Edit vertex/Fit/Spline/Decurve/
Ltype gen/Undo]: **S** ↵

A somewhat flatter shape, similar to the one shown in Figure 3.24, should replace the original polyline. Among other things, splined polylines are useful for creating contour lines on maps.

Now try the Width option.

Enter an option [Close/Join/Width/Edit vertex/Fit/Spline/Decurve/
Ltype gen/Undo]: **W** ↵
Specify new width for all segments: **5** ↵

The splined polyline is replaced with one with a 5 unit width. You will press ↵ to exit the Edit Polyline command.

Enter an option [Close/Join/Width/Edit vertex/Fit/Spline/Decurve/
Ltype gen/Undo]: ↵

Your drawing should look something like the one shown in Figure 3.25.

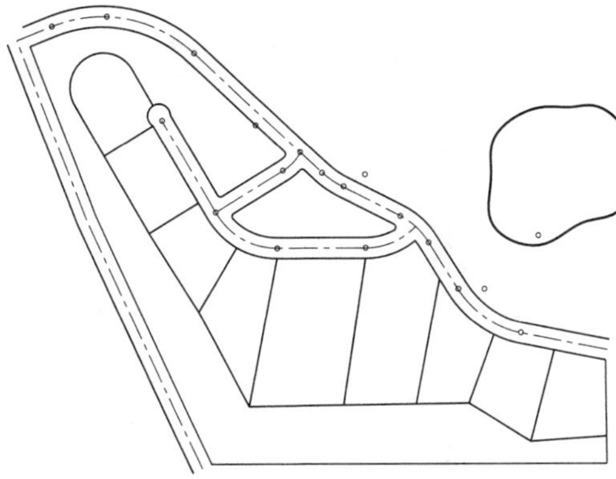

Figure 3.25

Using Spline

The Spline command lets you create quadratic or cubic spline (or NURBS) curves. The acronym NURBS stands for nonuniform rational B-spline, which is the name of the method used to draw the curves. These curves can be more accurate than spline-fitted polylines because you control the tolerance to which the spline curve is fit. Splines also take less space in your drawing file than do spline-fitted polylines.

You can also use the Object option of the Spline command to convert spline-fitted polylines to splines. (The variable Delobj controls whether the original polyline is deleted after it is converted.) The Spline command is on the Draw toolbar. You will draw a spline off to the side of the subdivision and then later erase it.

Pick: **Spline icon**
Specify first point or [Object]: **pick any point**
Specify next point: **pick any point**
Specify next point or [Close/Fit tolerance] <start tangent>: **pick any point**
Specify next point or [Close/Fit tolerance] <start tangent>: **pick any point**

Specify next point or [Close/Fit tolerance] <start tangent>: **pick any point**
Specify next point or [Close/Fit tolerance] <start tangent>: **C** ↵
Specify tangent: ↵

Pressing ↵ at the tangency prompt causes the AutoCAD software to calculate the default tangencies. You can make the spline tangent to other objects by picking the appropriate points at these prompts. The spline appears on your screen. Experiment by drawing splines on your own. You can edit Splines by using the Splinedit command on the Modify menu, under Object. When you have finished experimenting,

Erase all the splines that you created.
Pick: **to thaw layer TEXT**
Pick: **TEXT** to set it as the current layer
Use the Dtext command (Single Line Text) to add the label POND to the pond.
Set the height for the text to 30 units.

When you have finished these steps on your own, your screen should look like Figure 3.26.

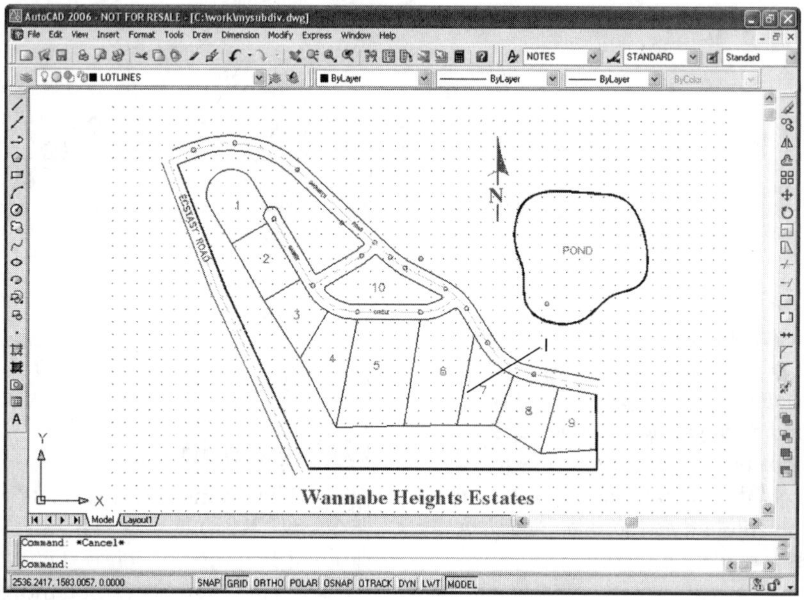

Figure 3.26

Getting Information about Your Drawing

Because your AutoCAD drawing database contains accurate geometry and has been created as a model of real-world objects, you can find information about distances and areas, as well as locate coordinates. You can also find volumes and mass properties of solid models, which you will learn to do in Tutorial 11. Next, you will use the AutoCAD commands to list objects and make calculations to determine information about the subdivision.

Using List

The List command shows information held in the drawing database about the object selected. Different information may be shown, depending on the type of object. The layer, coordinate location for the object, color and linetype (if different from the layer), and other information are listed. Refer to Figure 3.26 as you select.

Pick: **Tools, Inquiry, List**
Select objects: **pick line 1**
Select objects: ↵

The AutoCAD text window appears on your screen. If you want, you can resize it by picking on its corners and dragging it to a new size. You can also pick on the title bar and drag it to a new location. Refer to Figure 3.27 for the information listed about the line that you selected. You can use this information to make calculations or to label the lot lines of this subdivision.

Tip
You can get the same information by opening the Properties palette.

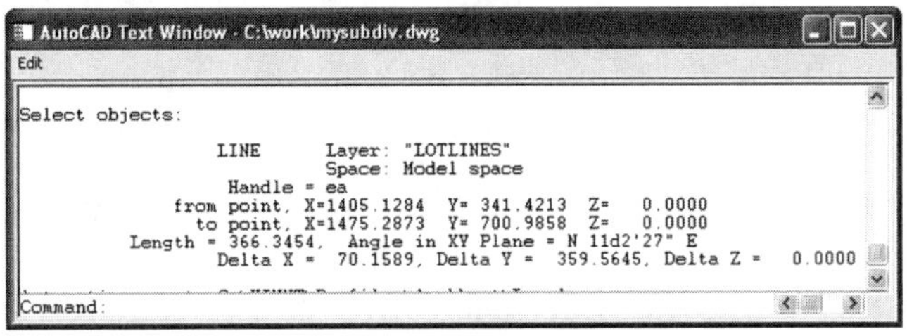

Figure 3.27

Close the text window by clicking on the close button in the upper right corner.

Pick: **Tools, Inquiry, List**
Select objects: **pick on the polyline representing the pond**
Select objects: ↵

The text window again appears on your screen as shown in Figure 3.28. It contains information about all the vertices of the polyline. Keep pressing ↵ until all the information has scrolled by. At the beginning of the information listed, you will see the area and perimeter of the polyline. This information can be very useful for calculating the area of irregular shapes like the pond.

Tip
You can turn on the Inquiry toolbar by right-clicking any toolbar and selecting Inquiry from the pop-up list.

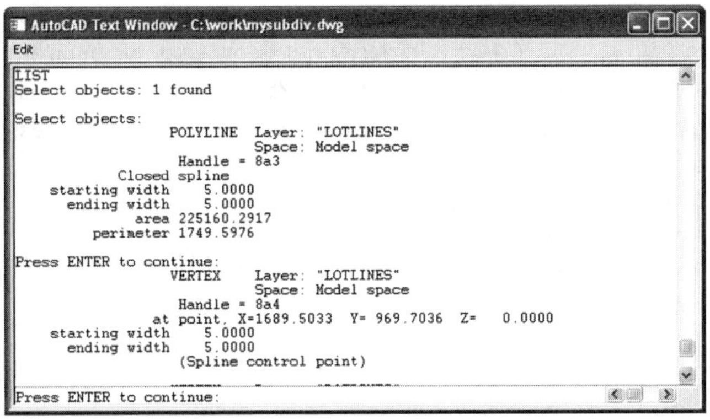

Figure 3.28

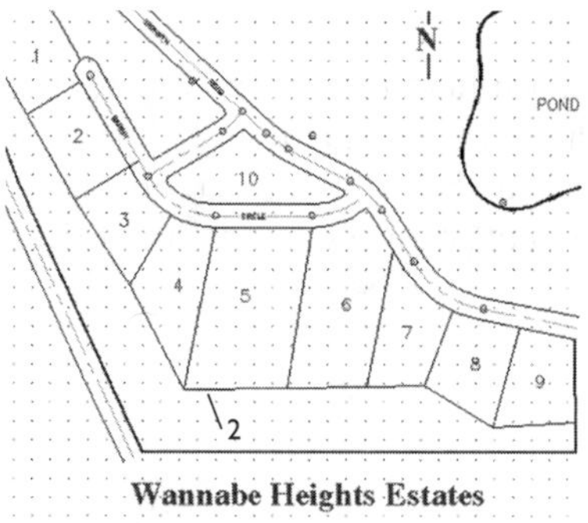

Figure 3.29

Tip

When the DYN button on the status bar is on, you will also see these values in the dynamic cursor.

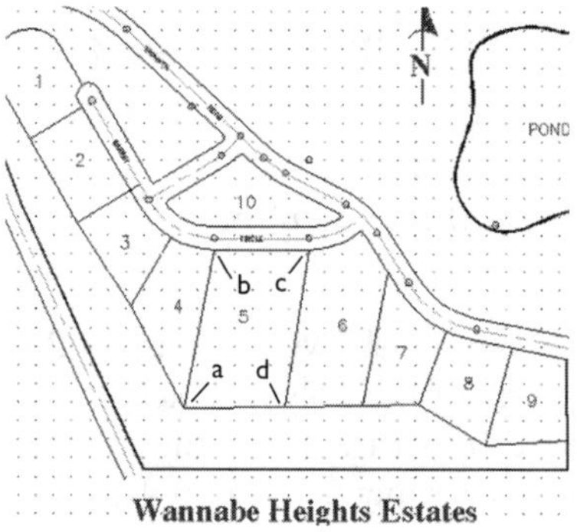

Figure 3.30

Tip

The area listed is in square units. If the drawing is in feet, the area will be in square feet. You can use the Quick Calc button on the Standard toolbar to convert to other units. To do so, use the Units Conversion area to set the Units (e.g., Area), what to convert from (e.g., square feet), and what to convert to (e.g., Acres). Type the area in the Value to convert box or cut and paste it from your Command area. The converted area will display in acres.

Locating Points

You will use the Endpoint running object snap with Locate Point to select accurate point locations for the next steps. Locate Point shows the coordinates of the location that you select. When you use this command in conjunction with object snaps, you can find the exact coordinates of an object's endpoint, center, midpoint, and other points.

Right-click: **OSNAP button and use the Settings tab of the dialog box to select Endpoint**

Pick: **to turn on OSNAP**

Pick: **Tools, Inquiry, ID Point**

Specify point: **pick on the left end of line 2 in Figure 3.29**

The command window displays the coordinates of the point, X=912.5026, Y=334.8196, and Z=0.0000.

Using Area

The Area command finds areas that you define by picking points to define a boundary, picking a closed object, or adding and subtracting boundaries. The options for the Area command are First point, Object, Add, and Subtract. To use the default method, First point, you begin by selecting points to define straight-line boundaries for the area that you want to measure. When you press ↵ to indicate that you have finished selecting, the AutoCAD software automatically closes the boundary for the area from the last point selected back to the first point. (You can also close the area by picking the first point again if you want.) The area inside the boundary that you specify is reported. By selecting the Object option, you can pick a closed object, such as a polyline, circle, ellipse, spline, region, or a solid object, and its area is reported. You could use this method to find the area of the pond instead of using List as you did previously. The Add and Subtract options let you define more complex boundaries by adding and subtracting from the first boundary selected. Next, you will use the Area command to find the area of lot 5. Remember that the Endpoint object snap is still active, so the nearest endpoint will be targeted when you select a line. This way the area calculation will be accurate.

Pick: **Tools, Inquiry, Area**

Specify first corner point or [Object/Add/Subtract]: **pick point a in Figure 3.30**

Specify next corner point or press ENTER for total: **pick b**

Specify next corner point or press ENTER for total: **pick c**

Specify next corner point or press ENTER for total: **pick d**

Specify next corner point or press ENTER for total: ↵

The area and perimeter values of lot 5 are listed in the command window: Area = 113884.6680, Perimeter = 1398.9121.

Pick: **EASEMENTS** as the current layer before continuing

Using Multilines

Next, you will create a Multiline style so you can add multiple lines to the drawing in one step. This feature is especially useful in architectural drawings (for creating walls) and in civil engineering drawings. For example, you can draw the centerline of the road and automatically add the edge of pavement and edges of right-of-way lines a defined distance away. Multiline also allows you to fill the area between two lines with a color. Using the command for Multiline Style, you can define as many as 16 lines, called *elements*, which you can use when drawing multilines. You can save multiline styles with different names so that you can easily recall them. You can also set the multiline justification so that you can create lines by specifying the top, middle, or bottom of the style. You do so by selecting the Justification option of the Multiline command or by directly setting the variable Cmljust to 0, 1, or 2, respectively.

Creating a Multiline Style

You select the Multiline Style command from the Format menu. Multiline Style creates the spacing, color, linetype, and name of the style, as well as the type of endcaps that will be used to finish off the lines.

Pick: **Format, Multiline Style**

The Multiline Styles dialog box appears on your screen, as shown in Figure 3.31. The default style name is STANDARD. Note that it is the current style.

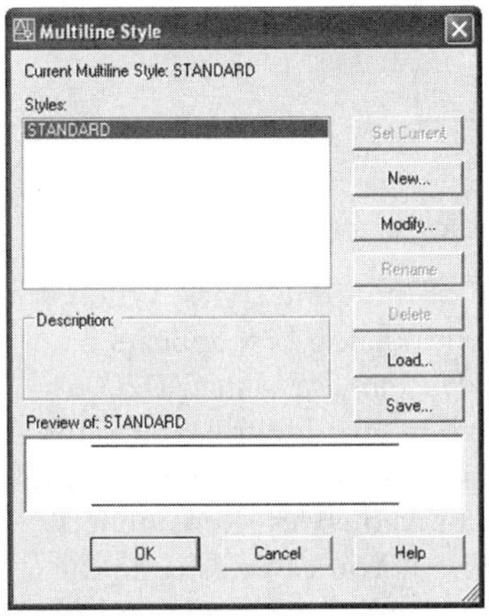

Figure 3.31

To create a new style,

Pick: **New**

Type: **EASEMENT** into the Create Multiline Style dialog box as shown in Figure 3.32.

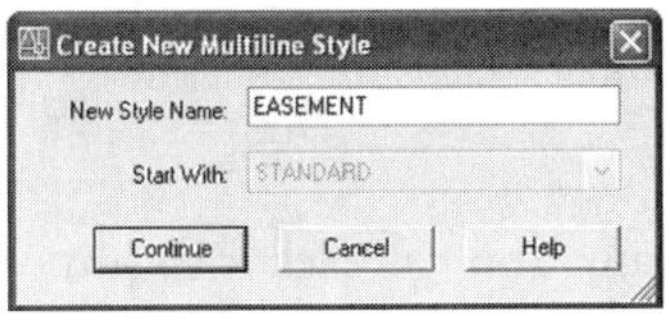

Figure 3.32

Pick: **Continue**

Use the New Multiline Style dialog box to set the spacing of the elements, as shown in Figure 3.33. The dialog box has two areas. You can use the Caps area to select different types of endcaps, including angled lines or arcs, to finish the multilines you create. You can also use this area to turn on Fill if you want the area between multiline elements to be shaded.

The Elements area is used to set the spacing, number, linestyle and color for the elements which make up the multiline. You will set the positive offset spacing to 15. To change the spacing for an element,

Pick: **on the top element shown in the list so that it becomes highlighted**

Pick: **in the input box to the right of the word Offset**

Type: **15**

You should notice the offset value for the top element change 15. Next, set the offset spacing for the second element to –15.

Pick: **on the second element in the list**

Pick: **highlight the text in the box to the right of the word Offset**

Type: **–15**

When you have set the element spacing, your dialog box should look like Figure 3.33. You will leave the color and linetype set to BYLAYER, as layer EASEMENTS already has these properties set to cyan and the DASHED linetype. If you want lines of different colors or different linetypes, you could use the appropriately named portions of the dialog box to set them. When you have finished,

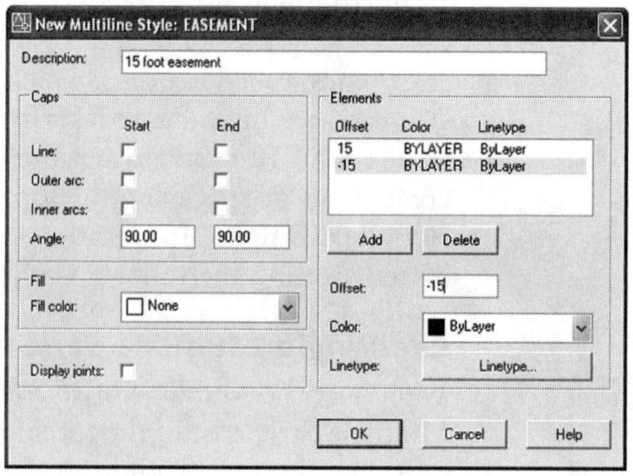

Figure 3.33

Pick: **OK** (to return to the Multiline Styles dialog box)

> **Tip**
>
> *If you do not see the* acad.mln *file in the* \support *subdirectory, you can click on the "Where are my Support Files" icon or use the Help system and select Locate Support Files.*

The Save button saves a style to the library of multiline styles. When you pick the Save button, the Save Multiline Styles dialog box appears on your screen. Multiline styles are saved to *c:\Program Files\AutoCAD2006\support\acad.mln* by default. You can create your own file for your multiline styles, if you want, by typing in a different name. The Load button loads saved multiline styles from a library of saved styles. Rename lets you rename the various styles you have created. You can't rename the STANDARD style. When you have finished examining the dialog box,

Pick: **Save**

Pick: **Set Current**

Pick: **OK** (to exit the Multiline Styles dialog box)

Drawing Multilines

The Multiline command is on the Draw menu. You will pick it to add some multilines for easements along the lot lines of the subdivision drawing. You will use the current multiline style, EASEMENT, that you created.

Pick: **Draw, Multiline**

Now you are almost ready to draw some multilines. Before you do, decide on the justification you will need to use. You can choose to have the multilines you draw align so that the points you select align with the top element, with the zero offset, or with the bottom element. You will set the justification so that the points you pick are the zero offset of the multiline, in this case the middle of the multiline.

Justification = Top, Scale = 1.00, Style = EASEMENT
Specify start point or [Justification/Scale/STyle]: **J** ↵
Enter justification type [Top/Zero/Bottom] <top>: **Z** ↵

Tip

Remember that the Endpoint running object snap should still be on.

Tip

If you want to trim a multiline, you must first use the Explode command to change it back into individual objects before you can trim it. Use the AutoCAD Help command for more information about using Explode.

Tip

Right-clicking on the MText window brings up a shortcut menu that you can use to select many useful MText symbols that you can insert by picking Symbol from the shortcut menu.

You will see the message Justification = Zero, Scale = 1.00, Style = EASEMENT. Now, you are ready to start drawing the easement lines. Refer to Figure 3.34 for the points to select.

Current settings: Justification = Zero, Scale = 1.00, Style = EASEMENT
Specify start point or [Justification/Scale/STyle]: **pick point 1**
Specify next point: **pick 2**
Specify next point or [Undo]: **pick 3**
Specify next point or [Close/Undo]: **pick 4**
Specify next point or [Close/Undo]: **pick 5**
Specify next point or [Close/Undo]: **pick 6**
Specify next point or [Close/Undo]: **pick 7**
Specify next point or [Close/Undo]: **pick 8**
Specify next point or [Close/Undo]: ↵

Your drawing should look like Figure 3.34.

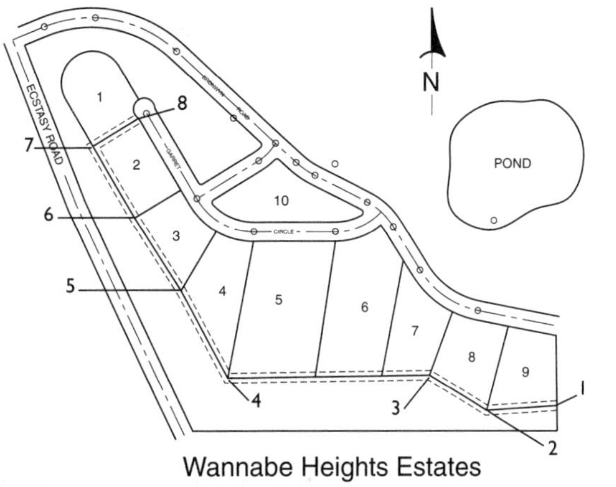

Figure 3.34

On your own, set TEXT as the current layer and use the Mtext (Multiline Text) command to add 15 unit tall text describing the location of the subdivision and the easements, as shown in Figure 3.35.

Save your drawing now.

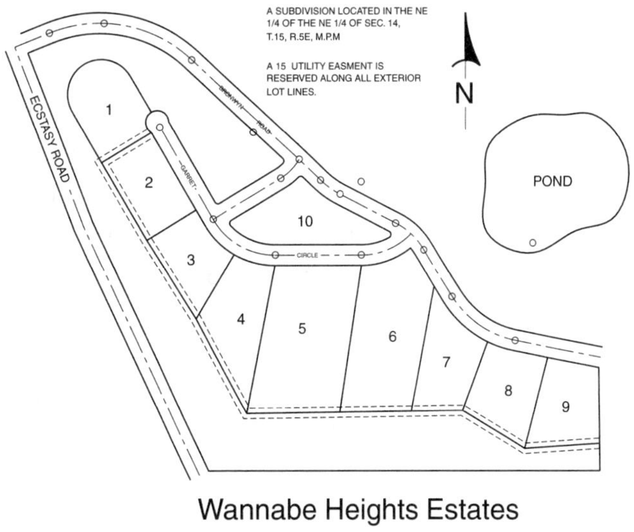

Figure 3.35

Warning

You should always save your drawing before you plot. If for some reason the plotter is not connected or there is another problem, you may not be able to continue. To go on, you would have to reboot the computer and would lose any changes that you had made to your drawing since the last time you saved.

Tip

To use the Plot command directly from the command prompt, type a hyphen (-) in front of the command (-plot). This also works for other commands.

The Plot Dialog Box

Depending on the types of printers or plotters you have configured with your computer system, the Plot command causes your drawing to be printed on your printer or plotted on the device that you configured for AutoCAD use. The same command is used for printing and for plotting. Selecting Plot causes the Plot dialog box (Figure 3.36) to appear on your screen.

Pick: **Plot icon** (from the Standard toolbar)

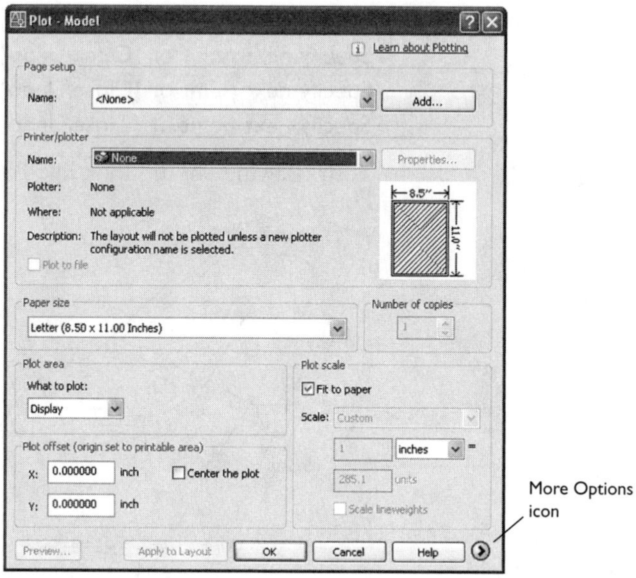

Figure 3.36

Among the things that the Plot dialog box lets you choose are:

- The plotter or printer where you will send the drawing (Printer/plotter);
- The portion of your drawing to plot or print (Plot area);
- The scale at which the finished drawing will be plotted (Plot scale);
- Where your plot starts on the sheet (Plot offset);
- Whether to use inches or millimeters as the plotter units;
- The pen or color, line weight, line fill, screening, dithering selections for the plotter or printer (Plot style);
- Whether the plot is portrait or landscape orientation.

Because there are so many factors, some of them are not always displayed. To see the additional options,

Pick: **More Options icon from the lower right of the dialog box**

When you are using the Plot dialog box, be careful not to change too many things about the plotter at once. That way you can see the effect that each option has on your plot.

The dialog box switches to show more options shown in Figure 3.37.

Plot Device

Use the printer/plotter area to select from the plotters that you have configured. If no printers or plotters are listed, you must use the Plotting tab in the Options dialog box to add a new printer or plotter configuration, or use the Windows operating system to install a printer. Refer to Chapters 1 and 2 for details about configuring your output device. To select a listed device, pull down the list of printers and click to highlight the name of the device you will use for your print. The options displayed for paper size and other items depend on your particular output device. If an item in the Plot dialog box appears grayed instead of black, it is not available for selection. You may not be able to choose certain items, depending on the limitations of your printer or plotter.

Make sure that your plotter or printer name is selected in the Printer/Plotter Name area of the dialog box.

Plot Style Table (Pen Assignments)

A plot style table lets you assign properties such as color, line weight, line fill, screening, and dithering for your printer or other output device. There are two main methods used to assign the plotting properties: color dependent plot styles (*.ctb*), and named plot styles (*.stb*). As you might guess, a color dependent plot style uses object color to determine the plot properties. A named plot style assigns a plot style property to objects or layers similar to the way the object color can be assigned. Plot style tables are independent of the output device selected. If a particular device does not have that property, say screening for example, that property is just skipped. This way a single plot style (or set of styles) can be used with a variety of printers or plotters. These plot styles are saved separately from the drawing. Changing the plot style changes how any drawing that uses that style will be output. For this example, you will use the default style named *acad.ctb*, which is a color dependent plot style. Refer to Figure 3.37.

Pick: **on the pull down menu in the Plot style table area of the dialog box**

Pick: ***acad.ctb***

Assign this plot table to all layouts?

Pick: **Yes**

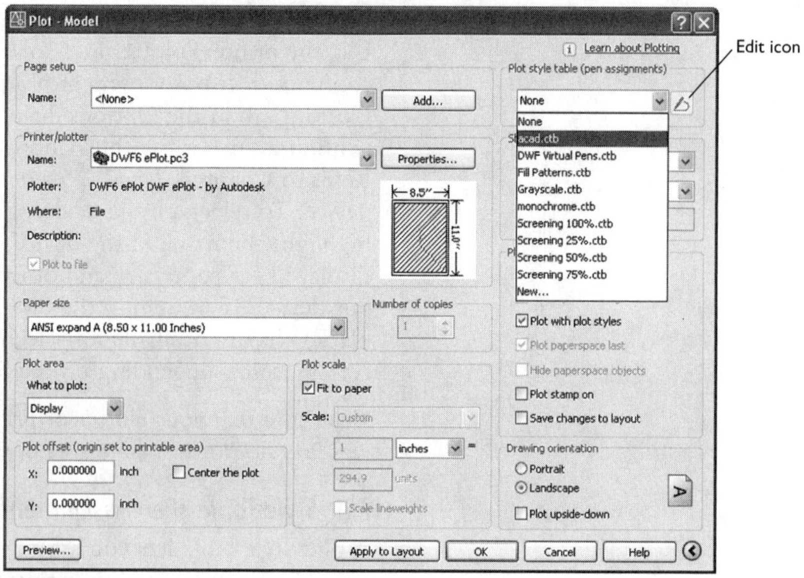

Figure 3.37

Pick: **Edit icon** (which looks like a pencil drawing a line)

The Plot Style Table Editor appears as shown in Figure 3.38. You can use it to set the parameters for the appearance of the plotted lines in the drawing. You will not change any of these settings at this time. You will learn more about plotting in Tutorial 5.

Pick: **Cancel**

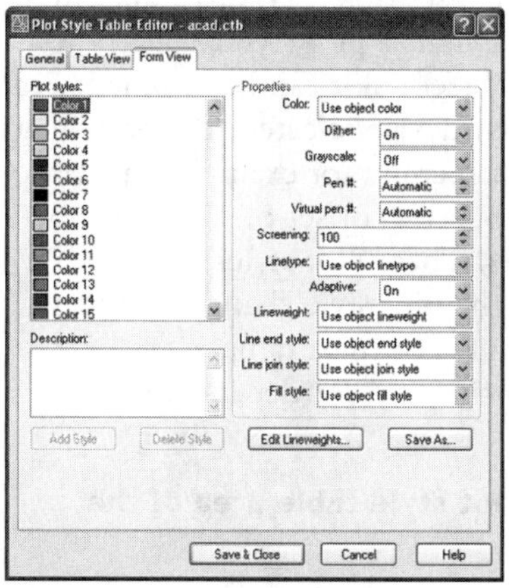

Figure 3.38

What to Plot

The Plot area portion of the dialog box lets you specify what area of the drawing will be printed or plotted. Display selects the area that appears on your screen as the area to plot. Extents plots any objects that you have in your drawing. Limits plots the predefined area set up in the drawing with the Limits command. View plots a named view that you have created with the View command. (If you have not made any views, this option will not appear.) Window lets you go back to the drawing display and create a window around the area of the drawing that you want to plot. You can do so by picking from your drawing or by typing in the coordinates. You will pick Limits to choose the area that was preset in the drawing (where the grid showed in model space.) If you have not set up the size with Limits, then Extents is often useful as it selects the largest area filled with drawing objects as the area to print. The What to Plot selections are shown in Figure 3.39.

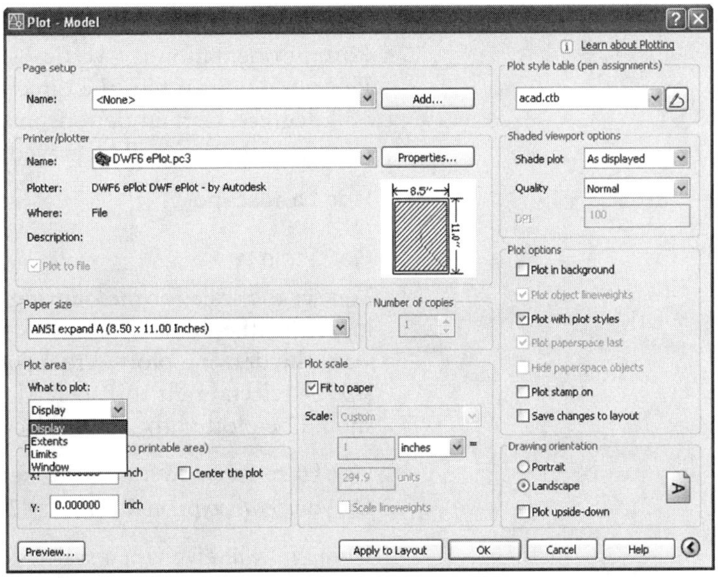

Figure 3.39

Pick: **Limits**

Paper Size

Pick: **the pull-down list under Paper Size**

A pull-down list similar to the one shown in Figure 3.40 appears so you can select the paper size. The paper sizes that you can select depend on your printer. Standard 8.5 x 11 paper is called size A; 11 x 17 paper is size B. (Smaller values indicate the image area that your printer can print on the sheet.) Max is the maximum size of paper that your printer will handle.

Tip

If you use the generic AutoCAD printer driver, DWF6 ePlot.pc3, you will see the paper sizes in Figure 3.40.

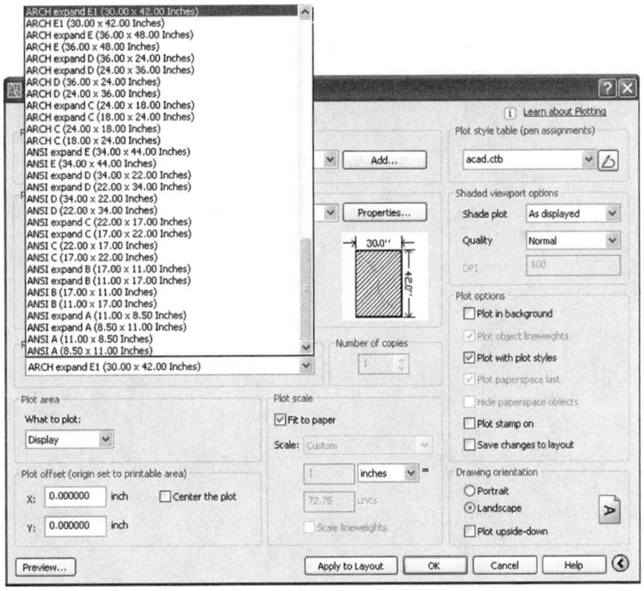

Figure 3.40

Drawing Orientation

Portrait orientation is a vertical sheet layout, and landscape is horizontal. Plot upside-down flips the direction that the plot starts on the sheet by 180 degrees. Certain options may not be available with your model of printer. If so, they will be grayed out. For this drawing,

Pick: **Landscape**

Plot Scale

You set the scale for the drawing by entering the number of plotted inches for the number of drawing units in your drawing. If you do not want the drawing plotted to a particular scale, you can fit it to the sheet size by selecting Fit to Paper. Most of the time an engineering drawing should be plotted to a known scale.

Pick: Fit to Paper so it is unchecked. Custom should appear in the Scale box. On your own, type in **1** inches = **250** units

Doing so will give you a scale of 1"=250' for your drawing, because the default units in the drawing represent decimal feet.

Plot Offset

You can use the Plot offset area of the dialog box to move the drawing to the right on the paper by using a positive value for X, and to move the drawing up on the paper by specifying a positive value for Y. You should be aware that moving the origin for the paper may cause the top and right lines of the drawing not to print if they are outside the printer limits. Center the plot automatically calculates X and Y values to center the plot on the paper.

Pick: **Center the plot** (so the check box is selected)

Plot Preview

You may preview your drawing as it will appear on the paper in the Preview window. If you have a very detailed drawing, obtaining a preview may take some time. The subdivision drawing is not too large to preview in a reasonable amount of time.

Pick: **Preview**

Your screen should look similar to Figure 3.41. The drawing orientation is set to landscape.

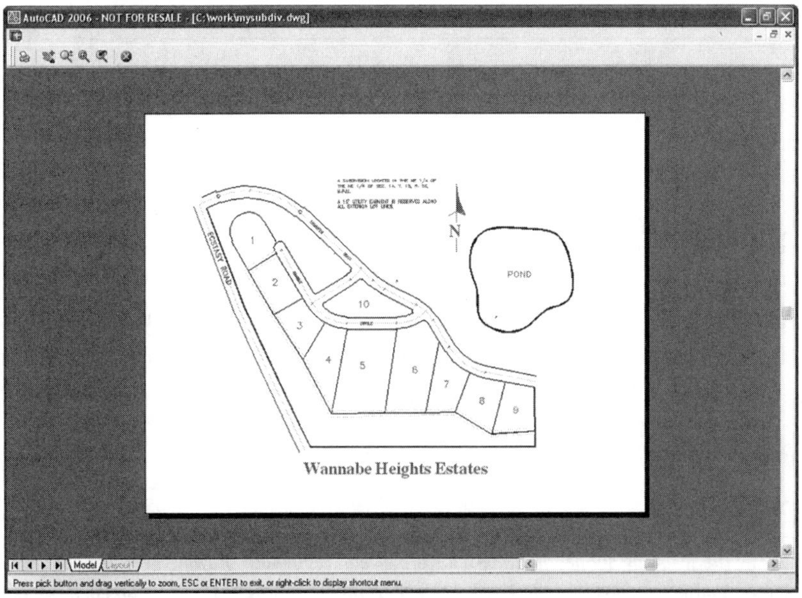

Figure 3.41

The cursor should take on the appearance of a magnifying glass with a plus sign above it and a minus sign below it. It is set on Zoom Realtime, allowing you to zoom in or out from the drawing. The following message should be at the command line:

Press pick button and drag vertically to zoom, ESC or ENTER to exit, or right-click to display shortcut menu.

The toolbar across the top of the Preview window offers different Zoom options, Pan, and Close.

On your own, select different commands to familiarize yourself with them. If the drawing appears to fit the sheet correctly, pick Close Preview Window from the toolbar or press the [Esc] or [↵] key. When you have returned to the Plot dialog box, pick OK to plot your drawing.

You will see a prompt similar to the following, depending on your hardware configuration:

Effective plotting area: 10.50 wide by 8.00 high
Plotting viewport 1.

If the drawing does not fit the sheet correctly, review this section and determine which setting in the Plot dialog box you need to change. You should have a print or plot of your drawing that is scaled exactly so that 1" on the paper equals 250' in the drawing.

When you have a successful plot of your drawing, you have completed this tutorial. To exit this session,

Pick: **File, Exit**

Key Terms

chamfer	elements	offset distance	through point
cutting edges	fillet	polyline	

Key Commands

Area	Fillet	Multiline Style	Print
Chamfer	List	Offset	Spline
Change Properties	Locate Point	Plot	Trim
Edit Polyline	Multiline	Polyline	

Exercises

Redraw the following shapes. If dimensions are given, create your drawing geometry exactly to the specified dimensions. The letter M after an exercise number means that the given dimensions are in millimeters (metric units). If no letter follows the exercise number, the dimensions are in inches. Don't include dimensions on the drawings.

3.1 Clearance Plate

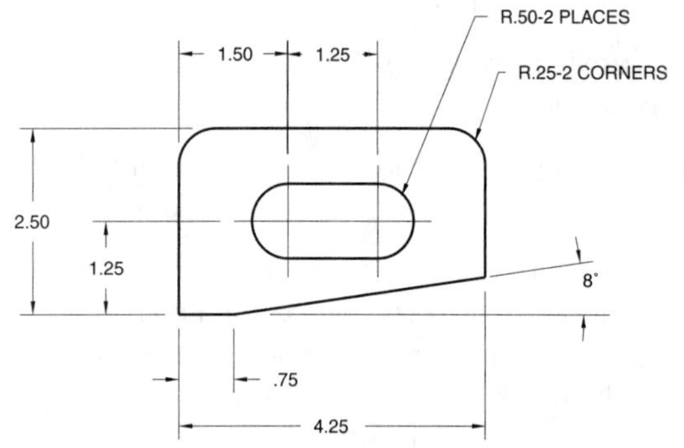

3.2M Bracket

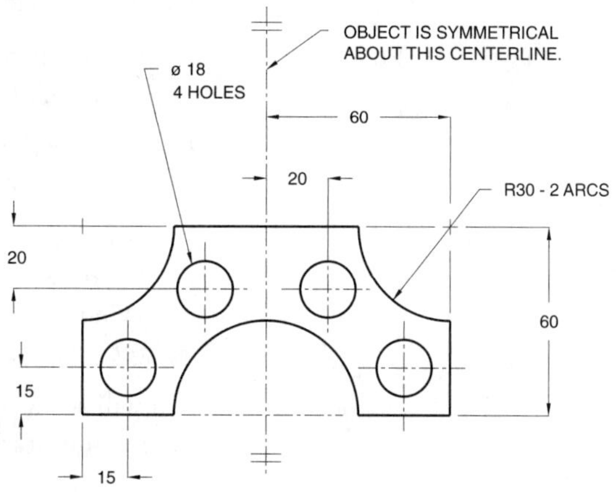

3.3 Roller Arm

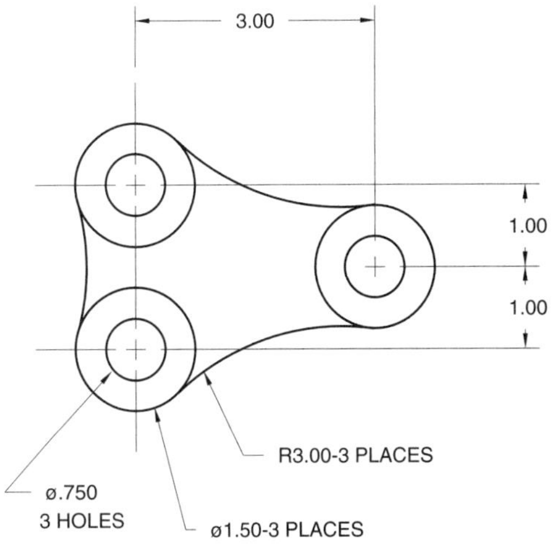

3.4 Outside Caliper

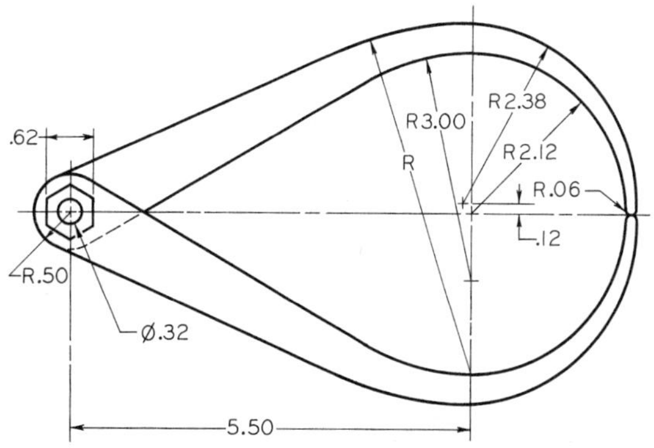

3.5 Roller Support

Hint: *Create construction geometry to locate the center of the upper arc of radius 1.16. Turn on the Object Snap modes for Endpoint and Intersection. Then offset the outer left-hand arc a distance of 1.16 to the outside. Draw a circle with radius 1.16 and its center at the left endpoint of the .56 horizontal line. Where the offset arc and the new 1.16 circle intersect will be the center of the needed arc.*

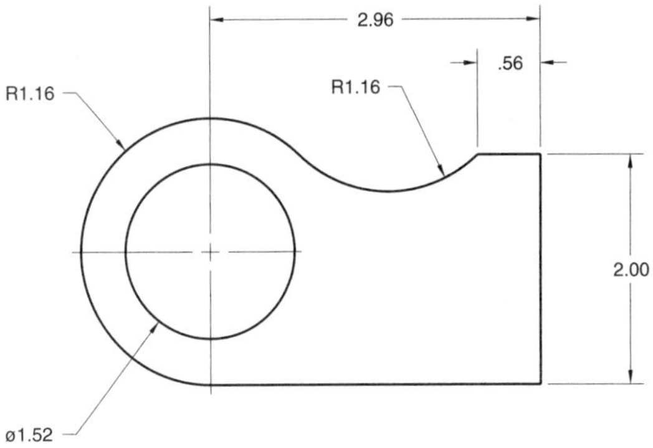

3.6 Special Cam

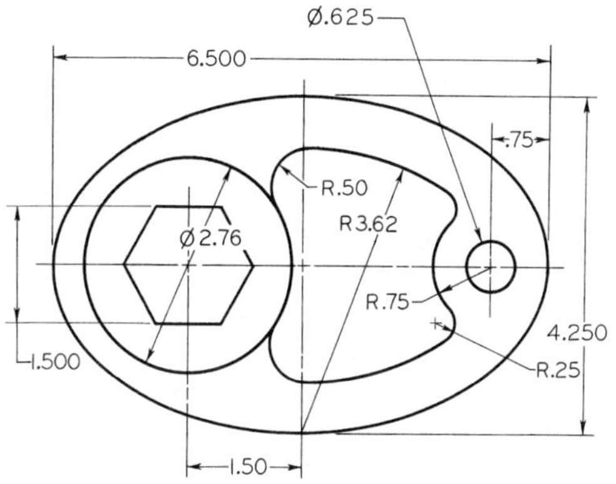

3.7 Slotted Ellipse

Draw the figure shown (note the symmetry). Do not show dimensions.

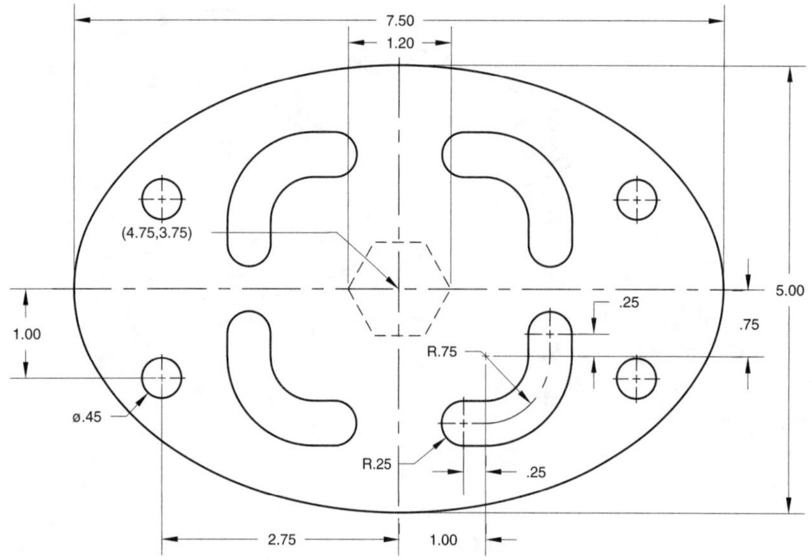

3.8 Roadway

Shown is a centerline for a two-lane road (total width is 20 feet). At each intersection is a specified turning radius for the edge of pavement. Construct the centerline and edge of pavement. Don't show any of the text.

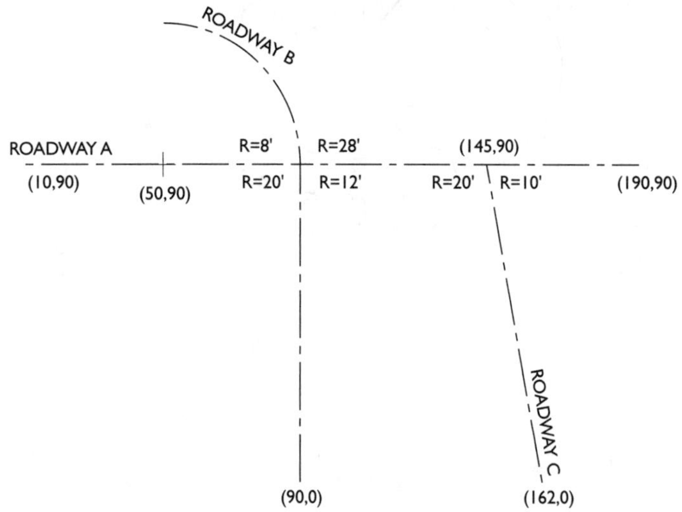

3.9 Circuit Board

Draw the following circuit board, using Polylines with the width option to create wide paths.

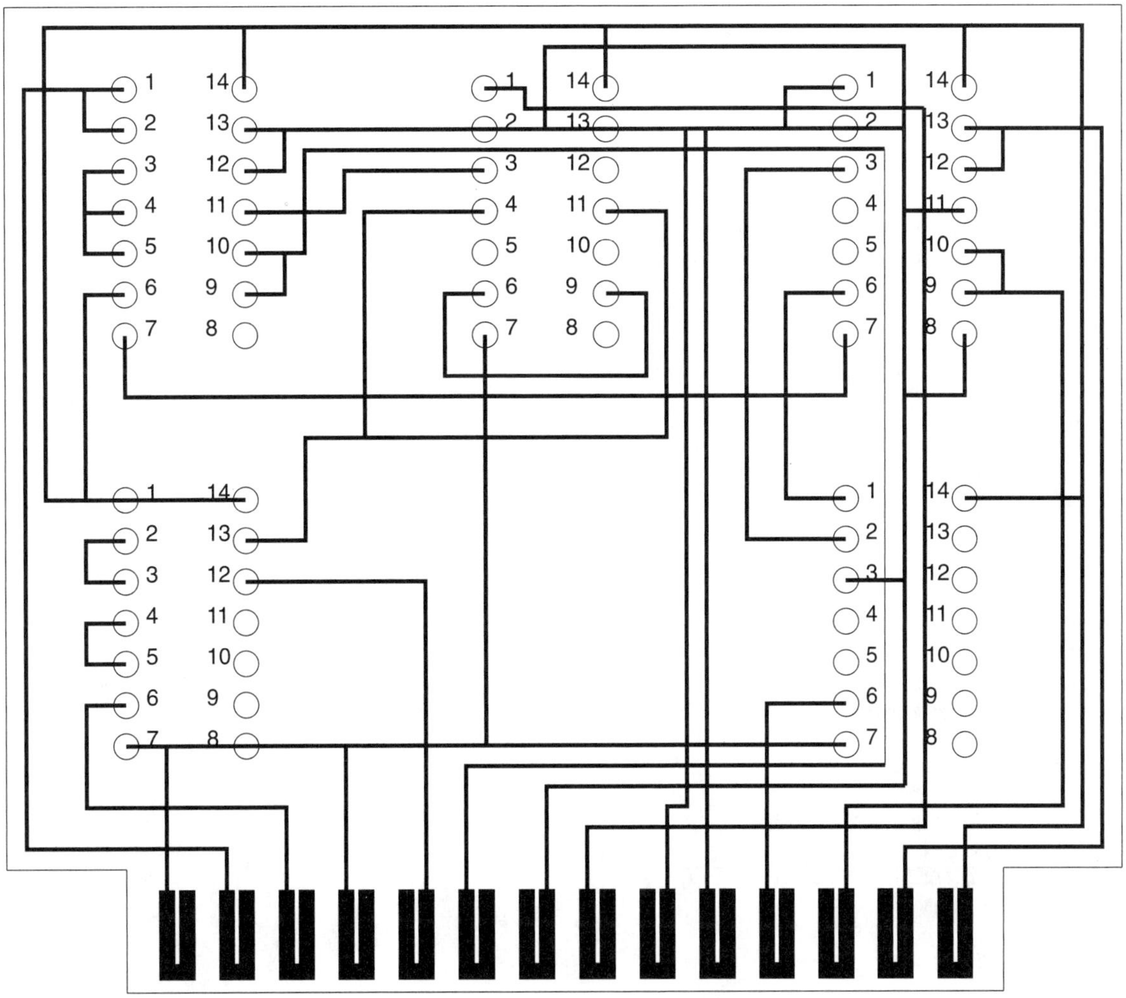

3.10M Shaft Support

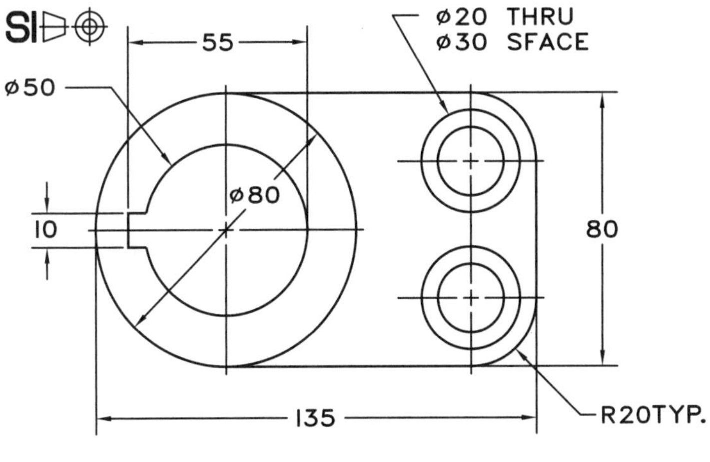

3.11M Puller Base

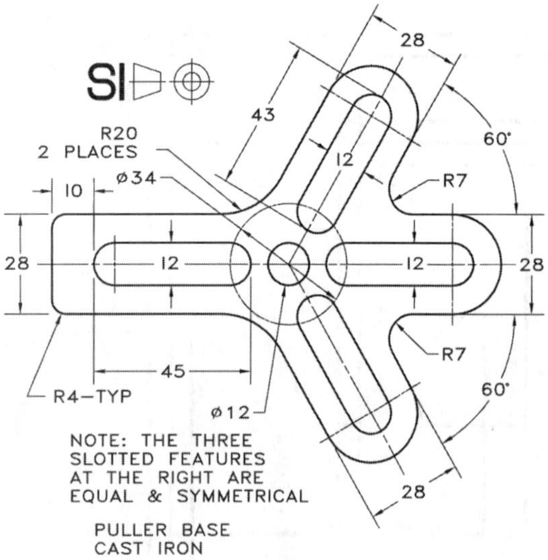

3.12 Concrete Walkway

Hint: *Construct the straight centerlines first. Then use a circle to construct the top R20 arc. Use Circle, TTR to construct the right-hand arc, tangent to the upper arc and a vertical line 45' from the left end. Trim the lines and offset them to finish.*

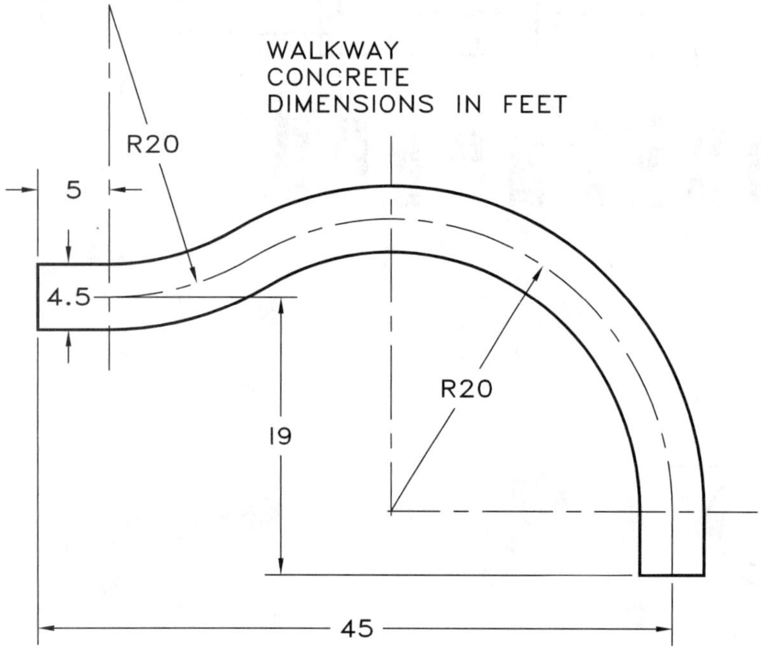

Tutorial

4 Geometric Constructions

Objectives

When you have completed this tutorial, you will be able to

1. Draw polygons and rays.
2. Use object snaps to pick geometric locations.
3. Load linetypes and set their scaling factors.
4. Use the Copy, Extend, Rotate, Move, Mirror, Array, and Break editing commands.
5. Build selection sets.
6. Use hot grips to modify your drawing.

Tip

You can turn on a startup dialog box by picking Tools, Options, the System tab, and choosing Show Startup dialog box from the list of options under the Startup item. The Startup dialog box lets you use a "Wizard" to set the Units and Limits of your drawing as you start a new drawing.

If you have trouble getting the Create New Drawing dialog box to appear, type FILEDIA at the command prompt and make sure its value is set to 1.

Introduction

This tutorial will help you expand your skills by introducing several techniques used to construct accurate geometry. You will learn more about how to use object snaps to select locations, such as intersections, endpoints, and midpoints of lines, based on your existing drawing geometry. You will also learn to use object snap tracking to draw objects at specific angles or in geometric relationships to existing drawing objects. This tutorial synthesizes the techniques you have learned so far by showing you how to coordinate the drawing commands to create shapes for technical drawings. In this tutorial you will create three drawings: a wrench, a coupler, and a geneva cam. You will learn how to apply editing commands to create drawing geometry quickly.

Starting

Launch the AutoCAD® 2006 software.
Pick: **File, New**
Double-click: **the *acad.dwt* template**

Setting the Units and Limits

You will create the wrench drawing using decimal inch measurements. For example, 4.5 units in your drawing will represent 4.5 inches on the real object. Although the AutoCAD software's decimal units can stand for any measurement system, here you will have them stand for inches. When you create drawing geometry, make the objects in your drawing the actual size. Do not scale them down as you would when drawing on paper. Keep in mind that one advantage of the accurate CAD drawing database is that you can use it directly to control machine tools to create parts. You would not want your actual part to turn out half-size because you created a half-size drawing of the part. When you plot the final drawing, you specify the ratio of plotted inches or millimeters to drawing units to produce scaled plots.

Use the Limits command to set up a larger drawing area whenever necessary and then Zoom All so that you see this larger drawing area on your screen.

Decimal units should be the default. If they are not, use the Units command and set them to decimal now.
Check to make sure that the limits for the drawing area is set to 12.0000 × 9.0000.
Use Zoom All to fit the drawing limits to your screen.
Turn on **Grid and Snap** (both should be set to 0.5 inches).
Turn off **OSNAP, POLAR, OTRACK** (if they are on).

Depending on the aspect ratio of your screen, the grid may not fill it in all directions.

Save your drawing in your ***c:\work*** directory as ***wrench.dwg***.

Warning

The Filedia system variable controls whether a dialog box is used for file selection. Setting this variable to 1 uses the dialog box. Setting the variable to 0 suppresses the use of the dialog box, so that the command line is used instead. Also, typing a hyphen (-) in front of a command name causes it to run from the command line instead of using a dialog box.

Drawing the Wrench

You will draw the basic shapes required for a wrench. You will do many of the steps on your own, using the commands you have learned in the previous tutorials. Pay careful attention to the directions, being sure that you complete each step before going on.

First, you will draw lines to use for construction that you will later change to centerlines. Refer to Figure 4.1.

On your own, use **Line** to draw a horizontal line **7.5** units long near the middle of your graphics window. You may want to turn on DYN and use dynamic entry to specify the line lengths.

The line does not have to be at the exact center because you can easily move your drawing objects later if they do not appear centered. You will learn how to move objects in this tutorial.

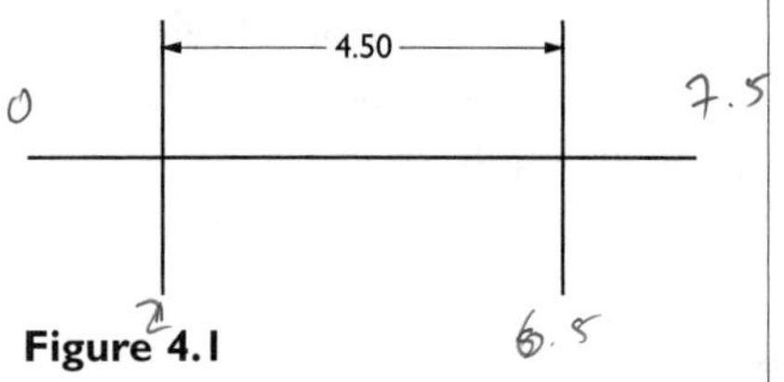

Figure 4.1

Draw two vertical lines that are **3.00** units long and **4.5** units apart, as shown in Figure 4.5.

The exact location of the vertical lines on the horizontal construction line is not critical, as long as they are 4.5 units apart.

Remember, you cannot select accurately unless you use Snap, an object snap, or type exact values.

Tip

Draw one line and then use the Offset command you learned in Tutorial 3, with an offset distance of 4.5, to create the other line.

Pick: **Circle icon**

Use Snap to draw a **1-inch radius circle** with its center at the intersection of the horizontal line and the right vertical line.

Using Copy Object

Copy Object copies an object or group of objects within the same drawing. The original objects remain in place, and during the command you can move the copies to a new location. You can pick Copy Object quickly from the Modify toolbar. You will pick Copy Object to create a second circle in your drawing.

Pick: **Copy Object icon**

Select objects: **select the circle**

Select objects: ↵

Tip

Getting the cursor to select the circle with Snap on might be difficult. Using implied Windowing or Crossing would allow you to easily select the circle. You might also find that turning Snap off makes selecting the circle easier. Be sure to turn it back on again before selecting the base point or displacement, or you may not pick the exact center point.

Pressing ↵ indicates that you have finished selecting objects and want to continue with the command. Be sure that Snap is on again so you can accurately select the center point of the circle, which you created on the snap increment.

Specify base point or [Displacement] <Displacement>: **select the center point of the circle**

The cursor switches to drag mode so that you can see the object move about the screen as you are prompted for the second point of displacement. You can define the new location by typing new absolute or relative coordinate values or by picking a location from the screen. Because

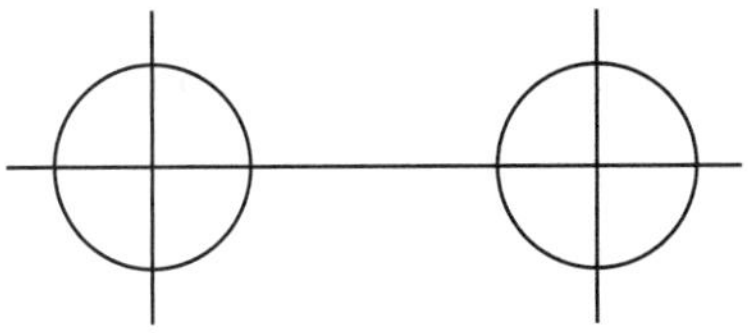

Figure 4.2

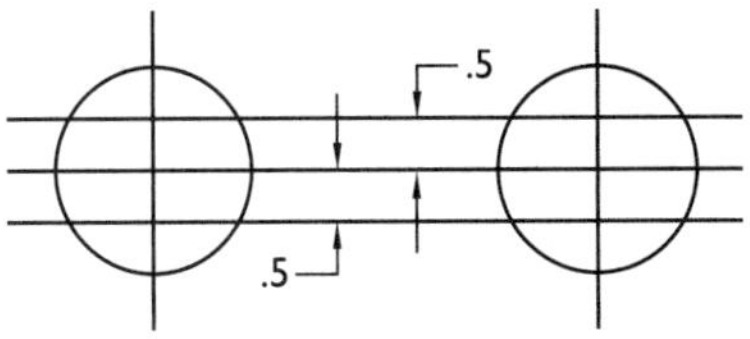

Figure 4.3

Tip

Trim the outer portions first. If you trim the inner lines first, the outer portions will no longer cross another object and therefore will not trim. You can erase the outer segments if you have already trimmed the inner lines.

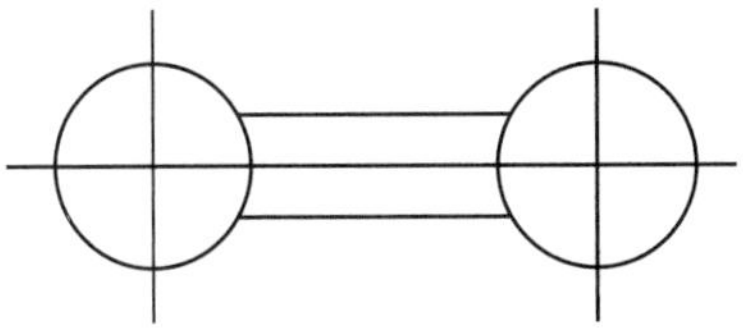

Figure 4.4

you created this object on the snap increment, use the snap and pick the second point of displacement.

The second circle must be centered at the intersection of the horizontal and left vertical lines, which should be a snap location.

Specify second point of displacement or <use first point as displacement>: **pick the left intersection**

Specify second point or [Exit/Undo] <Exit>: ↵

Your drawing should now look like Figure 4.2.

Next, use the Offset command on your own to offset the horizontal construction line a distance of 0.5 units to either side of itself to create the body of the wrench.

Your resulting drawing should look like Figure 4.3.

Now use the Trim command to trim the lines that you created with the Offset command so that they intersect neatly with the circles.

When you have finished, your drawing should look like Figure 4.4.

Effective Use of Layers

Recall from Tutorial 2 that layers behave like clear overlay sheets in your drawing. However, unlike a stack of overlays, the coordinate system always aligns exactly from one layer to the next. To use layers effectively, choose layer names that make sense and separate the objects you draw into logical groups. You will create a centerline layer and then use it to change the middle lines of the wrench onto that layer so that they take on its color and linetype properties.

Pick: **Layer Properties Manager icon**

The Layer Properties Manager appears on the screen, as in Figure 4.5.

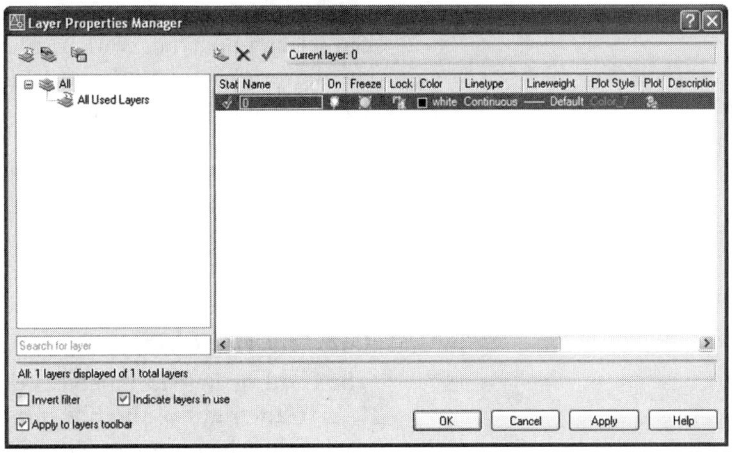

Figure 4.5

One layer name should be listed in the Name column, 0. Layer 0 is a special layer that is provided in AutoCAD. You cannot rename it or delete it from the list of layers. Layer 0 shows a green check indicating it is the current layer.

You will create a layer named, appropriately enough, Centerlines, for drawing the centerlines and set its color to green and linetype to center. Then, you will make it the current layer.

Pick: **New Layer icon** (located near the top middle of the dialog box)

A new Layer1 should be highlighted in the list of layer names.

Type: **Centerlines** ↵

To change the color for layer Centerlines,

Pick: **on the Color column box corresponding to layer Centerlines**

A dialog box containing color choices pops up on the screen with the color choices.

Pick: **Green** (Color 3 from the list of standard colors)
Pick: **OK**

Now the color for layer Centerlines is set to green.

Pick: **on Continuous in the Linetype column for layer Centerlines**

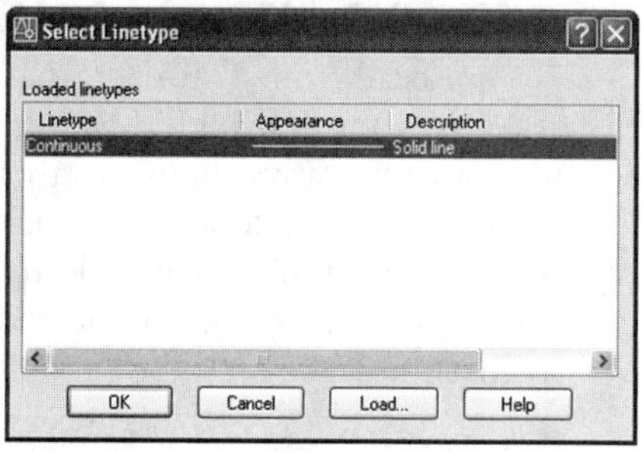

Figure 4.6

The Select Linetype dialog box shown in Figure 4.6 appears. Note that only one choice of linetype, CONTINUOUS, is available. Before you can select a linetype, you must load it. You need do so only one time in the drawing, and you do not need to load all the linetypes. To keep your drawing size small and get a shorter list of linetypes in the dialog box, load only the linetypes that you use frequently in your drawing. You can always load other linetypes as needed during the drawing process. You will select Load, the second button from the right at the bottom of the dialog box, to load the linetypes you want to use.

Pick: **Load**

Loading the Linetypes

The Load or Reload Linetypes dialog box appears, as shown in Figure 4.7. To the right of the File button is the name of the default file, *acad.lin*, in which the predefined linetypes are stored. You can also create your own linetypes, using the Linetype command. You can store your custom linetypes in the *acad.lin* file or in another file that ends with the extension **.lin*. Below the file name is the list of available linetypes and a picture of each. Use the scroll bar at the right of the list to move down the items until you see the selection CENTER.

Pick: **CENTER** (on the name so that it becomes highlighted)

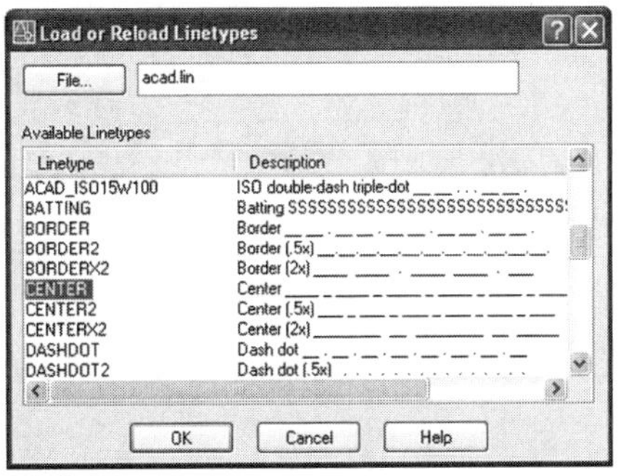

Figure 4.7

Pick: **OK** (to exit the Load or Reload Linetypes dialog box)

Pick: **Center** (so that it is the highlighted selection in the Select Linetype dialog box)

Pick: **OK** (to exit the Select Linetype dialog box)

The centerline pattern is selected for the layer and ready for use as shown in Figure 4.8

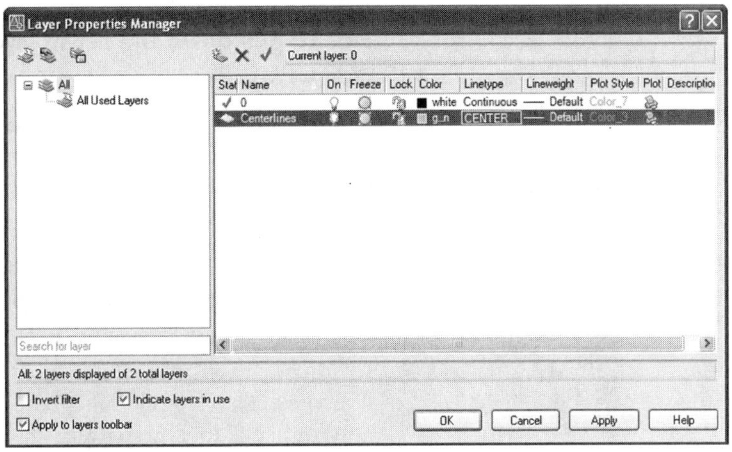

Figure 4.8

Pick: **OK** (to exit the Layer Properties Manager)

Tip

Objects that have had their color or linetype set to something other than BYLAYER will not be affected by changing the color or linetype of the layer they are on. In general, using layers to set the color and linetype is better.

Changing Properties

You will use the new layer you created to control the linetype and color of the centerlines.

Pick: **the middle horizontal line and the two vertical lines**

Small blue squares (called hot grips, which you will learn more about later in this tutorial) should be active on the endpoints and midpoints of each line as shown in Figure 4.9.

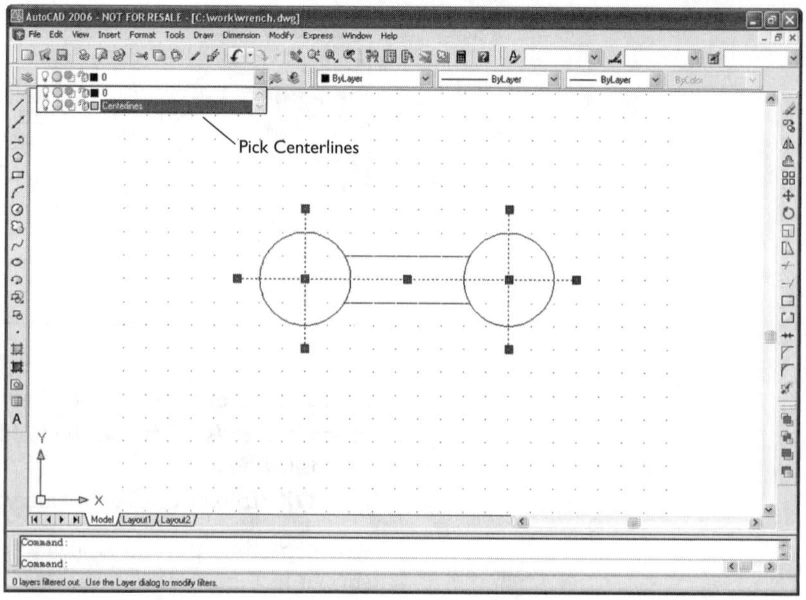

Figure 4.9

Pick: **to pull down the list of layers** (as shown in Figure 4.9)
Pick: **Centerlines**

The lines change to have the properties of that layer—the color green and linetype center. To remove the hot grips from your screen so that your drawing looks like Figure 4.10,

Press: Esc

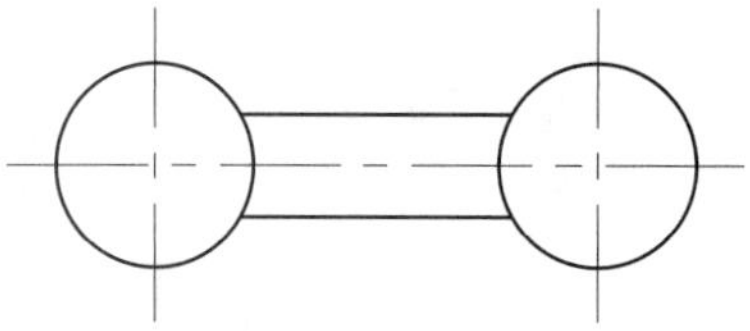

Figure 4.10

Setting the Global Linetype Scaling Factor

The *global linetype scaling factor* (LTScale command) is a value that you set to adjust the lengths of the lines and dashes used to make up various linetypes. This is very important for giving your drawings the correct appearance. Linetype patterns are stored in a file with the *.lin* file extension, which is external to your drawing. The lengths of the lines and dashes are set in that external file. But when you are working on large-scale drawings and the distances are in hundreds of units, a linetype with the dash length of 1/8 unit will not appear correctly. To adjust the linetypes, you specify a factor by which the length of the dashes in the *.lin* file should be multiplied. The global linetype scaling factor adjusts the scaling of all the linetypes in your drawing as a group.

When you are working on a large drawing such as the subdivision plat that you created in Tutorials 2 and 3, you must scale the dashed lines of the linetype up in order to make them visible. When you are working on a drawing that you will plot full scale, generally you should set the global linetype scaling factor to 1.00, which is the default. Setting the global linetype scaling factor to a decimal less than one (e.g., 0.75) results in a drawing with smaller dashes comprising the linetypes. In general, the linetype scaling factor you set in your drawing should be the reciprocal of the scale at which you will plot your drawing. When you learn about paper space in Tutorial 5, you will see that you can set the linetype scaling factor both in model space, where you are working

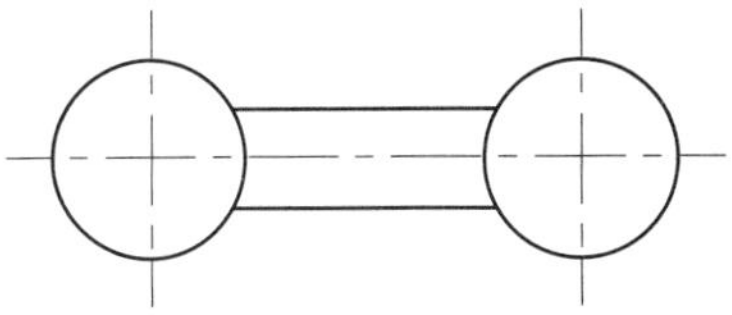

Figure 4.11

now, and in paper space. You will type the command to set the global linetype scale at the command prompt.

Command: **LTSCALE** ↵
New scale factor <1.0000>: **.75** ↵

The centerlines should now cross in the center of each circle, as shown in Figure 4.11.

Changing an Object's Linetype Scale

You can also use the Linetype Scale area of the Properties dialog box (CELTSCALE command) to set the linetype scale for any particular object, independent of the rest of the drawing. You should first adjust the general appearance of the lines using the global command LTSCALE and then use the next method if some lines still need further adjustment. The object linetype scale factor is multiplied by the global LTSCALE to determine the object's linetype scaling.

Next, you will set the linetype scale for the two vertical lines to 1.5, giving them a different linetype scale than the horizontal line. You will pick the Properties icon from the Standard toolbar in order to use the Properties palette.

Pick: **the two vertical lines so that they become selected** (their grips show)
Pick: **Properties icon**

The Properties palette appears on your screen as shown in Figure 4.12. You will use the box to the right of Linetype Scale to set the linetype scaling factor for the objects you selected to 1.5.

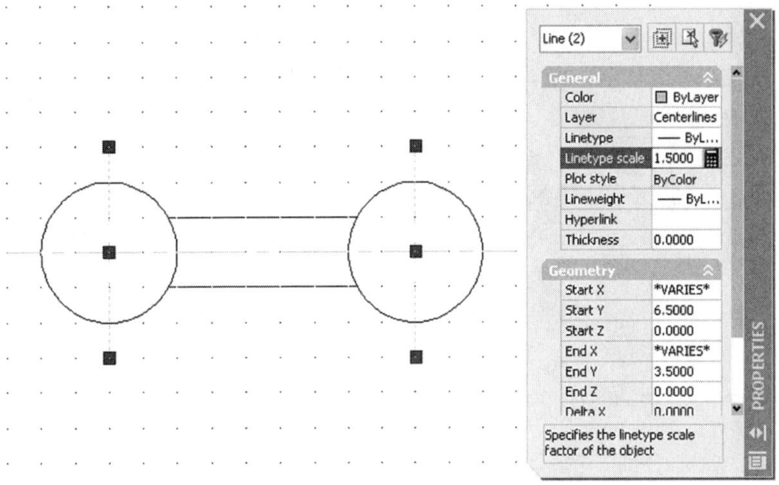

Figure 4.12

Tip

If you have trouble with the lines returning to their previous LTscale property, press ↵ after you type the value in the Properties palette before you close it.

Tip

The Dimcenter command creates correctly shown centerlines for circles. You will learn to use it in Tutorial 6.

Highlight the text in the box to the right of Linetype Scale and overtype the new value.

Type: **1.5** ↵
Pick: **the Close button (X) in the upper right of the Properties palette to close it**
Press: [Esc] **to unselect the object grips**

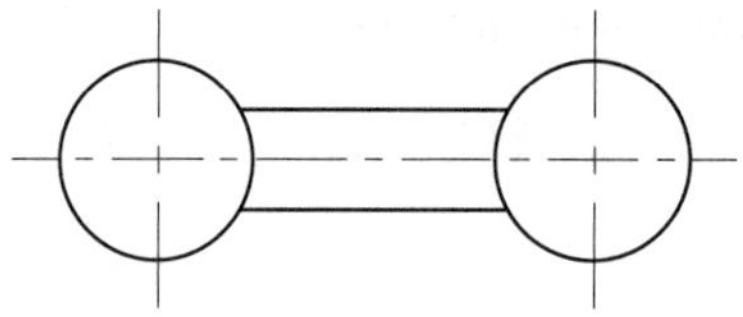

Figure 4.13

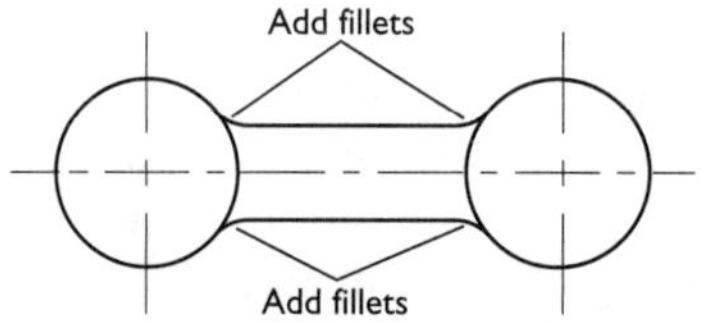

Figure 4.14

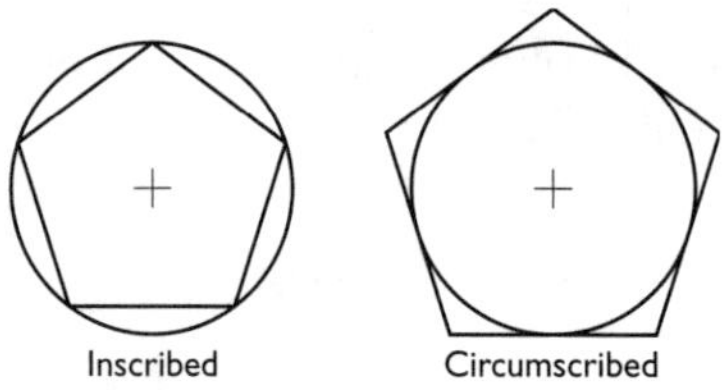

Figure 4.15

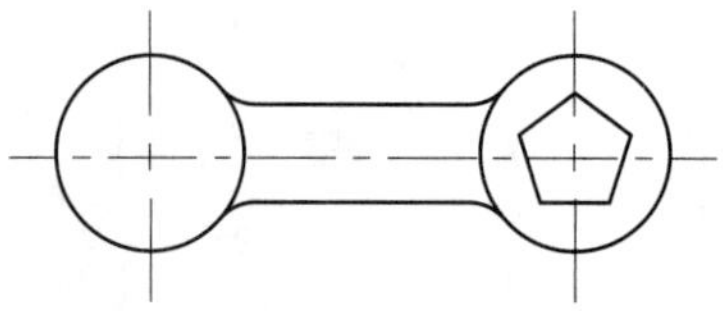

Figure 4.16

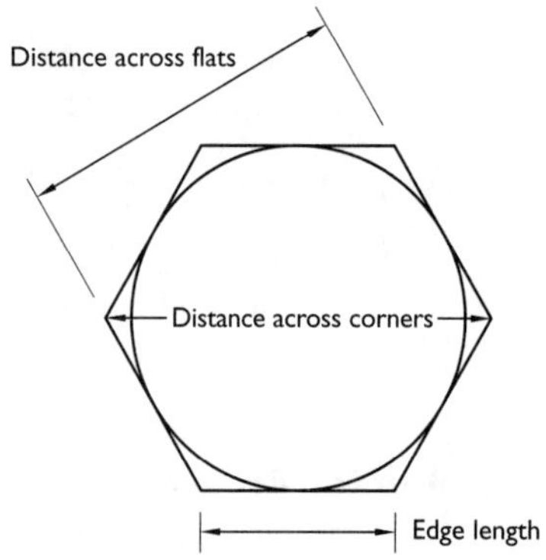

Figure 4.17

Now your drawing should look like Figure 4.13.

Save your drawing before continuing.

Now you are ready to add the fillets to your drawing, as shown in Figure 4.14. Refer to Tutorial 3 if you need to review Fillet.

Use the **Fillet** command, with a radius of **0.5**, to add the fillets on your own.

Using Polygon

The Polygon command draws regular polygons with 3 to 1024 sides. AutoCAD creates polygons as polyline objects, which you used in Tutorial 3. Polygons act as a single object because they are created as a connected polyline. A regular *polygon* is one in which the lengths of all sides are equal. The size of a polygon is usually expressed in terms of a related circle. This convention comes from the classic straightedge/compass construction techniques you probably learned in your first geometry course. Polygons are either *inscribed* in or *circumscribed* about a circle. A pentagon is a five-sided polygon. Figure 4.15 shows a pentagon inscribed within a circle and a pentagon circumscribed about a circle.

Polygon is on the Draw toolbar. You will add a pentagon to the right side of the wrench, circumscribed about a circle.

Pick: **Polygon icon**

Enter number of sides <4>: **5** ↵

Specify center of polygon or [Edge]: **select the center point of the right circle**

Enter an option [Inscribed in circle/Circumscribed about circle]<I>: **C** ↵

You are now in drag mode; observe that the pentagon changes size on the screen as you move your cursor. You must specify the radius of the circle, either by picking with the pointing device or by typing in the coordinates. For this object you will specify a radius of one-half inch.

Specify radius of circle: **.5** ↵

A five-sided regular polygon (a pentagon) is drawn on your screen. Your drawing should be similar to Figure 4.16.

Drawing Hexagons

Hexagons are six-sided polygons and are a common shape in technical drawings. The heads of bolts, screws, and nuts often have a hexagonal shape. The size of a hexagon is sometimes referred to by its *distance across the flats*. The reason is that the sizes of screws, bolts, and nuts are defined by the distance across their flat sides. For example, a 16-mm hexhead screw would measure 16 mm across its head's flats and would fit a 16-mm wrench. The distance across the flats of a hexagon is not the same as the length of an edge of the hexagon. Figure 4.17 illustrates the difference between the two distances. If a hexagon is circumscribed about a circle, the diameter of the circle equals the distance across the hexagon's flats. If a hexagon is inscribed in a circle, the diameter of the circle equals the distance across the corners of the hexagon.

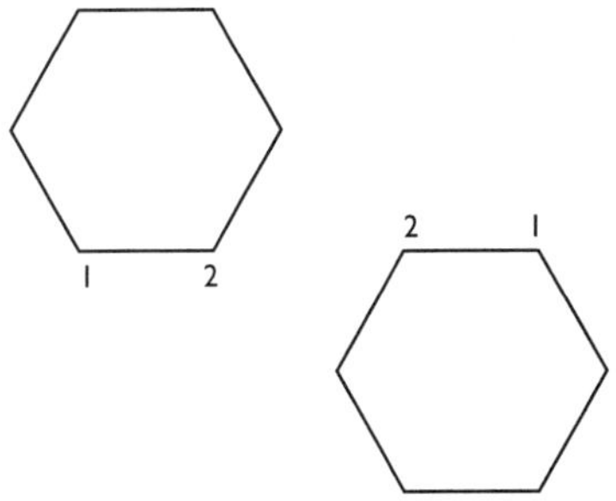

Figure 4.18

You can use the Polygon command's Edge option to draw regular polygons by specifying the length of the edge. This function is helpful when you are creating side-by-side hexagonal patterns (honeycomb patterns). Note that the AutoCAD software draws polygons counterclockwise. If you use the Edge option, the sequence in which you select points will affect the position of the polygon, as shown in Figure 4.18.

Next, you will add the hexagon to the other side of the wrench. You will use the circumscribed option again.

Command: ↵ (or press the return button on your mouse and select Repeat Polygon)
Enter number of sides <5>: **6** ↵
Specify center of polygon or [Edge]: **pick the center point of the left circle**
Enter an option [Inscribed in circle/Circumscribed about circle]<C>: ↵
Radius of circle: **.5** ↵

A hexagon measuring 1.00 across the flats appears in your wrench. The final drawing should be similar to Figure 4.19.

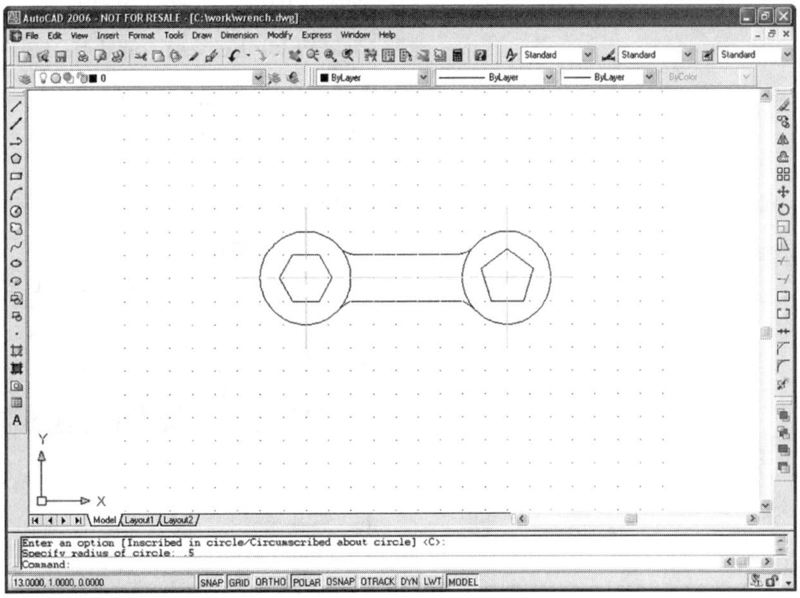

Figure 4.19

You have now completed your wrench. You will save this drawing and begin a new drawing to continue this tutorial. You will close drawing Wrench so that it does not stay available on your screen.

Pick: **Save icon**
Pick: **File, Close** (to close the Wrench drawing)

In this next section, you will practice with additional drawing commands and with object snaps. You will start a new drawing and name it *coupler.dwg*.

Pick: **New icon**
Pick: ***acad.dwt*** (as the template to use)
Pick: **OK**

Tip

If you see the Startup dialog box, pick Tools, Options and check to see that Do Not Show Startup dialog is selected on the System tab.

You return to the drawing editor.

Pick: **Grid** (to turn it on)
Set **Snap** to **.25** and turn it on.
Use **Zoom All** if necessary so that the grid area fills the graphics window.
Pick: **Save** icon
Type: ***coupler.dwg*** as the name of the new drawing

Using Polar Tracking

When you are in a command (such as Line or Circle) that prompts for a location such as From or To, you can use polar tracking to align the cursor along a path defined by a polar angle from the previous point. Polar tracking works along preset angle increments of 90°, 60°, 45°, 30°, 22.5°, 18°, 15°, 10°, and 5°, or you can specify other angles. The angles can be measured relative to the previous line segment or absolutely from the default of zero degrees to the East. So that you can see the effect of Polar tracking clearly,

Pick: **the DYN button** (to turn it off)

Next turn on polar tracking,

Pick: **Polar button** (on the status bar) or press F10

Like object snap, you will not notice any result until you select a command, such as Line or Circle, that prompts you to specify a location.

Next you will set the angle increment for polar tracking. To do this, you will right-click on the Polar button on the status bar.

Right-click: **Polar button**
Pick: **Settings** (from the pop-up menu)

The Drafting Settings dialog box appears on your screen with the Polar Tracking tab uppermost, as shown in Figure 4.20.

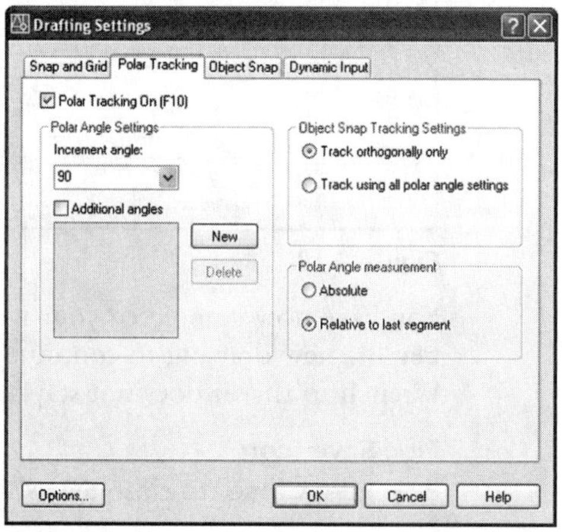

Figure 4.20

You will use the Increment angle pull-down selection box to choose an angle of 45 degrees for polar tracking.

Pick: **45**
Pick: **Relative to last segment radio button** (if not already selected)

Pick: **Options button** in the bottom left of the dialog box

The Options dialog box shows on your screen as in Figure 4.21.

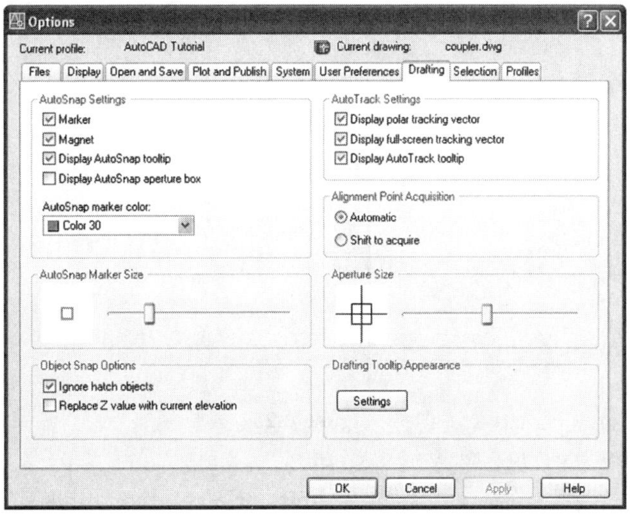

Figure 4.21

Make sure that Display AutoTrack tooltip is checked.
Pick: **OK**
Pick: **OK**

Tip

Ortho mode restricts the cursor to horizontal or vertical movement. Ortho mode and polar tracking cannot be turned on at the same time. When you select Ortho mode, polar tracking is automatically turned off and vice-versa, so that only one mode is available at any time.

The Polar button on the status bar should be on.

You will use polar tracking along with the Line and Circle commands to create lines 1–4 for the coupler shown in Figure 4.22.

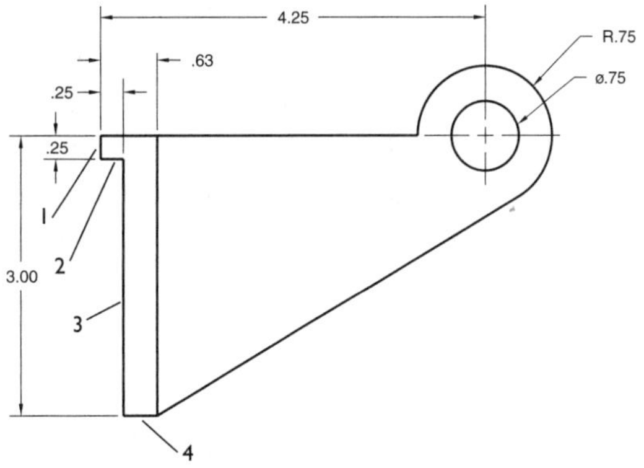

Figure 4.22

Pick: **Line icon**
Specify first point: **3.75,6.5** ↵

A line will rubberband from coordinate point (3.75, 6.5) on your screen. Move the crosshairs around so that you see the rubberband line. As you get near 0 degrees, 45 degrees, and any other angle increments of 45 degrees, you will notice a tracking line appear on your screen.

Position your cursor below the previous point, as shown in Figure 4.23, to draw a line **.25 units** long along the angle of **270 degrees.** When you see the tooltip appear with the correct value,
Press: **pick button** to select the location

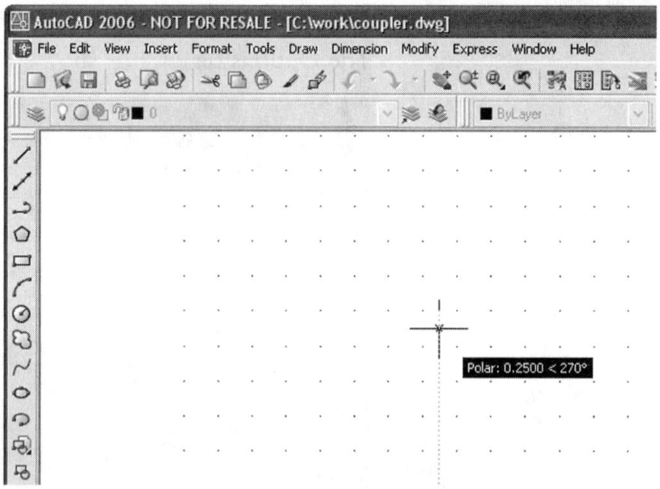

Figure 4.23

Tip

Polar tracking measures distances from the last point selected, so it is considered relative. An absolute measurement would be from the 0,0 point of the World Coordinate System. You can right-click on the Polar button and use the Drafting Settings dialog box to control whether angles are measured relative to the last point or absolutely. This is also true for Dynamic Input.

Specify next point or [Undo]: **use polar tracking to draw a line .25 units at a relative angle of 90 degrees**

Specify next point or [Undo]: **use polar tracking to draw a line 2.75 units at a relative angle of 270 degrees**

For the next point, you will type the length at the command prompt because it is not a point you can pick using the current Snap increment. Position your cursor to the right of the previous point so that the polar tracking angle of 90 degrees appears. Type the distance along the tracking angle at the command prompt,

Specify next point or [Close/Undo]: (use polar tracking at a relative angle of 90 degrees) **.375** ↵

Specify next point or [Close/Undo]: ↵

Pick: **Polar** (from Status bar or press F10) to turn Polar **off**

Pick: **Circle icon**

Specify center point for circle or [3P/2P/Ttr (tan tan radius)]: **8,6.5** ↵

Specify radius of circle or [Diameter]: **.75** ↵

When you have finished drawing these objects, your drawing should look like the one in Figure 4.24.

Figure 4.24

Pick: to turn **Snap off**

Next you will use object snaps to locate points accurately. Leaving Snap turned on may interfere with selection.

Using Object Snaps

As you learned in Tutorial 2, you use object snaps to select locations accurately in relation to other objects in your drawing. Object snaps can operate in two different ways: override mode and running mode.

Remember, when an object snap is active, the AutoSnap™ marker box appears whenever the cursor is near a snap point. When you select a point, it will select the object snap point if the marker box is present, *whether or not the cursor is within the marker box.*

Object Snap Overrides

You will finish drawing the coupler (Figure 4.22), using object snap overrides. You will use object snap overrides to position lines and circles relative to this figure. (You may see other ways that you could use editing commands to create parts of this figure, but in this example object snaps will be used as much as possible. When you are working on your own drawings, use a combination of the methods you have learned.)

Showing a Floating Toolbar

You will show the floating Object Snap toolbar to make selecting object snaps easy. Recall that the object snaps are also on the Standard toolbar as a flyout selection. You can turn toolbars on by right-clicking any toolbar.

Right-click: **anywhere on the Standard toolbar**
Pick: **Object Snap from the list of Toolbars that pops up**

The Object Snap toolbar appears on your screen, as shown in Figure 4.25. You can position it anywhere on the screen or dock it to the edge of the graphics window. Refer to Tutorial 1 if you need to review floating windows and how to dock toolbars.

Figure 4.25

Snap to Endpoint

The Endpoint object snap (END) locates the closest endpoint of an arc, line, or polyline vertex. You will draw a line from the endpoint of line 1, shown in Figure 4.26, to touch the circle at the quadrant point. The *quadrant points* are at 0°, 90°, 180°, and 270° of a circle or an arc. You will use the Endpoint and Quadrant object snaps to locate the exact points. You will use the floating Object Snap toolbar to select the object snaps.

Pick: **Line icon**
Specify first point: **pick Snap to Endpoint icon**

Note that AutoSnap shows a colored marker box reflecting the object snap you chose.

Endp of: **place the cursor on the upper end of line 1 shown in Figure 4.26 and press the pick button, using the AutoSnap Endpoint marker**

Note that the beginning of the line has jumped to the exact endpoint of the line you chose.

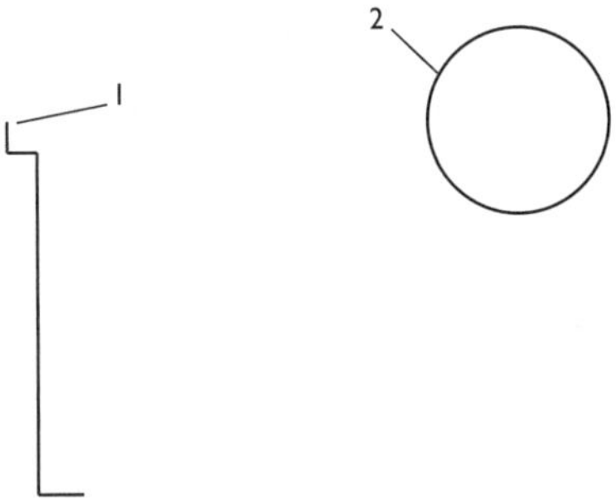

Figure 4.26

Tip

When an object snap running mode is active, you can still use a different object snap during a command. The object snap override takes precedence over the object snap running mode for that pick.

Tip

You can also type a three-letter code for the object snap at the Select objects prompt instead of picking an object snap mode from the toolbar.

The command-line equivalent of the Endpoint object snap is END.

Snap to Quadrant

The Quadrant object snap attaches to the quadrant point on a circle nearest the position of the crosshairs. The command-line equivalent of Snap to Quadrant is QUA. The quadrant points are the four points on the circle that are tangent to a square that encloses it. They are also the four points where the centerlines intersect the circle. Next you will finish the line, using the Quadrant object snap to pick the quadrant point of the circle as the second endpoint for your line. You should see the prompt for the next point of the Line command.

Specify next point or [Undo]: **pick Snap to Quadrant icon**
Qua of: **pick on the circle near point 2 in Figure 4.26**
Specify next point or [Undo]: ↵

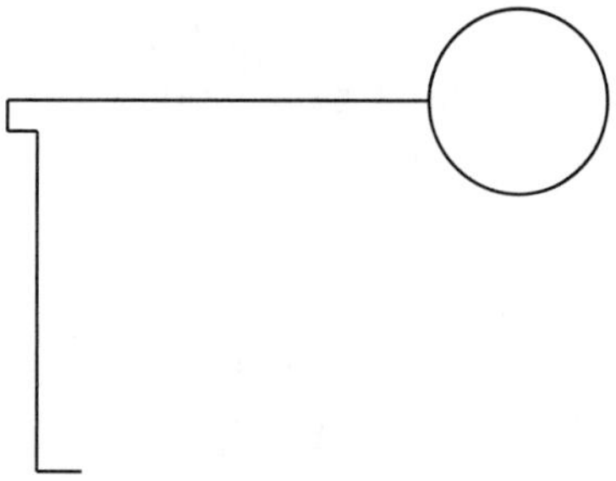
Figure 4.27

Your drawing should be similar to Figure 4.27.

Snap to Center

The Center object snap finds the center of a circle or an arc. You will use it to create concentric circles by selecting the center of the circle that you have drawn as the center for the new circle you will add. The command-line equivalent for Snap to Center is CEN.

Pick: **Circle icon**
Specify center point for circle or [3P/2P/Ttr (tan tan radius)]: **pick Snap to Center icon**
Cen of: **pick on the edge of the circle**

The AutoCAD software finds the exact center of the circle and a circle rubberbands from the center to the location of the crosshairs. Note the AutoSnap marker that appeared when your cursor was on the circle. Object snap overrides stay active for only one pick. You are now prompted to specify the radius.

Specify radius of circle or [Diameter]<0.7500>: **.375** ↵

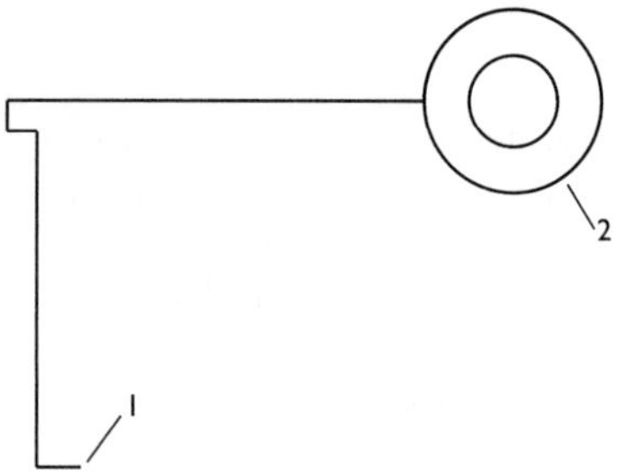

Figure 4.28

The circle should be drawn concentric to the original circle in the drawing, as shown in Figure 4.28.

To position the next line from the endpoint of line 1 in Figure 4.32 tangent to the outer circle, you will use the Endpoint object snap and then the Tangent object snap.

Pick: **Line icon**
Specify first point: **pick Snap to Endpoint icon**
Endp of: **pick near the right endpoint of line 1**

A line rubberbands from the endpoint of line 1 to the location of the crosshairs. Next, you will use the Tangent object snap to locate the second point of the line tangent to the circle.

Snap to Tangent

The Tangent object snap attaches to a point on a circle or an arc; a line drawn from the last point to the referenced object is drawn tangent to the referenced object. The command-line equivalent is TAN.

Specify next point or [Undo]: **pick Snap to Tangent icon**

Tan to: **pick the lower right side of the circle when you see the AutoSnap Tangent marker near point 2**

Specify next point or [Undo]: ↵

Your screen should be similar to Figure 4.29.

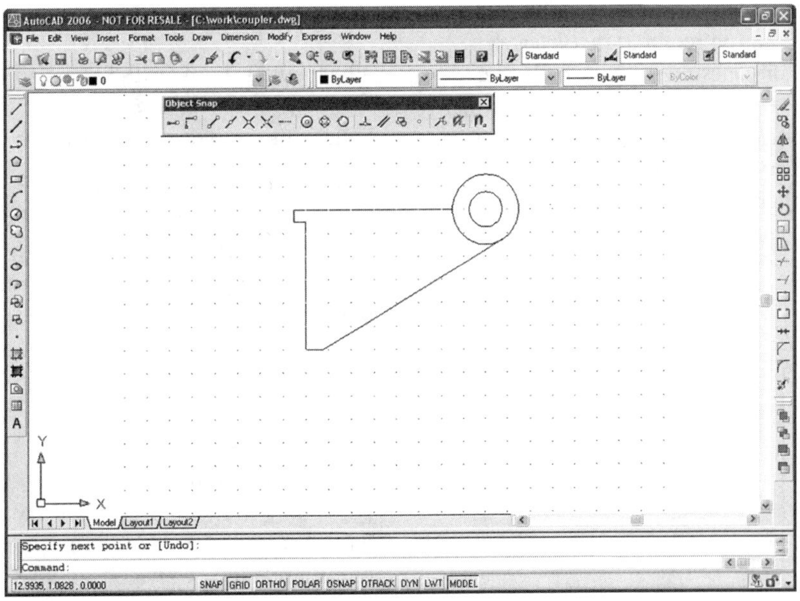

Figure 4.29

Tip

To draw a line tangent to two circles, pick Line. At the Specify first point prompt, pick Snap to Tangent and pick on one of the circles in the general vicinity of the tangent line you want to draw. You will not see a line rubberband. At the Specify next point prompt, pick Snap to Tangent again and pick the other circle. When you select the second object, the tangent is defined and will be drawn on your screen.

Next you will draw a line from the intersection of the short horizontal line and the angled line, perpendicular to the upper line of the object. You will use two more object snaps to draw this line.

Snap to Intersection

Snap to Intersection finds the intersection of two graphical objects. The command-line equivalent for Snap to Intersection is INT.

When you use 3D solid modeling in Tutorial 9, remember that when you are looking for the intersection of two objects with Snap to Intersection, the objects must actually intersect in 3D space, not just apparently intersect on the screen. (One line may be behind the other in the 3D model.) To select lines that do not intersect in space, use the Apparent Intersection object snap. It finds the intersection of lines that would intersect if extended and also the apparent intersection of two lines (where they appear to intersect in a view).

Refer to Figure 4.30 when selecting your points.

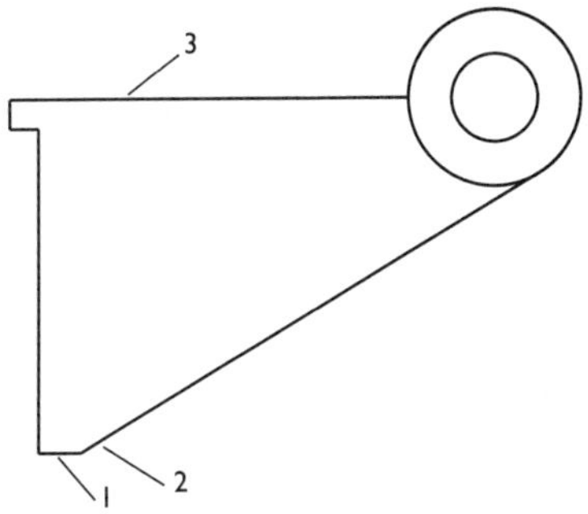

Figure 4.30

Pick: **Line icon**

Specify first point: **pick Snap to Intersection icon**

Int of: **pick so that the intersection of lines 1 and 2 is anywhere inside the target area**

A line rubberbands from the intersection to the current position of the crosshairs. To select the second endpoint of the line, you will use Snap to Perpendicular to draw the line perpendicular to the top horizontal line.

Tip

Note that when Snap to Intersection is on and the cursor passes over any object, the AutoSnap marker for intersection (an X) shows up with three dots to its right. These dots mean that if you select the line, you will be prompted for a second line or object that intersects with the first.

Tip

Remember, in order to draw a perpendicular line, you must define two points. When you are defining a perpendicular from a line, no line is drawn until you define the second point. The reason is that infinitely many lines are perpendicular to a given line, but only one line is perpendicular to a line through a given point. Your perpendicular line will be drawn after you have selected the second point.

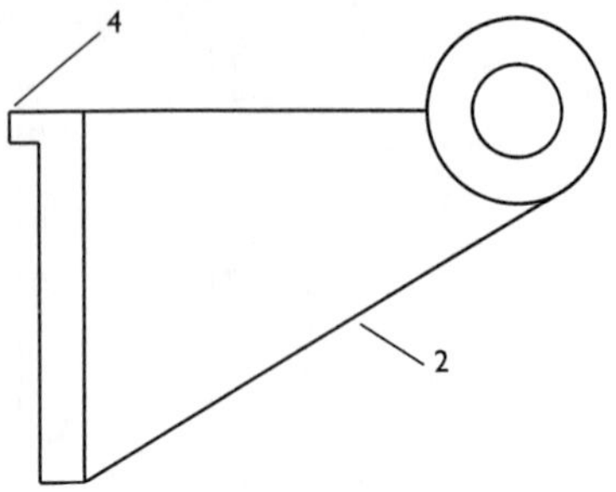

Figure 4.31

Snap to Perpendicular

The Perpendicular object snap attaches to a point on an arc, a circle, or a line; a line drawn from the last point to the referenced object forms a right angle with that object.

You will invoke the Perpendicular object snap by typing its command-line equivalent, PER.

Specify next point or [Undo]: **PER** ↵
Per to: **pick on line 3**
Specify next point or [Undo]: ↵

The line is drawn at a 90° angle, perpendicular to the line, regardless of where on the line you picked. The drawing on your screen should be similar to Figure 4.31. Although this example draws a perpendicular line that touches the target line, it need not touch it. If you choose to draw perpendicular to a line that does not intersect at an angle of 90°, the perpendicular line is drawn to a point that would be perpendicular if the target line were extended.

Snap to Parallel

The Parallel object snap acquires an object that your next pick will be parallel to. You will try it next and then undo the result. You will pick the override for the Parallel object snap from the toolbar. Its command-line equivalent is PAR.

Pick: **Line icon**
Specify first point: **pick Snap to Intersection icon**
Int of: **pick point 4 from Figure 4.31**
Specify next point or [Undo]: **pick Parallel icon**
Par to: **hold your cursor over line 2 until you see the AutoSnap marker Parallel appear but do not press the pick button**
Specify next point or [Undo]: **move your cursor so that the line rubberbanding from point 4 is roughly parallel to line 2.**

You should see a parallel tracking line appear as shown in Figure 4.32. When it does,

Pick: **a point along the tracking line parallel to line 2** ↵

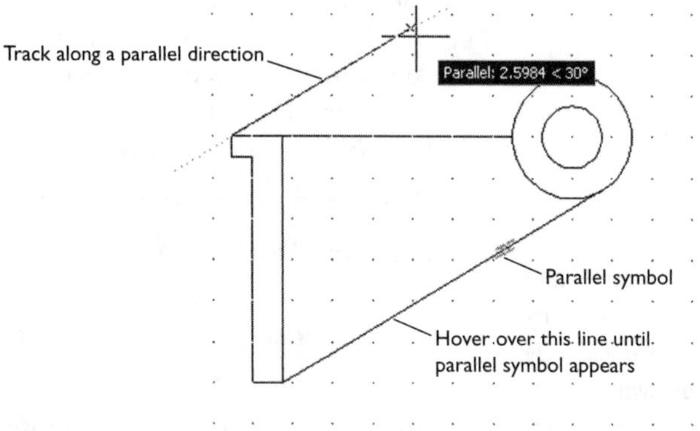

Figure 4.32

Tip

The Midpoint between Two Points (MTP) snap finds the midpoint between two points you select. You can right-click when prompted to select to pop up the shortcut menu showing the object snap modes, including Midpoint between Two Points.

Warning

When you are finished using running mode object snaps, be sure to turn them off. (You can do so by either deselecting them in the Object Snap Settings dialog box or toggling off the OSNAP button on the Status bar.) If you forget, you may have trouble with certain other commands. For example, if you turn on the running object snap for Perpendicular and leave it on and later try to erase something, you may have trouble selecting objects because the program will try to find a point perpendicular to every object you pick.

Tip

You can press F3 to toggle on and off the running object snap mode.

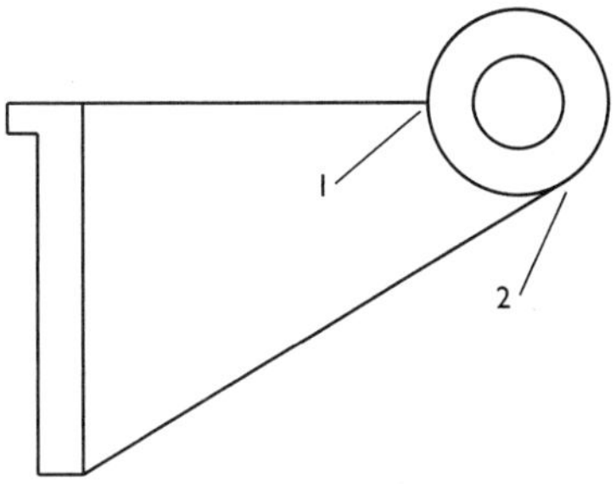

Figure 4.34

Next you will undo the parallel line.

Command: **U** ↵

Use the techniques that you have learned to **save your drawing** now.

Practice on your own with each of the object snaps. Try selecting the rest of the object snaps from the toolbar.

Practicing with Running Mode Object Snaps

You can also use object snap in the running mode, as you did in Tutorial 2 with Snap to Node. When you use object snaps this way, turn the mode on and leave it on. Any time that a command calls for the input of a point or selection, the current object snap is used when you pick. The running mode object snaps are very useful, as they reduce the number of times you must pick from the menu to achieve the desired drawing results. You can use any of the object snaps in either the running mode or the override mode.

Pick: **Object Snap Settings icon** (or right-click on OSNAP button and pick Settings)

The Drafting Settings dialog box appears on the screen with the Object Snap tab uppermost.

Pick: **Clear All** (to remove any current selections)

Pick: **Intersection**

A check appears in the box to indicate that you have selected Intersection. The Drafting Settings dialog box should appear as shown in Figure 4.33.

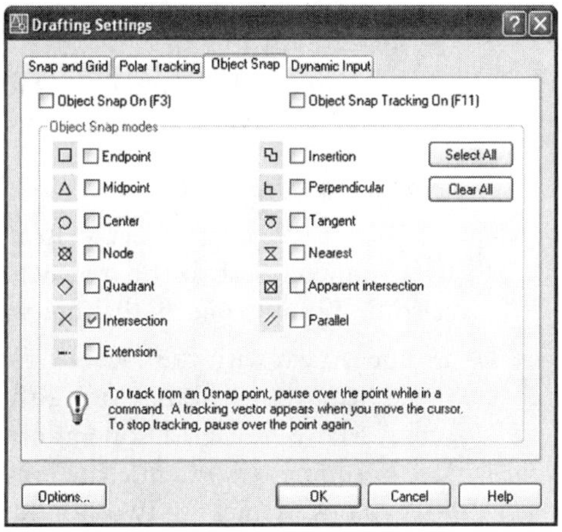

Figure 4.33

Pick: **Object Snap On** (F3) check box so that it is selected

Pick: **OK** (to exit the Drafting Settings dialog box)

Now Intersection is turned on. Anytime you are prompted to select, an AutoSnap marker box will appear when the cursor is near an intersection point.

You will use the Break command to break the circle between intersection 1 and intersection 2 in Figure 4.34. (Note that you could also accomplish the same thing by using Trim.)

Tip

Zoom in if necessary to see the intersections more clearly.

Tip

The Break at Point icon allows you to select to break a selected object at a specified point without erasing any portion of it.

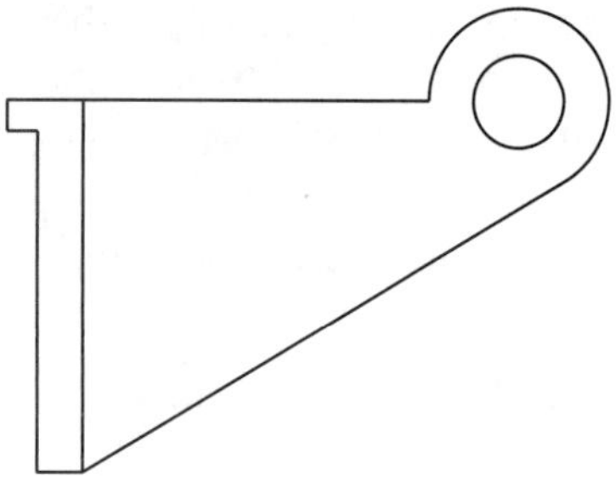

Figure 4.35

Using Break

The Break command erases part of an object (for example, a line, arc, or circle). The Break icon is on the Modify toolbar. When using the Break command, you can specify a single point at which to break the object or specify two points on the object and the Break command will automatically remove the portion between the points selected. You also can select the object and then specify the two points at which to break it. You will use the First point option after selecting the Break icon. Refer to Figure 4.34 to make your selections.

Pick: **Break icon**
Select object: **pick the large circle**
Specify second break point (or First point): **F** ↵
Specify first break point: **pick intersection 1**
Enter second point: **pick intersection 2**

When you select the second break point, the portion of the circle between the two selected points is removed. Your drawing should look like Figure 4.35. Save your coupler drawing.

Pick: **File, Save**

The other object snaps are described next. Try them on your own until you are familiar with how they work.

Snap to Apparent Intersection

The Apparent Intersection object snap finds two different types of intersections that the regular Intersection object snap wouldn't find. One type is the point at which two objects would intersect if they were extended. The other type is the point at which two 3D lines appear to intersect on the screen, when they do not in fact intersect in space. The command-line equivalents for Snap to Apparent Intersection are APPINT and APP.

Snap to Nearest

The Nearest object snap attaches to the point on an arc, circle, or line closest to the middle of the target area of your cursor. It will also find point objects that are within the target area.

A line drawn with the Nearest function may look like a line that could have been drawn simply using the Line command, but there is a difference. Many AutoCAD operations, such as hatching, require an enclosed area: All lines that define the area must intersect (touch). When you draw lines by picking two points on the screen, sometimes the lines don't actually touch. They appear to touch on the screen, but when you zoom in on them sufficiently, you will see that they don't touch. They may only be a hundredth of an inch apart, but they don't touch. When creating an AutoCAD drawing, you should always strive to create the drawing geometry accurately. The Nearest function ensures that the nearest object is selected. The command-line equivalent is NEA.

Snap to Node

The Node object snap finds the exact location of a point object in your drawing. You used it in Tutorial 2 to locate exact points that

Tip

The Locate Point (ID) command that you learned in Tutorial 3 lists the coordinates of a selected point. To find the exact insertion point of text or a block, pick Locate Point and then use the Insertion object snap and pick on the text or block. Similarly, you can find the coordinates of an endpoint or intersection by combining those object snaps with the Locate Point command.

Tip

You can turn on more than one object snap at the same time. For instance, you could select both Intersection and Nearest from the Drafting Settings dialog box. AutoSnap will show different marker boxes for each snap setting chosen.

Warning

When you have finished experimenting, return to the Drafting Settings dialog box and turn off any object snaps you may have left on.

had already been placed in the drawing with the Point command. The command-line equivalent is NOD.

Snap to Insertion

The Insertion object snap finds the insertion point of text or of a block. (You will learn about blocks in Tutorial 10.) This method is useful when you want to determine the exact point at which existing text or blocks are located in your drawing. The command-line equivalent is INS.

Snap From

The From object snap is a special object snap tool. It establishes a temporary reference point from which you can specify the point to be selected. Usually it is used in combination with other object snap tools. For example, you would use it if you were going to draw a new line that you want to start a certain distance from an existing intersection. To do so, pick the Line command; when prompted for the starting point of your line, pick the Snap From icon. You will then be prompted for a base point. It is the location of the reference point from which you want to locate your next input. At the base point prompt, pick Snap to Intersection. You will be prompted to select the intersection of two lines. Pick on the intersection. As the result of your having picked Snap From, you will see the additional prompt of <Offset>. At this prompt, use relative coordinates to enter the distance you want the next point to be from the base point you selected.

Snap to Extension

The Extension object snap also establishes a temporary reference. It displays a temporary extension line when you move the cursor over an object's endpoint, so that you can draw to an extension of the same line.

Object Tracking

Object Tracking is a unique snap tool allowing you to start a line with reference to other locations. For instance, if you have drawn a rectangle and want to draw a line from the middle of the rectangle, there is no snap for that point. With Tracking, you can start the line with reference to as many points as you select. Tracking will be covered in Tutorial 6.

Using Extend

The Extend command extends the lengths of existing lines and arcs to end at a selected boundary edge. Its function is the opposite of Trim's. Like Trim, Extend has two parts: First you select the object to act as the boundary, then you select the objects you want to extend. Extend is on the Modify toolbar.

Similar to the Trim command, the command-line options for the Extend command are Project, Edge, and Undo. The default option is just to select the objects to be extended. You can use the Edge option to extend objects to the point at which they would meet the boundary edge if it were longer. This method is useful when the boundary edge is short and the lines to be extended would not intersect it. The Project option allows you to specify the plane of projection to be used for extending. This option is useful when you're working in 3D drawings because it allows you to extend objects to a boundary selected from the current viewing direction or User Coordinate System. Often 3D objects may not actually intersect the boundary edge but just appear to do so in the view. You can use the Project option to extend them as they appear in the view. The Undo option lets you undo the last object extended, while remaining in the Extend command.

On your own, change your **Snap** setting to **0.25** before continuing.

Erase the lines labeled 1, 2, and 3 in Figure 4.36.

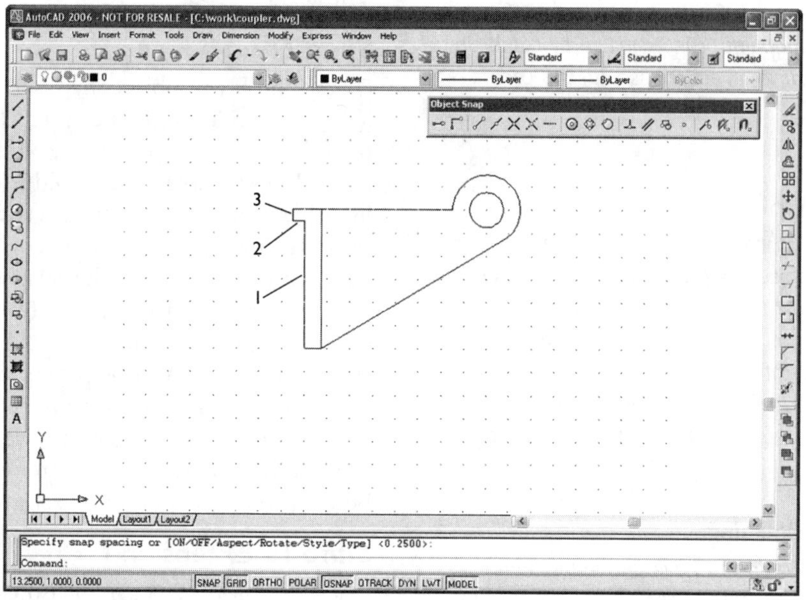

Figure 4.36

Draw a new line **0.5** units (two snap increments) from the previous left-most line as shown in Figure 4.37 (labeled Boundary edge).

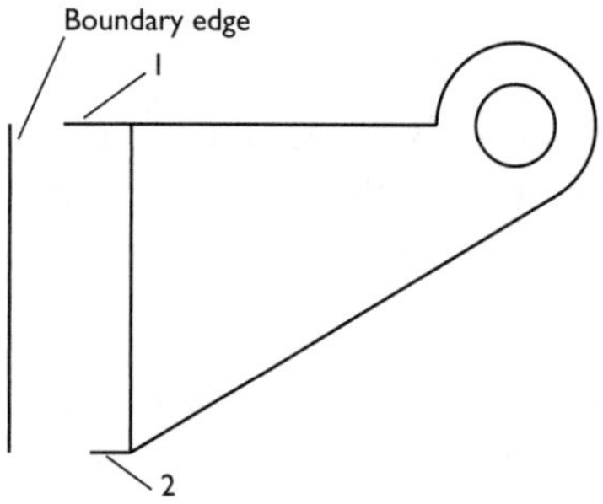

Figure 4.37

When you have completed this step, your drawing should be similar to Figure 4.37.

Now you will use the Extend command to extend the existing lines to meet the new boundary. Refer to Figure 4.37.

Pick: **Extend icon**

Current settings: Projection=UCS Edge=None
Select boundary edges ...
Select objects or <select all>: **select boundary edge**
Select objects: ↵

You have finished selecting boundary edges. To extend the horizontal lines, select them by picking points on them near the end closer to the boundary edge. (If the points are picked closer to the other end, you will get the message "No edge in that direction," and the lines won't be extended.)

Select object to extend or shift-select to trim or
[Fence/Crossing/Project/Edge/Undo]: **select lines 1 and 2**
Select object to extend or shift-select to trim or
[Fence/Crossing/Project/Edge/Undo]: ↵

The screen will look like Figure 4.38 once the lines have been extended.

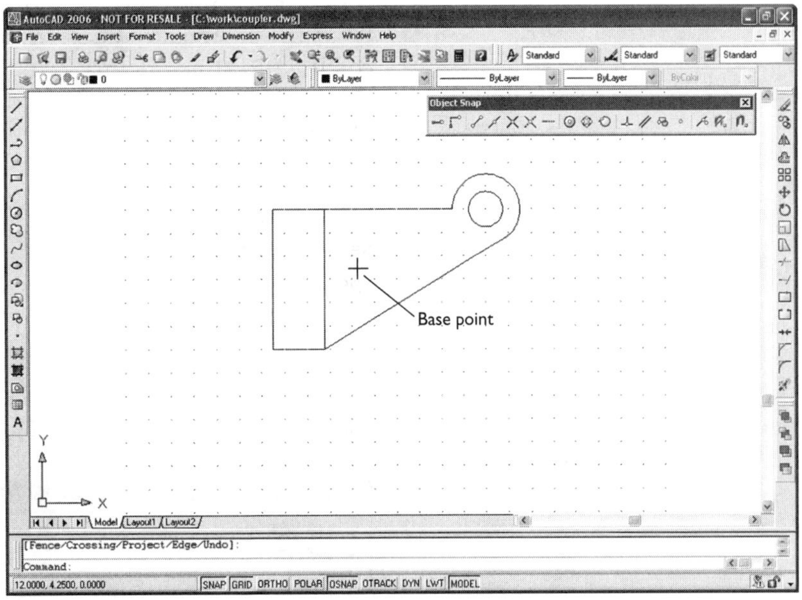

Figure 4.38

Using Rotate

The Rotate command allows you to rotate a drawing object or group of objects to a new orientation in the drawing. Rotate is on the Modify toolbar. In this section, you will use Rotate to rotate objects in your drawing.

Pick: **Rotate icon**
Current positive angle in UCS: ANGDIR=counterclockwise ANGBASE=0
Select objects: **select the entire coupler using a Crossing window**
7 found
Select objects: ↵

You are prompted for the base point. You will select the middle of the object as the base point, as shown in Figure 4.38.

Specify base point: **pick in the middle of the coupler**
Specify rotation angle or [Copy/Reference]: **45** ↵

Your coupler should be rotated 45 degrees, as shown in Figure 4.39. Positive angles are measured counterclockwise. A horizontal line to the right of the base point is defined as 0 degrees. You can also enter negative values.

Next you will restore the object to its original position before you continue.

Pick: **Undo icon**

The coupler should return to its original rotation.

Tip

The base point need not be part of the object chosen for rotation. You can use any point on the screen; the object rotates about the point you select. You may often find it useful to select a base point in the center of the object you want to rotate. As the object rotates, it stays in relatively the same position on the screen.

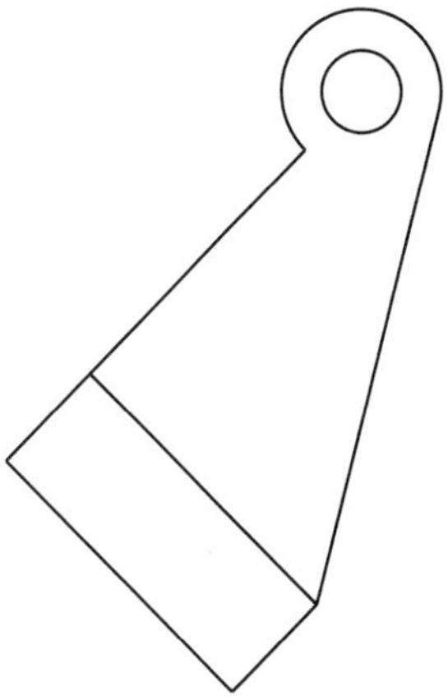

Figure 4.39

Using Move

The Move command moves existing objects from one location on the coordinate system in the drawing to another location. Do not confuse the Move command and the Pan command. Pan moves your view and leaves the objects where they were. Move actually moves the objects on the coordinate system. Move is on the Modify toolbar.

Pick: **Move icon**

Select objects: **use Crossing or Window to select the entire coupler**

Select objects: ↵

Specify base point or [Displacement] <Displacement>: **pick the Snap to Endpoint icon**

Endpoint of: **select the upper left corner of the coupler**

The cursor switches to drag mode so that you can see the object move about the screen, as shown in Figure 4.40.

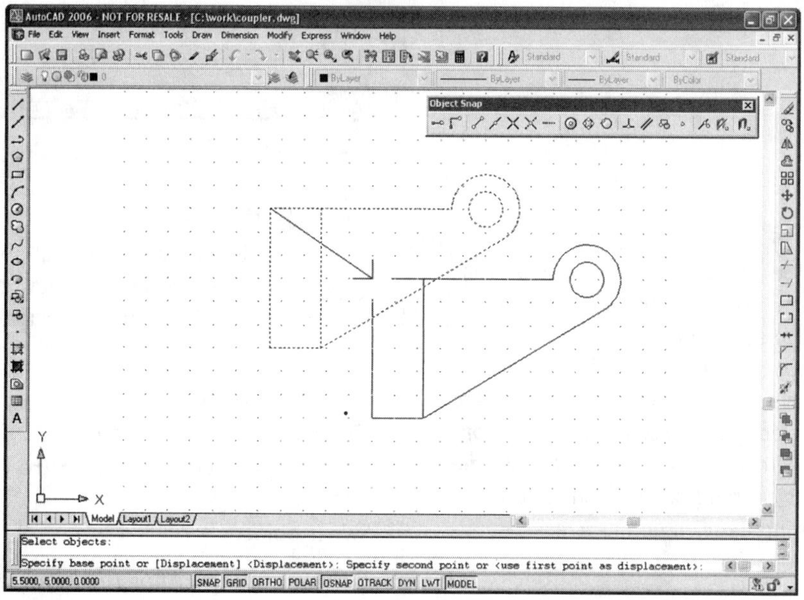

Figure 4.40

Specify second point or <use first point as displacement>: **select a point so the coupler is to the lower right of its old location**

Methods of Selecting Objects

One AutoCAD advantage is the many ways that you can select graphical objects for use with a command. You have already learned how to use Window and Crossing. You can save lots of time when creating and editing drawings by the clever use of the selection methods. Generally, whenever you are asked to select objects, you can continue selecting until you have all the objects that you want highlighted in one selection set. You can combine the various selection modes to select the objects you want. The command then operates on the selection set you have built.

At any Select objects: prompt, you can type the option letters for the method you want to use. You may continue selecting, using any of the methods in the following table, until you indicate that you have finished building the selection set by pressing ↵ or the return button. Then the command will take effect on the objects that you have selected.

Name	Option Letter(s)	Method
Picking	none	Selects objects by positioning cursor and pressing pick button
Select Window	W	Specifies diagonal corners of a box that only selects objects that are entirely enclosed
Select Window Crossing	C	Specifies diagonal corners of a box that selects all objects that cross or are enclosed in the box
Select Group	G	Selects all objects within a named group, prompts to enter group name
Select Previous	P	Reselects the previous selection set
Select Last	L	Selects the last object created
Select All	ALL	Selects all the objects in your drawing unless they are on a frozen layer
Select Window Polygon	WP	Similar to Window except you draw an irregular polygon instead of a box around the items to select
Select Crossing Polygon	CP	Similar to Window Polygon except that all objects that cross or are enclosed in the polygon are selected
Select Fence	F	Similar to Crossing except that you draw line segments through all the objects you want to select
Select Add	A	Use after Remove to add more objects to the selection set. Can continue with any of the other selection modes once Add has been chosen
Select Remove	R	Selects objects to remove from the current selection set; removal continues until Add or ↵ is used; you can use Window, Crossing, etc., while selecting items to remove
Undo	U	During object selection, deselects the last item or group of items you selected
Control	Ctrl	After you pick as close to the object as you can using the pick button, press Ctrl to cycle through objects that are close together or directly on top of one another. Continue to press Ctrl until the object you want is selected.

Additional methods of selecting are Auto, Box, Single, and Multiple. Consult AutoCAD Help for the Select command for definitions of their use.

Using Selection Filters

Selection filters are a special method of selecting objects. You can use them to select types of objects, such as all the arcs in the drawing or objects that you created by setting the color or linetype independently of the layer that they are on.

Command: **FILTER** ↵

The Object Selection Filters dialog box shown in Figure 4.41 appears on your screen. You can use this dialog box to filter the types of objects to select. You can save named filter groups for reuse.

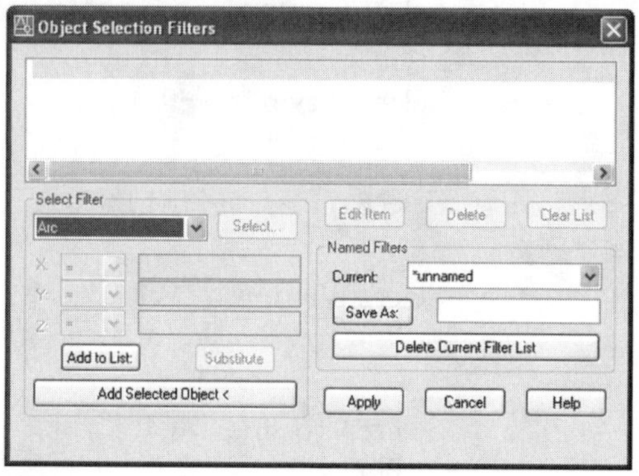

Figure 4.41

Pick: **Arc** (below the heading Select Filter)

The list of drawing object types pops up. You can use these drawing object types to filter the objects in your selection.

Pick: **Arc** (so that it is highlighted)
Pick: **Add to List**
Pick: **Apply**

You return to the command prompt to select the objects in your drawing. Note the message,

Applying filter to selection.
Select objects: **use Crossing to select all of the objects**

You should see the message "Applying filter to selection. 1 found." Only the arc object matched the filter list. The lines of the drawing were filtered out.

Select objects: Esc (to cancel)
Command: ↵ (to restart the FILTER command)

You should see the Object Selection Filters dialog box on your screen.

Pick: **Clear List**
Pick: **Windows Close button** (to close the dialog box)

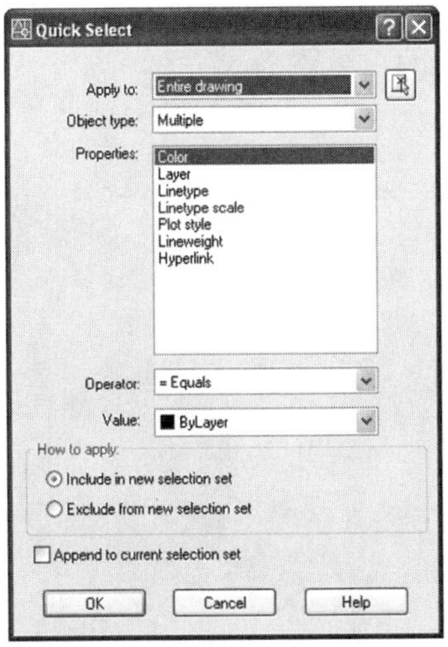

Figure 4.42

Tip

The Quick Select icon appears at the top of the Properties palette to provide quick selection functions when changing properties.

Using Quick Select

Quick Select (Qselect) allows you to create a selection set including or excluding matching objects and properties. You can apply Quick Select to your entire drawing or just to a previously created selection set. You can also append the Quick Select objects to the current selection set or replace the current selection. Quick Select is found on the Tools menu or you can pick it from the Properties palette. You can also right-click in the drawing window and pick Quick Select from the menu that pops up.

Next you will select all of the drawing so that the grips appear and all of the drawing objects become highlighted. Then you will remove the top arc from the selection set using Quick Select.

Pick: **Tools, Quick Select**

You should see the Quick Select dialog box as shown in Figure 4.42. The dialog box should display Entire drawing in the Apply to area. You will select Arc as the Object type to be selected.

Pick: **Arc** (from the pull-down list to the right of Object type)

The Properties area now displays properties of the arc which you could select for further filtering. In the How to apply area you can choose "Include in new selection set" which creates a new selection set of only objects that match the filtering criteria. Selecting "Exclude from new selection set" creates a new selection set composed only of objects that do not match the filtering criteria. In the How to apply area,

Pick: **Exclude from new selection set**

Make sure that Append to current selection set is not selected.

Pick: **OK** (to exit the dialog box)

All of the objects, with the exception of the top arc, should now be selected. Next you will use the color control to set the color for the selected objects to red.

Pick: **Red** (from the Color Control on the Properties toolbar)
Press: Esc

All but the arc should now appear in red on your screen.

Closing the Coupler Drawing

On your own, **close** the coupler drawing. **Discard** the changes to *coupler.dwg.*

Creating the Geneva Cam

You will create the geneva cam shown in Figure 4.43, using many of the editing commands you have learned in this tutorial. You will learn to use the Array command to create rectangular and radial patterns.

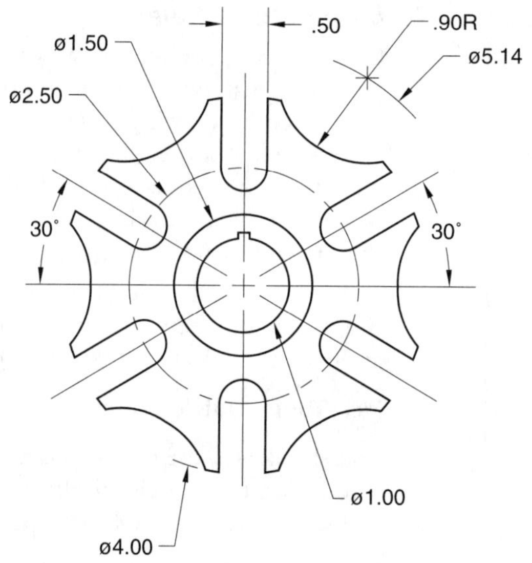

Figure 4.43

Tip

If you use Offset, remember to calculate the offset distance based on the diameters given. You will need to subtract the diameter of the inner circle from the diameter of the outer circle and then divide the result by 2 to find the value to use for the offset distance.

Start a new drawing from the ***acad.dwt*** template.
Save the drawing to your **c:\work** directory with the name ***geneva.dwg***.
Set the **Snap** to **0.25**.
Check the status bar to be sure that **Snap** and **Grid** are turned on.
Use **Zoom All** if needed so that the grid area fills the graphics window.

Next you will use the Circle command to create the innermost circle of diameter 1.00. Locate the center of the circle at (5.5, 4.5).

Pick: **Circle icon**
3P/2P/TTR/<Center point>: **5.5,4.5** ↵
Diameter/<Radius>: **D** ↵
Diameter: **1** ↵
Use Offset or the Circle command to draw a **1.5-diameter** circle and a **4-diameter** circle **concentric** to the circle you just drew.

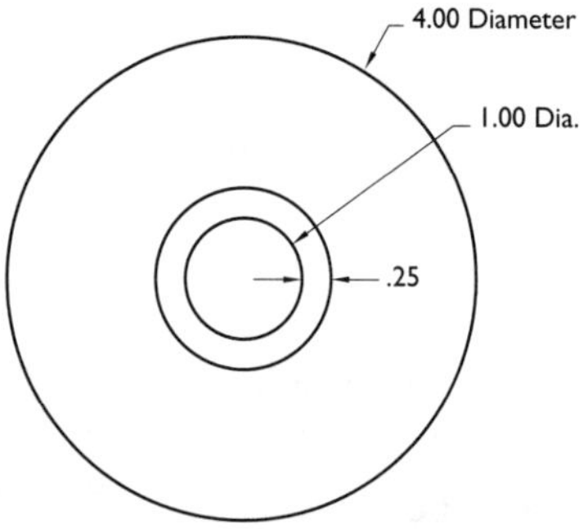

Figure 4.44

Your drawing should look like Figure 4.44.

Use Line to draw vertical and horizontal lines through the center of the circles.

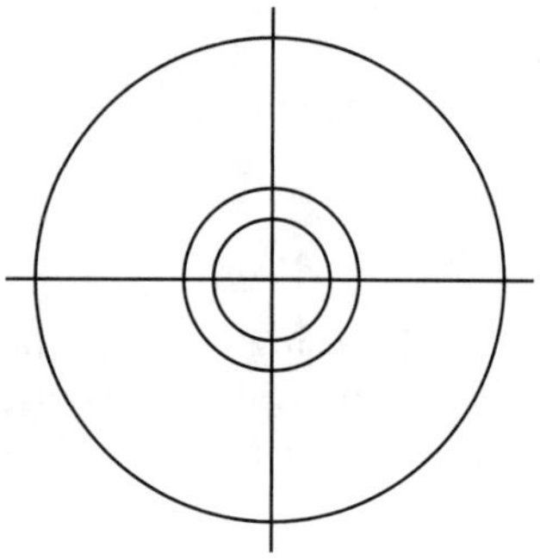

Figure 4.45

Your drawing should look like Figure 4.45.

Next you will use the Offset command to create lines parallel to the vertical centerline.

Pick: **Offset icon**
Specify offset distance or [Through/Erase/Layer] <2.50000>: **.25** ↵
Select object to offset or [Exit/Undo] <Exit>: **pick the vertical centerline**
Specify point on side to offset or [Exit/Multiple/Undo] <Exit>: **pick on the right side of the line**
Select object to offset or [Exit/Undo] <Exit>: **pick the same vertical centerline**
Specify point on side to offset or [Exit/Multiple/Undo] <Exit>: **pick on the left side of the line**
Select object to offset or [Exit/Undo] <Exit>: ↵

Next you will use the Construction Line command to draw a line angled at 60 degrees and infinitely long, as shown in Figure 4.46.

Using Construction Line

The Construction Line (XLine) and Ray commands create lines that extend infinitely and are very useful in creating construction geometry. Construction Line, on the Draw toolbar, creates a line (through a point that you select) that extends infinitely in both directions from the first point selected. The Ray command, on the Draw menu, draws a line which extends infinitely in only one direction.

Using the XLINE command, you can select options at the command prompt to draw a horizontal or vertical line, to bisect an angle that you specify, or to offset the construction line by a distance from the object you specify. You will use the Angle option from the command prompt to specify an angle of 60 degrees and a point for the line to pass through.

Pick: **Construction Line icon**

Specify a point or [Hor/Ver/Ang/Bisect/Offset]: **A** ↵

Enter angle of xline (0) or [Reference]: **60** ↵

Specify through point: **5.5,4.5** (or pick the center point of the circles, using Snap)

Specify through point: ↵

Use Zoom Window to enlarge your view as needed.

The construction line appears in your drawing, as shown in Figure 4.46.

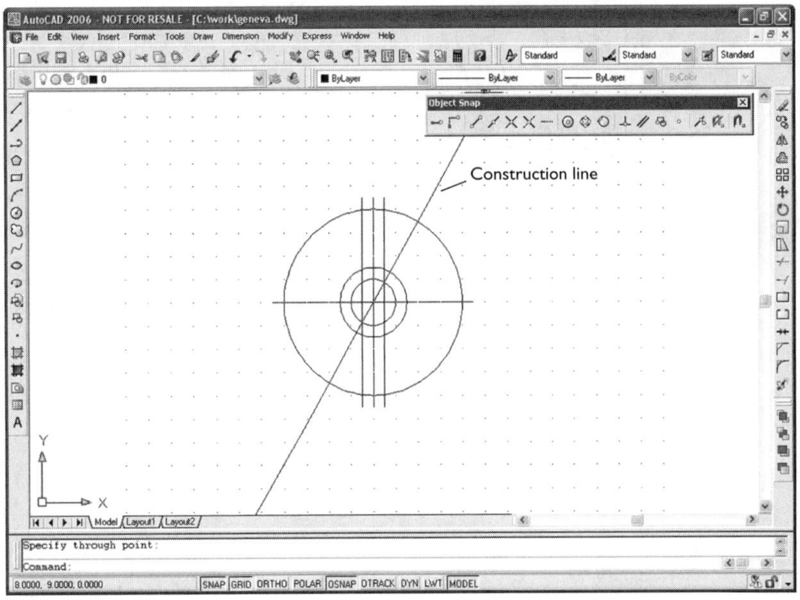

Figure 4.46

The line will extend as far as you pan your view in both directions of extension. If you trim a construction line at one end, it becomes a ray, extending infinitely in only one direction. If you trim it at both ends, it becomes a line.

Use Trim with the horizontal centerline as your cutting edge so that the construction line only extends upward from the center point.

Next you will use the Circle command to add the construction circles to your drawing.

On your own, make sure that the **running OSNAP** is **on** with **Center** and **Intersection** selected.

Pick: **Circle icon**

Specify center point for circle or [3P/2P/Ttr (tan tan radius)]: **select the center of the circles using the AutoSnap Center marker**

Specify radius of circle or [Diameter] <2.0000>: **2.57** ↵

Command: ↵ (or press the return button)

Specify center point for circle or [3P/2P/Ttr (tan tan radius)]: **select the center of the circles using the AutoSnap Center marker to pick the same center point as before**

Specify radius of circle or [Diameter] <2.5700>: **1.25** ↵

Command: ↵

Specify center point for circle or [3P/2P/Ttr (tan tan radius)]: **use AutoSnap Intersection to pick the point where the vertical centerline crosses the 1.25-radius construction circle (point A in Figure 4.51)**

Specify radius of circle or [Diameter] <1.2500>: **.25** ↵

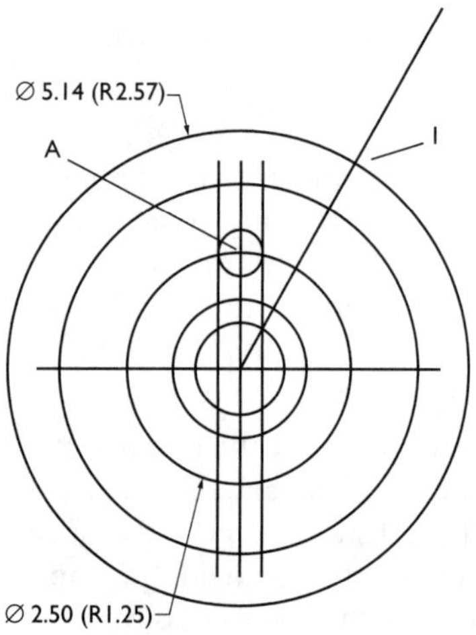

Figure 4.47

The small circle is added to your drawing between the two lines you offset. Your drawing should look like that in Figure 4.47.

Draw the final construction circle by specifying its center where the 60-degree ray and the outer circle intersect.

Command: ↵

Specify center point for circle or [3P/2P/Ttr (tan tan radius)]: **pick point I in Figure 4.47, using the AutoSnap Intersection marker**

Specify radius of circle or [Diameter]<.2500>: **.90** ↵

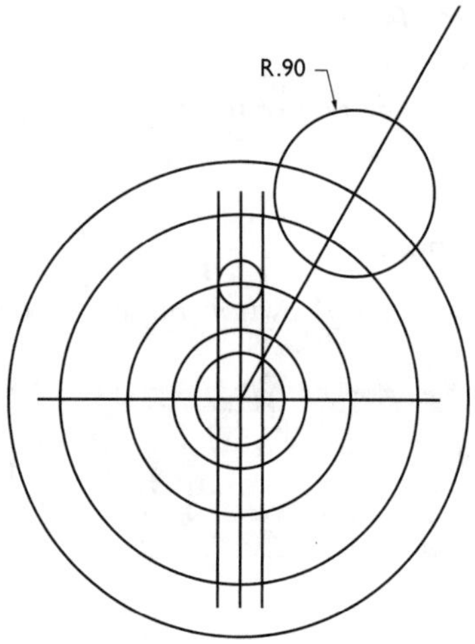

Figure 4.48

Your drawing should now look like that in Figure 4.48.

The next step is to remove the portions of the lines and circles that you won't need in the Array command.

Use Trim and Erase commands to remove the unwanted portions of the figure until your drawing looks like the one in Figure 4.49.

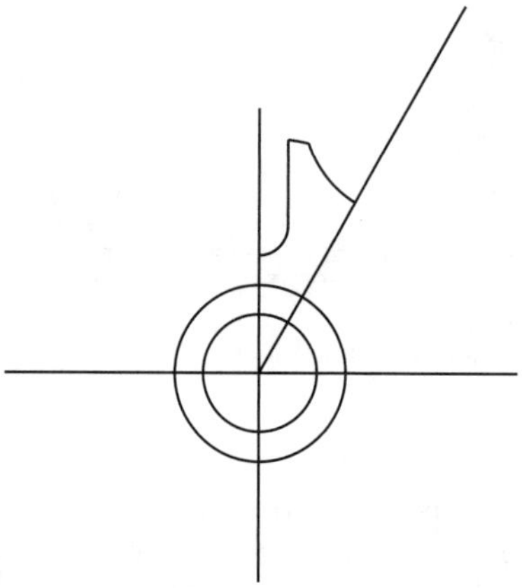

Figure 4.49

Tip

Try using Crossing to select several objects to trim at one time. Use the Erase option of the Trim command to remove any objects that no longer cross a cutting edge.

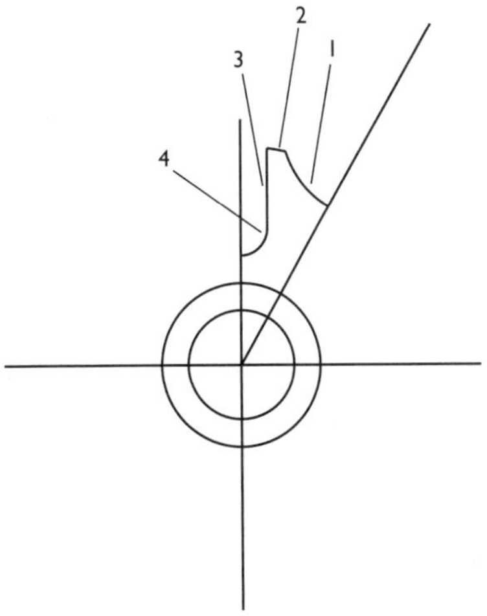

Figure 4.50

Tip

If you have a three button mouse, the override object snaps are available with the middle button. A pop-up menu appears on screen with the object snap settings as well as Running OSNAP.

Using Mirror

The Mirror command makes a mirror-image copy of the objects you select around a ***mirror line*** that you specify. Mirror is on the Modify toolbar. Its icon is the mirror image of a shape. The Mirror command also allows you to delete the old objects or to keep them.

To mirror an object, you must specify a mirror line, which can be horizontal, vertical, or slanted. A mirror line defines both the angle and the distance at which the mirror image is to be drawn. The mirrored image is drawn perpendicular to the mirror line. The mirrored object is the same distance from the mirror line as the original object is, but it's on the other side of the mirror line. The mirror line does not have to exist in your drawing; when asked to specify the mirror line, you can pick two points from the screen to define it.

The vertical centerline will serve as the mirror line as you mirror the lines and arcs of the geneva cam. Refer to Figure 4.50 as you pick points. Be sure that Snap is turned on or use object snaps before picking the mirror line.

Pick: **Mirror icon**
Select objects: **pick objects 1, 2, 3, and 4**
Select objects: ↵
Specify first point of mirror line: **select the exact center of the concentric circles**

Your cursor is now dragging a mirrored copy of the objects.

Specify second point of mirror line: **select a point straight below the center point**
Erase source objects? [Yes/No] <N> ↵

Your screen should look like Figure 4.51.

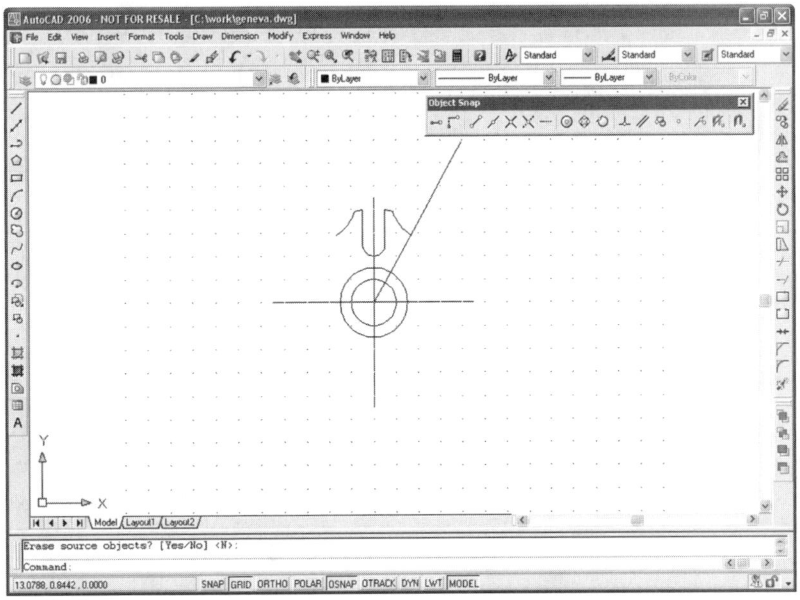

Figure 4.51

Tip

If you select objects that you do not want to mirror, you can use the Remove option to remove them from the selection set. To do so, type R ↵ or pick Remove from the Select Objects flyout on the Standard toolbar while still at the Select objects: prompt. Pick the object to be removed from the selection. If you want to add more objects after using Remove, pick Add or type A ↵ while still at the Select objects prompt. Press ↵ when you have selected the objects you want.

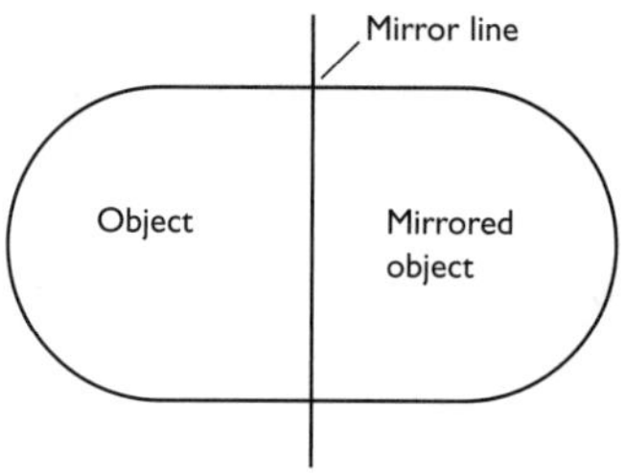

Figure 4.52

Tip

Figure 4.52 shows an object mirrored about one of its own edge lines. If you want, you can add mirror lines to the drawing and then erase them after completing the construction; or you can pick any two points from the screen that would define the line you want to specify.

Using Array

The Array command copies an object multiple times to form a regularly spaced rectangular or circular pattern. Anytime that you need to create a regularly spaced pattern of objects in your drawing, you can use the Array command to do so quickly. Examples are: creating a circular pattern of holes in a circular hub, creating rows of desks in laying out a classroom, or creating the teeth on a gear. The Array command is on the Modify toolbar.

Pick: **Array icon**

The Array dialog box appears on your screen as shown in Figure 4.53.

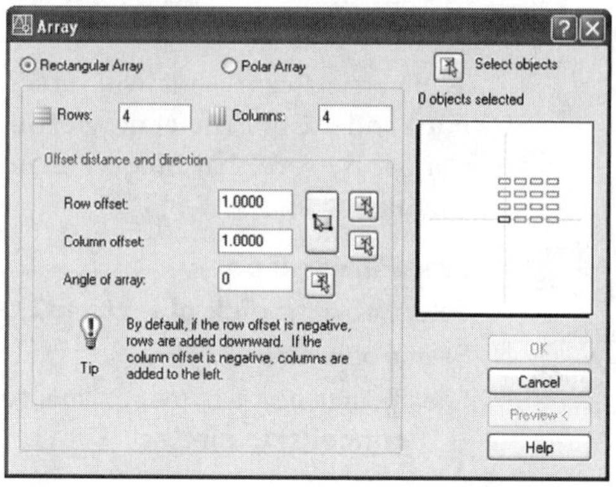

Figure 4.53

In the Array dialog box you can specify either a rectangular or polar array. A *rectangular array* is composed of a specified number of rows and columns of the items with a specified distance between them. In a *polar array*, the items are copied in a circular pattern around a center point that you specify.

Pick: **Polar Array button**

The dialog box changes to show the options for creating a polar array. It is shown in Figure 4.54.

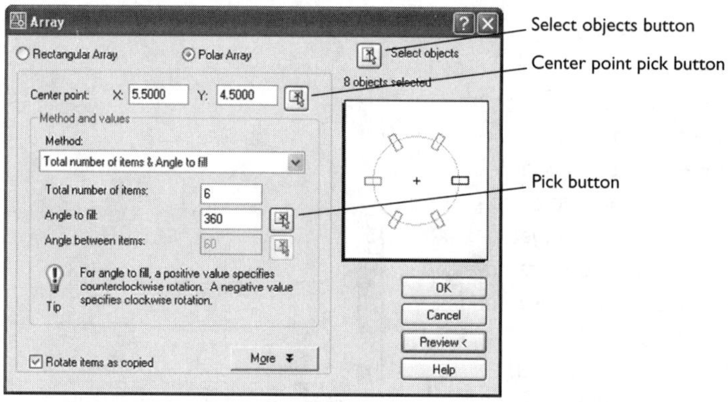

Figure 4.54

You can use the Method area to select from three methods of specifying the array: the Total number of items & Angle to fill, the Total number of items & Angle between items, or the Angle to fill & Angle between

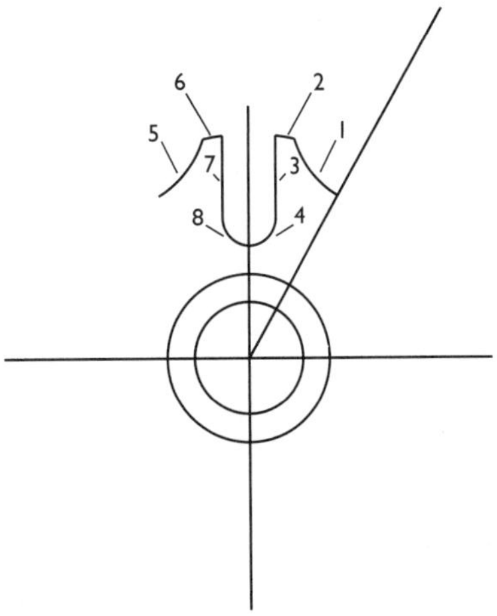

Figure 4.55

Tip

If you did not select the correct objects and your drawing does not look like Figure 4.60, you can restart the Array command and use the Select Objects pick button again to reselect. The other settings in the dialog box should remain the same until changed. You can also use the Preview option to see what the results will look like and then accept or change as needed.

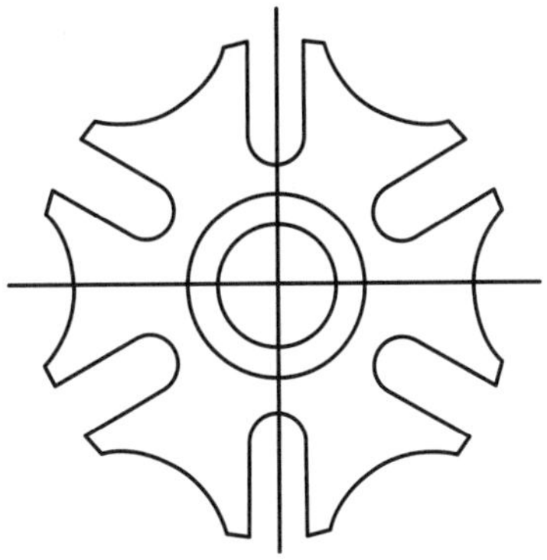

Figure 4.56

items. You will use the Total number of items & Angle to fill. The copies can fill 360 degrees of the circle or some portion of 360 degrees. You can use the check box near the bottom left of the dialog box to choose to rotate the items as they are copied with the Array command so that they have the proper orientation. The More/Less button expands/collapses the dialog box to show options for setting the rotation base point for the objects. You can find more information about changing the rotation base point in the on-line help.

You are now ready to use the Array command to copy the lines and arcs in a radial pattern to finish creating the geneva cam. Refer to Figure 4.55 for the items to select. Enter the information in the dialog box as listed below.

Total number of items: **6** ↵
Angle to fill: **360**
Rotate items as copied: **should be checked**
Pick: **Center point pick button from dialog box** (labeled in Figure 4.54)

You are returned to your drawing to select the center point.

Specify center point of array: **pick the center of the concentric circles**

You automatically return to the dialog box.

Pick: **Select objects pick button** (near the upper right of the dialog box)

You are returned to your drawing to select the objects.

Select objects: **pick the items 1–4 that you mirrored and the mirrored copies of them (5–8)**
Select objects: ↵

You return again to the dialog box.

Pick: **OK**
On your own, use **Erase** to erase the angled ray from the drawing.

Your drawing should look like that in Figure 4.56.

Your drawing is now complete; **save** it on your own.

Making Changes with Hot Grips

A quick way to make changes to your drawing is by using *hot grips*. Hot grips let you grab an object already drawn on your screen and use certain editing commands directly from the mouse or pointing device without having to select the commands from the menu or keyboard. To use the hot grips you must have a two- or three-button mouse. You will verify that hot grips are enabled.

Pick: **Tools, Options**

The Options dialog box appears on your screen. Pick on the **Selection tab** so that it becomes the uppermost tab in the dialog box, as shown in Figure 4.57. You should select the box to the left of Enable Grips at this time if it is not already selected.

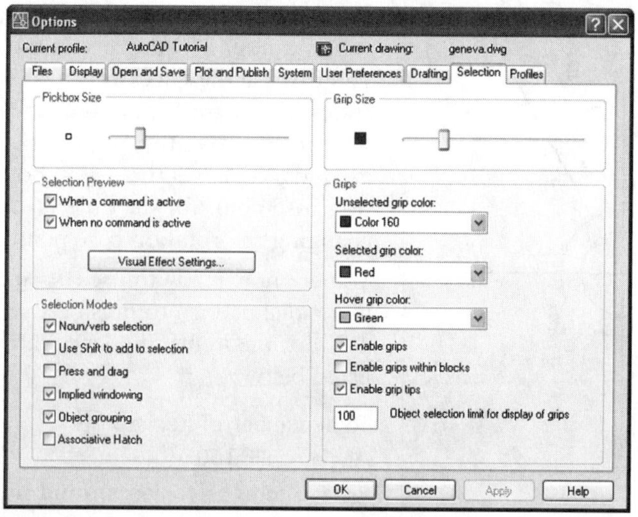

Figure 4.57

You can turn grips on or off in your drawing and change their color and size. To do so on your own, move the slider box near the top of the dialog box under Grip Size. When you have finished, restore it to its original size. You can also change the color of the grips and turn grips off completely if you do not want to use them.

To exit the Options dialog box,

Pick: **OK**

You return to the drawing editor.

Activating an Object's Grips

Move the crosshairs over the upper vertical centerline of the geneva cam and press the pick button to select the line. The line becomes dashed and small boxes appear at the endpoints, as shown in Figure 4.58.

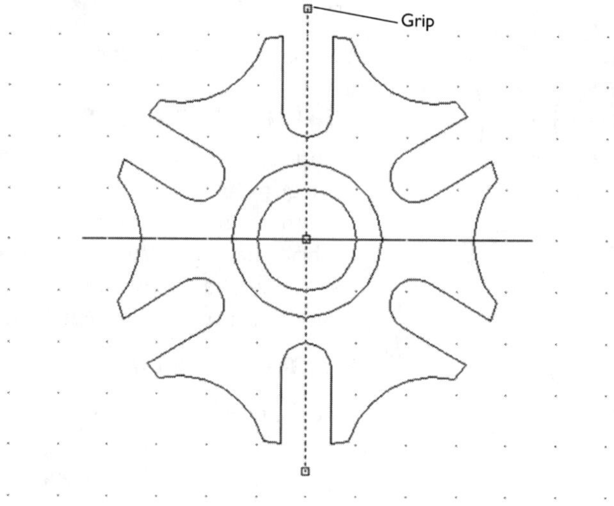

Figure 4.58

These boxes are called the hot grips. You can use them to stretch, move, rotate, scale, and mirror the object.

Selecting the Base Grip

Move the crosshairs to the grip at the upper end of the line and press the pick button to select it.

The selected grip changes to a filled solid in the highlighting color. This *base grip* will act as the base point for the command you will select by pressing the buttons on your pointing device.

Using Stretch with Hot Grips

In the command line area, you should see the prompt for the Stretch command.

STRETCH

Specify stretch point or [Base point/Copy/Undo/eXit]: **move the crosshairs to a point above and to the right of the old location of the endpoint and press the pick button**

The upper end of the line, where you picked the base grip, rubberbands from the position of the crosshairs. The point you selected should move to the new stretched location.

Tip

If you want to cancel using the hot grips, press [Esc] twice.

Using Move with Hot Grips

On your own make a crossing box that crosses the entire geneva cam.

The hot grips appear as small boxes on all the selected objects.

Select the center of the circles as the base grip by moving the crosshairs over the box and picking.

The base grip becomes highlighted. You will see the prompt for the Stretch command in the command line area.

Right-click: **(to activate the Hot Grips menu)**

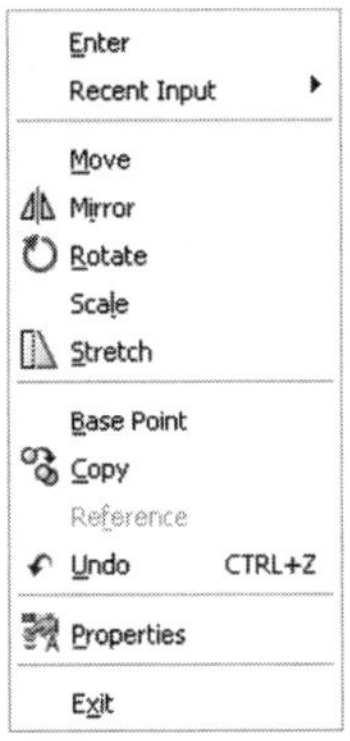

Figure 4.59

A pop-up Hot Grips menu similar to Figure 4.59 will appear. You will use the menu to

Pick: **Move**

The command prompt shows the following options for the Move command. You will move the geneva cam down and to the left. You will notice the shapes of the objects attached to the crosshairs during the move.

MOVE

Specify move point or [Base point/Copy/Undo/eXit]: **pick a new location for the center grip down and to the left of the previous location**

Using Move with the Copy Option

The hot grips should still be visible.

Tip

You can also press ↵ to cycle through the command choices that are available for use with hot grips.

Pick: **to highlight the grip at the center of the circles as the base grip**

Right-click: **(to activate the Hot Grips menu)**

Pick: **Move**

Specify move point or [Base point/Copy/Undo/eXit]: **C** ↵

A new prompt, similar to the previous one, appears.

MOVE (multiple)

Specify move point or [Base point/Copy/Undo/eXit]:

On your own, move the crosshairs to a location where you would like to make a copy of the object and press the pick button; repeat this procedure to make several copies.

When you are finished, press ⏎ or the return button and pick Exit to end the command.

If you were to choose Copy from the menu instead of Move, only the object that shares the Hot Grips box that you selected would be copied. To see how this alternative works, perform the same task on your own but select Copy from the menu without selecting Move first.

Use the Erase command to erase some of the copies if your screen is too crowded.

Using Rotate with Hot Grips

Now you will use implied Windowing to activate the hot grips for these lines.

Pick: **above and to the left of one of the copies of the geneva cam**

A window box will form as you move the crosshairs away from the point that you selected. Move downward and to the right to enclose all the lines in the drawing in the forming window. When you have the window sized correctly,

Pick: **a point below and to the right of the geneva cam**

The hot grips will appear on the objects in the drawing.

Select the grip at the center of the circles as the base grip by positioning the crosshairs over it and pressing the pick button.

You will see the base grip change color. The Stretch command appears at the command prompt.

Right-click: **(for the Hot Grips menu)**
Pick: **Rotate**

If Snap is turned on, turn it off so that you can see the effect of the rotation command clearly.

You will see the prompt

ROTATE

You will see the faint object rotating as you move the crosshairs around on the screen. You can press the pick button when the object is at the desired rotation or type in a numeric value for the rotation. Keep in mind that 0-degrees is to the right and positive values are measured counterclockwise.

Specify rotation angle or [Base point/Copy/Undo/Reference/eXit]: **45** ⏎

Note that the object rotated so that it is at an angle of 45°.

Using Scale with Hot Grips

The Scale command changes the size of the object in your drawing database. Be sure that you use Scale only when you want to make the actual object larger. Use Zoom Window when you just want it to appear larger on the screen in order to see more detail.

Activate the hot grips, using implied Crossing. To use Crossing, start your window box in the lower right of the drawing and select the first point. Move the crosshairs with the window up and to the left and press the pick button. A Crossing box selects anything that crosses the box or is enclosed. When you have done this successfully, the hot grips will appear at the corners and midpoints of the lines.

Pick: **the grip at the center of the circles as the base grip**

The grip becomes filled with the highlighting color. You will see the Stretch command in the command prompt area.

Right-click: **(to pop up the menu)**
Pick: **Scale**

You will see the prompt

SCALE
Specify scale factor or [Base point/Copy/Undo/Reference/eXit]:

Tip

To change the scale to known proportions, you can type in a scale factor. A value of 2 makes the object twice as large; a value of 0.5 makes it half its present size.

As you move the crosshairs away from the base point, the faint image of the object becomes larger; as you get closer to the base point, it appears smaller. When you are happy with the new size of the object,

Press: **the pick button**

Using Mirror with Hot Grips

On your own, activate the **hot grips** with implied Windowing again.
Select the **center grip** as the base grip.
Right-click: to pop-up the menu and select **Mirror**

The Mirror command uses a mirror line and forms a symmetrical image of the selected objects on the other side of the line. You can think of this line as rubberbanding from the base hot grip to the current location of the crosshairs. Note that, as you move the crosshairs to different positions on the screen, the faint mirror image of the object appears on the other side of the mirror line. You will see the prompt

MIRROR
Specify second point or [Base point/Copy/Undo/eXit]: **B** ↵

The Base point option lets you specify some other point besides the hot grip that you picked as the first point of the mirror line for the object.

Specify base point: **pick a point to the left of the geneva shape**

Move the crosshairs on the screen and note the object being mirrored around the line that would form between the base point and the location of the crosshairs. When you are happy with the location of the mirrored object, press the pick button to select it. The old object disappears from the screen and the new mirrored object remains. End the command by pressing ↵ or the return button.

Noun/Verb Selection

You can also use hot grips with other commands for noun/verb selection. *Noun/verb selection* is a method of selecting the objects that will be affected by a command first, instead of first selecting the command and then the group of objects. Think of the drawing objects as nouns, or things, and the commands as verbs, or actions. You will use this method with the Erase command to clear your screen.

Pick: **a point below and to the right of all your drawing objects**
Other corner: **pick a point above and to the left of the drawing objects**

You will see the hot grips for the objects that were crossed by the implied Crossing box appear in your drawing.

Pick: **Erase icon**

Note that you do not have to select the items. They were preselected with the hot grips, and as soon as you picked the Erase icon, the items that you had selected were erased.

You have completed Tutorial 4. Exit without saving your changes so that your finished geneva cam remains saved.

Pick: **File, Exit**

Key Terms

base grip	hot grips	noun/verb selection	quadrant point
circumscribed	inscribed	polar array	rectangular array
distance across the flats	mirror line	polygon	selection filters
global linetype scaling factor			

Key Commands

Array	Linetype	Scale	Snap to Intersection
Break	LTScale	Snap From	Snap to Nearest
CELTScale	Mirror	Snap to Apparent Intersection	Snap to Node
Construction Line (XLine)	Move	Snap to Center	Snap to Parallel
Copy Object	Polygon	Snap to Endpoint	Snap to Perpendicular
Extend	Quick Select	Snap to Extension	Snap to Quadrant
FileDIA	Ray	Snap to Insertion	Snap to Tangent
Grips	Rotate		Stretch

Exercises

The letter M after an exercise number means that the given dimensions are in millimeters (metric units). If no letter follows the exercise number, the dimensions are in inches. Don't include dimensions on the drawings.

4.1M Gasket

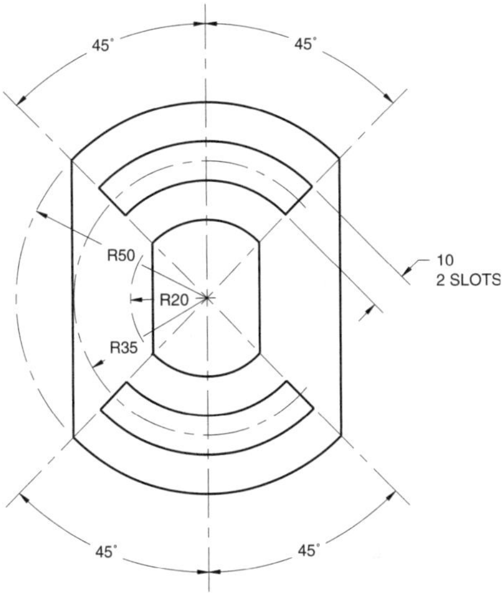

4.2 The Cycle

Starting with the parallelogram shown, use Object snap to draw the lines, arcs, and circles indicated in the drawing. Object snap commands needed are INT, END, CEN, MID, PER, and TAN.

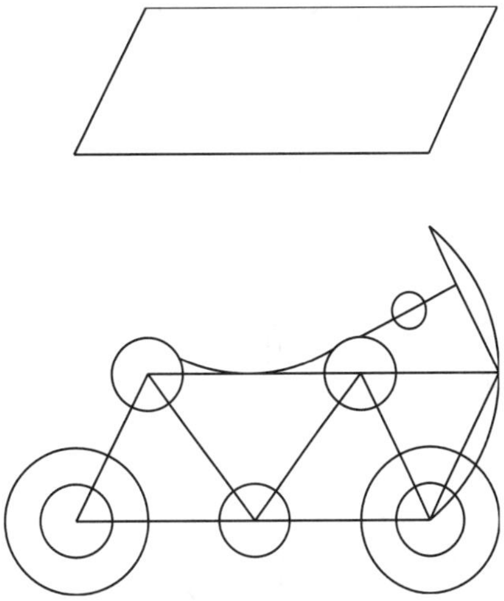

4.3 Starboard Rear Rib

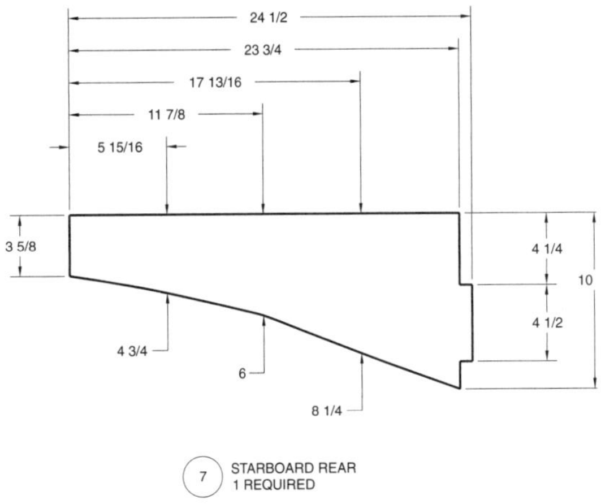

4.4 Park Plan

Create a park plan similar to the one shown here. Use Polyline and Polyline Edit, Spline to create a curving path. Note the symmetry. Add labels with Dtext.

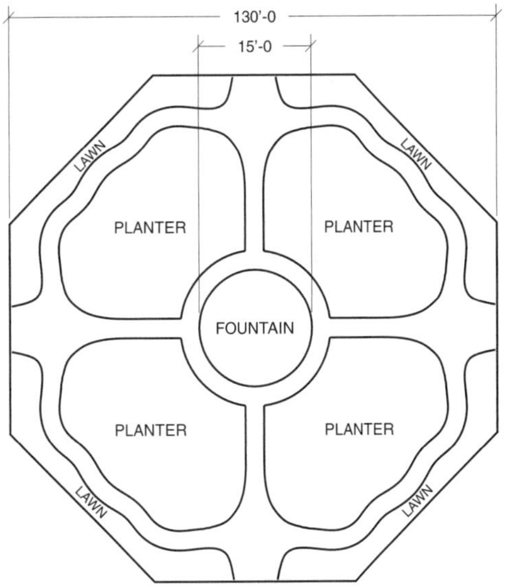

4.5 Floor Plan

Draw the floor plan according to the dimensions shown. Add text, border, and title block.

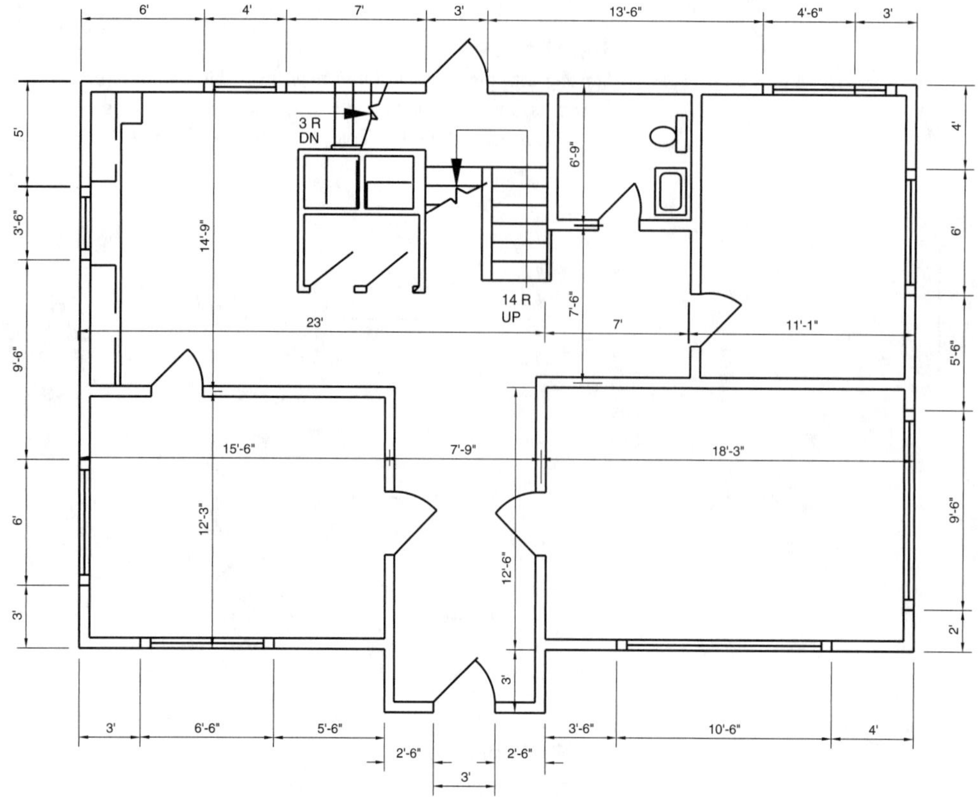

4.6 Interchange

Draw this intersection, then mirror the circular interchange for all lanes.

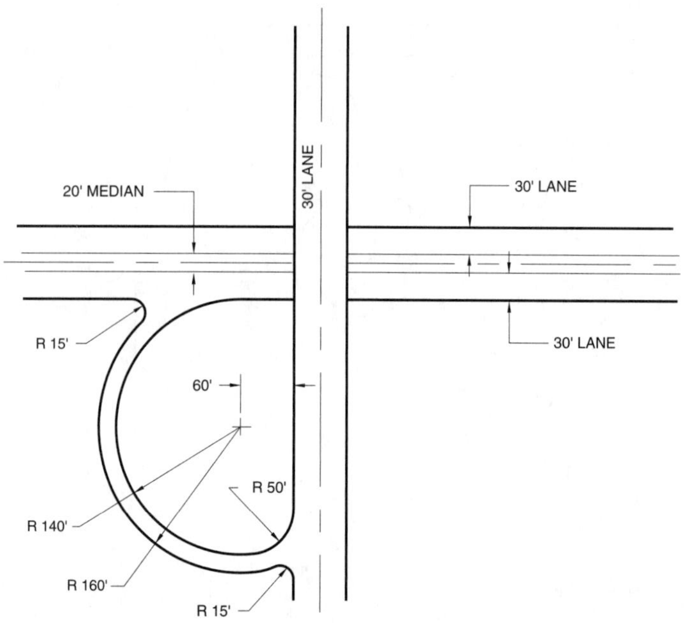

4.7M Plastic Knob

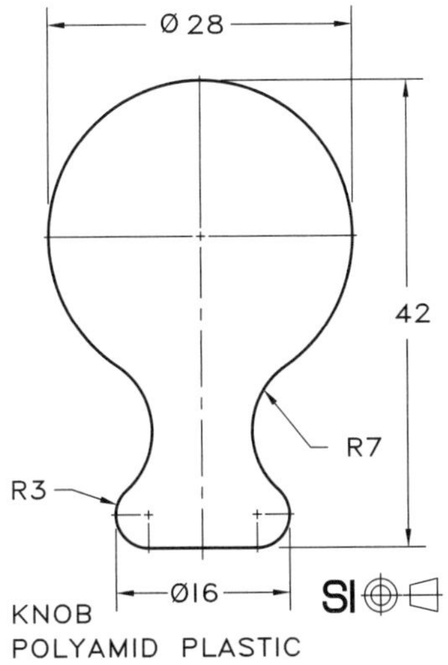

4.8M Foundry Hook

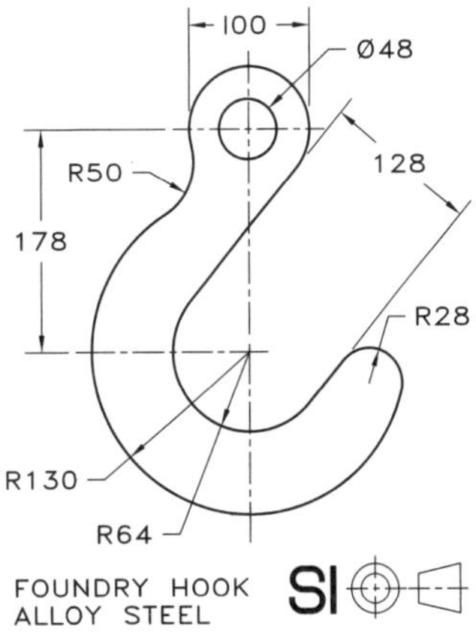

4.9M Support

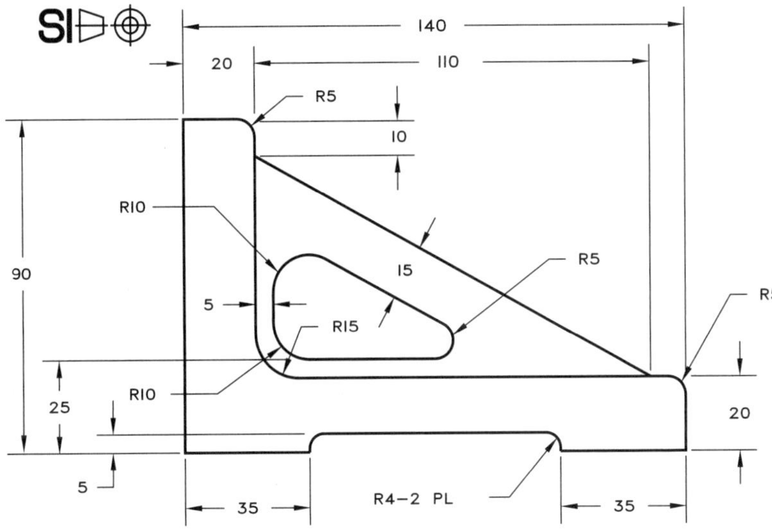

4.10 Hanger

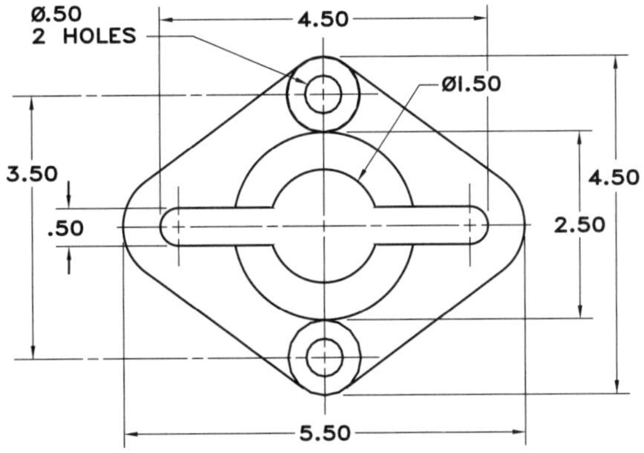

4.11 Slotted Ellipse

Draw the figure shown (note the symmetry). Do not show dimensions.

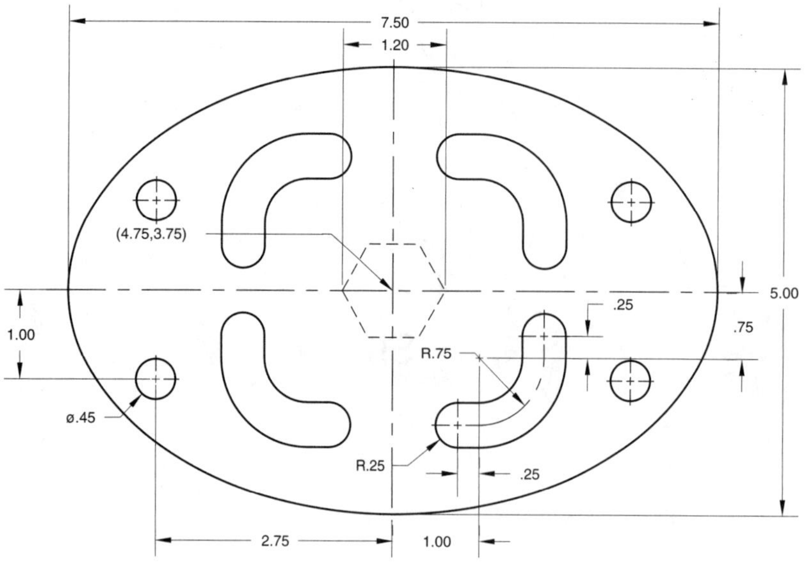

4.12 Shift Lever

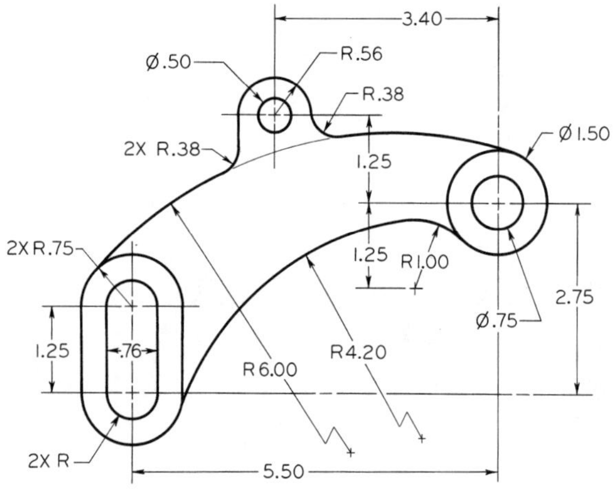

Tutorial

5 Template Drawings and More Plotting

Objectives

When you have completed this tutorial, you will be able to

1. Use a template drawing for standard sheet sizes.
2. Insert a drawing into another drawing as a block.
3. Zoom drawing views to scale for plotting.
4. Create and save a template drawing for later use.
5. Create a system of basic layers for mechanical drawings.
6. Use layer groups and filters.
7. Preset Viewres, Limits, and other defaults in a template drawing.
8. Set up paper space layouts in a template drawing.
9. Set the style for drawing points.
10. Use the Divide command.
11. Plot drawings using a layout.
12. Create a Sheet Set.

Introduction

One of the advantages of using the AutoCAD® software is that you can easily rescale, change, copy, and reuse drawings. Up to this point, most of the drawings that you have created began from a drawing called *acad.dwt*, which is part of the AutoCAD software. In *acad.dwt*, many variables are preset to help you begin drawing. A drawing in which specific default settings have been selected and saved for later use is called a *template drawing*. You can save any existing drawing as a template from which to start a new drawing.

You may want to create different template drawings to use for different sheet sizes and types of drawings. In this tutorial you will use a template for a C-sized sheet (22" × 17") to arrange views of the subdivision drawing for easy plotting. You will also make a drawing template containing default settings of your own from which you will start 8.5" × 11" drawings in succeeding tutorials.

Setting up template drawings can eliminate repetitive steps and help you work more efficiently. The amount of time you spend creating one template is roughly the amount of time you will save on each subsequent drawing that you start from the template drawing. You will use the layer commands to create your own drawing layers and the Drafting Settings dialog box to set up Grid, Snap, and other drawing tools. Your template drawing will contain your custom defaults for layers, limits, grid, snap, and text size and font for use in future drawings.

You will use paper space layouts to add views of your model space drawing as you want it to appear on the printed sheet. Using paper space layouts allows you to have more than one printed sheet format for a single model space drawing. You will also insert *c:\work\mysubdiv.dwg* into a new drawing as a block and use the settings there to plot it to scale.

Starting

Before you begin, **launch the AutoCAD 2006 program.**

Make sure the Layer, Properties, Draw, and Modify toolbars are available on your screen.

Using a Standard Template

You will create a new drawing using a standard AutoCAD template file: the ANSI-C template with color-dependent plot styles. This is set up to plot on a 22" × 17" sheet of paper following guidelines from the American National Standards Institute (ANSI). It will be used to demonstrate some features you can use to lay out plotted sheets.

Tip

You can show a Startup dialog box using Tools, Options and the System tab. From there, choose Show Startup dialog box.

Pick: **File, New**

Pick: **to change the file extension to .dwt** (from the pull-down at the bottom of the dialog box)

The Select Template dialog box changes to show the template selections.

Scroll down the list (as shown in Figure 5.1).

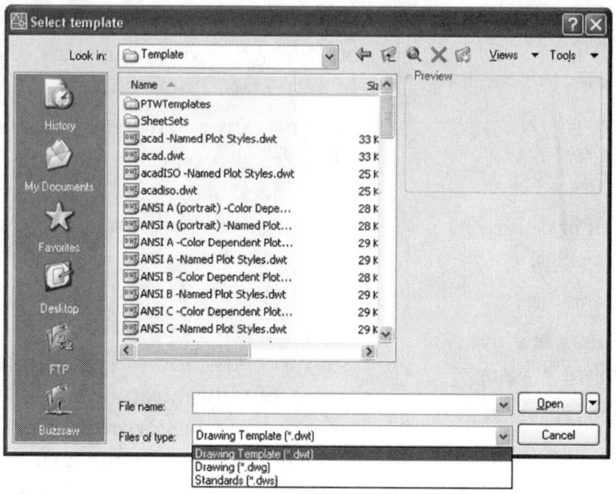

Figure 5.1

The templates stored in the default template location (set using the Files Tab of the Options dialog box) are listed alphabetically. You should see a list similar to that shown in Figure 5.1.

Tip

To change the default template directory pick Tools, Options, select the Files tab, and change the setting under Drawing Template File Location. To see the setting, pick the + (plus sign) to expand the list under Drawing Template Settings, and the items below it. You can use the Browse button at the right of the dialog box to select a new directory by picking.

Pick: **ANSI C–Color Dependent Plot Styles.dwt** (from the list of available templates)

Pick: **Open**

A new drawing should appear on your screen with a border and standard title block for a C-sized sheet. You will save it with a new name to your *c:\work* directory.

Pick: **File, Save**

Type: **Subd_Plot** (as the file name to save)

The file name Subd_Plot should show in the AutoCAD title bar. Notice that when you save a drawing created from a template it does not overwrite the template file. You supply a new name. This way you will not accidentally change your template file. Your screen should look similar to Figure 5.2.

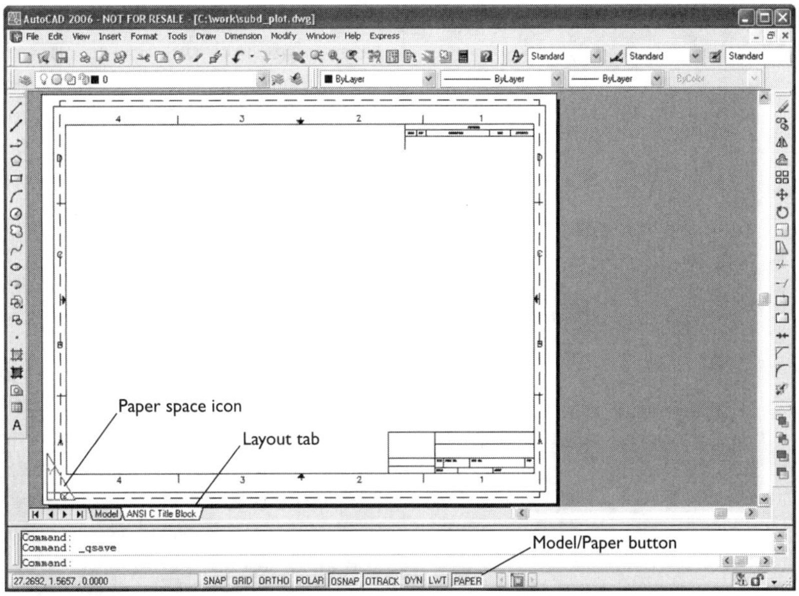

Figure 5.2

Paper Space

The AutoCAD 2006 software allows you to set up your drawings by using a method similar to hand drafting to create plots to any exact scale. Up to this point you have been working in ***model space*** to create your drawing geometry. As you have already seen in Tutorial 3, you can plot your drawing from model space if desired. A better method is to use ***paper space layouts*** to control the appearance of your plotted drawing.

Note the change in the UCS icon in the drawing on your screen. It shows the paper space icon, which looks like a triangle. Notice also that PAPER appears where MODEL used to be on the status bar. The ANSI-C template that you started from is a paper space drawing.

Using paper space layouts allows you to arrange views of your drawing on the "sheet of paper." Your drawing geometry is created in model space, whereas ***paper space*** is used for things like borders, title blocks, text notes, and viewports. (A viewport is like a window that you can look through to see your model space drawing on the sheet of paper).

At the bottom of the drawing window, notice the ANSI C Title Block layout tab shown in Figure 5.2.

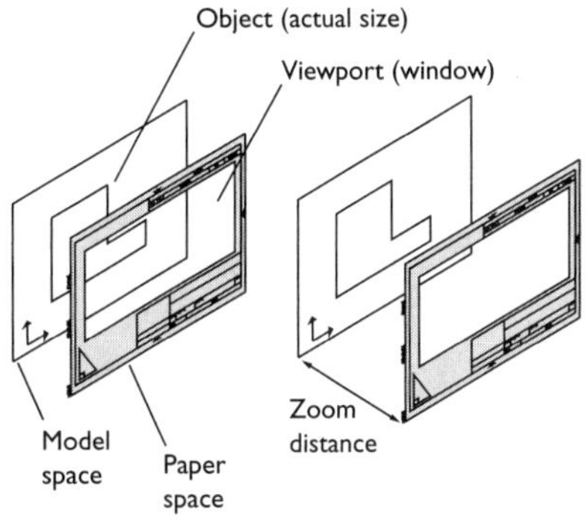

Figure 5.3

Layout tabs are like sheets of paper where you can specify page settings, borders, text, and drawing views. Figure 5.3 illustrates the concept of using paper space and model space. The page settings are used to control the plotter each time you plot the drawing. This way you do not have to reset the plotter requirements each time you print. You can also save the page settings and use that same named page setup with other drawings, or within a template file.

The paper space layout in this case already contains a border with zone numbers and letters which make it easy for you to refer to an area on the sheet when noting a revision or discussing the drawing with a client. It also contains a standard title block and revision block to which you can add your own text.

Printer Area

The white area on the screen (or shaded area in the illustration in Figure 5.3) represents the sheet of paper. The dashed line represents the limits of the printer. The distance from the edge that a printer can reach is different for each printer. The distance from the left edge isn't necessarily the same as it is from the right edge or the top and bottom edges. (When you preview a plot in the Plot dialog box, the outer line in the preview shows the printer limits.) The limits of a printer may also be different for each sheet size.

Viewport

The template drawing that you inserted also contains one viewport. A viewport is like a hole through the paper that you can look through to see model space. At this time there are no drawing objects in model space so nothing appears inside the viewport area on your screen. The viewport is drawn in paper space on a layer named Viewport. Next you will change the color for the viewport to magenta, so that it stands out on your screen.

Pick: **Layer Properties Manager icon**

The Layer Properties Manager appears on your screen. You will use it to set the color for layer Viewports to magenta as shown in Figure 5.4.

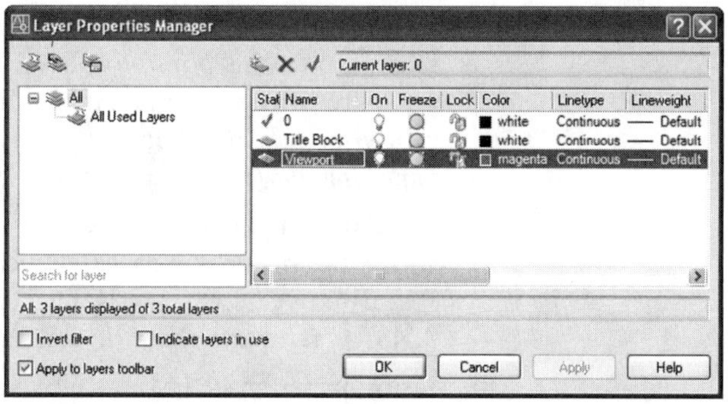

Figure 5.4

Pick: **the color box corresponding to layer Viewport**

Pick: **magenta** (from the top row of standard colors, number 6 from the left)

Pick: **OK**

Pick: **OK**

You should now see the lines that make up the viewport colored magenta. This viewport allows you to access your model space drawing from paper space.

Switching to Model Space

To access model space inside a viewport, you can pick the Paper/Model button on the status bar, or you can double-click inside the viewport. You can also type the alias MS at the command prompt to switch to model space. Type PS to switch back to paper space. To switch to model space,

Double-click: **anywhere inside the viewport**

The viewport border becomes highlighted as shown in Figure 5.5. The status bar button now displays MODEL instead of PAPER.

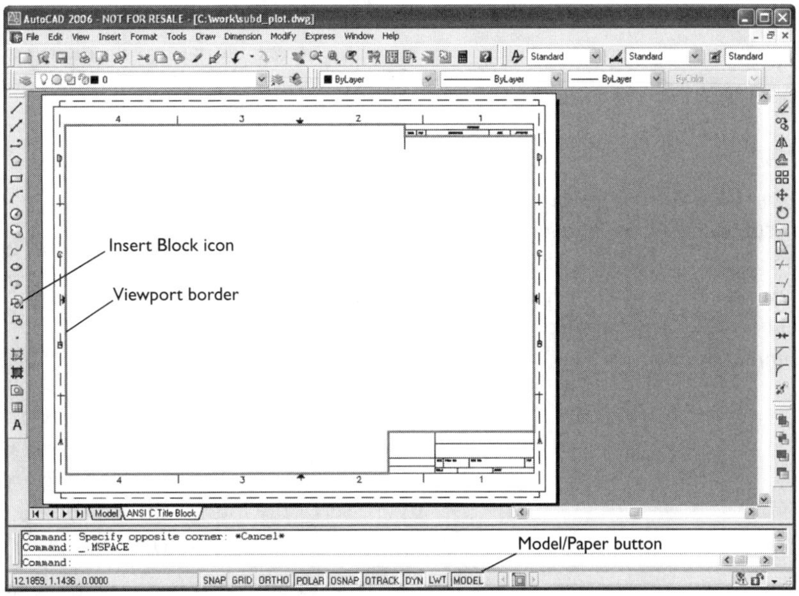

Figure 5.5

Inserting an Existing Drawing

You can insert any drawing into any other AutoCAD drawing. You will use Insert Block to insert the subdivision drawing that you finished in Tutorial 3 into the current template drawing so you can see the effects of using paper space viewports in the next steps.

First, check to see that layer 0 is the current layer.

Pick: **Layer 0** (in Layer Control to set it as the current layer if needed)

When a drawing is inserted into another drawing it becomes a Block. In other words, all of the objects in the drawing are made into a single symbol or Block object. This object resides on the layer that was current when it was inserted. (Blocks can be converted back to individual objects on their original layers using the Explode command.) The Insert Block icon on the Draw toolbar is shown in Figure 5.5.

Pick: **Insert Block icon**

The Insert dialog box appears on your screen, as shown in Figure 5.6.

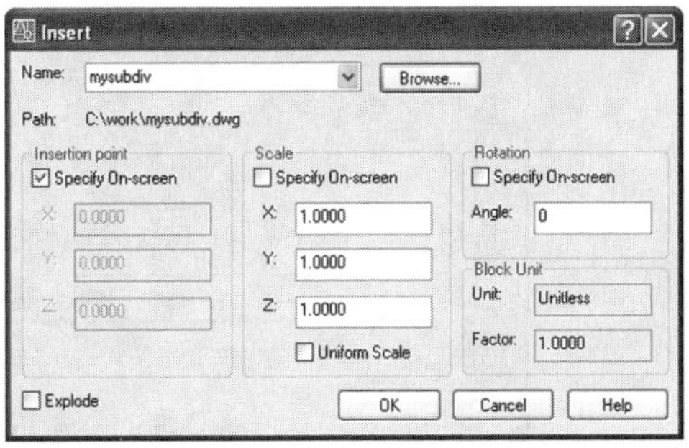

Figure 5.6

You will pick the Browse button to insert an existing drawing. Only the portion of the drawing created in model space will be inserted.

Pick: **Browse**

The Select Drawing File dialog box appears on your screen. You will select the file you created in Tutorial 3 named *mysubdiv.dwg*. You may need to change to the directory where it is located.

Tip

If you have not completed mysubdiv.dwg *from Tutorial 3, use the datafile* subdiv2.dwg *instead. It will not be complete, but you will be able to to see the effect of the commands.*

Pick: ***mysubdiv.dwg***
Pick: **Open**

You return to the Insert dialog box. Note the check to the left of the Specify On-screen box under the Insertion point heading. If there is no check, pick the box now.

This means you will return to your drawing to select the point where the subdivision drawing will be inserted. The Scale parameter is set to 1.0 for X, Y, and Z and the Rotation angle is set to 0. You can type a different value for the scale and rotation for inserted drawings if you want, or you can check to specify them on-screen. Typically you will insert drawings at the original size (a scale factor of 1.0 and the original rotation, 0-degrees).

Pick: **OK** (to return to the drawing)
Specify insertion point or [Basepoint/Scale/X/Y/Z/Rotate/PScale/PX/PY/PZ/PRotate]: **0,0** ↵

The image of the subdivision does not show in the viewport because, at the current zoom factor, the subdivision is much too large for the viewport. In order to see the subdivision, you must zoom out within the viewport. To make the subdivision fit inside the drawing window,

Pick: **Zoom All icon**

Now the entire subdivision drawing should appear inside the viewport, as shown in Figure 5.7.

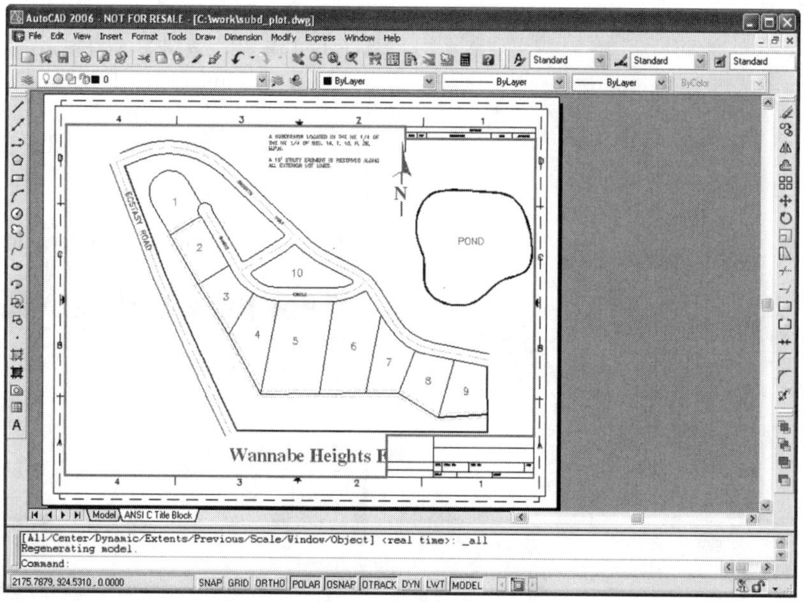

Figure 5.7

Properties of the Viewport

Next you will display the Properties window to view information about the viewport. The viewport is an object drawn in paper space. To select it, you must return to paper space.

Pick: **Model button** (so that it changes to Paper)
Pick: **Properties icon**

Tip

Double-clicking on a drawing object quickly pops up the Properties dialog box. Viewports are drawing objects in paper space. Try double-clicking on the viewport and using the Properties dialog box to quickly set its scale.

The Properties palette should appear on your screen. If it is not docked to the right side of the screen, drag it and dock it there on your own. Next you will select the viewport to display its properties.

Pick: **anywhere on a magenta line of the viewport**

The palette displays the general properties because more than one item is still selected. You will use the pull-down selection box at the top of the Properties palette to select just the viewport as shown in Figure 5.8.

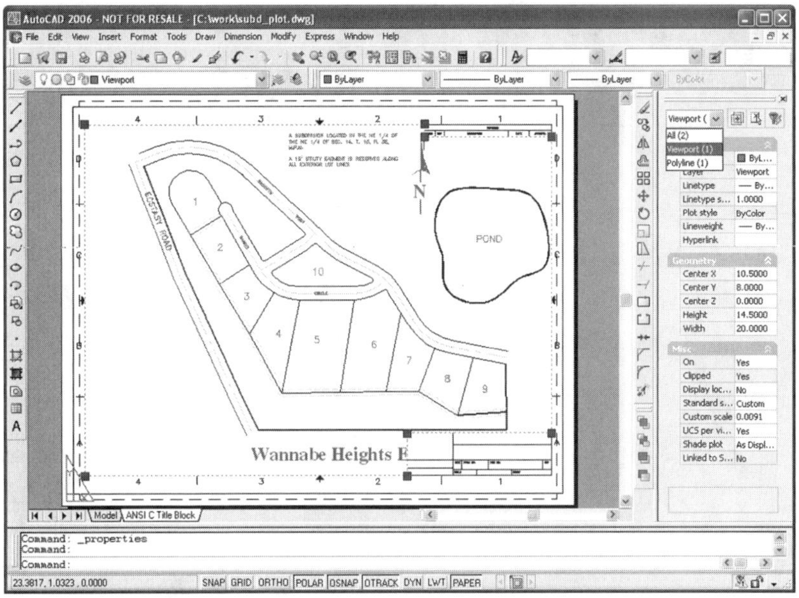

Figure 5.8

Pick: **Viewport (1)**

The dialog box changes to display the properties for the viewport, as shown in Figure 5.9. You can see the size, center point, linetype scale, layer, and other properties of the viewport. You can also use this dialog box to change these properties.

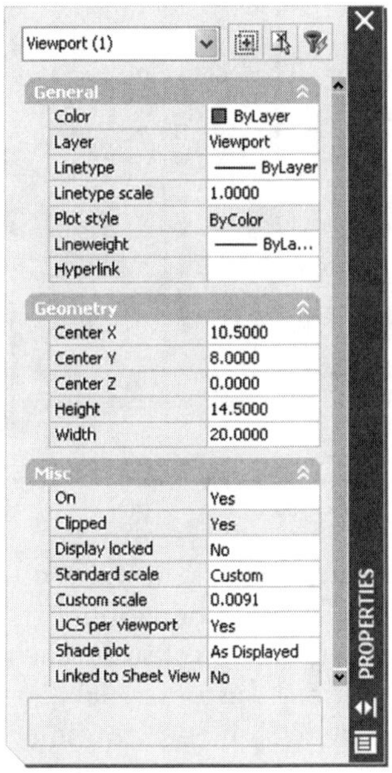

Figure 5.9

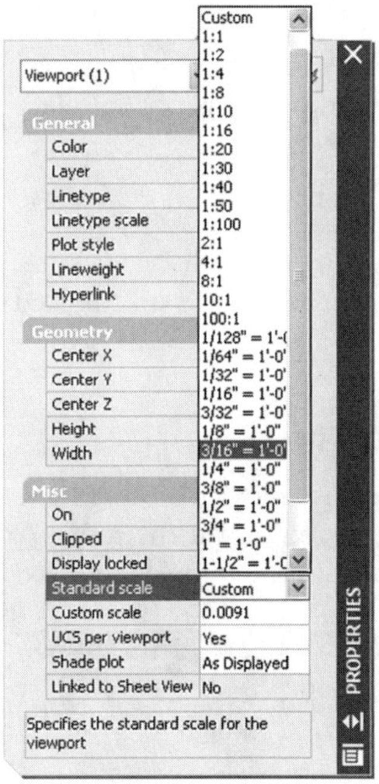

Figure 5.10

Setting the Viewport Zoom Scale

The next step is to set the scale for the drawing inside the viewport by establishing a relationship between the number of units in model space and the number of units in paper space. The standard scale area of the dialog box lets you choose from some likely relationships between paper space and model space. Figure 5.10 shows the Standard Scale choices expanded.

Scroll down to see all the Misc properties (if necessary).

Pick: **the input box relating to Standard Scale to expand its choices**

Pick: **1:100**

Your drawing should zoom inside the viewport as shown in Figure 5.11. The scale that you would note in the title block for this drawing is 1"=100'. That is because the paper space sheet is set up in inch units. The model space subdivision was drawn with decimal units where 1 unit equals 1 foot. The drawing is now zoomed so that when it plots, one paper space unit will equal 100 model space units, or a scale of 1"=100'.

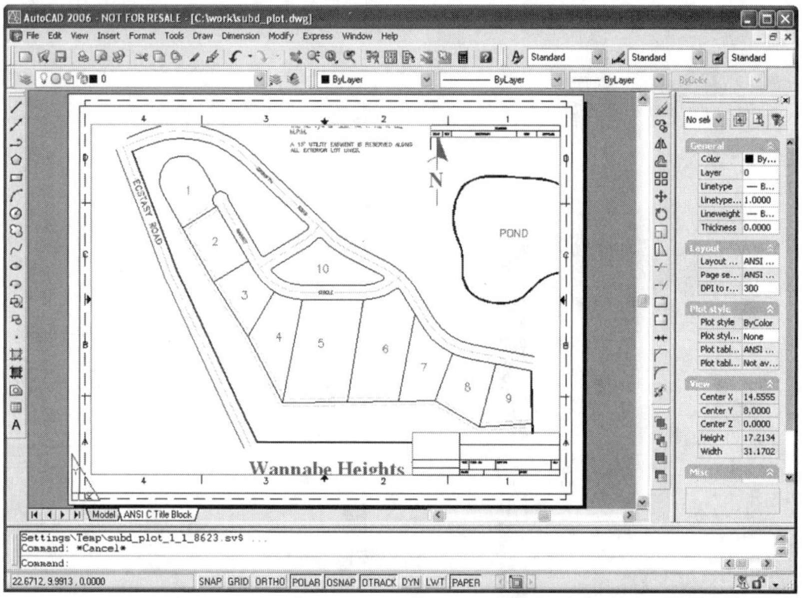

Figure 5.11

The entire subdivision does not fit inside the viewport, so you will use the custom scale area of the dialog box to fit the entire subdivision inside the viewport. It is preferred to plot drawings at typical scales such as the ones available on the standard scales selection. Custom scales should be used for drawings only when necessary to show the drawing clearly. You will use the dialog box to zoom the drawing so that one unit in paper space equals 150 units in the subdivision in model space (a scale of 1"=150'). The Custom Scale area of the dialog box specifies the zoom XP scale factor. You can also type the Zoom command and set this scale factor from the command prompt. The zoom XP scale factor is a ratio. It is the number of units from the object in paper space divided by the number of units in model space. For example, if you want the model space object to appear twice its size on the paper, specify 2XP as the scale factor (2 paper space units/1 model space unit). You can also

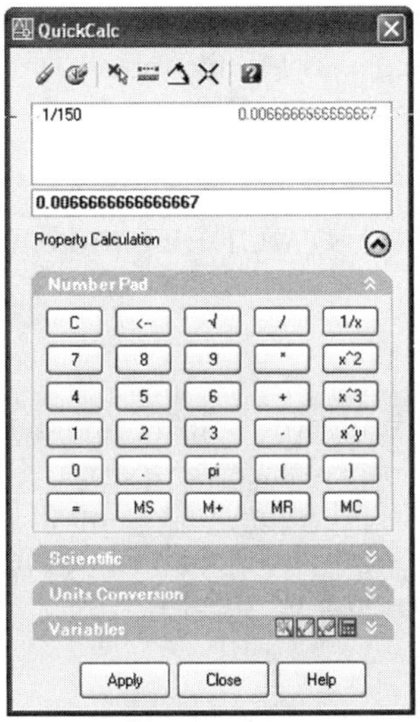

Figure 5.12

think of the zoom XP factor as the value or size of one model space unit when shown in paper space. To specify a scale of 1"=150' for the subdivision, you will set the XP scaling factor to 0.006667 (1 unit in paper space/150 units in model space). You will use QuickCalc to determine this value.

Pick: **in the Custom scale input area** of the Properties dialog box
Pick: **QuickCalc icon** that appears next to the values

The Quick Calculator appears on your screen as shown in Figure 5.12. The scale you will calculate for the drawing will be 1"=150', but the value in the input box must be the decimal equivalent for this expression. Use the QuickCalc buttons to

Pick: the downward arrow (if necessary) to show the buttons and use them to enter **1/150=**
Pick: **Apply**

Your screen should be similar to Figure 5.13. Note the image is now smaller. The scale you would note for the drawing is now 1"=150'.

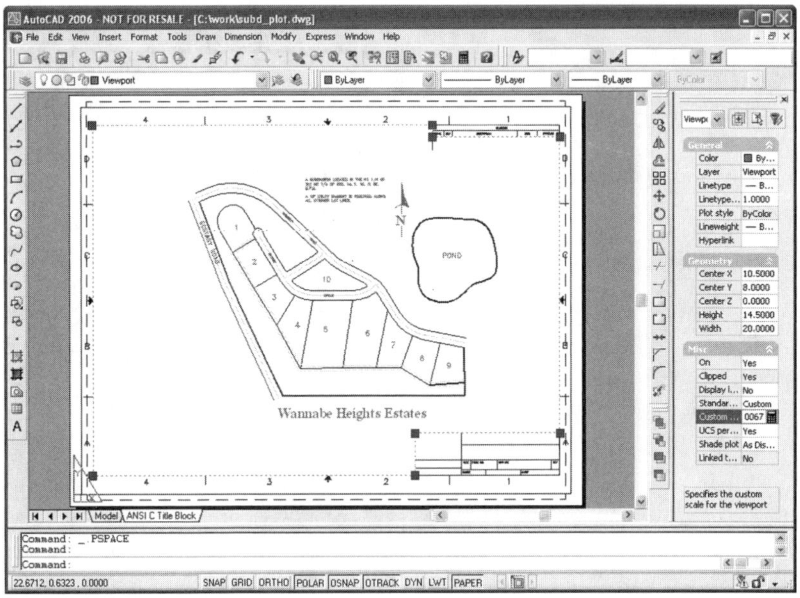

Figure 5.13

Press: [Esc] (to unselect the viewport border)
Pick: **Windows Close button** (to close the Properties palette)

You have set up the zoom scale for the viewport so that if you plot paper space at a scale of 1=1, the model space object is shown at a scale of 1"=150' on the paper. Remember, in the original subdivision drawing, each unit represented one foot.

In order to preserve the relationship between model space and paper space, be sure that if you use Zoom Window to enlarge your drawing, you use Zoom Previous, not Zoom All, to return to this XP size before you plot. Additionally, you can always return to this dialog box and specify the scale factor again if needed. Develop a habit of checking the viewport scale before you plot a drawing.

Tip

To avoid inadvertently changing the zoom scale for the viewport, you can switch to paper space and then select the viewport. Right-click and use the context menu to pick Display Locked and then Yes. This selection will manage zooming so that the zoom XP factor does not change.

Next you will switch to model space so that you can relocate the objects inside the viewport. You will type the command alias MS for model space.

Command: **MS** ⏎

The viewport becomes highlighted and the PAPER/MODEL button displays MODEL.

Using Pan Realtime

You can use the Pan command (on the Standard toolbar) to drag the model space drawing around in the paper space viewport without changing the scale or the location of the drawing on the model space coordinate system. Once you have selected the Pan command, the cursor will change to look like a hand as shown in Figure 5.14.

Pick: **Pan Realtime icon**

Pick a point near the top center of the subdivision and drag the image around until it is centered in the viewport.

Press: Esc (to exit the Pan command)

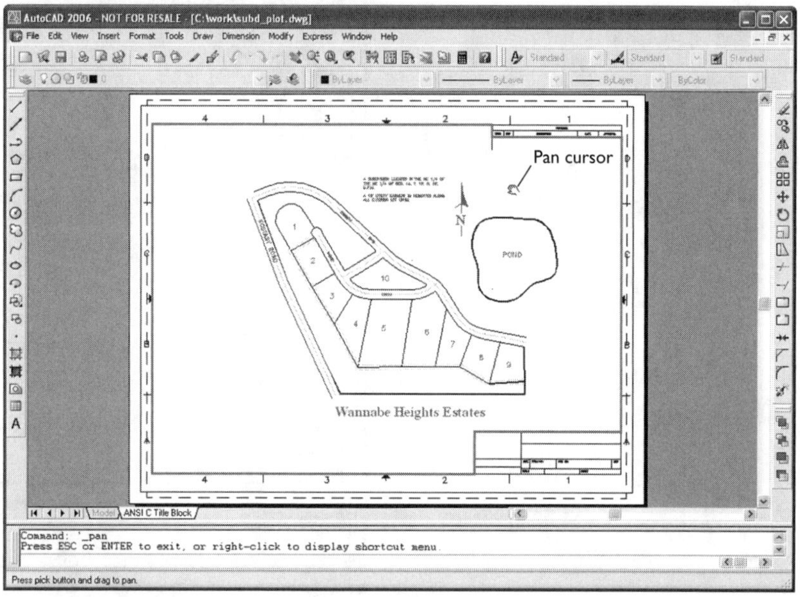

Figure 5.14

Tip

You can also exit the dynamic Pan or Zoom commands by pressing the return button on your pointing device and then selecting Exit from the pop-up menu. Another quick way is to press ⏎ to exit.

Next you will switch back to paper space to create another viewport. You will create this viewport in layer Viewport, so you will make that the current layer.

Pick: **MODEL button** (to change to paper space, or double-click outside the viewport border)

Pick: **to make the Viewport layer current using the Layer Control**

Pick: **to turn off OSNAP**

Creating a Second Floating Viewport

Viewports can be created in model space or in paper space. Model space viewports are called *tiled viewports* because their edges line up next to each other like floor tiles. Paper space viewports are called *floating viewports* because they can overlap each other or "float" on top of one another. Multiple paper space viewports can be printed on one layout sheet.

You can use floating viewports to create enlarged details, location drawings, or additional views of the same object. (You will learn more about this method when you create solid models in Tutorial 11.) You will use the View menu to select the command to create a single viewport. This menu selection starts the Mview command.

Pick: **View, Viewports, 1 Viewport**

At the command prompt you can see options for turning viewports on and off. You can't see any objects in viewports that are turned off, regardless of whether the objects' layers are frozen or thawed. The option Shadeplot allows you to select options for how objects in viewports are plotted; for example, rendered or with hidden lines removed. The Fit option fits a viewport to the available paper space graphics window. The options for 2, 3, and 4 viewports create patterns of multiple viewports in the drawing. Restore converts tiled viewports (in model space) to floating viewports (in paper space) of similar configurations.

At the corner prompt, you will pick a location for one corner of the viewport. Refer to Figure 5.15 for the placement of the viewport you will create.

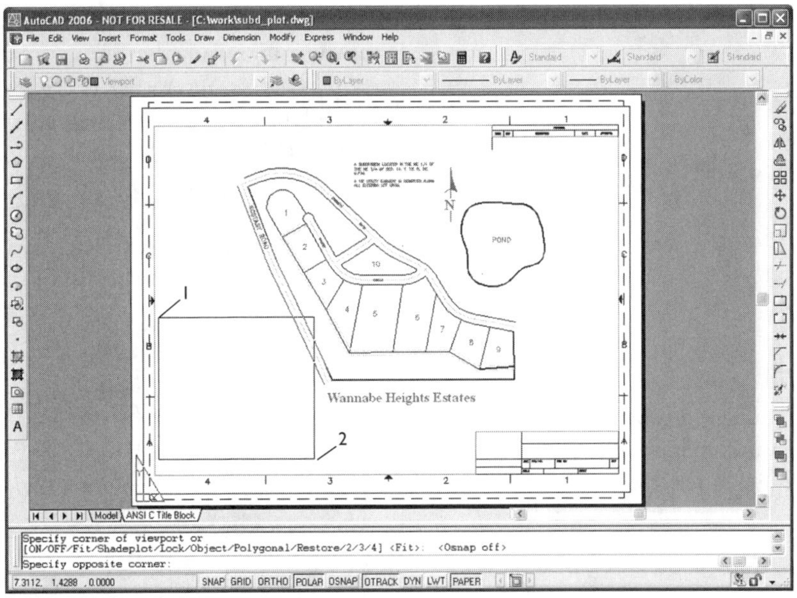

Figure 5.15

Specify corner of viewport or [ON/OFF/Fit/Shadeplot/Lock/Object/Polygonal/Restore/2/3/4] <Fit>: **pick near point 1 for the upper left corner of the viewport**

Specify opposite corner: **pick near point 2 for the lower right corner of the viewport**

A second viewport is added to the drawing as shown in Figure 5.16. It shows the entire subdivision drawing, zoomed so that all of the drawing limits fit inside the viewport.

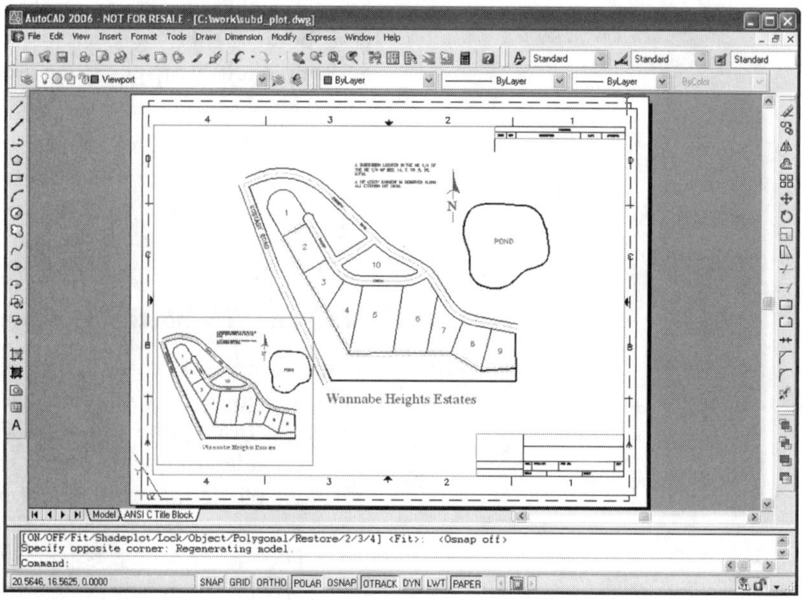

Figure 5.16

Making a Viewport Active

When you are in paper space, double-clicking inside a viewport will make the viewport active and switch to model space. Only one viewport can be active at a time. To make a different viewport active, move the arrow cursor into that viewport and press the pick button. When a viewport is active, its border becomes highlighted and the crosshairs appear completely inside it. Next you will switch to model space and make the new smaller viewport active.

Double-click: **inside the smaller viewport**

The smaller viewport border appears highlighted as shown in Figure 5.17. The crosshairs should be inside the viewport.

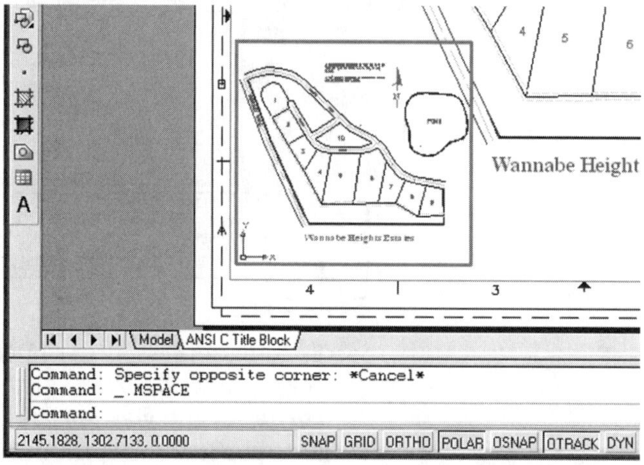

Figure 5.17

Tip

If you have trouble picking a viewport to make it active, press Ctrl*-R to select it.*

Next, you will use the Zoom Window command to enlarge an area inside the smaller viewport you created.

Pick: **Zoom Window icon**

Specify first corner: **pick the first corner so that you enlarge the rounded end of lot 1**

Specify opposite corner: **pick to create a window around lot 1**

Pick: **View, Regen All** (to make the rounded shape appear correctly)

The area inside the window you selected will be enlarged inside the viewport, as shown in Figure 5.18.

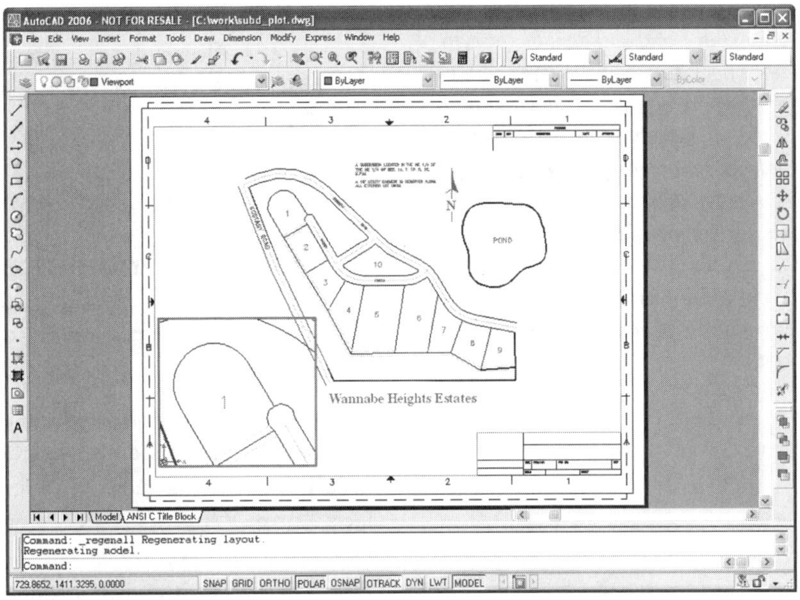

Figure 5.18

On your own, use the Pan Realtime command if needed to position the objects inside the viewport. Don't forget to press Esc to exit the Pan command.

Making the Viewport Layer Non-Plotting

Often you do not want to plot the actual viewport objects as they would appear as a box around the view. To do this, you will make the Viewport layer non-plotting.

Pick: **Layer Properties Manager icon**

The Layer Properties Manager appears on your screen. You will turn off plotting for layer Viewport as shown in Figure 5.19

Tip

You cannot edit a viewport when its layer is turned off. You can still edit the contents of the viewport, that is, the objects that are in model space. If at some time you are trying to change or erase a viewport while in paper space and you cannot get it to work, check to see if the layer where the viewport border was created is turned off, locked, or frozen. Making the layer non-plotting allows you to still see the layer so it is always available for editing but it will not plot. You can also use non-plotting layers to add notes to your drawing, such as reminders, that you do not want to print.

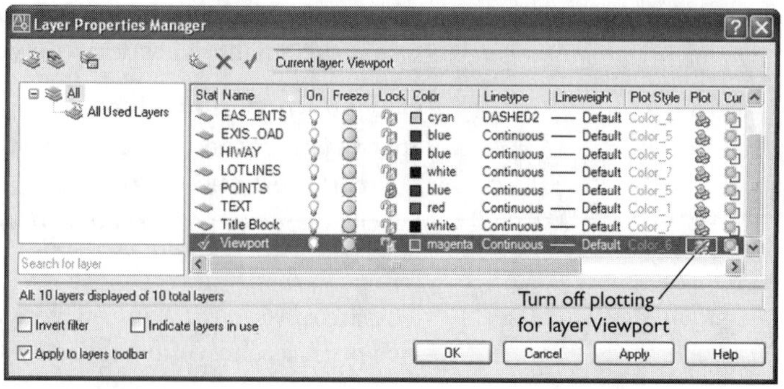

Figure 5.19

Pick: **on the Plot symbol adjacent to layer Viewport to turn off plotting for that layer**
Pick: **OK**

You should still see the magenta colored viewport on your screen. But you will notice later that this layer will not plot.

Adding Text and Notes to Paper Space

Things like borders and general notes belong on the sheet of paper and not in model space. First, you will switch to paper space, and then you will add text to the title block.

Pick: **to switch to paper space using the MODEL button, or double-click outside the viewport borders**
Pick: **TEXT as the current layer using the Layer Control**
Pick: **Zoom Window icon** and enlarge the title block on your screen.
Pick: **Format, Text Style**
Pick: **TITLES** (as the Style Name)
Pick: **to close the dialog box**
Pick: **Draw, Text, Single Line Text**
Specify start point of text or [Justify/Style]: **J** ↵
Enter an option [Align/Fit/Center/Middle/Right/TL/TC/TR/ML/MC/MR/BL/BC/BR]: **MC** ↵
Specify middle point of text: **pick the center of the title box shown as point 1 in Figure 5.20**
Specify height <31.2195>: **.16** ↵
Specify rotation angle of text <0>: ↵
Type: **Wannabe Heights Estates** ↵
Press: ↵
On your own, change the font styles and create text for the additional items in the title block as shown in Figure 5.20.

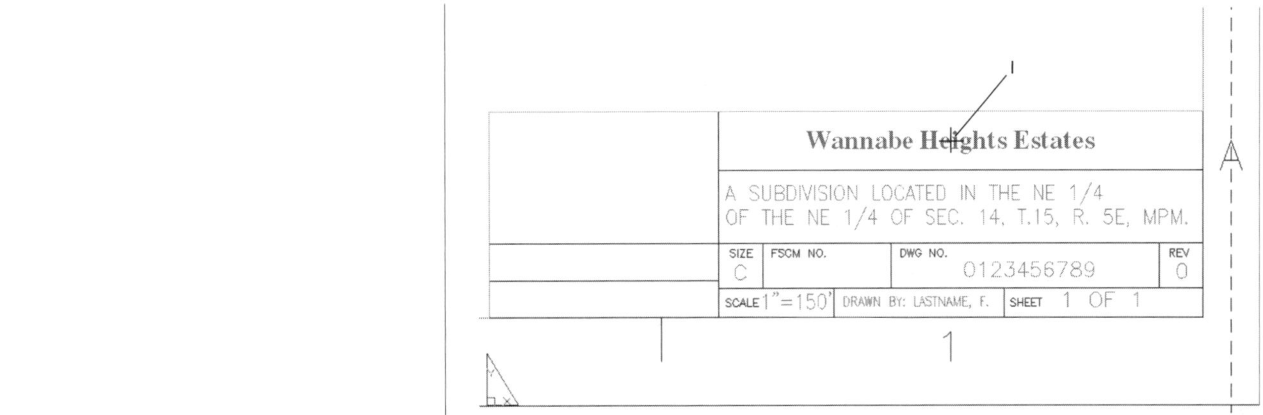

Figure 5.20

Next you will use the Circle command to draw a circle around the area shown in the second viewport, which is going to serve as a detail of lot 1. This circle will be drawn in paper space. Lines added to model space will show up in every viewport (unless you control the visibility with the viewport layer visibility control). Keep in mind that paper space represents the sheet of paper on which you are laying out the drawing.

Pick: **Zoom All icon**

On your own, use paper space and add a circle around the area that is zoomed in the detail. Use the circle's hot grips to stretch or move it as necessary so that it fits around area in the main drawing that is zoomed up in the detail. Add text SEE DETAIL A below the circle. Add text DETAIL A below the enlarged detail as shown in Figure 5.21.

Pick: **Save icon** (to save your drawing)

When you have finished these steps, your drawing should look like Figure 5.21.

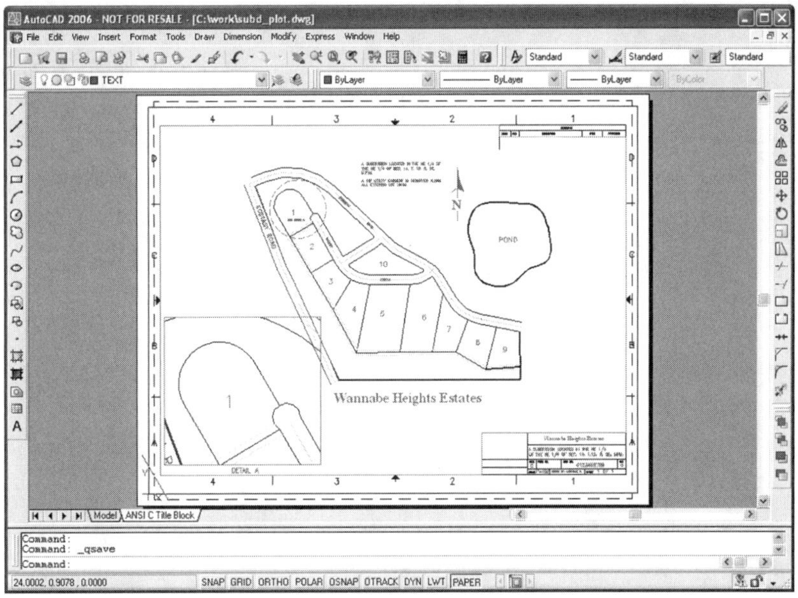

Figure 5.21

Figure 5.22

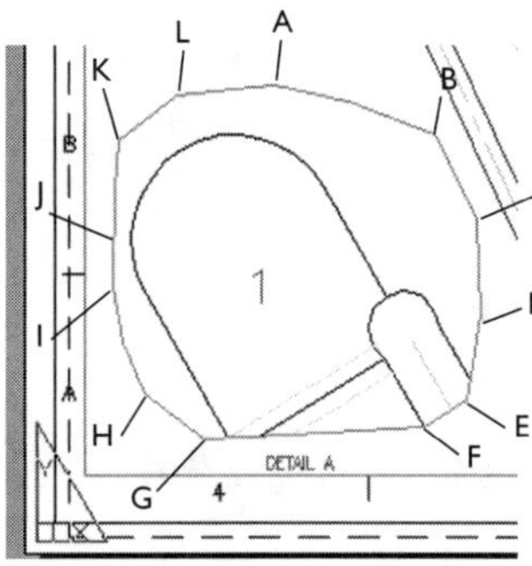

Figure 5.23

Using Irregularly Shaped Viewports

Viewports do not have to display a rectangular shape. You can use the VPClip command to create irregularly shaped viewports from viewports you have already created. Using the Object option, you can convert an existing paper space object into a viewport. The Polygonal option allows you to select points to define an irregular boundary. The boundary must have at least three points and must be closed. The AutoCAD software locates a viewport object using the points you specify and then clips the content of the viewport to the specified boundary. You will try each of these methods next.

Pick: to make **VIEWPORT** the current layer

Pick: on **the small magenta rectangular viewport so that its grips appear**

Right-click: **in the drawing area to pop up the context menu as shown in Figure 5.22**

Pick: **Viewport Clip**

Select clipping object or [Polygonal] <Polygonal>: ↵

Specify start point: **pick a point near A in Figure 5.23**

Specify next point or [Arc/Close/Length/Undo]: **pick points B through L to form an irregular boundary inside the circle**

Specify next point or [Arc/Close/Length/Undo]: **C** ↵

The contents of the viewport are clipped to the irregular polygon boundary as shown in Figure 5.23. Next you will use the option to clip the viewport to an object by drawing a circle in paper space and then clipping the viewport to that shape.

Draw a circle in paper space around the viewport you just clipped.

Command: **VPClip** ↵

Select viewport to clip: **pick the irregular viewport boundary**

Select clipping object or [Polygonal/Delete] <Polygonal>: **pick the circle around the small viewport**

The contents of the viewport are clipped to the shape of the circle as shown in Figure 5.24.

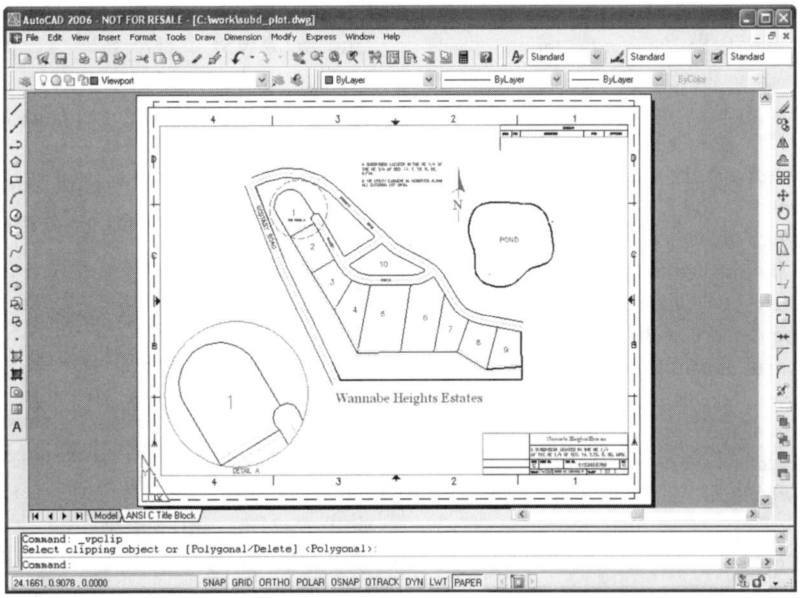

Figure 5.24

Plotting from Paper Space

You have set up your drawing in paper space and established the XP scaling factor (the number of units in model space that equal one unit in paper space). You are now ready to plot. Be sure that you are still in paper space. If you are not, your plotted drawing may not fit on the sheet and the title block won't be shown. Because you used a paper space layout and created a viewport that should fit exactly on your C-sized sheet, you will type 1=1 for the scaling in the Plot command.

Pick: **Plot icon**

The Plot dialog box will appear on your screen as shown in Figure 5.25.

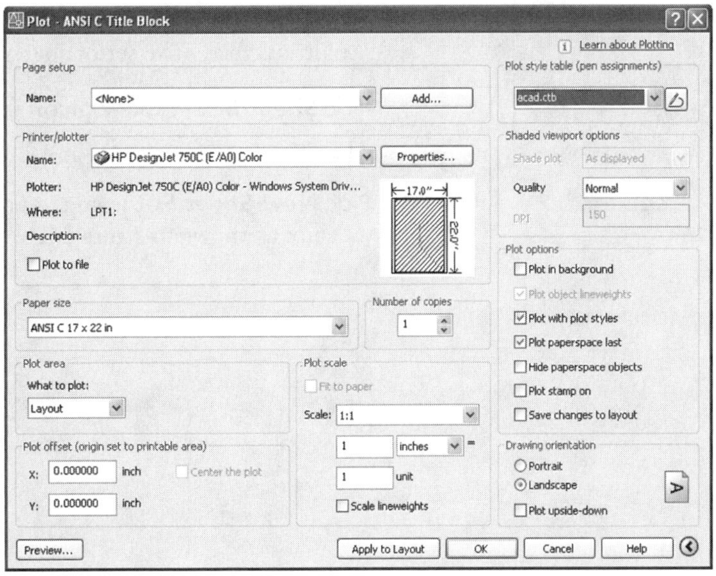

Figure 5.25

Tip

If you do not have a plotter capable of using the C-sized sheet, you can plot a check print to a standard 8.5" × 11" printer or plotter. To do this, select this sheet and choose Fit to paper in the Plot scale area. The entire drawing border and contents will be scaled to fit on the smaller sheet size. Of course this means that the drawing scale of 1"=150' no longer applies. Make sure that the Save changes to layout box near the top of the Plot dialog box is ***not*** *selected before you change your paper size.*

Tip

To learn more about the Sheet Set Manager, pick Help, New Features Workshop, and choose Sheet Set Manager from the list of items.

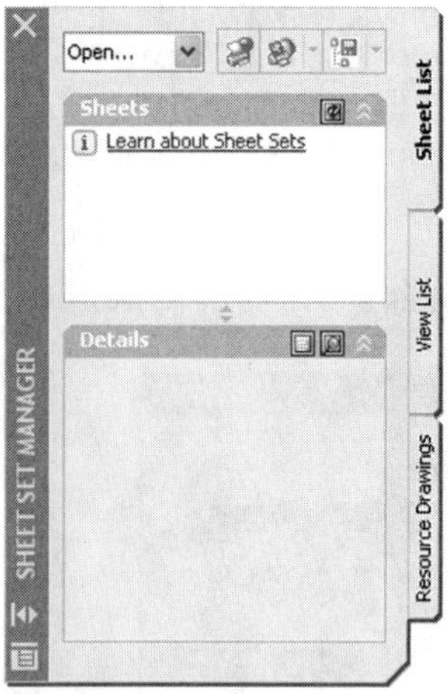

Figure 5.26

Choose: **Layout** (for Plot area)
Choose: **ANSI C** (17" × 22") paper size
Set: **1:1** as the Plot Scale
Make sure the Save changes to layout box is **not** checked.
Pick: **Preview**
Pick: **OK** to plot or Cancel to cancel plotting the drawing
Save and close drawing *Subd_plot.dwg.*

Sheet Sets

Large projects often have more than one drawing sheet associated with them. Sheets sets are a way to organize and publish drawing sets. Each sheet in a sheet set can show one layout at a time. Although it is possible to create multiple layout tabs for a single drawing, this is not useful when using the Sheet Set Manager.

Next you will create a sheet set that contains the layout for the subdivision drawing you just created along with other drawings.

Before creating a sheet set:

- Create your drawings with only one layout tab per drawing. Only one layout can function as a separate sheet within a single drawing. To create multiple sheets from the same drawing information, save the file with a new name and create a single new layout for that sheet. Using multiple layouts from a single drawing as separate sheets in a set makes it impossible for multiple users to access that sheet or layout at the same time. It also makes your sheet sets more complicated and harder to keep organized.
- Organize your drawing files. Generally you will want all of the drawings for a project to be in the same folder (or subfolders of one folder). The sheet set aids you in locating the files and publishing them but it will not overcome disorganized file storage habits.
- Think about which template file will be used to add new sheets to the set. You will specify this in the Sheet Set Properties dialog box.
- Consider the page setup file you will use to store page setups for plotting the entire set of sheets.

Pick: **Sheet Set Manager icon** from the Standard Toolbar

The Sheet Set Manager appears on your screen as shown in Figure 5.26.

Pick: **New Sheet Set** from the pull-down list near the top of the dialog box as shown in Figure 5.27

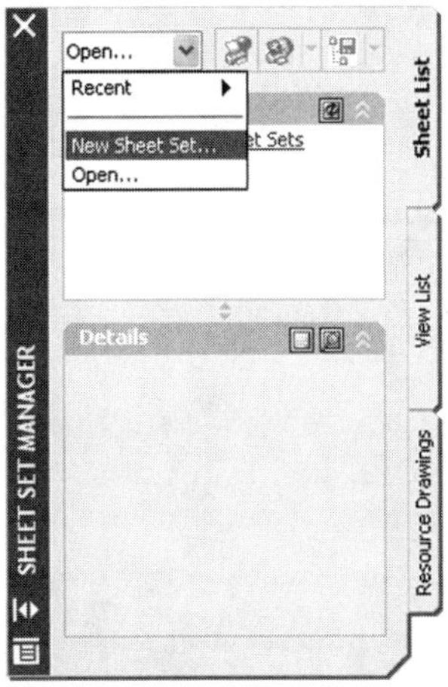

Figure 5.27

The Create Sheet Set wizard appears on your screen. You can begin a new sheet set from an example showing sheet organization or by adding your existing drawings.

Pick: **Existing Drawings** as shown in Figure 5.28

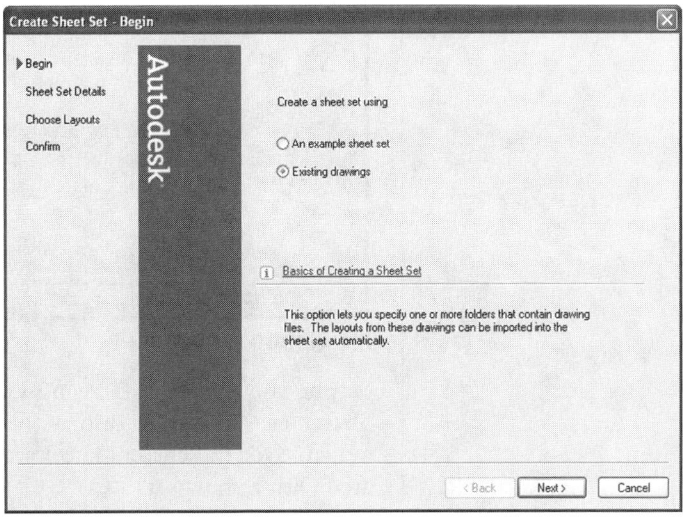

Figure 5.28

Pick: **Next**

Using the Sheet Set Details page shown in Figure 5.29, you can specify the name for the sheet set, a description, and the path where the sheet set file (which uses the *.dst* extension) will be stored. You can also set additional properties by picking on the Sheet Set Properties button.

Type: **Wannabe Estates** for the name of the new sheet set and add a description as shown in Figure 5.29

Change the path to ***c:\work*** in the Store sheet set data file here input box.

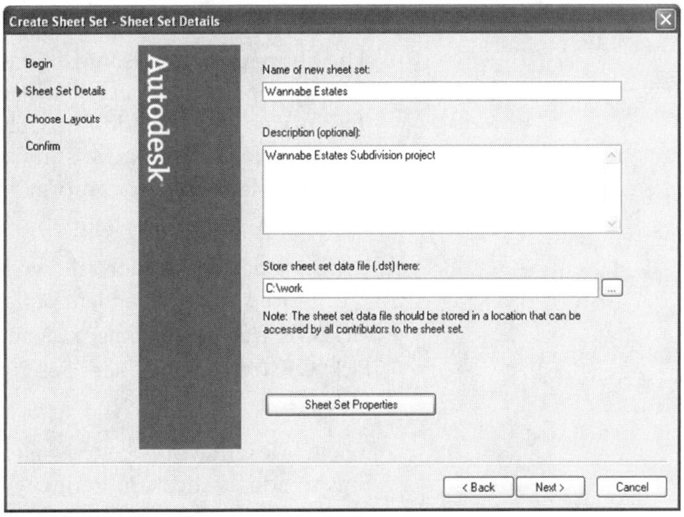

Figure 5.29

Pick: **Sheet Set Properties button**

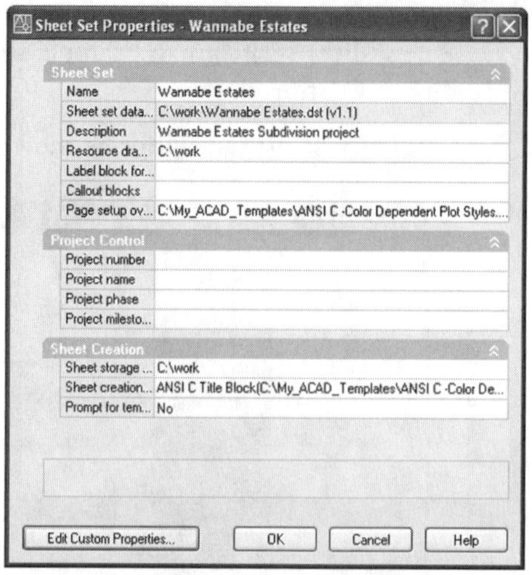

Figure 5.30

Setting the Resource Drawing Location(s) area causes that tab of the Sheet Set Manager to display the subfolders, drawings, and named views available for the current sheet set. More than one folder can be associated with a sheet set.

Pick: **the ellipsis button** that appears when you pick in the Resource Drawings Location input box
Pick: **Add button** in the dialog box
Navigate to ***c:\work***.
Pick: **Open**
Pick: **OK**

The Page Setup Overrides files area displays the path for the page setup file (containing the page size and other necessary printing information) that will override any different user settings when the sheet set is plotted as a batch.

Use your default location for your page setup files.

The Sheet Creation Template area displays the path for the template that will be used by default when a new sheet is added to the sheet set. This makes creating additional sheets that have the same sheet size and format quick and easy. Most drawing sets standardize on one sheet size and title block style for an organized appearance and ease of handling the printed sheets.

Use your default location (shown in the dialog box) and browse to select a C-sized color-dependent template.
Pick: **OK** (to exit the Select Layout as Sheet Template dialog box)
Pick: **OK** (to exit the Sheet Set Properties dialog box)
Pick: **Next**

The Choose Layouts page is used to select layouts from existing drawings to add as sheets in your organized sheet set.

Pick: **Browse**
Pick: ***c:\work***
Pick: **OK**

You should see a list of the drawings inside the folder *c:\work* that contain layouts that can be used as sheets as shown in Figure 5.31.

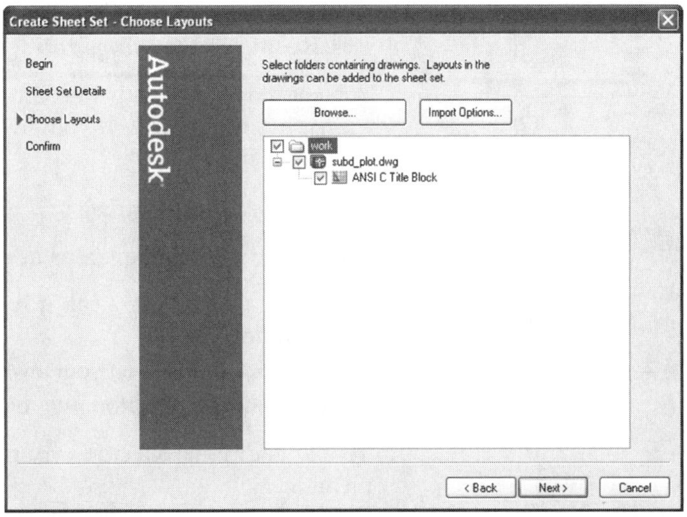

Figure 5.31

Pick: **the check box next to *c:\work* to deselect all**

Pick: ***subd_plot.dwg*** and its **ANSI C Title Block sheet** so they are checked

Pick: **Next**

Tip

*Make sure your **subd_plot.dwg** drawing is closed or you will see a message stating that the drawing file is locked.*

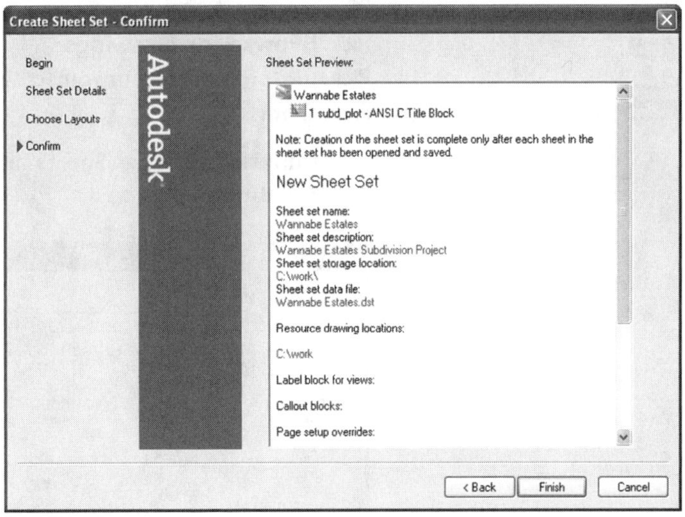

Figure 5.32

The Sheet Set Preview as shown in Figure 5.32 shows the drawings you have selected and the default paths you set for the sheet set to be defined.

Pick: **Finish**

You return to the drawing editor where the Sheet Set Manager shows the drawing layouts you have selected listed. Figure 5.33 shows the appearance of the Sheet Set Manager.

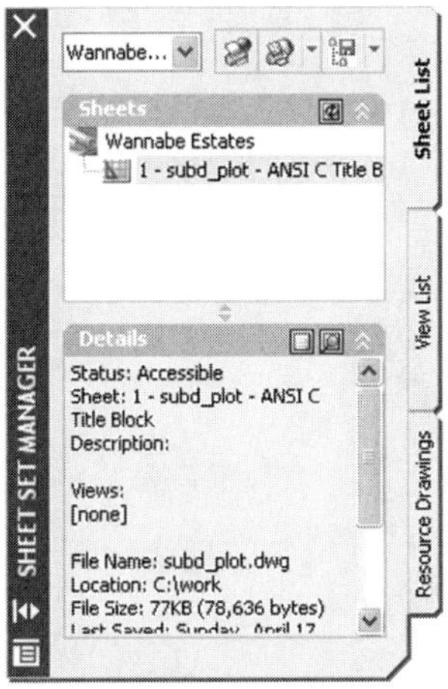

Figure 5.33

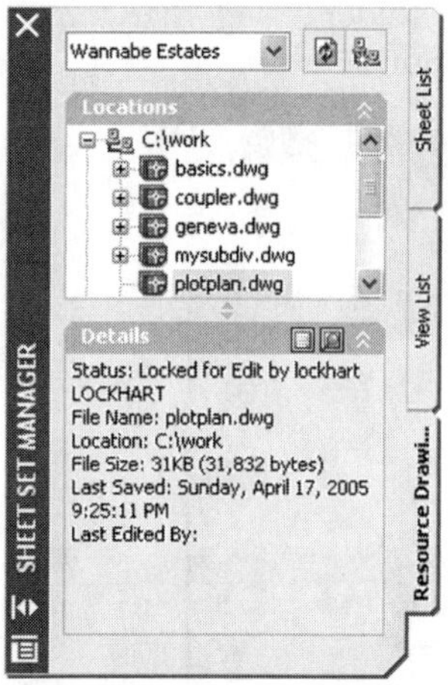

Figure 5.34

Figure 5.35

To open a sheet, you only need to double-click on its name in the Sheet Set Manager. To open a drawing from the sheet set you only need to double click on its file name.

Pick: **Resource Drawings tab**

You should see the drawings listed that are in your *c:\work* folder as shown in Figure 5.34. If you do not, pick the Add New Location icon and select it.

Double-click: ***plotplan.dwg***

The plot plan drawing opens in the drawing editor.

Right-click: **on Layout 2 tab if it appears and use the short-cut menu to delete it**

Switch to Layout 1 on your own to activate it.

Save and close *plotplan.dwg* on your own.

To add additional sheets to your sheet set, you can use the short-cut menu.

Pick: **Sheet List Tab**

Right-click: **Wannabe Estates sheet set name**

The short-cut menu pops up on your screen as shown in Figure 5.35.

Notice that you can use this menu to create new sheets, new subsets or categories of sheets, and to publish a sheet set.

Pick: **Import Layout as Sheet**

Pick: **Browse for Drawings**

Pick: ***plotplan.dwg*** from your ***c:\work*** directory

Pick: **Open**

The Import Layouts as Sheets dialog box shows on your screen as you see in Figure 5.36.

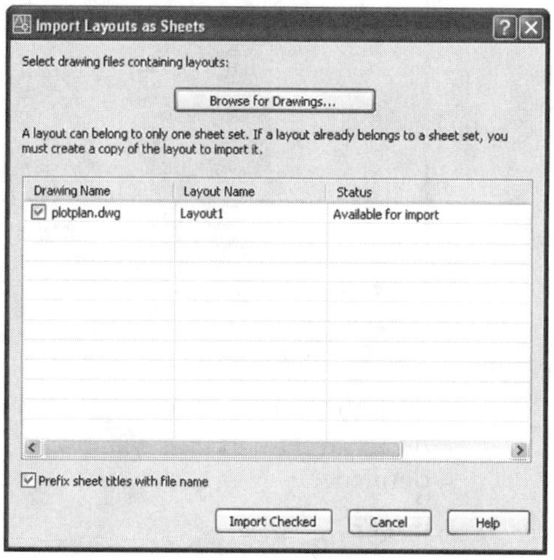

Figure 5.36

Make sure that *plotplan.dwg* is checked and then

Pick: **Import Checked button**

The plotplan layout is added to your sheet set.

Sheet sets can be a very important productivity and organization tool when you are working on large projects. You can explore sheet sets more using Help.

You are finished with this portion of the tutorial.

Pick: **to close the Sheet Set Manager**

Pick: **to close any drawings that remain open**

Creating a Template Drawing

Next you will create a template drawing that you will use for most of the remaining tutorials in this book. The file you will create is also provided as a template named *proto.dwt* in the datafiles for this book (in case you do not complete this portion of the tutorial).

Pick: **File, New**

Pick: ***acad.dwt*** (as the template to use)

You should be in the AutoCAD drawing editor with a blank drawing showing. Be sure that the Draw and Modify toolbars, as well as the Standard, Layer, and Properties toolbars, are turned on.

Pick: **Save icon**

The Save Drawing As dialog box should appear on the screen. Located at the bottom of the dialog box is a Files of type: option as shown in Figure 5.37. This pull-down menu allows you to save the drawing in Release 2000 format, as a Drawing Standards file (*.dws*), in several Drawing Exchange Formats (*.dxf*), and in Template format (*.dwt*).

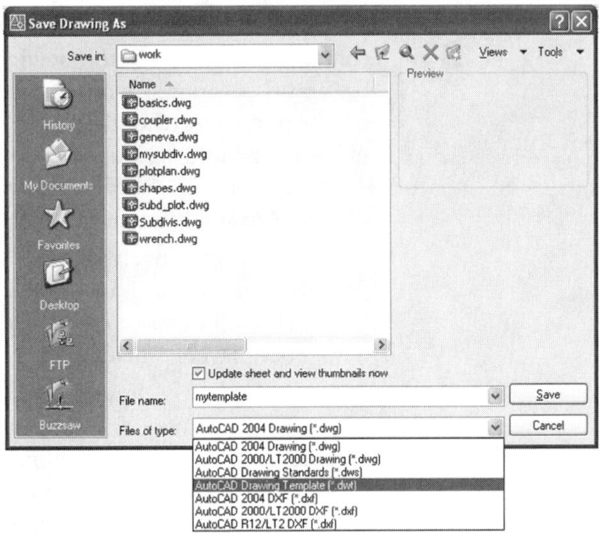

Figure 5.37

You will save your drawing as an AutoCAD template (**.dwt*) file. The only difference between a drawing file (**.dwg*) and a template file (**.dwt*) is the file extension. The default choice is to save files in Release 2004 (**.dwg*) format, so you must change the selection to Drawing Template (**.dwt*).

Tip

The drawing file format for AutoCAD and AutoCAD LT Release 2000, 2000i, and 2002 are the same. This means that drawing files can be directly exchanged between these versions without any translation between file types.

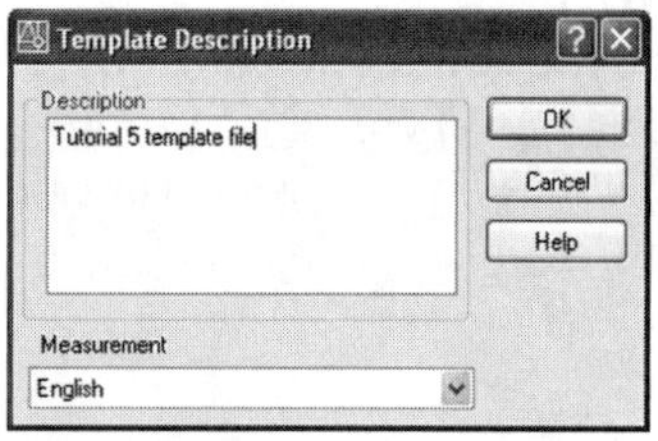

Figure 5.38

Tip

You can use the operating system to rename template files to drawing files and vice versa.

Pick: **AutoCAD Drawing Template (*.*dwt*)**
Type: **MYTEMPLATE** (as the File name)
Navigate to *c:\work*, if necessary.
Pick: **Save**

A Template Description dialog box is shown in Figure 5.38.

The Measurement pull-down menu at the bottom of the dialog box describes whether the template uses English units or Metric units. Make sure that English units are selected.

Type: **the description shown in Figure 5.38**
Pick: **OK** (to exit the Template Description dialog box)

The main AutoCAD drawing editor appears on your display screen, with Mytemplate in the title bar.

You will set the limits, grid, snap, layers, text size, and text style in this drawing, as well as set up the paper space limits, viewport, and linetype scale. This approach will save time, make plotting and printing easier, and provide a system of layers to help you keep future drawings neatly organized.

Creating Default Layers

Layers are similar to the system of *pin-registry* drafting, which was often used in drafting maps manually. In pin-registry drafting, a series of transparent sheets were punched with a special hole pattern along one edge, allowing the sheets to be fitted onto a metal pin bar. The metal pin bar aligned the drawings from one sheet to the next. Each sheet was used to show different information. For example, one sheet may have shown streets, another lot lines, and another political boundaries; yet another rivers and other geography. When preparing a map, only the sheets that contained the information needed would have been attached to the pin bar and then printed with a vacuum frame printer. You can use layers for similar purposes, to organize the information in your drawing and turn off or freeze information you do not want to show. Unlike pin-registry drafting, where the sheets of punched transparent paper sometimes slipped, causing misalignment, layers always stay aligned.

To use layers effectively, choose layer names that make sense and separate the objects you draw into logical groups. The AutoCAD Layer Manager allows you to create groups and use filters to manage large numbers of layers efficiently.

Object color in the drawing can be used to control the plotter's pen selection. The same control holds for line thickness on printers that are capable of printing different line weights. The AutoCAD default is to set color by layer. Using different layers helps standardize the colors of groups of objects in the drawing, which in turn helps standardize plotting the drawing. You should use different colors for different types of objects in order to plot more than one color or line thickness effectively when using color dependent plot styles. Layers are also used to associate named plot styles with the objects on that layer.

Using a template drawing helps you maintain a consistent standard for layer names. Using consistent and descriptive layer names allows more than one person to work on the same drawing without puzzling over the purpose of various layers. On networked computer systems, many different people can work on a single drawing. A template drawing is an easy way to standardize layer names and other basic settings, such as linetype.

Defining the Layers

Now you will use the Layer Properties Manager to create the remaining layers for your template drawing.

Pick: **Layer Properties Manager icon**

The Layer Properties Manager appears on the screen, as in Figure 5.39.

Tip

You can right-click on a heading in the Layer Properties Manager, and select Maximize Column Headings from the pop-up menu that appears.

Tip

If you selected dark lines on a light background when configuring your video display, white lines will be black on your monitor and color boxes indicating white will be black.

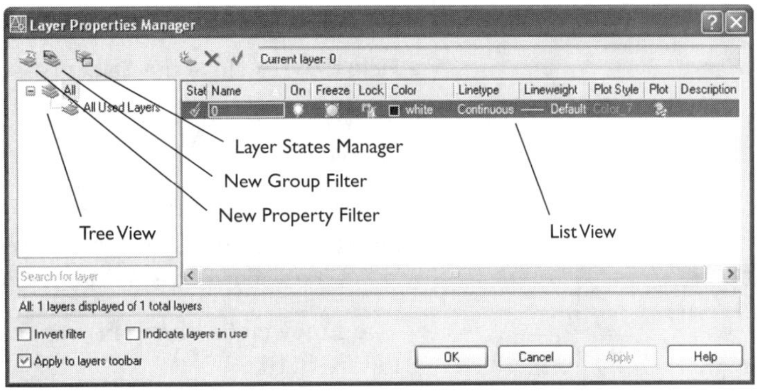

Figure 5.39

There are two panes in the Layer Properties Manager. The left one shows a tree-structured view of the layers. The right one shows the list view. You can use the New Property Filter and New Group Filter to display different groups of layers depending on layer properties or layer group membership. The Layer States Manager lets you save and restore various settings, such as on/off, frozen/thawed, color, linetype, lineweight, and the other layer properties.

From the keyboard, you will type in the new layer names followed by commas.

Tip

Many Windows programs identify typing shortcuts by use of an underlined letter. Note the underlined letter N on the tooltip for the New Layer icon. This indicates that you can quickly select this operation by typing the key combination Alt-N. Look for the quick key combinations in other dialog boxes.

Pick: **New Layer icon near the top of the dialog box**

Type: HIDDEN_LINES,TEXT,VISIBLE,THIN,CENTERLINE, CUTTING_PLANE,HATCH,PROJECTION, DIM,BORDER,VPORT ↵

Each time you type a comma (,) a new "Layer1" pops up on the list of layer names. Then the name you type replaces the name Layer1.

Tip

If the list of layer names is long; you may need to use the scroll bars located on the right-hand side of the dialog box.

Note that the layers you have created are turned on. The color for all the layers is white (or black depending on your system configuration). In addition to the color and linetype, you can also set a lineweight value in the default units of millimeters (mm) or inches. Lineweights in the drawing only show on the screen when paper space is enabled and when the LWT button on the status bar is turned on. You will set the lineweight for the HIDDEN LINES layer to .30 mm, the standard for plotting or sketching hidden lines. Lineweights should be used only to control the plotted appearance, not to represent the actual thickness of an object. Next you will set the color, linetype, and then lineweight for the hidden line layer.

Pick: **the white color box in the Color column across from the Hidden_Lines layer**

Pick: **Blue** from the Standard Colors boxes

Pick: **OK**

Pick: **Continuous in the Linetype area** (to the right of layer Hidden_Lines)

The Select Linetype dialog box appears on your screen.

Pick: **Load**

Pick: **HIDDEN**

Pick: **OK** (to exit the Load or Reload Linetypes dialog box)

You will see the linetypes HIDDEN and CONTINUOUS.

Pick: **HIDDEN**

Pick: **OK** (to close the Select Linetype dialog box)

Now you should see that the linetype for layer Hidden_Lines is set to linetype HIDDEN.

Pick: **Hidden_Lines** (in the layer name list if it is not already highlighted)

Pick: **the thin line with the word Default in the Lineweight area across from the Hidden-Line layer**

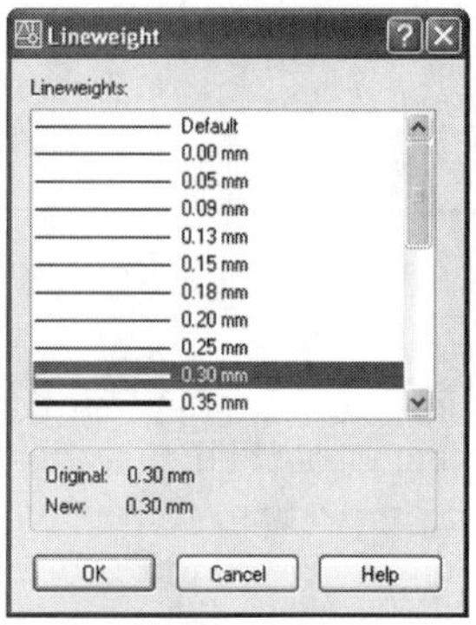

Figure 5.40

The Lineweight dialog box appears on your screen as shown in Figure 5.40.

Pick: **0.30 mm**

Pick: **OK**

The 0.30 lineweight is displayed as the setting for layer HIDDEN The list of layer names should now show layer Hidden_Lines having color blue, linetype HIDDEN, and a lineweight of 0.30.

Setting Up the Remaining Layers

Next, you will set the colors and linetypes for the reminaining layers that you have created. You can select more than one Layer name at the same time by using the [Ctrl] or [Shift] keys in conjunction with the mouse (as you would to select multiple files in other Windows programs).

Use the arrow cursor to move to the desired layer name.

Pick: **Thin**

Press: [Ctrl] (keep it depressed) and then

Pick: **Hatch** (keeping [Ctrl] depressed)

Pick: **Text** (keeping [Ctrl] depressed)

You should now have three layers selected.

Pick: **the Color box across from one of the selected layers**

The Select Color dialog box, which you used earlier in this tutorial, pops up on the screen. Use the standard colors as before. You will pick red as the color for the layers you selected.

Pick: **Red from the Standard Colors boxes**

Pick: **OK**

Pick: **the thin line with the word Default in the Lineweight area across from one of the selected layers**

Pick: **0.30 mm**

Pick: **OK**

Layers Thin, Hatch, and Text should now have their color set to red and lineweight set to 0.30 mm. Next, you will set the color, linetype, and lineweight for layer Centerline.

Pick: **Centerline** (to highlight the layer name)

Pick: **the Color box across from the Centerline layer**

Pick: **Green from the Standard Colors boxes**

Pick: **OK**

Pick: on **Continuous** in the Linetype column across from layer Centerline

The Select Linetype dialog box appears on your screen. You will need to load linetype CENTER before it can be used.

Pick: **Load**

On your own use the Load or Reload Linetypes dialog box and select the line pattern CENTER to use for layer Centerlines.

Pick: **the thin line with the word Default in the Lineweight area across from layer Centerline**

Pick: **0.30 mm**

Pick: **OK**

When you have finished, the Centerline layer should be color green, linetype CENTER, and lineweight .30 mm.

On your own, repeat these steps to set the colors and linetypes in the following table for the other layers that you have created. When you are setting the colors for the layers listed, remember that magenta is a purplish pink color (number 6 in the row of standard colors), and that the color white appears black if you have chosen to draw on a light background.

Tip

When you are selecting the color and linetype, be sure to highlight only the names of the layers you want to set.

Layer	Color	Linetype	Lineweight
0	WHITE	CONTINUOUS	default
HIDDEN LINES	BLUE	HIDDEN	0.30 mm
TEXT	RED	CONTINUOUS	0.30 mm
VISIBLE	WHITE	CONTINUOUS	0.60 mm
THIN	RED	CONTINUOUS	0.30 mm
CENTERLINE	GREEN	CENTER	0.30 mm
PROJECTION	MAGENTA	CONTINUOUS	default
HATCH	RED	CONTINUOUS	0.30 mm
CUTTING_PLANE	WHITE	DASHED	0.60mm
DIM	BLUE	CONTINUOUS	0.30 mm
BORDER	WHITE	CONTINUOUS	0.60 mm
VPORT	MAGENTA	CONTINUOUS	default

Before you exit the dialog box, you will set the current layer to VPORT.

Double-click: **Vport** (to set it as the current layer—it will show a green check mark)

Tip

You can click on the Name heading in the Layer Properties Manager to switch the list of layer names to reverse alphabetical order. Pick it again to restore it to A-Z order.

Tip

The variable Maxsort controls the number of layers that will be sorted in the Layer Control dialog box. It is set at 200 as the default. If you do not want your layer list to be sorted, you can type MAXSORT at the command prompt and then follow the prompts to set its value to 0.

Pick: **the Plot icon across from layer Vport** so that the layer becomes non-plotting

When you have finished creating the layers and setting the colors and linetypes, the dialog box should be similar to Figure 5.41.

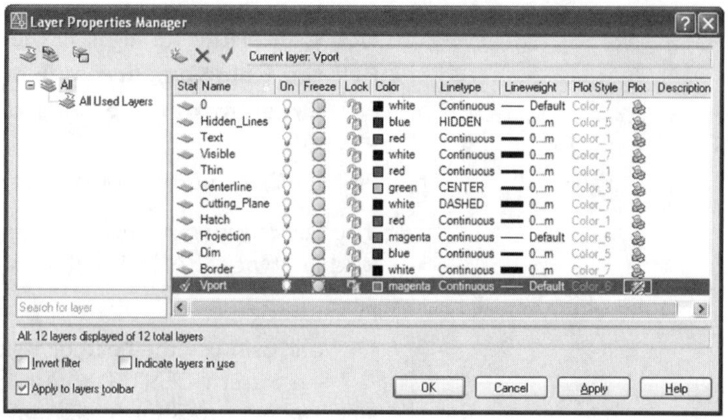

Figure 5.41

Remember that lineweights do not display unless the LWT button on the status bar is selected and paper space has been enabled. You will see the effect of the lineweight later in this tutorial.

Using layers to control the color and linetype of new objects that you create will work only if BYLAYER is active as the method for establishing object color, object linetype, and lineweight. It is the default, so you should not have to change anything. To check,

Examine the Color Control, Linetype Control, and the Lineweight Control on the Properties Toolbar. All three should be set to BYLAYER.

You have now created a basic set of layers for use in future drawings. Next you will explore the New Property Filter and New Group Filter.

Pick: **New Property Filter icon** (from the upper left of the dialog box)

The Layer Filter Properties dialog box appears as in Figure 5.42.

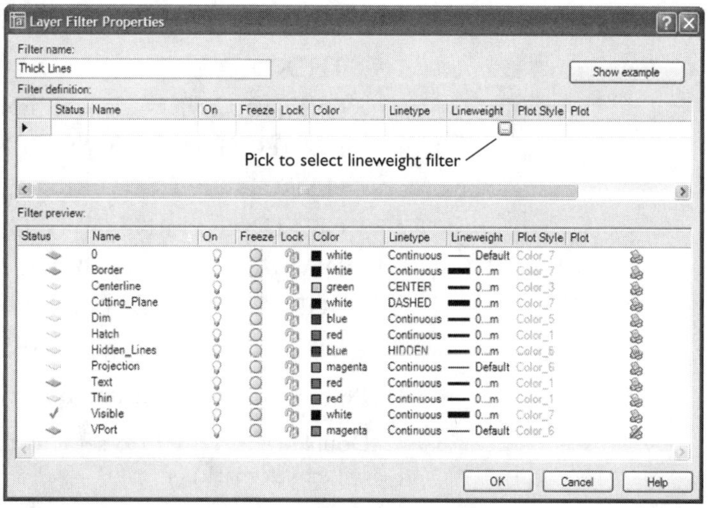

Figure 5.42

Type: **Thick Lines in the Filter Name area** (at the upper left of the dialog box)

Pick: **in the Lineweight area of the top part of the dialog box**

Pick: **the ellipsis box that appears**

Pick: **0.60 mm from the Lineweight dialog box that appears**

Pick: **OK**

The Layer Filter Properties dialog box changes as in Figure 5.43 to show a preview list that includes only the layers that have a 0.60 mm lineweight.

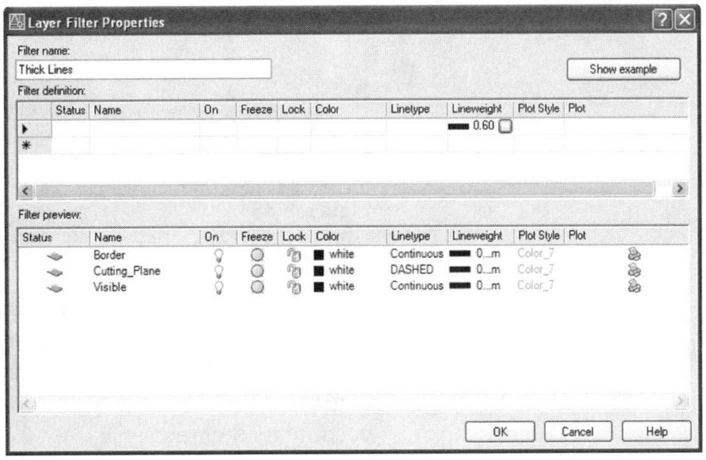

Figure 5.43

Pick: **OK**

You return to the Layer Properties Manager with the Thick Lines properties filter showing in the tree view as shown in Figure 5.44.

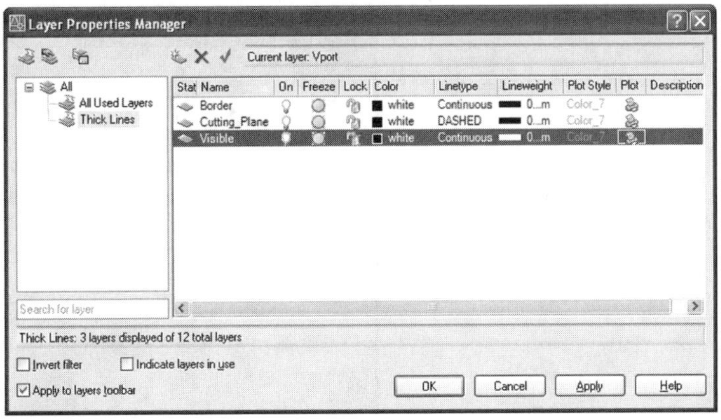

Figure 5.44

The only layers that appear in the list view are 0.60 mm lineweight. To see all of the layers,

Pick: **All** (from the top of the tree list)

All of the layers display in the list area now. You can select the Thick Lines filter whenever you want to display just the 0.60 mm lines.

Pick: **New Group Filter**

Group Filter1 is added as a group to the tree list as shown in Figure 5.45. It is highlighted so that you can overtype it with a descriptive name.

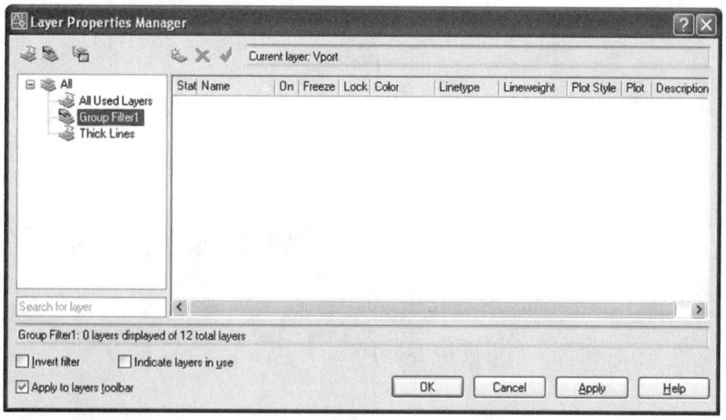

Figure 5.45

Type: **SECTION LAYERS** (as the Group name)

The group Section Layers appears in the tree view. Currently no layers are a member of this group, so nothing is displayed in the list view. Next you will display all of the layers and then drag the Hatch and Cutting_Plane layers onto the Section Layers group so that they will become its members.

Pick: **All** (from the top of the tree view)

Pick: **Cutting_Plane and then press** Ctrl **and pick Hatch so that they both become highlighted**

Pick: **and drag the highlighted layers onto the Section Layers group in the tree view** (as in Figure 5.46)

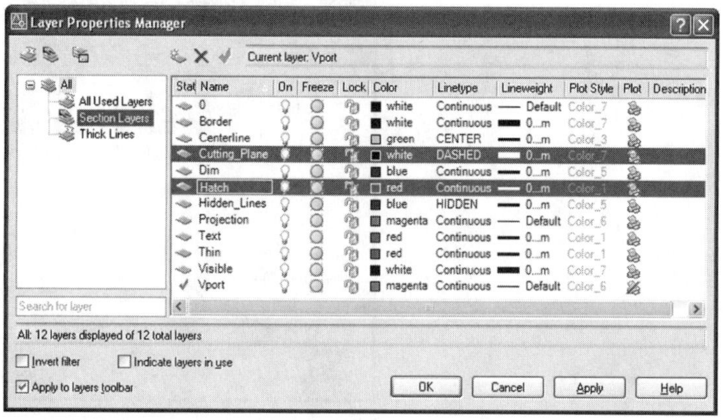

Figure 5.46

To see the layers that are a member of the group,

Pick: **Section Layers group from the tree list**

The list view now displays only Hatch and Cutting_Plane.

Pick: **All**

All of the layers now return to the list view.

Pick: **to Freeze layers 0 and Projection**
Pick: **Layer States Manager icon**
Pick: **New**
Type: **Frozen** (in the Layer State to Save dialog box)
Pick: **OK** (to return to the Layer States Manager
Pick: **Clear All**
Pick: **Frozen/Thawed**

You see the Layer States Manager as shown in Figure 5.47.

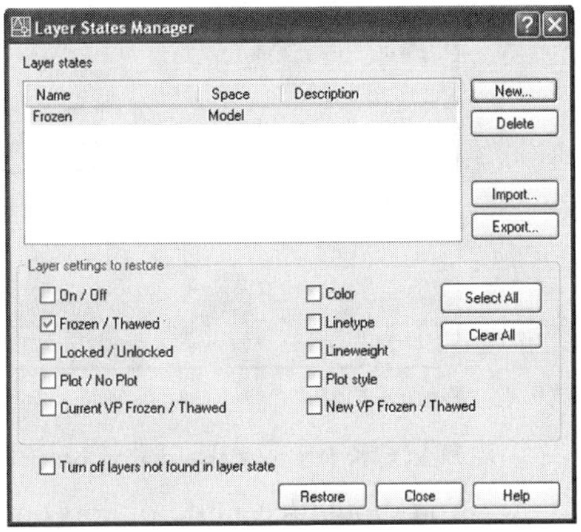

Figure 5.47

Pick: **Close**

You return to the Layer Properties Manager.

On your own, thaw Layer 0 and Layer Projection.
Pick: **Layer States Manager**
Pick: **Restore**

The thawed layers return to the frozen state. Now you will finish with the Layer Properties Manager and continue setting up your template file.

Pick: **OK**
Save your drawing before continuing.

Using the Drafting Settings Dialog Box

Next you will select the Drafting Settings dialog box and use it to set the Snap and Grid.

Tip

You can also right-click on the Snap, Grid, Polar, Osnap, or Otrack buttons to launch the Drafting Settings dialog box.

Pick: **Tools, Drafting Settings**
Pick: **Snap and Grid tab**

You will set the X and Y spacing for the snap to .25.

Pick: **to highlight the text in the input box next to Snap X spacing**
Type: **.25** [Tab]

The Snap Y spacing box automatically changes to match the Snap X spacing when you tab to (or click in) the Y box. If you press [↵], the dialog box automatically closes. If you want unequal spacing for X and Y, you can change the Snap Y spacing separately.

Leave the Grid set to **0.5**.
Use the check boxes to turn on Snap and Grid.

When you have finished, the Drafting Settings dialog box should appear as shown in Figure 5.48.

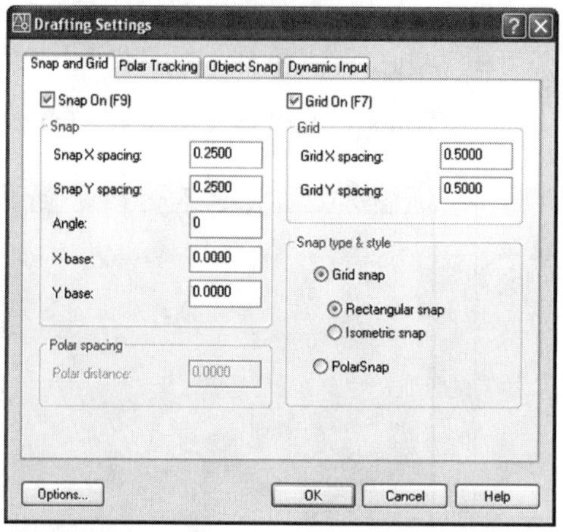

Figure 5.48

Tip

When the grid is turned on in both model space and paper space, two patterns of grid dots, which don't necessarily align, are produced, which can be confusing. Generally, you will want to turn off the paper space grid before you return to model space.

Pick: **OK** (to exit the dialog box)

You should see a grid of dots on your screen. You will use Zoom All if the grid does not fill the entire screen. Do not be concerned if the grid does not fill the screen entirely. Your drawing limits are currently set to 12" ×9". If your graphics window on the screen does not have the same *aspect ratio* (the ratio of the height to the width), only one dimension will be filled completely. If you want, you can figure out the aspect ratio of your graphics window and always set your drawing limits so that the grid fills the entire screen, but that really is unnecessary. When you start a drawing from your template, you will set the drawing limits at that time to a value large enough for the particular part you will draw. Then you can use the Zoom command to view the new drawing limits.
For now,

Tip

You can also set your drawing limits by picking from the screen the lower left corner and then the upper right corner. This way your limits will be sure to fill the screen area.

Pick: **Zoom All icon**

Selecting the Default Text Font

The AutoCAD software offers various fonts for different uses. The best font for lettering engineering drawings is called *romans*, for Roman Simplex. The *.shx* fonts are provided, so all other AutoCAD users will also have this font. True Type fonts and other system fonts may look great in your drawing, but may not be available on someone else's system, causing them to have to substitute another font which may make the lettering not fit correctly in the drawing.

Pick: **Format, Text Style**

The Text Style dialog box, which you used in Tutorial 1, appears, showing the Style name, Font, and Effects choices.

Pick: **New**
Type: **MYTEXT**
Pick: **OK** (or press ↵)

Pick: ***romans.shx*** (from the Font Name pull-down)

You will use the defaults in all other areas of the dialog box. Remember, accepting the defaults now means you will be prompted for these values when you create the text; this method offers you a lot of flexibility when drawing. Do not become confused between style names and font names. A font is a set of characters with a particular shape. When you create a *style*, you can assign it any name you want, but you must specify the name of a font that already exists for the style to use. Your dialog box should look like Figure 5.49.

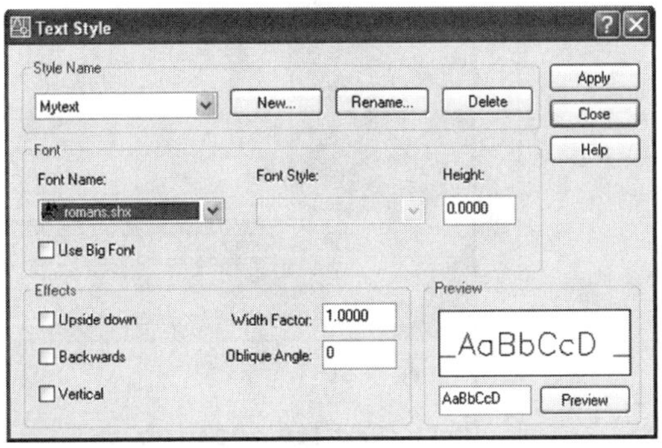

Figure 5.49

Pick: **Apply**
Pick: **Close**

Setting the Viewres Default

The *Viewres* command controls the number of line segments used to draw a circle on your monitor. It does not affect the way that circles are plotted—just how they appear on the screen. Have you noticed that when you use Zoom Window to enlarge a portion of the drawing, circles may appear as octagons? The reason is that Viewres is set to a low number. The default setting is low to save time when you draw circles on the screen. With faster processors and high-resolution graphics, you can use a larger value. You will type VIEWRES at the command prompt.

Tip

If you are using a slower computer system, you may notice that performance on your computer slows down. It may be because of this setting. If you need to, you can reset Viewres to a lower number. Type REGEN at the command prompt to regenerate circles that do not appear round.

Command: **VIEWRES** ↵
Do you want fast zooms? [Yes/No] <Y>: ↵
Enter circle zoom percent (1-20000)<1000>: **5000** ↵

To save your template drawing,

Pick: **Save**

Switching to a Paper Space Layout

Next you will switch to paper space and create a drawing layout that you will use for plotting.

Pick: **Layout1 tab**

Figure 5.50 shows the paper space layout as it appears on your screen.

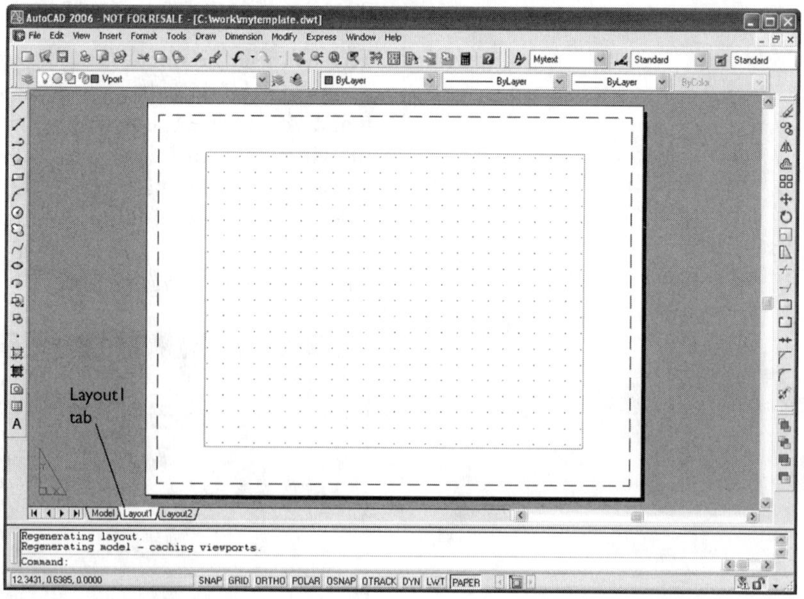

Figure 5.50

Right-click: **Layout2 tab**
Pick: **Delete** (from the short-cut menu)

At the message "The selected layouts will be permanently deleted ...",

Pick: **OK**

Layout 2 is deleted. Keep in mind that it is not a good practice to use multiple layouts in a single drawing if you are going to use the Sheet Set Manager.

The magenta box around the drawing view is the AutoCAD paper space viewport. You can think of it as a hole or window that you can use to look through the paper and see your model space drawing. Figure 5.51 shows another illustration of the concept of model space and paper space. The viewport border is a drawing object in paper space that defines the shape of the window to model space. The zoom factor determines the size at which the model space objects appear in the paper space viewport.

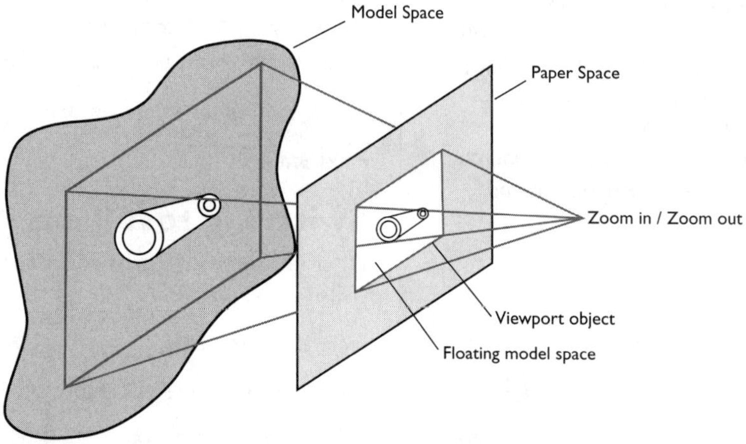

Figure 5.51

Adding a Title Block and Text to Paper Space

You can easily add a title block to your drawing using lines and text in paper space. The advantage of adding the title block, notes, and border to paper space is that the measurements there are the same as you would make them on a regular sheet of paper. For instance, the standard size for text on 8.5" × 11" drawings is 1/8". To add text of this height to paper space, you would set the text height to 1/8" and create the text. If you wanted to add text to model space so that it would appear 1/8" high on the final plot, it would only appear 1/8" tall on the final plot if the scale for the drawing is 1 to 1. Otherwise model space will be plotted at some portion (larger or smaller) of its actual size. For example in the subdivision drawing, you would need to create the text 18.75 units high in model space in order for it to be 1/8" high on the final plot if the subdivision is sized in the viewport to plot at a scale of 1"= 150' (when the drawing units represent feet).

You will draw the border on a separate layer so that you can turn on the display of lineweights to their effect in paper space.

Pick: **BORDER** (to set it as the current layer)
Pick: **to turn on the LWT button on the status bar**

You will use the commands you've learned to add a border and a title block on your own. You will draw the lines for the border of the drawing shown in Figure 5.52.

Pick: **Line icon**
Specify first point: **.5,.25** ↵
Specify next point or [Undo]: **10,.25** ↵
Specify next point or [Undo]: **10,7.75** ↵
Specify next point or [Close/Undo]: **.5,7.75** ↵
Specify next point or [Close/Undo]: **C** ↵

Now you will use the Offset command to offset a line across the bottom of the viewport.

Pick: **Offset icon**
Specify offset distance or [Through/Erase/Layer] <Through>: **.375**
Select object to offset or [Exit/Undo] <Exit>: **pick the bottom border line**
Specify point on side to offset or [Exit/Multiple/Undo] <Exit>: **pick above the bottom border line**
Select object to offset or [Exit/Undo] <Exit>: ↵

The border lines and title strip should appear in your drawing as shown in Figure 5.52.

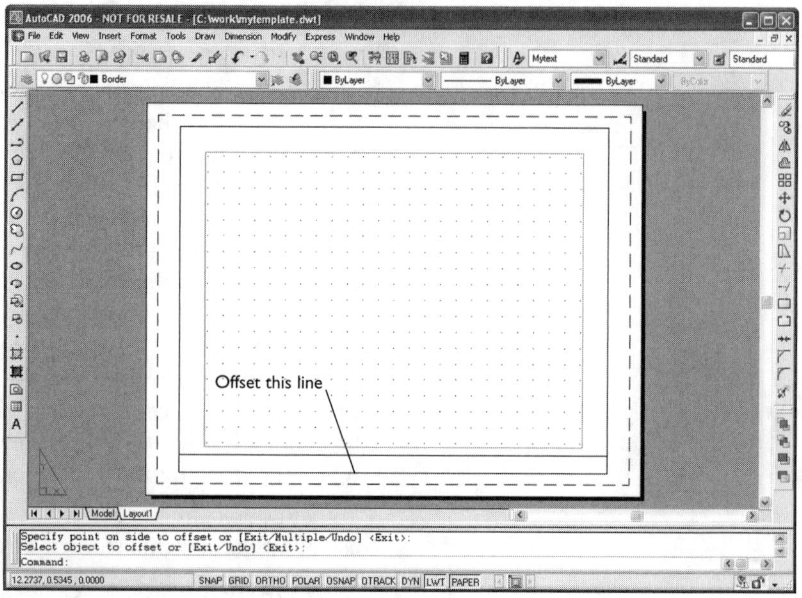

Figure 5.52

Pick: **Zoom Window icon**

Enlarge the lower left corner of the drawing as in Figure 5.53 so that you can see the lineweight used to represent the border.

Figure 5.53

Pick: **Zoom Previous icon**

Your view returns to show the entire drawing area.

Using Divide

The *Divide* command places points along the object that you select, dividing it into the number of segments you specify. You can also choose to have a block of grouped objects placed in the drawing instead of points. You will use the Divide command to place points along the line that you created using Offset, dividing it into three equal segments.

Type: **Divide**
Select object to divide: **pick the line above the bottom border line**
Enter the number of segments or [Block]: **3** ↵

Because the Point Style is set at just a dot, you probably won't be able to see the points that mark the equal segment lengths. You will use the Point Style dialog box to change the display of points in the drawing to a larger style so you can see them easily.

Pick: **Format, Point Style**

The Point Style dialog box shown in Figure 5.54 now appears on your screen. On your own, select one of the point styles that has a circle or target around the point so that it is easily seen. To exit the dialog box,

Pick: **OK**

The points should appear larger on the screen now. Your drawing should look similar to that in Figure 5.55.

Tip

The Measure command is similar to the Divide command. However, instead of specifying the number of segments into which you want to have an object divided, with Measure you specify the length of the segment you would like to have. Like Divide, Measure puts points or groups of objects called blocks (which you will learn about in Tutorial 10) at specified distances along the line.

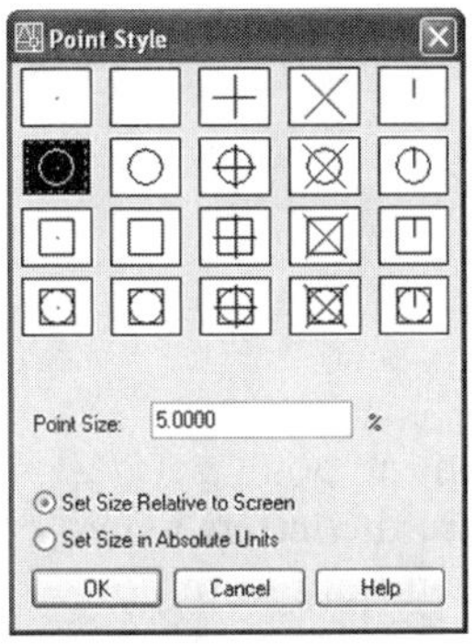

Figure 5.54

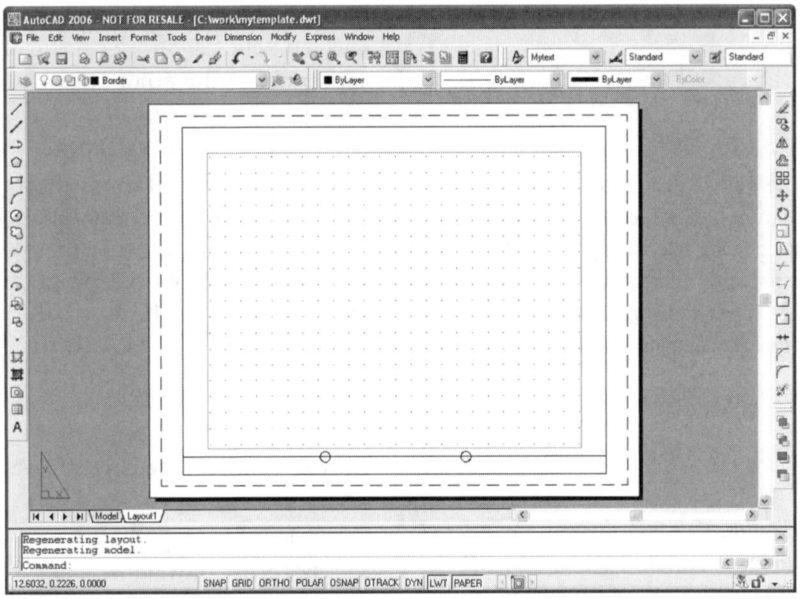

Figure 5.55

You can use the Node object snap to find point objects in your drawing. To draw lines dividing the title area exactly into thirds,

Right-click: **OSNAP button and pick Settings**
Pick: **Node and Perpendicular** (from the Object Snap tab)
Pick: **OK**
Pick: **OSNAP button on status bar to turn it on**

Tip

When the points are sized relative to the screen, they may appear large when you zoom in. To recalculate the display file for your drawing in order to resize them, use the Regen command on the View menu.

Pick: **Line icon**

Specify first point: **target one of the points with AutoSnap™ Node**

Draw a line straight down from the point by using the Perpendicular object snap.

Specify next point or [Undo]: **pick the bottom line of the border when the AutoSnap Perpendicular marker appears**

Now repeat this process on your own to draw another line at the other point.

Pick: **Format, Point Style**

On your own, use the Point Style dialog box to change the point style to a mode that does not display anything. When you are finished,

Pick: **OK** (to exit the Point Style dialog box)

Next you will use the Dtext command to add titles to the drawing.

Set **TEXT** as the current layer.

Make sure you are in **paper space**.

Type: **DTEXT**

Specify start point of text or [Justify/Style]: **C** ↵

Specify center point of text: **5.25, .375** ↵

Specify height <0.2000>: **.125** ↵

Specify rotation angle of text: **0** ↵

Type: **DRAWING TITLE** ↵

The words DRAWING TITLE appear, centered on the point you selected. The centering is horizontal only; otherwise the letters would appear above the point selected for the center. If you want both horizontal and vertical centering, pick the Justify option and then Middle.

Tip

The default justification for Dtext is Bottom Left, so you do not need to specifically select that option. If you want text to be justified bottom left, just select the start point and no other justification options.

Now, repeat this process using the Justify, BL (Bottom Left) option of the Dtext command to position the words DRAWN BY: YOUR NAME in the left part of the title block. You are prompted for the bottom left starting point for the text that you will enter. Use the Justify, BR (Bottom Right) option to right justify the words SCALE: 1=1 in the area to the right. The Justify BR option prompts you for the lowest, rightmost point for the text that you will enter.

Now you have completed a simple title block for your template drawing.

Tip

In AutoCAD 2006 drawings, a field storing information can be inserted into any text area except for tolerances. Fields store information that will update automatically, such as the date or sheet number. Pick Insert, Field from the pull-down menu and use the dialog box that appears to select the type of information to insert. From there follow the prompts similar to inserting text.

On your own, set the current layer to VISIBLE.

Command: **MS** ↵

Command: **Z** ↵

Specify corner of window, enter a scale factor (nX or nXP), or [All/Center/Dynamic/Extents/Previous/Scale/Window/Object] <real time>: **1XP** ↵

You will save this drawing in floating model space so that you can see the paper space border, but still create your new drawing objects in model space. You will leave the drawing zoomed to a scale of 1=1 and with VISIBLE set as the current layer. Then, when you begin a new drawing from this template, you will be ready to start drawing on the layer for VISIBLE lines.

Your drawing should look like Figure 5.56.

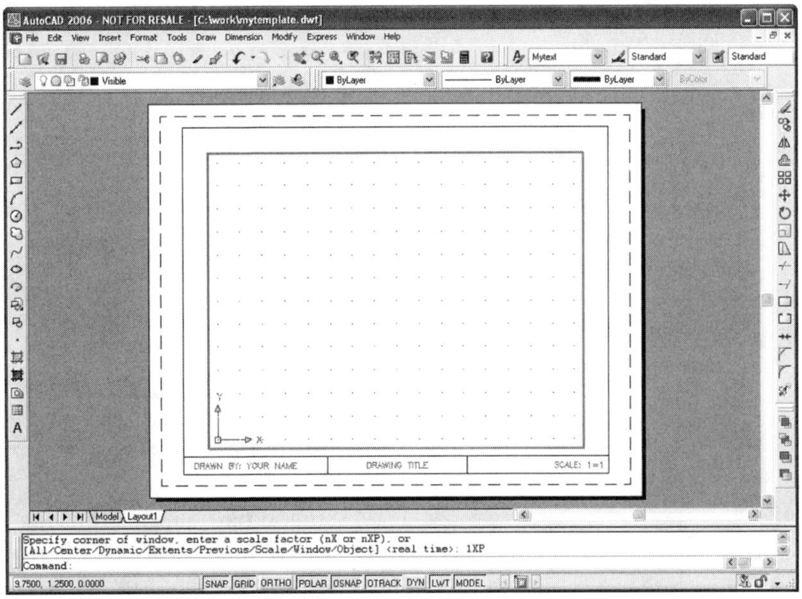

Figure 5.56

Now save your drawing to the file name *mytemplate.dwt*.

Pick: **Save icon**
Pick: **File, Close**

Now you have completed *mytemplate.dwt*. Be sure to keep a copy of the drawing on your own disk. You also should keep a second copy of your drawings on a backup disk, in case the first disk becomes damaged.

You can easily use the Edit Text command to make changes to the standard information you provide in the title block. Refer to Tutorial 1 if you need to review the Edit Text (Ddedit) command.

Tip

If you have access to several different printers or work with different sheet sizes, having several different template drawings is very useful. Or use a standard AutoCAD template and modify it for your uses. Then save it with a new template name.

Beginning a New Drawing from a Template Drawing

You can use any AutoCAD drawing as a starting point for a new drawing. The settings that you have made in drawing *mytemplate.dwt* will be used to start future drawings. An identical template drawing, called *proto.dwt*, is in your datafiles. If you want to use the template you just created, substitute *mytemplate.dwt* whenever you are asked to use *proto.dwt*. Next, you will start a new drawing from your template.

Pick: **New**

Use the dialog box shown in Figure 5.55 to select the correct drive and directory and pick *mytemplate.dwt*. (If you have not created the template in the previous steps, you may substitute the datafile *proto.dwt*.)

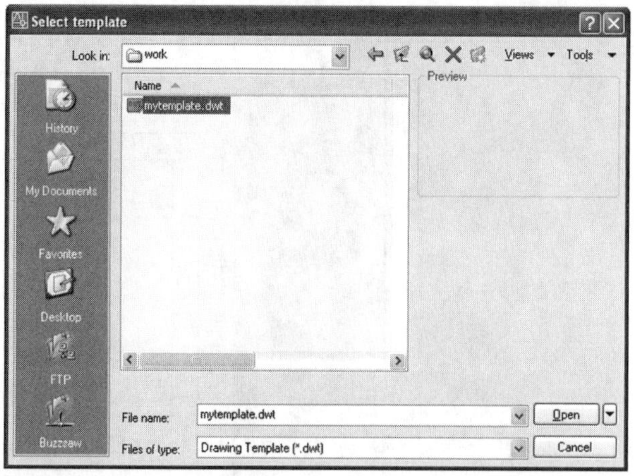

Figure 5.57

When you have finished making this selection, pick Open to return to the drawing editor. Now when you choose Save and are prompted for a new drawing name, the original template file will remain untouched.

Pick: **Save icon**
Type: **TRY1** (for File Name)
Pick: **Save**

Now you can work in the new drawing which is a copy of *mytemplate.dwt*. The drawing *mytemplate.dwt* remains unchanged so that you can use it to start other drawings. Your current drawing name is now *try1.dwg*. For future drawings in this book, use *proto.dwt* or your drawing *mytemplate.dwt* as a template drawing unless you are directed to do otherwise.

Changing the Title Block Text

You created the border, text, and lines of the title block in paper space. To make a change to any of them, you must first return to paper space. Then, you will double-click on the text or use the Edit Text selection (DDedit command) to change the title block text so that it is correct for the new drawing that you are starting.

Tip

You can rename a layout tab by right-clicking on it and picking Rename from the short cut menu.

Tip

You can change the style of text that has already been added to your drawing by picking Text Style from the Styles toolbar. Select a text object. Use the Text Style pull down to view the list of available styles and make a new selection. Remember that you must create styles with the Style command before you can use them. You can also use the Properties palette to change the style, height, width factor, rotation, and location of the text entry.

Command: **PS** ↵
Type: **DDEDIT** ↵
Select an annotation object or [Undo]: **select the text Drawing Title**

The Edit Text box appears in place containing the text you selected. Use the ←, Backspace and/or Delete keys to remove the words "Drawing Title." Change the entry to "Try1." When you have finished editing the text,

Select an annotation object or [Undo]: ↵ (to end the command)

When using a template, remember to make sure that you are in model space before creating drawing objects. Only items like the border, title-block, and general notes and keys should be placed in paper space.

Exit the AutoCAD program and discard the changes to drawing *try1.dwg*.

Key Terms

aspect ratio	paper space	template drawing
floating viewports	paper space layouts	text style
model space	pin-registry	tiled viewports

Key Commands

Divide	Measure	Pan Realtime	Tile
Insert Block	Model Space	Paper Space	Viewport Clip
Layer	Mview	Regen	Viewres

Exercises

Draw the following objects. The letter M after an exercise number means that the given dimensions are in millimeters (metric units).

5.1 Amplifier Circuit

Draw the amplifier circuit. Use the grid at the top to determine the sizes of the components. Each square = 0.0625.

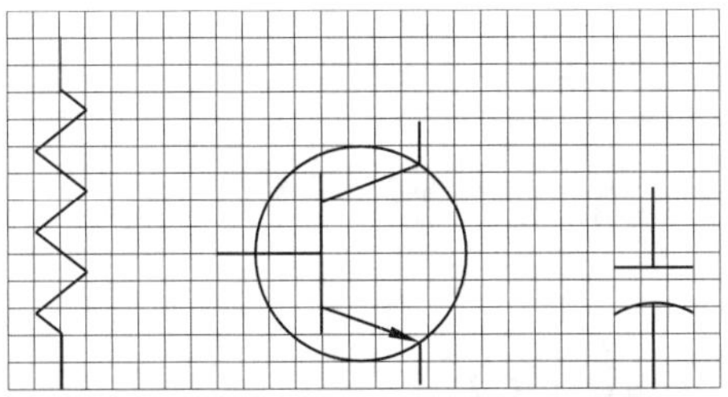

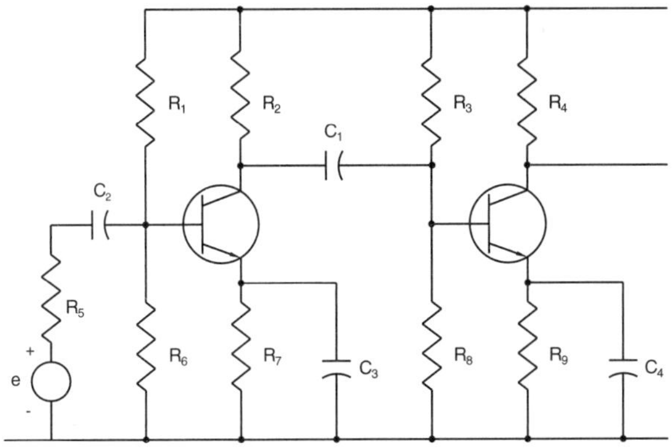

5.2 Support

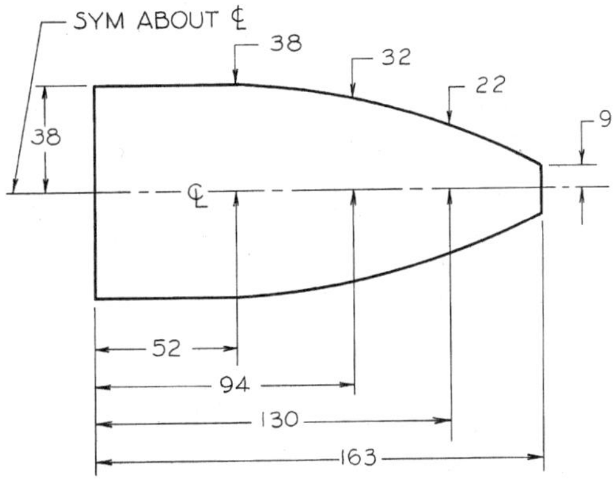

5.3 Vee Block

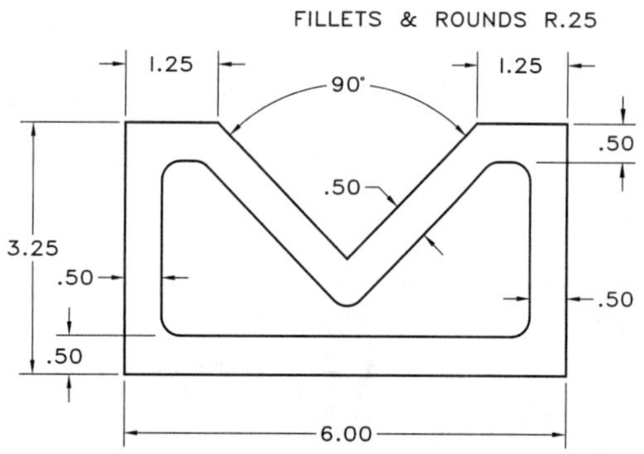

5.4M Grab Link

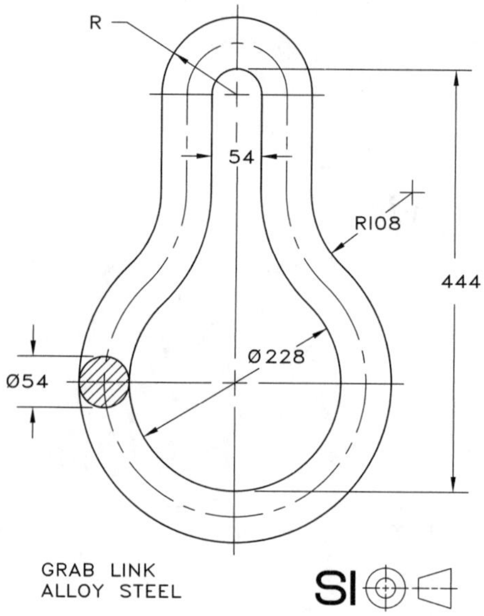

5.5M Tee Handle

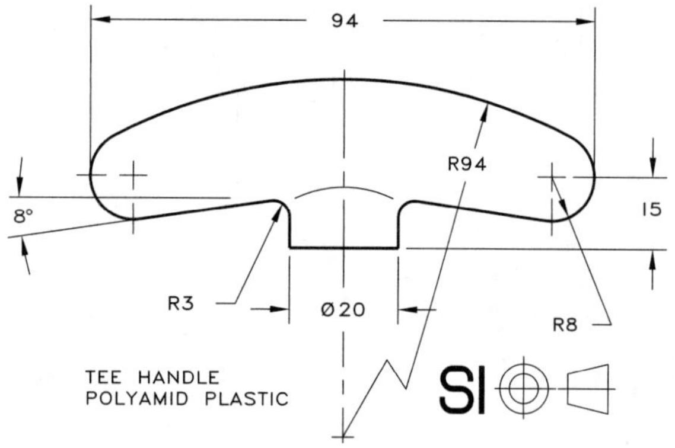

5.6 Idler Pulley Bracket

Create the front view for the object shown.

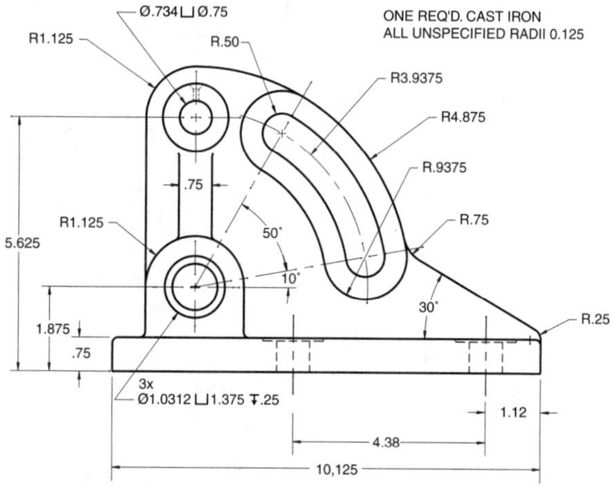

5.7 Hanger

Draw the object shown. Set Limits to (–4, –4) and (8, 5). Set Snap to 0.25 and Grid to 0.5. The origin (0, 0) is to be the center of the left circle. Do not include the dimensions.

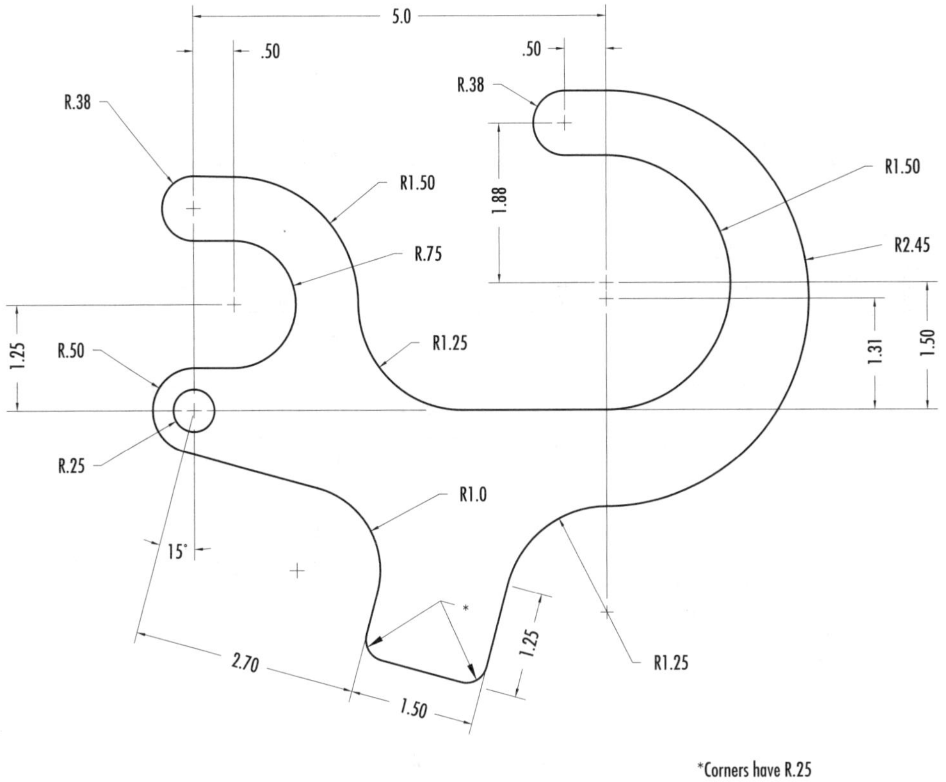

5.8 Title Block

Create this title block as a model space drawing. Explore using fields or attributes for the date, scale, and other changeable information. Use the Insert command to add this title block in paper space to other drawings.

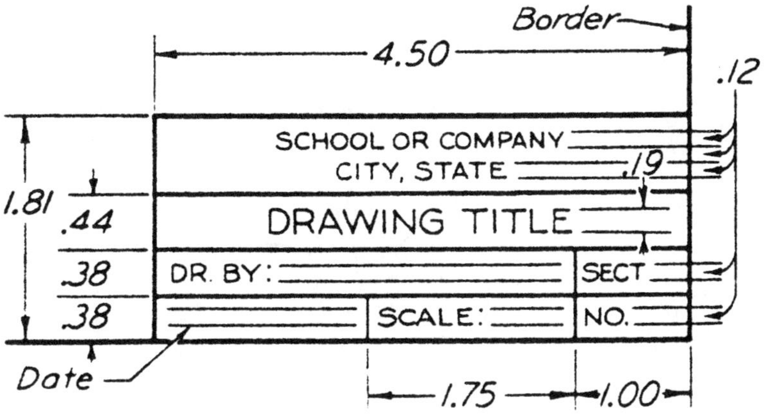

5.9 Window Schedule

Redraw the window schedule shown below. Experiment with different fonts.

WINDOW SCHEDULE

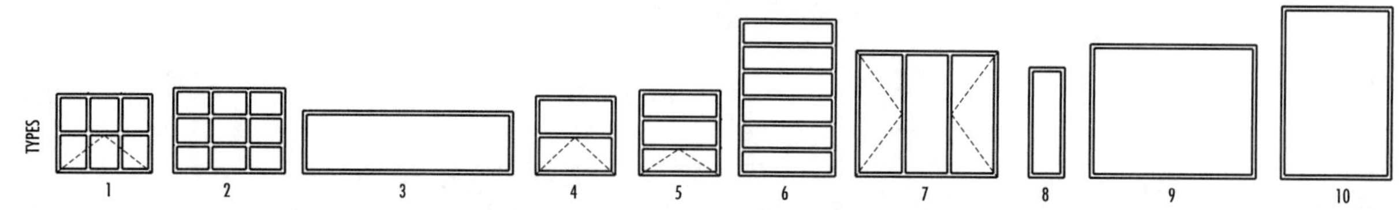

SYM	TYPE	SIZE		MATL FIN	FRAME	FIN SCRN AREA	AREA		VENT	GLAZING		DETAILS			REMARKS
		H	W								MAT'L	H	J	S	
A	1	5'-0"	6'-4"	MTL	ST	MTL	ST	Y	32.5 SF	65 SF					
B	2	5'-5"	7'-4"	MTL	ST	MTL	ST	N		40.5 SF					FIXED GLAZING
C	3	4'-0"	14'-8"	MTL	ST	MTL	ST	N		58.8 SF					FIXED GLAZING
D	4	7'-0"	5'-0"	MTL	ST	MTL	ST	N		70 SF					FIXED GLAZING
E	5	5'-5"	4'-6"	MTL	ST	MTL	ST	N		48.6 SF					FIXED GLAZING
F	6	5'-0"	5'-4"	MTL	ST	MTL	ST	Y	13.3 SF	26.5 SF					
G	7	5'-5"	5'-4"	MTL	ST	MTL	ST	Y	9.9 SF	29.7 SF					
H	8	8'-0"	6'-4"	MTL	ST	MTL	ST	N		100.8 SF					FIXED GLAZING
I	9	5'-6"	6'-4"	MTL	ST	MTL	ST	N		126.1 SF					FIXED GLAZING
J	10	8'-0"	9'-4"	MTL	ST	MTL	ST	Y	24.8 SF	74.4 SF					
K	11	5'-6"	4'-8"	MTL	ST	MTL	ST	N		25.3 SF					FIXED GLAZING
L	12	6'-0"	3'-0"	WD	ST	WD	ST	N		36 SF					FIXED GLAZING
M	13	7'-6"	11'-6"	WD	ST	WD	ST	N		86.3 SF					FIXED GLAZING WITH CURVED GLASS
N	14	10'-0"	8'-0"	MTL	ST	MTL	ST	N		160 SF					FIXED GLAZING
O	15	10'-0"	14'-0'	MTL	ST	MTL	ST	N		140 SF					FIXED GLAZING
P	16	6'-0"	6'-6"	WD	ST	WD	ST	N		32.5 SF					FIXED GLAZING

5.10 Saw Blade

Draw the saw blade shown below. Use Array and Polyline. Do not include dimensions. Use the Arc option of the Polyline command to create the thick arc. Add the arrow to the arc by making a Polyline with a beginning width of 0 and a thicker ending width to show the blade's rotation.

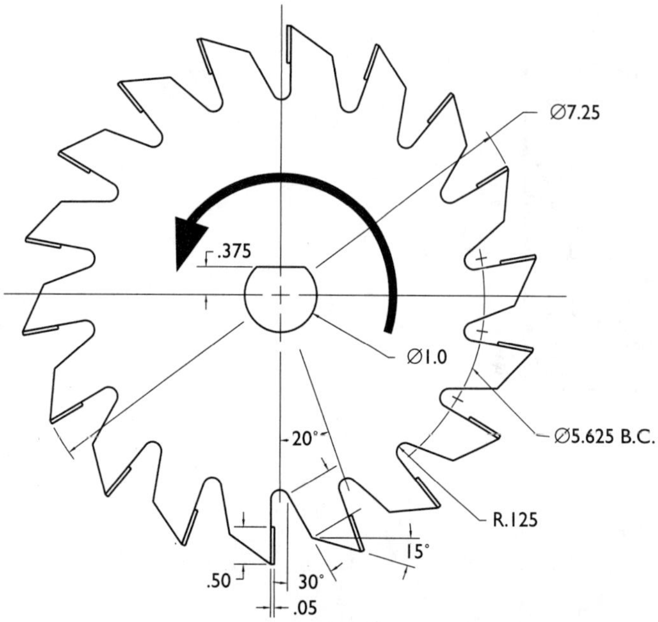

5.11 Five Lobe Knob

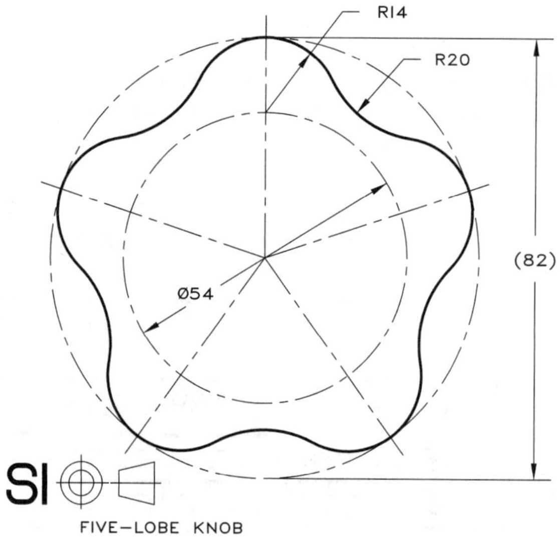

Tutorial

6 2D Orthographic Drawings

Objectives

When you have completed this tutorial, you will be able to

1. Create 2D orthographic drawings.
2. Use Ortho for horizontal and vertical lines.
3. Create construction lines.
4. Draw hidden, projection, center, and miter lines.
5. Set the global linetype scaling factor.
6. Add correctly drawn centermarks to circular shapes.

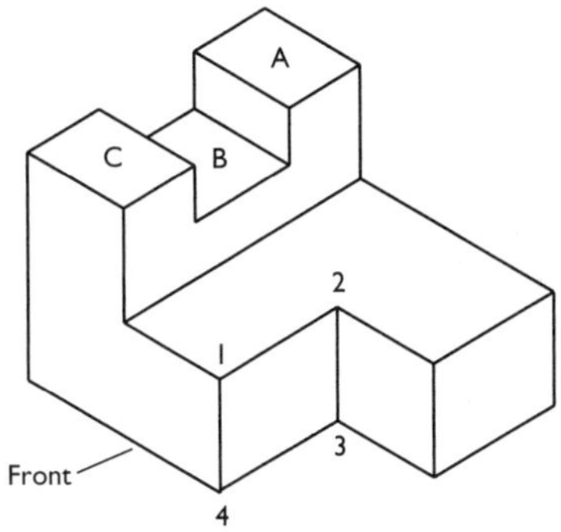

Figure 6.1

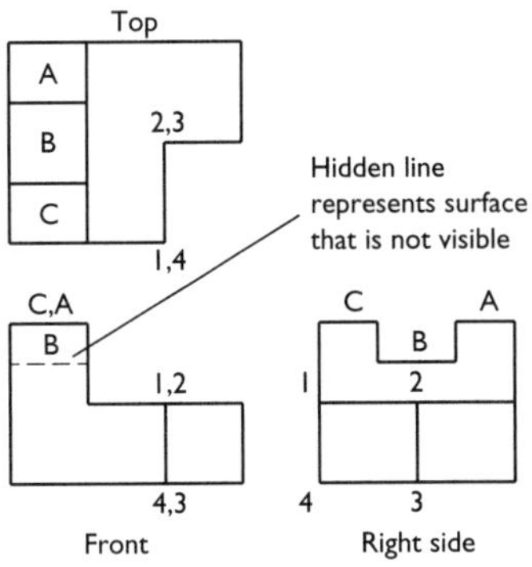

Figure 6.2

Introduction

In this tutorial you will apply many of the commands that you have learned to create orthographic views. *Orthographic views* are two-dimensional (2D) drawings that you use to depict accurately the shape of three-dimensional (3D) objects. You will learn to look at a 3D object and draw a set of 2D drawings that define it. In Tutorial 11 you will learn to create a 3D solid model of an object.

The Front, Top, and Right-Side Orthographic Views

Technical drawings usually require front, top, and right-side orthographic views to define completely the shape of an object. Some objects require fewer views and others require more. All the objects in this tutorial require three views. Each orthographic view is a 2D drawing showing only two of the three dimensions (height, width, and depth). Thus no individual view contains sufficient information to define completely the shape of the object. You must look at all three views together to comprehend the object's shape. For this reason it is important that the views be shown in the correct relationship to each other.

Figure 6.1 shows a part and Figure 6.2 shows the front, top, and right-side orthographic views of the part.

Three rectangular surfaces, labeled A, B, and C, are located on the left side of the top view. Which surface is the highest? The top view alone is not sufficient to answer this question. The three surfaces must be located on the other views for you to comprehend the relationships among them. The right-side view (often just referred to as the side or profile view) shows that surfaces A and C are the same height and that surface B is lower.

The side view shows the relative locations of surfaces A, B, and C, but the surfaces appear as straight lines; therefore, you need the top view to see the overall shape of the surfaces. You need both the top view and the side view to define the size, shape, and location of the surfaces.

Look at surface 1–2–3–4 in the right-side view of Figure 6.2. Its shape is shown in the right-side view, but it appears as a straight line in the front and top views because it's perpendicular to the views—like a sheet of paper viewed edge on. A plane surface appears as a straight line when viewed from a direction where the surface is perpendicular to the viewing plane. Surfaces that are perpendicular to two of the three principal orthographic views are called *normal surfaces* (normal meaning 90 degrees). Normal surfaces show the true size of the surface in one of the principal views. All surfaces in the object shown in Figure 6.1 are normal surfaces.

All surfaces should be drawn in all views or the view should be clearly labeled as a partial view. Surface B is shown in the front view of Figure 6.2 with a hidden line. A ***hidden line*** represents a surface not directly visible, that is, hidden from view by some other surface on the object.

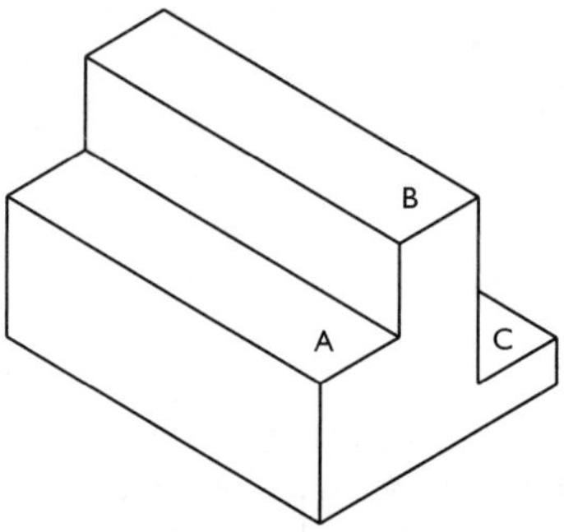

Figure 6.3

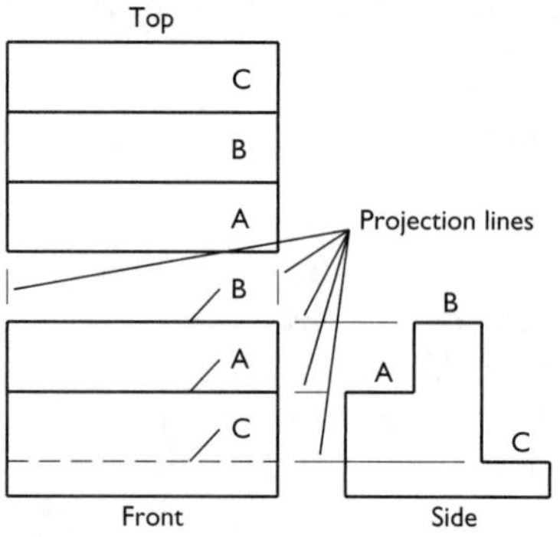

Figure 6.4

View Location

The locations of the front, top, and side views on a drawing are critical. The top view must be located directly above the front view. The side view should be located directly to the right of the front view. An alternative position for the side view is to rotate it 90° and align it with the top view. By aligning the views precisely with each other, you can interpret them together to understand the 3D object they represent. Because views are shown in alignment, you can project information from one view to another. Refer to Figures 6.3 and 6.4.

Surfaces A, B, and C in Figure 6.3 appear as three straight lines in the front view. Which line represents which surface? Because the front and side views are aligned, you can draw horizontal lines from the vertices of the surfaces in the front view to locate them in the side view. These lines are called ***projection lines*** and each surface is located between its projection lines in both views. You can locate surfaces between the front and top views by using vertical projection lines. Without exact view alignment, you couldn't relate the lines and surfaces of one view to those of another view, making it difficult or impossible to interpret the object shown in the drawing.

Starting

Before you begin, **launch AutoCAD® 2006.**

You will begin this tutorial by drawing an orthographic view for the adapter in Figure 6.6. The file *proto.dwt* has been provided with the datafiles so that you can be sure you are using the same settings as are used in the tutorial.

Tip

You can substitute your drawing mytemplate.dwt *if you have finished it correctly.*

To start a drawing from a template as you did at the end of Tutorial 5,

Pick: **File, New**

Use the dialog box that appears on your screen to select the file ***proto.dwt*** from the datafiles that accompany this text **in the Datafile 2006** folder. When you have finished selecting it,

Pick: **Open** (you should see the preview in the dialog box)

Pick: **Save icon**

Type: **ADAPTORT** and save to your ***c:\work*** directory

Pick: **Save**

The main AutoCAD drawing editor should reappear on your display screen with Adaptort in the title bar as shown in Figure 6.5.

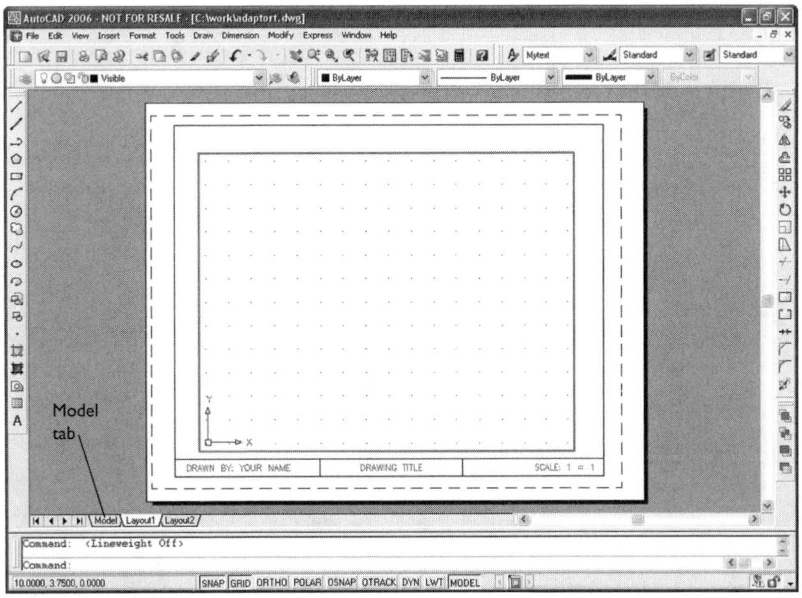

Figure 6.5

On your own, be sure that **Grid** and **Snap** are turned on. The grid should be set to **0.5** spacing and the snap set to **0.25** spacing and turned on; the grid should be on your screen and the Snap button should be selected on the status bar. You should be in floating **model space**. Make sure that **VISIBLE** is the current layer. Check that the **POLAR**, **OSNAP**, **OTRACK**, **LWT**, and **DYN** buttons on your status bar are turned **off**.

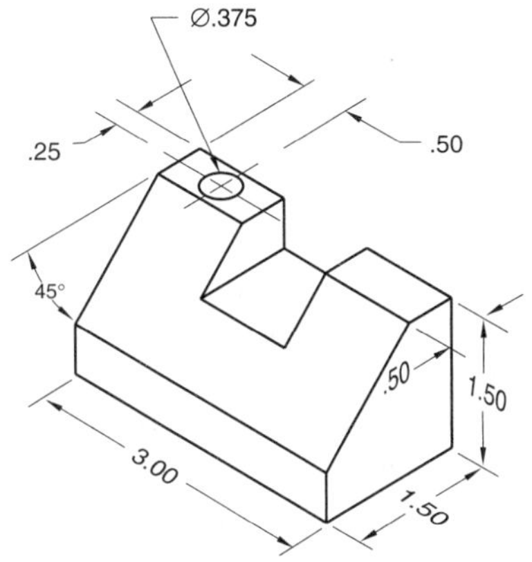

Figure 6.6

Figure 6.6 shows the adapter that you will create. All dimensions are in decimal inches.

Switching to Model Space

You can view and edit model space from a layout in the area inside a viewport (floating model space) as you see on your screen. You can also temporarily disable the paper space layout and work in model space alone. You will work in model space during this tutorial and then switch back to the layout for plotting.

Pick: **Model tab** (labeled in Figure 6.5)

The border and text should disappear from your screen leaving only model space, as shown in Figure 6.7. Notice that both the model tab and model space button are now highlighted.

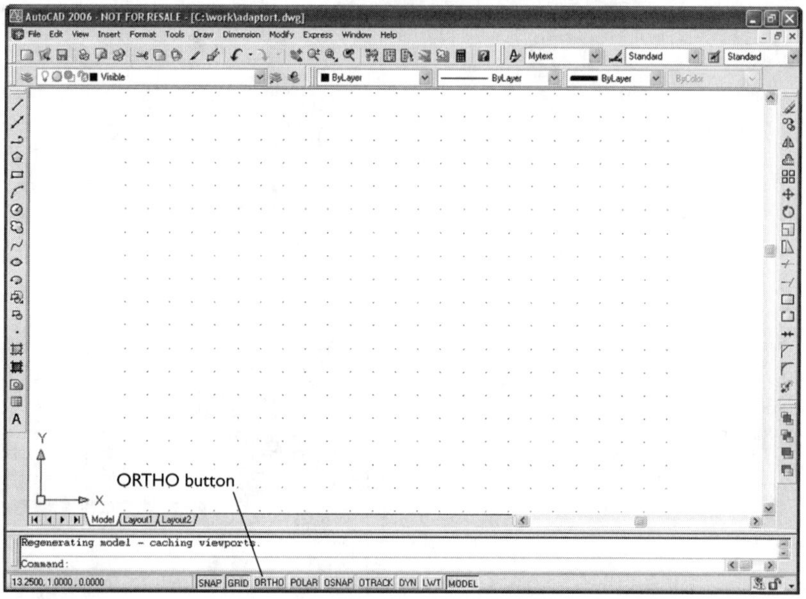

Figure 6.7

Deciding the Model Space Limits

Recall from Tutorial 5 that you can use the Limits command in paper space to set the limits of the paper area that you want to draw on. You can also use the Limits command in model space to set the limits of the area that you will use to create your real-world model of the object. The limits set in paper space and in model space do not have to be the same. Set the limits in model space to the value necessary to fit the views of the object that you are creating. You can change the limits at any time during a drawing session by using the Limits command.

Examine the size of the part and the amount of space the views will require. Then set the model space limits to allow a big enough area to create the views. The adapter is 3 inches wide, 1.5 inches high, and 1.5 inches deep. The slot in the top of the adapter is 0.5 inch deep. The default limits for model space are 12 × 9 units. The adapter that you will draw does not require much space; therefore, you will leave the limits set to 12 × 9 units.

Viewing the Model Space Limits

Use the command Zoom All in model space to show the drawing limits or extents (of the drawing objects), whichever is larger.

Pick: **Zoom All icon**

Move the cursor around inside the drawing area. You should see that the coordinates and grid match the limits of the drawing.

Using Ortho

You can use the Ortho command to restrict Line and other commands to operate only horizontally and vertically. This feature is very handy when you are drawing orthographic views and projecting information between the views. You toggle the Ortho mode on and off by picking the ORTHO button on the status bar or by pressing the F8 function key to easily activate it when you are in a different command.

Pick: **ORTHO button**

The ORTHO button on the status bar should now be highlighted to show that it is active.

Next, you will draw the horizontal and vertical construction lines, as shown in Figure 6.8. These lines will represent the leftmost and bottom-most margins of your orthogonal views. The coordinates are given for the lines you will create to ensure that your results will be the same as in the tutorial. In general, you can create the construction lines at any location and then move the views if necessary. Don't worry if the views are not perfectly centered when you begin your drawing. You will center the views after you've drawn them and seen how much room is needed.

Drawing Construction Lines

Construction lines extend infinitely. The default method for drawing a construction line is to specify two points through which it passes. When you use the Horizontal option, the line is drawn parallel to the X-axis through the point you select. The Vertical option is the same, but creates a line parallel to the Y-axis. Using the Angle option, you can specify the construction line by entering the angle and a point through which the line passes. The Bisect option lets you define an angle by three points and create a construction line that bisects it. Finally, the Offset option allows you to specify the offset distance or through point, as when you use the Offset command, to create an infinite construction line.

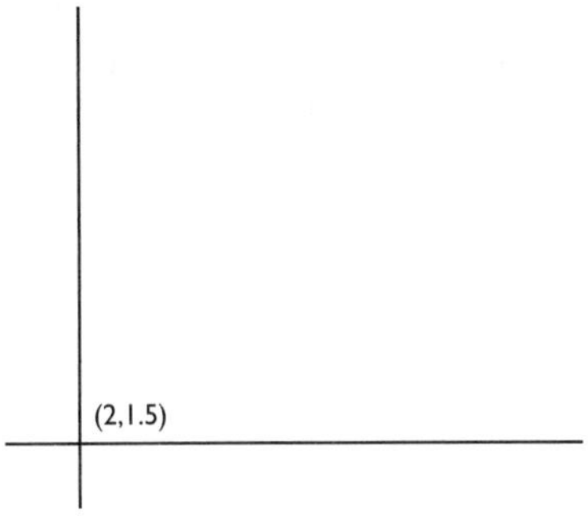

Figure 6.8

Pick: **Construction Line icon**
Specify a point or [Hor/Ver/Ang/Bisect/Offset]: **2,1.5** ↵
Specify through point: **pick to the right to define a horizontal line**
Specify through point: **pick above to define a vertical line**
Specify through point: ↵

Two infinite construction lines appear in your drawing similar to Figure 6.8: One is vertical through point (2,1.5), and the other is horizontal through the same point. They are on layer VISIBLE. You should have the LWT button turned off, which often makes it easier to work on the drawing.

Next, you will use the Offset command to create a series of parallel horizontal and vertical lines to define the overall dimensions of each view, as shown in Figure 6.9. Then, you will trim the lines to remove the excess portions. If you need to, review the Offset command in Tutorial 3.

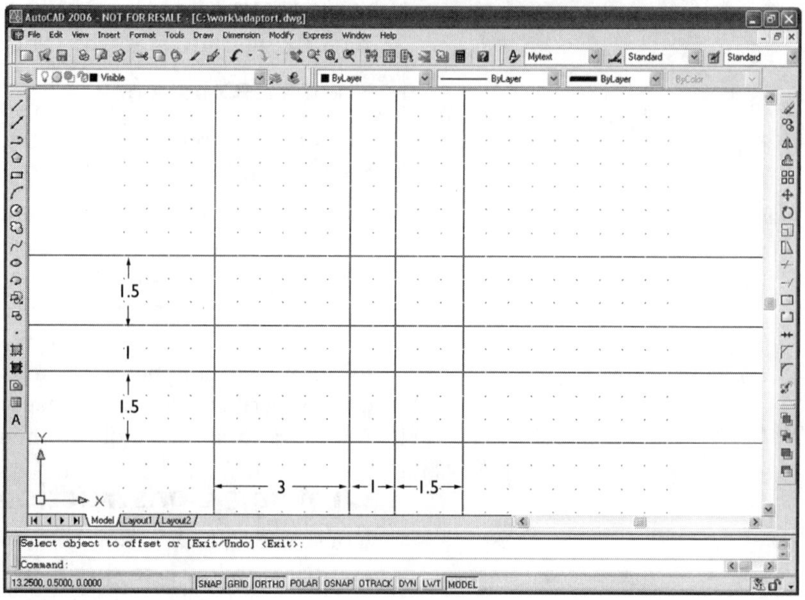

Figure 6.9

For the first horizontal line,

Pick: **Offset icon**
Specify offset distance or [Through/Erase/Layer] <Through>: **1.5** ↵
Select object to offset or [Exit/Undo] <Exit>: **pick the horizontal line**
Specify point on side to offset? **pick any point above the horizontal line**

A new line is created, parallel to the bottom line and exactly 1.5 units away. You will end the command with the ↵ key because the next line will be a different distance away.

Select object to offset or [Exit/Undo] <Exit>: ↵

You will restart the Offset command by pressing ↵ so that you are prompted again for the offset distance.

Command: ↵
Specify offset distance or [Through/Erase/Layer] <1.5000>: **1** ↵
Select object to offset or [Exit/Undo] <Exit>: **pick the newly offset line**
Specify point on side to offset? **pick any point above the line**

A line appears 1.00 unit away from the line you selected.

Select object to offset or [Exit/Undo] <Exit>: ↵
Now repeat this process on your own until you have created all the horizontal and vertical construction lines according to the dimensions shown in Figure 6.9. The lines are parallel to the horizontal line at distances of 1.5 (the given height of the object), 2.5 (the 1.5-inch height and an arbitrary 1-inch spacing between the front and top views), and 4 (the 1.5-inch height plus 1 plus the 1.5-inch depth of the object). Your screen should look like Figure 6.9.

You will define the areas for the front, top, and side views by using the Trim command to remove excess lines. You will pick Trim from the

Modify toolbar and use implied Crossing to select all the lines as cutting edges. Recall that, when construction lines have one end trimmed, they become rays. When trimmed again, they become lines. Use Figure 6.10 to determine which construction lines to trim.

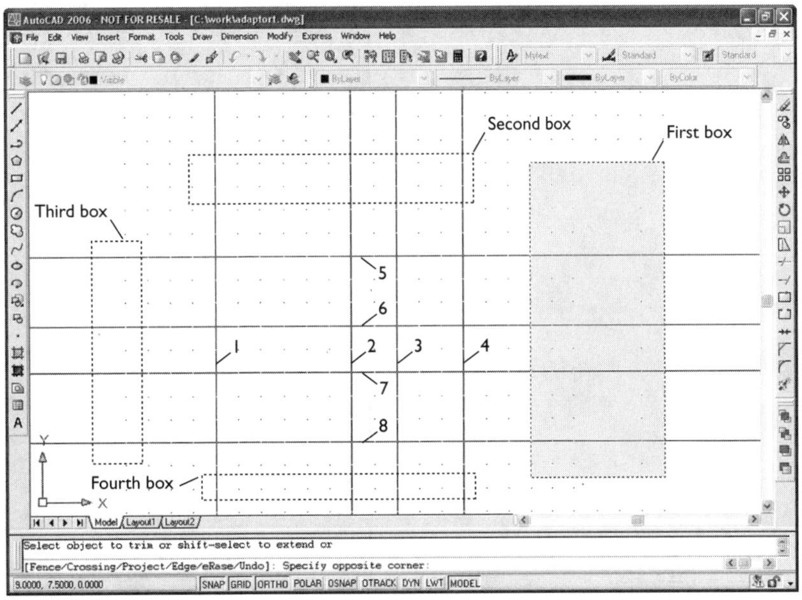

Figure 6.10

Pick: **Trim icon**

Select cutting edges

Select objects or <select all>: ↵

Select cutting edges ...

Select object to trim or shift-select to extend or
[Fence/Crossing/Project/Edge/eRase/Undo]: **pick to the right of the lines to create a crossing box as shown in Figure 6.10**

Select object to trim or shift-select to extend or
[Fence/Crossing/Project/Edge/eRase/Undo]: **create a crossing box to trim the vertical lines where they extend above the upper horizontal line**

Select object to trim or shift-select to extend or
[Fence/Crossing/Project/Edge/eRase/Undo]: **create a crossing box to trim the vertical lines where they extend below the lower horizontal line**

Select object to trim or shift-select to extend or
[Fence/Crossing/Project/Edge/eRase/Undo]: **create a crossing box to trim the horizontal lines where they extend to the left of the leftmost vertical line**

Select object to trim or shift-select to extend or
[Fence/Crossing/Project/Edge/eRase/Undo]: **pick lines 1–8 to trim** (see Figure 6.10)

Tip

Turn Snap off while trimming to make it easier to select lines.

Next use the Erase option of the Trim command to remove the lines in the upper right as shown in Figure 6.11. You should still have the Trim command active.

Select object to trim or shift-select to extend or [Fence/Crossing/Project/Edge/eRase/Undo]: **R** ↵

Select objects to erase or <exit>: **use a crossing box to select the upper right lines to erase as shown in Figure 6.11** ↵

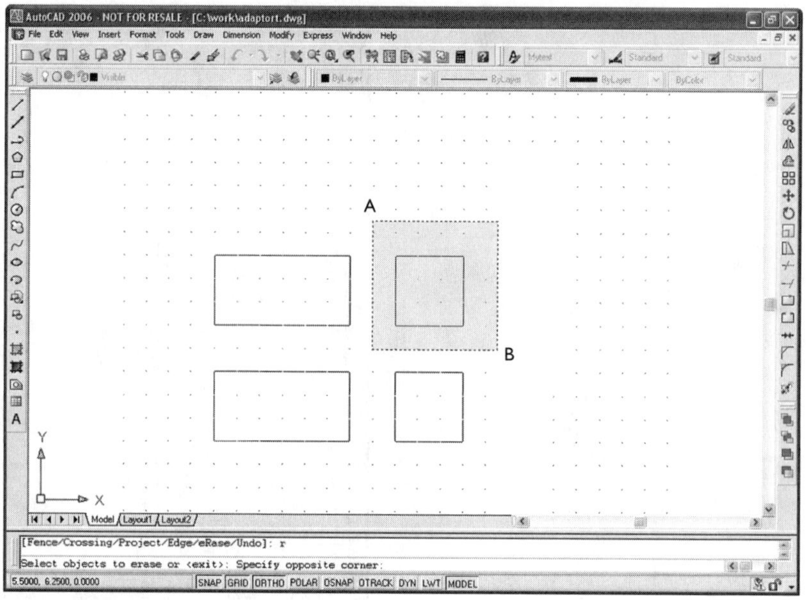

Figure 6.11

Use **Zoom Window** on your own to enlarge the drawing so that it fills the screen.

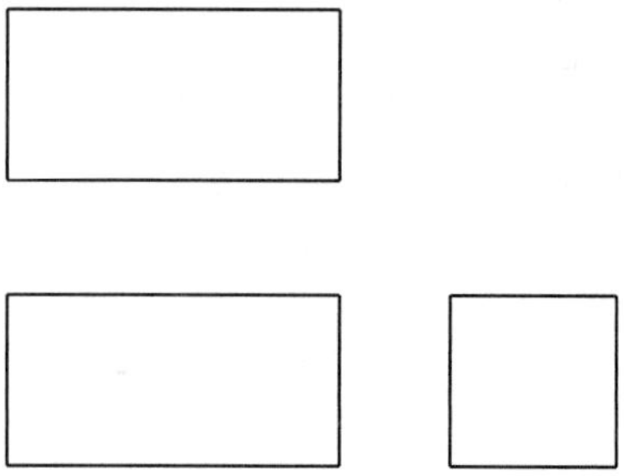

Figure 6.12

Your drawing should be similar to Figure 6.12. The overall dimensions of the views are established and aligned correctly.

Next, draw the slot in the front view. Use the following points or create the lines on your own by looking at the dimensions specified on the object in Figure 6.6.

Pick: **Line icon**

Specify first point: **3,3** ↵

Specify next point or [Undo]: **3,2.5** ↵

Specify next point or [Close/Undo]: **4,2.5** ↵

Specify next point or [Close/Undo]: **4,3** ↵

Specify next point or [Close/Undo]: ↵

On your own, use the **Trim** command and remove the center portion of the top horizontal line.

Your drawing should look like Figure 6.13.

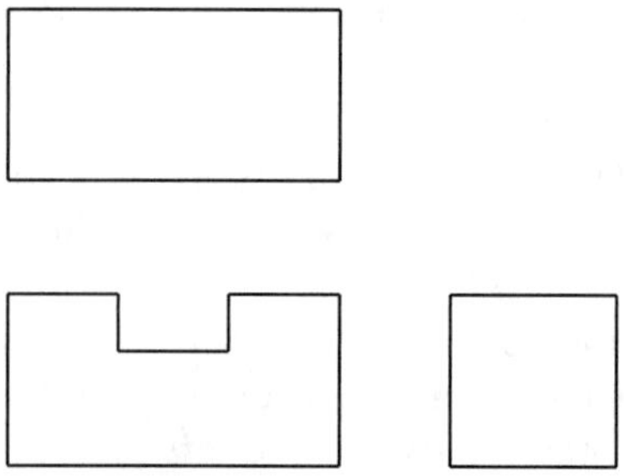

Figure 6.13

Hidden Lines

You will use hidden lines to represent the lines that are not visible in the side view. Remember, each view is a view of the entire object drawn from that line of sight. All surfaces are shown in every view. A hidden line in the drawing represents one of three things:

1. An intersection of two surfaces that is behind another surface and therefore not visible;

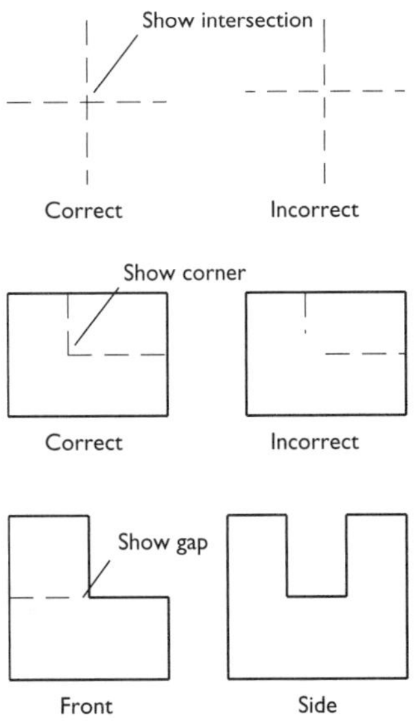

Figure 6.14

2. The *edge view* of a hidden surface; or
3. The hidden outer limit of a curved surface, also called the *limiting element* of a contour.

You should follow at least three general practices when drawing hidden lines to help prevent confusion and to make the drawing easier to read.

- Clearly show intersections, using intersecting line segments.
- Clearly show corners, using intersecting line segments.
- Leave a noticeable gap (about 1/16") between colinear continuous lines and hidden lines.

See Figure 6.14.

These hidden line practices are sometimes difficult to implement using CAD. If you change one hidden line using the global linetype scale command, so that it looks better, all the other hidden lines take on the same characteristics and may be adversely affected. As you saw in Tutorial 4, you can change individual lines to have different linetype scales than the general pattern. However, hidden line practices are not followed as strictly as they once were, partly because with CAD drawings plotted on a good-quality plotter, the thick visible lines can easily be distinguished from the thinner hidden lines. The results of a reasonable attempt to conform to the standard are considered acceptable in most drawing practices.

Hidden lines are usually drawn in a different color than the one used for the continuous object lines on the AutoCAD drawing screen. This practice helps distinguish the different types of lines on the screen and makes them easier to interpret. Also, you often control printers and plotters by using different colors in the drawing to represent different thicknesses or patterns of lines on the plot. You can use any color, but be consistent: Make all hidden lines the same color. The best approach is to set the color and linetype by layer and draw the hidden lines on that separate layer with the correct properties. That's why BYLAYER is the AutoCAD default choice for color, lineweight, and linetype. A separate layer for hidden lines already exists in the *proto.dwt* template drawing from which you started *adaptort.dwg*.

Tip

To improve the appearance of hidden lines, you can use the Linetype Control on the Properties toolbar to set the linetype scale for individual graphical objects. Another way to improve their appearance is by drawing polylines. For hidden lines drawn with a polyline, you can set the Plinegen variable to 1 to make the linetype a continuous pattern over the length of the polyline. When you set this variable to 0, each segment of the polyline begins and ends with a dash. Use the Pedit, Ltypegen command option to set this variable. This method can improve the appearance of intersecting hidden lines.

Drawing Hidden Lines

Now you will create a hidden line in the side view of your drawing to represent the bottom surface of the slot. You will use the Layer Control to set the current layer.

Pick: **HIDDEN_LINES** (to make it current using the Layer Control)

Next you will add a horizontal line from the bottom edge of the slot in the front view into the side view. This line will be used to *project* the depth of the slot to the side view. Verify that the ORTHO button on the status bar is highlighted. For drawing the following lines, the running object snap Intersection will be quite helpful.

Right-click: **OSNAP button**
Pick: **Settings**
Pick: **Clear All** (from the Object Snap tab of the dialog box)
Pick: **Intersection**

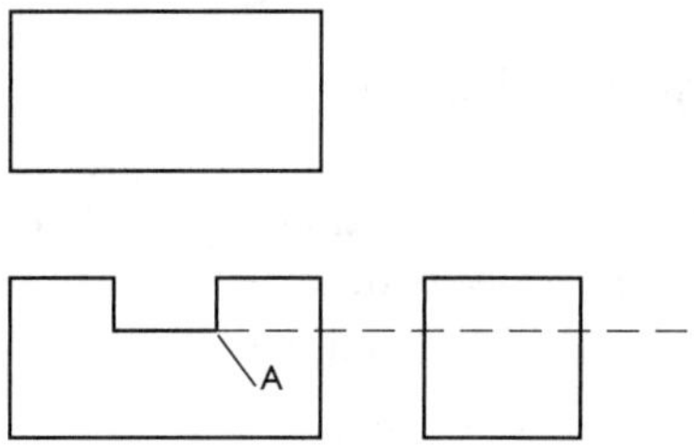

Figure 6.15

Pick: **OK** (to exit the dialog box)
Pick: **OSNAP button** (to turn it on)
Pick: **Line icon**
Specify first point: **pick the lower right corner (A) of the slot in the front view; an AutoSnap™ marker should appear at that point**
Specify next point or [Undo]: **pick any point to the right of the side view**
Specify next point or [Undo]: ↵

Your drawing should look like Figure 6.15.

On your own, trim the projection line so that only the portion within the side view remains.

Your screen should look like that shown in Figure 6.16.

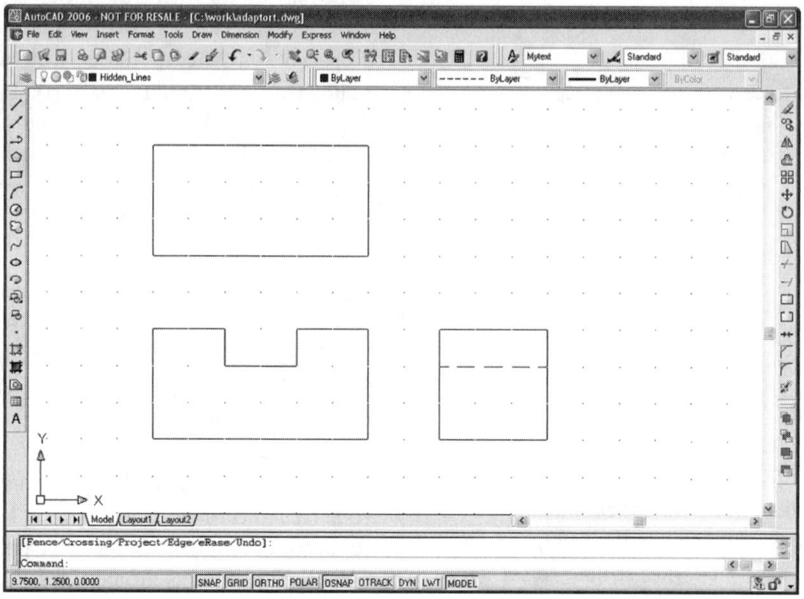

Figure 6.16

Next, you will use the Line command to project the width of the slot from the front view into the top view using vertical lines created on layer VISIBLE. You will also turn on the running object snap Perpendicular.

Pick: **VISIBLE** to set it current using the Layer Control
Right-click: **OSNAP button**
Pick: **Settings**
Pick: **Perpendicular** (from the Object Snap tab of the dialog box)
Pick: **OK** (to exit the dialog box)
On your own, make sure that **Ortho** is **on**, so that your projection lines will be straight. Now you are ready to draw the lines for the slot.
Pick: **Line icon**
Specify first point: **target the upper left corner of the slot in the front view, labeled 1 in Figure 6.17**
Specify next point or [Undo]: **pick a point on the upper line of the top view, labeled 2, using the AutoSnap Perpendicular marker**

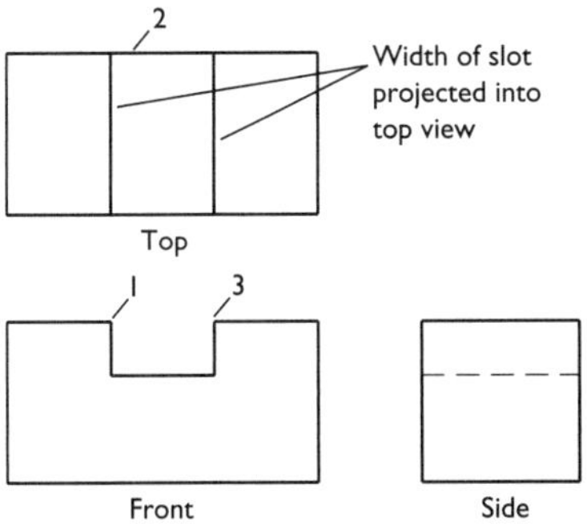

Figure 6.17

Specify next point or [Undo]: ↵
Command: ↵ (to restart the Line command)
Specify first point: **target the upper right corner of the slot in the front view, labeled 3**
Specify next point or [Undo]: **pick a point on the upper line of the top view, labeled 2, using the AutoSnap Perpendicular marker**
Specify next point or [Undo]: ↵
On your own, use the **Trim** command to remove the excess lines.

Your drawing should be similar to Figure 6.17.

Save *adaptort.dwg* before you continue.

Line Precedence

Different types of lines often align with each other within the same view, as illustrated in Figure 6.18.

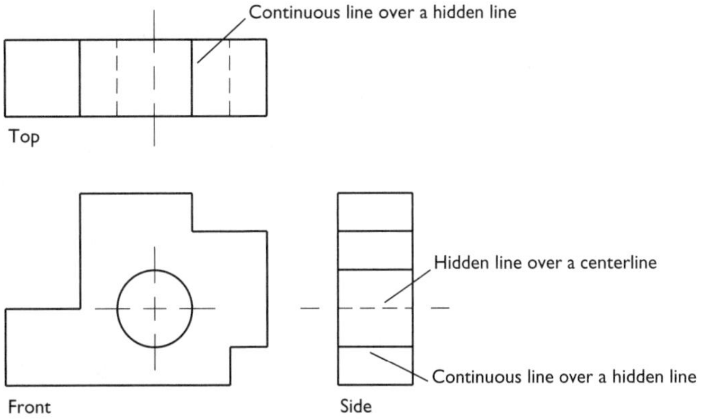

Figure 6.18

Which line should you draw when two overlap? The rule is that continuous lines take *precedence* over hidden lines, and hidden lines take precedence over centerlines. Note that in the side view of Figure 6.18, the short end segments of the covered-up centerline show beyond the edge of the object. This practice is sometimes used to show the centerline underlying the hidden line. If you show the short end segments where a centerline would extend, leave a gap so that the centerline does not touch the other line, as that makes interpreting the lines difficult.

The AutoCAD software doesn't determine line precedence for you. You must decide which lines to show in your 2D orthographic views. If you draw a line on top of another line, both lines will be in your AutoCAD drawing. If you are using a plotter, both will plot, making a darker or thicker line than should be shown. On your screen you may not notice that there are two lines because one line will be exactly over the other.

Slanted Surfaces

Orthographic views can only distinguish *inclined surfaces* (surfaces that are tipped away from one of the viewing planes) from normal surfaces (surfaces that are parallel to the viewing plane) if the surfaces are shown in profile. Inclined surfaces are perpendicular to one of the principal viewing planes and tipped away, or foreshortened, in the other views. As illustrated in Figure 6.19, you can't tell by looking at the top and side views which surfaces are inclined and which are normal.

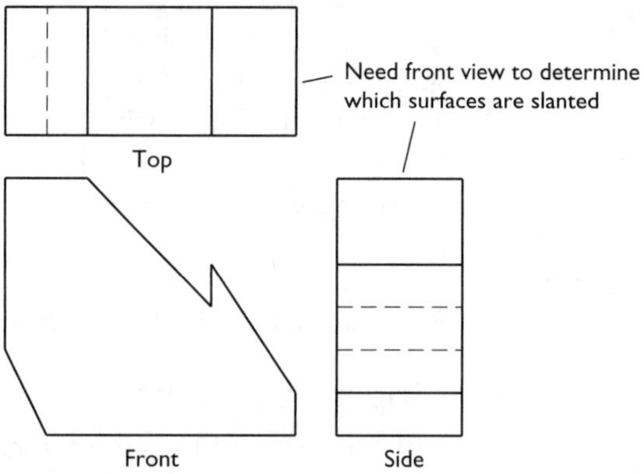

Figure 6.19

The front view is required, along with the other two views, to define the object's size and shape completely. In the next steps you will add a slanted surface to the adapter so that the object looks like Figure 6.20.

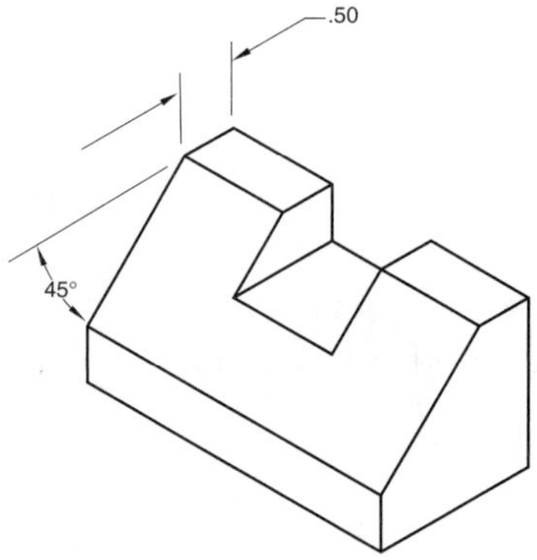

Figure 6.20

You will use the Line command to add the slanted surface to the side view using relative coordinates. You will locate a point 0.5 inch to the left of the top right corner of the right-side view and draw a slanted line from this point for the 45-degree surface.

Pick: **Line icon**

Specify first point: **7,3** ↵

Specify next point or [Undo]: **@3<–135** ↵

Specify next point or [Undo]: ↵

The distance 3 was chosen because the exact distance is not known and 3 is obviously longer than needed, as the entire object is only 1.5 inches high. Your screen should look like Figure 6.21.

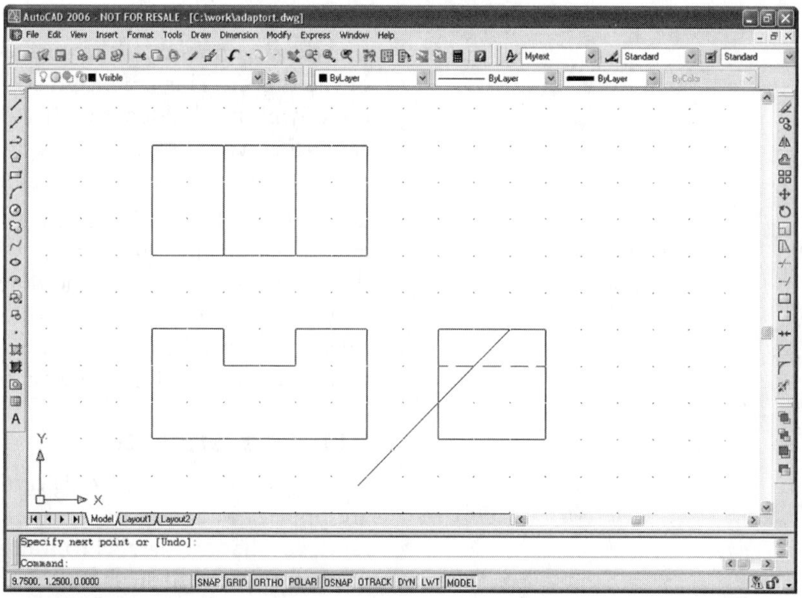

Figure 6.21

Tip

Use Zoom Window to zoom the side view to help you locate the points to trim. Return to your drawing with Zoom Previous when all the excess lines are removed. You may want to turn Snap and Ortho off to trim the lines.

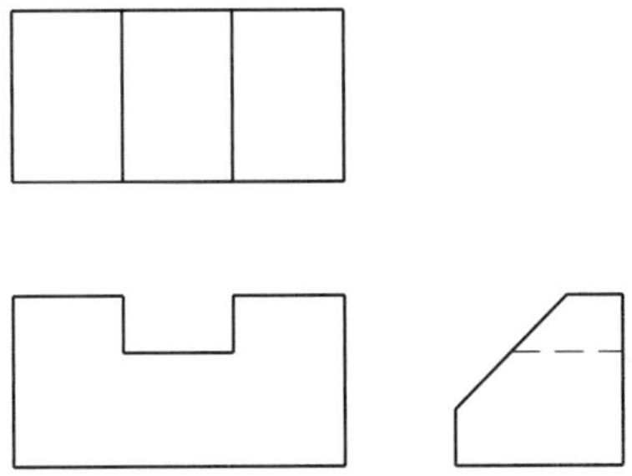

Figure 6.22

On your own, use the **Trim** command to remove any lines above the slanted surface.

When you have finished, your drawing should look like that in Figure 6.22.

Top-View to Side-View Projection

You can *project* information from the top view to the side view and vice versa by using a 45-degree *miter line*. You can draw the miter line anywhere above the side view and to the right of the top view, but it is often drawn from the top right corner of the front view, as shown in Figure 6.23.

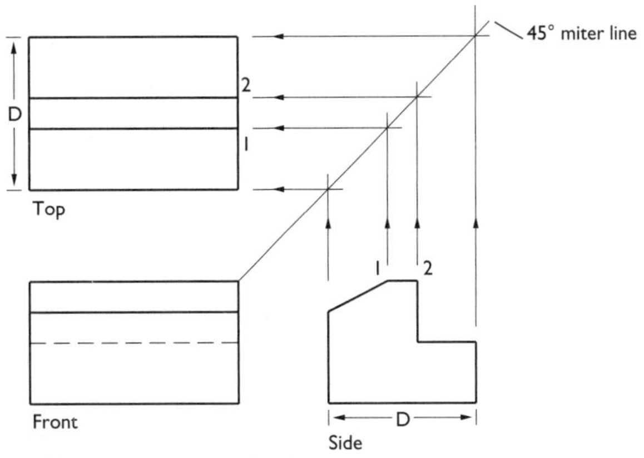

Figure 6.23

To project information from the side view to the top view, you would draw vertical projection lines from the points in the side view so that they intersect the miter line. In Figure 6.23, points 1 and 2 are projected. Then you would project horizontal lines from the intersection of the vertical lines and the miter line across the top view.

You will set layer PROJECTION current and then draw a miter line.

Pick: **PROJECTION** to set it current, using the Layer Control

Drawing the Miter Line

You will draw a 45-degree line, starting where the front edge of the top view and the front edge of the side view would intersect. So that you can draw angled lines,

Pick: **to turn ORTHO off**

Using Object Tracking

Object Tracking, or OTRACK, constrains your selections to line up with the X-, Y-, or Z-coordinates of an acquired tracking point. Object Tracking works with other commands such as Move and Copy. You can use the Tracking object snap to start a line from any point on the screen, based on reference points. This method helps you find an intersection where two objects would meet if extended. You will use it to find the point where the bottom edge of the top view and the left edge of the side view would intersect. To acquire an object tracking point, move the cursor over the object location temporarily. Do not pick with the mouse, just pause briefly over the object until you see the Osnap marker or a small plus sign (+) appear. Refer to Figure 6.24 for the objects you will use to acquire tracking points. Once the tracking points are acquired you will start to draw the line.

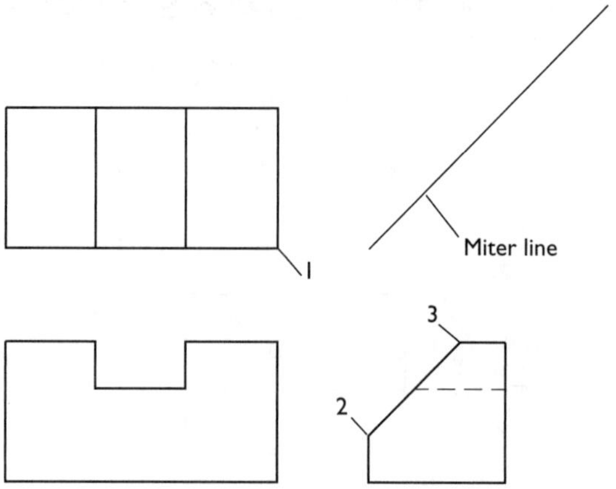

Figure 6.24

Tip

To clear an object tracking point once it has been acquired, move the cursor back over the point until the plus sign (+) marker is gone. Starting a new command will also clear the object tracking points, as will toggling the OTRACK button on the status bar.

Pick: **OTRACK button** from status bar to turn Object Tracking on

Make sure that **OSNAP Intersection** is turned **on**.

Pick: **Line icon**

Specify first point: **move the cursor over intersection 1 until it is acquired as an object tracking point, then move the cursor over point 2 until it is acquired**

You should see the tracking points acquired as in Figure 6.25.

Specify next point or [Undo]: **pick where the tracking lines intersect, as shown in Figure 6.25, to begin drawing the miter line**

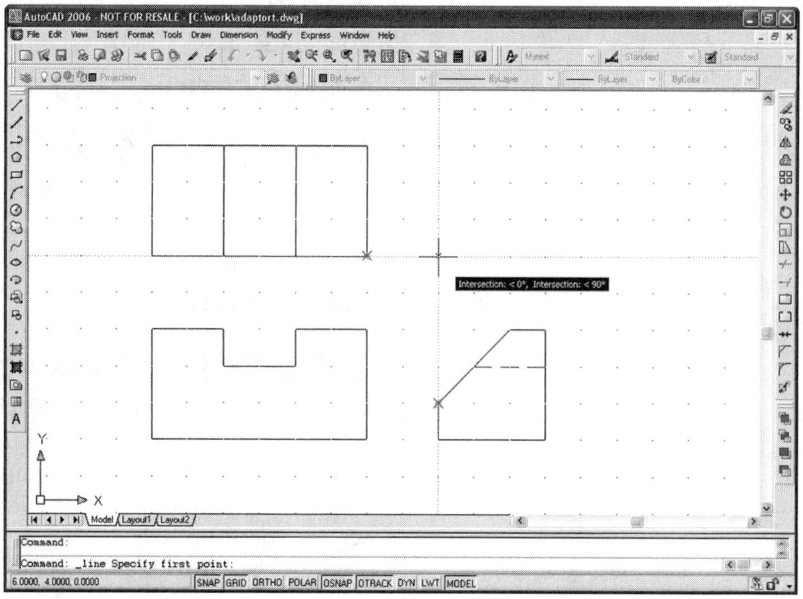

Figure 6.25

Specify next point or [Undo]: **@3<45** ↵
Specify next point or [Undo]: ↵
Pick: **OTRACK button** to turn it off

The line that you will use for the miter line is added to the drawing, as shown in Figure 6.26.

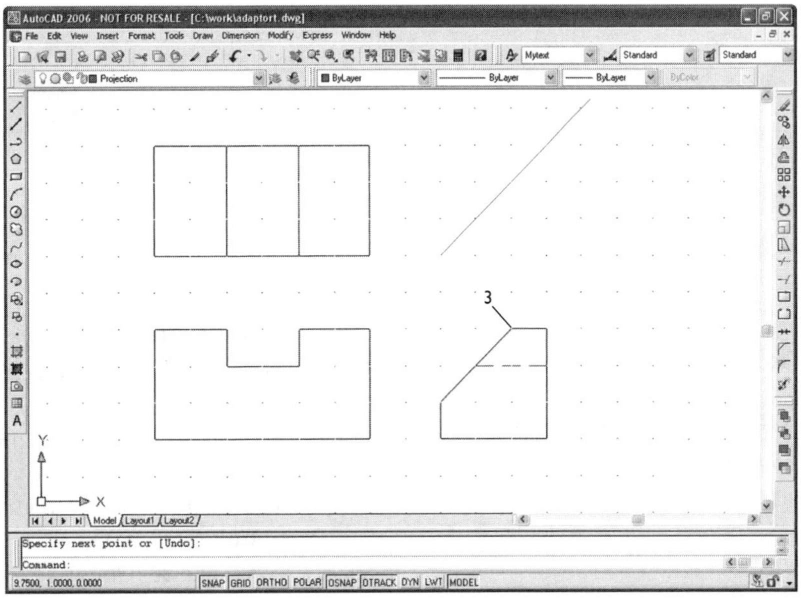

Figure 6.26

Next, you will project the corner point (point 3 in Figure 6.26) created by the slanted surface in the side view to the miter line by drawing a vertical ray from the intersection. The Ray command is on the Draw pull-down menu.

Pick: **ORTHO button** (to turn it on before you pick points)
Pick: **Draw, Ray**
Specify start point: **pick point 3 in Figure 6.26 (using Osnap Intersection)**
Specify through point: **pick anywhere above point 3**
Specify through point: ↵

The ray is added to your drawing, extending vertically from point 3. Next, you will project another ray from where the vertical ray intersects the miter line.

Pick: **Draw, Ray** (or press ↵ to restart the Ray command)
Specify start point: **pick where the vertical ray meets the miter line**
Specify through point: **pick a point to the left of the miter line**
Specify through point: ↵

Your drawing should look like Figure 6.27.

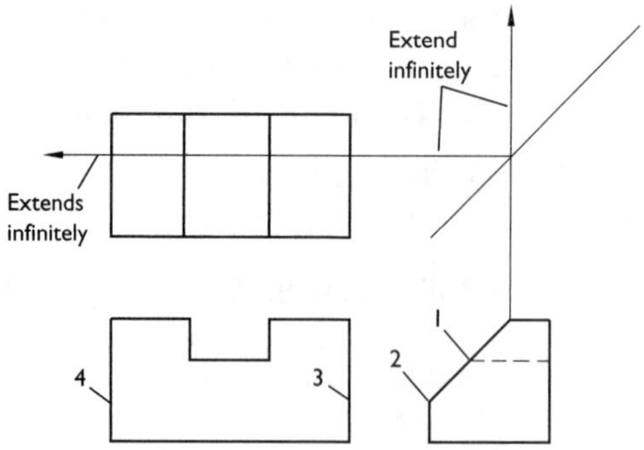

Figure 6.27

On your own, **project point 1** to the top view.

Next you will use Object Tracking to project point 2, shown in Figure 6.27, into the front view.

Make sure that **OSNAP** is **on** with **Perpendicular** selected.
Make sure that **SNAP** and **ORTHO** are toggled **off**, and **OTRACK** is on.
Pick: **Line icon**
Specify first point: **acquire tracking point 2 and pick line 3 using the AutoSnap Intersection marker to start the line**
Specify next point or [Undo]: **pick line 4 using the AutoSnap Perpendicular marker**
Specify next point or [Undo]: ↵

Tip

For a quick pop-up menu of Object Snaps, you can press the Shift key in combination with the right mouse button.

The front view should now have a solid line representing the lower part of the block's sloping surface. Now you only have to trim the Rays used in projecting the surface depths to the top view. Remember, when rays are trimmed they become regular lines.

On your own, trim the lines so that your screen looks like Figure 6.28.

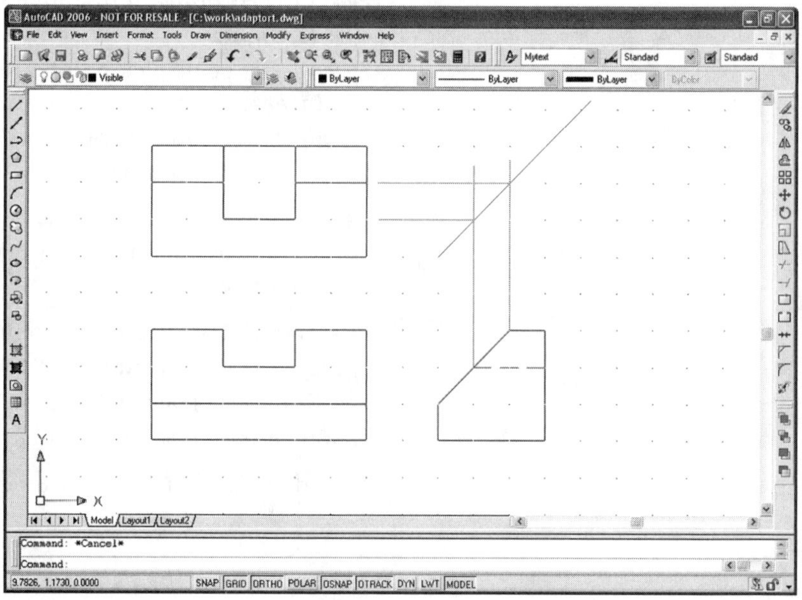

Figure 6.28

Now, you will change the new lines in the top and front views to the layer VISIBLE. Then you will set layer VISIBLE as the current layer and freeze layer PROJECTION. Leaving the projection lines frozen in the drawing is useful because, if you need to change something, you can just thaw the layer instead of having to re-create the projection lines.

Pick: **new lines in top and front views so that their grips appear**
Select: **layer VISIBLE** from the Layer Control
Press: Esc to remove the hot grips
Pick: **VISIBLE** to set it current using the Layer Control
Pick: **to Freeze layer PROJECTION** using the Layer Control

The selected lines change to reside on layer VISIBLE. The magenta projection lines disappear from your screen.

Sizing and Positioning the Drawing

Next you will switch to the paper space layout and verify the scaling factor for the drawing view, as you learned in Tutorial 5. When you used Zoom All in model space, the entire drawing or the limits area is fit on the screen, which does not give you any particular scale for the end drawing. You will check the viewing scale to make sure that the drawing will print so that 1 unit in paper space is equal to 1 unit in model space.

Pick: **Layout1 tab**
Right-click: **on any toolbar and use the list that pops up to select the Viewports toolbar**
Double-click: **inside the viewport to ensure that you are in floating model space inside the viewport**

Use the Viewports Toolbar to verify that the standard scale for the viewport is still set to 1:1 as shown in Figure 6.29.

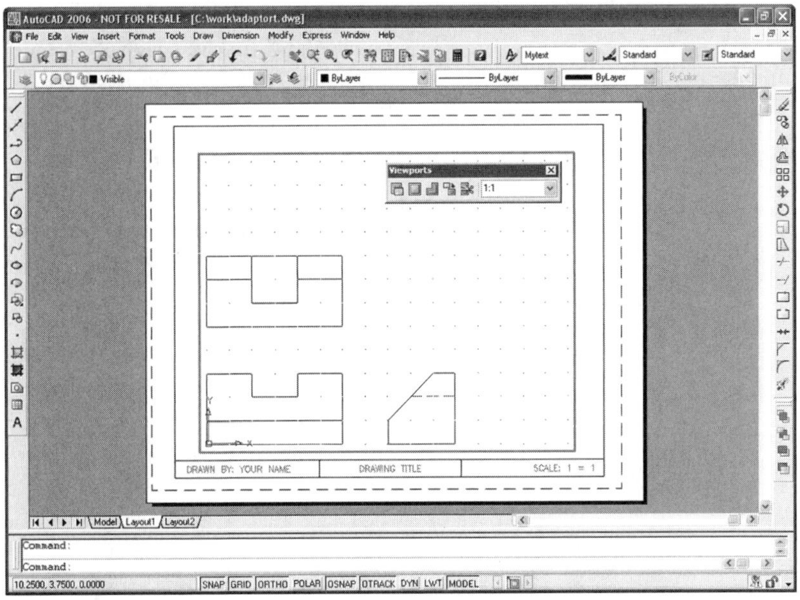

Figure 6.29

Next, you will use the Pan Realtime command to position the views you drew inside the viewport.

Pick: to close the Viewports toolbar

Pick: **Pan Realtime icon**

On your own, position the views so that they appear centered in the viewport.

Press: Esc to exit Pan Realtime

When you have finished, your screen should look like Figure 6.30.

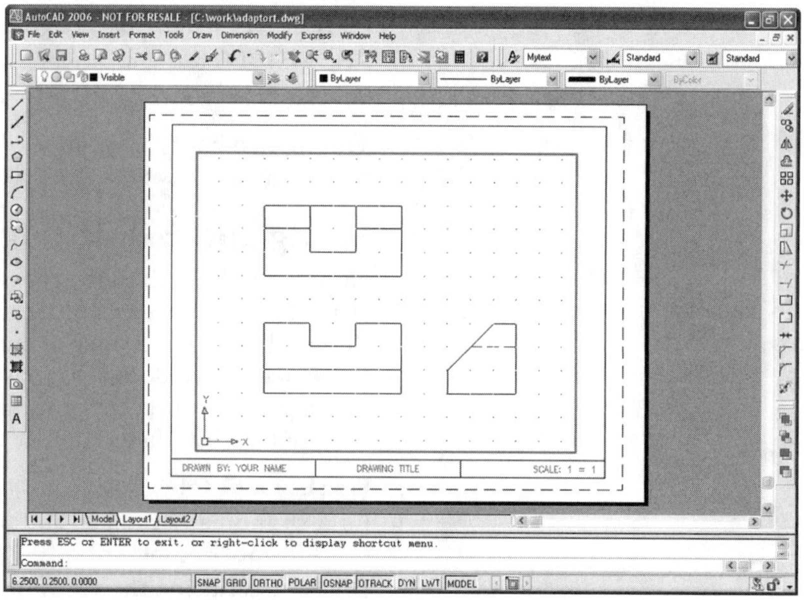

Figure 6.30

Locking the Viewport Scale

You can lock the scaling for the viewport so that zooming inside the floating viewport does not change the scale relationship between paper space and model space. You will use the short-cut menu to lock the scale as shown in Figure 6.31.

Double-click: **in the gray area outside the paper boundary to switch to paper space**

Pick: **on the magenta colored viewport so that its grips appear**

Right-click: **to show the short-cut menu**

Pick: **Display Locked**

Pick: **Yes**

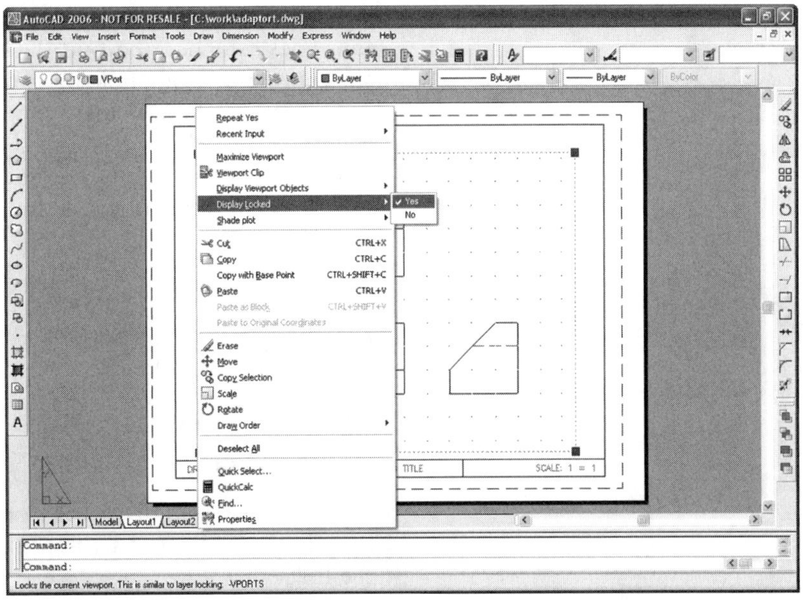

Figure 6.31

Tip

If your paper space layout does not fill the screen, switch to paper space and then use Zoom All. Make sure to return to model space.

Tip

It is good practice to frequently save your drawings on your disk. If your system experiences a power failure and you lose the drawing in memory, you can always retrieve a recent version from your disk.

Now that the viewport display is locked, when you zoom in or pan, it will not change the relationship between the model space drawing and its position or scale inside the viewport.

Pick: **Paper button to switch to Model space inside the viewport**

On your own, try using Zoom and Pan.

Did you notice that your view enlarges with the viewport staying at the same size relationship? And when you pan, the entire drawing moves on the screen? When the display is locked, the AutoCAD software zooms and pans by switching to paper space and performing the zoom or pan and then switching back to model space.

Pick: **OSNAP** on the status bar to turn it **off**

Pick: **OTRACK** to turn it **off**

Pick: **Save**

Drawing Holes

Figure 6.32 shows an object with two holes and the ways in which they are represented in front and top views.

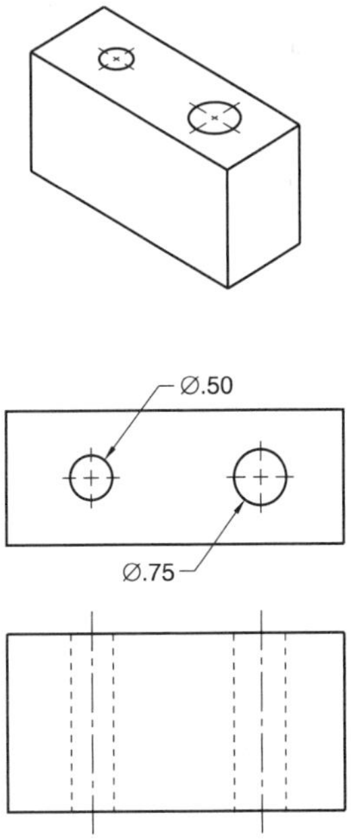

Figure 6.32

The *diameter symbol* indicates a diameter value. If no depth is specified for a hole, the assumption is that the hole goes completely through the object. As no depth is specified for these holes, the hidden lines in the front view go from the top surface to the bottom surface.

You will add a hole to the orthographic views that you have drawn to represent the adapter, as shown in Figure 6.33.

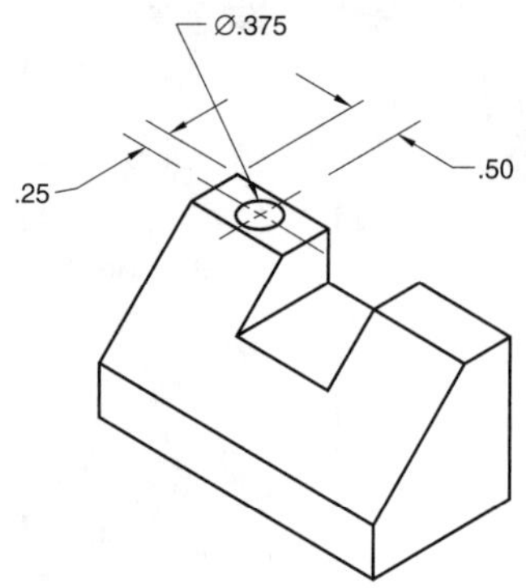

Figure 6.33

Centerlines for holes must be included in all views. A centermark and four lines extending beyond the four quadrant points are used to define the center point of a hole in its *circular view* (the view in which the hole appears as a circle). A single centerline, parallel to the two hidden lines, is used in the other views, called *rectangular views* because the hole appears as a rectangle. Centerlines should extend beyond the edge of the symmetrical feature by a distance of at least 3/16" on the plotted drawing.

You will start with the top view and add the circular view of the 0.375 diameter hole, as specified in Figure 6.33. As indicated in the figure, the hole's centerpoint is located 0.5 from the left surface of the view and 0.25 from the back surface.

First you will switch back so that you are working in model space.

Pick: **Model tab**

The border should disappear from your screen. Next check to see that Snap is turned on and set to .25 and draw the circle for the top view of the hole.

Pick: **to turn Snap on**
Pick: **Circle icon**
Specify center point for circle or [3P/2P/Ttr (tan tan radius)]: **2.5,5.25** (or pick using snap) ↵
Specify radius of circle or [Diameter]: **D** ↵
Diameter: **.375** ↵

Drawing Centerlines and Centermarks

Next, you will draw the centerlines for the circle. Engineering drawings involve the use of two different thicknesses of lines: (1) thick lines are used for visible lines, cutting plane lines, and short break lines; and (2) thin lines are used for hidden lines, centerlines, dimension lines, section lines, long break lines, and phantom lines. You typically use AutoCAD color or lineweight settings to tell the plotter or printer which thickness to use when printing lines.

Tip

You can also use the Properties icon to change the linetype for your centermarks to Continuous.

Because centerlines in the circular view should be thin, you will draw them on layer THIN. You could also use layer CENTERLINE, but it has a CENTER linetype. Because the Center Mark command automatically creates the dashes at the center of the circle by drawing short lines, centermarks will usually look better if they are not drawn with a linetype that already contains a dash (e.g., the centerline linetype). This is why you will use layer THIN, which has a continuous linetype.

Pick: **THIN to set it current using the Layer Control**

The Dimcen variable controls the size and appearance of the centermark that you add to the circle. The absolute value of the Dimcen variable determines the size of the centermark. The *sign* (positive or negative) determines the style of the centermark. Figure 6.34 shows the different styles of centermarks that you can create by setting Dimcen to a positive or negative value.

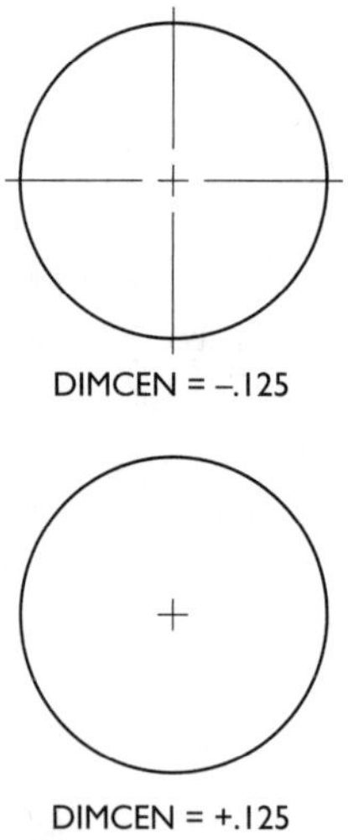

Figure 6.34

Setting Dimcen to zero will cause no centermark to be drawn. (This lack of a centermark is useful when using dimensioning commands such as Radial, which automatically add a centermark. You will learn more about dimensioning and adding centermarks in Tutorial 7.) Usually the cross at the center should be 1/8" wide, but as this hole is relatively small, you will need a smaller centermark; you will use the value –0.05. Then you will show the Dimension and Object Snap toolbars so that you can select the Center Mark command.

Command: **DIMCEN** ↵
Enter new value for DIMCEN <0.0900>: **–.05** ↵
Right-click: **on any toolbar and use the pop-up list to turn on the Dimension and Object Snap toolbars**

The added toolbars are shown in Figure 6.35. Position them so that they are convenient for you to use when selecting commands.

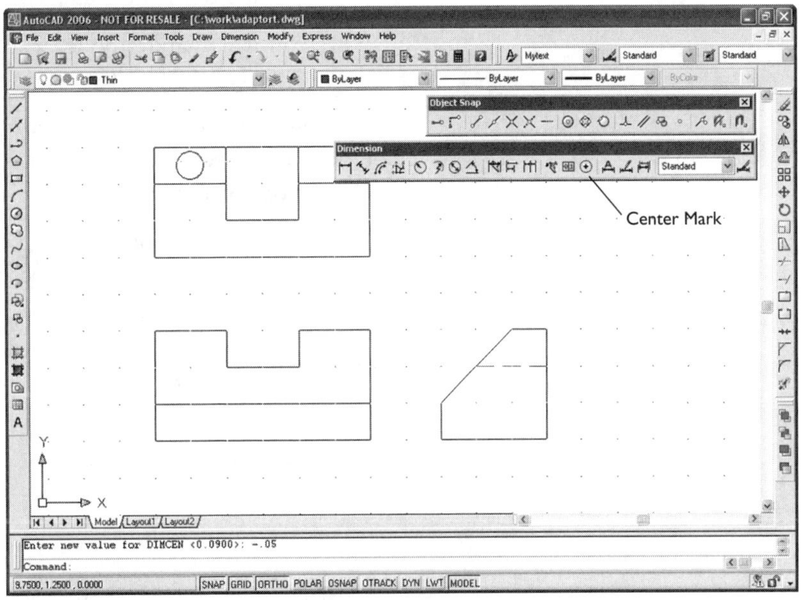

Figure 6.35

Next, you will use Center Mark to draw the circle's centerlines on layer THIN. Use the Center Mark icon from the Dimension toolbar whenever you are drawing a centerline in the circular view (where the hole appears round).

Tip

Use Zoom Window if you need to make targeting the objects and intersections easier.

Pick: **to turn Snap off**
Pick: **Center Mark icon**
Select arc or circle: **pick on the outer edge of the circle**

The circular view centerlines should appear in the drawing. Next, you will use hidden lines and the Intersection object snap to project the width of the hole into the front view.

Pick: **HIDDEN_LINES to set it current using the Layer Control**

Pick: **to turn on OSNAP and make sure that Intersection is on**

Pick: **ORTHO button** to turn it on

Pick: **Line icon**

Specify first point: **pick the intersection of the circle's horizontal centerline with the left edge of the circle**

Specify next point or [Undo]: **pick Snap to Perpendicular icon**

Per to: **pick any point on the lowest horizontal line in the front view**

Specify next point or [Undo]: ↵

On your own, repeat this procedure to draw the projection line for the right side of the hole and for the centerline.

Tip

Use Zoom Previous or Zoom All, if necessary, to return your screen to full size.

Next you will change the layer for the middle of the three lines you just drew to layer CENTERLINE.

Pick: **on the middle hidden line so that its grips appear**

Pick: **CENTERLINE** from the Layer Control

Pick: **Save icon** to save your drawing

The selected line should change to reside on layer CENTERLINE. The figure on your screen should be similar to Figure 6.36.

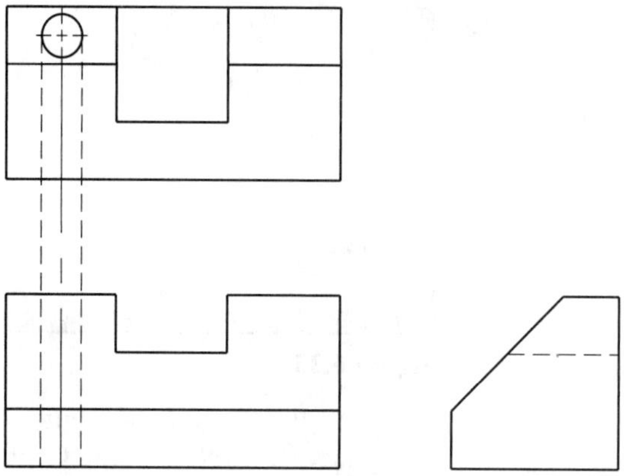

Figure 6.36

Next, you will break the line so that it is the right length for a centerline in the front view.

Breaking the Centerline

You will break the middle vertical line so that you can use it as a centerline by selecting the Break icon on the Modify toolbar. Centerlines should extend at least 0.1875" past the edge of the cylindrical feature when the drawing is plotted. You will extend the centerline 0.25" past the bottom of the front view to meet this criterion.

Pick: **Break icon**

Select object: **select the middle vertical line near where point 1 is labeled in Figure 6.37**

Tip

Be sure that Snap is on and that OSNAP is off to make selecting easier.

Tip

If you pick on the end of the line, you may not get a location past the end of the line for the second point of the break; instead, short segments of the line may remain and look like random points in your drawing.

Tip

You can use the Lengthen command and select the DElta option to lengthen a line by a specified amount.

The first point of the break is the point that you want to use as the top of the centerline. The second point is past the end, where the line extends into the top view, so that all of the centerline extending into the top view is broken off. Refer to Figure 6.37.

Specify second break point or [First point]: **select point 2, past the top end of the line**

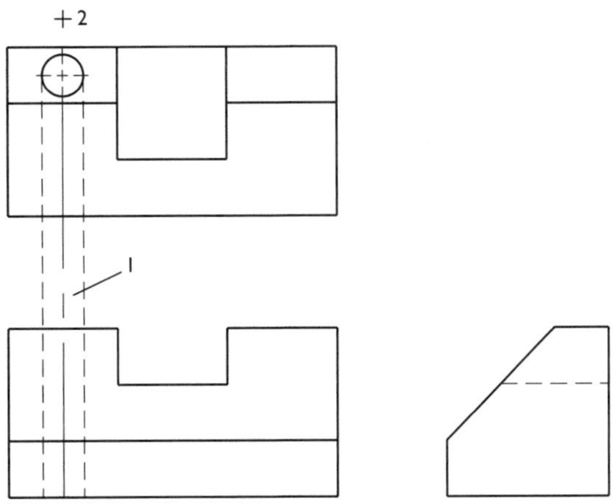

Figure 6.37

On your own, use hot grips with the **Stretch** command to stretch the centerline down **0.5" past the bottom of the front view**.

Refer to Tutorial 4 if you need to review using hot grips and Stretch.

Trim the two hidden lines where they extend past the front view of the object.

Your drawing should look like Figure 6.38.

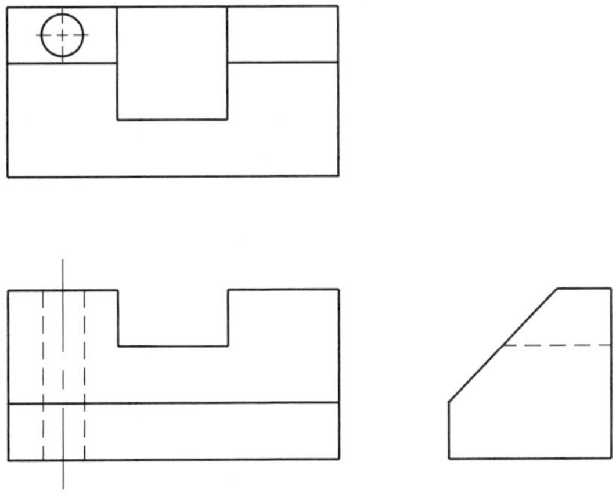

Figure 6.38

To complete the hole in the side view, you will project the location of the hole into the side view. Then you will use hot grips with the Move, Copy option to copy the lines from the front view to the side view.

Pick: **to close the Dimension toolbar**
Pick: **to thaw layer PROJECTION** using the Layer Control

Pick: **PROJECTION** (to set it current using the Layer Control)

On your own, draw a projection line from the top view where the vertical centerline intersects the circle to a point past the miter line. Refer to Figure 6.39. Use the Osnap (Intersection) mode and Ortho to help you.

Now project the intersection of the horizontal projection line with the miter line into the side view, creating a vertical projection line.

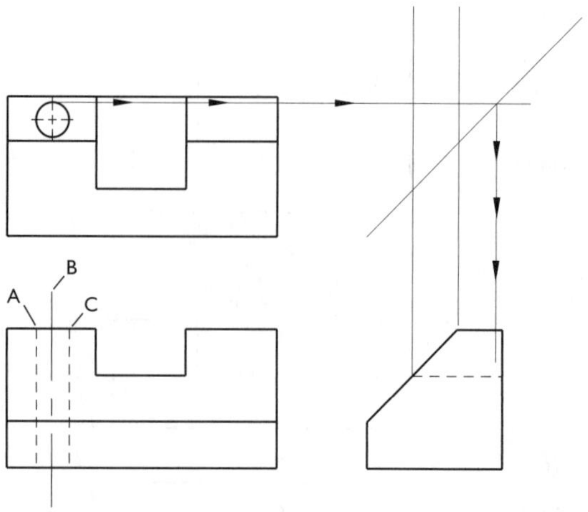

Figure 6.39

Because holes are symmetrical, the side view of the hole appears the same as the front view, except for the location. You will use hot grips with the Move, Copy option to copy the two hidden lines and the centerline from the front view to the side view.

Pick: **the two hidden lines and the centerline (A, B, and C) so that their grips appear as shown in Figure 6.40**

Pick: **the grip on the top endpoint of the right-hand hidden line as the base grip**

** STRETCH **

Specify stretch point or [Base point/Copy/Undo/eXit]: **right-click**

Pick: **Move**

** MOVE **

Specify move point or [Base point/Copy/Undo/eXit]: **right-click again**

Pick: **Copy**

** MOVE (multiple) **

Specify move point or [Base point/Copy/Undo/eXit]:

The lines you selected appear faintly, attached to the crosshairs. (OSNAP should still be active, with Intersection selected).

Target the intersection between the top line in the side view and the projection line locating the side of the hole (D), as shown in Figure 6.40.

You may want to use Zoom Window to help you choose the correct intersection. The three lines are copied to this location. To exit the command, press ↵ or the space bar,

Specify move point or [Base point/Copy/Undo/eXit]: ↵

Press: Esc **twice to remove the grips from the screen**

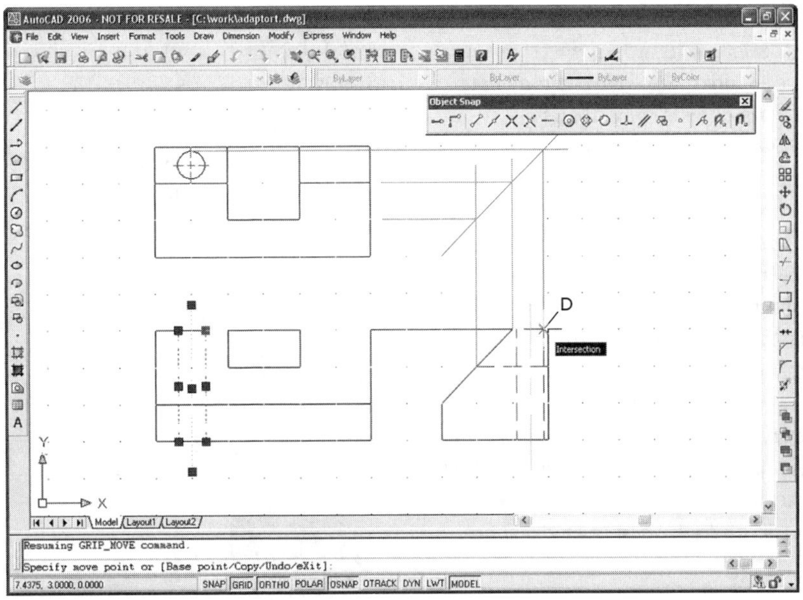

Figure 6.40

On your own,

Set **VISIBLE** as the current layer.

Freeze layer **PROJECTION** using the Layer Control.

Your drawing will look like that in Figure 6.41.

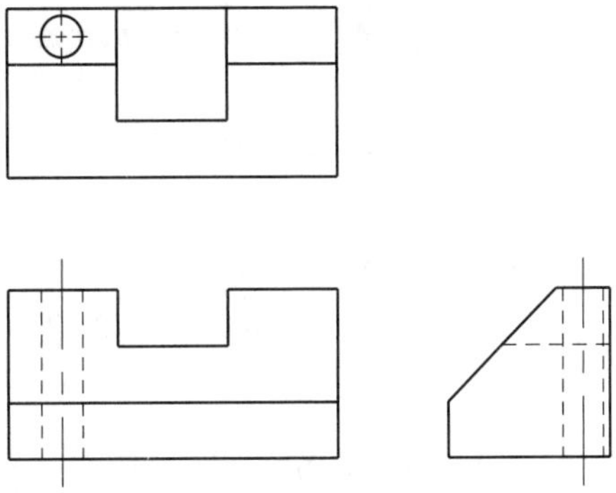

Figure 6.41

Setting the Global Linetype Scaling Factor

You can change the linetype scale factor for all linetypes at once by setting the global linetype scaling factor. Recall from Tutorial 4 that each linetype is defined by the distance that each dash, gap, and dot is to be drawn. Because linetypes are defined by specific distances, you may need to adjust the lengths of the dashes and gaps for use in your drawing. The LTscale command lets you adjust all the linetype lengths by the scaling factor you specify.

Since you will be plotting from a paper space layout, that is the best place to adjust the appearance of the line patterns, first using the LTscale command and then adjusting individual lines as needed.

Tip

The variable PSLTscale controls whether the Ltscale command in paper space controls the appearance of the linetypes over the same command in model space. By default PSLTscale is set to 1, so that the paper space LTscale has control.

Tip

Especially when you are working in metric units, the linetypes may not always appear correctly. Using a standard AutoCAD template for a metric drawing can help provide the proper settings. Sometimes a line may appear to be the correct color for the layer but not the correct pattern. The reason is that the lengths defined in the linetype file are defined in terms of inches. Incorrectly shown metric lines may have changed pattern, but the spacing is so small that you can't see it. Use LTscale to adjust the spacing. For metric units, try a value of 25.4 when in model space.

You will switch to paper space to adjust your lines with LTscale to make the CENTER linetype visible and the HIDDEN linetype have shorter dashes.

Pick: **Layout1 tab**
Pick: **MODEL button to switch to PAPER space if needed**
Command: **LTSCALE** ↵
Enter new linetype scale factor <1.0000>: **.65** ↵
Regenerating Layout

Your drawing should look like Figure 6.42.

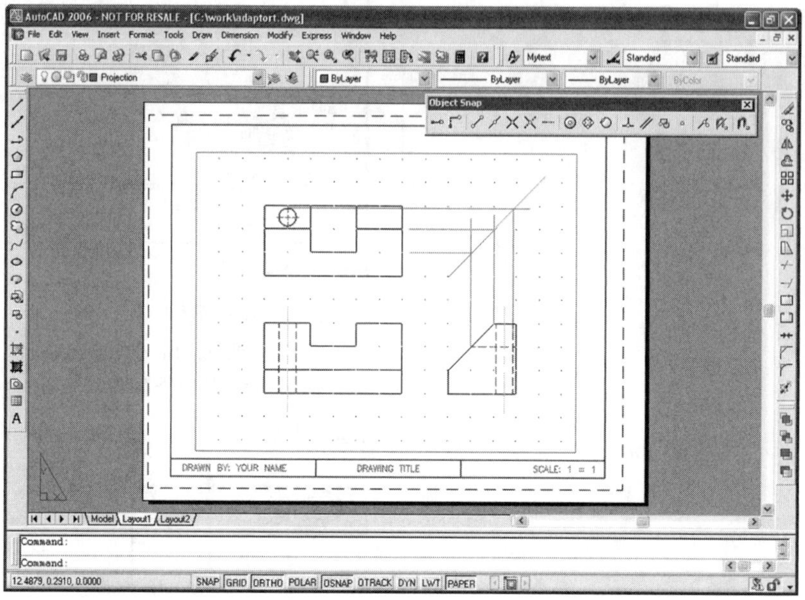

Figure 6.42

You have completed this orthographic drawing.

On your own, turn on the **LWT** button on the status bar.
Zoom in slightly so that you can see the effect of having the lineweights turned on.
Pick: **Zoom, Previous** (to restore your original view)
Close the Object Snap toolbar.
Save and close drawing *adaptort.dwg*.

Projecting Slanted Surfaces on Cylinders

Next, you will work with projecting slanted surfaces on cylinders. You will begin by using the template file *cyl1.dwt* from the datafiles for this text.

On your own, begin a new drawing called ***cyl1orth.dwg*** from the datafile template drawing ***cyl1.dwt***.
Pick: **Zoom All icon**

Your screen should be similar to Figure 6.43.

Tip

Your datafiles should be installed on the hard drive. Do not open files directly from your floppy disk. If you must open a file from a floppy, pick New and then use the file you want to open as a template. You should specify the new drawing file name so that it is created on the hard drive. These actions will prevent many problems and the likelihood of corrupted drawing files.

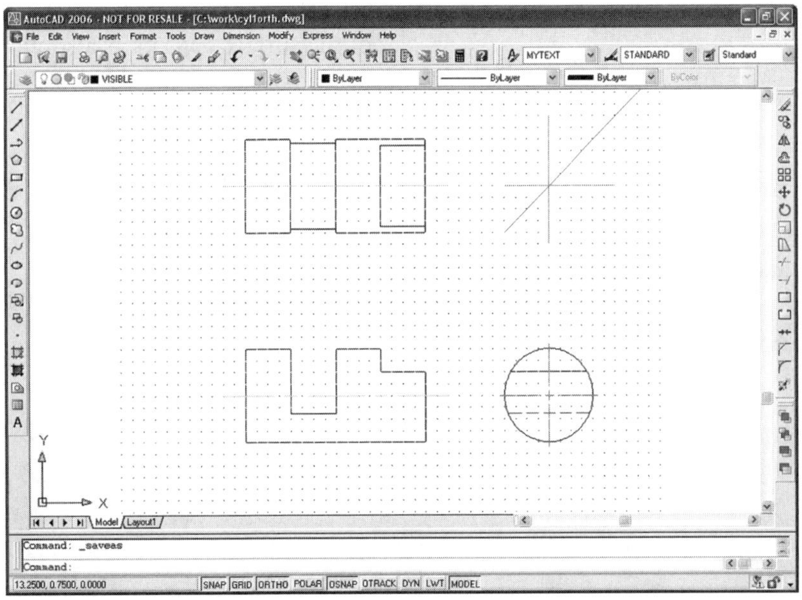

Figure 6.43

On your own, add a slanted surface to the front view and on edge in the side view, as shown in Figure 6.44.

The top of the slanted surface is located 1.5 inches from the right end of the cylinder, and the bottom of the surface is at the horizontal centerline. The top point of the slanted surface (the intersection of the vertical centerline and the edge of the cylinder in the side view) is labeled 1 in Figure 6.43. The bottom edge of the slanted surface is labeled 2, 3 and is located directly on the horizontal centerline in the side view.

On your own, remove all excess lines left from the shallow surface in the front view.

Remove the same surface from the top and side views; you will be creating a different surface in its place.

Your drawing should look like Figure 6.44.

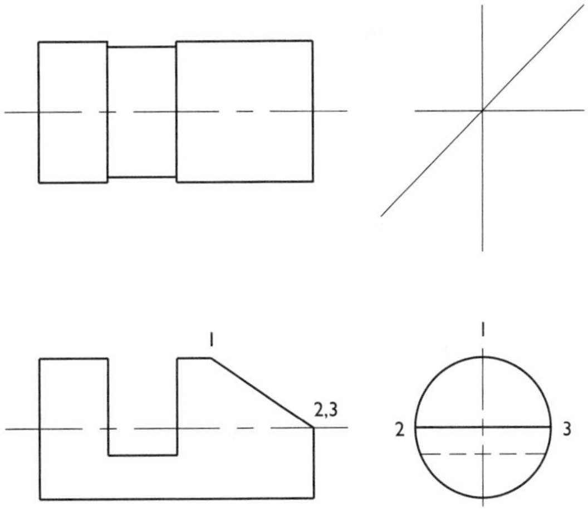

Figure 6.44

What is the shape of the slanted surface in the top view? The front view of the surface appears as a straight slanted line. The side view of the surface is a semicircle, but in the top view the surface is an ellipse, as shown in Figure 6.45. A circular shape seen from an angle other than straight on is an ellipse.

Since the locations of points 1, 2, and 3 on the ellipse are known, you can use the Ellipse command to draw the shape in the top view. Use Help or refer to Tutorial 2 to review Ellipse if necessary.

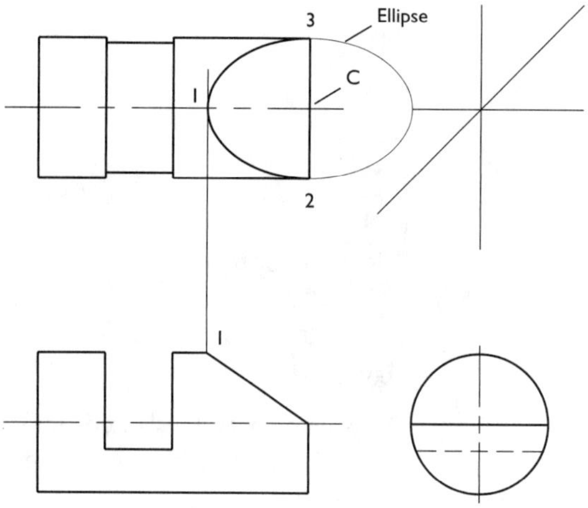

Figure 6.45

You will first project point 1 into the top view, as shown in Figure 6.45.

On your own, make layer **PROJECTION** current.

Use Osnap Intersection and the Line command to draw a vertical line from point 1 in the front view extending into the top view past the center.

Change the current layer back to layer **VISIBLE**.

Pick: **Ellipse icon**

Specify axis endpoint of ellipse or [Arc/Center]: **C** ↵

Specify center of ellipse: **pick the intersection marked C in Figure 6.45**

Specify endpoint of axis: **pick point 1 in the top view**, where your projection line crosses the centerline

Specify distance to other axis or [Rotation]: **pick point 2 in the top view**

Your ellipse should look like the one shown in Figure 6.46.

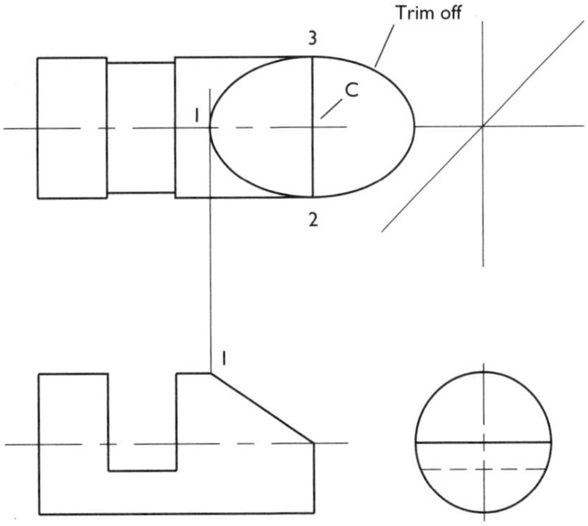

Figure 6.46

On your own, use the **Trim** command to remove the unnecessary portion of the ellipse.

Freeze layer **PROJECTION**.

The remaining curve represents the top view of the slanted surface. Your screen should be similar to Figure 6.47.

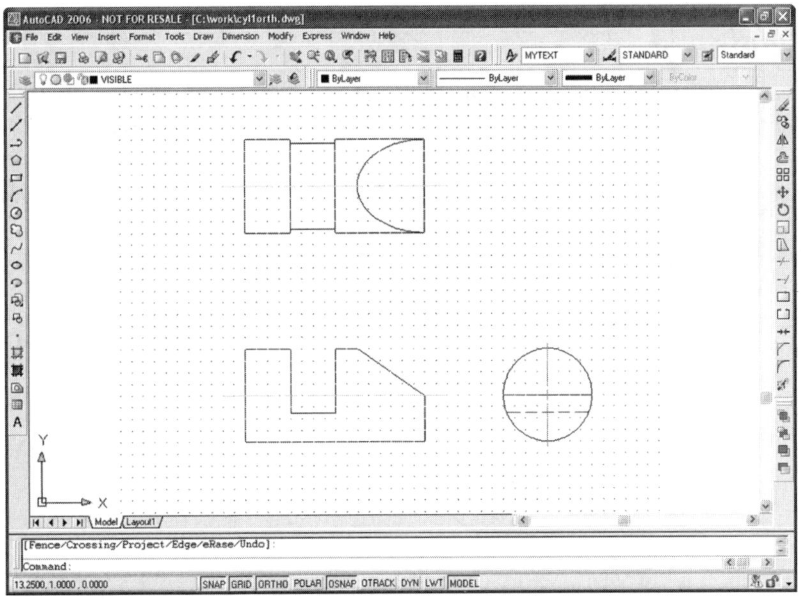

Figure 6.47

Circular shapes appear as ellipses when tipped away from the direction of sight. Not all curved surfaces are uniform shapes like circles and ellipses; some are irregular. You can create irregularly curved surfaces by using the Polyline command and the Spline option that you learned in Tutorial 3. To project an irregularly curved surface to the adjacent view, identify a number of points along the curve and project each point. Use the Polyline command to connect the points. Then use the Pedit, Spline option to create a smooth curve through the points.

You have now completed Tutorial 6.

Save the drawing as *cyl1orth.dwg* and **print** the drawing from the paper space layout. Turn off any extra toolbars that you may have open, leaving only the Draw and Modify toolbars on the screen. Exit the AutoCAD software.

Key Terms

circular view	inclined surface	orthographic views	rectangular view
diameter symbol	limiting element	precedence	sign
edge view	miter line	project	
hidden line	normal surface	projection lines	

Key Commands

Center Mark	Ellipse	OTrack
Dimcen	Ortho	Ray

Exercises

Draw front, top, and right-side orthographic views of the following objects. The letter M after an exercise number means that the problem's dimensional values are in millimeters (metric units). If no letter follows the exercise number, the dimensions are in inches.

6.1 Base Block

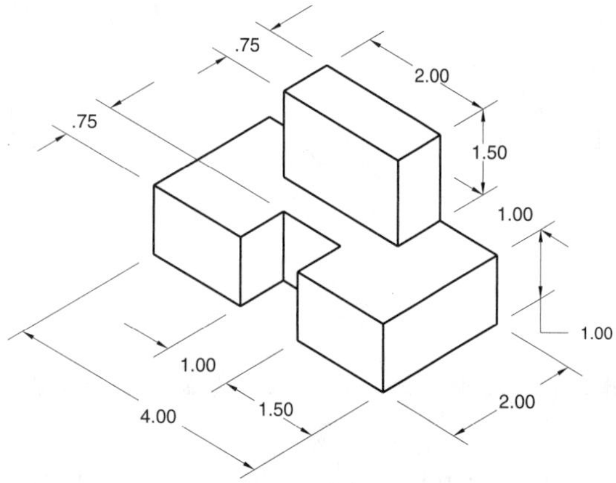

6.2 Piston Guide

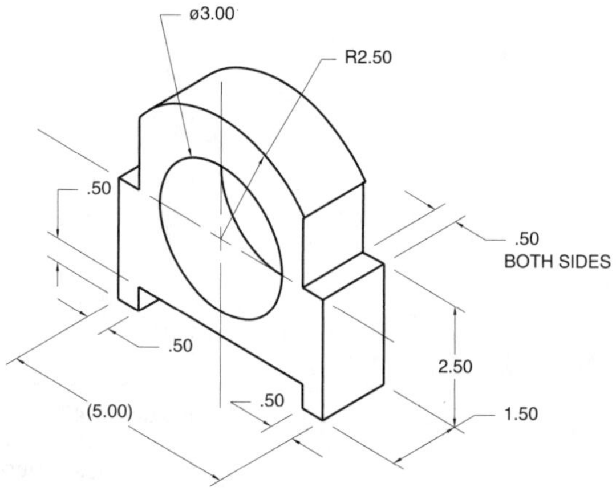

6.3M Shaft Guide

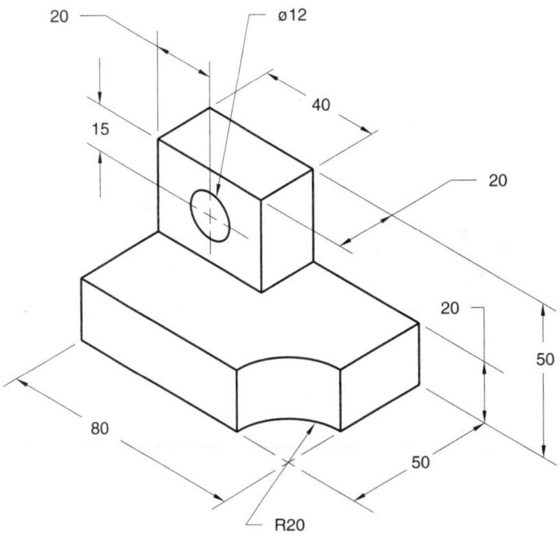

6.4M Lock Catch

The orthographic views are started for you. Add the missing lines and the top view.

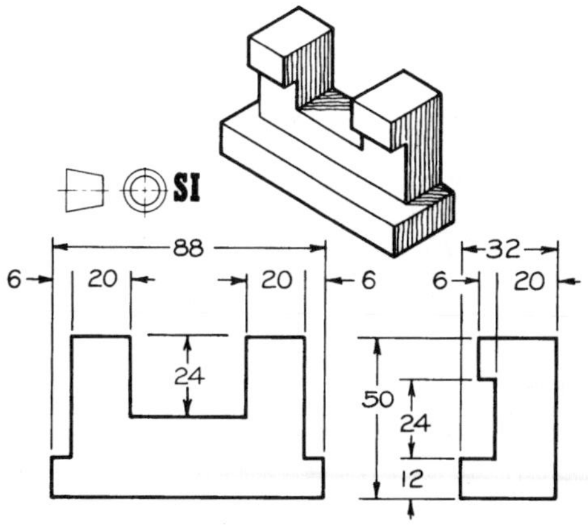

6.5 Bearing Box

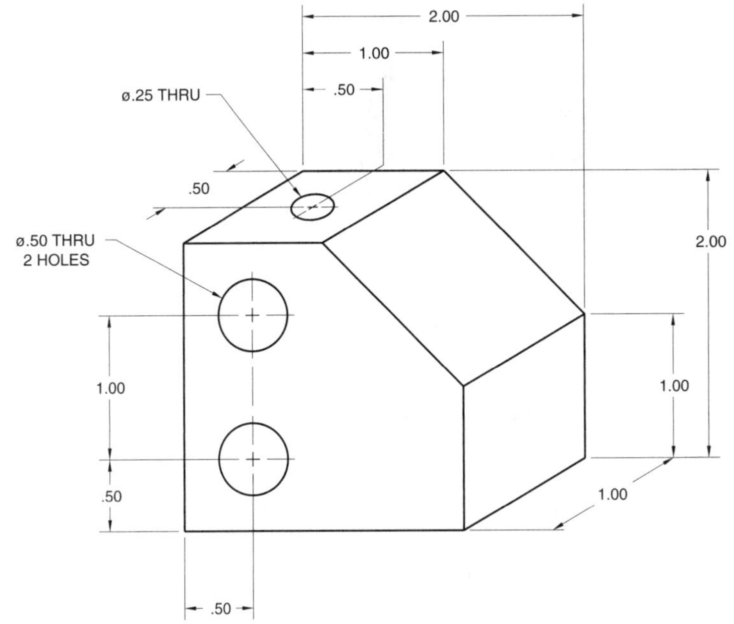

6.6M Bushing Holder

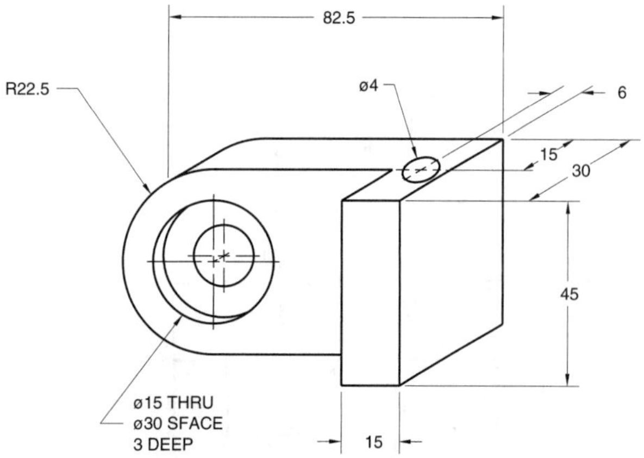

6.7 Lift Guide

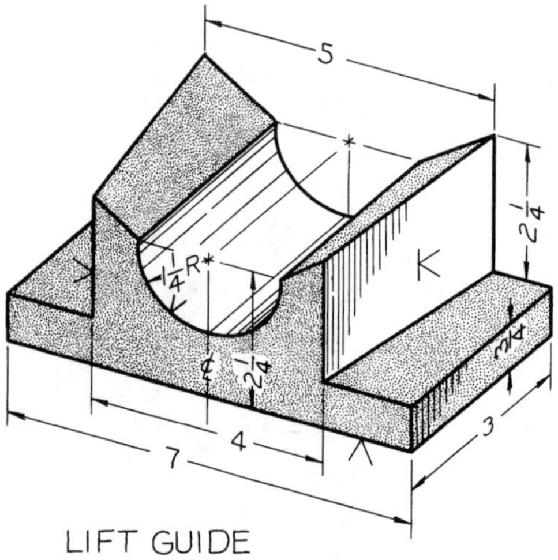

6.8M Stop Plate

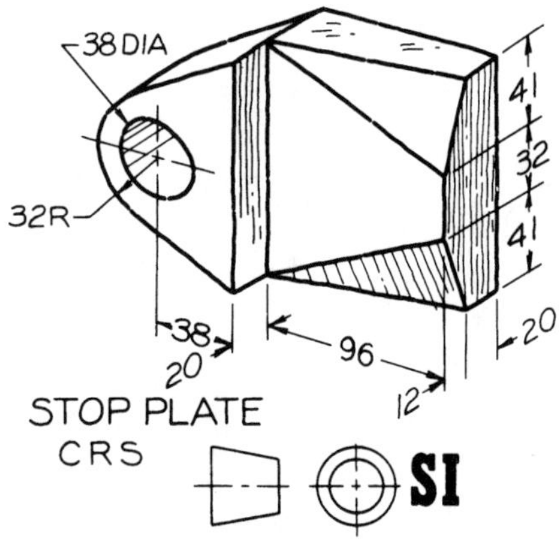

6.9M Clamp

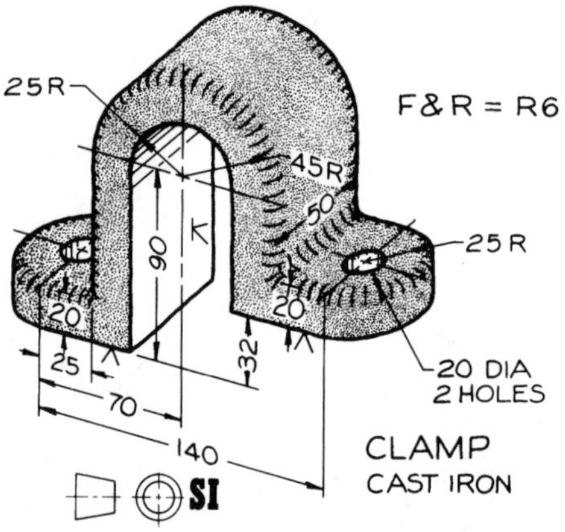

6.10M Holder Clip

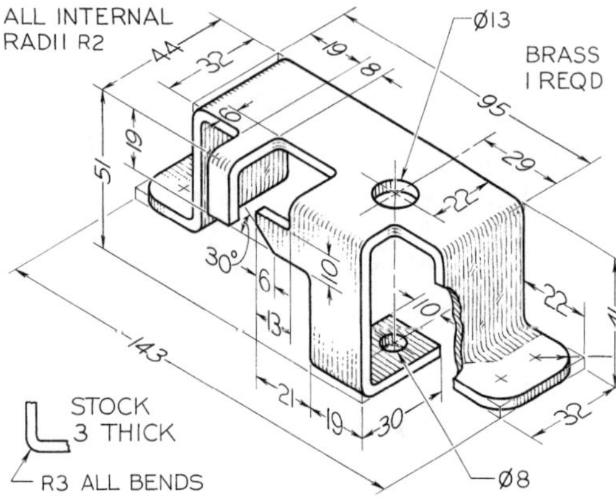

6.11M Rod Support

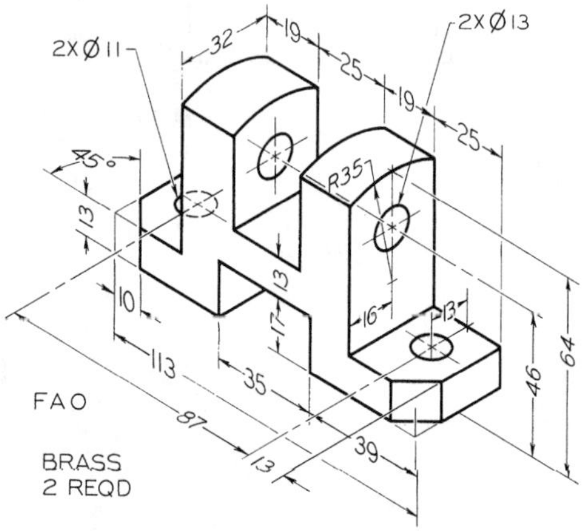

6.12 Shaft Support

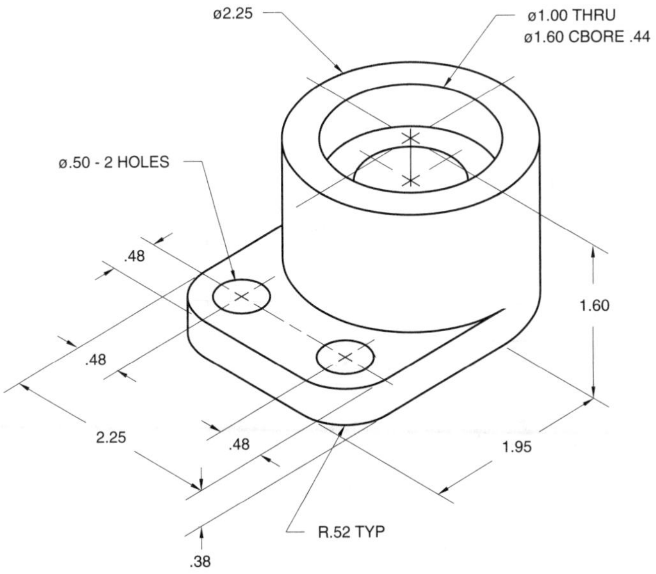

6.13 Manhole Junction

Draw standard orthographic views. Wall thickness is 6 inches throughout. The 10-inch hole is through the entire manhole junction (exits opposite side).

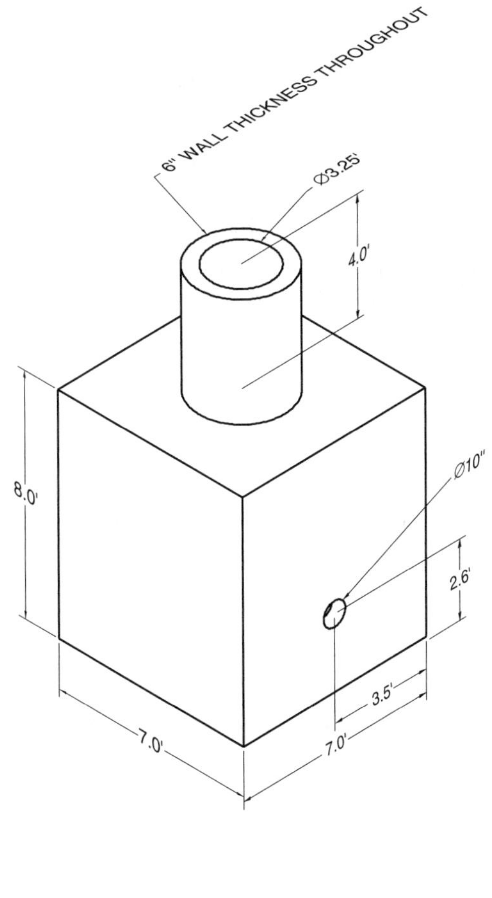

6.14 Missing View Problems

Redraw the given views and add the missing view as indicated.

1

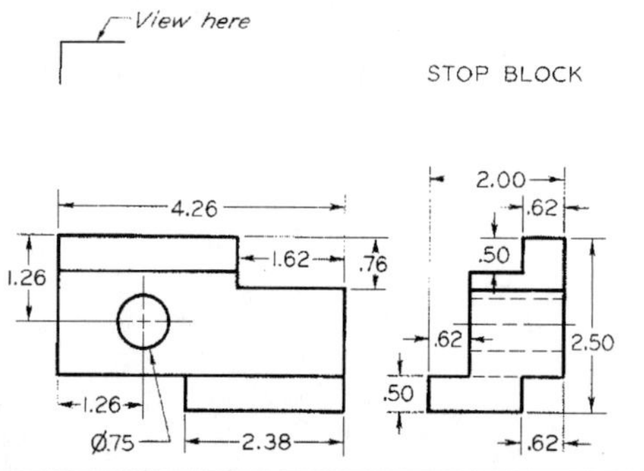

2

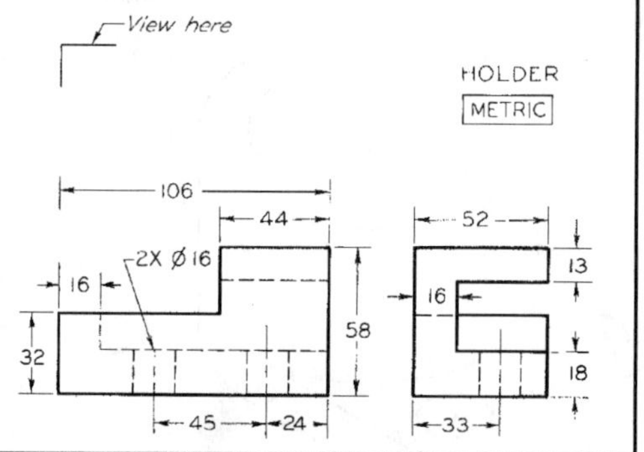

3

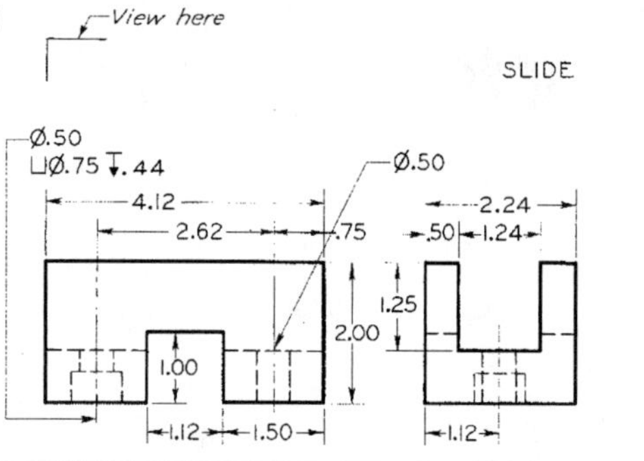

4

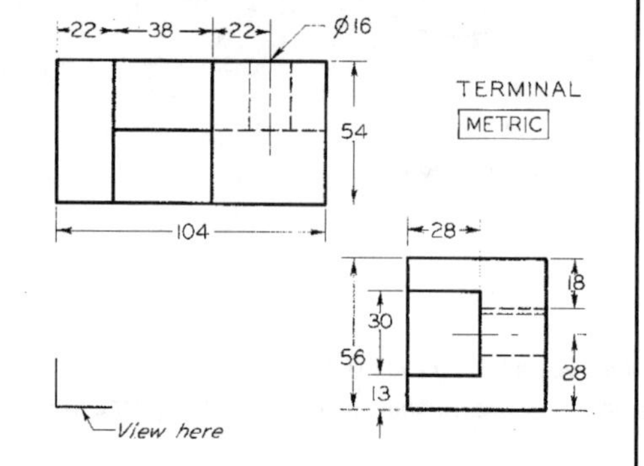

5

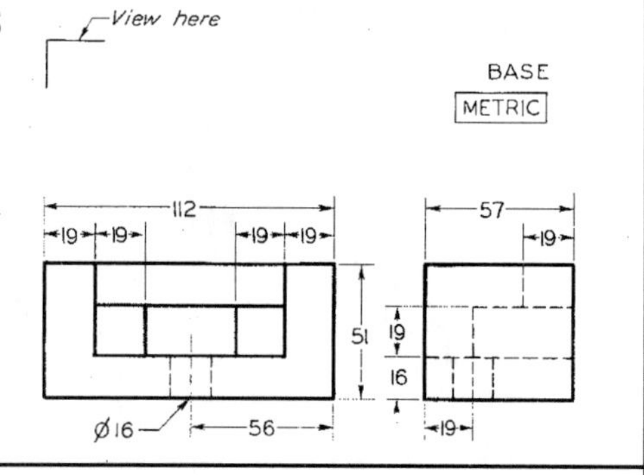

6

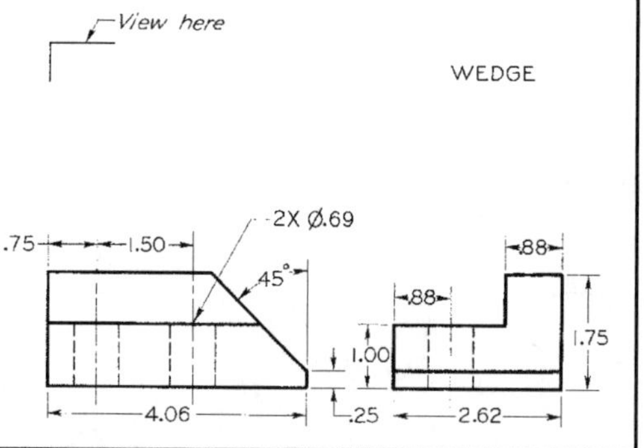

7

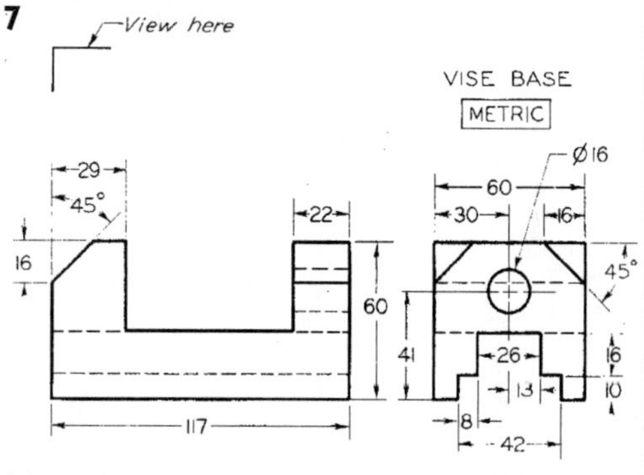

8

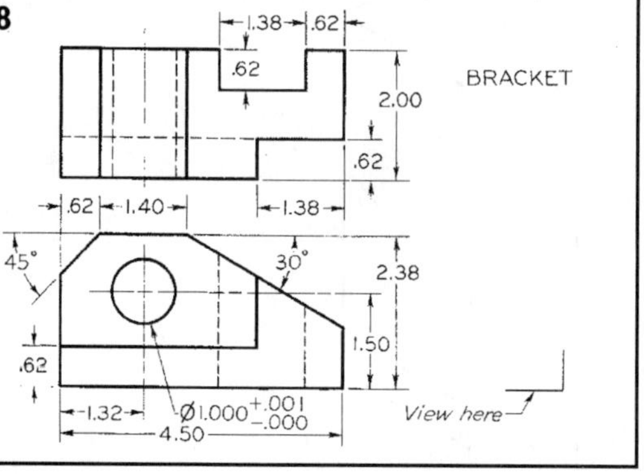

Tutorial 7 Dimensioning

Objectives

When you have completed this tutorial, you will be able to

1. Understand dimensioning nomenclature and conventions.
2. Control the appearance of dimensions.
3. Set the dimension scaling factor.
4. Locate dimensions on drawings.
5. Set the precision for dimension values.
6. Dimension a shape.
7. Use baseline and continued dimensions.
8. Use quick dimension.
9. Save a dimension style and add it to the template drawing.
10. Use associative dimensioning to create dimensions that can update.

Introduction

In the preceding tutorials you learned how to use the AutoCAD® program to define the shape of an object. Dimensioning is used to show the size of the object in your drawing. The ***dimensions*** you specify will be used in the ***manufacture*** and ***inspection*** of the object. Figure 7.1 shows a dimensioned drawing.

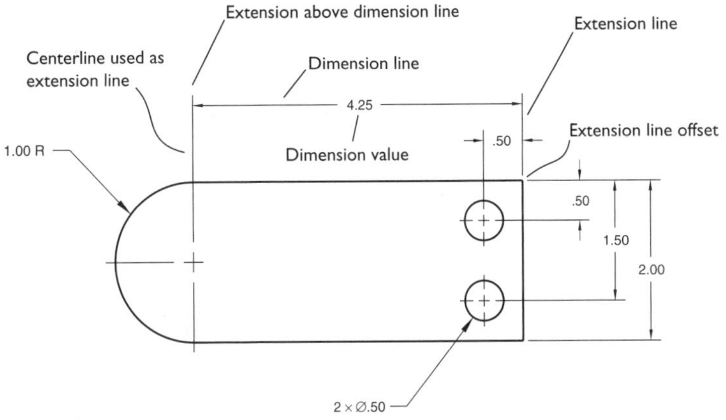

Figure 7.1

For the purpose of inspecting the object, a ***tolerance*** must be stated to define to what extent the actual part may vary from the given dimensions and still be acceptable. In this tutorial you will use a general tolerance note to give the allowable variation for all dimensions. Later, in Tutorial 8, you will learn how to specify tolerances for specific dimensions and geometric tolerances.

Terminology and Conventions

Dimensions are used to accurately describe the details of a part or object so that it can be manufactured. In engineering drawings, dimensions are always placed outside the object outline, unless placing the dimension on the object would result in a drawing that is easier to interpret. ***Extension lines*** relate the dimension to the feature on the part. On the plotted drawing, there should always be a gap of 1/16" between the feature and the beginning of the extension line, called the ***extension line offset***, as shown in Figure 7.1. Centerlines can be extended across the object outline and used as extension lines without leaving a gap where they cross object lines.

Dimension lines are drawn between extension lines and have arrowheads at each end to indicate how the dimension relates to the feature on the object. Keep these general rules in mind when you are dimensioning:

- Dimensions should be grouped around a view and evenly spaced to give the drawing a neat appearance.
- The *dimension values* should never touch the outline of the object.
- Dimension values are usually placed near the midpoint of the dimension line, except when it is necessary to stagger the numbers from one dimension line to the next so that all the values do not line up in a row. Staggering the numbers makes the drawing easier to read.
- Because dimension lines should not cross extension lines or other dimension lines, begin by placing the shortest dimensions closest to the object outline. Place the longest dimensions farthest out. In this way, you avoid dimension lines that cross extension and other dimension lines.
- It is perfectly acceptable for extension lines to cross other extension lines.
- When you are selecting and placing dimensions, think about the operations used to manufacture the part. When possible, provide *overall dimensions* that show the largest measurements for each dimension of the object. Doing so tells the manufacturer the starting size of the material to be used to make the part.
- The manufacturer should never have to add shorter dimensions or make calculations to arrive at the sizes needed for anything in the drawing.
- All necessary dimensions should be specified in your drawing. However, no dimensions should be duplicated, as this may lead to confusion, especially when an inspector is determining whether a part meets the specified tolerance.

Semiautomatic Dimensioning

The AutoCAD semiautomatic dimensioning feature does much of the work in creating dimensions for you. You can create the extension lines, arrowheads, dimension lines, and dimension values automatically. To get the most benefit from the dimensioning feature, use *associative dimensioning*. Associative dimensions are linked to their locations in the drawing by information stored on the DEFPOINTS layers that the program creates. As a result, associative dimensions automatically update when you modify the drawing. Although you can also use nonassociative dimensions, it isn't good practice because these dimensions are created from separate line, polyline, and text objects and do not contain information that allows them to update.

Associative dimensioning is the default in the AutoCAD 2006 program, which has fully associative dimensions. This allows for trans-spatial dimensioning, which makes it possible to add dimensions in paper space for an object that is in model space. When dimensions are associative, if the model space object is moved, the paper space dimension will update to the new location.

Starting

Start by **launching the AutoCAD 2006 program.**

Pick: **File, New**

Use the file ***proto.dwt*** located in the datafiles as a template.

Pick: **File, SaveAs**

Save your drawing as ***obj-dim.dwg***.

You return to the drawing editor with the border and settings you created in the template drawing on your screen.

Dimensioning a Shape

Review the object in Figure 7.1. You will draw this shape and then dimension it.

Layer **VISIBLE** should be the current layer in the drawing. If it is not, set layer VISIBLE as the current layer. Set **Grid** to **0.25** and **Snap** to **0.25**. Be sure that both are turned on.

Make sure that you are drawing in **model space.**

On your own, use the commands that you learned in the preceding tutorials to **draw the object shown in Figure 7.1** according to the specified dimensions.

You don't have to draw the centerlines now. Create the drawing geometry exactly, in order to derive the most benefit from the AutoCAD software's semiautomatic dimensioning capabilities. When you have finished, your screen should look like Figure 7.2.

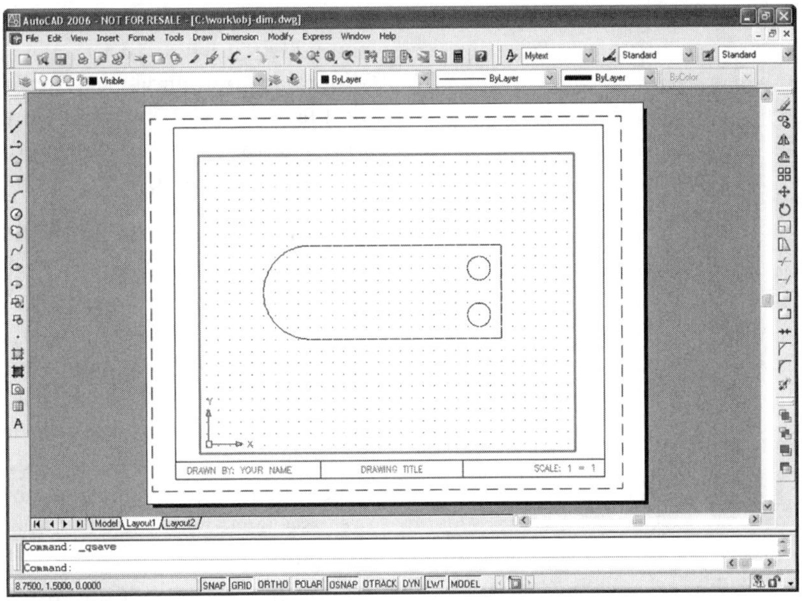

Figure 7.2

Tip

If your paper doesn't fill the drawing window, switch to paper space and use Zoom All to enlarge the paper area to fill the view. Then make sure to switch back to model space to create the drawing.

Using the DIM Layer

In order to produce a clear drawing of a subject, the outline and visible lines of the object are drawn with a thick-width pen when printing or plotting. The dimension, hidden, center, and hatch lines are plotted or printed with a thin-width pen. Thus your eye is drawn first to the bold shape of the object and then to the details of its size and other features. As you recall from previous tutorials, you use the color of the object on your AutoCAD drawing screen or a lineweight setting (usually set by layer) to set a thin width for the dimension lines when plotting.

Also, you will frequently want to turn off all of the dimensions in the drawing. Having dimensions on a separate layer makes plotting and turning off dimensions an easy task.

Pick: **DIM as the current layer**

Dimension Standards

There are standards and rules of good practice that specify how dimension lines, extension lines, arrowheads, text size, and various aspects of dimensioning should appear in the finished drawing. Mechanical, electrical, civil, architectural, and weldment drawings, among others, each have their own standards. Professional societies and standards organizations publish drawing standards for various disciplines. The American National Standards Institute (ANSI) publishes a widely used standard for mechanical drawings to help you create clear drawings that others can easily interpret.

For example, there should be a 1/16" space between the extension lines and the feature from which they are extended. The extension line should extend 1/8" past the last dimension line. Arrowheads and text should be approximately 1/8" tall on 8.5" × 11" drawings. The dimension line closest to the object outline should be at least 3/8" from the object outline on your plotted drawing. Each succeeding dimension line should be at least 1/4" from the previous dimension line.

Drawing Scale and Dimensions

Dimensions in the AutoCAD program are fully associated with the drawing objects. Versions of the program prior to Release 2004 created points in the non-printing layer, DEFPOINTS, with which to associate the dimension. The defpoints that were created coincided with the locations on the object that you selected for the dimension endpoints. Updating dimensions was accomplished by changing the location of these defpoints if they were selected when the object was moved or scaled, which did not fully associate the dimension. Now the dimensions are associated with the object geometry, but still use the created layer defpoints.

Also in past releases of the AutoCAD program, dimension objects when placed on the paper layout could display the correct value for the dimension of an object in model space, but when the view of that object was moved, for example, by panning the model space view inside the viewport, the dimension placed in paper space would not move with the object. This was a major drawback to placing the dimensions on the paper layout. Now dimensions placed in paper space are directly associated with the object and move with its view.

When adding dimensions to your drawing, it is important to have already determined the scale at which you will plot your drawing on the sheet of paper and established the zoom scaling factor. That way you can place the dimensions where they will show clearly on the layout for the final plot. If you are going to plot using a layout (paper space), you should set the scaling factor for the view before you dimension your drawing. Setting the scaling factor first allows you to place the dimensions around the drawing views where they will show clearly. If you change the scale, you will generally have to spend some time cleaning up the dimension placement. For this drawing the scale is already set to 1=1, as you started your drawing from *proto.dwt*, which had that setting. You should check it using the Viewports Toolbar, or by showing the viewport properties and checking that the standard scaling option is set to 1=1, or by typing MVSETUP and choosing Scale viewports from the command line options and selecting the viewport.

Tip

You can quickly display the Properties dialog box for an object by double-clicking on it or selecting it and then pressing Ctrl*-1.*

Tip

Dimensions take a lot of drawing space, especially between the views of a multiview drawing. Often you may need to zoom your drawing to half-size (.5XP) (standard scale of 2:1) or some other smaller scale to have room for dimensions. Keep this possibility in mind for future drawings. Do not change your XP scale factor for this tutorial.

The Dimension Toolbar

Dimensioning commands can be selected from one of two places, the Dimension pull-down menu or the Dimension toolbar. You can quickly select the dimensioning commands from the Dimension toolbar, which you will use for this tutorial.

Right-click: **on any toolbar and turn on the Dimension toolbar** (from the pop-up menu)

The Dimension toolbar floats on your screen, as shown in Figure 7.3.

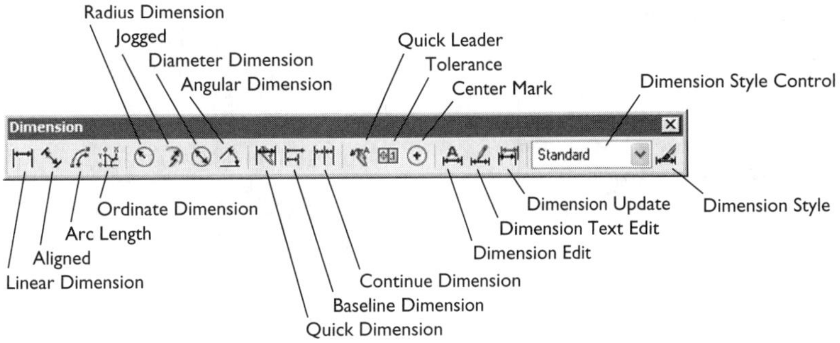

Figure 7.3

Using Dimension Styles

Many features controlling the appearance of the dimensions are set by *dimension variables (dim vars)*, which you can set using the Dimension Style dialog box. You can call this dialog box from the Format menu, by typing Dimstyle or DDIM at the command prompt, or by picking the Dimension Style icon from the Dimension or Styles toolbars. Dimension variables all have names, and you can set each one by typing its name at the command prompt. However, the dialog box allows you to set many dimension variables at the same time, so you will select it from the Dimension toolbar.

Pick: **Dimension Style icon**

The Dimension Style Manager appears on your screen, as shown in Figure 7.4.

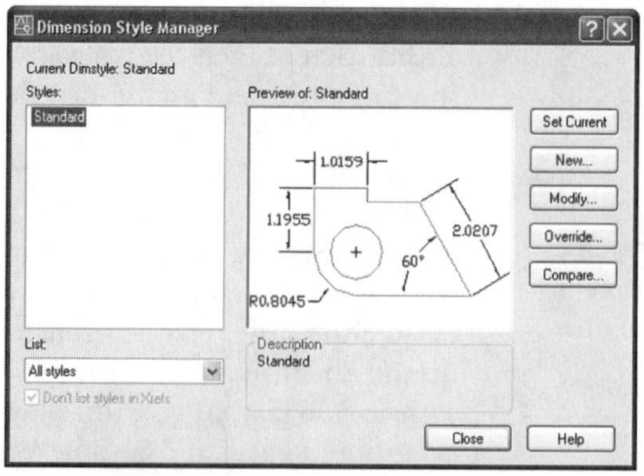

Figure 7.4

Creating a Named Dimension Style

The Dimension Style Manager allows you to change the dimension variables that control the appearance of the dimensions. Note that the current style name is STANDARD. It is displayed on the dimension toolbar. This basic set of features is provided as the default.

You can create your own *dimension style* with a name that you specify. This way you can save different sets of dimension features that will be useful for different types of dimensioning standards—such as mechanical or architectural. You will create a new dimension style named MECHANICAL. The new button is at the right side of the dialog box.

Pick: **New**

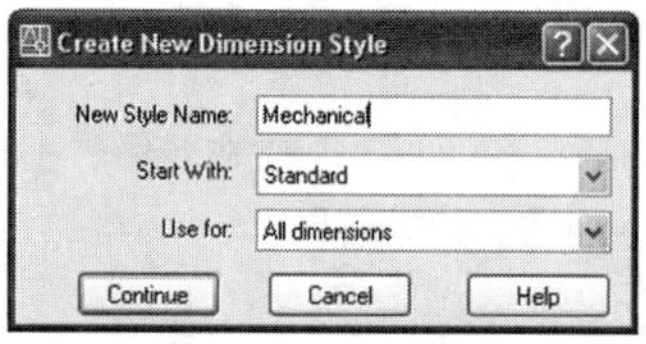

Figure 7.5

The Create New Dimension Style dialog box appears on your screen. In the New Style Name area, highlight the existing text, Copy of Standard, and

Type: **MECHANICAL**

MECHANICAL now appears as the new style name. See Figure 7.5. In the Start With area, STANDARD is listed as the style to use to begin the settings for the new MECHANICAL style. Near the bottom of the dialog box you will see the Use for area. This style will be used for all dimension types: linear, angular, radial, and so forth.

Pick: **Continue**

The New Dimension Style dialog box now appears. It has tabs for Lines, Symbols and Arrows, Text, Fit, Primary Units, Alternate Units, and Tolerances. You will use it to set the appearance of dimensions that use the style MECHANICAL.

The Lines tab should be uppermost as shown in Figure 7.6. This tab allows you to control how the dimension lines and extension lines are drawn.

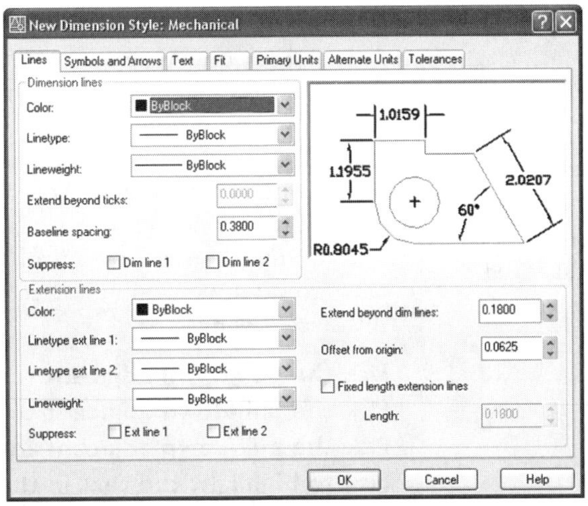

Figure 7.6

Setting the Line Features

In this dialog box you can change many features of dimensions. An important dimensioning variable is the scaling factor (Dimscale). It is on the Fit tab. You will see later that you can rescale as a group all of the values that control dimension appearance. You will set the sizes of dimension features to the size that should be plotted on a standard 8.5" ×11" mechanical drawing. You will use the Fit tab in a moment to tell the program that the sizes you have specified for dimensions are the sizes on the plotted layout, and not the size in model space. The settings that you will make are based on an 8.5" ×11" sheet size. Larger drawing sheets often use larger sizes.

Dimension Lines

In the Dimension Lines area at the upper left of the dialog box, you can control the appearance of the dimension lines. You can set the color, linetype, lineweight, and the distance for the baseline spacing. The value entered in the box to the right of baseline spacing controls the distance between successive dimensions added using *baseline dimensioning*. The default value, 0.38, will work for now. (The ANSI standard states that successive dimensions should be at least 1/4" or 0.25" decimal apart, so 0.38 will meet this criterion.) You can choose to suppress the first or second dimension line when the dimension value divides the dimension line into two parts by checking the boxes near the bottom of this area.

On your own make sure that none of the suppress dimension line boxes are checked. You will set the color, linetype, and lineweight for dimension lines so that they are controlled by the dimension's layer.

Pick: **the pull-down adjacent to Color and use it to select ByLayer**

Pick: **the pull-down adjacent to Linetype and select ByLayer**

Pick: **the pull-down adjacent to Lineweight and select ByLayer**

Tip

You can set the lineweight for extension and dimension lines so that it is controlled by layer or to a specified width using the Lineweight area of the Lines tab.

Tip

You can also use the downward arrow to set the value to .125.

Extension Lines

The Extension lines area lets you control the color, linetype and lineweight for extension lines. In addition, you can set the distance that extension lines extend beyond the dimension line drawn, and the distance from the selected dimension placement that the extension line will begin (offset from origin). You can also suppress either extension line. Make sure that neither box is checked to suppress the extension lines. You will use this area to control the color by layer, and then set the distance to extend beyond dimension lines to .125 (the ANSI standard for this size drawing).

Pick: **the pull-down adjacent to Color and use it to select ByLayer**
Pick: **the pull-down adjacent to Linetype and select ByLayer**
Pick: **the pull-down adjacent to Lineweight and select ByLayer**
Pick: **to highlight the text in the input box to the right of Extend beyond dim lines**
Type: **.125**

When you have made these settings the dialog box should look like Figure 7.7.

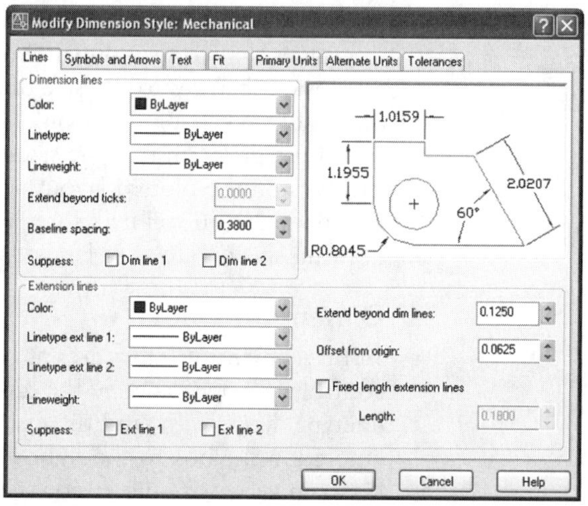

Figure 7.7

Symbols and Arrows

Use the Symbols and Arrows tab of the dialog box to set the arrow size, centermark size and style, arc length style, and jogged radius dimension angle.

Pick: **the Symbols and Arrows tab**
Pick: **to pull down the list of available arrow styles adjacent to the First Arrowhead box**

A list of the available arrowhead styles appears. When you select an arrowhead style from the list you will notice a change in the arrows shown in the *image tile*, or active picture near the top right of the dialog box. Scroll through the available styles. Return the setting to Closed filled when you are finished. Notice that when you select a style for the first arrowhead, the second arrowhead box automatically changes to reflect that. You can select a different style for the second arrowhead by choosing it last. Next set the size for the arrowhead.

Pick: **to highlight the value in the box below Arrow size**

Type: **0.125** to replace the value

Centermark Size and Style

When you create radius or diameter dimensions, you can use the Center Marks area to control the size and style of the centermark, or to suppress it so that no centermark is created. Selecting Line draws a full set of centermarks. Selecting Mark draws just a tick at the center of the circle. Selecting None will cause no centermarks to be drawn.

Pick: **the radio button to the left of Line**

Tip

If the value for the centermark size is too large, full centermarks will not be drawn even when the style is set to Line; instead, just the mark will appear in the center of the circle.

You can set the size of the centermark by using the box below the word Size. The value for Size sets the distance from the center to the end of one side of the center cross of the centermark. To make a smaller center cross, set it to a smaller value; for a larger center cross, set the size larger. Leave the value for your centermarks set to the default value, 0.09, for now. You can also control centermarks by typing Dimcen at the command prompt, as you did in Tutorial 6.

Notice the Arc length symbol and Radial dimension jog areas at the right of the dialog box. These can be used to set the placement for the arc length symbol used when adding an arc length dimension and for specifying the angle to use in creating a jogged radial dimension line, respectively. For now, leave these areas set at the defaults.

When you have finished making the selections described, the Symbols and Arrows tab should look like Figure 7.8.

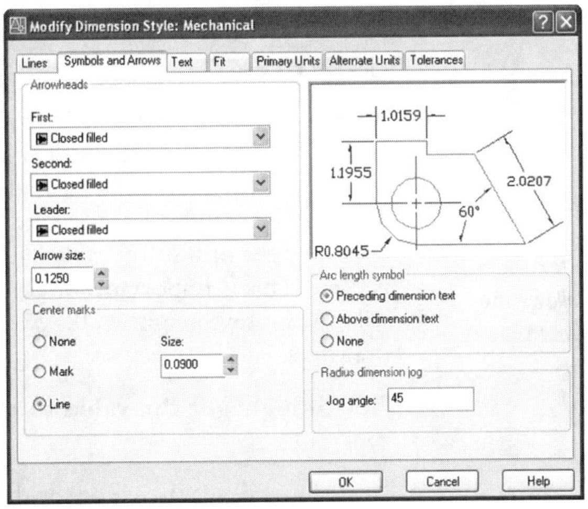

Figure 7.8

Text

The Text tab allows you to control the text style, height, color, background fill, and the gap between the end of the dimension line and the start of the dimension text.

Pick: **the Text tab** so that it appears uppermost

The Text Alignment area (bottom right) controls whether text always reads horizontally (i.e., is unidirectional text) or whether it will be aligned with the dimension line. The image tile changes to display the appearance for the selected setting.

On your own, choose Aligned with dimension line. Then choose ISO Standard. When you have finished experimenting, return the settings to **Horizontal** alignment.

The Text Placement area has a control for horizontal or vertical text placement. Use the pull-down menu adjacent to Horizontal to center text, place it near the first or second extension line, or place it over the first or second extension line. Usually, the default choice, Centered, is used for mechanical drawings.

On your own, try each setting and notice the effect of the selection on the image tile. When you are finished, return the setting to the default choice, **Centered**.

The pull-down menu adjacent to Vertical sets the placement of text relative to the dimension line. The options for vertical justification are Centered, Above, Outside, and JIS (Japanese Industrial Standard). For ANSI standard mechanical drawings, select Centered to create dimension values that are centered vertically, breaking the dimension line. The ISO (International Standards Organization) standard usually uses the options for text above or outside the dimension line. The JIS option orients the text parallel to the dimension line and to its left.

When you are finished examining this portion of the dialog box, return its setting to **Centered** on your own.

You will select style MYTEXT.

Pick: **to pull-down the style choices adjacent to Text Style**
Pick: **MYTEXT**

Remember, in order for styles to be listed here, you must have previously created them in the drawing with the Style command. Style MYTEXT was previously created in the template drawing you started from. Style MYTEXT was created with a text height of 0 (zero). Using a text height of 0 in the style allows you to set the text height when text is used. This is important for correct looking dimension text. Next you will set the text height to 0.125, the standard height for 8.5" × 11" drawings.

Tip

Using a text style with the text height set to 0 for dimensioning allows the dimension settings to control the text appearance.

Pick: **to highlight the value to the right of Text height**
Type: **.125**

Now you will set the color for the dimension text to BYLAYER.

Pick: **ByLayer** from the pull-down adjacent to Color

The Text tab should now appear as shown in Figure 7.9.

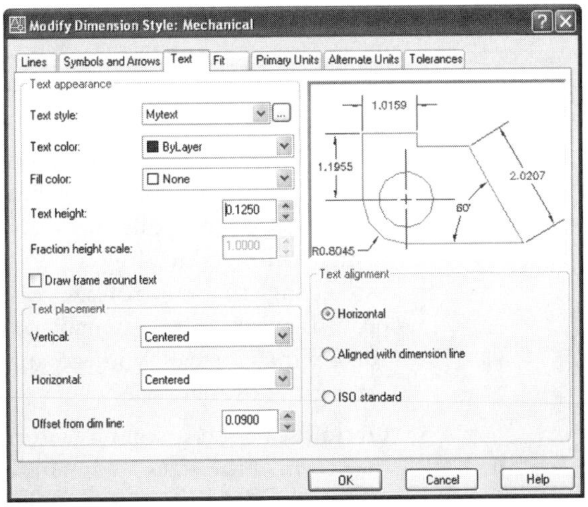

Figure 7.9

Fit

The Fit tab lets you set the options for how the dimensions will be placed in the drawing. These settings are especially helpful when there is not enough room to place both the dimension value and dimension lines and arrowheads inside the extension lines.

Pick: **the Fit tab**

The setting "Either text or arrows (best fit)", places both the text and arrows inside the extension lines, if possible. If that is not possible, either the text or the arrows will be placed inside the extension lines. If neither will fit, both the arrows and text are placed outside the extension lines. Generally, these are all accepted practices, as long as the dimension can be correctly interpreted. You can also set which will be moved outside first: the text, the arrows, or both text and arrows; or to always keep the text between the extension lines. You can also specify to suppress the arrows if they don't fit inside the extension lines.

On your own, choose **Either text or arrows (best fit)**.

The Text Placement area of this dialog box allows you to control how text is placed when it is not in the default location (between the extension lines). You can select to place it beside the dimension line, or over the dimension line, either with or without a leader.

The Fine Tuning area in the lower right of the dialog box lets you select either to place text manually or to force a line to be drawn between the extension lines, even when text and arrows are placed outside the extension lines. If you select Place text manually, when you pick or type the location for the dimension line, the dimension value will appear at that position. This can be important for creating radial and diameter dimensions that are placed outside the drawing outline. You will learn more about specific "child" dimension styles to do this in Tutorial 8 on advanced dimensioning.

Tip

To make radial dimensions that look like those shown in the exercises, choose the Place text manually selection in the Fine Tuning area of the Fit tab. Then you can drag the radial and diameter dimension value to place it around the outside of the object.

The Dimension Scaling Factor

There are essentially two ways to scale the dimension features: (1) use an overall scale factor (usually relative to model space) or (2) scale dimensions to the layout (paper space). Think about a drawing that is to be plotted to a scale of 1 plotted inch in paper space to 2 model units. If you want your arrowheads and text to be 1/8" on the plotted sheet, then at this scale the arrows need to be 1/4" high in model space so that when reduced by half they will be 1/8". You could double all the settings that control sizes of the dimension elements, such as arrowhead size, but there are many of them, so this method would be time-consuming. Instead, you can automatically scale all the size features by setting the overall scale.

Overall scale sets a scaling factor to use for all of the dimension variables that control the sizes of dimension elements. Its value appears in the box to the right of "Use overall scale of:." Setting the overall scale to 2 doubles the size of all the dimension elements in the drawing so that, when plotted half-size, your arrowheads, text, and other elements will maintain the correct proportions on the final plot. (You can also type Dimscale at the command prompt and enter the value by which the dimension elements are multiplied.)

Picking Scale dimensions to layout uses the paper space zoom factor to set the scaling for dimension elements so that the values you enter in the dialog box are the sizes on the drawing when paper space is plotted at a scale of 1=1.

For this tutorial,

Pick: **Scale dimensions to layout radio button**

Your Fit tab should appear as shown in Figure 7.10.

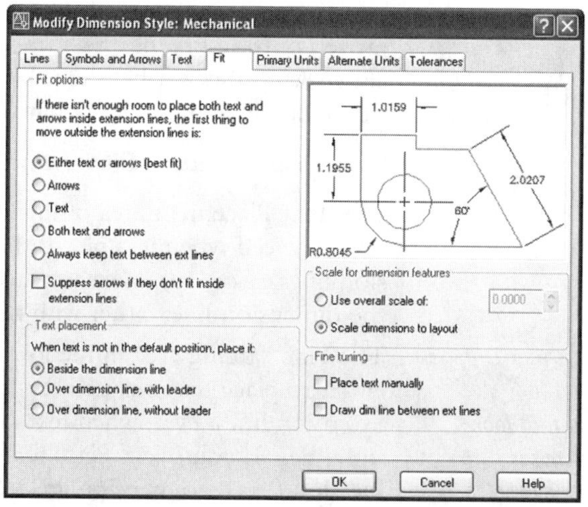

Figure 7.10

Next, you will set up the primary units for the dimensioning.

Pick: **Primary Units tab** (so that it appears uppermost)

Primary Units

You use the Primary Units tab to set up the number of decimal places, the prefix, and the suffix for dimensions. When dimensioning a drawing, you must consider the precision of the values to be used in the dimensions. Specifying a dimension to four decimal places, which is the AutoCAD default, implies that accuracies of 1/10,000th of an inch are appropriate tolerances for this part. Standard practice is to specify decimal inch dimensions to two decimal places (an accuracy of 1/100th of an inch) unless the function of the part makes a tighter tolerance desirable.

You can select the type of units and set the number of decimal places displayed for linear and angular dimension values. For this tutorial you will leave the linear dimension units set to Decimal.

To set the precision, you will pull down a list of decimal places, as shown in Figure 7.11.

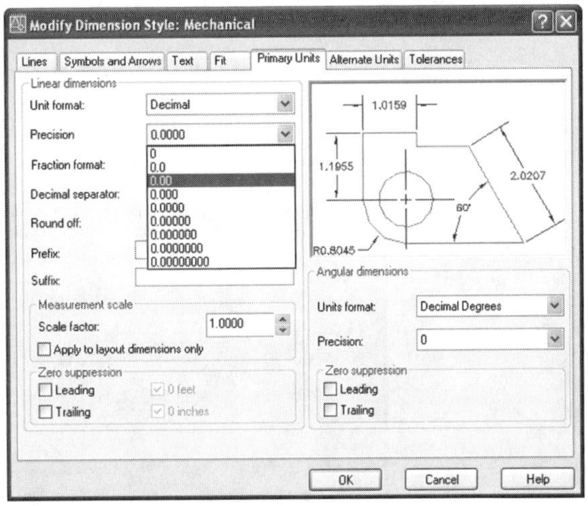

Figure 7.11

Pick: **to pull-down the choices adjacent to Precision**
Pick: **0.00**

Measurement Scale

The Measurement Scale area is used to specify a scaling factor by which all the actual dimension values are multiplied. This factor is different from the overall scaling factor because the dimension value is affected, not the size of the dimension elements. Leave the value to the right of Scale factor set to 1.0000.

You can use this area to scale only layout (paper space) dimensions by picking the check box.

Zero Suppression for Linear Dimensions

The Zero Suppression area allows you to suppress leading or trailing zeros in the dimension value. You can also suppress dimensions of 0 feet or 0 inches. In decimal dimensioning, common practice is to show leading zeros in metric dimensions and to suppress them in inch dimensions when dimensions are less than 1 unit. Zero Suppression is available for both linear dimensions and angular dimensions, in four categories:

leading zeros, trailing zeros, 0 feet, and 0 inches. Selecting the box to the left of any of these items suppresses those zeros; a check appears in the box when you select it. In the Linear Dimensions area under Zero Suppression,

Pick: **to suppress Leading zeros**

Angular Dimensions

The type of units used to dimension angles can be set using the Angular Dimensions area of the Primary Units tab. To select, pull down the list and choose from the types of units shown. (You can further control the appearance of angular dimensions by selecting the Angular child style in the Dimension Styles dialog box.)

Zero Suppression for Angular Dimensions

You will suppress the leading zeros for angular dimensions as you did for linear dimensions. In the Angular Dimensions area under Zero Suppression,

Pick: **to suppress Leading zeros**

When you have finished setting this tab of the dialog box, it should appear as shown in Figure 7.12.

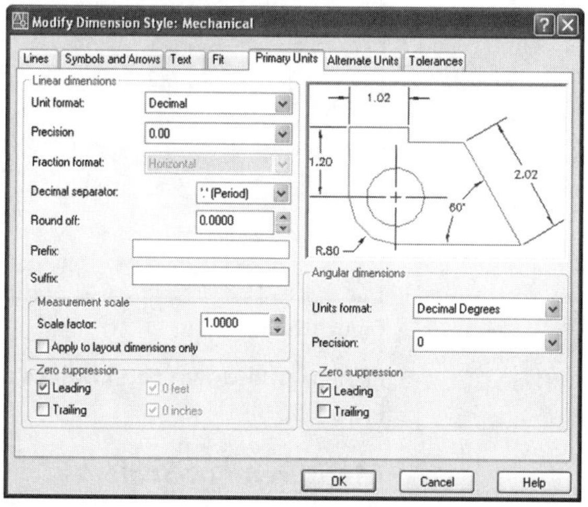

Figure 7.12

Next you will look at the settings that can be controlled using the Alternate Units tab.

Pick: **Alternate Units tab**

Alternate Units

Alternate units are useful when you want to dimension a drawing with more than one system of measurement. For example, dimensioning drawings with both metric and inch values is fairly common. When you use alternate units, the AutoCAD program automatically converts your drawing units to the alternate units, using the scaling factor you provide. You can enable alternate units by picking the box to the left of "Display alternate units" in the upper left of the Alternate Units tab. Until you select the box to display the alternate units, the remaining selections are grayed out.

Pick: **Display alternate units so that it is checked**

The Alternate Units tab appears on your screen as shown in Figure 7.13.

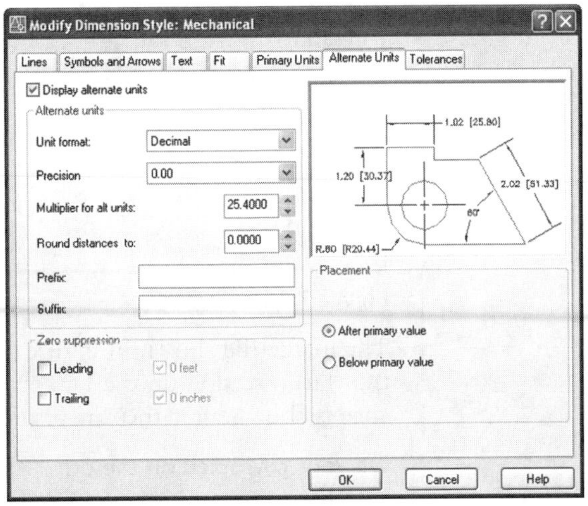

Figure 7.13

To set the scale for the alternate units, you set a Multiplier for alt units, by using the up/down arrows or typing in a scaling factor. You can also type a prefix and suffix for the alternate units in the appropriate boxes. The prefix you enter appears in front of the dimension value; the suffix appears after the dimension value.

You can control the appearance of the alternate units by picking the button to place them After primary value or Below primary value. The default places the alternate units inside square brackets following the normal units. For this drawing you will not use alternate units so,

Pick: **Display alternate units so that it is not checked**

Next you will select the Tolerances tab to see this area of the dialog box. You will learn more about setting tolerances in Tutorial 8.

Pick: **Tolerances tab**

The Tolerances tab appears on your screen.

Tolerances

You can use the Tolerances tab to specify limit or variance tolerances with the dimension value. You can set the tolerance method to Symmetrical, Deviation, Limits, Basic, or None.

Pick: **Deviation** (from the pull-down for Method)

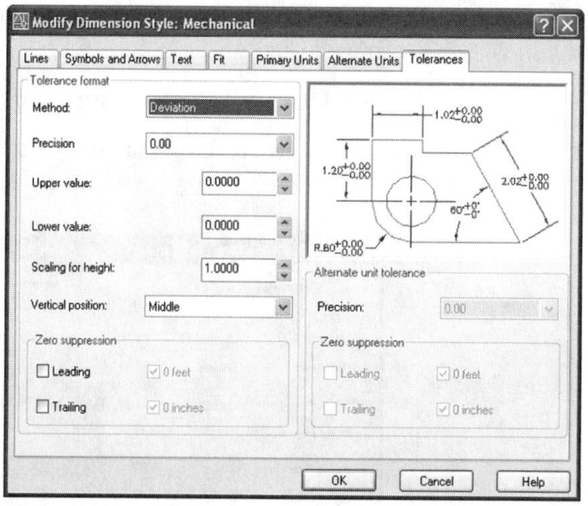

Figure 7.14

The image tile shown in Figure 7.14 reflects the choices you have made thus far in setting up the Dimension style. Notice that now the tolerance is shown after the dimension values.

On your own, pick on the other tolerance methods to view the effect of these settings in the image tile.

Pick: **None** (from the pull-down for Method) so that tolerances are not used

Now you have set up your basic style for the dimensions.

Pick: **OK**

You are returned to the Dimension Style Manager dialog box.

Setting the Current Style

In order to apply your dimension style MECHANICAL so that new dimensions use this style, pick the Set Current button near the top of the Dimension Style Manager.

Pick: **Set Current**

The selections you have made apply to dimension style MECHANICAL only. As you dimension your drawing, you can return to this dialog box and create a new style if you need to create dimensions with a different appearance.

When you change a style and pick OK, the changes are applied to all existing dimensions in the drawing that you created with that style. If you want to make changes to a style and not have them take effect on existing dimensions, you can pick the Override button to allow changes to take effect on newly created dimensions, but not on existing dimensions having that style. The Compare button lets you compare two different styles to view their differences.

Pick: **Close** (to exit the Dimension Style Manager)

Notice that the name MECHANICAL now appears in the Dimension toolbar as the current style as shown in Figure 7.15.

Figure 7.15

Checking Your Dimension Settings

As you have seen, you can change many settings to affect the appearance of the dimensions you add to your drawings. You can set these variables either through the Dimension Styles dialog box or by setting each individual dimension variable at the command line. Most commands that use dialog boxes to select settings can be run at the command prompt by typing a hyphen (-) in front of the command name.

You can use the -Dimstyle command to list and set dimension styles and variables at the command line. If any dimension variable overrides are set, they will be listed after the name of the dimension style. There should not be any overrides set for style MECHANICAL because you have saved your settings to the parent style.

Command: **-DIMSTYLE** ↵

Current dimension style: Mechanical

Enter a dimension style option [Save/Restore/STatus/Variables/
Apply/?]<Restore>: **ST** ↵

Tip

You can press F2 *to pop up the text window to scroll through the text entries.*

The dimension variables and their current settings are listed in the text window on your screen. On your own, use the scroll bars to scroll up and down to see all the entries.

To exit the text window, if it is still on your screen,

Pick: the **Windows Close button (X)**

Associative Dimensioning

The Dimassoc variable controls whether associative dimensioning is turned on or off. Associative dimensioning inserts each dimension as a block or group of drawing objects relative to the points selected in the drawing. If the drawing is scaled or stretched, the dimension values automatically update. Dimassoc was a new variable starting in the AutoCAD 2004 release, replacing the old Dimaso variable from prior releases. The Dimassoc variable has three settings for the associativity between dimensions and drawing objects. A setting of 2 causes dimensions to automatically adjust their locations, orientations, and measurement values when the geometric objects associated with them are modified. A setting of 1 causes dimensions to be nonassociative. This means that the dimension does not change when the geometric object it measures is modified. Finally, a setting of 0 causes the dimension to be a collection of separate objects (exploded) rather than a single dimension object. Dimensions created with Dimassoc set to 0 cannot be updated, but their individual parts, such as arrowheads or extension lines, can be erased or moved.

Dimensions created with Dimassoc set to 0 also do not automatically update when you change their dimension styles. When Dimassoc is set to 2 or 1, the entire dimension acts as one object in the drawing.

Make sure that Dimassoc is set to 2,

Command: **DIMASSOC** ↵

Tip

You do not have to type a new value for Dimassoc if the default <2> is set to 2.

Enter new value for DIMASSOC <2>: **2** ↵

Now you are ready to start adding dimensions to your drawing. Look at the status bar. You will see that the coordinates still display the cursor position with four decimal places of accuracy, even though you selected to display only two decimal places in your dimensions. The AutoCAD software can keep track of your drawing and the settings you have made in the drawing database to a precision of at least fourteen decimal places. However, the dimensions will be shown only to two decimal places, as set in the current style. The display of decimal places on the status bar is set independently of the dimension precision (using the Units command you learned in Tutorial 1). This feature is useful because you can still create and display an accurate drawing database while working on the design, yet dimension according to the often lower precision required to manufacture acceptable parts.

Adding Dimensions to the Layout or the Model

Tip

Dimensioning in Model Space is also perfectly acceptable. For this tutorial, add the dimensions to paper space. For future drawings, decide whether you prefer dimensions in model or paper space.

It is possible to add dimensions in model space, where your geometric objects reside, or to the layout, which is like the sheet of paper where notes, borders, and other such information are placed. Adding the dimensions to the layout may allow for easier updating of dimensions if the drawing scale is changed later. The Scale dimensions to layout option you chose on the Fit tab of the Dimension Style dialog box set the scaling for dimension elements so that the values you entered in the dialog box are the sizes on the drawing when paper space is plotted at a scale of 1=1. Even if you change the scale for the viewport, the dimensions will maintain their proper appearance. You will add dimensions to the layout, not to the model space object this time. (Prior to Release 2005, this was not preferred because dimensions added to the layout were not associated to the objects in a way that let them move as the model was panned inside the viewport.) Many factors influence the decision whether to add the dimensions to model space or to paper space. It can be easier to dimension a drawing in paper space when using multiple viewports, especially when they are at different scales. Even with the ability to associate paper space dimensions with the real life-sized model space drawing entities, sometimes there are problems updating the dimensions correctly. Dimensions can be reassociated if they fail to update correctly, but this can be an extra effort. All in all it depends on your particular drawing application, company practices, and downstream uses for the drawing which one you should ultimately choose. You will try each method in this tutorial. For this drawing you will add the dimensions to paper space.

Grid and Snap can be set differently for model space and for paper space. It can look confusing when both grids are turned on at the same time.

Tip

If you see two grids that don't align with one another, check to see that you have the grid turned off in model space before you turn the grid on in paper space.

Turn the **model space Grid off**.

Switch to paper space by picking on the Model/Paper button so that it shows **Paper**.

Set the paper space **Snap to .25** and turn it on.

Turn the paper space **Grid** on.

Notice that turning on the grid in paper space shows a grid that extends outside the viewport boundary to the edges of the layout sheet.

You will use the paper space grid to help you locate the dimensions 0.5 unit away from the object outline (thus meeting the criterion that a dimension must be at least 3/8", or 0.375, from the object outline).

Adding Linear Dimensions

The Linear Dimension command measures and annotates a feature with a horizontal or vertical dimension line. The value inserted into the dimension line is the perpendicular distance between the extension lines. If you use the Linear Dimension command and dimension a line drawn at an angle on the screen, the value returned is just the X- or Y-axis component of the length. The dimension is adjusted to horizontal or vertical, depending on the points selected.

You will use the intersection and quadrant modes to select the exact intersections in the drawing for the extension lines so that the dimensions will be drawn accurately. You will dimension the horizontal distance from the end of the block to the center of the upper hole. Refer to Figure 7.16 for your selections.

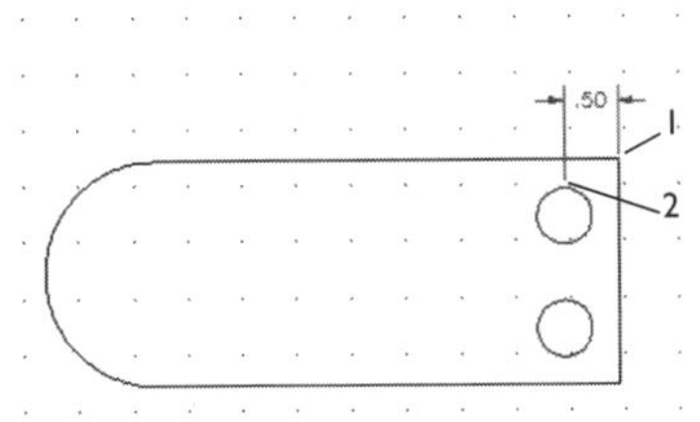

Figure 7.16

On your own, turn the **Intersection** and **Quadrant** running mode object snaps on and all other object snaps and tracking off.

Pick: **Linear Dimension icon**

Specify first extension line origin or <select object>: **pick point 1 at the top right-hand corner**

Specify second extension line origin: **pick on the upper small hole, using AutoSnap™ Quadrant to locate point 2**

Specify dimension line location or [Mtext/Text/Angle/Horizontal/Vertical/Rotated]: **pick a point two snap units above the top line of the object**

Dimension text = 0.50

The dimension should appear in your drawing, as shown in Figure 7.16. Next you will add the diameter dimensions for the two small holes.

Creating a Diameter Dimension

The Diameter Dimension selection adds the centermarks and draws the *leader line* from the point you select on the circle to the location you select for the dimension value. The leader line produced is a radial line, which, if extended, would pass through the center of the circle. Keep in mind that you can make changes to these appearances by setting the dimension style.

You will pick the Diameter Dimension icon from the Dimension toolbar. After you have entered the dimension, you will use the Text option of the Diameter Dimension command to add an additional line of text below the dimension value. Refer to Figure 7.17 for the placement of the dimension.

Tip

Be sure that Snap and Ortho are off to make selecting the circles and drawing angled leader lines easier.

Pick: **Diameter Dimension icon**

Select arc or circle: **pick on the lower of the two small circles**

Specify dimension line location or [Mtext/Text/Angle]: **M** ↵

The Text Formatting dialog box similar to Figure 7.17 appears on your screen.

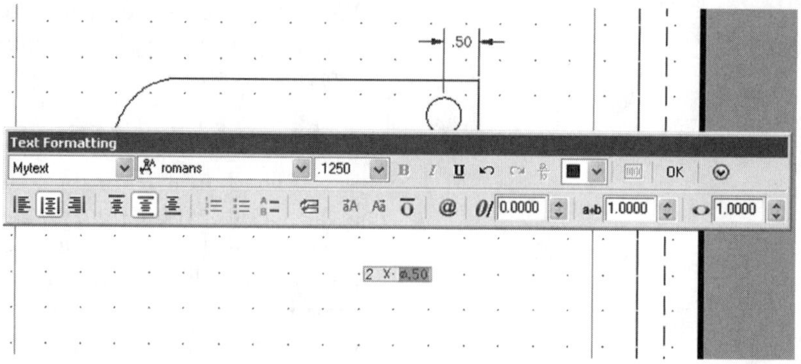

Figure 7.17

Tip

Take care that the text is not highlighted; you want to insert text, not replace the dimension value.

Tip

You can replace the default value for the dimension with a different value. If you do so, however, your dimension values won't automatically update when you change your drawing. A better practice is to create your drawing geometry accurately and accept the default value provided.

You will use the dialog box to add the text 2 × in front of the dimension value.

On your own, **position the cursor in front of the ∅.50 value.**
Type: **2 X**
Pick: **OK**

Next, you are prompted for the dimension line location.

Specify dimension line location or [Mtext/Text/Angle]: **pick a point below and to the left of the circle at about 7 o'clock, 0.5 outside the object outline**

Use the grid as a visual reference to help you position the dimension text 0.5 unit away from the object outline. See Figure 7.18.

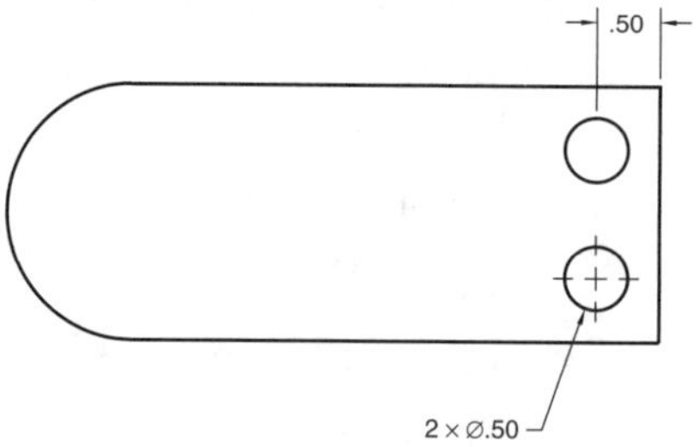

Figure 7.18

Tip

When dimensioning a full circle of 360 degrees (as opposed to an arc), use the diameter command rather than the radius. This is important because equipment used to manufacture and inspect holes and cylinders is designed to measure diameter, not radius. The machinist making the part should never have to calculate any dimensions, including not having to double the radius to arrive at the diameter. Measuring the radius of a hole is difficult because the center has already been drilled out.

Next, you will add a centermark for the upper of the two small holes.

Pick: **Center Mark icon**
Select arc or circle: **pick on the edge of the top circle**

The centermark is added to the drawing, as shown in Figure 7.19.

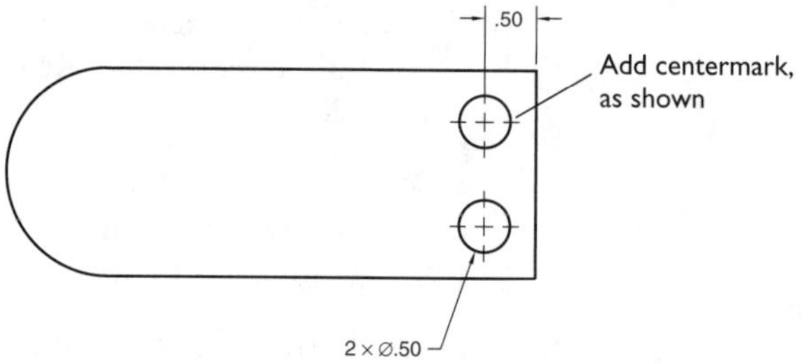

Figure 7.19

Now you will use the Radius Dimension command to create the radius dimension and centermarks for the rounded end. You will use the Radius Dimension icon on the Dimension toolbar to select the command.

Pick: **Radius Dimension icon**

Select circle or arc: **pick on the rounded end**

Specify dimension line location or [Mtext/Text/Angle]: **pick a point above and to the left of the circle at about 10 o'clock, .5 outside the object outline**

The radial dimension and centermark for the arc are added. Your drawing should look like that in Figure 7.20.

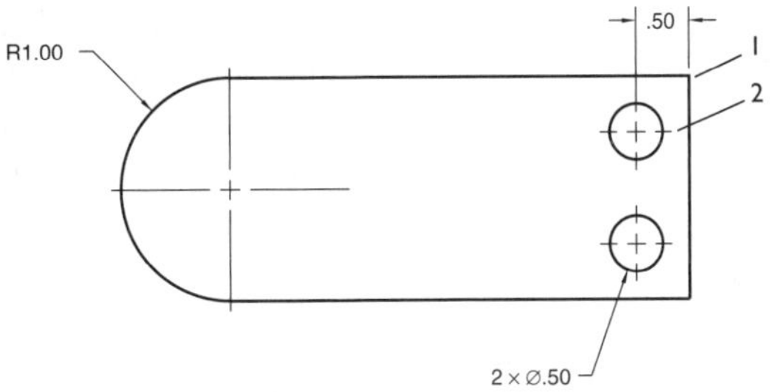

Figure 7.20

Next, you will add a linear dimension for the vertical distance from the upper edge of the part to the center of the top hole. Refer to Figure 7.20 as you make selections.

Tip

To add the linear dimension for the location of the hole and have the centermark appear correctly, pick the quadrant point of the circle, not the center. If you select the center, the extension line will extend into the circle and obscure the centermark.

Pick: **Linear Dimension icon**

Specify first extension line origin or <select>: **pick intersection 1 at the top right-hand corner**

Specify second extension line origin: **target quadrant point 2**

Specify dimension line location or [Mtext/Text/Angle/Horizontal/Vertical/Rotated]: **pick a point three snap units to the right of the object**

The dimension added to your drawing should look like that in Figure 7.21.

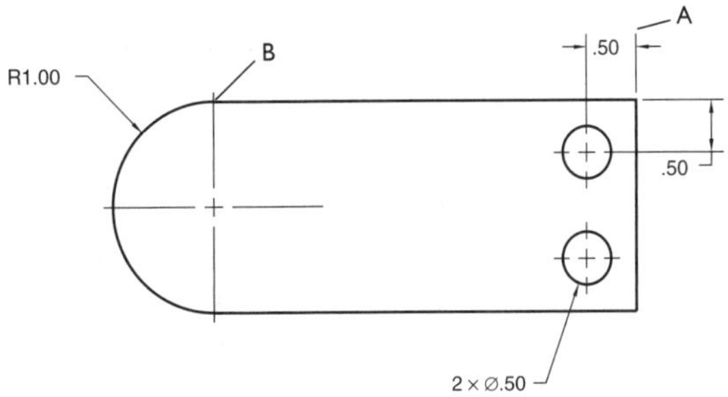

Figure 7.21

When you use the best fit method for placing text, the AutoCAD software automatically places the text value outside in instances where there is not enough space to fit the text cleanly. You can use hot grips to fine tune the placement if needed.

If the dimension value is not inside the extension lines, turn Snap off to make it easier to position the value.

On your own, pick on the linear dimension. Use the grips that appear and pick the grip centered in the dimension value to make it active. Use it to drag the text inside the extension lines.

Next, you will use baseline dimensioning to add the horizontal dimension between the edge of the part and the rounded end.

Baseline Dimensioning

Baseline and *chained dimensioning* are two different methods of relating one dimension to the next. In baseline dimensioning, as the name suggests, each succeeding dimension is measured from one extension line or baseline. In chained or *continued dimensioning*, each succeeding dimension is measured from the last extension line of the previous dimension. Baseline dimensioning can be the more accurate method because the tolerance allowance is not added to the tolerance allowance of the preceding dimension, as it is in chained dimensioning. However, chained dimensioning often may be preferred because the greater the tolerances allowed, the cheaper the part should be to manufacture. The more difficult the tolerance is to achieve, the more parts will not pass inspection. Figure 7.22 depicts the two different dimensioning methods. Note that, if a tolerance of ± 0.01 is allowed, the baseline dimensioned part can be as large as 4.26 or as small as 4.24. However, with chained dimensions, an acceptable part could be as large as 4.27 or as small as 4.23.

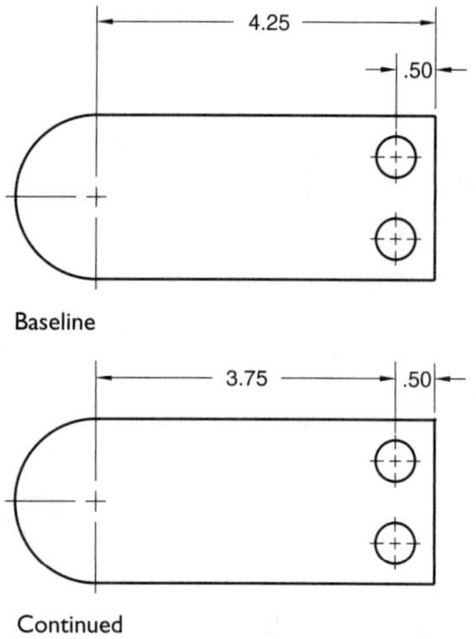

Figure 7.22

Adding dimensions with Baseline or Continue is preferable because adding a second dimension with the Linear Dimension command will draw the extension line a second time. That will give a poor appearance to your drawing when it is plotted.

Use the Baseline Dimension command to create the next dimension. Refer to Figure 7.21 as you make selections.

You will use the Select option to specify the dimension you want to use as the base dimension. As you have added several dimensions since determining the horizontal location for the upper small hole, you will need to specify that it is the base dimension before you can create the baseline dimension. If you were continuing from the previous dimension, you would not need to do this.

Pick: **Baseline Dimension icon**

Specify a second extension line origin or [Undo/Select] <Select>: ↵

Select base dimension: **pick A for the base dimension**

Specify a second extension line origin or [Undo/Select] <Select>: **pick intersection B**

Specify a second extension line origin or [Undo/Select] <Select>: ↵

Select base dimension: ↵

The new dimension appears, as in Figure 7.23. Note that the program located the dimensions automatically based on your dimension style settings.

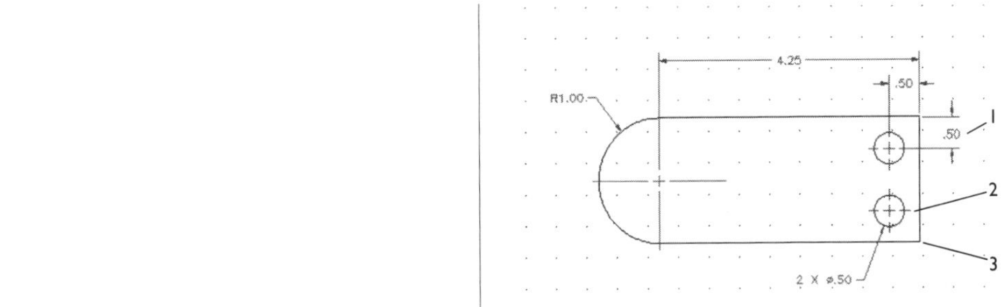

Figure 7.23

Next you will add baseline dimensions for the vertical location of the lower hole and for the overall height. Refer to Figure 7.23 for the points to select.

Pick: **Baseline Dimension icon**

Specify a second extension line origin or [Undo/Select] <Select>: ↵

Select base dimension: **pick 1 for the base dimension**

Specify a second extension line origin or [Undo/Select] <Select>: **pick the centerline endpoint 2**

Specify a second extension line origin or [Undo/Select] <Select>: **pick intersection 3**

Specify a second extension line origin or [Undo/Select] <Select>: ↵

Select base dimension: ↵

Save your drawing now.

Your drawing should now look like that in Figure 7.24.

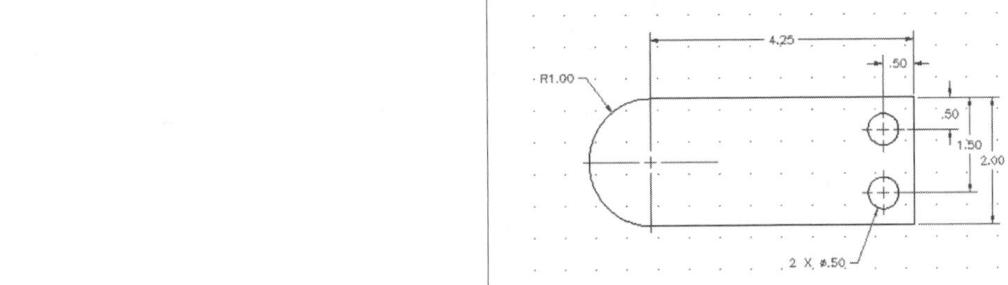

Figure 7.24

Using Xplode

The Xplode command lets you change dimensions, blocks, polylines, and other grouped objects back to their individual components; at the same time, you can control the color, layer, and linetype of the components. You will use Xplode to erase just the single right line of the centermark for the rounded end. You will select the Layer option of the Xplode command and the default layer, DIM, for the exploded object's layer.

Note that there is also a command named Explode that doesn't have any options. Explode simply changes the grouped objects back to individual objects, regardless of the X-, Y-, and Z-scaling factors. (In previous AutoCAD releases, the X-, Y-, and Z-scaling factors of a block had to be the same or it could not be exploded.) The Xplode command has suboptions that allow you to control the color, layer, linetype and other options as the object is changed back into its original components.

Explode and Xplode are different commands. Refer to on-line help to investigate the differences between these two commands further.

Because the rounded end is an arc, not a full circle, its centermark should extend only for the half-circle shown. The right portion of the centermark should be erased. Because associative dimensions are created as blocks, they are all one object: No part can be erased singly. To eliminate the extra portion of the centermark on the rounded end, you will type the Xplode command.

Command: **XPLODE** ↵
Select objects to XPlode.
Select objects: **pick on the dimension for the rounded end**
Select objects: ↵
[All/Color/LAyer/LType/LWeight/Inherit from parent block/
Explode] <Explode>: **LA** ↵
Enter new layer name for exploded objects <DIM>: ↵

You will see the message "Object exploded onto layer DIM" at the command prompt. The appearance of the drawing doesn't change, but now you are able to erase the individual line at the right of the centermark for the rounded end.

On your own, **erase** the extra line from the centermark for the rounded end and **save** your drawing at this time.

Adding Text with Special Characters

When you are using AutoCAD shape fonts (e.g., Roman Simplex) to create text, you can type in special characters during any text command and when entering the dimension text.

You can add special text characters by inserting the code %% (double percent signs) before the text. The most common special characters have been given letters to make them easy to remember. Otherwise, you can specify any special character by typing its ASCII number. (Most word processor documentation includes a list of ASCII values for symbols in an appendix.)

The most common special characters and their codes are listed in Table 7.1.

Table 7.1

Code	Character	Symbol
%%C	Diameter symbol	∅
%%D	Degree symbol	°
%%P	Plus/minus sign	±
%%O	Toggles on and off the overscore mode	$\overline{\text{On}}$
%%U	Toggles on and off the underscore mode	$\underline{\text{On}}$
%%%	Draws a single percent sign	%
%%N	Draws special character number *n*	*n*

Tip

You can double-click on text to edit it in place.

Add the note **"All tolerances ± .01 unless otherwise noted."** Type **%%P** to make the ± sign.

Below the tolerance note add notes indicating the material from which the part is to be made, such as **"MATERIAL: SAE 1020"** and a note stating **"ALL MEASUREMENTS IN INCHES."**

Use the **Edit Text** command to change the text in your title block, noting the name of the part, your name, and the scale, to complete the drawing.

Save your drawing.

Using Quick Dimension

Next you will erase the dimensions that you added and try using the Quick Dimension command to add them.

On your own, **erase** the dimensions that you added.

Switch to **Model Space** inside the viewport by toggling the Model/Paper button to Model.

Pick: **Quick Dimension icon**

Select geometry to dimension: **use implied Windowing to select all of the drawing lines** and press ↵

Specify dimension line position, or [Continuous/Staggered/Baseline/Ordinate/Radius/Diameter/datumPoint/Edit/seTtings: **pick two snap increments above the object**

Two dimensions are added to the drawing as shown in Figure 7.25.

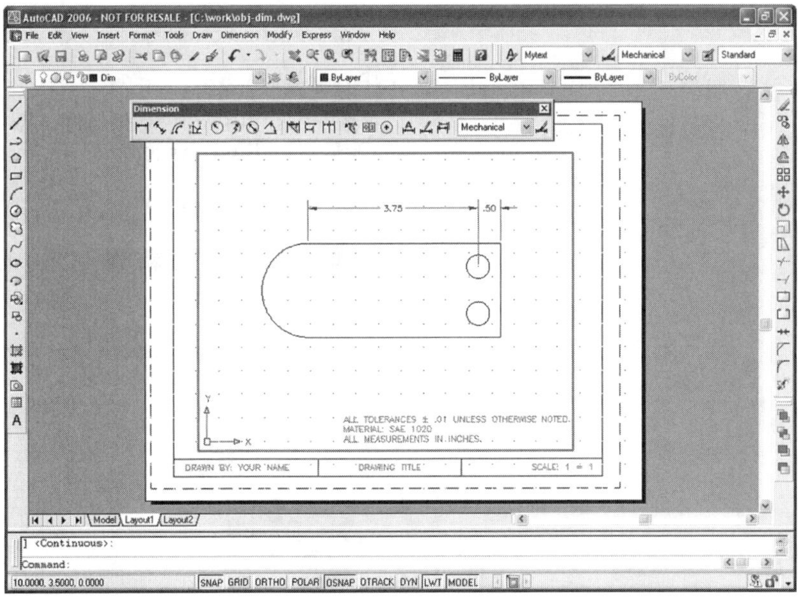

Figure 7.25

Next you will restart the Quick Dimension command and add the dime-sion for the rounded end.

Command: ↵

Associative dimension priority = Endpoint

Select geometry to dimension: **Pick on the rounded end**

Select geometry to dimension: ↵

Tip

You can use the AutoCAD DesignCenter™ to import dimension styles from an existing drawing into your current drawing. You will learn more about the DesignCenter in Tutorial 10.

Tip

Drawings started from dimtemplate.dwt *will have the dimension styles that you created earlier in this tutorial available for use.*

Specify dimension line position, or [Continuous/Staggered/Baseline/Ordinate/Radius/Diameter/datumPoint/Edit/seTtings] <Radius>: **pick to the left of the rounded end**

The dimension for the rounded end appears in your drawing as a radial dimension.

On your own, pick on the dimension for the rounded end and use its grips to position it so that the leader to the value is at an angle.

Saving As a Template

Any drawing that you have created can be used as a template from which to start new drawings. You will use Save As and save your *obj-dim.dwg* with a new name and file type so that you can use it as a template to start other drawings.

On your own, **erase** the object and all dimensions and set layer **VISIBLE** as the current layer.

Use **Save As** to save this drawing as ***dimtemplate.dwt*** (by changing the file type to a Drawing Template **.dwt*).

In the Template Description, describe this template as a dimensioning template and leave measurement with English units.

Close the file when you have finished saving it.

Dimensioning the Adapter

You will continue to work with the orthographic views of the adapter from Tutorial 6 by adding dimensions to the drawing.

Pick: **New icon**

Pick: Navigate to the ***datafile 2006*** folder and select the file ***adapter1.dwt***

Pick: **File, Save As** and name the drawing ***adapt-dm.dwg***.

Your screen should look like Figure 7.26.

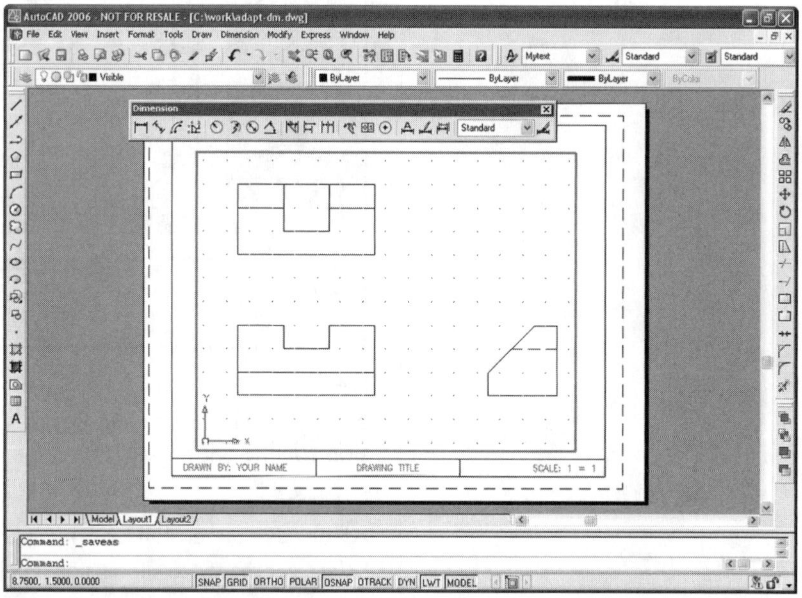

Figure 7.26

This drawing is similar to the one you did in Tutorial 6. Here, the hole has not been added and the views have been moved apart to make room for dimensions. You will be adding the dimensions to model space for this drawing.

Dimensions are usually placed between views when possible, except for the overall dimensions, which are often placed around the outside. You will use the dimension style list on the dimensioning toolbar to set the current style to MECHANICAL. To select it, pick on the name STANDARD, as shown in Figure 7.27 and then select MECHANICAL from the pull-down list of dimension styles.

Pick: **MECHANICAL** (to replace STANDARD as the current style)

Its name should then appear as the current style.

Figure 7.27

You will verify that associative dimensioning is turned on. Later in the tutorial you will use the feature to automatically update dimensions, and you can't update dimensions unless you created them with Dimassoc turned on. You will type Dimassoc at the command prompt.

Command: **DIMASSOC** ↵
Enter new value for DIMASSOC <2>: **2** ↵
On your own, check to see that the **Intersection** running object snap is turned on.
Check the Layer Control to be sure that you are on layer **DIM**.

Next you will add the horizontal dimension that shows the width of the left portion of the block. The shape of this feature shows clearly in the front view, so add the dimension to the front view between the views. You will use the Select object option, which allows you to pick an object from the screen instead of specifying the two extension line locations. The AutoCAD software will automatically locate the extension lines at the extreme ends of the object you select.

Pick: **Linear Dimension icon**

Specify first extension line origin or <Select object>: ↵

Select object to dimension: **pick the top left-hand line in the front view**

Specify dimension line location or [Mtext/Text/Angle/Horizontal/Vertical/Rotated]: **pick 0.5 unit above the object outline**

Your drawing should be similar to Figure 7.28.

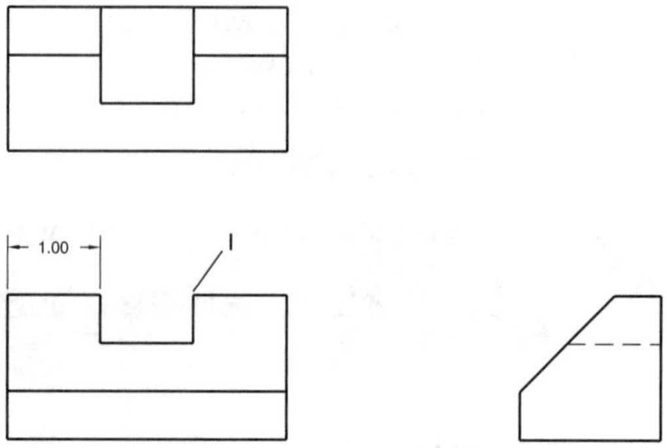

Figure 7.28

Using Continue Dimension

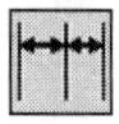

Now use the AutoCAD Continue Dimension command to add a chained dimension for the size of the slot. You will use the Select option again to choose which dimension is to be continued. (The Baseline Dimension command has a similar option.) When using this feature, pick near the extension line that you want to have continued. Refer to Figure 7.28.

Tip

When using the Continue Dimension command, you can press ↵ to select a different dimension to continue from.

Pick: **Continue Dimension icon**

Select continued dimension: **pick the right extension line of the dimension you just added**

Specify a second extension line origin or [Undo/Select]<Select>: **pick point I using AutoSnap Intersection**

Specify a second extension line origin or [Undo/Select] <Select>: ↵

Select continued dimension: ↵

The chained dimension should appear in your drawing, as shown in Figure 7.29.

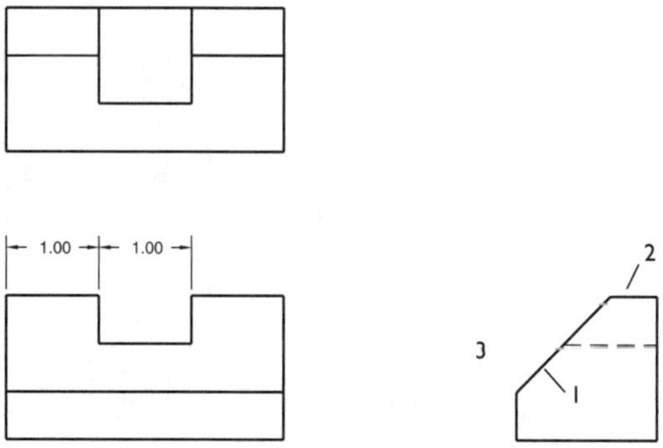

Figure 7.29

Angular Dimensions

Next, you will create the angular dimension for the drawing. Using the child settings makes it easy to make certain types of dimensions vary somewhat from the parent style. You will activate the Dimension Styles dialog box by using the Dimension toolbar.

Pick: **Dimension Style icon**

The Dimension Style Manager appears on your screen. You will use it to set the child styles for angular dimensions to be different from the parent style MECHANICAL. The style MECHANICAL should be listed as the current style at the top of the dialog box.

Setting a Child Style

To create a child style that is different from the parent,

Pick: **New**

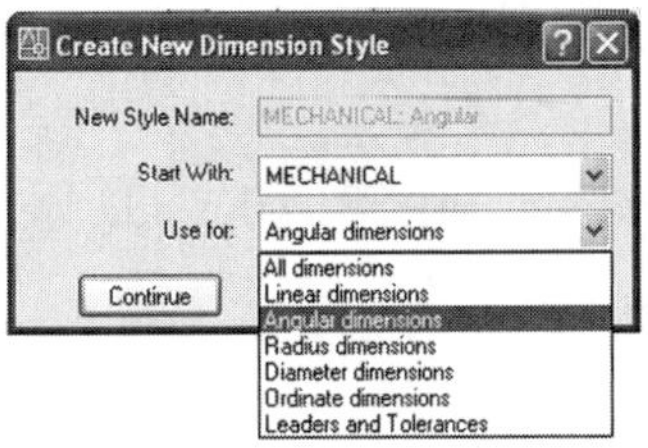

Figure 7.30

The Create New Dimension Style dialog box appears on your screen. Notice that this dimension style already has child styles for diameter and radius dimensions. You will add a child style to MECHANICAL that is only used for Angular dimensions. In the Use for area of the dialog box,

Pick: **Angular dimensions** as shown in Figure 7.30.
Pick: **Continue**

You will want most of the settings to remain the same as the parent style and change only the items that should differ for angular dimensions. You can think of parent styles and child styles as similar to inherited genetic characteristics. Children inherit appearance from their parents, but each child's appearance may be different from that of the parents. That is why you set the general appearance first using the Parent selection. Then you set the specific differences for each child's appearance after the parent style has been created. Once a child style has been set, changing the parent style will no longer change the child style.

Pick: **Primary Units tab**
Pick: **0** (as the Precision in the Angular Dimension area)
Pick: **OK**
Pick: **Close**

Adding the Angular Dimension

The Angular Dimension command lets you add an angular dimension by selecting two angled lines and then picking the location for the angle dimension. Depending on where you select, you will define the major angle or the minor angle between the lines. You also have the option during the command of pressing ↵ instead of selecting the first line. If you do so, you will be prompted for three points to define the angle. You do not have to use the %%D special character to make the degree sign; it is inserted automatically unless you override the default text.

Add the angular dimension for the angled surface in the side view, referring back to Figure 7.29.

Pick: **Angular Dimension icon**

Select arc, circle, line or <specify vertex>: **pick line 1**
Select second line: **pick line 2**
Specify dimension arc line location or [Mtext/Text/Angle]: **pick near point 3**

The angular dimension is added to the side view, as in Figure 7.31.

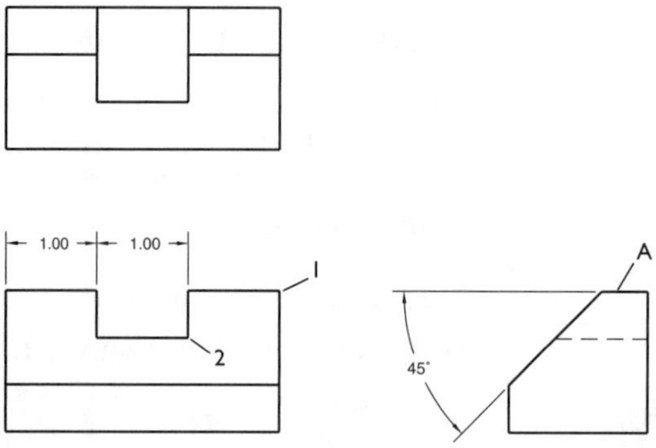

Figure 7.31

Next, add the dimension for the depth of the top surface in the side view.

Pick: **Linear Dimension icon**
Specify first extension line origin or <select object>: ↵
Select object to dimension: **pick the short horizontal line labeled A in Figure 7.31**
Specify dimension line location or [Mtext/Text/Angle/Horizontal/Vertical/Rotated]: **pick 0.5 unit above the top line of the side view**

Now add the dimension for the height of the slot in the front view. Refer to Figure 7.31.

Pick: **Linear Dimension icon**
Specify first extension line origin or <select object>: **pick the intersection labeled 1**
Specify second extension line origin: **pick the right-hand bottom corner of the slot, labeled 2**
Specify dimension line location or [Mtext/Text/Angle/Horizontal/Vertical/Rotated]: **pick 0.5 unit away from the right side of the front view**

The dimension for the slot should appear in your drawing, as shown in Figure 7.32.

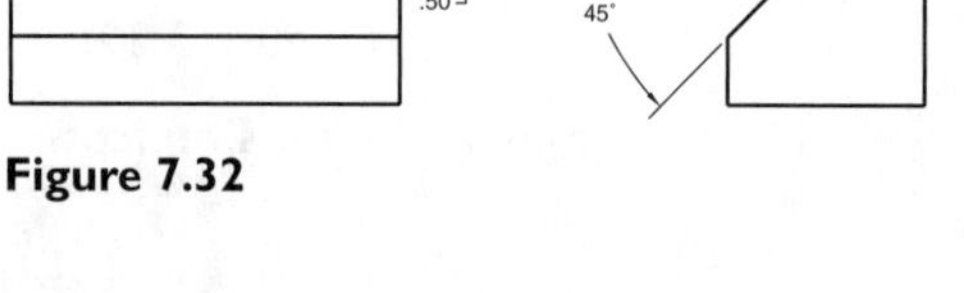

Figure 7.32

Tip

Note that you do not need dimensions for the short vertical line labeled A in the side view. Its length is already defined by the overall dimension for the height of the part, the 0.50 distance across the top surface, and the 45° angle. To include this dimension would be overdimensioning. You will learn more about why you must avoid overdimensioning later in this tutorial. If you want to give this dimension, include the value in brackets, or followed by the word REF, to indicate that it is a reference dimension only.

Tip

You can right-click on a dimension and use the pop-up menu to pick Flip arrows and quickly change whether the arrows are inside or outside the extension lines.

On your own, **add the overall dimensions** to the outsides of the views so that your drawing looks like Figure 7.33.

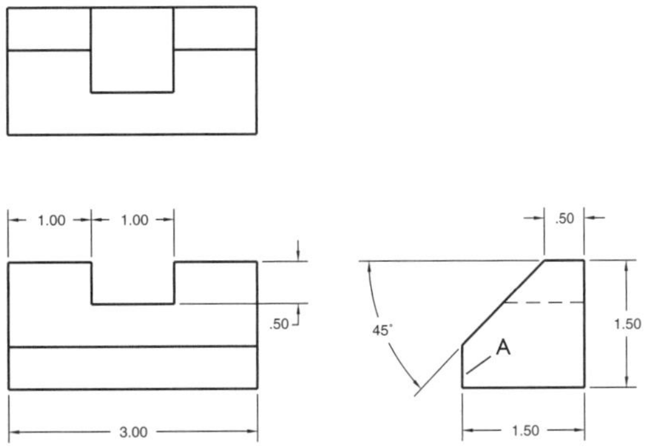

Figure 7.33

Centering the Views

Now you will use the Pan command to center the dimensioned drawing views inside the border. To do this you will use the Pan command in model space. Check that you are in model space.

Type: **MS** ↵ (if necessary)
Pick: **Pan Realtime icon**
Move view upward to center the dimensioned views inside the border.

Dimensions that are located in paper space sometimes do not pan with the drawing objects even with fully associated dimensions. That is why it is often better to locate the dimensions in model space. When you have located the view where you want it,

Press ESC or ENTER to exit, or right-click to display shortcut menu: Esc

Adding the Tolerance Note

Next you will add a note to paper space specifying a general tolerance for the drawing.

Pick: **MODEL/PAPER button** so that it displays PAPER
Pick: **TEXT as the current layer**
Pick: **Draw, Text, Single Line Text**
Use the Dtext command on your own to add 0.125" text stating ALL TOLERANCES ARE ± .01 UNLESS OTHERWISE NOTED. Use the %%P special text character to create the ± symbol.
Add a second note below the first stating MATERIAL: SAE 1020.
Add a third note that says ALL MEASUREMENTS ARE IN INCHES.
Double-click the drawing title to use the DDEDIT command or use the Properties palette to edit the text so that it says DIMENSIONED ADAPTER.

If you want, plot your drawing while in paper space with the drawing limits at the scale of 1=1.

Save your drawing *adapt-dm.dwg* before you continue.

Your finished drawing should be similar to Figure 7.34.

Tip

You can trim and extend linear and ordinate dimensions with the Trim and Extend commands. When trimmed or extended, the dimension acts as though there were a line between the endpoints of the extension line origins. Trimming and extending takes effect on the dimension at that location.

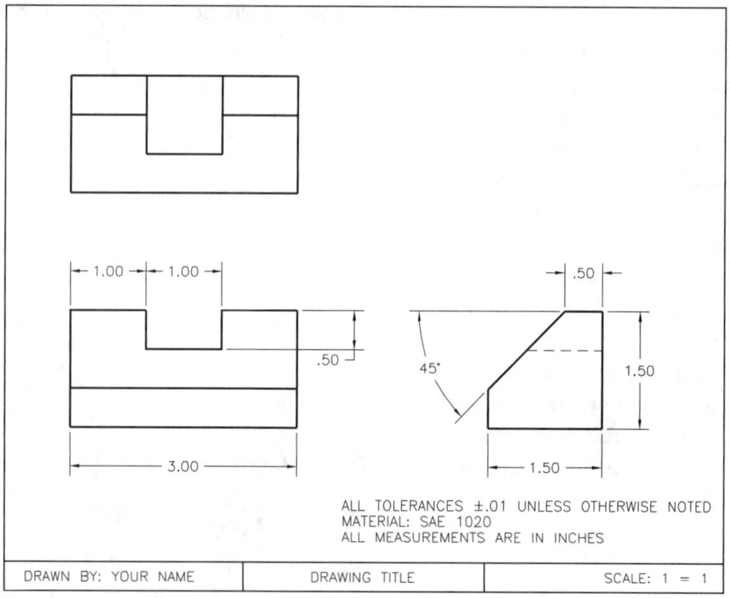

Figure 7.34

Updating Associative Dimensions

Dimensions created with associative dimensioning (Dimassoc) turned on are an AutoCAD block object. Blocks are a group of objects that behave as a single object. If you try to erase a dimension that you created with associative dimensioning on, the entire dimension is erased, including the extension lines and arrowheads. Because these dimensions have the special properties of a block, you can also cause them to be updated automatically.

As the geometric objects that you are going to change are in model space, you must return to model space in order to change them.

Pick: **MODEL/PAPER button** so that it displays MODEL

Using Stretch

The Stretch command is used to stretch and relocate objects. It is similar to stretching with hot grips, which you did in Tutorial 4. You must use implied Crossing, Crossing, or Crossing Polygon methods to select the objects for use with the Stretch command. As you select, objects entirely enclosed in the crossing window specified will be moved to the new location rather than stretched. Keep this in mind and draw the crossing box only around the portion of the object you want to stretch, leaving the other portion unselected to act as an anchor.

You will use the Stretch command to make the adapter wider. When you do so, the appropriate dimensions automatically update to the new size. Note that the overall width of the front view is currently 3.00. Refer to Figure 7.35.

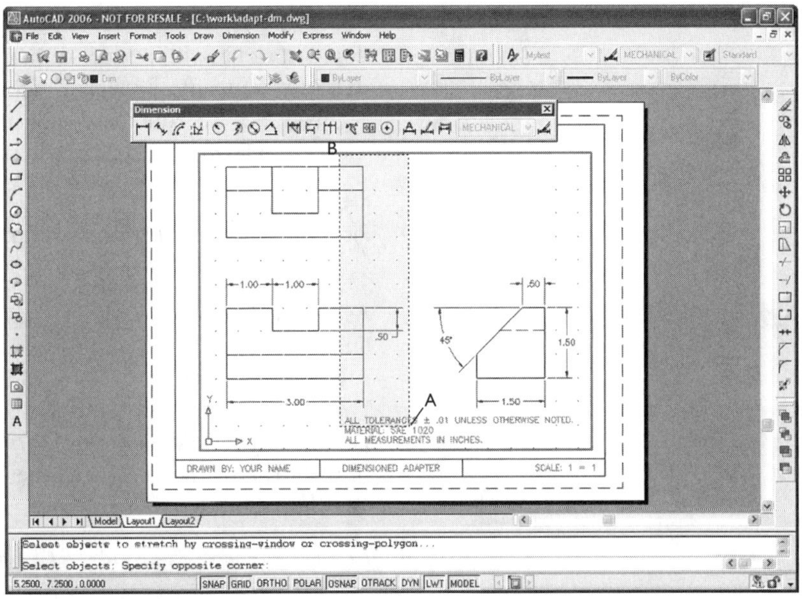

Figure 7.35

Tip

When a Crossing selection box is being drawn, it appears green or with a dashed outline depending on your settings. When a Window selection box is being drawn, it appears blue or has a solid outline. Use this visual cue. Crossing boxes are drawn from right to left.

Tip

If you have trouble stretching, double-check to be sure that you are not still in paper space. Also, the Stretch command works only when you use the Crossing option. If you type the command, you must be sure to select Crossing or type C and press ⏎ afterward, or use implied Crossing (by drawing the window box from right to left), as you did in the previous step.

Pick: **Stretch icon** (from the Modify toolbar)
Select objects to stretch by crossing-window or crossing-polygon
Select objects: **use Crossing and select point A**
Specify opposite corner: **select point B**
Select objects: ⏎
Specify base point or [Displacement] <Displacement>: **target the bottom right-hand corner of the front view**
Specify second point or <use first point as displacement>: **move the cursor over .5 units to the right and press pick button**

Note that the overall dimension now reads 3.50 and that it has updated automatically. The result is shown in Figure 7.36.

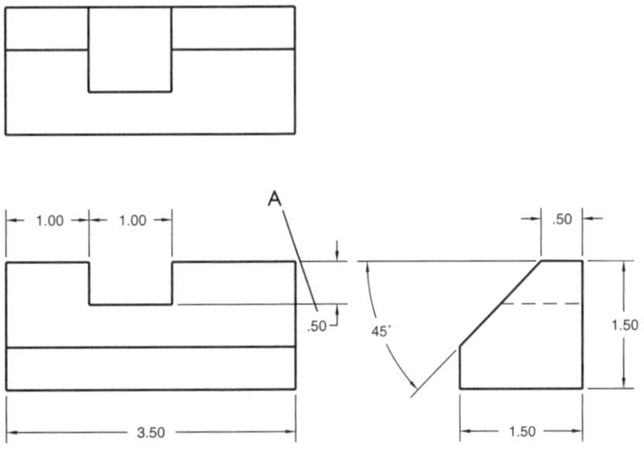

Figure 7.36

Modifying Dimensions

You can modify individual dimensions and override their dimension styles by using the Properties icon on the Standard toolbar. Refer to Figure 7.36. To edit the dimension properties, you must be in the same space (model/paper space) where the dimension resides.

Pick: **Properties icon**
Pick: **the vertical dimension labeled A so that its grips appear**

The Properties palette appears on your screen as shown in Figure 7.37. As with other objects, you can modify the layer, color, linetype, lineweight, and linetype scale of a dimension. Near the bottom of the palette are selections for Misc, Lines & Arrows, Text, Fit, Primary Units, Alternate Units, and Tolerances (just like the tabs in the Modify Dimension Style dialog box). You can pick on the arrows (v) to the right of the name to expand the list of dimension style features that you can change under that topic.

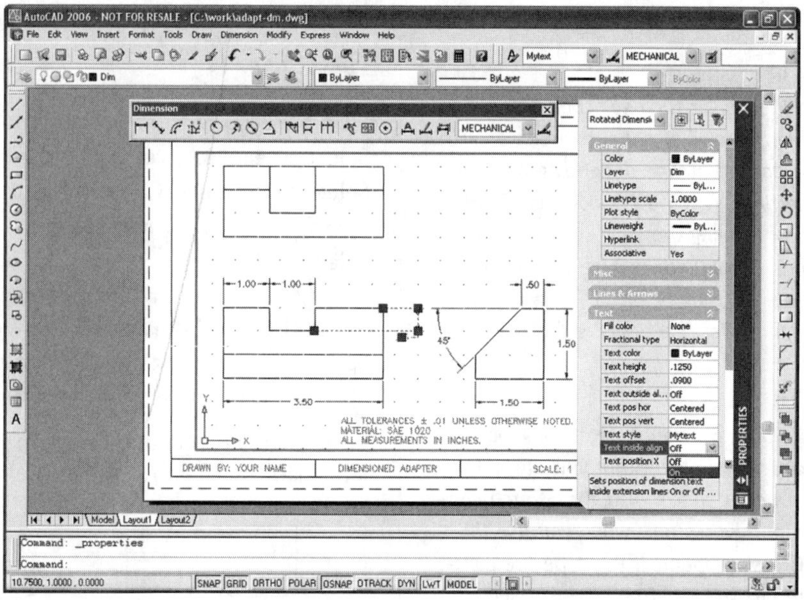

Figure 7.37

You will change the text orientation so that it is parallel to the dimension line.

Pick: **to expand Text selections** (using the down arrow)

The Text area should appear expanded as shown in Figure 7.38.

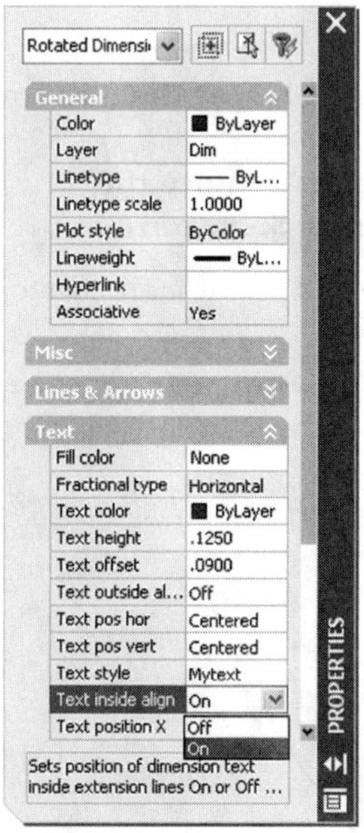

Figure 7.38

Pick: **the text box to the right of Text inside align**
Pick: **On** to align the dimension text inside the extension lines with the dimension line
Pick: **Windows Close button** to close the Properties palette
Press: [Esc] to remove hot grips from vertical dimension

The position of the 0.50 vertical dimension changes so that it is now parallel to the dimension line, as shown in Figure 7.39. The dimension style for MECHANICAL has not changed; only that single dimension was overridden to produce a new appearance.

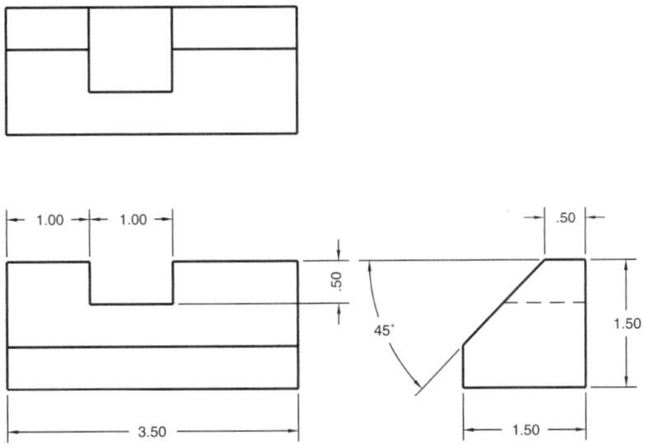

Figure 7.39

Updating a Dimension Style

When you change a dimension style, all the dimensions that you created with that style automatically take on the new appearance. (This method works only for dimensions created with associative dimensioning on.) You will change the arrow style to a new appearance for all the dimensions created with style MECHANICAL. Use the Dimension Styles dialog box to change the arrow style.

Pick: **Dimension Style icon**

The Dimension Style Manager appears on your screen.

Make sure that MECHANICAL is the style name highlighted.
Pick: **Modify**
Pick: **Symbols and Arrows tab**
Pick: **Right Angle** (for the First Arrowhead; notice that the image tile updates to show a right angle arrowhead)
Pick: **OK**
Pick: **Close** (to exit the Dimension Style Manager)

The dimensions in the drawing update automatically to reflect this change. The arrows are now right-angled arrows instead of filled arrows. Your drawing should be similar to Figure 7.40.

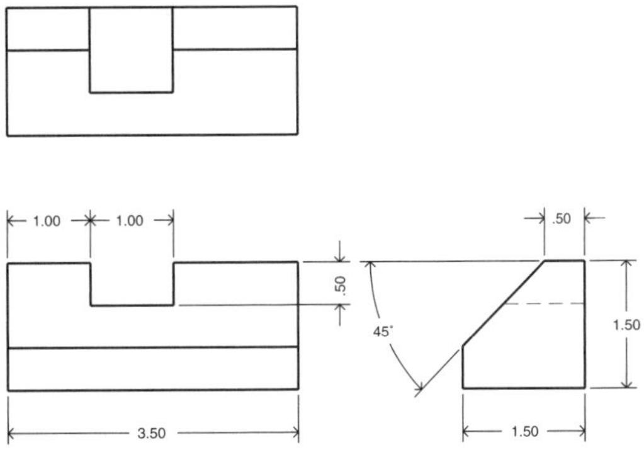

Figure 7.40

Tip

If you are not sure what dimension style and overrides you may have used when creating a particular dimension, use the List command and pick on the dimension. You will see a list of the dimension style and any overrides that were used for the dimension.

Now use the Edit Text (Ddedit) command or the Properties palette and edit the text in the title box to correct the date, name, and scale, as necessary.

Save the drawing when you have finished.

Close any open toolbars except the Draw and Modify toolbars, which should be docked to the edge of the graphics window, and exit the AutoCAD 2006 program.

You have completed Tutorial 7.

Key Terms

associative dimensioning
baseline dimensioning
chained (continued) dimensioning
dimension line
dimension style
dimension value
dimension variables (dim vars)
dimensions
extension line
extension line offset
image tile
inspection
leader line
manufacture
overall dimensions
tolerance

Key Commands

Angular Dimension
Baseline Dimension
Continue Dimension
Diameter Dimension
Dimassoc
Dimension Status
Dimension Style
Linear Dimension
Radius Dimension
Stretch
Xplode

Exercises

Draw and dimension the following shapes. The letter M after an exercise number means that the units are metric. Add a note to the drawing saying, "METRIC: All dimensions are in millimeters for metric drawings." Specify a general tolerance for the drawing.

7.1M Stop Plate

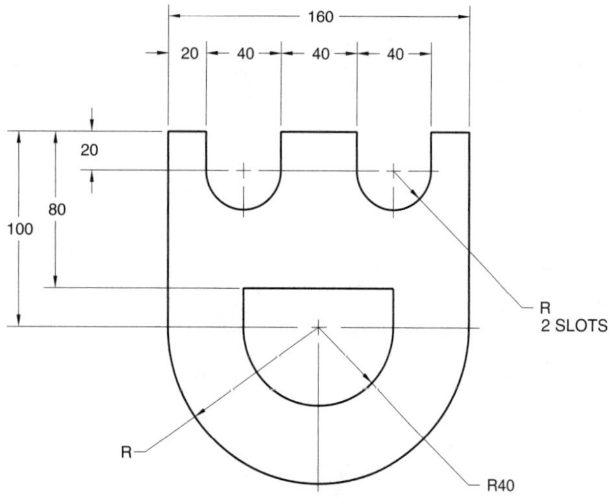

7.2M Hub

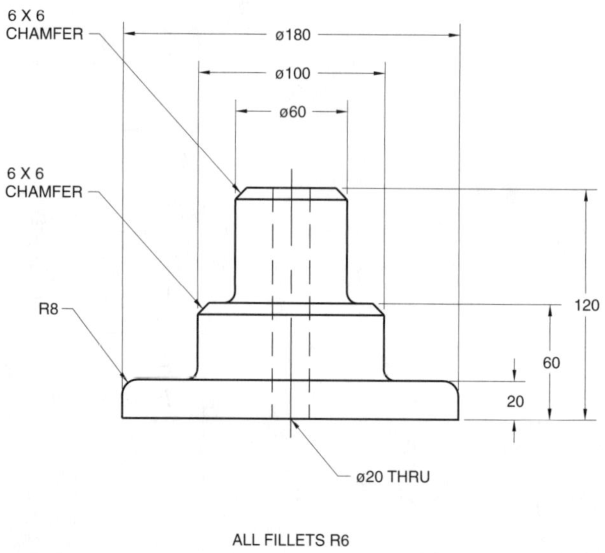

7.3 Guide Block

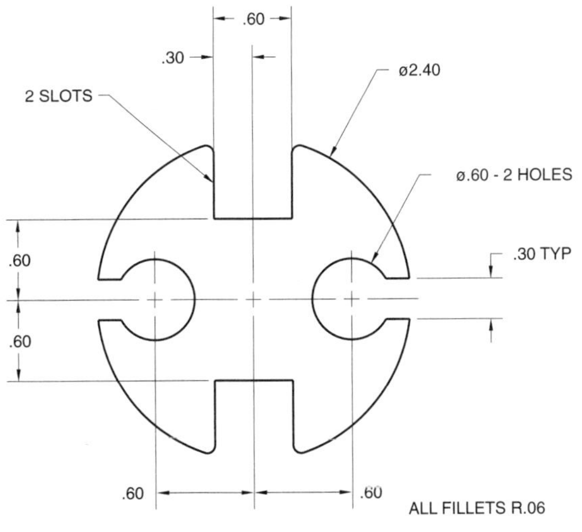

7.4 Interchange

Draw and dimension this intersection, then mirror the circular interchange for all lanes.

***Hint:** To make radial dimensions with placements as shown, you may need to use the Dimension Style, Fit tab and then select Place text manually in the Fine Tuning area of the dialog box.*

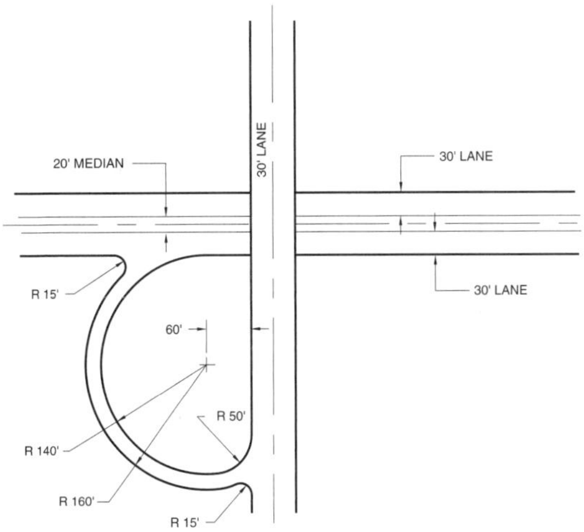

7.5 Angle Bracket

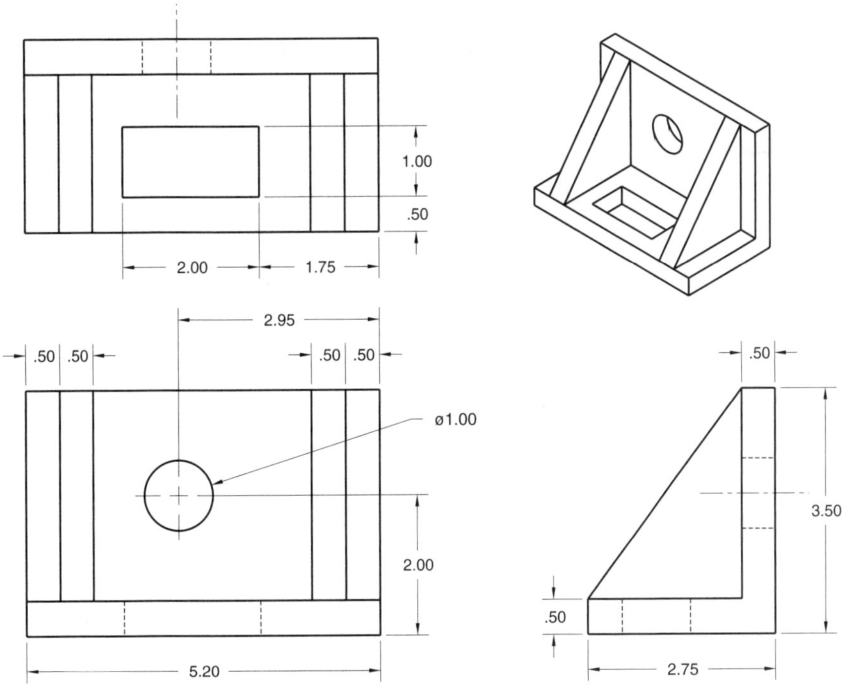

7.6 Bearing Box

Draw and dimension the following shape. Specify a general tolerance for the drawing.

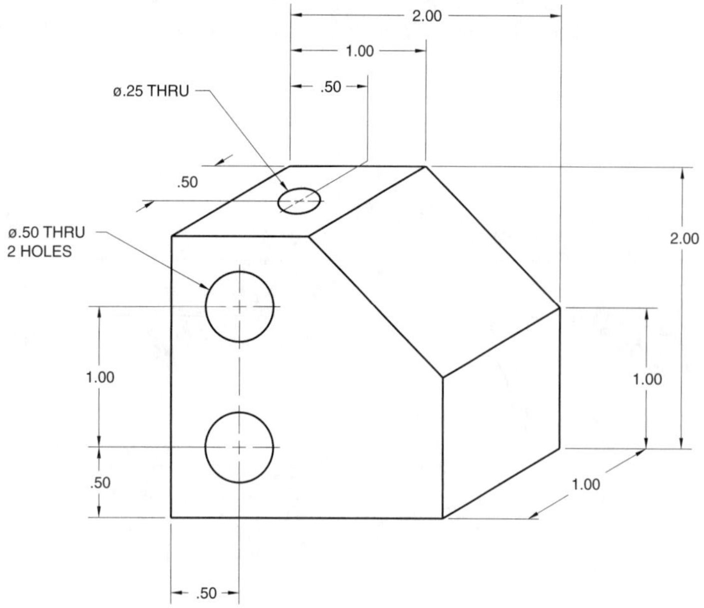

7.7 Plot Plan

Draw and dimension using the civil engineering dimensioning style shown, and find the missing dimensions.

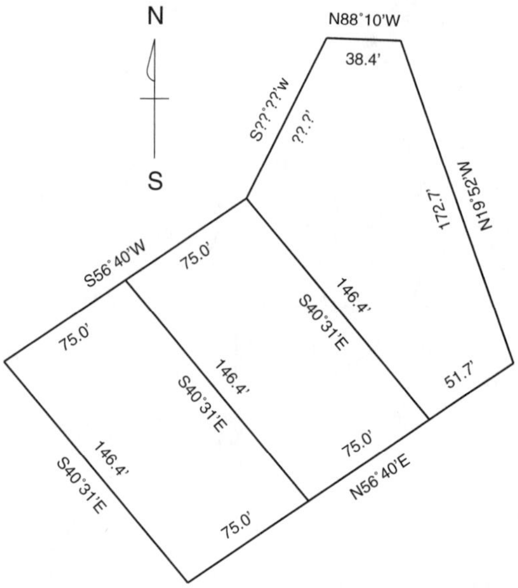

7.8 Hub

Draw and dimension the hub shown. Use 1 grid unit = .0125" for a decimal inch drawing or 25 mm for a metric drawing.

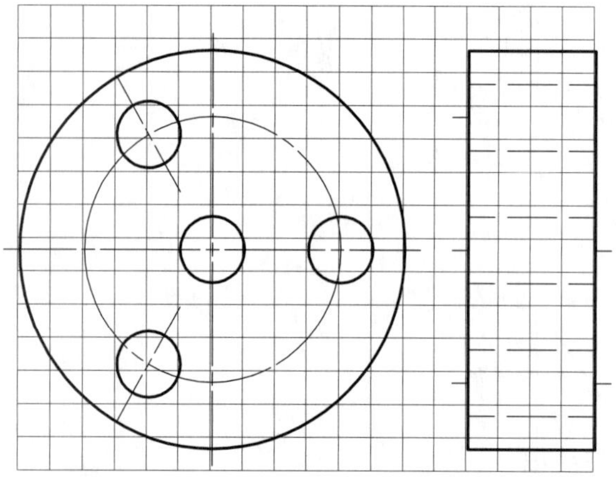

7.9 Support

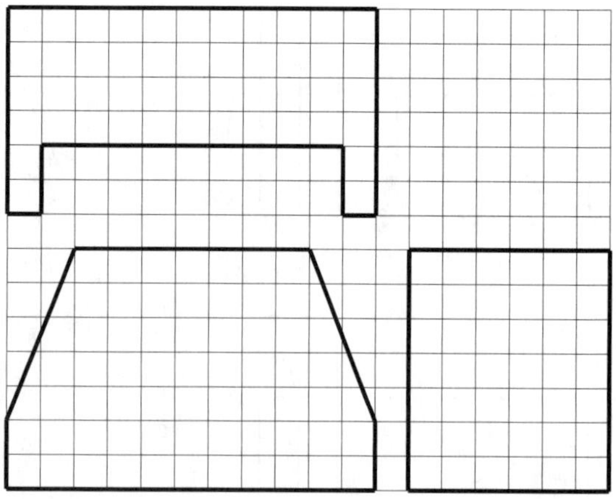

7.10 Index Feed

Draw dimensioned orthographic views of the part shown. Show only the necessary views.

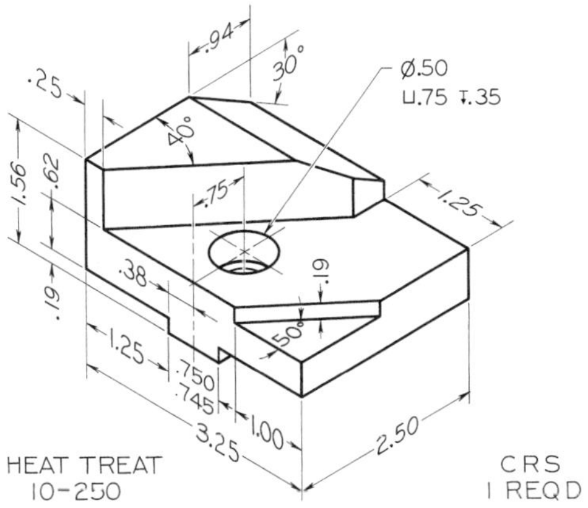

7.11M Socket Bearing

Draw dimensioned orthographic views of the part shown. Show only the necessary views.

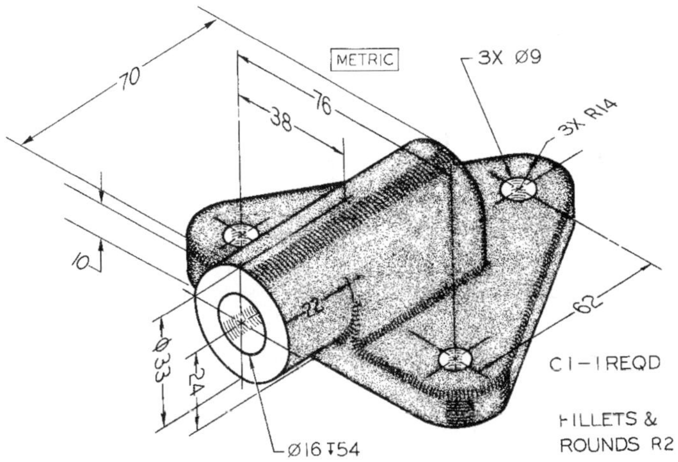

7.12 Floor Plan

Use architectural units to draw and dimension the floor plan shown, making good use of layers.

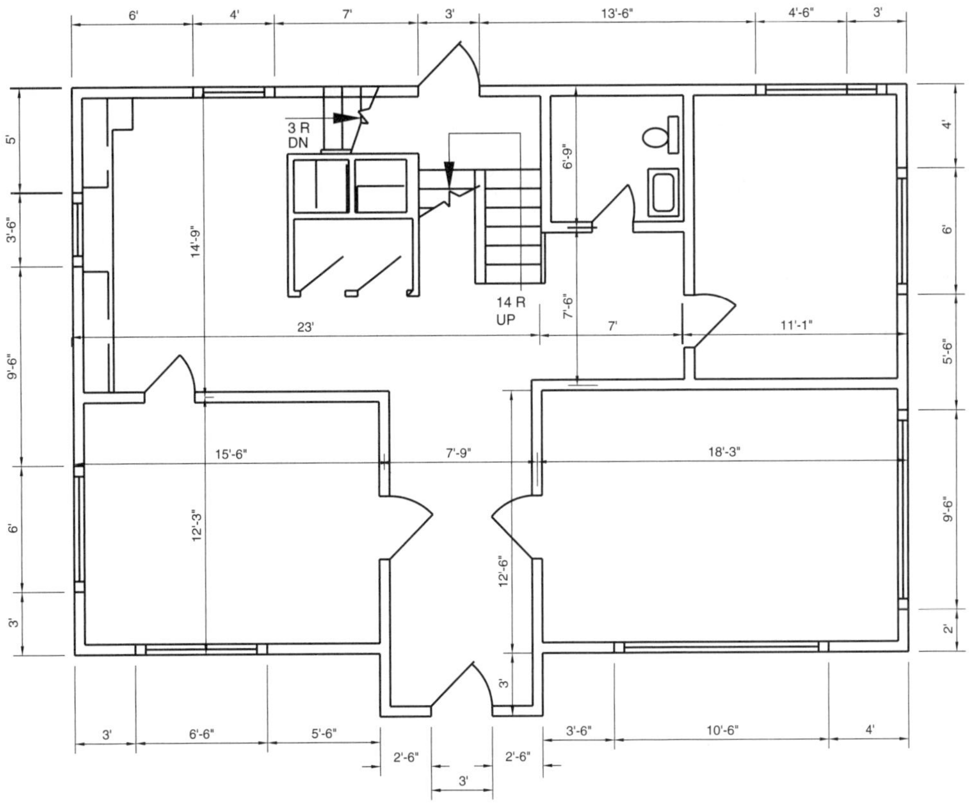

7.13 Control Block

Draw and dimension the views shown. Specify a general tolerance of ±.02 for lengths and ±1° for angles.

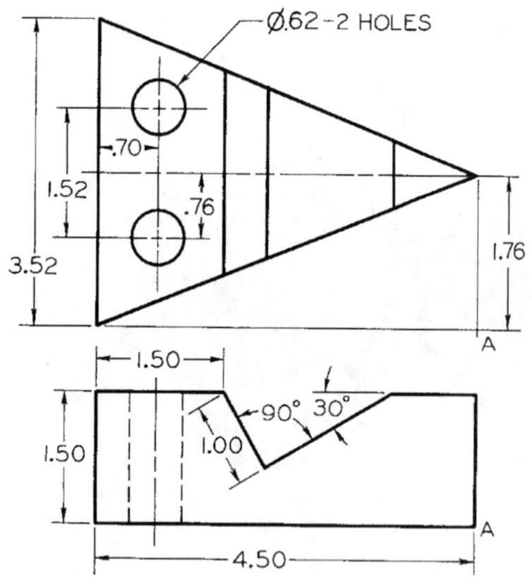

7.14 Trip Arm

Draw and dimension the views shown. Specify a general tolerance of ±.02 for lengths and ±1° for angles.

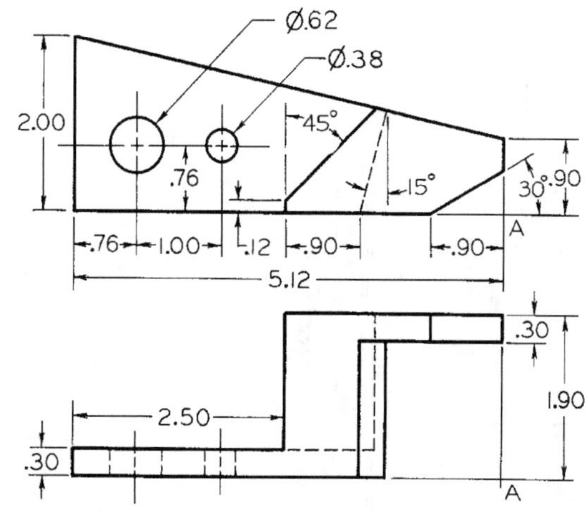

Tutorial 8 Advanced Dimensioning

Objectives

When you have completed this tutorial, you will be able to

1. Use tolerances in a drawing.
2. Set up the dimension variables to use limit tolerances and variance (plus/minus) tolerances.
3. Add geometric tolerances to your drawing.
4. Use dimension overrides.

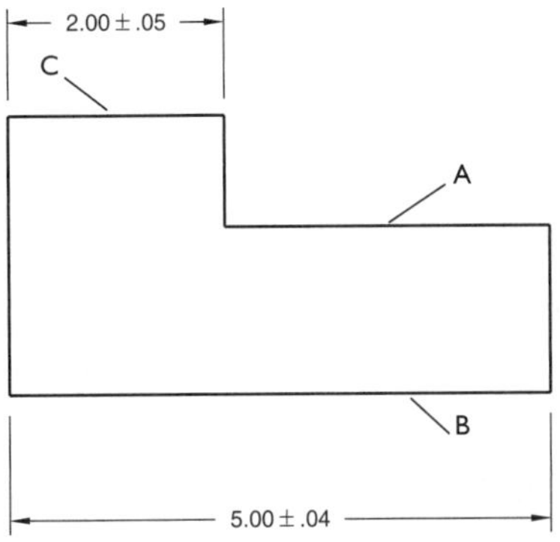

Figure 8.1

Tolerance

No part can be manufactured to exact dimensions. There is always some amount of variation between the size of the actual object when it is measured and an exact dimension specified in the drawing. To take this variation into consideration, tolerances are specified along with dimensions. A *tolerance* is the total amount of variation that an acceptable part is allowed to have.

The dimensions given in the drawing are used to make and inspect the part. Included with the dimension is the allowable amount of variation (tolerance) that the part can have and still be acceptable. In order to determine whether a part is acceptable, the measurements of the actual part are compared to the toleranced dimensions specified in the drawing. If the part falls within the tolerance range specified, it is an acceptable part.

To better understand the role that tolerances play in dimensioning, consider Figure 8.1. Surface A on the actual object is longest when the 5.00 overall dimension shown for surface B is at its largest acceptable value and when the 2.00 dimension shown for surface C is at its shortest acceptable value. Thus

$A_{max} = 5.04 - 1.95 = 3.09$

Surface A is shortest when surface B is at its smallest acceptable value and surface C is at its largest acceptable value. Thus

$A_{min} = 4.96 - 2.05 = 2.91$

In other words, the given dimensions with the added tolerances permit surface A to vary between 3.09 and 2.91 units.

Tolerance Formats

In Tutorial 7, you learned how to add a general tolerance note to your drawing to specify this allowable variation. The AutoCAD® program provides three ways to add a tolerance to the dimension for a feature: limit tolerances, variance tolerances, and geometric tolerances.

Limit tolerances specify the upper and lower allowable measurements for the part. A part measuring between the two limits is acceptable.

Variance tolerances or *plus/minus tolerances* specify the *nominal dimension* and the allowable range that is added to it. From this information you can determine the upper and lower limits. Add the plus tolerance to the nominal size to get the upper limit; subtract the minus tolerance from the nominal size to get the lower limit. (Or you can think of it as always adding the tolerance, but when the sign of the tolerance is negative, it has the effect of subtracting the value.) The plus and minus values do not always have to be the same. There are two types of variance tolerances: bilateral and unilateral. ***Bilateral tolerances*** specify a nominal size and both a plus and minus tolerance. ***Unilateral tolerances*** are a special case where either the plus or the minus value specified for the tolerance is zero. You can create both bilateral and unilateral tolerances.

Geometric tolerances use special symbols inside feature control frames that describe ***tolerance zones*** that relate to the type of feature being controlled. The Tolerance command allows you to create feature control frames quickly and select geometric tolerance symbols for them. You will learn to create these frames later in this tutorial.

Figure 8.2 shows the drawing from Tutorial 7 with tolerances added to the dimensions. Tolerances A, B, F, and G are examples of bilateral tolerances. Tolerances C, D, and E are limit tolerances.

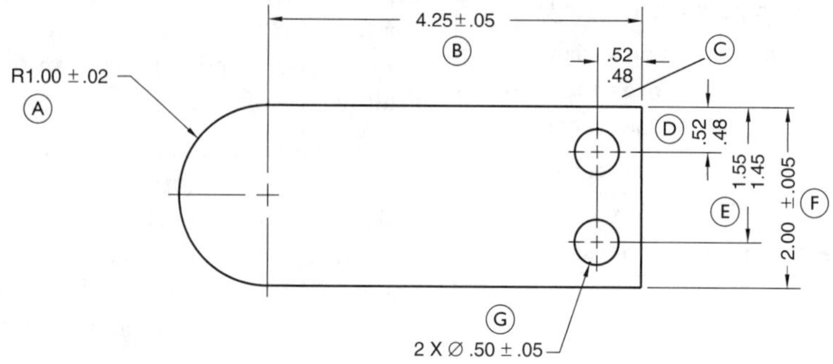

Figure 8.2

Starting

Start the AutoCAD program.

On your own, use ***obj-dim.dwt*** as the template for a new drawing.

Name your new drawing ***tolernc.dwg***.

Your screen should be similar to Figure 8.3. Be sure that layer DIM is set as the current layer.

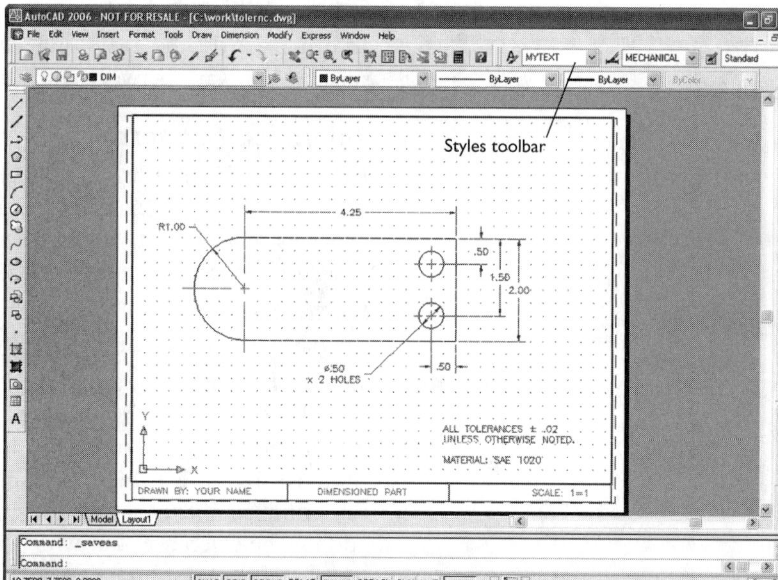

Figure 8.3

You will first set up the dimension variables to use tolerances.

Automatic Bilateral Tolerances

You can have the program automatically add bilateral tolerances by setting the dimensioning variables with the Dimension Styles dialog box. You will pick the Dimension Style Manager from the Styles toolbar. It should be docked near the top of your screen as shown in Figure 8.3.

Pick: **Dimension Style Manager icon**

The Dimension Style Manager appears on your screen, as shown in Figure 8.4. You will use it to set up the appearance of the tolerances to be added to the dimensions. The dimension style MECHANICAL is current. It is like the style you created in Tutorial 7. You will make changes to it so that the dimensions in the drawing created with that style will show a variance, or deviation, tolerance.

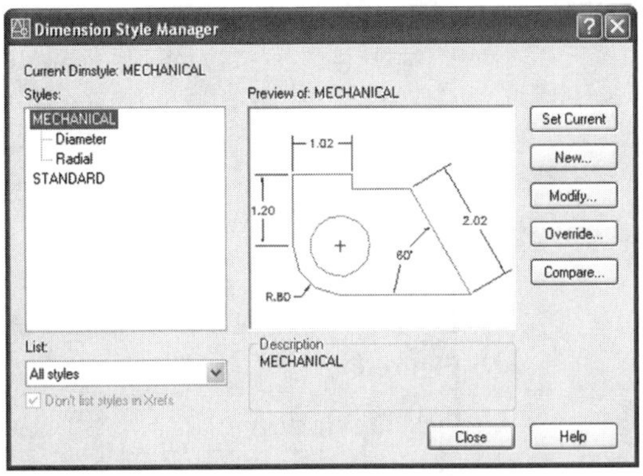

Figure 8.4

Recall from Tutorial 7 that you use the New button to create a new dimension style. You could create a new style, but this time you will change style MECHANICAL to include deviation tolerances. When you are done making the following changes to the dimension style, the dimensions in the drawing will automatically reflect the changes.

Pick: **Modify**

The Modify Dimension Style dialog box appears on your screen.

Pick: **Tolerances tab**

The Tolerances tab appears uppermost.

Pick: **in the box to the right of Method in the Tolerance Format area of the dialog box to pull down the list of available tolerance methods shown in Figure 8.5**

The choices of tolerance methods are None, Symmetrical, Deviation, Limits, and Basic.

- *None* uses just the dimension and does not add a tolerance, as your current dimensions reflect.
- *Symmetrical tolerances* are lateral tolerances with the same upper and lower values; these tolerances generally specify the dimension plus or minus a single value.

- *Deviation tolerances* are lateral tolerances that have a different upper and lower deviation.
- *Limit tolerances* show the maximum value for the dimension and the minimum value for the dimension.
- *Basic dimension* is a term used in geometric dimensioning and tolerancing to specify a theoretically exact dimension without a tolerance. Basic dimensions appear in your drawing with a box drawn around them.

If you choose any of the tolerance methods, you can preview what your dimensions will look like in the image tile.

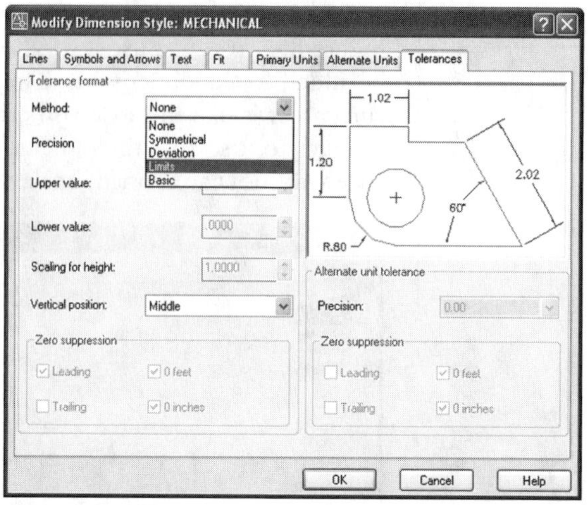

Figure 8.5

Pick: **Deviation**

Note the image tile at the right of the dialog box; it shows a dimension with a deviation style tolerance added.

Pick: **Limits** (as the tolerance Method)

Notice the change to the image tile. Continue picking the tolerance methods on your own until you cycle through all the options and return to Deviation tolerance, as shown in Figure 8.6.

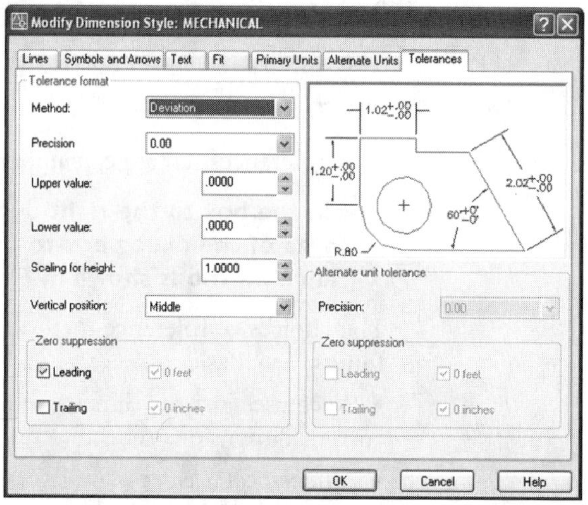

Figure 8.6

Setting the Tolerance Precision

The tolerance values can have a different precision from the dimension values. You control the precision by using the Precision pull-down near the top left of the dialog box.

Pick: **on the Precision list box**

A list of precision values pulls down as shown in Figure 8.7.

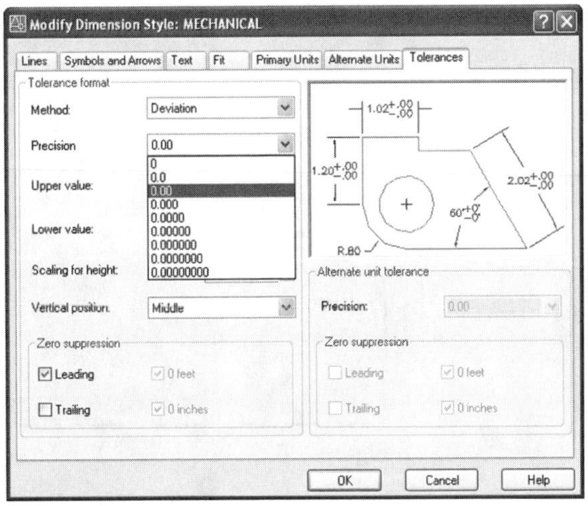

Figure 8.7

Pick: **0.00 from the list**

Specifying Tolerance Values

The text boxes for setting tolerance values were formerly grayed. Now that you have selected a tolerance method, they are available for input. You will use them to specify the upper and lower values that you want to use with the dimension to specify the allowable deviation. Both values will be positive. The upper value will be added to the dimension value; the lower value will be subtracted from the dimension value. The program will automatically add the plus or minus sign in front of the value when showing the tolerance.

Tip

You can press [Tab] to move to the next text entry box. Doing so will also highlight the text in that box.

Pick: **to highlight the text to the right of Upper Value**
Type: **.05**
Pick: **to highlight the text to the right of Lower Value**
Type: **.03**

Note that you can also control the vertical position of the tolerance. For now you will leave it set to Middle, the default.

Setting the Tolerance Text Height Scaling

The default setting of 1.0000 appears in the Scaling for height input box in the Tolerance Format area. This value is a scaling factor. A setting of 1.0000 makes the tolerance values the same height as the standard dimension text. For this tutorial you will set tolerance height to 0.8 (so that the height of the tolerance values will be 8/10 the height of the dimension values).

Pick: **to highlight the value in the Scaling for height input box**
Type: **.8**

The same text style used for the dimension text, MYTEXT, will also be used for the tolerance text. You can control the text style and the dimension text height, color, and gap using the Text tab of the dialog box. You will leave these features set as they are. The Tolerances tab should now appear as shown in Figure 8.8.

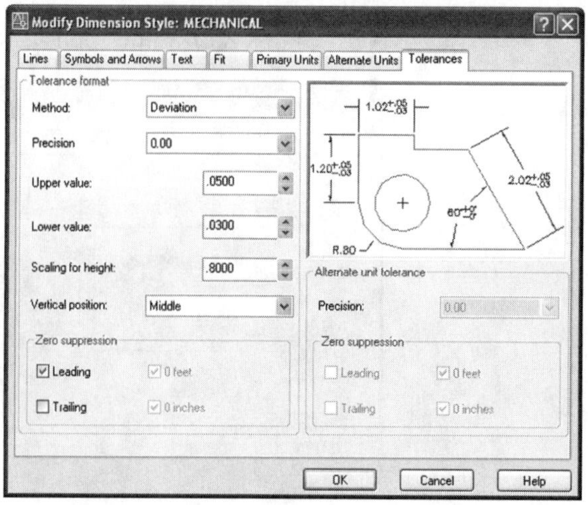

Figure 8.8

Pick: **OK** (to exit the Modify Dimension Style dialog box)
Pick: **Close** (to exit the Dimension Style Manager)

You return to your drawing. The dimensions created with style MECHANICAL automatically update to show the deviation tolerance. Your drawing should look like that in Figure 8.9.

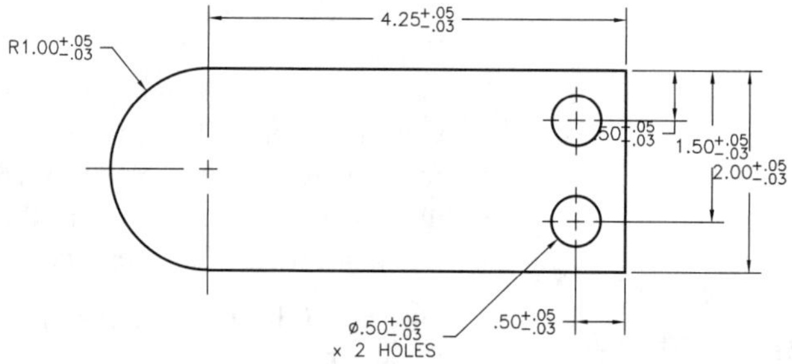

Figure 8.9

On your own, use hot grips editing to move the dimension values so that the text is not crossing drawing lines as shown in Figure 8.10.

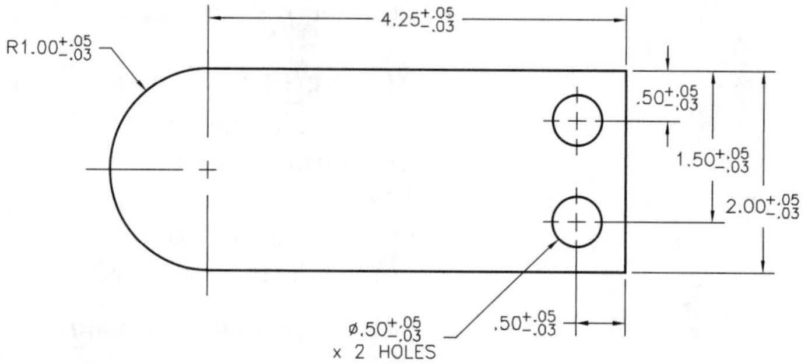

Figure 8.10

You can find information about the dimension using the List command.

Pick: **Tools, Inquiry, List**

Select objects: **pick the radial dimension at the left end of the object** ↵

Tip

Press F2 *to toggle the text window on if you do not see it.*

The List command displays the information shown in Figure 8.11 in a Text window.

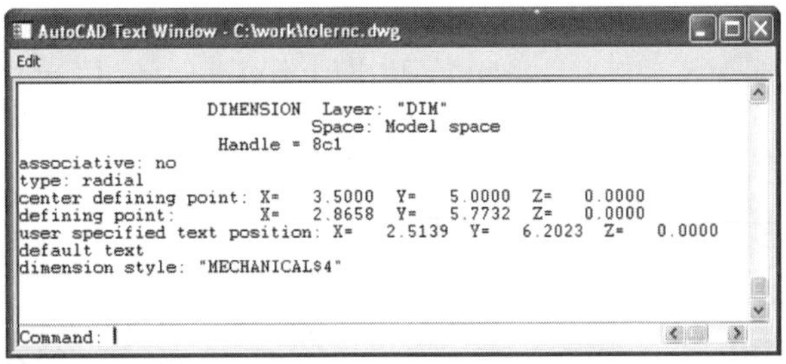

Figure 8.11

Note that the style name for this dimension is MECHANICAL$4. When you list a dimension, the $# code tells you that the dimension uses a child style different from the parent style. Here, it tells you that the dimension was created with a child style that has different settings than the parent style, MECHANICAL. If you need to review parent and child styles, refer to Tutorial 7. The codes for the child types are:

$0	Linear
$2	Angular
$3	Diameter
$4	Radial
$6	Ordinate
$7	Leader (also used for tolerance objects)

Using Dimension Overrides

Dimension overrides let you change the dimension variables controlling a dimension and leave its style as is. A good approach is to change the general appearance of the dimensions by changing the dimension style and to change individual dimensions that need to vary from the overall group of dimensions (to suppress an extension line, for instance) by using overrides.

You can change dimension variables by typing DIMOVERRIDE at the command prompt. Dimoverride has the alias Dimover. When you use Dimoverride at the command prompt, the program prompts you for the exact name of the dimension variable you want to control and its new value. Then you select the dimensions to which you will apply the override. The Clear option of the Dimoverride command lets you remove overrides from the dimensions you select. You can also use the Dimension Style command, and select the Override button from the Dimension Style Manager.

You can also use the Properties palette to do the same thing.

Double-click: **the radial dimension for the rounded end**

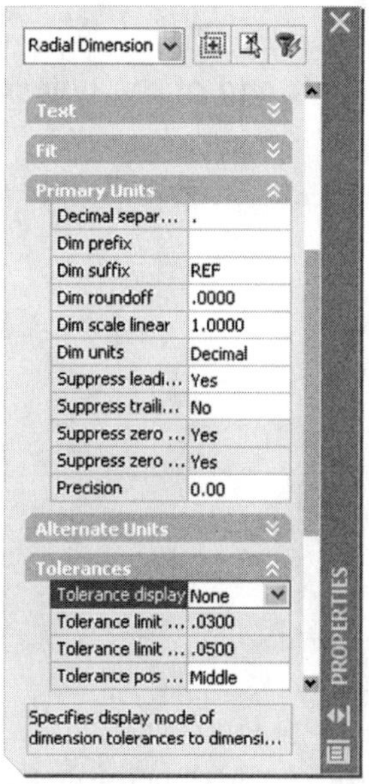

Figure 8.12

The Properties palette appears on your screen. You will use it to override the dimension style for the radial dimension. Because the 2.00 vertical dimension at the right side of the part controls the part's height, providing the radial dimension is an example of overdimensioning. When you want to call attention to the full rounded end, which is tangent to the horizontal surfaces at the top and bottom of the object, you can show the 1.00 radius value as a *reference dimension*. Or you can simply identify it with the letter R, indicating the radius but leaving its value to be determined by the other surfaces. You will turn off the tolerance and add REF to the end of the radial dimension value to indicate that it is provided as a reference dimension only.

You can also note reference dimensions by including the dimension value in parentheses ( ).

Pick: **to expand the Tolerances area**
Pick: **None** (as the selection in the Tolerance display area)
Pick: **to expand the Primary Units area**
Type: **REF** (in the Dim suffix text box)

When you have finished making these selections, your palette should look like Figure 8.12.

Pick: **to Close the Properties palette**
Press: Esc twice to unselect the radial dimension

You can also use the Properties palette to override the dimension text by picking to expand the Text area and using the Text override input box that appears to change the text. After you have overridden the text, your dimension values no longer update if you stretch or change the object. As usual with the Properties palette, you can change the layer, color, linetype, lineweight, and linetype scale. Your drawing should look like the one in Figure 8.13.

Tip

The Revcloud command creates cloud-shaped balloons used to call attention to drawing revisions. Use the Help command to read about its options.

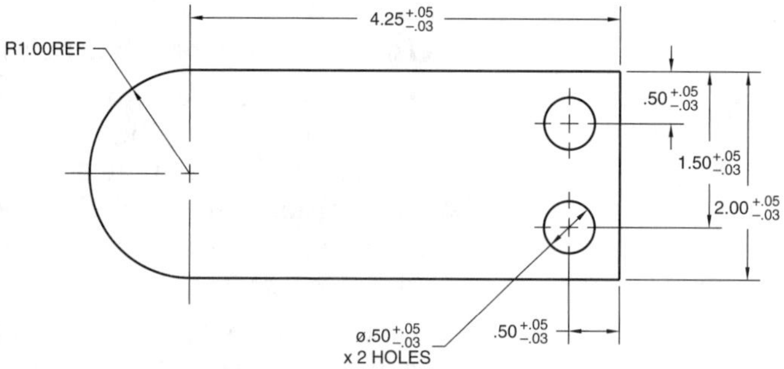

Figure 8.13

Next, use List again to list the radial dimension.

Pick: **Tools, Inquiry, List**
Select objects: **pick the radial dimension for the rounded end** ↵

A Text window appears, as shown in Figure 8.14, listing the information about the radial dimension. Note that overrides for the dimension variables Dimgap, Dimlim, Dimpost, and Dimtol are now listed. Dimpost displays the dimension suffix, which is set to REF. Dimlim is set to Off, so that no deviation tolerance is applied to the dimension.

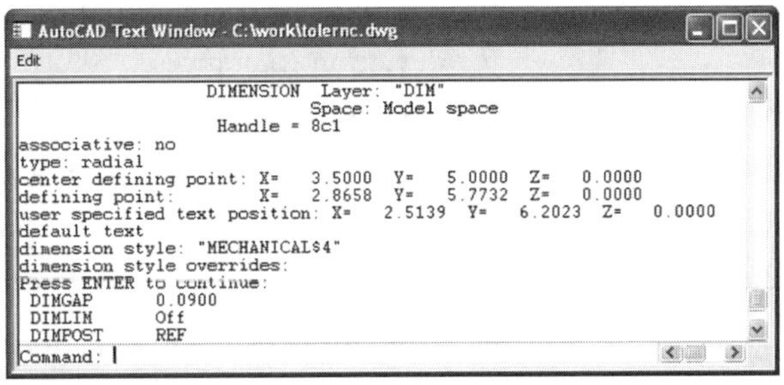

Figure 8.14

When dimensioning, keep your dimension styles organized by creating new dimension styles and controlling the child styles as needed. Use dimension overrides when certain dimensions need a different appearance than the general case for that type of dimension.

You can now close the Text window.

Using Limit Tolerances

Next you will create a new style for dimensions using limit tolerances, and then you will change the object's overall dimension to use that style.

Pick: **Dimension Style icon**

The Dimension Style Manager appears; you will create a new style.

Pick: **New**

The Create New Dimension Style dialog box appears. For the New Style Name,

Type: **LIMITTOL**

Be sure the Start With selection says **MECHANICAL**, and the Use for area says **All dimensions**.

Pick: **Continue button**

Pick: **Tolerances tab**

Pick: **Limits** as the tolerance method

The dialog box should now look like Figure 8.15.

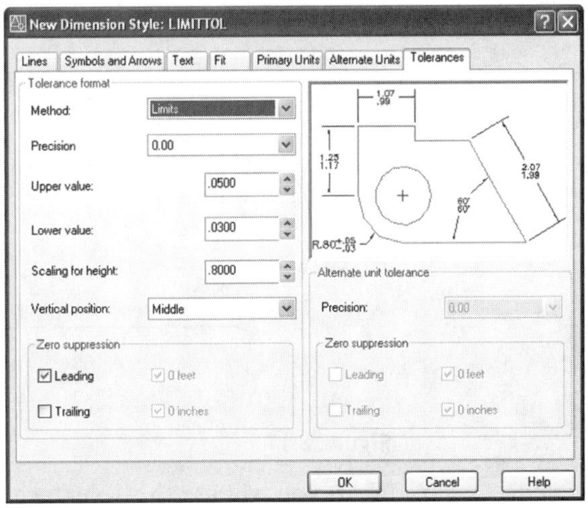

Figure 8.15

Tip

You can also use the Properties palette to change the selected dimension. Expand the MISC heading and select the desired style.

You can leave the upper and lower values and text height set as you did for deviation tolerances.

Pick: **OK** (to exit the dialog box)
Pick: **Close** (to exit the Dimension Style Manager)

Next, you will change the overall dimension of the object to use the new style, LIMITTOL. To do so, you will use the Styles toolbar.

Pick: **on the 4.25 overall dimension so that its grips appear**

To change the dimension to style LIMITTOL,

Pick: **to expand the dimension styles** (as shown in Figure 8.16)
Pick: **LIMITTOL** from the list of styles
Press: [Esc] to release the grips

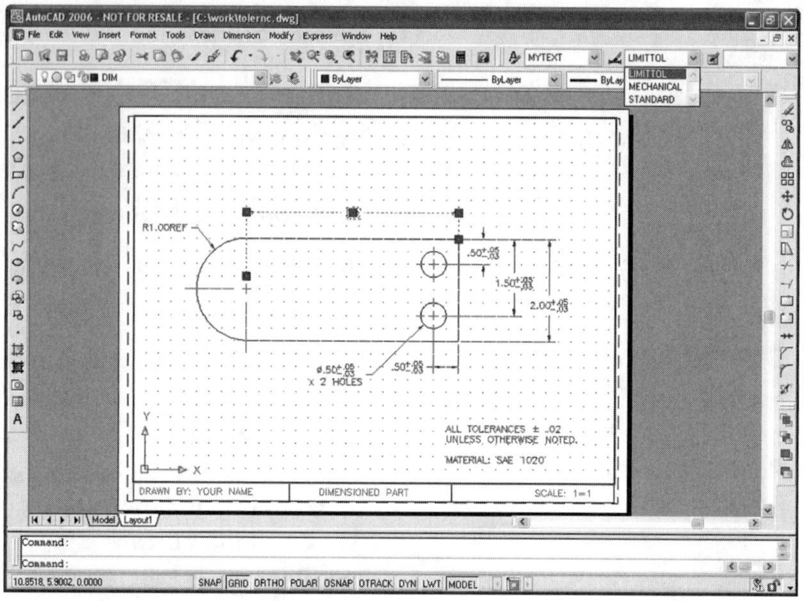

Figure 8.16

The limit tolerance appears, as shown in Figure 8.17.

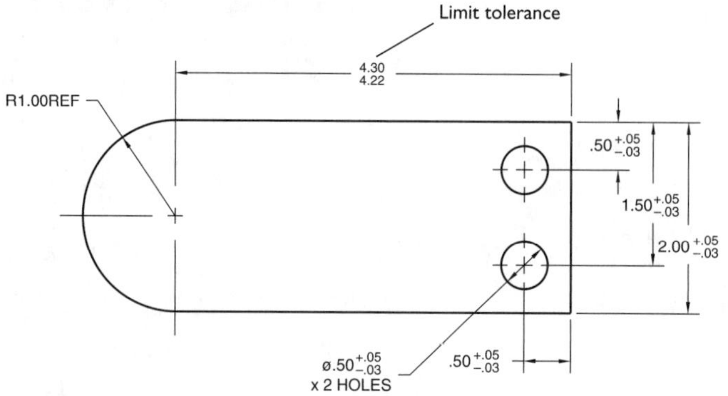

Figure 8.17

Next, you will use the Tolerance command to add a feature control frame specifying a geometric tolerance to the drawing.

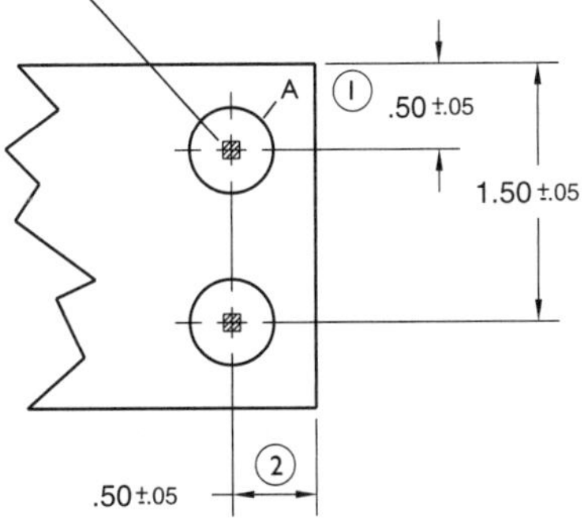

Figure 8.18

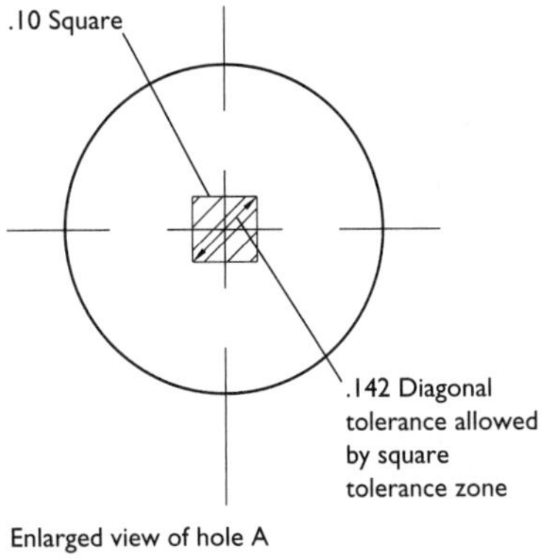

Figure 8.19

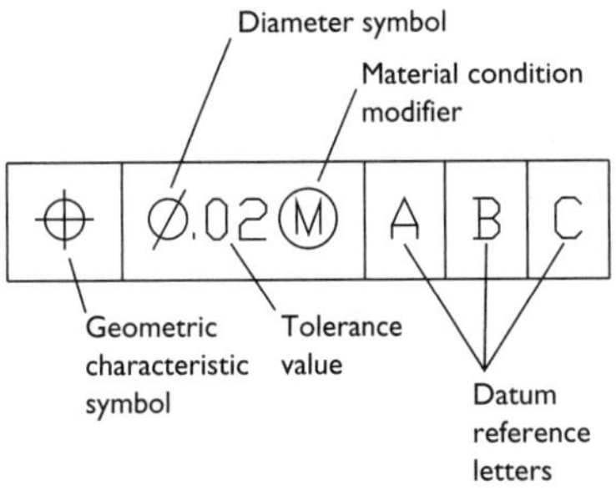

Figure 8.20

Creating Feature Control Frames

Geometric tolerancing allows you to define the shapes of tolerance zones in order to control accurately the manufacture and inspection of parts. Consider the location dimensions for the two holes shown in Figure 8.18. The location for the center of hole A is allowed to vary in a square zone 0.1 unit wide, as defined by the location dimensions 1 and 2 and the ± 0.05 tolerance applied to them.

This tolerance zone is not the same length in all directions from the true center of the hole. The stated tolerances allow the location for the center of the actual hole to be off by a larger amount diagonally, as shown in Figure 8.19.

In other words, some parts that should be rejected would be accepted because the tolerance stated for the location of the hole was considered to be only a horizontal or vertical dimension. Or, if the diagonal was considered when the tolerance was stated, some parts that are off horizontally or vertically, but could have been accepted because of the diagonal dimension, would be rejected. This realization, among others, led to the development of specific tolerance symbols for controlling the geometric tolerance characteristics for position, flatness, straightness, circularity, concentricity, runout, total runout, angularity, parallelism, and perpendicularity.

Geometric tolerances allow you to define a *feature control frame* that specifies a tolerance zone shaped appropriately for the feature being controlled (sometimes this method is called feature-based tolerancing). A feature control frame is shown in Figure 8.20.

The feature control frame begins with the *geometric characteristic symbol*, which tells the type of geometry being controlled. Figure 8.20 first shows a geometric characteristic symbol for positional tolerance. It next specifies the total allowable tolerance zone; in this case a diametral-shaped zone 0.02 wide around the perfect position for the feature. These two symbols are followed by any modifiers for material condition or projected tolerance zone. The circled M shown is the modifier for maximum material condition, meaning that at maximum material, in this case the smallest hole, the tolerance must apply, but when the hole is larger a greater tolerance zone may be calculated, based on the size of the actual hole measured. The remaining boxes indicate that the position is measured from datum surfaces A, B, and C. Not every geometric tolerance feature control frame requires a datum; for example, flatness can just point to the feature and control it, without respect to another surface. Features such as perpendicularity that are between two different surfaces require a datum.

Among other things, proper application of geometric tolerancing symbols requires that you understand

- the design intent for the part;
- the shapes of the tolerance zones specified with particular geometric characteristic symbols;
- the selection and indication of datum surfaces on the object; and
- the placement of feature control frames in the drawing.

In this tutorial, you will learn how to create feature control frames and add them to your drawing. To understand the topic of geometric tolerancing fully, refer to your engineering design graphics textbook or a specific text on geometric tolerancing. Merely adding feature control frames to the drawing will not result in a drawing that clearly communicates your design intent for the part to the manufacturer.

Right-click: **on any toolbar** (use the pop-up list to turn on the **Dimension** toolbar)

The Dimension toolbar appears on your screen.

Position the toolbar where it will be easily available but not in the way of your drawing.

Next you will create the feature control frame shown in Figure 8.20. To create a feature control frame, you will pick the Tolerance icon from the Dimension toolbar.

Pick: **Tolerance icon**

The Geometric Tolerance dialog box shown in Figure 8.21 appears.

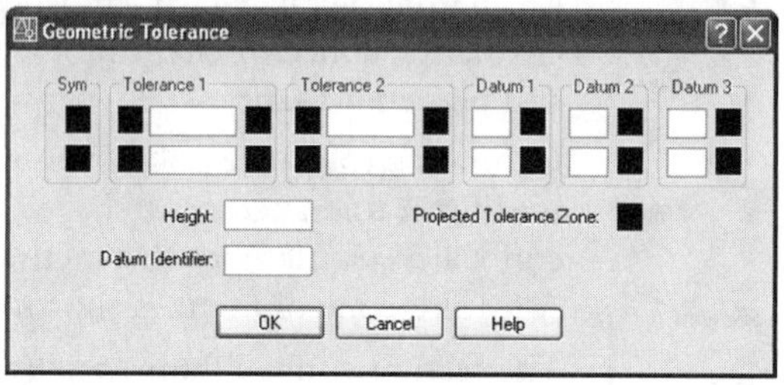

Figure 8.21

You will use it to create the geometric tolerance feature control frame by filling in tolerance values and selecting symbols.

Pick: **on the blank symbol area at the top left of the dialog box**

The Symbol palette appears on your screen as shown in Figure 8.22.

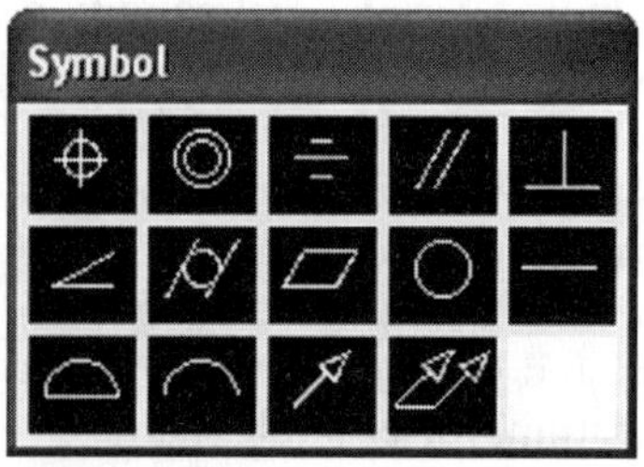

Figure 8.22

Pick: **the positional tolerance symbol in the upper left corner**

The symbol you selected appears in the box you picked. You will make selections so that the dialog box appears as shown in Figure 8.23. The positional tolerance symbol should already be shown at the left.

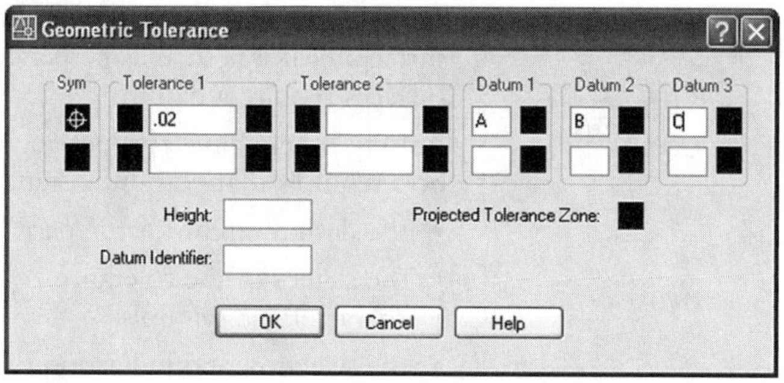

Figure 8.23

The box to the right of the positional tolerance symbol is a toggle.

Pick: in the empty box to **turn on the diameter symbol**

When you pick in the empty box, the symbol should appear.

Click in the empty input box and type **0.02**.

To add a modifier, **pick on the blank symbol tile** to the right of the value you typed.

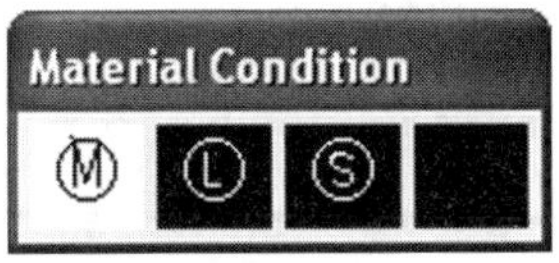

Figure 8.24

The Material Condition dialog box appears, as shown in Figure 8.24. To select the modifier for maximum material condition,

Pick: **on the circled M**

You return to the Geometric Tolerance dialog box. The modifier appears for the feature control frame. Next, you will specify datum surfaces A, B, and C. To do so,

Tip

Datum plane C would be identified in another view if used.

Pick: **in the empty text box below Datum 1**

Type: **A**

Repeat this process for **datum B** and **datum C** on your own.

Note that datums can also have modifiers. If you wanted to, you could pick on the empty symbol tile to add a modifier for the datum.

Now you are ready to add the feature control frame to your drawing.

Pick: **OK** (to exit the Geometric Tolerance dialog box)

You will locate the feature control frame below the 0.50 diameter dimension for the two holes.

Enter tolerance location: **pick the location for the tolerance symbol**

Your drawing should look like that shown in Figure 8.25.

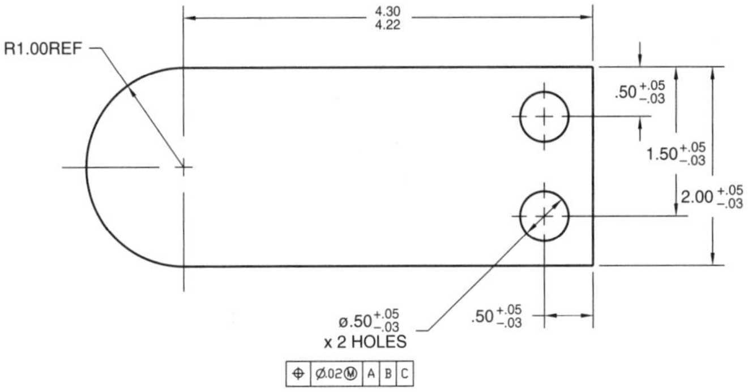

Figure 8.25

Using Leader with Tolerances

You can also use the Leader command to add a leader with an attached geometric tolerance symbol to your drawing. You will create the next feature control frame by starting with the Leader command. You will pick the Leader icon from the Dimension toolbar.

Turn on running OSNAP for **Nearest**.
Pick: **Quick Leader icon**
Specify first leader point, or [Settings] <Settings>: ↵
Pick: **Tolerance** in the Leader Settings dialog box, as shown in Figure 8.26

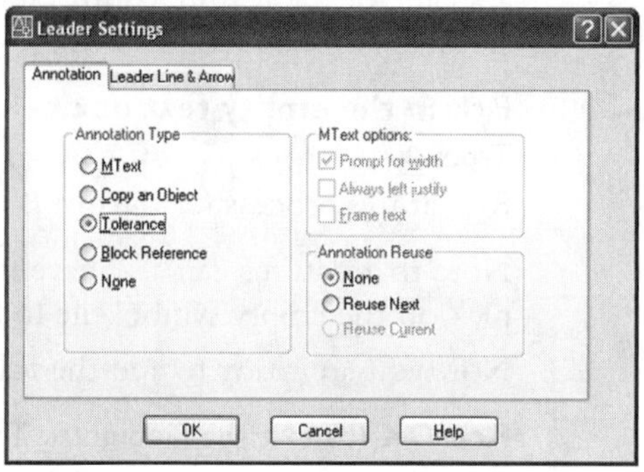

Figure 8.26

Pick: **OK**
Specify first leader point, or [Settings] <Settings>: **pick at about 2 o'clock on the upper hole, using AutoSnap™ Nearest**
Specify next point: **pick above and to the right of the drawing**
Specify next point: ↵

The Geometric Tolerance dialog box appears; from there you can start creating the feature control frame.

On your own, **create another feature control frame like the first one.**
After you've finished making selections in the Geometric Tolerance dialog box, pick OK.

The feature control frame is added to the end of the leader line, as shown in Figure 8.27.

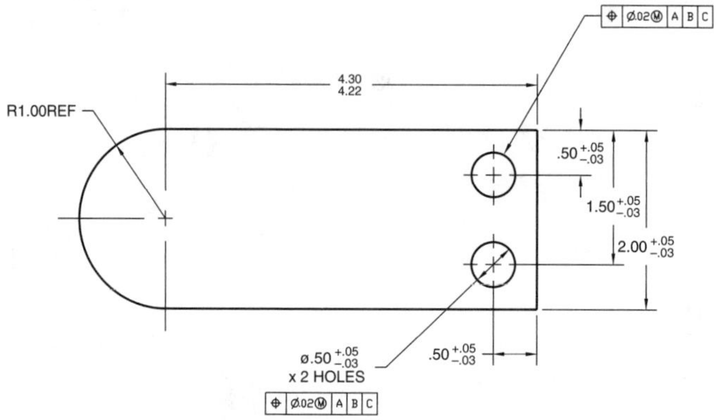

Figure 8.27

Next, you will override the location dimensions for the holes so that they appear as basic dimensions. When you specify a positional tolerance, the true position is usually located with basic dimensions, which are theoretically exact dimensions. The feature control frame for positional tolerance controls the zone in which the true position can vary. To create basic dimensions by overriding the dimension style,

Pick: **the 0.50 vertical dimension at the upper right of the object so that its grips appear**

Pick: **Properties icon**

The Properties palette appears on your screen.

Pick: **to expand the Tolerances area**

Pick: **Basic** as the tolerance display

When you have finished

Press: [Esc] twice to unselect the dimension

Figure 8.28 shows the drawing with the 0.50 basic dimension.

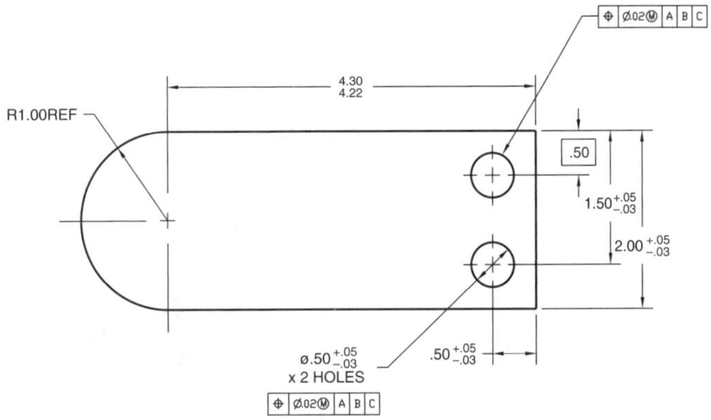

Figure 8.28

On your own, override the dimension style for the 0.50 horizontal dimension below the object, and then for the 1.50 vertical dimension so they are basic dimensions.

Pick: **to Close the Properties palette**

When you have finished, save your drawing on your own.

Next, you will add datum flags to identify datum surfaces A and B, from which the position feature can vary.

Creating Datum Flags

Datum flags are boxed letters identifying the feature on the object that is being used as a datum. Often they are attached to the extension line that is parallel to the surface being identified as the datum surface. To create a datum flag, you will use the leader command and then select to add the tolerance.

Pick: **Quick Leader icon**

Specify first leader point, or [Settings] <Settings>: ↵

Check to see that **Tolerance** is still selected on the Annotation tab.

Pick: **Leader Line & Arrow tab**

Pick: **Datum triangle filled** for the arrowhead style as shown in Figure 8.29

Pick: **OK**

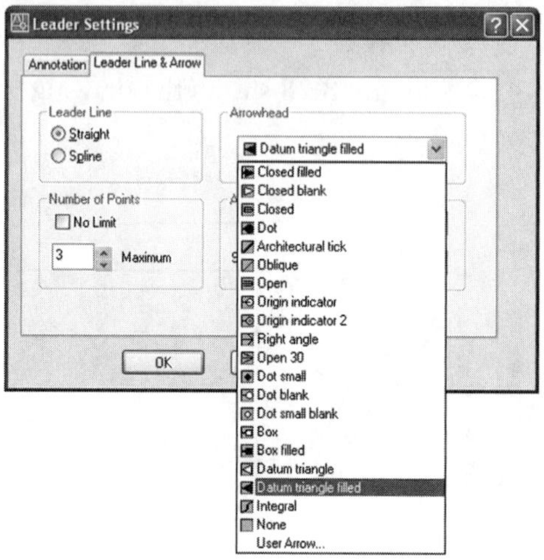

Figure 8.29

You will return to your drawing to select the location for the leader line that will attach the datum flag.

Turn on **ORTHO.**

Specify first leader point, or [Settings] <Settings>: **pick on the upper right extension line**

Specify next point: **pick a point above the previous point**

Specify next point: **pick a point to the right of the previous point**

The Geometric Tolerance dialog box appears on your screen. You will leave the selections blank, except for the datum identifier.

Pick: **in the input box to the right of Datum Identifier**

Type: **A**

When you have finished, the dialog box should look like Figure 8.30.

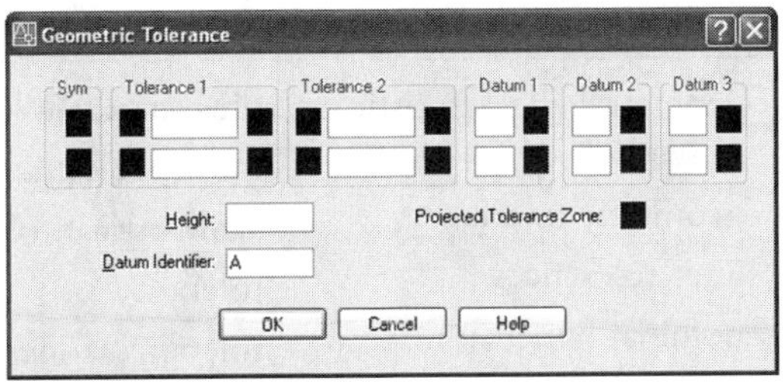

Figure 8.30

Pick: **OK**

The datum flag appears in your drawing as shown in Figure 8.31.

Add datum flag B to the drawing on your own.

Tip

If you have trouble making the straight leader segment for the datum flag, create the datum identifier separately using the Tolerance command. Use the leader command to draw the filled triangle and line or just use the Line command and add a filled triangle on your own.

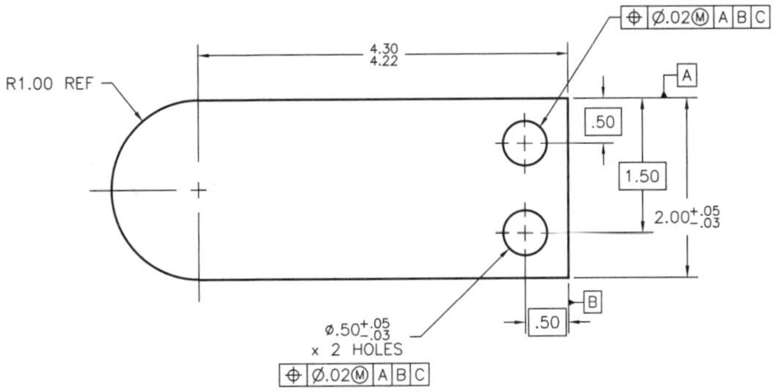

Figure 8.31

Close the Dimension toolbar.
Save your drawing, and exit the AutoCAD program.

You have completed Tutorial 8.

Key Terms

basic dimension
bilateral tolerances
datum flags
deviation tolerances
feature control frame
geometric characteristic symbol
geometric tolerances
limit tolerances
nominal dimension
plus/minus tolerances
reference dimension
symmetrical tolerances
tolerance
tolerance zones
unilateral tolerances
variance tolerances

Key Commands

Dimgap
Dimlim
Dimoverride
Dimpost
Dimtol
Leader
Tolerance

Exercises

Draw the necessary 2D orthographic views and dimension the following shapes. Include tolerances if indicated.

8.1 Stop Base

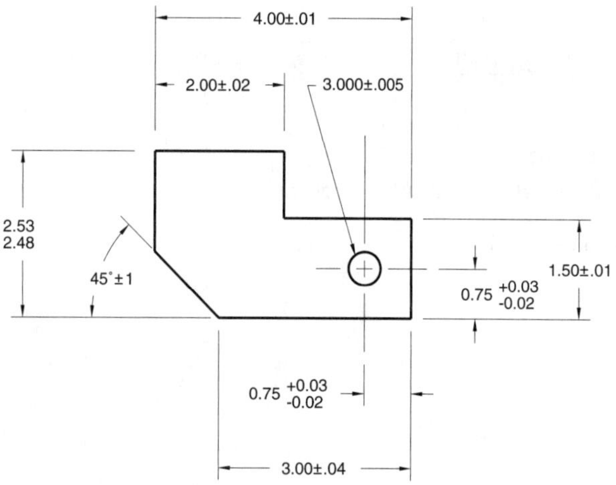

8.2 Tolerance Problem

Calculate the maximum and minimum clearance between Parts A and B and Part C as shown.

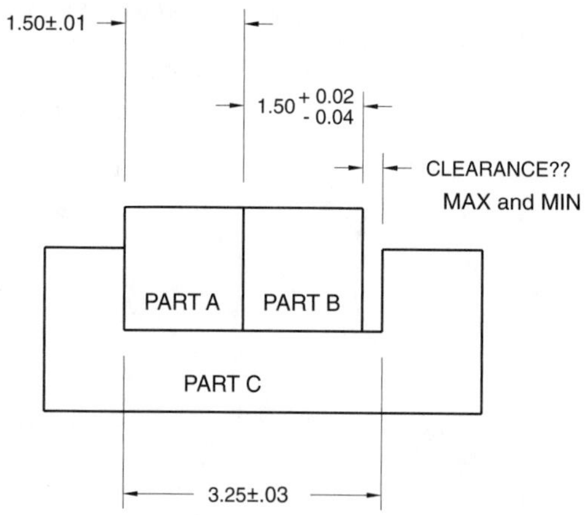

8.3M Lathe Stop

Show bilateral tolerances of ±.02 for the ∅.75 hole and the 1.50 upper slot.

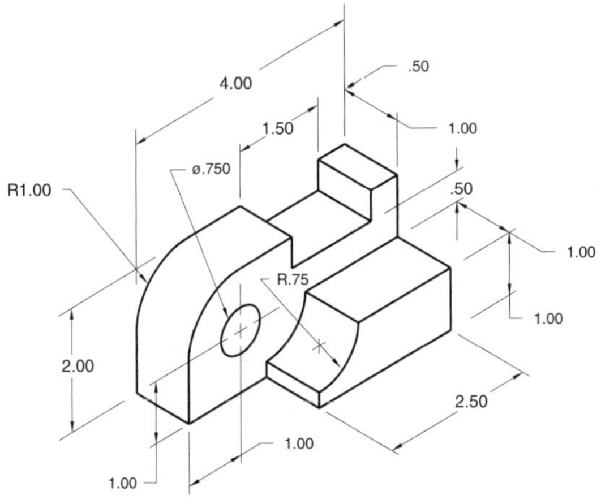

8.4M Mill Tool

Consider the symmetry of this part as you dimension the orthographic views.

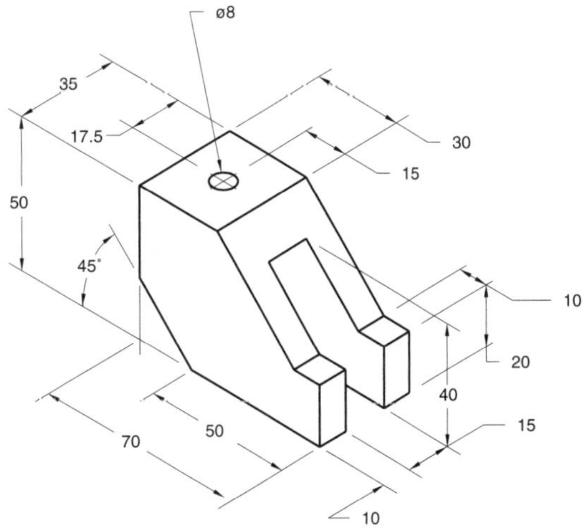

8.5M Shaft Bearing

Show a limit dimension for the ∅32 hole with an upper limit of ∅35 and a lower limit of ∅30.

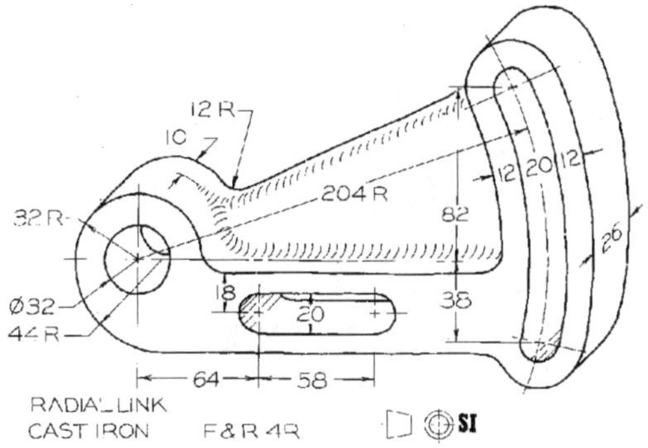

8.6 Angular Tolerance

Using a feature control frame and the necessary dimensions, indicate that the allowable variation from the true angle specified for the inclined plane is 0.7 mm, using the bottom surface of the object as the datum.

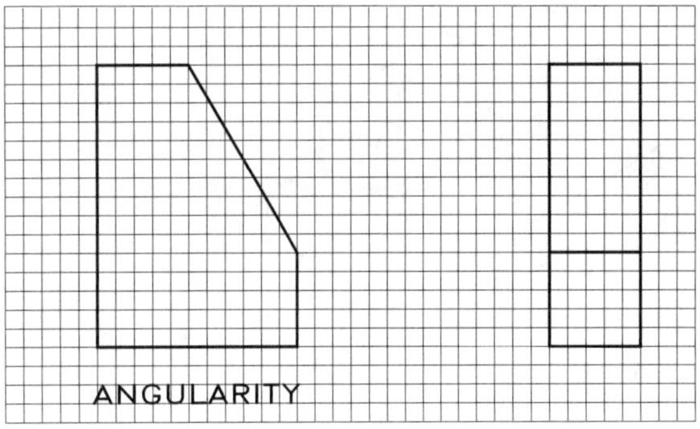

8.7 Positional Tolerance

Locate the two holes with an allowable size tolerance of 0.05 inches and a position tolerance of .02 inches DIA. Use the proper symbols and dimensions. Each square is .25 inches.

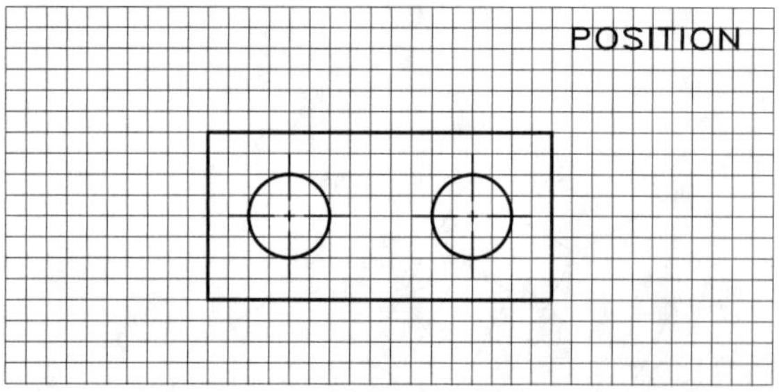

8.8 Hub

Create the drawing shown.

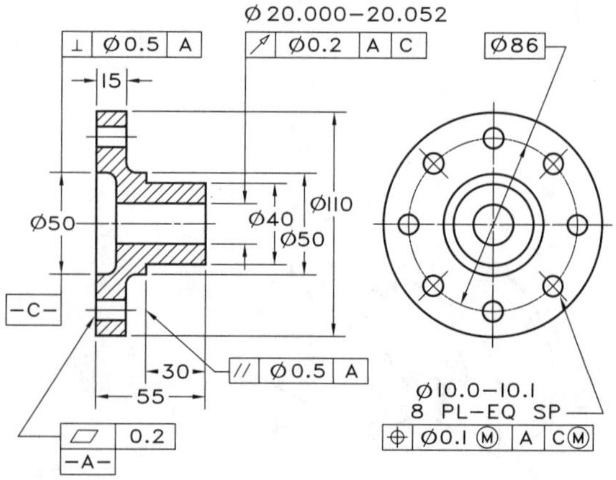

8.9 Chuck Jaw

Draw dimensioned orthographic views. Add limit tolerances as shown.

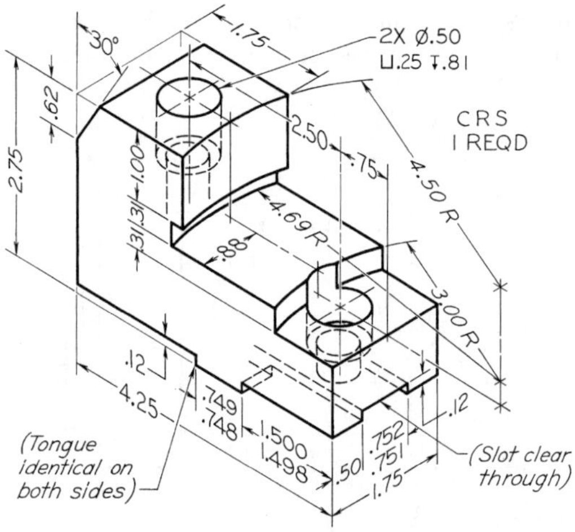

8.10M Roller Stud

Draw dimensioned orthographic views. Add limit tolerances as shown.

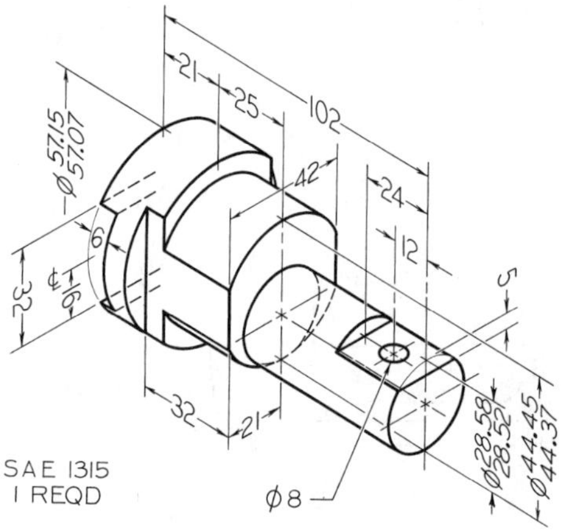

Tutorial

9 Section and Auxiliary Views

Objectives

When you have completed this tutorial, you will be able to

1. Show the internal surfaces of an object, using 2D section views.
2. Locate and draw cutting plane lines and section lines on appropriate layers.
3. Hatch an area with a pattern.
4. Edit associative hatching.
5. Draw auxiliary views, using 2D projection.
6. Set up a UCS to help create a 2D auxiliary view.
7. Rotate the snap to help create a 2D auxiliary view.
8. Draw auxiliary views of curved surfaces.

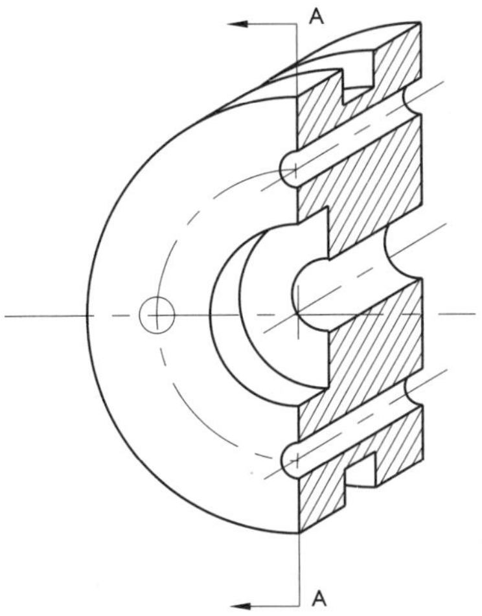

Figure 9.2

Introduction

In this tutorial you will learn first how to draw section views and, in the second half of the tutorial, how to draw auxiliary views.

Section Views

A *section view* is a special type of orthographic view used to show the internal structure of an object. Essentially, it shows what you would see if a portion of the object were cut away and you were to look at the remaining part. Section views are often used when the normal orthographic views contain so many hidden lines that they are confusing and difficult to interpret. In this tutorial you will learn to use two-dimensional (2D) projection to create section views. In Tutorial 14 you will learn to use solid modeling to generate a section view directly from a solid model.

Section View Conventions

Figure 9.1 shows the front and side views of a cylindrical object. The side view contains many hidden lines and is somewhat difficult to interpret.

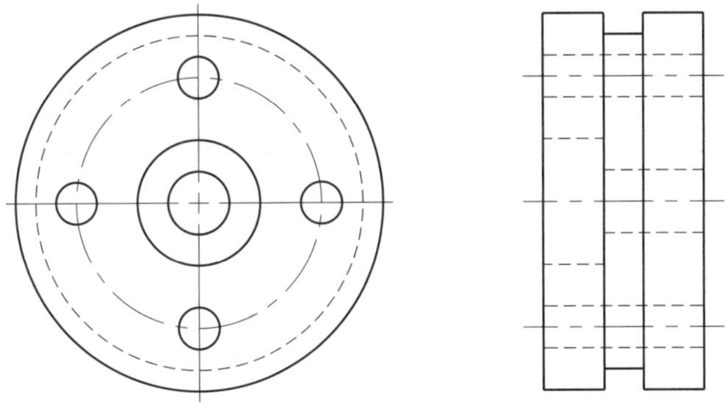

Figure 9.1

Figure 9.2 shows a pictorial drawing of the same object cut in half along its vertical centerline. This type of drawing is called a *pictorial full section*.

In many drafting applications, an area (such as the portion of an object that has been cut to show a section view) is filled with a pattern to make the drawing easier to interpret. The pattern can help differentiate components of an assembly, or it can indicate the material comprising the object. You can accomplish this *crosshatching* or pattern filling by using the AutoCAD® Hatch command.

In Figure 9.2, crosshatching shows the solid portions of the object; that is, where material was cut to make the section view.

Figure 9.3 shows front and section views of the same circular object. A *cutting plane line*, line A–A, defines where the sectional cut should be made and indicates the direction in which you should view the object to produce the section view.

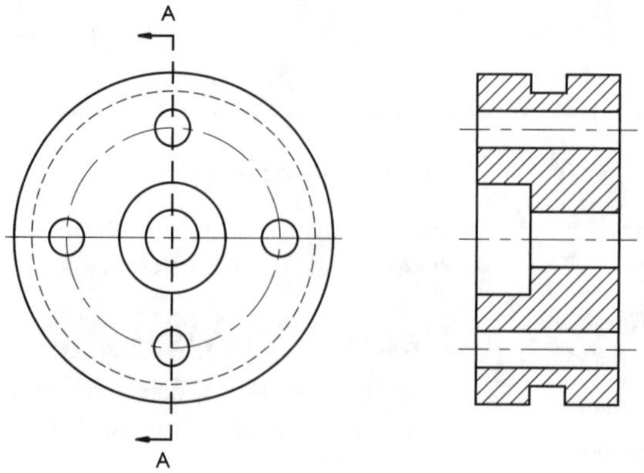

Figure 9.3

Compare the side view in Figure 9.1 with the section view in Figure 9.3 and the 3D section view shown in Figure 9.2. Figures 9.2 and 9.3 are easier to interpret than the front and side views shown in Figure 9.1.

Figure 9.4 shows a different object with a cutting plane line and the appropriate section view.

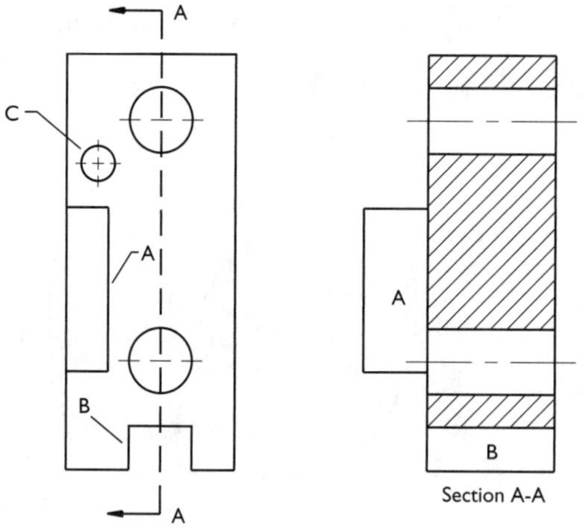

Figure 9.4

Crosshatching

Crosshatching is used to show where material has been cut. Note in Figure 9.4 that the surfaces labeled A and B are not crosshatched. Only material that has been cut by the cutting plane is crosshatched. Surfaces A and B are shown in section A–A because they are visible after the cut has been made, but they are not hatched because they were not cut by the cutting plane.

A section view shows what you would see if you looked at the object in the direction the arrows on the cutting plane line point, with all the material behind the arrows removed. When creating a section view, you should ignore the portion of the object that will be cut off. Draw the remaining portion, toward which the arrows on the cutting plane line point. Remember, once the object has been cut, some features that were previously hidden will be visible and should be shown. The hole labeled C in Figure 9.4 is in the remaining portion of the object, but is not visible in the section view, so it is not shown. The purpose of a section view is to show the internal structure without the confusion of hidden lines. You should use hidden lines only if the object would be misunderstood if the lines were not included. (To show hole C in the section view, you could use an offset cutting plane line—which bends 90° to pass through features that are not all in the same plane. Refer to any standard engineering graphics text to review conventions for cutting plane lines and types of section views.)

Starting

Start the AutoCAD 2006 program on your own.

Use the datafile ***cast2.dwt*** as a template file to begin a new drawing.

Save the drawing as ***bossect.dwg***.

Creating 2D Section Views

The top, front, and side orthographic views of a casting are displayed on your screen. The horizontal centerlines have been erased in the top view. Your screen should look like Figure 9.5.

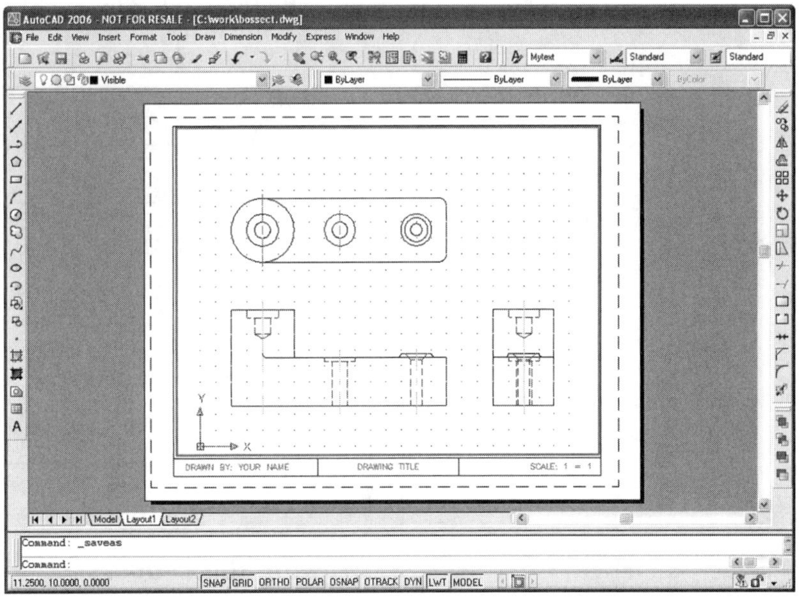

Figure 9.5

Often one or more of the orthographic views are replaced with section views. You will use the front orthographic view to draw a front section view. You will use the side view to draw a side section view through the boss.

Cutting Plane Lines

You can draw a cutting plane line by using one of two different line-types: long dashes (DASHED) or long lines with two short dashes followed by another long line (PHANTOM). You should use only one type of cutting plane line in any one drawing. You will make dashed cutting plane lines using the Cutting_Plane layer that was created in the template. Linetype DASHED has longer dashes than linetype HIDDEN. The Cutting_Plane layer has a different color than the Hidden_Line layer to help distinguish it. Also, cutting plane lines are drawn with a thick pen during plotting. The lineweight for the layer is set to a 0.6 mm thickness to produce a thick line.

Creating Dashed Lines

Set layer **Cutting_Plane** as the current layer.

Be sure that Snap is turned on and set to **0.25**.

Pick: **Line icon**

On your own, add a **horizontal dashed cutting plane line** in the top view of the boss that passes through the center of the holes in the top view between points A–A in Figure 9.6.

Now add a **vertical dashed cutting plane** line through the center of the top view of the boss between points B–B.

Save your drawing on your own.

The lines on layer Cutting_Plane should extend beyond the edges of the object by about 0.5 units as shown in Figure 9.6.

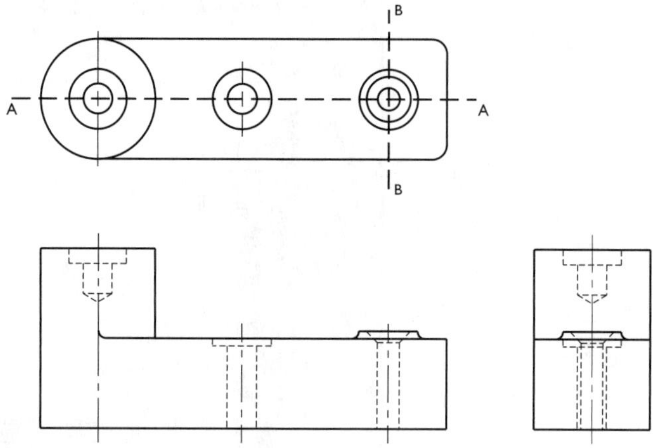

Figure 9.6

Drawing the Leaders

The Leader command lets you construct complex leaders. A leader is a line ending in an arrowhead (or sometimes a dot) that is used to locate specific notes and drawing information for an item. Leaders should generally be drawn at some angle other than horizontal or vertical.

In this case you will use the Leader command to add the line segments ending in arrows for the cutting plane lines. Because the arrowed line segments are part of the cutting plane lines, they should be drawn on layer Cutting_Plane. After you have drawn the leaders, you will use the Dtext command to place the text labeling the cutting plane lines.

Use **Ortho** to assist you in drawing straight lines.

Make sure OSNAP is turned on, with **Endpoint** selected.

Pick: **Dimension, Leader**

Specify first leader point or [Settings] <Settings>: ↵

Leader Command Options

The Leader command provides the Settings option to allow you to change the appearance of the leader before you start drawing one. The Leader settings dialog box appears with the Annotation tab uppermost.

Pick: **Leader Line & Arrow tab** (so that it appears uppermost)

The Leader Line & Arrow tab has further options that allow you to select the shape for the leader line: Splined or Straight. These options let you choose splined lines (so that you can make a curved leader) or straight lines (like the leaders you have drawn so far). Below the Leader Line area is the Number of Points area. This should be currently set to 3. This allows you to draw leaders with two line segments and then move on to the text prompt portion of the command. You can set the number higher to make more complicated leaders; however, most engineering leaders are straight line leaders with only two segments. The Arrowhead pull-down lets you select the style of arrowhead, including none. The Arrow option draws an arrow at the end of the leader and None draws a leader with no arrow. The Angle Constraints area lets you define the angles at which leaders must be drawn. For the Second Segment,

Pick: **Horizontal**

The Leader Line & Arrow tab should look like Figure 9.7.

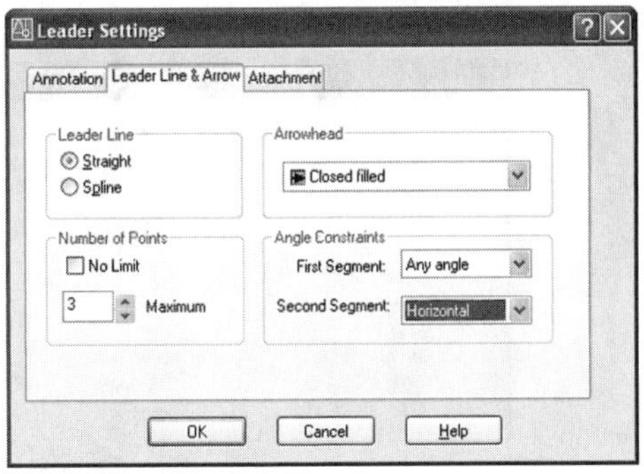

Figure 9.7

Pick: **Attachment tab** (so it appears uppermost)

The Attachment tab appears as shown in Figure 9.8. You can use this tab to determine how text at the end of a leader is placed in relation to the leader line you draw. Leave the selections set as shown.

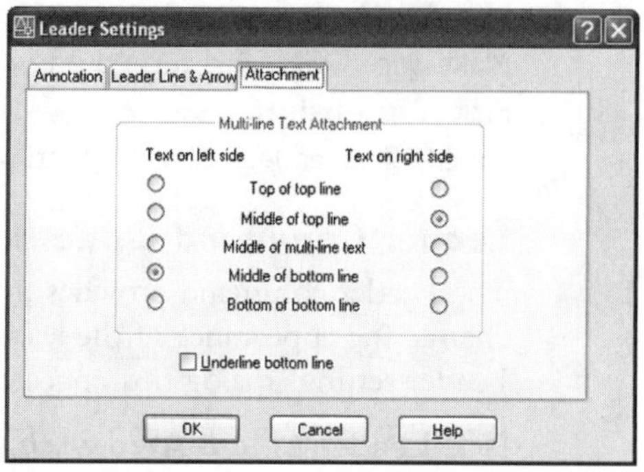

Figure 9.8

Pick: **Annotation tab**

The Annotation tab appears as the top tab as shown in Figure 9.9. It has the following options: Mtext, Copy an Object, Tolerance, Block Reference, and None. The default option is Mtext; you have used this option to create text at the end of the leader line, and you can also use it to create multiple lines of text. The Tolerance selection lets you add a geometric tolerance feature control frame to the end of the leader line. (You used this option in Tutorial 8 when you learned about advanced dimensioning features.) Copy an Object lets you pick on an existing feature control frame, block, or text object and copy it to the end of the new leader line. Choosing Block Reference lets you select a block to be added to the end of the leader, as you will in Tutorial 13. The None option lets you draw a leader line with no text added to the end. You will use the None option to end the Leader command when you draw the leaders for cutting plane lines.

Pick: **None**

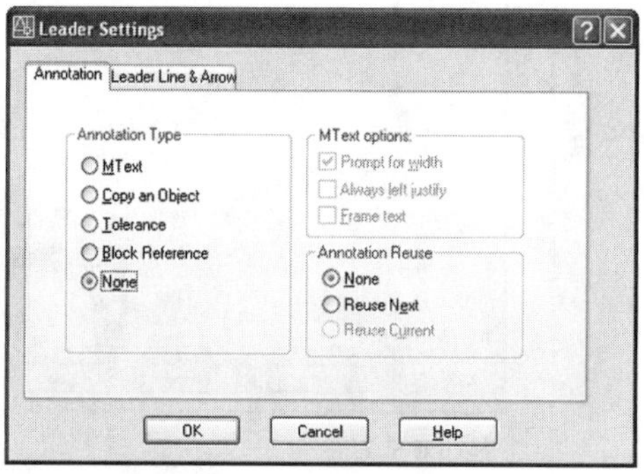

Figure 9.9

Tip

The Leader command will not draw the arrows if the first line segment of the leader is too short. The first line segment must be longer than the current arrowhead size. You can set the arrowhead size with the dimensioning variables that you learned to use in Tutorial 7.

Pick: **OK** (to exit the dialog box)

You will start the leader 0.5 unit to the left of the top end of cutting plane line B–B.

Specify first leader point, or [Settings] <Settings>: **select a point 0.5 unit to the left of, and even with, the top end of cutting plane line B–B**
Specify next point: **pick the top end of the cutting plane line B–B**
Specify next point: ↵

Repeat these steps to create a leader for the bottom of cutting plane line B–B.

Command: ↵

Specify first leader point, or [Settings] <Settings>: **select a point 0.5 unit above, and even with, the left endpoint of cutting plane line A–A**

Specify next point: **pick the left endpoint of cutting plane line A–A**

Specify next point: ↵

Command: ↵ (to restart the Leader command)

Specify first leader point, or [Settings] <Settings>: **pick a point 0.5 unit above, and even with, the right endpoint of cutting plane line A–A**

Specify next point: **pick the right endpoint of cutting plane line A–A**

Specify next point: ↵

Use the Dtext command to add the label A to both ends of cutting plane line A–A.

Add the label B to both ends of cutting plane line B–B.

When completed, your leader lines should look like the ones shown in Figure 9.10.

Tip

You can easily insert arrowheads at the end of a cutting plane line by making your own arrowhead block. A quick way to make a block for arrowheads is to explode a leader line and make a block from its arrowhead. You can also use a Polyline with a zero starting width and larger ending width to create an arrowhead from scratch.

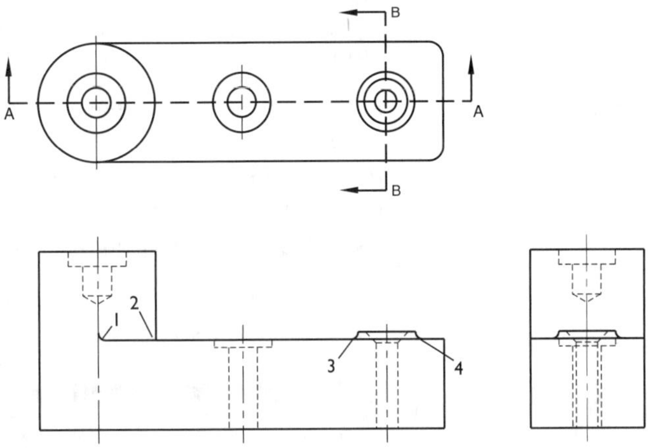

Figure 9.10

Next, you will remove the unnecessary lines from the front view. When you draw a section view, you do not want to see the lines that represent intersections and surfaces on the outside of the object.

On your own, turn **Snap off**.

Use **Zoom Window** to enlarge the view to help select the points.

Use the **Erase** command to remove the *runout* (or curve that represents the blending of two surfaces) labeled 1 in Figure 9.10.

Use **Trim** to remove the portion of the line to the left of point 2.

Use the **Erase** command to remove the solid line from point 3 to point 4, which defines the surface in front of the boss.

Your drawing should be similar to that in Figure 9.11.

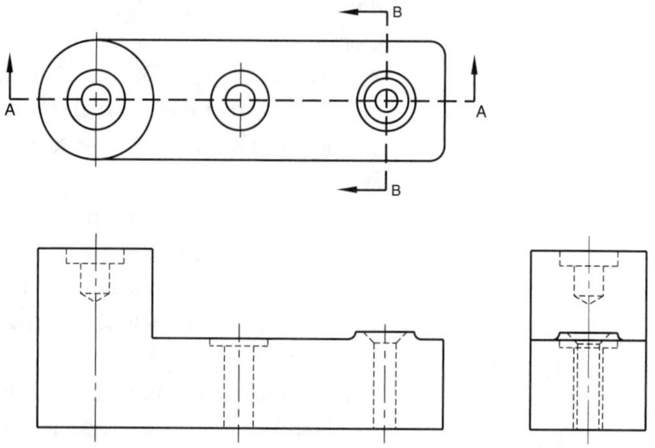

Figure 9.11

Changing Hidden Lines to Visible

When you section the drawing, the interior details become visible. You will use the Layer Control to change the layer of the hidden lines to VISIBLE.

Tip

Use a crossing box to make selecting the hidden lines in the front view easier.

Pick: **on all of the hidden lines in the front view** so that their grips appear

Pick: **to pull down the Layer Control**

Pick: **on Layer VISIBLE** to move the selected lines to that layer

Press: Esc to unselect the objects

Now all the hidden lines in the front view have been changed to layer VISIBLE. Your screen should now be similar to Figure 9.12.

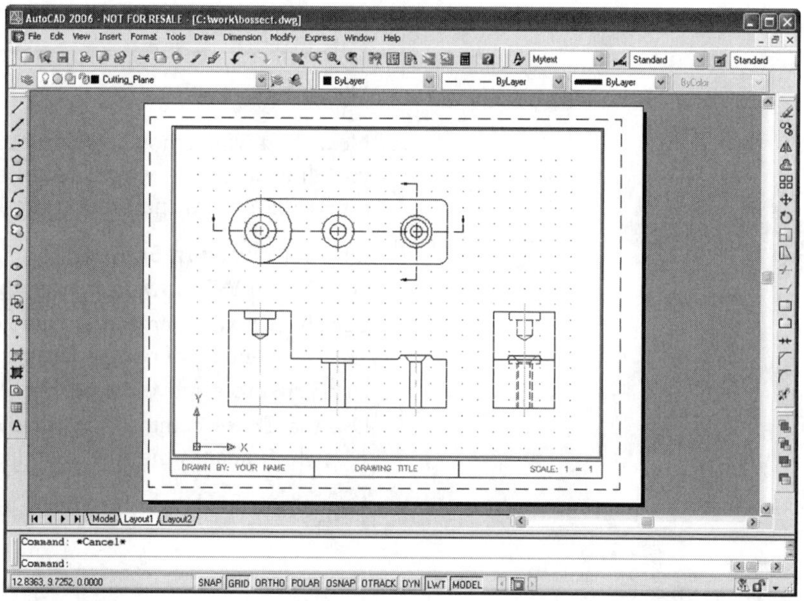

Figure 9.12

If you have zoomed your drawing, use Zoom Previous to return to the original size. You are almost ready to add the hatching to the drawing.

The hatching will fill the areas of the drawing where the solid object was cut by the cutting plane.

Hatching should be on its own layer and should be plotted with a thin line. Having the hatch on its own layer is useful so that you can freeze it if you do not want it displayed while you are working on the drawing. In the drawing you started from, a separate layer for the hatching has already been created. Its color is red, and its linetype is CONTINUOUS.

Pick: **HATCH** to set it current using the Layer Control

Using Hatch

Hatching comprises a series of lines, dashes, or dots that form a pattern. The Hatch command fills an area with a pattern or solid fill. It creates ***associative hatching***, which means that, if the area selected as the hatch boundary is changed, the hatching is automatically updated to fill the new area. Associative hatching is the default for the Hatch command. If you update the selected boundary so that it no longer forms a closed area, the hatching will no longer be associative. Hatch helps you choose the boundary for the pattern by selecting from its various boundary selection options. To activate Hatch, select the Hatch icon from the Draw toolbar.

Pick: **Hatch icon**

The Hatch and Gradient dialog box appears on your screen with the Hatch tab uppermost, as shown in Figure 9.13. The Associative check box in the Options area at the right of the dialog box should indicate that associative hatching is turned on.

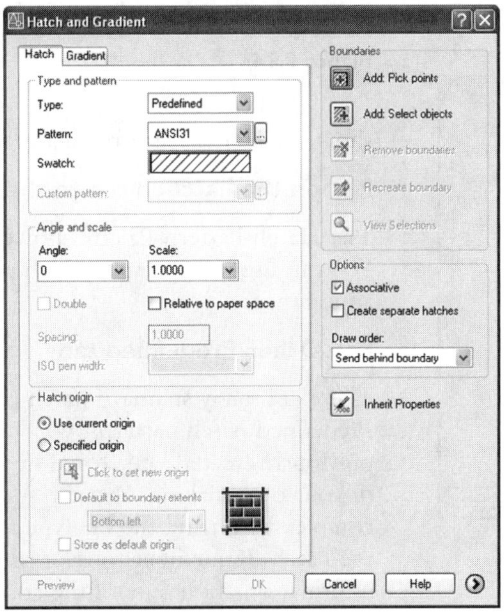

Figure 9.13

Selecting the Hatch Pattern

You can select predefined hatch patterns by pulling down the list next to Pattern. ANSI31 is the default hatch pattern. It consists of continuous lines angled at 45° and spaced about 1/16 apart, and is typically used to show cast iron materials. It is also used as a general pattern when you do not want to use the hatch pattern to specify a material. To select a hatch pattern, pick on the name ANSI31 in the box to the right of Pattern.

Pick: **ANSI31** (to the right of Pattern)

The list of predefined hatch patterns pulls down, as shown in Figure 9.14.

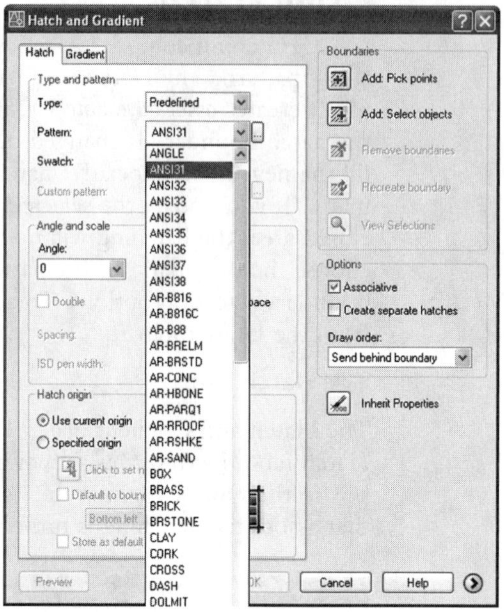

Figure 9.14

You can also select a hatch pattern by picking on the Swatch tile to show the Hatch Pattern Palette.

Pick: **on the hatched tile to the right of Swatch**

The Hatch Pattern Palette shown in Figure 9.15 appears on your screen. You can use it to preview hatch patterns by looking at a sample of their appearance.

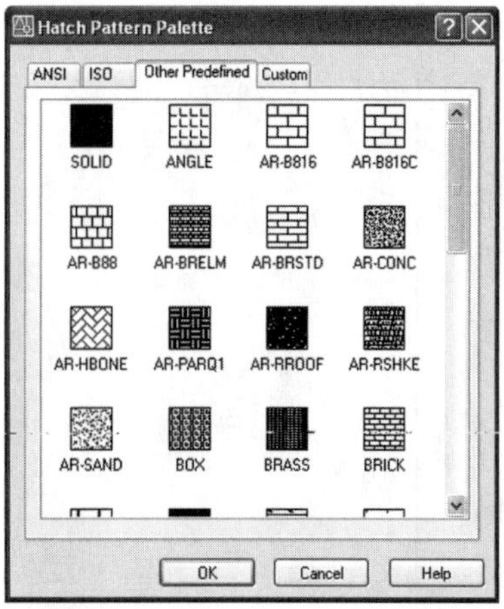

Figure 9.15

Pick: **Other Predefined tab**

There are many standard hatch patterns available. In addition to Predefined hatch patterns, you can use *custom hatch patterns* that you previously created and stored in the file *acad.pat* or another *.pat* file of your own making. You can make *user-defined hatch patterns* more complex by setting the linetype for the layer on which you will create the hatch. Remember to refer to the AutoCAD online help for more information about any of the commands described in these tutorials.

After you have looked at some of the hatch patterns,

Pick: **ANSI31** from the ANSI tab as the hatch pattern

Pick: **OK** to return to the Hatch and Gradient dialog box

Warning

Be cautious when specifying a smaller scale for the hatch pattern. If the hatch lines are very close together, the AutoCAD software will take a long time calculating them and may even run out of space on your hard disk, causing your system to crash.

Angling the Hatch Pattern

The Angle area of the Hatch and Gradient dialog box allows you to specify a rotation angle for the hatch pattern. The default is 0 degrees, or no rotation of the pattern. In the hatch pattern you selected, ANSI31, the lines are already at an angle of 45 degrees. Any angle you choose in the Angle area of the dialog box will be added to the chosen pattern; for example, if you added a rotation angle of 10 degrees to your current pattern, the lines would be drawn at an angle of 55 degrees.

Leave the default value of 0 degrees for now.

Scaling the Hatch Pattern

The Scale option on the Hatch tab determines the spacing for the hatched lines in your drawing. The hatch pattern is similar in some ways to a linetype. Hatch patterns are stored in an external file, with the spacing set at some default value. Usually the default scale of 1.0000 is the correct size for drawings that will be plotted full scale, resulting in hatched lines that are about 1/16 apart. If the views will be plotted at a smaller scale, half-size for instance, you will need to increase the spacing for the hatch by setting the scale to a larger value so that the lines of the hatch are not as close together.

For this drawing, you will not need to change the scale of the hatch pattern.

Options for Hatch Boundaries

The right side of the Hatch and Gradient dialog box lets you select among the different methods that you can use to specify the area to hatch. Add: Pick Points allows you to pick inside a closed area to be hatched; Add: Select Objects lets you select drawing objects to form a closed boundary for the hatching. Picking the right facing arrow at the bottom right of the dialog box lets you select more options for the creation of the hatch boundary.

Pick: **the right facing arrow at the bottom right of the dialog box** (to show more options)

Figure 9.16 shows the additional options for creating hatch boundaries. By picking the Retain boundaries box, you can save the AutoCAD generated hatch boundaries as one of two different types of objects: a polyline or a region (a region is a 2D enclosed area). When determining the hatch boundary, the software analyzes all the objects on the screen. This step can be time-consuming if you have a large drawing database. To define a different area to be considered for the hatch boundary, you would pick the New button in the Boundary set area. You would then return to your drawing, where you could select the objects to form the new set. Using implied Windowing works well for this procedure.

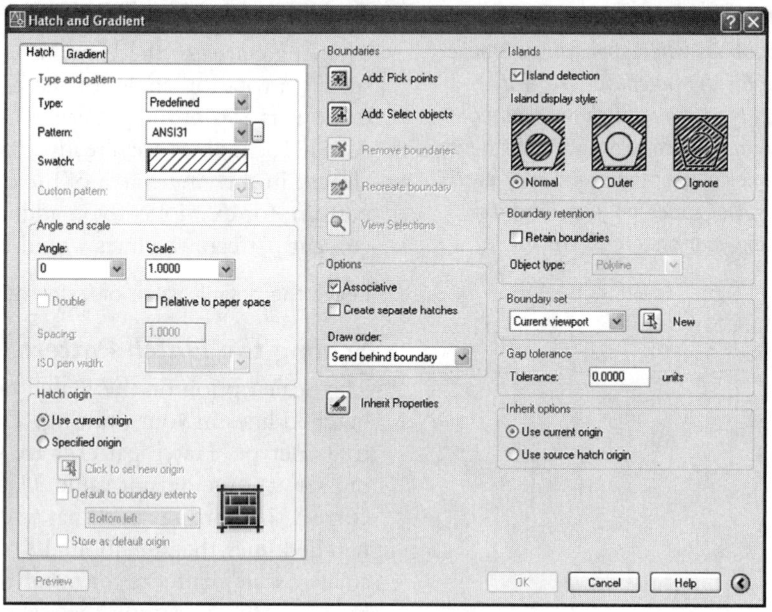

Figure 9.16

You can use the Islands area to change the way islands inside the hatch area are treated. Observe the pictures above the radio buttons that describe the options. The selection Normal causes islands inside the hatched area to be alternately hatched and skipped, starting at the outer area. Choosing Outer causes only the outer area to be hatched; any islands inside are left unhatched. You can also choose Ignore; then, the entire inside is hatched, regardless of the structure. Leave this area of the dialog box set to Normal.

Pick: **Help from the bottom right of the dialog box**

On your own **review the options for setting a Gap Tolerance** and **setting the Hatch Origin Points**.

Close the Help screen to return to the Hatch and Gradient dialog box.

Pick: **the leftward pointing arrow at the bottom right of the dialog box so the additional options no longer show**

Gradient Fills

A *gradient fill* fills an area with a smooth transition between darker and lighter shades of one color, or transitions between two colors. While gradients are not frequently used in engineering drawings, they can add the appearance of shading or interest to logos, maps, and other graphics.

Pick: **Gradient tab**

The Gradient tab appears at the top of the stack as shown in Figure 9.17.

The radio buttons at the top of the dialog box let you select whether you are using a one or two color gradient. Do not add any gradient fills to your drawing at this time.

Pick: **Hatch** tab

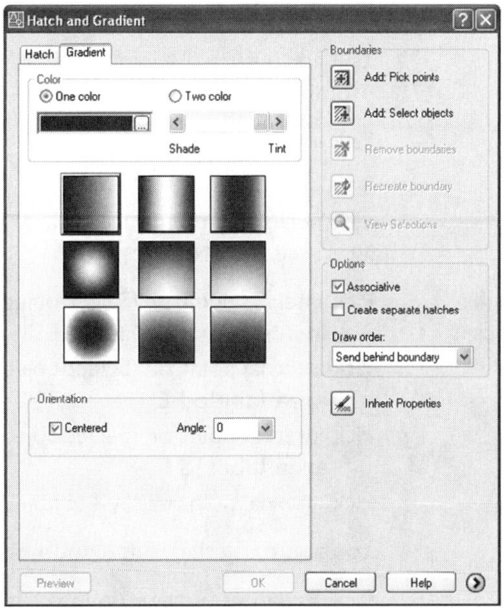

Figure 9.17

Adding the Hatch Pattern

You will specify Pick Points on the Hatch tab as the method for selecting the area to fill with the hatch pattern, then return to your drawing to select points inside the areas that you want to have hatched. (To use the Select Objects method, you would return to your drawing and pick on the objects that form the boundary.) The program will determine the boundary around the areas you picked. (If there are islands inside the area that you did not want hatched, you would use Remove Islands to pick them after you have picked the area to be hatched.) When you are finished selecting, you will press ⏎ to indicate that you are finished selecting and want to continue with the Hatch command. You can use any standard selection method to select the objects. Refer to Figure 9.18 as you make selections.

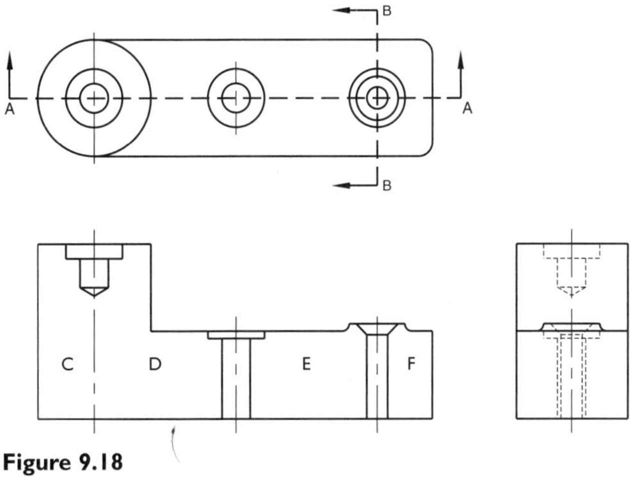

Figure 9.18

Pick: **Add Pick Points**

You are returned to your drawing screen and the following command prompt appears.

Pick internal point or [Select objects/remove Boundaries]: **pick a point inside the area labeled C**

The perimeter of the area that you have selected is highlighted, and you again see the prompt:

Tip

Turn Grid off before previewing, as it can make reading the hatch pattern difficult.

Tip

You can check the Create Separate Hatches box if you would like each area you pick to be created as a separate hatch, so that they can be edited individually later.

Pick internal point or [Select objects/remove Boundaries]: **pick a point inside the area labeled D**

Pick internal point or [Select objects/remove Boundaries]: **pick inside the area labeled E**

Pick internal point or [Select objects/remove Boundaries]: **pick inside the area labeled F**

Pick internal point or [Select objects/remove Boundaries]: ↵

You return to the Hatch and Gradient dialog box.

Pick: **Preview button** (in lower left corner)

You return to your drawing screen with the hatch showing so that you can confirm that the areas you selected are correct. If the area was not hatched correctly, return to the dialog box and make the necessary changes and then preview the hatch again. When what you see is correct, you will pick OK to apply the hatch. (Your screen may not show the preview perfectly, but if the areas are generally correct, they will probably hatch correctly.) If the hatch appeared correctly,

Pick or press Esc to return to dialog or <Right-click to accept hatch>: Esc

Pick: **OK**

The area that you selected becomes hatched in your drawing. Your drawing should now look like the one in Figure 9.19.

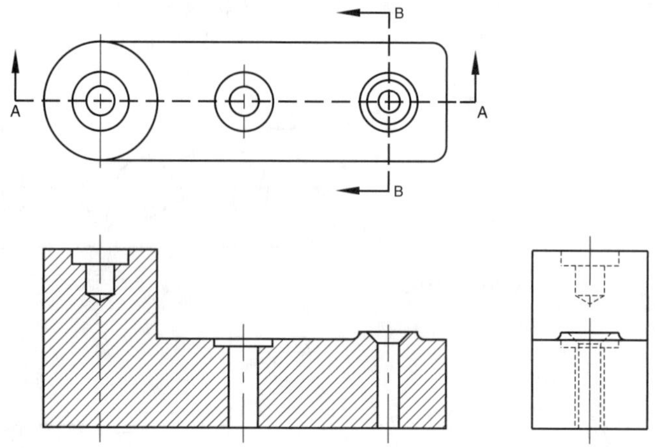

Figure 9.19

Creating the Side Section View

To draw section B–B, you will need to increase the space available to draw the side view on your screen. You will zoom out so that the drawing is shown to a smaller scale and more drawing area shows in the viewport. You will use the Viewports toolbar to set the zoom scale.

Right-click: **on any toolbar**
Pick: **Viewports** (from the pop-up menu) to turn on the **Viewports toolbar**

Figure 9.20

Changing the Viewport Scale

The Viewports toolbar is shown in Figure 9.20. You can use the selection box at its right to set the viewport zoom scale factor. The standard scale choices will pop down when you select on it. The scale you will use is not a standard scale, so you will type in the desired zoom XP scale.

Pick: to highlight the text at the right of the toolbar and type **.75** ↵

Your drawing appears smaller, so more of it fits into the viewport.

Next, you will use the Pan Realtime command to make more room to the right of the existing views.

Pick: **Pan Realtime icon** (move the image until it is close to the left hand side of the viewport)
Right-click: **to pop up menu**
Pick: **Exit**

Tip

You can also use the hot grips to rotate. Use implied Crossing to select all the objects you want to rotate. Once you've selected them and you see all the blue hot grips, pick a base grip that will be the base point in the Rotate command. After selecting the base grip, you will see the Stretch command echoed in the command prompt area. Press the right mouse button to activate the pop-up menu and select Rotate. Follow the prompts that appear on your screen to rotate the objects in the side view 90 degrees.

Reorienting and Hatching the View

Now you have space to create section B–B to the right of the top view. You will use the Rotate icon from the Modify toolbar to reorient the side view so that you can align it with the top view, as shown in Figure 9.21.

On your own, verify that Snap is on.
Pick: **Rotate icon**
Select objects: **select all of the objects in the side view with implied Crossing**
Select objects: ↵
Specify base point: **pick the top left corner of the side view**
Specify rotation angle or [Copy/Reference] <0>: **90** ↵

Now you will align the rotated side view with the top view.

Pick: **Move icon**
Select objects: **P** (for previous selection set) ↵
Select objects: ↵
Specify base point or [Displacement] <Displacement>: **pick the upper left corner of the rotated object**
Specify second point or <use first point as displacement>: **pick a point on the snap that lines up with the top line in the top view**

Your drawing should now look like that in Figure 9.21.

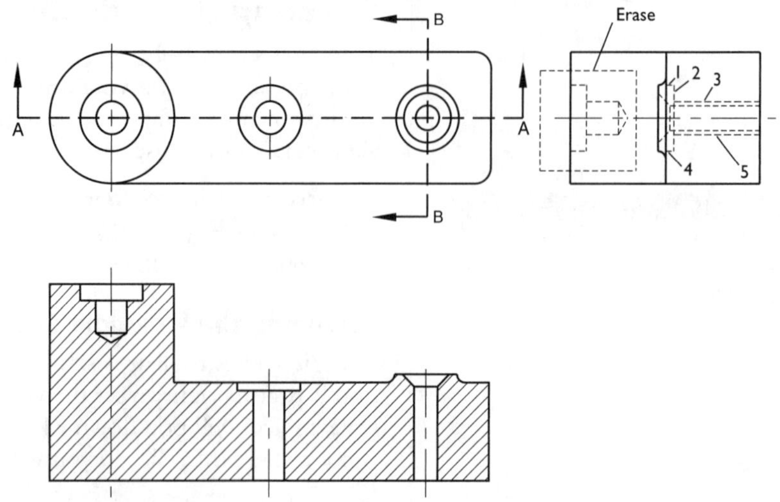

Figure 9.21

On your own, turn Snap off.

Use the **Erase** command to remove the unnecessary hidden lines (those for the counterbored hole and lines 1 through 5) from the rotated object.

Change the hidden lines for the countersunk hole in the rotated side view to layer VISIBLE.

Tip

You may need to use Zoom Window to enlarge the area on the screen. When you are finished erasing and changing the lines, use Zoom Previous to return the area to its original size.

The countersunk hole is the only one that will show in the section view. Refer to Figure 9.21 to help you make the selections.

Your screen should be similar to Figure 9.22 when you are finished.

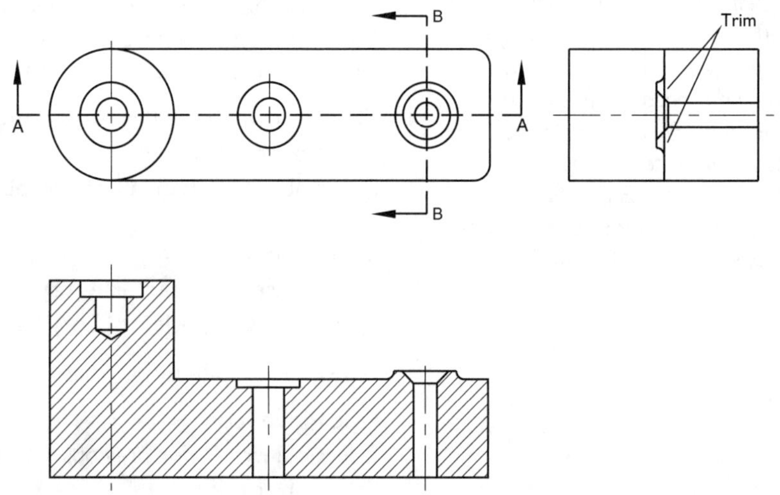

Figure 9.22

Next, use the **Trim** command on your own to remove the visible line that crosses the outer edge of the boss, as shown in Figure 9.22.

When you are finished trimming, your drawing should look like Figure 9.23.

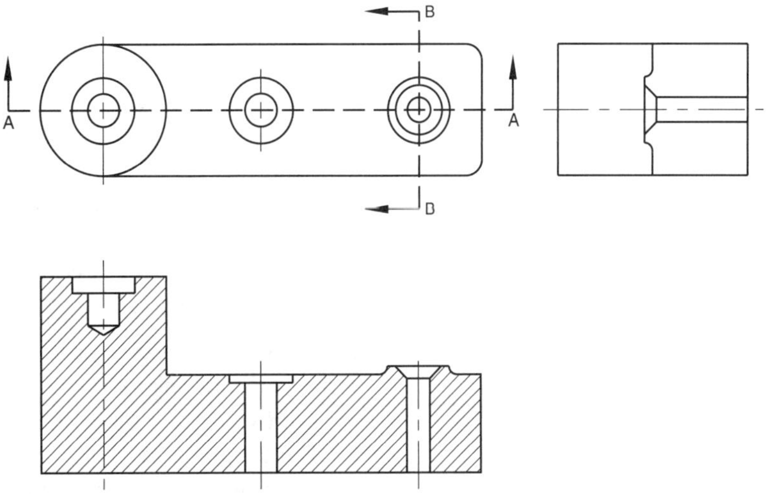

Figure 9.23

Now you are ready to add the hatching.

Pick: **Hatch icon**
Be sure the hatch pattern **ANSI31** is selected as the current pattern.
Pick: **Pick Points**
Select inside the areas you want to have hatched and press ↵.

You return to the Hatch and Gradient dialog box. To preview the hatching,

Pick: **Preview** button

If the hatching appears the way you want it to,

Pick or press Esc to return to dialog or <Right-click to accept hatch>: ↵

The hatching in your drawing should look like that in Figure 9.24.

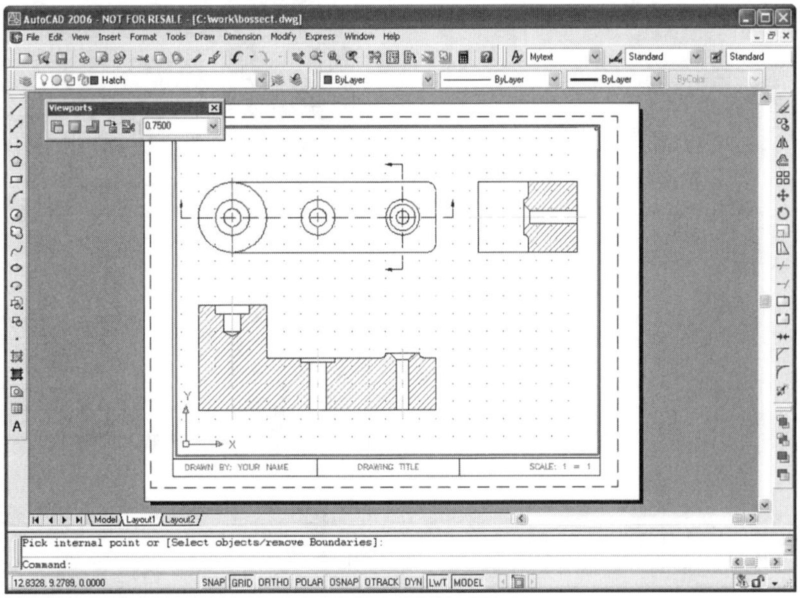

Figure 9.24

Tip

Although you won't always be instructed to do so, remember to save your work frequently while creating drawings. The AutoCAD autosave feature saves automatically to a file named auto.sv$. You set the time interval for the autosave feature with the system variable Savetime. The default is to save every 120 minutes. You would not want to lose two hours of work, so you should set Savetime to save automatically at shorter intervals. To make such a change, type SAVETIME at the command prompt and enter the new number in minutes. However, do not rely on automatic saves. Save your file whenever you have made a major change that you want to keep or about every 10 minutes otherwise.

Plot your drawing on your own. Before you plot, be sure to switch to paper space. If you need help plotting, refer to Tutorials 3 and 5.

Solid Fill

Sometimes you may want areas of the drawing to be filled in with a solid color instead of a hatch pattern. The Hatch command also allows you to make solidly filled areas. Use solid fill sparingly in your drawings because it is time consuming to plot, and some printers and plotters are not capable of showing it correctly. You will use solid fill inside a rectangle on layer DIM.

Turn off the Viewports toolbar.

Return your drawing to Model space if it is not selected.

Pick: **DIM** to make it the current layer using the Layer Control

Pick: **Rectangle icon**

Draw a small rectangle overlapping the lower right of the front section view.

Pick: **Hatch icon**

The Hatch and Gradient dialog box appears.

Pick: **Solid** (from the top of the Pattern pull-down list)

Pick: **Add Select objects**

Select objects or [picK internal point/remove Boundaries]: **pick the new rectangle** ↵

Pick: **Preview**

The rectangle is filled with a solid color, similar to Figure 9.25. The rectangle is on layer DIM, so it is blue.

Pick: Esc to return to the dialog box

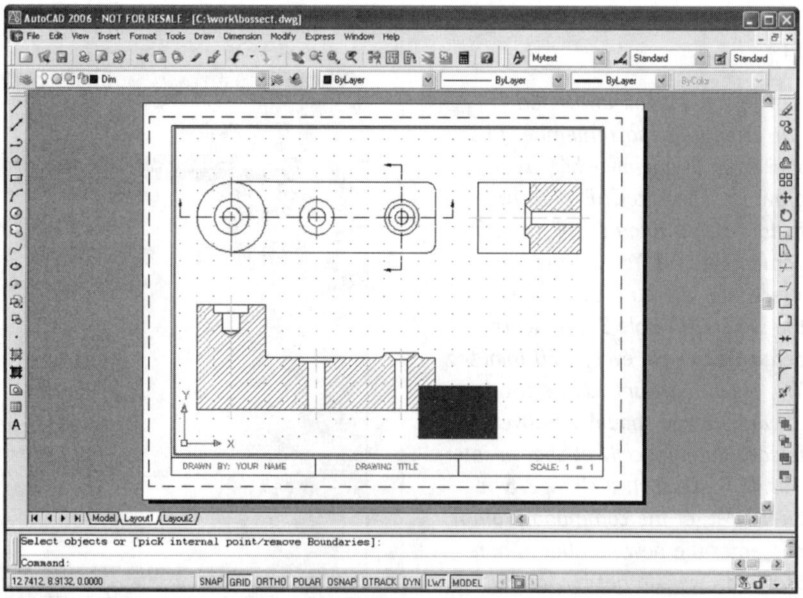

Figure 9.25

Tip

You can use the Draworder command from the Modify II toolbar, or by picking Tools, Display Order from the menu bar to change the draw order for objects that overlay.

Tip

To select hatches and solid fills, pick on their edges, not in the middle of the area.

Using Draworder with Hatch

The Draworder option can be used to specify which object is on top when two or more objects overlay one another.

Pick: **to pull down the Draw order selections** as shown in Figure 9.26
Pick: **Send to back**
Pick: **Preview**

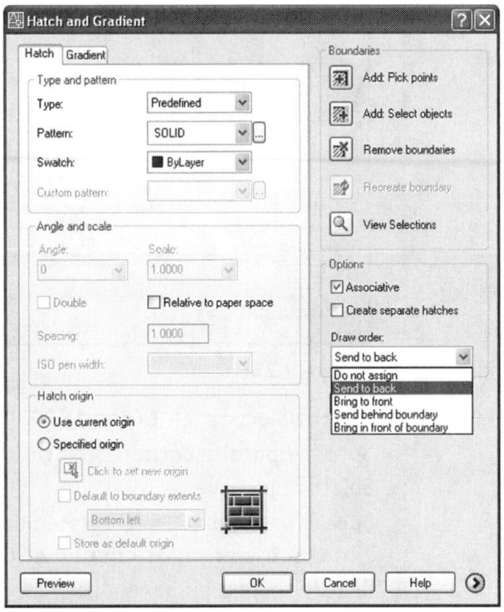

Figure 9.26

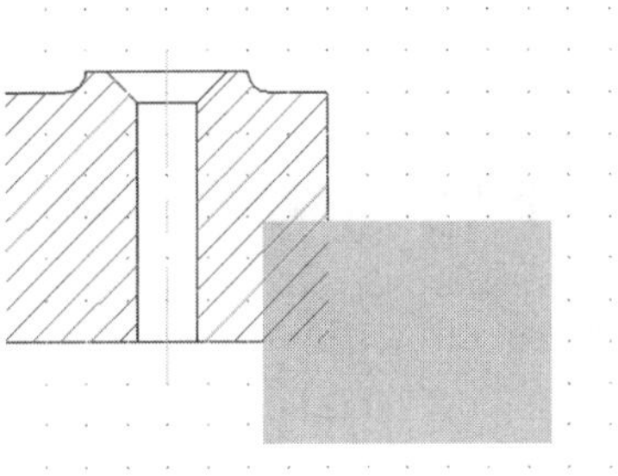

Figure 9.27

The section hatch should now be drawn over the solid blue hatch color as in Figure 9.27. Use Zoom Window for a closer view if needed.

Press: [Esc] to return to the dialog box
On your own, practice with the other draworder options: Send to Back, Bring to Front, etc.
Pick: **OK** to exit the dialog box
When you are done, restore the previous Zoom.
Erase the rectangle and solid hatch.
Change the current layer back to HATCH.

Changing Associative Hatches

The hatching created with the Hatch command is associative. In other words, it automatically updates so that it continues to fill the boundary when you edit the boundary by stretching, moving, rotating, arraying, scaling, or mirroring. You can also use grips to modify hatching that you've inserted into the drawing.

Next, you will stretch the top and front views of the drawing; the hatching will automatically update to fill the new boundary. Refer to Figure 9.28 for the points to select to create a crossing box.

Be sure that you are in model space and that Snap is turned on.
Pick: **Stretch icon**
Select objects to stretch by crossing-window or crossing-polygon…

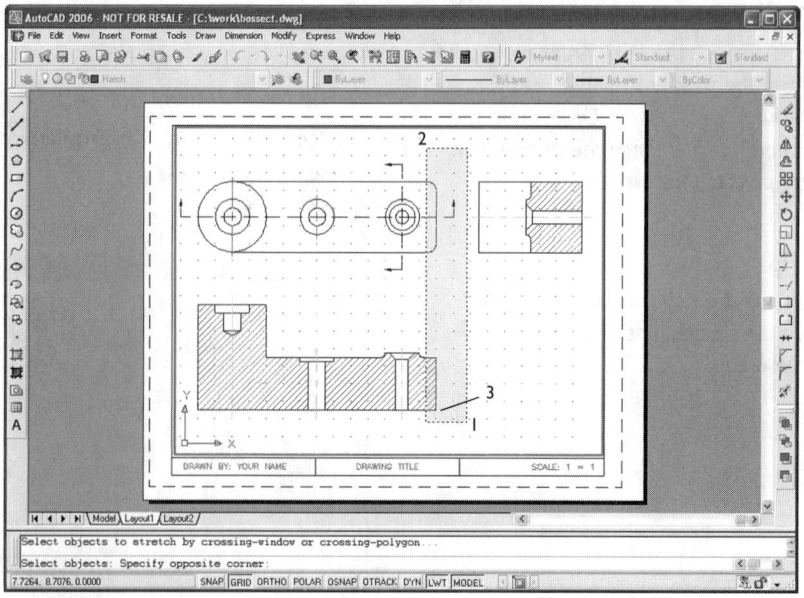

Figure 9.28

Select objects: **pick point 1**
Specify opposite corner: **pick point 2**
Select objects: ↵
Specify base point or [Displacement] <Displacement>: **use Snap to pick the lower right corner of the front view (point 3)**
Specify second point or <use first point as displacement>: **turn Snap off and pick to the right of the previous location**

The front and top views of the drawing are stretched to the right. Your screen should be similar to Figure 9.29.

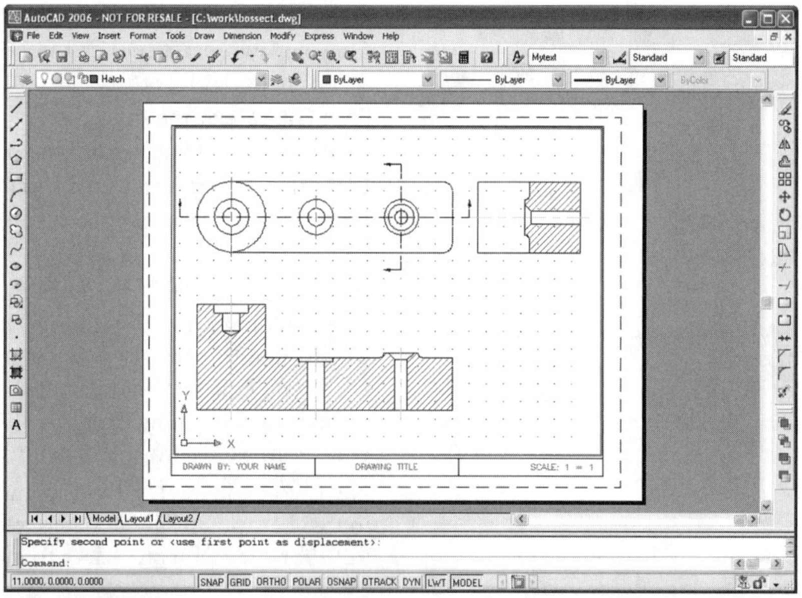

Figure 9.29

The objects selected by the crossing box are stretched, as shown in Figure 9.29. The hatching updates to fill the new boundary. You will now use the Hatchedit command to change the angle of the hatching. Because the angled edge of the countersunk hole is drawn at 45°, you will change the angle of the hatch pattern so that the hatch is not parallel to features in the drawing. (Having the hatch run parallel or perpendicular to a major drawing feature is not good engineering drawing practice.) You will turn on the Modify II toolbar and use it to select the Hatchedit command. You can also select Modify, Hatch from the menu bar to activate the command.

Figure 9.30

Right-click on any toolbar.
Pick: **Modify II from the list**

Figure 9.30 shows the Modify II toolbar with the Edit Hatch icon.

Pick: **Edit Hatch icon**
Select hatch object: **pick the hatching in the front view**

The Hatch Edit dialog box similar to Figure 9.31 appears on your screen. Its appearance is identical to the Hatch and Gradient dialog box. You can use this dialog box to edit hatching already added to your drawing.

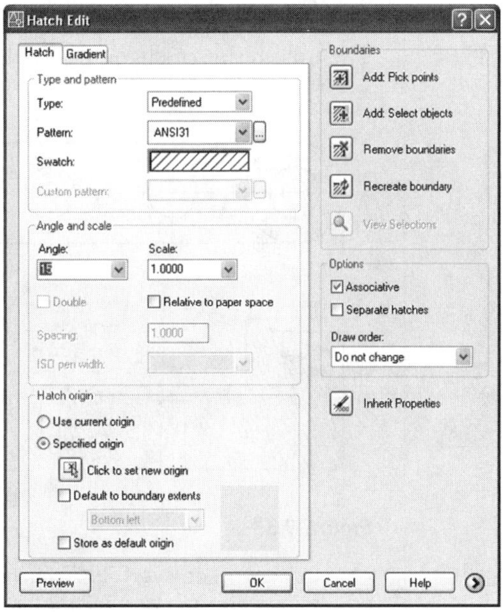

Figure 9.31

Type: **15** (for the Angle)
Pick: **OK**

The hatching updates so that it is angled an additional 15 degrees, as shown in Figure 9.32.

Tip

You can double-click on an existing hatch to edit it quickly.

Tip

You can create open, irregular hatch boundaries by typing the -Hatch command at the command prompt and selecting the W for the draW option. Irregular hatch boundaries are useful for hatching large areas where you do not want to fill the entire area—for example, to represent earth around a foundation on an architectural drawing, or in mechanical drawings to hatch only the perimeter of a large shape instead of filling in the entire area.

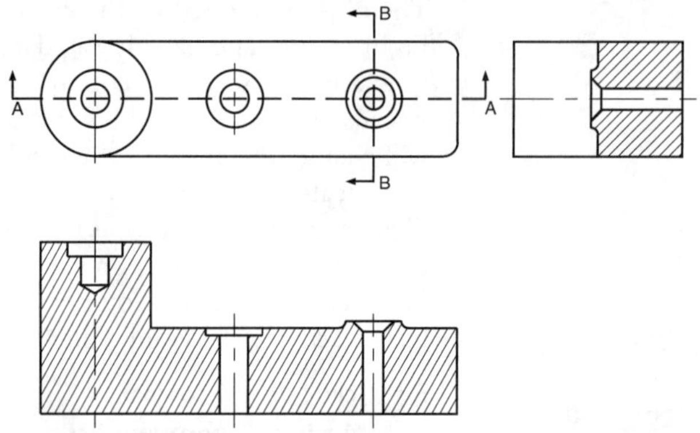

Figure 9.32

You will restart the Edit Hatch command by pressing ↵ at the command prompt.

Command: ↵
Select hatch object: **pick the hatching in the side view**

Again the Hatch Edit dialog box returns to your screen.

Type: **15** (for the Angle entry)
Pick: **OK**

The final result of changing the hatch angles is shown in Figure 9.33.

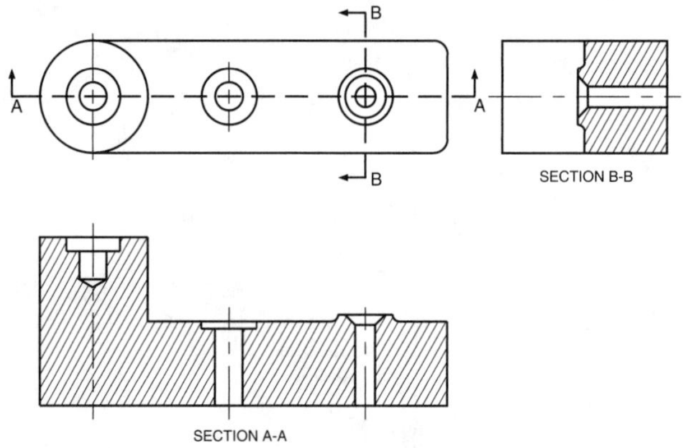

Figure 9.33

On your own, set layer TEXT current.
Use **Dtext** to label the section views SECTION A–A and SECTION B–B.
Place the text directly below the section views, as shown in Figure 9.33.
Turn off the **Modify II** toolbar.
Save and close your *bossect.dwg* drawing.

You have completed the section view portion of this tutorial. Next, you will learn how to create auxiliary views.

Auxiliary Views

An *auxiliary view* is an orthographic view of the object that has a line of sight different from the six *basic views* (front, top, right-side, rear, bottom, and left-side). Auxiliary views are most commonly used to show the true size of a slanted or oblique surface. Slanted and oblique surfaces are *foreshortened* in the basic views because they are tipped away from the viewing plane, causing their projected size in the view to be smaller than their actual size. An auxiliary view is drawn with its line of sight perpendicular to the surface, showing the true size and shape of a slanted or oblique surface.

You will learn to create auxiliary views first using 2D methods. You can project 2D auxiliary views from the basic orthographic views by rotating the snap or by aligning a new User Coordinate System.

Figure 9.34 shows three views of an object and an auxiliary view.

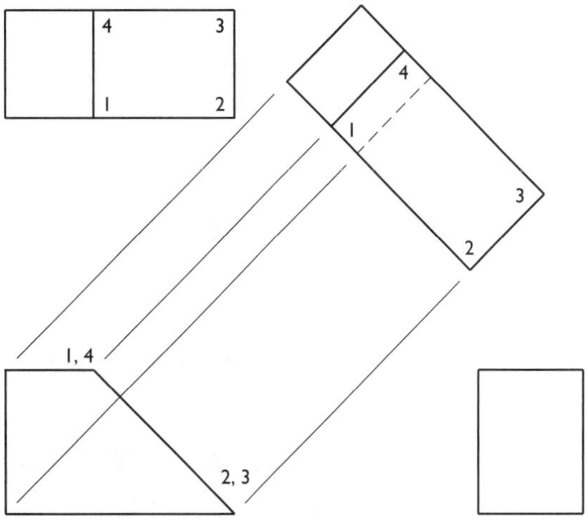

Figure 9.34

The surface defined by vertices 1–2–3–4 is inclined. It is perpendicular to the front viewing plane and shows on edge in the front view. Both the top and side views show foreshortened views of the surface; that is, neither shows the true shape and size of that surface of the object.

To project an auxiliary view showing the true size of surface 1–2–3–4, you create a new view by drawing projection lines perpendicular to the edge view of the surface, in this case the angled line in the front view. You transfer the width of the surface, measured from a *reference surface*, to the auxiliary view to complete the projection. Note that, as with the front, top, and side views, the auxiliary view shows the entire object as viewed from the line of sight perpendicular to that surface, causing the base of the object to show as a hidden line.

Drawing Auxiliary Views Using 2D

Open the drawing ***adapt4.dwg***, provided with the data files.

Save your drawing as ***auxil1.dwg***.

The AutoCAD drawing editor shows the drawing of the orthographic views for the adapter on your screen, similar to Figure 9.35.

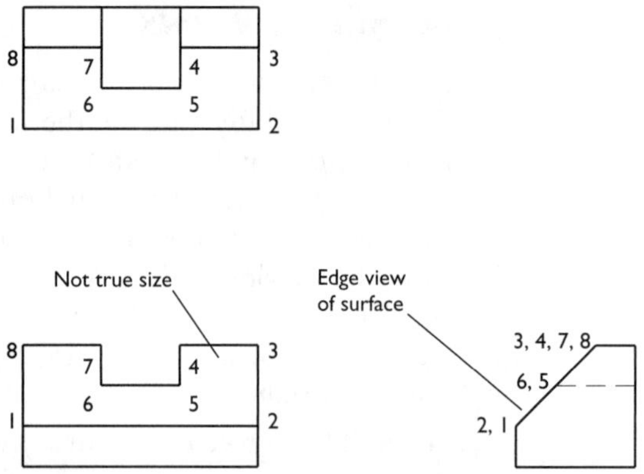

Figure 9.35

You will create an auxiliary view showing the true size of the inclined surface. The surface is labeled 1–2–3–4–5–6–7–8 in Figure 9.35.

You can create the auxiliary view by using information from any two of the views shown, as any two views with a 90-degree relationship provide all the principal dimensions. For this tutorial, you will erase the top view and use the front and side views to project the auxiliary view.

Pick: **Erase icon**

Select objects: **use implied Windowing to select the top view**

Select objects: ↵

Use Redraw as necessary.

Your drawing will look like Figure 9.36 after you have erased the top view.

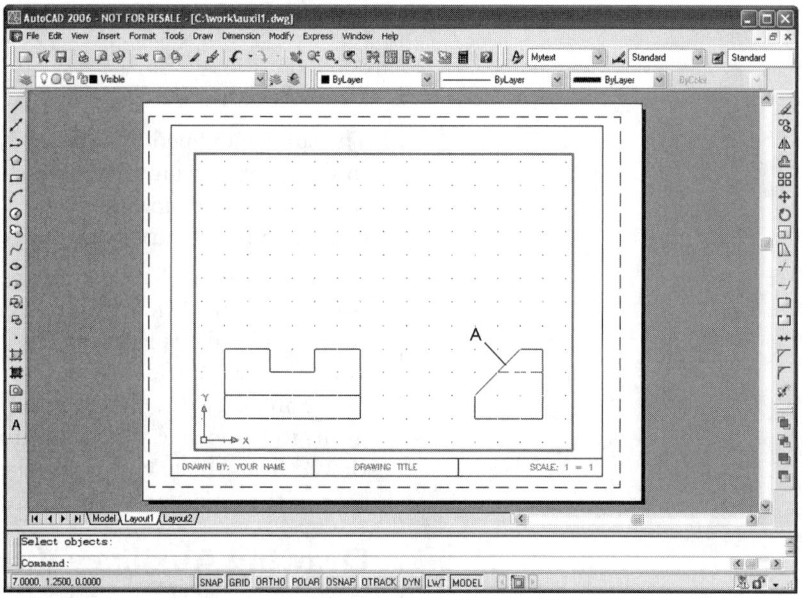

Figure 9.36

Next, you will draw projection lines perpendicular to surface 1–2–3–4–5–6–7–8 in the side view. You will create a new UCS and align it with the edge view to help you project these lines easily.

Aligning the UCS with the Angled Surface

You will set the UCS so that it is aligned with the angled surface. You will use the Object option to do so. The Object option prompts you for the existing drawing object with which you want to align the UCS. You will align the UCS with the angled line in the side view. You will pick the Object UCS icon from the Tools pull-down menu.

Pick: **Model tab** to show only model space
Pick to **turn off LWT button** on the status bar (if it is on).
Pick: **Tools, New UCS, Object**
Select object to align UCS: **pick the angled line in the side view,** identified as A in Figure 9.36

When you have finished aligning the UCS, your screen should look like Figure 9.37. Note that the crosshairs and grid, as well as the UCS icon, now align with the angled surface.

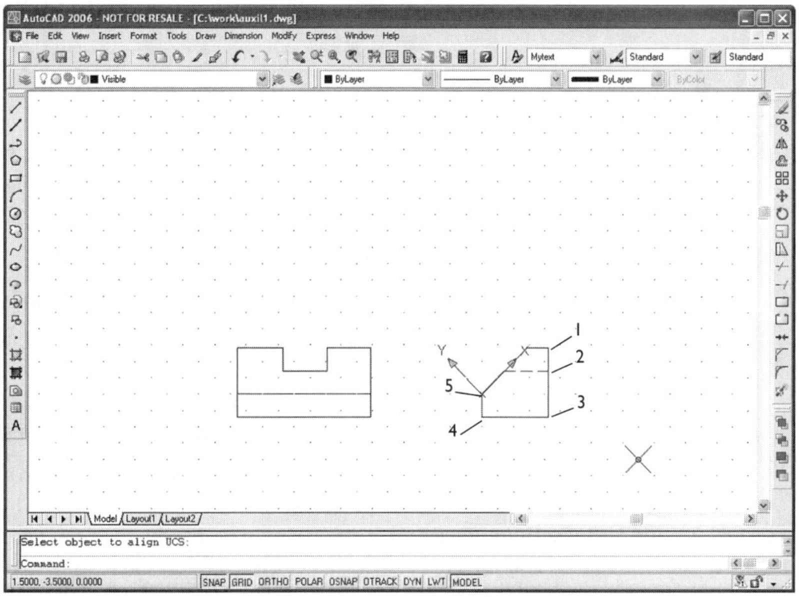

Figure 9.37

Pick: **PROJECTION** as the current layer using the Layer Control
Turn OSNAP on with the **Intersection** mode selected.
Turn **Ortho** on.
Make sure that Snap is off.

Now you will draw rays from each intersection of the object in the side view into the open area of the drawing above the front view. You will pick Ray from the Draw menu; if you need help creating rays, refer to Tutorial 4.

Pick: **Draw, Ray**
Specify start point: **pick intersection 1 in Figure 9.38**
Specify through point: **with Ortho on, pick a point above and to the left of the side view**
Specify through point: ↵

Restart the Ray command and **draw projection lines from points 2 through 5 in the right-side view.**

Pick: **Line icon**

On your own, use Snap and **draw a reference line perpendicular to the projection lines.**

The location of this line can be anywhere along the projection lines, but it should extend about 0.5 unit beyond the top and bottom projection lines.

Your drawing should look like that in Figure 9.38.

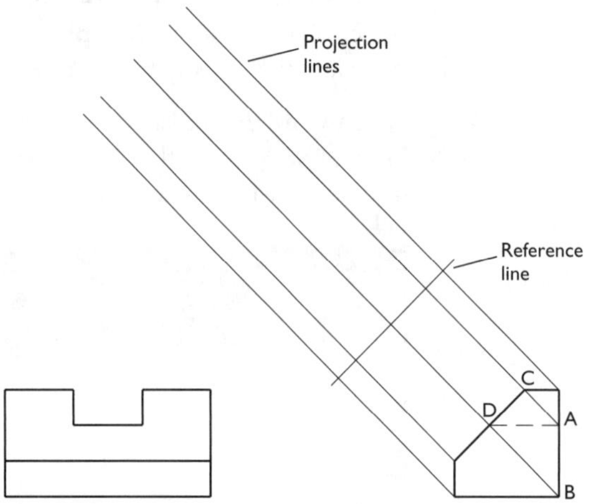

Figure 9.38

Note that the back edge of the slot (labeled A) and the lower right corner (labeled B) in the side view align with the projection lines through the corners of the angled surface (labeled C and D) to produce a single projection line. If points C and D did not align on the projection lines that you created, you would need to project them.

Tip

If you did not know the dimensions, you could use the Distance command (available from the Tools menu under Inquiry) with the Intersection object snap in the front view to determine the distance.

The width of the object is known to be 3. Next, you will use the Offset command to draw a line 3 units from and parallel to the reference line.

Pick: **Offset icon**

Specify offset distance or [Through/Erase/Layer] <Through>: **3** ↵

Select object to offset or [Exit/Undo] <Exit>: **pick the reference line**, as shown in Figure 9.38.

Specify point on side to offset or [Exit/Multiple/Undo] <Exit>: **pick a point anywhere to the left of the reference line**

Select object to offset or [Exit/Undo] <Exit>: ↵

Your drawing should look like the one in Figure 9.39.

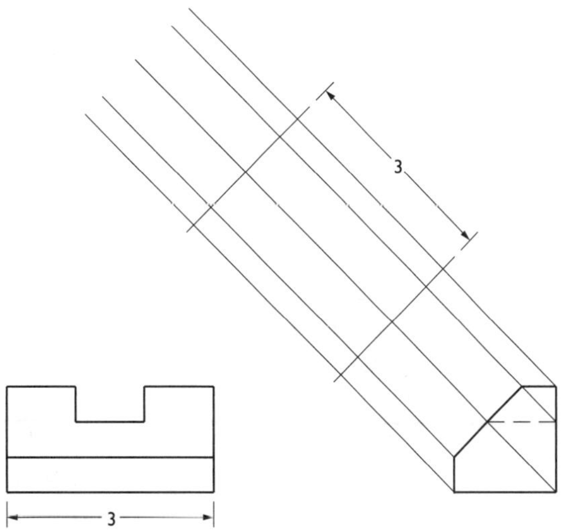

Figure 9.39

Add the width of the slot on your own by using Offset to create two more parallel lines, 1 unit apart.

Your drawing should look like that in Figure 9.40.

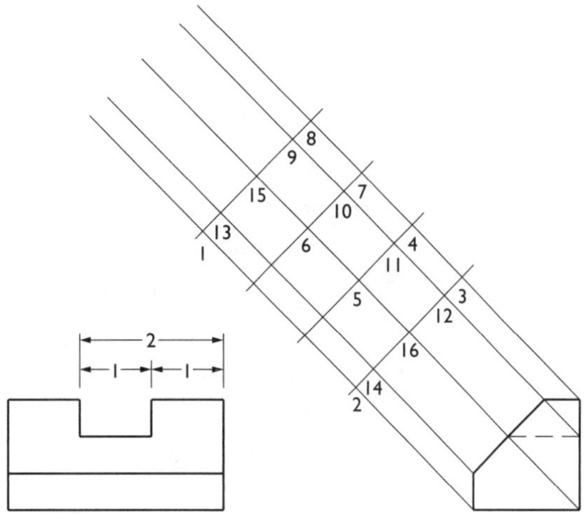

Figure 9.40

Next, you will draw the visible lines in the drawing over the top of the projection lines. Be sure to draw the correct shape of the object as it will appear in the auxiliary view. Refer to Figure 9.40 for your selections.

Pick: **VISIBLE** as the current layer using the Layer Control

Use AutoSnap™ **Intersection** when selecting points in the following steps.

Pick: **Line icon**

Specify first point: **pick the intersection of the projection lines at point 1**

Specify next point or [Undo]: **pick point 2**

Specify next point or [Close/Undo]: **pick point 3**

Specify next point or [Close/Undo]: **pick point 4**

Specify next point or [Close/Undo]: **pick point 5**

Specify next point or [Close/Undo]: **pick point 6**

Specify next point or [Close/Undo]: **pick point 7**
Specify next point or [Close/Undo]: **pick point 8**
Specify next point or [Close/Undo]: **C** ↵

Now you will restart the Line command and draw the short line segments where the two short top surfaces of the object intersect the slanted front surface:

Command: ↵
Specify first point: **pick point 9**
Specify next point or [Undo]: **pick point 10**
Specify next point or [Undo]: ↵
Command: ↵
Specify first point: **pick point 11**
Specify next point or [Undo]: **pick point 12**
Specify next point or [Undo]: ↵

Next, you will draw the line representing the back edge of the slot in the auxiliary view.

Command: ↵
Specify first point: **pick point 10**
Specify next point or [Undo]: **pick point 11**
Specify next point or [Undo]: ↵

Now you will add the line showing the intersection of the vertical front surface with the angled surface.

Command: ↵
Specify first point: **pick point 13**
Specify next point or [Undo]: **pick point 14**
Specify next point or [Undo]: ↵

Next you will set layer HIDDEN_LINES current and then draw the lines for the bottom and back surfaces that are hidden from that direction of sight.

Pick: **HIDDEN_LINES** as the current layer using the Layer Control
Command: **L** ↵
Specify first point: **pick point 15**
Specify next point or [Undo]: **pick point 16**
Specify next point or [Undo]: ↵

Next you will freeze the PROJECTION layer so that those lines do not appear.

Pick: **Freeze/Thaw icon for PROJECTION layer** (so that it looks like a snowflake)
Pick: **Trim icon**
On your own, trim the portion of the hidden line that coincides with the visible line from point 5 to point 6.

When you have finished, your screen should look like Figure 9.41.

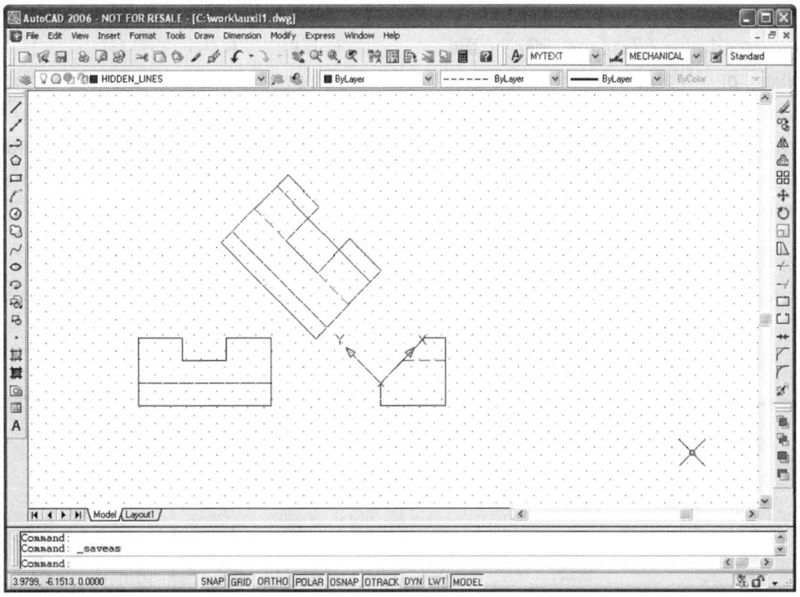

Figure 9.41

Adding Visual Reference Lines

Next, you will add two visual *reference lines* to your drawing from the extreme outside edges of the surface shown true size in the auxiliary view to the inclined surface in the side view. The lines will provide a visual reference for the angles in your drawing and help show how the auxiliary view aligns with the standard views. You can extend a centerline from the primary view to the auxiliary view or use one or two projection lines for the reference lines. In this case, as there are no centerlines, you will create two reference lines. Leave a gap of about 1/16" between the reference lines and the views.

Pick: **Freeze/Thaw icon for PROJECTION layer** (so that it looks like a sun)

Pick: **the two rays that project from the ends of the angled surface so that their grips appear**

Pick: **to pull-down the Layer Control list**

Pick: **THIN** layer, so that the selected lines change to that layer

Refer to Figure 9.42 if you are unsure which lines to select.

The rays should change to layer THIN. You can verify this result visually because the lines will turn red, the color for layer THIN.

Linetype Conventions

Two lines of different linetypes should not meet to make one line. You must always leave a small gap on the linetype that has lesser precedence. In the case of the visible and the reference lines, the reference line should have a small gap (about 1/16" on the plotted drawing) where it meets the visible line. In the case of the visible and the hidden lines, the hidden line should have a small gap (about 1/16" on the plotted drawing) where it meets the visible line. You can use the Break command to do this.

Tip

You could also offset the edge of the object by 1/16 in each view and use Trim to create the gap between the lines.

Pick: **to freeze layer PROJECTION**

Pick: **Break icon**

On your own, create a gap of about 1/16" between each view and the reference lines.

Create a similar gap where the hidden line extends from the visible line, forming the front of the slot in the auxiliary view.

Thaw layer PROJECTION and erase the extra portions of the rays where they extend past the side and auxiliary views.

Your drawing should look like the one in Figure 9.42.

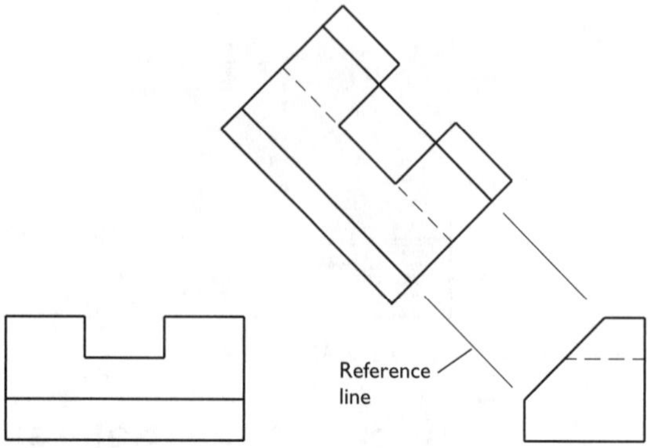

Figure 9.42

On your own, save and close your drawing.

Curved Surfaces

Now you will create an auxiliary view of the slanted surface in a cylinder drawing like the one you created at the end of Tutorial 6. The drawing has been provided for you as *cyl3.dwt* in the data files that came with this book.

On your own, begin a new drawing.

Use ***cyl3.dwt*** as a template.

Name your new drawing ***auxil3.dwg***.

You return to the AutoCAD drawing editor. Figure 9.43 shows the orthographic views of the cylinder with the slanted surface that should be on your screen.

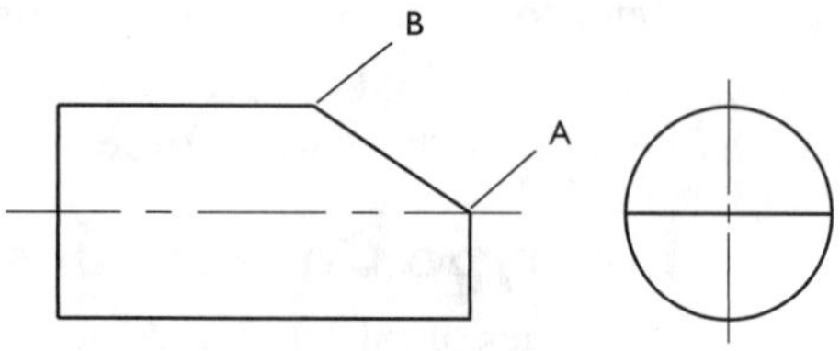

Figure 9.43

The drawing shows the front and side views of the slanted surface but not the true shape of the surface. You will draw a *partial auxiliary view* to show the true shape of the surface. Partial auxiliary views are often used because, in the auxiliary view, the inclined or oblique surface chosen is shown true size and shape, but the other surfaces are all foreshortened.

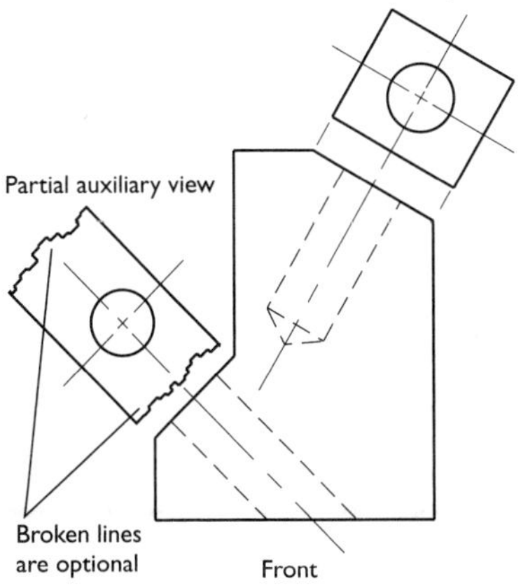

Figure 9.44

As these other surfaces have already been defined in the basic orthographic views, there is no need to show them in the auxiliary view. A partial auxiliary view shows only the inclined surfaces (leaving out the normal surfaces), thus saving time in projecting the view and giving a clearer appearance to your drawing.

Figure 9.44 shows a front view of an object, along with two partial auxiliary views.

Rotating the Snap

This time you will use the Rotate option of the Snap command to rotate the grid and snap so that they align with the inclined surface. Doing so lets you easily project the curved surface to the auxiliary view that you will create.

Turn running OSNAP Intersection on.
Make sure the grid is on.
Turn Ortho off.
Make sure that PROJECTION is the current layer.

Now you will rotate the snap angle with the Snap command. You will pick two points (A and B) in Figure 9.43 to define the angle.

Command: **SNAP** ↵
Specify snap spacing or [ON/OFF/Aspect/Rotate/Style/Type] <0.2500>: **R** ↵
Specify base point <0.0000,0.0000>: **pick the intersection labeled A**
Specify rotation angle <0>: **pick the intersection labeled B**

The message, Angle adjusted to 326, will appear. Your screen should be similar to Figure 9.45. Note that the crosshairs and grid have aligned with the inclined surface, but the UCS icon remains as it was previously, aligned with the World Coordinates.

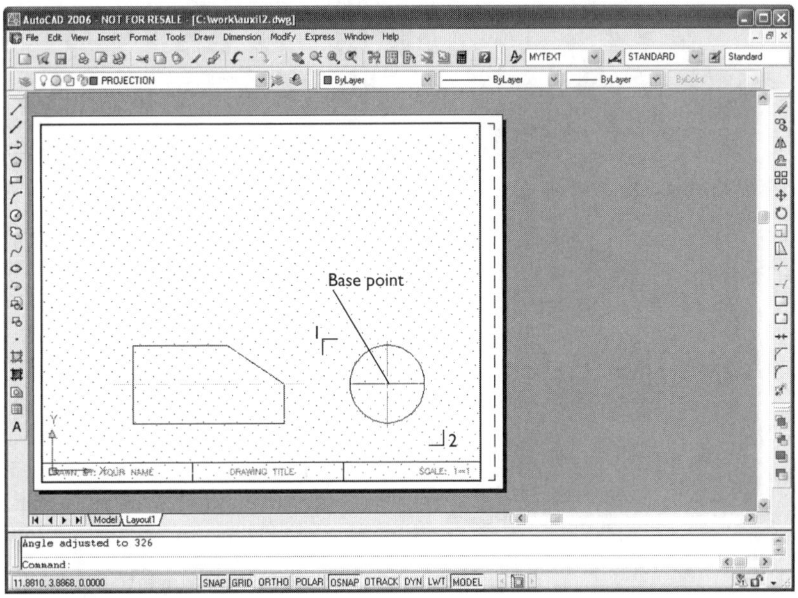

Figure 9.45

Next, you will copy the object in the side view and rotate it so that it aligns with the rotated grid and snap. Doing so makes projecting the depth of the object from the side view into the auxiliary view easy. Then you do not have to use a reference surface to make depth measurements, as you did in the previous drawing. The shapes in this drawing are simple, but these methods will also work for much more complex shapes.

For the next steps you will use Ortho and Snap. Be sure that they are turned on. Refer to Figure 9.45 for the points to select.

Pick: **Copy Object icon**

Select objects: **pick corner 1**

Other corner: **pick corner 2 to form a window around the side view**

Select objects: ↵

Specify base point or [Displacement] <Displacement>: **pick the intersection labeled Base point**

Specify second point of displacement or <use first point as displacement>: **pick a point on the snap above and to the right of the side view**

Specify base point or displacement: ↵

A copy of the side view should appear on your screen, as shown in Figure 9.46.

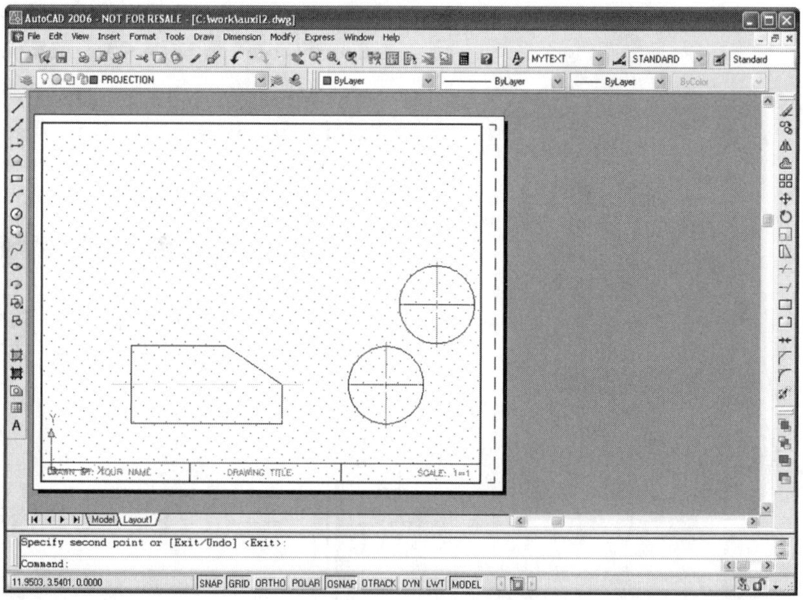

Figure 9.46

Now you will change the copy onto layer PROJECTION because it is part of the construction of the drawing, not something you will leave in the drawing when you are finished. You will freeze layer PROJECTION when you have finished the drawing.

On your own, change the copied objects to layer PROJECTION.

The objects that you selected are changed onto layer PROJECTION. Their color is now magenta, which is the color of layer PROJECTION.

Now you are ready to rotate the copied objects so that they align with the snap and can be used to project the auxiliary view. You will use the Rotate icon from the Modify toolbar.

Pick: **Rotate icon**

Select objects: **use Window or Crossing to select the copied objects**

Select objects: ↵

Specify base point: **pick the intersection of the centerlines of the copied objects**

Specify rotation angle or [Copy/Reference] <0>: **with Ortho turned on, select a point above and to the right of the base point you picked**, as shown in Figure 9.47.

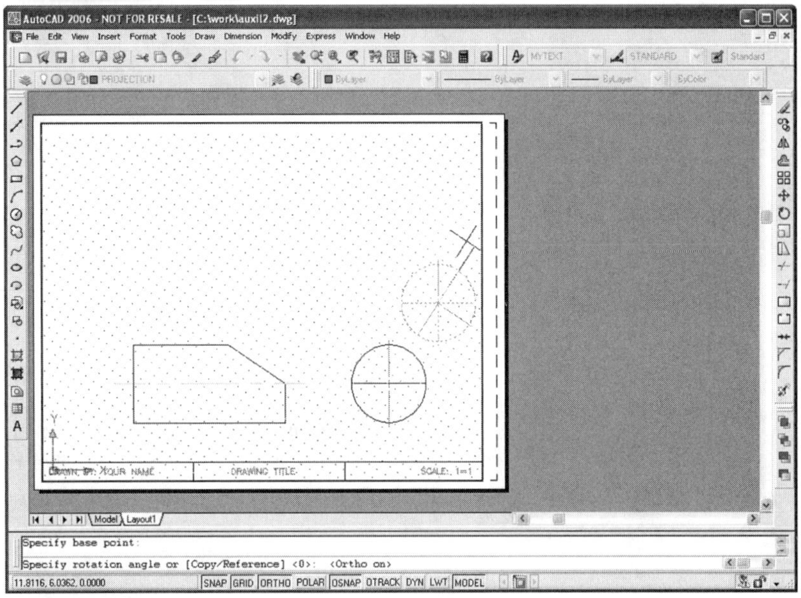

Figure 9.47

The objects that you copied previously should now be rotated into position so that they align with the snap and grid. Your drawing should look like that in Figure 9.48.

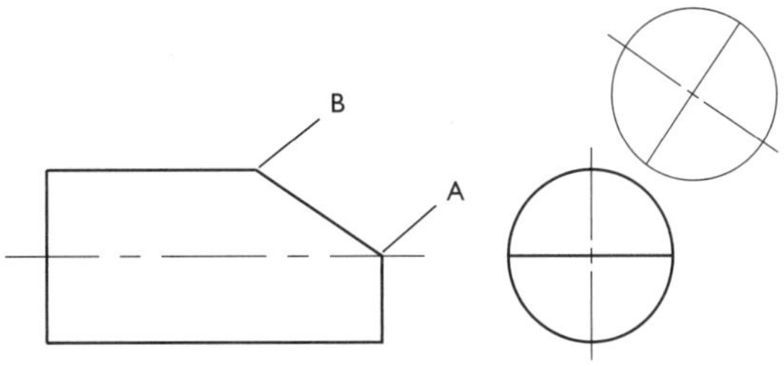

Figure 9.48

Next, you will draw projection lines from the front view to the empty area where the auxiliary view will be located. (Ortho and the Intersection running object snap should be on.) Refer to Figure 9.48 for the points to select.

Pick: **Draw, Ray**

Specify start point: **pick the intersection labeled A in Figure 9.48**

Specify through point: **pick a point above the front view, as in Figure 9.49**

Specify through point: ↵

Command: ↵ (to restart the Ray command)

Specify start point: **pick the intersection labeled B in Figure 9.48**

Specify through point: **pick a point above the front view**

Specify through point: ↵

Figure 9.49 shows an example of these lines.

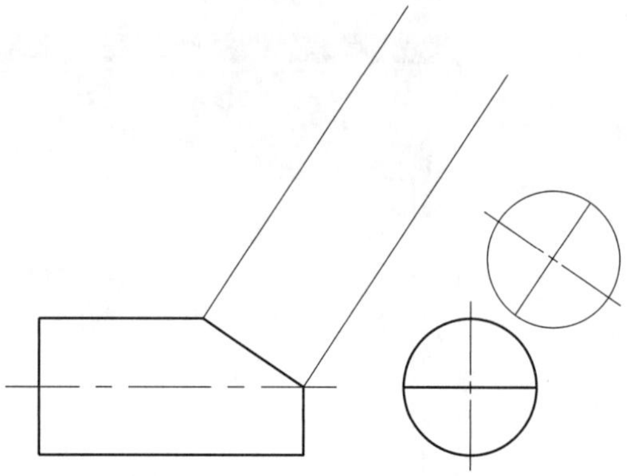

Figure 9.49

On your own, project rays from the intersections in the copied side view so that your drawing looks like the one in Figure 9.50.

Pick: **VISIBLE** as the current layer using the Layer Control

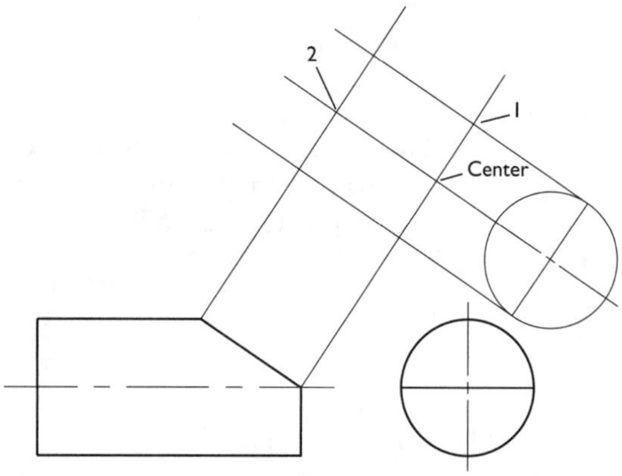

Figure 9.50

Drawing the Ellipse

Because the object appears as a circle in the side view and is tilted away in the front view, the true shape of the surface must be an ellipse. You will select the Ellipse icon from the Draw toolbar to create the elliptical surface in the auxiliary view. Refer to Figure 9.50 for your selections.

> **Tip**
>
> *If the surface in the side view were an irregular curve, you could project a number of points to the auxiliary view and then connect them with a polyline. After connecting them, you could connect them in a smooth curve, using the Fit Curve or Spline option of the Edit Polyline command. Although this method would also produce an ellipse, the Ellipse command is quicker.*

Pick: **Ellipse icon**

Specify axis endpoint of ellipse or [Arc/Center]: **C** ↵

Specify center of ellipse: **pick the intersection labeled Center**

Specify endpoint of axis: **pick intersection 1**

Specify distance to other axis distance or [Rotation]: **pick intersection 2**

The ellipse in your drawing should look like the one in Figure 9.51. You will need to trim the lower portion of it to create the final surface.

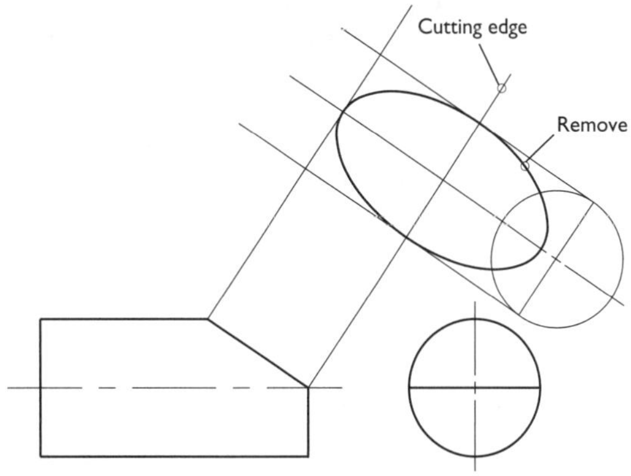

Figure 9.51

You will use the Trim command to eliminate the unnecessary portion of the ellipse in the auxiliary view.

Pick: **Trim icon**

Select cutting edges: **pick the cutting edge in Figure 9.51**

Select objects: ↵

Select object to trim or shift-select to extend or [Fence/Crossing/Project/Edge/eRase/Undo]: **pick on the ellipse to the right of the cutting edge**

Select object to trim or shift-select to extend or [Fence/Crossing/Project/Edge/eRase/Undo]: ↵

The lower portion of the ellipse is now trimmed off.

Change the two projection lines from the front view onto layer THIN on your own.

Use the Break command to break them so that they do not touch the views.

Draw in the final line across the bottom of the remaining portion of the ellipse on layer VISIBLE.

Freeze layer PROJECTION to remove the construction and projection lines from your display.

When you are finished, your screen should look like Figure 9.52.

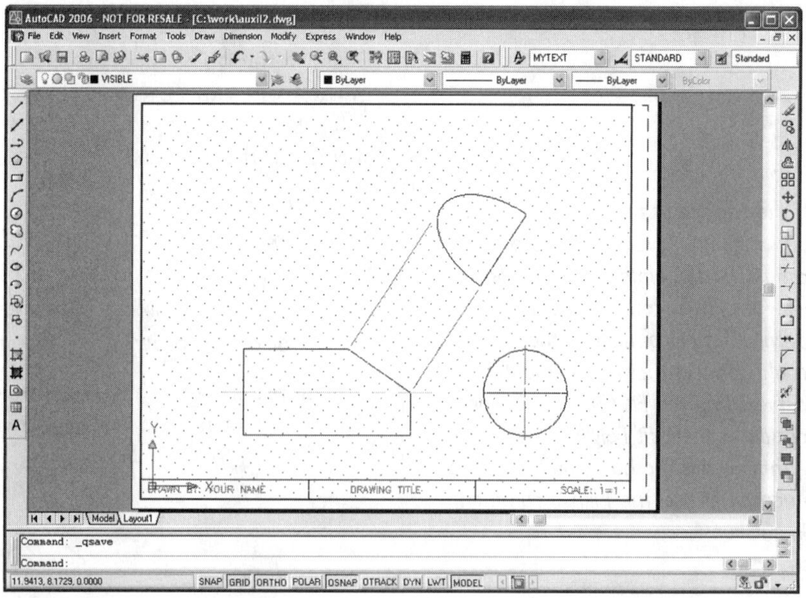

Figure 9.52

Save and close your drawing.

You have completed Tutorial 9.

Key Terms

associative hatching	custom hatch pattern	partial auxiliary view	runout
auxiliary view	cutting plane line	pictorial full section	section view
basic view	foreshortened	reference line	user-defined hatch pattern
crosshatching	gradient fill	reference surface	

Key Commands

Distance	Ellipse Center	Ray	UCS 3 Point
Edit Hatch	Hatch	Savetime	

Exercises

Redraw the given front view and replace the given right side view with a section view. Assume that the vertical centerline of the front view is the cutting plane line for the section view. The letter M after an exercise means that the given dimensions are in millimeters.

9.1 High-Pressure Seal

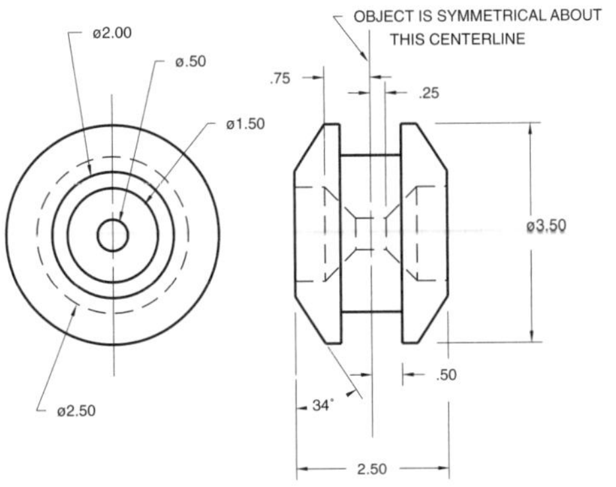

9.2 Valve Cover

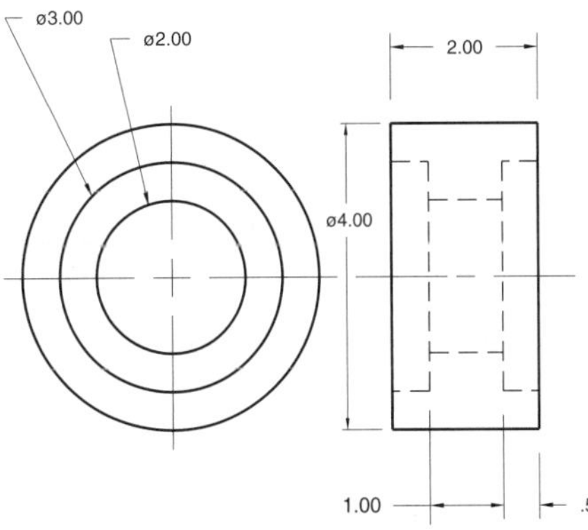

9.3M Pulley

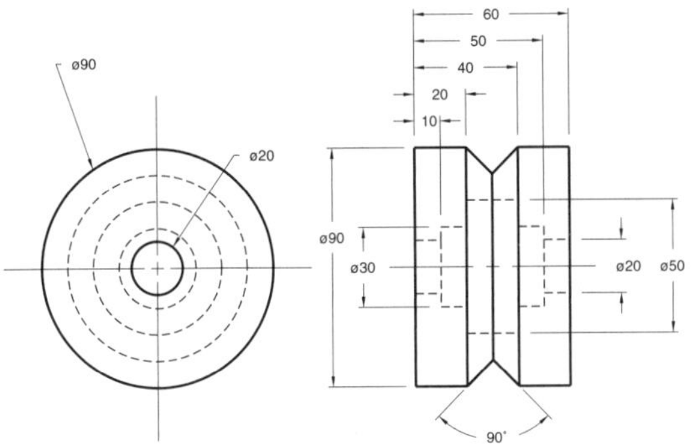

9.4 Control Bracket

Draw top and right orthographic views, a front section view, and a partial auxiliary view showing the true size of the angled feature. Add dimensions if so directed by your instructor.

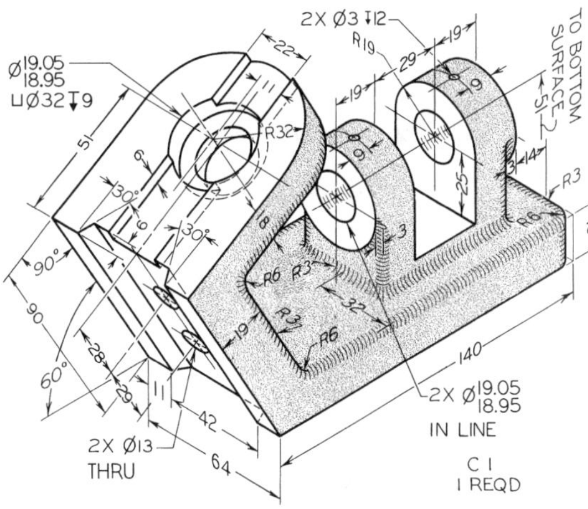

9.5 Double Cylinder

Use 2D techniques to draw this object; the grid shown is 0.25 inch. Show the front view as a half section and show the corresponding cutting plane in the top view. On the same views, completely dimension the object to the nearest 0.01 inch. Include any notes that are necessary.

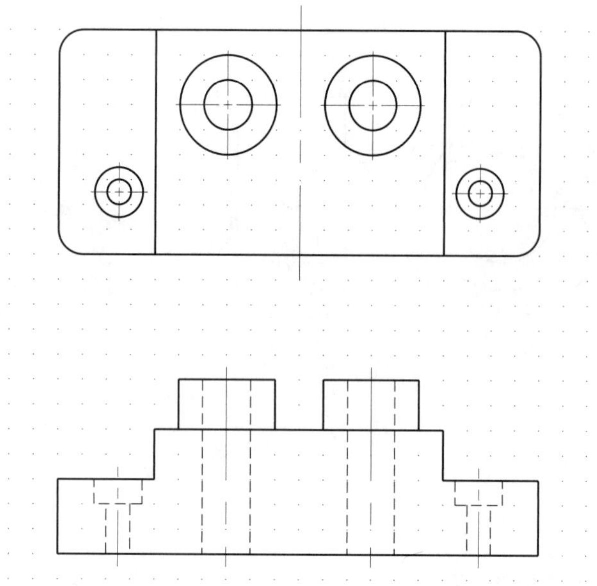

9.6 Manhole Junction

Draw standard orthographic views and show the front view in section. Wall thickness is 6 inches throughout. The 10-inch hole is through the entire manhole junction (exits opposite side).

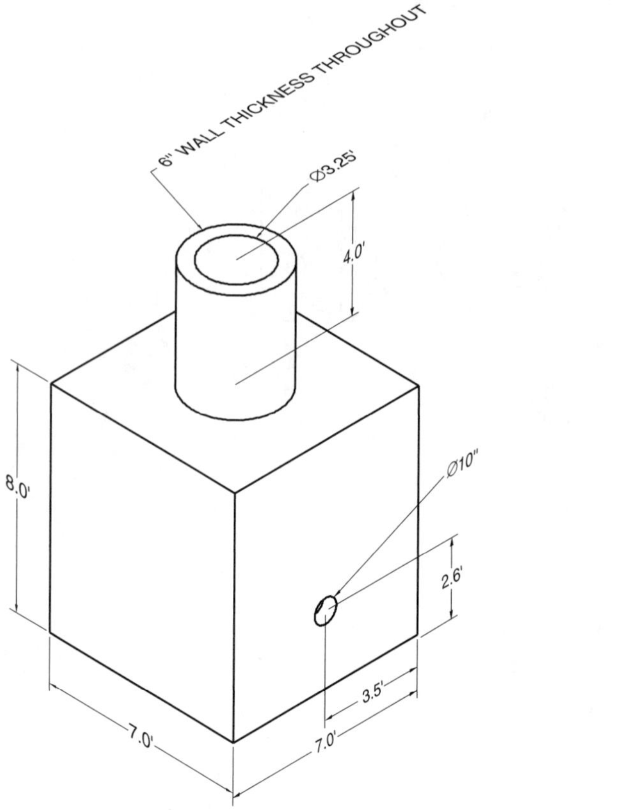

9.7 Plate

Use 2D to construct the top view with the cutting plane shown and show the front view in section.

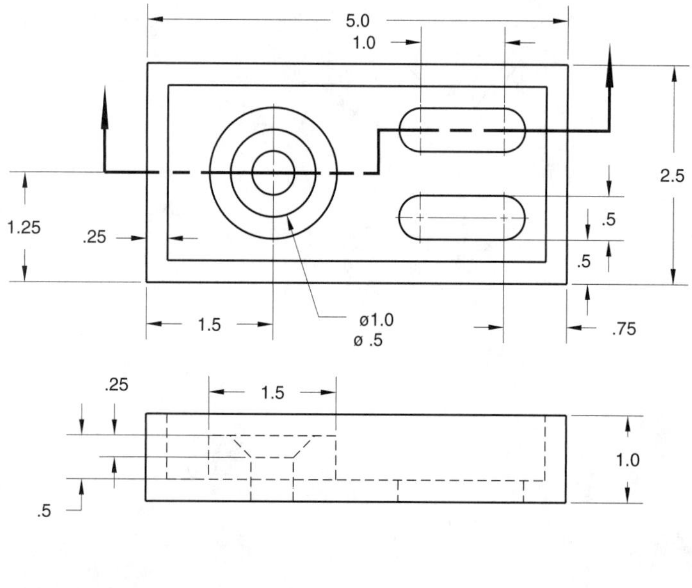

9.8 Support Bracket

Create a drawing of the object shown with a plan view and full section front view. Note the alternate units in brackets; these are the dimensions in millimeters for the part.

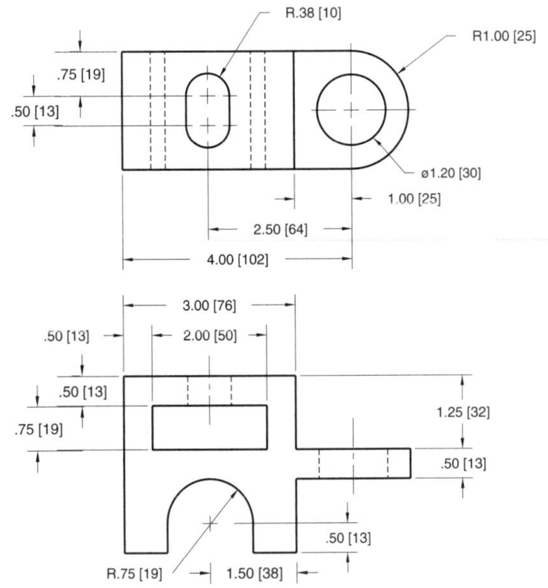

9.9 Shaft Support

Redraw the given front view and create a section view. Assume that the vertical centerline of the shaft in the front view is the cutting plane line for the section view.

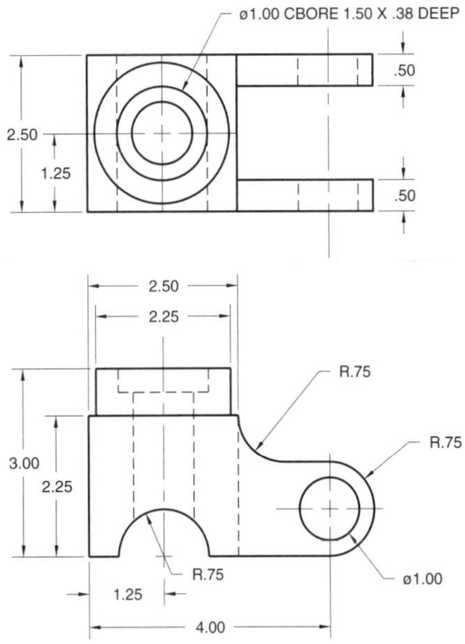

9.10 Turned Down Slab Detail

Use 2D methods to create the drawing shown. Use Boundary Hatch to fill the area with the pattern for concrete. Type the Hatch command and create the irregular areas to fill with patterns for sand and earth.

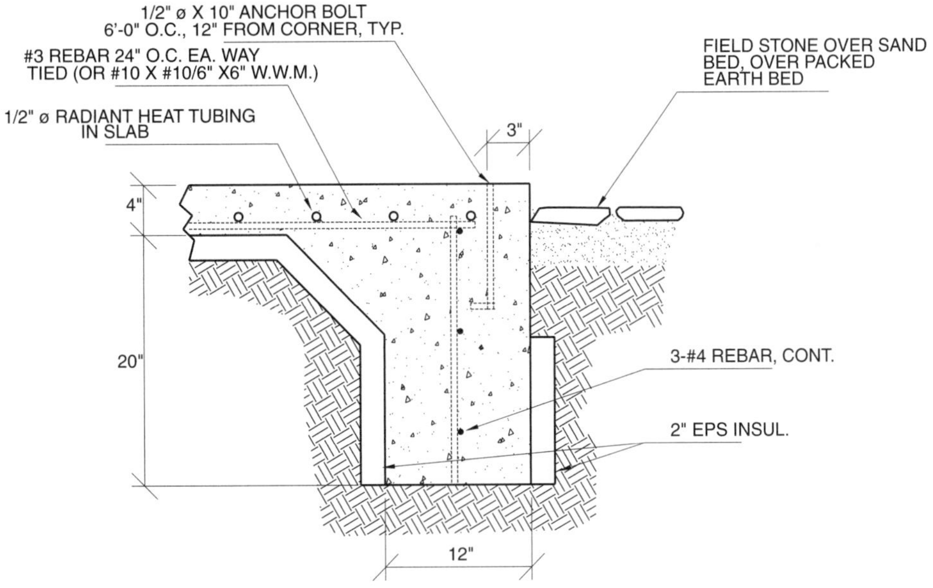

Use the 2D techniques you have learned in the tutorial to create an auxiliary view of the slanted surfaces for the objects below. The letter M after an exercise number means that the given dimensions are in millimeters.

9.11 Stop Block

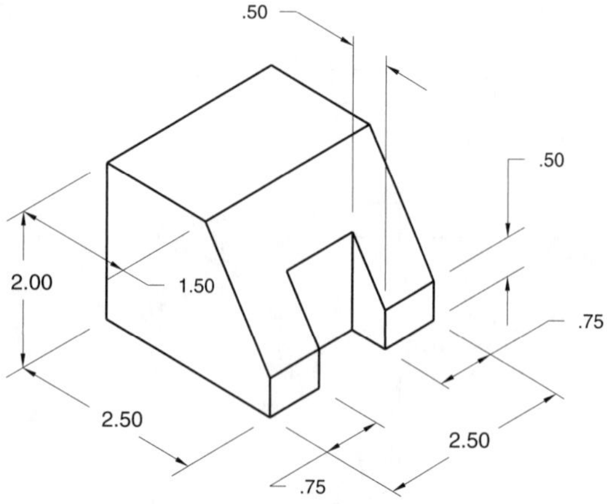

9.12 Bearing

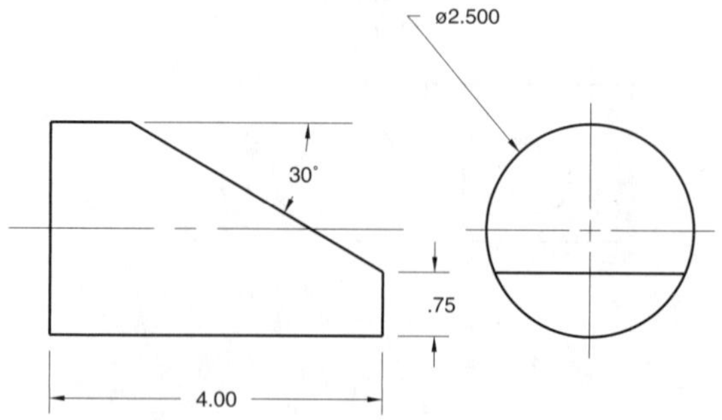

9.13 Tooling Support

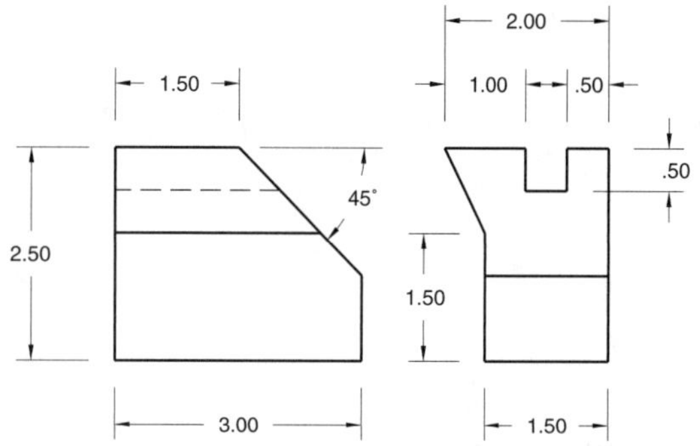

9.14M Level

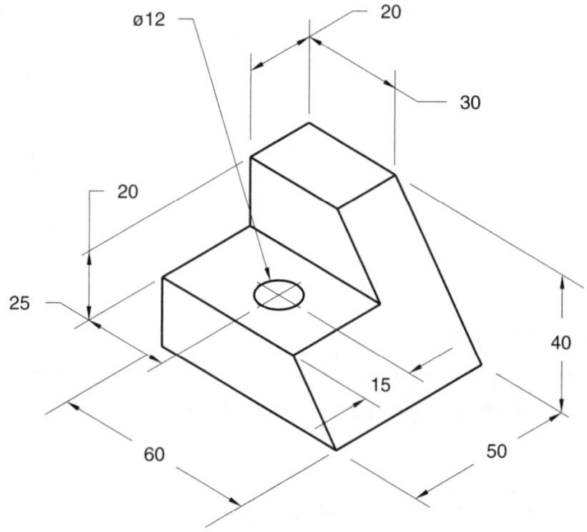

9.15 Mounting Clip

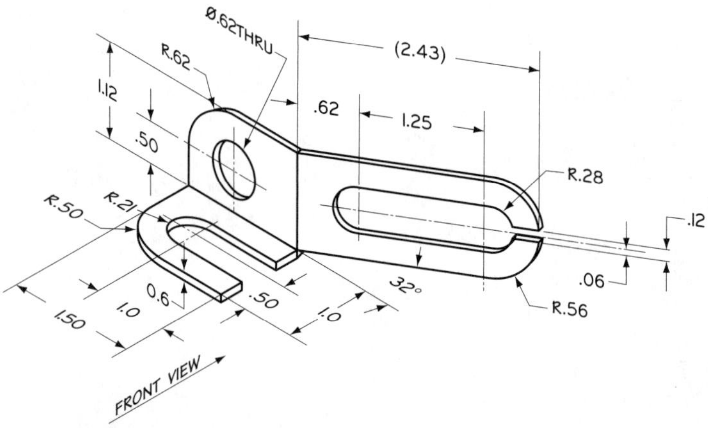

Tutorial

10 Blocks, DesignCenter™, and Tool Palettes

Objectives

When you have completed this tutorial, you will be able to

1. Use the Block, Write Block, Insert Block, and Donut commands.
2. Use the DesignCenter™.
3. Add blocks and commands to a Tool Palette.
4. Add your block symbols to toolbar buttons.
5. Create a logic circuit diagram using blocks.
6. Create named groups.
7. Create your own toolbars.
8. Customize your workspace.

Introduction

You can unify a collection of drawing objects into a single symbol by using the Block command. Using blocks can help you organize your drawing and make updating symbols easy. Blocks can have associated text objects called attributes, which can be visible or invisible. You can extract this attribute information to an external database or spreadsheet for analysis or record keeping. (You will learn more about using attributes in Tutorial 13.) The use of blocks has many advantages. You can construct a drawing by assembling blocks that consist of small details. You can draw objects that appear often once and then insert them as needed, rather than drawing them repeatedly. Inserting blocks rather than copying basic objects results in smaller drawing files, which saves time in loading and regenerating drawings. Blocks can also be nested, so that one block is a part of another block.

In this tutorial, you will create symbols used in drawing electronic logic gates: Buffer, Inverter, And, Nand, Or, and Nor. You will learn to use the Block and Insert Block commands to add symbols easily to your drawing. Using Write Block, you will make the symbols into separate drawings that can be added to any drawing. You will learn to use the DesignCenter™ to access blocks, layers, and other named entities from your existing drawings. You will also learn how to create a tool palette, which you can use to insert blocks into your drawing. Tool palettes make it easy to add blocks and hatches to your drawings, as well allow quick command selection. Finally, you will learn to create custom toolbars to which you can add your block symbols and save your custom work space.

You can create named groups using the AutoCAD® Object Group command. A ***group*** is a named selection set. You can also form ***selectable groups***. When a group is selectable, picking on one of its members selects all the members of the group that are in the current space and not on locked or frozen layers. An object can belong to more than one group. Groups are another powerful way of organizing the information in your drawing. Some CAD programs use groups instead of layers to organize drawing information. In many ways groups are like blocks, but groups differ because of their special use for selecting objects as named sets.

One case in which you might use blocks and groups together is in an architectural drawing. You could create each item of furniture—a table, chair, etc.—as a separate block and then insert it multiple times into the drawing. You could use several different layers to draw each block. You could then name all the tables as a group called TABLES and all the chairs as a group called CHAIRS. The TABLES and CHAIRS groups could belong to a group named FURNITURE. Unlike a block, which acts as a single object, you can still move or modify items in groups individually, but you can also quickly select the group (using the Select Group selection method) and modify it as a unit.

Starting

Begin the AutoCAD® program and open the drawing file ***electr.dwg*** provided with the datafiles. Save the drawing and name it ***eblocks.dwg***. When you have finished, it should appear as in Figure 10.1.

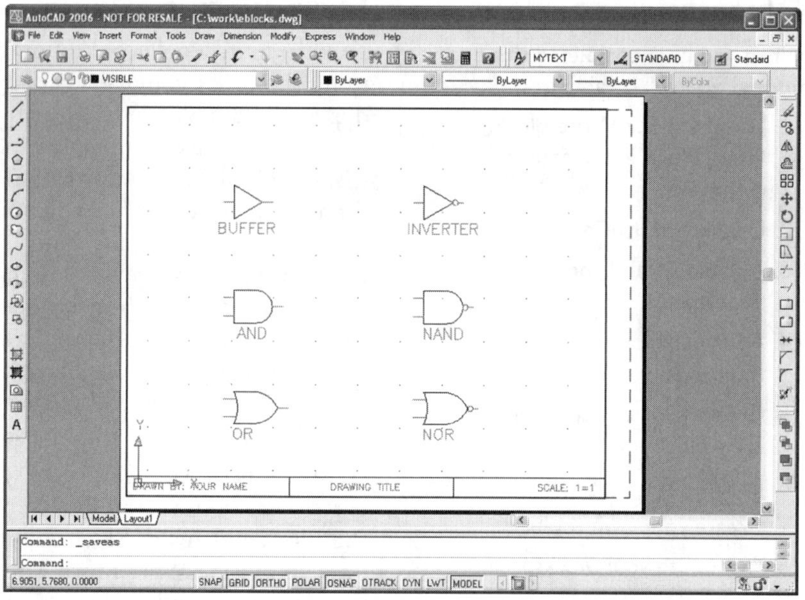

Figure 10.1

Figure 10.1 shows six symbols used in drawing electronic logic circuits: the *Buffer*, *Inverter*, *And*, *Nand*, *Or*, and *Nor gates*. You will make each symbol into a block.

Using the Block Command

A *block* is a set of objects formed into a compound object or symbol. You define a block from a set of objects in your current drawing. You specify the *block name* and then select the objects that will be part of the block. The block name is used whenever you insert the compound object (block) into the drawing. Each insertion of the block into the drawing, the *block reference*, can have its own scale factors and rotation. The AutoCAD software treats a block as a single object; you select the block for use with commands such as Move or Erase simply by picking any part of the block. You can explode blocks into their individual objects by using the Explode or Xplode commands, but doing so removes the blocks' special properties.

A block can be composed of objects that were drawn on several layers with several colors and linetypes. The layer, color, and linetype information of these objects is preserved in the block. Upon insertion, each object is drawn on its original layer with its original color and linetype, regardless of the current drawing layer, object color, and object linetype. There are three exceptions to this rule.

Tip

Block names can be as many as 255 characters long and can include spaces and any other characters that are not reserved for system use. The AutoCAD Release 14 software allowed for block names that were up to 31 characters long and which could contain letters, numbers, and the following special characters: $ (dollar sign), - (hyphen), and _ (underscore). If you will be saving back to older versions or converting information to other CAD software, it is a good idea to use simpler block names, especially ones that are different within the first 8 characters if possible. If a block with the name you choose already exists, the program tells you that it does. You can either exit without saving so that you do not lose the original block, or you can choose to redefine the block.

Tip

You can use the DesignCenter to import blocks from existing drawings into your current drawing.

1. Objects that were drawn on layer 0 are generated on the current layer when the block is inserted, and they take on the characteristics of that layer.
2. Objects that were drawn with color BYBLOCK inherit the color of the block (either the current drawing color when they are inserted or the color of the layer when color is set by layer).
3. Objects that were drawn with linetype BYBLOCK inherit the linetype of the block (either the current linetype or the layer linetype, as with color).

Blocks defined with the Block command are stored only in the current drawing and you can use them only in the drawing in which they were created. To use a block in another drawing, you need to use the Write Block command or the Windows Clipboard. You can use blocks in other drawings by copying vectors (graphical objects) to the Windows Clipboard and pasting them into another drawing, which results in a block. In addition, you can insert the drawing containing a block into another drawing. When you insert a drawing as you did in Tutorial 4 with the subdivision drawing, **subdivis.dwg**, any blocks it contains are then defined in the drawing in which it is inserted.

Unlike using the Windows Clipboard to copy a block, or inserting a file containing a block, using the Write Block command saves the selected block or drawing objects as a separate drawing file. This block file can then be inserted into any drawing. You will learn more about Write Block later in this tutorial.

Zoom up the area of the drawing showing the And gate so that your screen is similar to Figure 10.2.

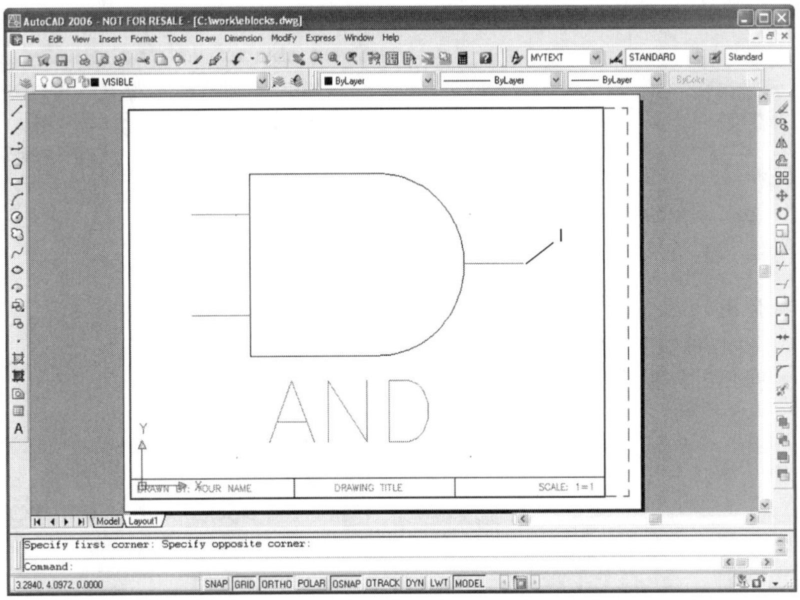

Figure 10.2

You will use the Make Block icon on the Draw toolbar to create a block from the objects making up the And gate on the screen. Be sure to select Make Block and not Insert Block on the same toolbar. Refer to Figure 10.2 to help you select point 1.

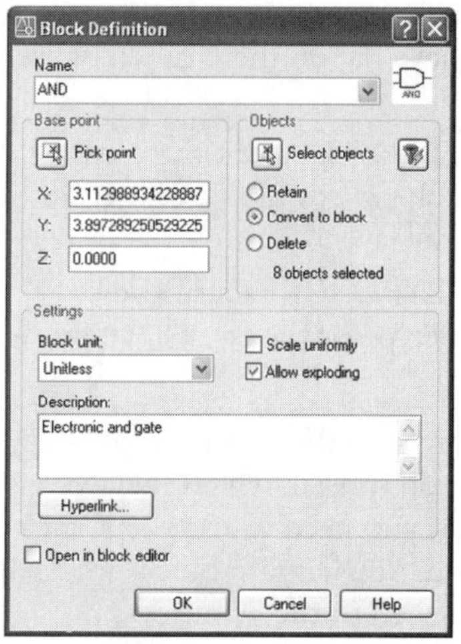

Figure 10.3

Turn on running object snap **Endpoint**.
Pick: **Make Block icon**

A Block Definition dialog box appears, similar to Figure 10.3.

The dialog box allows you to type in a block name, select a base point, select objects to be used in that group, and view existing blocks. The Objects area of the dialog box allows you to select whether the items you pick to make the block will be retained in your drawing (as individual objects), converted to a block (as a single object), or deleted.

Leave the Objects radio buttons set to **Convert to block**.

You can also add a description, and specify the default unit system you are using to define the sizes of the features in the block. These things will help you later find and size the blocks when you insert them into drawings.

Next you will type the block name, select a base point, and finally select the objects to be used.

Type: **AND** (for the Name)
Pick: **Pick Point** (located in the Base Point section of the dialog box)

Be sure to choose a base point that will be useful when you insert the block in another drawing. If you do not select a base point, the default base point coordinates (0,0,0) or whatever other coordinates appear in the dialog box will be used. Refer to Figure 10.2 and use AutoSnap™ Endpoint to pick the base point.

Specify insertion base point: **pick endpoint 1**

When you return to the dialog box, you will choose Select objects.

Pick: **Select objects**
Select objects: **use implied Crossing to select all of the objects making up the And gate, including the name AND** ↵
Pick: **Unitless** (as the Block Unit type under Settings)
Type: **Electronic and gate** (as the description)
Pick: **OK**

You are returned to the drawing editor and now have a block of the And gate to be used in later drawings.

Pick: **Zoom Previous**

This will restore the original view of the drawing, where you can see each symbol.

Pick: **Make Block icon**
On your own, create a block for each of the other electronic logic symbols.
Name the blocks NAND, OR, NOR, INVERTER, and BUFFER.
Select the right-hand endpoint of the lead from each electronic logic gate as the base point.

To see how you can use blocks within the current drawing, you will insert the And block you created.

Tip

You can reenter the Block Definition dialog box and update the selections for any of the blocks in the drawing. To do this, pick the Make Block icon and expand the list of names in the dialog box to select the block you want to redefine. Make any necessary changes to the dialog box and then pick OK.

Inserting a Block

The Insert Block command inserts blocks or other drawings into your drawing. When inserting a block, you use a dialog box to specify the block name, the insertion point (the location for the base point you picked when you created the block), the scale, and the rotation for the block. A scale of 1 causes the block to remain the original size. The scaling factors for the X-, Y-, and Z-directions do not have to be the same. However, using the same size ensures that the inserted block has the same proportions, or aspect ratio, as the original. Blocks (even those with different X-, Y-, and Z-scaling factors) can be exploded back into their original objects with the Explode command. A rotation of 0° ensures the same orientation as the original. You can also use Insert Block by typing INSERT at the command prompt.

You will select Insert Block from the Block flyout on the Draw toolbar and use the dialog box to insert the And gate into your drawing.

Pick: **Insert Block icon**

The Insert dialog box appears on your screen, as shown in Figure 10.4.

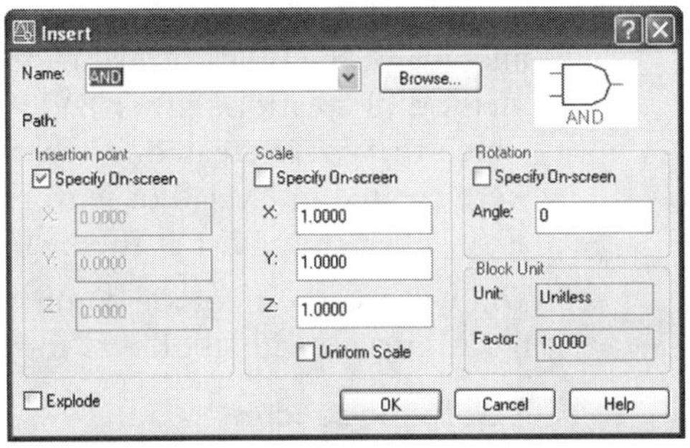

Figure 10.4

Pick: **AND** (from the list that pulls down adjacent to Name)

The dialog box lets you select whether you will be returned to your drawing to specify the Insertion point, Scale, and Rotation or whether you will type in a value for these (or use the defaults). You will leave the Scale factor set to 1 for the X, Y, and Z coordinate directions. This way the block will retain the same size in the drawing as where it was created. Also leave the Rotation set to an angle of 0 degrees so that the block retains its original angle.

Be sure that in the Insertion area the box to the left of Specify On-screen has a check in it. This feature allows you to pick the location for the block from your screen after you exit the dialog box. Otherwise, you must type in the coordinates for its location in the dialog box.

To exit the dialog box and begin specifying the insertion parameters on screen,

Pick: **OK**

The And block appears, attached to the crosshairs by its endpoint, the base point you specified. Continue with the Insert command.

Specify insertion point or [Basepoint Scale/X/Y/Z/Rotate/PScale/PX/PY/PZ/PRotate]: **pick a point anywhere to the right of the logic symbols**

The And block is added to your drawing.

On your own, try to erase one of the lines of the newly added block. Cancel the Erase command without erasing anything.

Note that the entire block behaves as one object. In Tutorial 7, when you added associative dimensions to your drawing, they were also blocks. That's why they behaved as a single object, even though they were a collection of lines, polylines, and text. Before you can change individual pieces of a block, you must use the Explode command, as you did with Xplode in Tutorial 7. However, exploding takes away a block's special properties.

Using Explode

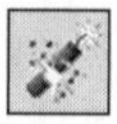

The AutoCAD software treats blocks as a single object. The Explode command replaces a block reference with the simple objects the block comprises. Explode also turns 2D and 3D polylines, associative dimensions, and 3D mesh back into individual objects. When you explode a block, the resulting image on the screen is identical to the one you started with, except that the color and linetype of the objects may change. That can occur because properties such as the color and linetype of the block return to the settings determined by their original method of creation, either BYLAYER or the set color and linetype with which they were created. There will be no difference unless the objects were created in layer 0 or with the color and linetype set to BYBLOCK, as specified in the list at the beginning of this tutorial.

You will use the Explode command to break the newly inserted And block into individual objects for editing.

Pick: **Explode icon**
Select objects: **pick any portion of the newly inserted And block**
Select objects: ↵

The block is now broken into its component objects.

On your own, try to erase a line from the block.

Notice that now you can erase one line at a time, rather than the whole block.

Erase the newly added AND block.

Tip

You can use Write Block to export part of any drawing to a separate file. This action can speed up your computer's response time by keeping file sizes smaller. When you are working in an extremely large file, but just need to work on a certain part of it, use Write Block to export that area to a new file. Work on the new, smaller file that contains only the part of the drawing you need. When done, use Insert Block to reinsert the finished work in the larger drawing. You will have to explode it after inserting it before you can edit it.

Using Write Block

The block you just created is only defined in the current drawing. You can use the Write Block command to make it into a separate drawing for insertion into other drawings. A drawing file made with the Write Block command is the same as any other drawing file. You can open it and edit it like any other drawing. You can use any AutoCAD drawing as a block and insert it into any other drawing, as you did in Tutorial 5. This is a great tool you can use when creating AutoCAD drawings.

You will use the Write Block command to write the AND block that you created to a new AutoCAD drawing file called *and-gate.dwg*. The alias for the WBLOCK command is W.

Command: **W** ↵

The Write Block dialog box similar to that shown in Figure 10.5 appears on the screen.

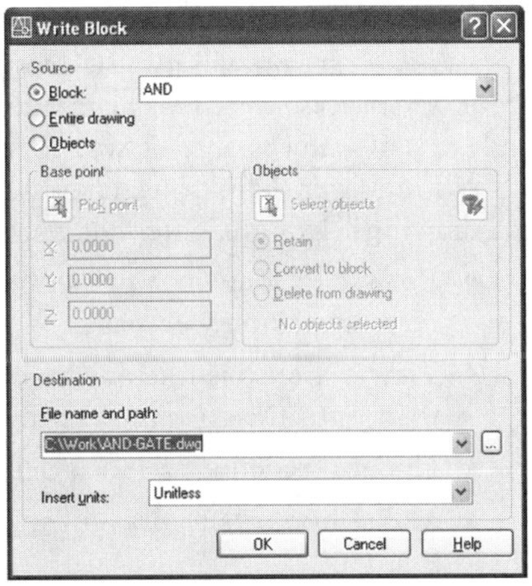

Figure 10.5

You can select the source information for the Wblock by picking one of the following three radio buttons:

- **Block** Pick the name of a block that already exists in the current drawing. The objects that make up the specified block are written to the drawing file being created.
- **Entire drawing** This saves the entire current drawing to the name specified as the Destination file name (as the Save command does), except that unused named objects, layers, and other definitions are eliminated.
- **Objects** Picking this allows you to specify the objects and the base point, similar to the Make Block options. You can choose whether the items you select are retained, deleted, or converted to blocks in the current drawing. The selected objects are written to the drawing file name that you specify in the Destination area.

In the Source area,

Pick: **the Block radio button**
Pick: **AND** (as the block name)

The middle area of the dialog box appears grayed out. Next you will set the destination file and default units for the block. You will name the new file that will be created *and-gate*. You do not need to include the file extension; the *.dwg* extension is automatically added. (Be sure to use the *c:\work* directory for the new file to keep your hard drive organized.)

Type: **AND-GATE** (for the File name)
Pick: **the ellipsis button** to the right of File name and path to navigate to ***c:\work*** as necessary
Pick: **Unitless** (for the Insert units)
Pick: **OK**

The block that you created, named AND, has been saved to the new AutoCAD drawing file *and-gate.dwg*.

Warning

Do not give the write block the same name as an existing drawing. If you do, you will see the message "This file already exists. Replace existing file?" Select No unless you are certain that you no longer want the old drawing file.

Tip

Write Block does not save views, User Coordinate Systems, viewport configurations, unreferenced symbols (including block definitions), unused layers or linetypes, or text styles. This compresses your drawing file size by getting rid of unwanted overhead.

On your own, use the Write Block command to create separate drawing files for each of the other blocks that you created. Name them *or-gate, nor-gate, nand-gate, inverter*, and *buffer*.

Using DesignCenter and Tool Palettes

Next you will use the DesignCenter and Tool Palettes to manage blocks so that you can add them easily to your drawings. The DesignCenter is an easy way to save time on drawings by copying and pasting layer definitions, layouts, and text and dimension styles between drawings. DesignCenter allows you to:

- Browse for drawings or symbol libraries on your computer, your network, or on web pages.
- View definitions for blocks and layers and insert, attach, copy or paste them into the current drawing.
- Update (redefine) a block definition.
- Make shortcuts to drawings, folders, and web pages that you use frequently.
- Add xrefs, blocks, and hatches to drawings.
- Open drawing files in a new window.
- Drag drawings, blocks, and hatches to a convenient tool palette.

Start a new drawing from the ***proto.dwt*** template provided with the datafiles. Name it ***hfadder.dwg***.

Pick: **DesignCenter icon** (from the Standard toolbar)

The DesignCenter appears on your screen similar to Figure 10.6.

On your own, use the Folder List area to show the list of files in your *c:\work* directory.

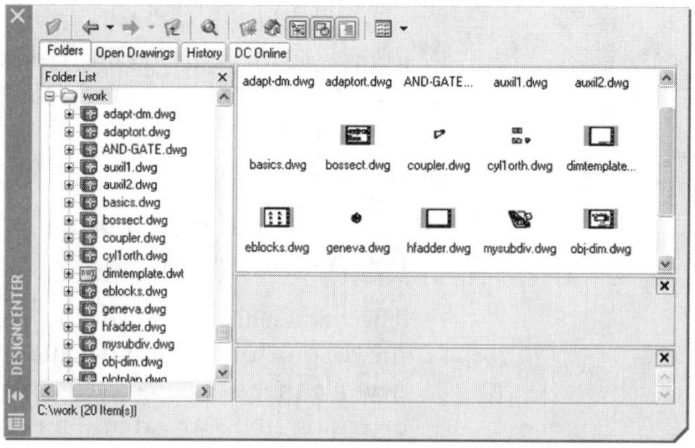

Figure 10.6

The DesignCenter shows a list of all of the files that are available in the selected directory. You can drag and drop named drawing objects, such as layers, blocks, text and dimension styles, layouts, linetypes, and xrefs into your drawing. Next, you will pick drawing *mysubdiv.dwg* so you can drag one of its layers into your current drawing.

Tip

You can also show the contents of a drawing by double-clicking on its thumbnail pictured in the list at the right.

Pick: **drawing *mysubdiv.dwg* from tree list at left** (if you don't have this drawing use the datafile named *subdiv2.dwt*)

In the DesignCenter, you should now see a list of the types of named objects that are available from within the Mysubdiv drawing as shown in Figure 10.7.

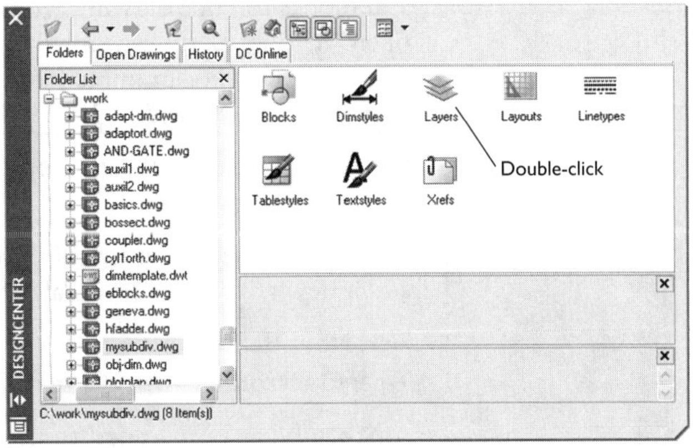

Figure 10.7

Double-click: on the **Layers icon in the DesignCenter**

The DesignCenter changes to show the list of layers that are available inside drawing Mysubdiv (see Figure 10.8). You will drag and drop layer Points into the current drawing.

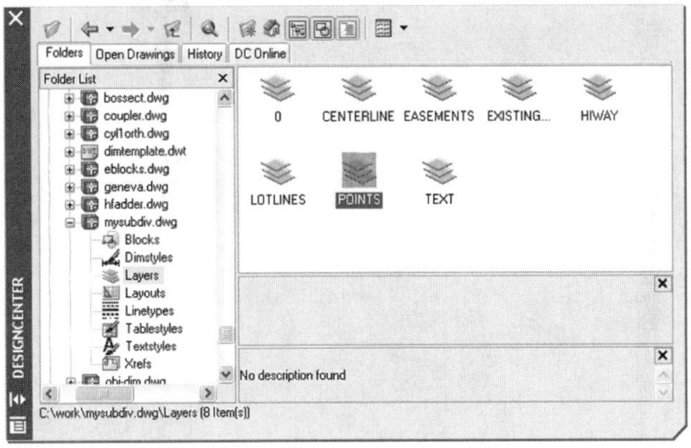

Figure 10.8

Drag layer Points to your current drawing.

Pick: **Layer Control**

You should see that your current drawing now has a new layer named Points as shown in Figure 10.9. It has all the same properties as the layer Points from drawing Mysubdiv, is locked, and has the color set to blue.

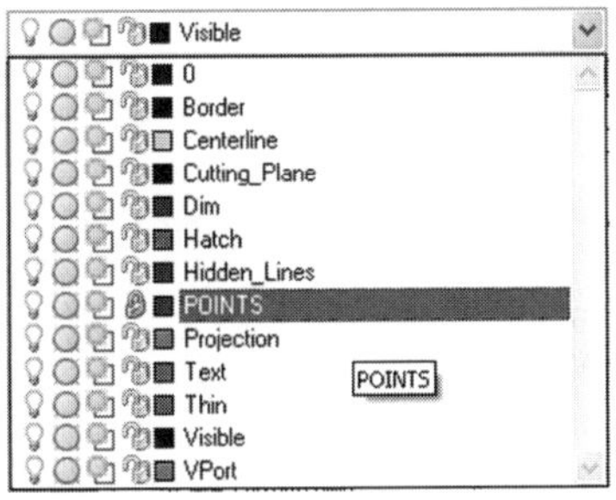

Figure 10.9

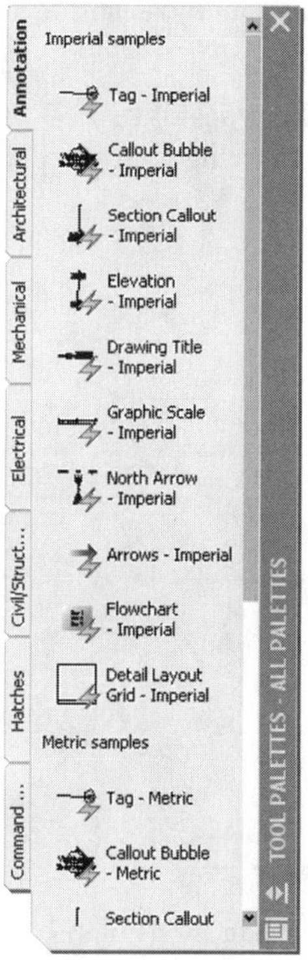

Figure 10.10

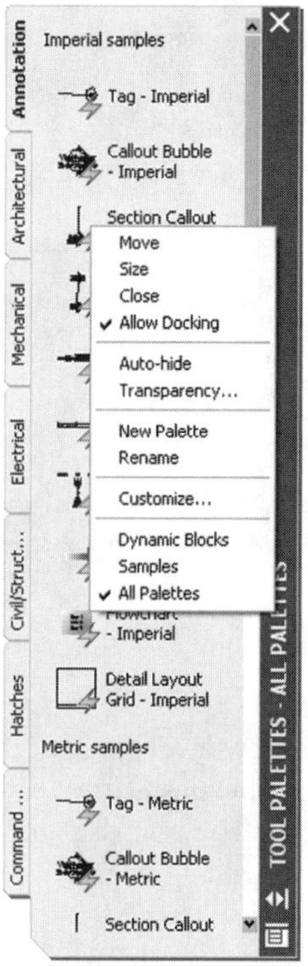

Figure 10.11

Next you will turn on the Tool Palettes and then add your electronic gates to it.

Pick: **Tool Palettes icon** (from the Standard toolbar)

You should see the Tool Palettes appear on your screen as shown in Figure 10.10. The Tool Palettes are an easy way to quickly add hatches and blocks to your drawing without having the entire DesignCenter open. A tool palette can only be used in the AutoCAD version in which it was created. For example, you cannot use an AutoCAD 2006 tool palette in the AutoCAD 2005 program.

Right-click on the dark band along the right edge of the Tool Palettes to pop up the menu choices.

The pop up menu appears as shown in Figure 10.11. You will use it to add a new tab to the Tool Palettes for your electronic blocks.

Pick: **New Palette**
Type: **Electronic** (when the text cursor appears) and press ↵

A new tab has been added to the Tool Palettes. It is shown in Figure 10.12. You will drag and drop your electronic gate drawings onto this new Tool Palette.

Figure 10.12

On your own, use the DesignCenter and drag and drop the logic gate drawings onto the Tool Palette as shown in Figure 10.13.

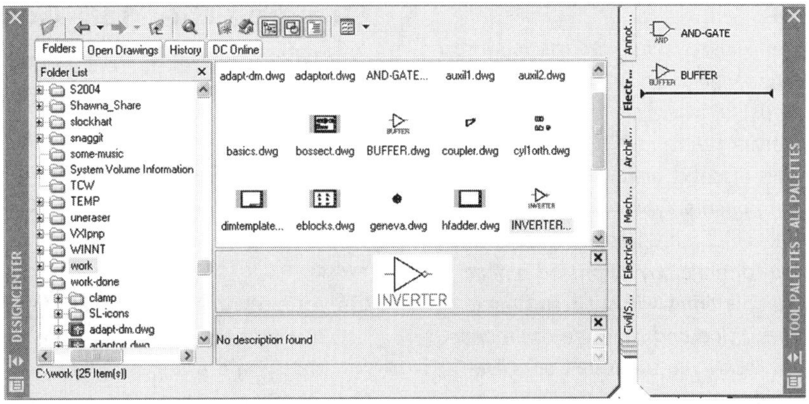

Figure 10.13

Continue until you have added all 6 logic gates so that your Tool Palette is similar to Figure 10.14.

Close the DesignCenter on your own.

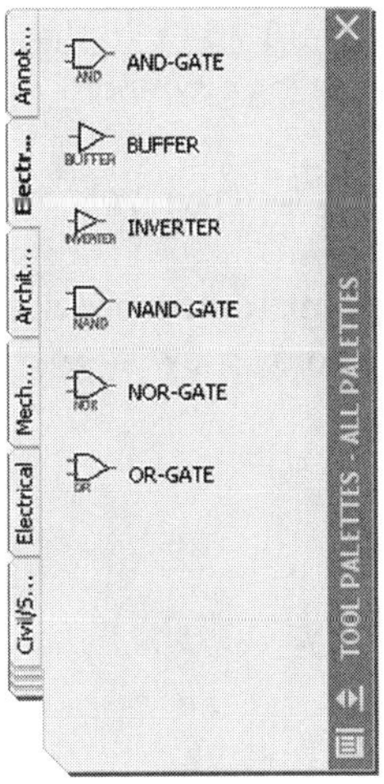

Figure 10.14

Next you will add the Explode command to this tool palette. You can drag tools (command icons) from a tool bar onto a palette when the Customize dialog box is open.

Right-click: on a blank area of the tool palette

Pick: **Customize** from the menu that pops up

The Customize dialog box appears on your screen.

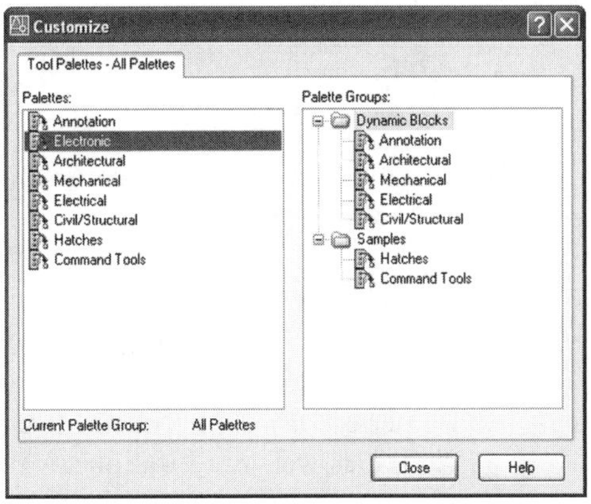

Figure 10.15

On your own, drag a copy of the Explode command from your Modify toolbar onto the tool palette.

Close the Customize dialog box when you have finished.

The Explode command is added to the tool palette as in Figure 10.16.

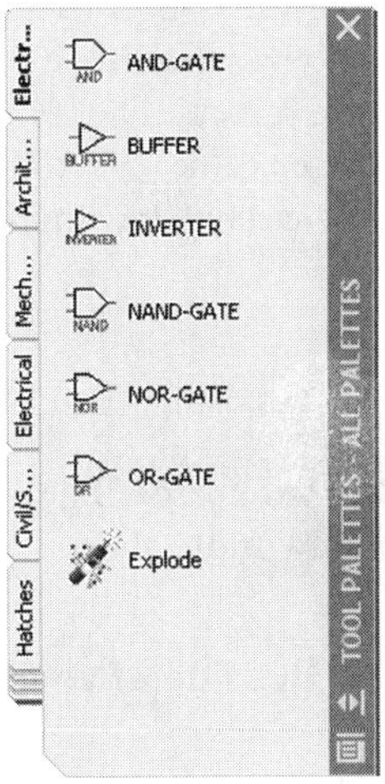

Figure 10.16

Now you have learned to create a customized AutoCAD tool palette. You can create your own blocks and add them to other tool palettes. You can also program your own commands onto toolbars and icons or modify existing toolbars and icons using the techniques that you will learn later in this tutorial.

You are ready to try adding some of the logic blocks to your drawing by dragging and dropping them from the Tool Palettes.

Tip

The Minsert command lets you insert a rectangular array of blocks. It can be useful when you're laying out drawings that have a pattern, such as rows of desks or rows of electronic components. Typing the command MULTIPLE and pressing enter allows you to make any command repeat multiple times without restarting it. The Divide and Measure commands also allow you to insert blocks. The Divide command divides an object that you select into the number of parts that you specify. You can either insert a point object where the divisions will be (as you did in Tutorial 5), or you can select the Block option and specify a block name. The Measure command works in much the same way, except that instead of specifying the number of divisions that you want to use, you specify the lengths of the divisions. Use the on-line Help facility to get more information about these commands.

Drawing the Half-Adder Circuit

You will use the new tool palette you created to draw a half-adder circuit with electronic logic symbols.

Switch to paper space and use the Edit Text command to change the text in the title block to HALF-ADDER CIRCUIT and type your name. Specify NONE for the scale, as electronic diagrams usually aren't drawn to scale.

Switch back to model space when you are finished.

On your own, set the current layer to **THIN** and **Snap** to **0.1042** so that it will align with the spacing between the leads on the logic symbols that you created.

Use the Electronic tool palette on your own to insert the logic symbols as shown in Figure 10.17.

Use the **Line** and **Arc** commands with **Snap to Endpoint** to connect the output from one logic circuit to the inputs of the next as shown.

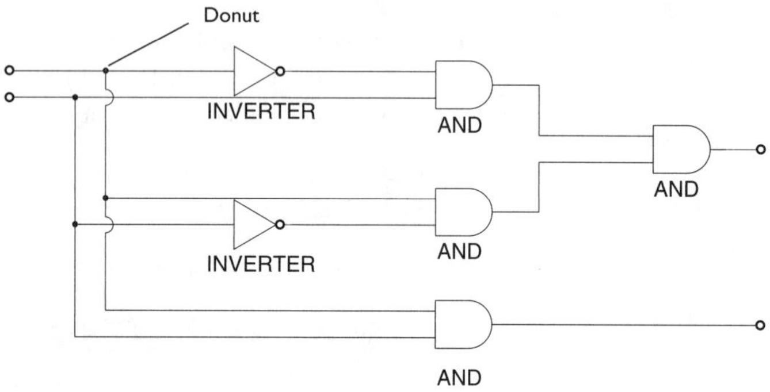

Figure 10.17

You will use the Donut command to make the filled and open circles for connection points.

Using Donut

The Donut command draws filled circles or concentric filled circles. See Figure 10.18. Found on the Draw menu, the Donut command requires numerical values for the inside and outside diameters of the concentric circles, as well as a location for the center point. If you enter a zero value for the inside diameter, a solid dot appears on the screen. The diameter of the dot will equal the stated outside diameter value. Next, you will draw some donuts off to the side of your logic circuit drawing.

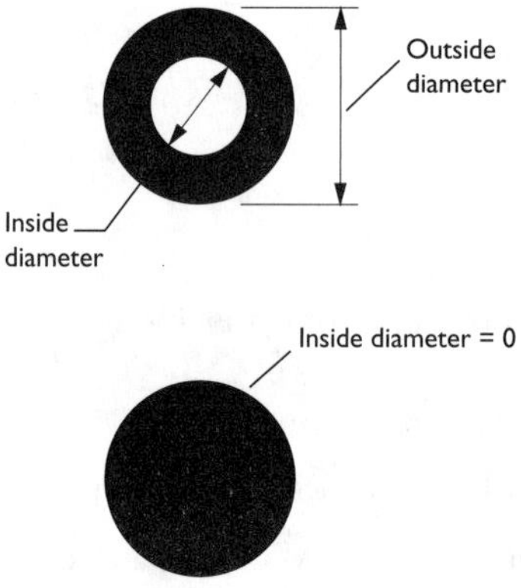

Figure 10.18

Pick: **Draw, Donut**

Specify inside diameterof of donut <0.5000>: ↵

Specify outside diameter of donut <1.0000>: ↵

Note that a doughnut-like shape is now moving with your cursor. The Center of donut prompt is repeated so that you can draw more than one donut. Select points on your screen.

Specify center of donut or <exit>: **select a point off to the side of your drawing**

Specify center of donut or <exit>: **select another point**

To exit the command when you have finished practicing drawing donuts of the same size, you will press ↵.

Specify center of donut or <exit>: ↵

On your own, **erase** the donuts that you drew to the side.

Restart the Donut command and set the inside diameter for the donut to **0**.

Set the outside diameter to **0.075**.

Draw the solid connection points for the logic circuit that you see in Figure 10.17.

Next add the open donuts at the ends of the lines.

Start the Donut command and set the inner diameter to **0.0625** and the outer diameter to **0.075**.

Create four donuts on the side of your drawing.

Place the four donuts by using the **Move** command so that each donut is attached at its outside edge, not its center. Use **Snap to Quadrant** to select the base point on the donut and then **Snap to Endpoint** to select the endpoint of the line.

When you have drawn and placed all the connection points, your drawing should look like that in Figure 10.17.

Freezing the TEXT Layer

The drawing *electr.dwg*, which you used to create the blocks for the logic gates, contained different layers for the text, lines, and shapes of the logic gates. You can freeze or turn off layers to control the visibility within parts of a block. You will freeze the text in the blocks because it is there to help identify the blocks while you are inserting them but would not ordinarily be shown on an electronic circuit diagram. The text in the blocks is on layer TEXT2. The text in the title block is on layer TEXT. You will use Layer Control to freeze the layer that holds the text showing the name of the type of gate.

Pick: **Layer Control icon**

Use the Layer Control list that appears on your screen to freeze layer TEXT2. The names of the gates should disappear from the screen.

Save your drawing on your own before continuing.

Your drawing should look like Figure 10.19.

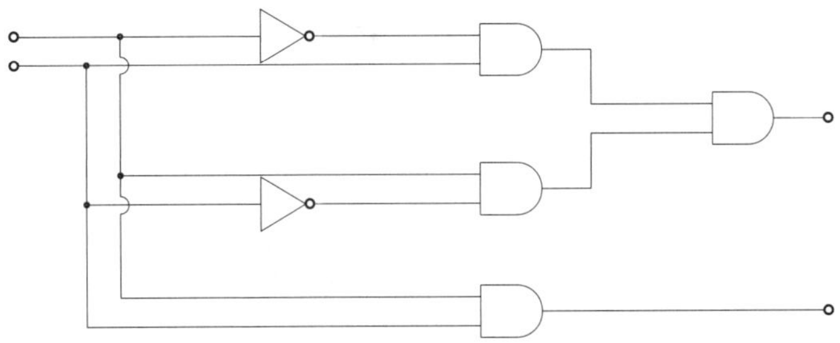

Figure 10.19

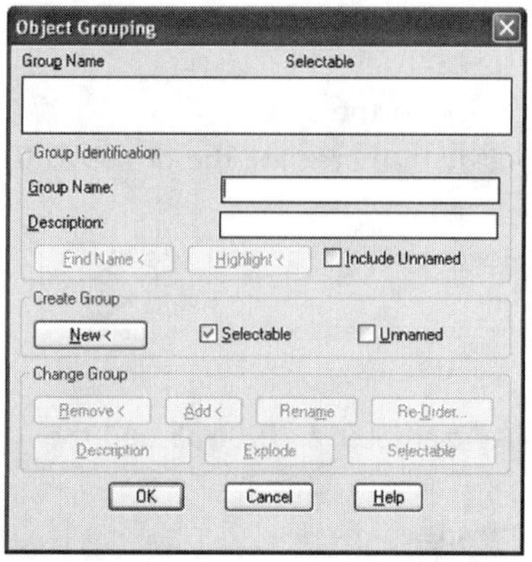

Figure 10.20

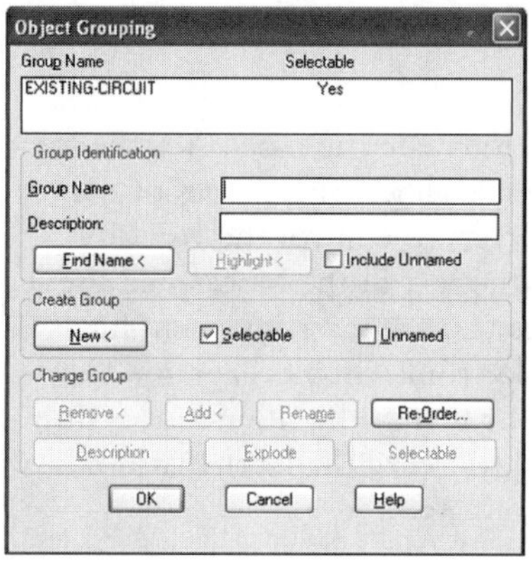

Figure 10.21

Creating Object Groups

Another powerful method of organizing your drawing is to use named groups. You can select these groups for use with other commands. You will type the Group command at the prompt.

Command: **GROUP** ↵

The Object Grouping dialog box appears on your screen, as shown in Figure 10.20. You will create a new group named EXISTING-CIRCUIT. For the existing circuit, you will select the upper Inverter and And gate and the two leads into each of them. Groups can be selectable, not selectable, named, or unnamed. When a group is selectable, the entire group becomes selected if you pick a member of the group when selecting objects. You can return to the dialog box and turn Selectable off at any time. Type the following information into the Group Identification area of the dialog box.

Group Name: **EXISTING-CIRCUIT**
Description: **Portions of the Existing Circuit**
Make sure **Selectable** is checked.
Pick: **New**
Select objects for grouping: **pick the upper Inverter and upper And gate and the two leads to the left of each of them**
Select objects: ↵

The dialog box returns to your screen as shown in Figure 10.21 so that you can continue creating groups. You will group the remainder of the circuit and give it the group name NEW-CIRCUIT.

Type: **NEW-CIRCUIT** as the Group Name
Pick: **New**
Select all the remaining objects to form the NEW-CIRCUIT group.
Press: ↵ when you are done selecting
Pick: **OK** to exit the dialog box

Now, you are ready to try your groups with drawing commands. Remember, you can pick on any member of a selectable group to select the entire group. You will change the linetype property for the NEW-CIRCUIT group to a HIDDEN linetype. To cause the Properties palette to appear on your screen,

Pick: **Properties icon**
Pick: **pick on one of the symbols from the NEW-CIRCUIT group**

The entire group becomes selected.

Pick: **Hidden** (from the pull-down list for Linetype)
Pick: **Windows Close button** (to remove the Properties dialog box from your screen)
Press: Esc twice

The wiring diagram for the new portion of the circuit becomes dashed lines.

Pick: **Undo** (from the Standard toolbar)

This will reverse this linetype change before you go on.

To be able to select each object individually, return to the Object Grouping dialog box on your own and turn Selectable off.

Your finished drawing should look like Figure 10.22.

Save and plot your drawing.

Close the Tool Palettes.

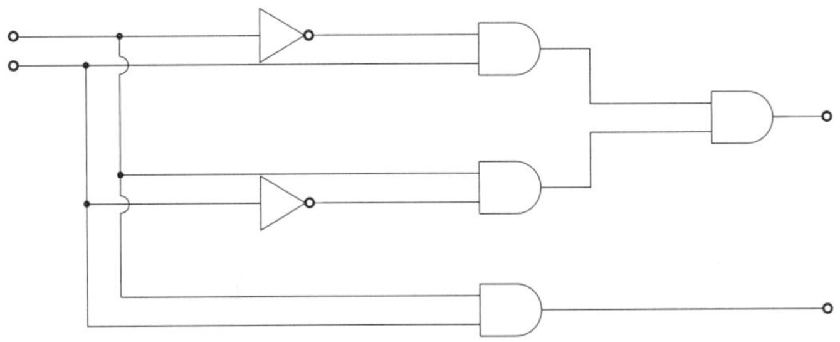

Figure 10.22

The DesignCenter and Tool Palettes are important tools for reusing your past work efficiently. Make the most of them! Reuse layers, blocks, dimension styles, and other named objects from your past drawings to create new drawings quickly.

Tip

You can quickly change blocks by redefining them. If you redefine a block, the appearance of all the blocks with that name will update. To redefine a block, make the changes you want to the block. Then use the Block command to save it as a block again, retaining the same file name. You will be prompted that the block already exists and asked if you want to redefine it. The appearance of all existing blocks that have the same name as the redefined block will update.

Creating Custom Interfaces

Another way in which you can *customize* your AutoCAD software is by creating new toolbars and programming the existing toolbars so that they contain the commands you use most frequently. You can also reprogram the individual buttons on the AutoCAD toolbars. You can save customized user interfaces called workspaces that display the toolbars, palettes and windows that you find useful.

To create a custom workspace,

Pick: **Tools, Customize, Interface**

The Customize User Interface dialog box appears on your screen as shown in Figure 10.23 showing the AutoCAD Default workspace.

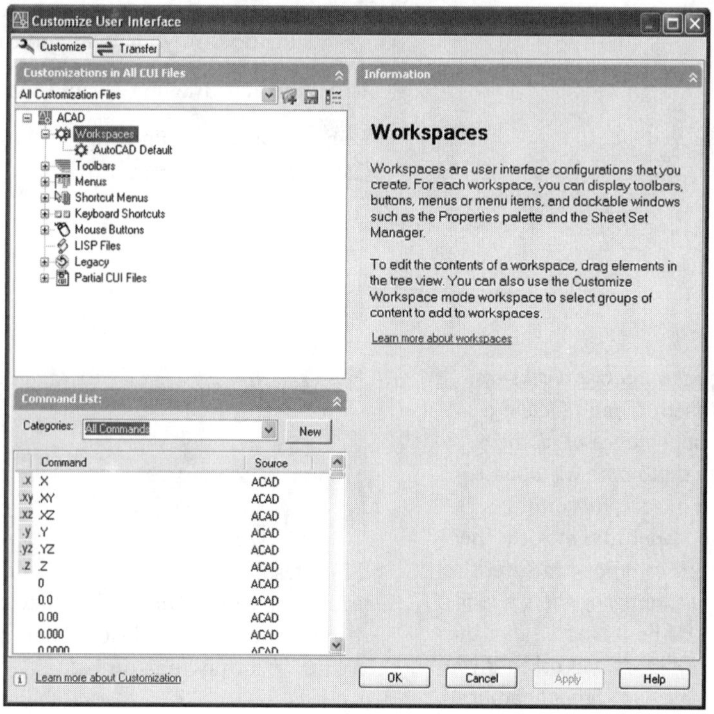

Figure 10.23

To create your custom workspace,

Right-click: on the **Workspaces** item highlighted in Figure 10.23 to show the pop-up menu

Pick: **New, Workspace**

A new workspace named Workspace1 is added to the list below the AutoCAD Default workspace. Figure 10.24 shows the top of the dialog box as it appears after the new workspace is added.

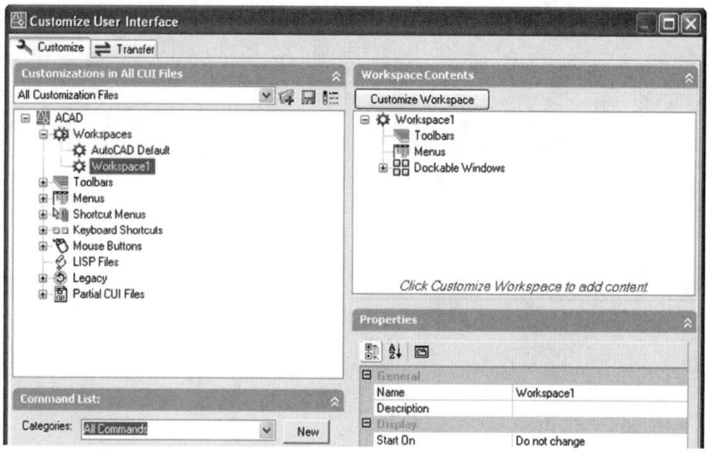

Figure 10.24

Right-click: **on Workspace1** highlighted in Figure 10.24 to show the pop-up menu

Pick: **Rename**

Type: **MyWay** as the name for your workspace

Tip

When you create a toolbar, it is added by default to all workspaces. This is controlled by the On By Default item in the Properties window for the toolbar.

Next, you will create your own toolbar for the logic symbols that you created. You will program the buttons on the new toolbar to insert the logic symbols. To create a new toolbar,

Right-click: on **Toolbars** in the top left window to show the pop-up menu
Pick: **New, Toolbar**

Toolbar1 is added to the end of the list of toolbars shown in the dialog box, as in Figure 10.25.

On your own, rename Toolbar1 to **Logic.**
Pick: **Apply**

Figure 10.25

Figure 10.26

You will see a small toolbar appear on your screen. (It does not have any buttons on it, so it may be hard to notice. You may have to move the dialog box around as it may be behind it.) It should be similar to Figure 10.26.

To create a new command, you will use the Command List area at the bottom left of the dialog box.

Pick: **New button** to the right of Categories

Command1 is added to the list of commands that appear in the lower left of the dialog box as shown in Figure 10.27

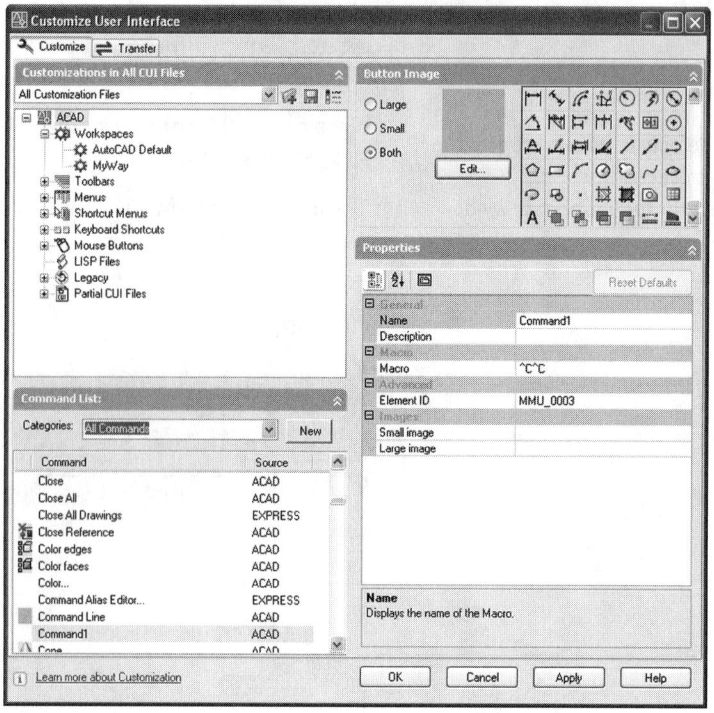

Figure 10.27

Rename Command1 in the list in the lower left to **And-gate** on your own.

Next you will program the command appearance and select the button icon file.

The input box to the right of Name in the Properties area allows you to specify the name of the command that you are creating. This name will appear as the tool tip for the button exactly as you type it. You use the input box to the right of Description to enter the help line for the button, which will appear in the status bar at the bottom of the screen. The area to the right of Macro lets you type in the AutoCAD command sequence that you want to use when you pick the button. Do not add any spaces between ^C^C and the first command you type. A space represents pressing ↵ or Spacebar.

You will program the button to insert your and-gate block into your current drawing. When you pick the button, the Insert Block command will be invoked to insert the specified block.

Tip

The block or file that you are inserting must be in the current path or you must specify where the block is located by adding the path name ahead of the block name. (You can change the current path in the Preferences dialog box.) The backslash has a special meaning in this dialog box: pause for user input. Therefore, when you add a path to a macro, you use the forward slash instead of the backslash to separate the directories (e.g., c:/work/and-gate.dwg). Finally, you can create a block library drawing and insert it into the drawing so that all the blocks are available in the current drawing prior to using the Logic toolbar that you just created.

Using Special Characters in Programmed Commands

There are some special characters that you can use in programming the toolbars. One of these is ^C. If you put ^C in front of the command name you are programming, it will cancel any unfinished command when you select its button from the toolbar. In programming menus and buttons, putting cancel twice before a command is often a good idea in case you have left a subprompt active (so that it would take two cancels to return to the command prompt). Putting cancel before the Insert Block command is useful because you cannot select this command during another command. Do not add cancel before the toggle modes or transparent commands (a ' must precede them) because, if you execute cancel before you use them, you can't use them during another command.

A space or ↵ is automatically added to the end of every command you program for the buttons. This way the command is entered when you select the button. You can enter a string of commands, or a command and its options, by separating them with a space to act as ↵. You can use the following special characters to program the toolbar buttons:

Character	**Meaning**
space	↵
;	↵
^Z	At the end of a line, suppresses the addition of a space to the end of a command string
+	At the end of a command string, allows it to continue to the next line
-	In front of a command name, causes it to operate at the command line (not using a dialog box)
\	Pauses for user input
/	Separates directories in path names, because \ (backslash) pauses for user input
^V	Changes current viewport
^B	Ctrl-B Snap mode toggle
^C	Ctrl-C Cancel
*^C^C	At the beginning of a line, automatically restarts command sequence (repeating)
^D	Ctrl-D Coordinates toggle
^E	Ctrl-E Isoplane toggle
^G	Ctrl-G Grid mode toggle
^O	Ctrl-O Ortho mode toggle

An _ (underscore) preceding a command or option automatically translates AutoCAD keywords and command options for use with foreign-language versions.

Pick: **in the input box to the right of Name**
Type: **AND-GATE**
Pick: **in the input box to the right of Description**
Type: **INSERTS AND-GATE SYMBOL**
Pick: **to the right of ^C^C, for Macro**
Type: **-INSERT c:/work/AND-GATE.dwg**

Pick: **to the right of Small Image**
Type: **c:\datafile2006\And.bmp** (or click ... and browse for the file)

Pick: **to the right of Large Image**
Type: **c:\datafile2006\And.bmp** (or click ... and browse for the file)

When you have finished making the selections, the dialog box appears as shown in Figure 10.28.

Tip

You may need to add the path to where your and-gate drawing is stored (i.e., ^C^C-Insert c:/work/and-gate). You must use a forward slash in the path. Do not add spaces between the ^C^C and the Insert command. Do not forget to type the hyphen (-) in front of the insert command so the command will run at the command prompt.

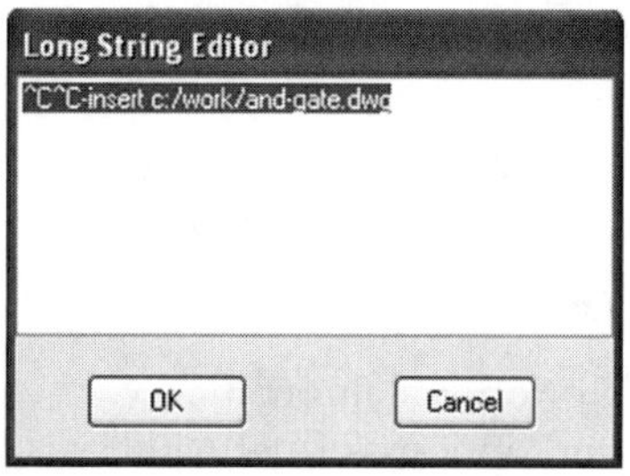

Figure 10.29

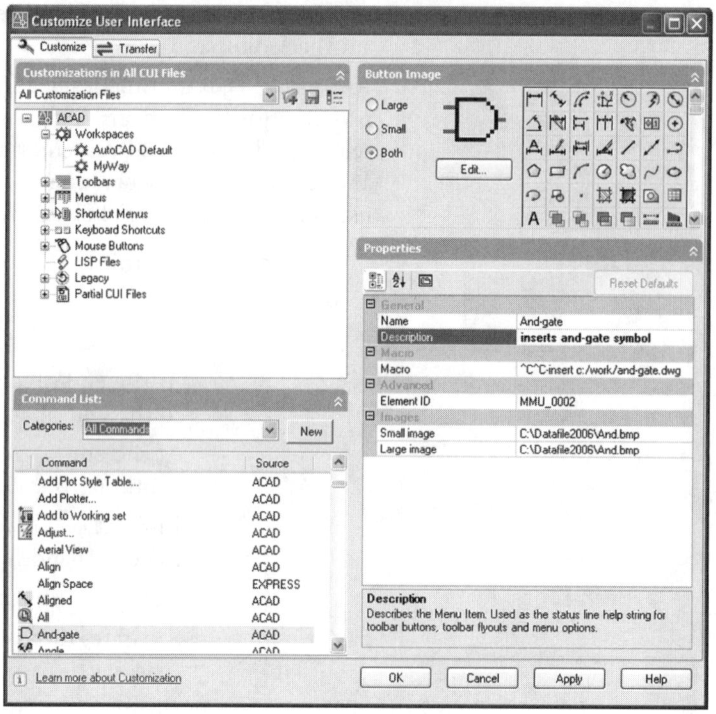

Figure 10.28

Pick: **in the text box next to Macro**

Pick: **...** (the ellipsis to the right of the Macro area)

The Long String editor appears on your screen as shown in Figure 10.29. You can use it to see and edit long macros for commands. Your command to insert the And-gate should look like the figure.

Pick: **OK** (to exit the Long String Editor)

Scroll down in the image list in the Button Image area and pick the new And icon if it does not appear as shown in Figure 10.28.

Pick: **Edit** (below the Button Image tile at the top right)

The Button Editor dialog box appears on your screen. (When the Toolbars dialog box is not open, if you double-click with the right button on an icon, the Toolbars dialog box opens and then the Button Editor dialog box opens.) The button editor works much like many paint-type drawing programs. Each little box in the button editor represents a pixel, or single dot, on your screen. You can select the drawing tool from the buttons at the top of the editor. The color of the drawing tool is selected from the colored buttons at the right of the editor.

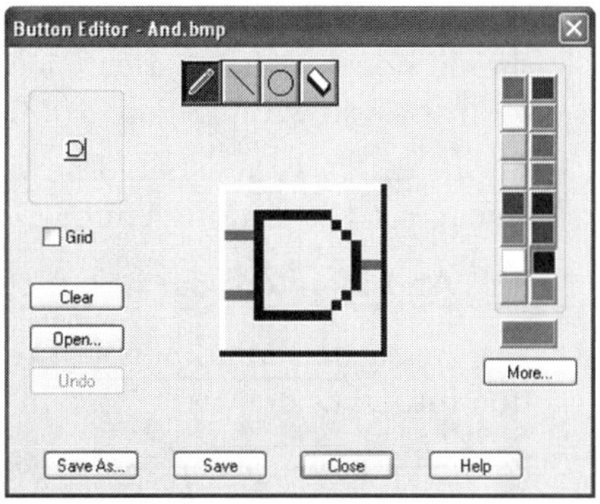

Figure 10.30

The And-gate button image was provided with the datafiles, but you can see how you could create your own button images using the button editor.

Pick: **Close**

Now you are ready to drag your command onto the Logic toolbar you created.

Pick: **the Logic toolbar in the upper left portion of the dialog box**

Drag the And-gate command onto it from the Command List as shown in Figure 10.31.

Pick: **the Logic toolbar** again (if needed) to see the preview in the top right

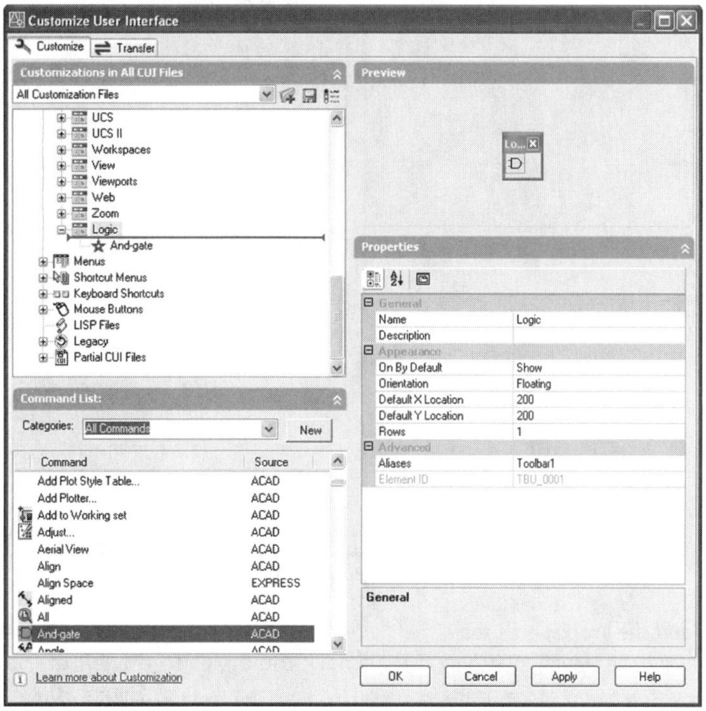

Figure 10.31

Pick: **Apply**

Pick: **OK** (to close the Customize User Interface dialog box)

Figure 10.32

When you pick Apply, your selections are applied to the icon. You should now see the And-gate icon that you made appear on your Logic toolbar as shown in Figure 10.32.

All the dialog boxes should now be closed. Close Tool Palettes if necessary to see the drawing editor.

Pick: **And icon** (on your new toolbar)

The And gate should now be attached to the crosshairs, ready for insertion into your drawing.

Position it as you like in your drawing and press the pick button. Press ↵ for the remaining prompts for scale and rotation.

Tip

If the And gate doesn't move with the cross hairs, press the Esc *key and try it again. If that doesn't fix the problem, return to the button properties dialog and check to see that you have the command entered with the correct syntax.*

The And-gate should appear in your drawing.

Next you will finish customizing the interface. You will add a selection of toolbars, windows, and palettes to your MyWay workspace.

Pick: **Tools, Customize, Interface**

Pick: **MyWay**

The Customize User Interface dialog box returns to your screen as shown in Figure 10.33.

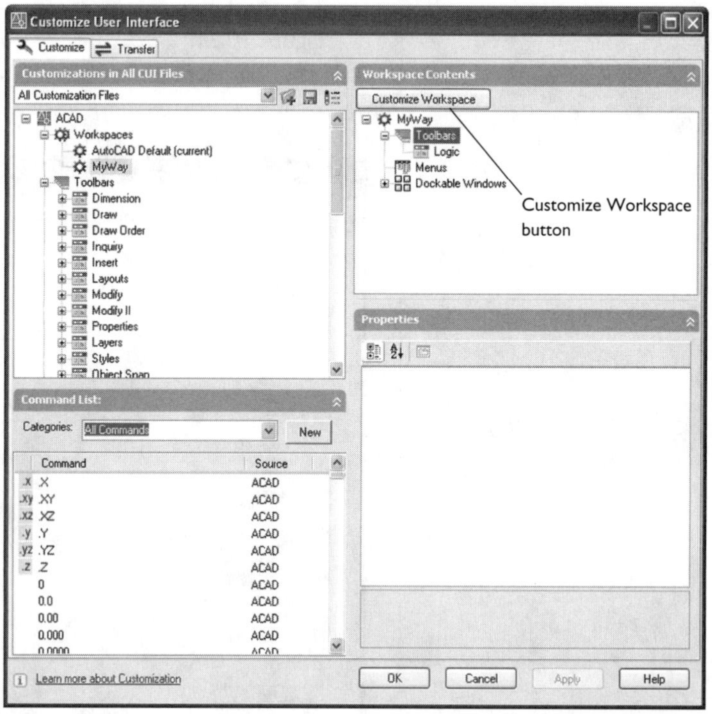

Figure 10.33

Pick: **Customize Workspace button**

Check the boxes to the left of toolbars you want to add to your MyWay workspace as in Figure 10.34. Be sure to add the Workspaces toolbar so that you can switch between workspaces quickly.

Warning

Be sure to add the Workspaces toolbar or you will have trouble switching back to the default workspace quickly.

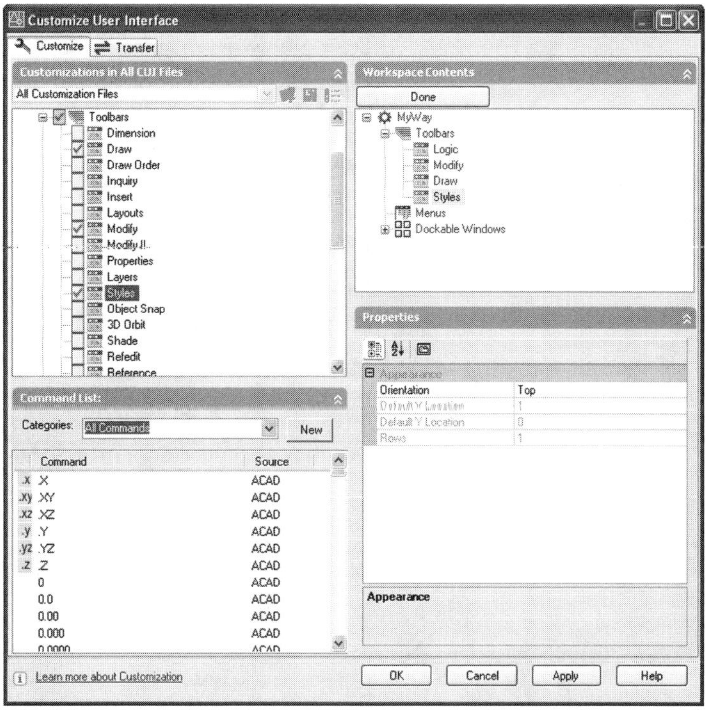

Figure 10.34

Own your own use the Menus listing shown in Figure 10.35 to select the File menu and any others you wish to add to your workspace.

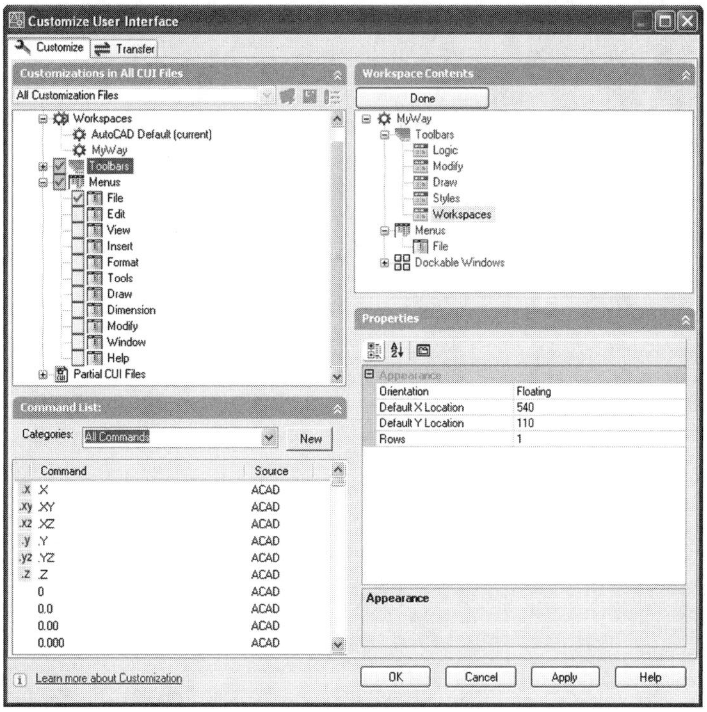

Figure 10.35

Pick: **Apply**

Pick: **OK**

Close any drawings and extra toolbars that you may have open.
Start a new drawing from the default template ***acad.dwt***
Right-click on any toolbar and use the pop-up list to turn on the Workspaces toolbar.

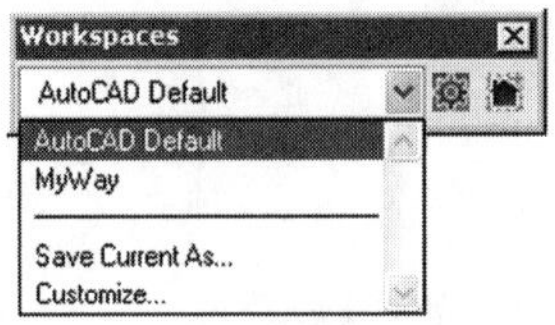

Figure 10.36

The Workspaces toolbar is shown in Figure 10.36. You will use it to select your custom MyWay workspace.

Pick: **MyWay** from the pull-down list on the Workspaces toolbar

The customizations you made to the interface now appear on the screen. To restore the default appearance,

Pick: **AutoCAD Default** from the Workspaces toolbar
Exit the AutoCAD program.

You have completed Tutorial 10.

Key Terms

And gate	block reference	group	Nor gate
block	Buffer gate	Inverter gate	Or gate
block name	customize	Nand gate	selectable group

Key Commands

Block	DesignCenter	Insert Block	Tool Palettes
Customize User Interface	Donut	Multiple Insert	Write Block
Customize Workspace	Explode	Object Group	

Exercises

10.1 Cup Washer

Draw a front orthographic view of the part shown. Create a block for the rounded arc-shaped feature. Practice inserting the block at different rotation angles. Add a right-side section view if so directed by your instructor.

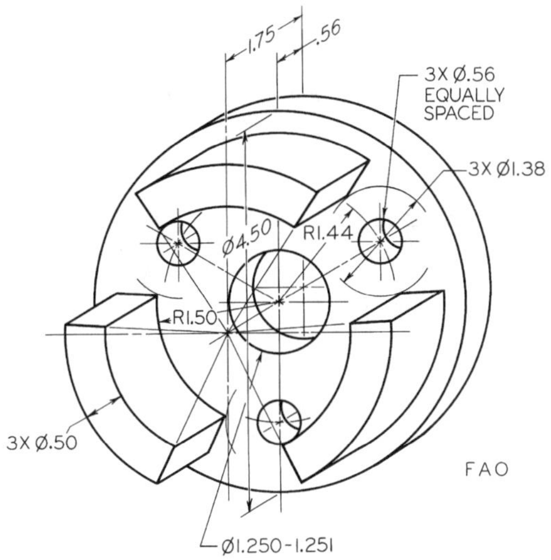

10.2 Stress Test Circuit

Create this circuit board layout, using Grid and Snap set to 0.2. Use donuts and polylines of different widths to draw the circuit.

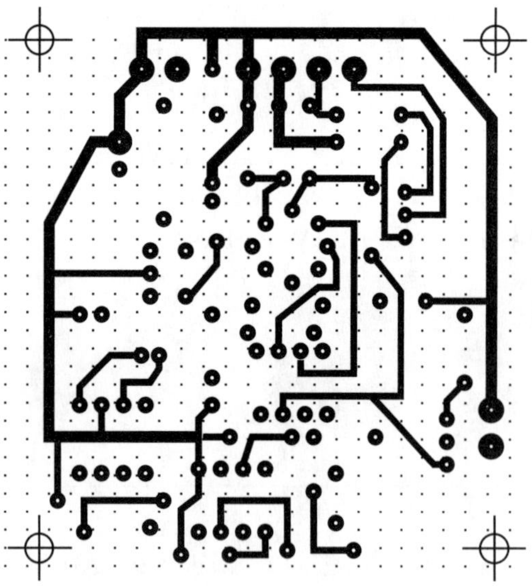

10.3M Decoder Logic Unit

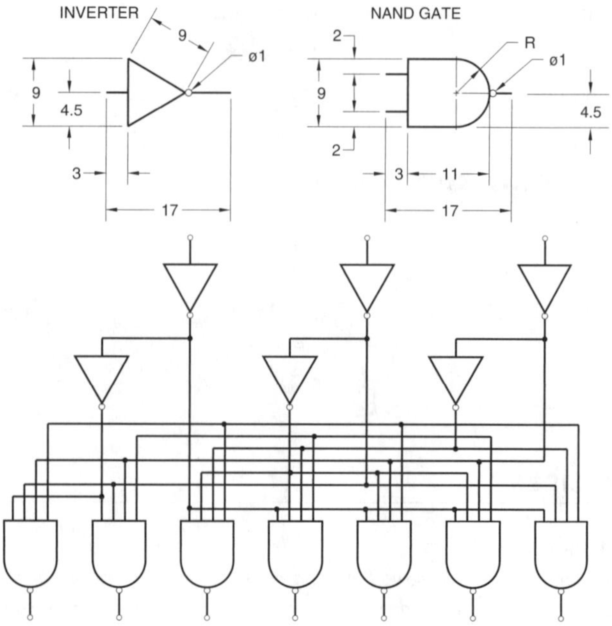

10.4 Floor Plan

Draw the floor plan shown for the first floor of a house. Create your own blocks for furniture and design a furniture layout for the house.

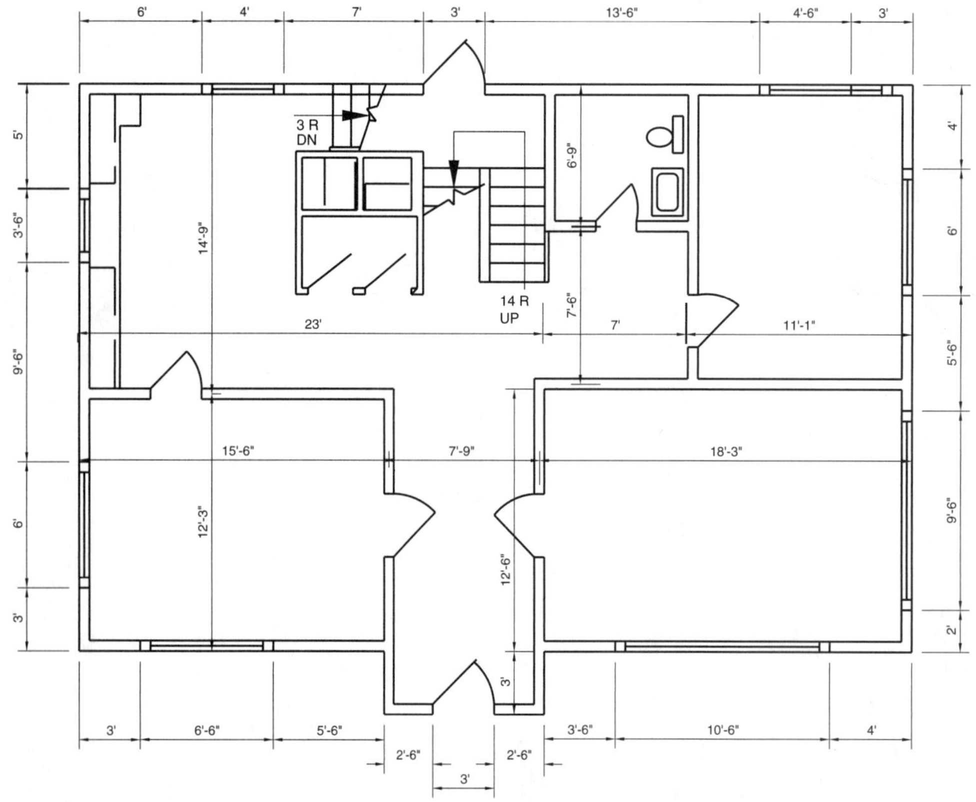

10.5M Arithmetic Logic Unit

Create blocks for the components according to the metric sizes shown. Use the blocks that you create to draw the circuit shown.

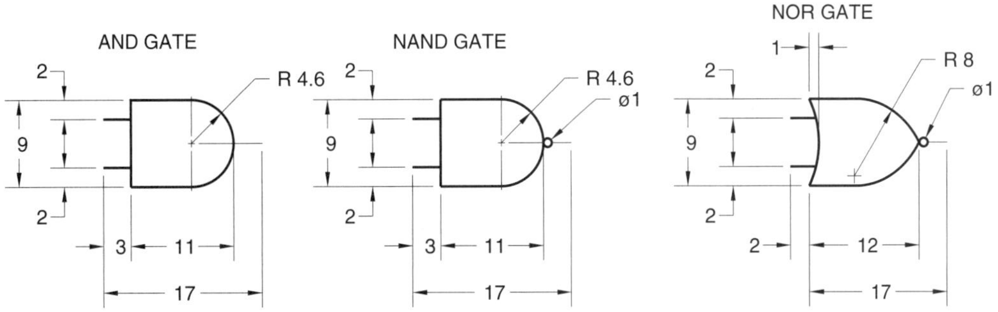

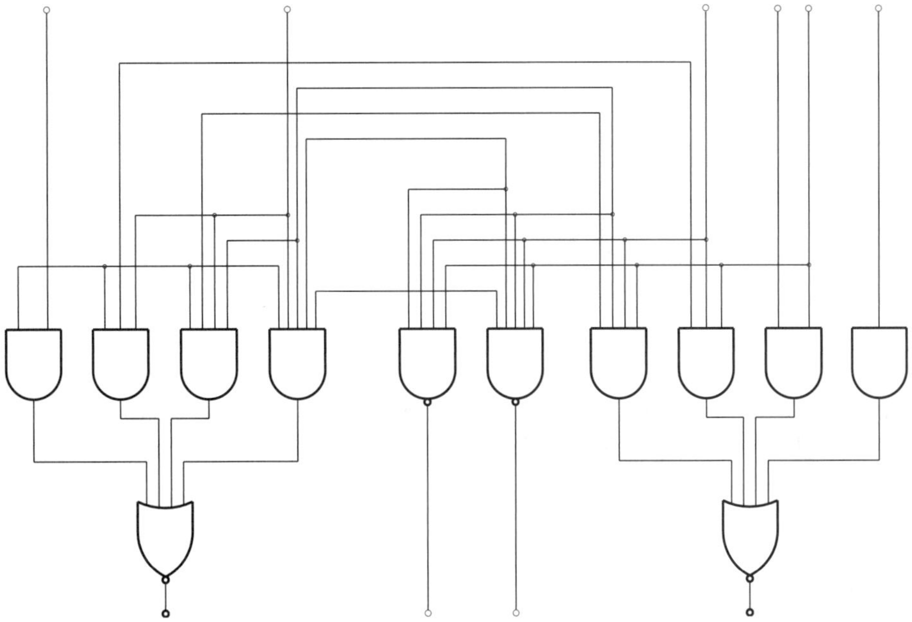

10.6 Amplifier Circuit

Use the grid at left to draw and create blocks for the components shown. Each square equals 0.0625. Use the blocks that you create to draw the amplifier circuit.

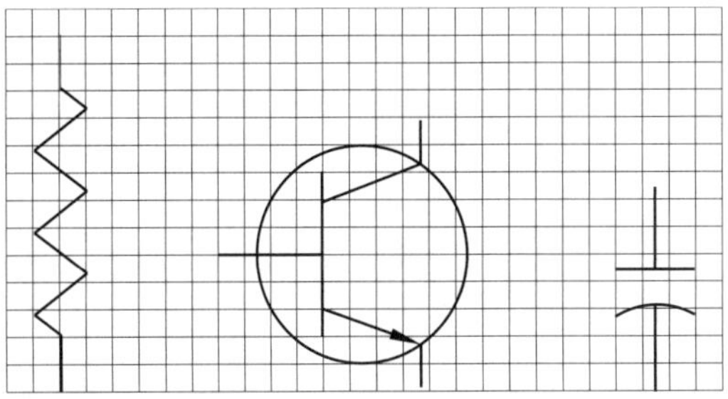

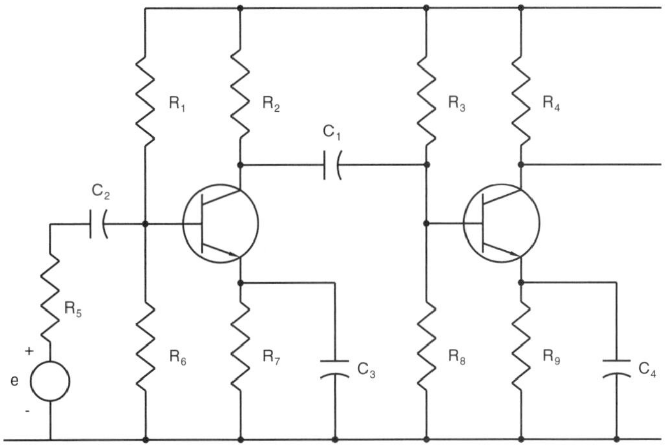

10.7 Piping Symbols

Draw the piping symbols at right to scale; the grid shown is 0.2 inch (you do not need to show it on your drawing). Use polylines 0.03 wide. Make each symbol a separate block and label it. Insert all the blocks into a drawing named pipelib.dwg.

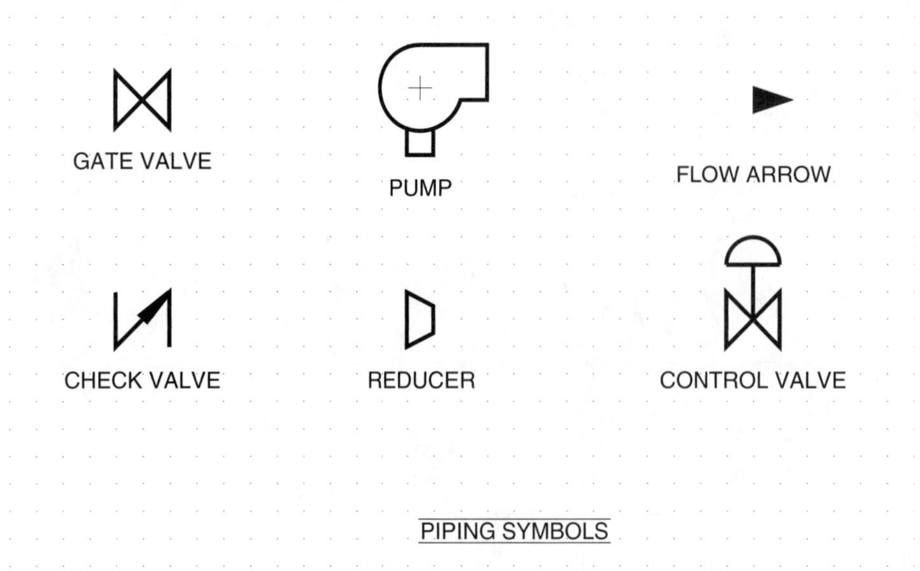

10.8 Utilities Layout

Construct this representation of the utilities layout for a group of city blocks (grid spacing is 0.25). Using Polylines 0.05 wide, construct and label the three main symbols shown. Then scale the symbols down to 1/4 size, make each one a block, and insert them in the proper locations.

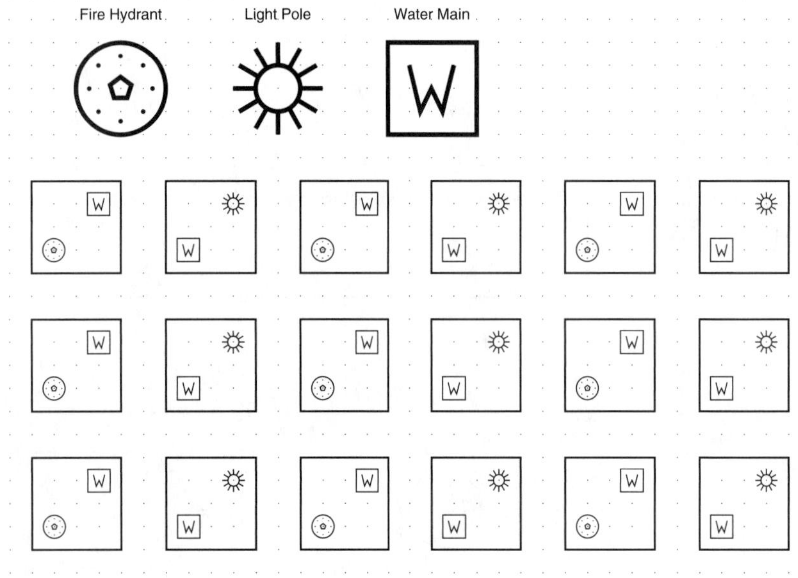

10.9 Office Plan

Draw the office furniture shown and create blocks for DeskA, DeskB, ChairA, ChairB, and the window. Use the floor plan shown as a basis for creating your own office plan.

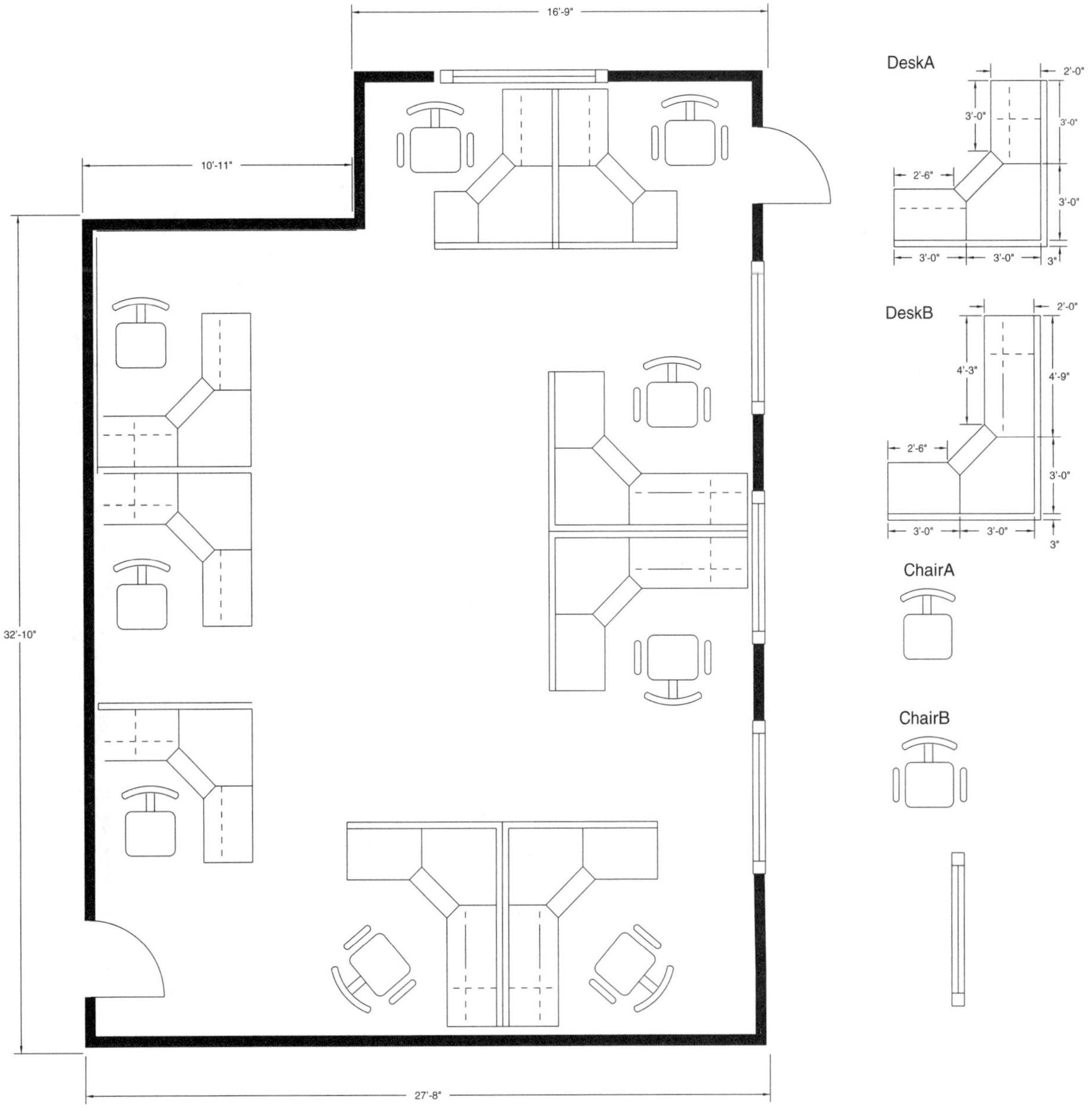

10.10 Wood Screws

Create blocks for each of the wood screws shown. The grid gives the proportions for drawing them. Make the diameter of each 1.00 so that you can easily determine the scale needed for inserting them at other sizes.

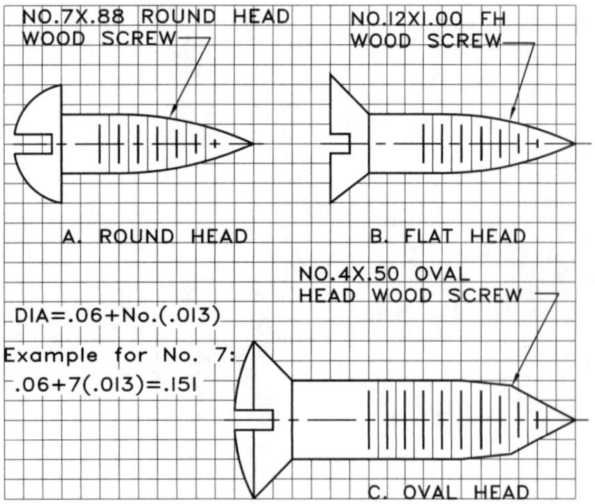

10.11 Mechanical Fasteners

Draw the hex head bolt, square head bolt, regular hex nut, and heavy hex nut according to the proportions shown. Make each into a block. Base the dimensions on a major diameter (D) of 1.00. This way when you insert the block you can easily determine the scaling factor that will be necessary to produce the correct major diameter. Insert each block into a drawing named fastenrs.dwg.

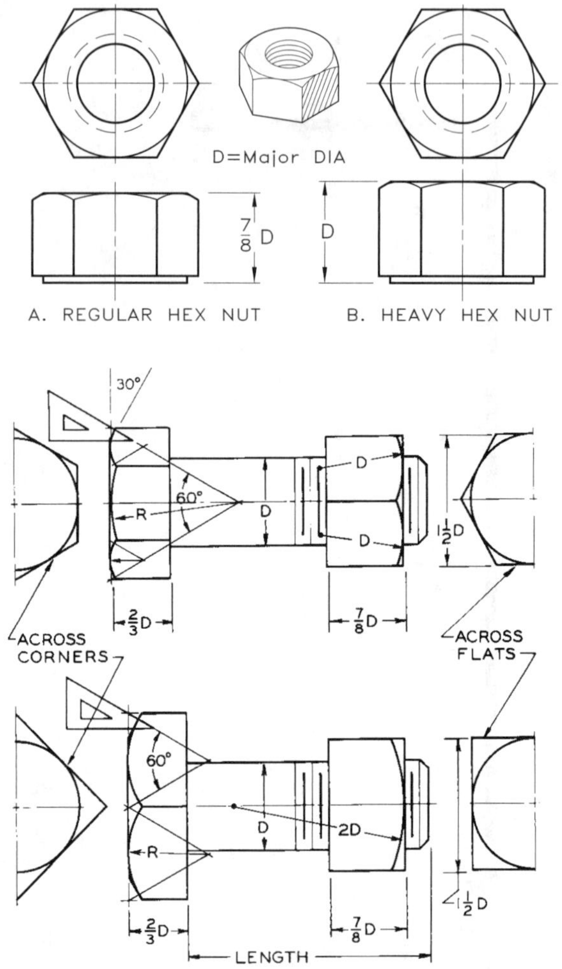

Tutorial

11 Introduction to Solid Modeling

Objectives

When you have completed this tutorial, you will be able to

1. Change the 3D viewport.
2. Work with multiple viewports.
3. Set individual limits, grid, and snap for each viewport.
4. Create and save User Coordinate Systems.
5. Set Isolines to control model appearance.
6. Create model geometry using primitives, extrusion, and revolution.
7. Use Boolean operators to add, subtract, and intersect parts of your model.
8. Use region modeling.
9. Create basic surface models.

Introduction

In Tutorials 1 through 10 you learned how to use the AutoCAD® software to model three-dimensional (3D) objects in two dimensions. When you create a multiview drawing, it is a model of the object that contains enough information within the various views to give the person interpreting it an understanding of the complete 3D shape. Your models have been composed of multiple two-dimensional (2D) views, which are used to convey the information. Now you will learn to use the AutoCAD program to create 3D models.

AutoCAD 3D models are of three types: wireframe, surface, and solid. *Wireframe modeling* uses 3D lines, arcs, circles, and other graphical objects to represent the edges and features of an object. It is called wireframe because it looks like a sculpture made from wires. *Surface modeling* takes 3D modeling one step further, adding surfaces to the model so that it can be shaded and hidden lines can be removed. A surface model is like an empty shell: There is nothing to tell you how the inside behaves. *Solid modeling* is the term for creating an accurate 3D model that describes a volume contained by the surfaces and edges making up the object. A solid model is most like a real object because it represents not only the lines and surfaces, but also the volume contained within. In this tutorial you will first learn to create solid models and then how to create surface models.

Using the computer, you can represent three dimensions in the drawing database; that is, you can create drawings by using X-, Y-, and Z-coordinates. When you create a solid model drawing database, in some ways it is as if the actual object were stored inside the computer. Benefits of solid models include the following: They are easier to interpret; they can be rendered (shaded) so that someone unfamiliar with engineering drawings can visualize the object easily; 2D views can be generated directly from them; and their *mass properties* can be analyzed. The need to create a physical prototype of the object may even be eliminated.

Creating a solid model is somewhat like sculpting the part in clay. You can add and subtract material with *Boolean operators* and create features by *revolution* and *extrusion*. Of course, when modeling with the AutoCAD software, you can be much more precise than when modeling with clay. At first, the AutoCAD software's solid modeling will look much like wireframe or surface modeling. The reason is that wireframe representation usually is used even in solid modeling and surface modeling to make many drawing operations quicker. When you want to see a more realistic representation, you can shade or hide the back lines of solid models and surface models.

Starting

Launch AutoCAD® 2006.

Begin a new drawing based on the AutoCAD default template drawing ***acad.dwt***. Save your new drawing as ***block.dwg***.

Check to see that you are in model space. The limits should be set to 12 × 9.

Set the grid to **2** and turn it on.

Use Zoom All so that the grid area fills the screen.

Tip

Setting the grid larger for now will help you see the Orbiter clearly.

The regularly spaced grid dots should appear every 2 units, filling your screen. When you are working in 3D, the grid can help you relate visually to the current viewing direction and coordinate system.

3D Coordinate Systems

The AutoCAD software defines the model geometry using precise X-, Y-, and Z-coordinates in what is called the *World Coordinate System (WCS)*. The WCS is fixed and is used to store both 2D and 3D drawing geometry in the database. Its default orientation on the screen is a horizontal X-axis, with positive values to the right, and a vertical Y-axis, with positive values above the X-axis. The Z-axis is perpendicular to the computer screen, with positive values in front of the screen. The default orientation of the axes is shown in Figure 11.1.

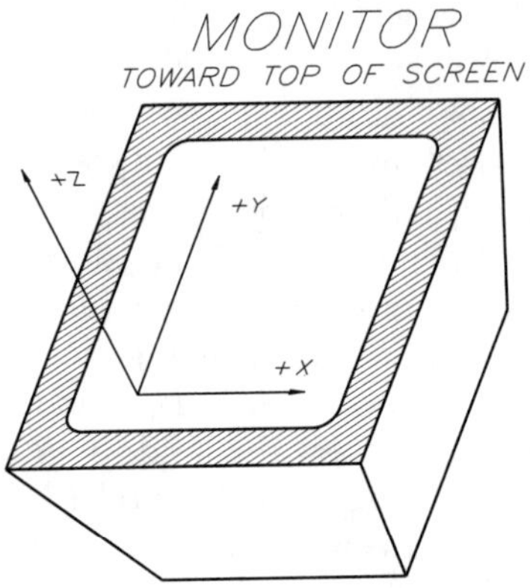

Figure 11.1

While creating 2D geometry, you have been using this default WCS. You have been looking straight down the Z-axis, so that a line in the Z-direction appears as a point. When you do not specify the Z-coordinate, the AutoCAD software uses the default elevation, which is zero. This method has made creating and saving 2D drawings easy.

Setting the Viewpoint

When creating 3D geometry, you will find it useful to establish a different direction, or several directions, from which to view the XY-plane, so that you can see the object's height along the Z-axis. You can do so with the 3DOrbit command (alias 3DO). You will turn on the 3D Orbit toolbar (shown in Figure 11.2) and use it to select the 3D Orbit icon to establish a new viewing direction.

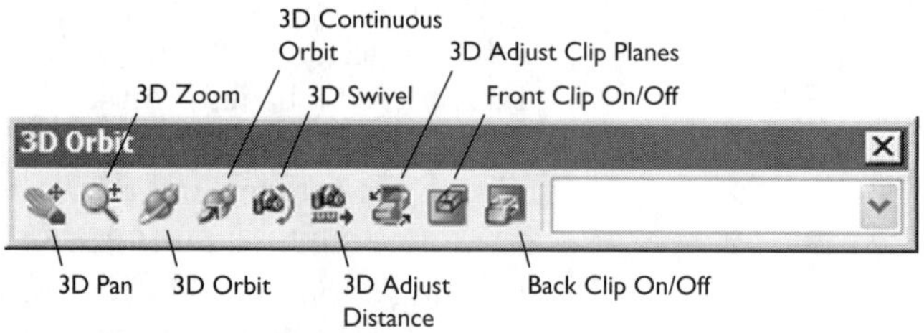

Figure 11.2

Right-click: on any toolbar and use the pop-up menu to turn on the **3D Orbit toolbar**

Pick: **3D Orbit icon**

The cursor changes to the orbiter cursor and the *arcball* appears on your screen, as shown in Figure 11.3. The arcball is a circle divided by four small circles into quadrants. In the 3DOrbit command, the center of the arcball (the target) stays stationary. The point from which you are viewing (the camera) moves around the target.

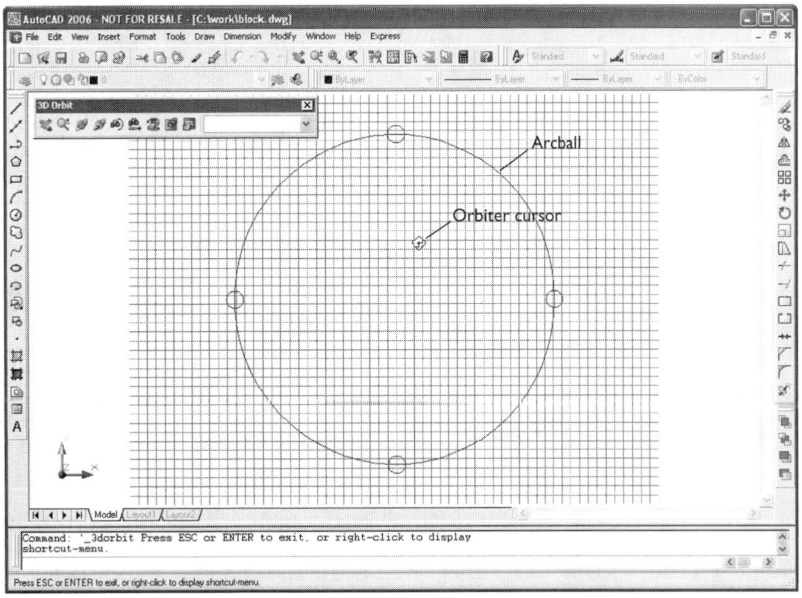

Figure 11.3

On your own, move your cursor over different parts of the arcball. Notice the change to the orbiter cursor.

Hold down the pick button and move your cursor inside the arcball circle.

Your view might appear something like that shown in Figure 11.4. The cursor appears as a sphere with circular orbits. Note that your view has changed. You are no longer looking straight down on the XY-plane, which is represented by the grid area. Your view is now from an angle. Notice that you can rotate the view freely, as if your cursor were grabbing a sphere surrounding the drawing objects and dragging it around the target point. Try rolling your mouse horizontally, vertically, and diagonally.

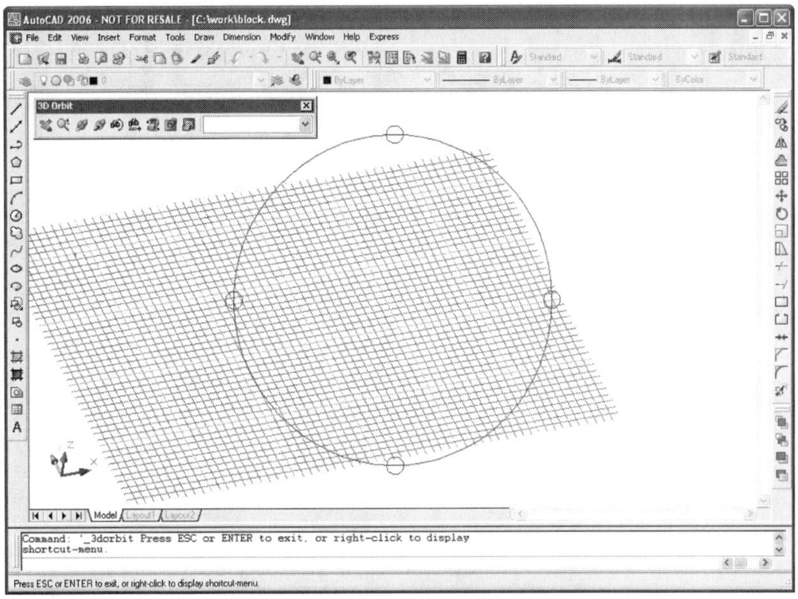

Figure 11.4

Now move the cursor outside the arcball. The cursor changes to a sphere circled by an arrow. Click and drag the cursor around, keeping it outside the arcball.

Notice that the view "rolls" around an axis that extends through the center of the arcball, perpendicular to the screen. Practice on your own rolling the view using this mode.

Move your cursor over the small circle at the left of the arcball.

The cursor now looks like a sphere surrounded by a horizontal ellipse with a horizontal line representing the Y-axis.

Click and drag your mouse from this point.

Notice that the view rotates around the Y-axis through the center of the arcball. The same thing results if you select the circle on the right side of the arcball.

Move the cursor to the small circle on the top of the arcball.

Click and drag your mouse here to see how the view rotates around the X-axis. The X-axis is shown as a horizontal line on the cursor icon.

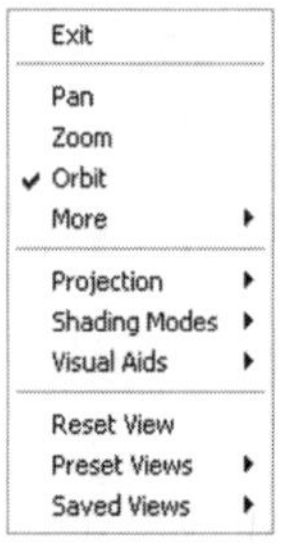

Figure 11.5

Right-click: **in the drawing area**

The pop-up menu shown in Figure 11.5 appears on your screen. You can use it to quickly select Realtime Pan and Zoom, change from parallel to perspective projection, change the shading method used, select default views, and reset the view, among other things.

Pick: **Preset Views, SE Isometric**

To exit the 3D Orbiter,

Press: Esc or ↵, or right-click to display the context menu and pick Exit

Set the grid to **.5** on your own.

Your screen should look like Figure 11.6. The Southeast isometric view that you have selected produces a *viewpoint* showing the coordinate system from above and to the right.

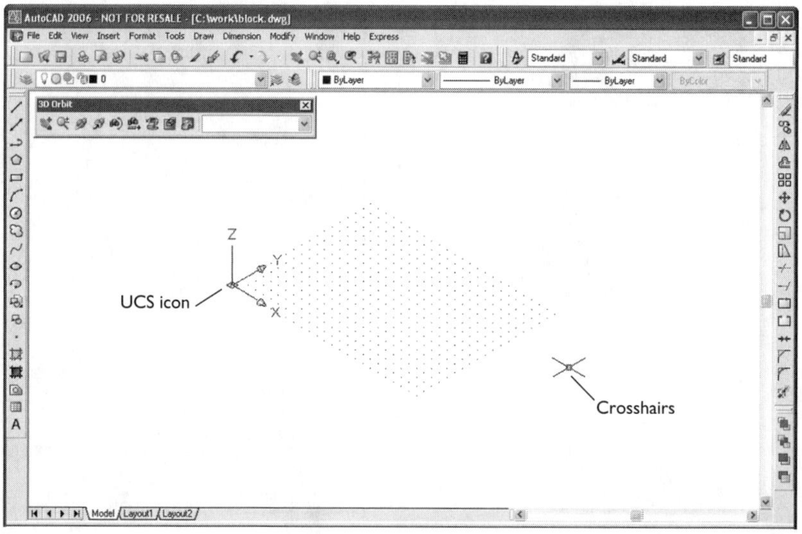

Figure 11.6

User Coordinate Systems

A *User Coordinate System (UCS)* is a set of X-, Y-, and Z-coordinates that you define to help you create your 3D models. You can define your own UCS, which may have a different origin and rotation from the WCS and may be tilted at any angle with respect to it. UCSs are helpful because your mouse moves in only two dimensions, and UCSs let you orient the basic drawing coordinate system at any angle in the 3D model space of the drawing, so you can continue using your mouse or other pointing device for drawing. You can define any number of UCSs, give them names, and save them in a drawing, but only one can be active at a time.

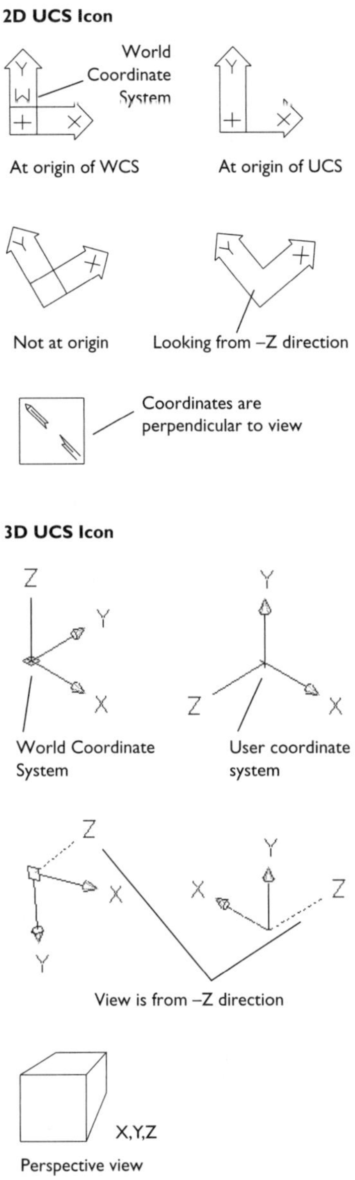

Figure 11.7

The UCS Icon

The UCS icon appears in the lower left of the screen. It will help you to orient yourself when looking at views of the object. The monitor screen is essentially flat so, even if the object is a 3D solid model in the database, only 2D views of it can be represented on the monitor. Because wireframe models look the same from front and back or from any two opposing viewpoints, keeping track of which view you are seeing on the screen is especially important.

Figure 11.7 shows some of the appearances of the 2D and 3D UCS icons. When you are displaying the 2D UCS icon, it is always drawn in the XY-plane of the current UCS. The arrows at the X- and Y-ends always point in the positive direction of the X- and Y-axes of the current UCS. A W appearing in the UCS icon tells you that the UCS is currently aligned with the WCS. The box in the lower corner of the icon indicates that you are viewing the UCS from above. A plus sign in the lower left of the icon indicates that the icon is positioned at the origin of the current UCS. When you start a drawing from the *acad.dwt* template, the origin (0,0,0) of the drawing is in the lower left of the screen. If the UCS were at the origin, it would be partially out of the view; thus the default for the 2D UCS icon is not at the origin. You can use the UCSICON command to reposition the icon so that it is at the origin of the X-, Y-, and Z-coordinate system.

A special symbol may appear instead of the UCS icon to indicate that the current viewing direction of the UCS is edgewise. (Think of the X- and Y-coordinate system of the UCS as a flat plane like a piece of paper; the viewing direction is set so that you are looking directly onto the edge of the paper.) In this case you can't use most of the drawing tools, so the icon appears as a box containing a broken pencil. Take special note of this icon.

The 3D UCS icon shows the X-, Y-, and Z-axis directions. When the Z-axis is viewed from the negative direction, it appears dashed. A box at the intersection of the X-, Y-, and Z-axes indicates the World Coordinate System is active. A small plus sign at the intersection indicates that the UCS icon is at the origin of the coordinate system.

The *perspective icon* replaces the UCS icon when perspective viewing is active; it appears as a cube drawn in perspective. Many commands are also limited when perspective viewing is in effect.

Next you will explore the options for setting the appearance of the UCS icon.

Command: **UCSICON** ↵

Enter an option [ON/OFF/All/Noorigin/ORigin/Properties] <ON>: **P** ↵

The UCS icon dialog box appears on your screen as shown in Figure 11.8.

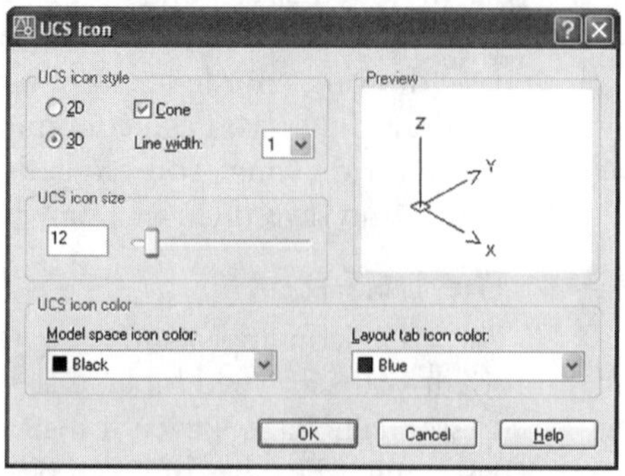

Figure 11.8

You can use this dialog box to switch between the 2D and 3D appearance of the UCS icon. You can also set the color, linewidth, and arrowhead appearance for the icon as well as its size. Test the effect of various settings on the image tile shown in the dialog box. When you are finished, leave the appearance set to show a 3D UCS icon.

Pick: **Cancel** (to exit the UCS icon dialog box)

Next you will create three new layers, one to contain the solid model, another for the viewports, and the third for the drawing's border.

Use the Layer Properties Manager to **create the following layers**:

MYMODEL	Blue	Continuous
VPORT	Magenta	Continuous
BORDER	White	Continuous

Set layer **MYMODEL** as the current layer.

Showing the Solids Toolbar

Right-click: on any toolbar and use the pop-up menu to turn on the **Solids toolbar**

The Solids toolbar will appear on your screen, as shown in Figure 11.9. Use the methods that you have learned to position it in an area of your screen where it will be accessible, but not in the way of your drawing.

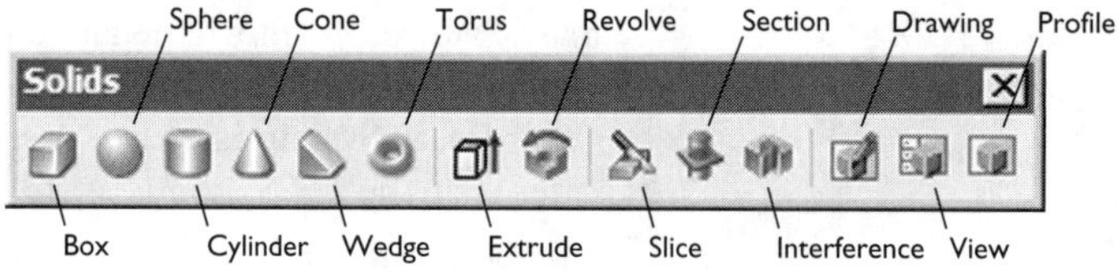

Figure 11.9

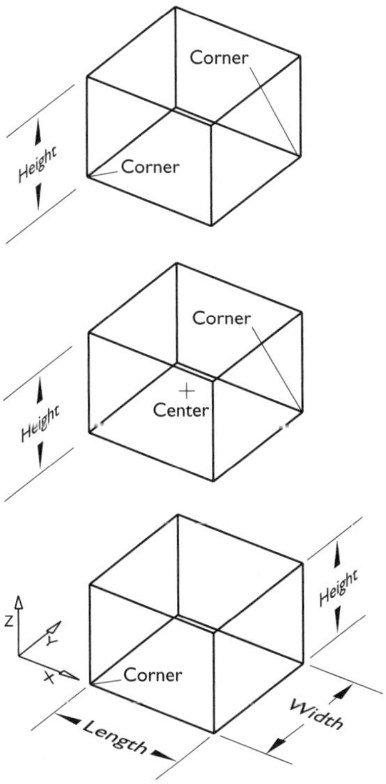

Figure 11.10

Creating an Object

The AutoCAD software provides three methods for creating model geometry: *primitives*, extrusion, and revolution. Primitives are basic shapes (e.g., boxes, cylinders, and cones) that can be joined to form more complex shapes. You will create a solid 3D box. Later in this tutorial you will learn how to join shapes by using Boolean operators and how to create other shapes with extrusion and revolution.

The Box command enables you to draw a solid rectangular prism. You can draw a box by specifying the corners of its base and its height, its center, corner, and height, or its location and length, width, and height. Figure 11.10 shows the information you specify to draw a box using these methods. The default method of defining a box is to specify two corners across the diagonal in the XY-plane and the height in the Z-direction.

You will use the Box selection on the Solids toolbar and draw a solid box by specifying the corners of the base and the height of the box.

Pick: **Box icon**

The prompt for the box primitive appears. You will type in the coordinates.

Specify corner of box or [CEnter] <0,0,0>: **2,2,0** ↵
Specify corner or [Cube/Length]: **8,6,0** ↵
Specify height: **3** ↵

Your screen should be similar to Figure 11.11.

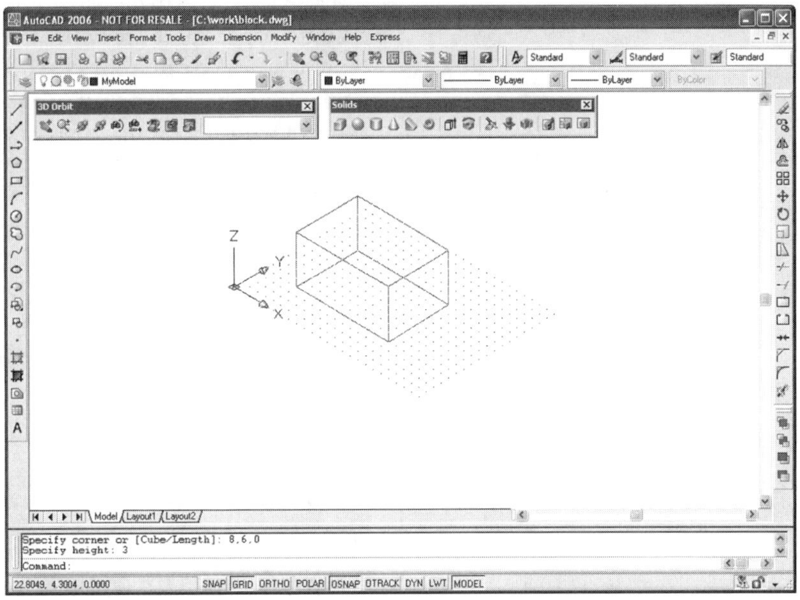

Figure 11.11

Next, shade the box, so that it appears as a more realistic solid. You are going to like this!

Pick: **View, Shade, Flat Shaded**

The box should now appear on your screen as shown in Figure 11.12.

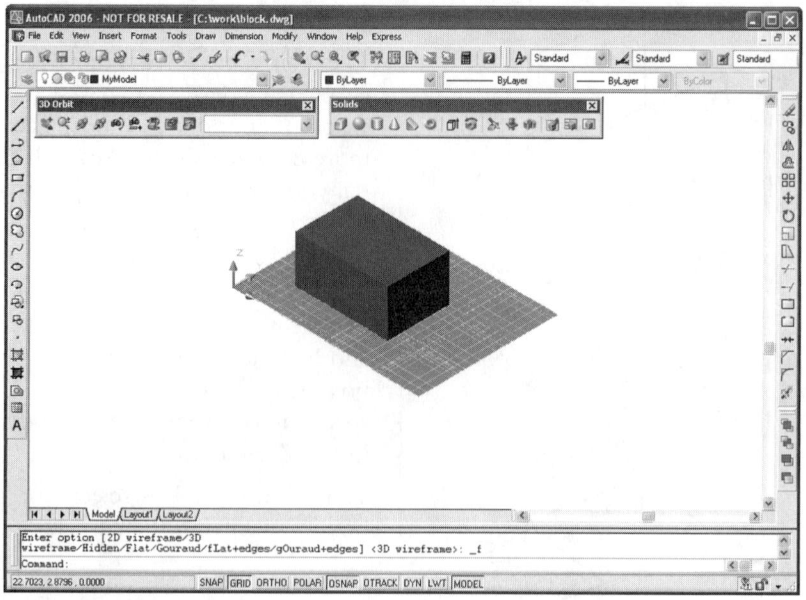

Figure 11.12

Creating Multiple Viewports

Now you have a 3D solid object on your screen. You will next create viewports to show several views of the object at the same time. This way you can create just one solid model and produce a drawing with the necessary 2D orthographic views directly from that 3D model. Having several views also makes creating the model easier. You have already used a single paper space viewport for printing and plotting in Tutorial 5. Now you will create four viewports and then change them so that they contain four different views of the model. You can think of the four separate viewports as four separate TV screens, each one of them showing the model. Each TV screen (viewport) can show a different view of the game (similar to watching the same televised event on several different stations at once). When watching several televisions, each cameraperson is looking at the game from a different angle, producing a different view on each TV set. Yet there is only one real event being televised. Multiple viewports work the same way. You can have many AutoCAD viewports, each of which contains a different view of the model, but there is only one model space and each object in it need be created only once. You will set layer VPORT current and then switch to paper space where you will create four viewports.

Pick: **VPORT to set it current using the Layer control**
Pick: **Layout1 tab**

When you switch to Layout1, note the triangular paper space icon in the lower left of your screen and shown in Figure 11.13. Recall from Tutorial 5 that paper space allows you to arrange views of your model, text, and other objects as you would on a sheet of paper.

If necessary, use Zoom All so that the paper space layout fills the graphics area.

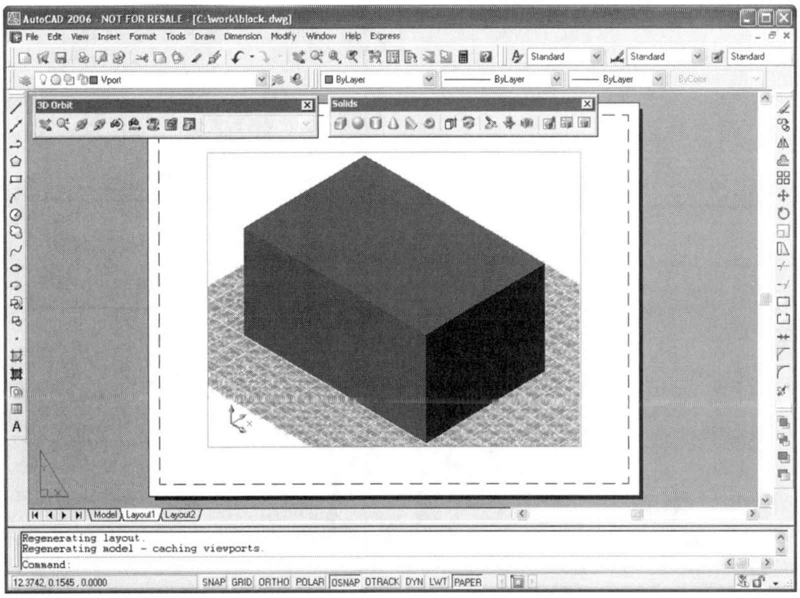

Figure 11.13

Tip

The type of viewports created depends on whether you are in model space or paper space. Paper space (or layout) viewports are called floating viewports, because they can be arranged on top of each other or with space between them. You can also create viewports in model space. These are called tiled viewports because they must always abut one another like floor tiles. In these tutorials you will use floating viewports. Tiled viewports can be a useful modeling tool. Experiment with them on your own.

You will erase the current viewport and create four viewports in its place. Check to make sure you are in paper space.

Pick: **Erase icon**
Select objects: **the magenta viewport border**
Select objects: ↵

The viewport and objects showing in it disappear from your layout. The block you created is still there. You will make four new viewports in which to show it. You use the Mview command to create viewports. You will pick it from the View menu on the menu bar.

Pick: **View, Viewports, 4 Viewports**

The Mview command is echoed in the command prompt area, and its prompts appear. You will place the viewports inside the area that you want to plot full size, centered on your page, as you did in Tutorial 5. You may find that the following values work for your printer. If you used a different setting in Tutorial 5, apply the one that works for your printer.

Specify first corner or [Fit] <Fit>: **.25,.25** ↵
Specify opposite corner: **10.25,7.75** ↵

Four viewports appear on your screen, each containing an identical view of the object.

Your screen should be similar to Figure 11.14.

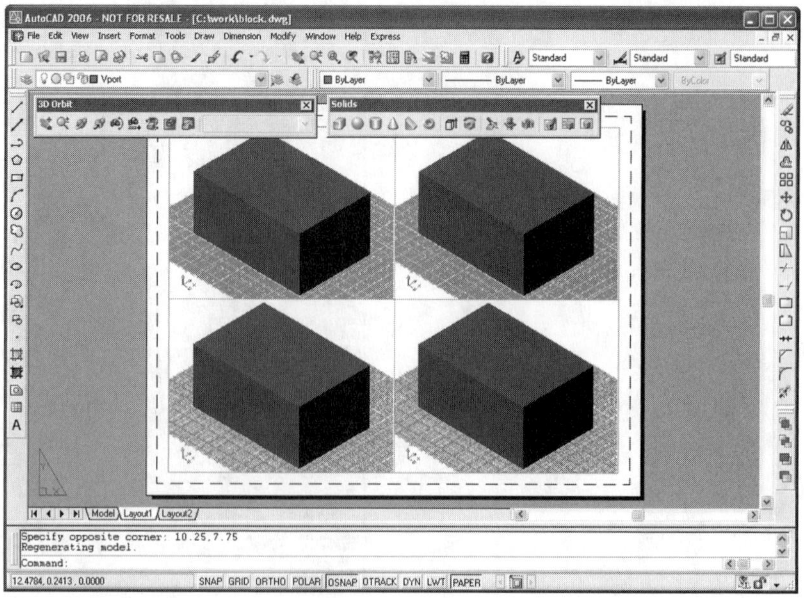

Figure 11.14

Next, you will change the viewing direction inside each viewport so that together they show a top, front, right-side, and isometric view of the model.

Remember, when you are in paper space, you cannot change things that are in model space. The original box was created in model space, where you create and make changes to your model, including the direction from which it is viewed. To switch back to model space,

Command: **MS** ↵

You know that you are in model space when the paper space icon disappears. You should still see a 3D UCS icon displayed in each viewport. Next you will switch each viewport to wireframe display.

Selecting the Active Viewport

To make the upper left viewport active, you will move the arrow cursor until it is positioned in the top left viewport and then press the pick button.

Pick: **anywhere in the upper left viewport**

The crosshairs will appear in the viewport and the viewport becomes highlighted, as shown in Figure 11.15. This indicates that it is now the active viewport.

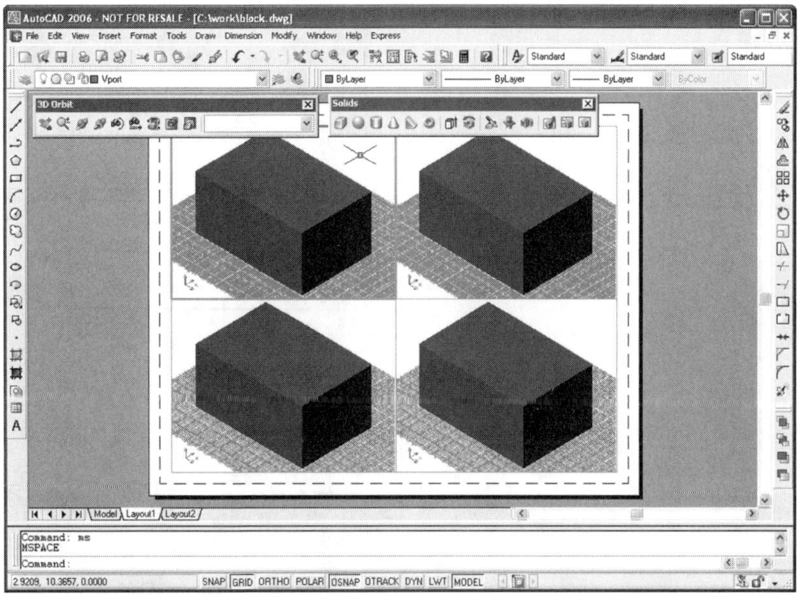

Figure 11.15

You can only draw in a viewport and pick points in it when it is active. After you create something, whatever you created is visible in all other viewports showing that area of the WCS, unless the layer that the object is on is frozen in another viewport. (Using the Vplayer command, you can freeze layers in specific viewports.) Keep in mind that, while you are using a certain viewport to access model space, there is only one model space. Thus, you can start drawing something in one viewport and finish drawing it in another.

Tip

You can press Ctrl-R to toggle the active viewport. This action is helpful when you are unable to pick in the viewport for some reason.

Command: **SHADEMODE** ↵

Enter option [2D wireframe/3D wireframe/Hidden/Flat/Gouraud/fLat+edges/gOuraud+edges] <2D wireframe>: **2** ↵

The upper left viewport shows the wireframe display of the box you created, and the UCS icon appears standard.

On your own, make the lower left and lower right viewports active and set Shademode equal to 2 in those viewports.

When you are finished your screen should look similar to Figure 11.16.

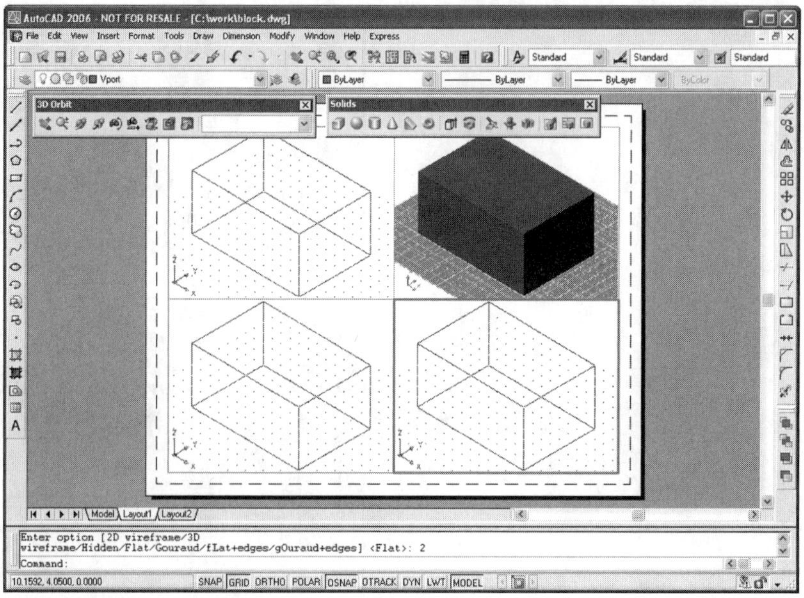

Figure 11.16

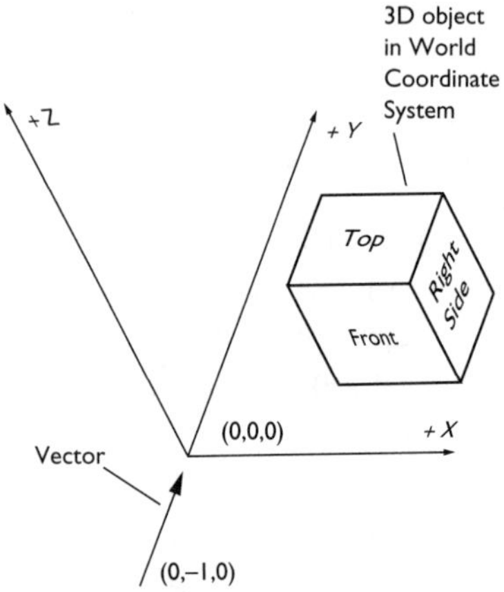

Front view is produced by Vpoint (0,–1,0), which looks perpendicular to the ZX-plane.

Figure 11.17

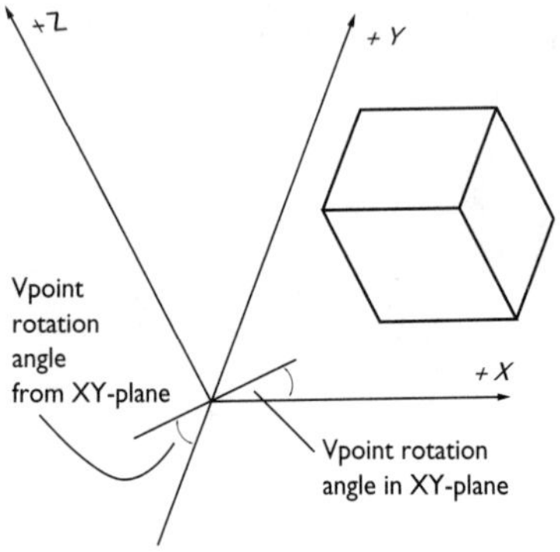

Figure 11.18

Next, you will change the upper left viewport to show the view of the model looking straight down from the top.

Changing the Viewpoint

You will change the viewpoint for the upper left viewport so that it shows the top view of the object. By controlling the viewpoint with the Vpoint (Viewpoint) command, you can create a view from any direction. The numbers you enter in the Vpoint command are the X-, Y-, and Z-coordinates of a point that defines a ***vector***, or directional line. The other point defining the vector is the origin (0,0,0). Your line of sight, or ***viewpoint***, is defined by this vector, or imaginary line, toward the origin from the coordinates of the point you enter. The actual size of the number you enter does not matter—only the direction it establishes. Thus entering 2,2,0 is the same as entering 1,1,0, as only the direction of sight is determined by this number. See Figure 11.17.

You can also select the Rotate option and establish the viewing direction by specifying the rotation angle in the XY-plane from the X-axis and then the rotation above the XY-plane for the viewpoint. See Figure 11.18. Experiment with these options on your own.

Using the View Toolbar

The View toolbar is shown in Figure 11.19. You can use it to pick different viewing directions for the active viewport. The selections on the View toolbar use the Vpoint command to select commonly used viewing directions. You will use the toolbar to pick the Top View icon.

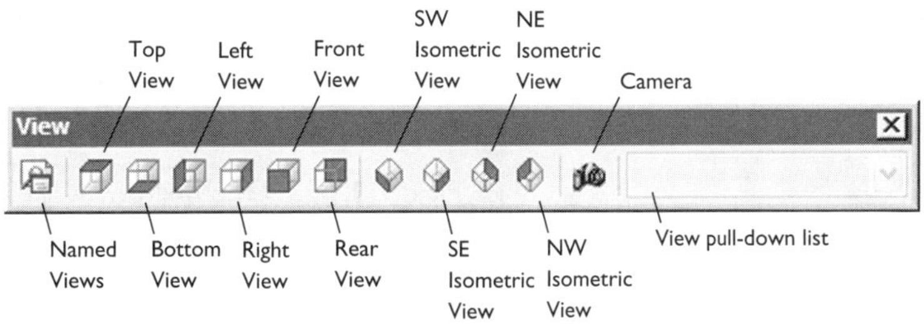

Figure 11.19

Right-click: on any toolbar and select to turn on the **View toolbar**
Make sure the **upper left viewport** is active.
Pick: **Top View icon**

The view in the upper left viewport changes. Now you are looking straight down on top of the box. Your screen should look like Figure 11.20, which shows the 3D box viewed from the top in the upper left viewport. Note that the view of the UCS icon is straight down the Z-axis now that you have changed the viewing direction.

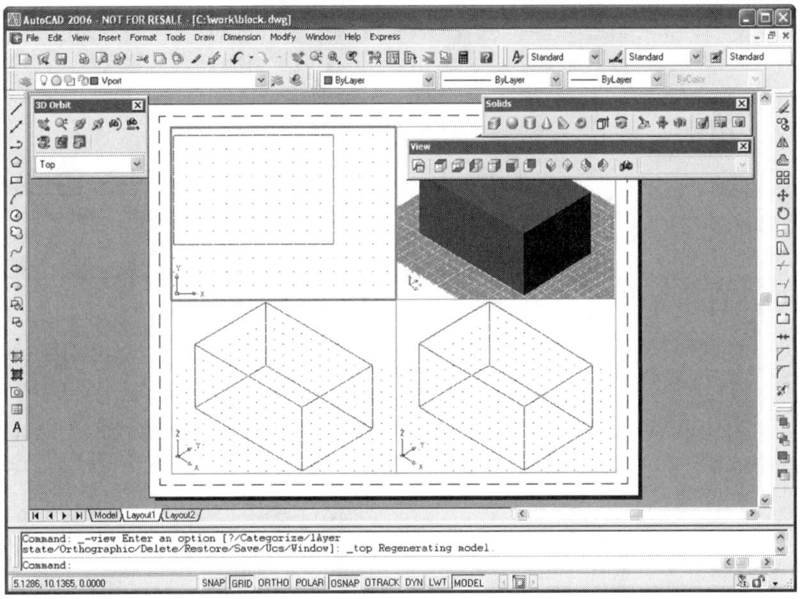

Figure 11.20

You will turn on the Viewports toolbar and set the viewing scale for the viewport so that the object appears half-size in paper space.

Double-click: **outside the viewports on the layout sheet to switch to paper space**

Tip

Or press Ctrl*-1 to pop up the properties dialog box.*

The paper space icon should appear in the lower left corner of the graphics area.

Right-click: **on any toolbar and use the menu to turn on the Viewports toolbar**

The Viewports toolbar appears on your screen.

Pick: **the upper left viewport border**

The area at the right of the toolbar lists the scale.

Pick: **1:2** (using the pull-down list at the right of the Viewports toolbar)
Press: [Esc] twice to remove the grips from the viewport

The top view of the box should fit into the viewport at half paper space scale. Your drawing screen should look like that in Figure 11.21.

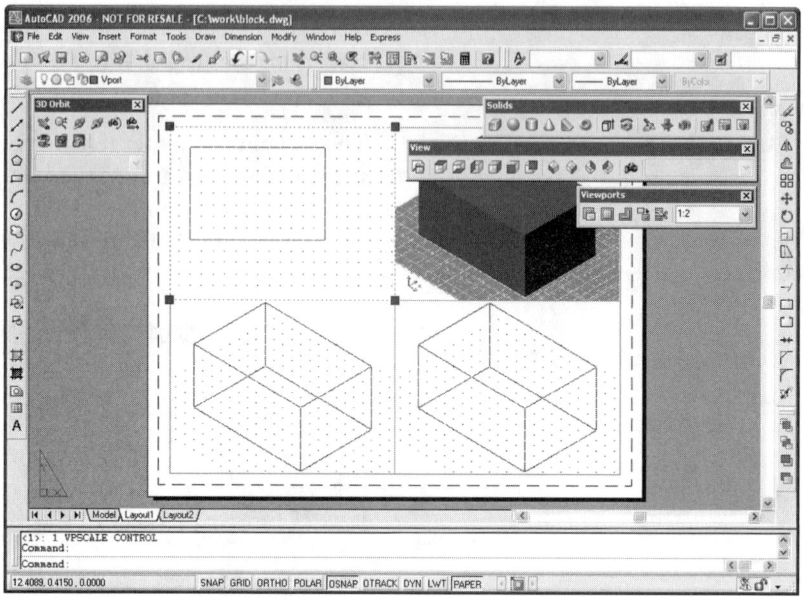

Figure 11.21

Each viewport can contain its own setting for Grid, Snap, and Zoom. Now make the lower left viewport active and switch to model space.

Double-click: **anywhere in the lower left viewport to make it active and switch to model space**

The crosshairs appear in the lower left viewport and its border becomes highlighted. You should see the UCS icon in each viewport.

You will use the Front View icon to change the view of the lower left viewport.

Pick: **Front View icon**

Now the view in this viewport is of the front of the object, as though you had taken the top view and tipped it 90° away from you. (Imagine that the original Y-axis is projecting straight into your monitor.) The object is again too large to fit in the viewport. Think of the distance of the object from the viewport or drawing screen as determined by the zoom set by the Standard scale using the Viewport toolbar. Once again you will set the Standard viewing scale to 1:2. This time, you will use the quick method of setting the scale inside the viewport.

Pick: **1:2** (using the Viewport toolbar pull-down list of standard scales)

Now you see the entire front view of the object in the viewport at half size related to the paper units. Your screen should be similar to Figure 11.22.

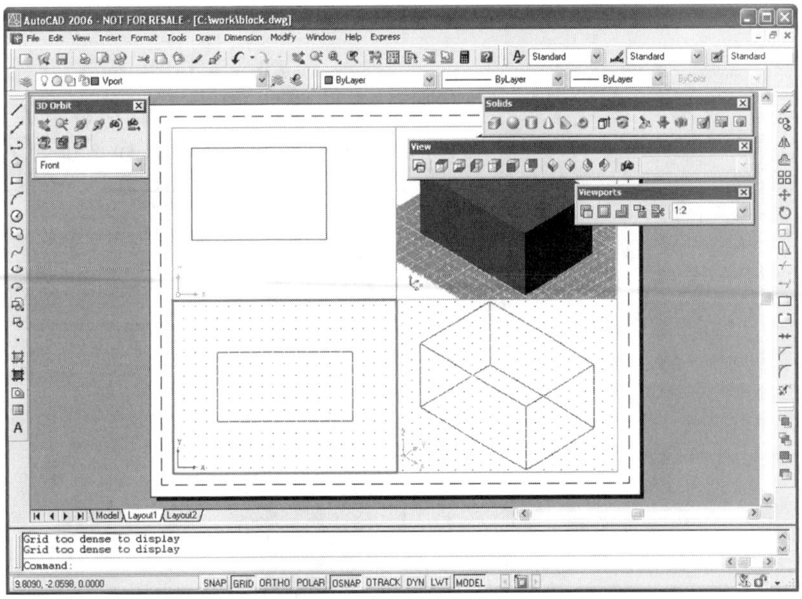

Figure 11.22

Notice that the grid aligned so that it is parallel to the surface in the front view. Previously the grid was parallel to the bottom surface of the block in the top view. The UCS icon no longer has a box drawn where the axes meet. This tells you that your drawing's current XY-plane has changed so that it is not the original World Coordinate System. This is a convenient feature to help you create 3D drawings. The coordinate system can automatically align with surfaces parallel to the view. Think about what would happen if it did not. It would be like looking at a piece of paper edgewise at eye level and then trying to draw on it. If the user coordinates were not parallel to your view, you could not pick points in the viewport to draw objects.

Save your drawing *block.dwg* at this time.

Viewports Using Different UCSs

The ability to display more than one UCS at a time in different viewports is controlled by system variable UCSVP. When UCSVP is set to 1 in a viewport, the viewport is locked so that it does not change to match the display of the current UCS. It retains its original UCS. When UCSVP is set to 0, the viewport always displays the current UCS. Next you will set the UCSVP variable for the upper right (isometric view) to 0, so that it always displays the current UCS.

Pick: **the upper right viewport so that it becomes active—its border will be highlighted**

Command: **UCSVP** ↵

Enter new value for UCSVP <1>: **0** ↵

The upper right viewport should now no longer retain its original UCS. It should change to display the active UCS. In general this is useful so that you can use this isometric view to see your current drawing plane. Next you will make the lower left viewport (front view) active and change the UCS. You will check the effect this has in the isometric view.

Pick: **the lower left viewport to make it active**

The grid shows in the lower left viewport and the grid in the shaded upper right viewport switches so that it is parallel to the front surface of the object, as shown in Figure 11.23.

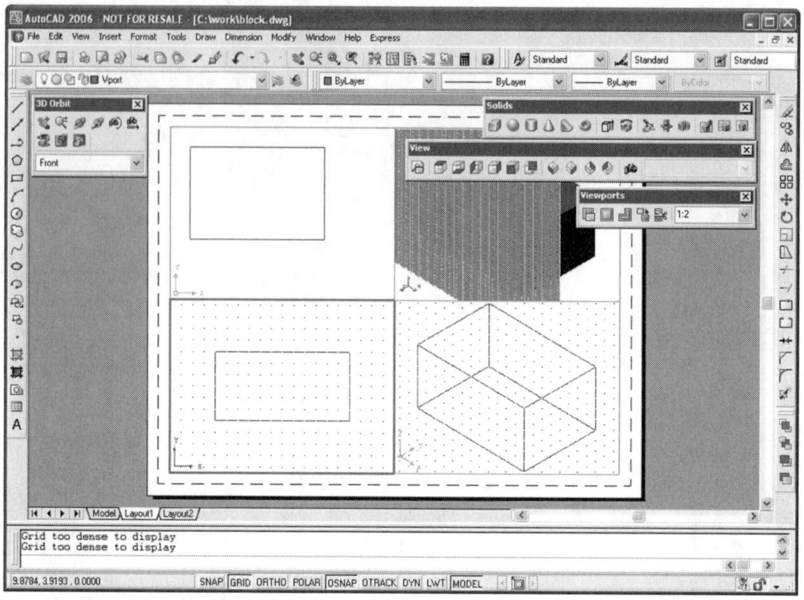

Figure 11.23

Pick: **inside the upper left viewport**

Notice that the grid displays in the upper left viewport and becomes parallel to the bottom surface of the object once again in the upper right viewport.

Pick: **inside the lower left viewport**

The UCS returns to the one set for the front view (parallel to the view in the lower left viewport)

Setting Up the Right-Side View

You will continue to set the viewing direction and create a UCS for the right-side view.

Pick: **the lower right viewport to make it active**

Now the crosshairs appear in the lower right viewport. You will create a side view of the model in this viewport. You will use the Right View icon to select the viewing direction for this view.

Pick: **Right View icon**

Tip

If you have trouble lining up the views, use the Pan command to make them line up approximately while you are working. To line them up exactly, use MVSETUP and use the Align option. Select Horizontal or Vertical alignment. Then pick a point in one viewport (using Snap to Endpoint or some other object snap) and pick a point that should align in the other viewport (again using an object snap). The view in the viewport that you pick second will be shifted to align with the point you selected in the first viewport. You can use Pan in the first viewport to position the view where you want it before you begin the MVSETUP command.

The view changes to show a right-side view of the object. You will zoom the view relative to paper space, as you did with the first two views. This time you will set the viewing scale using the Zoom Scale icon (see Figure 11.24) with the Zoom XP command option.

Pick: **Zoom Scale icon** from the Zoom flyout on the Standard toolbar
Enter Scale factor (nX or nXP): **.5XP** ⏎

Now the right-side view matches the size of the other orthographic views and the UCS and grid are parallel to this viewport. The upper right viewport where UCSVP has been set so that it shows the current user coordinate system has the grid parallel to the side of the object. Notice that just because the UCS is parallel to the right side view does not mean that it is on the right side of the object. The automatic UCS for the viewport is created so that it goes through the origin (0,0,0) of the original world coordinate system. You can create user coordinate systems with any other orientation you want. You will learn more about it later in this tutorial.

When you are finished, your screen should look like Figure 11.24.

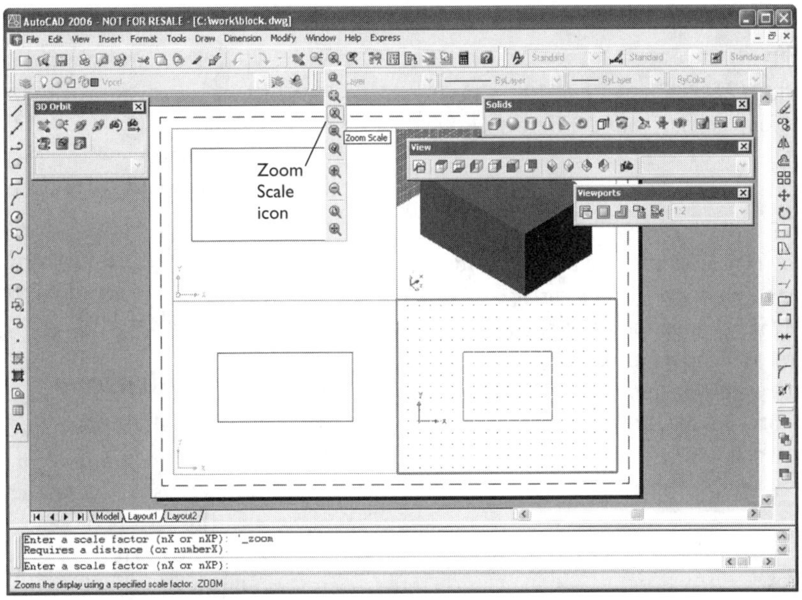

Figure 11.24

Make the upper right viewport, in which the box appears 3D, active by picking in the viewport.

The crosshairs will appear in the viewport when you select it.

Command: **Z** ⏎
Specify corner of window, enter a scale factor (nX or nXP), or [All/Center/Dynamic/Extents/Previous/Scale/Window/Object] <real time>: **.8X** ⏎

Next you will make the upper left viewport active and restore the WCS as the active coordinate system.

Pick: **to make the upper left viewport active**

Your screen should look like Figure 11.25.

Tip

The scale in the isometric viewport need not match the scale in the top, front, and side orthographic views. Isometric views are often shown at a different, visually pleasing scale.

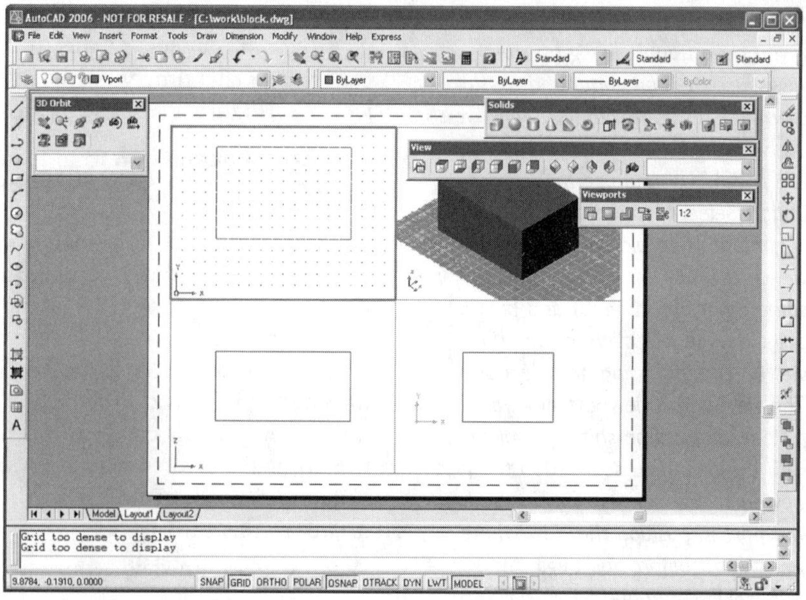

Figure 11.25

Tip

The PLAN command produces a view looking directly onto the current UCS.

Tip

You can quickly create this standard arrangement of views by using MVSETUP and then selecting to create standard engineering views, or by starting from the template file, proto-3d.dwt*, provided with these tutorials.*

Tip

If you do not specify a Z-coordinate, it is assumed to be your current elevation, which should be 0.

Now the UCS icon appears parallel to the top view in the upper left viewport. The box around the origin of the UCS tells you that it is the WCS. The default AutoCAD XY-plane is considered to be the *plan view* of the WCS. A plan view is basically a top view, which may sound familiar if you have worked with architectural drawings.

In the next portion of the tutorial, you will familiarize yourself with the basic solid modeling primitives that you can use to create drawing geometry. You will add and subtract them with Boolean commands to create more complicated shapes.

Creating Cylinders

Next, you will add a cylinder to the drawing. Later, you will turn the cylinder into a hole by using the Subtract command. You create cylinders by specifying the center of the circular shape in the XY-plane and the radius or diameter, then giving the height in the Z-direction of the current UCS. The Elliptical option allows you to specify an elliptical shape instead of circular and then give the height.

Instead of giving the height, you can use the Cylinder command's Center of other end option to specify the center of the other end by picking or typing coordinates.

Set layer MYMODEL as the current layer.
Pick: **Cylinder icon**
Specify center point for base of cylinder or [Elliptical] <0,0,0>: **4,4** ↵
Specify radius for base of cylinder or [Diameter]: **.375** ↵
Specify height of cylinder or [Center of other end]: **3** ↵

Next, you will change the color of the cylinder. For many drawings the best approach is to make objects on separate layers and use the layer to determine the color, but that is not always the case with solid modeling. When you use a Boolean operator to join two objects, the result of that operation will always be on the current layer of the first item picked,

Tip

You can change the color of a single face of a model by using the Solidedit command and then selecting the Face and Color options. You can use a similar method to recolor single edges. Turn on the Solids Editing toolbar to quickly select Color Faces or Color Edges.

unless you change it later. Sometimes seeing features is easier if they are different colors, so you may want to set the color for an object before you join it with another object. To change the color of the cylinder, which you will use to create a hole,

Pick: **select the cylinder**
Pick: **Red** (from the Color Control pull-down list on the Properties toolbar)
Press: [Esc] to unselect the cylinder

The cylinder should be changed to the new color. Your screen should look like Figure 11.26.

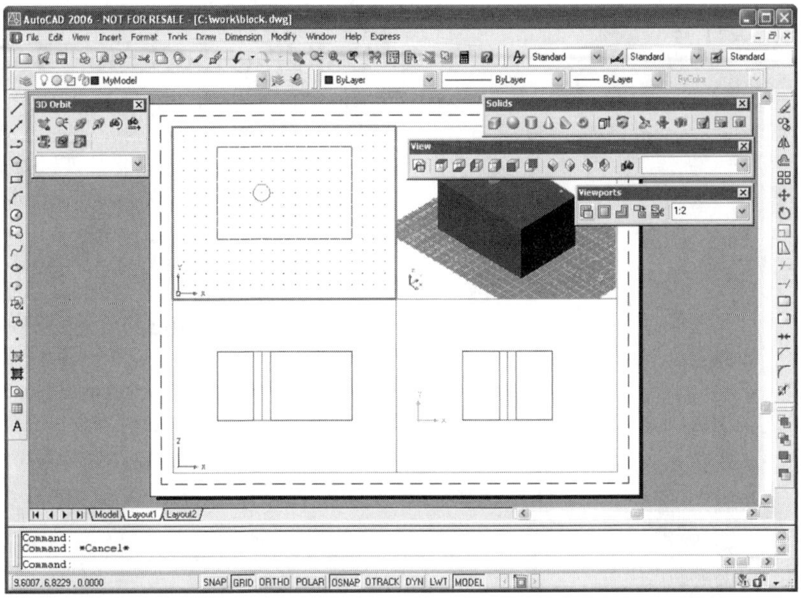

Figure 11.26

Now you have a box and a cylinder, each occupying the same space. Although they could not do so in the real world, in the drawing database these two objects are both occupying the volume inside the cylinder.

Setting Isolines

Before you continue, you will set the variable called Isolines. This variable controls the wireframe appearance of the cylinders, spheres, and tori (3D "donuts") on the screen. You can set the value for Isolines between 4 and 2047, to control the number of tessellation lines used to represent rounded surfaces. Displayed on a curved surface, tessellation lines help you better visualize the surface. The number of *tessellation lines* that you set will be shown on the screen, representing the contoured surface of the shape. The higher the value for Isolines, the better the screen appearance of rounded wireframe shapes will be. The default setting of 4 looks poor but saves time in drawing. The highest setting may look best, but more time is needed for the calculations, especially for a complex drawing.

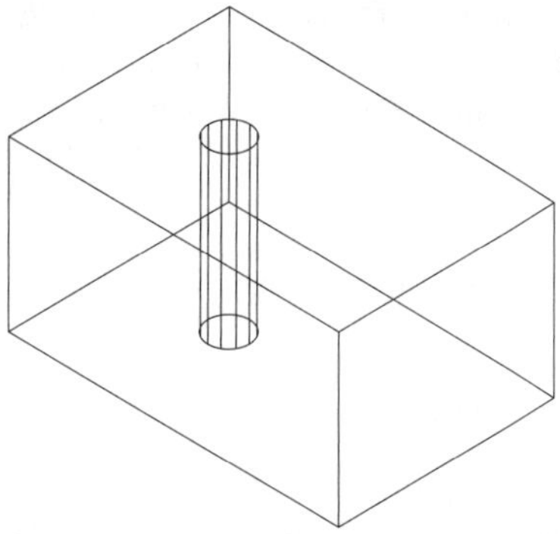

Figure 11.27

You will set the value to 12. You can change the setting for Isolines and regenerate the drawing at any time. You will use the Regenall command to regenerate all of the viewports to show the new setting for Isolines.

Command: **ISOLINES** ↵
Enter new value for ISOLINES <4>: **12** ↵
Pick: **View, Regen All**

The cylinder should be redrawn with more tessellation lines, similar to Figure 11.27.

Next you will use the Boolean operator Subtract to remove the cylinder from the box so that it forms a hole.

Building Complex Solid Models

You can create complex solid models with Boolean operators, which find the *union* (addition), *difference* (subtraction), and *intersection* (common area) of two or more sets. These operations are named for Irish logician and mathematician George Boole, who formulated the basic principles of set theory. In the AutoCAD software the sets can be 2D areas (called regions) or they can be 3D solid models. Often *Venn diagrams* are used to represent sets and Boolean operations. Figure 11.28 will help you understand how the Union, Subtract, and Intersection commands work. The order in which you select the objects is important only when you're subtracting (i.e., A subtract B is different from B subtract A). Keep in mind that when objects are on different layers, the solid resulting from a Boolean operation will reside on the layer of the first item picked.

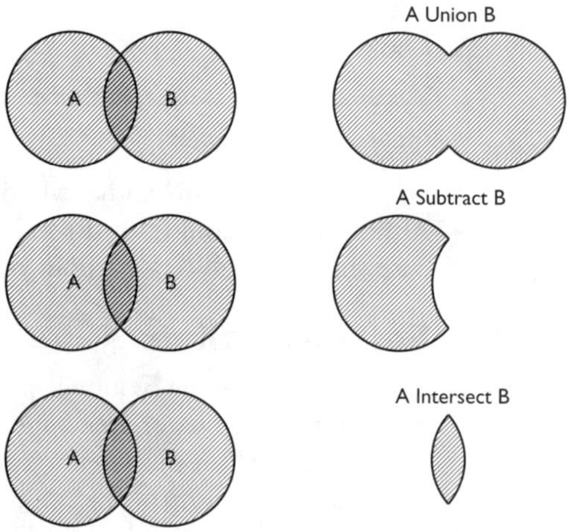

Figure 11.28

The Boolean operators are on the Modify menu, under Boolean. To make the commands for editing solids easily available, you will turn on the Solids Editing toolbar.

Right-click: on any toolbar and use the menu to turn on the **Solids Editing** toolbar and turn off the 3D Orbit, Viewports, and View toolbars

The Solids Editing toolbar shown in Figure 11.29 appears.

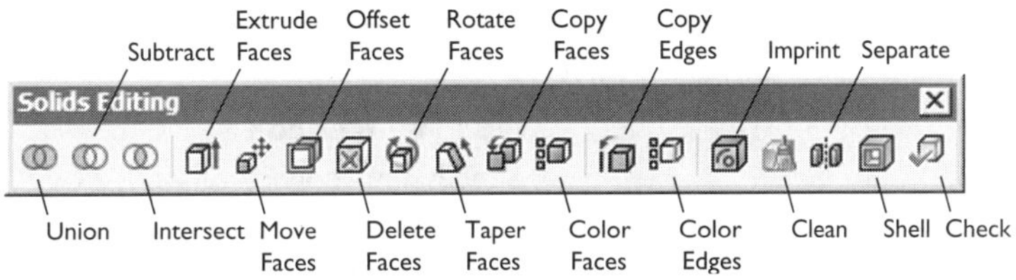

Figure 11.29

Next you will remove the volume of the cylinder from the box, thereby forming a new solid model with a hole in it. You will pick the Subtract command from the Solids Editing toolbar.

Pick: **Subtract icon**
Select solids and regions to subtract from...
Select objects: **pick the box and press** ↵
Select solids and regions to subtract...
Select objects: **pick the cylinder and press** ↵

The resulting solid model is a rectangular prism with a hole through it. If you selected the items in the wrong order (i.e., picked the cylinder and subtracted the box from it) the result would be a null solid model or one that has no volume. If you picked both the box and the cylinder and then pressed ↵, the command would not work unless you picked something else to subtract. If you make a mistake, you can back up by typing U ↵ at the command prompt to use the Undo command and then try again.

Figure 11.30

Note that you can now see that the cylinder has formed a hole in the block. The color inside the hole is red and the rest of the block is blue. Your drawing in the upper right viewport should look like that in Figure 11.30.

You will restore the wireframe appearance of the isometric view. Objects are easier to select when they are not shaded. Also, overlapping solids are much easier to see when they are not shaded.

Make the upper right viewport current if it is not already.
Pick: **View, Shade, 3D Wireframe**
Save your drawing, *block.dwg*, before continuing.

Saving periodically will prevent you from losing your drawing in the event of a power failure or other hardware problem. Also, saving your work after you've completed a major step and before you go on to the next step is useful. That way, if you want to return to the preceding step, you can open the previous version of the drawing, discarding the changes that you have made.

Tip

The Facetres variable adjusts the smoothness of shaded objects and objects from which hidden lines have been removed. Its value can range from .01 to 10. Viewres controls the number of straight segments used to draw circles and arcs on your screen. Viewres can be set between 1 and 20000. You can type these commands at the command prompt and set their values higher to improve the appearance of rendered objects.

Creating Wedges

Now you will add a Wedge primitive to the drawing and then subtract it from the main block. The Wedge command has two options: Corner (the default) and Center. Drawing a wedge by specifying the corner first lets you draw the rectangular base of the wedge, and prompts you for two points that define the diagonal of the rectangular base. The height you enter starts at the first point specified for the base and gets smaller in the X direction toward the second point. The Center option asks you to specify the center point of the wedge you want to draw.

Pick: **Wedge icon**
Specify first corner of wedge or [CEnter]: **8,6** ↵
Specify corner or [Cube/Length]: **6,2** ↵
Specify height: **3** ↵

Now you will use the Boolean operators to subtract the wedge from the object.

Pick: **Subtract icon**
Select solids and regions to subtract from...
Select objects: **pick the box with the hole and press** ↵
Select solids and regions to subtract...
Select objects: **pick the wedge and press** ↵

With the wedge subtracted, your drawing should look like that in Figure 11.31.

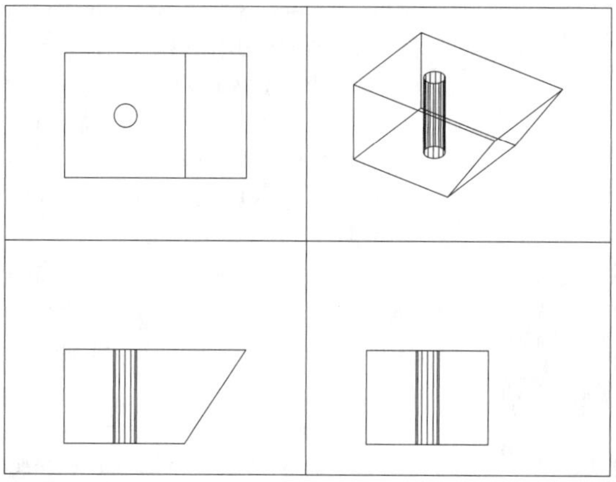

Figure 11.31

Next, use Hide to remove hidden lines from the upper right view.

Tip

You can type HIDE at the command prompt.

Be sure that the upper right viewport is active.
Pick: **View, HIDE**

The 3D object will appear on your screen with the hidden lines removed. The shape in the upper right viewport should look like that in Figure 11.32.

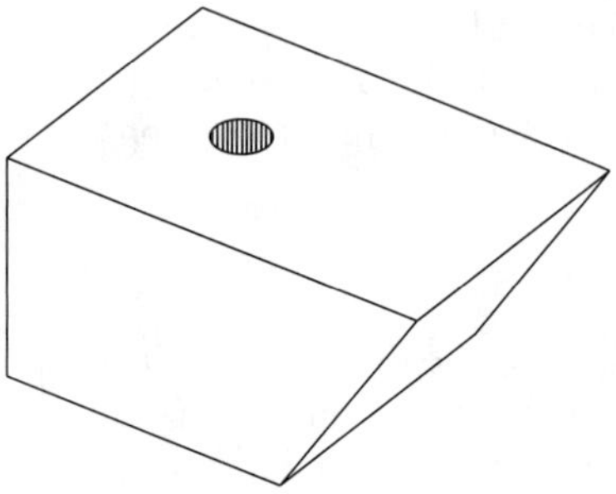

Figure 11.32

You will continue to work with wireframe representation for the isometric view.

Pick: **View, Shade, 3D Wireframe**

Creating Cones

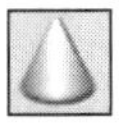

The cone primitive creates a solid cone, defined by a circular or elliptical base and tapering to a point perpendicular to the base. It is similar to the cylinder primitive that you have already used. The circular or elliptical base of the cone is always created in the XY-plane of the current UCS. The height is along the Z-axis of the current UCS.

Now you will create a cone using the cone primitive and then subtract it from the block to make a countersink for the hole. It will have a circular base and a negative height. Specifying a negative height causes the cone to be drawn in the opposite direction from a positive height (i.e., in the negative Z-direction).

Pick: **Cone icon**
Specify center point for base of cone or [Elliptical] <0,0,0>: **4,4,3** ↵
Specify radius for base of cone or [Diameter]: **.625** ↵
Specify height of cone or [Apex]: **–.75** ↵
On your own, change the color for the cone to Green.

Use the Boolean operator to subtract the cone from the block to make a countersink for the hole.

Pick: **Subtract icon**
Select solids and regions to subtract from...
Select objects: **pick the block and press** ↵
Select solids and regions to subtract...
Select objects: **pick the cone and press** ↵

Next, shade the object in the upper right viewport as you did before.

Pick: **View, Shade, Gouraud Shaded**

The upper right viewport now displays a view of the shaded object. Your screen should look like Figure 11.33.

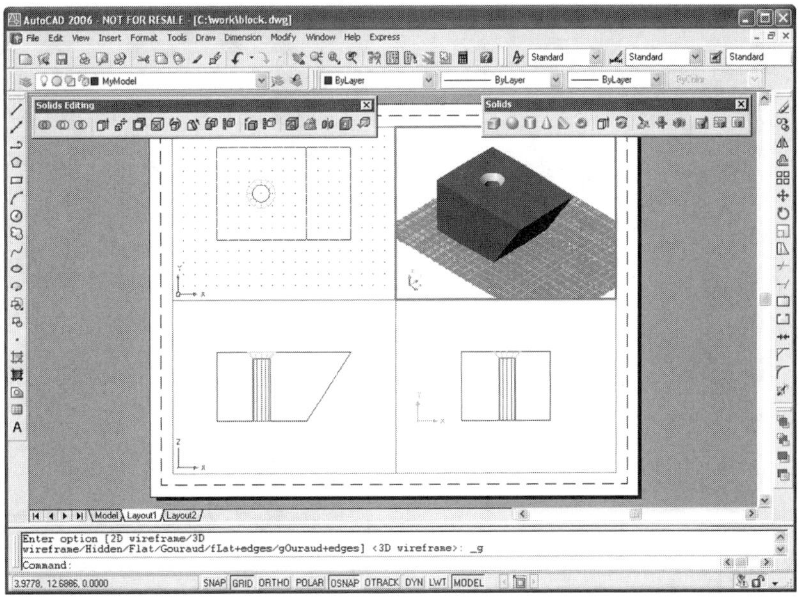

Figure 11.33

Next, you will use the cylinder primitive to add a rounded surface to the top of the block.

Creating User Coordinate Systems

You can have more than one coordinate system in the AutoCAD environment. The object is stored in the WCS, which stays fixed, but you can use the UCS command to create a User Coordinate System oriented any way you want. The UCS command allows you to position a User Coordinate System anywhere with respect to the WCS. You can also use it to change the origin point for the coordinate system and to save and restore named coordinate systems. You will create a new UCS that aligns with the left side of the block. To make it easy to select back edges,

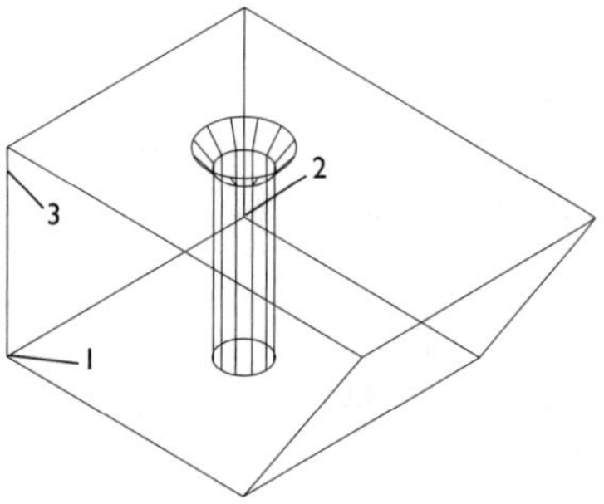

Figure 11.34

Make sure the upper right viewport is active.
Right-click: **OSNAP button**
Pick: **Settings**
Pick: **Clear All** (from the Object Snap tab of the Drafting Settings dialog box)
Pick: **Endpoint and Midpoint**
Pick: **OK**
Pick: **View, Shade, 3D Wireframe**
Pick: **Tools, New UCS, 3 Point**
Specify new origin point <0,0,0>: **target endpoint 1 in Figure 11.34**
Specify point on positive portion of X-axis <3.0000,2.0000,0.0000>: **target endpoint 2**
Specify point on positive-Y portion of the UCS XY plane <1.0000,2.0000,0.0000>: **target endpoint 3**

Now there is a grid in your drawing parallel to the side view (lower right viewport) that is aligned with the left surface of the object as shown in Figure 11.35.

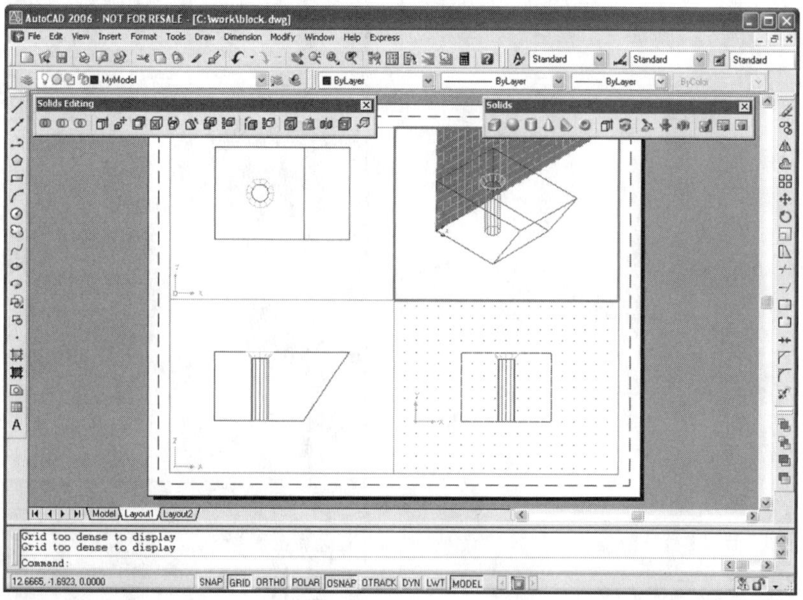

Figure 11.35

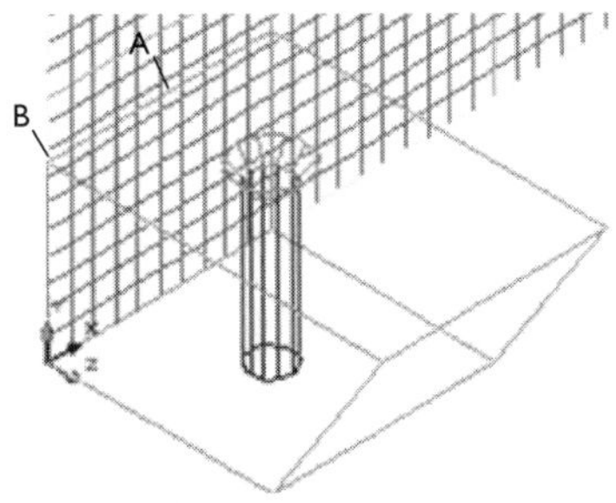

Figure 11.36

You will save the new UCS that you created parallel to the left side of the part and give it a name so that you can select it again later.

Command: ↵ (to restart the UCS command)
Enter an option [New/Move/orthoGraphic/Prev/Restore/Save/Del/Apply/?/World] <World>: **S** ↵
Enter name to save current UCS or [?]: **LEFT** ↵
On your own, verify that the upper right viewport is active.

Next, you will use the Cylinder icon and choose to draw a cylinder by specifying its center. Refer to Figure 11.36 for the points to select.

You will use the object snaps for Midpoint and Endpoint to aid in selecting locations from the object.

On your own, make sure that running object snap (OSNAP) is turned on.
Pick: **Cylinder icon**
Specify center point for base of cylinder or [Elliptical] <0,0,0>: **pick the midpoint of the back top line A**
Specify radius for base of cylinder or [Diameter]: **pick the endpoint of edge B**
Specify height of cylinder or [Center of other end]: **1** ↵

Your drawing should look like the one shown in Figure 11.37.

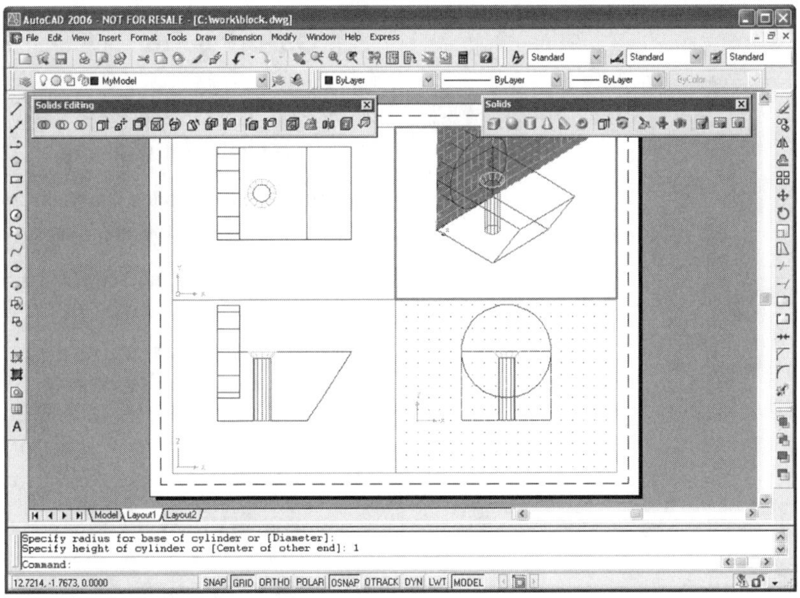

Figure 11.37

Next, you will use the Boolean operator Union to join the cylinder to the block.

Pick: **Union icon**
Select objects: **pick the new cylinder and the block**
Select objects: ↵
Pick: **View, Shade, Gouraud Shaded**

When the objects are joined, your drawing should be similar to Figure 11.38.

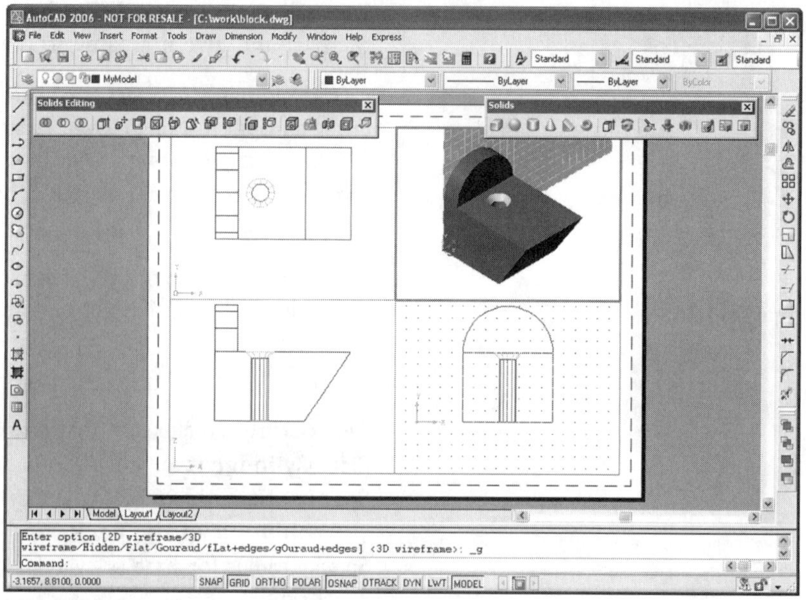

Figure 11.38

On your own, use the Pan command to **pan the view** of the object in the upper right viewport so that the entire object fits the available space.

Save your completed *block.dwg* drawing.

Pick: **OSNAP button** on the Status bar to turn it off

Plotting Solid Models from Paper Space

Next, you will plot your multiview drawing of the block.

Change to paper space on your own by typing **PS** ↵ at the command prompt or double-clicking outside the viewport borders.

When you have done so, the paper space icon appears.

You will use the Mview command with the Hideplot option so that when you plot your drawing from paper space, the back surface lines will be automatically removed. When selecting the objects for the Hideplot option of the Mview command, remember that you are selecting which viewports to show with hidden lines removed. To select a viewport, pick on its border, not inside it.

Command: **MVIEW** ↵
Specify corner of viewport or
[ON/OFF/Fit/Shadeplot/Lock/Object/Polygonal/Restore/2/3/4] <Fit>: **S**
Shade plot? [As displayed/Wireframe/Hidden/Rendered] <As displayed>: **H**
Select objects: **pick on the border of the upper right viewport**
Select objects: ↵

Nothing noticeable happens when you finish the command. However, when you plot your drawing, the back surface lines will automatically be removed from this viewport. You can also print shaded views with the shading shown by choosing the Rendered option. Using Wireframe leaves the back edges showing like the wireframe model. You will learn more about printing shaded drawings in Tutorial 15.

Tip

To quickly add the border and title strip, you can open a drawing that contains one, copy it from that drawing, and paste it into the current drawing. Make sure that you are in paper space in each drawing, so that you only copy the border and titles.

To make it so that the four viewport borders won't print on your drawing,

Make **BORDER the current layer** and **freeze layer VPORT** on your own.

Use the Line command to **draw a border** around all the viewports while you are in paper space.

Add a title strip and notes if you want to, as you did in Tutorial 5.

Be sure that you are in paper space and plot the drawing limits at a scale of 1=1. The orthographic views that you have drawn should be exactly half-size on the finished plot because the Zoom XP scale factor was set to 0.5. Your plotted drawing should be similar to that in Figure 11.39.

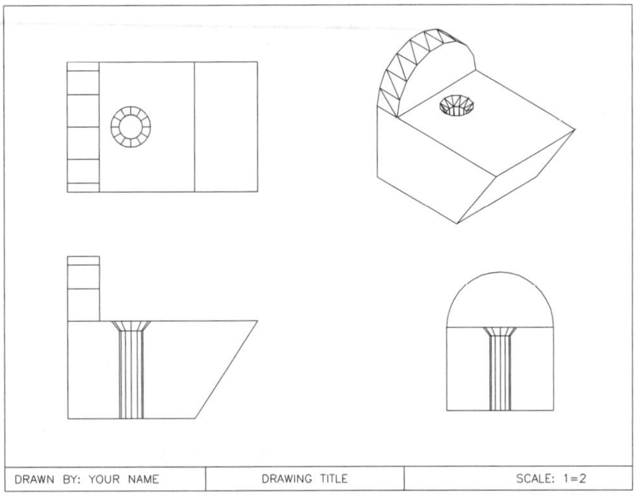

Figure 11.39

Saving Your Multiview Setup as a Template

Next you will switch back to model space, so that when the template is saved, the 3D model space will be active.

Command: **MS** ↵ (or pick the Paper button to switch to model space)

The UCS icons are restored to all the viewports.

Pick: **MYMODEL** to be the current layer using the Layer Control

Now you will erase the object and save the basic settings to use as a template for new 3D drawings. Type the alias for Erase.

Command: **E** ↵
Select objects: **pick the solid block object you have drawn**
Select objects: ↵

It is erased from all viewports.

Next, you will restore the World Coordinate System, by typing the UCS command.

Command: **UCS** ↵
Enter an option [New/Move/orthoGraphic/
Prev/Restore/Save/Del/Apply/?/World] <World>: **W** ↵

Warning

Do NOT explode 3D models after you have created them, as it converts them back to 3D lines and surfaces. Once you've exploded a 3D solid, you can't rejoin the resulting objects to form the 3D object again. If you need to make changes to a solid and can't do so with the techniques used in these tutorials, re-creating the 3D solid is the best option.

Next you will use Save As to create a template file named *soltemplate.dwt*.

Pick: **File, Save As**
Pick: **AutoCAD Drawing Template .dwt** (in the Files of Type area)
Name the file ***soltemplate.dwt***.
Description: **3D template with 4 viewports**
Select: **English** (as the measurement units)
Pick: **OK**
Pick: **File, Close** to close the current drawing

Creating Solid Models with Extrude and Revolve

Next, you will learn how to create new solid objects using the extrusion and revolution methods.

Tip

Switch to paper space and use Zoom All if necessary so that the paper area fills the graphics window. Be sure to switch back to model space.

Pick: **New icon**
Pick: **Use a Template icon** (from the Startup dialog box)
Use the drawing *proto-3D.dwt* provided with your datafiles or *soltemplate.dwt* that you just created.
Use **Save As** and name the new drawing ***extrusn.dwg***.

Your screen should be similar to Figure 11.40.

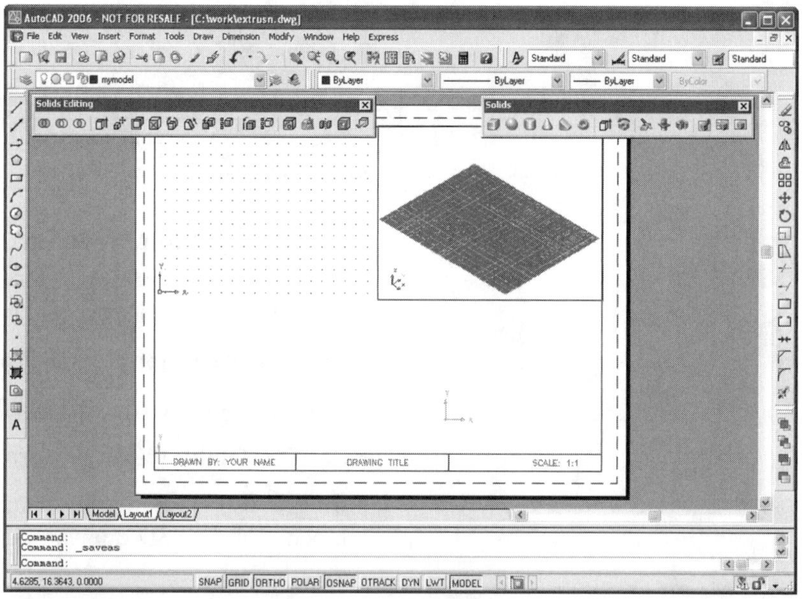

Figure 11.40

Tip

If you want to see the viewports, you can thaw the layer VPORT and make it a non-plotting layer, so that it will not print.

Because you started your new drawing from the solid modeling template, the viewports already exist. The viewports themselves are on layer VPORT, which is currently frozen. You can still make each viewport active by picking inside it. The UCS called LEFT that you saved previously is still available by selecting it from the Views toolbar, by using the UCS Restore option, or by picking Tools, Named UCS.

Make sure layer MYMODEL is the current layer.

Pick: **the upper left viewport to make it active**

Verify that Grid and Snap are active and that Snap is set to .5 and turned on.

You will draw the I shape shown in Figure 11.41 using the 2D Polyline command. The coordinates have been provided in Figure 11.41 to make selecting the points easier for you.

Pick: **Polyline icon**

Specify start point: **pick point A**

Current line-width is 0.0000

Specify next point or [Arc/Halfwidth/Length/Undo/Width]: **pick points B-L in order**

Specify next point or [Arc/Close/Halfwidth/Length/Undo/Width]: **C** ↵

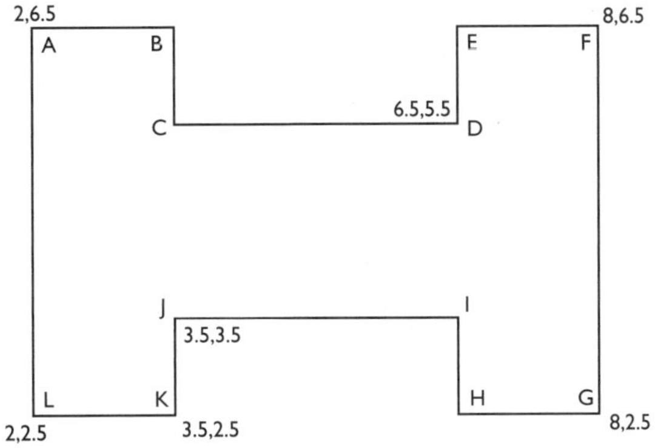

Figure 11.41

You will set the fillet radius to 0.25 and then use the Fillet command's Polyline option to round all the corners of the polyline. Use the alias for the Fillet command.

Tip

If you did not close your object by typing C, you will get the message 11 lines were filleted. In this case, undo the last two commands and redraw your I shape, closing the polyline with the Close option.

Command: **F** ↵

Select first object or [Undo/Polyline/Radius/Trim/Multiple]: **R** ↵

Specify fillet radius <0.0000>: **.25** ↵

Select first object or [Undo/Polyline/Radius/Trim/Multiple]: **P** ↵

Select 2D polyline: **pick the polyline you just created**

12 lines were filleted

On your own, use the Snap spacing to draw the two circles shown in Figure 11.42.

Tip

Each viewport can have a different grid setting. In the figure, the grid in the upper right viewport is set to 4 to make it easier to see the shape. In later figures, the grid is turned off for the same reason.

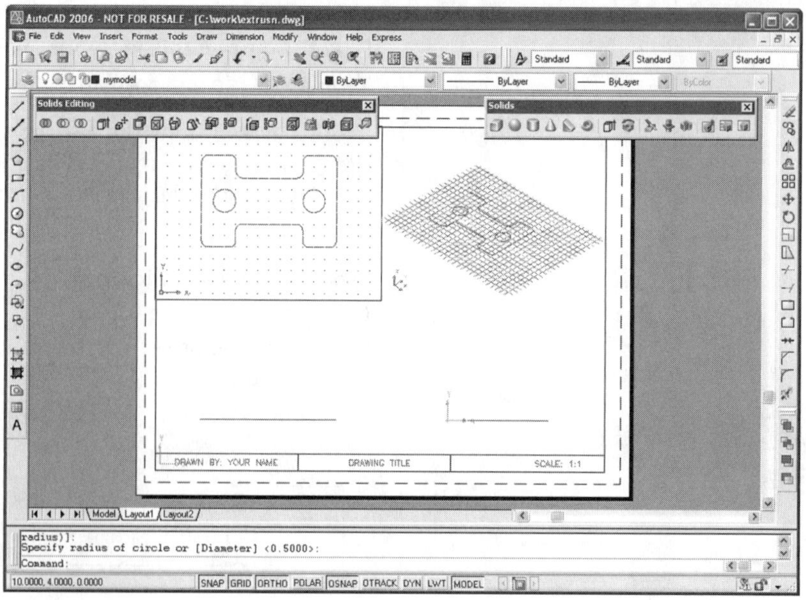

Figure 11.42

Tip

If the upper right viewport is not shaded, make it active and then pick View, Shade, Flat Shaded. Be sure to make the top left viewport active when finished.

Region Modeling

You can also use the Boolean operators with the closed 2D shapes made by circles, ellipses, and closed polylines. You can convert closed 2D shapes to *regions*, which essentially are 2D solid models, or areas. Use the Region icon from the Draw toolbar. Region modeling and extrusion can be combined effectively to create complex shapes.

Turn Snap off on your own to make selecting easier.

Pick: **Region icon**

Select objects: **use implied Crossing to pick the polyline and both circles; then press** ↵

3 loops extracted

3 regions created

Now you are ready to subtract the two circles from the polyline region to form holes in the area.

Pick: **Subtract icon**

Select solids and regions to subtract from...

Select objects: **pick the polyline region and press** ↵

Select solids and regions to subtract...

Select objects: **pick the circles and press** ↵

Now there is only one region, which has two holes in it. Notice that in the shaded view in the upper right viewport, the circles now appear as holes in a shaded flat region, as shown in Figure 11.43.

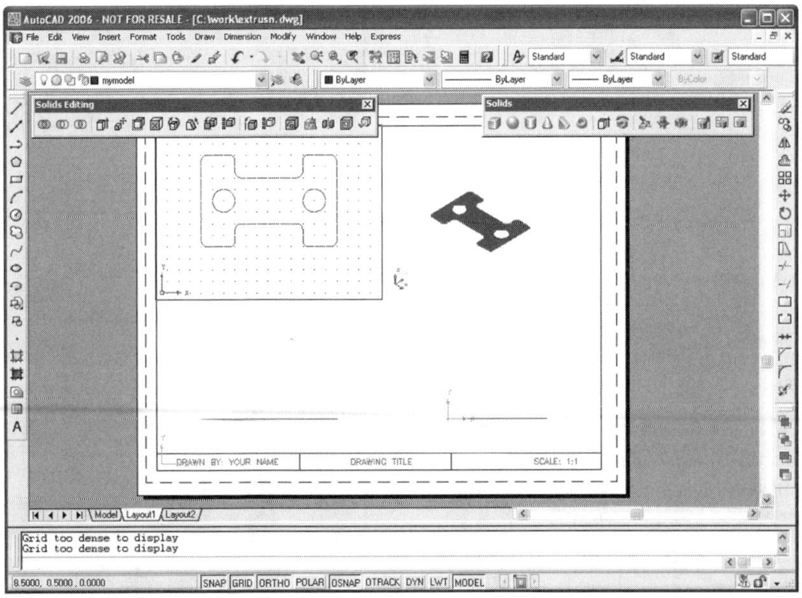

Figure 11.43

Extruding a Shape

Now you can extrude this shape to create a 3D object. Extrusion is the process of forcing material through a shaped opening to create a long strip that has the shape of the opening. The Extrude command works similarly to form a 3D shape. Closed 2D shapes such as splines, ellipses, circles, donuts, polygons, regions, and polylines can be given a height, or extruded.

Polylines must have at least three vertices in order to be extruded. You can specify a taper angle if you want the top of the extrusion to be a different size than the bottom. You can use the Path option to extrude a shape along a path curve that you have previously drawn. Path curves can be lines, splines, arcs, elliptical arcs, polylines, circles, or ellipses. (You may encounter problems when trying to extrude along path curves with a large amount of curvature and where the resulting solid would overlap itself.) The Extrude icon appears on the Solids toolbar. Make sure to pick it there and not the similar looking Extrude Faces icon from the Solids Editing toolbar.

Pick: **Extrude icon**
Select objects: **pick the region and press ↵**
Specify height of extrusion or [Path]: **2 ↵**
Specify angle or taper for extrusion <0>: ↵

Your screen should look like that in Figure 11.44.

Tip

Using the Boundary or Pedit commands to join objects into a closed polyline is an effective way to create 2D shapes to extrude. You can also use the Join command to connect line segments.

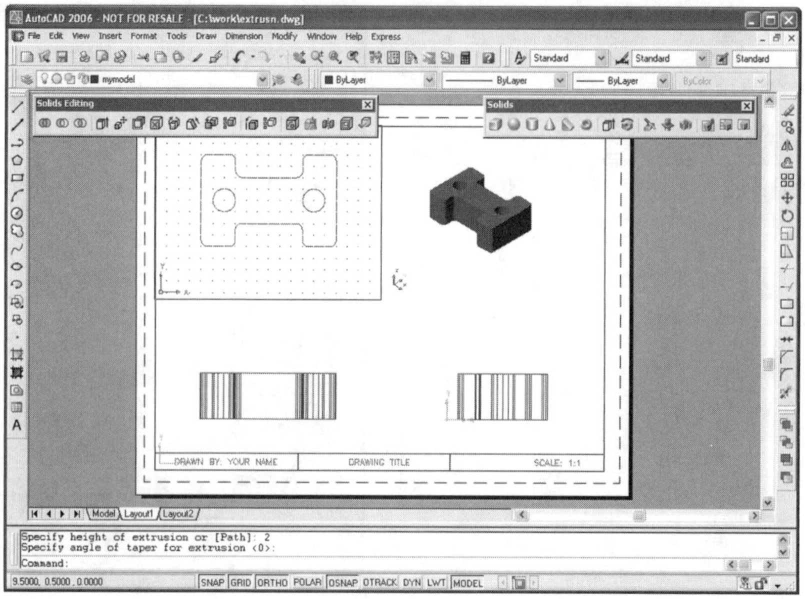

Figure 11.44

On your own, save and close your drawing, *extrusn.dwt.*

Pick: **New icon**

Pick: **Use a Template**

Use your *soltemplate* file or the datafile *proto-3D.dwt.*

Call your new drawing ***revolutn.dwg***.

Make sure that Snap is on and that Osnap is turned off.

Creating Solid Models by Revolution

Creating a solid model by revolution is similar in some ways to creating an extrusion. You can use it to sweep a closed 2D shape about a circular path to create a symmetrical solid model that is basically circular in cross section. You can revolve closed polylines, polygons, circles, ellipses, closed splines, donuts, and regions to form solid objects.

Use the 2D Polyline command on your own to draw a closed shape like that shown in Figure 11.45.

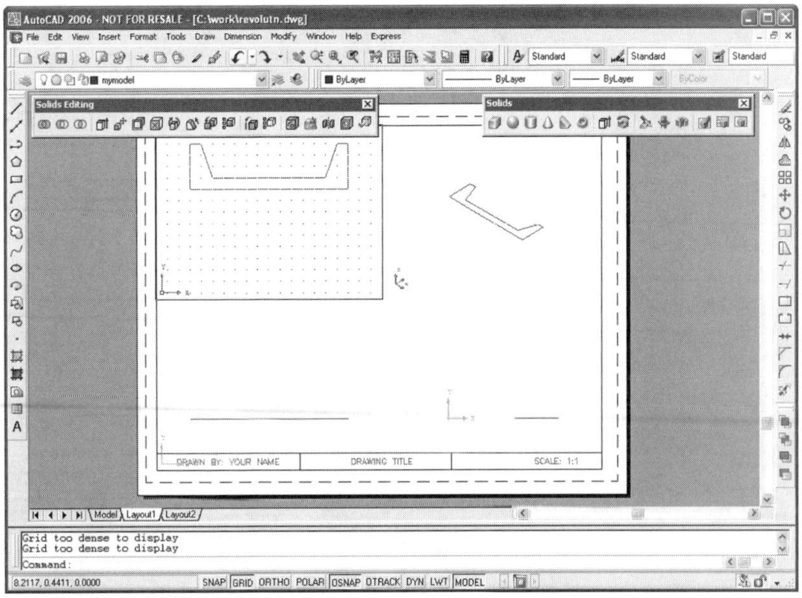

Figure 11.45

Now you will revolve the polyline about an axis to create a solid model. You don't need to draw the axis line; you can specify it by two points. The Revolve icon is on the Solids toolbar.

Pick: **Revolve icon**

Select objects: **pick the polyline and press** ↵

Specify start point for axis of revolution or define axis by [Object/X (axis)/ Y (axis)]: **pick one endpoint of the bottom line**

Specify endpoint of axis: **pick the other endpoint**

Specify angle of revolution <360>: ↵

Aligning the Views

Next, you will use the Pan Realtime command and Mvsetup to help align the views in the lower left, lower right, and upper left viewports.

Pick: **the lower left viewport to make it active**

Pick: **Pan Realtime icon**

On your own, pan the view so that the solid appears centered in the lower left viewport.

Press: Esc to exit the Pan command

Your screen should now be similar to Figure 11.46.

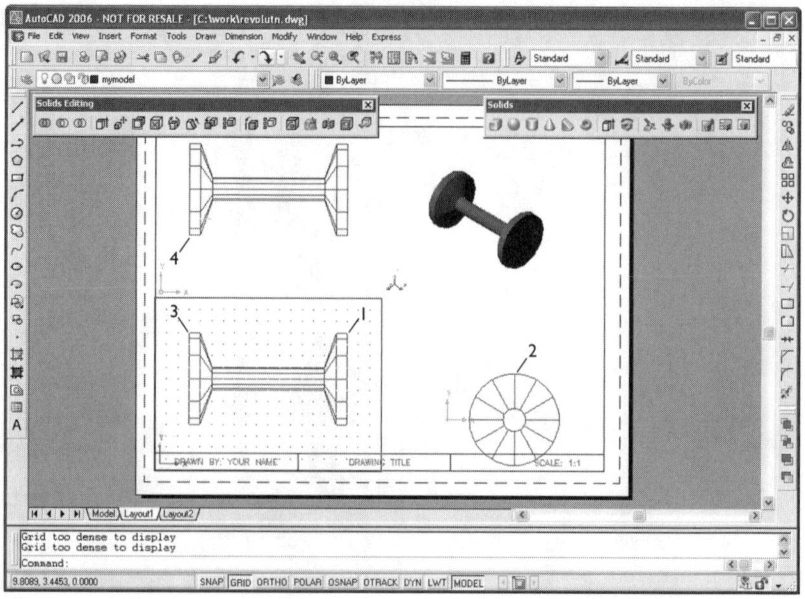

Figure 11.46

Next, you will type the command Mvsetup and align the lower right and upper left views relative to the lower left viewport using Osnap Quadrant. Use Figure 11.46 to help in making the selections.

On your own, be sure that OSNAP is turned on, with Quadrant selected.
Type: **MVSETUP** ↵
Enter an option [Align/Create/Scale viewports/Options/Title block/Undo]: **A** ↵
Enter an option [Angled/Horizontal/Vertical alignment/Rotate view/Undo]: **H** ↵
Specify basepoint: **select point 1, using the AutoSnap Quadrant marker to help**
Specify point in viewport to be panned: **select the lower right viewport and point 2, using the AutoSnap Quadrant marker**

The view in the lower right viewport should align with the view in the lower left viewport relative to the points you selected. Now you will repeat these steps for the upper left viewport.

Tip

If this option line is not active, then press the return button to reactivate MVSETUP and choose align again.

Enter an option [Angled/Horizontal/Vertical alignment/Rotate view/Undo]: **V** ↵
Specify basepoint: **select point 3 using the AutoSnap Quadrant marker to help**
Specify point in viewport to be panned: **select the upper left viewport and point 4, using the AutoSnap Quadrant marker to help**

When you have finished aligning the view in the upper left viewport, use the Pan Realtime command again in the upper right viewport so that the view looks similar to Figure 11.47.

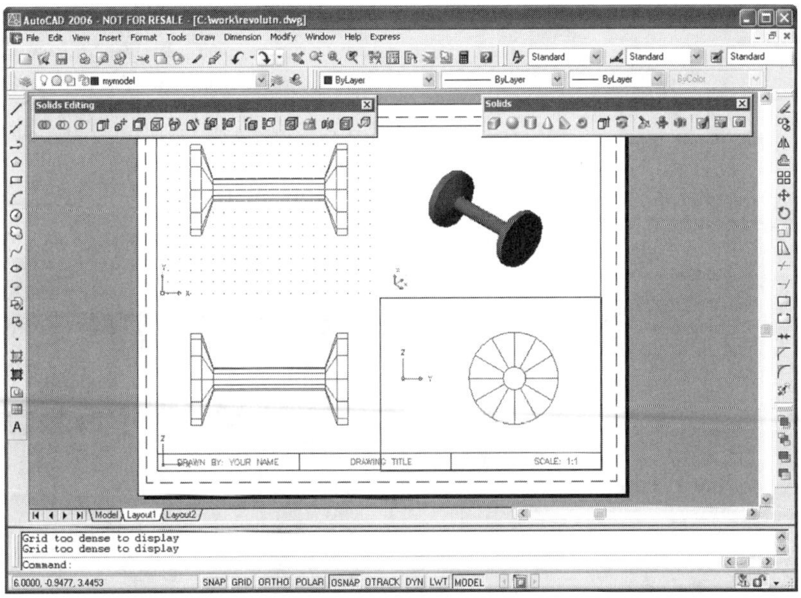

Figure 11.47

Save your drawing.
Pick: **Save As command**
Name your new drawing ***intersect.dwg***.
On your own, erase the solid model that you just revolved.

Using the Boolean Operator Intersection

Like the Union and Subtract Boolean operators, Intersection lets you create complex shapes from simpler shapes. Intersection finds only the area common to the two or more solid models or regions that you have selected. You will create the shape shown in Figure 11.48 by creating two solid models and finding their intersection.

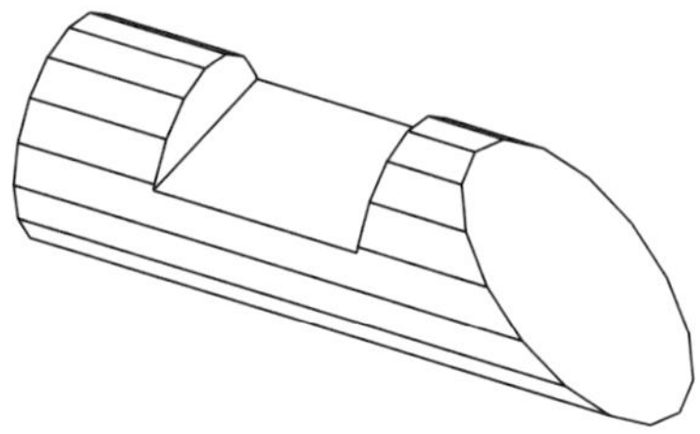

Figure 11.48

First, you will select to work in the lower left viewport and create a UCS parallel to this viewport.

Pick: **the lower left viewport to make it active**
Pick: **Tools, New UCS, View**

A UCS is created parallel to the view in the lower left viewport. The grid shows in the lower left viewport.

Next, you will create the shape of a surface in the front view that you will extrude to create the angled face and notch. You will use the Polyline command to create a polyline that defines the shape of the object in the front view.

Pick: **Polyline icon**
Specify start point: **2.5,0** ↵
Current line-width is 0.0000
Specify next point or [Arc/Close/Halfwidth/Length/Undo/Width]: **2.5,1.5** ↵
Specify next point or [Arc/Close/Halfwidth/Length/Undo/Width]: **3.5,1.5** ↵
Specify next point or [Arc/Close/Halfwidth/Length/Undo/Width]: **3.5,1** ↵
Specify next point or [Arc/Close/Halfwidth/Length/Undo/Width]: **5,1** ↵
Specify next point or [Arc/Close/Halfwidth/Length/Undo/Width]: **5,1.5** ↵

Specify next point or [Arc/Close/Halfwidth/Length/Undo/Width]: **5.5,1.5** ↵
Specify next point or [Arc/Close/Halfwidth/Length/Undo/Width]: **7,0** ↵
Specify next point or [Arc/Close/Halfwidth/Length/Undo/Width]: **C** ↵

After you've drawn the shape of the object in the front view, you may need to use the Pan Realtime and Mvsetup commands so that you can see it in the top and side views and align them with the front view.

When you have finished, your drawing will look like the one shown in Figure 11.49.

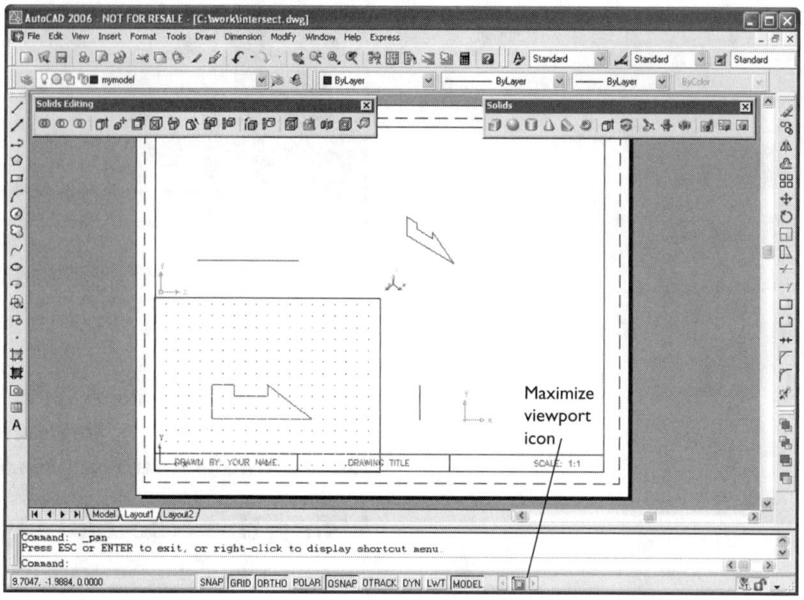

Figure 11.49

Now extrude this shape to form a solid model.

Pick: **Extrude icon**
Select objects: pick the polyline ↵
Specify height of extrusion or [Path]: **–3** ↵
Specify angle of taper for extrusion <0>: ↵

The solid model shown in Figure 11.50 has been created.

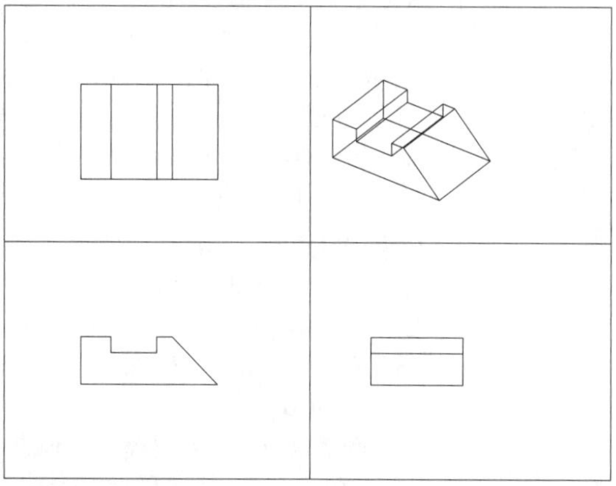

Figure 11.50

Next, you will pick the upper right viewport to be active and then switch so that you are only working in model space. Often when you are modeling it is useful to disable the paper space layouts temporarily and work only in the model view.

Pick: **the upper right viewport to make it active**
Pick: **to turn the Grid off in the upper right viewport**
Pick: **Maximize viewport icon from the status bar**

Your screen should show a single view of the object in model space as shown in Figure 11.51.

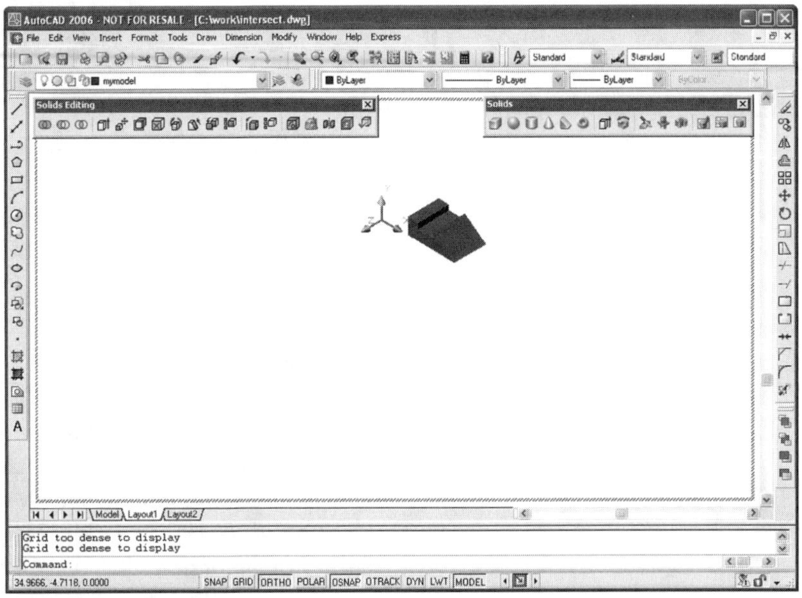

Figure 11.51

Pick: **Zoom Object icon from the Zoom flyout**
Select objects: **pick on the extruded shape**
Select objects: ↵

The object is zoomed so that it fills the view area as in Figure 11.52.

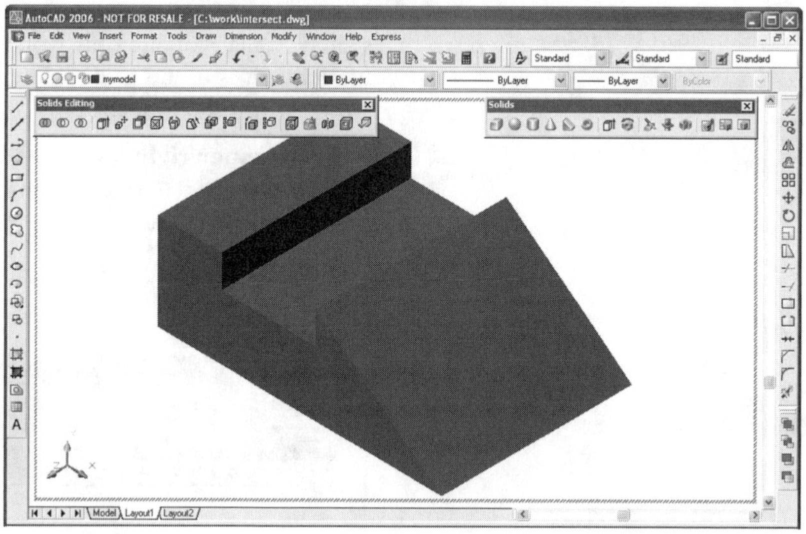

Figure 11.52

Next you will create a UCS that is parallel to the vertical back side of the object.

Set the Grid to 2 and turn it on.

Command: **UCS** ↵

Enter an option [New/Move/orthoGraphic/Prev/Restore/Save/Del/Apply/?/World] <World>: **W** ↵

Command: ↵ (to restart the UCS command)

Enter an option [New/Move/orthoGraphic/Prev/Restore/Save/Del/Apply/?/World] <World>: **N** ↵

Specify origin of new UCS or [ZAxis/3point/OBject/Face/View/X/Y/Z] <0,0,0>: **Y** ↵

Specify rotation angle about Y axis <90>: **90** ↵

The grid and coordinates appear as shown in Figure 11.53.

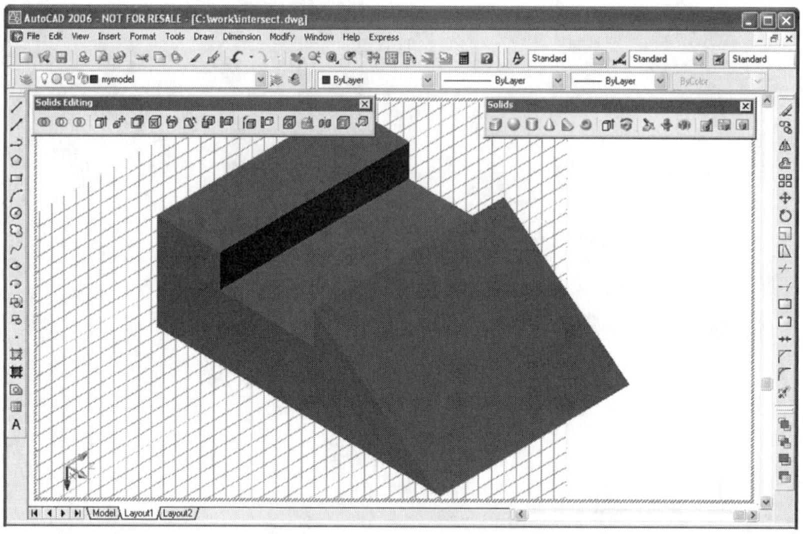

Figure 11.53

Next you will create the circular shape of the object, as shown in Figure 11.54. First you will zoom to a percentage of the current size so that you can see more of the drawing area.

Command: **Z** ↵
Specify corner of window, enter a scale factor (nX or nXP), or [All/Center/Dynamic/Extents/Previous/Scale/Window/Object] <real time>: **.8X** ↵
Pick: **Circle icon**
Specify center point for circle or [3P/2P/TTR (tan tan radius)]: **–.75,1.5** ↵
Specify radius of circle or [Diameter]: **0.75** ↵

The circle is drawn a distance away from the previously drawn solid model in the plane of the UCS, where the grid shows. You will use the Extrude command to elongate the circle into a cylinder.

Pick: **Extrude icon**
Select objects: **pick the circle** ↵
Specify height of extrusion or [Path]: **10** ↵
Specify angle of taper for extrusion <0>: ↵

The drawing in model space should look like that in Figure 11.54.

Experiment by typing DELOBJ at the command prompt and changing the setting to 0. Create a polyline and extrude it in one direction using a taper angle. The original polyline will remain. Select it again and extrude it in the other direction using the same taper angle. This way you can create a surface that tapers in both directions.

Tip

The Delobj variable controls whether the 2D object is automatically deleted after being extruded or revolved. A value of 1 means delete the object that was used to create the other object (the circle that created the cylinder, for example); a value of 0 means do not delete the object. The default AutoCAD setting is 1 (delete).

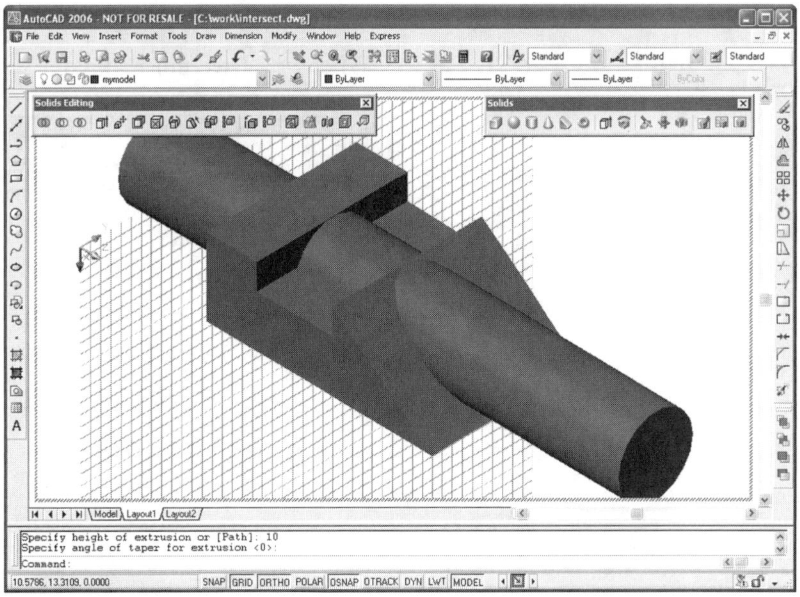

Figure 11.54

Now you are ready to use the Intersection command to create a new solid model from the overlapping portions of the two solid models that you have drawn.

Pick: **Intersect icon**
Select objects: **pick the cylinder and the extruded polyline** ↵
Save your *intersect.dwg* drawing.

The solid model is updated. Your drawing should look like Figure 11.55.

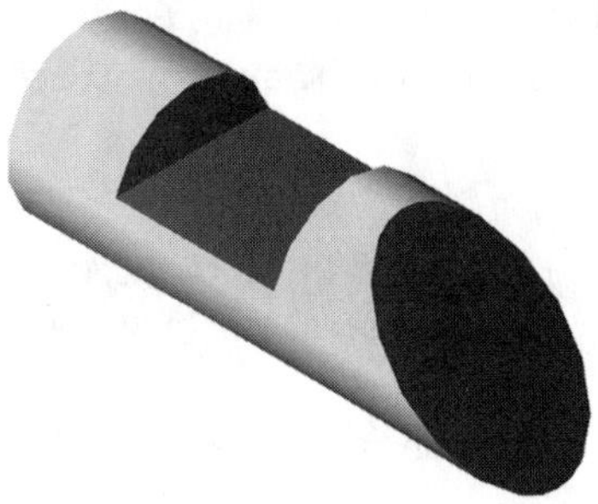

Figure 11.55

On your own, close the Solids and Solids Editing toolbars.

Close *intersect.dwg*.

Creating Surface Models

You can also use the AutoCAD software to create surface models. AutoCAD surface models are composed of a faceted polygonal mesh that approximates curved surfaces. Surface modeling can be more difficult to use than solid modeling and provides less information about the object. The reason is that only the surfaces and not the interior volumes of the object are described in the drawing database. However, surface modeling is well suited to applications such as modeling 3D terrain for civil engineering applications.

In general you should not mix solid modeling, surface modeling, and wireframe modeling, as you can't edit them in the same ways to create a cohesive single structure. Select the single method that is best for your application.

You can convert solid models to surface models by using the Explode command. Surface models can be likewise converted to wireframe models. However, because they do not contain the same information, you can't go from wireframe to surface models or from surface models to solid models.

Start a new drawing from ***contrdat.dwg***, which was provided with the datafiles.

Name your new drawing ***surf1.dwg***.

When you have finished, your screen should look like Figure 11.56.

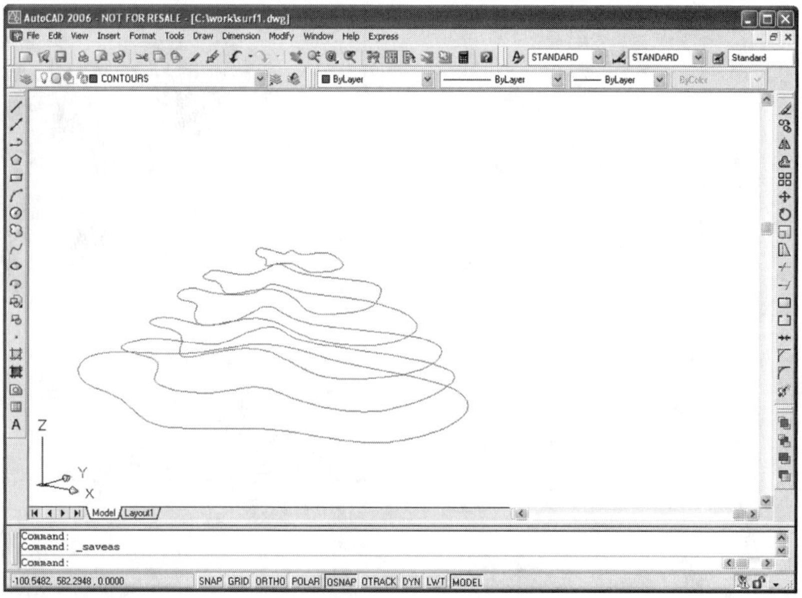

Figure 11.56

Next, you will show the Surfaces toolbar.

Right-click: **on any toolbar and open the Surfaces toolbar**

The Surfaces toolbar appears on the screen as shown in Figure 11.57.

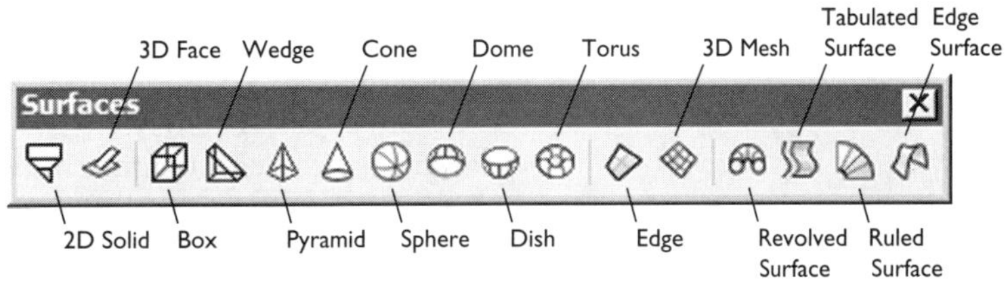

Figure 11.57

The Surfaces toolbar contains selections for 2D Solid, 3D Face, Box, Wedge, Pyramid, Cone, Sphere, Dome, Dish, Torus, Edge, 3D Mesh, Revolved Surface, Tabulated Surface, Ruled Surface, and Edge Surface. Many of the selections are similar to the selections on the solids toolbar. However, the objects created with surface modeling are like empty shells. They do not contain information about the volume and mass properties of the object, as solid models do. An important consideration is that you cannot use Boolean operators to join surface models. You must edit the mesh that creates surface models differently.

Because using Box, Wedge, Pyramid, Cone, Sphere, Dome, Dish, Torus, Revolved Surface, and Tabulated Surface is basically similar to the method you used earlier in the tutorial to create solid models, they will not be covered here. Instead, on your own, refer to AutoCAD Help for further information about creating these shapes.

The 2D Solid selection lets you create a solid surface using four points. When this surface is parallel to the screen, it is filled with a solid color.

The 3D Face selection lets you add a three- or four-sided surface anywhere in your drawing. It can be used to create surfaces on top of wireframe drawings.

The Edge command lets you change the visibility of an edge of a 3D face created with the previous command. You can use it to hide edges that join with other 3D faces or to hide back edges that may not hide correctly when you use the Hide command.

In this tutorial, you will learn to create a 3D Mesh, an Edge Surface, and a Ruled Surface. Understanding how to create these objects will allow you to create a wider variety of shapes that are especially useful for modeling 3D terrain, such as mountainous topography.

On the screen are 2D splines representing contours (lines of equal elevation on a contour map). The splines have been moved along the Z-axis so that they are at different heights. The bottom line is at Z 200, the next at Z 220, the next at Z 240, and so on. You can create these contour lines on your own by drawing splines (or polylines) through your data points, joining points of equal elevation. Then use Move to relocate the resulting spline. Specify a base point of (0,0,0) and a displacement of (0,0,200) (or whatever your elevation may be).

If needed, change the viewpoint and use Zoom to see the lines clearly.

On your own, make layer **MESH** current.

Creating a Ruled Surface

Using the Ruled Surface selection from the Surfaces toolbar, you can create a surface mesh between two graphical objects. The objects can be lines, points, arcs, circles, ellipses, elliptical arcs, 2D polylines, 3D polylines, or splines. The objects can either be both open (like lines) or both closed (like circles). Points can be connected to either open or closed objects.

Controlling Mesh Density

The mesh comprising a surface is defined in terms of a *matrix* of M and N vertices; M and N specify the column and row locations of vertices. Two system variables control the density of the mesh for creating surfaces. Surftab1 controls the density of the mesh in the M direction, and Surftab2 controls the density of the mesh in the N direction. The larger the value for Surtab1 and Surftab2, the more tightly the generated mesh will fit the initial objects selected. As with other commands, increasing the density of the mesh increases the time for calculation and display of the object.

The Surftab1 variable controls the density of the mesh for Ruled Surfaces because they are always a 2 ×Surftab1 +1 mesh. To set the value for Surftab1,

Command: **SURFTAB1** ↵
Enter new value for SURFTAB1 <6>: **40** ↵

Next, you will create a ruled surface between the two bottom splines. Use the Surfaces toolbar to select Ruled Surface. Refer to Figure 11.58 for the lines to select.

Pick: **Ruled Surface icon**
Select first defining curve: **pick curve 1**
Select second defining curve: **pick curve 2**

The ruled surface will be added between the two splines as shown in Figure 11.58.

Tip
When you are picking the defining curves, pick in a similar location on each curve. If you pick on the opposite end of the second curve, the generated mesh will be intersecting.

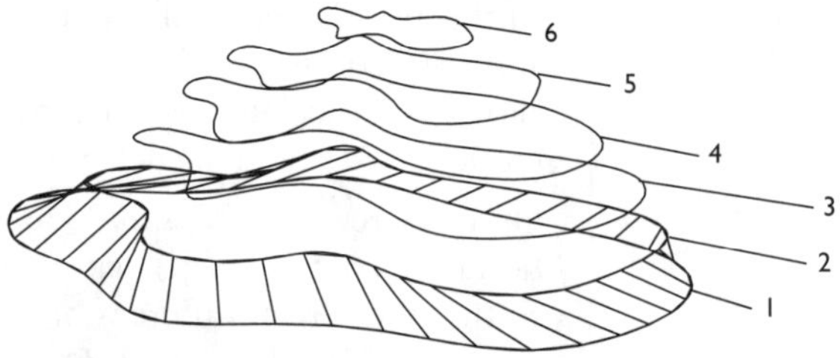

Figure 11.58

On your own, repeat the command for Ruled Surfaces between curves 2 and 3, 3 and 4, 4 and 5, and 5 and 6 shown in Figure 11.58.
You may need to zoom in so that you can pick the red splines.

If you pick on the blue mesh, you will not be able to use it as a defining curve. Note that for the upper curves, half the mesh for the ruled surface is connected to each curve. To create an accurate model, sometimes you must change Surftab1 to vary the mesh refinement to avoid so much interpolation.

Tip
Remember, 'Zoom is transparent and can be used during the command.

On your own, use the 3D Orbiter to spin your view of the surface created. Change to a shaded view.

When you have finished, the drawing will look like Figure 11.59.

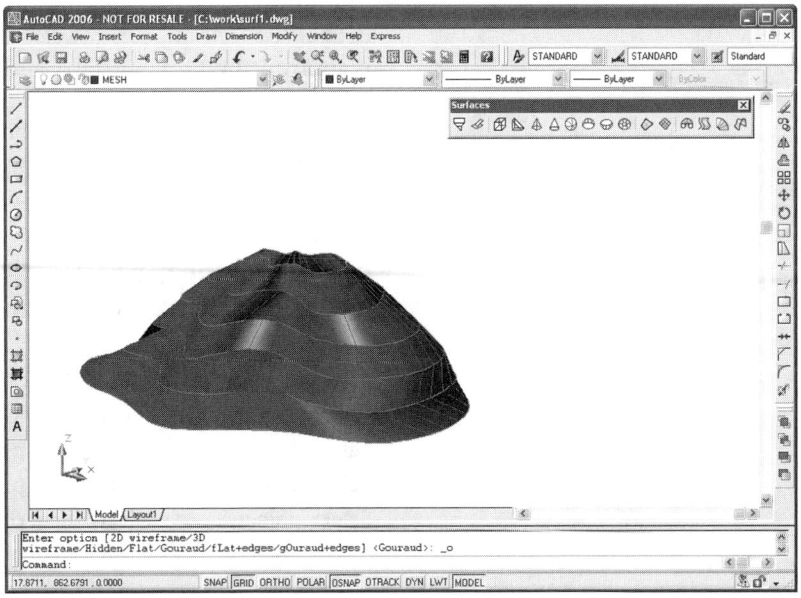

Figure 11.59

Now freeze layer CONTOURS to remove the original splines from the screen.

Save and close your drawing.

Start a new drawing on your own from ***edgsurf.dwg***.

Name your new drawing ***surf2.dwg***.

On your own, make **MESH** the current layer.

Your screen should look like Figure 11.60.

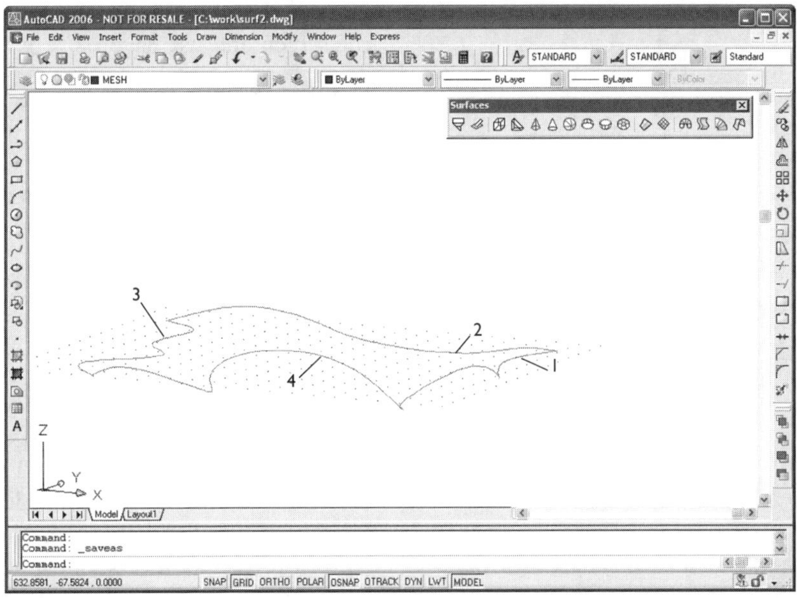

Figure 11.60

You will use the four 3D splines shown on the screen to define an edge surface.

Creating an Edge Surface

The Edge Surface selection from the Surfaces toolbar creates a mesh defined by four edges you select. The mesh density for an edge surface is controlled by the Surftab1 and Surftab2 variables. The Edge Surface selection creates a *Coons patch mesh*. A Coons patch mesh is a *bicubic surface* interpolated between the four edges. First, you will set the values for Surftab1 and Surftab2 to control the mesh density. Then you will select Edge Surface from the Surfaces toolbar. Refer to Figure 11.60 for the splines to select.

Command: **SURFTAB1** ↵
New value for SURFTAB1 <6>: **20** ↵
Command: **SURFTAB2** ↵
New value for SURFTAB2 <6>: **20** ↵
Pick: **Edge Surface icon**
Select object 1 for surface edge: **pick curve 1**
Select object 2 for surface edge: **pick curve 2**
Select object 3 for surface edge: **pick curve 3**
Select object 4 for surface edge: **pick curve 4**

The edge surface appears in your drawing as shown in Figure 11.61.

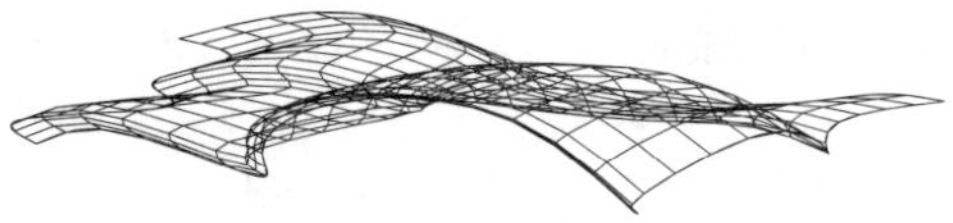

Figure 11.61

On your own, shade the view and use the 3D Orbiter to change your viewpoint.
Save your drawing.

Next, you will define a rectangular mesh. You will erase the objects from the screen and use Save As to give the drawing a new name.

Pick: **Erase icon**
Select objects: **ALL** ↵
Select objects: ↵
Use Save As to save the empty drawing with the name ***mesh.dwg***.

The name mesh appears in the title bar at the top of the current drawing.

Creating 3D Mesh

The 3D Mesh command lets you construct rectangular polygon meshes by entering the X-, Y-, and Z-coordinates of the points in the mesh. First, you define the number of columns (M) and then the number of rows (N) for the mesh matrix. The values for M and N must fall between 2 and 256. After you define M and N, you are prompted to type the values for the vertices defining the mesh. You can often use an AutoLisp® program or script in conjunction with the 3DMesh command to automate creation of the mesh.

Pick: **3D Mesh icon**

Enter size of mesh in M direction: **3** ↵

Enter size of mesh in N direction: **3** ↵

Specify location for vertex (0, 0): **0,0,0** ↵

Specify location for vertex (0, 1): **15,0,1** ↵

Specify location for vertex (0, 2): **30,5,2** ↵

Specify location for vertex (1, 0): **0,15,0** ↵

Specify location for vertex (1, 1): **18,18,3** ↵

Specify location for vertex (1, 2): **30,15,0** ↵

Specify location for vertex (2, 0): **0,30,2** ↵

Specify location for vertex (2, 1): **15,30,0** ↵

Specify location for vertex (2, 2): **30,34,3** ↵

The mesh appears in your drawing. You will use Zoom, Extents so that you can see the entire drawing.

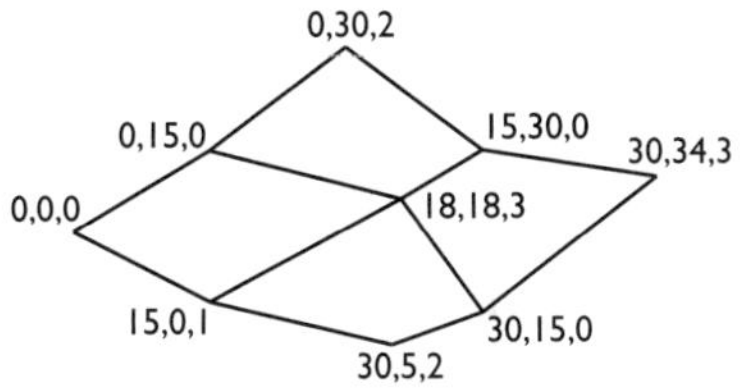

Figure 11.62

Pick: **Zoom Extents icon**

Pick: **View, Shade, 3D Wireframe**

Your drawing should appear similar to Figure 11.62, although you won't see the coordinates of the vertices. Use the 3D Orbiter and shade and spin the view on your own.

Now you know how to establish viewports and viewing directions and create and join the basic shapes used in solid modeling. With these tools you can create a variety of complicated shapes. In Tutorial 12, you will learn how to change solid models further, as well as to plot them.

Practice creating shapes and working with the User Coordinate Systems on your own.

You have now completed Tutorial 11.

Close toolbars and save and close all drawings before exiting.

Key Terms

arcball
bicubic surface
Boolean operators
Coons patch mesh
difference
extrusion
intersection
mass properties
matrix
perspective icon
plan view
primitives
regions
revolution
solid modeling
surface modeling
tessellation lines
union
User Coordinate System (UCS)
vector
Venn diagrams
viewpoint
wireframe modeling
World Coordinate System (WCS)

Key Commands

3DMesh
3DWireframe
Box
Cone
Cylinder
Delobj
Edge Surface
Extrude
Facetres
Front View
Hide
Intersection
Isolines
Mview
Mvsetup
Named UCS
Plan
Regenerate All
Region
Revolve
Right View
Ruled Surface
SE Isometric View
Shademode
Subtract
Surftab1
Surftab2
Top View
UCS
Union
Viewres
View UCS
Vpoint
Wedge Center
Wedge Corner
World UCS

Exercises

Use solid modeling to create the parts shown according to the specified dimensions.

11.1 Connector

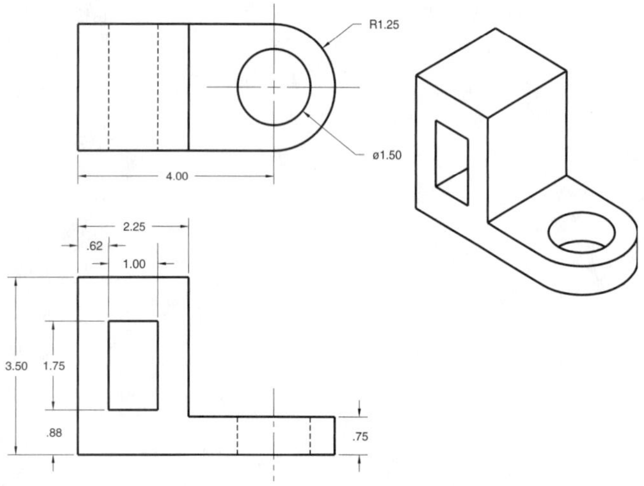

11.2 Support Base

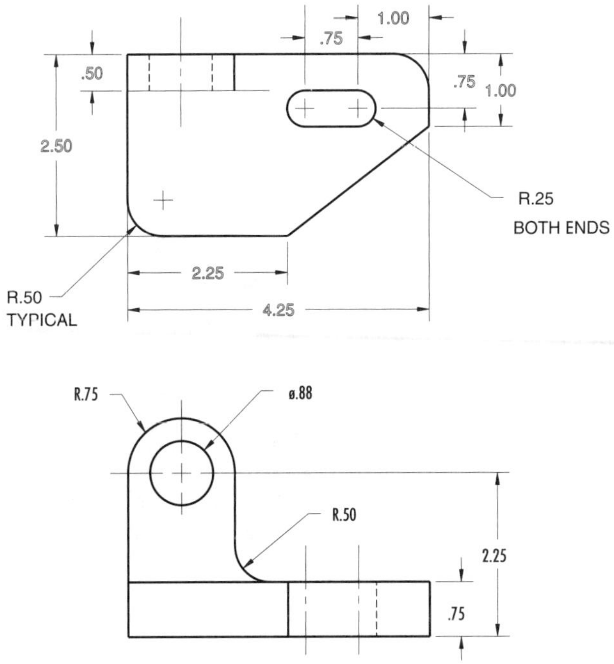

11.3 Hold Down

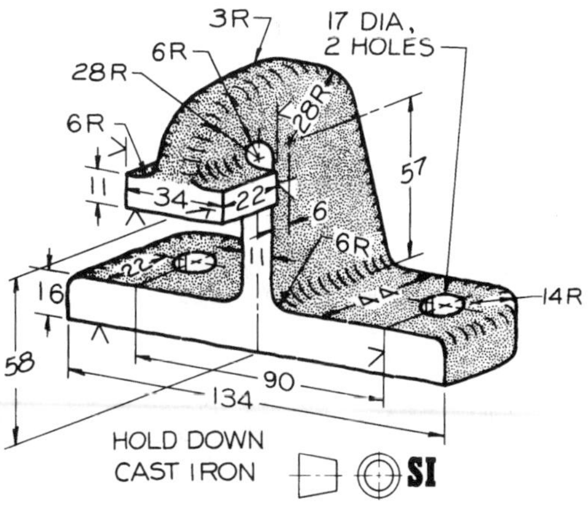

11.4 Angle Link

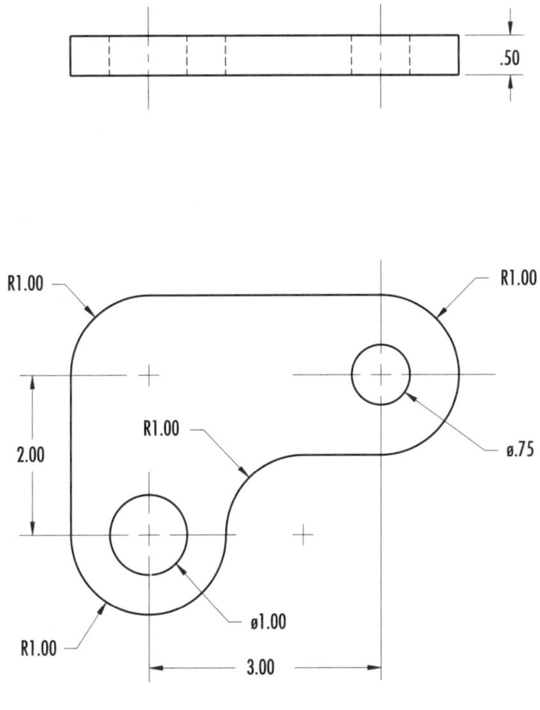

11.5 Chess Piece

Create the rook chess piece body by revolving a polyline. Use Subtract to remove box primitives to form the cutouts in the tower. Add an octagon for the base. Extrude it to a height of 0.15 and use a taper angle of 15°. (Use your soltemplate.dwt as the template from which you start the rook.)

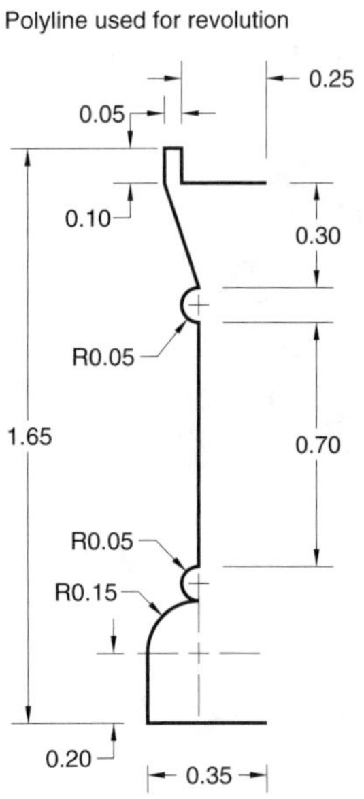

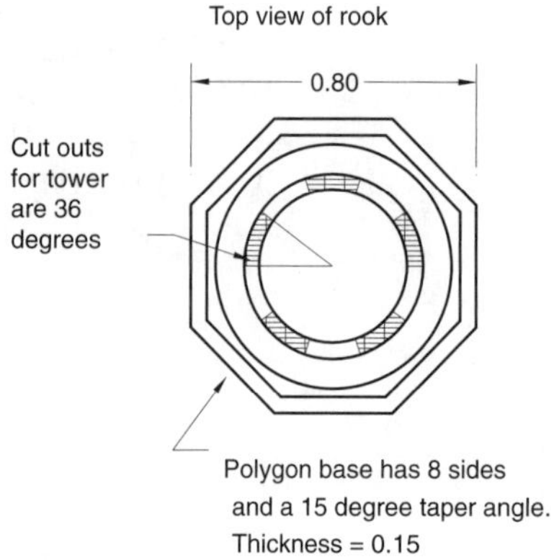

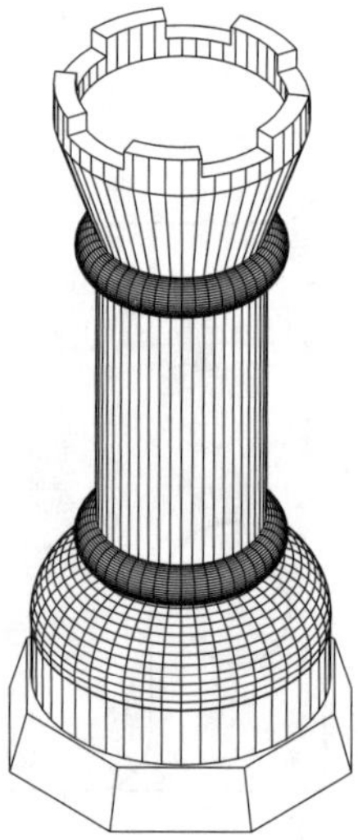

Draw the following shapes by using solid modeling techniques. The letter M after an exercise number means that the units are in millimeters.

11.6M Bushing Holder

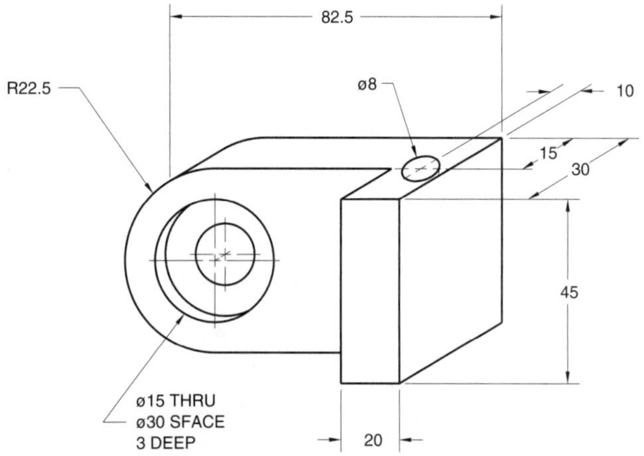

11.7 Shaft Support

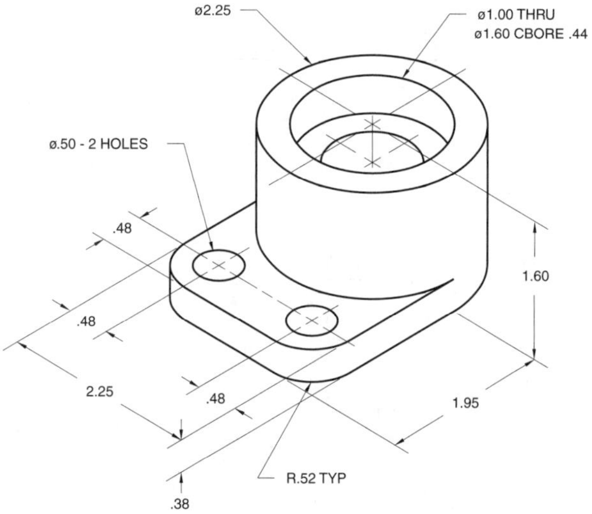

11.8 Balcony

Design a balcony like the one shown here, or a more complex one, using the solid modeling techniques you have learned. Use "two-by-fours" (which actually measure 1.5" x 3.5") for vertical pieces. Use Divide to ensure equal spacing.

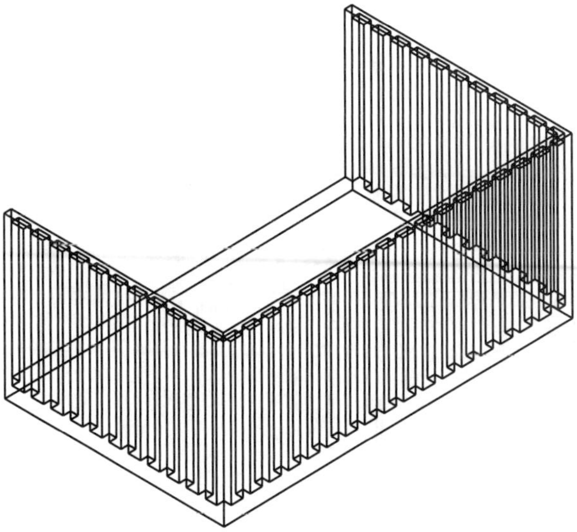

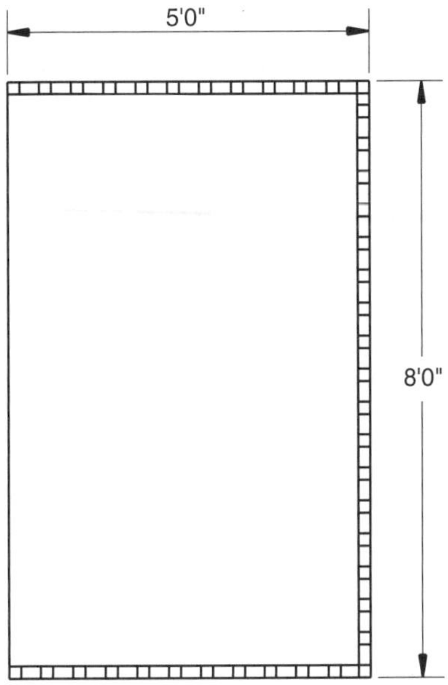

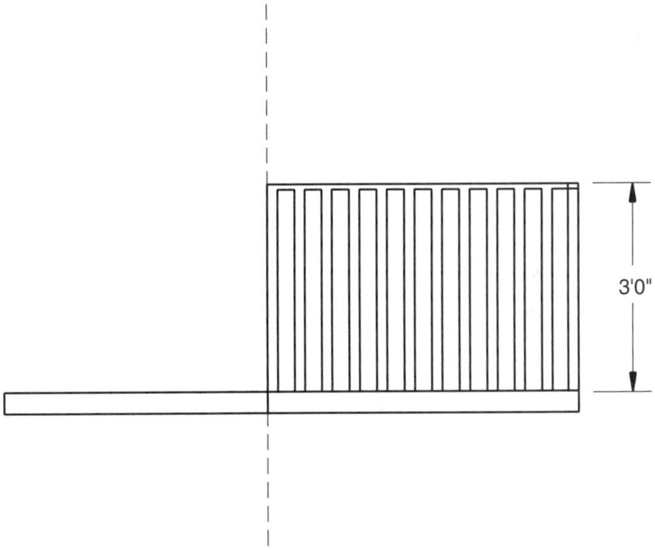

11.9 Bridge

Create the bridge shown. First, determine the size of the bridge that you want and the area to be left open with the arc. Use extrusion to create the arc. Add the structure of the bridge, making sure that the supports are evenly spaced and of sufficient height. (You can enter one-half of the supports and then use Mirror.)

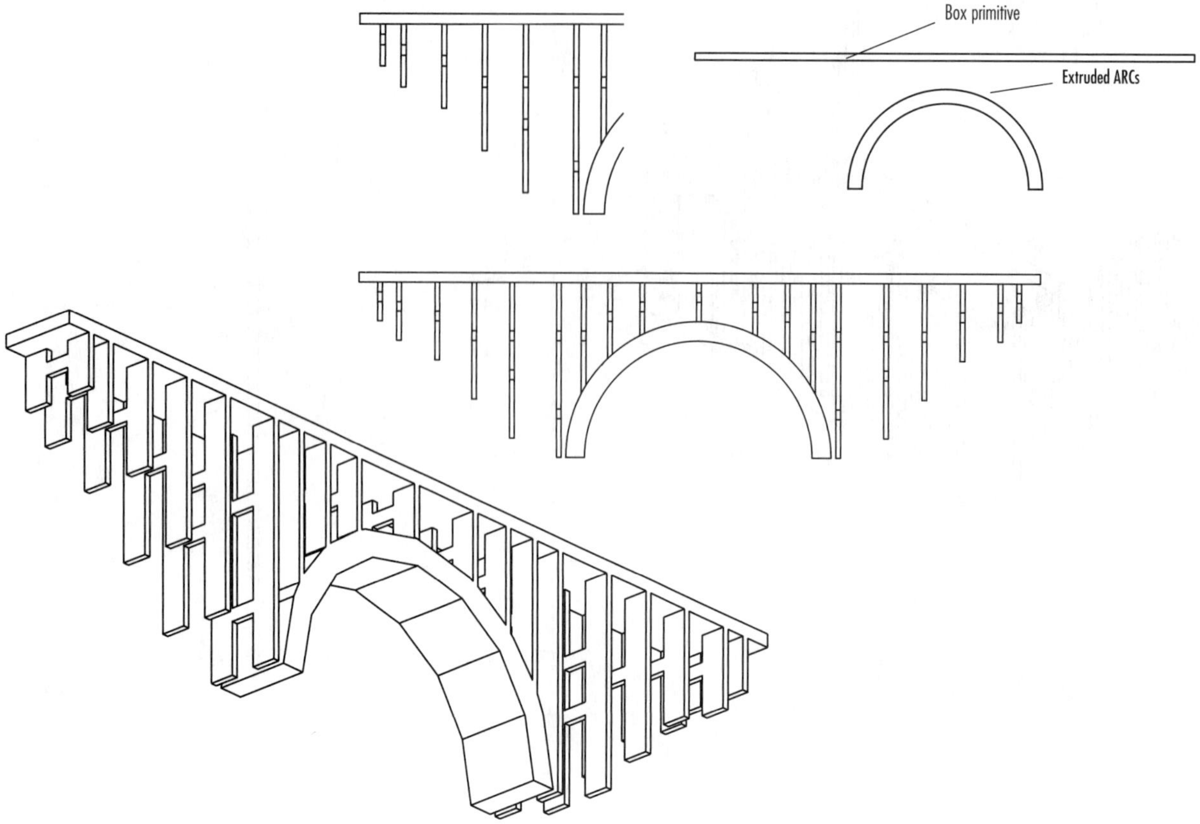

11.10 Rock Plan

Use the information in the file rockplan.pts to create the plan and profile drawings for the railroad bed as shown below. The file has the information in the following order: point number, northing (the y-coordinate to the north from the reference point), easting (the x-coordinate to the east from the last reference point), elevation, and description. Start by locating each point at the northing and easting given. Extrapolate between elevations and draw polylines for the contour lines at 1' intervals. Make the contour lines for 95' and 100' wide, so that they stand out. Create a 3D mesh using the information in the file rockplan.pts modeling the terrain shown.

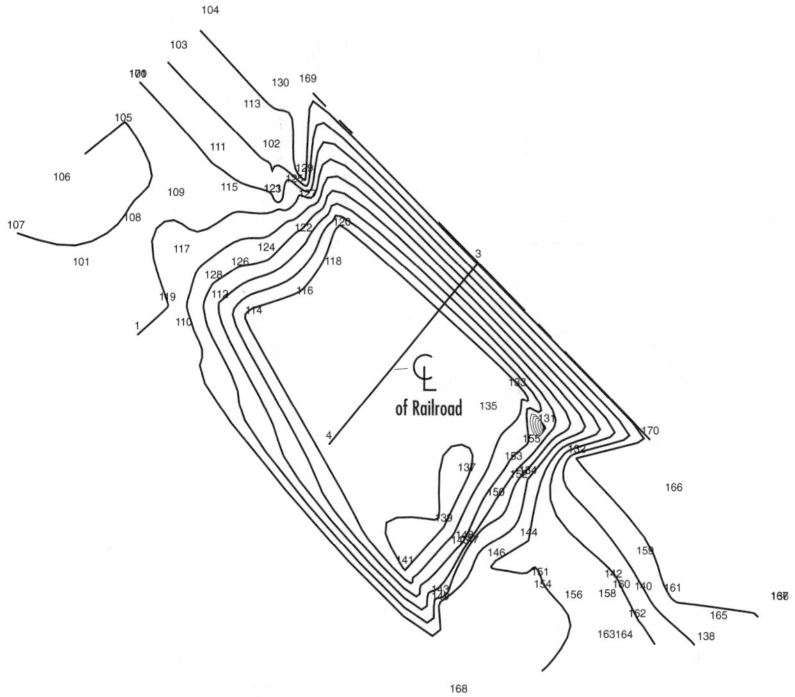

Tutorial

12 Changing and Plotting Solid Models

Objectives

When you have completed this tutorial, you will be able to

1. Add a rounded fillet between two surfaces.
2. Add an angled surface or chamfer to your model.
3. Remove a portion from a solid.
4. List the solid information and tree structure.
5. Plot 2D views of the model with hidden lines shown correctly.
6. Control visibility of layers within each viewport.

Introduction

You have learned how to create solid models and use multiple viewports. In this tutorial you will learn to use the solid modeling editing commands to make changes and create a larger variety of shapes. You can create solid models for many engineering drawing needs. From these models you can directly generate two-dimensional (2D) orthographic views that correctly show hidden lines. You will learn a method for controlling layer visibility that allows you to add centerlines so that they appear in a single view. You can also use this method for adding dimensions that appear only in a single viewport. In future tutorials you will learn how to apply solid modeling to create many different standard types of engineering drawings.

Starting

Launch the AutoCAD® software.

Open your drawing ***block.dwg*** that you created in Tutorial 11 or the datafile ***solblock.dwg***.

Save it with the name ***soledit.dwg***

Make the World coordinate system current if it is not already.

Make the upper right viewport active.

Open the Solids and Solids Editing toolbars on your own.

Your screen should be similar to Figure 12.1.

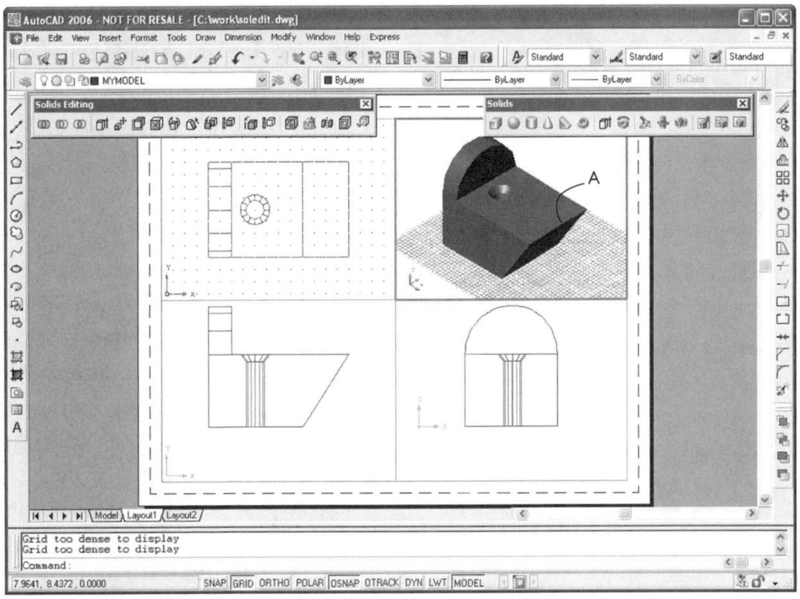

Figure 12.1

Tip

As you work through this tutorial, you may need to redraw or regenerate the drawing to eliminate partially shown lines or shading. Use Redraw to eliminate partially shown lines in a single viewport. Use RedrawAll to redraw all the viewports at the same time. The Redraw commands refresh the screen from the current display file. The Regen commands recalculate the display file from the drawing database and refresh the screen. Use Regen to regenerate the current viewport or RegenAll to regenerate all the viewports at once.

Tip

To make selecting easier, remember the 'Zoom Window command. Transparent zooming allows you to zoom a view during another command. You can use it to enlarge an area to make selecting easier. To return the area to the original size, always use 'Zoom Previous, not 'Zoom All. To use the transparent version of Zoom, don't forget to add the apostrophe in front of the command (or select it from the toolbar or from the View menu).

Using Fillet on Solids

The Fillet command lets you add concave or convex rounded surfaces between plane or cylindrical surfaces on an existing solid model. You have already used it to create rounded corners between 2D objects. Now you will use it to create a rounded edge for the front, angled surface of the object. Refer to Figure 12.1 for your selection of line A.

Pick: **Fillet icon**

Select first object or [Undo/Polyline/Radius/Trim/Multiple]: **pick on line A**

Enter fillet radius: **.5** ↵

Select an edge or [Chain/Radius]: ↵

Your drawing with the rounded edge should look like Figure 12.2.

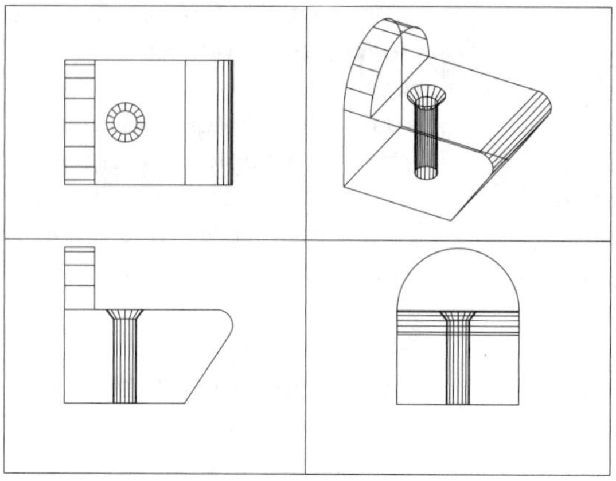

Figure 12.2

Next, you will undo the fillet and then use the Chamfer command to add an angled surface.

Command: **U** ↵

The fillet that you added to your drawing is eliminated.

Using Chamfer on Solids

The Chamfer command works on solid models in a way similar to the Fillet command, except that it adds an angled surface instead of a rounded one. Its Loop option allows you to add a chamfer to all edges of a base surface at once.

Pick: **Chamfer icon**

Select first line or [Undo/Polyline/Distance/Angle/Trim/mEthod/Multiple]: **D** ↵

Specify first chamfer distance <0.5000>: **.75** ↵

Specify second chamfer distance<0.7500>: ↵

Select first line or [Undo/Polyline/Distance/Angle/Trim/mEthod/Multiple]: **pick line A in Figure 12.1**

Base surface selection...

Enter surface selection option [Next/OK/(current)] <OK>: **if the top surface of the object is highlighted, press ↵; if not, type N so that the next surface becomes highlighted**

Specify base surface chamfer distance<0.7500>: ↵

Tip

When you are picking on the solid model, you may have trouble at first deciding which surface to select because each wire of the wireframe represents not one surface, but the intersection of two surfaces. Many commands have the Next option to allow you to move surface by surface until the one you want to select is highlighted. If the surface you want to select is not highlighted, use the Next option until it is. When the surface you want to select is highlighted, press ↵*, You can also cycle through surfaces by pressing the* Ctrl *key when selecting.*

Specify other surface chamfer distance<0.7500>: ↵
Select an edge or [Loop]: **pick line A again** ↵
Select an edge or [Loop]: ↵

Your screen should look like Figure 12.3.

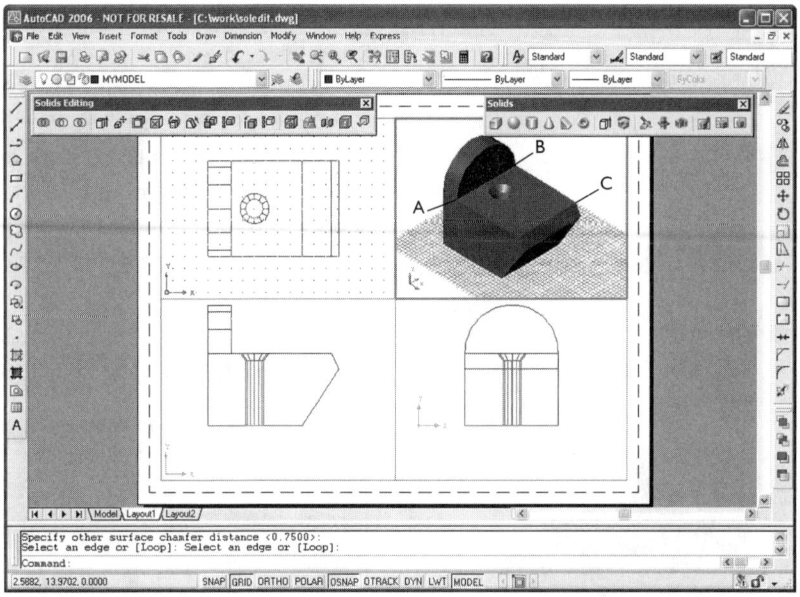

Figure 12.3

Command: **U** ↵

The chamfer that you added to your drawing is eliminated.

Using Slice

Using the Slice command, you can cut a solid using a specified *cutting plane*, also called the *slicing plane*. The cutting plane does not have to be an existing drawing entity. You can specify the cutting plane in several ways.

Option	Function
Object	Select an existing planar entity
Zaxis	Specify a point for the origin and a point that gives the direction of the Z-axis of the cutting plane
View	Align a plane parallel to the current view and through a point
XY, YZ, ZX	Choose a plane parallel to the XY-, YZ-, or ZX-coordinate planes and through a point
3points	Choose three points to define a plane

When you have specified the cutting plane, you are prompted to pick a point on the side of the plane where you want the object to remain. The portion of the object on the other side is then deleted. You can choose the Both sides option so that the object is cut into two pieces, with neither side being deleted.

In this example you will use the 3points option of the Slice Command to separate the rounded top surface from the block itself. Refer to Figure 12.3 for your selections.

On your own, be sure that running object snap **Endpoint** is on.
Pick: **Slice icon**
Select objects: **select the block**
Select objects: ↵
Specify first point on slicing plane by [Object/Zaxis/View/XY/YZ/ZX/
3points] <3points>: ↵
Specify first point on plane: **pick endpoint A using AutoSnap™**
Specify second point on plane: **pick endpoint B using AutoSnap**
Specify third point on plane: **pick endpoint C using AutoSnap**
Specify a point on the desired side of the plane or [keep Both sides]: **B** ↵

Now if you select the half-cylinder that used to be the top surface of the block, it will be separate from the block. The grips on the cylinder appear separate from the block, as shown in Figures 12.4 and 12.5.

Figure 12.4

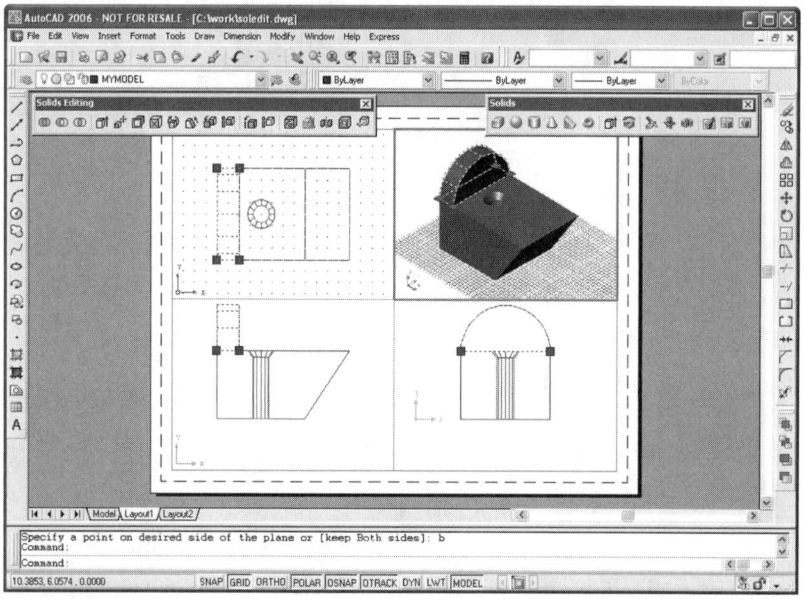

Figure 12.5

Next, you will move the half-cylinder up one unit in the Z-direction and then create a new rectangular piece beneath it.

Pick: **Move icon**
Select objects: **pick on the half-cylinder that you separated from the block, unless it is already selected**
Select objects: ↵
Specify base point or Displacement <Displacement>: **0,0,1** ↵
Specify second point of displacement or <use first point as displacement>: ↵

The cylinder is moved upward 1 unit in the Z direction, as shown in Figure 12.6.

Tip

Many of the editing commands that you learned in the 2D tutorials are still effective in solid modeling. Don't be afraid to try them when they would be useful.

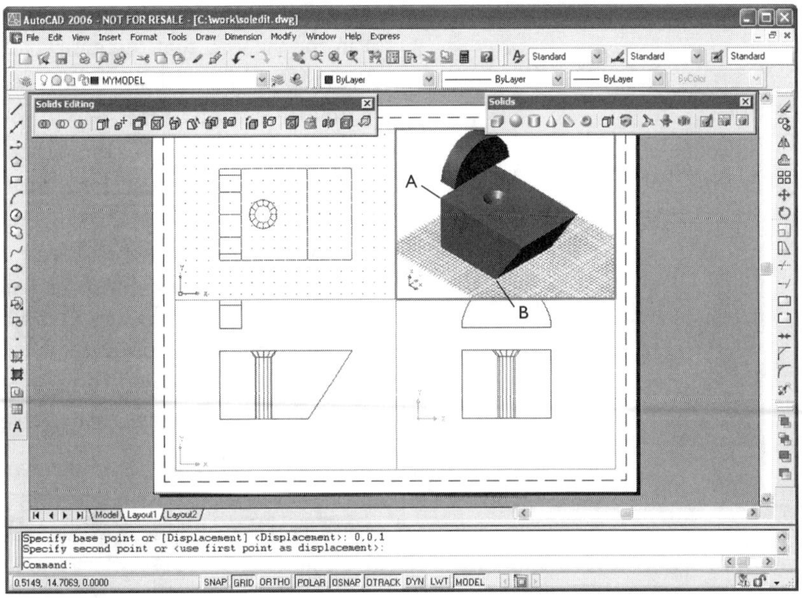

Figure 12.6

Now you will create two rectangular boxes. One will be immediately below the cylinder and the second will be where you subtracted a wedge in Tutorial 11. The WCS should still be active. Use Figure 12.6 for your selections.

Pick: **Box icon**

Specify corner of box or [CEnter] <0,0,0>: **pick corner A in Figure 12.6, using the AutoSnap Endpoint marker**

Specify corner or [Cube/Length]: **L** ↵

Specify length: **1** ↵

Specify width: **4** ↵

Specify height: **1** ↵

Command: ↵

Specify corner of box or [CEnter] <0,0,0>: **pick corner B in Figure 12.6, using the AutoSnap Endpoint marker**

Specify corner or [Cube/Length]: **L** ↵

Specify length: **2** ↵

Specify width: **4** ↵

Specify height: **3** ↵

Pick: **View, Shade, 3D Wireframe** to show the wireframe view in the upper right viewport

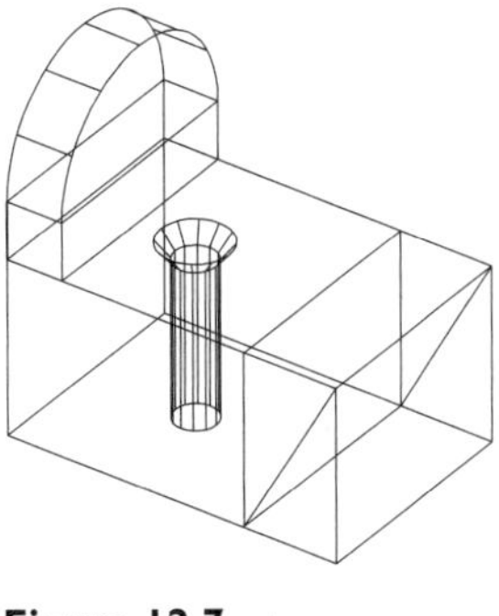

Figure 12.7

The boxes should appear on your screen as shown in Figure 12.7. Note that the object is not centered well in the viewports. You will use the Pan command to position the view within the upper right viewport.

Be sure that the upper right viewport is active before continuing.

Pick: **Pan Realtime icon**

On your own, position the view so that the entire object is visible inside the viewport.

Press: Esc to exit the Pan command

Pick: **inside the lower right viewport to make it active**

Pick: **Pan Realtime icon**

Pan the view so that the entire view fits inside the lower right viewport.

Press: Esc to exit the Pan command

Command: **MVSETUP** ↵

Enter an option [Align/Create/Scale viewports/Options/Title block/Undo]: **A** ↵

Enter an option [Angled/Horizontal/Vertical alignment/Rotate view/Undo]: **H** ↵

Specify basepoint: **use Osnap Endpoint and pick the lower left corner of the object in the lower right viewport**

Specify point in viewport to be panned: **make the lower left viewport active and then use Osnap Endpoint and pick the lower right corner of the object**

Enter an option [Angled/Horizontal/Vertical alignment/Rotate view/Undo]: ↵

Enter an option [Angle/Create/Scale viewports/Options/Title block/Undo]: ↵

Your screen should be similar to Figure 12.8.

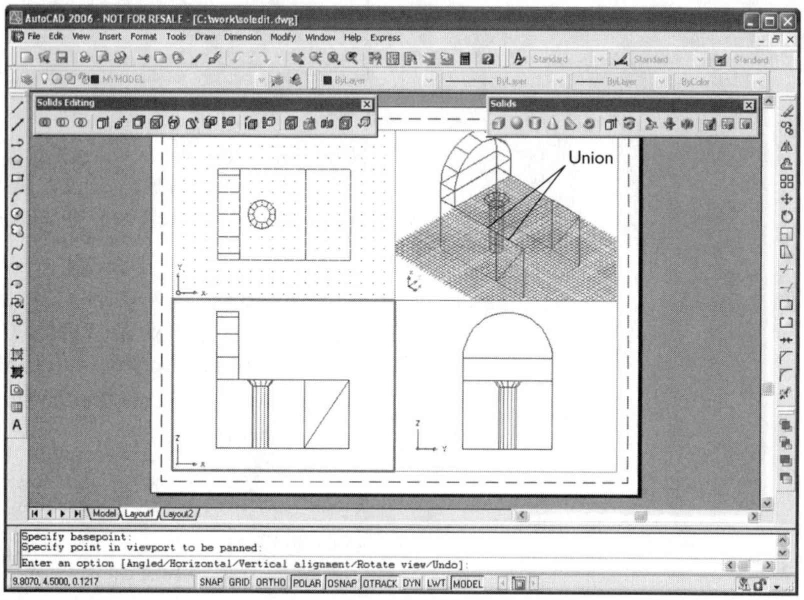

Figure 12.8

Now you will use Union to join the block and the second box you created (where you subtracted the wedge in Tutorial 11). The Union command is on the Solids Editing toolbar, or you can select it from the menu bar under Modify, Solids Editing.

Pick: **Union icon**

Select objects: **used implied Crossing to select ONLY the block and the second box, using Figure 12.8 for reference**

Select objects: ↵

Pick: **View, Shade, Gouraud Shaded**

The two objects should now be joined, forming one object similar to that in Figure 12.9.

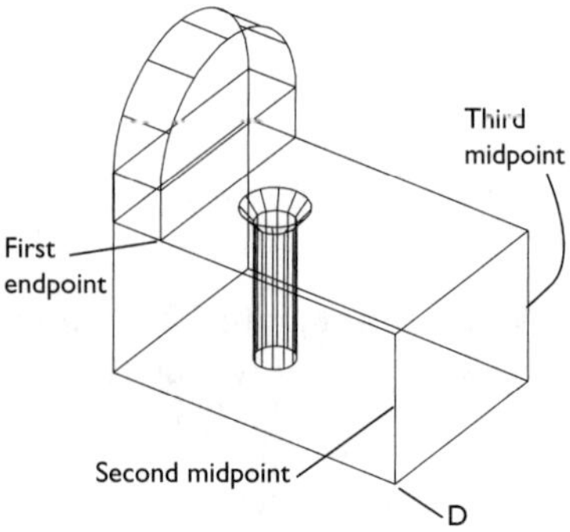

Figure 12.9

Now you will use the 3points Slice option again to slice an angled portion from the block. Select the Slice command from the Solids toolbar. Refer to Figure 12.9 for the three points.

Pick: **Slice icon**
Select objects: **select the block object**
Select objects: ↵
Specify first point on slicing plane by [Object/Zaxis/View/XY/YZ/ZX/3points] <3points>: **target the endpoint labeled First endpoint, using the AutoSnap Endpoint marker**
Specify second point on plane: **target the front vertical edge labeled Second midpoint, using the AutoSnap Midpoint marker**
Specify third point on plane: **target the front vertical edge labeled Third midpoint, using the AutoSnap Midpoint marker**
Specify point on the desired side of the plane or [keep Both sides]: **pick on the bottom left corner, labeled D**

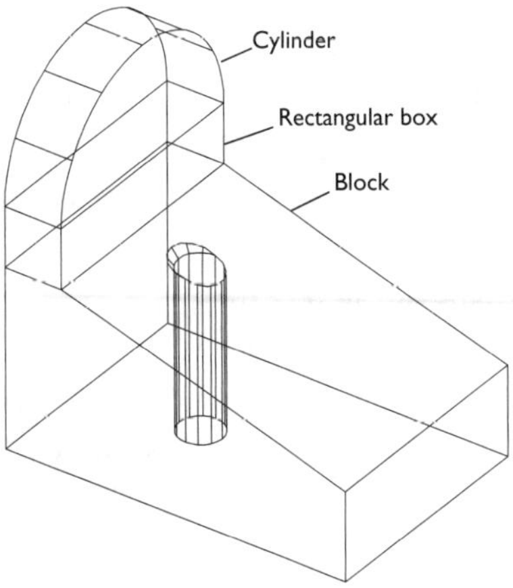

Figure 12.10

The upper portion of the block is cut off, leaving an angled surface, as shown in Figure 12.10.

Now use the Union command to join the three parts.

Pick: **Union icon**
Select objects: **use implied Crossing to select all three objects**
Select objects: ↵

Your drawing should look like that in Figure 12.11.

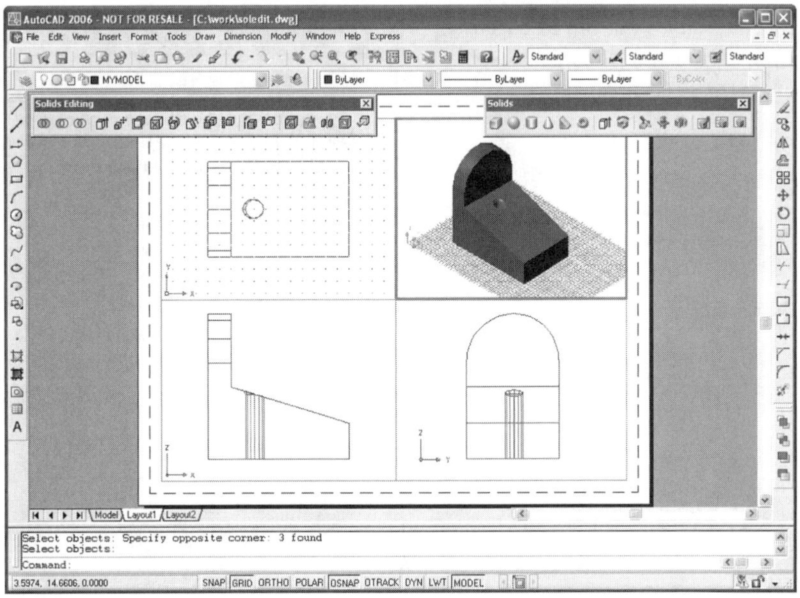

Figure 12.11

Next, you will add a 0.375 deep hole of diameter 0.5, perpendicular to the angled surface.

To create a hole perpendicular to the angled surface, you will create a User Coordinate System that aligns with the angled surface. To do so, you will use the UCS 3 point command to locate the origin and X- and Y-axes. Refer to Figure 12.12 as you pick points.

Tip

You can also pick Tools, New UCS, 3 point from the pull-down menu to start the UCS 3 point command.

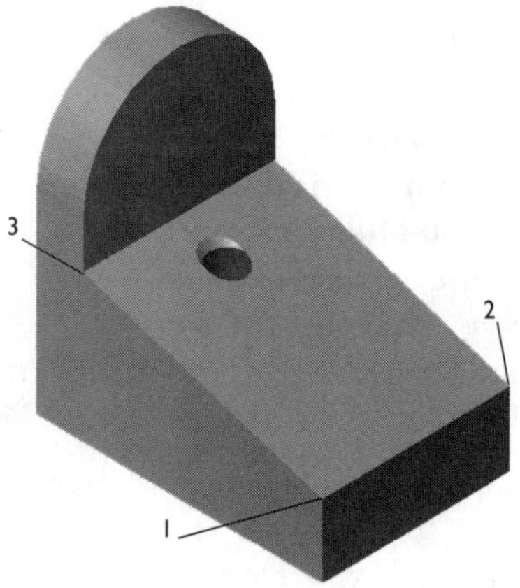

Figure 12.12

Tip

Always keeping the grid turned on helps you see how the UCS is aligned. You can also look at the UCS icon, but often the grid is more noticeable.

Pick: **to make the upper right viewport active**

Turn on running OSNAP for Endpoint.

Turn on the UCS toolbar on your own.

Pick: **3 Point UCS icon** (from the UCS toolbar)

Specify new origin point <0,0,0>: **target the lower left corner of the angled surface, point 1 in Figure 12.12**

Specify point on positive portion of the X axis <9.0000, 2.0000, 1.5000>: **target the lower right corner of the angled surface, point 2**

Specify point on positive-Y portion of the UCS XY plane <7.0000, 2.0000, 1.5000>: **target the upper left corner of the angled surface, point 3**

The grid changes so that it now aligns with the angled surface.

Next you will turn the shading off so that you can see the back surfaces of the object, then use the Plan command to align your view so that you are looking straight down the Z-axis. The resulting view shows the XY-plane of the new UCS that you created in the previous step. The Plan command will fit the drawing extents to the viewport.

Pick: **View, Shade, 3D Wireframe**

Command: **PLAN** ↵

Enter an option [Current ucs/Ucs/World] <Current>: ↵

The view in the upper right viewport should now be directly perpendicular to the angled surface of the object. Your drawing should look like that in Figure 12.13.

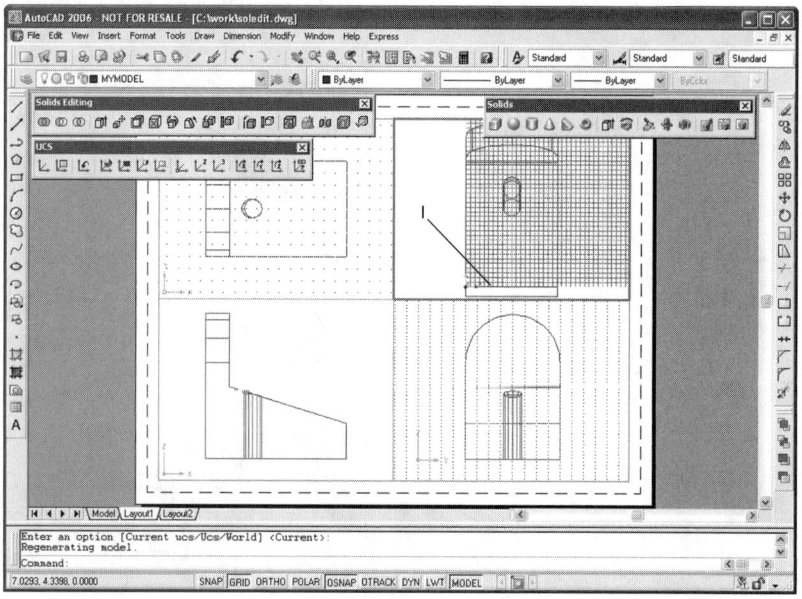

Figure 12.13

Next, you will save the view and the UCS so that you can restore them later if you want to.

Pick: **UCS icon**

Enter an option [New/Move/orthoGraphic/Prev/Restore/Save/
Del/Apply/?/World] <World>: **S** ↵

Enter name to save current UCS or [?]: **ANGLE** ↵

Command: **VIEW** ↵

On your own pick the Named Views tab if it is not uppermost.

The View dialog box is shown in Figure 12.14. You will use it to create a new named view.

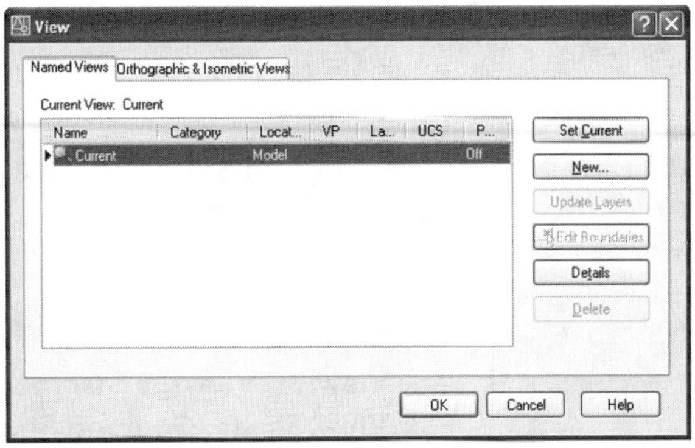

Figure 12.14

Pick: **New**

The New View dialog box appears on your screen. Use it to make the settings shown in Figure 12.15.

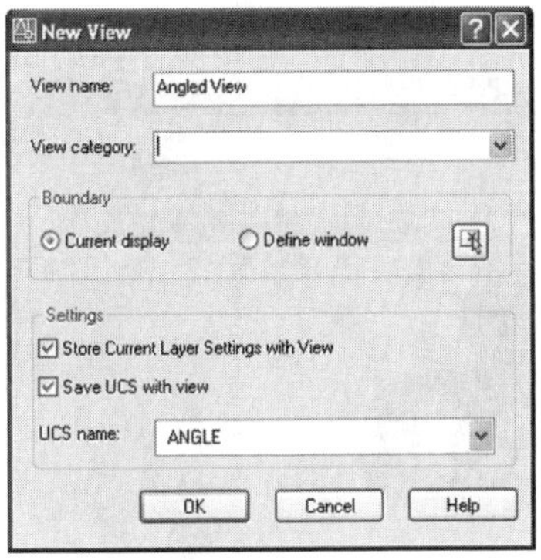

Figure 12.15

Type: **Angled View** for the view name

Pick: **Current Display**

Pick: **Save UCS with view** (so that it appears checked)

UCS name: **angle** (should be selected)

Pick: **OK**

You return to the View dialog box.

Pick: **OK**

Creating the Hole

You will use the cylinder primitive and then subtract it to create the hole. You will also use OTRACK to aid in the location of the cylinder. Refer to Figure 12.13 for your selection of point 1.

Make sure that the running object snap **Midpoint** is active.

Turn off the Grid in the upper right viewport to make it easier to see the selections.

Turn on **OTRACK**.

Pick: **Cylinder icon**

Specify center point for base of cylinder or [Elliptical] <0,0,0>: **Otrack point 1, using AutoSnap Midpoint** as shown in Figure 12.16.

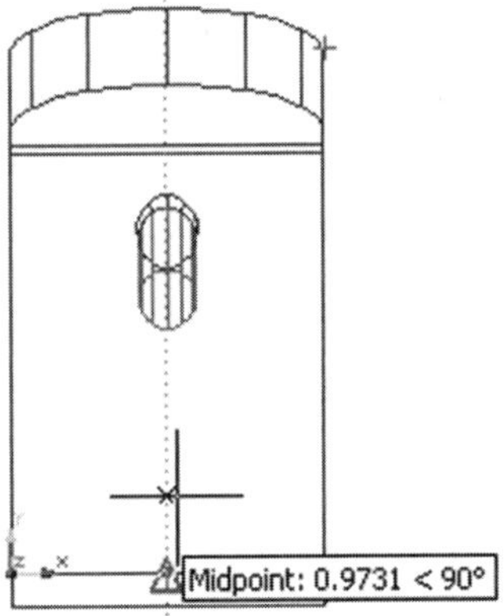

Figure 12.16

Specify center point for base of cylinder or [Elliptical] <0,0,0>: **positioning cursor along temporary tracking line that appears, type 1** ↵ **to specify a distance of 1 along the tracking line**

Specify radius for base of cylinder or [Diameter]: **D** ↵

Tip

*The AutoCAD 2006 software has a handy new Quick Calculator function that can be very useful in specifying points that would be impossible to specify by other drawing means. Whenever you see a prompt requesting input of a point, real number, integer, or vector, you can use the Quick Calculator or the transparent command 'CAL. 'CAL lets you write an expression in infix notation, such as 112*sin(30), at the prompt and the resultant value is used. You can also use OSNAP functions and acquire points from your drawing in combination with the Quick Calculator. This is very useful in creating complex models.*

Specify diameter for base of cylinder: **.5** ↵
Specify height of cylinder or [Center of other end]: **–.375** ↵
On your own, change the color for the small cylinder you just created to Red.

Next, subtract the cylinder to form a hole in the object.

Pick: **Subtract icon**
Select objects: **pick the large block**
Select objects: ↵
Select solids and regions to subtract...
Select objects: **pick the short cylinder you just created**
Select objects: ↵

Now you will use the World UCS icon to change back to World Coordinates.

Pick: **World UCS icon**

Next, reset the viewpoint for the upper right viewport,

Pick: **View, 3D Views, SE Isometric**
Pick: **View, Shade, Gouraud Shaded**
Use Save As to name your drawing ***anglblok.dwg***.
Turn off the Solids Editing and UCS toolbars.

Your drawing should now look like the one shown in Figure 12.17.

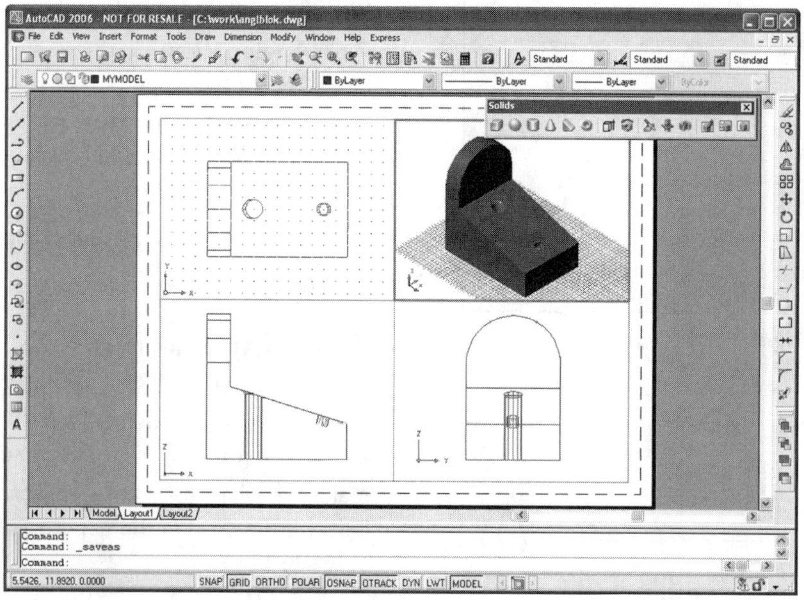

Figure 12.17

Plotting with Hidden Lines

To generate views that plot correctly using hidden lines, you can use the Setup Profile (SOLPROF) command to create a 2D projection, or *profile*, of each view. The Profile icon is located on the Solids toolbar. When you use Setup Profile, separate layers for hidden and visible lines are automatically generated for each viewport. The tangential edges, or multiple lines, that make up circular features can also be automatically deleted. You will project a 2D profile of the object in each viewport using the Setup Profile command. First, verify that the Solids toolbar is turned on. Next,

Pick: **in the upper left viewport so that it becomes active**
Pick: **Profile icon**
Select objects: **pick on an edge of the object in the upper left viewport**
Select objects: ↵
Display hidden profile lines on separate layer? [Yes/No] <Y>: ↵
Project profile lines onto a plane? [Yes/No] <Y>: ↵
Delete tangential edges? [Yes/No] <Y>: ↵

You will see lines drawn over the original colored lines that designate the edges of your model in the current viewport. The default color for the profile lines is white (which appears black on a light background).

Pick: **to pull-down the list of layers**

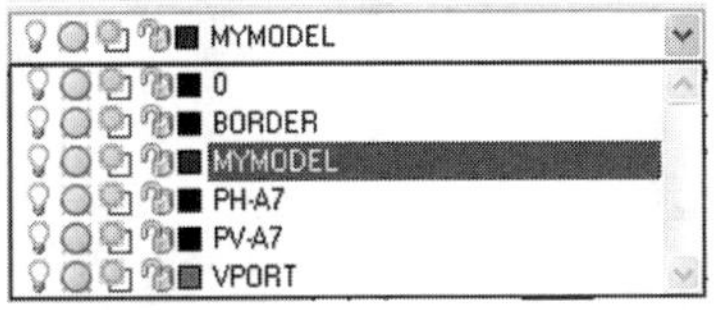

Figure 12.18

You should now have two new layers that were created by the Setup Profile command during the last step. Setup Profile creates new layers for the lines of the profile, and the default color setting is white (or black). Because you responded "Yes" to the prompt for displaying hidden profile lines on a new layer, two new types of layers exist in the drawing—one for *visible profile lines* and one for *hidden profile lines*. Figure 12.18 shows the Layer Control list with the new layers.

The AutoCAD software automatically names the layers for visible profile lines. The layer names for profiled visible lines start with the letters PV-. The layer names for profiled hidden lines start with the letters PH-. The remaining portion of the layer name is based on the handle number of the viewport that the object was profiled in. You will work more with these layers after you create profiles for the other views.

Next, you will create a 2D profile for the front view.

Pick: **the lower left viewport to make it active**
Pick: **Profile icon**
Select objects: **pick on an edge of the object in the lower left viewport**
Select objects: ↵
Display hidden profile lines on separate layer? [Yes/No] <Y>: ↵
Project profile lines onto a plane? [Yes/No] <Y>: ↵
Delete tangential edges? [Yes/No] <Y>: ↵
On your own, **repeat this process** for the two remaining viewports.

Again, lines appear over the original colored lines in this viewports. When you have completed profiling the object in each viewport, you will see only white lines (which appear black on a light background) and colored tessellation lines on the screen, except in the shaded view, where they may be hard to see.

Controlling the Generated Layers

The layers that were created using the Setup Profile command were named with two parts: PV or PH, describing whether they were the visible or hidden profile lines, and a handle number for the viewport. To find the handle number for each viewport, switch to paper space and use the List command. Later you will use this information selectively to freeze and thaw the profiled lines for the desired layers.

On your own, switch to paper space.
Thaw layer Vport if it is not already thawed.

Note that the paper space icon, a triangle, is now displayed in the lower left corner of your screen. Next, you will list the information for the viewports. To select a viewport, you must pick on its border and not just somewhere inside the viewport.

Pick: **Tools, Inquiry, List**
Select objects: **pick the border of the upper right viewport**
Select objects: ↵

The information shown in Figure 12.19 is displayed on your screen.

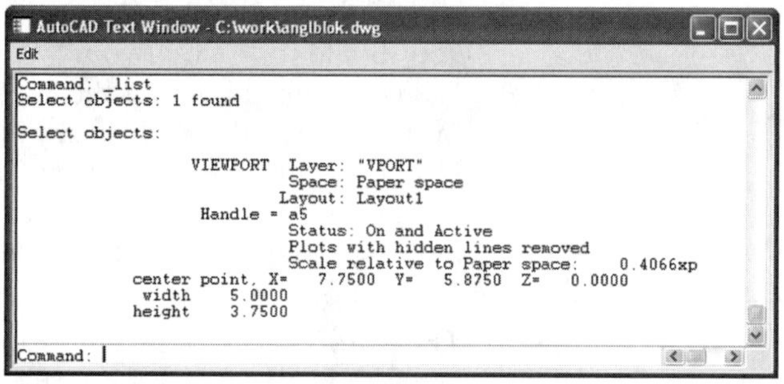

Figure 12.19

Write the handle number for the upper right viewport in the space provided on the next page. The handle numbers begin with hexadecimal number 1, which is assigned to the first object you create in your drawing, and then proceed with hexadecimal numbers for each additional entity. (Hexadecimal representation for decimal number 10 is A; 11 is B; and so on.) The handle number that you see in your drawing may be different from that listed in Figure 12.19, depending on how you created each object in the drawing.

Pick: **the Close button to remove the text window**
Pick: **Tools, Inquiry, List**
Select objects: **pick the border of the upper left viewport**
Select objects: ↵

The information and handle number for the upper left viewport are listed on the text screen.

Write the handle number for the upper viewports in the space provided. Then write the handle numbers for the lower left and lower right viewports on your own.

Upper Right Viewport Handle Number:
Upper Left Viewport Handle Number:
Lower Left Viewport Handle Number:
Lower Right Viewport Handle Number:

You will need to keep track of these numbers in order to easily freeze and thaw profile layers in any particular viewport.

Setting the Linetypes and Colors for Generated Layers

Now you will use the Layer Properties Manager to set the color and linetype for the new layers.

Pick: **Layer Properties Manager icon**

The Layer Properties Manager appears on your screen. Note that eight more layers are listed in the dialog box than were previously. These are the generated layers for the profiles that were created when you used the Setup Profile (SOLPROF) command. You will use the dialog box to set the color and linetype of the generated hidden line layers. Remember to hold down the Shift key in order to select more than one layer name at a time.

Pick: **each of the layer names that start with PH-**
Pick: **on Continuous** (under the heading Linetype, across from one of the selected layers)
Pick: **Load**
Pick: **Hidden** (from the Load or Reload Linetypes dialog box)
Pick: **OK**
Pick: **Hidden**
Pick: **OK** (to exit the Select Lineweight dialog box)
Pick: **the Color box** (across from one of the selected layers)
Pick: **Blue**
Pick: **OK** (to exit the Select Color dialog box)
Pick: **Default** (under the Lineweight listing)
Pick: **0.30 mm** (from the list of Lineweights)
Pick: **OK**

You have finished setting the color blue and linetype HIDDEN for the generated hidden line layers. The PH- and PV- layers are frozen in the current viewport, which was done automatically when you generated the layers; otherwise, each 2D profile would appear in every viewport, creating a lot of confusion.

Using the techniques you have learned, set the lineweight for all PV layers to 0.60 mm and freeze these layers.
Set layer 0 as the current layer.
Freeze and lock layer MYMODEL so that you will not see the original solid model that you created underneath the hidden lines.
Pick: **OK** (to exit the Layer Properties Manager box)

You have frozen the visible lines to make selecting specific lines easier as you continue to work on your drawing. When you have made these changes the list of layers appears as shown in Figure 12.20.

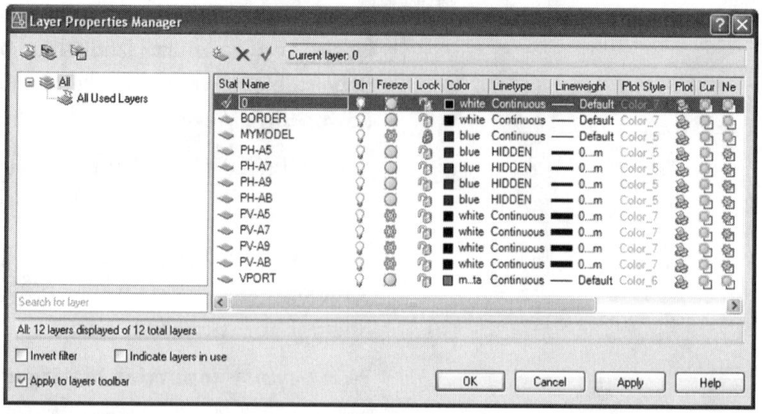

Figure 12.20

When you return to your drawing, only blue hidden lines and the viewport borders should be visible on the screen, as shown in Figure 12.21.

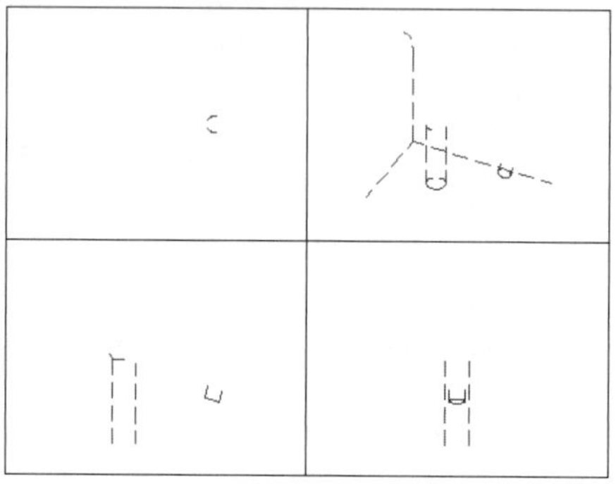

Figure 12.21

Eliminating Unnecessary Hidden Lines

Hidden lines are not usually shown in pictorial or isometric views unless they are needed to show the depth of a hole or some other feature that cannot be inferred without them. In an isometric view, holes are assumed to be through holes unless the depth is indicated in the drawing by hidden lines, a visible back surface showing the depth, or a note. Because they are generated automatically, the isometric view has hidden lines shown that are not necessary.

Before you can erase the unwanted hidden lines, you will use the Xplode command to turn the block of hidden lines back into single entities. Xplode has an option to let the individual entities inherit their settings from the parent object. This provides an easy way to ensure that the exploded objects stay on the correct layer. Remember, you shouldn't explode the actual model, as you can't rejoin the separate objects to form the model again. To ensure that this does not happen, you have frozen and locked layer MYMODEL, on which you created the actual model. The lines remaining on your screen are the hidden profile lines.

On your own, switch to Model space inside the upper right viewport.

Command: **XPLODE** ↵

Select objects: **pick on the blue lines in the upper right viewport**

Select objects: ↵

Enter an option [All/Color/LAyer/LType/LWeight/Inherit from parent block/Explode] <Explode>: **I** ↵

Object exploded.

The lines should now be separate entities, and you can select any one of them. Now you can erase the outer hidden lines and any other unnecessary hidden lines.

On your own, erase all of the lines in the isometric view except those showing the depth of the blind hole.

When you have finished, your drawing should look like Figure 12.22.

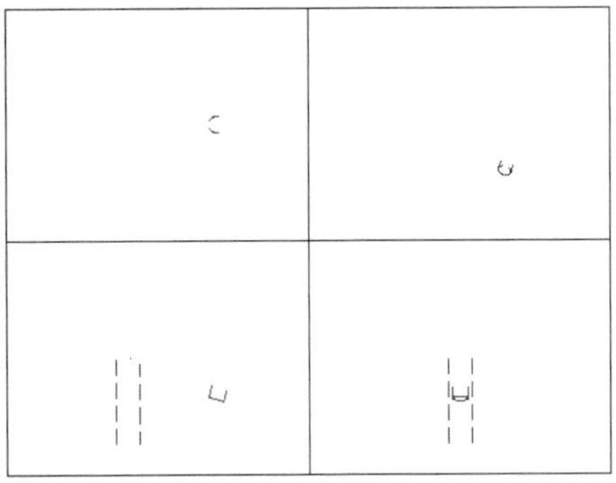

Figure 12.22

Now you will thaw the profile visible layers.

Pick: **the Layer Control list and thaw all of the layers with names starting with PV** (profile visible lines)

Pick on the lower left viewport to make it active before continuing.

Next, you will restore the UCS for the front view.

Pick: **Tools, Orthographic UCS, Front**

When you have restored the UCS for the front view, the grid will appear in the lower left viewport. Now you are ready to draw the centerline for the front view.

Your screen should look like Figure 12.23.

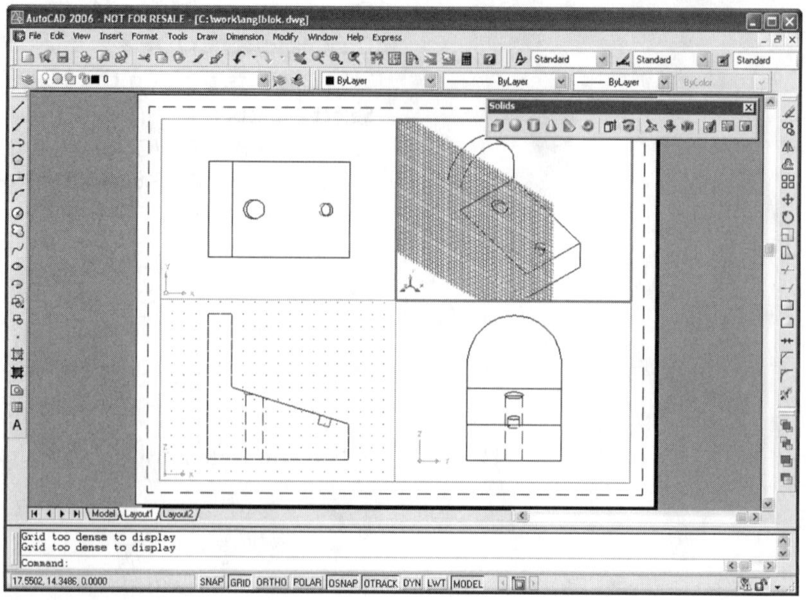

Figure 12.23

Adding the Centerlines

Next you will draw the centerlines for the front view. First you will create a new layer named CL-FRONT for the front view centerlines, using the Layers Properties Manager.

Pick: **Layer Properties Manager icon**
Pick: **New**
Type: **CL-FRONT**
Pick: **the Color box** to the right of the new layer
Pick: **Green** (from within the Select Color dialog box)
Pick: **OK** (to exit the Select Color dialog box)
Pick: **linetype CONTINUOUS** to the right of the new layer
Pick: **Load**
Pick: **CENTER** (from the Load or Reload Linetypes dialog box)
Pick: **OK**
Pick: **CENTER**
Pick: **OK** (to exit the Select Linetype dialog box)
Pick: to set the **lineweight** for the new layer
Pick: **0.30 mm**
Pick: **OK** (to exit the Lineweight dialog box)
Pick: **Set Current icon** (to make CL-FRONT the current layer)
Pick: **OK** (to exit the Layer Properties Manager dialog box)
On your own, be sure that Snap is turned on.
Use Snap and the Line command to draw a centerline for the through hole in the front view.
Switch to paper space and set LTSCALE to .5 if the centerline pattern does not appear correctly.

When you have finished, your drawing should be similar to Figure 12.24.

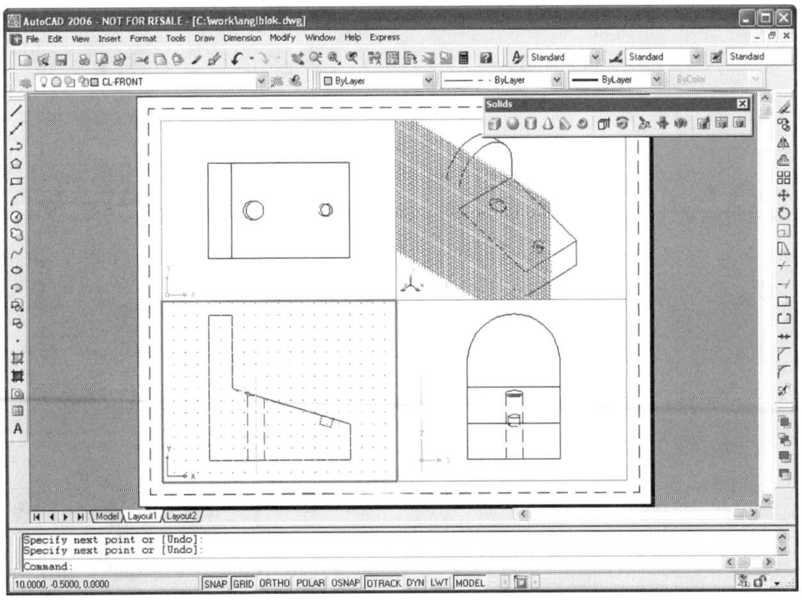

Figure 12.24

What happened? The line that you drew appears in the other viewports. Anything you add in model space will be visible in all the views unless you specify otherwise. You can use Freeze/Thaw in the Current Viewport selection in the Layer Properties Manager to freeze the layer in specific viewports so that the centerline does not appear in them.

Using Freeze/Thaw in Current Viewport

When you add lines such as centerlines and dimensions to 3D drawings, you usually have to create layers for each viewport. Using the Freeze/Thaw in Current Viewport selection, you can turn off the visibility of the layers in the viewports in which you do not want the lines to show. The AutoCAD software did this for you with the generated layers for profile visible and profile hidden. You must control the visibility of layers that you create unless you want them to show in every viewport. Imagine putting dimensions in the front view and having them show up edgewise in the top and side views.

Pick: **to make the lower right viewport active**
Pick: **Layer Properties Manager icon**

The Layer Properties Manager appears on your screen. You will use it to Freeze layer CL-FRONT in the current viewport (the lower right viewport at this time).

The Current Viewport Freeze selection is shown in Figure 12.25. You may find it necessary to expand the headings so that you can see their full names. (You can right-click in the heading row and select Maximize column headings from the pop-up menu.)

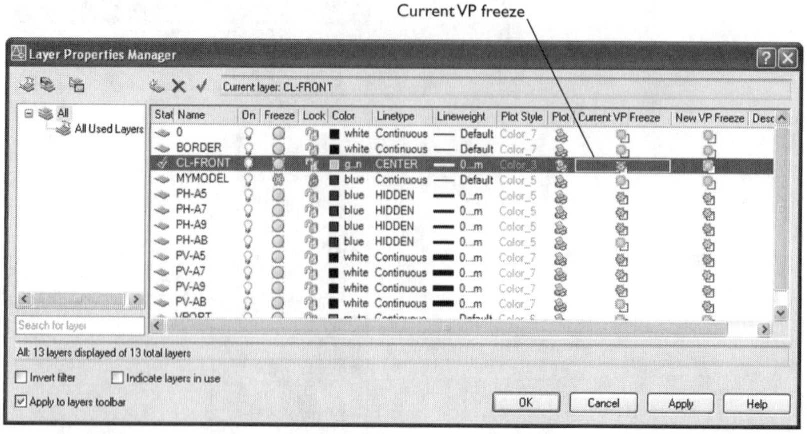

Figure 12.25

Pick: **Current VP Freeze** (adjacent to layer CL-Front so that it appears like Figure 12.25)

Pick: **OK** (to exit the dialog box)

Now the centerline you drew should be visible only in the front and isometric views (you can see it only as a point in the Top view because it is a line perpendicular to the page). Next you will freeze layer CL-Front in the upper right viewport using the layer list.

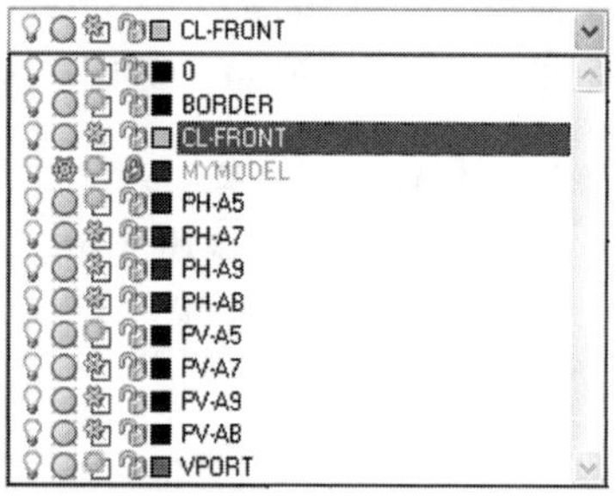

Figure 12.26

Pick: **to make the upper right viewport active**

Pick: **to pull down the layer list**

Pick: **Current VP Freeze adjacent to layer CL-FRONT as shown in Figure 12.26**

The centerline you drew should now be visible only in the front view.

Now that you have set the layer visibility,

Draw the centerline for the smaller hole on your own.

Next, you will use the Layer Properties Manager to create centerline layers for the top and side view. Then you will set their visibility and draw the appropriate centerlines.

Pick: **the upper left viewport to make it active**

Pick: **Layer Properties Manager icon**

Use the Layer Properties Manager to create **two new layers, CL-SIDE and CL-TOP.**

Set their linetypes to **CENTER** and their colors to **green.**

The Layer Properties Manager appears on your screen as shown in Figure 12.27.

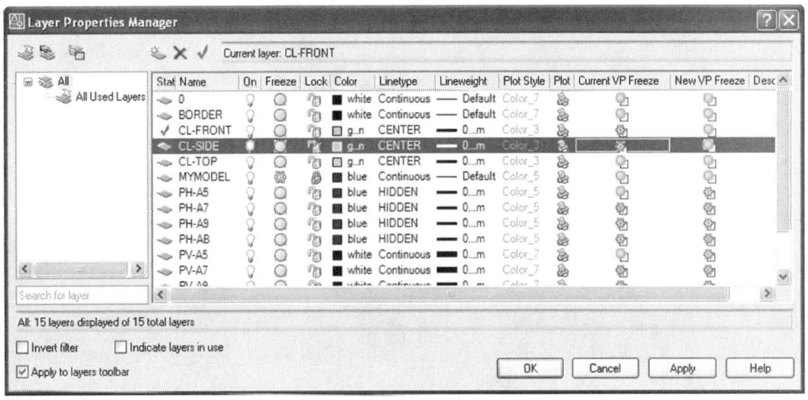

Figure 12.27

When you have finished creating the layers, you are ready to control their visibility.

You have already made the top view the active, or current, viewport. You will freeze the layers that you created so that your list looks like the one shown. Layer CL-FRONT should already be frozen for the current viewport because you froze it previously with the Layer Control pull-down list. You will freeze CL-SIDE in the current viewport.

Pick: **on layer name CL-SIDE so that it becomes highlighted**
Pick: **the Current VP Freeze selection**

The sun with the small viewport becomes a snowflake with a small viewport, signifying that the layer has been frozen in the current viewport.

Pick: **OK** (to exit the dialog box)

On your own, restore the UCS for the side view. Make the lower right viewport current and draw the side view centerlines. The lines will not appear in the top view because the current layer is frozen in that viewport.

On your own, make the lower left viewport (containing the front view) current and then return to the Layer Properties Manager. This time, use the dialog box to freeze layers CL-SIDE and CL-TOP in the lower left viewport. Make layer CL-TOP current by double-clicking it. When you have finished, pick OK to exit the dialog box.

Next, use the UCS command to restore the WCS. Draw the top view centerlines.

Make the lower right viewport active and use the Layer Control pull-down list to freeze all of the centerline layers in that viewport except CL-SIDE. Then make the isometric viewport active and freeze all the centerline layers in that viewport.

Your drawing should be similar to the one in Figure 12.28. You can also create dimensions that appear in only one viewport by controlling layer visibility as you did for the centerlines.

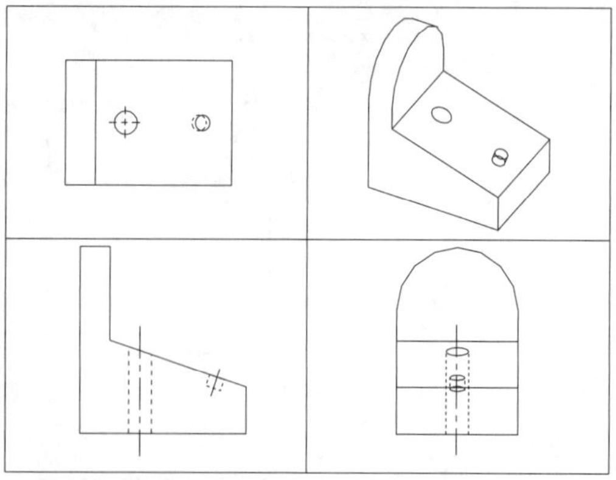

Figure 12.28

Plotting

Now you are ready to plot your drawing. You will switch to paper space next to set up your drawing for plotting.

Command: **PS** ↵

Now you will adjust the LTSCALE so that the centerlines and hidden lines in the drawing appear at an appropriate scale.

Tip

Try various values for LTScale until you are pleased with the results.

Command: **LTSCALE** ↵
New scale factor <1.000>: **.5** ↵

Usually, multiview engineering drawings do not have border lines between the views. This is why you created the layer VPORTS when you created the viewport boundaries. Now you will freeze this layer so that the views of your drawing plot correctly, with no lines dividing the views.

Pick: **to freeze the layer VPORTS**

The viewport border lines disappear from the screen.

On your own, use Save As to save your drawing to the file name ***angl_plt.dwg*** before you plot.
Use the **Plot icon** to plot your drawing.
Close all drawings and exit the AutoCAD software.

You have now completed Tutorial 12.

Key Terms

cutting plane	hidden profile line	slicing plane
handles	profile	visible profile line

Key Commands

Calculator	Fillet	Setup Profile
Chamfer	List	Slice

Exercises

12.1 Angled Support

Create this figure as a 3D solid model. Create necessary views and plot with correct hidden lines and centerlines.

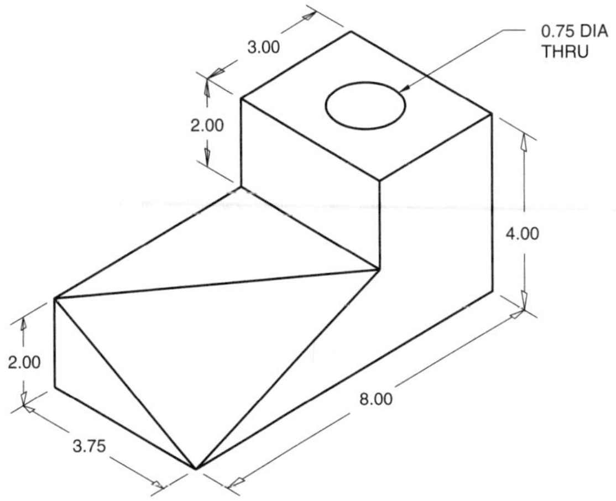

12.2 Gland

Create a 3D solid model of the part shown in the orthographic views.

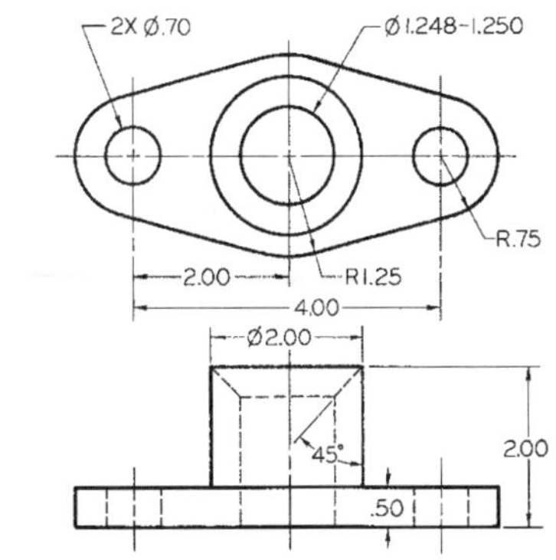

12.3 Step Model

Construct a solid model of this object. Grid spacing is 0.25 inch. Use a viewpoint of (3,–3,1) in the upper right viewport.

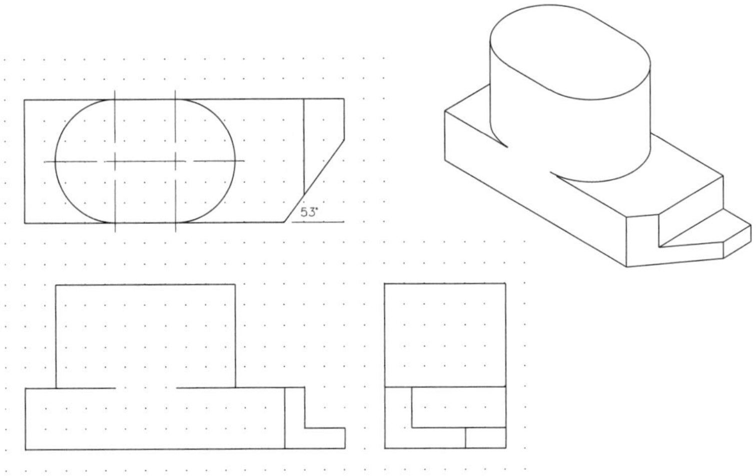

12.4M Rack

Create a 3D solid model of this metric part.

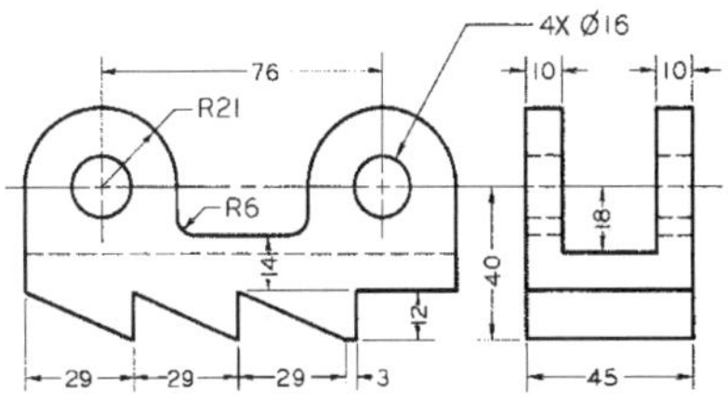

Create solid models for the objects shown. Show the necessary orthographic views in the correct viewports. Use SOLPROF to generate hidden lines.

12.5 Rod Holder

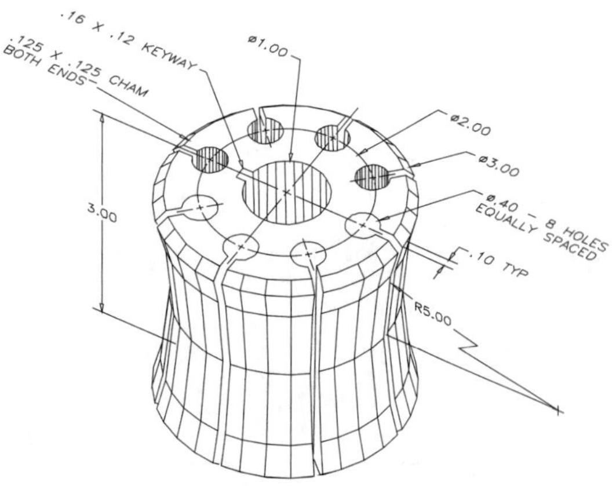

12.6 Gear

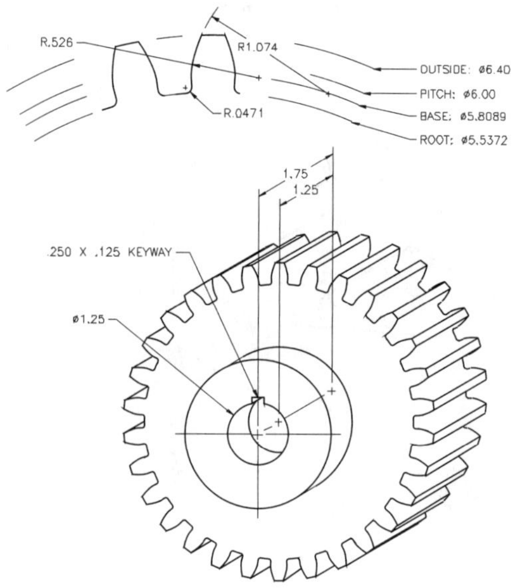

12.7 Router Guide

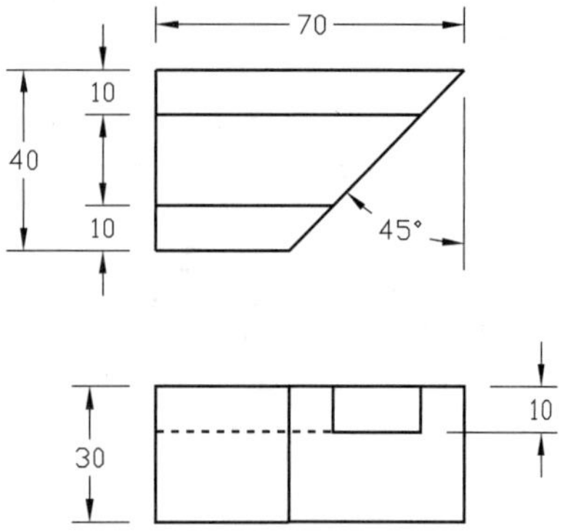

12.8 Slide Support

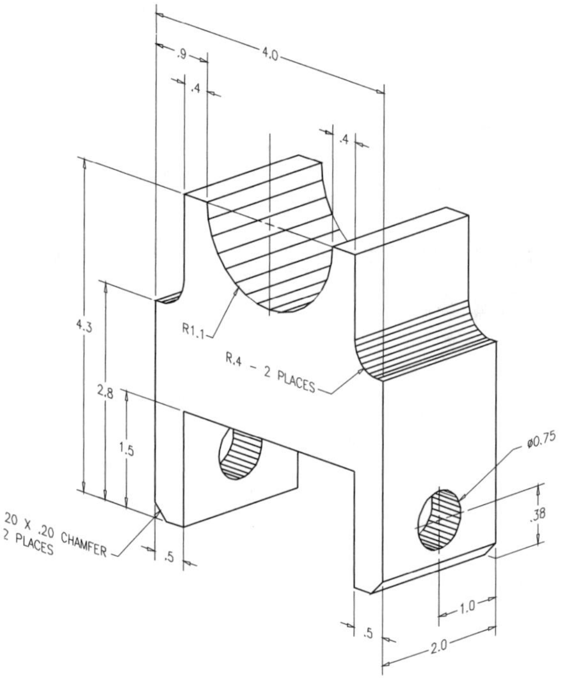

12.9 Spacer

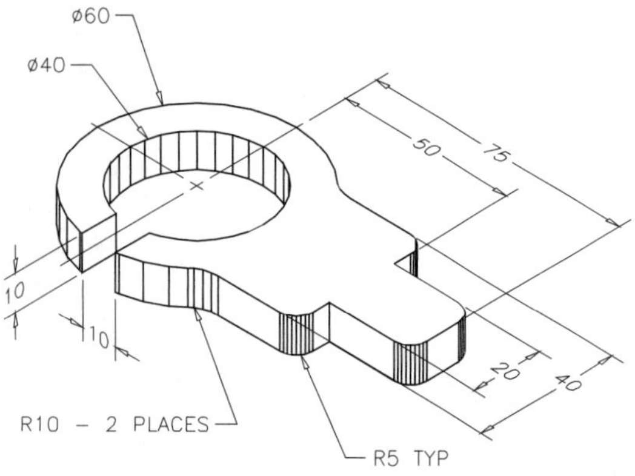

Tutorial

13 Creating Assembly Drawings from Solid Models

Objectives

When you have completed this tutorial, you will be able to

1. Create an assembly drawing from solid models.
2. Use external references.
3. Check for interference.
4. Analyze the mass properties of solid models.
5. Create an exploded isometric view.
6. Create and insert ball tags.
7. Create and extract attributes.
8. Create a parts list.

Introduction

In previous tutorials you created solid models of objects and projected 2D views to create orthographic drawings. To make a set of working drawings using solid modeling, you will create an assembly drawing of a clamp, similar to the one shown in Figure 13.1. The parts for the assembly drawing have been created as solid models and are included with the datafiles. You will proceed directly to creating the assembly drawing. The purpose of an assembly drawing is to show how the parts go together, not to describe completely the shape and size of each part. Assembly drawings usually do not show dimensions or hidden lines.

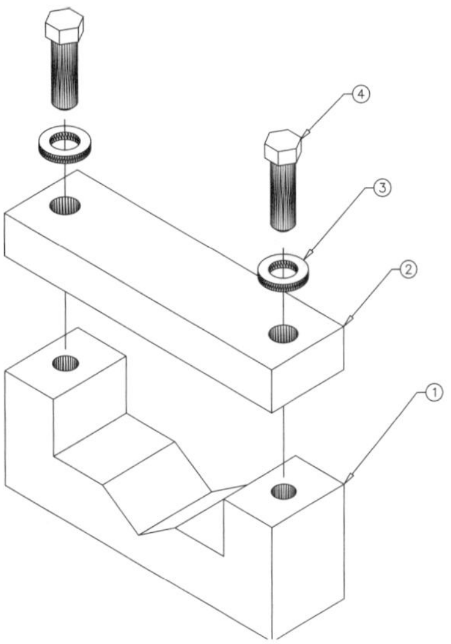

Figure 13.1

Attaching Solid Models

In this tutorial you will learn how to use the External Reference commands to attach part drawings to create an assembly drawing. When you use external references to attach a part drawing to the assembly drawing, the AutoCAD® software will automatically update the assembly drawing whenever you make a change to the original part drawing. You can use this same method to attach any drawing information into any other drawing as well, for example, to include the outline of a floor plan of a house in a site plan drawing.

You will also learn more about how to use the Insert command and Tool Palettes, as you did in Tutorial 10 when inserting the electronic logic symbols. Objects added to a drawing with the Insert command or dragged from a Tool Palette are included in the new drawing, but if you update the

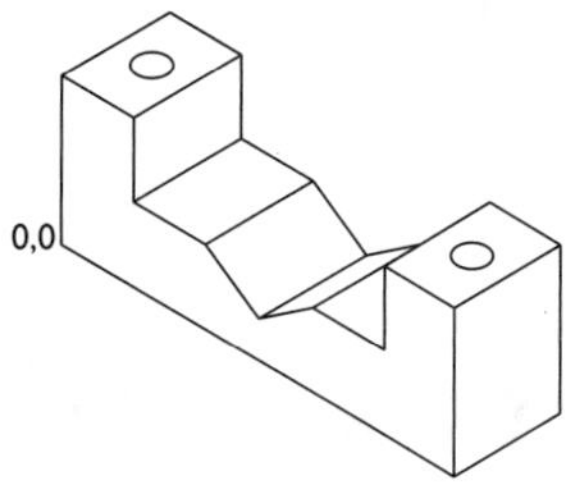

Figure 13.2

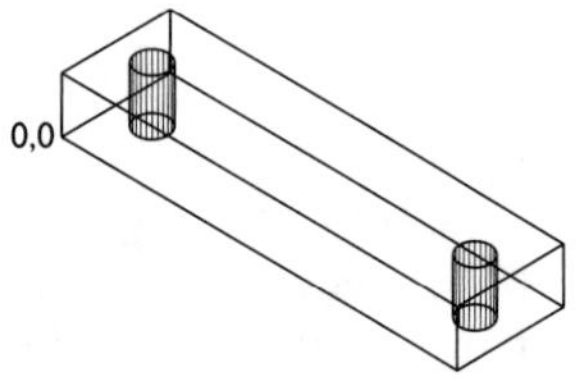

Figure 13.3

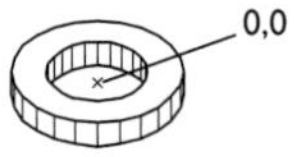

Figure 13.4

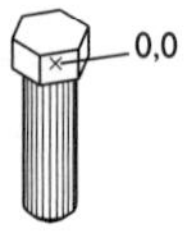

Figure 13.5

original drawing, the AutoCAD software doesn't automatically update the drawing where the copy was inserted.

The parts in Figures 13.2, 13.3, 13.4, and 13.5 are the parts provided with the datafiles. The insertion points are identified as 0,0 in the figures.

Starting

Start the AutoCAD program and begin a new drawing using the drawing template called ***proto-iso.dwt*** (provided with the datafiles).

Name the drawing ***asmb-sol.dwg***.

On your own, turn on the **Reference toolbar**

The drawing editor appears on your screen with the settings from a template drawing for 3D isometric views.

If necessary, switch to paper space and use Zoom All, so that the layout area fills the available graphics window. Your screen should be similar to Figure 13.6.

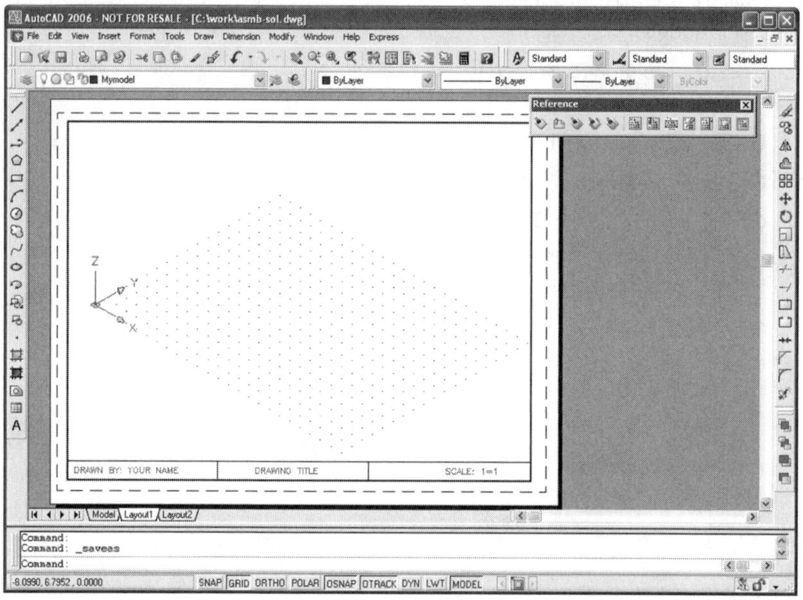

Figure 13.6

The icons on the Reference toolbar are shown in Figure 13.7.

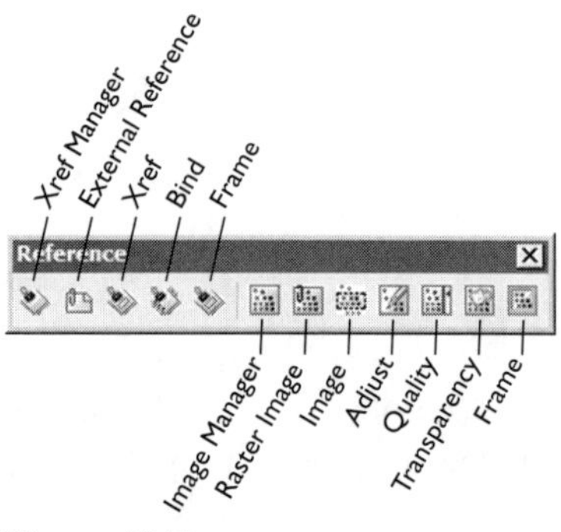

Figure 13.7

Using External References

The External Reference command lets you use another drawing without adding it to your current drawing. The advantage of this is that if you make a change to the referenced (original) drawing, any other drawing to which it is attached updates automatically the next time you open that drawing. As with blocks, you can attach external references anywhere in the drawing; you can also scale and rotate them. You can quickly select the External Reference command options from the Reference toolbar. As with any other AutoCAD command, you can also type the command name, -XREF, and select the option you want. You will begin your drawing by attaching the base of the clamp to your assembly drawing as an external reference.

Pick: **Xref Manager icon** from the Reference toolbar

The Xref Manager appears, as shown in Figure 13.8.

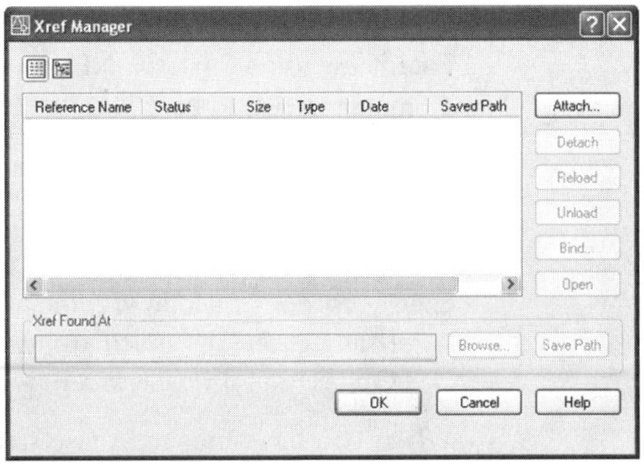

Figure 13.8

Pick: **Attach** (which is equivalent to the External Reference Attach command)

The Select Reference File dialog box appears on your screen.

Pick: ***base-3d.dwg***, which is in the *c:\datafile2006* directory
Pick: **Open**

The External Reference dialog box appears, similar to Figure 13.9.

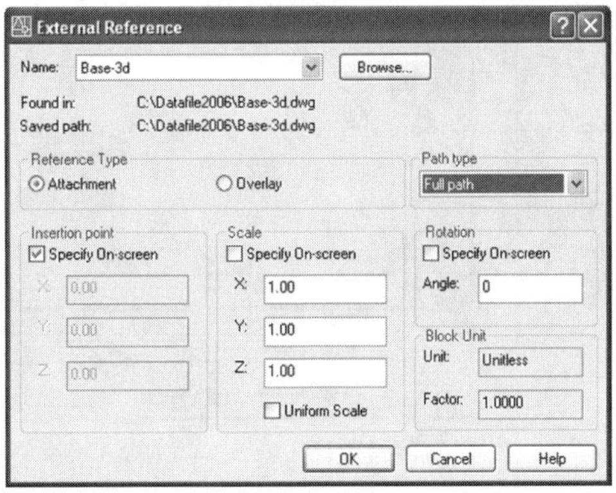

Figure 13.9

Note the options available for Reference Type. Xrefs can be used as an attachment or used as an overlay. If Overlay is selected, when the drawing containing the Xref overlay is inserted into a new drawing, the Xref will NOT be carried along. When Attachment is selected, the Xref-ed file comes along with it.

In the Insertion point area of the dialog box,

Deselect: **Specify On-screen** (remove the check)

The Insertion point of 0,0,0 should no longer be grayed out. If you wanted you could overtype these with new values. The scale will remain as 1 for X, Y, and Z, and the Rotation will remain at angle 0.

Pick: **OK**

Tip

The command alias for Regen is RE. You can type this shortcut instead of typing REGEN.

The base part appears in your drawing. Next you will set the Isolines variable to a larger value to produce more tessellation lines and improve the appearance of the rounded surfaces.

Command: **ISOLINES** ↵
Enter new value for ISOLINES <4>: **12** ↵
Command: **REGEN** ↵

Next, you will use the Zoom command with the XP option to set the paper space zoom factor.

Command: **Z** ↵
Specify corner of window, enter a scale factor (nX or nXP), or
[All/ Center/Dynamic/Extents/Previous/Scale/Window/
Object] <real time>: **.5XP** ↵

When you have finished these steps, your screen should be similar to Figure 13.10.

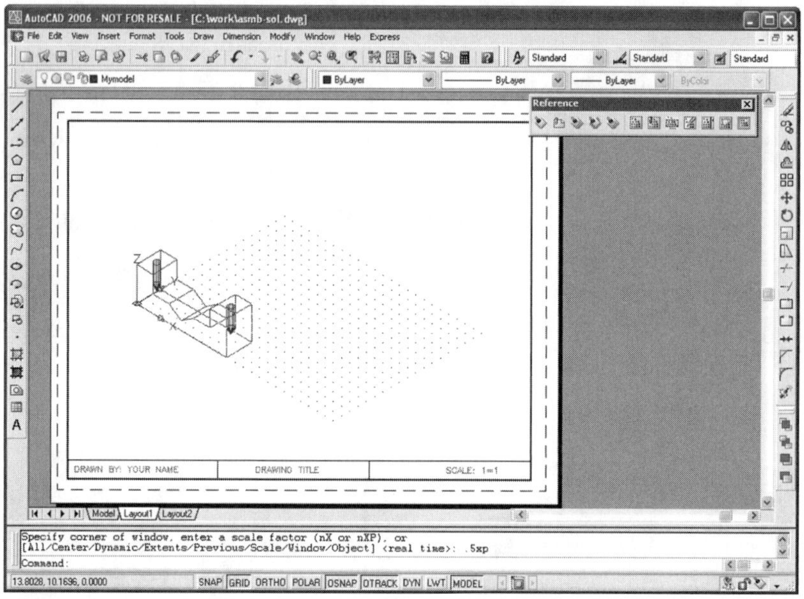

Figure 13.10

Layers and External References

When you attach a drawing to another drawing by using External Reference Attach, all its subordinate features (e.g., layers, linetypes, colors, blocks, and dimensioning styles) are attached with it. You can control the visibility of the layers attached with the referenced drawing, but you cannot modify anything or create any new objects on these layers. The Visretain system variable controls the extent to which you can make changes in the visibility, color, and linetype. If Visretain is set to 0, any changes that you make in the new drawing apply only to the current drawing session and will be discarded when you end it or reload or attach the original drawing. A new feature in AutoCAD Release 2004 let you use the Refedit command to make minor changes to an Xref'd object in the current drawing. Making major changes using Refedit is not advisable as your file size will be significantly larger during in-place

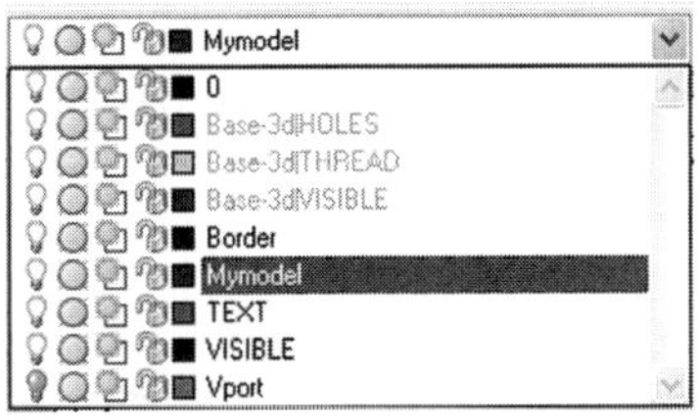

Figure 13.11

editing. You can easily open the referenced drawing in a separate window to edit it to avoid this.

Use Layer Control from the Layer toolbar to pull down the list of available layers.

Scroll to the top of the list, if necessary, to see the result of attaching the base as an external reference.

The list should be similar to that in Figure 13.11.

Note that the layer names attached with the external reference have the name of the external reference drawing in front of them.

Pick: **to freeze layer BASE-3D|VISIBLE**

The base externally referenced to the drawing disappears from the screen.

Pick: **to thaw layer BASE-3D|VISIBLE**

You can also control which portions of an external reference are visible by using the External Reference Clip command. This command creates a paper space viewport that you can use as a window to select the portion of the external reference that you want to be visible in the drawing.

On your own, use the Help command to obtain more information about the Xrefclip command.

Inserting the Solid Part Drawings

Next, you will insert the solid model drawing *cover-3d.dwg* into the assembly drawing as a block. You will use the Insert command, as you did in Tutorial 10 when inserting the electronic logic symbols.

Turn on running mode **OSNAP** for **Endpoint** and **Center**.

Pick: **Insert Block icon**

Pick: **Browse**

Double-click: to select ***cover-3d.dwg*** from the datafiles directory

When you have selected the file, you will be able to set the parameters for how the file is inserted. You will use the Specify On-screen option for the Insertion point. Leave the Scale set to the default values of 1 for X, Y, and Z, and the Rotation set to the default of angle 0.

Pick: **Specify On-screen** (so that it appears checked in the Insertion point area)

Pick: **OK** (to exit the Insert dialog box)

You return to the command prompt for the remaining prompt.

Specify insertion point or [Basepoint/Scale/X/Y/Z/Rotate/PScale/PX/PY/PZ/PRotate]: **pick anywhere in the drawing editor**, away from the base part

The solid model of the clamp cover appears in your drawing, as shown in Figure 13.12.

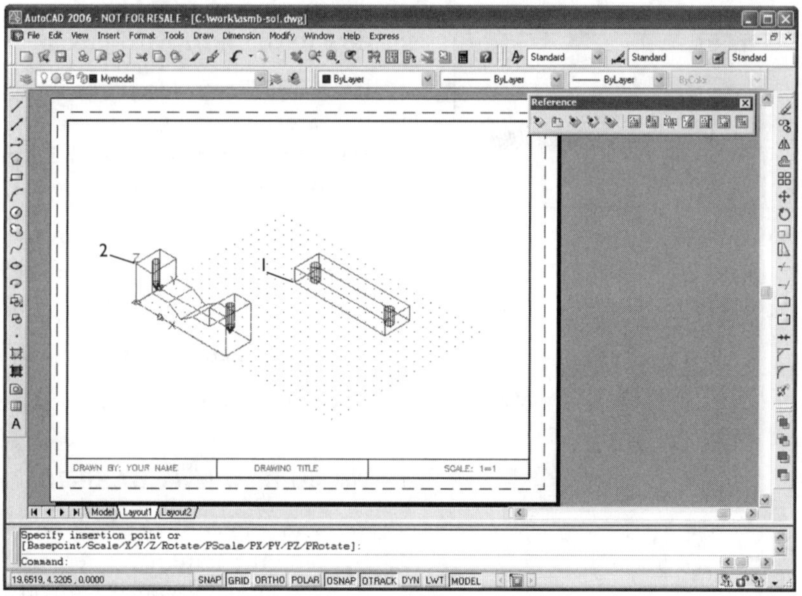

Figure 13.12

You will now use the Align command to align the edge of the cover with the edge of the base.

Command: **ALIGN** ↵
Select objects: **select the cover that you just inserted**
Select objects: ↵
Specify first source point: **use AutoSnap™ Endpoint to select point 1 in Figure 13.12**
Specify first destination point: **use AutoSnap Endpoint to select point 2 in Figure 13.12**
Specify second source point: ↵
Save your drawing.

Tip

The Align command can also be used with more than one point. For example, you can select additional points to align two points along an edge or three points defining a plane. When you have aligned all of the desired points press ↵ to have the command take effect.

The solid model of the clamp cover moves to align with the base.

Next you will insert the washers and screws into the assembly. You will select the Attach button from the External Reference dialog box.

Make sure that Snap is off.
Pick: **Model tab** (to disable paper space and switch to viewing only the model)
Pick: **View, Shade, 3D Wireframe**
Use Zoom Window to enlarge the view.
Pan to position it near the center of the screen.

Your drawing should look like Figure 13.13.

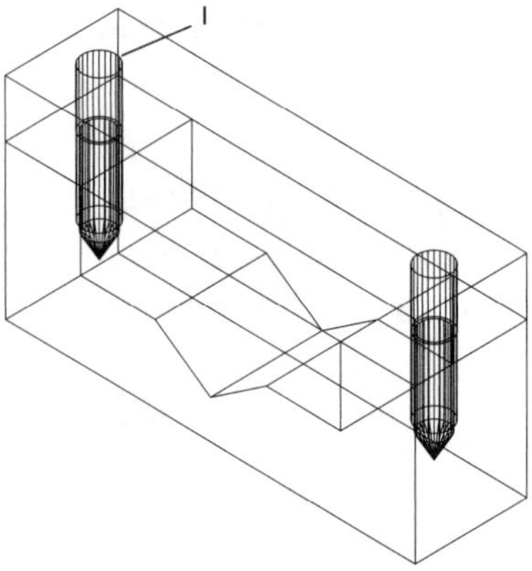

Figure 13.13

Pick: **External Reference icon**
Pick: ***washr-3d.dwg*** (being sure to select the drive and directory for your datafiles)
Pick: **Open**

The External Reference dialog box appears on your screen. You will now select Specify On-screen for the Insertion point selection. You will leave the Scale and Rotation set to the defaults.

Pick: **Specify On-screen** (so that it is checked in the Insertion point area)
Pick: **OK** (to exit the dialog box)
Specify insertion point or [Scale/X/Y/Z/Rotate/PScale/PX/PY/PZ/PRotate]:
target the top edge of hole 1 in Figure 13.13, using the AutoSnap Center marker
Insert the washer for the right side of the part on your own.

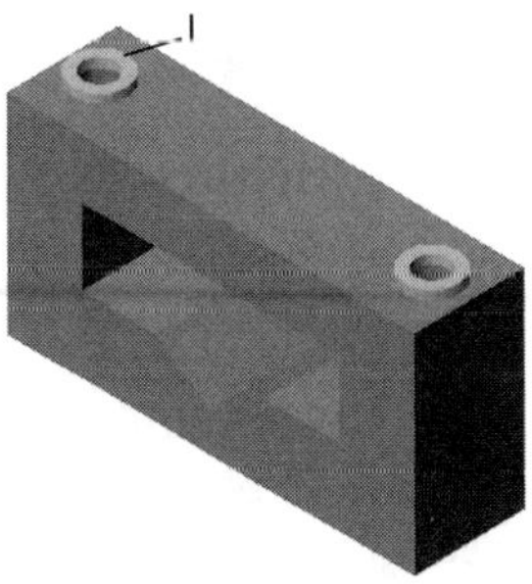

Figure 13.14

The following message appears: Xref "Washr-3d" has already been defined. Using existing definition. If you knew that drawing *washr-3d.dwg* had changed and you wanted to update it without having to exit the drawing, you could use the Reload option of the Xref command. Reload is especially useful if you are working on a networked system and sharing files with other members of a design team. At any point you can use the Reload option to update the definition of the referenced objects in your drawing. In this case, you want to insert another copy of the same drawing, so you can just ignore this message. (You could also use the Copy command to create the other washer.)

Once you have inserted the washers, switch to Gouraud shading on your own so your drawing looks like that in Figure 13.14.

Next, you will add the two screws to the assembly to finish inserting the parts that you will need. You will make a new Tool Palette that has the screw and washer to see another way that you can insert parts.

Pick: **Tool Palettes icon**
Right-click: **on the Tool Palettes**
Pick: **New Palette** (from the pop-up menu)
Type: **3D Parts** (for the name of the new Tool Palette) ↵
Pick: **DesignCenter™ icon**
Use the **Folders** list in the DesignCenter on your own to select the Datafile2006 directory and drag and drop ***Screw-3D*** and ***Washr-3D*** onto the Tool Palettes as shown in Figure 13.15.

Tip

You can right-click on the DesignCenter to pop up a context menu of useful options, including changing how the items are viewed. You can right-click the DesignCenter title bar and choose to Auto-hide it.

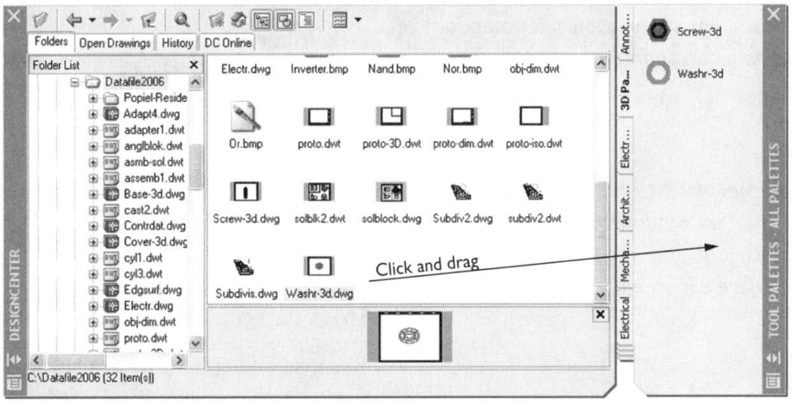

Figure 13.15

Pick: to close **DesignCenter**
Drag ***Screw-3d*** from the Tool Palettes and drop it into the hole location in the washer in your drawing using **OSnap Center**.
Repeat this process on your own for the second screw.
Pick: to close **Tool Palettes and the Reference toolbar**

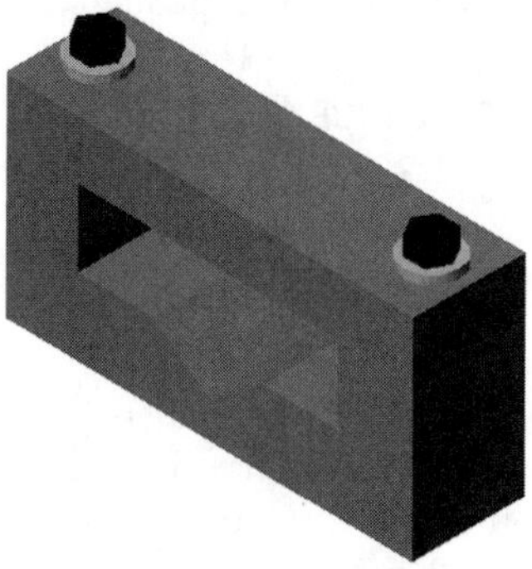

Figure 13.16

Tip

If you didn't close the Solids toolbar from the last tutorial, it may already be on your screen.

Tip

Only explode the objects one time. Exploding them more will turn them into surfaces or just 3D lines & arcs, which you cannot check for solid interference.

Tip

You may need to use Zoom Window to select the screw. If you list the cover and screws and they are regions, not solids, use Undo to undo the Explode command.

Tip

You may need to drag on the corner of the text window to see the full message for the results of the Interfere command.

Tip

If you want to try this, move one of the screws so that it overlaps the cover and then use the Interfere command again. After you have tested this, Undo the drawing to where the screw is in the correct position.

Now your drawing should depict the parts in completely assembled form, as shown in Figure 13.16.

Checking for Interference

When you are designing a device, you often want to know whether the parts will fit correctly. You can use the AutoCAD software's Interfere command to determine whether two parts overlap. If they do, Interfere creates a new solid showing where they do. You can use this command to determine whether the objects fit together as intended.

On your own turn on the **Solids toolbar**.
Locate the Solids toolbar where it is convenient for you to use.

You will determine whether the screws in the assembly will fit the holes in the cover. The Interfere command will only analyze solids, but objects that you've inserted in the drawing are now blocks. To return the cover and screws to solids, you will explode them. When you explode an object, doing so removes one level of grouping at a time, so exploding the block will return it to a solid. If you explode the solid, it will become a region or surface model. First, you will check to see what type of objects they are.

On your own, **List** the cover and two screws (they should show as block references).
Pick: **Explode icon**
Select objects: **pick the cover and the two screws**
Select objects: ↵

The cover and two screws are now exploded.

List the cover and two screws again on your own (they should now be listed as 3DSOLID objects).

Next you will determine whether the screws interfere with the cover. From the Solids toolbar,

Pick: **Interference icon**
Select first set of solids:
Select objects: **pick on the cover**
Select objects: ↵
Select second set of solids:
Select objects: **pick on the two screws**
Select objects: ↵
Comparing 1 solid against 2 solids.
Solids do not interfere.

Because the solids do not interfere, you know that the screws fit through the cover. If the solids did interfere, you would see a message similar to "Interfering solids: 2 Interfering pairs: 1 Create interference solids? [Yes/N] <N>:" You can type Y ↵ if you want the AutoCAD software to create a new solid on the current layer from the overlap between the interfering solids.

Determining Mass Properties

The AutoCAD software enables you to inquire about the mass properties of solids. One of the advantages of the solid modeler used in the AutoCAD 2006 release is the accuracy with which volumes and mass properties are calculated. Like Interfere, the Mass Properties command works only on solids, not on external references.

Pick: **Tools, Inquiry, Region/Mass Properties**
Select objects: **pick the clamp cover**
Select objects: ↵

The AutoCAD text window opens displaying the mass property information, as shown in Figure 13.17.

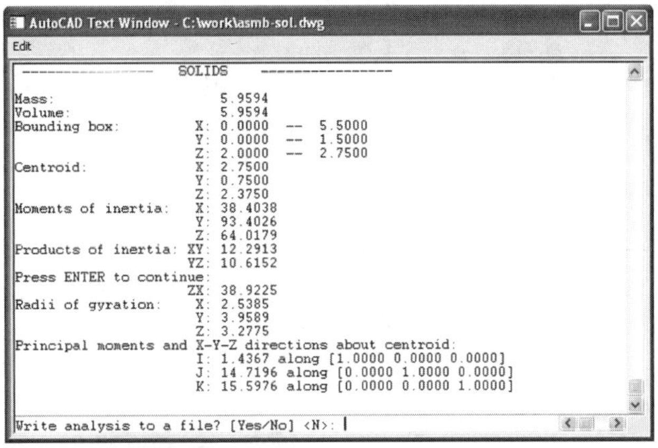
```
AutoCAD Text Window - C:\work\asmb-sol.dwg
Edit
 ----------------   SOLIDS   ----------------

Mass:                       5.9594
Volume:                     5.9594
Bounding box:            X: 0.0000  --  5.5000
                         Y: 0.0000  --  1.5000
                         Z: 2.0000  --  2.7500
Centroid:                X: 2.7500
                         Y: 0.7500
                         Z: 2.3750
Moments of inertia:      X: 38.4038
                         Y: 93.4026
                         Z: 64.0179
Products of inertia:    XY: 12.2913
                        YZ: 10.6152
Press ENTER to continue:
                        ZX: 38.9225
Radii of gyration:       X: 2.5385
                         Y: 3.9589
                         Z: 3.2775
Principal moments and X-Y-Z directions about centroid:
                         I: 1.4367 along [1.0000 0.0000 0.0000]
                         J: 14.7196 along [0.0000 1.0000 0.0000]
                         K: 15.5976 along [0.0000 0.0000 1.0000]

Write analysis to a file? [Yes/No] <N>:
```

Figure 13.17

Scroll through the information in the text window if necessary.
Press: ↵ to close the AutoCAD text window

You can also write the mass properties information to a file. Once you have closed the text window, you will see the prompt,

Press ENTER to continue: ↵
Write analysis to a file? [Yes/No] <N>: ↵

Creating an Exploded Isometric View

Exploded views show the parts removed from their assembled positions yet still aligned, as though the assembly had exploded. Exploded views are often used for assembly drawings to show how parts are to be assembled. You will create an exploded view from your assembly drawing by moving the parts away from each other. Because the exploded parts should be aligned with their assembled positions, you will move them only along one axis. You will use the Move icon on the Modify toolbar to move the screws from their assembled positions.

Pick: **Move icon**
Select objects: **pick the two screws** ↵
Specify base point or [Displacement] <Displacement>: **0,0,5** ↵
Specify second point or <use first point as displacement>: ↵

The screws move up in the drawing and off the view. You will use the Zoom Extents command to fit the entire drawing on the screen.

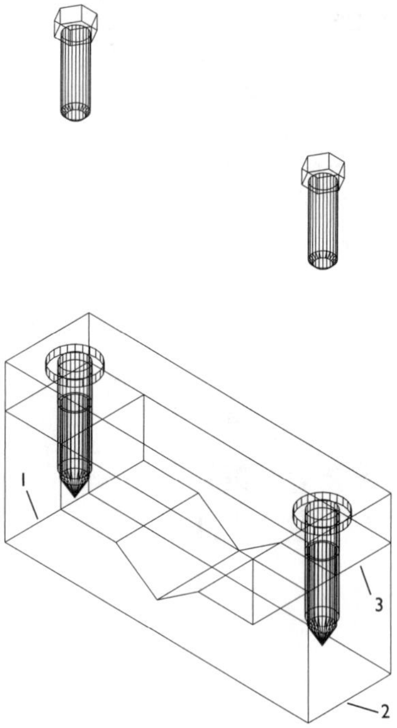

Figure 13.18

Tip

Another useful technique in aligning 3D objects in an assembly drawing is to use the Tracking command. You can Attach or move the solids with reference to locations on other solids.

Pick: **Zoom Extents icon**

Your drawing should be similar to that in Figure 13.18.

You will continue to use the Move command and relocate the washers, keeping them aligned with their present position but three units above, along the Z-axis.

Pick: **Move icon**
Select objects: **pick the two washers** ↵
Specify base point or [Displacement] <displacement>: **0,0,3** ↵
Specify second point or <use first point as displacement>: ↵

The washers align below the screws and all remain aligned with the holes in the object. Next, move the clamp cover up two units, along the Z-axis.

Command: ↵
Select objects: **pick the cover** ↵
Specify base point or [Displacement] <Displacement>: **0,0,2** ↵
Specify second point or <use first point as displacement>: ↵

When you create an exploded view, you should add thin lines to show how the parts assemble.

To create lines in the same plane as the objects' centers, you need to define a UCS that aligns through the middle of the objects. You will make a new layer for the lines. As usual, zoom in if necessary to pick the correct locations on the part.

Turn on OSnap for **Midpoint**.
Create a new layer called ALIGN that has color cyan and linetype CONTINUOUS.
Set ALIGN as the current layer.
Turn on the Grid.
Pick: **Tools, New UCS, 3 Point**
Specify new origin point <0,0,0>: **pick the middle of line 1 in Figure 13.18**
Specify point on positive portion of X-axis <1.0000,0.7500,0.0000>: **pick the middle of line 2**
Specify point on positive-Y portion of the UCS XY plane <1.0000,0.7500,0.0000>: **pick the middle of line 3**

The UCS icon and grid change to align with the plane through the middle of the parts as shown in Figure 13.19. If they do not, repeat the command and try again.

On your own, verify that Snap is on.
Draw the lines, showing how the parts align, by picking points on the Snap or using Object Snap.
Save your drawing before you continue.
Pick: to close the Solids toolbar

When you have finished, your drawing should look like Figure 13.19.

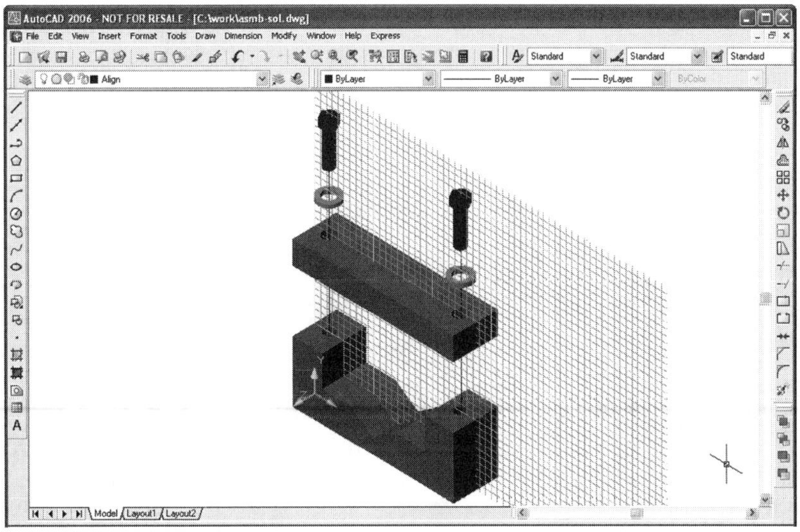

Figure 13.19

Creating a Dynamic Block for the Ball Tags

Ball tags identify the parts in the assembly. They are made up of the item number in the assembly enclosed in a circle, hence the name ball tags. You can easily add ball tags to the drawing by making a block. You will make a block that has one visible attribute and several invisible attributes. An *attribute* is basically text information that you can associate with a block. It is an effective method of adding information to the drawing. You can also extract attribute information from the drawing and import it into a database or word processing program for other uses.

Dynamic Blocks

A new feature of the AutoCAD 2006 software is the ability to create *dynamic blocks*. These are blocks which have custom properties that allow you to adjust inserted blocks within your drawing instead of having to redefine them or insert another block. Dynamic blocks must have at least one parameter and one action associated with the parameter. The types of parameters that can be associated with the block are:

Parameter	Control Location	Associated Actions
Point	Defines an X and Y location	Move, Stretch
Linear	Defines a distance between two anchor points	Move, Scale, Stretch, Array
Polar	Defines a distance between two anchor points and an angle value	Move, Scale, Stretch, Polar Stretch, Array,
XY	Defines X and Y distances from a base point	Move, Scale, Stretch, Array
Rotation	Defines an angle	Rotate
Flip	Defines a reflection line about which objects can be flipped	Flip

Parameter	Control Location	Associated Actions
Alignment	Defines an X and Y location and an angle which applies to the entire block	No action needs to be associated with this parameter. The alignment parameter allows the block reference to automatically rotate around a point to align with another object in the drawing. An alignment parameter affects the rotation property of the block reference.
Visibility	Controls visibility of objects in the block	No action is assigned, but a list of visibility states for the block is created which can be controlled.
Lookup	Defines a custom property used to look up or evaluate a value from a defined list or table	Lookup
Base	Defines a base point for the dynamic block	Cannot be associated with any actions, but can belong to an action's selection set.

Tip

You can also use the Block Editor to add dynamic properties and attributes to blocks you have previously created with the block command. Attributes can also be added to blocks using the Attdef command and then selecting the attribute you have defined when you create a block.

You will add dynamic properties to your ball tag block so that you can flip the leader to the opposite side of the block and stretch the leader extending from it wherever the block has been inserted. You can create the dynamic block and add its attribute using the Block Editor.

Figure 13.20 shows ball tags like the ones you will create. You will use the Block Editor to create the "smart" block for the ball tag.

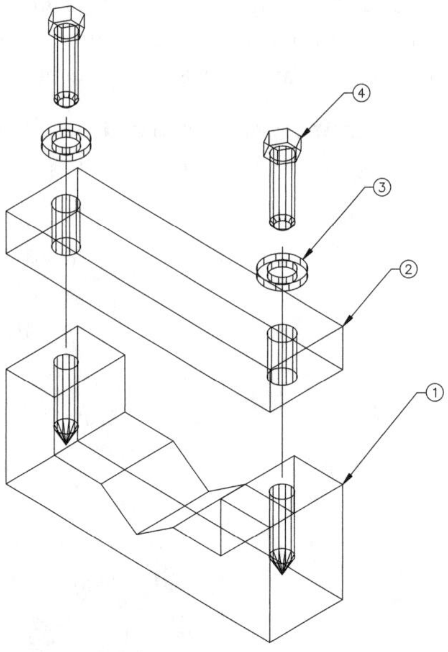

Figure 13.20

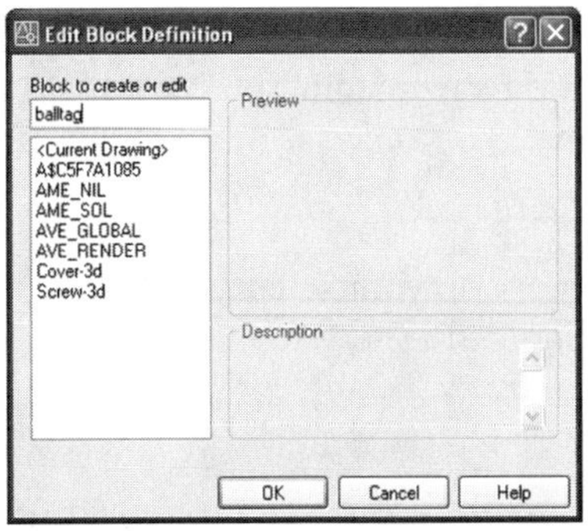

Figure 13.21

Pick: **TEXT as the current drawing layer**
Pick: **Block Editor icon** from the Standard toolbar

The Block Editor appears on your screen similar to Figure 13.21.

Type: **BALLTAG** in the input box for Block to create or edit, as shown in Figure 3.21
Pick: **OK**

Your screen appearance changes so that it looks like Figure 13.22 once you are inside the Block Editor. You may see the message, "Do you want to see how dynamic blocks are created?" If you pick Yes, the New Features workshop will be displayed and you can use it to see a demonstration of the dynamic block functions. For now, pick No or explore the New Features workshop and then return to the Block Editor screen.

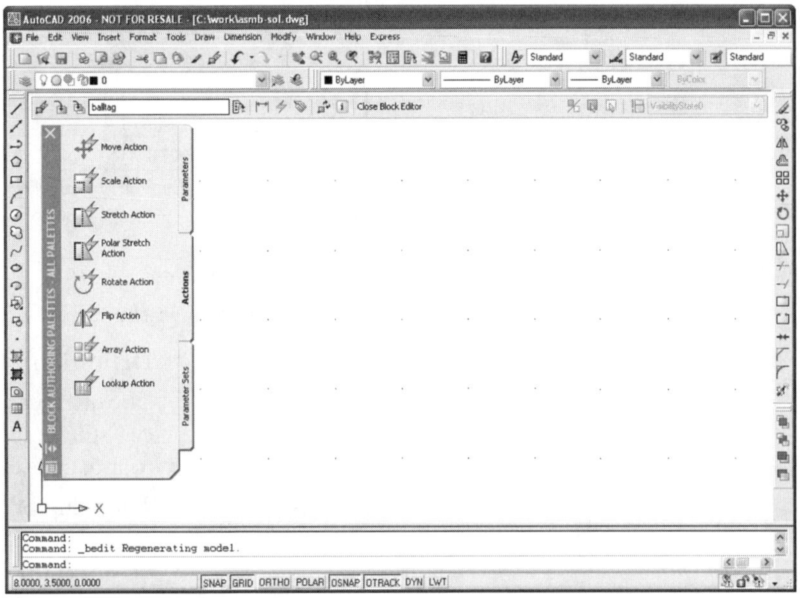

Figure 13.22

A new toolbar appears at the top of the screen and the Block Authoring palettes is open.

Pick: **Circle icon**

Draw a circle of diameter 0.25 to the side of the Block Authoring Palettes in the blank area of the drawing editor as shown in Figure 13.23.

Pick: **Dimension**, **Leader**

Draw a leader with the arrow pointing to the left and connected to the left quadrant of the circle as shown in Figure 13.23. Do not add any text at this time.

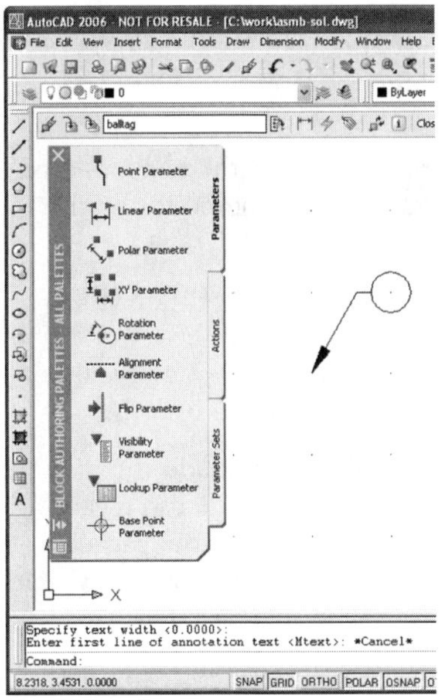

Figure 13.23

Defining Attributes

The Define Attributes command is on the Draw menu. You can use Define Attributes to create special attribute text objects.

Pick: **Draw, Block, Define Attributes**

The Attribute Definition dialog box appears on your screen. You will use it to make the selections shown in Figure 13.24.

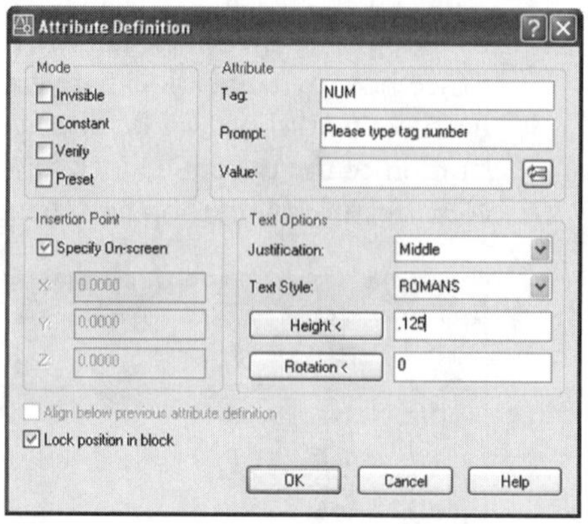

Figure 13.24

Attribute Modes

Attributes can have the following special modes, or properties.

Mode	**Definition**
Invisible	The attribute does not appear in the drawing, but can still be used for other purposes, such as extracting to a database.
Constant	The value of the attribute is set at the beginning of its definition, so you are not prompted for a value on insertion of the block.
Verified	You can make sure that the value is correct after typing the value.
Preset	You can change the attribute later, but you will not be prompted for the value when you insert it.

You will now use the Attribute Definition dialog box to add the number in the center of the ball tag as a visible attribute. You will also create attributes for the other information commonly shown in the parts list (such as the part name, part number, material, and quantity) as invisible attributes.

Leave each of the Mode boxes unchecked to indicate that you want this attribute to be visible, variable, not verified, and typed in, not preset.

Attribute Tag

The *attribute tag* is a variable name that is replaced with the value that you type when prompted as you insert the attribute block. The tag appears when the block is exploded or before the attribute is made into a block. You will use NUM for the attribute tag.

On your own, type **NUM** in the Tag input box.

Attribute Prompt

The *attribute prompt* is the prompt that appears in the command area when you insert the block into a drawing. Make your prompt descriptive, so it clearly identifies the information to be typed and how it should be typed. For instance, "Enter the date (dd/mm/yy)" is a prompt that specifies not only what to enter—the date—but also the format—numeric two-digit format, with day first, then month and year.

On your own, type **Please type tag number** in the Prompt input box.

Default Attribute Value

Value defines a default value for the attribute. Leaving the box to the right of Value empty results in no default value for the tag. As every tag number will be different, there is no advantage to having a default value for the ball tag attribute. If the prompt would often be answered with a particular response, that response would be a good choice for the default value.

Attribute Text Options

Attributes and regular text use the same types of options. You can center, fit, and align attributes just like any other text.

Select the **Middle** option from the Justification pull-down menu.

Selecting Middle will cause the middle of the text to appear in the center of the ball tag when you type it.

Set the text style to **ROMANS**.

You do not need to change the Text Style setting.

Set the text height to **0.125**.

Leave the rotation set at 0° for this attribute. You do not want the attribute rotated at an angle in the drawing.

Attribute Insertion Point

You can select Specify On-screen in the Insertion Point section to select the insertion point on your screen, or you can type the X-, Y-, and Z-coordinates into the appropriate boxes.

Make sure that Specify On-screen is checked.
Pick: **OK**
Check that OSnap is on with Center selected.

Your drawing returns to the screen.

Specify start point: use OSnap to **pick the center of the circle**

Tip

The prompt appears with a colon (:) after it to indicate that some entry is expected. The colon is included automatically; you do not need to type a colon in the dialog box.

Tip

You can create a title block for your drawings that uses attributes. For the drafter's name, you make the attribute prompt "Enter drafter's name". In the Value text box, you put your own name as the default value. When you insert the block into a drawing, the default value after the prompt within the AutoCAD default angle brackets will be your own name. To accept the default values press ⏎ instead of having to type in your name each time.

You can also use Fields to display information, such as the current date in the title block.

Tip

Clicking on the Height or Rotation buttons lets you set the height or rotation, either by picking from the screen or by typing at the command prompt.

Figure 13.25

The tag NUM is centered in the circle. The circle and the attribute tag should look like Figure 13.25. If the attribute is not in the center of the circle, use the Move command to center it in the circle on your own.

Next you will make the attributes for part name (description), part number, material, and quantity. These attributes will be invisible, to avoid making the drawing look crowded, but they can still be extracted for use in a spreadsheet or database.

Command: ↵ (to restart the Define Attributes command)

The Attribute Definition dialog box appears on your screen. Continue to use it to create an invisible attribute with the following settings.

Select: **Invisible mode** so that a check appears in the box to its left
Tag: **PART**
Prompt: **Please type part description**
Value: (leave Value blank so that there is no default value)
Justification: **Left**
Text Style: **ROMANS**
Height: **.125**
Rotation: **0**
Make sure that **Specify On-screen** is checked.

When you have entered this information into the dialog box, you are ready to select the location in the drawing for your invisible attribute.

Pick: **OK**

Your drawing returns to the screen.

Specify start point: **pick a point to the right of the ball tag circle**
Command: ↵

The tag PART should appear at the location you selected.

On your own, use this method to create the following three invisible attributes. Choose the box to the left of **Align below previous attribute** to locate each new attribute below the previous attributes.
Select: **Invisible**
Tag: **MATL**
Prompt: **Please type material**
Value: **Cast Iron**
Justification: **Left**
Text Style: **ROMANS**
Height: **.125**
Rotation: **0**

Select: **Invisible**
Tag: **QTY**
Prompt: **Please type quantity required**
Value: (leave blank)
Justification: **Left**
Text Style: **ROMANS**
Height: **.125**
Rotation: **0**

Select: **Invisible**
Tag: **PARTNO**
Prompt: **Please type part number, if any**
Value: (leave blank)
Justification: **Left**
Text Style: **ROMANS**
Height: **.125**
Rotation: **0**

Figure 13.26

When you have finished, each of the tags should appear in the drawing below the Part tag as shown in Figure 13.26.

Defining the Parameters

Now you will add the parameters for the block for the features you will control dynamically.

Pick: **Point Parameter** from the Block Authoring Palette
Specify parameter location or [Name/Label/Chain/Description/Palette]: **pick the endpoint of the leader arrow**
Specify label location: **pick a location near the leader arrow as shown in Figure 13.27**

Tip

The Block Attribute Manager command (Battman) lets you edit a block definition's attributes. You can pick it from the Modify II toolbar.

The parameter is added to the block definition as in Figure 13.27.

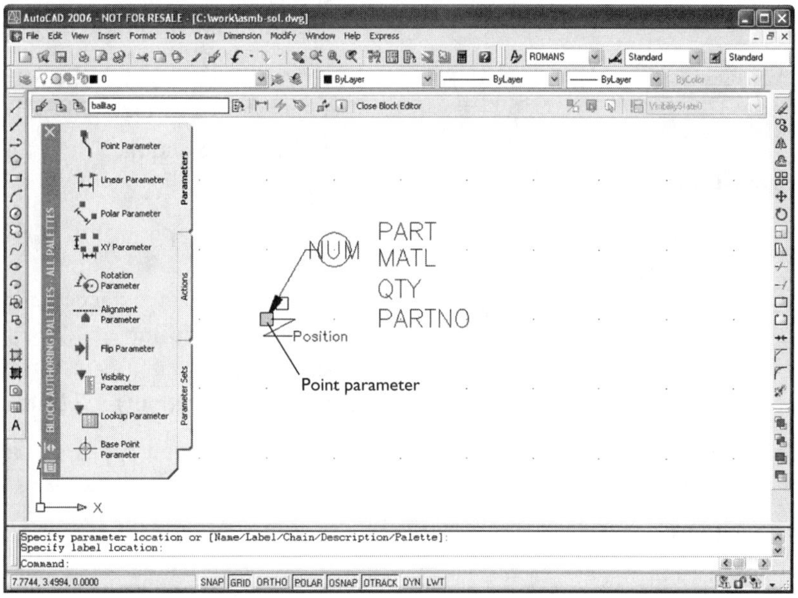

Figure 13.27

Pick: **Flip Parameter** (from the Block Authoring Palette)
Specify base point of reflection line or [Name/Label/Description/Palette]: **use OSnap to pick the center of the circle**
Specify endpoint of reflection line: **use Ortho or OTrack to specify a point directly above the center point you picked**
Specify label location: **pick a point above and to the right of the circle as shown in Figure 13.28.**

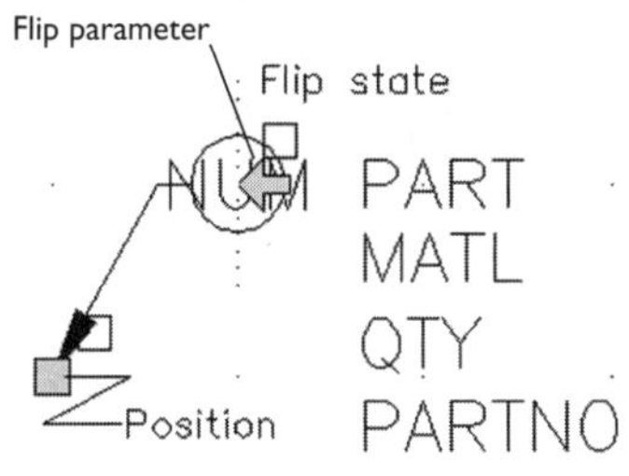

Figure 13.28

The Flip parameter should appear on screen as in Figure 13.28.

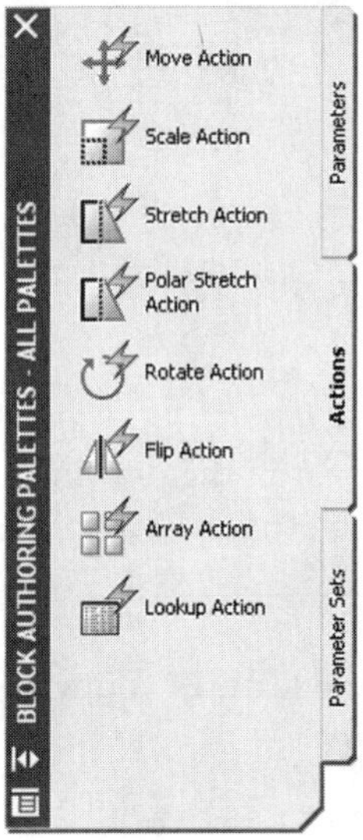

Figure 13.29

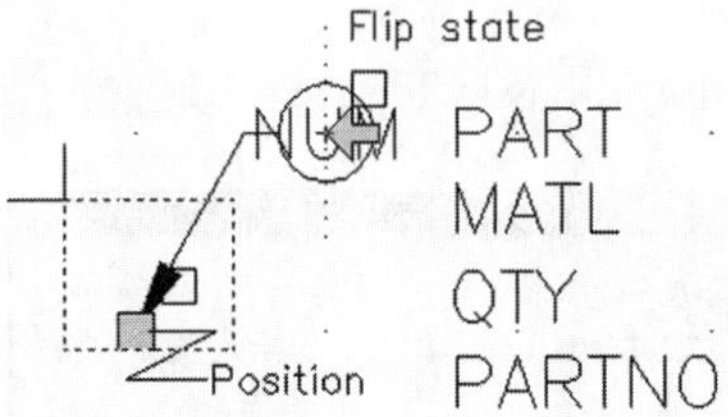

Figure 13.30

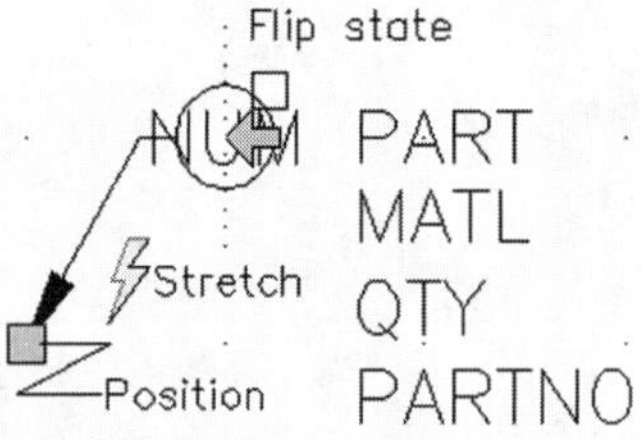

Figure 13.31

Defining the Actions

Now that you have the parameters defined, you are ready to add actions to them.

Pick: **Actions Tab of the Block Authoring palette**

The Actions tab should appear uppermost on the Block Authoring palette as shown in Figure 13.29.

The Actions tab shows the actions that you can add to control blocks dynamically. You will add the stretch action to the point parameter at the end of the leader and the flip action to the flip parameter to allow the leader to flip to the opposite side of the block.

Pick: **Stretch Action**
Select parameter: **pick on the Point parameter icon that appears as a small square near the end of the leader**
Specify first corner of stretch frame or [CPolygon]: **pick below and to the right of the leader**
Specify opposite corner: **pick toward the left of the leader at about its midpoint as shown in Figure 13.30** (you only want to stretch this portion)
Specify objects to stretch: **pick the leader line**
Select objects: ↵
Specify action location or [Multiplier/Offset]: **pick a location for the action text and icon to appear to the right of the leader line**

When you have finished, the Stretch action icon will appear on your screen as shown in Figure 13.31.

To add the Flip action,

Pick: **Flip Action**
Select parameter: **pick on the Flip parameter icon** (the square with the arrow)
Specify selection set for action: **pick the leader**
Select objects: **1 found**
Select objects: ↵
Specify action location: **pick below the words Flip state**

The Flip action icon appears as in Figure 13.32.

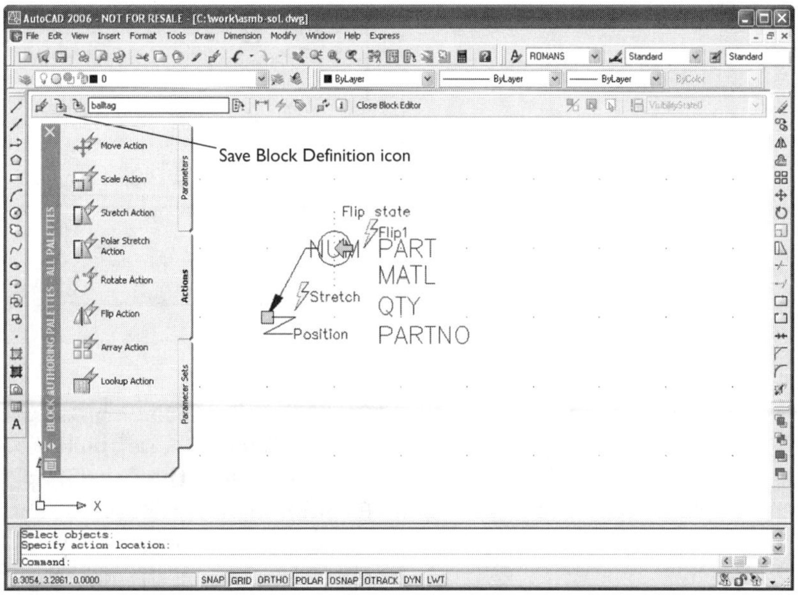

Figure 13.32

Pick: **Parameters tab** (from the Block Authoring palette)
Pick: **Base Point Parameter**
Specify parameter location: **pick the endpoint of the leader arrow**

An icon will be added to the dynamic block indicating the base point for the block.

Tip

You may want to use the Write Block command (Wblock) so that the block is available for other drawings. Remember, without Write Block, the block is defined only in the current drawing.

Pick: **Save Block Definition icon** (from the toolbar identified in Figure 13.32)
Pick: **Close Block Editor** (from the toolbar)

Inserting the Ball Tags

You will use the Insert Block command from the Draw toolbar to insert the BALLTAG block. You can use Figure 13.34 as your guide as you insert the ball tags.

Turn **OSnap Nearest** on.
Make sure Ortho is off.
Command: **PLAN** ↵
Enter an option [Current ucs/Ucs/World] <Current>: ↵

Your view changes to so that the direction of sight is perpendicular to the front of the block and the user coordinate system is parallel to the screen.

Pick: **Insert Block icon**

The Insert dialog box appears on your screen.

Pick: **Balltag** (from the pulldown list in the Name area)

The dialog box should look like Figure 13.33. You will specify the location for the block on screen.

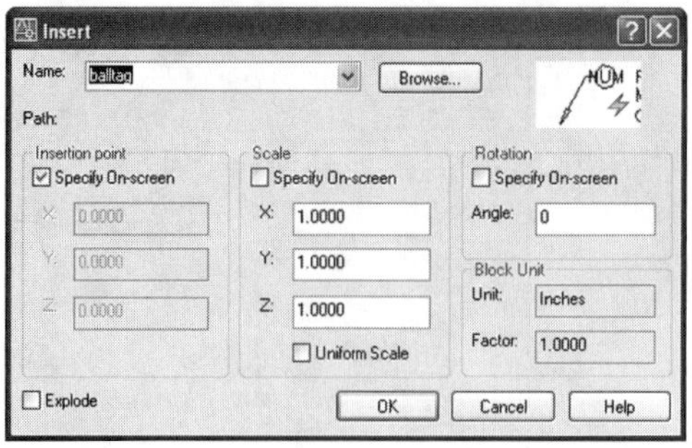

Figure 13.33

Pick: **OK**

Specify insertion point or [Basepoint/Scale/X/Y/Z/Rotate/PScale/PX/PY/PZ/PRotate]: **pick a point on the right edge of part 1, the base, using the AutoSnap™ Nearest marker**

Enter attribute values

Please type tag number: **1** ↵

Please type part description: **BASE** ↵

Please type material <Cast Iron>: **STEEL** ↵

Please type quantity required: **1** ↵

Please type part number, if any: **ADD1** ↵

Tip

Remember, the space bar does not act as ↵ when you are entering text. Because text may include spaces, when you are entering text commands, press ↵ to end the command.

The circle and number 1 appear on your screen. Your prompts for attribute information may have appeared in a different order. If you made a mistake, you can correct it in the next section.

Tip

If the attribute values are not replaced with the text that you typed and do not become invisible, try opening the Block Editor from the icon on the standard toolbar and then resaving the block and closing the Block Editor.

Continue to insert the balltag block for parts 2 (the cover), 3 (the washers), and 4 (the hex head) on your own. The tip of the leader can start anywhere on the edge of the part. Try to place the ball tags in the drawing where they are accessible and easy to read. When adding the ball tags, refer to the following table showing the information for each part.

Item	Name	Mat'l	Q'ty	Number
1	BASE	STEEL	1	ADD1
2	CLAMP TOP	1020ST	1	ADD2
3	.438 X .750 X .125 FLAT WASHER	STOCK	2	ADD3
4	.375-16 UNC X .50 HEX HEAD	STOCK	2	ADD4

When completed, your drawing should look similar to Figure 13.34.

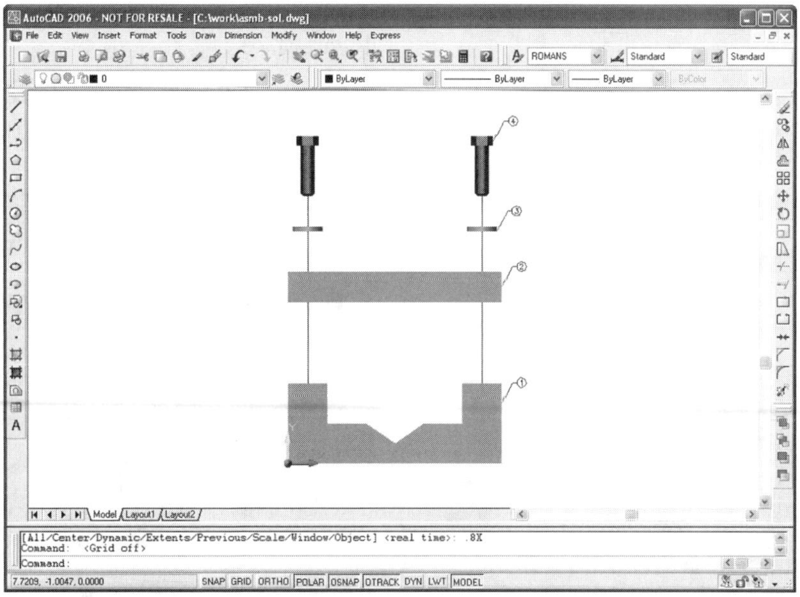

Figure 13.34

Save your drawing before you continue.

Use Zoom Window to enlarge ball tag 1 attached to the base part so that it appears larger on your screen

Pick: **on the ball tag**

The ball tag block become highlighted and icons appear indicating its dynamic properties as shown in Figure 13.35.

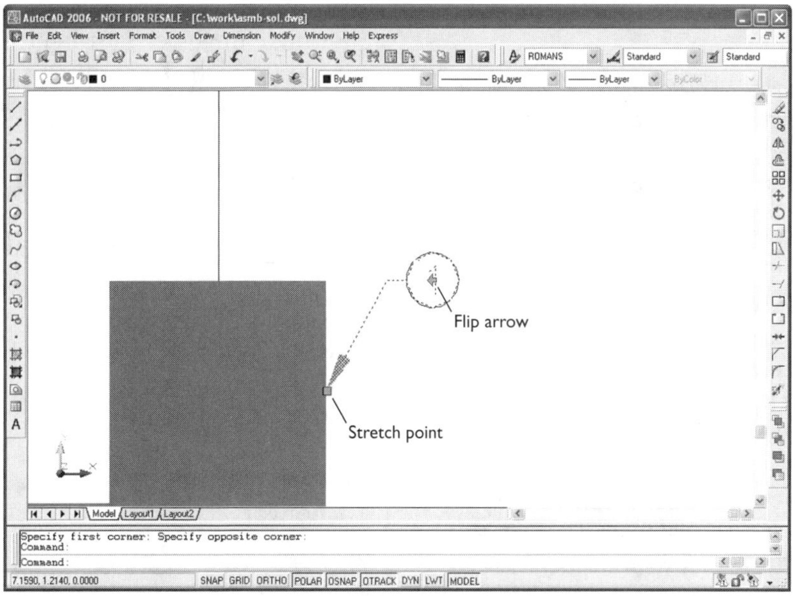

Figure 13.35

Now it is time to check out your smart block!

Pick: **on the Flip arrow**

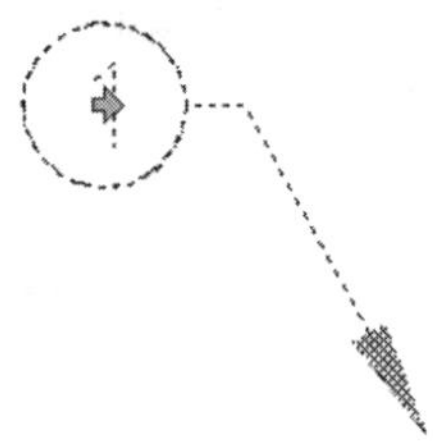

Figure 13.36

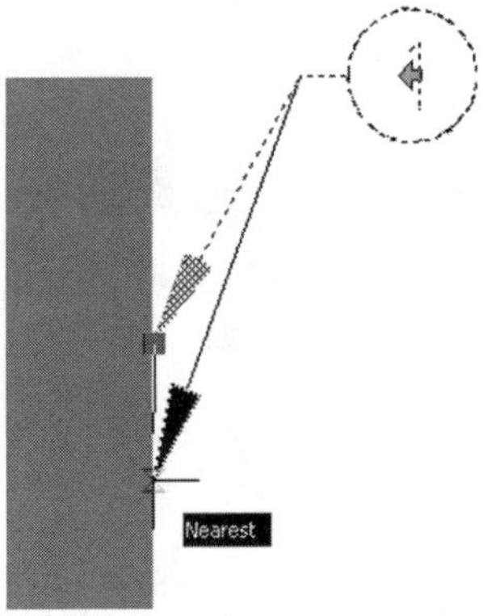

Figure 13.37

The leader on the ball tag flips to the right side of the block as shown in Figure 3.36.

Pick: **on the Flip arrow again to return it to the right side**

Pick: **on the Stretch point on the tip of the arrow and stretch it to a new location** as shown in Figure 13.37

Using these and the other features of dynamic blocks you can make some very useful and sophisticated blocks for use with your drawings.

Changing an Attribute Value

The Edit Attribute command is very useful for changing an attribute value. If you mistyped a value or you want to change an existing attribute value, select Attribute from the Modify menu.

Pick: **Modify, Object, Attribute, Single**

The Enhanced Attribute Editor dialog box appears, as shown in Figure 13.38. Your attributes may appear in a different order.

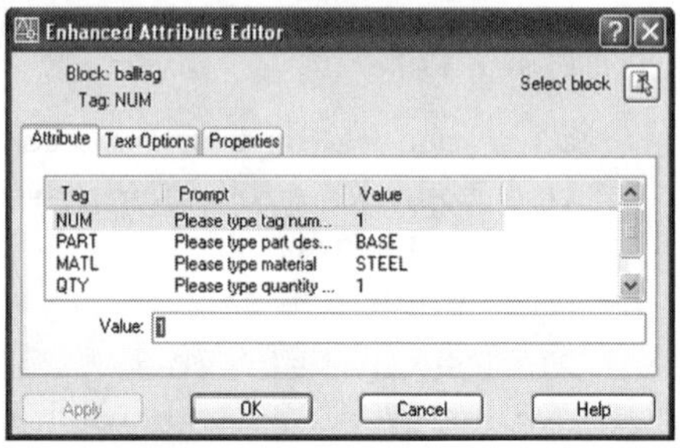

Figure 13.38

Tip

You can start the Enhanced Attribute Editor by double-clicking on a block that has attributes if you have Noun Verb selection turned on in the Options dialog box.

Shown are the block's attributes, their prompts, and the values you entered for each. To change a value, pick on an attribute and use the input box at the bottom of the dialog box to change its value. To exit the dialog box,

Pick: **OK or Cancel**

Tip

If you have added the datafile base-3d.dwg *from a directory where it is "read only" on your network, you will not be able to edit it. Use the Windows Explorer to copy the* base-3d.dwg *file from the datafile2006 directory to* c:\work. *Use the XREF command and select the reference for* base-3d. *Browse to select the file from* c:\work *(where you should have permission to change files). Select Reload to reload the external reference from this location.*

Changing an Externally Referenced Drawing

The primary difference between blocks and externally referenced drawings is that external references are not really added to the current drawing. A pointer is established to the original drawing (external reference) that you attached. If you change the original drawing, the change is also made in any drawing to which it is attached as an external reference. You will try this feature by editing the referenced drawing *base-3d.dwg* in place. You will change the *base-3d.dwg* drawing by filleting its exterior corners.

Pick: **Zoom All**

Pick: **View, 3D Views, SE Isometric**

Double-click: **on the Base-3d part** in your drawing to quickly start the Reference Edit command or, pick Tools, Xref and Block In-place Editing, Edit Reference In-Place

The Reference Edit dialog box appears on your screen as shown in Figure 13.39.

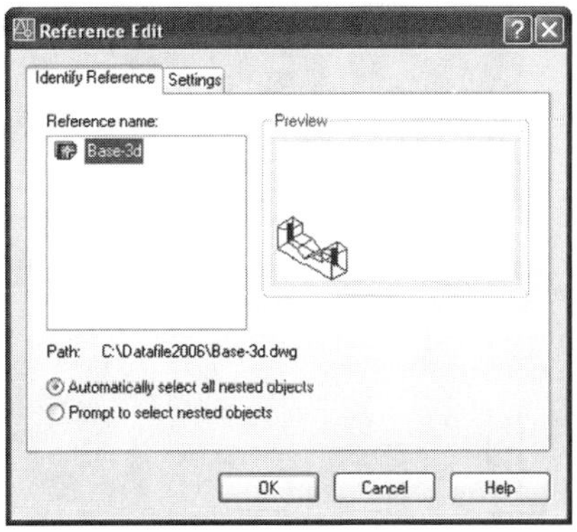

Figure 13.39

Tip

If you cannot open base-3D, *check to see that your file is not "read-only." Also be sure that the file is not open in another AutoCAD window or session. If it is, you may need to Refclose to close it.*

If the base part is selected as shown,

Pick: **OK**

The Refedit toolbar appears on your screen along with the message, "Use REFCLOSE or the Refedit toolbar to end reference editing session."

Now the base part is open for editing in place.

Use the commands that you have learned to add a fillet of radius 0.25 to all four exterior corners of the base so that it looks like Figure 13.40.

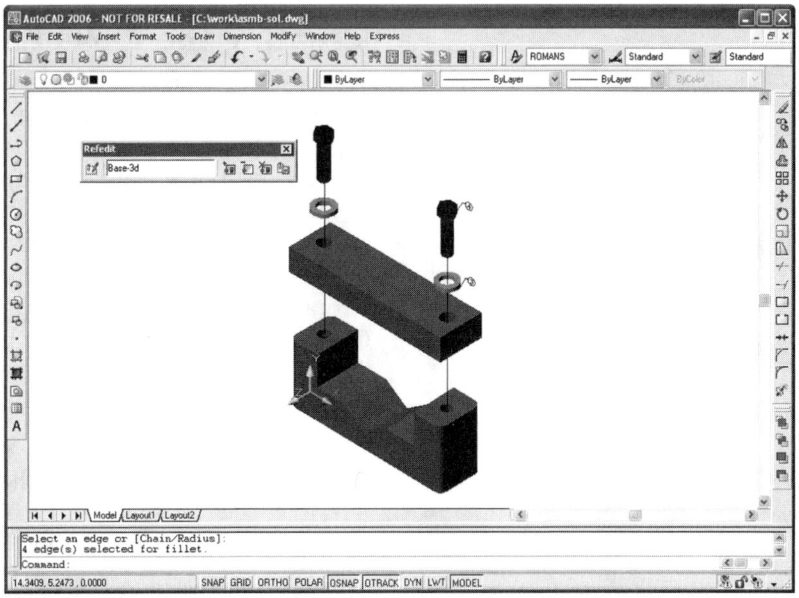

Figure 13.40

Pick: **Save reference edits** from the Refedit toolbar

Pick: **OK** (at the message that "All reference edits will be saved.")

Open the *base-3d* part you attached as a reference.

Observe that the changes you made in the assembly also have been made to the referenced drawing *base-3d.dwg*.

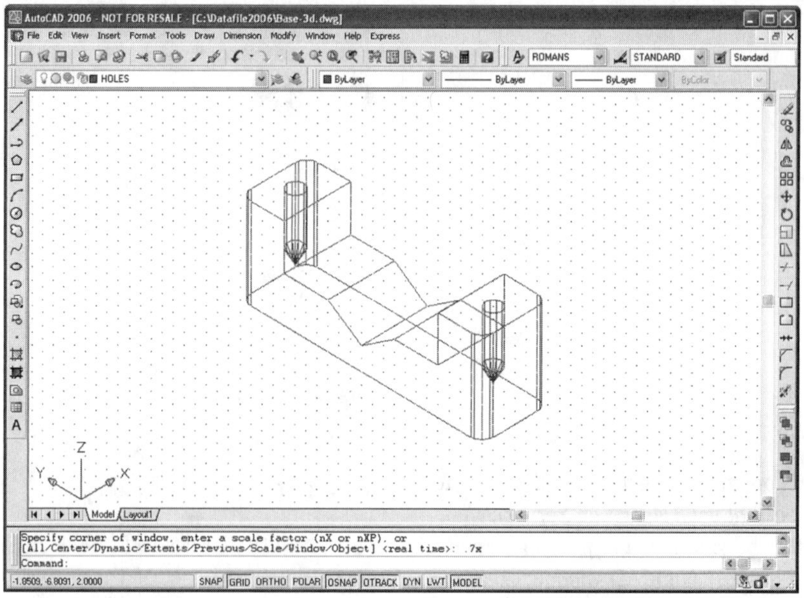

Figure 13.41

Tip

You must carefully keep track of your drawings when using external references. If you did not intend to change the assembly but made a change to its externally referenced drawing, the assembly will change. If you want to change an externally referenced drawing but not the assembly, use Save As and save the changed drawing to a new file name. If you move an externally referenced drawing to a different directory, you will have to Reload the external reference and supply the new path in order for the AutoCAD program to find it.

Close *base-3d.dwg* again.

Verify that *asmb-sol.dwg* is your current drawing before continuing.

Its name should appear in the title bar near the top of the screen.

Creating the Parts List

The next task is to create a parts list for your drawing. The required headings for the *parts list* are Item, Description, Material, Quantity, and Part No. The item number is the number that appears in the ball tag for the part on your assembly drawing. Sometimes a parts list is created on a separate sheet; but often in a small assembly drawing, such as the clamp assembly, it is included in the drawing. This method is preferable because having both in one drawing keeps the parts list from getting separated from the drawing that it should accompany. The parts list is usually positioned near the title block or in the upper right corner of the drawing.

There is no standard format for a parts list; each company may have its own standard. You can loosely base dimensions for a parts list on one of the formats recommended in the MIL-15 Technical Drawing Standards or in the ANSI Y14-2M Standards for text sizes and note locations in technical drawings. Next you will use the Modify II toolbar.

On your own, switch to Layout 1 and paper space.

Turn on the **Modify II toolbar.**

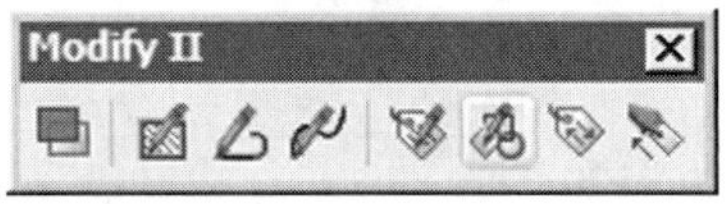

Figure 13.42

The Modify II toolbar appears on your screen as shown in Figure 13.42.

Extracting Attribute Information

You will extract the attribute information that you created to generate the parts list. This data can also be saved to an external file, imported into a spreadsheet or word processing program, and reinserted into your AutoCAD drawing using Windows Object Linking and Embedding (OLE). For this tutorial, you will create the table within the AutoCAD program. You will use the Modify II toolbar to pick the EATTEXT command for extracting attributes.

Pick: **Attribute Extraction icon**

The Attribute Extraction wizard appears. You can start from scratch or use a template previously created using this wizard. Templates allow you to extract block attributes using a format previously established.

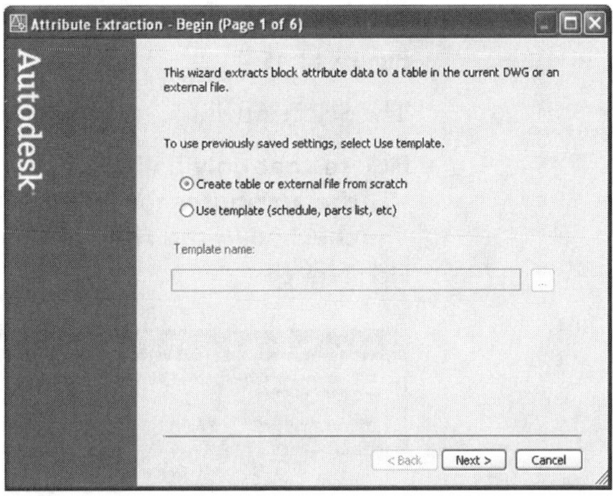

Figure 13.43

Pick: **the Create table or external file from scratch button** as shown in Figure 13.43

Pick: **Next**

The next page of the wizard appears.

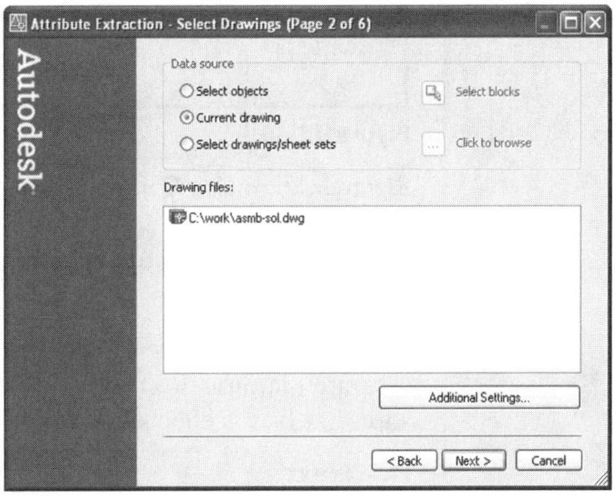

Figure 13.44

Pick: **Current drawing** as shown in Figure 13.44.

Pick: **Next**

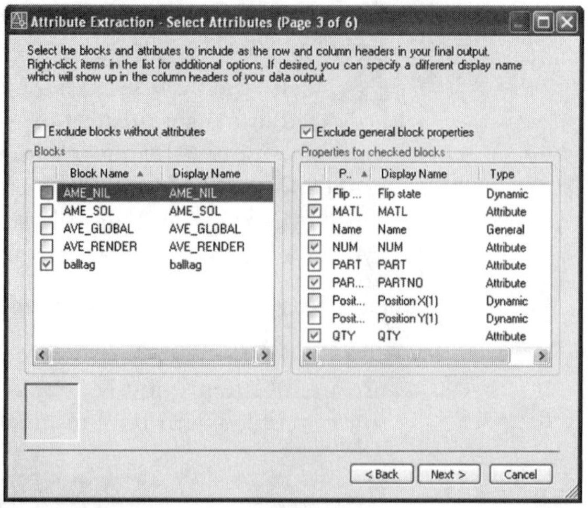

Figure 13.45

The Select Attributes page appears as shown in Figure 13.45.

Pick: **so that only balltag is checked from the left column and only the attributes for NUM, PART, PARTNO, QTY, and MATL are checked in the right column**

Pick: **Next**

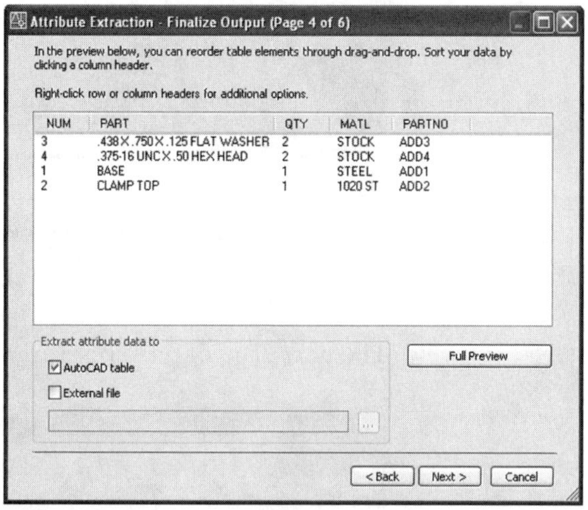

Figure 13.46

Right-click: **on the Quantity column and pick Hide so that it does not display**

Drag and drop the other columns so that they appear as in Figure 13.46.

If you check the External file box, your attributes would be saved to a separate file. For this tutorial, you will create an AutoCAD table, so be sure that box is checked.

Pick: **Next**

The Table Style page of the wizard shows on your screen as shown in Figure 13.47.

Tip

You will usually insert parts lists, notes, and other similar items into the paper space layout, depending on how your drawing is organized.

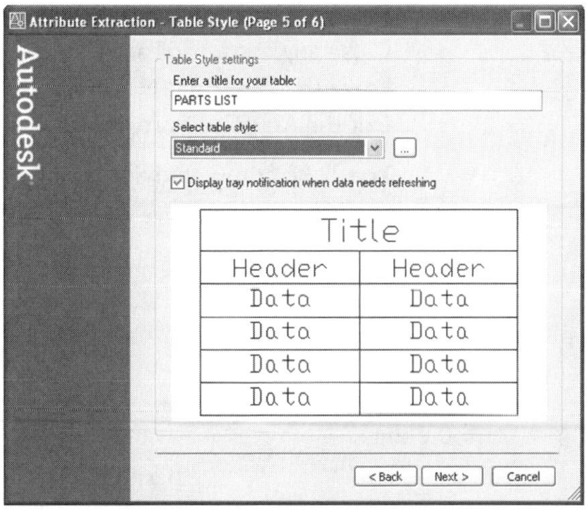

Figure 13.47

Type: **PARTS LIST** in the title box
Pick: **Next**
Pick: **Finish** to extract the data

The Save Template pick on the Finish page allows you to save these settings as a template for extracting similar attributes. You return to the drawing screen. The message "Any manual edits you make to a data extraction table will be lost when you refresh the data in this table. Continue Inserting Table?"

Pick: **Yes**

The table appears in your drawing attached to the crosshairs.

On your own, position the table near the top of the drawing and press the pick button to insert it. Then use the Scale command with a scaling factor of .5 to resize the table. Use Move and locate the parts list in the upper right corner of the drawing.

Your drawing should look similar to Figure 13.48.

Tip

If you are going to send a drawing to someone on a disk, you must be sure to send any externally referenced drawings too. Otherwise the recipient will not be able to open the referenced portions of the drawing. A good way to avoid this problem is to use the External Reference command with the Bind option at the command prompt to link the two drawings. Doing so makes the referenced drawing a part of the drawing to which it is attached. Also, it prevents you from unintentionally deleting the original drawing. However, once you have done so, the external reference will no longer update. To use the External Reference Bind option, after you have attached the drawing, pick the External Reference icon, select the referenced objects you want to bind, select the Bind option, and then choose the Bind type (Bind or Insert). One drawback to binding the files is that the file size for the assembly drawing will be larger.

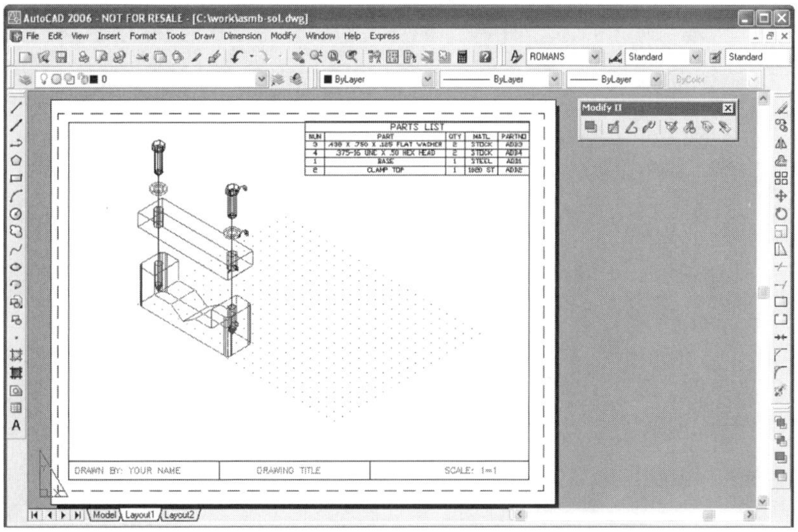

Figure 13.48

Save your drawing.
Close any extra toolbars you may have on your screen.
Leave the Draw and Modify toolbars showing.
Exit the AutoCAD program.

You have completed Tutorial 13.

Key Terms

attribute	attribute tag	dynamic block
attribute prompt	ball tag	parts list

Key Commands

Define Attribute	External Reference Attach	Flip Parameter	Point Parameter
Edit Attribute	External Reference Clip	Interfere	Reference Edit
Edit Block Definition	Extract Attributes	Mass Properties	Zoom Extents
External Reference			

Exercises

13.1 Clamping Block

Prepare assembly and detail drawings and a parts list based on the following information, using solid modeling techniques. Create solid models of Parts 1 and 2. Join Part 2 to Part 1, using two .500-3UNC × 2.50 LONG HEX-HEAD BOLTS. Include .500-13UNC NUTS on each bolt. Locate a .625 × 1.250 × .125 WASHER under the head of each bolt between Parts 1 and 2 and between Part 1 and the NUT. (Each bolt will have three washers and a nut.)

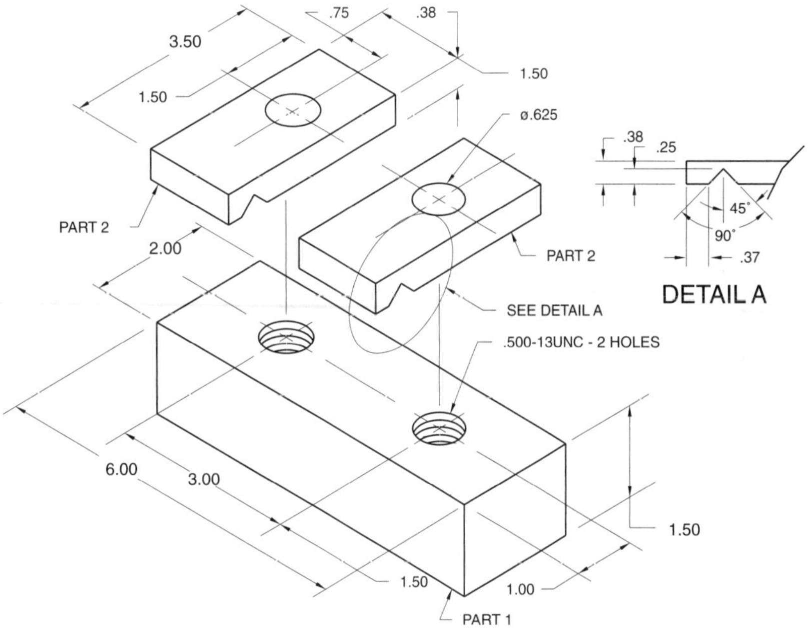

13.2M Hand Rail Column

Use solid modeling to create an assembly drawing for the hand rail column shown. Thread is typically only modeled as a cylinder showing the major diameter.

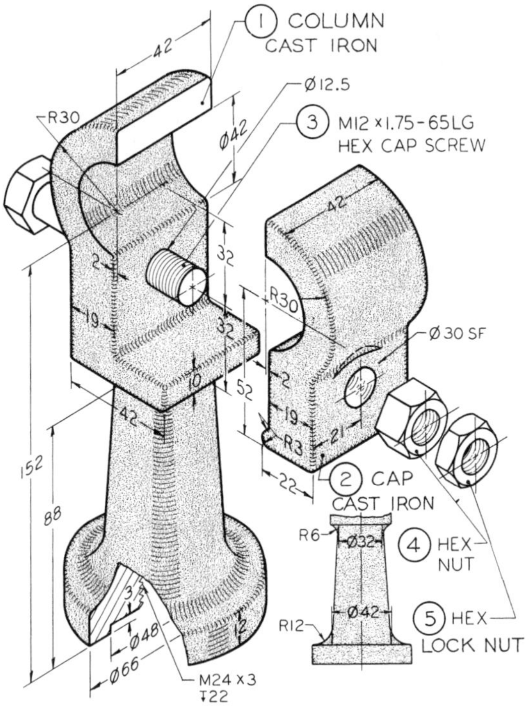

13.3 Pressure Assembly

Prepare assembly and detail drawings and a parts list of the pressure assembly, using solid modeling techniques. Create solid models of the BASE, GASKET, and COVER shown. Use four .375-16UNC × 1.50 HEX-HEAD SCREWS to join the COVER, GASKET, and BASE. The GASKET assembles between the BASE and COVER.

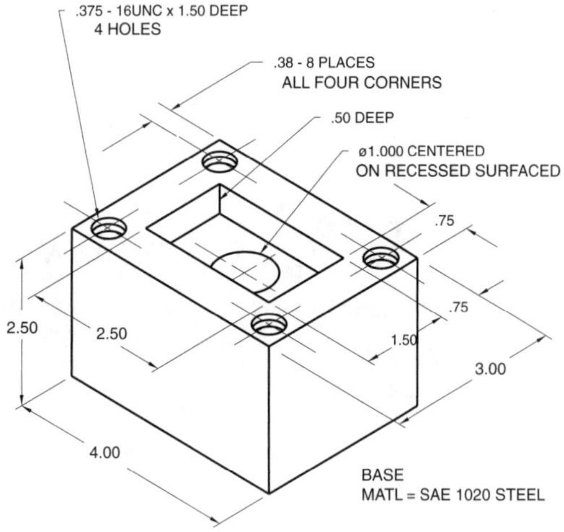

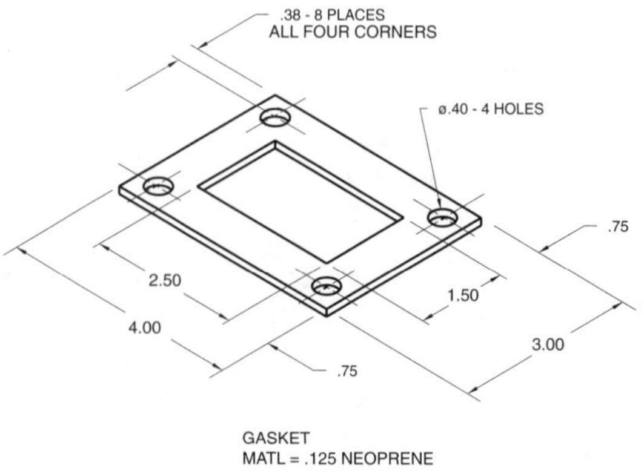

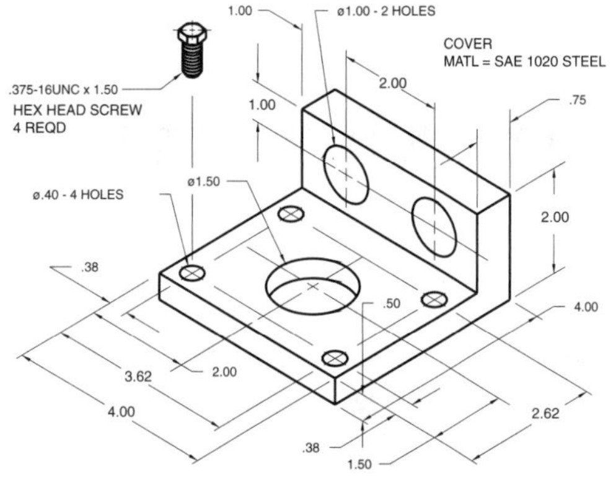

13.4 Hub Assembly

Create an assembly drawing for the parts shown. Use eight bolts with nuts to assemble the parts.

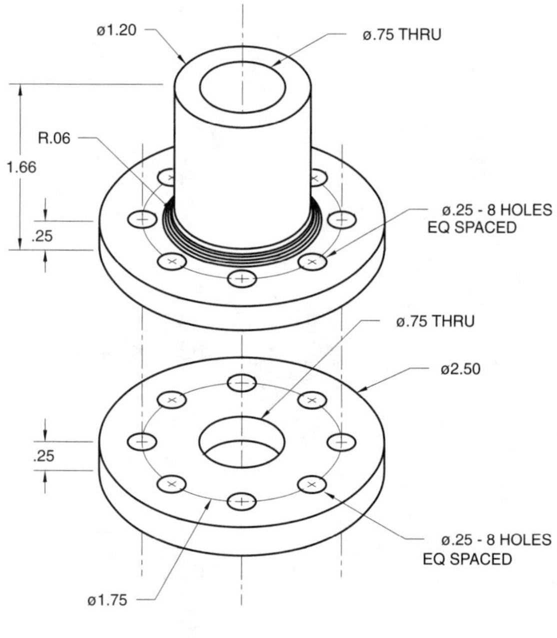

13.5 Turbine Housing Assembly

Create detail drawings for the two parts shown and save each as a Wblock. Insert each block to form an assembly.

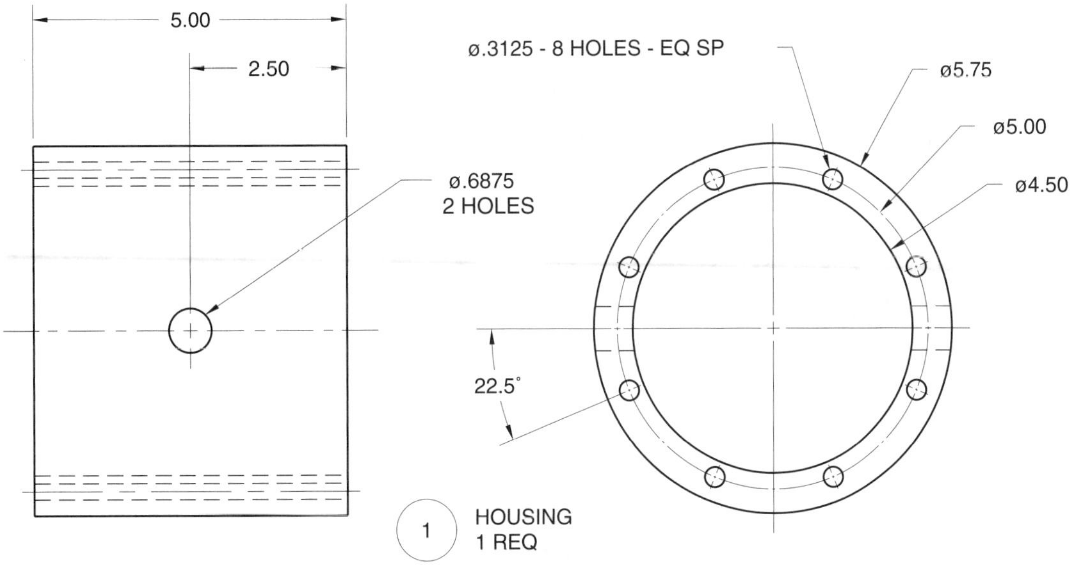

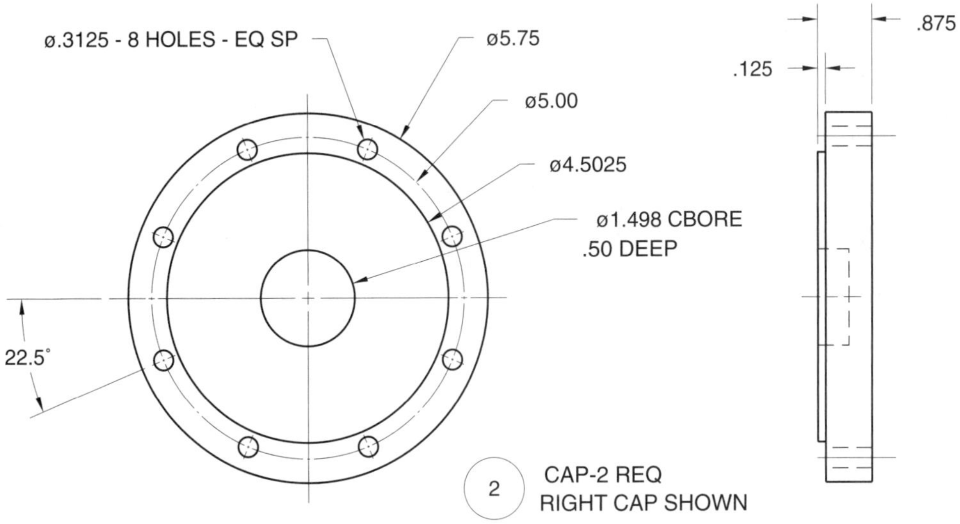

13.6 Geneva Wheel Assembly

Create an assembly drawing for the parts shown, using solid modeling techniques. Experiment with different materials and analyze mass properties.

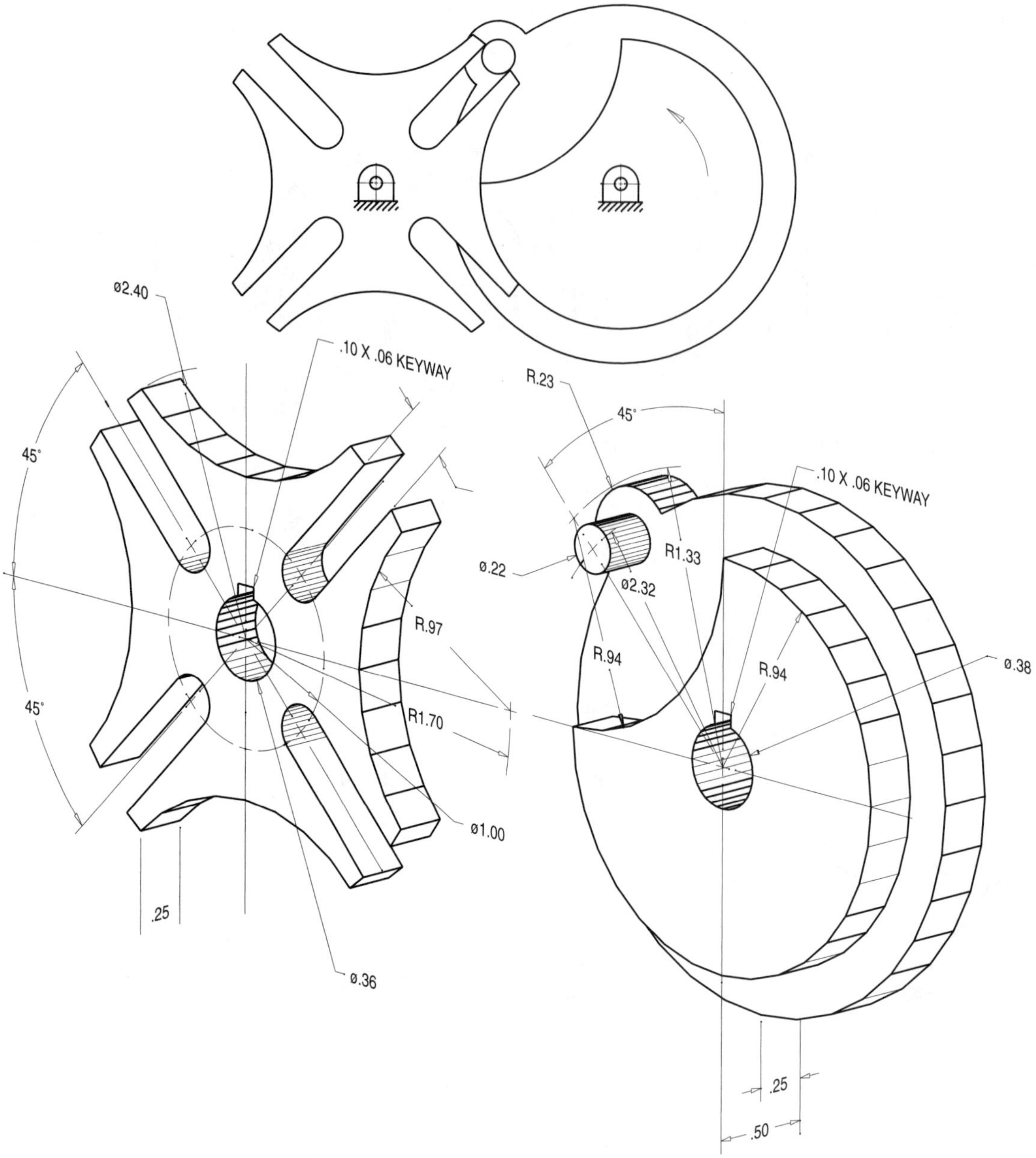

13.7 Staircase

Use solid modeling to generate this staircase assembly detail.

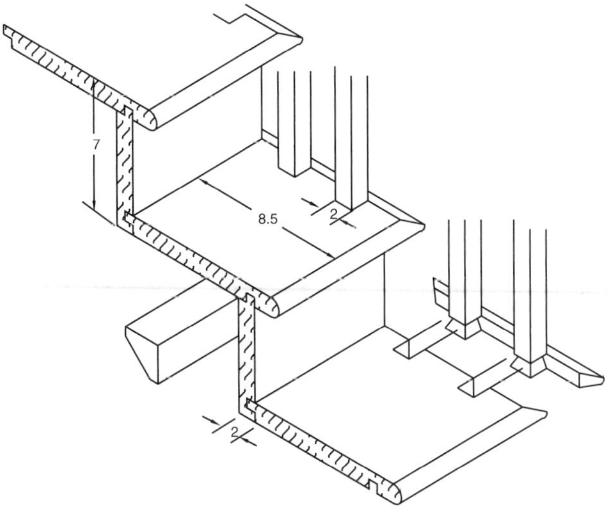

13.8 Milling Jack

Create a 3D assembly model for the milling jack. Do not model thread. When a tolerance is shown for a size, model the feature at the smallest hole size.

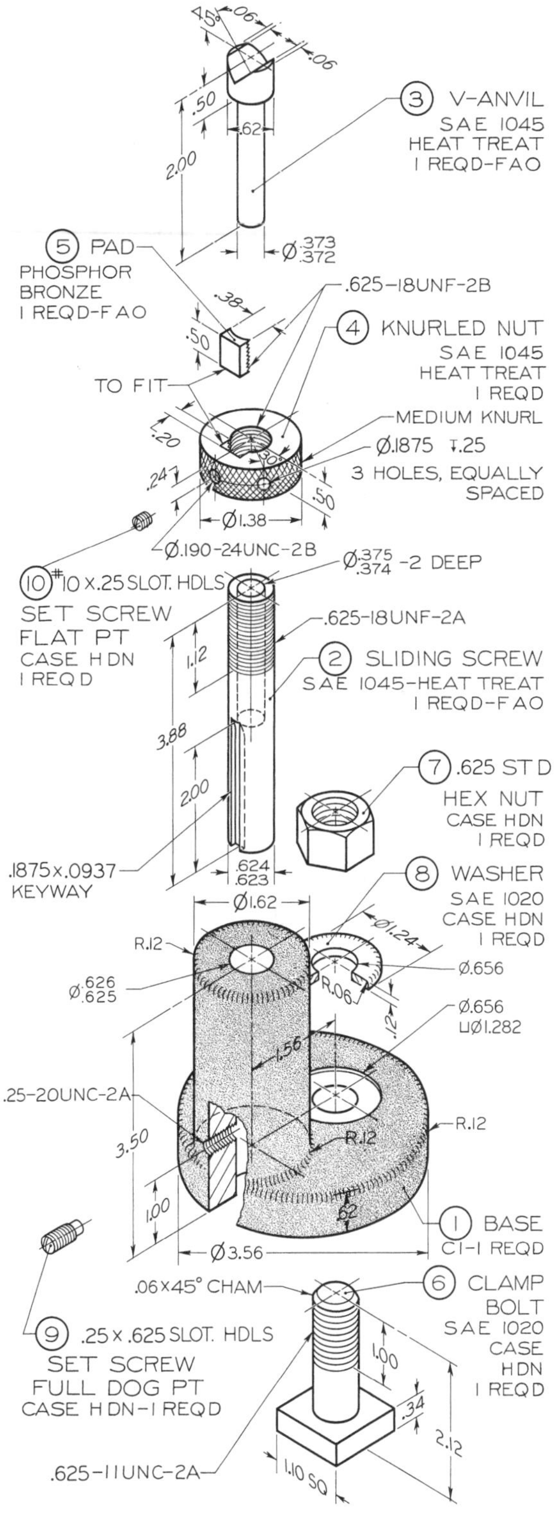

13.9M Step Bearing

Use solid modeling to create an assembly drawing of this step bearing.

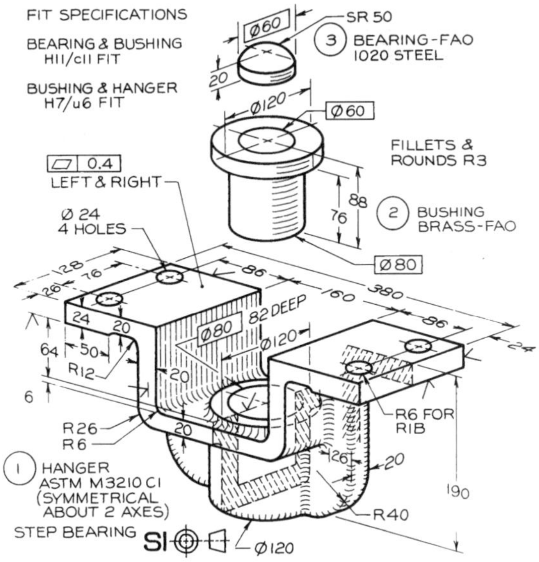

13.10M Universal Joint

Create an assembly drawing for the parts shown, using solid modeling techniques. Analyze the mass properties of the parts.

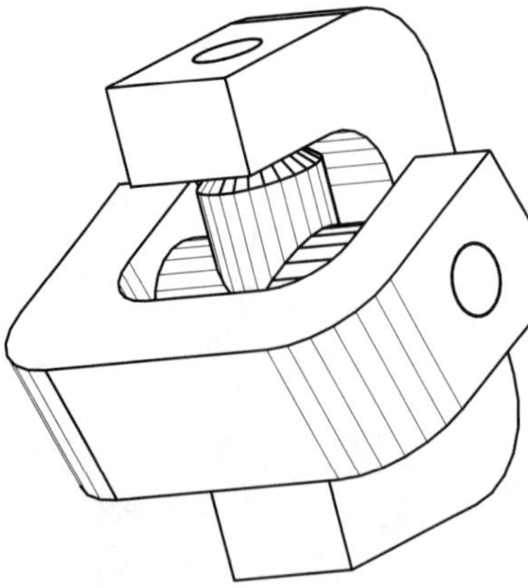

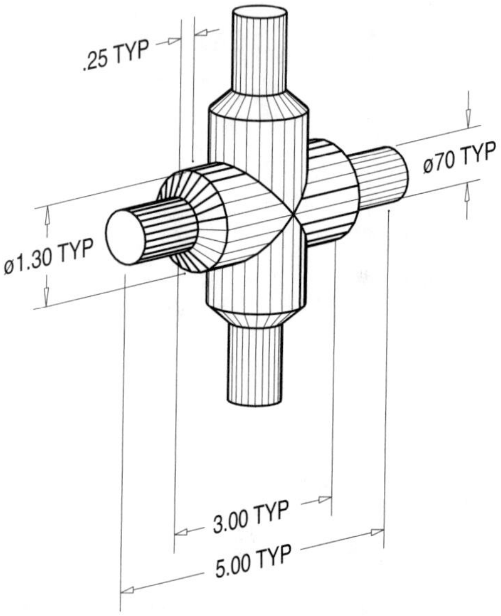

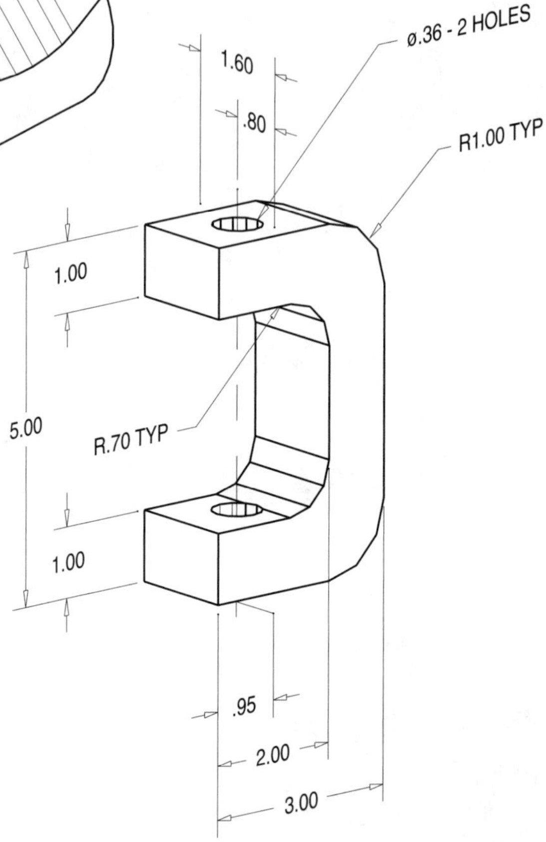

13.11M Tensioner

Create an assembly drawing of this tensioner, using solid modeling.

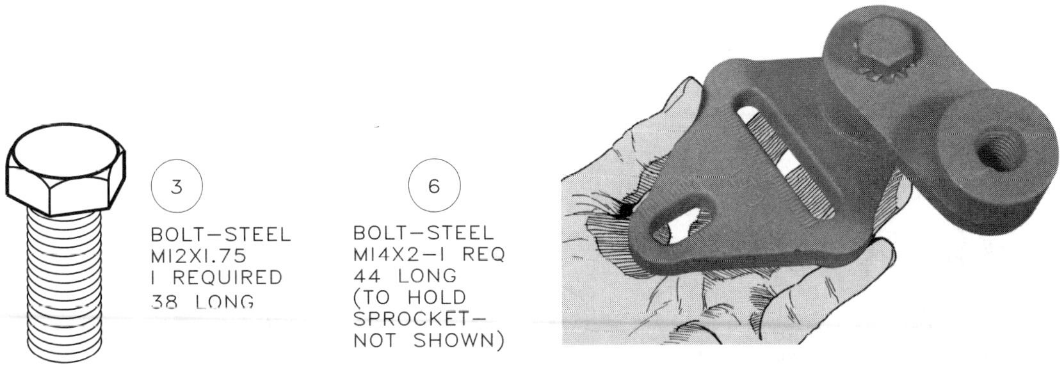

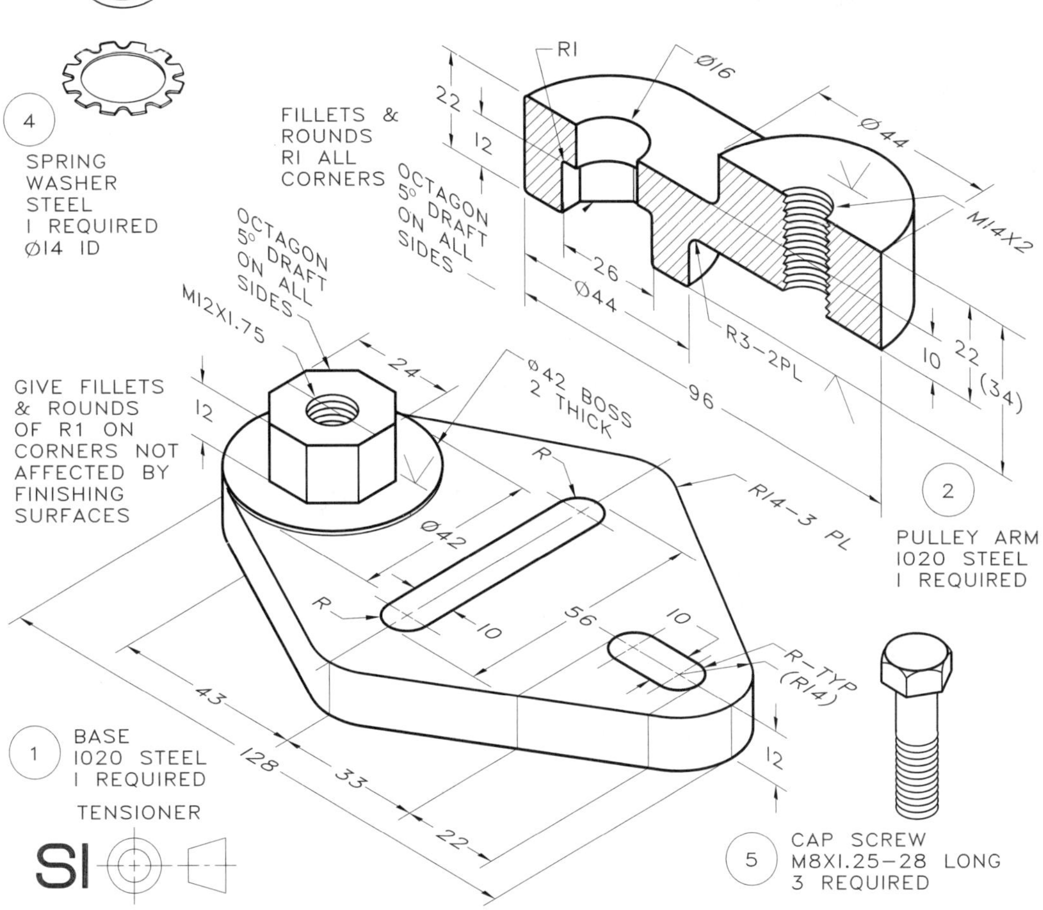

13.12M Trailer Hitch

Make an assembly drawing of this trailer hitch, using solid modeling.

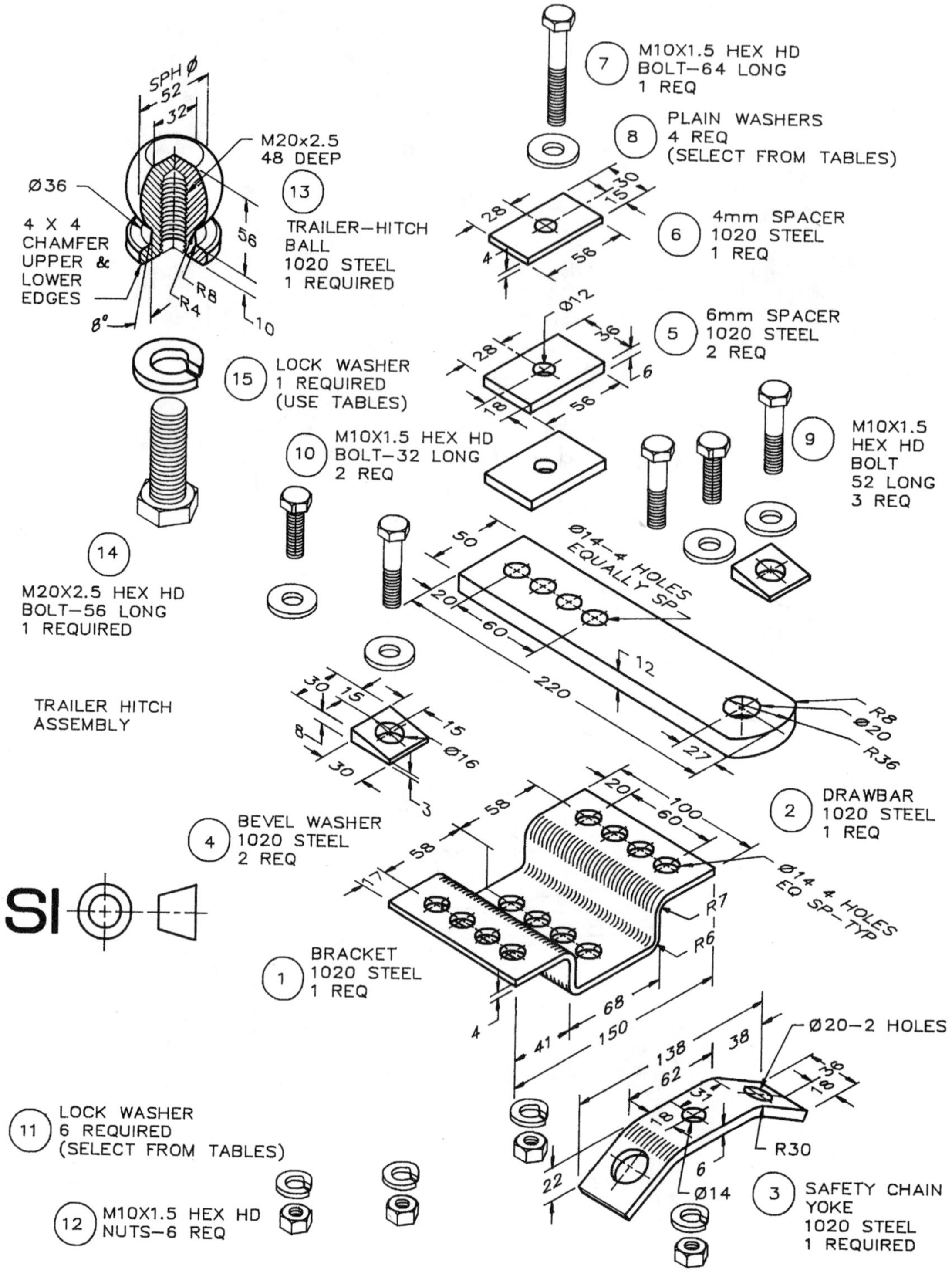

Tutorial

14 Solid Modeling for Section and Auxiliary Views

Objectives

When you have completed this tutorial, you will be able to

1. Show the internal surfaces of an object, using 3D section views.
2. Section and slice a solid model.
3. Control layer visibility within a viewport.
4. Create an auxiliary view of a 3D solid model.

Tip

If necessary, switch to paper space and use Zoom All to enlarge the layout inside the graphics area.

Introduction

In this tutorial you will learn how to draw section and auxiliary views from 3D solid models. You can generate section and auxiliary views directly from solid models. Refer to Tutorial 9 for review.

Creating Sections from a Solid Model

This time you will start your drawing from a solid model template provided with the datafiles. It is similar to the object that you created in Tutorial 11.

Launch the AutoCAD® 2006 software.
Pick: **New icon**
Use the datafile *solblk2.dwt* as a template for your new drawing.
Save it as ***blksect.dwg***.

A drawing similar to the one you created and modified in Tutorials 11 and 12 appears on your screen, as shown in Figure 14.1.

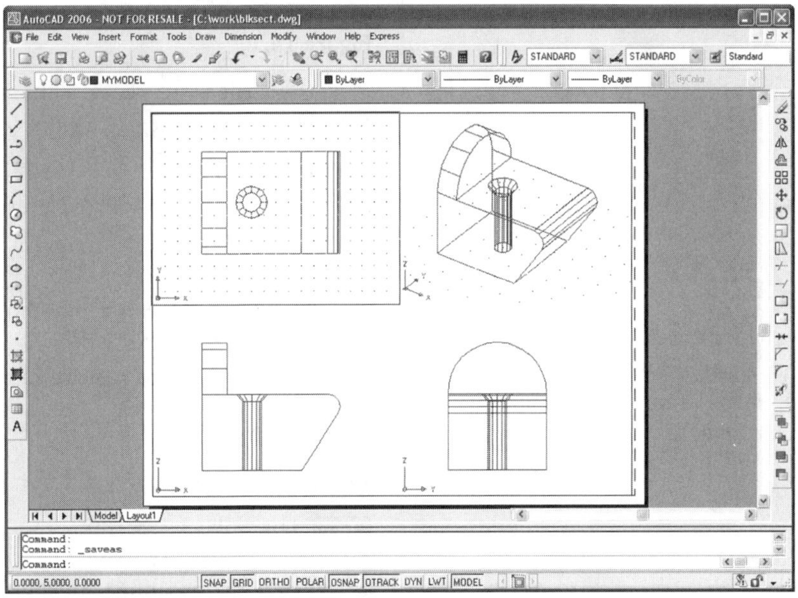

Figure 14.1

You will use SOLVIEW to create a section view. The section view created will take the place of the lower left viewport image. You will erase the lower left viewport by selecting its border. Even though you can switch between viewports at present, the layer that contains their borders is frozen. Before you can erase the viewport, you must thaw the VPORT layer on which the borders reside.

Pick: **to Thaw layer VPORT using the Layer Control**
Pick: **to Freeze layer BORDER**
Switch to paper space.
Pick: **Erase icon**
Select objects: **select the magenta border of the lower left viewport**
Select objects: ↵

The front view should disappear, as in Figure 14.2.

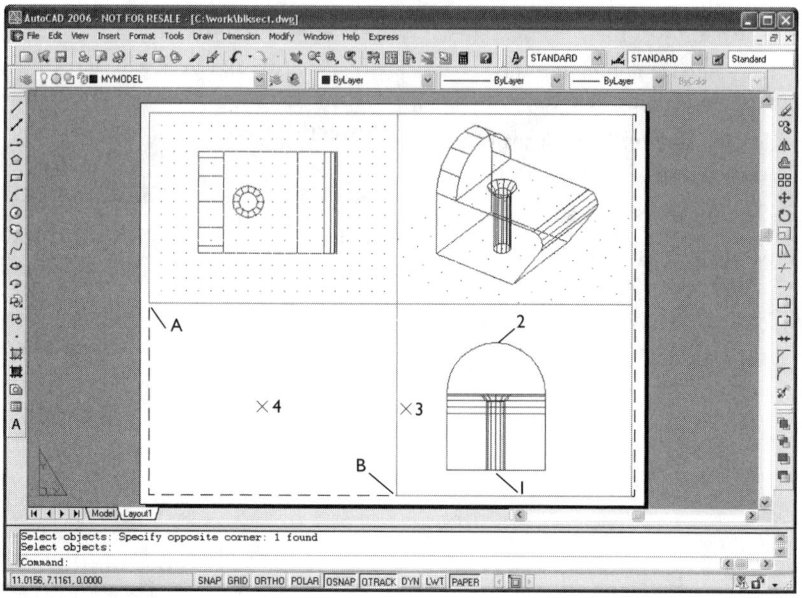

Figure 14.2

Next you will switch back to model space by typing the command, MS, and then restore the UCS previously saved as SIDE.

Command: **MS** ↵
Pick: **inside the lower right viewport to make it active**
Command: **UCS** ↵
Current ucs name: *WORLD*
Enter an option [New/Move/orthoGraphic/Prev/Restore/Save/Del/Apply/?/World] <World>: **R** ↵
Enter name of UCS to restore or [?]: **SIDE** ↵

Tip

If you want to select in a viewport that is not active, press Ctrl-R to toggle the active viewport during commands.

Now you are ready to create the section view.

Using Solview and Soldraw

The Solview (Setup View) and Soldraw (Setup Drawing) commands are used to generate section and auxiliary views. To create a section view, you must specify the cutting plane, the side to view from, the view scaling factor, where to place the section view, and the size of the paper space viewport. Then you use the Soldraw command to view the section hatch. The AutoCAD software automatically generates four new layers for the section view and freezes them where necessary. Use Figure 14.2 to aid in selecting points.

Tip

You can also pick the Solview and Soldraw commands from the Solids Toolbar.

On your own, make sure that running OSnap for Endpoint and Midpoint is on.
Make sure the lower right viewport is active.

Command: **SOLVIEW**
Enter an option [UCS/Ortho/Auxiliary/Section]: **S**
Specify first point of cutting plane: **pick using AutoSnap™ Midpoint at point 1**
Specify second point of cutting plane: **pick the AutoSnap Midpoint at point 2**
Specify side to view from: **pick near point 3**
Enter view scale <0.5000>:
Specify view center: **pick near point 4**
Specify view center <specify viewport>:
Specify first corner of viewport: **pick A**, targeting the viewport Endpoint
Specify opposite corner of viewport: **pick B**, targeting the viewport Endpoint
Enter view name: **SECTION**
Enter an option [UCS/Ortho/Auxiliary/Section]:

Your screen should be similar to Figure 14.3.

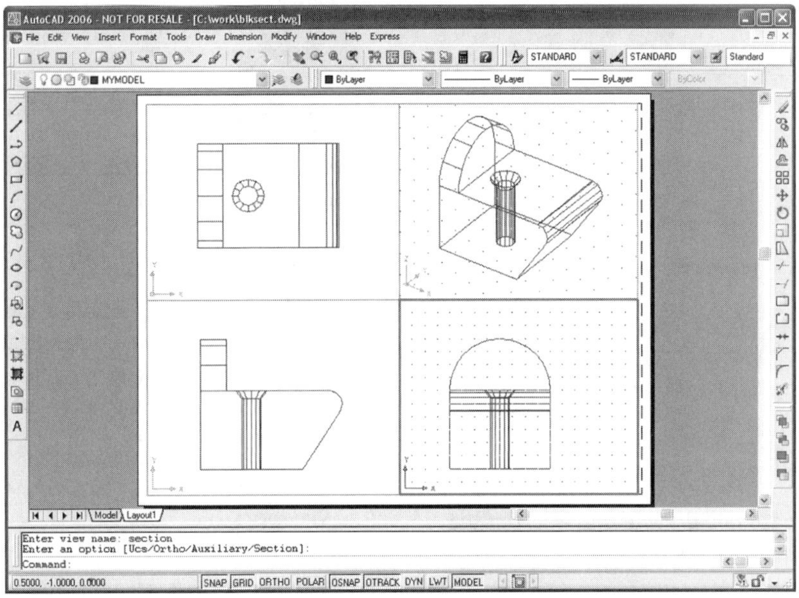

Figure 14.3

Note that the section hatch pattern is not shown in the front view. You will use Soldraw to show the hatch.

Command: **SOLDRAW**
Select viewports to draw...
Select objects: **pick the border of the lower left viewport**
Select objects:
One solid selected.

The section hatch should have appeared in the lower left viewport on the screen, similar to Figure 14.4.

If you look at the Layer Control pull-down list, you will see that the Solview command has created a number of new layers with the proper visibilities set for each viewport.

On your own, **change the color for layer SECTION-HAT to Red and set its lineweight to 0.30 mm**. Change the **lineweight for layer SECTION-VIS to 0.60 mm**.

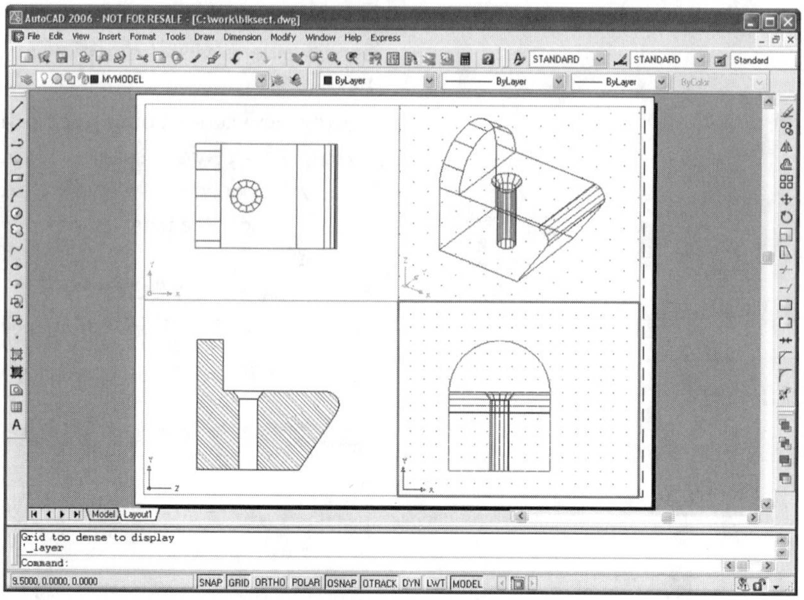

Figure 14.4

Setup Profile

As you learned in Tutorial 12, Setup Profile, or the Solprof command, eliminates lines on the back surfaces of the object from the screen and inserts hidden lines where necessary in the drawing. Next, you will use the Solprof command to generate 2D profiles in the upper left and lower right viewports.

Tip

Don't forget you can switch to model space and activate a viewport at the same time by double-clicking inside a viewport.

On your own, switch to model space if needed and activate the upper left viewport.

Command: **SOLPROF** ↵

Select objects: **pick on an edge of the object in the upper left viewport**

Select objects: ↵

Display hidden profile lines on a separate layer? <Y>: ↵

Project profile lines onto a plane? <Y>: ↵

Delete tangential edges? <Y>: ↵

One solid selected.

Pick: **the lower right viewport to make it active**

Command: ↵ (to restart the Solprof command)

Select objects: **pick on an edge of the object in the lower right viewport**

Select objects: ↵

Display hidden profile lines on a separate layer? <Y>: ↵

Project profile lines onto a plane? <Y>: ↵
Delete tangential edges? <Y>: ↵
One solid selected.

On your own, **change the linetype and color of the PH- layers to hidden and blue with lineweight 0.30 mm. Set the lineweight for the PV- layers to 0.60 mm.**

Using techniques used earlier in this manual, **freeze layer MYMODEL in the upper left and lower right viewports only**. (Remember to use the Current VP Freeze selection in the Layer Control.)

Black visible lines created by the Solprof command should be visible, with blue hidden lines as shown in Figure 14.5.

Restore the World Coordinate System and add a cutting plane line to the top view to show where the section was taken if you want. (It is optional because is clear where the section was created.)

Add centerlines on your own, remembering to control layer visibility in other viewports.

Save and close your drawing before continuing.

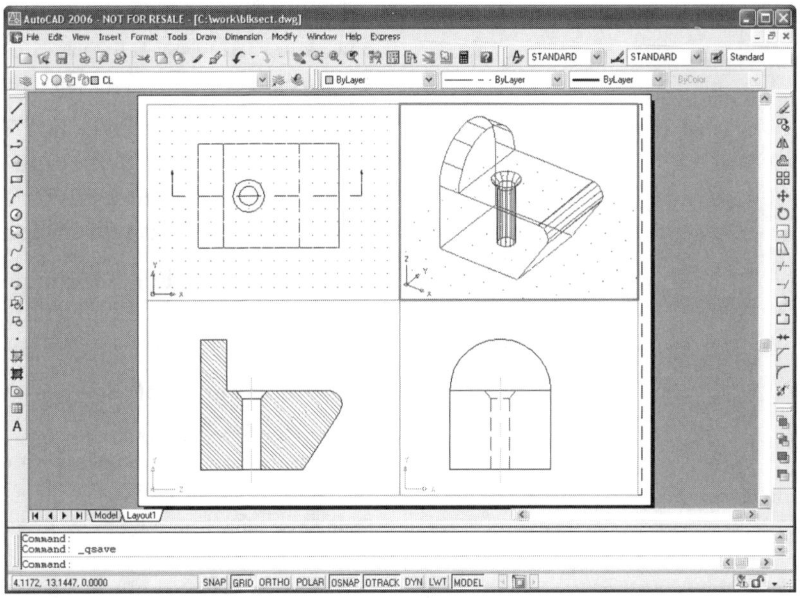

Figure 14.5

Next you will create an isometric section view using the Section and Slice commands.

Using Section and Slice

You will start a new drawing, using the same prototype previously used.

Pick: **New**

Use the datafile drawing *solblk2.dwt* as a template.

Save your drawing as ***blksect2.dwg***.

A drawing similar to the one you just used appears on your screen as shown in Figure 14.6.

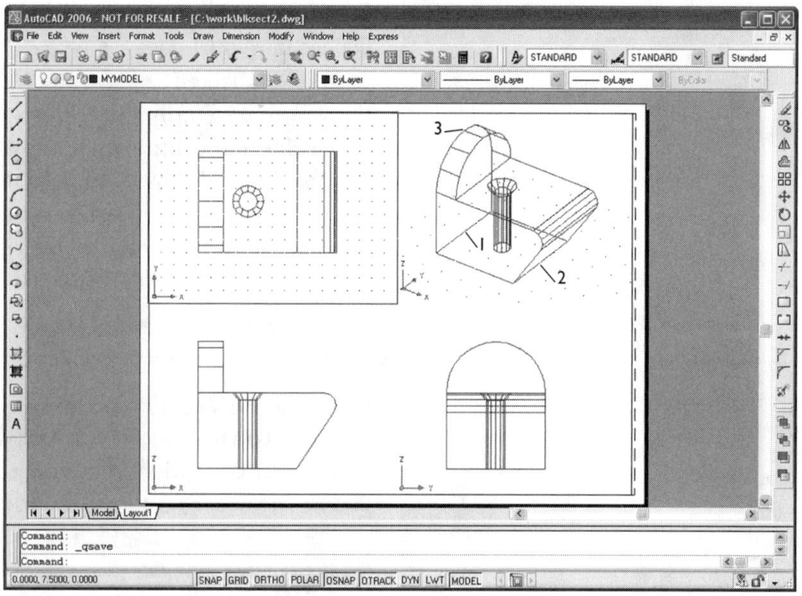

Figure 14.6

The AutoCAD program places the region it generates during the Section command on the current layer.

On your own, **create layer HATCH**.
Assign it **color red** and **linetype CONTINUOUS**.
Make **HATCH** the current layer.
Turn on running OSnap for **Midpoint**.

You will use the Midpoint running object snap to create a UCS through the center of the part. You will type the UCS command at the prompt. Refer to Figure 14.6 to make your selections.

Pick: **the upper right viewport to make it active**
Command: **UCS** ↵
Enter an option [New/Move/orthoGraphic/Prev/Restore/Save/Del/Apply/?/World]: **N** ↵
Specify origin of new UCS or [ZAxis/3point/OBject/Face/View/X/Y/Z] <0,0,0>: **3** ↵
Specify new origin point <0,0,0>: **pick near point 1**
Specify point on positive portion of the X-axis <3.0000,4.0000,0.0000>: **pick near point 2**
Specify point on the positive-Y portion of the UCS Xyplane <2.0000,5.0000,0.0000>: **pick near point 3**

The UCS changes so that it is through the middle of the object. Next, you will type the UCSICON command to show the UCS icon at the origin of the newly created UCS. This helps you see whether the correct coordinate system has been selected.

Command: **UCSICON** ↵
Enter an option [ON/OFF/All/Noorigin/ORigin/Properties] <ON>: **OR** ↵

The UCS icon should appear in the middle of the part in the upper right view. Your screen should look like Figure 14.7. If it does not, repeat the preceding steps, being careful to select the midpoints indicated in Figure 14.6.

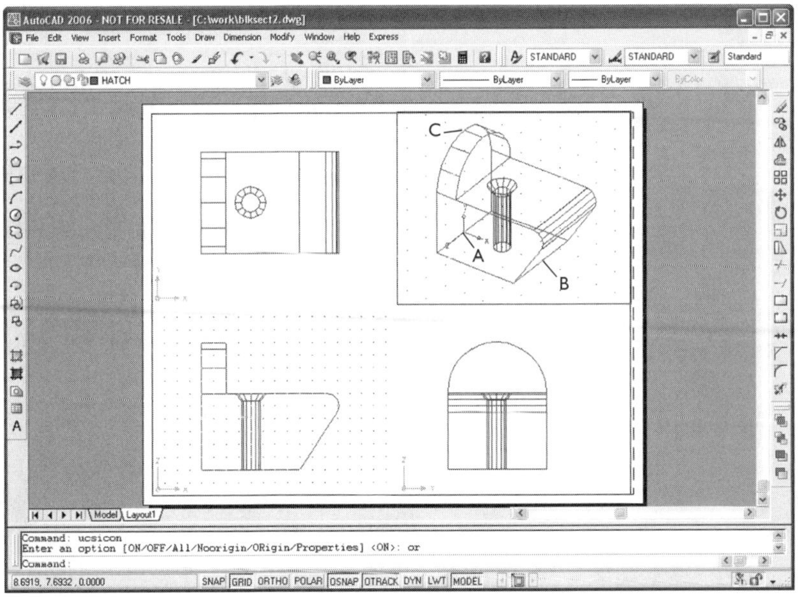

Figure 14.7

Next, turn on the Solids toolbar,

Right-click on any toolbar.
Pick: **Solids from the menu**
Pick: **to make the upper right viewport active if needed**

Using Section

The Section command generates a region (a closed 2D area) from a solid and a cutting plane that you specify. The region is inserted on the current layer and at the location of the cross section you specified by selecting the cutting plane. You can pick the Section icon from the Solids toolbar.

Pick: **Section icon**
Select objects: **pick the object displayed in the upper right viewport**
Select objects: ↵
Specify first point on Section plane by [Object/Zaxis/View/XY/YZ/ZX/3points] <3points>: ↵

You can specify the cutting plane by choosing:

Object	Aligns the cutting plane with a circle, ellipse, arc, 2D spline, or 2D polyline that you select.
Zaxis	Prompts you for two points that determine the edge view of an XY plane. The cutting plane is the Z-axis plane through the first point you select and is normal (perpendicular) to the line defined by the two points selected.
View	Aligns the cutting plane parallel to the current viewing plane through the point you specify.

XY, YZ, or ZX	Aligns the cutting plane parallel to the specified UCS plane through the point you specify.
3 points	Prompts you for three points, through which the desired cutting plane passes.

You will specify three points to define the cutting plane, which will pass through the middle of the object. The Midpoint running object snap, which you turned on earlier, will select the midpoint of the lines you pick. Refer to Figure 14.7 for selections.

Specify first point on plane: **pick the midpoint of line A**
Specify second point on plane: **pick the midpoint of line B**
Specify third point on plane: **pick the midpoint of line C**

The Section command creates a region or a block in your drawing. You should see it appear in your drawing, as shown in Figure 14.8.

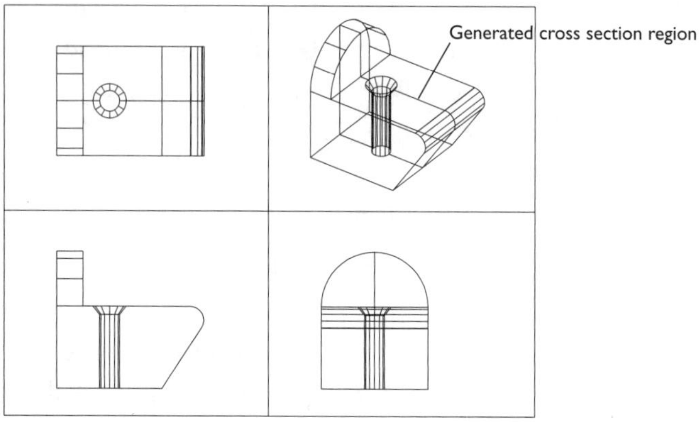

Figure 14.8

Next, use the Hatch command to hatch the section boundary that you created.

Pick: **Hatch icon**

The Hatch and Gradient dialog box appears on your screen.

On your own, choose the button for Select Objects to define the boundary.
Pick: **the boundary that you created with the Section command and press** ↵ to return to the dialog box.
Preview the hatching to make sure that the correct area will be hatched.
Press: Esc **to return to dialog box** (or right-click to accept Hatch)
Pick: **OK** (to apply the hatch and exit the Hatch and Gradient dialog box)

The hatching appears in your drawing, as shown in Figure 14.9.

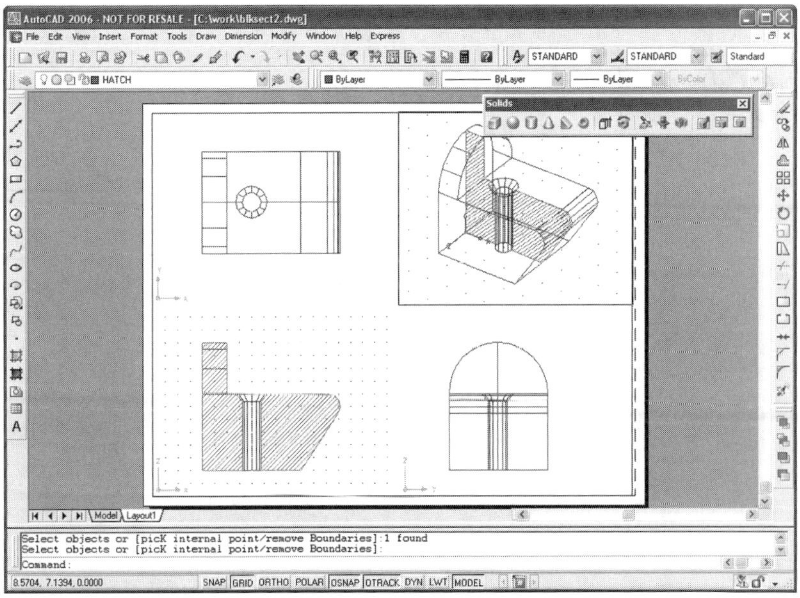

Figure 14.9

The hatching should only be drawn in the section view (in this case, the front view) according to good engineering drawing practice, but at this point it is still visible in every view. (It is on edge in the top and side views, so it just appears as a single line through the center of the part.) You will control the visibility for layer HATCH so that the hatching only shows in the front view and isometric view.

Tip

Remember that you can use Draworder to locate the hatch behind or in front of the object outline.

Controlling Layer Visibility

You will use the Layer Control to freeze the hatching in individual viewports.

On your own, make the top left viewport current.

Pick: **Layer Control**

Pick: **the Freeze or Thaw in Current Viewport icon to the left of layer name HATCH**

Pick: **anywhere in the drawing to end using the Layer Control**

The icon changes from a sun with a little viewport to a snowflake with a little viewport as shown in Figure 14.10.

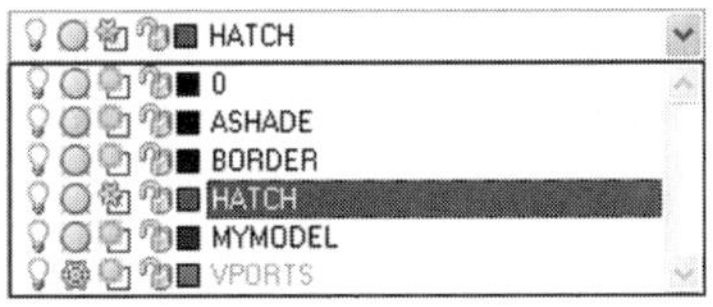

Figure 14.10

The line representing the edge view of the hatching should no longer be visible in the upper left viewport.

Repeat this process on your own to freeze the hatching in the lower right viewport.

When you have finished, your screen should look like Figure 14.11.

Tip

You can use Solprof to generate the correct 2D top and side views before you slice the model.

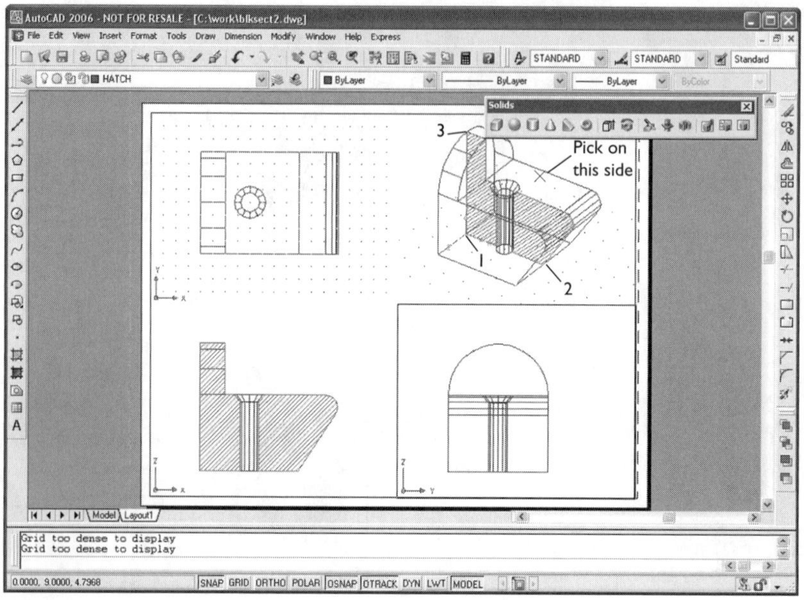

Figure 14.11

Using Slice

The Slice command lets you remove a portion of a solid by specifying a slicing plane similar to the cutting plane in the Section command. You can use the Section command in conjunction with the Slice command to create pictorial section views from solid models. Next, you will slice the model and cut away the front half. Refer to Figure 14.11 for the points to select. (They will be the same points you selected last time to define the section.) You can pick the Slice icon from the Solids toolbar.

Pick: **to make the upper right viewport active**
Pick: **Slice icon**
Select objects: **pick the object displayed in the upper right viewport**
Select objects: ↵

The methods by which you selected the cutting plane for a section are very similar to the methods for using the Slice command. You will specify three points to define the cutting plane, which will pass through the middle of the object. The Midpoint running object snap will select the midpoint of the lines you pick. Refer to Figure 14.11 for the lines to select.

Specify first point on slicing plane by [Object/Zaxis/View/XY/YZ/ZX/3points] <3points>: **use OSnap Midpoint to target line 1**
Specify second point on plane: **use OSnap Midpoint and target line 2**
Specify third point on plane: **use OSnap Midpoint and target line 3**
Specify a point on desired side: **pick near the point shown**

The front half of the object is sliced away.

Using Hide

As you saw in Tutorial 13, the Hide command removes lines defining the back surfaces of the object from the display so that the object appears correctly in the viewport. Next you will hide the back surface lines with the Hide command.

Pick: **View, Hide**

When you are finished, your screen should look like Figure 14.12.

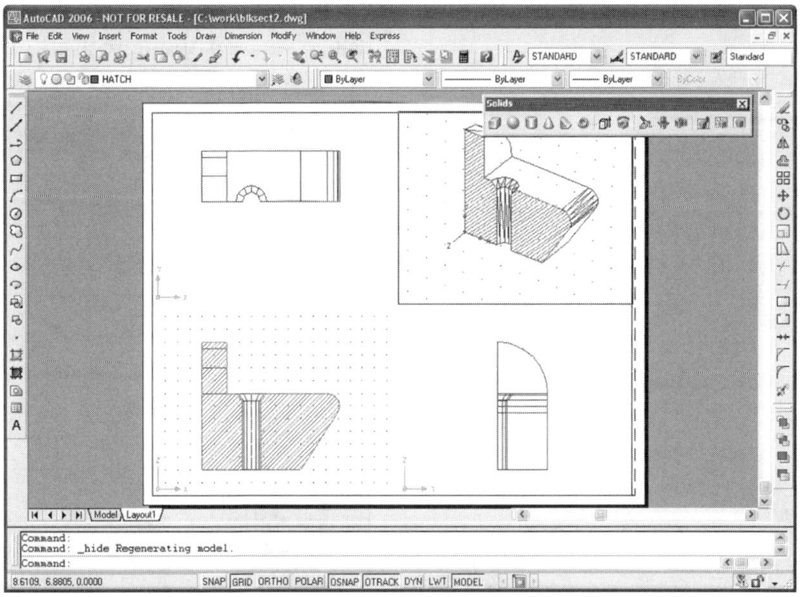

Figure 14.12

Plot the upper right viewport from model space, if you wish. Select the Hide Object box in the Plot Options area of the Plot dialog box. To plot from paper space with hidden lines removed, use the Mview command and select the Hideplot option, and pick the viewports in which you want back surface lines removed when plotting.

Turn off the Midpoint running object snap on your own.

Close the Solids toolbar.

Save and close your drawing.

Creating an Auxiliary View of a 3D Solid Model

You can easily create auxiliary views of 3D solid models by changing the viewpoint in any viewport to show the desired view. You can view the model from any direction inside any viewport. However, good engineering drawing practice requires that adjacent views align; otherwise, interpreting the drawing can be difficult or impossible. In general, you should show at least two principal orthographic views of the object. Additional views are sometimes placed in other locations on the drawing sheet or on a separate sheet. If you use a separate sheet, you should clearly label on the original sheet the view that is located elsewhere. When placing auxiliary views in other locations, you should show a viewing plane line, similar to a cutting plane line, that indicates the direction of sight for the auxiliary view. You should clearly label the auxiliary view and preserve its correct orientation, rather than rotate it to a different alignment.

On your own, start a new drawing.

Use the drawing *anglblok.dwt* provided with the data files as the template.

Name the new drawing ***aux3d.dwg***.

Switch to paper space and use Zoom All so that the drawing fills the available viewing area, then switch back to model space.

The solid model shown in Figure 14.13 appears on your screen. You will continue working with this drawing, creating an auxiliary view that shows the true size of the inclined surface.

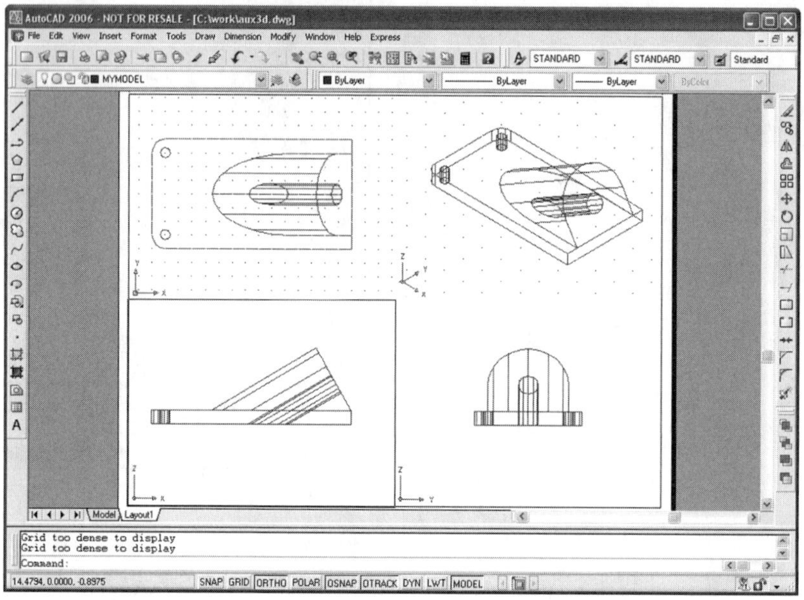

Figure 14.13

You will use hot grips to stretch the viewports to different sizes in order to make room for the auxiliary view. To do so, you will need to thaw the layer containing the viewports because it is turned off in the data file.

Pick: **to thaw layer VPORT**

Pick: **to freeze layer BORDER**

When layer VPORT is thawed, you should see the outlines of each viewport in your drawing.

Now you are ready to stretch the viewports to different sizes to make room for a new viewport that will show the auxiliary view.

Pick: **to switch to paper space**

Tip

To activate the grip for each of the four viewports, make an implied Crossing box where the viewports come together at the center of the screen.

You should see the paper space icon in the lower left of the screen. Next you will select the viewports so that you can stretch them. (Remember, viewports are paper space objects, and you can modify them by using Scale, Rotate, Stretch, and Copy, among other commands, but only when you are in paper space.)

Pick: **on each of the viewport borders so that their grips appear**

The grips are activated, as shown in Figure 4.14.

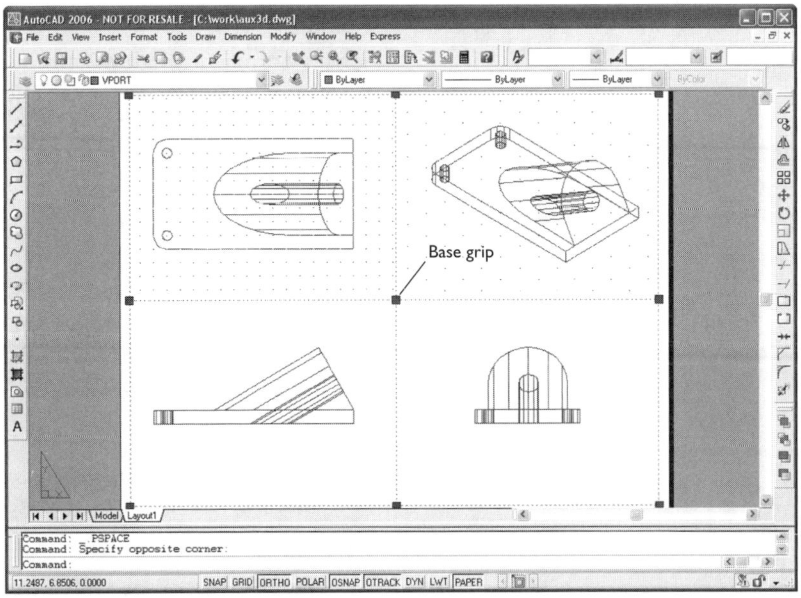

Figure 14.14

Pick: **the grip in the center of the four viewports as the highlighted base grip**

You will stretch the viewports to the right, making the viewports containing the pictorial view and side view smaller.

On your own, use ORTHO and stretch the viewports to the right so that the final result on the screen looks like Figure 14.15.

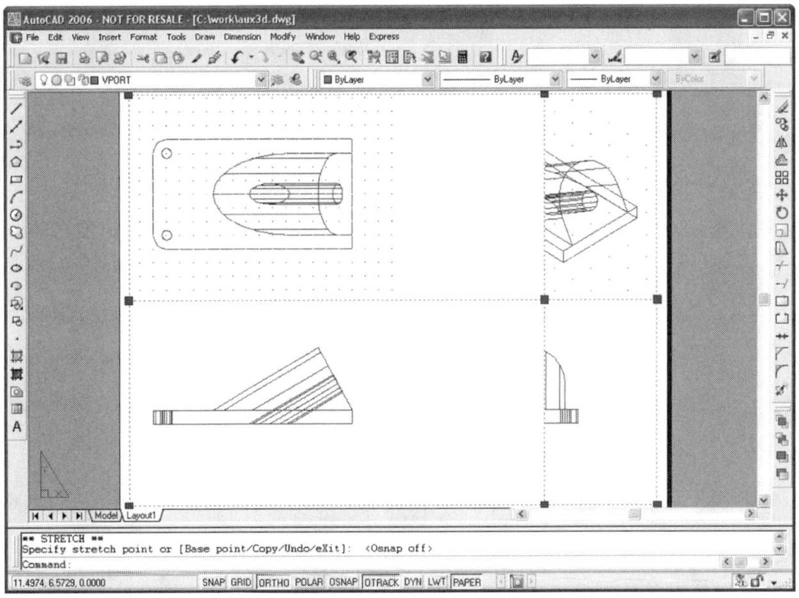

Figure 14.15

Next you will switch to model space and take the following steps.

Command: **MS** ↵
Pick: **the top right view to make it active**
Command: **Z** ↵
Specify corner of window, enter a scale factor (nX or nXP), or [All/Center/Dynamic/Extents/Previous/Scale/Window/Object] <real time>: **.6X** ↵

Now the pictorial view should be shown at 6/10 of its previous size.

Pick: **Pan Realtime icon**
On your own, pan the view of the angled block until it is centered in the upper right viewport.
Then use Pan Realtime and MVSETUP's Align option to move the views in the lower right and upper left viewports to make room for a new viewport and realign them with the lower left viewport.
Pick: **to switch to paper space**
Pick: **VPORT** as the current layer

The paper space icon is displayed in the lower left corner of your screen. You will now create your new viewport, using the View menu.

Make the upper right viewport active.
Pick: **View, Viewports, 1 Viewport**
Specify corner of viewport or [ON/OFF/Fit/Shadeplot/Lock/Object/Polygonal/Restore/2/3/4] <Fit>: **pick point A in Figure 14.16**
Specify opposite corner: **pick point B**

The new viewport appears, as shown in Figure 14.16. The overlapping viewport borders don't matter because you will turn their layer off before plotting your drawing. Depending on which viewport was active when you switched to paper space, you may see a different view in the viewport. This is okay. You will create the auxiliary view in the viewport after a few more steps.

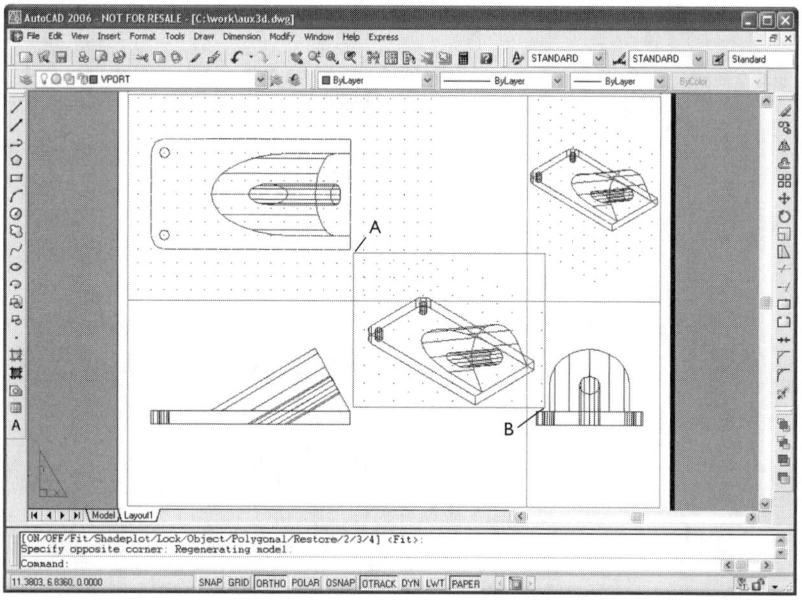

Figure 14.16

Rotating the View

You will rotate the view in the new center viewport so that you can see the angled face clearly.

Switch to model space inside the center viewport.
Pick: **View, 3D Orbit**
On your own, rotate the view of the angled face so that it is clearly visible.
Press: [Esc] when you have finished to exit the Orbiter

Next you will align the UCS with the angled surface and then use the Plan command inside the new viewport to show the view looking straight toward the UCS. The points you will select are shown in Figure 14.17.

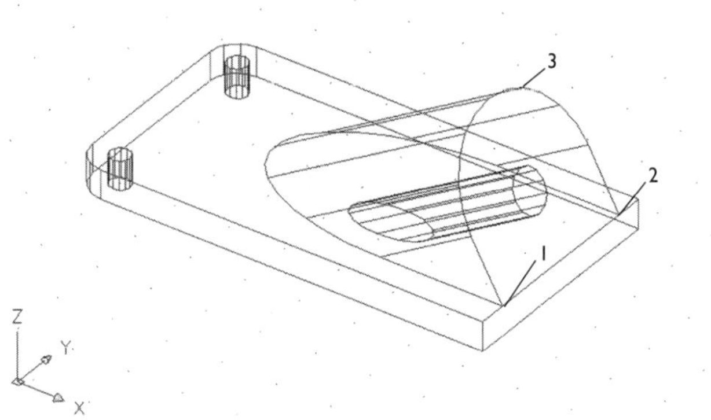

Figure 14.17

3 Point UCS

The 3 Point option of the UCS command creates a User Coordinate System that aligns with the three points you specify. You are prompted to pick the origin, a point in the positive X-direction, and a point in the positive Y-direction. Refer to Figure 14.17 for the points to select.

On your own, be sure that OSnap is active with **Endpoint** and **Quadrant** selected.
Right-click: **on any toolbar**
Pick: **UCS** from the pop-up menu to turn on the UCS toolbar
Pick: **3 Point UCS icon**
Specify new origin point <0,0,0>: **pick Endpoint 1**
Specify point on positive portion of the X-axis <14.000,4.5000,0.5000>: **pick Endpoint 2**
Specify point on positive-Y portion of the UCS XY plane <12.0000,4.5000,0.5000>: **pick on the upper curved line labeled as point 3, using the AutoSnap Quadrant marker**
Command: **UCSICON** [Enter]
Enter an option [ON/OFF/All/Noorigin/ORigin/Properties] <ON>: **OR** [Enter]

The UCS icon should appear at the origin and aligned with the angled face as shown in Figure 14.18.

The UCS icon is important because it tells you that the User Coordinate System is correctly aligned with the angled surface. Make sure that the coordinate system appears parallel to the angled face.

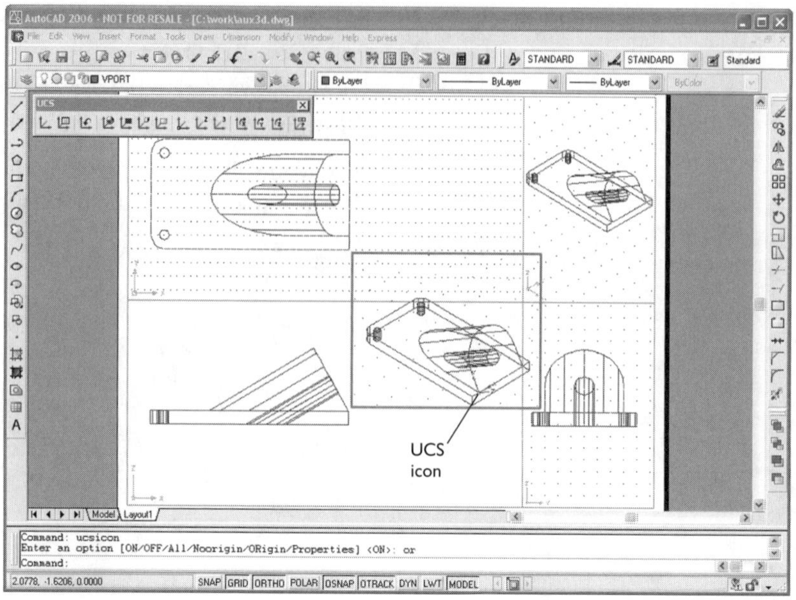

Figure 14.18

Using Plan

Tip

If you have trouble picking inside a viewport because it overlaps other viewports, type Ctrl*-R to toggle the viewport.*

The Plan command aligns the viewpoint in the active viewport so that you are viewing the current UCS, a named UCS, or the WCS straight on. You will accept the default, the current UCS, to show the true size view of the angled surface, with which you have already aligned the coordinate system. You will type the Plan command at the command prompt, but it is also available from the View menu under 3D Views, Plan View.

Make sure the center viewport is active.

Command: **PLAN** ↵

Enter an option [Current ucs/Ucs/World] <Current>: ↵

Tip

If your viewport is not large enough to show the entire view zoomed to .5XP, switch back to paper space and use hot grips to stretch the viewport so that it is slightly larger than before. Switch back to model space when you are finished and use Pan once again to position the view.

The view in the center viewport changes so that you are looking straight at the angled surface. Next you will use the Zoom command with a .5XP scaling factor to size the view. (The original views were zoomed to .5XP in the data file.)

Command: **Z** ↵

Specify corner of window, enter a scale factor (nX or nXP), or [All/ Center/Dynamic/Extents/Previous/Scale/Window] <real time>: **.5XP** ↵

Use the Pan Realtime command to center the view inside the viewport on your own.

When you have finished these steps, your screen should look like Figure 14.19.

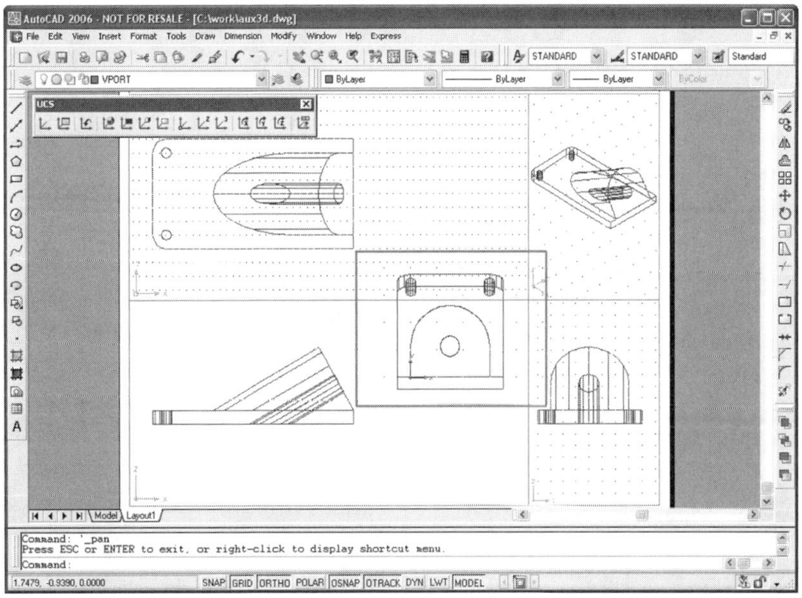

Figure 14.19

Now the view shows the true size of the angled surface, but it is not aligned correctly with the front view. Remember, to show a true-size view of the surface, you use a line of sight that is perpendicular to the view in which the surface shows on edge, as in the front view.

Tip

You can set the Ucsfollow variable to generate the plan view of the current UCS automatically. Pick in a viewport to make it active and then set Ucsfollow to 1. The AutoCAD software automatically generates a plan view of the current UCS in that viewport whenever you change the UCS.

Using 3D Dynamic View

The 3D Dynamic View command uses the metaphor of a camera and a target, where your viewing direction is the line between the camera and the target. It is called 3D Dynamic View because while you are in the command, you can see the view of the selected objects change dynamically on the screen when you move your pointing device. If you do not select any objects for use with the command, you see a special block shaped like a 3D house instead. Use AutoCAD Help to discover more information about the options of the 3D Dynamic View command.

In the next steps you will use the 3D Dynamic View command with the Twist option to twist the viewing angle. You will type DVIEW at the command prompt. The angled surface is at 60° in the front view. You will type 30 for the twist angle, which will produce a view that is aligned 90° to the front view.

On your own, verify that the center viewport is active.

Command: **DVIEW** ↵

Select objects or <use DVIEWBLOCK>: **pick on the solid model** ↵

Enter option [CAmera/TArget/Distance/POints/PAn/Zoom/TWist/
    CLip/Hide/Off/Undo]: **TW** ↵

Specify view twist angle <0.00>: **30** ↵

CAmera/TArget/ Distance/POints/PAn/Zoom/TWist/CLip/Hide/
    Off/Undo/<eXit>: ↵

The view is twisted 30° to align with the edge view of the angled surface. Your screen should look like Figure 14.20.

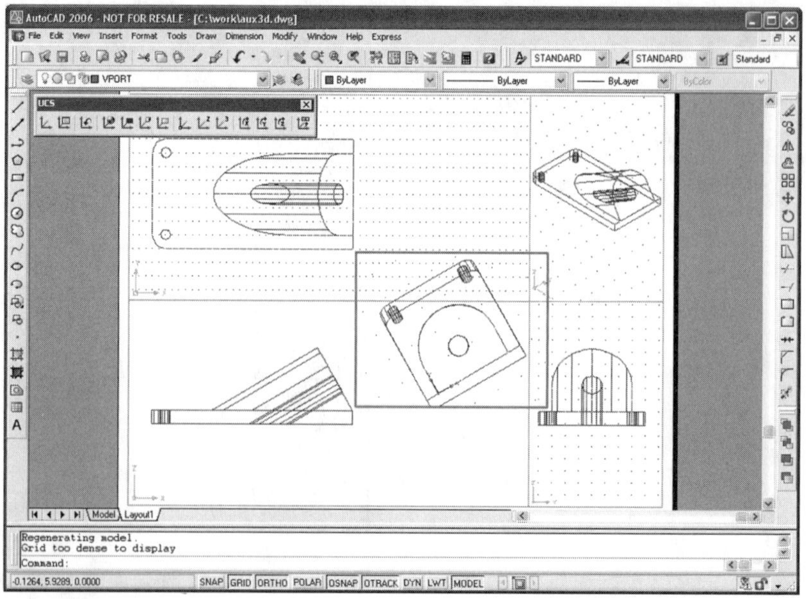

Figure 14.20

On your own, return to paper space and use hot grips to stretch the center viewport so that it is large enough to show the entire object.

When you have it sized as you want, set layer MYMODEL as the current layer.

Freeze layer VPORT.

When you have finished, your screen should be similar to Figure 14.21.

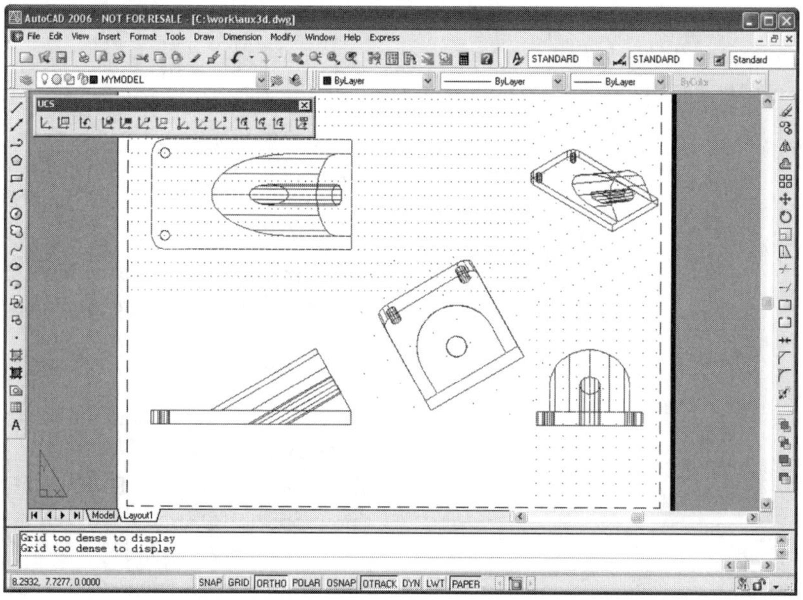

Figure 14.21

Next, you will create an Auxiliary view with the Solview command.

Save your drawing.
Use Save As to save the drawing with the new name ***aux3D-2.dwg.***
On your own, thaw layer VPORT.
Switch to paper space.
Erase the center viewport showing the auxiliary view.

Using Solview

This time you will use Solview to create your Auxiliary view. After performing the previous tasks, your screen should look like Figure 14.22.

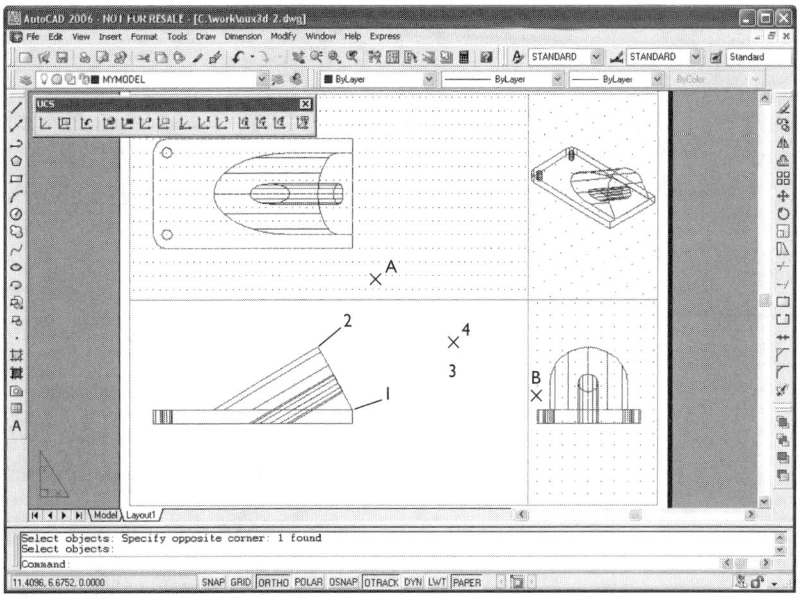

Figure 14.22

Command: **SOLVIEW** ↵
Enter an option [Ucs/Ortho/Auxiliary/Section]: **A** ↵
Specify first point of inclined plane: **select point 1 using AutoSnap Endpoint**
Specify second point of inclined plane: **select point 2 using AutoSnap Quadrant**
Specify side to view from: **pick point 3**
Specify view center: **pick near point 4**
Specify view center <specify viewport>: ↵
Specify first corner of viewport: **select point A**
Specify opposite corner of viewport: **select point B**
Enter view name: **AUXILIARY** ↵
Enter an option [Ucs/Ortho/Auxiliary/Section]: ↵

Your drawing should appear on the screen as shown in Figure 14.23.

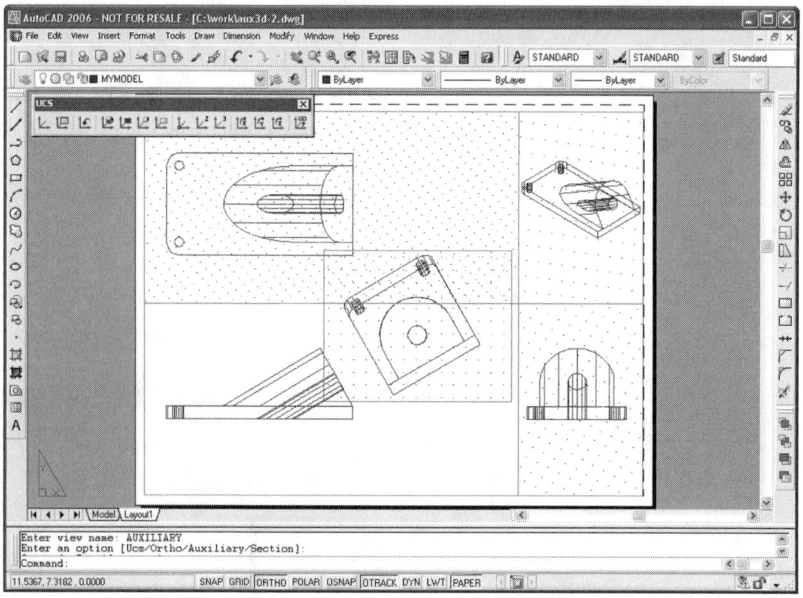

Figure 14.23

Switch to model space.

Turn the grid off in your new viewport.

Switch to paper space.

Make layer MYMODEL current.

Freeze layer VPORT and layer VPORTS created by the Solview command.

When you have finished, your screen should look like Figure 14.24.

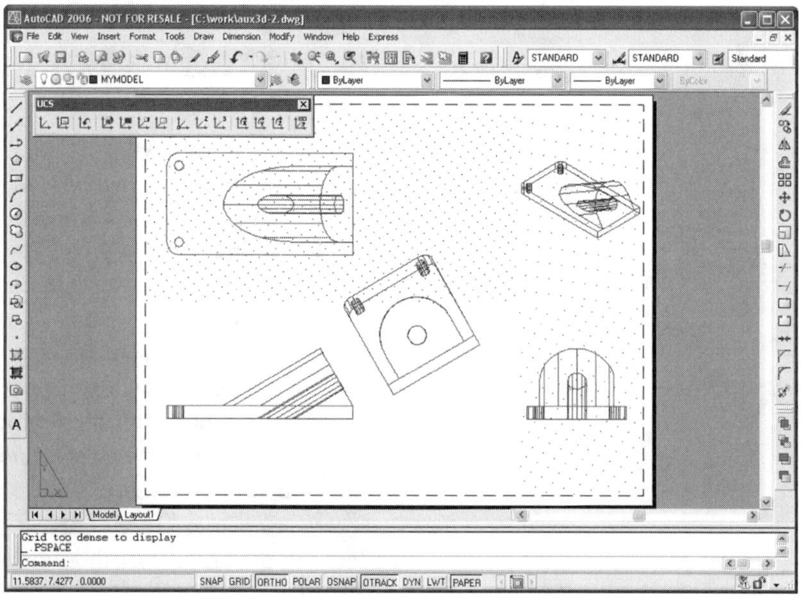

Figure 14.24

You have completed Tutorial 14. You can use the techniques you learned previously to project 2D views from the solid with hidden lines shown correctly. Dimensions can be added in paper space to complete the drawing.

Key Terms

cutting plane line	pictorial full section	section view

Key Commands

3 Point UCS	Hide	Setup Drawing (Soldraw)
3D Dynamic View (Dview)	Object UCS	Setup View (Solview)
	Section	Slice

Exercises

Use solid modeling to create the parts shown. Section the part along the vertical centerline in the front view. The letter M after an exercise means that the given dimensions are in millimeters.

14.1 High-Pressure Seal

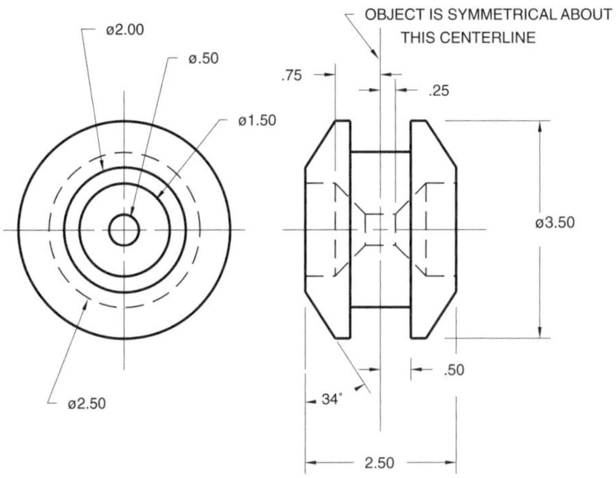

14.2 Valve Cover

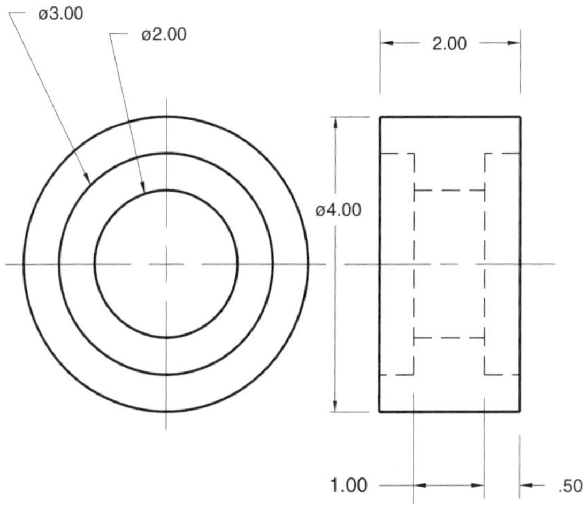

14.3M Pulley

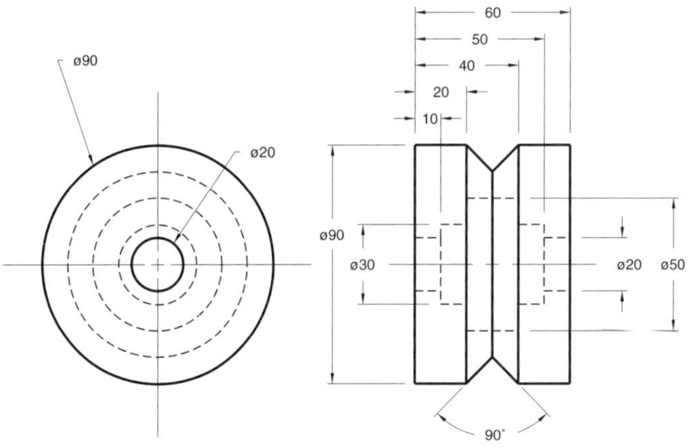

14.4 Double Cylinder

Use solid modeling to draw this object; the grid shown is 0.25 inch. Show the front view as a half section and show the corresponding cutting plane in the top view. On the same views, completely dimension the object to the nearest 0.01 inch. Include any notes that are necessary.

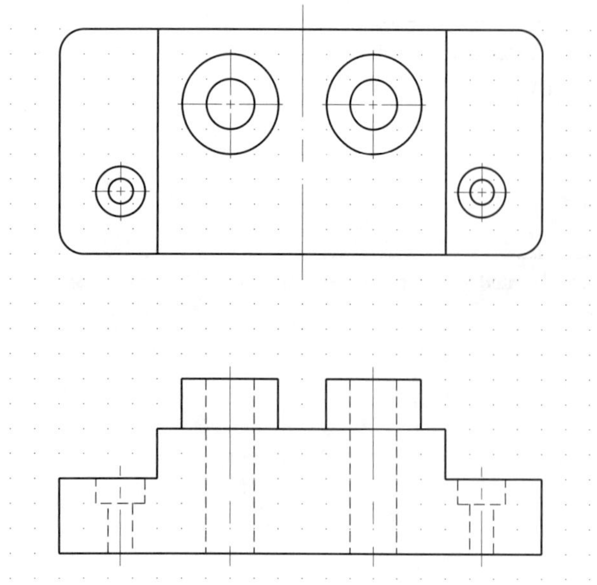

14.5 Plate

Use solid modeling to construct the top view with the cutting plane shown and show the front view in section.

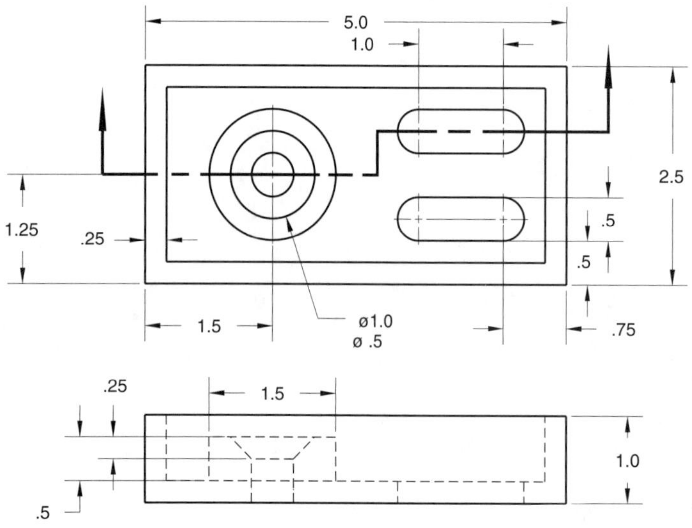

14.6 Support Bracket

Create a solid model of the object shown, then produce a plan view and full section front view. Note the alternate units in brackets; these are the dimensions in millimeters for the part.

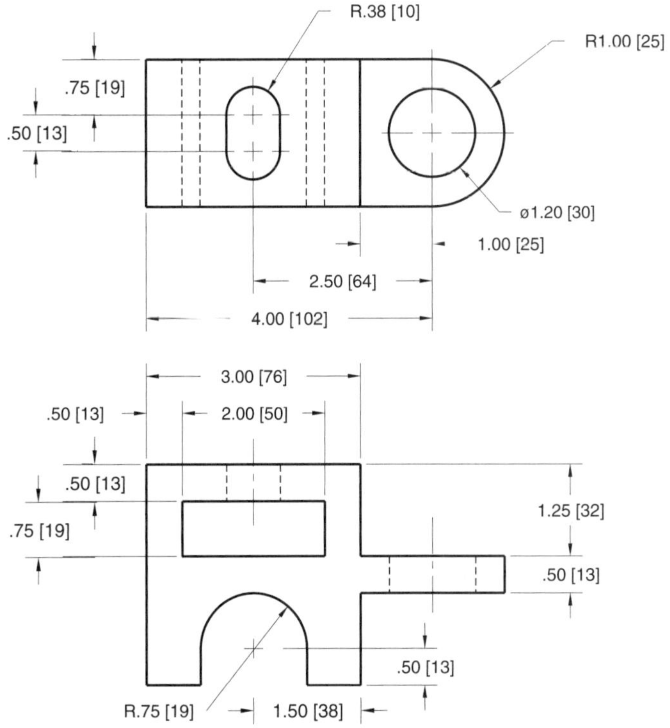

14.7 Shaft Support

Generate the given front view from your solid model and create a section view. Assume that the vertical centerline of the shaft in the front view is the cutting plane line for the section view.

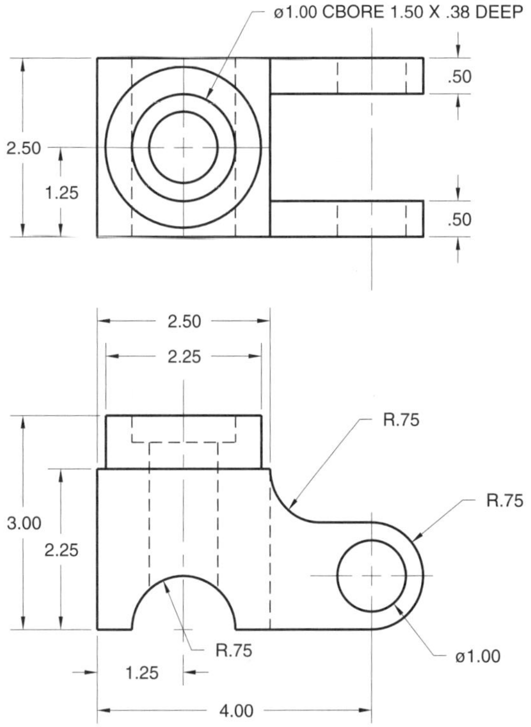

14.8 Wedge

Make a solid model based on the given views, then produce a plan view and a full-section front view. Align the sectioned front view with the plan view. Hidden lines and/or cutting planes are not needed in the plan view.

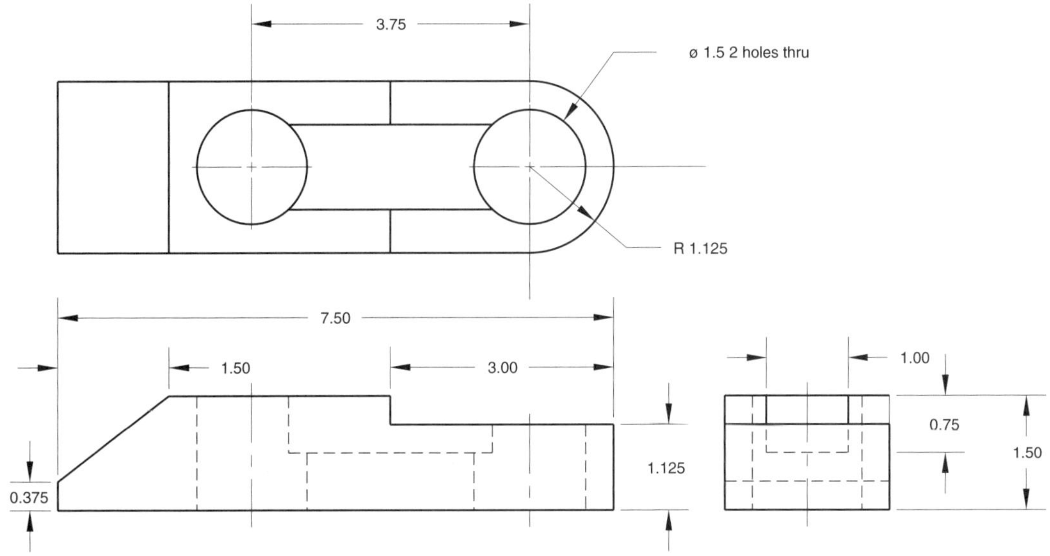

14.9M Pulley Arm

Use solid modeling to create a pictorial view like the one shown.

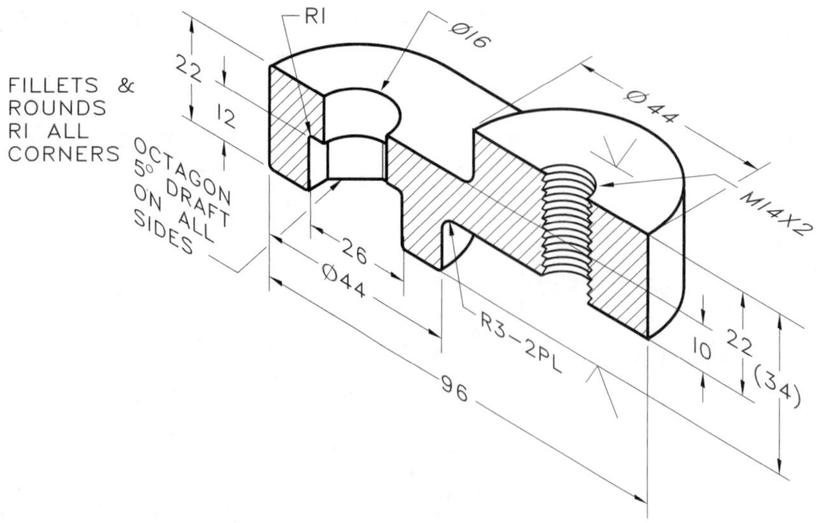

Use the 2D or solid modeling techniques you have learned in the tutorial to create an auxiliary view of the slanted surfaces for the objects below. The letter M after an exercise number means that the given dimensions are in millimeters.

14.10 Stop Block

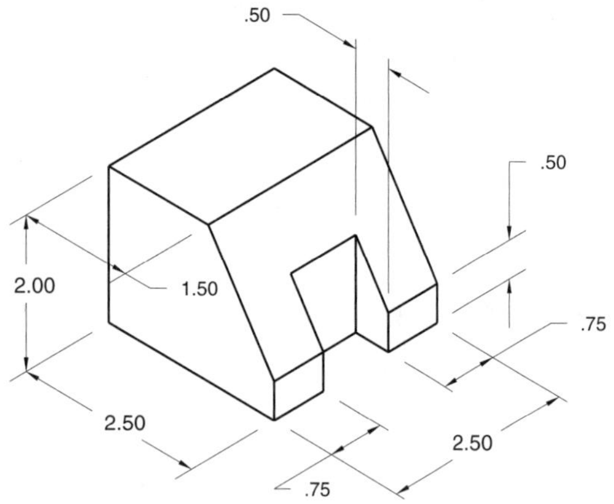

14.11 Bearing

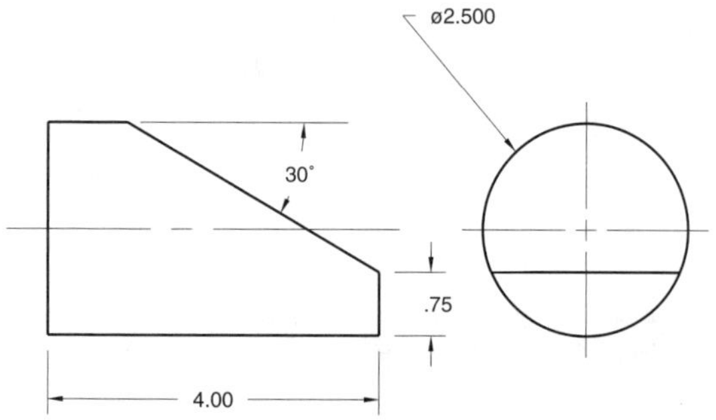

14.12 Tooling Support

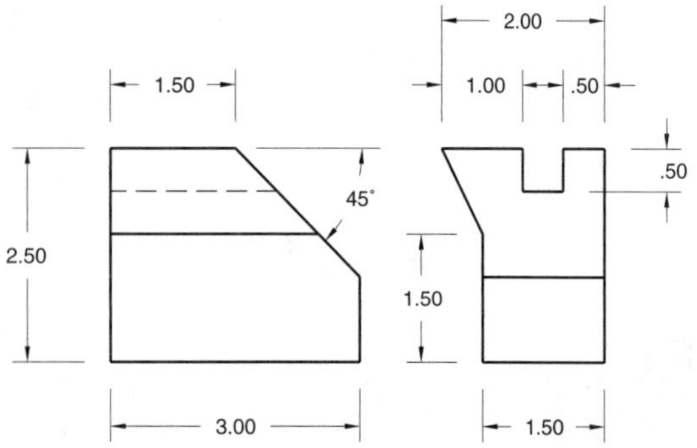

14.13M Level

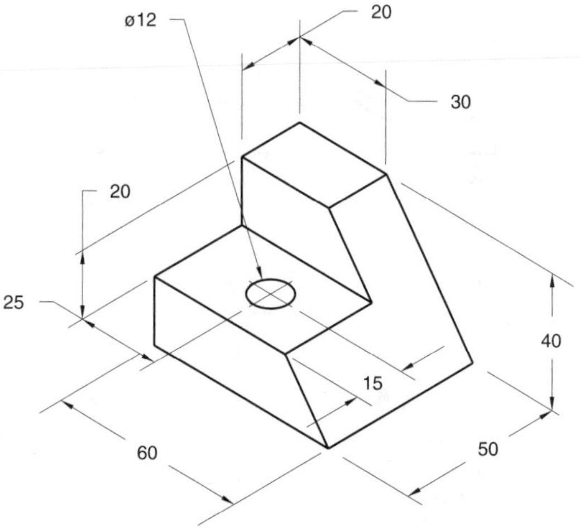

Tutorial

15 Rendering

Objectives

When you have completed this tutorial, you will be able to

1. Realistically shade a solid model or surface-modeled drawing.
2. Set up and use lighting effects.
3. Apply materials and finishes.
4. Save rendered files for use with other programs.
5. Plot a shaded drawing.

Introduction

The *Render* command allows the creation of rendered images of AutoCAD® objects that have surfaces. Rendering is the process of calculating the lighting effects, color, and shape of an object in a single two-dimensional (2D) view. A rendered view adds greatly to the appearance of the drawing. It makes the object appear more real and aids in interpretation of the object's shape, especially for those unfamiliar with engineering drawings. Rendered drawings can be used very effectively in creating presentations.

AutoCAD objects that have surfaces can be rendered. Objects that have surfaces include solid models, regions, and objects created with the AutoCAD surface modeling commands.

Rendering is a mathematically complex process. When you are rendering, the capabilities of your hardware, such as speed, amount of memory, and the resolution of the display, are particularly noticeable. The complex rendering calculations demand more of your hardware than just running the AutoCAD program, so you may notice that your system seems slower. Resolution affects not only the speed with which objects are rendered, but also the quality of the rendered appearance. Better appearance can be gained by rendering to a higher resolution and more colors; however, increased resolution and more colors take longer to render.

In this tutorial you will learn to apply materials, surface maps, and lighting to your drawing and to render views of an object. Applying a material to a surface in your drawing gives the surface its color and shininess; it is similar to painting the surface. Materials can also reflect light like a mirror or be transparent like glass. Adding a surface map is similar to adding wallpaper; surface maps are patterns or pictures that you can apply to the surface of an object. Lighting illuminates the surfaces. Lighting is a very important factor in creating the desired effect in your rendered drawing.

Starting

In this tutorial you will use Render to shade the solid model of the assembly that you created in Tutorial 13.

Launch the AutoCAD 2006 program.

Start a new drawing from the template drawing *assemb1.dwt* provided with the datafiles.

Save your drawing as ***asmshade.dwg***.

The drawing appears on your screen, as shown in Figure 15.1.

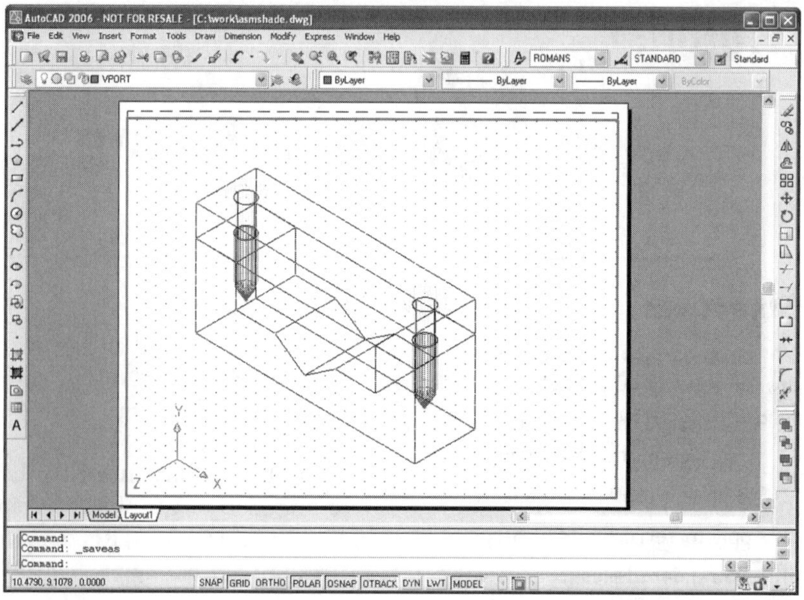

Figure 15.1

Render has its own submenu and toolbar.

Pick: **View, Render**

The Render menu selections pull down from the menu bar, as shown in Figure 15.2.

Figure 15.2

Next, you will turn on the Render toolbar so that you can use it to select commands.

Right-click: on any toolbar and pick **Render** from the list that appears

The Render toolbar appears on your screen, as shown in Figure 15.3. Pick on its title bar and, holding the pick button down, drag it to a location where it will be handy but not in the way of your drawing.

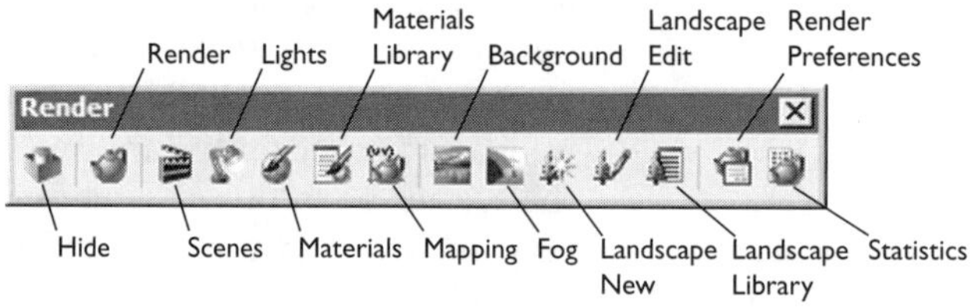

Figure 15.3

You will use Render to render the solid model so that it appears realistically shaded on your screen.

The Render Dialog Box

The Render icon opens the Render dialog box to allow you to set rendering options for your drawing.

Pick: **Render icon**

The Render dialog box appears on your screen.

Rendering Algorithms

Photo Real should be shown as the default Rendering Type. The other rendering types available are Render and Photo Raytrace. The Render rendering type uses either Gouraud or Phong shading to add smooth shading and materials, but not *surface maps* or shadows. *Gouraud shading* calculates the shading value for each vertex of a surface and then averages the color across the surface. This method is faster, but less accurate, than Phong shading, which calculates the shading value for each pixel on the surface. *Phong shading* takes longer, but produces more realistic highlights. (When you select Render as the rendering type, you can use the More Options selection to choose between the Gouraud and Phong rendering algorithms.)

The Photo Raytrace rendering type uses a *ray-tracing* algorithm to produce rendered images that have reflections, refractions, and detailed shadows. This method can produce a more realistic result, but because it is more complex, it takes more time to render. The Photo Real rendering algorithm falls somewhere between Render and Photo Raytrace in complexity. It can render objects with surface maps and shadows but not transparent materials or reflections and refractions.

Pick: **Photo Real** as the Rendering Type (if necessary)

When you are rendering, the best approach often is to start with the least complex method and a lower resolution and progress to more complex renderings. This way, while you are working out details of how to set up the lighting and surfaces for a realistic appearance, you do not have to wait a long time for a complex rendering. For this tutorial, you will use Photo Real and the settings shown in Figure 15.4.

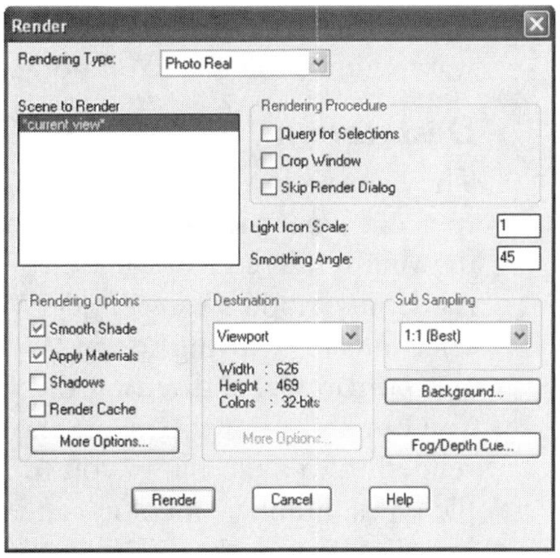

Figure 15.4

Scene to Render

A *scene* establishes a direction from which you will view the model and the lights you will use for that scene. You make and name scenes with Render's Scenes command. (You can select it by picking the Scenes icon from the Render toolbar.) To select a view for use in the Scenes command, you must first use the AutoCAD View command and save a named view. Then select the Scenes command and associate that named view with the new scene name. The default selection, current view, always appears and can be used to render the current view on your screen even if you have not created any named scenes.

Background

Picking the Background button displays the Background dialog box, which lets you select colors, bitmapped images, gradient backgrounds (that blend from one color to the next), and merge, which uses the current image as a background for your rendered image.

Fog/Depth Cue

Selecting the Fog/Depth Cue button displays the Fog dialog box, which you can use to turn on and adjust this effect. The fog cue provides visual cues about the distance that the object is from the camera, as if you were looking at the object through a fog. As the distance to the object increases, the amount of fog between you and the object increases. Fog uses a white color to obscure more of the object as it gets farther from the camera. The depth cue has the same effect as Fog, but uses black to achieve the visual cue.

Query for Selections

If you check this box, when you choose Render you are returned to your drawing screen to select the objects that you want to render. When you press ↵ to end the selection, the objects that you have selected are rendered. You do not return to the Render dialog box.

Crop Window

If you check the Crop Window box, when you choose Render you are returned to your drawing to pick a window defining the area that you want to render. Once you've defined the window, the AutoCAD software renders the area. You do not return to the Render dialog box.

Destination

The Destination pull-down list allows you to send the rendered output to a viewport, the Render Window, or a file. For now you will have the drawing rendered to your viewport. Choosing to send the output to the rendering window uses Render Window, which has its own menu bar selections for copying to the Windows Clipboard, saving the rendering as a bitmap file, and setting the resolution for the rendering window. You can also print the image shown in the rendering window. Selecting rendering to a file allows you to select more options, such as different file types, number of colors, and resolution for the rendered image saved in a file. Be sure that Viewport is selected under the heading Destination.

Rendering Options

Smooth Shade causes rounded surfaces to be shaded so that they appear round. If it is off, rounded surfaces will appear faceted (made up of flat surfaces). The Smoothing Angle value controls which surfaces are shaded as smoothed, rounded surfaces and which are shaded as flat surfaces. The value 45 smoothes all surfaces that meet with a change in angle of less than 45 degrees and considers surfaces with a greater change in angle to be flat, intersecting surfaces.

Apply Materials tells Render to apply materials to objects. Verify that Smooth Shade and Apply Materials are turned on under Rendering Options. As you have not selected any finishes, the AutoCAD Color Index (ACI) will be used in the scene that you will render, giving your shaded objects a color similar to their original AutoCAD color. Later, when you apply materials to the surfaces of the objects in your drawing, selecting Apply Materials will cause the surfaces to be rendered with the material appearance, not the AutoCAD color.

Selecting Shadows causes shadows to be generated when you use Photo Real or Photo Raytrace as the rendering algorithm. (This option is not available with the Render algorithm.) Using shadows can create drawings that have a more realistic appearance but take longer to render.

The Render Cache option allows you to Render the drawing to a cache file that it will use again. This option is useful when you will be rendering a drawing a number of times without changing any of the parameters, view positions, and the like. The AutoCAD software then uses the Rendered cache file, taking less time to calculate the Rendering.

The More Options button displays additional options that you can use in the Render Options dialog box. When you pick it, different dialog boxes appear depending on which rendering type you have selected: Photo Real, Render, or Photo Raytrace.

One of the additional options that you can set is anti-aliasing, which produces a smoother appearance on edges of surfaces by blending additional pixels along the edge with a color between the edge color and the surface color. You can set the level of anti-aliasing, which is helpful because rendering takes longer when you use high levels of anti-aliasing. Because additional pixels are blended along edges, edge lines appear thicker when you use anti-aliasing.

Options for Texture Map Sampling control the projection of bitmaps onto objects that are smaller than the bitmaps.

Another of the additional selections lets you control the shading of back surfaces of the object, called *back faces*. Picking Discard back faces causes the back surfaces to be ignored. Doing so speeds up rendering time when there are no surfaces in back of the object that you can see. You would not want to select Discard back faces when you are looking into an open box and can see the back surface. Back face normal is Negative controls the direction for the back surface of the objects. A *normal* is a vector perpendicular to a surface, used to indicate which is the top side of the surface. Selecting Back face normal is negative tells the program to shade the back surface inside a shape, such as an open box, not the outside back surface.

On your own, pick Cancel if necessary to close the Render Options dialog box and return to the Render dialog box.

Help

You can get help for the items in the Render dialog box by picking the Help button at the lower right of the dialog box.

Pick: **Help**

The Help window appears on your screen, as shown in Figure 15.5.

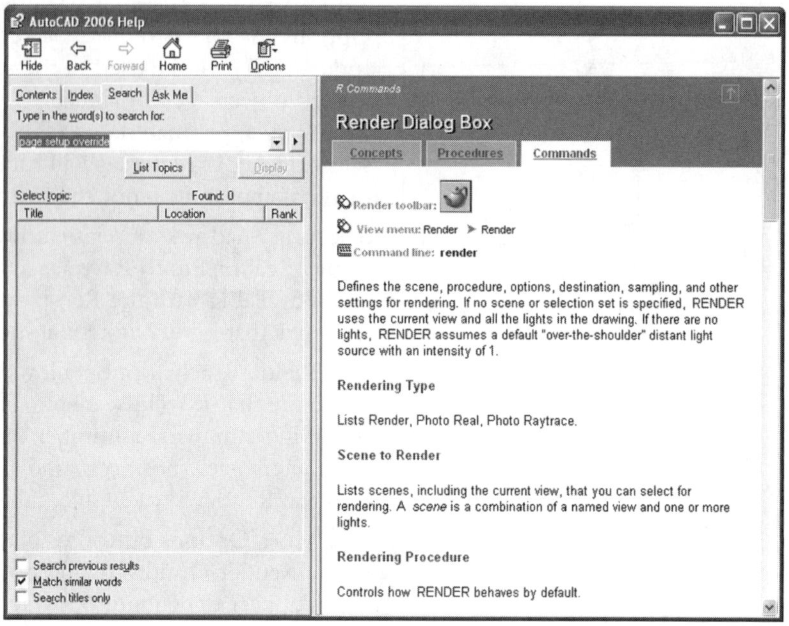

Figure 15.5

Review Tutorial 1 if necessary for directions on how to use the AutoCAD Help window. You can pick an item that is highlighted in the Help window to get help for that topic. Use the tabs and buttons above the menu bar to go to the Help Contents or to move back to the previous Help screen. Experiment with Help for the Render commands on your own. When you are finished,

Pick: **the Close button to close the Help window**

You return to the Render dialog box. If you experimented with any of the settings, return the Render dialog box to the selections shown in Figure 15.4.

Pick: **Render button**

Your drawing is rendered to the display. It should appear on your screen as shown in Figure 15.6.

Tip

You can turn off the grid before you render if you do not like its appearance.

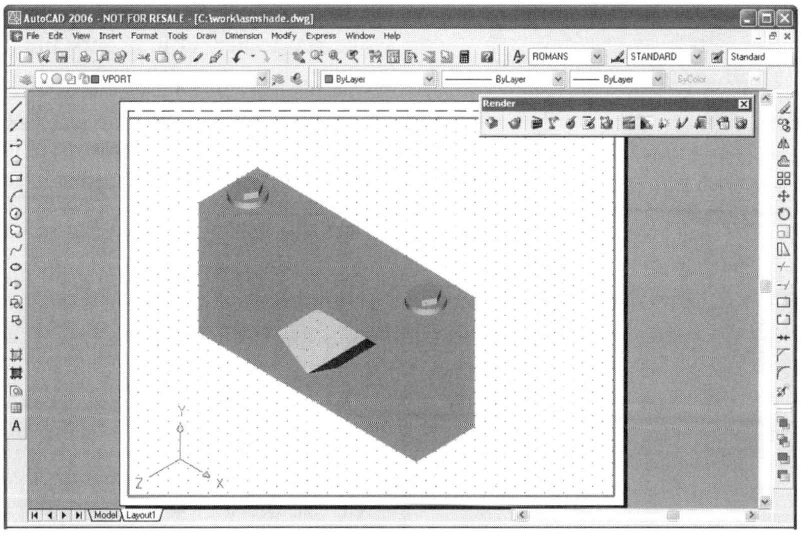

Figure 15.6

Adding Lights

Note that some of the surfaces in your rendered drawing blend into one another and are hard to see. The reason is that you have not set up any lighting in the drawing. The default lighting is ambient lighting with an intensity of 0.30, which is not very much illumination. *Ambient lighting* illuminates every surface equally, so distinguishing one surface on the object from the next is difficult. The best use for ambient lighting is to add some light to back surfaces of the object so that they do not appear entirely dark. You can improve the look of your rendered drawing by using Render to add additional lights. Lighting is very important in achieving good-looking rendering results.

Pick: **Light icon**

The Lights dialog box appears on your screen, as shown in Figure 15.7. You will use it to create lighting for your drawing.

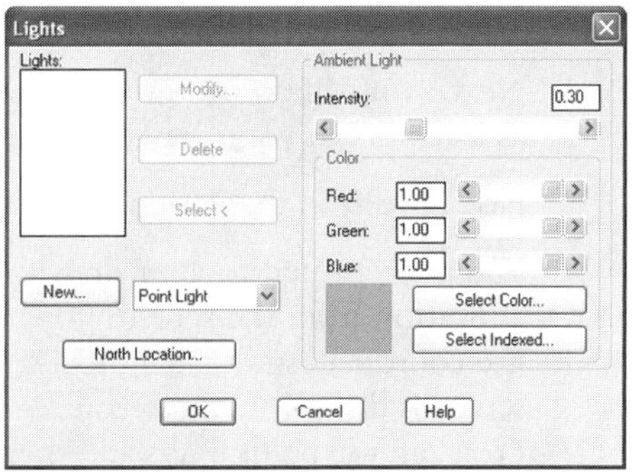

Figure 15.7

In addition to ambient light, Render allows three different types of lights. A *point light* is like a bare light bulb that casts light in every direction (i.e., it is omnidirectional). A *distant light* is like sunlight. It illuminates with equal brightness all the surfaces on which it shines. A *spotlight* highlights certain key areas and casts light only toward the selected target. Point lights and spotlights create indoor lighting effects.

Render provides a sun angle calculator to help you establish the location of the sun or distant light. This feature is particularly useful for architectural applications. You will learn how to use the sun angle calculator later in this tutorial. To see the other Lights options,

Pick: **the arrow next to Point Light to pull down the lighting choices**

The list of light types appears. Next, you will add a point light to your drawing. Because it is the default, it is already selected in the box to the right of the New button. Leave this selection set to Point Light.

To create a new light for the drawing, you will use the New button.

Pick: **New**

The New Point Light dialog box appears, as shown in Figure 15.8. You will use this dialog box to name the new light and select the features that determine its appearance, such as *intensity* (brightness), location, color, attenuation (strength), and shadows, in the drawing. You will name the light FILL because you are using it to fill the area where your object is located with more lighting.

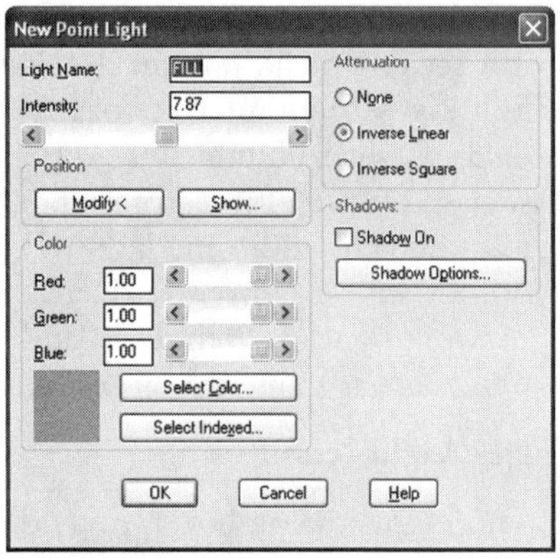

Figure 15.8

Type: **FILL** in the text box to the right of Light Name

Next, you will position the light in your drawing. Render places a block as a symbol in your drawing to represent the light.

Pick: **Modify** in the Position area of the dialog box

You are returned to your drawing. You can position the light by picking a location from the screen; however, for this example you will type in the coordinates for the light. Positioning the light by picking from the screen is difficult because you are selecting only the X- and Y-coordinates. (You can use point filters and then set the Z-location if you want. Use Help to find out more about point filters.) When specifying the coordinates for the light position, do not position it too close to the object.

Enter light location <current>: **3,5,10** ↵

You return to the New Point Light dialog box.

Pick: **Show**

The Show selection opens the Show Light Position dialog box and reveals the coordinates of the light's location. This step allows you to determine whether you made an error or to identify the coordinates for lights that you placed previously or located by picking from the screen.

Pick: **OK** (to exit the Show Light Position dialog box)

Next, you will adjust the intensity, or brightness, of the light. You can think of intensity as the wattage of a bare light bulb (a 100-watt bulb is brighter than a 60-watt bulb). You will type the value in the box provided. You can also use the slider bar to adjust the intensity of the light.

Select: **the value in the text box to the right of Intensity**
Type: **9** (or use the slider to set the value close to 9)

You can use the Color area of the dialog box to select a different color for the light. Setting the light to a yellowish color will give a warmer effect, like indoor lamps. For this example, you will leave it white.

Pick: **OK** (to exit the New Point Light dialog box)
Pick: **OK** (to exit the Lights dialog box)

Whenever you make changes that will affect the rendered appearance of your object—adding lights or materials, for instance—you need to rerender your drawing. You are now ready to use the Render command to see the effect of adding the point light to your drawing.

Pick: **Render icon**

The Render dialog box appears on your screen. Be sure that the options you set earlier are still current: Rendering Type should be Photo Real, Smooth Shading and Apply Materials should be on, and Destination should be Viewport. When you have verified these selections,

Pick: **Render button**

The added lighting should improve the appearance of your rendered drawing on the screen so that it looks like Figure 15.9.

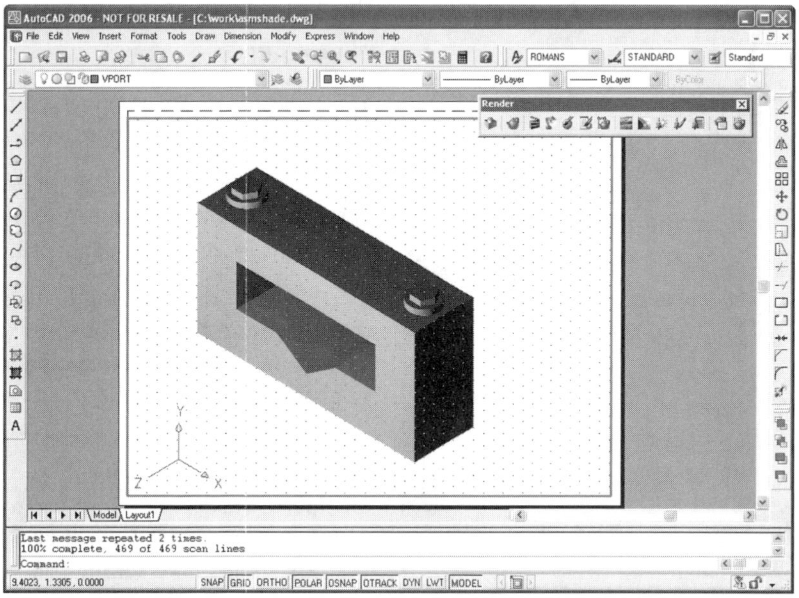

Figure 15.9

The right surface of the object is still not very well lit; not much light is striking that surface. Next, you will add a spotlight behind the object to light that surface and provide highlights in the drawing. You will use the Lights dialog box again to add a new light.

Pick: **Light icon**
Pick: **on the name Point Light and from the list that appears,**
Pick: **Spotlight**
Pick: **New**

The New Spotlight dialog box appears on your screen. You will use it to name and select the attributes for the spotlight, so that it appears as shown in Figure 15.10.

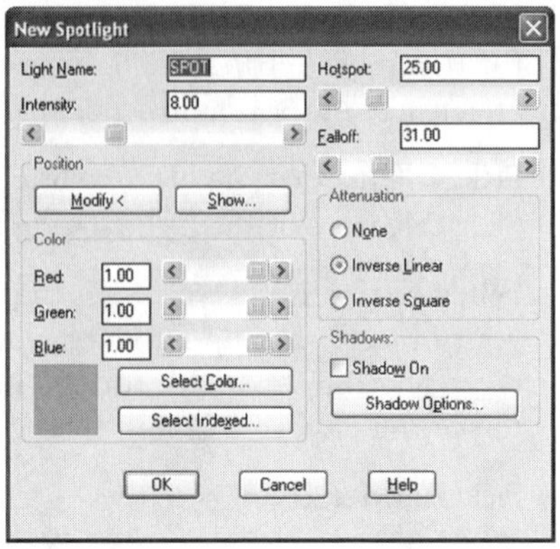

Figure 15.10

Type: **SPOT** in the text box to the right of Light Name
Set the intensity for the spotlight by moving the scroll bar to enter a value near 8 in the box to the right of Intensity.

Now you are ready to position the light in your drawing. When positioning a spotlight, you first specify the target toward which it will point. Then you give the location of the light. In the Position area of the dialog box,

Pick: **Modify**

You will press ↵ to accept the current location for the target (near the center of the object), then type in the location for the light at the next prompt:

Enter light target <current>: ↵
Enter light location <current>: **10,6,–6** ↵

The New Spotlight dialog box returns to your screen. Next, you will set the falloff and hotspot for the spotlight. *Falloff* is the angle of the cone of light from the spotlight. *Hotspot* is the angle of the cone of light for the brightest area of the beam. The angles for the falloff and hotspot must be between 0° and 160°. Render won't let you set Hotspot to a greater value than Falloff.

On your own, use the slider bar to set the value for **Hotspot to 25.00** and the value for **Falloff to 31.00**. When you are finished, your dialog box should have settings similar to those shown in Figure 15.10.

Pick: **OK** to exit the New Spotlight dialog box
Pick: **OK** to exit the Lights dialog box

You return to the AutoCAD drawing editor. You will use the Render dialog box to render your drawing again to see the effect of adding the spotlight to the drawing.

Pick: **Render icon**

Check the settings in the dialog box to be sure that they are the same ones that appear in Figure 15.4. Then,

Pick: **Render button**

The drawing is rendered to your screen and should be similar to Figure 15.11. Note the bright area of the spotlight beam, which you set using Hotspot. The size of the entire circle of light from the spotlight is determined by the setting you entered for Falloff.

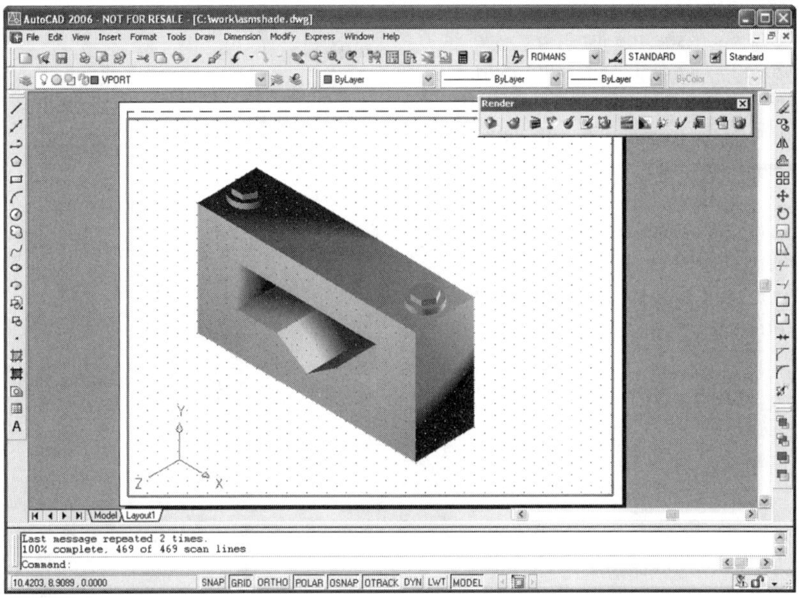

Figure 15.11

Choosing Materials

You can also improve your rendered drawing by selecting or creating realistic-looking *materials* for the objects in it. You can either use the materials that are provided in the Materials Library or create your own materials with Render. As with lights, a block is added to the drawing to represent materials. To add materials,

Pick: **Materials icon**

The Materials dialog box appears on your screen, as shown in Figure 15.12.

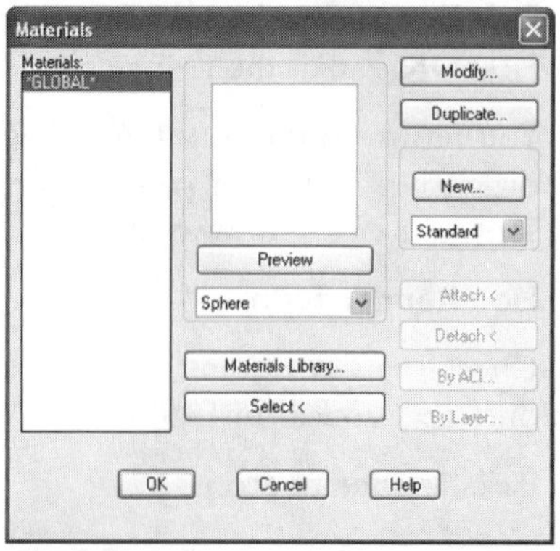

Figure 15.12

You will use the Materials dialog box to select materials from the Materials Library for the objects in your drawing. A single block or solid object in the drawing can have only one material assigned. This limitation usually isn't a problem in engineering drawings because you will typically make each part in an assembly a separate object or block in the drawing. Do not use Boolean operators to join parts to which you want to assign different materials.

To select from the library of premade materials,

Pick: **Materials Library** from the lower center of the dialog box

Warning

If you don't see the list of materials shown in Figure 15.13, you may not have the path set correctly to tell the AutoCAD software where to look for texture files. To change the path, pick Tools, Options. Use the Files tab of the dialog box to set the path to where your texture files are stored. Make sure that you have loaded the materials files.

The Materials Library dialog box shown in Figure 15.13 appears on your screen. You will choose materials for your assembly drawing from the list of materials shown at the right in the dialog box.

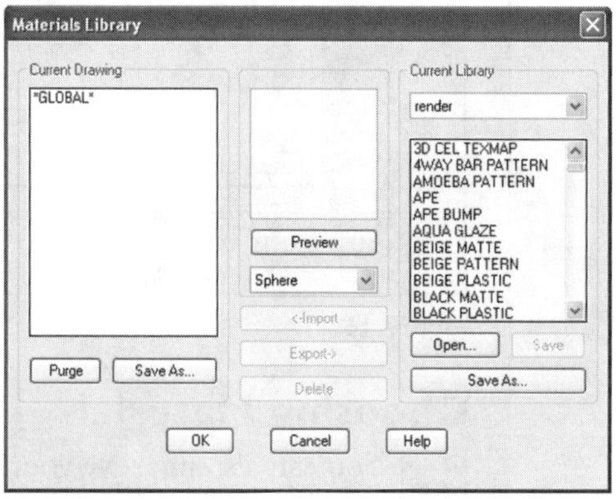

Figure 15.13

Use the scroll bar or pick on the arrows to scroll through the list of materials until you see the selection BRASS VALLEY, which you will use for the washers in the assembly drawing.

Pick: **BRASS VALLEY** so that it becomes highlighted

Many of the materials dialog boxes allow you to preview the selection to see approximately what the material will look like. This preview saves you time if you decide not to use the particular material once you see it or if your system is not capable of displaying it. Remember, rendering a complex drawing can be time consuming. Use the Preview function to see what different materials look like.

Pick: **Preview**

The material that you selected is applied to a spherical shape in the Preview box, as shown in Figure 15.14.

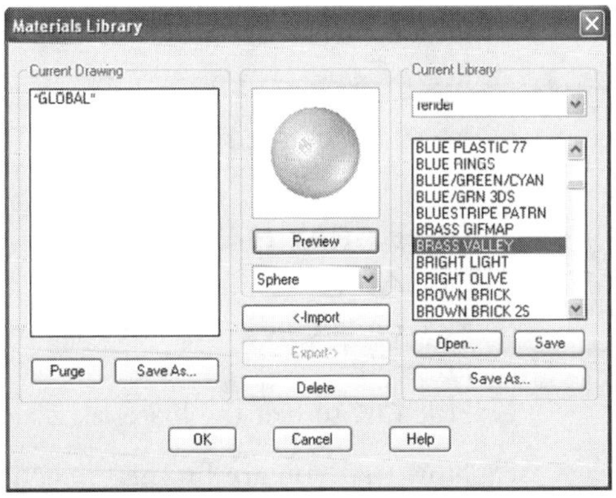

Figure 15.14

Pick: **Sphere selection shown below the Preview button and change it to Cube**
Pick: **Preview**
Return the selection to **Sphere** on your own.

Once you have previewed the materials, you will import BRASS VALLEY so that it is available for use in your drawing. Note that you can preview only one material at a time but that you can select several materials to import at the same time.

Pick: **Import**

The selected material is shown in the list at the left of the dialog box. Now you are ready to select another material.

Pick: **to highlight the materials GRAY MATTE and GRAY SEMIGLOSS**
Pick: **Import**

Now those materials are available for use in the current drawing. The names are added to the list at the left. When you have finished importing the materials,

Pick: **OK** to exit the Materials Library dialog box

You return to the Materials dialog box, where you will attach the materials to the objects in your drawing.

Select: **BRASS VALLEY** from the Materials list at the left of the dialog box
Pick: **Attach** at the right of the dialog box

You are returned to your drawing to select the objects, in this case the two washers. If you accidentally select something else, use the Select Remove option to remove it from the selection set or use Detach later in the dialog box to detach the wrong material. If you have trouble selecting, try to pick on an edge, not in the center of an object, or use implied Windowing.

Pick: **on the edge of each of the two washers**
Press: ↵

The Materials dialog box returns to your screen so that you can continue attaching materials.

Select: **GRAY SEMIGLOSS**
Pick: **Attach**
Pick: **on the edge of the two screws**
Press: ↵

Next, attach the material GRAY MATTE to the base and cover of the assembly.

Select: **GRAY MATTE**
Pick: **Attach**
Pick: **on the edge of the base and the cover**
Press: ↵
Pick: **OK** to exit the Materials dialog box

Now that you are finished selecting the materials, you will render the drawing again to view the results of the changes that you made.

Pick: **Render icon**

Accept the same defaults that you used previously.

Pick: **Render button**

Your drawing should now show the new materials. Your screen should look like Figure 15.15.

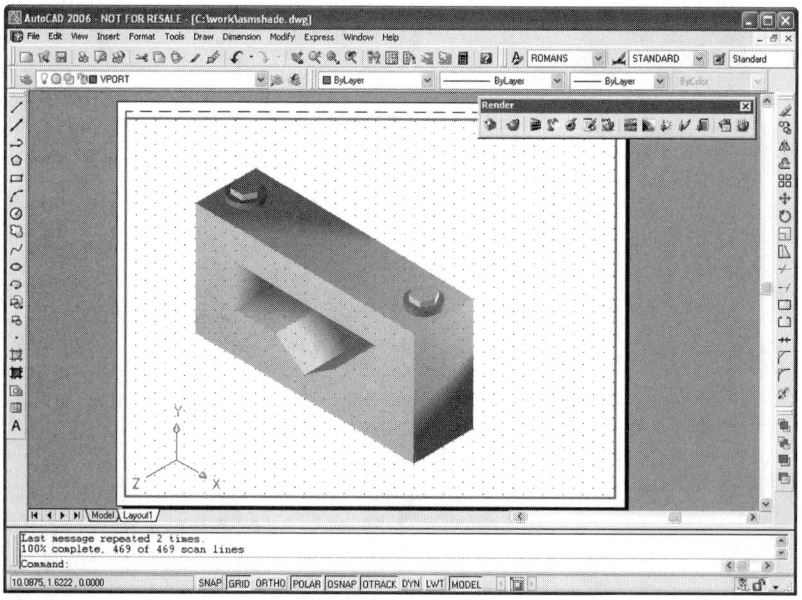

Figure 15.15

You can also use Render to create your own materials. Next, you will create a material that looks like steel to use for the base and cover of the assembly.

Pick: **Materials icon**

When the Materials dialog box appears,

Pick: **New** from the right-hand side of the dialog box

The New Standard Material dialog box shown in Figure 15.16 appears on your screen.

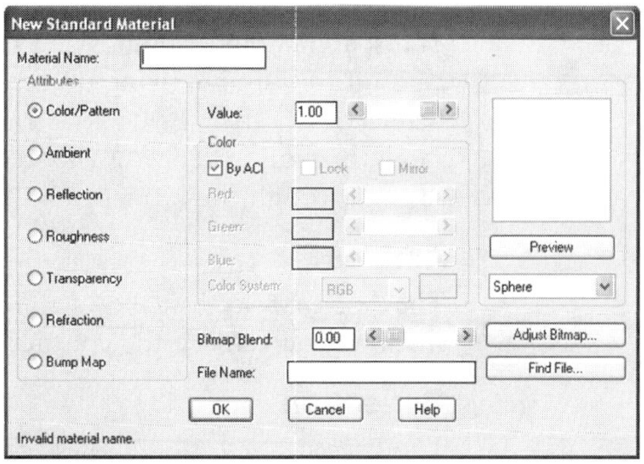

Figure 15.16

Type: **STEEL** in the text box to the right of Material Name

At the left in the New Standard Material dialog box are the various qualities, or material attributes: Color/Pattern, Ambient, Reflection, Roughness, Transparency, Refraction, and Bump Map. These are the attributes that you can control to create materials with different appearances. In general, these qualities indicate how the surface or material responds when light strikes it. To change attributes, pick in the circle to the left of the attribute for which you want to set the values.

Color/Pattern

The Color/Pattern selection determines the color for the material. The default selection for color is By ACI (AutoCAD Color Index), which results in the object being rendered in the color assigned to its lines in the AutoCAD model. You saw this when you rendered the assembly for the first time and the objects were shown in the original layer colors.

Pick: **to unselect By ACI in the Color area**

Now you can select other Color options. Near the bottom of the Color area the selection RGB appears, which represents red, green, and blue, the primary colors of light.

On your own, use the slider bars in that section of the dialog box to set the amount of each color of light to use to make up the material color. As you move the slider bars, the resulting color is shown in the empty box at the bottom of the Color area. It is called the color swatch.

Keep in mind that colors on your computer screen are made of the primary colors of light (red, green, and blue), not the primary colors of pigment (red, blue, and yellow) that you may be used to using. Changing the selection at the bottom of the Color area from RGB to HLS (hue, lightness, and saturation) lets you use the same slider bars to define the color in terms of these qualities instead of RGB.

When you have changed the color slightly,

Pick: **Preview**

In addition, you can use a bitmap (a pattern or picture), such as a scanned image or drawing created with a paint-style program, instead of just solid color. To do so, in the lower center area of the dialog box, type the name of a bitmap file in the text box to the right of File Name. You can use bitmaps with the selections Color/Pattern, Reflectivity, Transparency, and Bump Map. The Bitmap Blend value determines the amount of the underlying object color that shows through the bitmap. Values of less than 1.00 allow some of the underlying object color to show through. The lower the value, the more the underlying color shows through the bitmap.

Ambient

The *Ambient* selection allows you to set the color for the object's shadow. You can use the color controls just discussed.

Reflection

The *Reflection* selection allows you to adjust the color of the material's reflective highlight. When you select ray tracing, you can specify the value for the material's reflectivity from 0, where it does not reflect any light, to 1, where it is perfectly reflective, like a mirror.

Roughness

The *Roughness* selection lets you specify the surface roughness of the material. Roughness is also related to reflectivity. The less rough the surface is, the more reflective it will be. Change the value and use Preview to see how roughness changes the size of the material's highlight.

Transparency

The settings for *transparency* allow you to make objects that are clear, like glass, or somewhat clear, like colored liquids. Keep in mind that completely transparent objects, which you can't even see in the drawing when they are rendered, still take time to render.

Refraction

The *Refraction* control is used only with transparent objects. Refraction is the amount that light is bent when entering and leaving a transparent object. You must use the Photo Raytrace rendering algorithm in order to see the effect of this setting. *Ray tracing* uses a more sophisticated rendering algorithm to generate reflections, refractions, and detailed shadows. In ray tracing, the result is calculated for each "ray" of light striking the object. This produces very realistic and detailed effects, but increases the complexity and rendering time.

Bump Map

The Bump Map selection allows you to enter the file name of a bump map. *Bump maps* convert the color intensity or grayscale information to heights to give the appearance that features are raised above the surface, like embossed letters.

Next, you will set the attributes for the material steel that you are going to create.

On your own, be sure that Color/Pattern is selected and that By ACI is turned off.

Use the slider bars to adjust the colors for Red, Green, and Blue so that Red and Green are each set to a value of 0.88 and Blue is set to a value of 0.92.

Note how the color swatch changes as you move the slider bars. The resulting color should be gray.

Preview the result on your own.

Next, you will make the surface somewhat reflective and assign a small value for surface roughness so that the material will look like steel.

Pick: **Reflection**
Use the slider bar to set the value for Reflection to 0.65.
Pick: **Roughness**
Set the value for Roughness to 0.30.

To see the effects of your selections on the material being created,

Pick: **Preview**

Your screen should be similar to Figure 15.17.

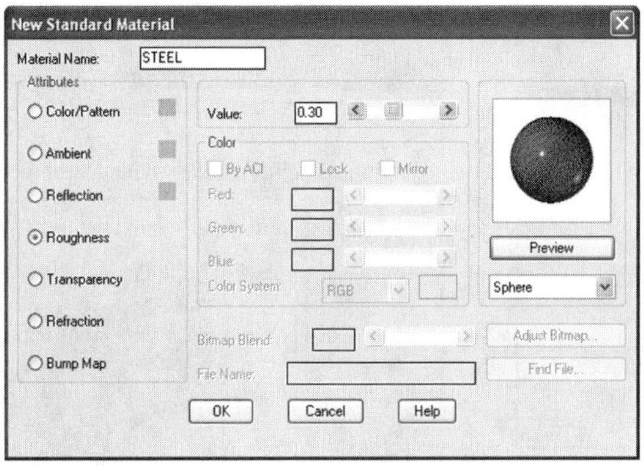

Figure 15.17

Pick: **OK** to exit the New Standard Material dialog box

You return to the Materials dialog box. Next, you will attach this material to the base and cover in the assembly drawing in place of GRAY MATTE.

Pick: **STEEL**
Pick: **Attach**
On your own, attach the material to the base and cover.

When you have attached the material,

Pick: **OK** (to exit the dialog box)
Pick: **Render icon**
Pick: **Render button**

Adjusting Mapping

When bitmaps or materials that use bitmapped patterns are applied to surfaces in your drawing, you can control the type of mapping, coordinates, scale, repeat, and other aspects of the maps' appearance. Next, you will apply a bitmapped material to the base of the assembly to see these effects, then use Mapping to adjust them.

Warning

The AutoCAD software keeps track of the location (path) for the textures and bitmapped materials. If your options do not show this location correctly for where your files are stored, you will not be able to see materials that contain textures (bitmaps) correctly. To check this,

Pick: **Tools, Options**

The Options dialog box appears on your screen as shown in Figure 15.18. The Texture Maps Search Path should be set to the location where your texture map files are stored. You may need assistance from your network administrator or computer support person to determine the correct location.

Pick: **OK**

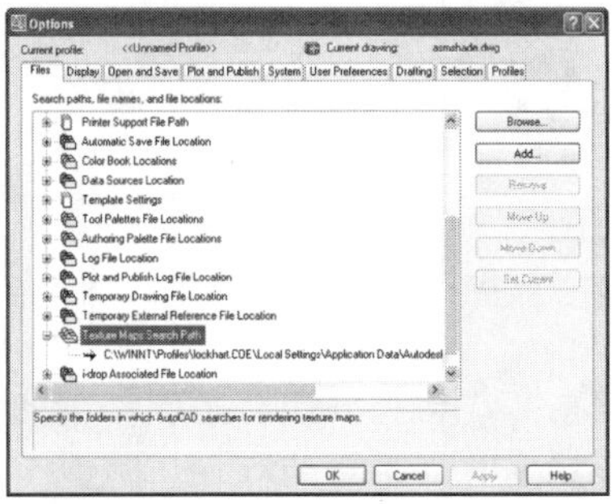

Figure 15.18

Tip

Double-clicking on a material name in the Materials dialog box brings up the dialog box so you can edit its appearance.

Pick: **Materials icon**
Pick: **Materials Library**
Pick: **V Pattern** (from the list of materials at the right)
Pick: **Import**
Pick: **OK** (to exit the Materials Library dialog box)
Pick: **Attach**
Select objects to attach "V PATTERN" to: **pick the base** ↵
Pick: **OK** (to exit the Materials dialog box)

The V Pattern material is attached to the base part of the drawing. Render the current scene to the viewport, but this time choose Photo Raytrace as the rendering type.

Pick: **Render icon**
Pick: **Photo Raytrace** (from the pull-down menu to the right of Rendering Type)
Pick: **Render**

Your screen should look like Figure 15.19. If the V Pattern material doesn't show correctly, pick Tools, Options and check to see that your Texture Map Search Path is set correctly.

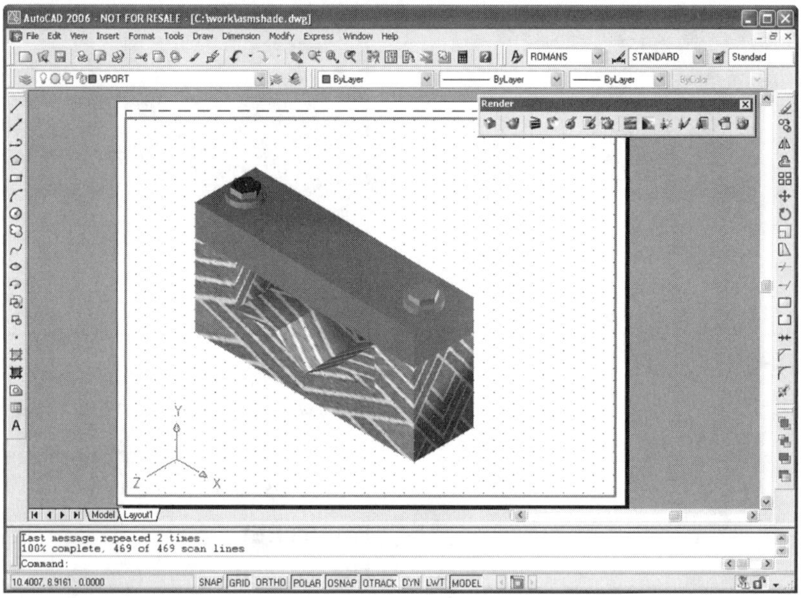

Figure 15.19

Pick: **Mapping icon**

The Setuv command is echoed at the command prompt, followed by the prompt,

Select objects: **pick the base**
Select objects: ↵

The Mapping dialog box appears on your screen, as shown in Figure 15.19. To preview the mapping for the Planar method of projection, which is currently selected,

Pick: **Preview**

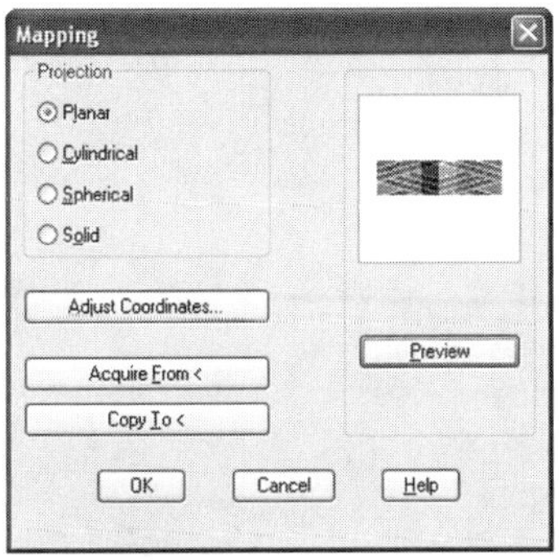

Figure 15.20

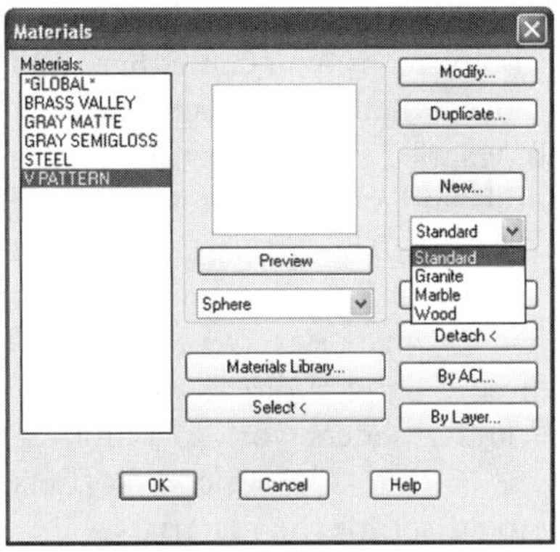

Figure 15.21

The preview of the bitmapped material in planar projection is shown in the upper right of the dialog box in Figure 15.20.

To adjust the mapping for a cylindrical or spherical object, you can pick the Cylindrical, Spherical, or Solid radio buttons from the left of the dialog box.

Try each one on your own and then use Preview to see the effect of that projection method.

In general, you would use cylindrical mapping for cylindrical objects, spherical mapping for spherical objects, and so on.

As the base is composed of plane surfaces, return the selection to Planar.

Solid mapping is a special type that you should use to represent granite, marble, and wood solid materials. Figure 15.21 shows the Materials dialog box with the list of these materials pulled down. Picking one of these materials and then the New button from the Materials dialog box displays a dialog box that you can use to create that type of custom material.

If you experimented with the solid materials, return to the Mapping dialog box on your own.

Next, you will adjust the mapping coordinates to change the direction for the pattern.

Pick: **Adjust Coordinates**

The Adjust Planar Coordinates dialog box appears on your screen.

Pick: **WCS XZ Plane**

Pick: **Preview**

The preview of the object with the pattern applied in the XZ-direction appears, as shown in Figure 15.22.

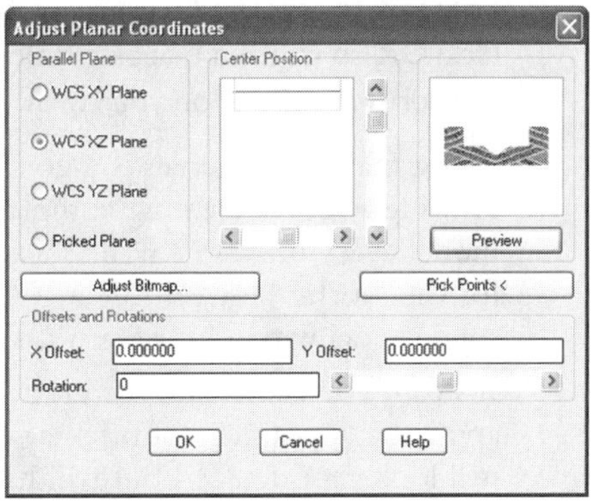

Figure 15.22

Next, you will change the scale of the pattern.

Pick: **Adjust Bitmap**

The Adjust Object Bitmap Placement dialog box appears on your screen. On your own, use it to change the scale to 2.5 and preview the result, shown in Figure 15.23.

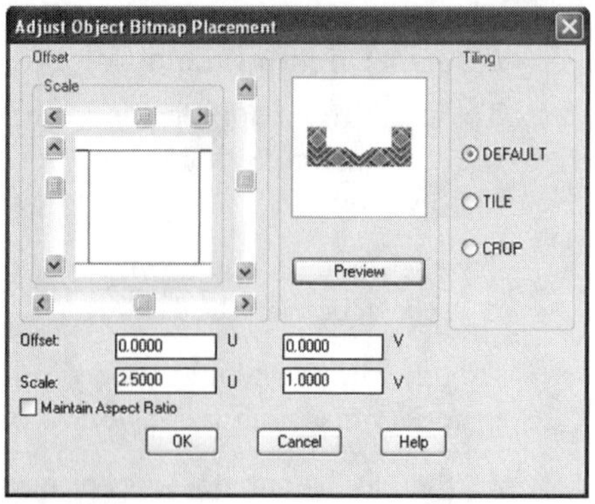

Figure 15.23

In addition to changing its scale, you can select the radio buttons at the right of the dialog box to tile or crop the bitmapped image. Tiling causes it to repeat its pattern across the object. Crop uses the bitmapped image like a decal: It appears only at the single location specified by the offsets. When you create materials that use bitmaps, you can either tile or crop them. The DEFAULT selection uses whatever you set for the material as a whole when you created it. Mapped coordinates are given relative to the U- and V-directions. The U- and V-coordinates are equivalent to X- and Y-coordinates for the map. The letters U and V are used to indicate that they are part of a local coordinate system for the map that is independent of the X- and Y-coordinate system of the drawing. You specify offset and scale using these U- and V-directions. When you select Maintain Aspect Ratio, the U and V sliders work as a unit to maintain the proportion of the bitmapped pattern. The scale and offsets set in this dialog box are additive to the ones set for the material as a whole. The offset is added to the materials offset, and the scale is multiplied by the scale for the material. To exit the dialog box,

Pick: **OK**
Pick: **OK** to exit the Adjust Planar Coordinates dialog box
Pick: **OK** to exit the Mapping dialog box
Render the drawing on your own.

Using mapped materials is a good way to add detail to your rendered drawing without creating complex models. For example, you could model every brick in a wall as a separate solid and create a different solid for the mortar between them. Doing so would create a very complex solid model with a lot of vertices.

Instead, you can create the entire wall as a single flat surface and then apply the appearance of brick to it as a bitmapped pattern. The drawing will look very detailed but will have far fewer vertices and take less file space than the previous example. You can also combine bitmaps and bump maps in the same drawing to give a raised appearance to parts of the material.

Rendering to a File

Rendering your drawing to a file allows you to use it in other programs. For example, you can render your drawing to a Windows metafile format and paste it into various Windows applications.

Pick: **Render icon**

Using the Destination area,

Pick: on **Viewport** to pull down the selection list
Pick: **File**
Pick: **More Options** below Destination

The File Output Configuration dialog box appears on your screen, as shown in Figure 15.24. You can use the selection at its upper left to save your drawing in many different file formats, among them TGA (TARGA), TIFF, Postscript, PCX, and BMP. If you have a paint-style program that uses one of these formats, you may be able to edit and print the saved image file. You can often also use these formats to insert the drawing in a word processing program. You can set the ***resolution*** for the output file by using the selection below File Type, where you see 640 × 480 (VGA) and the number of colors for the resulting file. You do not need to change the resolution.

Pick: **TIFF** as the File Type
Pick: **OK**

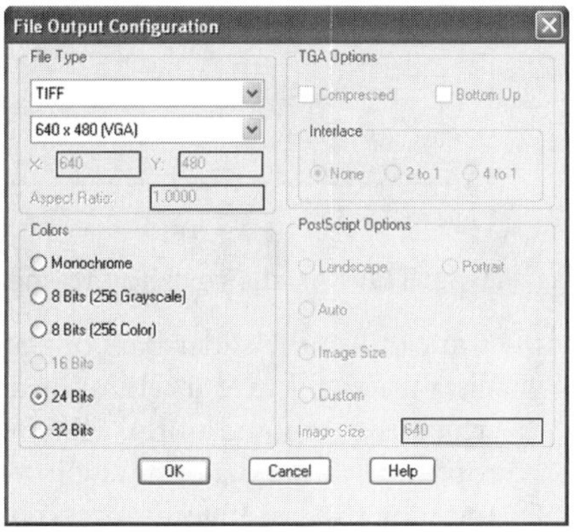

Figure 15.24

The file will be saved with the extension *.tif* to your working directory. To render to the file,

Pick: **Render button**

Use the Rendering File dialog box that appears to specify the name and directory in which to save the file.

On your own, try importing your rendered drawing as a graphic into your word processor. Then return to your AutoCAD drawing session.

Using the Sun Angle Calculator

The sun angle calculator is particularly useful in architectural drawings for showing the different effects that sunlight has on the rendered scene at different times of the day and year. You can use the sun angle calculator to obtain these effects easily, instead of going through the laborious process of looking up the information in tables and adding the correct lighting effects to your drawing. You can even set the geographic location by picking it from the map. The sun will be added as a distant light in your rendered drawing, so

Pick: **Light icon**

Pick: **Distant Light** (from the list that pulls down to the right of New)

Pick: **New**

The New Distant Light dialog box shown in Figure 15.25 appears on your screen.

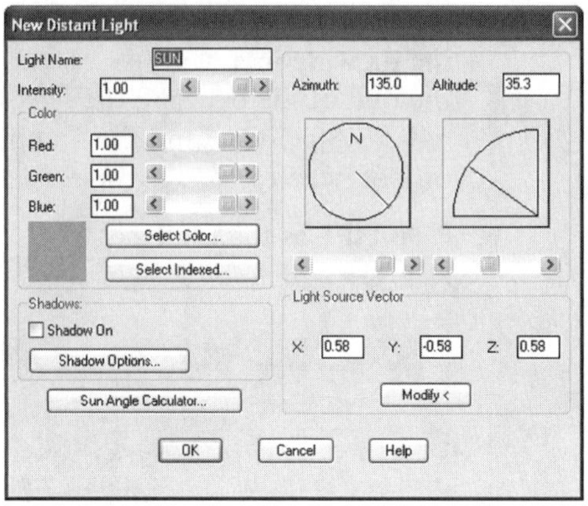

Figure 15.25

Type: **SUN** (in the text box to the right of Name)

You can use the slider bars or the color wheel to set the color for the distant light. Leave it white for now, as the sun usually casts white light, which is composed of the full spectrum of light colors. The area at the top right of the dialog box allows you to specify the azimuth and altitude for the sun if you want to do so. You can use the Sun Angle Calculator button at the bottom left of the dialog box and let it determine these values for you. You will do that now.

Pick: **Sun Angle Calculator**

The Sun Angle Calculator dialog box appears on your screen. You can use it to specify the date, time of day, time zone, latitude, and longitude to determine the angle of the sun.

On your own, set the date to December 20 (12/20) and the clock time to 6:00 hours (6 a.m.) MST. Turn Daylight Savings on by picking in the box to its left so that a check is displayed. Note that the azimuth and altitude settings change as you make selections.

When you are finished, the dialog box should look like Figure 15.26.

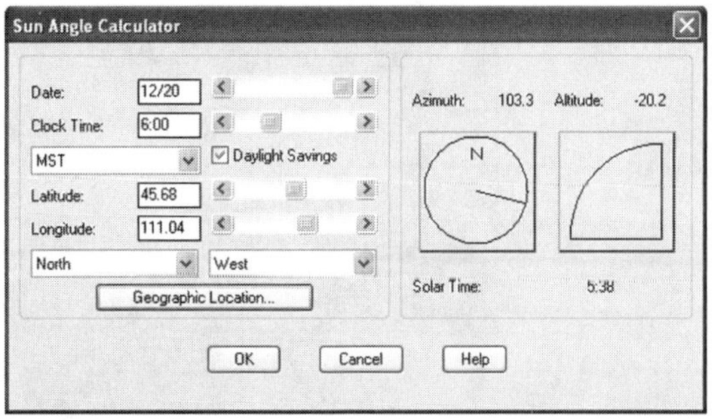

Figure 15.26

Next, you will specify the geographic location because it works with the date and time of day to determine the angle of the sun.

Pick: **Geographic Location**

The Geographic Location dialog box shown in Figure 15.27 appears on your screen.

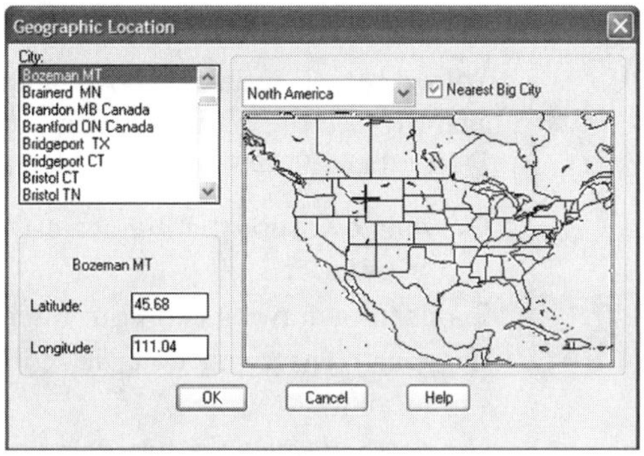

Figure 15.27

Move the cursor over the map until it is positioned as shown in Figure 15.27 and press the pick button.

Note that Bozeman, MT (cultural Mecca and center of the universe) appears as the Nearest Big City in the list at the left. Below, the latitude and longitude for Bozeman are displayed. You can also scroll down the list of cities to make a selection. Note the words North America at the upper left of the map area.

Pick: **on the words North America**

A list of the other continents pulls down, as shown in Figure 15.28. You can use the scroll bar to select from the other continents. The major cities of other continents are stored in the database, and you can select them by picking from the map or by scrolling down the list of cities.

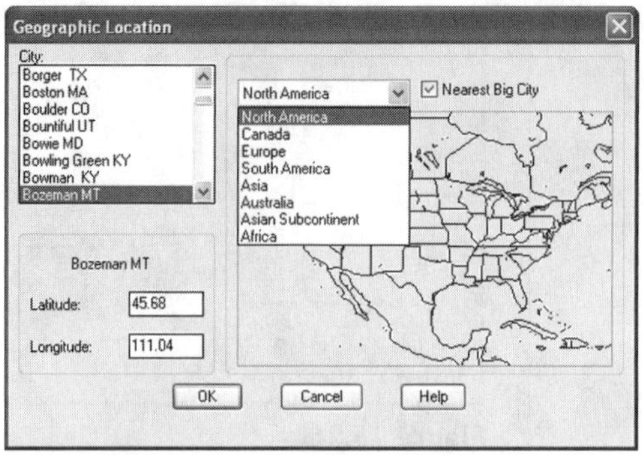

Figure 15.28

Do not change the continent selection at this time. Leave it set to North America.

Pick: **OK** to exit the Geographic Location dialog box
Pick: **OK** to exit the Sun Angle Calculator dialog box
Pick: **OK** to exit the New Distant Light dialog box
Pick: **OK** to exit the Lights dialog box

Your drawing returns to the screen. Now, you will render the drawing again to see the part as though the sun were shining on it at 6 a.m. on December 20 in Bozeman, Montana.

On your own, use the Render dialog box and set the Destination back to **Viewport**.
Render the drawing and note the effect of the sunlight.
On your own, select the Light icon and pick **SUN** as the light you want to modify.
Use the Sun Angle Calculator to change the time of day to **4 p.m.** (The time-of-day clock is a 24-hour clock.)
Render the drawing again and note the change.

Although this assembly is not an architectural drawing, you can imagine what a great advantage the sun angle calculator is for architectural uses. You can also use it to evaluate the suitability of a site for solar power and other types of heat transfer analysis.

Adding Backgrounds

You can add a background to your rendering by using the Background icon on the Render toolbar. Backgrounds can be solid colors, gradient colors (which blend one to three colors), images (bitmaps), or the current AutoCAD image (selected using Merge).

Pick: **Background icon**

You will set up the Background dialog box so that it looks like Figure 15.29. You will use it to select an image as the background.

Pick: **Image** radio button in the top row
Pick: **Find File** button in the lower left of the dialog box

Use the dialog box that appears to select the file to be used as the background image. Be sure to change the file type to **.tga*, since it defaults to **.bmp*.

Pick: ***cloud.tga***

Pick: **Open** to return to the Background dialog box

You can adjust the appearance of the bitmap, as you did earlier in this tutorial, by picking Adjust Bitmap. Environment lets you use an image that Render maps onto a sphere surrounding your drawing. This environment is then reflected onto other objects when you use reflective and refractive materials in your drawing. When you use the Photo Real renderer, reflective objects mirror the background image. When you use the Raytrace renderer, the environment is raytraced.

Tip

Make sure to return the selection to Viewport for the Render dialog box destination area.

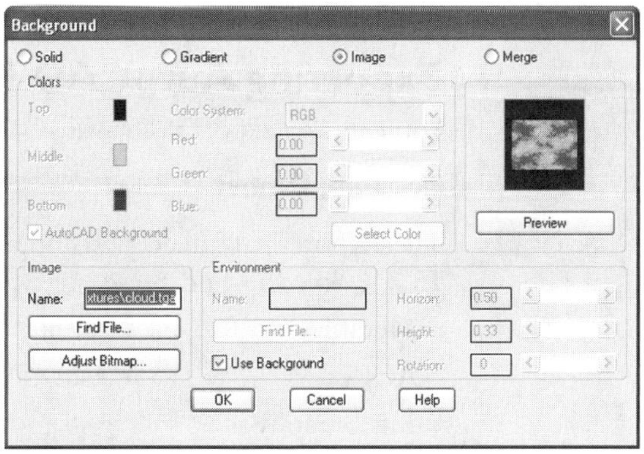

Figure 15.29

Pick: **OK** (to exit the Background dialog box)

On your own, render your drawing to show the cloud background.

Next, you will restore the world coordinate system so that the landscape objects you add will have the correct orientation.

Pick: **World UCS**

The UCS icon changes back to the WCS.

Using Landscape Objects

Landscape objects are bitmapped images that are applied to extended entity objects and added to your drawing. Landscape objects have grips at the base, top, and corners that you can use to move, scale, rotate, and otherwise edit them. You can create your own landscape objects and add them to the landscape library. To add a landscape object to the drawing,

Figure 15.30

Pick: **Landscape New icon**

The Landscape New dialog box appears on your screen, as shown in Figure 15.30. On your own, select People #2. Change Height to 6.0 and pick Preview to preview the person that you will add to your drawing.

To locate the landscape object in your drawing,

Pick: **Position**

Choose the location of the base of the landscape object: **5,5,0** ↵

You return to the Landscape New dialog box.

Pick: **OK** (to add the landscape object and exit the dialog box)

The landscape object is added to your drawing. It appears as a triangular shape.

On your own, use Zoom All to zoom out so that you can see the entire landscape object. If necessary, use Zoom Window afterwards to size your view of the landscape object and the assembly.

Render the drawing on your own.

Although the effects of the background and person are not particularly applicable to this engineering assembly drawing, you can easily imagine creating realistic effects in the rendering by using backgrounds and landscape objects.

Exporting AutoCAD Files

You can also export your AutoCAD drawings for use with other software.

Pick: **File, Export**

The Export Data dialog box appears on your screen, as shown in Figure 15.31. You will find these file types:

Metafile	**.wmf*
ACIS	**.sat*
Lithography	**.stl*
Encapsulated PS	**.eps*
DXX Extract	**.dxx*
Bitmap	**.bmp*
3D Studio®	**.3ds*
Block	**.dwg*

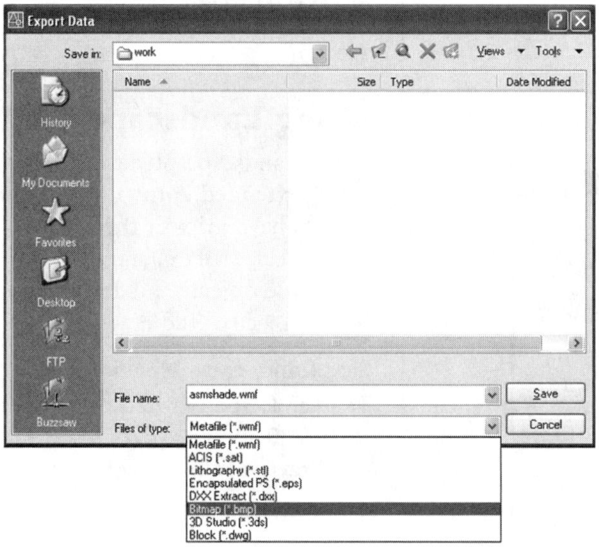

Figure 15.31

Pick: **Cancel**

Tip

You can use SaveAs and change the Save As Type area to save your drawing files back to previous AutoCAD versions.

Drawing Web Format

The Drawing Web Format allows you to convert an AutoCAD drawing so that it can be viewed on the Web. To create a DWF™ file (*.dwf* extension), you use the Plot command and create an ePlot file.

Pick: **Plot icon**

You will select the *DWF ePlot.pc3* file as the output device for the plot.

Pick: **to expand the list of plotter configurations to the right of Name**

The list of plotter choices pulls down as shown in Figure 15.32.

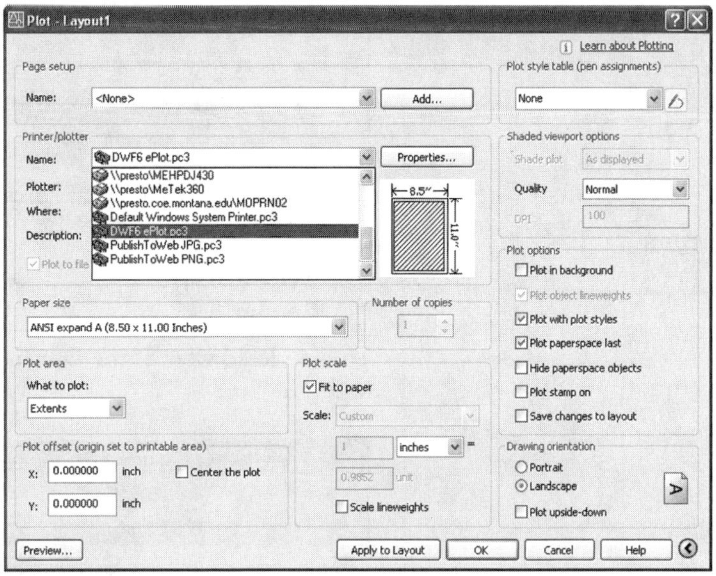

Figure 15.32

Pick: **DWF6 ePlot.pc3**
Pick: **OK**

The DWF file is created in your default directory. You can publish this file to the Web for others to view. They must have installed the WHIP!® plug-in version 4.0 or later on their system to view DWF files with a browser such as Netscape Communicator or Microsoft Internet Explorer.

Tip

You can create electronic drawing sets using the Publish command found on the Standard toolbar. Other people, such as your clients, can view the published set of drawings using a free download of Autodesk Express Viewer available at www.Autodesk.com.

You can also use the File, Publish to Web menu selection to create a web page to display images from one or more drawing files.

On your own, save and close the file.

Plotting Shaded Views

You can also choose to directly plot (or print) shaded views.

On your own, use the **template file *asmb-sol.dwt*** from the data files provided to start a new drawing.
Name your drawing ***asmb-ren.dwg***.

A drawing similar to the assembly you created in Tutorial 13 should appear on your screen as shown in Figure 15.33.

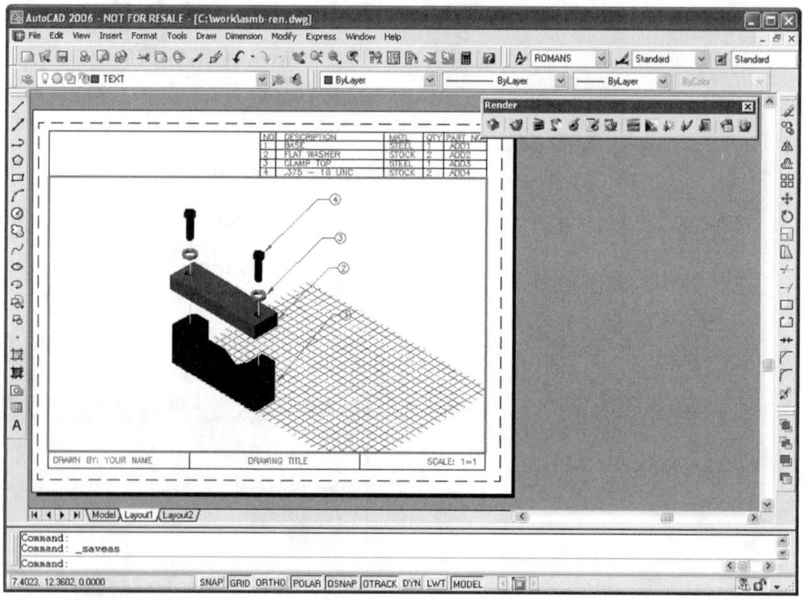

Figure 15.33

Pick: **Render icon**
Pick: **Render**

The rendered view of the drawing should appear on your screen similar to Figure 15.34.

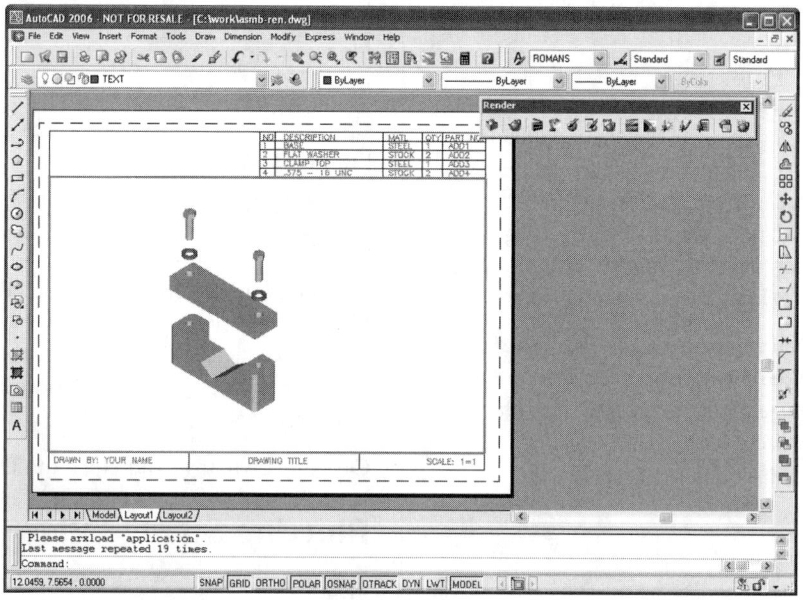

Figure 15.34

On your own, switch to paper space.
Pick: **on the magenta viewport**
Pick: **Properties icon**
On your own, expand the options in the Misc area as shown in Figure 15.35.

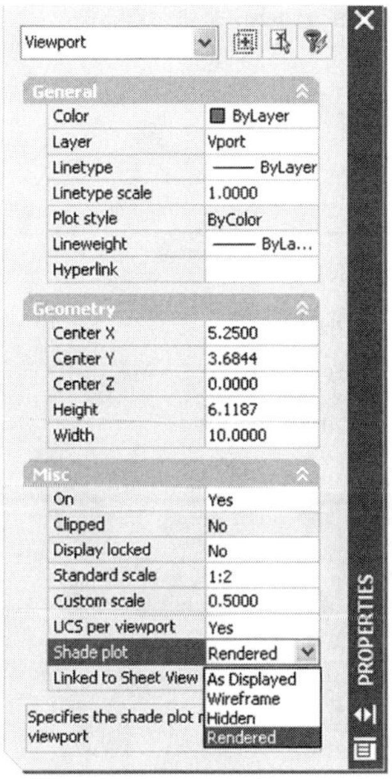

Figure 15.35

Notice that the plot area is set to Rendered. You can also select to have the objects in the viewport plot As Displayed, Wireframe (so that the back edges would show), or Hidden (with the back lines removed). Leave this set to Rendered.

Pick: **Plot icon**

The Plot dialog box appears on your screen. Notice that the Shaded Viewport options area is set to Rendered as shown in Figure 15.36.

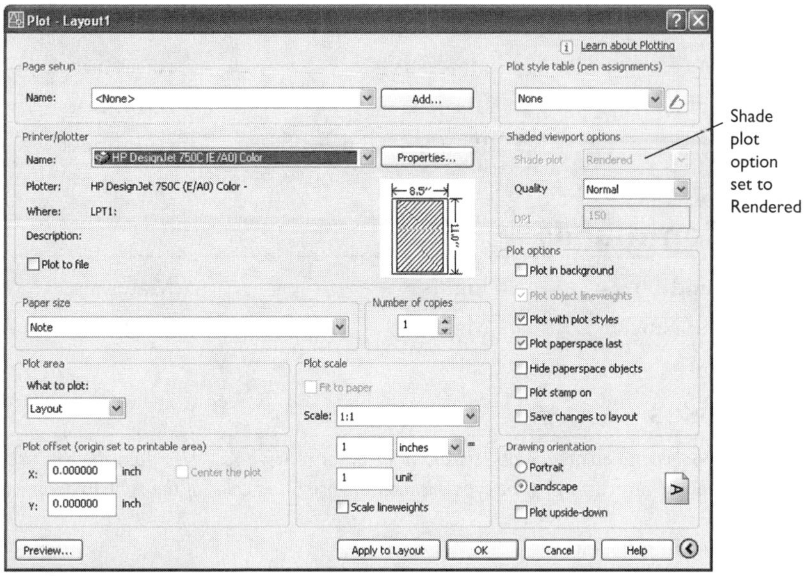

Figure 15.36

Pick: **Preview**

The preview of the plot appears on your screen, as shown in Figure 15.37.

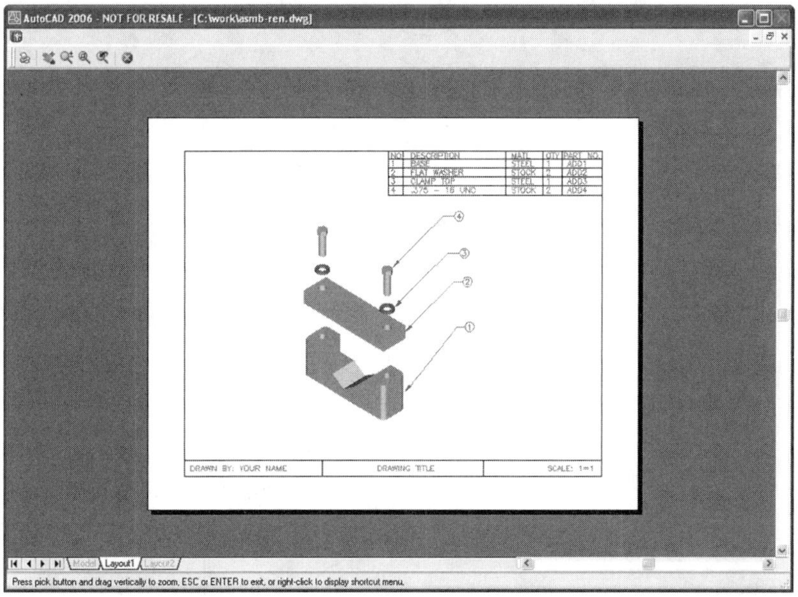

Figure 15.37

Save your drawing and print it using the paper space layout.

You have completed Tutorial 15 and this tutorial guide!

Exit the AutoCAD program.

Key Terms

ambient	Gouraud shading	point light	scene
ambient lighting	hotspot	ray tracing	spotlight
back faces	intensity	reflection	surface map
bump map	materials	refraction	transparency
distant light	normal	resolution	
falloff	Phong shading	roughness	

Key Commands

Background	Lights	Materials	Render
Landscape New	Mapping	Publish	Scenes

Exercises

Use solid modeling to create the objects shown below or retrieve your files from the exercises you did for Tutorial 13. Produce three different renderings of the object, varying the type, location, intensity, and color of the light. Experiment with different materials and backgrounds.

15.1 Clamping Block

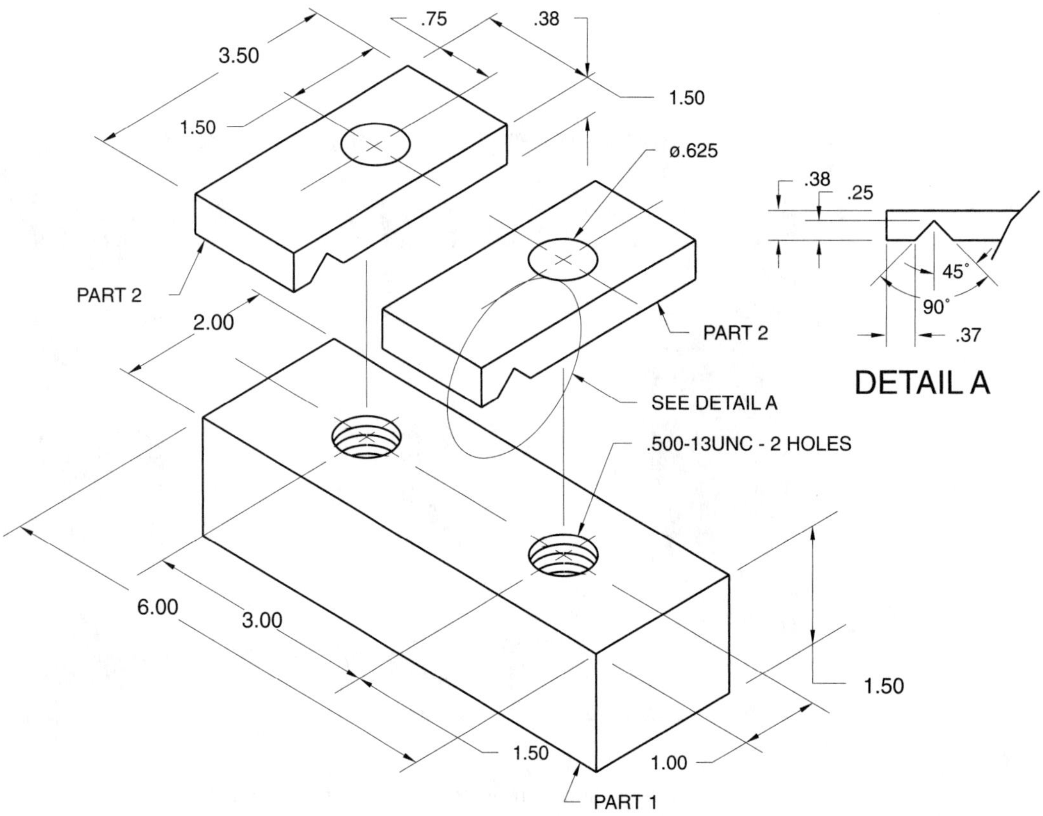

15.2 Pressure Assembly

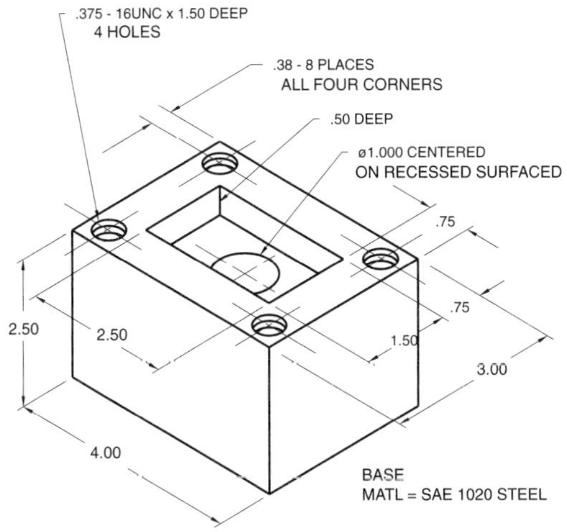

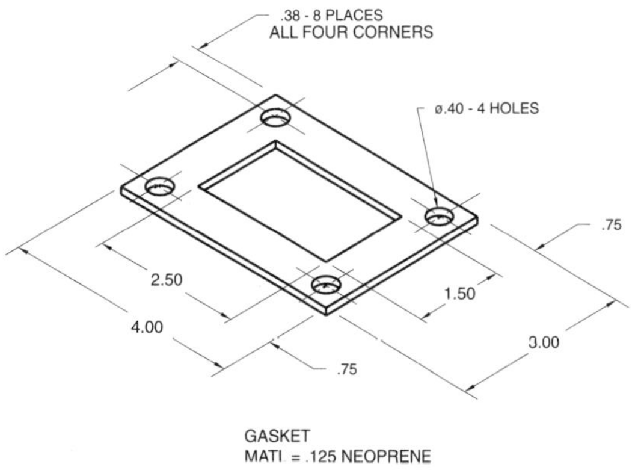

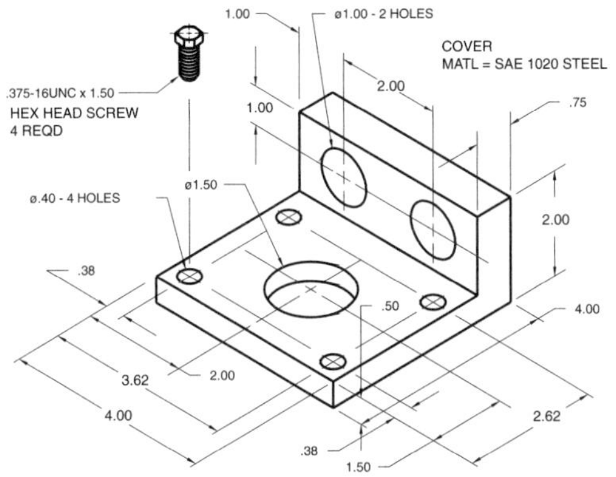

15.3 Hub Assembly

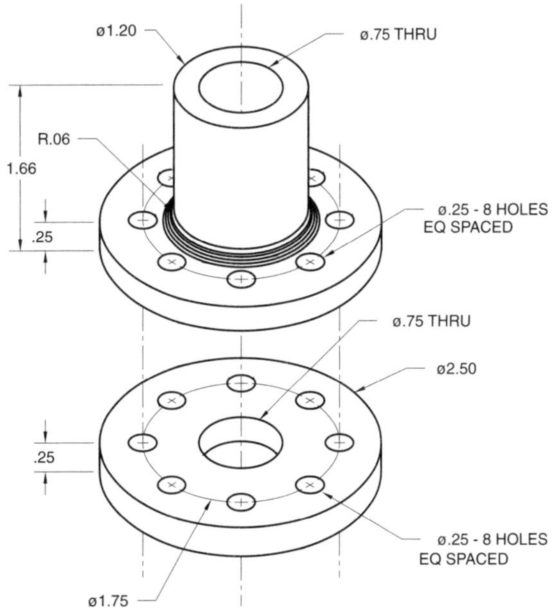

15.4 Turbine Housing Assembly

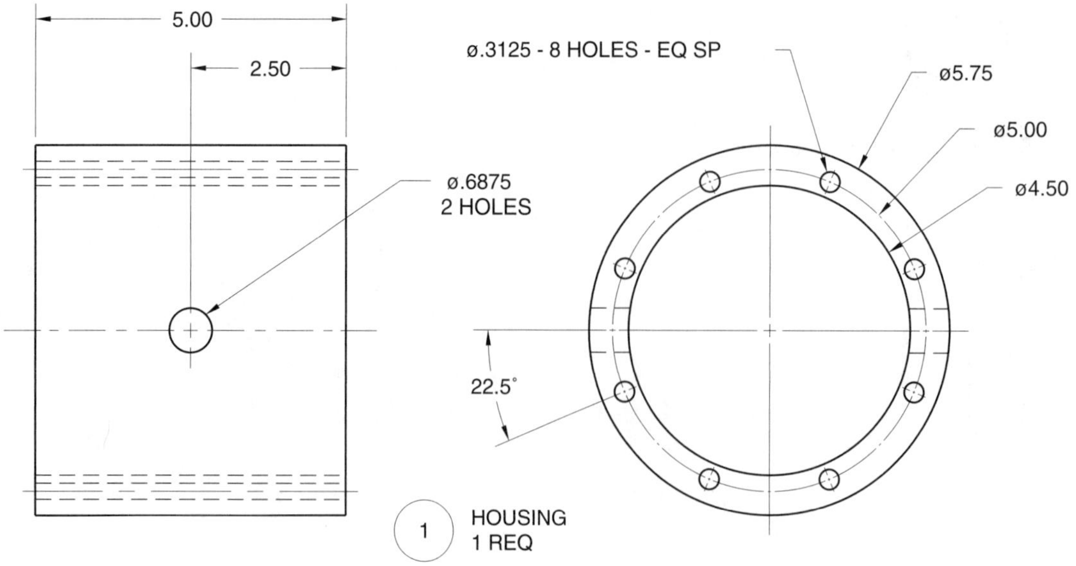

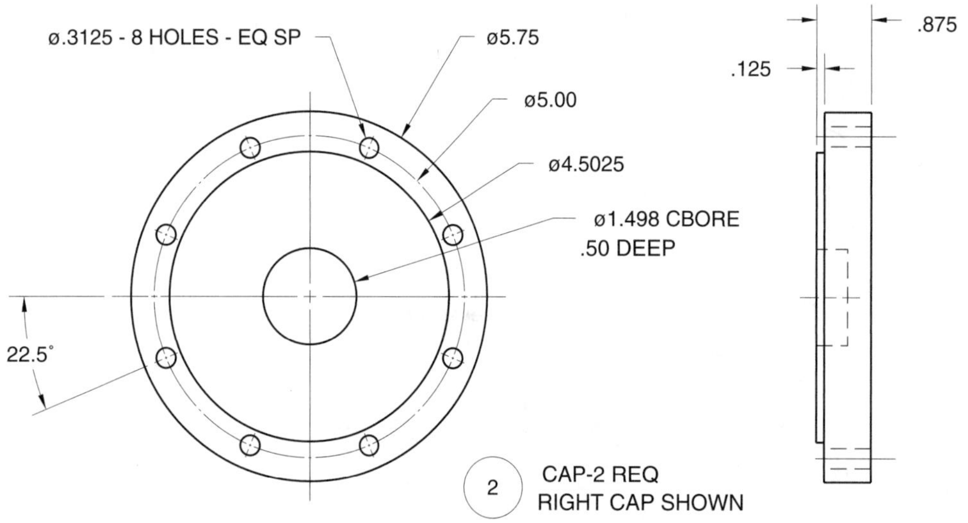

15.5 Geneva Wheel Assembly

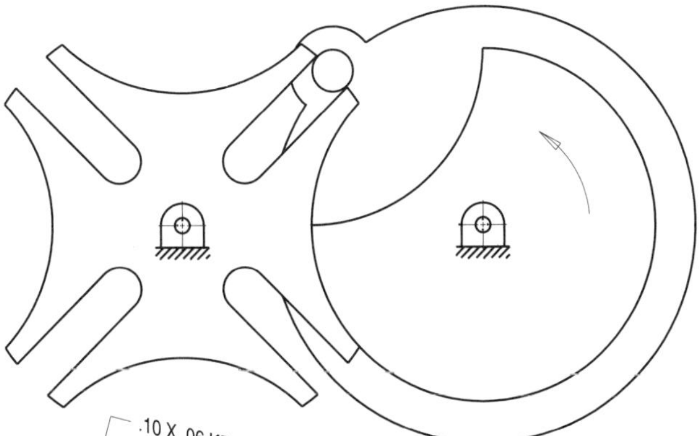

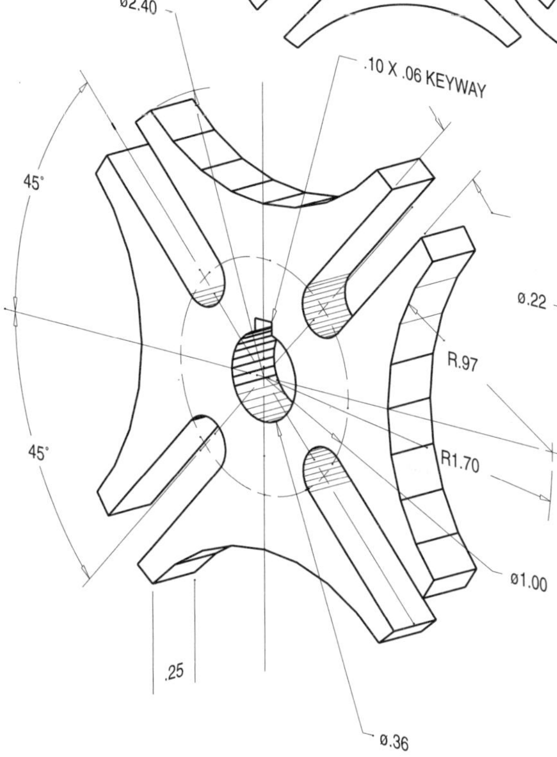

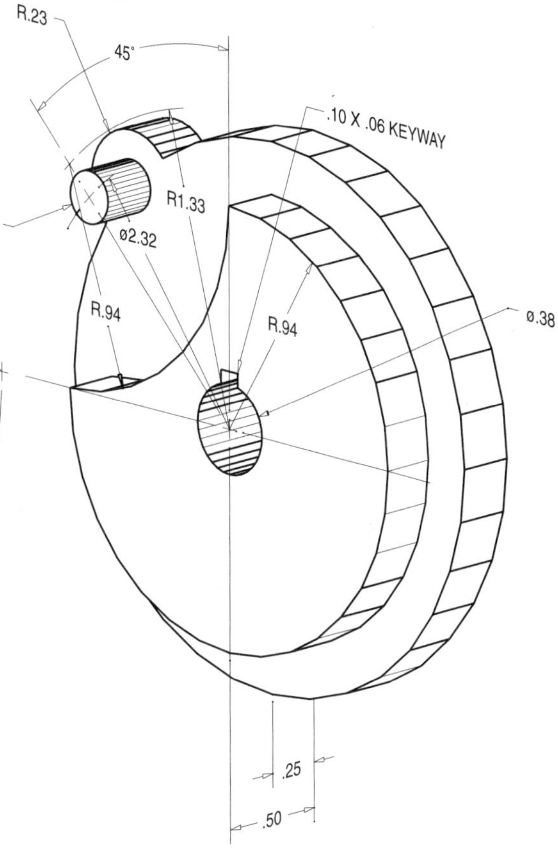

15.6M Universal Joint

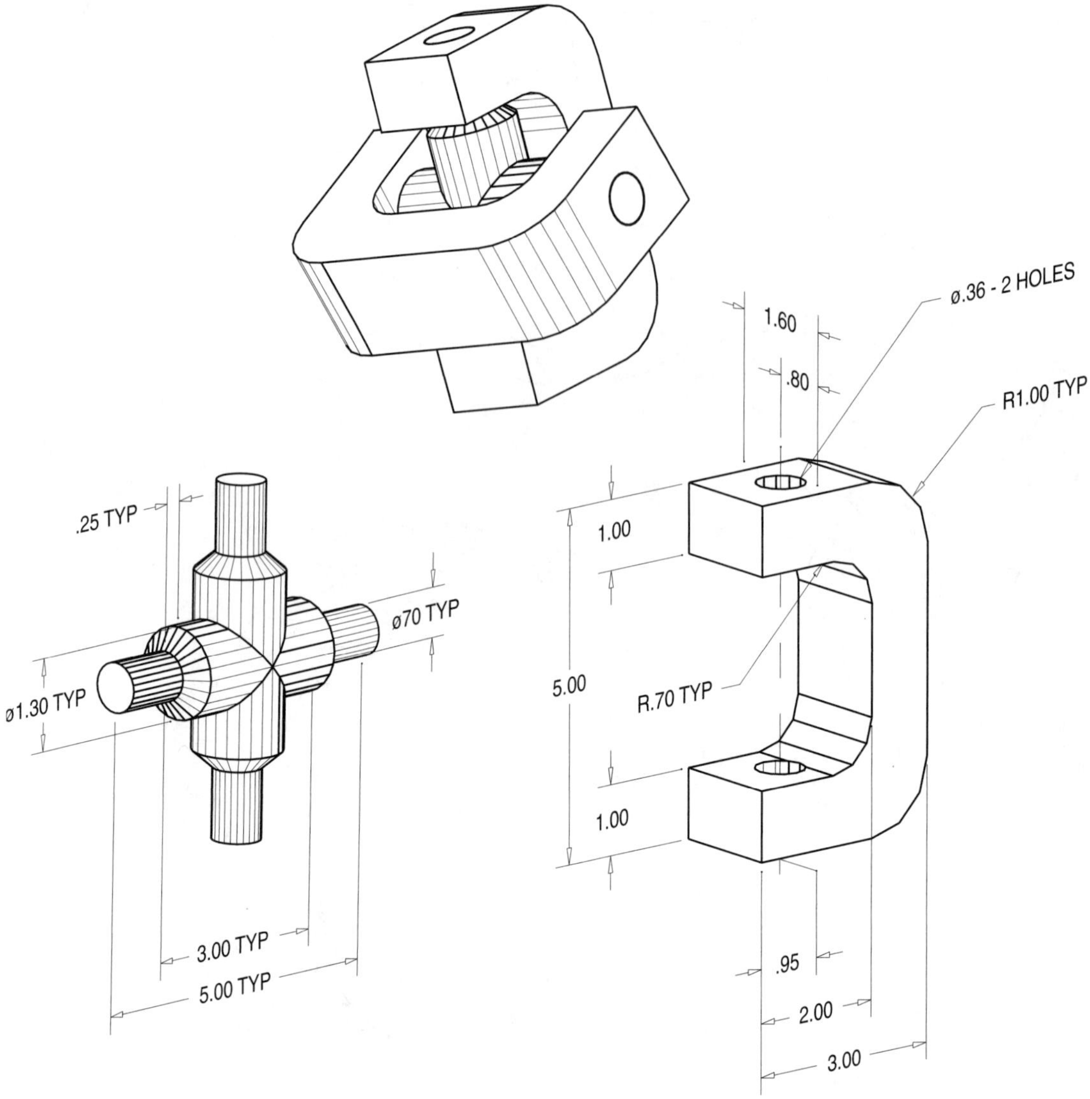

15.7 Staircase

Retrieve your file from Exercise 13.7 and render the stairs using wood materials and a distant light source.

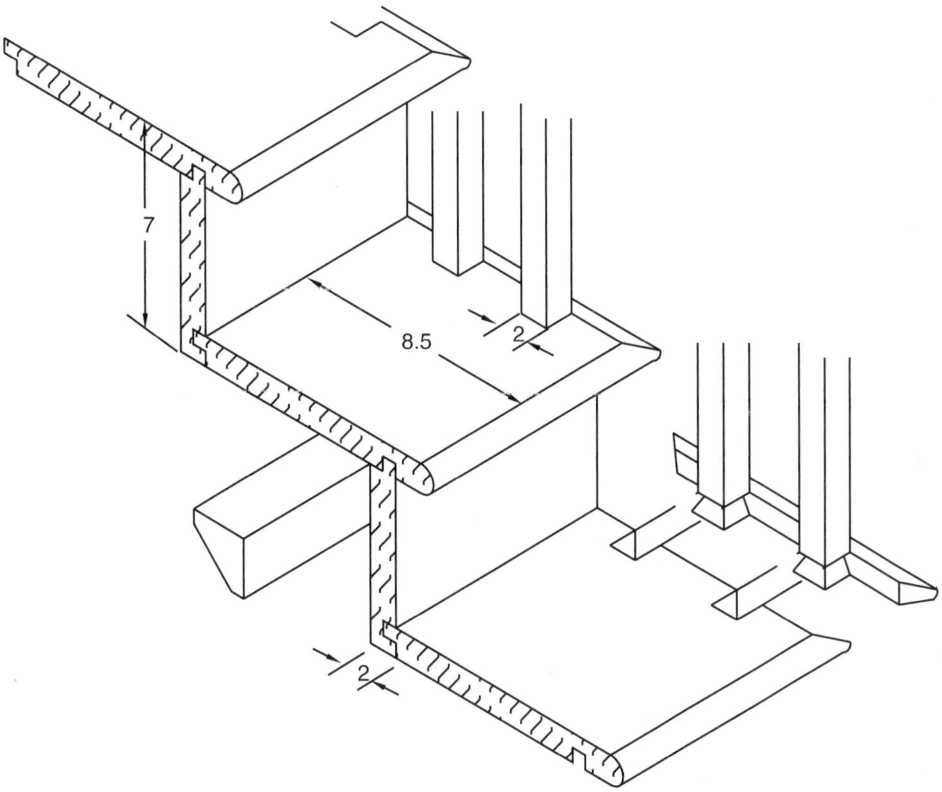

15.8M Pulley Arm

Use solid modeling to create a pictorial view like the one shown. Render the model to create a pictorial section.

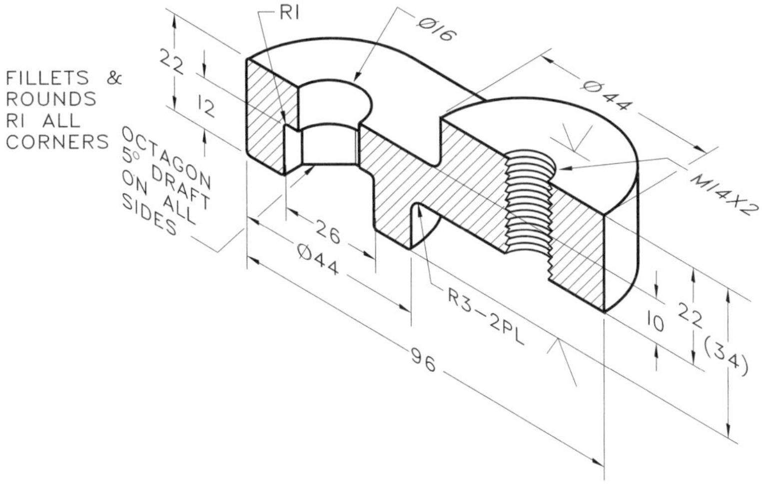

15.9M Step Bearing

Retrieve your file from Exercise 13.9M. Assign materials, create lighting and render your drawing to a file. Import the rendered drawing into your Windows word processor and add ball tags and a parts list to create a rendered isometric assembly drawing.

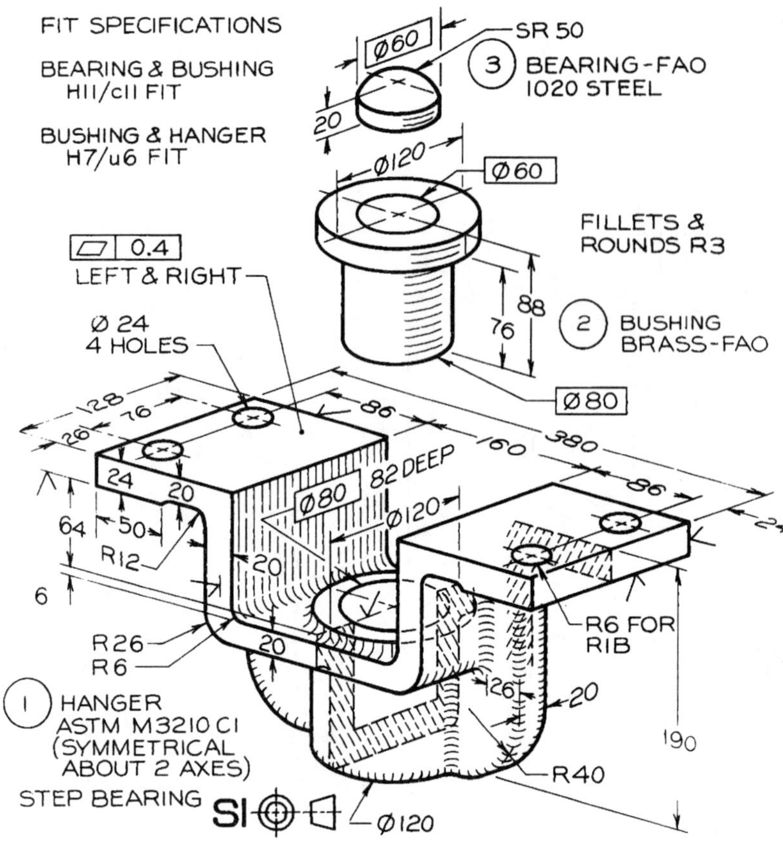

15.10M Tensioner

Retrieve your file from Exercise 13.11M. Assign materials, create lighting and render your drawing to a file. Import the rendered drawing into your Windows word processor and add ball tags and a parts list to create a rendered isometric assembly drawing.

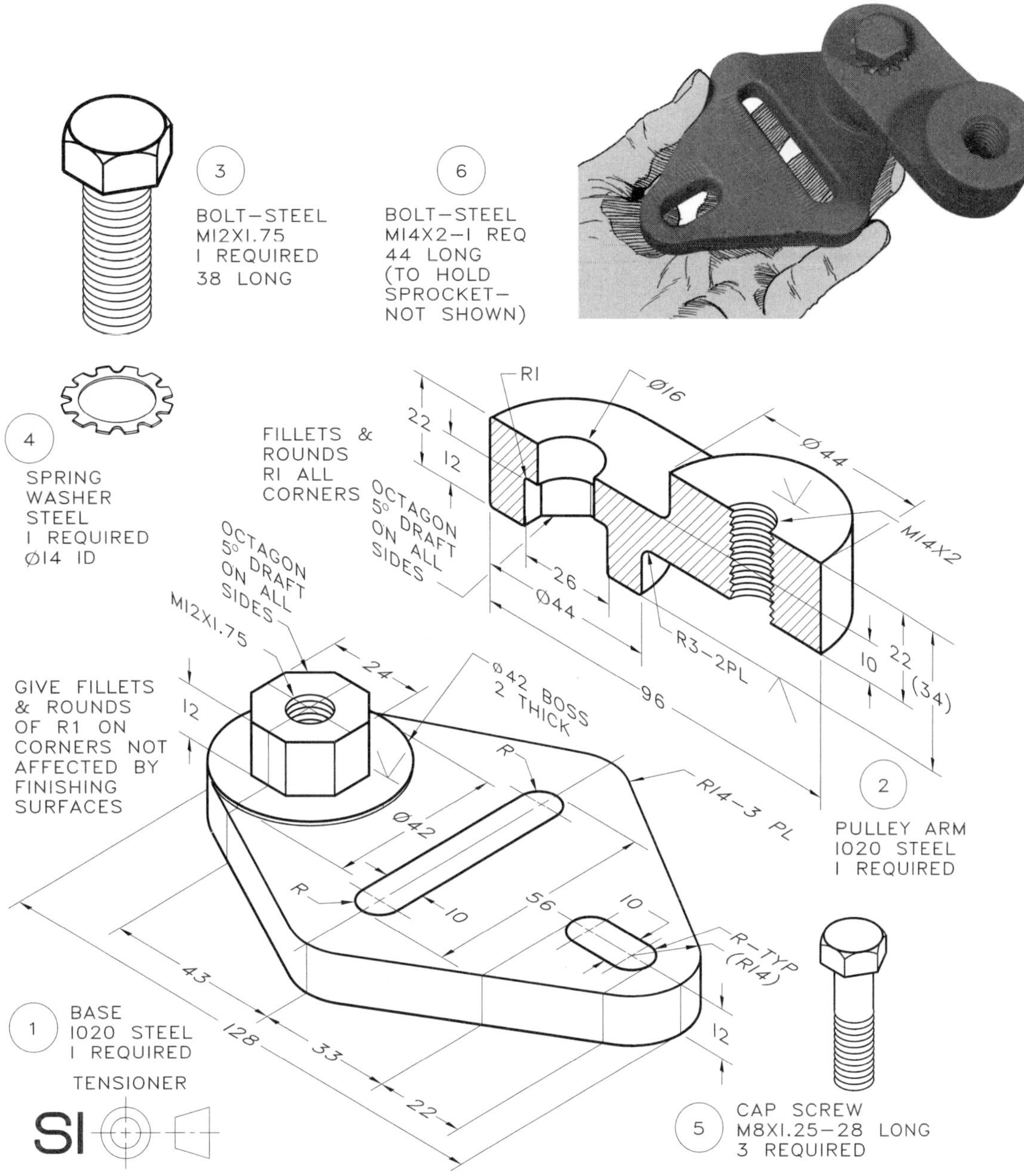

AutoCAD® Command Summary

This grid includes most commands available for use with the AutoCAD 2006 software. You should use the AutoCAD on-line Help feature for complete information about the commands and their options. Most commands can be run at the command line by typing a hyphen (-) in front of the command name. Many commands have keyboard shortcuts that are displayed alongside their names on the menu bar.

Command or Icon Name	Description	Toolbar	Icon	Menu Bar	Command or Alias
2D Wireframe Shade	Displays objects using lines and curves to represent boundaries.	Shade	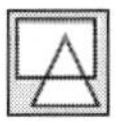	View, Shade, 2D Wireframe	SHADEMODE
2D Solid	Creates solid-filled polygons.	Surfaces		Draw, Surfaces, 2D Solid	SOLID, SO
3 Point UCS	Selects a user coordinate system based on any three points in the graphics window.	Standard (UCS flyout) or UCS		Tools, New UCS, 3 Point	UCS
3D	Creates three-dimensional mesh objects.	N/A		Draw, Surfaces, 3D Surfaces	3D
3D Array	Creates a three-dimensional array.	N/A		Modify, 3D Operation, 3D Array	3DARRAY, 3A
3D Clip	Interactive 3D view and to adjust clipping planes.	3D Orbit		N/A	3DCLIP
3D Continuous Orbit	Interactive 3D view showing continuous motion.	3D Orbit		N/A	3DCORBIT
3D Distance	Make objects appear closer or farther in the interactive 3D view.	3D Orbit		N/A	3DDISTANCE
3D Dynamic View	Changes the 3D view of a point.	N/A		N/A	DVIEW, DV
3D Face	Creates a three-dimensional surface.	Surfaces		Draw, Surfaces, 3D Face	3DFACE, 3F
3D Mesh	Creates a free-form polygon mesh.	Surfaces		Draw, Surfaces, 3D Mesh	3DMESH

Command or Icon Name	Description	Toolbar	Icon	Menu Bar	Command or Alias
3D Mirror	Creates a mirror image of objects about a plane.	N/A		Modify, 3D Operation, Mirror 3D	MIRROR3D
3D Orbit	Interactive 3D viewing.	3D Orbit		View, 3D Orbit	3D ORBIT, 3DO
3D Polyface Mesh	Creates a 3D polyface mesh by vertices.	N/A		N/A	PFACE
3D Polyline	Creates a 3D polyline of straight line segments.	N/A		Draw, 3D Polyline	3DPOLY, 3P
3D Rotate	Rotates an object in a 3D coordinate system.	N/A		Modify, 3D Operation, Rotate 3D	ROTATE3D
3D Studio In	Imports a 3D Studio® (*.*3ds*) file into an AutoCAD drawing.	N/A		Insert, 3D Studio	3DSIN
3D Studio Out	Saves a file formatted for use in 3D Studio (*.*3ds*).	N/A		N/A	3DSOUT
3D Web Publish	Creates 3D DWF™ files of 3D models (when installed).	N/A	N/A	N/A	3DDWFPUB-LISH
3D Wireframe Shade	Displays objects using lines and curves to represent boundaries. Displays shaded 3D UCS icon. Material colors applied to objects are shown.	Shade		View, Shade, 3D Wireframe	SHADEMODE
About	Displays information about the AutoCAD software.	N/A		Help, About	'ABOUT, ABOUT
Acadlspasdoc	System variable controlling whether or not the *acad.lsp* file is loaded into every drawing.	N/A		N/A	ACADLSPAS-DOC
Acadprefix	System variable that stores the directory path, if any, specified by the ACAD environment vari-able. (read only)	N/A		N/A	ACADPREFIX
Acadver	System variable that stores the AutoCAD version number. (read only)	N/A		N/A	ACADVER
ACIS In	Imports an ACIS (*.*sat*) file into an AutoCAD drawing.	N/A		Insert, ACIS File	ACISIN

Command or Icon Name	Description	Toolbar	Icon	Menu Bar	Command or Alias
ACIS Out	Saves a file formatted in ACIS (*.*sat*).	N/A		N/A	ACISOUT
Active Assistance	Displays Quick Help about the current command in the Info Palette.	N/A		Help, Info Palette	ASSIST, 'ASSIST
Adcclose	Closes the DesignCenter™ window.	N/A		N/A	ADCCLOSE
Adcenter	Manages and inserts blocks, xrefs, hatch patterns, and more.	Standard		Tools, DesignCenter	ADCENTER
Adcnavigate	Lets you specify a path or drawing file name to load in the Folders tree view of the DesignCenter.	N/A		N/A	ADCNAVIGATE
Administration	Performs administrative functions with external database commands.	N/A		Tools, dbConnect	DBCONNECT, AAD
Aerial View	Opens the Aerial View window.	N/A		View, Aerial View	DSVIEWER, AV
Align	Moves and rotates objects to align with other objects.	N/A		Modify, 3D Operation, Align	ALIGN, AL
Align Dimension Text, Edit	Aligns dimension text to Home, Left, Right or Angle position.	Dimension		Dimension, Align Text	DIMTEDIT, DIMTED
Aligned Dimension	Creates an aligned linear dimension.	Dimension		Dimension, Aligned	DIMALIGNED, DAL, DIMALI
AME Convert	Converts AME solid models to AutoCAD solid objects.	N/A		N/A	AMECONVERT
Angular Dimension	Dimensions an angle.	Dimension		Dimension, Angular	DIMANGULAR, DAN, DIMANG
Aperture	Controls the size of the object snap target box.	N/A		N/A	'APERTURE, APERTURE
Aperture Box	System variable controlling display of the object snap target box.	N/A		N/A	APBOX
Application Load	Loads AutoLISP® (*.*ads*), and (*.*arx*) files.	N/A		Tools, Load Application	'APPLOAD, AP

Command or Icon Name	Description	Toolbar	Icon	Menu Bar	Command or Alias
Arc	Draws an arc based on three points.	Draw		Draw, Arc, 3 Points	ARC, A
Arc Center Start Angle	Draws an arc of a specified angle based on the center and start points.	N/A		Draw, Arc, Center Start Angle	ARC, A
Arc Center Start End	Draws an arc based on the center, start, and endpoints.	N/A		Draw, Arc, Center Start End	ARC, A
Arc Center Start Length	Draws an arc of a specified length based on the center and start points.	N/A		Draw, Arc, Center Start Length	ARC, A
Arc Continue	Draws an arc from the last point of the previous line or arc drawn.	N/A		Draw, Arc, Continue	ARC, A
Arc Length Dimension	Dimensions the length of an arc, using the symbol set using Dimension Style.	Dimension		Dimension, Arc Length	DIMARC
Arc Start Center Angle	Draws an arc of a specified angle based on the start and center points.	N/A		Draw, Arc, Start Center Angle	ARC, A
Arc Start Center End	Draws an arc based on the start, center, and endpoints.	N/A		Draw, Arc, Start Center End	ARC, A
Arc Start Center Length	Draws an arc of a specified length based on the start and center points.	N/A		Draw, Arc, Start Center Length	ARC, A
Arc Start End Angle	Draws an arc of a specified angle based on the start and endpoints.	N/A		Draw, Arc, Start End Angle	ARC, A
Arc Start End Direction	Draws an arc in a specified direction based on the start and endpoints.	N/A		Draw, Arc, Start End Direction	ARC, A
Arc Start End Radius	Draws an arc of a specified radius based on the start and endpoints.	N/A		Draw, Arc, Start End Radius	ARC, A
Area	Finds the area and perimeter of objects or defined areas.	Inquiry		Tools, Inquiry, Area	AREA, AA
Array	Creates multiple copies of objects in a regularly spaced circular or rectangular pattern.	Modify		Modify, Array	ARRAY, AR
Attdia	System variable that controls whether the Insert command uses a dialog box for attribute value entry.	N/A		N/A	ATTDIA

Command or Icon Name	Description	Toolbar	Icon	Menu Bar	Command or Alias
Attedit	Allows you to change attribute information.	N/A		Modify, Object, Attribute	ATTEDIT
Attribute Display	Globally controls attribute visibility.	N/A		View, Display, Attribute Display	'ATTDISP, ATTDISP
Attribute Editor, Enhanced	Edits attributes of a block reference.	Modify II		Modify, Object, Attribute, Single	EATTEDIT
Attribute Redefine	Redefines a block and updates its attributes.	N/A		N/A	ATTREDEF
Audit	Evaluates the integrity of a drawing.	N/A		File, Drawing Utilities, Audit	AUDIT
AutoCAD Runtime Extension	Provides information, loads/unloads ARX applications.	N/A		N/A	ARX
Back View	Sets the viewing direction for a three-dimensional visualization of the drawing to the back.	View		View, 3D Views, Back	VPOINT, -VP, DDVPOINT, VP
Background	Sets a background for a rendered scene.	Render		View, Render, Background	BACK-GROUND
Base	Specifies the insertion point for a block or drawing.	N/A		Draw, Block, Base	'BASE, BASE
Baseline Dimension	Continues a linear, angular, or ordinate dimension from the baseline of the previous or selected dimension.	Dimension	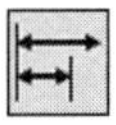	Dimension, Baseline	DIMBASELINE, DBA, DIMBASE
Bitmap Out	Saves AutoCAD objects in a bitmap (*.*bmp*) format.	N/A		N/A	BMPOUT
Blipmode	System variable that controls the display of blip marks.	N/A		N/A	'BLIPMODE, BLIPMODE
Block Attribute Manager	Allows editing of block attribute properties.	Modify II		Modify, Object, Attribute, Block Attribute Manager	BATTMAN
Block Editor	Adds dynamic behavior to blocks.	Standard		Tools, Block Editor	BEDIT
Block Icon	Generate preview images for blocks created with R14 or earlier.	N/A		File, Drawing Utilities, Update Block Icons	BLOCKICON

Command or Icon Name	Description	Toolbar	Icon	Menu Bar	Command or Alias
Bottom View	Sets the viewing direction for a three-dimensional visualization of the drawing to the bottom.	View		View, 3D Views, Bottom	VPOINT, -VP, DDVPOINT, VP
Boundary	Creates a region or polyline of a closed boundary.	N/A		Draw, Boundary	BOUNDARY, BO, -BOUND-ARY, -BO
Boundary Hatch	Automatically fills the area you select with a pattern. Same as HATCH.	N/A		N/A	BHATCH, BH, H
Box	Creates a three-dimensional rectangular-shaped solid.	Solids		Draw, Solids, Box	BOX
Break	Removes part of an object or splits it in two.	Modify		Modify, Break	BREAK, BR
Browser	Launches the Web browser defined in the system registry.	Web		N/A	BROWSER
Calculator	Calculates mathematical and geometrical expressions.	N/A		N/A	'CAL, CAL
Calculator, Quick	Performs calculations, converts units, and more.	Standard		Tools, QuickCalc	QUICKCALC
Cancel	Exits current command without performing operation.	N/A		N/A	Esc
Celtype	System variable that sets the linetype of new objects.	N/A		N/A	CELTYPE
Center Mark	Draws center marks and center-lines of arcs and circles.	Dimension	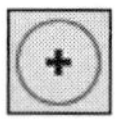	Dimension, Center Mark	DIMCENTER, DCE
Chamfer	Draws a straight line segment (called a chamfer) between two given lines.	Modify		Modify, Chamfer	CHAMFER, CHA
Change	Changes the properties of exist-ing objects.	N/A		N/A	CHANGE, CH, CHPROP
Check Standards	Checks the current drawing for CAD Standards violations.	CAD Standards		Tools, CAD Standards, Check	CHECKSTAN-DARDS
Circle	Draws circles based upon center point and radius.	Draw		Draw, Circle, Center Radius	CIRCLE, C

Command or Icon Name	Description	Toolbar	Icon	Menu Bar	Command or Alias
Circle Center Diameter	Draws circles based upon center point and diameter.	N/A		Draw, Circle, Center Diameter	
Circle Tan Tan Radius	Draws circles based upon two tangent points and a radius.	N/A		Draw, Circle, Tan Tan Radius	
Circle Tan Tan Tan	Draws circles based upon three tangent points.	N/A		Draw, Circle, Tan Tan Tan	
Circle 3 Points	Draws circles based upon 3 points.	N/A		Draw, Circle, 3 Points	
Circle 2 Points	Draws circles based upon 2 points.	N/A		Draw, Circle, 2 Points	
Close	Closes the current drawing; prompts to save or discard the changes if it was modified.	N/A		File, Close	CLOSE
Close All	Closes all open drawings.	N/A		Window, Close All	CLOSEALL
Cmddia	System variable controls whether dialog boxes are enabled some commands.	N/A		N/A	CMDDIA
Color Control	Sets the color for new objects.	Properties		Format, Color	'COLOR, COLOR, 'DDCOLOR, DDCOLOR, COL
Command Line	Displays the command window when it has been hidden.	N/A		Tools, Command Line	COMMAND-LINE
Compile	Compiles PostScript font files and shape files.	N/A		N/A	COMPILE
Cone	Creates a three-dimensional solid primitive with a circular base tapering to a point perpendicular to its base.	Solids		Draw, Solids, Cone	CONE
Construction Line	Creates an infinite line.	Draw		Draw, Construction Line	XLINE
Continue Dimension	Adds the next chained dimension, measured from the last dimension.	Dimension	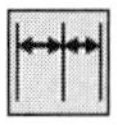	Dimension, Continue	DIMCONTINUE, DIMCONT, DCO
Convert	Converts associative hatches and 2D polylines created in Release 13 or earlier.	N/A		N/A	CONVERT

Command or Icon Name	Description	Toolbar	Icon	Menu Bar	Command or Alias
Convert Color Dependent Plot Style	Converts color-dependent plot style table to a named plot style table.	N/A		N/A	CONVERTCTB
Convert Plot Styles	Converts the current drawing to a named or color dependent plot style.	N/A		N/A	CONVERTP-STYLES
Copy	Copies an existing shape from one area on the drawing to another area.	Modify		Modify, Copy	COPY, CP, CO
Copy Link	Copies the current view to the Windows Clipboard for linking to other OLE applications.	N/A		Edit, Copy Link	COPYLINK
Copyclip	Copies objects to the Windows Clipboard.	Standard		Edit, Copy	COPYCLIP
Copyhist	Copies all text in the command line history to the Clipboard.	N/A		N/A	COPYHIST
Customize	Allows customization of toolbars, buttons, and shortcut keys	N/A		Tools, Customize, Interface	CUSTOMIZE
Cutclip	Copies objects to the clipboard and erases them from the drawing.	Standard		Edit, Cut	CUTCLIP
Cylinder	Creates a three-dimensional solid primitive similar to an extruded circle, but without a taper.	Solids		Draw, Solids, Cylinder	CYLINDER
Data Base Close	Closes the dbConnect Manager and removes dbConnect menu from the menu bar.	N/A		Tools, dbConnect	DBCLOSE
Data Base Connect	Interfaces with external database tables.	N/A		Tools, dbConnect	DBCONNECT
Database List	Lists database information for drawing objects.	N/A		N/A	DBLIST
Define Attribute	Creates attribute text.	N/A		Draw, Block, Define Attributes	ATTDEF, -AT, DDATTDEF
Delay	Adds a timed pause (33 seconds maximum) within a script.	N/A		N/A	'DELAY, DELAY
Delobj	Controls whether objects used to create other objects are retained or deleted from the drawing database.	N/A		N/A	DELOBJ

Command or Icon Name	Description	Toolbar	Icon	Menu Bar	Command or Alias
DesignCenter	Manage drawing content.	Standard		Tools, Design-Center	ADCENTER
DesignCenter Navigate	Controls path for AutoCAD DesignCenter.	N/A		N/A	ADCNAVIGAT, CTRL-1
Detach	Removes an externally referenced drawing.	N/A		N/A	XREF, XR, -XREF, -XR
Detachurl	Removes hyperlinks from a drawing.	N/A		N/A	DETACHURL
Diameter Dimension	Adds center marks to a circle when providing its diameter dimension.	Dimension		Dimension, Diameter	DIMDIAMETER, DIMDIA, DDI
Diastat	System variable that stores the exit method of the most recently used dialog box. (read only)	N/A		N/A	DIASTAT
Dimalt	System variable that enables alternate units.	N/A		N/A	DIMALT
Dimaltd	System variable that sets alternate unit precision.	N/A		N/A	DIMALTD
Dimaltf	System variable that sets alternate unit scale.	N/A		N/A	DIMALTF
Dimalttd	System variable that stores the number of decimal places for the tolerance values of an alternate units dimension.	N/A		N/A	DIMALTTD
Dimalttz	System variable that toggles the suppression of zeros for tolerance values.	N/A		N/A	DIMALTTZ
Dimaltu	System variable that sets the units format for alternate units of all dimension style family members, except angular.	N/A		N/A	DIMALTU
Dimaltz	System variable that toggles suppression of zeros for alternate units dimension values.	N/A		N/A	DIMALTZ
Dimapost	System variable that specifies the text prefix and/or suffix to the alternate dimension measurement for alternate types of dimensions except angular.	N/A		N/A	DIMAPOST

Command or Icon Name	Description	Toolbar	Icon	Menu Bar	Command or Alias
Dimaso	System variable that controls the creation of associative dimension objects.	N/A		N/A	DIMASO
Dimassoc	System variable which controls the associativity of dimensions. Set to 0, it creates dimensions with no association between dimension elements—lines, arrows, etc. are all separate objects. Set to 1, it forms elements into non-associative dimension objects, whose values update. Set to 2, it creates fully associative dimension objects.	N/A		N/A	DIMASSOC
Dimasz	System variable that controls the size of dimension line and leader line arrowheads.	N/A		N/A	DIMASZ
Dimaunit	System variable that sets the angle format for angular dimensions.	N/A		N/A	DIMAUNIT
Dimblk	System variable that sets the name of a block to be drawn instead of the normal arrowhead at the end of the dimension line or leader line.	N/A		N/A	DIMBLK
Dimblk1	System variable that, if Dimsah is on, specifies the user-defined arrowhead block for the first end of the dimension line.	N/A		N/A	DIMBLK1
Dimblk2	System variable that, if Dimsah is on, specifies the user-defined arrowhead block for the second end of the dimension line.	N/A		N/A	DIMBLK2
Dimcen	System variable that controls the drawing of circle or arc centermarks or centerlines.	N/A		N/A	DIMCEN
Dimclrd	System variable that assigns colors to dimension lines, arrowheads, and dimension leader lines.	N/A		N/A	DIMCLRD
Dimclre	System variable that assigns colors to dimension extension lines.	N/A		N/A	DIMCLRE
Dimclrt	System variable that assigns color to dimension text.	N/A		N/A	DIMCLRT
Dimdec	System variable that sets the decimal places for the tolerance values of a primary units dimension.	N/A		N/A	DIMDEC

Command or Icon Name	Description	Toolbar	Icon	Menu Bar	Command or Alias
Dimdle	System variable that extends the dimension line beyond the extension line when oblique strokes are drawn instead of arrowheads.	N/A		N/A	DIMDLE
Dimdli	System variable that controls the dimension line spacing for baseline dimensions.	N/A		N/A	DIMDLI
Dimension, Arc Length	Dimensions the length of an arc, using the symbol set using Dimension Style.	Dimension		Dimension, Arc Length	DIMARC
Dimension Edit	Edits dimensions.	Dimension		N/A	DIMEDIT, DIMED, DED
Dimension Status	Shows the dimension variables and their current settings.	N/A		N/A	DIMSTATUS
Dimension Style	Controls dimension styles.	Dimension, Styles		Dimension, Dimension Style	DDIM, D, DIMSTYLE, DST, DIMSTY
Dimension Update	Updates the dimensions based on changes to the dimension styles and variables.	Dimension	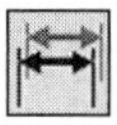	Dimension, Update	DIM (w/update), STYLE
Dimexe	System variable that determines how far to extend the extension line beyond the dimension line.	N/A		N/A	DIMEXE
Dimexo	System variable that determines how far extension lines are offset from origin points.	N/A		N/A	DIMEXO
Dimfit	System variable that controls the placement of text and attributes inside or outside extension lines.	N/A		N/A	DIMFIT
Dimgap	System variable that sets the distance around the dimension text when you break the dimension line to accommodate dimension text.	N/A		N/A	DIMGAP
Dimjust	System variable that controls the horizontal dimension text position.	N/A		N/A	DIMJUST
Dimlfac	System variable that sets the global scale factor for linear dimensioning measurements.	N/A		N/A	DIMLFAC
Dimlim	System variable that, when on, generates dimension limits as the default text.	N/A		N/A	DIMLIM

Command or Icon Name	Description	Toolbar	Icon	Menu Bar	Command or Alias
Dimoverride	Allows you to override dimensioning system variable settings associated with a dimension object, but will not affect the current dimension style.	N/A		N/A	DIMOVERRIDE, DIMOVER, DOV
Dimpost	System variable that specifies a text prefix and/or suffix to the dimension measurement.	N/A		N/A	DIMPOST
Dimrnd	System variable that rounds all dimensioning distances to the specified value.	N/A		N/A	DIMRND
Dimsah	System variable that controls the use of user-defined attribute blocks at the ends of the dimension lines.	N/A		N/A	DIMSAH
Dimscale	System variable that sets overall scale factor applied to dimensioning variables that specify sizes, distances, or offsets.	N/A		N/A	DIMSCALE
Dimsd1	System variable that, when on, suppresses drawing of the first dimension line.	N/A		N/A	DIMSD1
Dimsd2	System variable that, when on, suppresses drawing of the second dimension line.	N/A		N/A	DIMSD2
Dimse1	System variable that, when on, suppresses drawing of the first extension line.	N/A		N/A	DIMSE1
Dimse2	System variable that, when on, suppresses drawing of the second extension line.	N/A		N/A	DIMSE2
Dimsho	System variable that, when on, controls redefinition of dimension objects while dragging.	N/A		N/A	DIMSHO
Dimsoxd	System variable that, when on, suppresses drawing of dimension lines outside the extension lines.	N/A		N/A	DIMSOXD
Dimtad	System variable that controls the vertical position of text in relation to the dimension line.	N/A		N/A	DIMTAD
Dimtdec	System variable that sets the number of decimal places to display the tolerance values for a dimension.	N/A		N/A	DIMTDEC
Dimtfac	System variable that specifies a scale factor for the text height of tolerance values relative to the dimension text height.	N/A		N/A	DIMTFAC

Command or Icon Name	Description	Toolbar	Icon	Menu Bar	Command or Alias
Dimtih	System variable that controls the position of dimension text inside the extension lines for all dimension types except ordinate dimensions.	N/A		N/A	DIMTIH
Dimtix	System variable that draws text between extension lines.	N/A		N/A	DIMTIX
Dimtm	System variable that, when Dimtol or Dimlim is on, sets the minimum (or lower) toler ance limit for dimension text.	N/A		N/A	DIMTM
Dimtofl	System variable that, when on, draws a dimension line between the extension lines even when the text is placed outside the extension lines.	N/A		N/A	DIMTOFL
Dimtoh	System variable that, when turned on, controls the position of dimension text outside the extension lines.	N/A		N/A	DIMTOH
Dimtol	System variable that generates plus/minus tolerances.	N/A		N/A	DIMTOL
Dimtolj	System variable that sets the vertical justification for tolerance values relative to the nominal dimension text.	N/A		N/A	DIMTOLJ
Dimtp	System variable that, when Dimtol or Dimlim is on, sets the maximum (or upper) tolerance limit for dimension text.	N/A		N/A	DIMTP
Dimtsz	System variable that specifies the size of oblique strokes drawn instead of arrowheads for linear, radius, and diameter dimensioning.	N/A		N/A	DIMTSZ
Dimtvp	System variable that adjusts text placement relative to text height.	N/A		N/A	DIMTVP
Dimtxsty	System variable that specifies the text style of a dimension.	N/A		N/A	DIMTXSTY
Dimtxt	System variable that specifies the height of the dimension text, unless the current text style has a fixedheight.	N/A		N/A	DIMTXT
Dimtzin	System variable that controls the suppression of zeros for tolerance values.	N/A		N/A	DIMTZIN

Command or Icon Name	Description	Toolbar	Icon	Menu Bar	Command or Alias
Dimunit	System variable that sets the units format for all dimension family members, except angular.	N/A		N/A	DIMUNIT
Dimupt	System variable that controls the cursor functionality for User Positioned Text.	N/A		N/A	DIMUPT
Dimzin	System variable controlling the suppression of the inch portion of a feet-and-inches dimension when distance is an integral number of feet, or the feet portion when distance is less than a foot.	N/A		N/A	DIMZIN
Disassociate Dimension	Removes associativity from selected dimensions.	N/A		N/A	DIMDISASSO-CIATE
Dispsilh	System variable that controls the display of silhouette curves of body objects in wire-frame mode.	N/A		N/A	DISPSILH
Distance	Reads out the value for the distance between two selected points.	Inquiry		Tools, Inquiry, Distance	'DIST, DIST, DI
Divide	Places points or blocks along an object to create segments.	N/A		Draw, Point, Divide	DIVIDE, DIV
Donut	Draws concentric filled circles or filled circles.	N/A		Draw, Donut	DONUT
Double-click Edit	Turns on and off double-click editing mode used to automatically launch the Properties palette and other editing features.	N/A		N/A	DBLCLKEDIT
Drafting Settings	Sets Snap mode, grid, polar and object snap tracking.	N/A		Tools, Drafting Settings	DSETTINGS
Drafting Settings	Sets the drawing aids for the drawing.	N/A		Tools, Drafting Settings	'DSETTINGS
Dragmode	Controls the way dragged objects are displayed.	N/A		N/A	'DRAGMODE, DRAGMODE
Drawing Properties	Set and display properties of the current drawing.	N/A		N/A	DWGPROPS
Draworder	Changes the display order of images and objects.	Modify II		Tools, Draw Order	DRAWORDER, DR

Command or Icon Name	Description	Toolbar	Icon	Menu Bar	Command or Alias
DWF Out	Saves drawing objects in Drawing Web format (*.*dwf*).	N/A		N/A	DWFOUT, PLOT
DXB In	Imports coded binary files (*.*dxb*).	N/A		Insert, Drawing Exchange Binary	DXBIN
DXF In	Imports drawing saved in DXF™ Drawing Interchange (*.*dxf*) format.	N/A		File, Open, .DXF	DXFIN
DXF Out	Saves drawing objects in DXF™ Drawing Interchange (*.*dxf*) Format.	N/A		File, Export	DXFOUT
DWG Props	Sets and displays properties of the current drawing.	N/A		File, Drawing Properties	DWGPROPS
Edge	Changes the visibility of three-dimensional face edges.	Surfaces		Draw, Surfaces, Edge	EDGE
Edge Surface	Creates a three-dimensional polygon mesh.	Surfaces		N/A	EDGESURF
Edit Attribute	Edits attribute values.	Modify II		Modify, Object, Attribute, Single	EATTEDIT, ATTEDIT, -ATE
Edit Attribute Globally	Edits attribute values.	N/A		Modify, Object, Attribute, Global	DDATTE, ATTEDIT, ATE
Edit Hatch	Modifies an existing associative hatch block.	Modify II		Modify, Object, Hatch	HATCHEDIT, HE
Edit Links	Updates, changes, and cancels existing links.	N/A		Edit, OLE Links	OLELINKS
Edit Multiline	Edits multiple parallel lines.	N/A		Modify, Object, Multiline	MLEDIT
Edit Polyline	Changes various features of polylines.	Modify II		Modify, Object, Polyline	PEDIT, PE
Edit Scale List	Modifies the list of scales displayed in view and plot scale lists.	N/A		Format, Scale List	SCALELIST-EDIT
Edit Spline	Edits a spline object.	Modify II		Modify, Object, Spline	SPLINEDIT, SPE

Command or Icon Name	Description	Toolbar	Icon	Menu Bar	Command or Alias
Edit Text	Allows you to edit text inside a dialog box.	Text		Modify, Object, Text, Edit	DDEDIT, ED
Electronic Transmit	Creates a set of drawings and related files for transmittal.	N/A		N/A	ETRANSMIT
Elev	Sets elevation and extrusion thickness of new objects.	N/A		N/A	'ELEV, ELEV, ELEVATION
Ellipse	Used to draw ellipses.	Draw		Draw, Ellipse, Center	ELLIPSE, EL
Ellipse Axis End	Used to draw ellipses.	N/A		Draw, Ellipse, Axis End	ELLIPSE
Ellipse Arc	Used to draw ellipses.	N/A		Draw, Ellipse, Arc	ELLIPSE
End Startup Dialog	Turns off use of the Startup dialog box.	N/A		Tools, Options, System, Do not show startup dia.	
Erase	Erases objects from drawing.	Modify		Modify, Erase	ERASE, E
Explode	Separates blocks or dimensions into component objects so that they are no longer one group and can be edited.	Modify	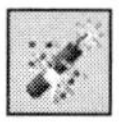	Modify, Explode	EXPLODE, X
Export	Exports a drawing to a file of type DXF so that another application can use it.	N/A		File, Export	EXPORT, EXP
Export Links	Exports link information for selected objects.	N/A		Tools, dbConnect	DBCONNECT
Express Tools	Activate Express Tools if needed.	N/A		N/A	EXPRESS-TOOLS
Extend	Extends the length of an existing object to meet a boundary.	Modify		Modify, Extend	EXTEND, EX
Extract Attributes	Extracts attribute data to an external file.	Modify II		Tools, Attribute Extraction	EATTEXT, ATTEXT, DDATTEXT

Command or Icon Name	Description	Toolbar	Icon	Menu Bar	Command or Alias
External Reference	Attaches, Detaches, Reloads, Unloads, Binds, etc. other drawings as external references, without really adding them to your current drawing.	Reference		Insert, Xref Manager	XREF, XR, -XREF, -XR
External Reference Attach	Uses another drawing as an external reference, without really adding it to your current drawing.	Reference		Insert, External Reference	XATTACH, XA
External Reference Bind	Binds symbols of an xref to a drawing.	Reference		Modify, Object, External Reference, Bind	XBIND, XB, -XBIND, -XB
External Reference Clip	Defines an xref clipping boundary.	Reference		N/A	XCLIP, XC
External Reference Clip Frame	System Variable that controls visibility of clipping boundaries.	Reference		Modify, Object, External Reference, Frame	XCLIPFRAME
Extrude	Extrudes a two-dimensional shape into a three-dimensional object.	Solids		Draw, Solids, Extrude	EXTRUDE, EXT
Facetres	System variable that adjusts the smoothness of shaded and hidden line-removed objects.	N/A		N/A	FACETRES
Filedia	System variable that suppresses the display of the file dialog boxes.	N/A		N/A	FILEDIA
Fill	Controls the filling of multilines, traces, solids, and wide polylines.	N/A		N/A	'FILL, FILL
Fillet	Connects lines, arcs, or circles with a smoothly fitted arc.	Modify		Modify, Fillet	FILLET, F
Find	Finds, replaces, selects, or zooms to specified text.	N/A		Edit, Find	FIND
Flat Shading	Shades flat polygon faces on 3D objects.	Shade		View, Shade, Flat Shaded	SHADEMODE
Flat Shading, Edges On	Shades flat polygon faces on 3D objects and highlights edges.	Shade		View, Shade, Flat Shaded Edges On	SHADEMODE
Fog	Provides visual information about the distance of objects from the camera.	Render		View, Render, Fog	FOG
Front View	Sets the viewing direction for a three-dimensional visualization of the drawing to the front.	View		View, 3D Views, Front	VPOINT, VP, DDVPOINT, -VP

Command or Icon Name	Description	Toolbar	Icon	Menu Bar	Command or Alias
Global Linetype	System variable that sets the current global linetype scale factor for objects.	N/A		N/A	LTSCALE
Gouraud Shade	Shades with smoothed edges between polygon faces for a realistic appearance.	Shade		View, Shade, Gouraud Shaded	SHADEMODE
Gouraud Shading, Edges On	Shades with smoothed edges between polygon faces for a realistic appearance. Highlights edges.	Shade		View, Shade, Gouraud Shaded Edges On	SHADEMODE
Graphics Screen	Switches from the text window back to the graphics window.	N/A		N/A	'GRAPHSCR, GRAPHSCR, F2
Grid	Displays a grid of dots at desired spacing on the screen.	Status bar		N/A	'GRID, GRID, or toggle off and on with F7
Grips	Enables grips and sets their color.	N/A		Tools, Options, Selection	'GRIPS, GRIPS, 'DDGRIPS, DDGRIPS, GR
Group	Creates and manages grouped objects.				GROUP
Handles	System variable that displays the setting for the use of handles in solid models.	N/A		N/A	HANDLES
Hatch	Automatically fills the area you select with a pattern.	Draw	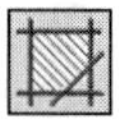	Draw, Hatch	HATCH, -H
Help	Displays information explaining commands and procedures.	Standard		Help	'HELP, '?, HELP, ?, or toggle on with F1
Hidden	Displays the objects using 3D wireframe hiding the lines representing back faces.	Shade		View, Shade, Hidden	SHADEMODE
Hide	Hides an object.	Render		View, Hide	HIDE, HI
Highlight	System variable that controls object highlighting.	N/A		N/A	HIGHLIGHT
Hyperlink	Attaches/modifies a hyperlink to an object.	N/A		Insert, Hyperlink	HYPERLINK
Identify Point	Displays the coordinate of a location.	Inquiry		Tools, Inquiry, ID Point	ID

Command or Icon Name	Description	Toolbar	Icon	Menu Bar	Command or Alias
Image	Opens the Image Manager.	Draw (Insert flyout) or Reference		Insert, Image Manager	IMAGE, IM, -IMAGE, -IM
Image Adjust	Controls the fade, contrast, and brightness of a selected image.	Reference		Modify, Object, Image, Adjust	IMAGEAD-JUST, IAD
Image Attach	Attaches a new image to the drawing.	Reference		Insert, Raster Image	IMAGEAT-TACH, IAT
Image Clip	Creates clipping boundaries for image objects.	Reference		Modify, Clip, Image	IMAGECLIP, ICL
Image Frame	Controls whether an image frame is displayed or not.	Reference		Modify, Object, Image, Frame	IMAGE-FRAME
Image Quality	Controls the quality of images.	Reference		Modify, Object, Image, Quality	IMAGE-QUALITY
Image Transparency	Controls whether the back-ground of an image is opaque or clear.	Reference		Modify, Object, Image, Trans-parency	TRANS-PARENCY
Import	Imports many different file formats.	Draw (Insert flyout) or Insert		Insert	IMPORT, IMP
Insert Block	Places blocks or other drawings into a drawing via the com-mand line or via a dialog box.	Draw (Insert flyout) or Insert		Insert, Block	INSERT, -I, DDINSERT, I
Insert Multiple Blocks	Inserts multiple instances of a block in a rectangular array.	N/A		N/A	MINSERT
Insert Objects	Inserts a linked or embedded object.	N/A		Insert, OLE Object	INSERTOBJ, IO
Interfere	Shows where two solid objects overlap.	Solids		Draw, Solids, Interference	INTERFERE, INF
Intersect	Forms a new solid from the area common to two or more solids or regions.	Solids Editing		Modify, Solids Editing, Intersect	INTERSECT, IN
Isolines	System variable that specifies the number of isolines per surface on objects.	N/A		N/A	ISOLINES
Isometric Plane	Controls which isometric draw-ing plane is active: left, top, or right.	N/A		N/A	'ISOPLANE, ISOPLANE, or Ctrl-E or F5

Command or Icon Name	Description	Toolbar	Icon	Menu Bar	Command or Alias
Join	Joins lines, circles, arcs, or splines into a single object.	Modify		Modify, Join	JOIN
Jpeg out	Saves selected objects to a file in JPEG file format.	N/A		N/A	JPEGOUT
Justify Text	Changes the justification point of text.	Text		Modify, Object, Text, Justify	JUSTIFYTEXT
Landscape Edit	Allows you to edit a landscape object.	Render		View, Render, Landscape Edit	LSEDIT
Landscape Library	Maintains libraries of landscape objects.	Render		View, Render, Landscape Library	lSLIB
Landscape New	Lets you add realistic landscape items, such as trees and bushes, to your drawings.	Render		View, Render, Landscape New	lSNEW
Layer Properties Manager	Creates layers and controls layer color, linetype, and visibility.	Layers		Format, Layer	'LAYER, LAYER, 'LA, LA, 'DDLMODES, DDLMODES, -LAYER, -LA
Layer Translator	Changes a drawing's layers to specified layer standard.	CAD Standards		Tools, CAD Standards, Layer Translator	LAYTRANS
Layout	Create, rename, copy, save, or delete layouts for managing plotted views.	Layouts		Insert, Layout	LAYOUT
Layout Wizard	Starts the layout wizard which you can use to create and control layouts.			Insert, Layout, Wizard or Tools, Wizards, Create Layout	LAYOUT-WIZARD
Leader	Creates leader lines for identifying lines and dimensions.	Dimension		Dimension, Leader	LEADER, Lead, LE, QLEADER
Left View	Sets the viewing direction for a three-dimensional visualization of the drawing to the left side.	View		View, 3D Views, Left	VPOINT, -VP, DDVPOINT, VP
Lengthen	Lengthens an object.	N/A		Modify, Lengthen	LENGTHEN, LEN
Light	Controls the light sources in rendered scenes.	Render		View, Render, Light	LIGHT
Limits	Sets up the size of the drawing.	N/A		Format, Drawing Limits	'LIMITS, LIMITS

Command or Icon Name	Description	Toolbar	Icon	Menu Bar	Command or Alias
Line	Draws straight lines of any length.	Draw		Draw, Line	LINE, L
Lineweight	Sets the line thickness for objects.	Properties		Format, Lineweight	LWEIGHT, 'LWEIGHT, Right-click LWT button, pick Settings
Linear Dimension	Creates linear dimensions.	Dimension	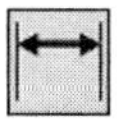	Dimension, Linear	DIMLINEAR, DIMLIN, DLI
Linetype	Changes the pattern used for new lines in the drawing.	Properties		Format, Linetype	'LINETYPE, LINETYPE, -LT 'DDLTYPE, DDLTYPE, LT
Linetype Scale	System variable that changes the scale of the linetypes in the drawing.	N/A			'LTSCALE, LTSCALE, LTS
List	Provides information on an object, such as the length of a line.	Inquiry		Tools, Inquiry, List	LIST, LI, LS
List Variables	Lists the values of system variables.	N/A		Tools, Inquiry, Set Variable	'SETVAR, SETVAR, SET
Load	Makes shapes available for use by the Shape command.	N/A		N/A	LOAD
Locate Point	Finds the coordinates of any point on the screen.	Inquiry		Tools, Inquiry, ID Point	'ID, ID
Log File Off	Closes the log file.	N/A		Tools, Options, Open and Save	LOGFILEOFF
Log File On	Writes the text window contents to a file.	N/A		Tools, Options, Open and Save	LOGFILEON
Make Block	Groups a set of objects together so that they are treated as one object.	Draw		Draw, Block, Make	BMAKE, B, BLOCK, -B
Make Slide	Creates a bitmapped slide file of the current viewport or layout	N/A		N/A	MSLIDE
Mapping	Lets you map materials onto selected geometry.	Render		View, Render, Mapping	SETUV

Command or Icon Name	Description	Toolbar	Icon	Menu Bar	Command or Alias
Markup Set Manager	Displays and allows you to add notes to markup drawings.	Standard		Tools, Markup Set Manager	MARKUP
Match Properties	Copies the properties of one object to other selected objects.	Standard		Modify, Match Properties	'MATCHPROP, MATCHPROP, MA, PAINTER
Materials	Controls the material a rendered object appears to be made of, and allows creation of new materials.	Render		View, Render, Materials	RMAT
Materials Library	Manages all the materials available for your drawing.	Render		View, Render, Materials Library	MATLIB
Mass Properties	Calculates and displays the mass properties of regions and solids.	Inquiry		Tools, Inquiry, Mass Properties	MASSPROP
Measure	Marks segments of a chosen length on an object by inserting points or blocks.	N/A		Draw, Point, Measure	MEASURE, ME
Menu	Loads a menu file.	N/A		N/A	MENU
Menu Load	Loads partial menu files.	N/A		Tools, Customize, Interface	MENULOAD
Menu Unload	Unloads partial menu files.	N/A		N/A	MENUUN-LOAD
Mirror	Creates mirror images of shapes.	Modify		Modify, Mirror	MIRROR, MI
Mirror3d		N/A		Modify, 3D Operation, Mirror 3D	MIRROR 3D
Model Space	Enters model space.	Status bar		N/A	MSPACE, MS
Modify Properties	Controls properties of existing objects.	Standard		Modify, Properties	PROPERTIES, DDMODIFY, MO
Move	Moves an existing shape from one area on the drawing to another area.	Modify		Modify, Move	MOVE, M
Mtprop	Changes paragraph text properties.	N/A		N/A	MTPROP

Command or Icon Name	Description	Toolbar	Icon	Menu Bar	Command or Alias
Multiline	Creates multiple, parallel lines.	N/A		Draw, Multiline	MLIne, ML
Multiline Style	Defines a style for multiple, parallel lines.	N/A		Format, Multiline Style	MLSTYLE
Multiline Text	Creates a paragraph that fits within a nonprinting text boundary.	Draw or Text		Draw, Text, Multiline Text	MTEXT, MT, T, -MTEXT, -T
Multiple	Repeats the next command until canceled.	N/A		N/A	MULTIPLE
Multiple Redo	Reverses the effects of previous UNDO commands.	Standard		N/A	MREDO
MV Setup	Helps set up drawing views using a LISP program.	N/A		N/A	MVSETUP
Mview	Creates viewports in paperspace (when Tilemode = 0).	N/A		View, Viewports New (all options)	MVIEW, MV
Named UCS	Selects a named and saved user coordinate system.	UCS II		Tools, Named UCS	UCSMAN, DDUCS, UC
Named Views	Sets the viewing direction to a named view.	View		View, Named Views	'VIEW, VIEW, -V, 'DDVIEW, DDVIEW, V
NE Isometric View	Sets the viewing direction for a three-dimensional visualization of the drawing.	View		View, 3D Views, NE Isometric	VPOINT, -VP, DDVPOINT, VP
New Drawing	Sets up the screen to create a new drawing.	Standard		File, New	NEW
NW Isometric View	Sets the viewing direction for a three-dimensional visualization of the drawing.	View		View, 3D Views, NW Isometric	VPOINT, -VP, DDVPOINT, VP
Object Group	Creates a named selection set of objects.	N/A		N/A	GROUP, G, -GROUP, -G
Object Selection Filters	Creates lists to select objects based on properties.	N/A		N/A	'FILTER, FILTER, FI
Object Selection Settings	Defines Selection Mode.	N/A		Tools, Options, Selection	'DDSELECT, DDSELECT, SE

Command or Icon Name	Description	Toolbar	Icon	Menu Bar	Command or Alias
Object Snap Settings (Running Object Snap)	Sets running objects snap modes and changes target box size.	Object Snap or Status Bar		Tools, Drafting Settings, Object Snap	'OSNAP, OSNAP, 'DDOSNAP, DDOSNAP, OSNAP, -OS, OS
Object UCS	Selects a user coordinate system based on the object.	UCS		Tools, New UCS, Object	UCS
Offset	Draws objects parallel to a given object.	Modify		Modify, Offset	OFFSET, O
OLE Properties	Allows you to control properties of linked objects.	N/A		Right-click an OLE object and pick Scale	OLESCALE
Oops	Restores erased objects.	N/A		N/A	OOPS
Open Drawing	Loads a previously saved drawing.	Standard		File, Open	OPEN
Options	Customize the AutoCAD software for your use.	N/A		Tools, Options	OPTIONS
Ordinate Dimension	Creates ordinate point dimensions.	Dimension	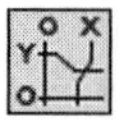	Dimension, Ordinate	DIMORDINATE, DIMORD, DOR
Origin UCS	Creates a user-defined coordinate system at the origin of the view.	UCS		Tools, New UCS, Origin	UCS
Ortho	Restricts movement to only horizontal and vertical.	Status bar		N/A	'ORTHO, ORTHO, or toggle with F8
Page Setup	Specifies the layout page, plotting device, paper size, and settings for new layout.	Layouts		File, Page Setup or right-click Model tab and pick Page Setup	PAGESETUP
Pan Down	Moves the drawing around on the screen without changing the zoom factor.	N/A		View, Pan, Down	
Pan Left	Moves the drawing around on the screen without changing the zoom factor.	N/A		View, Pan, Left	
Pan Point	Moves the drawing around on the screen without changing the zoom factor.	N/A		View, Pan, Point	'-PAN, -PAN, '-P, -P
Pan Right	Moves the drawing around on the screen without changing the zoom factor.	N/A		View, Pan, Right	

Command or Icon Name	Description	Toolbar	Icon	Menu Bar	Command or Alias
Pan Realtime	Moves the drawing around on the screen without changing the zoom factor.	Standard		View, Pan, Real Time	'PAN, PAN, 'P, P,
Pan Up	Moves the drawing around on the screen without changing the zoom factor.	N/A		View, Pan, Up	
Paper Space	Enters paper space when TILE-MODE is set to 0.	Status bar		View, Paper Space	PSPACE, PS
Paper Space Linetype Scale	System variable that causes the paper space LTSCALE factor to be used for every viewport.	N/A		N/A	PSLTSCALE
Paste From Clipboard	Places objects from the Windows Clipboard into the drawing using the Insert command.	Standard		Edit, Paste	PASTECLIP
Paste Special	Inserts and controls data from the Clipboard.	N/A		Edit, Paste Special	PASTESPEC, PA
PC In Wizard	Displays a wizard to import PCP and PC2 configuration file plot settings into the Model tab or current layout.	N/A		Tools, Wizards, Import Plot Settings	PCINWIZARD
Perimeter	System variable that stores the last perimeter value computed by the Area or List commands. (read only)	N/A		N/A	PERIMETER
Plan	Creates a view looking straight down along the Z-axis to see the XY coordinates.	N/A		View, 3D Views, Plan View	PLAN
Plot Stamp	Places information on a specified corner of each drawing and logs it to a file.	N/A		N/A	PLOTSTAMP
Plot Style	Sets or assigns current plot style.	Properties		N/A	PLOTSTYLE
Plotter Manager	Allows you to add or edit plotter configurations.	N/A		File, Plotter Manager	PLOTTER-MANAGER
Point	Creates a point object.	Draw		Draw, Point, Single Point	POINT, PO
Point Filters (.X, .Y, .Z, .XY, .XZ, .YZ)	Lets you selectively find single coordinates out of a point's three-dimensional coordinate set.	N/A		N/A	(used within other commands) .X or .Y or .Z or .XY or .XZ or .YZ

Command or Icon Name	Description	Toolbar	Icon	Menu Bar	Command or Alias
Point Style	Specifies the display mode and size of point objects.	N/A		Format, Point Style	'DDPTYPE, DDPTYPE, PDMODE
Polygon	Draws regular polygons with 3 to 1024 sides.	Draw		Draw, Polygon	POLYGON, POL
Polyline	Draws a series of connected objects (lines or arcs) that are treated as a single object called a polyline.	Draw		Draw, Polyline	PLINE, PL
Polyline edit (Pedit)	Edits polylines and three-dimensional polygon meshes.	Modify II		Modify, Object, Polyline	PEDIT
Preferences	Customizes the AutoCAD settings.	N/A		Tools, Options	PREFERENCES, OPTIONS
Preset UCS	Selects a preset UCS.	UCS		Tools, Orthographic UCS, Preset	DDUCSP, UCSMAN
Previous Layer	Undoes the last change or set of changes to the layer settings.	Layers		N/A	LAYERP
Previous Layer Mode	Enables/disables the tracking of layer changes.	N/A		N/A	LAYERP-MODE
Previous UCS	Returns you to the previously used user coordinate system.	UCS		N/A	UCS
Print/Plot	Prints or plots a drawing	Standard		File, Plot	PLOT, PRINT
Print Preview	Previews the drawing before printing or plotting.	Standard		File, Plot Preview	PREVIEW, PRE
Projmode	System variable that sets the current projection mode for trim or extend operations.	N/A		N/A	PROJMODE
Properties	Used to change the properties of an object.	Properties		Modify, Properties	PROPERTIES, CHPROP, DDCH-PROP, CH
PS Drag	Controls the appearance of a PostScript image as it is dragged into place.	N/A		N/A	PSDRAG
PS Fill	Fills a 2D outline with a PostScript pattern.	N/A		N/A	PSFILL

Command or Icon Name	Description	Toolbar	Icon	Menu Bar	Command or Alias
PS In	Imports a file in PostScript (*.*eps*) format.	N/A		N/A	PSIN
PS Out	Saves drawing objects in PostScript (*.*eps*) format.	N/A		N/A	PSOUT
Publish	Creates multi-sheet drawing sets for publishing to a single multi-sheet DWF™ (Design Web Format) file, a plotting device, or a plot file.	Standard		File, Publish	PUBLISH
Publish to Web	Includes images of selected drawings in HTML page format.	Standard		File, Publish to Web	PUBLISH-TOWEB
Purge	Removes unused items from the drawing database.	N/A		File, Drawing Utilities, Purge	PURGE, PU
Qtext	Controls the display and plotting of text and attribute text.	N/A		N/A	'QTEXT, QTEXT
Quick Calculator	Performs calculations, converts units, and more.	Standard		Tools, QuickCalc	QUICKCALC
Quick Dimension	Quickly creates dimensions.	Dimension		Dimension, Quick Dimension	QDIM
Quick Leader	Quickly creates leaders and annotations.	Dimension		Dimension, Leader	QLEADER
Quick Select	Quickly creates selection sets based on filtering criteria.	Tools, Quick Select		N/A	QSELECT
Quit	Exits with the option not to save your changes, and returns you to the operating system.	N/A		File, Exit	QUIT, EXIT
Radius Dimension	Adds centermarks to an arc when providing its radius dimension.	Dimension		Dimension, Radius	DIMRADIUS, DIMRAD, DRA
Ray	Creates a semi-infinite line.	N/A		Draw, Ray	RAY
Reassociate Dimension	Associates dimension to drawing object.	N/A		Dimension, Reassociate Dimensions	DIMREASSO-CIATE
Recover	Repairs a damaged drawing.	N/A		File, Drawing Utilities, Recover	RECOVER

Command or Icon Name	Description	Toolbar	Icon	Menu Bar	Command or Alias
Rectangle	Creates rectangular shapes.	Draw		Draw, Rectangle	RECTANG, REC
Redefine	Restores AutoCAD internal commands changed by the Undefine command.	N/A		N/A	'REDEFINE, REDEFINE
Redefine Attribute	Redefines a block and updates associated attributes.	N/A		N/A	ATTREDEF
Redo	Reverses the effect of the most recent UNDO command. MRedo has multiple redo capability.	Standard		Edit, Redo	MREDO, REDO, Ctrl-Y
Redraw All	Redraws all viewports at once.	Standard		View, Redraw	'REDRAWALL, REDRAWALL, RA
Redraw View	Removes blip marks added to the drawing screen and restores objects partially erased while you were editing other objects.	N/A		N/A	'REDRAW, REDRAW, 'R, R
Reference, Close	Saves back or discards changes made during in-place xref editing.	N/A		Tools, Xref & Block In Place Editing, Save Reference Edit, Close Reference	REFCLOSE
Reference Edit	Selects a reference for editing.	Refedit		Tools, Xref & Block In Place Editing, Edit Reference in Place	REFEDIT
Refset	Adds or removes objects from a working set during in-place editing of an xref or block.	N/A		Tools, Xref & Block In Place Editing, Add/Remove from Working Set	REFSET
Regenauto	Controls the automatic regeneration of a drawing.	N/A		N/A	'REGENAUTO, REGENAUTO
Regenerate	Recalculates the display file in order to show changes.	N/A		View, Regen	REGEN, RE
Regenerate All	Regenerates all viewports at once.	N/A		View, Regen All	REGENALL, REA
Regenerate Dimensions	Updates the locations of associated dimensions.	N/A		N/A	DIMREGEN

Command or Icon Name	Description	Toolbar	Icon	Menu Bar	Command or Alias
Region	Creates a two-dimensional area object from a selection set of existing objects.	Draw		Draw, Region	REGION, REG
Reinit	Reinitializes the digitizer, input/output port and program parameters.	N/A		N/A	REINIT
Rename	Changes the names of objects.	N/A		Format, Rename	RENAME, DDRENAME, REN, -REN
Render	Produces a realistically shaded 2D view of a 3D model.	Render		View, Render, Render	RENDER, RR
Render File Options	Sets the render to file options for rendering.	N/A		N/A	RFILEOPT
Render Preferences	Lets you control how images are rendered and how you use the Render commands.	Render		View, Render, Preferences	RPREF, RPR
Render Screen	Renders to a full-screen display only.	N/A		N/A	RENDSCR
Render Statistics	Provides rendering information, such as rendering type, scene, and time.	Render		View, Render, Statistics	STATS
Replay	Displays a BMP, TGA, or TIFF image.	N/A		Tools, Display Image, View	REPLAY
Restore UCS	Restores a saved user coordinate system.	UCS		Tools, Named UCS	UCS UCSMAN
Resume	Continues an interrupted script.	N/A		N/A	'RESUME, RESUME
Revision Cloud	Creates a polyline of sequential arcs to form a cloud shape.	Draw		Draw	REVCLOUD
Revolve	Creates a three-dimensional object by sweeping a two-dimensional polyline, circle or region about a circular path to create a symmetrical solid.	Solids		Draw, Solids, Revolve	REVOLVE, REV
Revolved Surface	Creates a rotated surface about a selected axis.	Surfaces		Draw, Surfaces, Revolved Surface	REVSURF
Right View	Sets the viewing direction for a three-dimensional visualization of the drawing to the right side.	View		View, 3D Views, Right	VPOINT, DDVPOINT, VP, -VP

Command or Icon Name	Description	Toolbar	Icon	Menu Bar	Command or Alias
Rotate	Rotates all or part of an object.	Modify		Modify, Rotate	ROTATE, RO
Rscript	Creates a continually repeating script.	N/A		N/A	RSCRIPT
Ruled Surface	Creates a polygon mesh between two curves.	Surfaces		Draw, Surfaces, Ruled Surface	RULESURF
Save	Saves a drawing using Quick Save.	Standard		File, Save	QSAVE
Save	Saves a drawing to a new file name, without changing the name of the drawing on your screen.	N/A		N/A	SAVE
Save As	Saves a drawing, allowing you to change its name or location, or to a previous version.	N/A		File, Save As	SAVEAS
Save Image	Saves a rendered image to a file.	N/A		Tools, Display Image, Save	SAVEIMG
Save Slide	Creates a slide file of the current viewport.	N/A		N/A	MSLIDE
Save Time	System variable that controls how often a file is automatically saved.	N/A		N/A	SAVETIME
Save UCS	Saves a user coordinate system.	UCS		N/A	UCS, UCSMAN
Scale	Changes the size of an object in the drawing database.	Modify		Modify, Scale	SCALE, SC
Scale Text	Changes the scale of text objects without changing location.	Text		Modify, Object, Text, Scale	SCALETEXT
Scenes	Saves and recalls named scenes, making it easier to quickly change to a different viewpoint and lighting.	Render		View, Render, Scene	SCENE
Script	Executes a sequence of commands from a script.	N/A		Tools, Run Script	SCRIPT, SCR
SE Isometric View	Sets the viewing direction for a three-dimensional visualization of the drawing.	View		View, 3D Views, SE Isometric	VPOINT, DDVPOINT, VP, -VP

Command or Icon Name	Description	Toolbar	Icon	Menu Bar	Command or Alias
Section	Uses the intersection of a plane and solids to create a region.	Solids		Draw, Solids, Section	SECTION, SEC
Select	Selects objects with a selection method listed below. Commands must be typed following the Select command.	N/A		N/A	'SELECT, SELECT
Select Add	Places selected objects in the previous selection set (default method).	N/A		N/A	ADD (at Select Objects: prompt)
Select All	Places all objects in the selection set.	N/A		N/A	ALL (at Select Objects: prompt)
Select Auto	Selects objects individually, objects within a left-to-right window, and objects crossing and within a right-to-left window (default selection method).	N/A		N/A	AUTO (at Select Objects: prompt)
Select Box	Selects objects within a left-to-right window, and/or objects crossing and within a right-to-left window (default selection method).	N/A		N/A	BOX (at Select Objects: prompt)
Select Crossing	Selects all objects within and crossing the selection box (default selection from right to left).	N/A		N/A	Crossing (at Select Objects: prompt); C
Select Crossing Polygon	Selects all objects within and crossing a user-defined polygon boundary.	N/A		N/A	CPolygon (at Select Objects: prompt); CP
Select Fence	Selects objects crossing a user-defined polyline.	N/A		N/A	Fence (at Select Objects: prompt); F
Select Group	Selects all objects within a specified group.	N/A		N/A	Group (at Select Objects: prompt); G
Select Last	Re-highlights last selection.	N/A		N/A	Last (at Select Objects: prompt); L
Select Multiple	Selects objects without highlighting them.	N/A		N/A	Multiple (at Select Objects: prompt); M
Select Previous	Places previously selected objects in the selection set.	N/A		N/A	Previous (at Select Objects: prompt); P
Select Remove	Removes selected objects in the previous selection set.	N/A		N/A	Remove (at Select Objects: prompt); R

Command or Icon Name	Description	Toolbar	Icon	Menu Bar	Command or Alias
Select Single	Selects a single object.	N/A		N/A	Single (at Select Objects: prompt); S
Select Undo	Cancels the selection of the most recently selected object.	N/A		N/A	Undo (at Select Objects: prompt); U
Select Window	Selects all objects within a user-defined window.	N/A		N/A	Window (at Select Objects: prompt); W
Select Window Polygon	Selects all objects within a user-defined polygon.	N/A		N/A	WPolygon (at Select Objects: prompt); WP
Set Variables	Changes the values of system variables.	N/A		Tools, Inquiry, Set Variable	'SETVAR, SETVAR, SET
Setup Drawing	Generates Profiles and sections in viewports created with SOLVIEW.	Solids		Draw, Solids, Setup, Drawing	SOLDRAW
Setup Profile	Creates profile images of 3D solids.	Solids		Draw, Solids, Setup, Profile	SOLPROF
Setup View	Creates floating viewports for orthographic projection, section views, and multi-views of 3D solids.	Solids		Draw, Solids, Setup, View	SOLVIEW
Shade	Creates a shaded view of a model.	Shade		View, Shade, (select mode)	SHADE, SHA
Shade Mode	Controls the display of solid object shading in the current viewport.	N/A		View, View Shade	SHADEMODE
Shape	Inserts a shape into the current drawing.	N/A		N/A	SHAPE
Sheet Set Manager	Organizes, displays, and manages named collections of sheets.	Standard		N/A	SHEETSET
Shell	Accesses operating system commands.	N/A		N/A	SHELL
Show Materials	Shows you the material and attachment method for the selected object.	N/A		N/A	SHOWMAT
Single Line Text	Adds text to a drawing.	N/A		Draw, Text, Single Line Text	DTEXT, DT

Command or Icon Name	Description	Toolbar	Icon	Menu Bar	Command or Alias
Sketch	Creates a series of freehand line segments.	N/A		N/A	SKETCH
Slice	Slices a set of solids with a plane.	Solids		Draw, Solids, Slice	SLICE, SL
Snap	Limits cursor movement on the screen to set interval so objects can be placed at precise locations easily.	Status bar		N/A	SNAP, SN, or toggle off and on with F9
Snap From	Establishes a temporary reference point as a basis for specifying subsequent points.	Object Snap		N/A	'OSNAP, OSNAP, 'DDOSNAP, DDOSNAP, OS, -OS, OSNAP
Snap to Apparent Intersection	Snaps to a real or visual three-dimensional intersection formed by objects you select or by an extension of those objects.	Object Snap		N/A	'APP, APP, EAPPINT, APPINT
Snap to Center	Snaps to the center of an arc, circle, or ellipse.	Object Snap		N/A	'CEN, CEN
Snap to Endpoint	Snaps to the closest endpoint of an arc, elliptical arc, ray, multiline, or line, or to the closest corner of a trace, solid, or three-dimensional face.	Object Snap		N/A	'ENDP, ENDP, END
Snap to Insertion	Snaps to the insertion point of text, a block, a shape, or an attribute.	Object Snap		N/A	'INS, INS
Snap to Intersection	Snaps to the intersection of a line, arc, spline, elliptical arc, ellipse, ray, construction line, multiline, or circle.	Object Snap		N/A	'INT, INT
Snap to Midpoint	Snaps to the midpoint of an arc, elliptical arc spline, ray, solid, construction line, multiline, or line.	Object Snap		N/A	'MID, MID
Snap to Nearest	Snaps to the nearest point of an arc, elliptical arc, ellipse, spline, ray, multiline, line, circle, or point.	Object Snap		N/A	'NEA, NEA
Snap to Node	Snaps to a point object.	Object Snap		N/A	'NOD, NOD
Snap to None	Turns object snap mode off.	Object Snap		N/A	'NONE, NONE
Snap to Parallel	Aligns new drawing vector parallel to an acquired object.	Object Snap		N/A	PAR

Command or Icon Name	Description	Toolbar	Icon	Menu Bar	Command or Alias
Snap to Perpendicular	Snaps to a point perpendicular to an arc, elliptical arc, ellipse, spline, ray, construction line, multiline, line, solid, or circle.	Object Snap		N/A	'PER, PER
Snap to Quadrant	Snaps to a quadrant point of an arc, elliptical arc, ellipse, solid, or circle.	Object Snap		N/A	'QUA, QUA
Snap to Tangent	Snaps to the tangent of an arc, elliptical arc, ellipse, or circle.	Object Snap		N/A	'TAN, TAN
Solid Edit	Edits faces and edges of 3D solid objects.	Solids Editing		Modify, Solids Editing	SOLIDEDIT
Space Translation	Converts length values between model space and paper space.	Text			SPACETRANS
Spelling	Checks spelling in a drawing.	N/A		Tools, Spelling	'SPELL, SPELL, SP
Sphere	Creates a three-dimensional solid sphere.	Solids		Draw, Solids, Sphere	SPHERE
Spline	Fits a smooth curve to a sequence of points within a specified tolerance.	Draw		Draw, Spline	SPLINE, SPL
Standards	Manages CAD standards files associated with AutoCAD drawings.	Standards		Tools, CAD Standards, Configure	STANDARDS
Statistics	Displays information about your last rendering.	Render		View, Render, Statistics	STATS
Status	Displays drawing statistics, modes, and extents.	N/A		N/A	'STATUS, STATUS
STL Out	Stores solids in an ASCII or binary file.	N/A		N/A	STLOUT
Stretch	Stretches the objects selected.	Modify		Modify, Stretch	STRETCH, S
Style	Lets you create new text styles and modify existing ones.	Styles		Format, Text Style	'STYLE, STYLE, ST
Styles Manager	Uses dialog box to manage plot styles.	N/A		File, Plot Style Manager	STYLES-MANAGER

Command or Icon Name	Description	Toolbar	Icon	Menu Bar	Command or Alias
Subtract	Removes the set of a second solid or region from the first set.	Solids Editing		Modify, Solids Editing, Subtract	SUBTRACT, SU
Surftab1	System variable that sets the number of tabulations to be generated for Rulesurf and Tabsurf.	N/A		N/A	SURFTAB1
Surftab2	System variable that sets mesh density in the N direction for Revsur and Edgesurf.	N/A		N/A	SURFTAB2
SW Isometric View	Sets the viewing direction for a three-dimensional visualization of the drawing.	View		View, 3D Views, SW Isometric	VPOINT, DDVPOINT, VP, -VP
Synchronize Attributes	Updates all instances of specified block to current attributes.	Modify II			ATTSYNC
System Windows	Arranges windows and icons on screen.	N/A		N/A	SYSWINDOWS
Tablet	Calibrates the tablet with a paper drawing's coordinate system.	N/A		Tools, Tablet	TABLET, TA
Tabmode	System variable that controls the use of tablet mode.	N/A		N/A	TABMODE
Tabulated Surface	Creates a tabulated surface from a path curve and direction vector.	Surfaces		Draw, Surfaces, Tabulated	TABSURF
Target	System variable that stores location (in UCS coordinates) of the target point for the current viewport (read only).	N/A		N/A	TARGET
Text	Creates a single line of user-entered text.	N/A		N/A	TEXT
Text Screen	Switches from the graphics screen to the text screen.	N/A		View, Display, Text Window	'TEXTSCR, or toggle back and forth with F2
Thickness	Sets the current 3D solid thickness.	N/A		N/A	THICKNESS, TH
Tiled Viewports	Divides the graphics window into multiple tiled viewports and manages them.	N/A		View, Viewports	VPORTS
Tilemode	When set to 1, allows creation of tiled viewports in model space; when set to 0, enables use of paper space.	Status bar		N/A	TILEMODE, TI or pick model/layout tabs

Command or Icon Name	Description	Toolbar	Icon	Menu Bar	Command or Alias
Time	Displays the date and time statistics of a drawing.	N/A		Tools, Inquiry, Time	'TIME, TIME
Tolerance	Creates geometric tolerances and adds them to a drawing in feature control frames.	Dimension		Dimension, Tolerance	TOLERANCE, TOL
Tool Palettes	Opens the Tool Palettes window.	Standard		Tools, Tool Palettes Window	TOOL-PALETTES
Toolbar	Displays, hides, and positions all toolbars.	N/A		View, Toolbars	TOOLBAR, TO
Tooltips	System variable that controls the display of Tooltips.	N/A		N/A	TOOLTIPS
Top View	Sets the viewing direction for a three-dimensional visualization of the drawing to the top.	View		View, 3D Views, Top	VPOINT, DDVPOINT, VP, -VP
Torus	Creates a donut-shaped solid.	Solids		Draw, Solids, Torus	TORUS, TOR
Trace	Creates solid lines.	N/A		N/A	TRACE
Transparency	Controls transparency of background in a bitmap image.	Reference		Modify, Object, Image, Transparency	TRANS-PARENCY
Treestat	Displays information on the drawing's current spatial index.	N/A		N/A	TREESTAT
Trim	Removes part of an object at its intersection with another object.	Modify		Modify, Trim	TRIM, TR
UCS	Manages User Coordinate Systems.	UCS		Tools, UCS	UCSMAN, UCS, DDUCS, UC
UCS Follow	System variable that allows you to generate a plan view of the current UCS in a viewport whenever you change the UCS.	N/A		N/A	UCSFOLLOW
UCS Icon	System variable that repositions and turns on and off the display of the UCS icon.	N/A		N/A	UCSICON
UCS Manager	Manages defined user coordinate systems.	UCS		Tools, Named UCS	USCMAN

Command or Icon Name	Description	Toolbar	Icon	Menu Bar	Command or Alias
Undefine	Allows an application-defined command to override an AutoCAD command.	N/A		N/A	UNDEFINE
Undo	Reverses the effect of previous commands.	Standard		Edit, Undo	UNDO, U
Union	Adds two separate sets of solids or regions together to create one solid model.	Solids Editing		Modify, Solids Editing, Union	UNION, UNI
Units	Controls the type and precision of the values used in dimensions.	N/A		Format, Units	'UNITS, UNITS, -UN 'DDUNITS, DDUNITS, UN
View	Saves views of an object to be plotted, displayed, or printed.	N/A		N/A	'VIEW, VIEW, 'DDVIEW, DDVIEW, -V
Viewport Clip	Clips viewport objects.	N/A		N/A	VPCLIP
View Resolution	Sets the resolution for object generation in the current viewport.	N/A		N/A	VIEWRES
View Slide	Displays a raster-image slide file in the current viewport.	N/A		N/A	VSLIDE
View UCS	Selects a user coordinate system aligned to a specific view.	UCS		Tools, New UCS, View	UCS
Viewport Layer	Controls the visibility of layers within specific viewports in paper space.	N/A		N/A	VPLAYER
Visual Basic Editor	Display the Visual Basic Editor.	N/A		Tools, Macro, Visual Basic Editor	VBAIDE
Visual LISP	Display Visual LISP® interactive development environment (IDE).			Tools, AutoLISP, Visual LISP Editor	VLISP
Wedge	Creates a three-dimensional solid with a closed face tapering along the X-axis by specifying the center.	Solids		Draw, Solids, Wedge	WEDGE, WE
Who Has	Display ownership info. for open drawing files.	N/A		N/A	WHOHAS
WMF In	Imports a file saved in Windows Metafile (*.*wmf*) format.	N/A		Insert, Windows Metafile	WMFIN

Command or Icon Name	Description	Toolbar	Icon	Menu Bar	Command or Alias
WMF Options	Sets options for importing a Windows Metafile.	N/A		N/A	WMFOPTs
WMF Out	Saves drawing objects in Windows Metafile (*.*wmf*) format.	N/A		File, Save As, (set file as type *.*wmf*)	WMFOUT
World UCS	Selects the world coordinate system as the user coordinate system.	UCS		Tools, New UCS, World	UCS
Write Block	Saves a block as a separate file so that it may be used in other drawings.	N/A		N/A	WBLOCK, W
X Axis Rotate UCS	Selects a user coordinate system by rotating the X-axis.	UCS		Tools, New UCS, X	UCS
Xplode	Breaks a component object into its component objects; see also Explode.	N/A		N/A	XPLODE
Y Axis Rotate UCS	Selects a user coordinate system by rotating the Y-axis.	UCS		Tools, New UCS, Y	UCS
Z Axis Rotate UCS	Selects a user coordinate system by rotating the Z-axis.	UCS		Tools, New UCS, Z	UCS
Z Axis Vector UCS	Selects a user coordinate system defined by a vector in the Z direction.	UCS		Tools, New UCS, Z-Axis Vector	UCS
Zoom All	Resizes to display the entire drawing in the current view-port.	Standard (Zoom flyout) or Zoom		View, Zoom, All	'ZOOM, ZOOM, 'Z, Z
Zoom Center	Resizes to display a window by entering a center point, then a magnification value or height.	Standard (Zoom flyout) or Zoom		View, Zoom, Center	'ZOOM, ZOOM, 'Z, Z
Zoom Dynamic	Resizes to display the generated portion of the drawing with a view box.	Standard (Zoom flyout) or Zoom		View, Zoom, Dynamic	'ZOOM, ZOOM, 'Z, Z
Zoom Extents	Resizes to display the drawing extents.	Standard (Zoom flyout) or Zoom		View, Zoom, Extents	'ZOOM, ZOOM, 'Z, Z
Zoom In	Resizes areas of the drawing in the screen to make it appear closer or larger.	Standard (Zoom flyout) or Zoom		View, Zoom, In	'ZOOM, ZOOM, 'Z, Z
Zoom Object	Resizes display to fit one or more selected objects centered in drawing area.	Standard (Zoom flyout) or Zoom		View, Zoom, Object	'ZOOM, ZOOM, 'Z, Z

Command or Icon Name	Description	Toolbar	Icon	Menu Bar	Command or Alias
Zoom Out	Resizes areas of the drawing in the screen so that more of the drawing fits in the screen.	Standard (Zoom flyout) or Zoom		View, Zoom, Out	'ZOOM, ZOOM, 'Z, Z
Zoom Previous	Resizes to the previous view.	Standard		View, Zoom, Previous	'ZOOM, ZOOM, 'Z, Z
Zoom Realtime	Resizes the view in a real-time fashion.	Standard		View, Zoom, Realtime	'ZOOM, ZOOM, 'Z, Z
Zoom Scale	Resizes to display at a specified scale factor.	Standard (Zoom flyout) or Zoom		View, Zoom, Scale	'ZOOM, ZOOM, 'Z, Z
Zoom Vmax	Resizes so that the drawing is viewed from as far out as possible on the current viewports virtual screen without forcing a complete regeneration of the drawing.	N/A		N/A	'ZOOM, ZOOM, 'Z, Z
Zoom Window	Resizes to display an area specified by two opposite corner points of a rectangular window.	Standard (Zoom flyout) or Zoom		View, Zoom, Window	'ZOOM, ZOOM, 'Z, Z

Glossary

absolute coordinates	The exact location of a specific point in terms of x, y, and z from the fixed point of origin.
absolute value	The numerical value or magnitude of the quantity, without regard to its positive or negative sign.
alias	A short namc that can be used to activate a command; you can customize command aliases by editing the file *acad.pgp*.
ambient	The overall amount of light that exists in the environment of a rendered scene.
And gate	An electronic logic symbol; if either input is zero, the output is zero.
angle brackets	A value that appears in angle brackets < > is the default option for that command, which will be executed unless it is changed.
aperture	A type of cursor resembling a small box placed on top of the crosshairs; used to select in the object snap mode.
architectural units	Drawings made with these units are drawn in feet and fractional inches.
aspect ratio	The relationship of two dimensions to each other.
associative dimensioning	Dimensioning where each dimension is inserted as a group of drawing objects relative to the points selected in the drawing. If the drawing is scaled or stretched, the dimension values automatically update.
associative hatching	The practice of filling an area with a pattern which automatically updates when the boundary is modified.
attribute	Text information associated with a block.
attribute prompt	The prompt, which you define, that appears in the command area when you insert the block into a drawing.
attribute tag	A variable name that is replaced with the value that you type when prompted as you insert the attribute block.
AutoSnap™	A feature which displays a marker and description to indicate which object snap location will be selected.
auxiliary view	An orthographic view of an object using a direction of sight other than one of the six basic views (front, top, right side, rear, bottom, left side).
ball tag	A circled number identifying each part shown in an assembly drawing; also called a balloon number.
base feature	In a feature-based model, the main feature from which other features are defined based on the constraints put on the model.

base grip The selected grip, used as the base point for hot grip commands.

baseline dimensioning A dimensioning method in which each successive dimension is measured from one extension line or baseline.

basic dimension A theoretically exact dimension to which no tolerance is applied.

basic view One of the six standard views of an object: front, top, right side, rear, bottom, or left side.

bearing The angle to turn from the first direction stated toward the second direction stated.

bicubic surface A sculptured plane, mathematically describing a sculptured surface between three-dimensional curves.

bidirectional associativity Describes the link between the drawing and the model. If a change is made to the model, the drawing is automatically updated to reflect the change; if a change is made to the parametric dimensions in the drawing, both the drawing and the model update automatically.

bilateral tolerances Tolerances specified by defining a nominal dimension and the allowable range of deviation from that dimension, both plus and minus.

blip marks Little crosses that appear on the screen, indicating where a location was selected.

block A set of objects that have been grouped together to act as one, and can be saved and used in the current drawing and in other drawings.

block name Identifies a particular named group of objects.

block reference A particular insertion of a block into a drawing (blocks can be inserted more than once).

Boolean operators Find the union (addition), difference (subtraction), and intersection (common area) of two or more sets.

Buffer An electronic logic symbol.

bump map Converts color intensity or grayscale information to heights to give the appearance that features are raised above the surface, like embossed letters.

buttons A method of selecting options by picking in a defined area of the screen resembling a box or push button.

Cartesian coordinate system A rectangular coordinate system created by three mutually perpendicular coordinate axes, commonly labeled x, y, and z.

chained (continued) dimensioning A dimensioning method in which each successive dimension is measured from the last extension line of the previous dimension.

chamfer A straight line segment connecting two otherwise intersecting surfaces.

chord length The straight line distance between the start point and the endpoint of an arc.

circular view A view of a cylinder in which it appears as a circle (looking into the hole).

circumscribed Drawn around the outside of a base circle.

clearance fit The space available between two mating parts, where the greatest shaft size always is smaller than the smallest hole size, thus producing an open space.

colinear constraint Lying on the same straight line.

command aliasing The creation and use of alternative short names for commands, such as LA for Layer.

command prompt — The word or words in the command window that ask for the next piece of information.

command window — The lines of text below the graphics window that indicate the status of commands and prompt for user input.

construction plane — A plane that is temporarily defined during commands for creating new drawing objects.

context sensitive — Recognizes when you are in a command, and displays information for that command.

Coons patch — A bicubic surface interpolated between four edges.

coordinate system locator — An icon to help you visually refer to the current coordinate system.

coordinate values — Used to identify the location of a point, using the Cartesian coordinate system; x represents the horizontal position on the X axis, and y represents the vertical position on the Y axis. In a three-dimensional drawing, z represents the depth position on the Z axis.

crosshatching — The practice of filling an area with a pattern to differentiate it from other components of a drawing.

current layer — The layer you are working on. New drawing objects are always created on the layer that is current.

cursor (crosshairs) — A mark that shows the location of the pointing device in the graphics window of the screen; used to draw, select, or pick icons, menu items, or objects. The appearance of the cursor may change, depending on the command or option selected.

custom hatch pattern — A design that you have previously created and stored in the file *acad.pat* or another *.pat* file of your own making to use to fill an area.

customize — To change the toolbars, menus, and other aspects of the program to show those commands and functions that you want to use.

cutting edges — Objects used to define the portions to be removed when trimming an object.

cutting plane line — Defines the location on the object where the sectional view is taken.

datum surface — A theoretically exact geometric reference used to establish the tolerance zone for a feature.

default — The value that AutoCAD will use unless you specify otherwise; appears in angle brackets < > after a prompt.

default directory — The directory to which AutoCAD will save all drawing files unless instructed otherwise.

delta angle — The included angular value from the start point to the endpoint.

diameter symbol ∅ — Indicates that the value is a diameter.

difference — The area formed by subtracting one region or solid from another.

dimension line — Drawn between extension lines with an arrowhead at each end; indicates how the stated dimension relates to the feature on the object.

dimension style — A group of dimension features saved as a set.

dimension value — The value of the dimension being described (how long, how far across, etc.); placed near the midpoint of the dimension line.

dimension variables — Features of dimensions that can be altered by the user; you control the features by setting the variables using the Dimension Style dialog box.

dimension Describes the size and location of a part or object so that it can be manufactured.

distance across the flats A measurement of the size of a hexagon from one flat side to the side opposite it.

docked Attached to any edge of the graphics window, as a toolbar can be.

draft angle The taper on a molded part that makes it possible to easily remove the part from the mold.

drag To move an object on the screen and see it at the same time, in order to specify the new size or location.

edge view A line representing a plane surface shown on its end.

elements Parts of a multiline, which can be made up of up to 16 lines.

engineering units Drawings made with these units are drawn in feet and decimal inches.

export To save a file from one application as a different file type for use by another application.

extension line Relates a dimension to the feature it refers to.

extension line offset Specifies a distance for the gap between the end of the extension line and the point that defines the dimension.

extrusion Creates a long three-dimensional strip with the shape of a closed two-dimensional shape, as if material had been forced through a shaped opening.

falloff The angle of the cone of light from a spotlight.

feature Any definable aspect of an object—a hole, a surface, etc.

feature control frame Geometric dimensioning and tolerancing specification that uses rectangular boxes with symbols to specify allowable variations in the manufactured part.

file extension The part of a file name that is composed of a period, followed by one to three characters, and that helps you to identify the file type.

fillet An arc of specified radius that connects two lines, arcs, or circles, or a rounded interior corner on a machined part.

floating Refers to the toolbar's or command window's ability to be moved to any location on the screen.

floating viewport A window, created in paper space, through which you can see your model space drawing; very useful for plotting the drawing, adding drawing details, showing an enlarged view of the object, or showing multiple views of the object.

flyout A sub-toolbar that becomes visible when its representative icon on the main toolbar is chosen.

font A character pattern defined by the text style.

foreshortened Appears smaller than actual size, due to being tipped away from the viewing plane.

fractional units Drawings made with these units express lengths less than 1 as fractions (e.g., 15 1/4).

freeze Make a layer invisible and exclude it from regeneration and plotting.

generated layer A layer created automatically (instead of by the user) during commands such as SOLPROF.

geometric characteristic symbol Form, orientation, profile, runout, and locational symbols used to specify allowable variations in the manufactured part.

geometric tolerance Specialized tolerance symbols based on geometric form.

global linetype scaling factor The factor of the original size at which all lines in the drawing are displayed.

globe Used to select the direction for viewing a three-dimensional model.

graphics window The central part of the screen, which is used to create and display drawings.

grid Regularly spaced dots covering an area of the graphics window to aid in drawing.

group A named selection set of objects.

handle number A unique identifier assigned to each AutoCAD drawing object, including viewports.

heads-up Entering a command while looking at the screen; by picking an icon, for example, you do not need to look down to the keyboard to enter the command.

hidden line A line that represents an edge that is not directly visible because it is behind or beneath another surface.

highlight A change of color around a particular command or object, indicating that it has been selected and is ready to be executed or worked on in some way.

hot grips A method for editing an already drawn object using only the pointing device, without needing to use the menus, toolbars, or keyboard.

hotspot The angle of the cone of light for the brightest area of the beam of a spotlight.

image tile An active picture which displays dialog box choices as graphic images rather than words.

implied Crossing mode When this mode is activated, the first corner of a box is started when you select a point on the screen that is not on an object in the drawing. If the box is drawn from right to left, everything that partially crosses as well as items fully enclosed by the box are selected.

implied Windowing mode When this mode is activated, the first corner of a box is started when you select a point on the screen that is not on an object in the drawing. If the box is drawn from the left to right, a window is formed that selects everything that is entirely enclosed in the box.

import To open and use a file created by a different application than the one being used.

inclined surface Slanted at an angle, a surface that is perpendicular to one of the three principal views and tipped away from the other principal views.

included angle The angular measurement along a circular path.

inscribed Drawn inside a base circle.

inspection The act of examining the part against its specifications.

instance Each single action of a command.

intensity The brightness level of a light source.

intersection The point where two lines or surfaces meet, or the area shared by overlapping regions or solid models.

Inverter gate A symbol used to draw an electronic logic circuit; for inputs of 1, the output is 0, for inputs of 0, the output is 1.

layer A method of separating drawing objects so that they can be viewed individually or stacked like transparent acetates, allowing all layers to show. Used to set color and linetype properties for groups of objects.

leader line A line from a note or radial dimension that ends in an arrowhead pointing at the feature.

limiting element The outer edge of a curved surface.

limiting tolerances Tolerances specified by defining an upper and lower allowable measurement.

lock To prohibit changes to a layer, although the layer is still visible on the screen.

major arc An arc which comprises more than 180° of a circle.

major axis The long axis of symmetry across an ellipse.

manufacture To create a part according to its specifications.

mass properties Data about the real-world object being drawn, such as its mass, volume, and moments of inertia.

matrix An array of vertices used to generate a surface.

menu bar The strip across the top of the screen showing the names of the pull-down menus, such as File, Edit, etc.

minor axis The short axis of symmetry across an ellipse.

mirror line A line that defines the angle and distance at which a reflected image of a selected object will be created.

miter line A line drawn above the side view and to the right of the top view, often drawn from the top right corner of the front view, used to project features from the side view onto the top view of an object.

model space The AutoCAD drawing database, when an object exists as a three-dimensional object.

Nand gate A symbol used to draw an electronic logic circuit; when both inputs are 1, output is 0, when any input is 0, output is 1.

nominal dimension The general identification for the size of a typical feature, for example a 1/2" diameter hole.

Nor gate A symbol used to draw an electronic logic circuit; when both inputs are 0, output is 1, any input of 1, output is 0.

normal surface A surface that is perpendicular to two of the three principal orthographic views and appears at the correct size and shape in a basic view.

noun/verb selection A method for selecting an object first and then the command to be used on it.

nurb A cubic spline curve.

offset distance Controls the distance from an existing object at which a new object will be created.

options The choices associated with a particular command or instruction.

Or gate A symbol used to draw an electronic logic circuit; any input of 1 results in output of 1, when both inputs are 0, output is 0.

orthographic view A two-dimensional drawing used in representing a three-dimensional object. A minimum of two orthographic views are necessary to show the shape of a three-dimensional object, because each view shows only two dimensions.

output file The file to which attribute data is extracted.

overall dimensions The widest measurements of a part; needed by manufacturers to determine how much material to start with.

override mode When the desired object snap mode is selected during each command it is to be used for.

palette A type of toolbar, usually divided into areas, that allows for quick selection of items. AutoCAD Tool Palettes are used to organize blocks, hatches, and more in a location where they can be dragged into a drawing (similar to the way paint is held on an artist's palette for quick access).

paper space A mode that allows you to arrange, annotate, and plot different views of a model in a single drawing, as you would arrange views on a piece of paper.

parametric A modeling method that allows you to input sizes for and relationships between the features of parts. Changing a size or relationship will result in the model being updated to the new appearance.

partial auxiliary view An auxiliary view that shows only the desired surfaces.

parts list Provides information about the parts in an assembly drawing, including the item number, description, quantity, material, and part number.

perspective icon A cube drawn in perspective that replaces the UCS icon when perspective viewing, activated by the 3D Dynamic View command, is in effect.

pictorial full section A section view showing an object cut in half along its vertical center line.

pin registry A process in which a series of transparent sheets are punched with a special hole pattern along one edge, allowing the sheets to be fitted onto a metal pin bar. The metal pin bar keeps the drawings aligned from one sheet to the next. Each sheet is used to show different map information.

plan view The top view or view looking straight down the Z axis toward the XY plane.

plus/minus tolerances Another name for variance tolerances.

point filter Option that lets you selectively find single coordinates out of a point's three-dimensional coordinate set.

point light A light source similar to a bare light bulb that casts light in every direction.

pointer An indicator established from the current drawing to the original drawing, or external reference.

polar array A pattern created by repeating objects over and over in a circular fashion.

polar coordinates The location of a point, defined as a distance and an angle from another specified point, using the AutoCAD input format @DISTANCE<ANGLE.

polygon A closed shape with sides of equal length.

polyline A series of connected objects (lines or arcs) that are treated as a single object.

precedence When two lines occupy the same space, precedence determines which one is drawn. Continuous lines take precedence over hidden lines, and hidden lines take precedence over center lines.

primitives Basic shapes that can be joined together or subtracted from each other to form more complex shapes.

profile A two-dimensional view of a three-dimensional solid object created using the Solprof (Setup Profile) command.

project To transfer information from one view of an object to another by aligning them and using projection lines.

projection lines Horizontal lines that stretch from one view of an object to another to show which line or surface is which.

Properties toolbar Contains the icons whose commands control the appearance of the objects in your drawing.

prototype drawing A drawing saved with certain settings that can be used repeatedly as the basis for starting new drawings.

quadrant point Any of the four points that mark the division of a circle or arc into four segments: 0°, 90°, 180°, and 270°.

ray tracing The method of calculating shading by tracking reflected light rays hitting the object.

real-world units Units in which drawings in the database are drawn; objects should always be drawn at the size that the real object would be.

rectangular array A pattern created by repeating objects over and over in columns and rows.

rectangular view A view of a cylinder in which it appears as a rectangle (looking from the side).

reference surface A surface from which measurements are made when creating another view of the object.

reflection The degree to which a surface bounces back light.

refraction The degree to which an object changes the angle of light passing through it.

regenerate To recalculate from the drawing database a drawing display that has just been zoomed or had changes made to it.

region A two-dimensional area created from a closed shape or a loop.

relative coordinates The location of a point in terms of the X and Y distance, or distance and angle, from a previously specified point @X,Y.

rendered Lighting effects, color, and shape applied to an object in a single two-dimensional view.

resolution Refers to how sharp and clear an image appears to be and how much detail can be seen; the higher the resolution, the better the quality of the image. This is determined by the number of colors and pixels the computer monitor can display.

revolution Creating a three-dimensional object by sweeping a two-dimensional polyline, circle, or region about a circular path to create a symmetrical solid that is basically circular in cross-section.

roman A font.

root page The original standard screen menu column along the right side of the screen, accessed by picking the word AutoCAD at the top of the screen.

roughness The apparent texture of a surface. The lower the surface roughness, the more reflective the surface will be.

round A convex arc, or a rounded external corner on a machined part.

running mode When the current object snap mode is automatically used any time a command calls for the input of a point or selection.

scale factor The multiple or fraction of the original size of a drawing object or linetype at which it is displayed.

section lines Show surfaces that were cut in a section view.

section view A type of orthographic view that shows the internal structure of an object; also called a cutaway view.

selectable group A named selection set in which picking on one of its members selects all members that are in the current space, and not on locked or frozen layers. An object can belong to more than one group.

selection filters A list of properties required of an object for it to be selected.

selection set All of the objects chosen to be affected by a particular command.

session Each use, from loading to exiting, of the AutoCAD program.

shape-compiled font Character shapes drawn by the AutoCAD software using vectors.

sign Positive or negative indicator that precedes a centermark value.

slicing plane A plane that is defined for use in slicing a solid object. During the Slice command, the object can be removed on either side of the slicing plane or the selected object can be parted along the slicing plane and both sides can be retained.

solid modeling A type of three-dimensional modeling that represents the volume of an object, not just its lines and surfaces; this allows for analysis of the object's mass properties.

spotlight A light source used to highlight certain key areas and cast light only toward the selected target.

Standard toolbar Contains the icons which control file operation commands.

status bar The rectangular area at bottom of screen that displays time and some command and file operation information.

style Controls the name, font file, height, width factor, obliquing angle, and generation of the text.

submenu A list of available options or commands relating to an item chosen from a menu.

surface modeling A type of three-dimensional modeling that defines only surfaces and edges so that the model can be shaded and have hidden lines removed; resembles an empty shell in the shape of the object.

swatch An area that shows a sample of the color or pattern currently selected.

sweeping Extrusion along a non-linear path rather than a straight line.

target area The square area on an object snap aperture, in which at least part of the object to be selected must fit.

template drawing A drawing with the extension *.dwt* having certain settings that can be used repeatedly as the basis for starting new drawings. Any drawing can be renamed and used as a template.

template file Specifies the file format for the Extract Attribute command as *.cdf* of *.sdf*.

tessellation lines To cover a surface with a grid or lines, like a mosaic. Tessellation lines are displayed on a curved surface to help you visualize it; the number of tessellation lines determines the accuracy of surface area calculations.

threshold value Determines how close vertices must be in order to be automatically welded during the rendering process.

through point The point through which the offset object is to be drawn.

tiled viewports Multiple viewports that cannot overlap. They must line up next to each other, like tiles on a floor.

tilemode An AutoCAD system variable that controls the use of tiled or floating viewports or paper space.

title bar The rectangular area at the top of the screen which displays the application and file names.

toggle A switch that turns certain settings on and off.

tolerance The amount that a manufactured part can vary from the specifications laid out in the plans and still be acceptable.

tool tip The name of the icon that appears when you hold the cursor over the icon.

toolbar A strip containing icons for certain commands.

transparency A quality that makes objects appear clear, like glass, or somewhat clear, like colored liquids.

transparent command A command that can be selected while another command is operating.

typing cursor A special cursor used in dialog boxes for entering text from the keyboard.

UCS icon Indicates the current coordinate system in use and the direction in which the coordinates are being viewed in 3D drawings.

unidirectional dimensioning The standard alignment for dimension text, which is to orient the text horizontally.

unilateral tolerance A tolerance that is applied in one direction from a specified dimension.

union The area formed by adding two regions or solid models together.

units The type of metric, decimal, scientific, engineering, or architectural measurement scales used in AutoCAD drawings. These are set with the Units command.

update To regenerate the active part or drawing using any new dimension values or changed sketches.

User Coordinate System (UCS) A set of x, y, and z coordinates whose origin, rotation, and tilt are defined by the user. You can create and name any number of User Coordinate Systems.

user-defined hatch pattern A predefined hatch pattern for which you have specified the angle, spacing, and/or linetype.

variance tolerances Tolerances specified by defining a nominal dimension and the allowable range of deviation from that dimension; includes bilateral and unilateral tolerances.

vector A directional line. Also, a way of storing a graphic image as a set of mathematical formulas.

Venn diagram — Pictorial description named after John Venn, an English logician, where circles are used to represent set operations.

viewpoint — The direction from which you are viewing a three-dimensional object.

viewport — A "window" showing a particular view of a three-dimensional object.

virtual screen — A file containing only the information displayed on the AutoCAD screen. Used to allow fast zooming without having to regenerate the original drawing file.

Windows close button — A button in the upper right corner of a window that closes the window.

wireframe modeling — A type of three-dimensional modeling that uses lines, arcs, circles, and other objects to represent the edges and other features of an object; so called because it looks like a sculpture made from wires.

World Coordinate System (WCS) — The AutoCAD system for defining three-dimensional model geometry using x, y, and z coordinate values; the default orientation is a horizontal X axis with positive values to the right, a vertical Y axis with positive values above the X axis, and a Z axis that is perpendicular to the screen and has positive values in front of the screen.

World Coordinates — The basis for all user coordinate systems.

Index

Terms beginning with numbers such as 3D are indexed as if the number was spelled out.

A

@ symbol, last point command, 50

About command/icon
  summary, 564

Absolute coordinates, 49

acad.dwt, 185

Acadlspasdoc command/icon
  summary, 564

Acadprefix command/icon
  summary, 564

Acadver command/icon
  summary, 564

ACIS In command/icon
  summary, 564

ACIS Out command/icon
  summary, 565

Action buttons, 24

Active Assistance command/icon
  summary, 565

Adcclose command/icon
  summary, 565

Adcenter command/icon
  summary, 565

Adcnavigate command/icon
  summary, 565

Add a Plotter Wizard, 12

Add Profile dialog box, 10

Adjust Object Bitmap Placement dialog box, 543–544

Adjust Planar Coordinates dialog box, 543

Administration command/icon
  summary, 565

Aerial View command/icon
  summary, 565
  using, 101–102

Aerial Viewer, 101–102

Alias, 36, 46

Align command/icon
  summary, 565
  using for assembly line drawings, 470

Align Dimension Text, Edit command/icon
  summary, 565

Aligned Dimension command/icon
  summary, 565

Ambient lighting, 531

Ambient material selection, 540

AME Convert command/icon
  summary, 565

And gate, 364, 366, 369–370, 381–384

Angle brackets, 43

Angling, hatch pattern, 333

Angular Dimension command/icon
  summary, 565
  using, 276, 291–293

Angular dimensions, 276, 291–293

ANSI-C template, 186

ANSI dimension standards, 266

ANSI31 hatch pattern, 332

ANSI Y14-2M Standards, 488

Anti-aliasing, 529

Aperture Box command/icon
  summary, 565

Aperture command/icon
  summary, 565

Application Load command/icon
  summary, 565

Arcball, 394–396

Arc Center Start Angle command/icon
  summary, 566

Arc Center Start End command/icon
  summary, 566

Arc Center Start Length command/icon
summary, 566

Arc command/icon
summary, 566
using, 93–94

Arc Continue command/icon
summary, 566
using, 97

Architectural units, 59

Arc Length Dimension command/icon
summary, 566

Arc 3 Points command/icon, 93–94

Arcs, 15
drawing, 93–98

Arc Start Center Angle command/icon
summary, 566

Arc Start Center End command/icon
summary, 566
using, 95

Arc Start Center Length command/icon
summary, 566
using, 96

Arc Start End Angle command/icon
summary, 566
using, 96

Arc Start End Direction command/icon
summary, 566

Arc Start End Radius command/icon
summary, 566
using, 97

Area command/icon
summary, 566
using, 130

Array command/icon
summary, 566
using, 174–175

Arrowheads, 327–329
ANSI dimension standards, 266
setting size and style, 270

Ask Me (help), 25, 47

Aspect ratio, 216

Assembly drawings
attaching solid models, 465–470
changing externally referenced drawing, 486–488
checking for interference, 472–473
creating ball tags, 475–477
exploded isometric views, 473–475
inserting solid part drawings, 469–472
mass property determination, 473
parts list creation, 488–491
using spreadsheet word processors, 489–492
using Windows OLE, 489–492

Associative dimensioning, 264, 279–280
updating, 294–298

Associative hatching, 331, 341–344

Attaching
materials for rendering, 537–538, 541, 542
solid models to assembly drawings, 465–470

Attdia command/icon
summary, 566

Attedit command/icon
summary, 567

Attenuation
rendered objects, 532

Attribute Definition dialog box, 478, 480

Attribute Display command/icon
summary, 567

Attribute Editor, Enhanced command/icon
summary, 567
using, 486

Attribute insertion point, 479–481

Attribute modes, 478

Attribute prompt, 479

Attribute Redefine command/icon
summary, 567

Attributes, 476–481
blocks, 363
changing values, 486
extracting information about, 489–492

Attribute tag, 479

Audit command/icon
summary, 567

AutoCAD. *See also* Commands; Dialog boxes; Drawing; Templates
autosave feature, 339
backing up, 20
backing up defaults, 4
commands and menu options, 16–17
commands not case-sensitive, 36
command summary, 563–601
configuring Windows for, 3–4
customizable support files, 5
documents, 28
exiting, 28–29
minimizing and restoring, 14
mouse techniques, 1
multiple shortcuts, 6–7
new features for AutoCAD 2006, 28
on-line help, 25–28
pointing techniques, 15–17
repeating commands, 21
screen, 31–35
starting, 13, 31
typographical conventions, 2–3
user profiles, 10
using Save As Type to save drawings in previous versions, 550
working directory creation, 6–7, 29

AutoCAD 2005
can't use tool palette from AutoCAD 2006 in, 372

AutoCAD 2006
block names, 365
can't use tool palette in AutoCAD 2005 program, 372
dynamic blocks feature, 475–477
fields storing information, 222
fully associative dimensioning, 264
long file names supported, 29
new features for, 28
Quick Calculator feature, 452
solid modeler advantages, 473
using Save As Type to save drawings in previous versions, 550

AutoCAD 2006 Tutorial shortcut, 7

AutoCAD Color Index (ACI), 529, 539

AutoCAD graphics window, 14

AutoCAD Runtime Extension command/icon
summary, 567

AutoCAD tutorials
assembly drawings, 465–492
auxiliary views, 345–358
auxiliary views, solid modeling for, 511–520
basic construction techniques, 79–107
basic editing and plotting techniques, 111–139
blocks, 363–370
configuration for, 8–12
custom toolbars, 377–386
data file installation, 7
DesignCenter, 370–377
dimensioning, 263–298
dimensioning, advanced, 303–319
geometric constructions, 145–180
introduction, 31–74
orthographic drawings, 229–258
rendering, 525–554
section views, 323–344
section views, solid modeling for, 501–511
solid modeling, assembly drawings from, 465–492
solid modeling, changing, 443–461
solid modeling, for section and auxiliary views, 501–520
solid modeling, introduction, 393–437
solid modeling, plotting, 462
templates, 185–224
Tool Palettes, 370, 372–374

Autodesk Express Viewer, 551

Autohide, 121

Automatic bilateral tolerances, 305–311

Autosave feature, 339

AutoSnap, 91–93, 156, 159
with circles, 103

Autostack Properties dialog box, 72

Auxiliary views, 345–346
adding visual reference lines, 351
aligning UCS with angled surface, 347–350
curved surfaces, 352–353
3D solid models, 511–514
linetype conventions, 351–352
rotating snap, 353–356
rotating using 3D Dynamic View, 517–519
rotating using Plan, 516–517
rotating using 3 Point UCS, 515–516
using Solview, 519–520

B

Back, option of Undo command, 58

Back faces, 529

Background command/icon
summary, 567
using, 528, 548–549

Backgrounds, adding in rendering, 528, 548–549

Backing up, 20
defaults, 4

Backspace key, 20

Back View command/icon
summary, 567

Ball tags, 475–477

Base command/icon
summary, 567

Base grip, 177

Baseline Dimension command/icon
summary, 567
using, 284–285

Baseline dimensioning, 269, 284–285

Basic dimensions, 306

Basic views, 345

Bearings, 59, 61

Bicubic surface, 436

Bilateral tolerances, 304

Bitmap Out command/icon
summary, 567

Blip marks, 53

Blipmode command/icon
summary, 567

Block Attribute Manager command/icon
summary, 567
using, 481

Block Authoring palette, 481–483

Block Definition dialog box, 366

Block Editor command/icon
summary, 567
using, 476–477, 484

Block Icon command/icon
summary, 567

Block names, 364, 365

Block reference, 364

Blocks, 363–366
inserting, 367–368
using Explode, 368
writing, 368–370

Boolean operators, 393
  complex model creation using, 412–413
  result always on current layer of first item picked, 412

Bottom View command/icon
  summary, 568

Boundary command/icon
  for joining objects, 424
  summary, 568

Boundary Hatch command/icon. *See also* Hatch command/icon
  summary, 568

Box command/icon
  summary, 568
  using in solid modeling, 399, 447

Break command/icon
  summary, 568
  using, 162–163
  using in auxiliary views, 351–352
  using in orthographic views, 250–251

Browser command/icon
  summary, 568

Buffer gate, 364, 366, 370

Bump map material selection, 540

Button Editor dialog box, 382

Buttons
  Depth Cue, 528
  in dialog boxes, 23–24
  highlighted, 44
  left mouse, 1, 15
  maximize, 14
  minimize, 14, 15
  pick button, 1, 15
  return button, 1, 2, 36, 49
  right mouse, 1, 2, 15
  windows control, 32

Buzzsaw icon, 40

C

Calculator, Quick command/icon
  summary, 568
  using, 452

Calculator command/icon
  summary, 568
  using, 452

Cancel button, 24

Cancel command/icon
  summary, 568
  using, 24

Cartesian coordinate system, 48

Cascaded drawings, 40, 41

Case-sensitive, AutoCAD commands not, 36

CELTScale command/icon
  using, 151

Celtype command/icon
  summary, 568

Centerlines
  adding in solid models, 458–459
  breaking, 250–253
  orthographic views, 248–253

Center Mark command/icon
  summary, 568
  using in dimensioning, 270, 282
  using in orthographic views, 249–250

Centermarks
  in dimensioning, 270, 282
  orthographic views, 248–253

Chained dimensioning, 284

Chamfer, 124–125

Chamfer command/icon
  rectangle, 62
  summary, 568
  using, 124–125
  using for solid model editing, 444–445

Change command/icon
  summary, 568
  using, 121–123

Changing
  associative hatching, 341–344
  blocks by redifining, 377
  externally referenced drawing for assembly drawing, 486–488
  layers in section views, 330–331
  object properties, 121–123
  properties in geometric constructions, 149–152
  solid models, 443–461
  title block text, 224
  viewpoint in solid modeling, 404

Check buttons, 24

Check Standards command/icon
  summary, 568

Child style, for dimensions, 291

Chord length, 96

Circle Center Diameter command/icon
  summary, 569

Circle Center Radius command/icon
  using, 63, 64

Circle command/icon
  options for, 38
  summary, 568
  using, 63–64
  using for complex object creation, 431

Circle 2 Points command/icon
  summary, 569
  using, 63–64, 103

Circle 3 Points command/icon
  summary, 569
  using, 63–64, 104–195

Circles, 15
  copying, 146
  distortion when zooming, 116

drawing, 63–64, 103–105
trimming, 117

Circle Tan Tan Radius command/icon
summary, 569
using, 63–64, 105

Circle Tan Tan Tan command/icon
summary, 569
using, 105

Circular view, 248

Circumscribed polygon, 152

Click (mouse action), 1

Close All command/icon
summary, 569

Close button, dialog boxes, 14, 23, 48

Close command/icon
summary, 569

Cmddia command/icon
dialog box settings, 12
summary, 569

Color Control command/icon
summary, 569
using, 83–84

Color/Pattern material selection, 539–540

Colors
controlling in layers, 83–84, 88
generated layers in solid models, 455–456
rendered objects, 532
templates, 210–211

Command aliasing, 36, 46
summary of commands and their aliases, 563–601

Command Line command/icon
summary, 569

Command option letter, 36, 38

Command options, 20

Command prompt, 17, 36

Commands
aliasing, 36, 46
backing out of, 20–21
canceling, 33, 35
picking, 15
picking from menu bar, 35
repeating, 21
summary of, 563–601
transparent, 46
typing, 17–18, 36–38

Command Summary Table, 563–601

Command window, 32

Compile command/icon
summary, 569

Complex solid models, 412–413

Concave arc, 95

Cone command/icon
summary, 569
using, 415–416

Cones, 415–416

Configuring
AutoCAD for tutorials, 8–12
Windows, 3–4

Construction. *See also* Drawing
opening existing drawing, 79–81
saving as new file, 81–82
using Arc commands, 93–98
using layers, 82–90
using object snap, 90–93

Construction Line command/icon
summary, 569
using, 171–172
using in orthographic views, 233–236

Construction lines, 233–236

Contents (help), 25, 47

Context-sensitive help, 25, 46

Context-sensitive menu, 56

Continued dimensioning, 284, 290

Continue Dimension command/icon
summary, 569
using, 290

Convert Color Dependent Plot Style command/icon
summary, 570

Convert command/icon
summary, 569

Convert Plot Styles command/icon
summary, 570

Convex arc, 95

Coons patch mesh, 436

Coordinates, 48–49
rendered objects, 543–544

Coordinate values, 48

Copyclip command/icon
summary, 570

Copy command/icon
summary, 570
text, 66
using, 146

Copyhist command/icon
summary, 570

Copy Link command/icon
summary, 570

Corrupted files, recovering, 40

Create New Dimension Style dialog box, 268, 291, 311

Create New Drawing dialog box, 145

Create Sheet Set Wizard, 203

Cropping
rendered objects, 544

Crop Window, 528

Crosshairs, 15–16, 32

Crosshatching, 323, 324–325

Current layer, 82, 86

Curved surfaces, in auxiliary views, 352–353

Custom hatch patterns, 332

Custom interfaces, 377–386

Customizable support files, 5

Customize command/icon
summary, 570
using, 377–386

Customize User Interface dialog box, 377, 384

Customize Workspace button, 384–386

Custom toolbars, 377–386
using Design Center and Tool Palettes, 370–374

Cutclip command/icon
summary, 570

Cutting edges, 114

Cutting plane, 445

Cutting plane lines, 324, 326–330
section views, 502, 507

Cylinder command/icon
complex object creation, 417
creating holes in solid models, 451–452
summary, 570
using, 410–411

Cylinders, 410–411

Cylindrical mapping, 543

D

Dashed lines, 326

DASHED linetype, 326

Data Base Close command/icon
summary, 570

Data Base Connect command/icon
summary, 570

Database List command/icon
summary, 570

Data file installation, 7

Datum flags, 318–319

DDEdit, *See* Edit Text command/icon

Default
attribute value, 479
backing up, 4
directory, 40
text font, 216–217
units, 58–59

Define Attribute command/icon
summary, 570
using, 476

DEFPOINTS, 266

Delay command/icon
summary, 570

Delobj command/icon
summary, 570
using, 431

Delta angle, 95

Depth Cue button, 528

DesignCenter, 363
for importing dimension styles, 288
right click to bring up useful options, 471

DesignCenter command/icon
summary, 571
using, 370–374

DesignCenter Navigate command/icon
summary, 571

Desktop icon, 40

Detach command/icon
summary, 571

Detachurl command/icon
summary, 571

Deviation tolerances, 306

Dialog boxes, 22–24
settings, 12

Diameter dimension, 281–284

Diameter Dimension command/icon
summary, 571
using, 281–282

Diameter symbol, 247

Diastat command/icon
summary, 571

Difference (Boolean operator), 412

Dimalt command/icon
summary, 571

Dimaltd command/icon
summary, 571

Dimaltf command/icon
summary, 571

Dimalttd command/icon
summary, 571

Dimalttz command/icon
summary, 571

Dimaltu command/icon
summary, 571

Dimaltz command/icon
summary, 571

Dimapost command/icon
summary, 571

Dimaso command/icon
summary, 572

Dimassoc command/icon
summary, 572
using, 279–280, 289

Dimasz command/icon
summary, 572

Dimaunit command/icon
summary, 572

Dimblk command/icon
summary, 572

Dimblk1 command/icon
summary, 572

Dimblk2 command/icon
summary, 572

Dimcen command/icon, 151
summary, 572
using in orthographic views, 248–249

Dimclrd command/icon
summary, 572

Dimclre command/icon
summary, 572

Dimclrt command/icon
summary, 572

Dimdec command/icon
summary, 572

Dimdle command/icon
summary, 573

Dimdli command/icon
summary, 573

Dimension (menu bar), 35

Dimension, Arc Length command/icon
summary, 573

Dimension alternate units, 276–277

Dimension Edit command/icon
summary, 573

Dimension fit, 273

Dimensioning
adding linear dimensions, 281, 283, 292
adding tolerance note, 293–294
associative, 264, 279–280, 294–298
automatic bilateral tolerances, 305–311
baseline, 269, 284–285
centering views, 293
datum flags, 318–319
diameter dimension, 281–284
feature control frames, 313–315
limit tolerances, 303, 311–313
saving as template, 288
semiautomatic, 264–265
shapes, 265
tolerance formats, 303–304
using Angular Dimension, 291–293
using Continue Dimension, 290
using dimension styles, 267–278
using DIM layer, 266
using overrides, 309–311
using Xplode, 285–286

Dimension lines, 263–264, 269
ANSI dimension standards, 266

Dimension measurement scale, 275

Dimension modification, 296–297

Dimension primary units, 275

Dimensions, 263

Dimension scaling factor, 274

Dimension standards, 266–267

Dimension Status command/icon
summary, 573
using, 279

Dimension Style command/icon
summary, 573
using, 267–278, 297
using with automatic bilateral tolerances, 305
using with limit tolerances, 311

Dimension Style Manager, 267–268, 291

Dimension Style Manager dialog box, 22–23, 278

Dimension styles, 267–278
updating, 297–298

Dimension Styles dialog box, 279

Dimension tolerances, 277–278

Dimension toolbar, 267

Dimension Update command/icon
summary, 573

Dimension values, 264

Dimension variables, 267

Dimension zero suppression, 275–276

Dimexe command/icon
summary, 573

Dimexo command/icon
summary, 573

Dimfit command/icon
summary, 573

Dimgap command/icon
override, 310
summary, 573

Dimjust command/icon
summary, 573

Dimlfac command/icon
summary, 573

Dimlim command/icon
override, 310
summary, 573

Dimoverride command/icon
summary, 574
using, 309–311

Dimpost command/icon
override, 310
summary, 574

Dimrnd command/icon
summary, 574

Dimsah command/icon
summary, 574

Dimscale command/icon
summary, 574
using, 269

Dimsd1 command/icon
summary, 574

Dimsd2 command/icon
summary, 574

Dimse1 command/icon
summary, 574

Dimse2 command/icon
summary, 574

Dimsho command/icon
summary, 574

Dimsoxd command/icon
summary, 574

Dimtad command/icon
summary, 574

Dimtdec command/icon
summary, 574

Dimtfac command/icon
summary, 574

Dimtih command/icon
summary, 575

Dimtix command/icon
summary, 575

Dimtm command/icon
summary, 575

Dimtofl command/icon
summary, 575

Dimtoh command/icon
summary, 575

Dimtol command/icon
override, 310
summary, 575

Dimtolj command/icon
summary, 575

Dimtp command/icon
summary, 575

Dimtsz command/icon
summary, 575

Dimtvp command/icon
summary, 575

Dimtxsty command/icon
summary, 575

Dimtxt command/icon
summary, 575

Dimtzin command/icon
summary, 575

Dimunit command/icon
summary, 576

Dimupt command/icon
summary, 576

Dimzin command/icon
summary, 576

Display, of units, 59–60

Display Properties dialog box, 3

Display tab, 9, 11

Dispsilh command/icon
summary, 576

Dissociate Dimension command/icon
summary, 576

Distance across the flats, hexagons, 152

Distance command/icon
summary, 576
using with auxiliary views, 348

Distant light, 531–532, 546

Divide command/icon
summary, 576
using, 221–223
using to insert blocks, 374

Docked toolbars, 19, 32

Documents, 28

Donut command/icon
summary, 576
using, 374–375

Double-click Edit command/icon
summary, 576

Double-click (mouse action), 1, 24

Drafting Settings command/icon
summary, 576

Drafting Settings dialog box, 37, 45, 91–92
and geometric constructions, 154
template drawings, 215–216

Drafting tab, 9

Dragging, 1, 32
objects, 16, 18
to resize windows, 14

Dragmode command/icon
summary, 576

Draw (menu bar), 35

Drawing. *See also* Auxiliary views; Construction; Dimensioning; Geometric constructions; Orthographic views; Rendering; Section views; Solid modeling
arcs, 93–98
circles, 63–64, 103–105
cones, 415–416
ellipses, 105–107
rectangles, 62–63
setting units, 58–60
using grid and snap, 49–50
using last point, 50
using polar coordinates, 51–52
using relative coordinates, 50
wedges, 413–414

Drawing Properties command/icon
summary, 576

Drawings. *See also* Assembly drawings; Templates
adding text, 64–72
getting information about, 128–130

multiple, 28, 40–42
naming files, 29, 39–40
orientation, 138
regenerating, 101
saving, 63, 73
sizing, 60
starting from templates, 111–114
starting new, 38–39

Drawing session, 58

Drawing Web Format (.dwf), 551

Draworder command/icon, 341
summary, 576
using with hatching, 509

Draw toolbar, 18

Dtext (Dynamic Text), *See* Single Line Text command/icon

.dwf extension, 551

DWF Out command/icon
summary, 577
using, 551

.dwg files, 29, 40, 207

DWG Props command/icon
summary, 577

.dws files, 207

.dwt files, 207

DXB In command/icon
summary, 577

.dxf files, 207

DXF In command/icon
summary, 577

DXF Out command/icon
summary, 577

Dynamic blocks, 475–477

Dynamic entry, 36–38

Dynamic input, 20

Dynamic Input table, 37

E

Edge command/icon
summary, 577

Edge Surface command/icon
summary, 577
using, 436

Edge surface creation, 436

Edge view, in orthographic views, 237

Edit (menu bar), 34

Edit Attribute command/icon
summary, 577
using, 486

Edit Attribute Globally command/icon
summary, 577

Edit Hatch command/icon
summary, 577
using, 343–344

Editing, 111–114. *See also* Geometric constructions
changing object properties, 121–123
solid models, 443–461
text, 67
using Chamfer, 124–125
using Fillet, 123–124
using Offset, 118–120
using Polyline, 125–127
using Spline, 127–128
using Trim, 114–118

Edit Links command/icon
summary, 577

Edit Multiline command/icon
summary, 577

Edit Polyline command/icon
summary, 577
using, 126–127
using for producing auxiliary views, 357

Edit Scale List command/icon
summary, 577

Edit Spline command/icon
summary, 577

Edit Text command/icon
summary, 578
using, 67

Electronic Transmit command/icon
summary, 578

Element Properties dialog box, 131

Elements, 15, 131

Elev command/icon
rectangle, 62
summary, 578

Ellipse Arc command/icon
summary, 578

Ellipse Axis End command/icon
summary, 578

Ellipse command/icon
summary, 578
using, 105–107
using for producing auxiliary views, 357–358
using in orthographic views, 256–258

Ellipses, 105–107

Ellipsis (...), after pull-down menu, 22

End Startup Dialog command/icon
summary, 578

Engineering units, 59

Enhanced Attribute Editor dialog box, 486

Enter key, 2

ePlot files, 551

Erase command/icon
getting rid of unwanted lines, 235–236
summary, 578
trimming lines, 119
use in drawing auxiliary views, 346
use in drawing section views, 338
using, 52–56
using with construction lines, 172

Erasing, 52–56
unwanted lines, 235–236
with windowing or crossing, 53–56

Escape key
for backing out of commands, 20–21
canceling commands, 33, 35
restarting commands, 49
to return to command prompt, 46

Exiting, 28–29

Explode command/icon
adding to tool palette, 373
with blocks, 368
checking assembly line drawings for interference, 472
summary, 578
for surface model creation, 432
trimming multilines, 133
Xplode contrasted, 285

Exploded isometric views, 473–475

Export command/icon
summary, 578
using, 550

Export Data dialog box, 550

Exporting files
in rendering, 550

Export Links command/icon
summary, 578

Express (menu bar), 35

Express Tools command/icon
summary, 578
using, 8

Extend command/icon
summary, 578
using, 163–165
using with dimensions, 294

Extension line offset, 263

Extension lines, 263, 270
ANSI dimension standards, 266

Externally referenced drawings, 466–468
changing for assembly drawing, 486–488
layers, 468–469

External Reference Attach command/icon
summary, 579
using, 467, 470–471

External Reference Bind command/icon
summary, 579

External Reference Clip command/icon
summary, 579
using, 469

External Reference Clip Frame command/icon
summary, 579

External Reference command/icon
summary, 579
using, 466–468, 486–488

External Reference dialog box, 467, 470

Extract Attributes command/icon
summary, 578
using, 489–492

Extrude command/icon
summary, 579
using, 420–423
using in complex object creation by intersection, 428–429

Extrusion, 393, 399
complex object creation, 420–424

F

F1 key, to bring up Help Window, 25, 46

F2 key, for returning to Graphics Window, 18

F3 key, for toggling Running Object Snap mode, 161

Facetres command/icon
summary, 579
using, 413

Falloff, 534

Favorites icon, 40

Feature control frames, 313–315

File (menu bar), 34

Filedia command/icon
dialog box settings, 12, 146
summary, 579

File extension, 40

File Output Configuration dialog box, 545

Files tab, 9

File transfer, 73

Fill command/icon
summary, 579

Fillet command/icon
rectangle, 62
summary, 579
using, 123–124
using for solid model editing, 444
using in geometric constructions, 152

Fillets, 122, 123–124

Find command/icon
summary, 579
using, 80–81

Find dialog box, 80–81

Flat Shading command/icon
summary, 579
using, 422

Flat Shading, Edges On command/icon
summary, 579

Flip Parameter (Block Authoring palette), 481, 482

Floating toolbars, 19, 32
showing, 157

Floating viewports, 195–198, 401

Floating window, 32

Floppy drives
avoid opening files directly from, 254
must include externally referenced drawings if sending drawing to someone, 491
saving files on, 29, 40
transferring files, 73

Flyouts, 19, 33

Fog command/icon
summary, 579
using, 528

Fonts, 67–70
templates, 216–217

Foreshortened surfaces, 345

Format (menu bar), 35

Fractional units, 59

Freeze option, 85

Freeze/Thaw command/icon
with auxiliary views, 351
with layers, 85, 375
with section views, 502
solid models, 459–461

Front orthographic view, 229–230

Front View command/icon
summary, 579
using, 406

FTP icon, 40

G

Geneva cam, 169–171

Geographic Location dialog box, 547

Geometric characteristic symbol, 313

Geometric constructions, 145
changing properties, 149–152
effective use of layers, 147–149
hot grips, 149, 175–180
loading linetypes, 148–149
object selection methods, 166–169
setting units and limits, 145–146
using Array, 174–175
using Break, 162–163
using Construction Line, 171–172
using Copy Object, 146
using Extend, 163–165
using Mirror, 173
using Move, 166
using Object Snap, 156–161
using polar tracking, 154–156
using Polygon, 152–154
using Rotate, 165

Geometric Tolerance dialog box, 314–315, 316

Geometric tolerances, 304

Global Linetype command/icon
summary, 580
using, 150–151

Global linetype scaling factor, 150–151
orthographic views, 253–254

Gouraud Shade command/icon
summary, 580
using, 415, 417

Gouraud shading, 415, 417, 451, 527

Gouraud Shading, Edges On command/icon
summary, 580

Gouraurd Shade command/icon
using in solid model editing, 451

Gradient fill
in section views, 334–335

Graphics cursor, 32

Graphics Screen command/icon
summary, 580

Graphics window, 32

Grayed items, in dialog boxes, 23

Grid, 42–43
drawing using, 49–50

Grid command/icon
with Limits, 61
summary, 580
toggling on/off, 44
using, 42–43

Grid toggles, 44

Grips command/icon. *See also* Hot grips
summary, 580
using, 175–180

Group command/icon
summary, 580
using, 376–377

Groups, 363
creating, 376–377

H

Half-adder circuit, 374

Handles, 454

Handles command/icon
summary, 580
using, 454

Hatch and Gradient dialog box, 331, 333
using with Section, 508

Hatch boundaries, 333–334

Hatch command/icon
summary, 580
using, 323, 331–336, 339–340
using Draworder with, 341
using with Section, 508–509

Hatch Edit dialog box, 343

Hatching, 162

Hatch Pattern Palette, 332

Hatch patterns, 332
associative hatching, 331, 341–344
crosshatching, 323, 324–325

Help (menu bar), 35

Help command/icon
summary, 580
using, 25, 46–48

Hexagons, 152–154

Hidden command/icon
summary, 580

Hidden lines
auxiliary views, 350
changing to visible in section views, 330–331
eliminating unnecessary in solid models, 456–458
orthographic views, 230, 236–239
plotting with, 453–456
section views, 330–331, 504–505
with templates, 209–210

Hidden profile lines, 453

Hide command/icon
summary, 580
using, 511
using in complex object creation, 414

Highlight command/icon
summary, 580

Highlighted buttons, 44

History icon, 40

HLS (hue, lightness, saturation) color, 539

Holes
creating in solid models, 451–452
orthographic views, 247–248

Horizontally tiled drawings, 40

Hot grips, 149, 175–180
with orthographic views, 252
for rotating in section views, 337

Hotspot, 534

Hyperlink command/icon
summary, 580

I

Icons, 18–20. *See also* Commands

Identify Point command/icon
summary, 580

Image Adjust command/icon
summary, 581

Image Attach command/icon
summary, 581
Image Clip command/icon
summary, 581

Image command/icon
summary, 581

Image Frame command/icon
summary, 581

Image Quality command/icon
summary, 581

Image tile, 270

Image Transparency command/icon
summary, 581

Implied Crossing mode, 53–54

Implied Windowing mode, 53–54

Import command/icon
materials for rendering, 537
summary, 581

Import Layouts as Sheets dialog box, 206

Inclined surfaces, 239

Included angular value, 95

Index (help), 25–26, 47

Input buttons, 24

Inscribed polygon, 152

Insert (menu bar), 35

Insert Block command/icon
summary, 581
using, 363, 367–368, 380
using in templates, 189–190

Insert Block flyout, 33

Insert dialog box, 189–190

Insert Multiple Blocks command/icon
summary, 581
using, 374

Insert Objects command/icon
attaching solid models to assembly drawings, 465, 469–470
summary, 581

Inspection, 263

Intensity, in rendered objects, 532

Interfere command/icon
summary, 581
using, 472–473

Interference, checking assembly drawings for, 472–473

Internet Explorer, 7

Intersect command/icon
summary, 581
using, 431–432

Intersection (Boolean operator), 412, 427–432

Inverter gate, 364, 366, 370

Isolines
  assembly line drawings, 468
  setting in solid modeling, 411–412

Isolines command/icon
  summary, 581
  using, 412
  using for assembly line drawings, 468

Isometric Plane command/icon
  summary, 581

Isometric views
  exploded, for assembly drawings, 473–475

J

Join command/icon
  in complex object creation, 424
  summary, 582

Jpeg out command/icon
  summary, 582

Justification, of dimension text, 272

Justify Text command/icon
  summary, 582
  using, 272

L

Landscape Edit command/icon
  summary, 582

Landscape Library command/icon
  summary, 582

Landscape New command/icon
  summary, 582
  using, 549–550

Landscape objects, 549–550

Last point command/icon
  using, 50

Layer Control, 83

Layer Filter Properties dialog box, 212–213

Layer Properties Manager, 188, 197, 209, 215, 459, 460
  in geometric construction, 147

Layer Properties Manager command/icon
  summary, 582
  using, 87–88

Layers, 82–90
  changing in section views, 330–331
  externally referenced drawings, 468–469
  in geometric constructions, 147–149
  in section views, 330–331, 509–510
  in solid models, 454–456
  in templates, a97, 188, 208–215

Layers command/icon
  using in solid model editing, 455–456
  using in templates, 188, 197, 208–215

Layer States Manager, 209, 215

Layer toolbar, 18, 34

Layer Translator command/icon
  summary, 582

Layout command/icon
  summary, 582
  using, 245

Layouts, 187–188. *See also* Model space layouts; Paper space layouts
  adding dimensions to, 279–280
  plotting, 136

Layout Wizard command/icon
  summary, 582

Leader command/icon
  cutting plane lines, 326–330
  summary, 582
  using with tolerances, 317

Leader line, 281

Leader Settings dialog box, 316

Left mouse button, 1, 15

Left View command/icon
  summary, 582

Lengthen command/icon
  summary, 582

Lights, 531–535

Lights command/icon
  summary, 582
  using, 531–535
  using with sun angle calculator, 546–548

Lights dialog box, 531–532

Limiting element, 237

Limits, 61–62

Limits command/icon
  setting for geometric constructions, 145–146
  summary, 582
  using, 61–62
  using for plotting, 136–137

Limit tolerances, 303, 304, 306, 311–313

Linear Dimension command/icon
  summary, 583
  using, 280–281, 283, 290, 292

Linear dimensions, 280–281, 283, 292

Line command/icon, 2
  summary, 583
  Undo option, 56–57
  using, 45–46, 49–51
  using for hidden lines, 238
  using for slanted surfaces, 240
  using in orthographic views, 233–236
  using with Arc, 97

Line precendence, 239

Lines, 15

Linetype command/icon
  summary, 583

Linetypes
in auxiliary views, 351–352
generated layers in solid models, 455–456
in layers, 89–90
in layers in templates, 210

Linetype Scale command/icon
plotting solid models, 462
summary, 583
using, 151–152, 253

Lineweight command/icon
summary, 583

List command/icon
finding information about tolerances, 309
summary, 583
using, 129
using in solid model editing, 454

List Variables command/icon
summary, 583

Load command/icon
summary, 583

Loading AutoCAD, 13

Locate Point command/icon
summary, 583
using, 130, 163

Location
points, 130, 161
rendered objects, 532
textures and bitmapped materials, 542

Locked layers, 85–86

Lock/Unlock command/icon, 85

Log File Off command/icon
summary, 583

Log File On command/icon
summary, 583

M

Major axis, ellipse, 106

Make Block command/icon
summary, 583

Make Object's Layer Current button, 86

Make Slide command/icon
summary, 583

Manufacturing, 263

Mapping command/icon
summary, 583
using, 541–544

Mapping dialog box, 542

Marking, 58

Markup Set Manager command/icon
summary, 584

Mass properties, 393
determination in assembly drawings, 473

Mass Properties command/icon
summary, 584
using, 473

Match Properties command/icon
summary, 584

Material Condition dialog box, 315

Materials
choosing in rendering, 535–544

Materials command/icon
summary, 584
using, 535–544

Materials dialog box, 535–536

Materials Library command/icon
summary, 584
using, 535–536, 542

Materials Library dialog box, 536–537

Matrix, 434

Maximize button, 14

Measure command/icon
summary, 584
using, 221
using to insert blocks, 374

Menu bar, 34–35
picking commands from, 35

Menu command/icon
summary, 584

Menu Load command/icon
summary, 584

Menu options, 16–17

Menu Unload command/icon
summary, 584

Mesh density, in ruled surface, 434–436

Midpoint Between Two Points (MTP) snap, 161

MIL-15 Technical Drawing Standards, 488

Minimize button, 14, 15

Minor axis, ellipse, 106

Mirror command/icon
summary, 584
using, 173
using with hot grips, 178

Mirror3D command/icon
summary, 584

Mirror line, 173

Miter line, 241, 242

Model Space command/icon
summary, 584
using, 187, 188–189

Model space layouts
auxiliary views, 512
rendered drawing plotting, 551–552
switching to in orthographic views, 231–232
templates, 187, 188–189

Modify (menu bar), 35
Modify Dimension Style dialog box, 23
using with automatic bilateral tolerances, 305–308
Modify Properties command/icon
summary, 584
Modify toolbar, 18
Modify II toolbar, 488
Mouse techniques, 1
Move command/icon
adjusting viewing area in section views, 337–338
creating exploded isometric view, 473–474
summary, 584
using, 166
using for solid model editing, 446–447
using with hot grips, 177–178
Moving text, 67
Mtprop command/icon
summary, 584
Multiline command/icon
summary, 585
using, 132–133
Multiline Style command/icon
summary, 585
using, 131–132
Multiline Styles dialog box, 131
Multiline Text command/icon
using, 71–72, 133
Multiple command/icon
summary, 585
Multiple drawings, 28, 40–42
Multiple Redo command/icon
summary, 585
Multitasking options, in Windows, 15
Mview command/icon
summary, 585
using, 401–402, 418–419
using with templates, 197
MV Setup command/icon
summary, 585
using, 409, 410, 419
using in complex object creation by intersection, 428
using in complex object creation by revolution, 426
My Documents icon, 40

N

Named UCS command/icon
summary, 585
using, 420
Named Views command/icon
summary, 585
Naming files, 29, 39–40
Nand gate, 364, 366, 370
NE Isometric View command/icon
summary, 585
Nested blocks, 363
Netscape Navigator, 7
Network configuration, 13
New Dimension Style dialog box, 268
New Distant Light dialog box, 546
New Drawing command/icon
summary, 585
using, 38–39
New Features Workshop, 28
New Multiline Styles dialog box, 131
New Point Light dialog box, 532–533
New Spotlight dialog box, 534–535
New Standard Material dialog box, 539
New View dialog box, 451
Nominal dimension, 303
Non-plotting Viewport layer, 197–198
Nor gate, 364, 366, 370
Normal, 529
Normal surfaces, 229
Notes
adding dimensioning note, 292–293
adding to paper space templates, 198–199
Noun/verb selection, 180
NURBS (nonuniform rational B-spline) curves, 127
NW Isometric View command/icon
summary, 585

O

Object Group command/icon
summary, 585
using, 363, 376–377
Object Grouping dialog box, 376
Objects, 15
selection, 16
selection methods, 166–169
Object Selection Filters command/icon
summary, 585
using, 168
Object Selection Filters dialog box, 168
Object Selection Settings command/icon
summary, 585
Object snaps, 90–93
for geometric constructions, 156–161
overrides, 157
Object Snap Settings dialog box, 161

Object Snap Settings (Running Object Snap) command/icon
summary, 586
turning off when drawing circles, 63
turning on when attaching solid part drawings to assembly drawings, 469
using, 90–93, 161

Object Snap toolbar, 90–91

Object tracking, 163
and hole creation in solid models, 451
orthographic views, 241–245

Object UCS command/icon
aligning UCS with angled surface in auxiliary view, 347
summary, 586
using with section views, 506

Offset command/icon
aligning UCS with angled surface in auxiliary view, 348–350
summary, 586
using, 118–120, 234

Offset distance, 118

OK button, dialog boxes, 23

OLE Properties command/icon
summary, 586

On-line help, 25–28

OOPS command/icon
summary, 586
using, 53

Open and Save tab, 9

Open Drawing command/icon, 79–81
summary, 586
using, 79–81

Options command/icon
summary, 586

Options dialog box, 8–9, 92
changes affect more than just current drawing, 24

Ordinate Dimension command/icon
summary, 586

Or gate, 364, 366, 370

Origin, 49

Origin UCS command/icon
summary, 586

Ortho command/icon
can't use with polar tracking, 155
summary, 586
turning off when drawing circles, 63
using, 232–233
using in auxiliary views, 355, 513

Orthographic views. *See also* Rendering
centerlines and centermarks, 248–253
construction lines, 233–236
front, top, and right-side, 229–230
global linetype scaling factor, 253–254
hidden lines, 230, 236–239
holes, 247–248
line precendence, 239
locking viewport scale, 246–247
replacing with section views, 325
sizing and positioning drawing, 245–246
slanted surface projection on cylinders, 254–258
slanted surfaces, 239–241
switching to model space, 231–232
top-view to side-view projection, 241
using Ellipse, 256–258
using object tracking, 241–245
using Ortho, 232–233

Otrack button, 242

Overall dimensions, 264

Override mode (object snap), 91

P

Page Setup command/icon
summary, 586

Pan Down command/icon
summary, 586
using, 409

Pan Left command/icon
summary, 586

Pan Point command/icon
summary, 586

Pan Realtime command/icon
adjusting viewing area in section views, 337
summary, 587
using, 102
using in complex object creation by intersection, 428
using in complex object creation by revolution, 425
using in dimensioning, 293
using in solid model editing, 447–448
using with auxiliary views, 514
using with orthographic views, 245–246
using with templates, 194, 197

Pan Right command/icon
summary, 586

Pan Up command/icon
summary, 587

Paper size, 137

Paper Space command/icon
summary, 587
using, 187–188

Paper space layouts
auxiliary views, 512
plotting from templates, 201–202
rendered drawing plotting, 552–554
solid model plotting, 418–420
templates, 187–188, 217–218

Paper Space Linetype Scale command/icon
summary, 587

Partial auxiliary views, 352–353

Parts list, 488–491

Paste From Clipboard command/icon
summary, 587

Paste Special command/icon
summary, 587

Pattern filling, 323

PC In Wizard command/icon
summary, 587

Pen assignments, 135

Perimeter command/icon
summary, 587

Perspective icon, 397

PHANTOM linetype, 326

Phong shading, 527

Pick, 2

Pick button, 1, 15

Pick (mouse action), 1

Pictorial full section, 323

Pictorial section views, 510

Pin-registry drafting, 208

Plan command/icon
summary, 587
using in solid modeling, 410, 450
using with auxiliary views, 516–517

Plan view, 410

Plot and Publish tab, 9, 11

Plot command/icon
rendered drawings, 551–554
using, 134–139
using with paper space templates, 201–202

Plot device, 135

Plot dialog box, 134–139
changes affect more than just current drawing, 24

Plot offset, 138

Plot preview, 138–139

Plot scale, 138

Plot Stamp command/icon
summary, 587

Plot Style command/icon
summary, 587

Plot Style Table Editor, 136

Plot style tables, 135–136

Plotter Manager command/icon
summary, 587

Plotting, 134–139
with hidden lines, 453–456
from paper space templates, 201–202
solid models, 462

Plus/minus tolerances, 303

Point command/icon
summary, 587

Pointer, from original externally referenced drawing, 486

Point Filters (.X, .Y, .Z, .XY, .XZ, .YZ) command/icon
summary, 587

Pointing techniques, 15–17

Point light, 531–532

Point (mouse action), 1

Point Parameter (Block Authoring palette), 481, 482

Point Style command/icon
summary, 588
using, 221

Point Style dialog box, 221

Polar array, 174–175

Polar coordinates, 51–52

Polar tracking, 154–156

Polygon command/icon
summary, 588
using, 152–154

Polygons, 152–154

Polyline command/icon
in complex object creation, 421, 427–428
for creating arrowheads from scratch, 329
summary, 588
using, 125–127

Polyline edit command/icon
for joining objects, 424
summary, 588

Polylines, 125–127

Postscript fonts, 68

Precendence, lines, 239

Preferences command/icon
summary, 588

Preset UCS command/icon
summary, 588

Press, 2

Preview
materials for rendering, 536–537

Previous Layer command/icon
summary, 588

Previous Layer Mode command/icon
summary, 588

Previous UCS command/icon
summary, 588

Primitives, 79, 399

Print/Plot command/icon
summary, 588
using, 134

Print Preview command/icon
summary, 588

Profile, 453

Profile lines, 453

Profiles tab, 9, 10

Projecting, hidden lines for, 237
Projection lines
orthographic views, 230
Projmode command/icon
summary, 588
Properties command/icon
summary, 588
using, 121–123
Properties palette, 121–122, 129
Properties toolbar, 18, 34
PS Drag command/icon
summary, 588
PS Fill command/icon
summary, 588
PS In command/icon
summary, 589
PS Out command/icon
summary, 589
Publish command/icon
summary, 589
using, 551
Publish to Web command/icon
summary, 589
using, 551
Pull-down menus, 21–22
Purge command/icon
summary, 589

Q

Qtext command/icon
summary, 589
Quadrant points, 157
Quick Calculator, 452
Quick Calculator command/icon
summary, 589
using with templates, 193
Quick Dimension command/icon
summary, 589
using, 287–288
Quick Leader command/icon
summary, 589
using with tolerances, 317
Quick Select command/icon
summary, 589
using, 169
Quit command/icon
to exit without saving file, 29
summary, 589

R

Radio buttons, 24
Radius Dimension command/icon
summary, 589
using, 283
Ray command/icon
summary, 589
using, 171
using with auxiliary views, 347–348, 356
using with orthographic views, 243–244
Rays, 171
auxiliary views, 347–348, 356
orthographic views, 243–244
Ray tracing, 527, 540
Real-world units, 60
Reassociate Dimension command/icon
summary, 589
Recover command/icon
summary, 589
Rectangle command/icon
summary, 590
using, 62–63
Rectangles, 62–63
Rectangular array, 174
Rectangular views
holes in orthographic views, 248
Redefine command/icon
summary, 590
Redefine Attribute command/icon
summary, 590
Redo command/icon
summary, 590
using, 49, 56, 57
Redraw All command/icon, 444
summary, 590
using, 53
Redraw View command/icon, 444
summary, 590
Reference, Close command/icon
summary, 590
Reference dimension, 310
Reference Edit command/icon
summary, 590
using, 468–469, 486–487
Reference Edit dialog box, 486–487
Reference lines, 351
Reference surface, 345
Reference toolbar, 466

Reflection material selection, 540, 541

Refraction material selection, 540

Refset command/icon
summary, 590

Regenauto command/icon
summary, 590

Regenerate command/icon, 444
summary, 590
using for assembly line drawings, 468
using with templates, 217

Regenerate All command/icon, 444
for setting isolines, 412
summary, 590

Regenerate Dimensions command/icon
summary, 590

Regenerating drawings, 101

Region command/icon
summary, 591
using, 422

Regions, 422

Reinit command/icon
summary, 591

Relative coordinates, 50

Rename command/icon
summary, 591

Render command/icon
summary, 591
using, 525–554

Render dialog box, 527–531

Render File Options command/icon
summary, 591
using, 529–530

Rendering, 393, 525–530
adding backgrounds, 548–549
adding lights, 531–535
algorithms, 527
choosing materials, 535–544
Drawing Web Format, 551
exporting files, 550
to file, 545
options, 529–530
shaded view plotting, 551–554
using landscape objects, 549–550
using sun angle calculator, 546–548

Rendering File dialog box, 545

Render Preferences command/icon
summary, 591

Render Screen command/icon
summary, 591

Render Statistics command/icon
summary, 591

Render toolbar, 526

Replay command/icon
summary, 591

Resizing
toolbars, 19
windows, 14

Resolution
AutoCAD screen, 3
rendering, 525, 545

Restore UCS command/icon
summary, 591

Resume command/icon
summary, 591

Return button, 1, 2, 36
restarting commands, 49

Return key, 2, 15, 20, 24, 36
Continue option, 97

Revision Cloud command/icon
summary, 591
using, 310

Revolution, 393, 399
complex object creation, 424–427

Revolve command/icon
summary, 591
using, 424–427

Revolved Surface command/icon
summary, 591

RGB (red, green, blue) color, 539

Right-click (mouse action), 1, 2

Right mouse button, 1, 2, 15

Right-side orthographic view, 229–230

Right-side solid model view, 408–410

Right View command/icon
summary, 591
using, 408–409

Roman Simplex, 68, 216

Rotate command/icon
adjusting viewing area in section views, 337
summary, 592
text, 67
using, 165
using in auxiliary views, 355
using with hot grips, 178

Roughness material selection, 540, 541

Rscript command/icon
summary, 592

Ruled Surface command/icon
summary, 592
using, 434–436

Ruled surfaces, 434–436

Running mode, Object Snap, 91

Running Object Snap command/icon, *See* Object Snap Settings command/icon

Runout, 329

S

Save As command/icon
summary, 592
using, 81–82, 107
using Save As Type to save drawings in previous AutoCAD versions, 550

Save command/icon
summary, 592
using, 39–40, 52, 73

Save Drawing As dialog box, 28–29, 39, 52, 81–82, 107, 207

Save Image command/icon
summary, 592

Save Multiline Styles dialog box, 132

Save Slide command/icon
summary, 592

Save Time command/icon
summary, 592
using, 339

Save UCS command/icon
summary, 592

Saving, 28–29

Scale
and dimensioning, 266–267
dimension scaling factor, 274
hatch pattern, 333
locking viewport in orthographic views, 246–247
plots, 138
templates, 190, 192–194
tolerance text height, 307–309

Scale command/icon
summary, 592
using with hot grips, 179
Zoom All command/icon contrasted, 43

Scale factors, 99

Scale Text command/icon
summary, 592

Scaling, *See* Scale

Scene rendering, 528

Scenes command/icon
summary, 592
using, 528

Scientific units, 59

Screen resolution, 3

Script command/icon
summary, 592

Scroll bars, 32
in dialog boxes, 24
in on-line help, 28

Search (help), 25, 27, 47

Section command/icon
summary, 593
using, 505–509

Section views, 323–325
adjusting viewing area, 337–340
associative hatching, 331, 341–344
changing layers, 330–331
creating from solid models, 501–502
crosshatching, 323, 324–325
cutting plane lines, 324, 326–330
gradient fills, 334–335
solid fill, 340
using Draworder, 341
using Hatch, 323, 331–334
using hide, 511
using Section, 505–509
using Slice, 505, 510
using Solprof, 504–505
using Solview and Soldraw, 502–504

SE Isometric View command/icon
summary, 592
using, 396

Select command/icon
summary, 593

Selectable groups, 363

Select Add command/icon, 167
summary, 593

Select All command/icon, 167
summary, 593

Select Auto command/icon
summary, 593

Select Box command/icon
summary, 593

Select Color dialog box, 84, 88, 210

Select Crossing command/icon, 54, 55
summary, 593

Select Crossing Polygon command/icon, 167
summary, 593

Select Drawing File dialog box, 190

Select Fence command/icon, 167
summary, 593

Select File dialog box, 80–81

Select Group command/icon, 167
summary, 593

Selection filters, 168

Selection set, 16, 53, 166

Selection tab, 9

Select Last command/icon, 167
summary, 593

Select Linetype dialog box, 89, 148, 210

Select Multiple command/icon
summary, 593

Select Previous command/icon, 167
summary, 593

Select Reference File dialog box, 467

Select Remove command/icon, 167
  summary, 593

Select Single command/icon
  summary, 594

Select Template dialog box, 111–112, 186

Select Undo command/icon
  summary, 594

Select Window command/icon, 54, 55, 167
  summary, 594

Select Window Crossing command/icon, 167

Select Window Polygon command/icon, 167
  summary, 594

Semiautomatic dimensioning, 264–265

Setup Drawing command/icon
  summary, 594
  using with section views, 502–504

Setup Profile command/icon
  summary, 594
  using, 453–456
  using with section views, 504–505

Setup View command/icon
  summary, 594
  using with auxiliary views, 519–520
  using with section views, 502–504

Set Variables command/icon
  summary, 594

Shade command/icon
  summary, 594

Shaded view plotting, 551–554

Shade Mode command/icon
  summary, 594
  using, 403

Shadows, on rendered objects, 532

Shape command/icon
  summary, 594

Shape-compiled fonts, 68

Shape dimensioning, 265

Sheet Set Manager command/icon
  summary, 594
  using, 8, 32, 202–207

Sheet Set Properties dialog box, 202

Sheet sets, 202–207

Shell command/icon
  summary, 594

Shortcuts, creating multiple, 6–7

Show Light Position dialog box, 533

Show Materials command/icon
  summary, 594

Sign, of centermark, 248

Single Line Text command/icon
  summary, 594
  using, 64–65

Sizing, 60
  orthographic views, 245–246
  toolbars, 19

Sketch command/icon
  summary, 595

Slanted surfaces
  orthographic views, 239–241
  projection on cylinders, 254–258

Slice command/icon
  summary, 595
  using for solid model editing, 445–451
  using in section views, 505, 510

Slicing plane, 445

Slider box, 28

Smart blocks, 476

Snap, 44. *See also* Object snap
  drawing using, 49–50
  and object selection, 52

Snap command/icon
  summary, 595
  toggling on/off, 44
  using, 44
  using in auxiliary views, 353–356

Snap From command/icon
  summary, 595
  using, 163

SnapTip, 91

Snap to Apparent Intersection command/icon
  summary, 595
  using, 162

Snap to Center command/icon
  summary, 595
  using, 158

Snap to Endpoint command/icon
  summary, 595
  using, 157
  using for circles, 103

Snap to Extension command/icon
  using, 163

Snap toggles, 44

Snap to Insertion command/icon
  summary, 595
  using, 163

Snap to Intersection command/icon
  summary, 595
  using, 159

Snap to Midpoint command/icon
  summary, 595
  using, 510

Snap to Nfarest command/icon
  summary, 595
  using, 162

Snap to Node command/icon
  summary, 595
  using, 92, 104, 162–163

Snap to None command/icon
summary, 595

Snap to Parallel command/icon
summary, 595
using, 160–161

Snap to Perpendicular command/icon
summary, 596
using, 160

Snap to Quadrant command/icon
summary, 596
using, 158

Snap to Tangent command/icon
summary, 596
using, 158–159

Soldraw command/icon, *See* Setup Drawing command/icon

Solid Edit command/icon
summary, 596
using to change color of model face, 411

Solid fill, 340

Solid mapping, 543

Solid model editing, 443
adding centerlines, 458–459
creating holes, 451–452
eliminating unnecessary hidden lines, 456–458
Freeze/Thaw in current viewpoint, 459–461
using Chamfer command, 444–445
using Fillet command, 444
using Slice command, 445–451

Solid modeling, 393–394
attaching solid models to assembly drawings, 465–469
auxiliary views, 511–514
changing viewpoint, 404
complex models, 412–413
cone creation, 415–416
creating surface models, 432–437
cylinder creation, 410–411
3D coordinate systems, 394
edge surface creation, 436
inserting solid part drawings into assembly drawings, 469–472
multiple viewport creation, 400–402
object creation, 399
plotting from paper space, 418–420
regions, 422
section view creation, 501–502
selecting active viewport, 402–404
setting isolines, 411–412
setting viewpoint, 394–396
User Coordinate System, 397–398
User Coordinate System creation, 416–418
using Extrude, 420–423
using Intersect, 427–432
using Revolve, 424–427
viewports using different UCSs, 407–410
View toolbar, 404–407
wedge creation, 413–414

Solids Editing toolbar, 411, 412–413

Solids toolbar, 398

Solprof command/icon, *See* Setup Profile command/icon

Solview command/icon, *See* Setup View command/icon

Spacebar, 2, 20
Continue option, 97
repeating commands, 21
restarting commands, 49
toggling operations on/off, 24

Space Translation command/icon
summary, 596

Special text characters, 65–66
for dimensioning, 286–287
in programmed commands, 380–386

Spell checking, 72

Spelling command/icon
summary, 596
using, 72

Sphere command/icon
summary, 596

Spherical mapping, 543

Spline command/icon
summary, 596
using, 127–128

Spline curves, 127–128

Spotlight, 532

Spreadsheet word processors
using for assembly drawings, 489

Standards command/icon
summary, 596

Standard toolbar, 18, 33–34

Start menu, adding shortcut to, 6

Statistics command/icon
summary, 596

Status bar, 34

Status command/icon
summary, 596

STL Out command/icon
summary, 596

Stretch command/icon
summary, 596
using, 294–295
using with associative hatching, 341–342
using with hot grips, 177

Style, 18, 67–68, 217

Style command/icon
summary, 596
using, 67–68

Styles Manager command/icon
summary, 596

Styles toolbar, 18

Subcommands, 20

Subtract command/icon
summary, 597
using for complex object creation, 413, 414, 415, 422
using to create holes, 452

Sun angle calculator, 546–548

Sun Angle Calculator dialog box, 546–547

Support files, customizable, 5

Surface maps, 527

Surface modeling, 393, 432–437

Surfaces toolbar, 432–433

Surftab1 command/icon
  summary, 597
  using, 434–436

Surftab2 command/icon
  summary, 597
  using, 435, 436

Surveyor units, 59–60

SW Isometric View command/icon
  summary, 597

Symmetrical tolerances, 305

Synchronize Attributes command/icon
  summary, 597

System tab, 9, 12

System variables, 12

System Windows command/icon
  summary, 597

T

Tab key, 24

Tablet command/icon
  summary, 597

Tabmode command/icon
  summary, 597

Tabulated Surface command/icon
  summary, 597

Tangent, 105

Target, 91

Target command/icon
  summary, 597

Template drawing, 185

Templates, 38, 111–114, 185
  adding text and notes to paper space, 198–199
  adding title block and text to paper space, 219–220
  beginning new drawing from, 223–224
  changing title block text, 224
  creating from scratch, 207–208
  default text font, 216–217
  inserting existing, 189–190
  making Viewport layer non-plotting, 197–198
  model space, 187, 188–189
  paper space, 187–188
  plotting from paper space, 201–202
  saving dimensions as, 288
  saving multiview setup as, 419–420
  second floating Viewport, 195–198
  setting viewport zoom scale, 192–194
  setting viewres default, 217
  sheet sets, 202–207
  standard template, 186–187
  switching to paper space, 217–218
  use of layers, 208–215
  using Divide, 221–223
  using Drafting Settings dialog box, 215–216
  using in extracting attribute information, 492
  using Pan Realtime, 194

Tessellation lines, 411, 468

Text, 15
  adding to drawings, 64–72
  adding tolerance note, 293–294
  adding to paper space templates, 198–199
  adding to templates, 216–217, 219–220
  ANSI dimension standards, 266
  attributes, 479
  changing title block text, 224
  default text font, 216–217
  in dimensioning, 271–272
  freezing text layer, 375
  special formatting characters, 286–287
  spell checking, 72
  tolerance text height scaling, 307–309

Text boxes, 24

Text command/icon
  summary, 597
  using, 64–72

Text Formatting dialog box, 71–72

Text Screen command/icon
  summary, 597

Text style, 67–70

Texture Maps Search Path, 542

Thickness command/icon
  rectangle, 62
  summary, 597

3D Array command/icon
  summary, 563

3D Clip command/icon
  summary, 563

3D command/icon
  summary, 563

3D Continuous Orbit command/icon
  summary, 563

3D coordinate systems, 394

3D Distance command/icon
  summary, 563

3D Dynamic View command/icon
  summary, 563
  using with auxiliary views, 517–519

3D Face command/icon
  summary, 563

3D Mesh command/icon
  summary, 563
  using, 436–437

3D Mesh surface creation, 436–437

3D Mirror command/icon
summary, 564

3D Orbit command/icon
summary, 564
using, 394–395
using with auxiliary views, 515

3D Polyface Mesh command/icon
summary, 564

3D Polyline command/icon
summary, 564

3D Rotate command/icon
summary, 564

3D solid models, *See* Solid modeling

3D Studio In command/icon
summary, 564

3D Studio Out command/icon
summary, 564

3D UCS icon, 397

3D Web Publish command/icon
summary, 564

3D Wireframe Shade command/icon
summary, 564
using for complex object creation, 413, 414, 437
using in solid model editing, 447, 450

3 Point UCS command/icon
summary, 563
using in assembly drawings, 474
using in solid model editing, 449–450
using with auxiliary views, 515–516

Through point, 118

Tiled viewports, 195, 401

Tiled Viewports command/icon
summary, 597
using, 195

Tilemode command/icon
summary, 597

Tiling
rendered objects, 544

Time command/icon
summary, 598

Title bars, 14, 32–33

Toggles
coordinates, 52
grid and snap, 44

Tolerance command/icon
summary, 598
using, 304

Tolerance precision, 307

Tolerances, 263
automatic bilateral, 305–311
datum flags, 318–319
in dimensioning, 277–278, 293–294
feature control frames, 313–315
formats, 303–304
limit, 303, 304, 306, 311–313
specifying values, 307
text height scaling, 307–309
using Leader command with, 316–317

Tolerance zones, 304

Toolbar command/icon
summary, 598

Toolbars, 18–20, 32–35
picking commands from, 17
quick way to select commands, 46

Tool palettes, 32, 363, 370, 372–374

Tool Palettes command/icon, 8
attaching solid models to assembly drawings, 465, 471
summary, 598
using, 372–374

Tools (menu bar), 35

Tool tips, 19, 32

Tooltips command/icon
summary, 598

Top orthographic view, 229–230

Top View command/icon
summary, 598

Torus command/icon
summary, 598

Trace command/icon
summary, 598

Tracking command/icon
aligning 3D objects, 474

Transferring files, 73

Transparency command/icon
summary, 598

Transparency material selection, 540

Transparent commands, 46

Treestat command/icon
summary, 598

Trim command/icon
adjusting viewing area in section views, 338–339
summary, 598
using, 114–120
using for producing auxiliary views, 357
using with construction lines, 171–172
using with dimensions, 294
using with orthographic views, 234–235, 241

True Type fonts, 68–69, 216

Tutorials, *See* AutoCAD tutorials

2D orthographic drawings, *See* Orthographic views

2D Solid command/icon
summary, 563

2D UCS icon, 397

2D Wireframe Shade command/icon
summary, 563

Typographical conventions, 2–3

U

UCS command/icon
summary, 598
using, 416–417, 419

UCS Follow command/icon
summary, 598

Ucsfollow variable, 517

UCS icon, 32, 397–398

UCS Icon command/icon
summary, 598
using in complex object creation, 427
using in solid model editing, 451
using with auxiliary views, 515–516
using with section views, 506
using with solid models, 397, 398

UCS Manager command/icon
summary, 598

Undefine command/icon
summary, 599

Undo command/icon, 167
summary, 599
using, 49, 56–58

Unicode fonts, 68

Unidirectional text, 65

Unilateral tolerances, 304

Union (Boolean operator), 412

Union command/icon
summary, 599
using, 417, 448–449

Units, 58–60, 274–275
in geometric constructions, 145

Units command/icon
summary, 599
using, 59–60, 274–275
using for geometric constructions, 145

User Coordinate System (UCS), 32, 397–398
creating, 416–418
viewports using different, 407–410

User-defined hatch patterns, 332

User Preferences tab, 9

User profiles, 10–12

V

Variance tolerances, 303–304

Vector, 404

Venn diagrams, 412

Vertically tiled drawings, 40

View (menu bar), 35

View command/icon
summary, 599
using in solid modeling, 399, 451

View dialog box, 451

Viewpoint, 394–396
changing, 404

Viewpoint command/icon, 404

Viewport Clip command/icon
summary, 599
using, 200

Viewport Layer command/icon
summary, 599
using, 400, 403

Viewports
auxiliary views, 511–514
changing scale in section views, 337
creating multiple in solid modeling, 400–402
freezing hatching in section views, 509
generated layers in solid models, 454
irregularly shaped, 200
locking in orthographic views, 246–247
making active, 196–197
making layer non-plotting, 197–198
rendered files, 545, 552–553
selecting active in solid modeling, 402–404
setting zoom scale, 192–194
templates, 188, 191–200
using different UCSs, 407–410

View Resolution command/icon
summary, 599
using, 217
using in complex object creation, 413

View Slide command/icon
summary, 599

View toolbar, 404–407

View UCS command/icon
summary, 599
using, 427

Virtual screen, 101

Visibility of layers, 84–85

Visible profile lines, 453

Visual Basic Editor command/icon
summary, 599

Visual Effects Settings dialog box, 54

Visual LISP command/icon
summary, 599

W

Wedge command/icon
summary, 599
using, 413–414

Wedges, 413–414

Who Has command/icon
summary, 599

Width command/icon
rectangle, 62

Window (menu bar), 35

Window border, 14

Window Cascade, 41

Windows control buttons, 32

Windows Explorer
file transfer using, 73

Windows 2000/NT/XP
configuring AutoCAD, 3–4
conventions, 13–14
multitasking options, 15
navigating, 14

Windows OLE (Object Linking and Embedding)
using for assembly drawings, 489–492

Window Tile Horizontally, 40

Window Tile Vertically, 40

Wireframe modeling, 393

WMF In command/icon
summary, 599

WMF Options command/icon
summary, 600

WMF Out command/icon
summary, 600

Working directory
creation, 6–7, 40
saving files to, 29

World coordinate system (WCS), 48, 394, 397

World UCS command/icon, 397
summary, 600
using in solid model editing, 452

Write Block command/icon
summary, 600
using, 363, 365, 368–370
using for assembly drawings, 483

Write Block dialog box, 369

X

X Axis Rotate UCS command/icon
summary, 600

X-coordinate values, 48
drawing using relative, 50

Xplode command/icon
for eliminating unnecessary hidden lines, 456–458
Explode contrasted, 285
summary, 600
using for dimensioning, 285–286

Y

Y Axis Rotate UCS command/icon
summary, 600

Y-coordinate values, 48
drawing using relative, 50

Z

Z Axis Rotate UCS command/icon
summary, 600

Z Axis Vector UCS command/icon
summary, 600

Z-coordinate values, 48

Zero suppression, dimensions, 275–276

Zoom, 43, 98–101
distortion resulting from, 116
using Aerial Viewer, 101–102
using Pan Realtime, 102

Zoom All command/icon
with landscape objects, 550
with Limits, 61
with orthographic views, 232
summary, 600
use in dimensioning, 265
using, 43, 101
using for geometric constructions, 145
using with orthographic views, 247

Zoom Center command/icon
summary, 600

Zoom Dynamic command/icon
summary, 600
using, 102

Zoom Extents command/icon
summary, 600
using, 473–474

Zoom In command/icon
summary, 600
using, 98–99

Zoom Object command/icon
summary, 600

Zoom Out command/icon
adjusting viewing area in section views, 337
summary, 601
using, 99

Zoom Previous command/icon
adjusting viewing area in section views, 338
summary, 600
using, 101
using with orthographic views, 241
using with templates, 193–194

Zoom Realtime command/icon
with auxiliary views, 516
summary, 601
using, 101

Zoom Scale command/icon, 409
summary, 601
using, 99
using with templates, 192–194
Zoom Vmax command/icon
summary, 601
Zoom Window command/icon
adjusting viewing area in section views, 338
with landscape objects, 550
summary, 601
using, 99–100
using for solid model editing, 444
using with orthographic views, 241
using with templates, 193–194, 197

Art Credits

Exercises 1.2, 1.3, 1.6, 2.2, 2.3M, 2.5, 3.5, 4.1M, 4.3, 4.4, 5.1, 6.4M, 6.5, 6.12, 6.6M, 7.1, 7.2, 7.3, 7.6, 7.7, 10.2, 10.4, 10.5, 10.8, 11.6M, 11.7, 12.5, 12.6, 12.8, 12.9, 13.4, 13.5, 13.6, 13.10M, 15.3, 15.4, 15.5, 15.6M courtesy of the Spocad Centers of Gonzaga University School of Engineering.

Exercises 1.9, 3.7, 3.8, 10.7, 10.9, 12.3, 14.4, 14.5, and 14.6 courtesy of Karen L. Coen-Brown, Engineering Mechanics Department, University of Nebraska-Lincoln.

Exercises 1.10, 2.6, 2.8, 2.9, 2.10, 3.10M, 3.11M, 3.12, 4.7M, 4.8M, 4.9M, 4.10, 5.2, 5.3, 5.4M, 5.5M, 5.11, 6.7, 6.8M, 6.9M, 7.9, 7.12, 8.5, 8.6, 8.7, 8.8, 10.10, 10.11, 11.3, 13.9M, 13.11M, 13.12M, 14.9, 15.8M, 15.9M, 15.10M courtesy of James H. Earle.

Exercises 1.11, 3.4, 3.6, 4.12, 5.8, 6.10, 6.11, 6.14, 7.10. 7.11, 7.13, 7.14, 8.9, 8.10, 9.4, 9.15, 10.1, 12.2, 12.4, 13.2, and 13.8 reprinted with permission from *Modern Graphics Communication, Third Edition*, by F. E. Giesecke, A. Mitchell, H. C. Spencer, I. L. Hill, J. T. Dygdon, J. E. Novak, and S. Lockhart (Pearson Prentice Hall, 2004).

Exercise 4.2 courtesy of D. Krall, Norfolk State University.

Exercises 4.6, 7.4, 7.5, 11.1, 11.2, 11.4, 9.9, 9.10, and 14.7 courtesy of Tom Bryson, University of Missouri-Rolla.

Exercise 5.9 courtesy of Kyle Tage.

Exercises 6.13 and 9.6 courtesy of Amy E. Monte, Michigan Technological State University.

Exercise 11.5 courtesy of Mary Ann Koen, University of Missouri-Rolla.

Exercise 12.1 courtesy of Kevin Berisso.

Figure 5.3 courtesy of Mary Tolle, South Dakota State University.